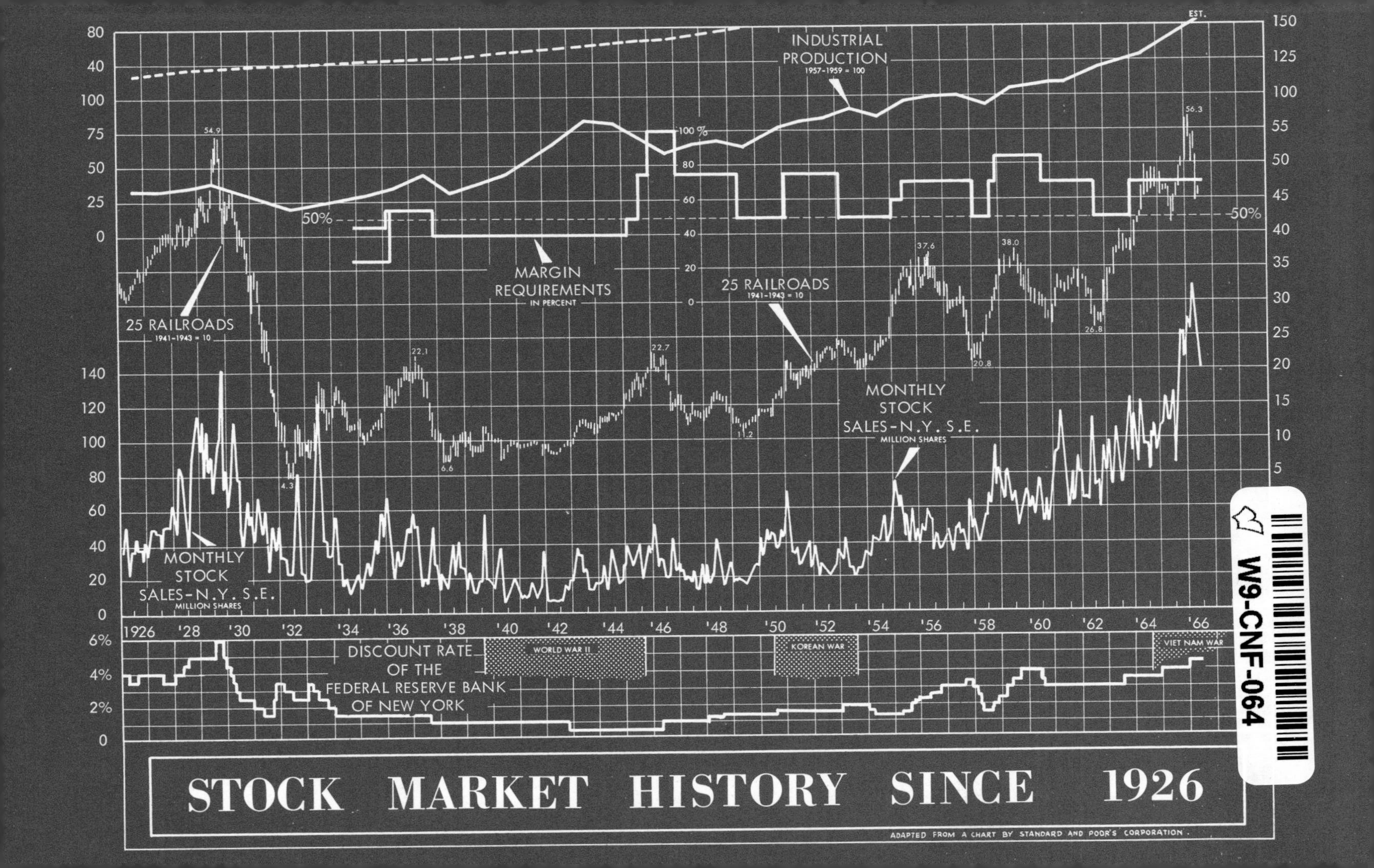


# STOCK MARKET HISTORY SINCE 1926

ADAPTED FROM A CHART BY STANDARD AND POOR'S CORPORATION.

# Investment Analysis and Portfolio Management

# INVESTMENT ANALYSIS AND PORTFOLIO MANAGEMENT

JEROME B. COHEN, Ph.D.
*Professor of Finance and*
*Associate Dean of Graduate Studies*
*Bernard M. Baruch School of Business and*
*Public Administration*
*The City University of New York*

EDWARD D. ZINBARG, Ph.D.
*Chief Economist and Director of*
*Investment Research*
*Prudential Insurance Company of America*
*Adjunct Associate Professor of Finance*
*Bernard M. Baruch School of Business and*
*Public Administration*
*The City University of New York*

1967
DOW JONES—IRWIN, INC.
Homewood, Illinois

First printing, April, 1967
Second printing, October, 1967
Third printing, March, 1968

Printed in the United States of America

Library of Congress Catalog Card No. 67–17044

*To Mina, Barbara, and our children,*

*for whose patience and encouragement*

*we are deeply grateful*

# PREFACE

"Thrift is a wonderful virtue, especially in an ancestor," someone once said. If one of your forebears had bought 100 shares of IBM in 1913 for $44½ per share and held, it would, through stock dividends and stock splits, by the end of 1966 have grown to 28,936 shares worth about $10.8 million. Or more recently, $1,000 invested in Polaroid in the mid-1950's would, by the end of 1966, have increased to $137,700. Happy developments of this sort make investments a fascinating subject. On the other hand, there is a real danger of losing your slowly and painfully accumulated resources through ignorance and stupidity. A recent book, *Wiped Out*, tells the sad story of an investor whose resources evaporated from $62,000 in October, 1957, to $297.78 in May, 1964, during the course of a major bull market.

For the individual, investments is not only an intriguing subject, it's a very confusing and difficult one as well. There are so many choices. Whether you have $500 or $5,000, or $50,000 or $500,000 to place, the alternatives are so many and the decisions so perplexing that the process may become nerve-racking. Is the time to invest now or should you wait? Should you plunge ahead and act on the tip you got yesterday, or should you try to check it out, or should you forget about it? Is this the time to buy stocks, or bonds, or nothing? Is real estate a better hedge against inflation than common stocks, or paintings, or postage stamps? Should you use analytic techniques to select and buy common stocks directly or should you buy mutual fund shares and let the professional managers worry about investment selection and timing? But if it's to be mutual funds, then which one? There are now more than 500. How do you find the limited number of effective ones among the many mediocre ones? Or, to be sure of preserving principal, should you play it safe and put your money in U.S. Savings Bonds, or in a savings account? Should the savings account be in a commercial bank, in a savings bank, or in a savings and loan association? Or perhaps you should increase your life insurance or buy an annuity? But these are fixed dollar investments. What about inflation? What about the variable annuity?

Perhaps this *is* the time to buy common stock, but what kind, in what industry, and in what company? What really are your investment objectives? Are you timid or aggressive; conservative or a speculator? Do you want safety of principal or appreciation of capital or both? Should you choose blue chips or speculative special situations? Income stocks or growth stocks or performance stocks? Cyclical issues or defensive stocks? Should you invest in airline stocks, in electronics, in color-TV manufacturers, in foods, or chain stores, or tobacco or utilities? And when you decide upon an industry, then which company? For the institutional investment manager the questions may be a bit different and more complex, but they are perplexing and involved with no easy answers.

We have tried to write a book which we think and hope will be useful to both categories of investors, present and prospective. It starts out simply and then grows in complexity. It ends with the computer and a peering into the future. We hope it reflects our own involvement over the years with the investment process. More importantly, however, we hope it reflects some of the advice, counsel, guidance and wisdom offered to us by many "pros" in the field.

We are particularly indebted to Mr. Morris Goldstein, partner in Francis I. du Pont & Co.; Mr. Leo C. Bailey, Vice-President of A. G. Becker and Company; Dr. Leo Barnes, Chairman, Department of Finance and Investments, Hofstra University; Mr. George A. Chestnutt, Jr., of the Chestnutt Corp. of Greenwich, Connecticut; Mr. John F. Bridges, Senior Vice-President of First Investors Annuity Corporation; Mr. Sidney Homer, partner in Salomon Bros. & Hutzler; Mr. Leon Kilbert, Vice-President of Lionel D. Edie; Mr. Wade Smith, Vice-President of Dun & Bradstreet; Mr. Louis Brand and Mr. Bernard H. Stiefel of Standard & Poor's Corporation; Mr. Manown Kisor, Jr. of Paine, Webber, Jackson & Curtis; Mrs. Lucille Tomlinson Wessman, partner in Arthur Wiesenberger & Co.; Mr. William D. Horgan, editor, *The Exchange;* Miss Janet Low of Merrill Lynch, Pierce, Fenner & Smith; Mr. Berton W. Godnick of Godnick and Son, Inc.; and Dr. Allen O. Felix of the New York Stock Exchange, as well as a number of colleagues at the Prudential Insurance Company.

Over the years, stimulating conversations with numerous experts have enhanced our understanding of the investment process. To list them all would fill more space than is available. But the names of several must be noted with deep appreciation: Mr. Louis C. Fieland of the New York Bar; Dr. John W. Harriman, Economist of Union Service Corporation; Dr. Gabriel Kerekes of Goodbody & Co.; Mr. John Rice of McDonnell & Co.; Mr. Frederic L. Simmons, retired Economist of the Morgan Guaranty Trust Company; and Dr. Stanley Tunick, C.P.A. Vice-Chairman of the New York State C.P.A. Examining Board.

Professor Harold G. Fraine of the University of Wisconsin and Professor Kenneth A. Romey of San Jose State College read the entire manuscript and offered many valuable suggestions for improvement. Needless to say, for the numerous errors which doubtless will still be found we assume full and apologetic responsibility.

NEW YORK, N.Y.

JEROME B. COHEN
EDWARD D. ZINBARG

March, 1967

# TABLE OF CONTENTS

CHAPTER PAGE

## PART I. THE SETTING



## PART II. SECURITY VALUATION

## PART III. INVESTMENT TIMING

# PART I

# THE SETTING

# 1

# THE INVESTMENT SETTING

October. This is one of the peculiarly dangerous months to speculate in stocks. The others are July, January, September, April, November, May, March, June, December, August and February.

—Mark Twain

Investment has many facets. It may involve putting money into bonds, or common stock, or paintings, or real estate, or mortgages, or oil ventures, or cattle, or the theater. It may involve speculating in bull markets or selling short in bear markets. It may involve choosing growth stocks, or blue chips, or defensive stocks, or income stocks, or even penny cats and dogs. It may involve puts and calls, straddles, rights, warrants, convertibles, margin, Monthly Investment Plan, mutual funds, etc., and result in accumulation of wealth or dissipation of resources. Diversity and challenge characterize the field. For the able or the lucky, the rewards may be substantial. For the uninformed, results can be disastrous.

Investment could mean buying 100 shares of IBM in 1913 for $44½ per share, and watching it appreciate, through stock dividends and stock splits, to 28,936 shares by the end of 1966, worth about $10.8 million. Or it could have meant buying Du Pont in 1929 at $503 per share and seeing it fall to $22 per share by 1932. It could mean buying Xerox at $2¼ per share and seeing it go to $295¾ per share. Or it could mean buying Brunswick at the peak of its popularity in 1961 at 74⅞ and watching it fall to 7⅛ in 1965. In the raging bull market of 1965 one could have bought A.T.&T., the bluest of the blue chips, at 70 and seen it decline to 60, a two-year low, by the end of the year, despite the market rise. Thus, of course, you would have a $1,000 loss for each 100 shares held. On the other hand, that same year you could have quadrupled your funds by buying SCM at 15⅝ and watching it rise to 62⅝. Little-known

Western Equities rose from 7⅝ to 44¾.[1] As you will learn, usually in the latter stages of a bull market, many high-grade quality issues tend to lose favor, even decline, while the low-priced, very speculative shares, receive the play and spurt ahead. Thus, during 1965 Du Pont fell from 261 to 225 and Sears, Roebuck declined from 77 to 62, while Noramco, Inc., advanced from 3⅛ to 8½, Solitron rose from 35½ to 154½, and Fairchild Camera soared from 27¼ to 165¼.

### Common Stock and Inflation

To most individuals investment means buying common stock. There are several reasons why this is so. First, the bull market over the last 15 years has provided substantial capital gains for many of those "in the market." The fever spreads, and the next fellow wants to duplicate the feat of his friend, who after all isn't any brighter or more knowledge-

FIGURE 1–1

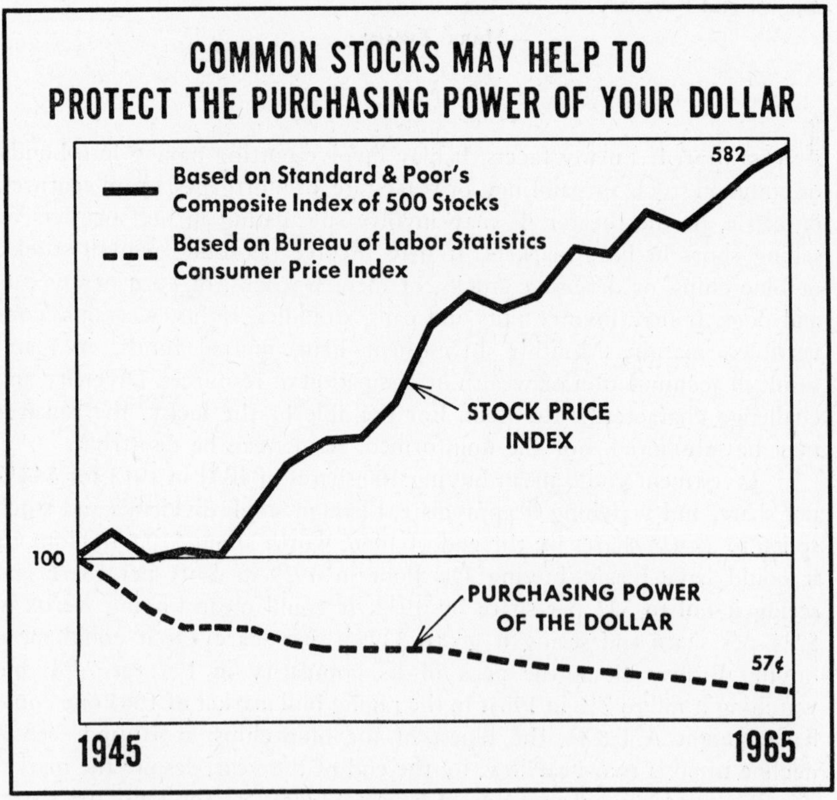

COMMON STOCKS MAY HELP TO PROTECT THE PURCHASING POWER OF YOUR DOLLAR

Based on Standard & Poor's Composite Index of 500 Stocks
Based on Bureau of Labor Statistics Consumer Price Index
582
STOCK PRICE INDEX
100
PURCHASING POWER OF THE DOLLAR
57¢
1945
1965

Source: Prepared by Merrill Lynch, Pierce, Fenner & Smith, Inc.

[1] But went into reorganization in 1966.

able than he is. As a result the number of those owning common stock rose from 6.5 million in 1952 to over 20 million persons by 1966.

In fact, over a longer period, a study[2] conducted by the Center for Research in Security Prices of the University of Chicago found that anyone who had invested in common stock broadly from 1926 on and had held through 1960 would have realized substantial capital appreciation.[3]

A second important reason is that the value of the dollar seems to have fallen steadily since the end of World War II, and investment in common stock has appeared to be an excellent hedge against inflation. As a matter of fact, as Figure 1–1 shows, since 1946 the dollar has lost over one third of its purchasing power, but the Standard & Poor's Index of Common Stocks has increased fivefold. Over a longer period the steady, relentless decline in the purchasing power of the dollar and the secular rise in common stock prices may be seen in Figures 1–2 and 1–3.

The extent of the deterioration of fixed dollar income may be shown in another way. Figure 1–4 shows "The Two-Way Squeeze" over two time periods, 1939/1965 and 1949/1965. The $10,000-a-year man of 1939 would have had to earn $26,309 in 1965 to retain the same purchasing power as his 1939 income yielded after taxes. Of the 1965 income of $26,309, $4,395 would have gone in taxes, compared to $269 in 1939, while $12,183 of purchasing power would have been lost due to inflation. The $10,000-a-year man of 1949 would have had to earn $13,430 in 1965 to retain the same purchasing power, largely because some $2,782 of purchasing power would have been lost due to inflation.

Ours has not, fortunately, been the experience of some countries that have experienced hyperinflation. France, for example, experienced hyperinflation. In 1914 the French franc was worth 19½ cents (in U.S. currency). By 1920 it was worth only 7 cents. When France returned to the gold standard in 1928, the franc was worth only 4 cents. With the Nazi invasion of France in 1940, the franc went down to 2 cents. By 1946 the official rate was down to less than a cent: 0.84 cents. By 1948, in the free market, it had declined to less than one third of a cent. In the 10 years from 1954 to 1964, France had a compounded annual rate of inflation of about 4½%, the value of the buying power of the franc dropping more than one third from the 1954 level.

What we have had may be called creeping inflation: a steady whittling away of the value of the dollar. During the first half of this century,

---

[2] Lawrence Fisher and James H. Lorie, "Rates of Return on Investments in Common Stocks," *Journal of Business*, University of Chicago, January, 1964.

[3] Conflicting views over the Fisher-Lorie study may be found in Leo Barnes, "What Difference Does Knowledge Make to Investors," *Financial Analysts Journal* September–October, 1965; and James H. Lorie and Lawrence Fisher, "Knowledge Makes A Difference: A Reply to Dr. Leo Barnes," *Financial Analysts Journal*, November–December, 1965.

FIGURE 1–2

**Purchasing Power of the Dollar**

(1939 Dollar equals 100 Cents)

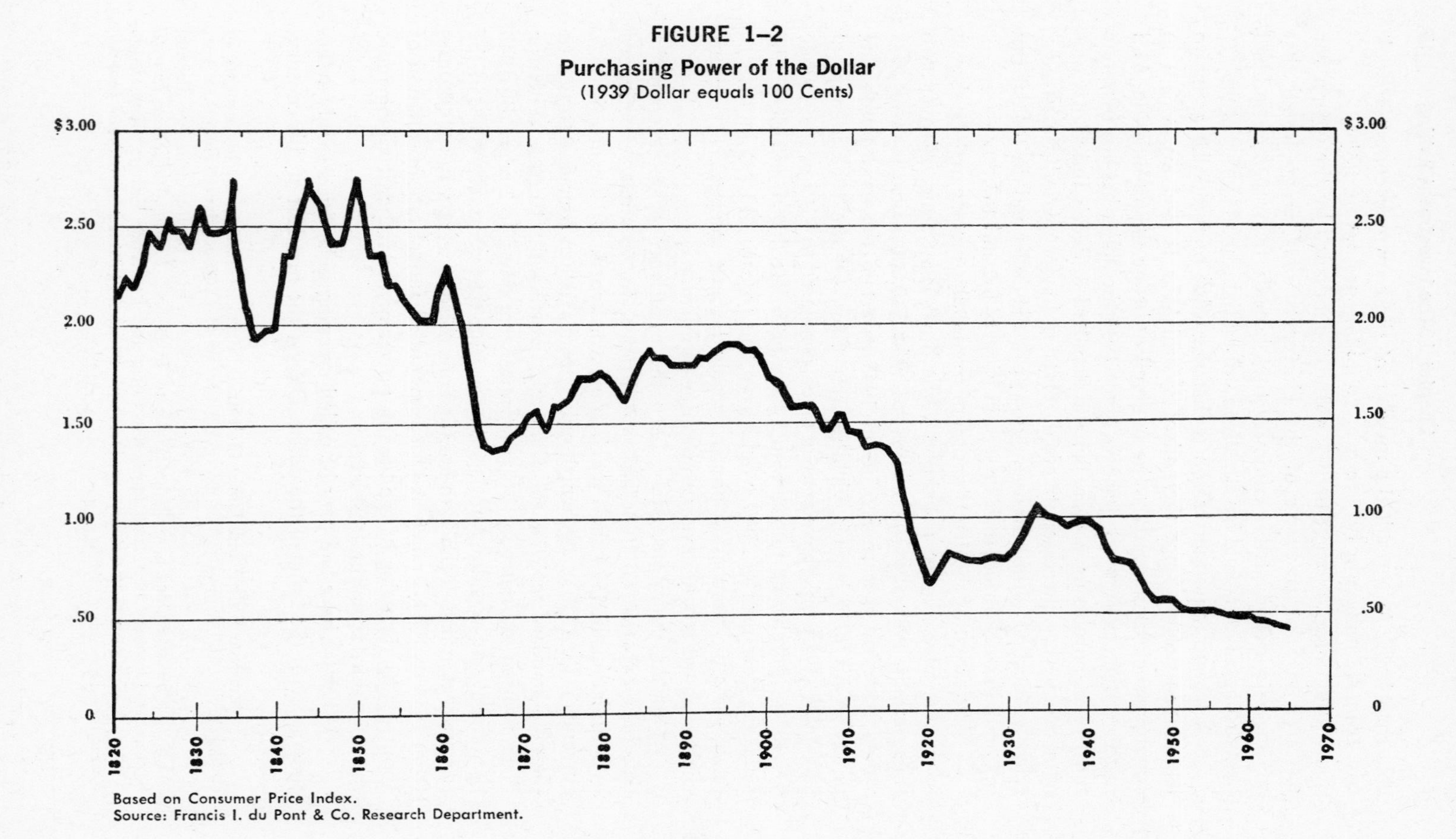


Based on Consumer Price Index.
Source: Francis I. du Pont & Co. Research Department.

FIGURE 1–3

Trading Range of Dow-Jones Industrial Stock Average

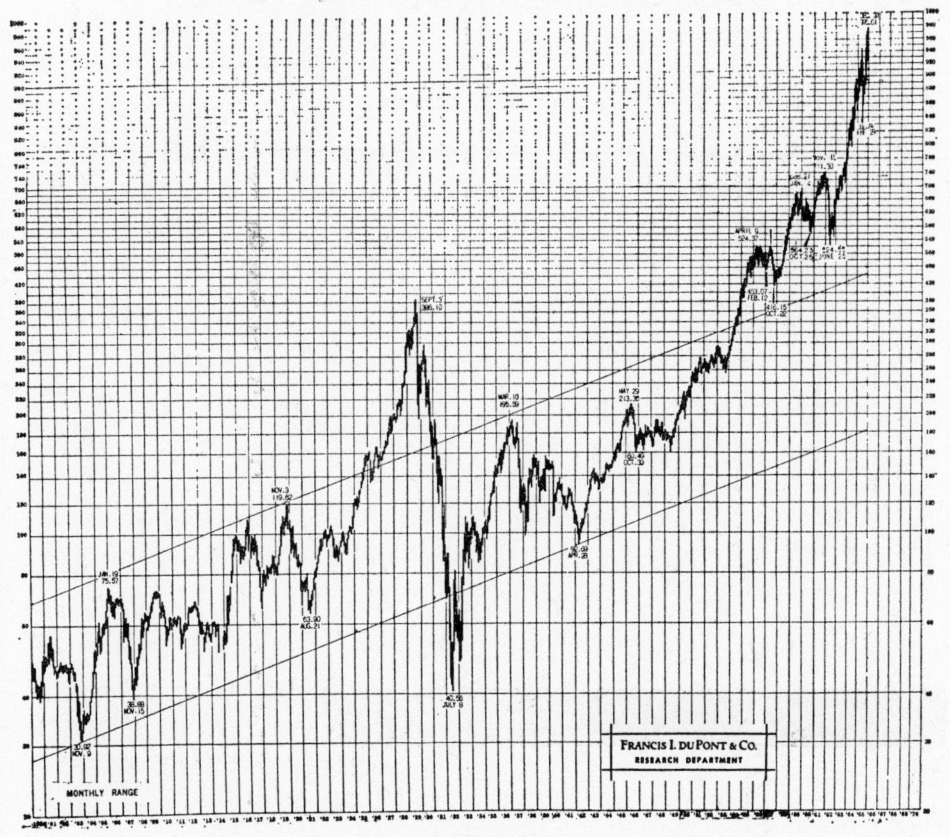


Source: Francis I. du Pont & Co. Research Department.

the purchasing power of the dollar declined about two thirds. Since 1939 the dollar has lost about half its purchasing power. Over the last decade, U.S. prices have been rising by 1% to 2% a year. At this rate the dollar will lose over a third of its current value in a quarter of a century. Yet, as Figure 1–3 shows, most of the time that the value of the dollar has been declining, the prices of common stocks (as an index) have been rising. This is one major factor that has led investors into common stock.

## Types of Common Stock

Yet the point should quickly be made that while common stock prices have been rising, some common stocks have fallen even in the bull market atmosphere. For example, during 1964, while sulphur stocks rose 74% and stocks of cigar manufacturers 34%, sugar stocks fell 23% and savings and loan association holding companies declined by 30%. In 1964

## FIGURE 1–4
## The Two-Way "Squeeze," 1965

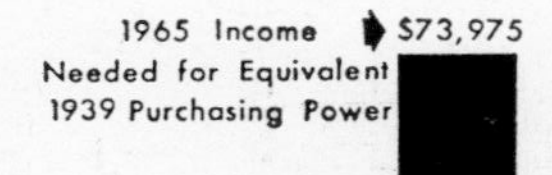


As might be expected, the decline in purchasing power of like amounts of gross income has been much more pronounced over the longer 1939-65 period than between 1949-65. A married man with two children has to earn nearly $12,800 this year to equal the purchasing power of the $5,000 he received in 1939. If he made $5,000 in 1949, he needs almost $6,800 this year to match his 1949 buying power.

The two main causes of this "squeeze" on personal income are price inflation and higher income taxes. The 1939-65 period was one in which the economy was subjected to the shock of two wars with their attendant inflation. Only the Korean War interjected something more than moderate price increases in the 1949-65 span.

The Federal income tax bite, also war affected, similarly had a greater impact over the longer period with effective tax rates higher for all levels of income in 1965 compared to 1939. With the reduced rates and more liberal deductions introduced in the Internal Revenue Act of 1964, however, some higher income brackets are now bearing a lighter tax burden than the same money income in 1949.

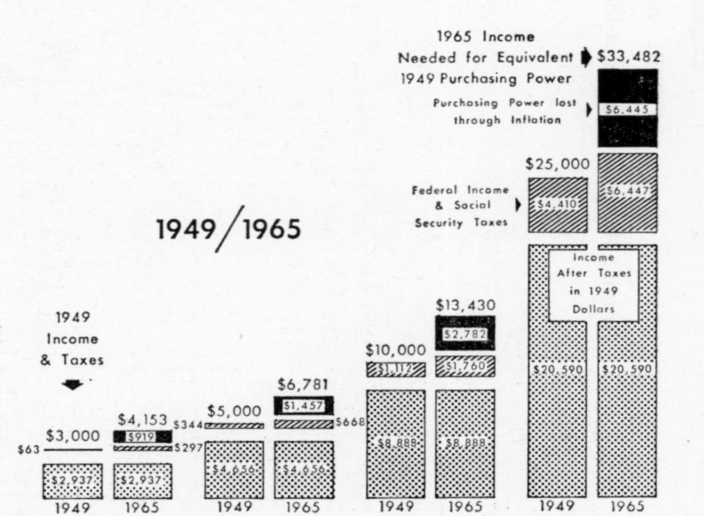


Source: National Industrial Conference Board, Inc., Road Maps of Industry No. 1523.

the common stocks of radio and TV manufacturers fell 11.4%, while in 1965 they rose 132%. There is a diversity in common stock which extends not only to industry and to company but to type of stock as well. In the loose and flexible language of the Street, it is customary to speak of blue chip stocks, of growth stocks, of cyclical stocks, of income stocks, of defensive stocks, and of speculative stocks—both high flyers and low-priced issues. Lines of demarcation between types are not precise and clear, but investors have a general notion of what is meant by each of these imprecise categories.

*Blue chip* stocks are high-grade investment quality issues of major companies which have long and unbroken records of earnings and dividend payments. Stocks like American Telephone & Telegraph, General Motors, Du Pont, Standard Oil of New Jersey, United States Steel, and so on, are generally considered "blue chip." The term is generally used to describe the common stock of large, well-established, stable and mature companies of great financial strength. The term was undoubtedly originally derived from poker, where blue chips (in contrast to white and red) had the greatest money value.

The financial press is replete with the term. "Blue Chips Losing Some Following. Stocks With More Potential for Growth Gain Favor," read one headline in the financial section of *The New York Times*. One mutual fund, Keystone S–1, invests only in "The Royal Blue Chips," in contrast to its other series which are devoted to income stocks, speculative stocks, etc. Each year the brokerage firm of Paine, Webber, Jackson & Curtis issues a compilation, entitled *Heirloom Stocks*, of one hundred companies paying dividends from 40 to 180 years. These blue chip or "heirloom" stocks are shown in Table 1–1. The figure in parenthesis after each company indicates the year since which dividends have been paid uninterruptedly to date. The ability to pay steady dividends over bad years as well as good for a long period is, of course, an indication of financial stability. Some of the "blue chips" of yesteryear have fallen from greatness. Of the top 20 stocks (by asset value) of 1909, for example, number 4 was J. P. Morgan's International Mercantile Marine, later reorganized as United States Lines. Number 7 was Central Leather Company, reorganized in 1926 as U.S. Leather and in 1953 as Keta Oil & Gas Company. By and large, however, investors who seek safety and stability and are conservative in their approach to the market turn to the blue chips. So, too, do institutional investment managers, particularly those who are involved in longer term investing.

Many of the blue chips may also be considered growth stocks. A *growth stock* is one of a company whose sales and earnings are expanding faster than the general economy and faster than the average for the industry. The company is usually aggressive, research minded, plowing back earnings to facilitate expansion. For this reason growth companies,

## TABLE 1–1

## "Heirloom" Stocks

*DIVIDENDS PAID FOR 150 YEARS OR MORE*

Bank of New York (1785)
First National Bank of Boston (1784)
First National City Bank of New York (1813)

*DIVIDENDS PAID FOR 100 YEARS OR MORE*

Chase Manhattan Bank (1848)
Chemical Bank New York Trust Co. (1827)
Cincinnati Gas & Electric (1853)
Continental Insurance (1854)
First Pennsylvania Bank & Trust Co. (1828)
Manufacturers Hanover Trust (1852)
Travelers Insurance Co. (1864)

*DIVIDENDS PAID FOR 75 YEARS OR MORE*

American Telephone & Telegraph (1881)
Chesebrough-Pond (1883)
Consolidated Edison (1885)
Corning Glass Works (1881)
Great American, N.Y. (1873)
Hartford Fire Insurance (1873)
Home Insurance, N.Y. (1874)
Insurance Co. of North America (1874)
Irving Trust, N.Y. (1865)
Eli Lilly Co. (1885)
New England Tel. & Tel. (1886)
Phoenix Insurance of Hartford (1874)
Security First National Bank of Los Angeles (1881)
Sherwin Williams (1885)
St. Paul Fire & Marine (1872)
Standard Oil Co. (N.J.) (1882)

*DIVIDENDS PAID FOR 50 YEARS OR MORE*

Aetna Life Insurance (1908)
American Electric Power (1909)
Anchor Hocking Glass (1914)
Borden Co. (1899)
Boston Edison (1890)
Bristol-Myers Co. (1900)
Campbell Soup (1902)
Caterpillar Tractor (1914)
Central Hudson Gas & Electric (1913)
Coca-Cola (1893)
Commonwealth Edison (1890)
Consumers Power (1913)
R. R. Donnelly & Sons (1911)
Dow Chemical (1911)
E. I. du Pont de Nemours (1904)
Duquesne Light (1913)
Eastman Kodak (1902)
Fireman's Insurance Fund (1908)
General Electric (1899)
Hercules Powder (1913)
Kroger Company (1902)
May Department Stores (1911)
Miles Laboratories (1894)
Morgan Guaranty Trust (1892)
Mountain States Telephone & Telegraph (1911)
National Biscuit (1899)
National Fuel Gas (1903)
National Lead (1906)
Norfolk & Western Ry. (1901)
Northern States Power (1910)
Otis Elevator (1903)
Owens-Illinois Gas (1907)
Pacific Lighting (1909)
Chas. Pfizer & Co. (1901)
Philadelphia Elec. (1902)
Pittsburgh Plate Glass (1899)
Potomac Elec. Power (1904)
Procter & Gamble (1891)
Public Service Electric & Gas (1907)
Rex Chainbelt (1894)
Socony Mobil Oil (1902)
Southern N. E. Telephone (1891)
Standard Brands (1899)
Standard Oil of Calif. (1912)
Standard Oil Co. (Ind.) (1894)
Sterling Drug (1902)
Sun Oil Co. (1904)
Texaco, Inc. (1903)
Union Electric (1906)
Union Pacific R.R. (1900)

TABLE 1–1 (Continued)

*DIVIDENDS PAID FOR 40 YEARS OR MORE*

| | |
|---|---|
| Amerada Petroleum (1922) | Idaho Power (1917) |
| American Home Products (1919) | International Business Mach. (1916) |
| Avon Products (1919) | Kansas Power & Light (1915) |
| Champion Spark Plug (1919) | Minnesota Mining & Manufacturing (1916) |
| Connecticut Light & Power (1922) | National Dairy Prod. (1924) |
| Corn Products (1920) | Pacific Gas & Electric (1919) |
| Delaware Power & Light (1921) | J. C. Penney Co. (1922) |
| Firestone Tire & Rubber (1924) | Pet Milk (1922) |
| General American Transp. (1919) | Pillsbury Co. (1924) |
| General Foods (1922) | Scott Paper (1915) |
| General Motors (1915) | Texas Utilities (1917) |
| Houston Light & Power (1922) | Union Carbide (1918) |

Source: Paine, Webber, Jackson & Curtis, 1966.

intent on financing their own expansion from retained earnings, pay relatively small dividends and their yield is generally low. Over time, however, substantial capital gains may accrue from the appreciation of the value of the common as a result of the plowback and expansion.

Growth stocks are usually quite volatile. They go up faster and farther than other stocks, but at the first hint that the high rate of earnings is either leveling off or not being sustained, prices can come tumbling down. For example, Texas Instruments, a high-flying growth company of the late 1950's saw earnings fall from some $15 million in 1960 to about $9 million in 1961. The common price fell from $256 a share in 1960 to $95 a share in 1961. In 1966 Fairchild Camera fell from a high of 216¾ to 101¼; Motorola dropped from 233½ to 92¾; Xerox from 267¾ to 132⅜; Polaroid from 175 to 118; SCM from 91⅞ to 44⅛, and Pan American Airways from 79⅜ to 40⅞. Smaller and newer "growth companies" are especially vulnerable when earnings fail to live up to expectations or promise. Thus Farrington Manufacturing, once highly touted as a growth stock, fell from 57½ to 11, while NAFI Corp. dropped from 66⅞ to 26⅝ and Transitron Electronics from 60 to 18¾, this in a year (1961) in which older, more established growth stocks like IBM, Litton, and Zenith went up 46%, 45% and 90% respectively. See Table 1–2.

In an effort to define the term "growth" stock with more precision, several services have developed statistical tests to identify and select growth stocks. Standard & Poor's, for example, has developed a list of "200 Rapid Growth Stocks" by screening over 6,000 issues by electronic data processing methods. The resultant list of 200 stocks, obtained by a purely mechanical process, is not to be regarded as a "buy list." The major criteria employed in selection are (*a*) if the growth in share earnings over the previous five years is steady, it must have amounted to at least 7% per annum compounded; (*b*) if the trend had been interrupted in only one

TABLE 1–2

Fallen from Grace*

| | 1960–61 High | Recent Price (Nov., 1961) | Percent Decline |
|---|---|---|---|
| COSMETICS | | | |
| Hazel Bishop | 10⅞ | 4⅝ | −58% |
| Bourjois | 33⅞ | 17¾ | −48 |
| Helene Curtis Industries | 74¼ | 51¼ | −31 |
| Lanolin Plus | 19 | 14¼ | −25 |
| Helena Rubenstein | 67½ | 52¼ | −23 |
| Chesebrough-Pond's | 65¾ | 52 | −21 |
| Nestle-LeMur Co. | 26⅝ | 21⅛ | −21 |
| ELECTRONICS | | | |
| Transitron Electronic | 60 | 18¾ | −69 |
| Avnet Electronics | 68¼ | 28⅛ | −59 |
| Texas Instruments | 256¼ | 110¾ | −57 |
| Ampex Corp. | 42¼ | 19½ | −54 |
| General Instrument | 55½ | 29 | −48 |
| Varian Associates | 77¾ | 42⅛ | −46 |
| International Rectifier | 35⅞ | 19¾ | −45 |
| Laboratory for Electronics | 70½ | 39 | −45 |
| Packard-Bell Electronics | 26⅜ | 14½ | −45 |
| Hewlett Packard | 53 | 32 | −40 |
| Cubic Corp. | 35⅜ | 23 | −35 |
| Standard Hollsman | 53¼ | 36⅛ | −32 |
| High Voltage Engineering | 230 | 162 | −30 |
| Loral Electronics | 46¼ | 33¾ | −27 |
| AMP, Inc. | 34¼ | 27 | −21 |
| LEISURE TIME | | | |
| NAFI Corp. | 66⅞ | 26⅝ | −60 |
| Bowl-Mor Co. | 51 | 25½ | −50 |
| Outboard Marine | 37¼ | 18¾ | −50 |
| Diners' Club | 33¼ | 20¼ | −39 |
| American Machine & Foundry | 63⅝ | 39⅝ | −38 |
| Bell & Howell | 69⅞ | 49¾ | −29 |
| Polaroid Corp. | 261¾ | 199 | −24 |
| Fairchild Camera & Instrument | 201¾ | 161 | −20 |
| PUBLISHING | | | |
| Pocket Books, Inc. | 41 | 23¾ | −42 |
| Crowell-Collier Publishing | 50⅞ | 37½ | −26 |
| Ginn & Co. | 35½ | 26¼ | −26 |
| American Book | 82 | 64 | −22 |
| International Textbook | 66 | 52 | −21 |
| VENDING MACHINES | | | |
| Universal Match | 80¾ | 33¼ | −59 |
| Seeburg | 48½ | 26¾ | −45 |
| Automatic Canteen | 52⅛ | 32 | −39 |
| ABC Vending | 30 | 19¼ | −36 |
| Vendo Co. | 77¾ | 49⅜ | −36 |

TABLE 1–2 (Continued)

| MISCELLANEOUS | | | |
|---|---|---|---|
| Farrington Manufacturing | 57½ | 11 | −81 |
| Collins Radio | 76 | 32 | −58 |
| Ryder System | 34¼ | 14⅝ | −57 |
| General Dynamics | 53⅜ | 27 | −49 |
| Hudson Vitamin Prod. | 41 | 29½ | −28 |
| Cenco Instruments | 87¾ | 65 | −26 |
| American Hospital Supply | 35 | 26⅝ | −24 |

* Many of the old-line "growth" stocks are at, or near, their all-time high. But a large number of smaller, and newer, "growth" stocks have suffered severe declines this year (1961).

Source: *Forbes*, November 1, 1961.

year and the decline was less than 5%, annual growth must have been at least 10%; (*c*) if growth had been interrupted in more than one year, or in one year the decline was more than 5%, annual growth rate must have been at least 12%. Selections are limited to issues with more than 500,000 shares outstanding and to those with earnings of at least $0.25 a share in the last full year. The screening is reported monthly. Thus the composition of the list changes from time to time as some stocks are added and others removed. At times companies are removed from the list even though they still qualify, if other firms with more desirable characteristics such as better marketability and/or better earnings records are unearthed. Sample pages from the Standard and Poor's *200 Rapid Growth Stocks* are shown in Table 1–3.

Another service, John S. Herold's *America's Fastest Growing Companies*, uses somewhat different criteria. A company is listed as a growth company by Herold if its annual profits per share have grown without interruption over the most recent three years at a minimum compound rate of 10% a year and if there is evidence of continued growth at the time of listing. A company is removed from the list (*a*) when profits in any 12-month period decline more than 10% from its most recent fiscal year period or when a reliable forecast reveals that such a decline is in prospect or (*b*) if annual growth in earnings over the most recent two years averages less than 5% and growth in the latest reporting is less than 10% over the like period of the prior year. A sample page from *America's Fastest Growing Companies* is shown in Table 1–4.

In his anually issued *Your Investments*, Dr. Leo Barnes develops a checklist of selected growth stocks. His basic criteria for inclusion in his list is an average yearly growth in after-tax earnings per share of 25% over the past five years. In order to minimize the results of one or two extraordinary years, gains of 20% or more in after-tax earnings per share must have been achieved by the company in at last three of the past five years. Nonrecurring income is, of course, excluded from the calculations. A company can have one year in which its earnings per share do not rise

TABLE 1–3

Sample Pages from Standard and Poor's *200 Rapid Growth Stocks*

STANDARD & POOR'S

*The* OUTLOOK®

**The S&P 200 Rapid Growth Stocks**

**Section 2** **February 20, 1967**

## Growth Stocks Lead on Rebound

FEW stocks manage to swim upstream against a current of the severity of last year's bear market. It is hardly surprising, therefore, that most growth stocks showed net declines in price between February 9 and October 7, 1966, the dates marking the beginning and end of the eight-month decline.

Exceptional volatility is a normal characteristic of high price-multiple issues, which abound in the growth stock list. The pattern of above-average sensitivity to an adverse turn in investor psychology was clearly visible in 1961-62, just as it was last year. By the same token, such stocks have shown striking leadership on market rebounds. This is highlighted in the recent history of the group.

As a group, the 200 Rapid Growth Stocks performed very little better than the market as a whole during the 1966 bear market. Against a 22.1% decline for the S & P 500, the growth group fell 21.5% from top to bottom, using only prices on the two terminal dates for comparison.

### Some Outstanding Performances

A profile study of the group, however, shows a number of outstanding performances. Of the total, 8% actually rose on balance in this period, and an additional 12% were down less than 10% in price. In all, 45% were bracketed in a group showing either gains or maximum price declines of 15%.

During the past four months, the high volatility characteristic and the pull of exceptional earnings growth were markedly demonstrated, as shown in the accompanying chart (based on a like dollar amount invested in each of the growth stocks). Between early October and early February, the rapid growth stocks

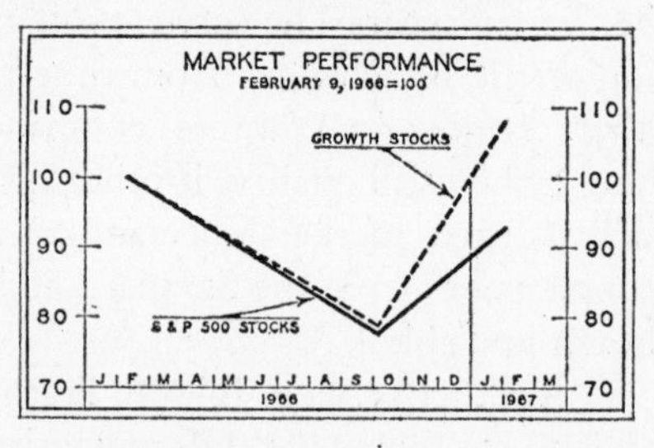


rose an average of 37.4%, while the S & P 500 was advancing 19.3%.

*As in other sectors of the market, the price comeback for growth stocks has been highly selective, with a few issues doubling in price since early October and a far greater number showing moderate gains. The four stocks analyzed below are among the latter, but earnings prospects in each case suggest an above-average market performance from here on.*

### BLACK & DECKER

Development of new products, increases in capacity, strong marketing, broadening foreign operations and expanding and diversified markets are the building blocks on which this leading maker of portable electric tools has based a strong growth record. The current year, ending September 30, got off to a fast start. In the December quarter, a widening of profit margins coupled with a 15.7% gain in sales produced earnings of $0.75 a share against a year-earlier $0.63. With no worse than a flattening of industrial activity in pros-

# TABLE 1–3 (Continued)

## Criteria for Selection: Definition of Terms

This list of 200 stocks is the end product of the screening of a much larger number of issues by electronic data processing methods. As such it represents a purely mechanical process and is not to be regarded as a "buy list." The major criteria employed are: (1) if growth in share earnings over the past years has been steady, it must have amounted to at least 7% per annum, compounded; (2) if growth has been interrupted in only one year and the decline has been less than 5%, annual growth must have been at least 10%; (3) if growth has been interrupted in more than one year, or in one year the decline was more than 5%, annual growth rate must have been at least 12%.

Selections have been limited to issues with more than 500,000 shares outstanding, and those with earnings of at least $0.25 a share in the last full years. Other criteria have been applied, aiming at the elimination of stocks with highly erratic earnings, and those with adverse recent trends despite good overall performance.

The screening is repeated periodically. The composition of the list will thus be subject to change from time to time, as some stocks no longer meet our growth criteria. Stocks may also be removed from the list, even though they still qualify, if other issues have more desirable characteristics such as better marketability and/or better earnings records.

*Five Year Growth Trend*—This shows the compounded annual rate of per-share earnings growth for the past five years.

*P/E Ratio*—Recent price divided by 1966 earnings or the earnings for the later 12 month period.

*Adjustments*—All data adjusted where necessary for stock splits and stock dividends. All earnings exclude non-recurring items.

## Large Companies

| Stock | Year Ends | Shares (000) | *Earnings Per Share ($) 1959 | 1960 | 1961 | 1962 | 1963 | 1964 | 1965 | 1966 | Latest 12 Mos. | Latest Interim Mos. | 1965 | 1966 | Price Range 1966-67 | Recent Price | Ind. Div. ($) | Yield (%) | Five Year Growth Trend (%) | P/E Ratio |
|---|---|---|---|---|---|---|---|---|---|---|---|---|---|---|---|---|---|---|---|---|
| ◆[7]AMP Inc. | Dec. | 6,086 | 0.83 | 0.96 | 1.10 | 1.28 | 1.41 | 1.60 | 2.05 | P2.45 | 2.46 | ...... | ... | ... | 72¼- 42⅜ | 70⅞ | [5]0.72 | 1.0 | 17 | 28.6 |
| ◆Air Products & Chemicals | Sep. | 4,381 | 0.45 | 0.75 | 1.18 | 1.33 | 1.41 | 1.45 | 1.70 | 2.07 | 2.07 | 3 Dec. | 0.53 | 0.53 | 43½- 22¼ | 38 | [2]0.20 | 0.5 | 12 | 18.4 |
| ◆American Electric Power | Dec. | 46,249 | 1.06 | 1.17 | 1.19 | 1.39 | 1.50 | 1.62 | 1.74 | P1.94 | 1.89 | ...... | ... | ... | 43½- 32¼ | 40⅝ | [8]1.44 | 3.5 | 9 | 20.9 |
| ◆American Enka Corp. | Dec. | 5,327 | 1.08 | 0.13 | 1.12 | 1.61 | 1.76 | 2.56 | 2.91 | 3.60 | 3.60 | ...... | ... | ... | 44¾- 27½ | 31⅝ | 1.60 | 5.1 | 26 | 8.8 |
| ◆American Home Products | Dec. | 23,682 | 2.09 | [3]2.07 | [3]2.15 | [3]2.33 | [3]2.49 | 2.74 | 3.10 | P3.65 | 3.65 | ...... | ... | ... | 92½- 61½ | 89½ | 2.15 | 2.4 | 11 | 24.5 |
| ◆American Hospital Supply | Dec. | 9,297 | [3]0.59 | 0.61 | 0.70 | 0.73 | 0.75 | 0.92 | 1.09 | P1.34 | 1.34 | ...... | ... | ... | 52¼- 35⅝ | 51 | 0.50 | 1.0 | 20 | 38.1 |
| ◆Ampex Corp. | Apr. | 9,451 | 0.53 | d0.51 | 0.48 | 0.65 | 0.76 | 0.83 | 0.90 | E1.10 | 1.03 | 9 Jan. | [9]0.61 | [9]0.74 | 31¾- 17 | 31 | ... | .. | 16 | 30.1 |
| ◆Amphenol Corp. | Dec. | 2,939 | 1.25 | 0.80 | 0.23 | 0.85 | 0.80 | 1.05 | 1.29 | P1.98 | 1.98 | ...... | ... | ... | 29½- 15¾ | 24½ | 0.70 | 2.9 | 42 | 12.4 |
| ◆Automatic Retailers of Amer. | Sep. | 3,513 | 0.50 | 0.54 | 0.96 | 1.39 | 1.48 | 1.73 | 2.01 | 2.22 | 2.29 | 3 Dec. | 0.60 | 0.67 | 58⅝- 42½ | 58⅛ | 0.60 | 1.0 | 17 | 25.4 |
| ◆Avon Products | Dec. | 28,690 | 0.50 | 0.61 | 0.73 | 0.88 | 1.03 | 1.39 | 1.66 | P1.92 | 1.92 | ...... | ... | ... | 89½- 66 | 82⅜ | 1.40 | 1.7 | 22 | 42.9 |
| ◆Beatrice Foods Co. | Feb. | 8,565 | 1.71 | 1.77 | 1.83 | 1.91 | 2.11 | 2.49 | 2.95 | E3.20 | 3.10 | 9 Nov. | 1.89 | 2.04 | 58¾- 40 | 46 | 1.50 | 3.3 | 11 | 14.4 |
| ◆Beech-Nut Life Savers | Dec. | 6,624 | 1.27 | 1.40 | 1.58 | 1.76 | 1.94 | 2.22 | 2.44 | E2.78 | 2.52 | 9 Sep. | 1.83 | 1.91 | 60 - 40½ | 43½ | 1.40 | 3.2 | 12 | 15.6 |
| ◆Beneficial Finance | Dec. | 14,408 | 1.77 | 1.96 | 2.28 | 2.49 | 2.65 | 3.03 | 3.35 | E3.45 | 3.44 | 9 Sep. | 2.37 | 2.46 | 55½- 28⅝ | 41½ | 1.60 | 3.9 | 11 | 12.0 |
| ◆Black & Decker Mfg. | Sep. | 4,838 | 1.12 | 1.19 | 1.23 | 1.38 | 1.54 | 1.92 | 2.37 | 2.75 | 2.87 | 3 Dec. | 0.63 | 0.75 | 68¾- 45¼ | 59¼ | 1.40 | 2.4 | 18 | 20.6 |
| Blue Bell, Inc. | Sep. | 1,337 | 1.80 | 1.61 | 1.94 | 1.97 | [3]2.48 | 2.64 | 3.38 | 4.28 | 4.12 | 3 Dec. | 0.54 | 0.38 | 51¾- 28 | 42¼ | 1.20 | 2.8 | 20 | 10.3 |
| ◆Boise Cascade Corp. | Dec. | 9,053 | [1]1.03 | [1]0.77 | [1]0.45 | [1]0.81 | [1]1.12 | [1]1.27 | 1.65 | E1.65 | 1.53 | 9 Sep. | 1.30 | 1.18 | 37½- 17¼ | 25⅞ | 0.25 | 1.0 | 23 | 15.7 |
| ◆Bristol-Myers Co. | Dec. | 25,173 | 0.43 | 0.52 | 0.62 | 0.77 | 0.91 | 1.12 | 1.32 | P1.57 | 1.57 | ...... | ... | ... | 59⅞- 41⅜ | 59⅛ | 0.85 | 1.4 | 20 | 37.7 |
| ◆Carolina Power & Light | Dec. | 11,567 | 1.08 | 1.12 | 1.20 | 1.34 | 1.41 | 1.60 | 1.80 | 1.87 | 1.87 | ...... | ... | ... | 49¾- 38¼ | 43¾ | 1.34 | 3.1 | 10 | 23.4 |
| ◆Celanese Corp. | Dec. | 13,308 | 2.44 | 2.07 | 2.22 | 3.00 | 3.42 | 4.25 | 5.10 | E4.60 | 4.82 | 9 Sep. | 3.79 | 3.51 | 89¾- 41½ | 57¼ | 2.00 | 3.5 | 21 | 12.4 |
| ◆Chemetron Corp. | Dec. | 3,144 | 1.23 | 1.75 | 1.61 | 1.56 | 2.17 | 2.83 | 4.51 | E5.05 | 5.02 | 9 Sep. | 3.27 | 3.78 | 64¾- 34 | 47½ | 1.80 | 3.8 | 21 | 9.4 |
| ◆Chesebrough-Ponds, Inc. | Dec. | 10,372 | 0.46 | 0.50 | 0.64 | 0.73 | 0.81 | 0.97 | 1.08 | P1.21 | 1.21 | ...... | ... | ... | 32 - 20 | 31⅝ | 0.76 | 2.4 | 15 | 26.1 |
| ◆Coca-Cola Co. | Dec. | 28,501 | 1.31 | 1.43 | 1.54 | 1.69 | 1.91 | 2.30 | 2.66 | E3.10 | 3.02 | 9 Sep. | 2.14 | 2.50 | 97 - 71½ | 95 | 1.90 | 2.0 | 13 | 30.6 |
| ◆Consolidated Freightways | Dec. | 5,226 | 0.57 | d0.51 | 0.05 | 0.66 | 0.54 | 1.16 | 1.69 | P2.20 | 2.20 | ...... | ... | ... | 25⅝- 14⅛ | 21⅛ | 0.80 | 3.8 | 90 | 9.6 |
| ◆Cook Coffee | Dec. | 1,668 | 0.89 | 0.90 | 0.74 | 1.15 | 1.64 | 2.28 | 2.86 | P3.27 | 3.27 | ..... | ... | ... | 35⅝- 25 | 32½ | 6% Stk. | .. | 35 | 9.9 |
| ◆Crown Cork & Seal | Dec. | 4,119 | 0.97 | 1.09 | 1.42 | 1.84 | 2.03 | 2.53 | 3.55 | E4.05 | 3.95 | 9 Sep. | 2.70 | 3.10 | 66⅜- 44¾ | 49½ | ... | .. | 25 | 12.2 |
| ◆Delta Airlines, Inc. | Jun. | 6,375 | 0.72 | 0.51 | 0.83 | 1.09 | [4]2.17 | 2.46 | 3.61 | 5.42 | 7.29 | 6 Dec. | 2.26 | 4.14 | 129½- 66¼ | 120 | 1.00 | 0.8 | 45 | 16.5 |
| ◆Diamond International | Dec. | 9,456 | 1.16 | 1.29 | 1.40 | 1.58 | 1.70 | 2.16 | 2.73 | E3.15 | 3.07 | 9 Sep. | 1.92 | 2.26 | 42½- 23⅜ | 40½ | 1.60 | 4.0 | 16 | 12.9 |
| ◆Disney (Walt) Productions | Sep. | 2,013 | 1.75 | d0.70 | 2.37 | 2.71 | 3.39 | 3.62 | 5.73 | 6.16 | 6.09 | 3 Dec. | 1.10 | 1.03 | 94½- 40¾ | 81½ | [5]0.40 | 0.5 | 23 | 13.4 |
| ◆Donnelley (R.R.) & Sons | Dec. | 12,913 | 0.76 | 0.84 | 0.83 | 1.02 | 1.14 | 1.35 | 1.59 | P1.60 | 1.60 | ..... | ... | ... | 47 - 29¼ | 45 | 0.60 | 1.3 | 15 | 28.1 |
| ◆Duke Power Co. | Dec. | 23,033 | 1.08 | 1.10 | 1.14 | 1.26 | 1.33 | 1.48 | 1.66 | 1.72 | 1.72 | ..... | ... | ... | 43¼- 35½ | 42⅞ | 1.20 | 2.8 | 9 | 24.9 |
| ◆Eastman Kodak Co. | Dec. | 80,773 | 1.55 | 1.57 | 1.61 | 1.74 | 1.79 | 2.32 | 3.07 | E3.85 | 3.65 | 9 Sep. | 3.06 | 2.64 | 141¾-105⅛ | 138 | 2.15 | 1.6 | 14 | 35.8 |
| ◆Emerson Electric Co. | Sep. | 8,887 | 1.07 | 1.33 | 1.54 | 1.68 | 1.80 | 2.04 | 2.53 | 2.97 | 3.07 | 3 Dec. | 0.65 | 0.75 | 67½- 47½ | 66 | 1.50 | 2.3 | 14 | 21.5 |

◆Listed on N.Y.S.E. ●Listed on A.S.E. All others listed on regional exchanges or traded over the counter. *Figures for years ended through May shown in prior year's column. A—Actual. E—Estimated. d—Deficit. P—Preliminary. [1]Pro-forma. [2]Plus 2% stock. [3]Plus 3% stock. [4]Includes approximately $0.50 per share attributable to Eastern Airlines strike. [5]Part of dividend subject to Puerto Rican tax. [7]Vote Apr. 27 on 2 for 1 split. [8]Plus 2½% stock. [9]Interim 1966 & 1967.

Page 4

February 20, 1967

Source: Standard & Poor's.

## TABLE 1–4

### Sample Page from John S. Herold's *America's Fastest Growing Companies*

| | Thous. Shares | Exch. | Fiscal Year Ends | Net Income - Dollars Per Share ............Annual.......... | | | | | ......Interim...... | | | Latest 12 Mo. | Fiscal Year Forecast |
|---|---|---|---|---|---|---|---|---|---|---|---|---|---|
| | | | | 1961 | 1962 | 1963 | 1964 | 1965 | Period | 1964 | 1965 | | |
| DOW-JONES INDUSTRIALS | | | | 31.91 | 36.43 | 41.21 | 46.43 | 53.78E | | | | 53.78 | 57.50 |
| Gulf & Western Industries, Inc. | 3,298[a] | NYS | Jul | .87 | 1.27 | 1.52 | 1.97 | 2.53 | 6 Mo Jan | 1.38[f] | 2.81[f] | 3.96 | 5.80 |
| Hercules, Inc. | 19,029 | NYS | Dec | 1.51 | 1.69 | 1.72 | 1.98 | 2.06 | | | | 2.06 | 2.25 |
| Heublein, Inc. | 4,916[b] | NYS | Jun | .80 | .91 | 1.03 | 1.21 | 1.50 | 3 Mo Dec | .78 | .84 | 1.56 | 1.85 |
| Howard Johnson Company | 2,366 | NYS | Dec | 1.86 | 2.09 | 2.40 | 3.24 | 3.80 | | | | 3.80 | ---- |
| Huston, Tom Peanut | 1,645 | OTC | Aug | 1.36 | 1.56 | 1.76 | 1.99 | 2.32 | 12 Wk Nov | .50 | .54 | 2.36 | ---- |
| Illinois Power Company | 12,840 | NYS | Dec | 1.57 | 1.64 | 1.80 | 1.98 | 2.12 | | | | 2.12 | 2.25 |
| International Business Machines | 35,180 | NYS | Dec | 7.35 | 8.76 | 10.44 | 12.30 | 13.54 | | | | 13.54 | 15.50 |
| Int'l. Minerals & Chemical Corp. | 6,307 | NYS | Jun | 1.49 | 1.53 | 1.77 | 2.48 | 3.19 | 6 Mo Dec | 1.07 | 1.28 | 3.40 | 3.80 |
| Jonathan Logan, Inc. | 3,262 | NYS | Dec | .92 | 1.02 | 1.30 | 1.83 | 2.41 | | | | 2.41 | 3.15 |
| Koehring Co. | 2,126 | NYS | Nov | .71 | 1.71 | 2.29 | 3.08 | 3.75 | 3 Mo Feb | .67[f] | 1.08[f] | 4.16 | 4.80 |
| X Kusan, Inc. | 416 | OTC | Nov | (.76) | .23 | .30 | .74 | .96 | 12 Mo Nov | .96 | 1.40 | 1.40 | 1.60 |
| Litton Industries | 22,681 | NYS | Jul | .52 | .78 | 1.09 | 1.35 | 1.73 | 6 Mo Jan | .79[f] | 1.05[f] | 1.99 | 2.15 |
| Loeb, M. Ltd. | 2,532 | TOR | Jan | .23 | .24 | .32 | .45 | .63 | 40 Wk Oct | .45 | .53 | .71 | .75 |
| Londontown Mfg. Co. | 1,576 | OTC | Feb | .22 | .35 | .52 | 1.02 | 1.71 | 9 Mo Nov | 1.34 | 1.55 | 1.93 | 2.00 |
| MCA, Inc. | 4,687 | NYS | Dec | 2.14 | 2.52 | 2.74 | 2.95 | 3.31 | | | | 3.31 | ---- |
| Magnavox Co. | 7,675 | NYS | Dec | 1.19 | 1.73 | 1.54 | 1.88 | 3.00 | | | | 3.00 | 4.00 |
| Manpower, Inc. | 1,421 | OTC | Jun | .59 | .72 | .82 | 1.17 | 1.30 | 6 Mo Dec | .78 | .93 | 1.45 | ---- |
| Mary Carter Paint Co., Class B | 2,433 | ASE | Dec | .49 | .62 | .70 | .79 | | 9 Mo Sep | .63 | .71 | .87 | ---- |
| Maryland Cup | 2,893 | NYS | Sep | 1.09 | 1.22 | 1.43 | 1.69 | 2.04 | 3 Mo Dec | .13 | .16 | 2.07 | 2.25 |
| Masco Corp. | 1,702[a] | ASE | Dec | .45 | .82 | 1.07 | 1.49 | 1.87 | | | | 1.87 | 2.25 |
| Matheson Co., Inc. | 781[a] | OTC | Dec | .76 | 1.05 | 1.09 | 1.37 | 1.72 | | | | 1.72 | 1.95 |
| McDonnell Aircraft | 8,045 | NYS | Jun | 1.72 | 1.88 | 2.28 | 3.26 | 4.01 | 6 Mo Dec | 1.70 | 2.09 | 4.40 | 4.80 |
| Medco, Inc., Class A | 860[a] | ASE | Mar | .19 | .38 | .47 | .60 | .81 | 9 Mo Dec | .78 | .98 | 1.01 | ---- |
| Medtronic, Inc. | 577 | OTC | Apr | (.13) | (.35) | .16 | .26 | .35 | 6 Mo Oct | .16 | .23 | .42 | .50 |
| Miles Laboratories | 4,100 | NYS | Dec | 1.37 | 1.33 | 1.54 | 1.70 | 1.97 | | | | 1.97 | 2.25 |
| Millmaster Onyx Corp. | 2,273 | ASE | Mar | NA | .39 | .50 | .55 | .71 | 9 Mo Dec | .48 | .67 | .90 | ---- |
| Minn. Mining & Mfg. | 53,407 | NYS | Dec | 1.46 | 1.60 | 1.75 | 1.92 | 2.18 | | | | 2.18 | 2.45 |
| Morse Shoe, Inc. | 1,813 | NYS | Dec | .80 | .82 | 1.04 | 1.76 | 2.40 | | | | 2.40 | 2.70 |
| X Murray Ohio Mfg. Co. | 617 | ASE | Dec | 2.74 | 3.31 | 3.32 | 3.86 | 2.63 | | | | 2.63 | ---- |
| National Periodical Pub. | 1,285 | NYS | Sep | .66 | .85 | 1.02 | 1.49 | 1.71 | 3 Mo Dec | .47 | .49 | 1.73 | 2.05 |
| New Jersey Natural Gas | 2,326 | OTC | Sep | .77 | .84 | .95 | 1.06 | 1.19 | 12 Mo Dec | 1.13 | 1.22 | 1.22 | 1.25 |
| Nielsen (A.C.) Co. | 5,130 | OTC | Aug | .47 | .58 | .63 | .74 | .87 | 6 Mo Feb | .37[f] | .51[f] | 1.01 | ---- |
| Norplex Corp. | 715 | OTC | Sep | .27 | .60 | .73 | .92 | 1.48 | 3 Mo Dec | .29 | .35 | 1.54 | 1.85 |
| Northern Illinois Gas Co. | 11,661 | MSE | Dec | 1.49 | 1.77 | 1.96 | 2.08 | 2.23 | 12 Mo Feb | 2.07[f] | 2.20[f] | 2.20 | 2.30 |
| Northwest Airlines | 4,574 | NYS | Dec | 1.11 | 2.39 | 2.86 | 5.86 | 9.99 | 1 Mo Jan | .47[f] | .81[f] | 10.33 | 13.00 |
| Norwich Pharmacal | 3,819 | NYS | Dec | 1.63 | 1.70 | 1.78 | 1.98 | 2.29 | | | | 2.29 | 2.64 |
| Opticks, Inc. | 479 | OTC | Sep | .40 | .67 | .98 | .98 | 1.27 | 3 Mo Dec | .18 | .25 | 1.34 | 1.55 |
| Orange & Rockland Utilities | 4,151 | NYS | Dec | .87 | .98 | 1.02 | 1.18 | 1.32 | | | | 1.32 | 1.45 |
| Oshawa Wholesale, Ltd. | 2,370 | TOR | Jan | .21 | .30 | .39 | .51 | .67 | 52 Wk Jan | .67[f] | .89[f] | .89 | 1.07 |
| Pabst Brewing Company | 4,671 | OTC | Dec | 1.10 | 1.38 | 1.71 | 2.11 | 2.62 | | | | 2.62 | 2.90 |
| Paddington Corp., Class A | 2,666 | ASE | Dec | 1.01 | 1.50 | 1.80 | 2.16 | 2.67 | | | | 2.67 | 3.10 |
| Pargas, Inc. | 2,415 | OTC | Dec | .25 | .43 | .56 | .94 | 1.26 | | | | 1.26 | 1.70 |
| Parkview Drugs, Inc. | 779[a] | OTC | Jul | .52 | .61 | .89 | 1.45 | 1.85 | | | | 1.85 | 2.10 |
| Peabody Coal | 9,797 | NYS | Dec | 1.37 | 1.49 | 1.74 | 2.16 | 2.27 | | | | 2.27 | 2.50 |
| Pennsalt Chemcials | 4,558 | NYS | Dec | 1.40 | 1.61 | 1.78 | 2.03 | 2.27 | | | | 2.27 | 2.60 |
| Peoples Gas Light & Coke | 15,798 | NYS | Dec | 1.83 | 1.96 | 2.14 | 2.35 | 2.62 | | | | 2.62 | 2.80 |
| PepsiCo., Inc. | 10,332 | NYS | Dec | 2.00 | 2.20 | 2.43 | 2.76 | 3.21 | | | | 3.21 | 3.65 |
| Perkin-Elmer Corp. | 2,906 | NYS | Jul | .62 | .75 | .82 | .98 | 1.23 | 6 Mo Jan | .52[f] | .62[f] | 1.33 | 1.50 |
| Petrolane Gas Service | 1,764 | NYS | Sep | 1.02 | 1.20 | 1.28 | 1.40 | 1.63 | 3 Mo Dec | .61 | .64 | 1.66 | 1.80 |
| Pickwick International | 337[d] | OTC | Apr | .19 | .43 | .55 | .65 | .91 | 6 Mo Oct | .39 | .55 | 1.07 | 1.18 |

* IMPORTANT, see explanatory notes at end of table.

(a) Includes provision for full conversion of convertible securities, warrants or options currently outstanding. (b) Excludes substantial number of shares reserved for conversion of preferred stock. Elimination of dividends on latter, however, would approximately offset dividend effect of conversion into common at current level of company earnings. (d) Includes stock reserved for options, warrants and/or convertible debentures. (f) Refers to 1965 and 1966 years. (h) Includes N.J. Zinc.

Source: John S. Herold's *America's Fastest Growing Companies.*

and still win inclusion in Dr. Barnes's list but only if the five-year average growth per year in earnings per share, including the one relatively poor year, was 25% or more. Some of the leading growth stocks on Dr. Barnes' list are shown in Table 1–5.

The larger brokerage houses also publish lists of growth stocks from time to time. They do not always, however, explicitly indicate the statisti-

## TABLE 1–4 (Continued)

| Growth Rate | | | | | Stock | P/E Ratio | | | | | | Write-up |
|---|---|---|---|---|---|---|---|---|---|---|---|---|
| Avg. An'l. | Interim Period | Latest Qtr. | Fore-cast | 4-1 Price | Price Trend | Latest 12 Mo. | Fore-cast | Current Progress | AFGC Rating | Cash Div. | % Yield | Month & Year |
| 14% | 16% | 8% | 7% | $920 | Down | 17 | 16 | Average off 3.4% in March. | - | 28.17 | 3.1 | -------- |
| 30 | 103 | NA | 130 | 101 | Flat | 25 | 17 | Sales are up. | B | .50 | 0.5 | 4-66 |
| 7 | 4 | 0 | 10 | 39 | Down | 19 | 17 | Sales are up. | B- | 1.00 | 2.6 | |
| 17 | 8 | 19 | 23 | 34 | Down | 22 | 18 | Sales up. | B | 1.00 | 2.9 | 2-66 |
| 19 | 17 | 57 | -- | 92 | Up | 24 | -- | Sales up. | B+ | 0 | --- | 3-66 |
| 14 | 8 | 9 | -- | 50 | Flat | 21 | -- | Selling out to Gen'l. Mills. | - | 1.00 | 2.0 | 12-65 |
| 8 | 10 | NA | 6 | 42 | Flat | 20 | 19 | Revenues up. | B | 1.60 | 3.8 | 3-65 |
| 17 | 10 | 9 | 15 | 519 | Up | 38 | 33 | No information available. | B | 6.00 | 0.1 | 2-66 |
| 21 | 20 | 16 | 20 | 79 | Flat | 23 | 21 | Sales up. | B+ | 1.20 | 1.5 | 4-66 |
| 27 | 32 | 55 | 31 | 45 | Up | 19 | 15 | Sales up. | A | .80 | 1.8 | 3-66 |
| 52 | 61 | 61 | 28 | 44 | Up | 11 | 9 | Feb. backlog up 50%. | A | 1.60 | 3.6 | 4-66 |
| 58 | 46 | 29 | 15 | 16 | Up | 11 | 10 | Feb net/sh. flat. | B- | .30 | 1.9 | 2-66 |
| 35 | 33 | 40 | 24 | 80 | Up | 40 | 37 | Sales are up. | B | 0 | 0 | 9-65 |
| 29 | 18 | 13 | 19 | 16 | Flat | 23 | 21 | Sales are up. | B | .10 | 0.6 | 2-66 |
| 67 | 15 | 29 | 17 | 22 | Flat | 11 | 11 | Bookings up 20%. | A | .20 | 0.9 | 4-66 |
| 12 | 12 | 11 | -- | 57 | Up | 17 | -- | No information available. | B | 0 | 0 | 12-65 |
| 26 | 60 | 47 | 33 | 110 | Up | 37 | 28 | Sales and profits are up. | B | 1.60 | 1.4 | 4-66 |
| 24 | 19 | 15 | -- | 35 | Down | 24 | -- | Revenues are up. | B | .48 | 1.4 | 3-66 |
| 17 | 13 | 38 | -- | 11 | Flat | 13 | -- | Progress unknown. | B | 0 | 0 | 3-66 |
| 17 | 23 | 23 | 10 | 46 | Flat | 22 | 20 | Unknown. | B | .50 | 1.1 | 2-66 |
| 43 | 25 | 32 | 20 | 30 | Flat | 16 | 13 | Sales and profits are up. | A | .32 | 1.1 | 3-66 |
| 22 | 25 | 68 | 13 | 23 | Flat | 13 | 12 | Sales up 15%. | A | .20 | 0.9 | 4-65 |
| 24 | 23 | 17 | 20 | 60 | Flat | 14 | 12 | Backlog is up. | A | .60 | 1.0 | 2-66 |
| 44 | 25 | 23 | -- | 11 | Flat | 11 | -- | Sales are up. | B+ | 0 | 0 | 4-65 |
| 42 | 44 | NA | 43 | 13 | Up | 31 | 26 | Sales are up. | B | 0 | 0 | 1-66 |
| 10 | 16 | 7 | 10 | 38 | Down | 19 | 17 | Sees moderate growth this year. | B | 1.00 | 2.6 | 3-66 |
| 22 | 39 | 35 | -- | 11 | Flat | 12 | -- | Sales up. | B | 0 | 0 | |
| 11 | 14 | 18 | 13 | 67 | Flat | 31 | 27 | Sales are up. | B | 1.20 | 1.8 | 2-66 |
| 32 | 36 | 47 | 12 | 24 | Flat | 10 | 9 | Sales and profits are up. | A | .50 | 2.1 | 4-65 |
| 0 | - 32 | -- | -- | 31 | Up | 11 | -- | Strike reduces profits. | B- | 1.40 | 4.7 | |
| 23 | 4 | 4 | 20 | 37 | Up | 21 | 18 | Sales up. | B+ | .80 | 2.2 | 4-66 |
| 11 | 8 | 20 | 5 | 20 | Flat | 16 | 16 | Sales up. | B | .80 | 4.0 | 2-66 |
| 17 | 38 | 40 | -- | 27 | Flat | 27 | -- | Revenues up. | B | .30 | 1.1 | 1-66 |
| 53 | 21 | 21 | 25 | 21 | Flat | 14 | 11 | Earns. up 25% in first 5 mos. | A | .40 | 1.9 | 2-66 |
| 11 | 6 | NA | 3 | 43 | Flat | 19 | 19 | Reduces rates. | B | 1.24 | 2.9 | 4-66 |
| 73 | 72 | 72 | 30 | 199 | Up | 19 | 15 | Adds 12% to jet fleet. | A | 1.20 | 0.6 | 3-66 |
| 8 | 16 | 7 | 15 | 55 | Flat | 24 | 21 | Moderate growth continuing. | B | 1.25 | 2.2 | 2-66 |
| 48 | 39 | 39 | 22 | 21 | Flat | 16 | 14 | Sales up. | A | .64 | 3.0 | 4-66 |
| 11 | 12 | 11 | 8 | 29 | Flat | 22 | 20 | Revenues up. | B | .96 | 3.3 | 4-66 |
| 33 | 33 | 28 | 20 | 27 | Flat | 30 | 25 | Sales up sharply. | B | .20 | 0.7 | 3-66 |
| 24 | 24 | NA | 11 | 37 | Flat | 14 | 13 | Sales up. | B | .50 | 1.3 | 2-66 |
| 27 | 23 | 13 | 16 | 30 | Flat | 11 | 10 | 1st. qtr. profits up 20%-25%. | B+ | 1.40 | 4.6 | 11-65 |
| 50 | 34 | NA | 35 | 25 | Flat | 20 | 15 | Sales up. | B+ | .40 | 1.6 | 3-66 |
| 37 | 28 | NA | 14 | 22 | Flat | 12 | 10 | Plans merger with Gem Int'l. | - | 0 | - | 1-66 |
| 14 | 5 | 4 | 10 | 34 | Down | 15 | 14 | First quarter sales up. | B+ | 1.00 | 2.9 | 2-66 |
| 13 | 12 | 3 | 15 | 46 | Flat | 20 | 18 | Acquires S.S. White Co. | B | 1.15 | 2.5 | 3-66 |
| 9 | 11 | NA | 7 | 40 | Flat | 15 | 14 | Studies merger with No. Ill. Gas. | B | 1.72 | 4.3 | 4-66 |
| 12 | 16 | 12 | 14 | 80 | Flat | 25 | 22 | Acq. Pepsi-Long Island/$7.5 mill. | B | 1.60 | 2.0 | 2-66 |
| 19 | 19 | 17 | 22 | 47 | Up | 35 | 31 | Sales up, record backlog. | B | 0 | - | 4-66 |
| 13 | 5 | 5 | 10 | 21 | Down | 13 | 12 | Revenues up. | B | .70 | 2.9 | 2-66 |
| 48 | 41 | NA | 30 | 11 | Flat | 10 | 9 | Sales up. | A | 0 | - | 4-66 |

cal basis for their selection. Merrill Lynch, Pierce, Fenner & Smith, Inc., once issued an elaborate study of "101 Growth Stocks" and from time to time publishes select lists of growth stocks. A recent example may be seen in Table 1–6. By and large the Merrill Lynch growth stock selections are of the larger, more mature, and more conservative growth companies, whereas the selections in *America's Fastest Growing Companies* tend more to the newer, smaller, and more obscure companies, such as Astrodata, Inc., Coffee-Mat, Coleco Industries, Consultants & Designers, Gulf & Western Industries, Londontown Manufacturing Company, Masco

TABLE 1–5

Some Leading Growth Stocks of the Past Five Years

| | Average Annual Percent Gain in Earnings per Share 1961–65 |
|---|---|
| Bangor Punta Alegre Sugar | 120% |
| W. H. Rorer | 30 |
| Brenco | 162 |
| International Industries | 342 |
| Litton Industries | 37 |
| American Safety Table | 138 |
| Oshawa Wholesale | 32 |
| Coffee-Mat | 104 |
| Quality Importers | 213 |
| Beeline Fashions | 125 |
| Russ Togs | 34 |
| Reeves Bros. | 144 |
| Swank | 53 |
| Automatic Data Processing | 99 |
| Consultants & Designers | 55 |
| Waltham Watch | 243 |
| New York Shipbuilding | 205 |
| Coastal States Gas Prod. | 33 |
| Smith Industries Int'l. | 205 |
| Solitron Devices | 154 |
| Xerox | 88 |
| Londontown Mfg. | 54 |
| Masco | 43 |
| McDonald's Corp. | 439 |
| Syntex | 129 |
| American Enka | 175 |
| Unarco Industries | 327 |
| Koehring | 381 |
| Polaroid | 30 |
| Northwest Airlines | 101 |

Source: Leo Barnes, *Your Investments* (American Research Council, 1967 ed.)

Corporation, Swank, Inc., Valve Corporation, and so on. Of the 20 stocks on the Merrill Lynch list, only two, FMC Corporation and IBM, are to be found on the AFGC list. Thus, growth stocks can mean different things to different people, and it makes a big difference whether psychologically you take a conservative or adventurous view of the market.

Some people, particularly the elderly and retired, buy stock for current income. While in recent years stocks have yielded less, on the average, than bonds or than the return on savings accounts, there are some stocks which may be classed as *income stocks* because they pay a higher than average return. Income stocks are those that yield generous current

**TABLE 1–6A**

**How Growth Stocks Grow***

| | Mid-1953 | Mid-1963 | End 1965 | End 1966 |
|---|---|---|---|---|
| American Cyanamid | $1,000 | $ 2,615 | $ 3,866 | $ 2,726 |
| Bristol-Myers | 1,000 | 15,671 | 30,308 | 34,727 |
| Caterpillar Tractor | 1,000 | 5,356 | 12,358 | 8,694 |
| Corning Glass Works | 1,000 | 5,548 | 7,419 | 10,033 |
| Factor (Max) | 1,000 | 23,484 | 26,182 | 30,188 |
| General Electric | 1,000 | 3,320 | 4,960 | 3,720 |
| Grumman Aircraft | 1,000 | 2,540 | 5,053 | 5,619 |
| Gulf Life Insurance | 1,000 | 4,336 | 3,875 | 2,695 |
| International Business Machines | 1,000 | 14,557 | 20,822 | 23,256 |
| Magnavox | 1,000 | 18,556 | 36,085 | 32,458 |
| Minneapolis-Honeywell | 1,000 | 3,500 | 5,228 | 4,658 |
| Minnesota Mining & Manufacturing | 1,000 | 7,235 | 8,612 | 9,879 |
| Pacific Gas & Electric | 1,000 | 2,601 | 2,990 | 2,929 |
| Pitney-Bowes | 1,000 | 7,557 | 7,461 | 7,442 |
| Polaroid | 1,000 | 33,777 | 101,168 | 137,700 |
| Procter & Gamble | 1,000 | 5,071 | 4,644 | 4,887 |
| Radio Corporation of America | 1,000 | 3,106 | 7,028 | 6,478 |
| Safeway Stores | 1,000 | 4,857 | 5,245 | 4,070 |
| Texaco | 1,000 | 5,646 | 6,759 | 6,012 |
| Union Bank (Los Angeles) | 1,000 | 8,681 | 5,639 | 3,573 |

*The table shows how a $1,000 cash investment in any of 20 different stocks regarded as growth stocks in 1953 would have grown since mid-1953. Full adjustment has been made in this tabulation for splits and stock dividends. But no account has been taken of cash dividends or rights offerings, and no allowance has been made for brokerage fees.

Source: Merrill Lynch, Pierce, Fenner & Smith, Inc.

returns. They are often sought by trust funds, pension funds, university and college endowment funds, charitable and educational foundations, and so on. Selecting income stocks can be a very tricky business. The stock may be paying a high return because price has fallen due to the fact that there is considerable uncertainty as to whether the dividend can be maintained in the light of declining earnings. Or the stock may be that of a lackluster company in an unpopular industry, with little future. Or the company may be located in a foreign area where there is a large risk due to political instability. On the other hand, there may be perfectly good overlooked stocks which are paying high yields because the public has not bid them up due to lack of knowledge.

Examples of each of these types may be illustrated. Baltimore Transit yields over 7% because there is some uncertainty that the dividend can be maintained. O'okiep Copper yields over 15%, Roan Selection Trust over 9%, Telephonos de Mexico over 9%, possibly because of political factors of foreign location. Erratic earnings may be said to account for Florida Capital's yield of over 9%. Real estate companies have disappointed stock investors in the last few years, and this factor may account for the yield of over 6% for First Mortgage Investors, over 7% for First National Real Estate Trust, over 6% for First Union Realty and

**TABLE 1–6B**

**Twenty Stocks for Long-Term Growth**

| Name of Stock | Approximate Price 1/12/67 | Current Annual Dividend Rate | Yield % | Consecutive Years Dividends Paid | 1966–67 Price Range High | 1966–67 Price Range Low |
|---|---|---|---|---|---|---|
| Amer. Electric Power | 39 | $1.44 | 3.7 | 58 | 42⅜* | 31½* |
| Chesebrough-Pond's | 29 | 0.76 | 2.6 | 84 | 32 | 20 |
| Corn Products | 47 | 1.70 | 3.6 | 48 | 53⅞ | 35½ |
| Du Pont | 152 | 5.75† | 3.8 | 63 | 242 | 143¼ |
| FMC Corporation | 31 | 0.75 | 2.4 | 32 | 42 | 29½ |
| General Electric | 87 | 2.60 | 3.0 | 69 | 120 | 80 |
| General Foods | 74 | 2.20 | 3.0 | 45 | 83 | 62¾ |
| Gen. Tel. & Electronics‡ | 46 | 1.28 | 2.8 | 32 | 46⅜ | 35⅝ |
| Goodyear Tire & Rubber | 43 | 1.35 | 3.1 | 31 | 57⅛ | 40¼ |
| Honeywell | 72 | 1.10 | 1.5 | 39 | 96 | 53½ |
| Insurance Co. of No. Amer. | 85 | 2.40 | 2.8 | 94 | 90½ | 68 |
| Int. Business Machines | 392 | 4.40 | 1.1 | 51 | 396½ | 289½ |
| Merck | 75 | 1.40§ | 1.9 | 33 | 81⅞ | 64⅝ |
| Minnesota Mining & Mfg. | 80 | 1.20 | 1.5 | 51 | 86¾ | 61 |
| Radio Corp. of America | 44 | 0.80 | 1.8 | 28 | 61* | 36* |
| Reynolds Metals | 55 | 0.90 | 1.6 | 25 | 66¼ | 38¼ |
| Scott Paper | 27 | 1.00 | 3.7 | 53 | 39⅞ | 25⅜ |
| Sears, Roebuck | 46 | 1.00§ | 2.2 | 33 | 65¾ | 44⅛ |
| Standard Oil Co. of Calif. | 61 | 2.50‖ | 4.1 | 55 | 81⅞* | 52½* |
| Xerox | 225 | 1.00 | 0.4 | 40 | 267¾ | 125¼ |

* Adjusted for stock dividend. † Paid last year.
‡ Offering of issue based on data contained in prospectus. § Excludes extra. ‖ Plus stock.
Source: Merrill Lynch, Pierce, Fenner & Smith, Inc.

for Levitt & Sons, and over 9% for Futterman. On the other hand, you probably never heard of Belknap Hardware. It has paid dividends each year since 1880 and sells at 9¾, yielding over 8.20%. Union Stockyards has paid dividends since 1884 and yields over 6%. A substantial list of stocks yielding 6% or more could be provided. There would be a substantial element of risk involved in some. At the 5% to 6% level, more conservative selections may be found. In its Annual Forecast for 1966, Standard & Poor's recommended the following five stocks yielding 5% in December, 1965:

| | December, 1965 | | October, 1966 | |
|---|---|---|---|---|
| Chesapeake & Ohio | 77 | 5.2% | 61½ | 6.5 |
| General Motors | 101 | 5.2 | 73 | 7.2 |
| Kansas City Southern Industries | 39 | 5.1 | 33⅞ | 6.0 |
| U.S. Gypsum | 64 | 5.0 | 46¾ | 6.4 |
| U.S. Tobacco | 32 | 5.2 | 28⅛ | 5.7 |

In addition, for the conservative investor a number of public utility preferred stocks are available yielding 5% or more. For those who seek current income, there are even companies such as American Home Products, Scott & Fetzer, Winn-Dixie Stores, Wrigley, and so on, that pay dividends monthly so that a portfolio may be arranged providing regular monthly income.

Some stocks are characterized as "*defensive.*" By this is meant stocks which are regarded as stable and relatively safe, especially in a period of declining business activity. In a period of economic weakness these stocks tend to decline less than other more glamorous market leaders, and some types may actually rise. The shares of electric utility and gas companies are generally regarded as the best defensive issues. Selected issues which have combined stability and growth over the years are shown in Table 1–7. In fact, a number of these issues can be said also to be blue chip or growth stocks or both. Texas Utilities, for example, has paid dividends

**TABLE 1–7**
**Selected Electric Utility "Defensive Stocks"**

| | *% Compound Growth Rate 1961–65* | *1965 Price Range* | |
|---|---|---|---|
| | | *High* | *Low* |
| American Electric Power | 10 | 48 | 41 |
| Arizona Public Service | 3½ | 43 | 34 |
| Boston Edison | 8 | 50 | 43 |
| Carolina Power and Light | 11 | 52 | 41 |
| Central Illinois Electric and Gas | 10 | 33 | 27 |
| Commonwealth Edison | 8 | 58 | 51 |
| Consumers Power | 10 | 61 | 54 |
| Detroit Edison | 9½ | 39 | 35 |
| Florida Power | 8 | 52 | 45 |
| Hartford Electric | 16 | 58 | 50 |
| Houston Lighting and Power | 18 | 57 | 50 |
| Kansas City Power and Light | 8 | 50 | 44 |
| Nevada Power | 12 | 53 | 42 |
| Niagara Mohawk Power | 9 | 30 | 25 |
| Oklahoma Gas and Electric | 14 | 34 | 28 |
| Orange and Rockland Utilities | 11 | 35 | 29 |
| Pacific Gas and Electric | 9 | 40 | 34 |
| Pacific Power and Light | 7 | 28 | 26 |
| Public Service of Colorado | 4 | 35 | 28 |
| Public Service Electric and Gas (N.J.) | 8 | 44 | 38 |
| Rochester Gas and Electric | 9 | 40 | 35 |
| Southern California Edison | 8 | 43 | 36 |
| The Southern Company | 9 | 72 | 63 |
| Tampa Electric | 15 | 30 | 25 |
| Texas Utilities | 9 | 68 | 59 |
| Virginia Electric and Power | 9 | 53 | 45 |

Source: Bear, Stearns & Co., "Monthly Comparison of Electric Utility Common Stocks."

uninterruptedly since 1917 and has risen in price from 4¾[4] to 66 over recent decades. A brokerage house study, "Investing in Electric Utilities"[5] compared the earnings per share of Moody's electric utility average with the record of earnings for Moody's industrial average and found that over the period 1950–64, earnings per share for the utilities rose 106.5%, while the comparable figure for industrials was 70.3%.

Other defensive issues are found among companies whose products suffer relatively little in recession periods. These include shares in companies producing tobacco, snuff, soft drinks, gum, candy bars, and so forth. Also, companies that provide essentials of life, particularly food and drugs, tend to hold up well. Packaged food and grocery chain companies are examples. One type of company that is preeminently defensive is the gold mine. In a recession or depression, while all other prices may go down, the price of gold either remains fixed or is raised, while costs of mining decrease. As a result, in bear markets gold-mining shares have tended to rise. In the Great Depression, for example, the price of the old Homestake Mining stock, the foremost gold producer in the United States went from 81 in 1931 to 544 in 1936, mainly as a result of the increase of the price of gold and the devaluation of the dollar.

Considerably different from the defensive stocks are the *cyclical shares*. A cyclical company is one whose earnings fluctuate with the business cycle and are accentuated by it. When business conditions improve, the company's profitability is restored and enhanced. The common stock price rises. When conditions deteriorate, business for the cyclical company falls off sharply, and its profits are greatly diminished. One brokerage house, Goodbody & Company, in a monthly letter discussed "Automobiles and Heavy Trucks—Growth Prospects in a Cyclical Industry." Another, Thomson & McKinnon, in a bulletin entitled "Profit Opportunities in Cyclical Stocks," reviewed six machine tool and heavy machinery manufacturers.

One of *Forbes*' market commentators declared:

Cyclical stocks for months have been "unwanted" stocks. The business cycle has been against them. Earnings have been declining. Most of them are not "growth" stocks, and most of them lack the glamour people have been seeking in issues representative of the electronics and advanced science industries. It is my opinion that traders and cyclical investors should take a long look at equities of the type tabulated below. I reason: (1) that the business cycle is near a probable turning point, (2) that these stocks are way down while the glamour issues are way up and (3) that investors this year will begin to look more at neglected values than at the overromanced shares. The tabulation

---

[4] Adjusted for stock splits.

[5] Shearson, Hammill & Co. Inc., New York, 1965.

speaks for itself. It shows that many cyclical issues, while up a little from their lows are selling at 20% to 60% under their former bull market highs.[6]

This was a remarkable case of a forecast of the upturn in the business cycle. It was written in January, 1961, and the National Bureau of Economic Research dated the upturn as starting in February, 1961. Over the next four years many of the stocks in the industries listed as cyclical—the building industry, chemicals, coppers, machinery, paper, rails, steels, and so forth—moved up sharply in the ensuing business expansion.

Webster defines "speculation" as a "transaction or venture the profits of which are conjectural. . . ." In this sense all common stock investment is speculative. When you buy shares you have no promise, no certainty that the funds you receive ultimately when you sell the stock will be more, less, or the same as the dollars you originally paid. Since they provide a variable rather than a fixed dollar outcome, common shares are speculative in Webster's sense. Yet in the accepted parlance of the Street, *speculative* shares or *speculative* stock has a more limited meaning. High-flying glamour stocks are speculative. Likewise, hot new issues and penny mining stocks are speculative. Other types could be identified as they come and go from time to time. Some are easy to identify, some more difficult. The high-flying glamour stocks can usually be identified by their very high price-earnings ratios. For example, at a time when the Dow-Jones Industrials were selling at about 18.5 times earnings, 12 leading runaway stocks were selling at the following multiples of their then most recent 12 months' earnings:

| *Stock* | *Price-Earnings Ratio** |
|---|---|
| National Video | 121 |
| Molybdenum | 103 |
| Polaroid | 85 |
| Xerox | 89 |
| Packard Bell | 79 |
| Syntex | 70 |
| Solitron | 66 |
| Fairchild Camera | 58 |
| Technical Operations | 57 |
| Texas Gulf Sulphur | 55 |
| Rollins Broadcasting | 52 |
| Electronics Associates | 50 |

* With the decline of the market in 1966, by October the price-earnings ratio for National Video was down to 16.4, for Molybdenum to 27.1, for Polaroid to 37.5, for Xerox to 33.9, for Packard Bell to 11.8, for Syntex to 29.5, for Solitron to 27.4, and for Fairchild Camera to 18.4.

[6] L. O. Hooper, "Time to Look at Cyclical Stocks," *Forbes*, January 15, 1961, p. 36.

The average price-earnings ratio for this group was 65! Speculative buying of these shares would appear to be discounting the future quite far ahead. As a famous Dow Theory disciple, William P. Hamilton, wrote back in the 1920's: "A bull market runs until it outruns values: in the final stage it is discounting possibilities only."

There usually comes a point in a bull market when small, hitherto unknown companies go public, or little new companies are formed, and the offering of their low-priced shares finds a fierce speculative demand. Prices double, triple, or even quadruple within a few days after issuance. Dynatronics issued at 7½, went to 25 overnight. Resitron Laboratories went from 1 to 3⅞. Cove Vitamin soared from 3⅛ to 60. Simulmatics, a two-year-old company with a net worth of minus $21,000 offered stock to the public at 2, and within a few hours it was quoted at 9. While stocks in companies with names ending in "tron" or "ics" were particularly coveted, even prosaically named issues like Leaseway Transportation and Mother's Cookie Company leaped 50 percent or more in price.

*Business Week* wrote of a new company devoted to ocean treasure hunts, Treasure Hunters, Inc., of Washington, which registered 1.9 million shares with the SEC. The company proposed to offer stock at $1 per share. According to its prospectus, the company "will primarily engage in the search for, and the recovery and sale of, sunken cargoes and buried treasure." Treasure Hunters' first project was to have been "to search for the unsalvaged silver, gold, and jewels that went to the bottom of Vigo Bay, Spain, in October, 1702." If all went well, its second undertaking was to have been a hunt for the "dozen wrecks of the Spanish treasure fleet which were lost during a violent storm off the Bahamas in November, 1643." In periods of intense excitement in the market, shares of this type sell readily, often soar in price, and then in due course, in most cases—but not all—fall drastically or disappear.

Perhaps the lowest level of speculative stocks are the penny mining and oil shares. A broker specializing in such shares circulated his market report and offers extensively by mail, and his combination packets read almost like a stamp dealer's. In one report he plugged Trans-Mountain Uranium Company, Globe Hill Mining Company, and Santa Fe International. His write-up on the first two companies was as follows:

*Trans-Mountain Uranium Co.:* Company has ore stockpiled at the Lucky Boy tungsten mine and are anxious to make shipments to the new Min-Con mill located about 14 miles distant. This mill is now in final stages of completion and am told they had expected to be ready for milling ores by October 15th. However, believe will take a little extra time before completed. We are all hoping to hear soon that Trans-Mountain is again shipping tungsten ore. The shares of stock are low at present price of 2¢.

*Globe Hill Mining Company:* has been doing development work on their Beryllium claims located near the U.S. Beryllium mine at Badger Flats and are planning to make ore shipment in near future. A stockholder letter from the company is expected to be mailed out at any time and this report should carry much information as to development of properties. Globe Hill shares active and present price $6.00 a thousand.

The mail-order broker's packet offer read:

*Combination Offer*—Following combination orders will be filled for whatever number combinations desired while can locate stock in above 3 companies to fill at price shown below: (bonus 1000 United Empire Gold with each combination order)

1,000 Trans-Mountain, 1,000 Santa Fe and 5,000 Globe Hill Mining, $63.75.

Thus common stock investment can range from buying shares in the staid and stable First National Bank of Boston, which has paid dividends uninterruptedly for the past 180 years, to buying Trans-Mountain Uranium at 2 cents per share. Obviously, with so wide a diversity in common stock, generalizations are both difficult and hazardous. It is fairly clear, however, that in recent years both individuals and institutional investment managers have been turning increasingly to common stock investment, both for capital gains and to hedge against inflation.

### Who Buys What

What they have been buying may in part be ascertained from lists of the most popular stocks of various types of investors. Table 1–8 compares the selections of the small investors (Monthly Investment Plan and Odd-Lot-Favorites) with those of the large investors (Savings Banks and Institutional Favorites). The first two listings show the preferences of the small investors as compiled by the New York Stock Exchange: the top 25 favorites of the Monthly Investment Plan participants who buy stocks regularly for as little as $40 every three months, and the favorite 25 stocks of the odd-lotters, those who buy less than 100 shares at a time. The choices of the pros make up the other two lists. The savings banks group comprises the 25 stocks most favored by the New York State savings banks as reflected in the portfolio of the banks' fund, the Institutional Investors Mutual Fund. The final list, compiled by *Data Digest,* is made up of the favorites of more than 2,100 financial institutions—insurance companies, investment companies, common trust funds, etc.

The lists (in Table 1–8) show the pros and the small investors in agreement on five blue chips—IBM, A.T.&T., Sears, Roebuck, Standard Oil of New Jersey, and General Electric. Five other stocks appear on three of the four lists—Ford, General Motors, Eastman Kodak, Texaco, and Xerox. Neither Ford nor General Motors was on the savings banks list, although they were on the other three lists. Texaco and Kodak were on both "Big Investors" lists. Institutional buyers showed marked preference for oil and chemical stocks, with more than half of their top 25 stocks in those categories. Interestingly, 14 stocks appear on both the MIP and the Institutional Favorites lists.

TABLE 1–8

| THE SMALL INVESTOR | | THE BIG INVESTOR | |
|---|---|---|---|
| *MIP FAVORITES* | *ODD-LOT FAVORITES* | *SAVINGS BANKS FAVORITES* | *INSTITUTIONAL FAVORITES* |
| American Tel. & Tel. Co. | American Tel. & Tel. Co. | Beneficial Finance Co. | General Motors Corp. |
| General Motors Corp. | General Motors Corp. | General Cable Corp. | Standard Oil (N.J.) |
| General Tel. & Electronics | Radio Corp. of America | Peoples Gas Light & Coke Co. | American Tel. & Tel. Co. |
| Radio Corp. of America | Xerox Corp. | Caterpillar Tractor Co. | General Electric Co. |
| Int'l. Business Machines | Chrysler Corp. | U.S. Fidelity & Guaranty Co. | Int'l. Business Machines |
| Sears, Roebuck & Co. | Texas Gulf Sulphur Co. | Merck & Co. | Texaco, Inc. |
| General Electric Co. | Ford Motor Co. | American Electric Power Co. | Du Pont de Nemours (E.I.) & Co. |
| Tri-Continental Corp. | Gen. Tel. & Electronics | American Tel. & Tel. Co. | Union Carbide Co. |
| Standard Oil (N.J.) | Int'l. Business Machines | Sunbeam Corp. | Socony Mobil Oil Co. |
| Minnesota Mining & Mfg. Co. | Westinghouse Electric Corp. | Sears, Roebuck & Co. | Gulf Oil Corp. |
| Pacific Gas & Electric Co. | Sperry Rand Corp. | Hartford Fire Insurance Co. | Sears, Roebuck & Co. |
| Eastman Kodak Co. | Control Data Corp. | Standard Oil (N.J.) | Eastman Kodak Co. |
| Standard Oil of Calif. | Pan American World Airways | Celanese Corp. of America | Ford Motor Co. |
| Dow Chemical Co. | Standard Oil (N.J.) | May Department Stores | Phillips Petroleum Co. |
| Safeway Stores | Communications Satellite Corp. | Socony Mobil Oil Co. | Standard Oil of Calif. |
| Scott Paper Co. | U.S. Steel Corp. | Burlington Industries, Inc. | Monsanto Co. |
| Gulf Oil Corp. | Bethlehem Steel Corp. | Continental Oil Co. | Internat'l. Paper |
| Pfizer (Chas.) & Co. | American Motors Corp. | Texaco, Inc. | First Nat'l. City Bank |
| Texaco, Inc. | Reynolds (R.J.) Tobacco Co. | Xerox Corp. | National Lead |
| Du Pont de Nemours (E.I.) & Co. | American Tobacco Co. | Cluett, Peabody & Co. | American Electric Power |
| Xerox Corp. | Sears, Roebuck & Co. | Coca-Cola Co. | General Foods |
| Phillips Petroleum Co. | General Electric Co. | General Electric Co. | American Cyanamid |
| Merck & Co. | Continental Air Lines, Inc. | Eastman Kodak Co. | Standard Oil (Ind.) |
| Lehman Corp. | Parke, Davis & Co. | Monsanto Co. | Dow Chemical |
| Ford Motor Co. | Brunswick Corp. | Int'l. Business Machines | Southern Calif. Edison |

Latest available data: New York Stock Exchange, Institutional Investors Mutual Fund, *Data Digest.*
Source: *Forbes,* October 1, 1965.

Each quarter it is possible to ascertain on a continuing and comparable basis what one large segment of institutional investors—the investment companies—are buying, selling, and holding. The 50 most popular listed stocks held by investment companies, ranked by dollar value, are shown in Table 1–9. Blue chips and major growth stocks predominate, with oil and

## TABLE 1–9

### Vickers Favorite Fifty

| RANK BY $ VALUE | | | | | STOCKS | $ Value (Millions) | § No. Fds. Holding | Number Shares Held | % Outst. Stk. Held by Fds. |
|---|---|---|---|---|---|---|---|---|---|
| Dec. 31 1963 | Dec. 31 1964 | Dec. 31 1965 | Mar. 31 1966 | June 30 1966 | | | | | |
| 1 | 1 | 1 | 1 | 1 | INTERNATIONAL BUSINESS MACHINES | 1256 | 219 | 3,582,800 | 6.6 |
| 9 | 12 | 5 | 3 | 2 | XEROX CORPORATION | 534 | 124 | 2,174,100 | 10.3 |
| - | 44 | 8 | 5 | 3 | POLAROID CORPORATION | 504 | 102 | 3,549,200 | 22.5 |
| 4 | 3 | 2 | 2 | 4 | GENERAL MOTORS CORPORATION | 497 | 182 | 6,177,000 | 2.2 |
| 14 | 13 | 7 | 7 | 5 | EASTMAN KODAK COMPANY | 450 | 115 | 3,499,700 | 4.3 |
| 3 | 4 | 3 | 4 | 6 | TEXACO INC. | 449 | 144 | 6,384,800 | 4.7 |
| - | 49 | 20 | 8 | 7 | NORTHWEST AIRLINES, INC. | 424 | 80 | 3,748,300 | 41.0 |
| 2 | 2 | 4 | 6 | 8 | STANDARD OIL COMPANY (NEW JERSEY) | 418 | 171 | 6,080,100 | 2.8 |
| 10 | 10 | 6 | 9 | 9 | GENERAL ELECTRIC COMPANY | 330 | 115 | 3,112,300 | 3.4 |
| - | 22 | 18 | 14 | 10 | AVON PRODUCTS, INC. | 257 | 56 | 3,104,900 | 10.8 |
| 8 | 7 | 10 | 12 | 11 | GULF OIL CORPORATION | 254 | 100 | 5,088,300 | 4.9 |
| 13 | 11 | 13 | 10 | 12 | INTERNATIONAL NICKEL OF CANADA | 254 | 123 | 2,890,500 | 9.8 |
| 11 | 8 | 9 | 11 | 13 | MOBIL OIL CORPORATION | 253 | 105 | 5,889,500 | 5.8 |
| 6 | 5 | 11 | 13 | 14 | ROYAL DUTCH PETROLEUM COMPANY | 250 | 100 | 6,430,100 | 6.6 |
| 18 | 14 | 17 | 19 | 15 | INTERNATIONAL TELEPHONE & TELEGRAPH | 245 | 80 | 3,306,800 | 16.2 |
| - | - | 22 | 18 | 16 | BOEING COMPANY | 225 | 87 | 3,130,000 | 16.1 |
| - | - | - | 26 | 17 | PAN AMERICAN WORLD AIRWAYS | 224 | 64 | 3,167,200 | 20.4 |
| 5 | 19 | .14 | 20 | 18 | AMERICAN TELEPHONE & TELEGRAPH | 217 | 123 | 3,952,600 | 0.8 |
| - | - | - | - | 19 | *TRANS WORLD AIRLINES | 216 | 61 | 2,404,800 | 27.0 |
| 37 | 24 | 19 | 24 | 20 | GENERAL TELEPHONE & ELECTRONICS | 214 | 94 | 5,094,300 | 5.6 |
| 28 | - | - | 41 | 21 | MINNESOTA MINING & MANUFACTURING | 211 | 70 | 2,861,200 | 5.4 |
| - | - | 16 | 17 | 22 | WESTINGHOUSE ELECTRIC CORPORATION | 200 | 86 | 3,817,000 | 10.2 |
| - | - | 33 | 22 | 23 | UNITED AIR LINES, INC. | 196 | 74 | 3,060,700 | 18.9 |
| - | - | 35 | 25 | 24 | ANACONDA COMPANY | 188 | 76 | 2,256,500 | 20.6 |
| - | - | - | 30 | 25 | TEXAS INSTRUMENTS, INC. | 185 | 52 | 1,614,800 | 16.0 |
| 20 | 21 | 47 | 39 | 26 | COLUMBIA BROADCASTING SYSTEM | 185 | 57 | 3,340,800 | 16.3 |
| - | - | 28 | 15 | 27 | MOTOROLA, INC. | 183 | 63 | 1,073,400 | 17.6 |
| 29 | 20 | 15 | 23 | 28 | UNION CARBIDE CORPORATION | 181 | 85 | 3,077,100 | 5.1 |
| - | - | 39 | 35 | 29 | UNITED AIRCRAFT CORPORATION | 176 | 83 | 2,042,500 | 17.8 |
| 7 | 6 | 12 | 16 | 30 | FORD MOTOR COMPANY | 176 | 77 | 3,872,200 | 3.5 |
| 38 | 38 | 34 | 33 | 31 | MERCK & COMPANY | 173 | 51 | 2,242,000 | 6.9 |
| 21 | 23 | 21 | 21 | 32 | STANDARD OIL COMPANY OF CALIFORNIA | 173 | 79 | 2,702,000 | 3.6 |
| - | - | - | 43 | 33 | DELTA AIR LINES, INC. | 167 | 55 | 1,518,000 | 23.8 |
| - | 46 | 36 | 31 | 34 | AMERICAN AIRLINES, INC. | 166 | 58 | 2,213,100 | 24.7 |
| - | - | - | 44 | 35 | REYNOLDS METALS COMPANY | 166 | 70 | 3,030,300 | 18.2 |
| - | - | - | - | 36 | *EASTERN AIR LINES | 165 | 53 | 1,585,700 | 35.9 |
| - | - | 31 | 34 | 37 | LITTON INDUSTRIES, INC. | 163 | 70 | 2,177,600 | 10.7 |
| 26 | 25 | 38 | 49 | 38 | GOODYEAR TIRE & RUBBER COMPANY | 160 | 56 | 3,166,200 | 8.9 |
| 23 | 9 | 23 | 27 | 39 | MONSANTO COMPANY | 157 | 81 | 2,378,700 | 7.5 |
| 15 | 17 | 42 | 46 | 40 | AMERADA PETROLEUM CORPORATION | 156 | 45 | 1,942,000 | 15.2 |
| 41 | 50 | 30 | 32 | 41 | LOCKHEED AIRCRAFT CORPORATION | 155 | 76 | 2,497,600 | 22.5 |
| 16 | 16 | 25 | 36 | 42 | SOUTHERN COMPANY | 153 | 58 | 4,975,300 | 10.5 |
| 19 | 15 | 24 | 42 | 43 | CONTINENTAL OIL COMPANY | 152 | 57 | 2,435,600 | 11.2 |
| 34 | - | 40 | 29 | 44 | RADIO CORPORATION OF AMERICA | 150 | 76 | 3,037,000 | 5.1 |
| 27 | 27 | 26 | 37 | 45 | SOUTHERN PACIFIC COMPANY | 140 | 60 | 4,059,200 | 15.0 |
| - | - | - | - | 46 | **ALCAN ALUMINIUM LTD. | 138 | 102 | 3,897,300 | 12.5 |
| - | - | 50 | 47 | 47 | KENNECOTT COPPER CORPORATION | 136 | 62 | 3,758,200 | 11.3 |
| - | - | - | 48 | 48 | ZENITH RADIO CORPORATION | 135 | 54 | 1,948,600 | 10.4 |
| 36 | 45 | - | - | 49 | **LOUISIANA LAND & EXPLORATION | 135 | 37 | 2,747,400 | 15.2 |
| - | - | - | - | 50 | **DEERE & COMPANY | 132 | 44 | 1,949,000 | 13.2 |

* NEWCOMER ** RETURNEE

DISPLACED: Armco Steel Corporation - Chrysler Corporation - Pennsylvania Railroad - Syntex Corporation - Union Oil Company of California

§ The figures in this column have been adjusted for late reporting funds and may not agree completely with RANK BY NUMBER OF INVESTMENT COMPANIES.

### SUMMARY OF FAVORITE FIFTY BY INDUSTRY

dollar value of stocks by industry to total dollar value of favorite fifty

| | 6/30/66 | 3/31/66 | 12/31/65 | 12/31/64 | 12/31/63 |
|---|---|---|---|---|---|
| OIL & NATURAL GAS | 18.0% | 19.1% | 22.6% | 31.0% | 30.1% |
| OFFICE EQUIPMENT | 14.4 | 13.4 | 12.7 | 10.1 | 11.7 |
| ELECTRIC & ELECTRONICS | 12.8 | 13.5 | 10.5 | 4.3 | 6.4 |
| AIRLINES | 12.5 | 8.5 | 4.3 | 2.0 | - |
| LEISURE | 9.2 | 8.3 | 6.9 | 4.6 | 3.6 |
| METALS & MINING | 7.1 | 6.1 | 4.6 | 2.4 | 2.1 |
| CHEMICALS & DRUGS | 6.2 | 7.7 | 7.7 | 11.5 | 9.3 |
| MOTORS | 5.4 | 8.4 | 9.8 | 11.0 | 8.4 |
| MISCELLANEOUS | 14.4 | 15.0 | 20.9 | 23.1 | 28.4 |
| | 100.0% | 100.0% | 100.0% | 100.0% | 100.0% |

Source: *Vickers Guide to Investment Company Portfolios.* 

## TABLE 1–9 (Continued)

### CANDIDATES

| STOCKS | $ Value (Mil.) | No. Fds Holding | Number Shares Held | STOCKS | $ Value (Mil.) | No. Fds. Holding | Number Shares Held |
|---|---|---|---|---|---|---|---|
| Union Oil Co. of California | 129.4 | 48 | 2,435,200 | National Airlines, Inc. | 110.0 | 49 | 1,302,000 |
| Texas Utilities Co. | 129.1 | 63 | 2,341,100 | Burlington Industries | 108.4 | 48 | 2,753,100 |
| Shell Oil Co. | 129.0 | 31 | 2,159,800 | W. R. Grace & Co. | 108.2 | 50 | 2,326,000 |
| Honeywell, Inc. | 127.7 | 65 | 1,507,200 | Standard Oil Co. (Indiana) | 107.5 | 56 | 2,349,500 |
| Florida Power & Light | 126.3 | 50 | 1,732,500 | International Paper | 107.1 | 70 | 3,930,000 |
| Chrysler Corp. | 125.8 | 92 | 3,224,600 | American Electric Power | 105.5 | 52 | 2,730,700 |
| Atlantic Richfield Co. | 124.8 | 52 | 1,659,000 | Sinclair Oil Corp. | 104.8 | 62 | 1,717,500 |
| Aluminum Co. of America | 123.5 | 62 | 1,494,600 | Massey-Ferguson, Ltd. | 103.5 | 73 | 3,234,400 |
| Armco Steel Corp. | 121.4 | 47 | 2,273,600 | E. I. duPont | 101.4 | 75 | 540,100 |
| Sears, Roebuck & Co. | 120.5 | 71 | 2,176,100 | Fairchild Camera & Instrument | 100.6 | 27 | 597,000 |
| Magnavox Co. | 119.9 | 44 | 2,404,100 | Corning Glass Works | 100.6 | 47 | 350,400 |
| Central & South West Corp. | 119.4 | 52 | 2,713,400 | Burroughs Corp. | 99.7 | 38 | 1,416,600 |
| Pennsylvania Railroad Co. | 119.2 | 53 | 2,060,400 | Arkansas Louisiana Gas | 98.9 | 37 | 2,254,300 |
| Gillette Co. | 118.1 | 55 | 3,203,700 | Federated Department Stores | 98.3 | 46 | 1,545,100 |
| Syntex Corp. | 113.6 | 55 | 1,224,300 | Chas. Pfizer & Co., Inc. | 95.3 | 52 | 1,466,600 |

### SELECTED STOCKS GAINING FAVOR

| STOCKS | $ Value (Mil.) | No. Fds. Holding | Number Shares Held | STOCKS | $ Value (Mil.) | No. Fds. Holding | Number Shares Held |
|---|---|---|---|---|---|---|---|
| Addressograph-Multigraph | 40.9 | 32 | 639,000 | Kaiser Aluminum & Chemical | 66.7 | 36 | 1,502,000 |
| Allegheny Ludlum Steel | 38.3 | 20 | 814,600 | KLM Royal Dutch Airlines | 28.5 | 16 | 233,500 |
| Armour & Co. | 45.9 | 27 | 1,232,300 | Martin-Marietta Corp. | 47.2 | 26 | 1,988,700 |
| Canteen Corp. | 22.2 | 12 | 836,600 | Otis Elevator | 28.5 | 17 | 615,900 |
| Continental Air Lines | 24.2 | 19 | 341,500 | Parke, Davis & Co. | 41.6 | 29 | 1,335,000 |
| General Aniline & Film | 3.2 | 8 | 135,300 | Pitney-Bowes, Inc. | 17.8 | 17 | 326,300 |
| General Precision Equipment | 15.0 | 13 | 293,400 | Revlon, Inc. | 41.5 | 43 | 882,700 |
| Gulf & Western Industries | 47.0 | 24 | 1,503,600 | SCM Corp. | 35.6 | 17 | 459,100 |
| International Harvester | 65.0 | 36 | 1,436,200 | Swift & Co. | 47.2 | 29 | 910,000 |
| Johnson & Johnson | 42.2 | 14 | 225,200 | Swingline, Inc. | 23.2 | 20 | 533,900 |

### COMMENTS

The 48th issue of Vickers Favorite 50 covers the common stock holdings of about 485 investment companies with combined assets of approximately $48 billion. The market value on June 30, 1966 of the 50 stocks was $12.4 billion, approximately 25% of total fund assets, against $12.6 billion as of March 31, 1966. The number of shares totalled 164 million and the average market price per share was $75¾ compared with approximately $82⅝ on March 31st and $78⅛ on December 31, 1965.

Vickers Favorite 50 Index stood at 781.23 as of June 30, 1966 against 793.29 at the end of March, a drop of 1.5%. This compares with a drop of 5.9% in the Dow-Jones Industrials from 924.77 to 870.10. Going a step further, at December '65 our Index was 728.74 and on June 30, 1965 was 600.81, representing increases to June '66 of 7.2% and 30.0%. The DJI was 969.26 at '65 year-end and 868.03 on June 30, 1965, representing a decrease of 10.2% from December to June '66 and an increase of 0.2% for the year.

TRANS WORLD AIRLINES, INC. - More investment companies bought more shares....1,559,300....of TWA in the June quarter than they have ever bought of any stock in a three-month period. At the end of the March 1966 quarter, 33 investment companies owned 845,500 shares of TWA worth $59 million, representing 9.7% of the outstanding common. As of June 30, 1966, they owned 2,404,800 shares worth $216 million, representing 27%....up 17.3%. As a result of this buying, TWA bypassed the Candidates and moved into 19th spot.

Why such interest? We contacted some of the major buyers for the answer. They were unanimous in stating that not only did they like TWA stock, but because of the size of the secondary offering they were able to buy a very substantial block at one fell swoop. These fund executives put it this way ....the market is thin on the offering side as well as on the bid side, and it is extremely difficult for a large block buyer to pick up a worthwhile quantity of a stock in which he has a real interest.

SUMMARY BY INDUSTRY - Our Summary by Industry Group shows a further decline in Oil & Natural Gas to 18%. Two leading oil stocks, TEXACO and STD. OIL (N.J.), both down approximately 300,000 shares, along with displaced UNION OIL were responsible. Airlines showed the sharpest gain from 8.5% to 12.5%, the result of two Newcomers, TWA and EASTERN AIR LINES. The total market value of the seven airline stocks now in the Favorite 50 is $1.6 billion, a dollar increase since March of $493 million or 46%. On the other hand, Motors had the sharpest drop from 8.4% to 5.4%, caused by sizable selling in G.M. (-717,300 shares), FORD (-859,000 shares) the most heavily sold stock, and Displaced CHRYSLER (-360,100 shares). This resulted in a dollar decrease since March of $390 million or 37%.

LEADERS - I.B.M.'s hold on first place is stronger than ever, with a dollar value of $1.3 billion, more than double the $534 million invested in 2nd-place XEROX. POLAROID moved into 3rd place on an increase in holdings of 239,000 shares.

LARGEST GAINERS IN RANK - M.M.M. showed the biggest gain, moving up 20 places from 41st to 21st spot, largely because of an increase in fund holdings of 568,300 shares. C.B.S. (+264,500 shares) was up 13 positions, from 39th to 26th. Next in line were GOODYEAR and DELTA with gains of 11 and 10 places respectively, both bucking the downward market trend.

LARGEST LOSERS IN RANK - R.C.A. (-262,600 shares) showed the biggest drop in rank, falling 15 places from 29th to 44th, followed by FORD, down 14 spots. MOTOROLA and MONSANTO lost 12 places each, casualties of market action.

NEWCOMERS AND RETURNEES - Newcomer TWA has been discussed above. Increase in holdings of EASTERN AIR LINES (+493,700 shares) moved it into 36th position. Returnee ALCAN, in 46th place, was one of the more heavily bought issues (+531,000 shares). LA. LAND and DEERE moved into 49th and 50th positions respectively, the main boost from good market action.

DISPLACED - Displaced stocks other than CHRYSLER and UNION OIL, mentioned above, were PENNSYLVANIA RR. (-416,500 shares), SYNTEX (-278,200 shares) and ARMCO, the latter off 10 points in market.

Source: *Vickers Guide to Investment Company Portfolios.* Copyright © 1966 by Vickers Associates, Inc. Reproduced by permission.

natural gas representing over 25% of the total dollar investment of the top 50 companies. As the tabulation shows, office equipment, principally IBM, accounted for another 12.5%, utilities 11%, automobiles 11%, and chemicals and drugs 10%.

Generally, the smallest individual and the largest institutional investors tend to be the most conservative. Left to them the market might not perhaps witness the wide swings in popularity and the ever changing surges of choice which seem continually to sweep across the investment scene.

### Styles in Stock

Fads and enthusiasms can be either very costly or very profitable to investors, or both, depending on their footwork. Or, as one Wall Street pundit put it, "If you want to make your pile, you got to be in style." Styles in common stocks, Eldon Grimm of Walston & Company pointed out, change almost as rapidly as women's fashions. Reviewing past enthusiasms which in due course faded one can go back as far as World War I, during the course of which Bethlehem Steel was in high fashion. It jumped from $10 a share in 1914 to $200 in one year. In the 1920's, talking pictures and radio swept the country. Warner Bros. Pictures soared from 9¾ in 1927 to 138 in 1928. RCA skyrocketed from 12½ in 1922 to 573 in 1929. Bank stocks took off in the mid 1920's. The ordinarily conservative National City Bank of New York, for example, jumped from the equivalent of 131 in 1926 to 580 in 1929. Even in the Great Depression there were fads and fancies. With the repeal of Prohibition, National Distillers became a magic word, and the stock jumped from 13 in 1932 to a peak of 124⅞ one year later and then went out of style.

In more recent years, aluminum stocks were very much in style in the early 1950's. ALCOA went from 46 in 1949 to the equivalent of 352 in 1955. Reynolds Metals rose from 19 to the equivalent 300 over the same period. As a group, the aluminum stocks rose some 430% in the early 1950's and then fell out of bed in 1957, declining by more than 50%. The advent of the computers helped push IBM from 40 to over 600 and Control Data from 2 to over 100. The ephemeral popularity of Metrecal as a dieting fad sent Mead Johnson shares up by 230%, but when the style changed and sales fell 31% in 1962, net fell 90% to just 3 cents a share, and Mead Johnson stock went down to its 1958 pre-Metrecal level.

Electronics shares boomed in the late 1950's. For example, when Lehman Bros. decided to back Litton Industries and raise the $1.5 million needed, they created a unique financial package. They divided the sum into 52 units requiring a cash investment of $29,200 each. The makeup of each unit was:

| | |
|---|---|
| 20 bonds @ $1,200 per bond | $24,000 |
| 50 shares of 5% preferred | 5,000 |
| 2,000 shares of common stock (10¢ par) | 200 |
| | $29,200 |

The bonds were subsequently converted into common stock at $10.75 per share. The preferred shares were converted into common at $1 per share.

There followed, after conversion, a 2½% stock dividend, a 2 for 1 stock split, and another 2½% stock dividend. When LIT common hit a high of $143 per share by 1961, each $29,200 unit had grown to 29,416 shares of common worth $4.2 million.

Other investors were not so fortunate. Toward the end of 1961 *Business Week* reported "Glamour industry takes its lumps. Shakeout among electronics companies is starting as industry matures after a decade of fast, youthful growth. To survive, a company will need sharp management." *The Wall Street Journal* headed its story "Fading Glamour. Sales Growth Slows, Competition Tightens for Electronics Firms. Transistor Prices Drop 44%." Transitron Electronic Corporation shares fell from 60 to 4. Fairchild Camera, which had risen from 38½ cents (adjusted) to $100⅞ per share, fell to 20, though if investors held on during the deep gloom, the stock rose again during 1965 from 27¼ to 165¼.

"Airlines Fighting Financial Storm" read a headline in *The New York Times* in 1961. The transition from the 28-passenger, 180-mile-an-hour DC–3 to the 100-plus passenger, 600-mile-an-hour DC–8 and 707 in less than two decades was not made without intense strain on the earnings and finances of the airlines. From the beginning of 1959 through mid-1962, the airlines acquired more than 350 four-engine jets at a cost of as much as $7 million per plane. As a result, the long-term debt of the domestic trunk lines plus Pan American rose from $765 million at the end of 1958 to $1.75 billion in mid-1962. Interest charges rose accordingly and affected earnings adversely. Whereas the domestic trunk lines had been profitable in the 1950's, they were just able to break even in 1960 and recorded a loss of $34.6 million in 1961. They made modest profits of $8.2 million in 1962, $10.7 million in 1963, then netted $136.5 million in 1964 and over $200 million in 1965. With the turnaround in earnings they came into high style. Braniff rose from a low of 7¼ in 1962 to 81¼ in 1965, Delta from a low of 8 in 1960 to 79⅛ in 1965, Eastern from a low of 15⅞ in 1962 to 98¼ in 1965, Northwest Airlines from a low of 6⅞ in 1960 to 142½ in 1965, and United from 18¾ in 1962 to 118⅝ in 1965. In the latter year alone, Northeast Airlines jumped from a low of 4⅛ to 39, almost a tenfold increase. In 1960 and 1961, institutional investors sold off the airlines. In 1964 and 1965, they acquired them extensively.

Keeping up with styles in stocks is, then, in many cases, an important part of the selection process.

### Investment Evaluation and Timing

Although the investor must be sharply attuned to the changing fads of the marketplace, the selection of specific stocks for purchase or sale should be based upon a thorough analysis of investment *values*. This involves an attempt to determine the growth potential of corporate earnings and dividends and to determine a price which will provide a reasonable rate of return if the growth potential is realized. Many techniques have been developed to assist the investor in his selection efforts, and these will be explored in detail in subsequent chapters.[7]

Perhaps as important as the choice of what stocks to buy is the decision as to when to buy—and when to sell. Investment timing is possibly even more difficult a task than investment choice. But the competent analyst must constantly make a judgment as to the trend and level of the market as a whole to provide the appropriate environmental setting for his portfolio additions or deletions. The level and trend of the market

**FIGURE 1–5**
**Industrial Common Stock Prices, 1871–1965**
(Cowles Commission to 1918; Standard and Poor's Thereafter) 1941–43 = 10

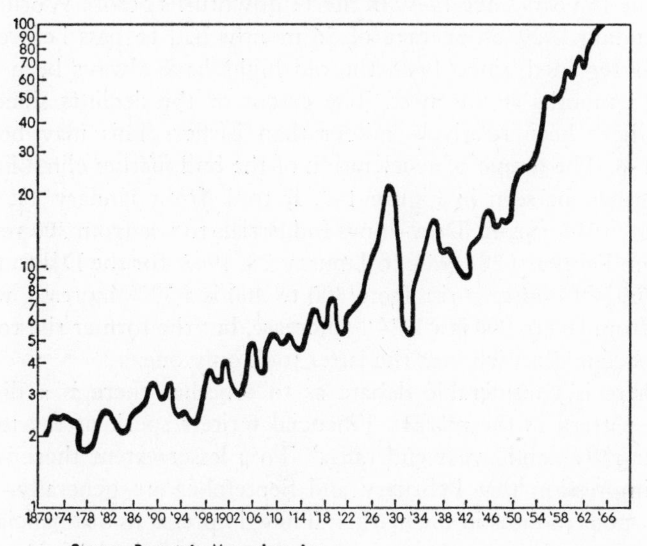


Source: Bernstein-Macaulay, Inc.

may be considered in three time dimensions: the secular, the cyclical, and the seasonal.

The secular trend is the long-run course of the market over a 10-, 25-, or 50-year period. Generally the trend has been upward for reasons indicated earlier—the continuing decline in the purchasing power of the dollar, the gradual inflation in the economy, the rise in demand for common stock as compared to a relatively limited supply, and the relatively steady growth in national income and corporate profits. The rising secular trend in common stock prices may be seen in Figure 1–5. As Bernstein-Macaulay point out, if you draw a line touching the lows of 1884–1908–1919–1942, this clearly defines the long-term uptrend. Extend

[7] Chapters 5 through 9.

that line to 1965 and it hits 16. The even steeper uptrend touching 1908–1914–1918–1949 only reaches 25 in 1965. This shows that prices could fall 75%–80% from their peak 1966 level and still leave the basic upward pattern intact. The postwar bull market far outshadowed anything in our history. Prices rose at an average annual rate of 12.6% between 1949 and 1966, more than quadruple the rate of growth from 1871 to 1949.

Cyclical trends in the market are also reflected in Figure 1–5. By cyclical trends we mean the alternation of bull and bear markets. In recent years bear market downturns have become milder than they were in earlier years, and the bull market uptrend has tended to last longer and go higher than earlier. The uptrend, as Bernstein-Macaulay note, during the 78 years prior to 1949 was a much more labored affair than it has been during the 16 years since 1949. In the 11 downturns before World War II, but excluding 1929, an average of 56 months had to pass before the old high was regained; since 1949, the old highs have always been regained within 15 months at the most. The extent of the declines since World War II have been relatively milder than earlier. This may be seen in Figure 1–6. The tempo of acceleration of the bull market climb in the past 20 years may be seen in Figure 1–7. It took from January 11, 1946, to March 11, 1954, for the Dow-Jones Industrials to rise from 300 to 400, but only from February 28, 1964, to January 28, 1965, for the DJI to rise from 800 to 900. Of course, a rise from 300 to 400 is a 33% increase, whereas a change from 800 to 900 is a 12½% increase, but the former rise took eight years to accomplish whereas the latter took only one.

There is considerable debate as to whether there is a discernible seasonal pattern in the market. Financial writers speak of the traditional "summer rally" and "year-end rally." To a lesser extent there is a widespread impression that February and September are generally—but not always—poor months in the market. These impressions of financial writers and observers of the market are based upon tabulations of advances and declines, by months, of long past periods of time. Such a tabulation covering the period 1897–1965 is shown in Table 1–10 and Figure 1–8. The summer rally period—July and August—is clearly apparent, as is the turn of the year—December and January—advance. Less well defined but nevertheless shown is the tendency of February and September to witness declines in stock prices.

Statistical analysts have taken issue with these conclusions on seasonality. Using a sophisticated technique, called spectral analysis, for examining economic time series, two Princeton professors found very little evidence of a seasonal pattern. They declared: "For no series so far studied has there been a significant twelve-month component, although in several of them its harmonics have been just visible, yet it is commonly assumed that the New York stock market possesses a significant seasonal

## FIGURE 1–6

### THE DOW JONES STOCK AVERAGES

1917-1966

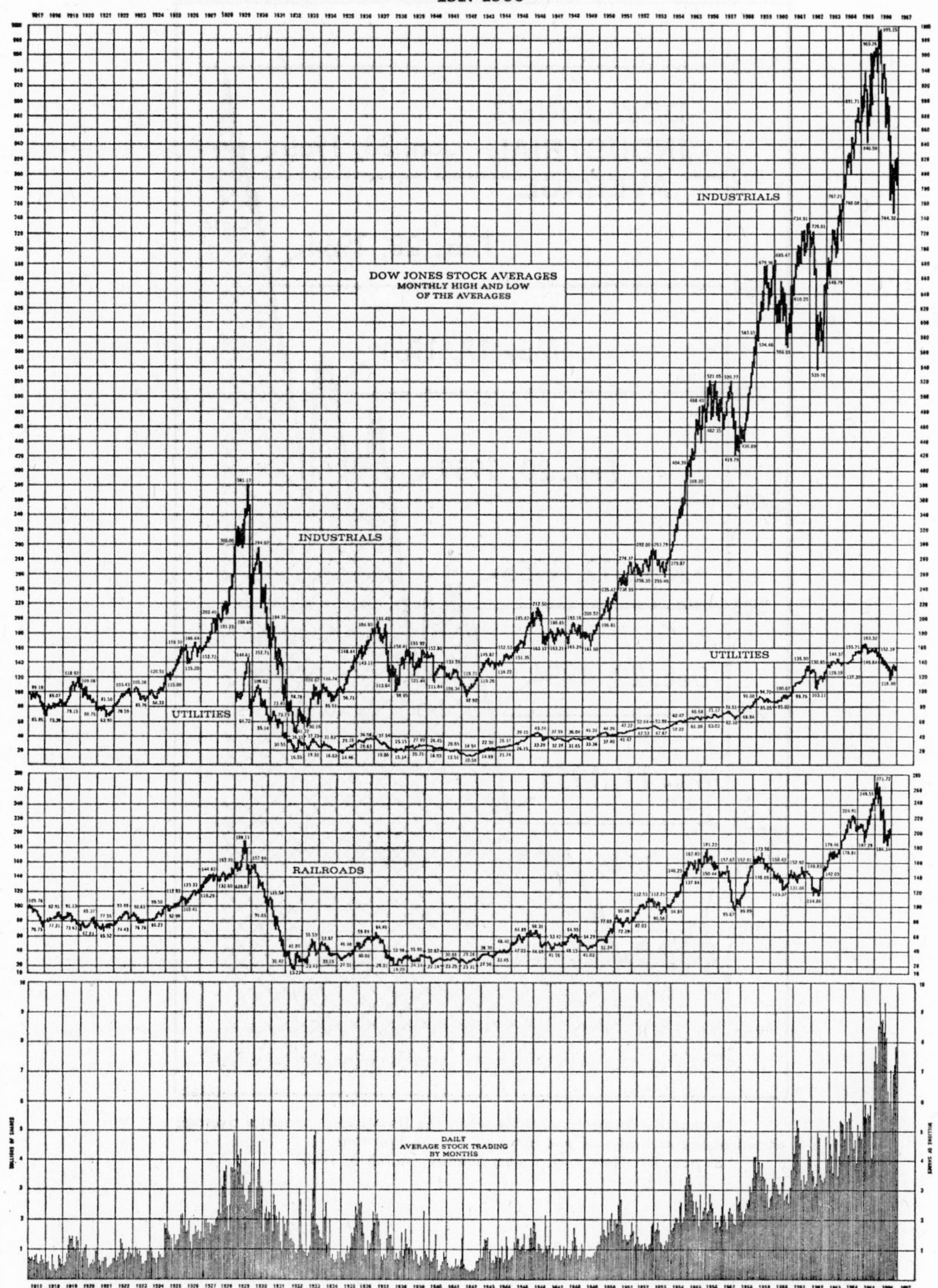


Source: Dow Jones & Company, Inc.

FIGURE 1–7

The Bull Market Climb, 1946–65

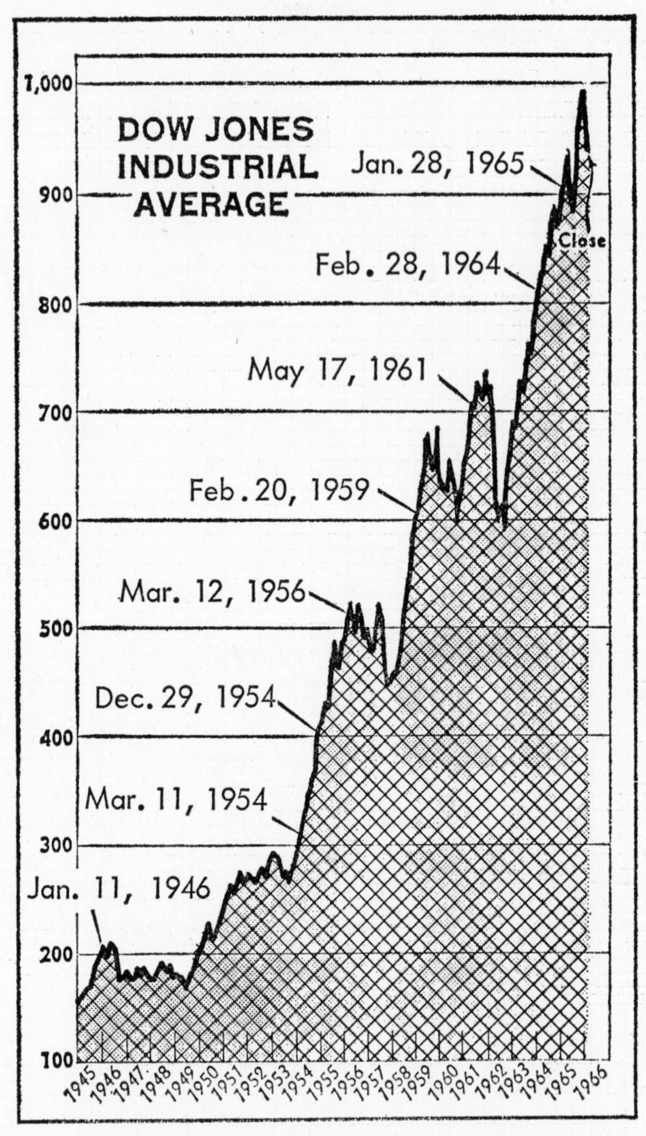


Note: The dates above show when the Dow-Jones industrial average closed above multiples of one hundred for the first time.

Source: *The New York Times*, Sunday, March 6, 1966.

## TABLE 1–10

### Seasonal Probabilities in the Stock Market
### Advances vs. Declines (in Respective Months, 1897–1965)

| | *Industrials* | | | *Rails* | | |
|---|---|---|---|---|---|---|
| *Month* | *Advances* | *Declines* | *Ratio* | *Advances* | *Declines* | *Ratio* |
| January | 44 | 25 | +1.76 | 43 | 26 | +1.65 |
| February | 34 | 35 | −1.03 | 31 | 38 | −1.23 |
| March | 39 | 30 | +1.30 | 39 | 30 | +1.30 |
| April | 36 | 33 | +1.09 | 34 | 35 | −1.03 |
| May | 38 | 31 | +1.23 | 38 | 31 | +1.23 |
| June | 35 | 34 | +1.03 | 39 | 30 | +1.30 |
| July | 48 | 21 | +2.29 | 48 | 21 | +2.29 |
| August | 48 | 20 | +2.40 | 42 | 26 | +1.62 |
| September | 31 | 37 | −1.19 | 28 | 40 | −1.43 |
| October | 37 | 31 | +1.19 | 34 | 34 | — |
| November | 41 | 27 | +1.52 | 35 | 33 | +1.06 |
| December | 51 | 18 | +2.83 | 42 | 27 | +1.56 |

Source: Francis I. du Pont & Co.

## FIGURE 1–8

### Seasonal Probabilities in the Stock Market

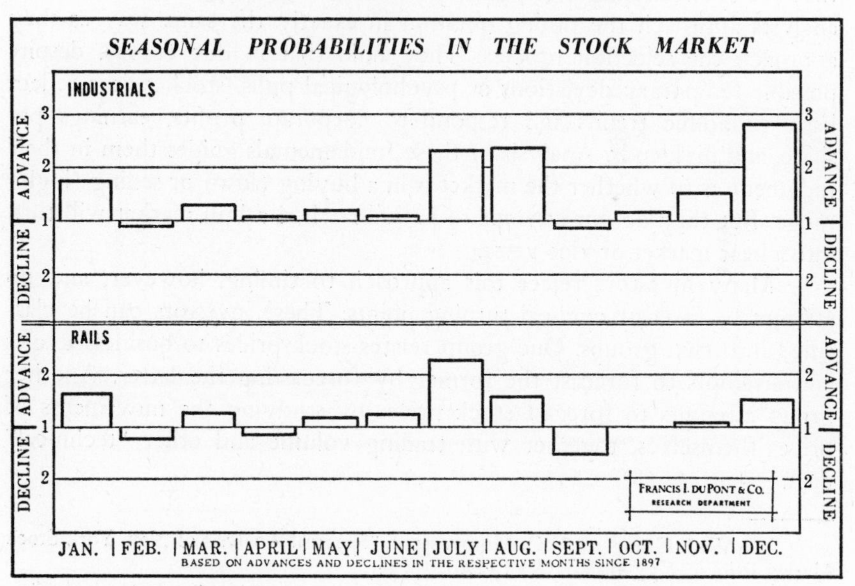


Source: Francis I. du Pont & Co.

movement."[8] In another statistical investigation, Zinbarg and Harrington reached the same conclusion. They declared:

> Although stock market commentators make frequent references to seasonal patterns of price change, they seldom define their terms meaningfully. When greater precision is given to the phrase "seasonal patterns," and when stock price data are examined using appropriate statistical procedures, the existence of a seasonal pattern becomes extremely suspect. On the basis of the evidence presened here, we cannot say dogmatically that stock prices do not have a recurring seasonal pattern. But we feel quite confident in stating that investors should not consider price seasonality in deciding when to buy or sell stocks. It is insignificant in relation to the many other factors affecting stock prices.[9]

This study, however, deals with movements of stock prices in the aggregate rather than with individual stock issues. Recent investigations by the firm of Merrill Lynch, Pierce, Fenner & Smith suggest that in a few industries, such as meat-packing and air conditioning, stock prices have exhibited very pronounced seasonal fluctuations.[10]

The problem of investment timing, as opposed to selection, is mostly concerned with the *cyclical* dimension of the stock market. Ideally, the investor who can buy stocks when prices are cyclically low and sell when they are cyclically high, will greatly enhance his profits. Traditional value analysts approach the timing question in exactly the same way as they approach the selection process. They hold that in due course, despite possible temporary deviations or psychological pulls, stock prices reflect basic economic trends and respond to corporate profits, earnings per share, and dividends. Analysis of these fundamentals guides them in their judgment as to whether the market is in a buying (low) or selling (high) range. But they do not attempt to *forecast* when a bull market will turn into a bear market or vice versa.

Many investors reject this approach to timing, however, and do attempt to forecast cyclical turning points. These investors can be classified into two groups. One group relates stock prices to business cycles and attempts to forecast the former by forecasting the latter. Another group attempts to forecast stock prices by studying the movements of prices themselves, together with trading volume and other "technical" data.

---

[8] C. W. J. Granger and O. Morgenstern, "Spectral Analysis of New York Stock Market Prices," *Kyklos*, Vol. XVI (1963), p. 14.

[9] Edward D. Zinbarg and John J. Harrington, Jr., "The Stock Market's 'Seasonal Pattern,'" *Financial Analysts Journal*, January–February, 1964.

[10] See *Fortune*, March, 1965, p. 62. There is also evidence of an interest rate seasonal pattern, particularly on securities of short maturity. Rates tend to be lower in the first half of the year than in the second half, notwithstanding efforts of the Federal Reserve authorities to smooth out seasonal influences.

Common stock prices are one of the 12 leading indicators developed during the course of years of business cycle study by the National Bureau of Economic Research. Leading indicators are those economic series, such as new orders for durable goods, commercial and industrial building contracts, business failures, and so on, basic changes in whose trend or direction tends, on the average, to precede and signal basic cyclical changes in business activity as a whole. Based on a study of past business cycles from 1870 to date, it has been found that basic cyclical changes in common stock prices tend to precede cyclical changes in business as a whole by about five months.

The designation of common stock prices as a leading indicator was based on performance on the average over preceding business cycles. It does not mean that common stock price trends *by themselves* forecast business changes, nor does it mean that a downtrend in stock prices preceded every recession since 1870. But the relationship between stock price cycles and business cycles has been close enough frequently enough to encourage investors to utilize the relationship for forecasting purposes. This effort will be examined at length in a later chapter.[11]

Likewise, the "technical" approach will be examined in detail.[12] The tools of the technical analyst are numerous, and an elaborate and exotic jargon has been evolved. Technical factors examined and interpreted include odd-lot trading, the short interest, volume of trading indicators, breadth-of-market analysis, advance-decline lines, ratios and indexes, disparity measures, high-low indexes and ratios, moving average lines, the confidence index, and so on.[13] The complete market technician's kit would also have to include chart jargon involving support and resistance, heads and shoulders, double tops and bottoms, line and saucer formations, V formations, measured move, first leg, the corrective phase, second leg, the coil or triangle, continuation patterns, reversal days, gaps, islands, bear traps, bull traps, and so on.[14] A *Fortune* article on "The Mystique of Point-and-Figure" began "Question: Does this look like reaccumulation preparatory to a new upthrust? Answer: No—because fulcrum characteristics are not present."[15]

This sort of jargon has convinced many observers that technical analysis is sheer rubbish. Indeed, a group of academicians has given

---

[11] Chapter 13.

[12] Chapter 14.

[13] For a detailed description see Chapters 14 and 31 of Leo Barnes, *Your Investments* (1966 ed.; Larchmont, N.Y.: American Research Council).

[14] For a detailed description, see William L. Jiler, *How Charts Can Help You in the Market* (New York: Commodity Research Publications Corp., 1962).

[15] See Daniel Seligman, "The Mystique of Point-and-Figure," *Fortune*, March, 1962; see also Daniel Seligman, "Playing the Market with Charts," *Fortune*, February, 1962.

prominence to a theory that short-term stock price movements are *random,* and that no amount of analysis of historical data on prices, volume, and the like can enable one to forecast future stock price swings around their long-term trends.[16] On the other hand, large numbers of Wall Street practitioners are equally convinced that price movements are not random and that technical analysis can improve one's chances of making correct timing decisions.

Why, if stock prices are random in the short run, do so many brokerage houses employ technicians and analysts who profess to find meaningful patterns in the fluctuations of stock prices, patterns that may be discerned and utilized? Cootner suggests the answer when he quotes Julian Huxley to the effect that superstitions are always apt to flourish when men must make decisions about matters they cannot control, and he adds:

> Whether or not that is the reason, it is hard to find a practitioner, no matter how sophisticated, who does not believe that by looking at the past history of prices one can learn something about their prospective behavior, while it is almost as difficult to find an academician who believes that such a backward look is of any substantial value.

It should be noted that scholars holding the random-walk view usually qualify it by observing that the random movement takes place within the framework of a long-term "drift"—i.e., over long periods of time, stock prices do move higher; hence a belief in randomness is not inconsistent with a "buy and hold" policy for stocks.

No one analyst uses all of the technical approach methods. If he did he would be more confused than a psychiatrist. He becomes intrigued with several and comes to rely upon them. A more interesting approach, however, is that of indicator consensus technique. Since individual indicators have given false signals from time to time in the past, the idea occurred to use a consensus of indicators for greater reliability. A number of services now use this technique. One of the more widely known is the *Indicator Digest,* which achieved some prominence as a result of the "sell" signal which it gave in January, 1962, thereby correctly anticipating the subsequent sharp drop in the market in the spring of 1962.

Indicator Digest, Inc., uses a composite index consisting of 11 techni-

---

[16] E. Philip Howrey, "Are Stock Prices Random or Predictable?" *Business Economics,* Summer, 1965; see also James E. Walter, "The Information Content of Stock Prices," *ibid;* also Paul H. Cootner (ed.), *The Random Character of Stock Prices* (Cambridge, Mass.: M.I.T. Press, 1964); also M. D. Godfrey, C. W. J. Granger, and Oskar Morgenstern, "The Random-Walk Hypothesis of Stock Market Behavior," *Kyklos,* XVII (1964); also C. W. J. Granger and Oskar Morgenstern, "Spectral Analysis of New York Stock Market Prices," *Kyklos,* XVI (1963); and Harry V. Roberts, "Stock Market Patterns and Financial Analysis: Methodological Suggestions," *Journal of Finance,* March, 1959.

cal indicators at any one time, varying several of them depending on whether a bull or a bear market is under way. These are then given weights of 1 or ½ for a total weight of 9. Whenever the composite total is 5 or more, a favorable signal is being given and stocks should be purchased. If the score sinks to 4½ or less, this is an unfavorable signal and stocks should be sold. If projected backwards this technique would have called all the major market turns from 1929 to 1962.[17] After 1962, however, it did not seem to be quite as effective. In 1965, for example, the composite index gave a sell signal in June when the DJIA dropped below 860. This turned out to be just the time to buy, however, because the DJIA began its renewed sharp rise in June, which carried through to a new all-time high of 969 by the end of the year. The "buy" signal in the composite index came in September, 1965, three months after the sell signal. See Figure 1–9.

The limitations of the technical approach bring some investors to use mechanical timing techniques. Not only do the technical methods have varying degrees of effectiveness from time to time but they are often in conflict with respect to the signals they are exuding. Even the composite techniques, of which there are several, are not always in agreement. At such times an investor can well become confused.

Three varieties of mechanical timing techniques can be distinguished.[18] There is dollar-cost averaging; there are formula plans, either constant dollar, constant ratio, or variable ratio; and there is automatic trend following. The broad purpose of these automatic techniques is to induce caution in bull markets and bravery in bear markets, to achieve the investor's long-sought but seldom achieved goal of buying low and selling high.

Dollar-cost averaging involves the regular purchase of securities—monthly or quarterly—in equal dollar amounts. The very obvious fact that the same amount of money will buy a greater number of shares of any stock when the price is low than it will when the price is high is the basis of the success of dollar averaging. You put the same fixed amount of money periodically into the same stock or stocks regardless of the price of the stock. Your fixed amount of money buys more shares when the stock is low, less shares when it is high. The important thing is to stick to your schedule—to buy, even though the price keeps falling, which, psychologically, is usually hard to do. This brings your average cost down, and any subsequent rise will yield a significant capital gain. To engage in dollar-cost averaging successfully, you must have both the funds and the courage to continue buying in a declining market when prospects may seem bleak.

---

[17] Publication of the *Indicator Digest* only began in May, 1961.

[18] These are discussed at greater length in Chapter 15.

FIGURE 1–9

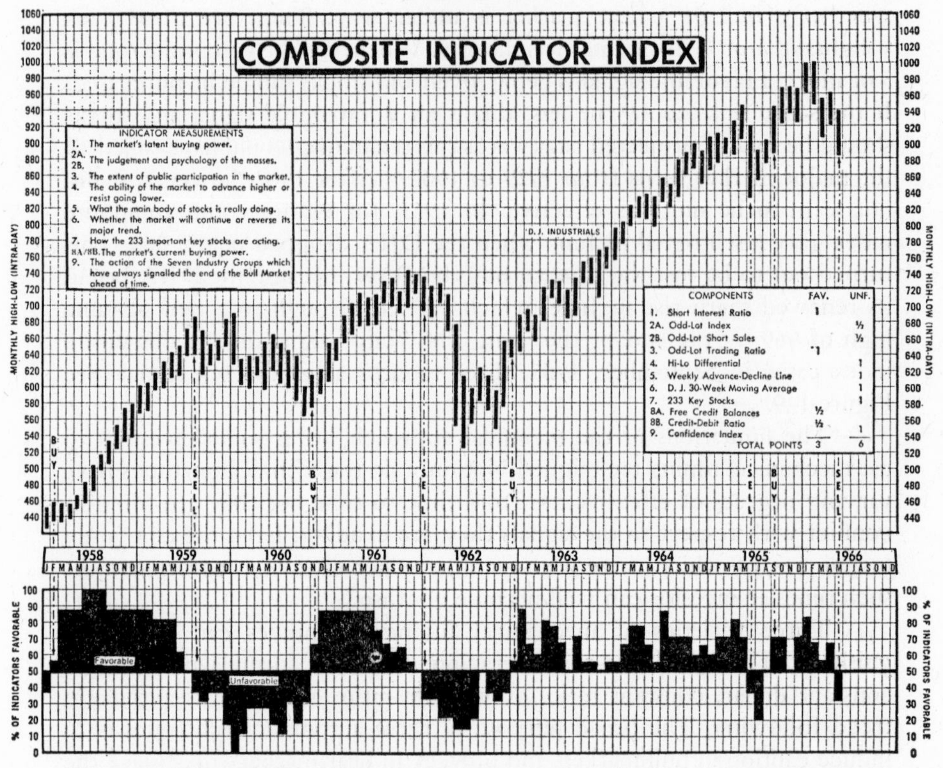


Source: *Indicator Digest*, published twice monthly by Indicator Digest, Inc., Palisades Park, New Jersey 07650. Publication began in May 1961.

In a bull market the average investor hates to sell and take his profit, both because he does not want to pay the capital gains tax and because he is afraid the market will continue to rise and he will, by selling, forego added gain. Thus he misses the top, for which most investors aim but rarely achieve, and continues to hold well into the downturn. He is reluctant to sell during the early stages of the downturn because he mourns the profit he missed by not selling at or near the peak (which only hindsight now permits him to recognize as a peak), and he holds hoping the market will reverse itself and return to the peak. It usually does not, but he continues to hold until, well on the downside, he loses patience and sells. In this way emotion and bad judgment play a real role in lack of investment success. Formula plans have been designed to overcome such human failing.

In the simple and somewhat naïve constant dollar plan, you divide your funds between stocks and cash or savings. You keep the dollar amount in stocks constant. If the market rises you sell enough stock to hold your total dollar amount invested in stock to your predetermined level. If the market falls, you draw from cash or savings and buy stock. In the constant ratio plan you decide in advance what percent of your resources you want to keep in stocks—40%, 50%, 60%—and then at regular intervals, if the market rises, you sell stock so that your stock investments are maintained at the predetermined ratio to your total resources. If the market falls, you buy stocks out of your other resources to maintain the ratio. Under the variable ratio plan you change your ratio of stocks to cash, or stocks to bonds, or stocks to total resources as the level of the market changes. For example, toward the end or peak of a bull market, you hold 10% in stocks and 90% in other resources. If the market declines you increase your percentage of stocks until near the end of a bear market you are 90% in stocks and 10% in other resources.

There are tough problems to solve. How do you determine your bench marks? How often and by what magnitude do you determine your ratios? How often do you buy or sell? Some of the mutual funds have tried the variable ratio plan and have come up with different answers, which have been changed from time to time. One thing is obvious, however. The variable ratio plan must provide better results than the constant ratio plan because under the variable ratio plan you buy significantly more stock at low prices and sell substantially more at high prices than under a constant ratio plan. If you have the resources, can cope with the intricacies and problems of a variable ratio plan, can bring yourself to buy as the market slides, you can get close to the objective of buying low and selling high.

Automatic trend following has been called investment timing without forecasting. The formula plans described above assume a fluctuating market which comes around full cycle from time to time. Automatic trend following makes no such assumption. You simply follow a trend until it reverses by a certain predetermined percentage. In a bull market, for example, you remain fully invested in common stock as long as some given market index does not decline by your predetermined percentage. If it does, you sell. To illustrate: all your funds are in common stock. The DJIA is 900. You determine that you will sell if the DJIA drops 10%. Thus if it falls to 810 (90 points—10% of 900), you sell. If it continues to go up, however, to 950, you raise your selling point to 855 (10% of 950 = 95; 950 − 95 = 855). If the DJIA rises to 1000, your new selling point would be 900.

This method, a sort of stop-loss–order approach, follows an old Wall Street adage: "Cut your losses but let your profits run." It can also be used in bear markets, although there is a danger of being whipsawed in shallow bear markets. You stay out of the market until your given index rises by your predetermined percentage, say 10%. Then you buy. If the market continues to drop, you move your buy point down with it. To illustrate assume you sold out at 855 and the DJIA drops to 800. You place orders to buy when the DJIA hits 880. If it doesn't go up to 880 but continues to fall to 750, you reduce your buy level to 825. The farther the market falls the lower your buy point. You miss the first 10% of a new bull market, but then you let your gains run. You can set your percentage at any level 10%, 12%, 15%, etc. You also miss out on the last 10% of the bull market, but this is a modest price to pay for the gains which may result from a careful and experienced use of this timing technique.

### Bond Investment

When a bull market begins to near its peak, when blue chips begin to sag, when speculative high flyers and low-priced cats and dogs begin to get the play, when stock yields fall to 3% or less and the yield spread between stocks and high-grade bonds widens to 1.5% in favor of bonds, when business is booming and interest rates are tight, the shrewd institutional investment manager who has choice and flexibility will quietly withhold funds from new common stock commitments and place the funds in high-grade bonds.

When prosperity tops out into recession, when business and common stock prices begin to slide, high-grade bonds come into favor. As interest rates decline high-grade bond prices rise. High-grade bond prices tend to vary inversely with interest rates and with common stock prices. As recession turns into recovery, reverse trends set in. Interest rates and common stock prices which have fallen start to rise and high-grade bond prices tend to weaken. Generally speaking, by high-grade bonds are meant those rated AAA or AA by the rating services.

The primary investment interest in bonds comes from institutions such as banks and insurance companies which must pay obligations in fixed number of dollars. If you have a $50,000 life insurance policy, for example, at some point in the future—whether 5 years or 35 years hence—the company will have to pay $50,000. If it invests in securities—bonds—which will return it a fixed number of dollars—it is in a position to meet its obligation. It does not matter in this case whether the dollars it gets back buy half as little as when they were invested. It has a fixed dollar obligation, not a purchasing power obligation. The individual investor may shy away from high-grade bonds because of the purchasing power risk, but most institutional investors have less need to worry about this problem. Individual investors, particularly wealthier ones, find a special interest in several types of bonds, particularly tax-exempts and convertibles. As a hedge against recession and deflation, however, switching from common stock to high-grade bonds as a boom tops out may be an excellent, profitable move for any investor.

### Bond Prices and Interest Rates

The principal price risk in high-grade bonds is related to the trend of interest rates. If a commercial bank holds high-grade bonds, and interest rates, which had been low, start to rise, and the bank must sell its bonds because funds are needed for some other purpose, such as expanding business loans, then a capital loss results. Why? If the bonds carry a coupon rate of interest of, say, 4%, and similar quality bonds now are being issued with coupons of 4½% or higher, no one will be willing to purchase the 4% bond at par value. The unwillingness of buyers to pay the previously prevailing prices, coupled with the actual selling pressure of investors who are seeking to raise funds for other investments, forces the price of the old 4% issue down, and it will fall to the point where its price in the market yields the new purchaser approximately the same rate of return as the average new, higher level of rates in the market. Thus, as the boom moves ahead, the demand for funds expands, and interest rates rise, high-grade bond prices will fall as stock prices rise.

At the peak of the expansion, when the central banking authorities are pursuing a tight money policy, which has driven interest rates up, bond prices down, the institutional investment manager may start switching from common stocks to high-grade bonds. As expansion turns to recession, tight money will be relaxed, interest rates will be allowed to fall, and they will go down because the demand for funds slackens, and high-grade bond prices will rise. In fact, the deeper the recession, the higher will go the prices of high-grade bonds as institutional investment demand switches to them and thus bids up their prices.

### Types of Bonds

Bonds may be either secured or unsecured and may range from first-mortgage bonds on the one hand to subordinated debentures on the other. The security behind a bond, while important, is not crucial. The earning power, financial condition, and quality of management is vital. Because of this, one company's unsecured bonds may be rated higher than another company's secured obligations. For example, the debentures of A.T.&T. are rated higher than the first-mortgage bonds of Indianapolis Power and Light. The debentures of Commonwealth Edison have a higher rating than the first-mortgage bonds of Missouri Power and Light Company.

Mortgage bonds are secured by a conditional lien on part or all of a company's property. If the company defaults (fails to pay interest or repay principal), the bondholders, through the trustee appointed to represent them and look after their rights, may foreclose the mortgage and take over the pledged property. Some corporate mortgages have what is known as an "*after-acquired*" property clause, which provides that all property thereafter acquired will become subject to the mortgage and automatically be pledged to secure the bond issue. While this is not widely found, it is very favorable to the investor, and where it exists, if the company wishes to float another bond issue secured by a mortgage on its property, this *second* mortgage will be a *junior lien*, subordinate to the first mortgage or *senior lien* on the property. Usually, when companies float junior issues, secured by junior liens, they do not clearly label them as such. They call them "general" or "consolidated," or some other ambiguous name, and the only way an investor can determine the security status of the bonds exactly is to read the *indenture*. The *indenture* is the formal, and usually lengthy, legal contract between the borrowing company and the creditor bondholders, spelling out all the detailed terms and conditions of the loan. The indenture will also indicate whether more bonds may be issued with the same security or under the same mortgage. If so, the mortgage is said to be "*open-end*." Additional issues of bonds under an "open-end" mortgage will naturally dilute the security available for earlier issues. If the mortgage is "closed-end," no additional bonds may be issued under the same mortgage, and the issue therefore has better protection.

A bond secured by a pledge of specific securities is known as a "*collateral trust bond*." These are issued mainly by holding companies, closed-end investment companies, and finance companies. They have not been popular in recent years, particularly after the passage of the Public Utility Holding Company Act in 1935. The *equipment trust bond or certificate* is usually used to finance the purchase of rolling stock by railroads. Under the Philadelphia Plan, title to equipment (freight cars, locomotives, passenger cars, etc.) being bought by a railroad rests in a trustee who holds it for the benefit of certificate holders. The railroad makes a down payment (perhaps 20%), and the trustee issues equipment trust certificates to cover the balance of the purchase price of the equipment. The trustee then leases the equipment to the railroad under an agreement whereby the railroad obtains title to the equipment only when all obligations have been met. Since the rolling stock can be moved anywhere in the country, should the railroad default, the equipment may be sold or leased to another railroad. Defaults have therefore been very rare in the case of equipment trust certificates.

*Debentures* are unsecured bonds protected only by the general credit of the borrowing corporation. They may contain a "covenant of equal coverage" which means that if any mortgage bond is issued in the future, which ordinarily would take precedence over the debentures, the issuer agrees to secure the debentures equally. In some states the law requires that this be done. All direct domestic obligations of federal, state, and municipal governments in the United States are debentures. Since this type of security is protected only by the general promise to pay, and in the event of default, the debenture holder is merely a general creditor, debentures can usually be sold only by corporations enjoying high credit standings. The value of a debenture must be judged wholly in terms of the earning power and overall financial status and outlook of the issuer, which is the best basis for evaluating any bond. *Subordinated* debentures are very junior issues ranking after other unsecured debt, as a result of explicit provisions in the indenture. Finance companies have made extensive use of subordinated debentures. Because of these companies' high liquidity and their need for large sums of capital, they have tended to develop layers of debt of which subordinated debentures are the lowest.

*Convertible bonds* are bonds which may be exchanged, at the option of the holder, for a specified amount of other securities, usually common stock. Usually the bond is convertible into a fixed number of shares of common. For example, the Phillips Petroleum 4¼s of 1987 were convertible into 20 shares of common per $1,000 bond. The conversion price of the common was thus $50 per share. When the common sold above this price, the convertible bond would move up with the common. When the common sold below the conversion parity of $50 per share, the bond would rest upon its investment value as a bond without reference to the conversion feature.

There are some exceptions to the rule of straight convertibility. For example, the holder of the A.T.&T. 4¼s of 1973 may exchange each bond for 30 shares of common stock but must also make a cash payment of $420 per bond upon conversion. The convertible bond would appear theoretically to have the best of two worlds, since it affords, on the one hand, the safety of a fixed income creditor obligation, and, on the other, an opportunity to share in the prospective growth and profits of the company. Thus it would seem, at one and the same time, to provide safety and stability, as well as a hedge against inflation and opportunity for significant capital gains. Indeed, large capital gains have been obtained in recent years in some convertibles. For example, the Brunswick-Balke second series of convertibles came out in April, 1958, at par when the common was selling at about 39, having been split two for one in 1957. There was a four-for-three split in the common in 1958, and the convertible was called for redemption in November, 1959, at a time when it was selling at 397. Thus the investor who paid $1,000 for the bond realized a $2,970 capital gain just 18 months later. Convertibles are particularly attractive to wealthy investors since they can be margined at about 20% compared to the 70% margin requirement for the common.[19] It must not be assumed, however, that convertible securities provide the best of two worlds automatically. As with any other investment, the potential rewards must be judged in relation to the price paid. Some investors have lost substantial capital in convertibles by ignoring the price factor.[20]

An *income bond* is a debt instrument whose distinguishing characteristic is that interest need be paid only if earned. Originally many income bonds arose out of railroad reorganizations and reflected the effort

---

[19] See Louis Brand, *Investing for Profit in Convertible Bonds* (rev. ed.; New York: Standard & Poor's Corporation, 1964); see also *A Guide to Convertible Bonds* (New York: Kalb, Voorhis & Co., 1965).

[20] For a more detailed analysis, see Chapter 12.

to reduce the burden of fixed charges to manageable proportions. Most income bonds require sinking funds; interest must be paid if earned, in contrast to preferred stock dividends; and interest is often cumulative for three years or longer, depending on the terms of the individual bond issue. Income bonds as an alternative to preferred stock have been taken up and utilized by industrial companies like Armour, Monsanto, Corning Glass, McLouth Steel, and National Can. Interest payments are a deductible expense for corporate income tax purposes. The Atchison, Topeka, and Santa Fe Railroad adjustment 4s of 1955 issued in the railroad's reorganization of 1895 are rated AA. This issue is an exception, however. Most income bonds are rated in the C category because as a group they are regarded as speculative.

*Tax-exempt bonds* are of special interest to wealthy investors and to certain institutional investors.[21] The income from state and municipal bonds is not subject to the U.S. federal income tax. This may mean that a nontaxable yield of 3.5% on a state or municipal bond may be equivalent to twice or three times as much on a taxable security, depending on the investor's income tax bracket. Rules of analysis for bonds, which will be explored later,[22] vary somewhat for state and municipal issues. There is, however, a simple formula which will show an investor the percentage yield which a bond or other security with fully taxable income must give in order to provide an after-tax yield equivalent to a given tax-exempt yield. The formula is as follows:

$$\text{Tax-exempt yield} \div (100\% - \text{tax bracket } \%) = \text{Taxable equivalent yield}$$

Assume an investor is in the 60% tax bracket. If he can buy a 3.5% tax-exempt, what would an alternate investment with fully taxable income have to yield to provide 3½% after taxes?

$$3.50\% \div (100\% - 60\%) = ?$$

$$\frac{3.50\%}{40\%} = 8.75\%$$

A fully taxable investment would have to yield 8.75% to give an after-tax return of 3.5% for an investor in the 60% tax bracket.

Since trading costs are high and liquidity often poor, tax-exempts are usually bought by the individual investor for the long pull. Occasionally, shrewd investors will abandon a speculative stock commitment and seek the safety of municipals. *Fortune* cites the case of the Bakalar Brothers, original owners of Transitron Electronic Corporation. "After selling over $75 million of Transitron stock in 1959 and 1960, at around $34 a share, they put much of the money into municipal bonds; since Transitron later

---

[21] See Goodbody & Co., *Investor's Tax Exempt Bond Guide* (New York, 1966).

[22] See Chapters 10 and 11.

sold under $6 a share, and their bonds are intact, this surely rates as one of the great investment switches in history."[23]

### Bond Analysis and Ratings

For the individual investor and smaller institutional investor, an initial step in bond analysis is to go to one of the financial services such as Standard & Poor's or Moody's and see what rating they have assigned to the bond. While these financial services are not infallible, their experts are accustomed to judging the relative merits of fixed income securities, and the rating will give you a clear idea of the approximate quality of the bond. It is a useful orientation for looking further into the merits, or lack of them, of the proposed purchase. It may be that when the rating assigned is seen, there may be no further interest in the bond.

In one sense bond evaluation is not very different from stock evaluation. The real basis for evaluation lies in the financial status and earning power of the borrowing corporation or governmental unit.[24] The farsightedness and efficiency of management, the outlook for the industry, the position of the particular firm in the industry, the company's earning power and the soundness of its internal finances as reflected in its balance sheet and income account, all must be carefully considered.

The security behind a bond is, in itself, no guaranty of soundness, since the value of the pledged property is usually dependent on earning power. If the company fails, its fixed assets may prove to be worth very little. A good example is the Seaboard-All Florida Railway's first mortgage 6s, which sold in 1931 at one cent on the dollar, soon after the completion of the road. In selecting any security, but especially bonds, it makes sense to try and choose a company which is likely to avoid trouble rather than seek to protect yourself in the event of trouble.

### Conclusion

Investors are subject to major types of investment risks. These include:

1. Business risk (i.e., a decline in earning power), which reduces a company's ability to pay interest or dividends.
2. Market risk (i.e., a change in "market psychology"), which causes a security's price to decline irrespective of any truly fundamental change in earning power.
3. Purchasing power risk (i.e., a rise in prices), which reduces the buying power of income and principal.
4. Interest rate risk (i.e., a rise in interest rates), which depresses the prices of fixed income type securities.

---

[23] Carol J. Loomis, "You May Be Missing a Bet in Bonds," in *Fortune's Guide to Personal Investing* (New York: McGraw-Hill Book Co., 1963).

[24] With the exception of the U.S. government.

5. Political risk (for example, price-wage controls, tax increases, changes in tariff and subsidy policies, etc.).

Common stocks are most vulnerable to (1), (2), and (5). Bonds are most vulnerable to (1), (3), (4), and (5). No securities are free of all risks. Even U.S. government bonds are subject to (3) and (4).

## SUGGESTED READINGS

Leo Barnes. "What Difference Does Knowledge Make to Investors?" *Financial Analysts Journal*, September–October, 1965.

Leo Barnes. *Your Investments—1967*. Rye, N.Y.: American Research Council; Englewood Cliffs, N.J.: Prentice-Hall, Inc.

Louis Brand. *Investing for Profit in Convertible Bonds*. Rev. ed. New York: Standard & Poor's Corporation, 1964.

Paul H. Cootner (ed.). *The Random Character of Stock Prices*. Cambridge, Mass.: M.I.T. Press, 1964.

Burton Crane. *The Sophisticated Investor*. Rev. ed. New York: Simon and Schuster, Inc., 1964.

*Encyclopedia of Stock Market Practices*. 2nd ed. Larchmont, N.Y.: Investors Intelligence, Inc., 1965.

Lawrence Fisher. "Outcomes of Random Investments in Common Stocks Listed on The New York Stock Exchange," *Journal of Business*, Vol. XXXXVIII, No. 2 (April, 1965).

Lawrence Fisher and James H. Lorie. "Rates of Return on Investments in Common Stock," *Journal of Business*, University of Chicago, January, 1964.

Benjamin Graham. *The Intelligent Investor*. 3rd ed. New York: Harper & Row, Publishers, 1965.

M. D. Godfrey, C. W. J. Granger, and O. Morgenstern. "The Random-Walk Hypothesis of Stock Market Behavior," *Kyklos*, Vol. XVII (1964).

John S. Herold, Inc. *Profitable Common Stocks: A Guide to America's Fastest Growing Companies*. 3rd ed. Greenwich, Conn., April, 1965.

E. Philip Howrey. "Are Stock Prices Random or Predictable?" *Business Economics*, Summer, 1965.

Kalb, Voorhis & Co. *A Guide to Convertible Bonds*. New York, 1965.

James H. Lorie and Lawrence Fisher. "Knowledge Makes A Difference: A Reply to Dr. Leo Barnes," *Financial Analysts Journal*, November–December, 1965.

Janet Low. *The Investor's Dictionary*. New York: Simon and Schuster, Inc., 1964.

Alfred T. Mahan. "What Price 'Defensive Stocks'?" *Financial Analysts Journal*, September–October, 1965.

James E. Walter. "The Information Content of Stock Prices," *Business Economics*, Summer, 1965.

# 2

# HOW THE SECURITIES MARKETS WORK

Money doesn't bring happiness, but it calms the nerves.

—French proverb

On May 28, 1962, news of extraordinary activity in the stock market flashed across the country on radio and television and occupied the front pages of America's leading newspapers. A heavy wave of selling sent stock prices tumbling. The DJIA declined 35 points (5.7%). Over the next two trading days the market recovered. About 35 million shares changed hands in three days, an all-time record. The reported volume of 14,-750,000 shares for May 29 represented a peak of activity second only to the 16.4 million shares traded on October 29, 1929.[1] This time, with new techniques and new equipment, the market took the large volume in stride. There were no difficulties or problems. The New York Stock Exchange, the world's largest competitive auction market, functioned well.

The investment process encompasses a number of markets and many institutions. There is a money market and a capital market. There are primary markets and secondary markets. There are organized exchanges and over-the-counter markets. There are both borrowers and lenders of short- and long-term funds. There are corporations and individuals with surplus funds who may decide either to invest, lend, or save them. There are a variety of financial intermediaries who facilitate the transfer of funds from those who have surpluses to those who need resources for a variety of purposes, ranging from productive investment to speculative trading.

---

[1] See *The Stock Market Under Stress*, a Research Report by the New York Stock Exchange, March, 1963.

## Sources and Uses of Funds

Perhaps the best overview of the flow of funds in financial markets is obtained from a sources-and-uses-of-funds analysis. One of the best of these is published each year by the Bankers Trust Company of New York.[2] The purpose of the detailed and elaborate analysis, which encompasses 26 tables covering different sectors, is to assess the investment outlook, to study demand and supply conditions in each of the sectors, and to form a basis for judging the probable trend of interest rates in various markets.

A summary of sources and uses of funds is given in Table 2–1. The volume of investment funds raised exceeded by far the volume of short-term funds. Savings institutions, both contractual type and deposit type, provided about half of the funds supplied; commercial banks were the next largest source. Individuals and others provided about one seventh and business corporations approximately one ninth of total sources of funds. The commercial banks and business corporations channeled their funds into short-term uses in large part, although not wholly, while savings institutions, including life insurance companies, pension funds, savings banks, savings and loan associations, and so forth, funneled their resources largely into investment uses.

The short-term sources and uses of funds are shown in Table 2–2. Short-term funds change hands in the money market. It is customary to distinguish between the money and capital markets by saying that the money market is the arena in which claims to funds change hands for from one day up to one year, but not beyond. Money-market instruments include promissory notes and bills of exchange, commercial paper, bankers' acceptances, Treasury bills, short-term tax-exempts, dealer paper, and negotiable time certificates of deposit. Institutions participating in the money market include the commercial banks, corporations large and small, the Federal Reserve, U.S. government securities dealers, and indeed anyone who lends or borrows on short term, including those who borrow on the collateral of securities to speculate. Activities in the money market range from a one-day loan of several millions by one commercial bank with surplus reserve funds to another which is short of reserves—the federal funds market—to an investor borrowing to buy securities on margin. Corporations with temporarily surplus funds place them in Treasury bills for 91 or 182 days or in time certificates of deposit tailored to their financial time requirements. The money market is the vital arena in which the Federal Reserve influences the reserve positions of commercial

---

[2] See *The Investment Outlook—1967*. A free copy may be obtained by writing to Economics Department, Bankers Trust Company, Box 318, New York, N.Y. 10015.

## TABLE 2–1

### Summary of Sources and Uses of Funds

(In Billions of Dollars)

| | 1958 | 1959 | 1960 | 1961 | 1962 | 1963 | 1964 | 1965 (*Est.*) | 1966 (*Proj.*) |
|---|---|---|---|---|---|---|---|---|---|
| *Uses (funds raised)* | | | | | | | | | |
| Investment funds | 28.3 | 28.9 | 25.4 | 30.4 | 33.9 | 38.9 | 42.0 | 45.3 | 47.4 |
| Short-term funds | 6.2 | 17.3 | 14.5 | 11.0 | 19.3 | 22.1 | 27.4 | 33.0 | 31.3 |
| U.S. government and agency publicly-held securities | 6.2 | 10.5 | −2.7 | 5.9 | 6.0 | 2.5 | 3.3 | 0.4 | 5.8 |
| Total Uses | 40.7 | 56.7 | 37.2 | 47.3 | 59.2 | 63.5 | 72.7 | 78.7 | 84.5 |
| *Sources (funds supplied)* | | | | | | | | | |
| Savings institutions: | | | | | | | | | |
| Life insurance companies | 5.1 | 5.2 | 5.4 | 5.6 | 6.4 | 6.6 | 7.4 | 8.1 | 8.5 |
| Corporate pension funds | 2.8 | 3.2 | 3.3 | 3.4 | 3.5 | 3.7 | 3.9 | 4.8 | 5.4 |
| State and local government retirement funds | 1.6 | 2.0 | 2.2 | 2.1 | 2.5 | 2.6 | 2.8 | 3.1 | 3.8 |
| Fire and casualty insurance companies | 0.8 | 1.5 | 1.1 | 1.3 | 1.2 | 1.3 | 1.1 | 0.9 | 1.2 |
| Contractual-type savings institutions | 10.3 | 11.9 | 12.0 | 12.4 | 13.6 | 14.2 | 15.2 | 16.9 | 18.9 |
| Savings and loan associations | 6.2 | 8.3 | 7.2 | 9.3 | 10.3 | 13.2 | 11.0 | 9.4 | 8.2 |
| Mutual savings banks | 2.5 | 1.4 | 1.5 | 2.1 | 3.1 | 3.5 | 4.2 | 3.8 | 3.6 |
| Credit unions | 0.3 | 0.7 | 0.6 | 0.4 | 0.6 | 0.7 | 0.9 | 1.1 | 1.3 |
| Deposit-type savings institutions | 9.0 | 10.4 | 9.3 | 11.8 | 14.0 | 17.4 | 16.1 | 14.3 | 13.1 |
| Investment companies | 1.6 | 1.4 | 1.1 | 1.4 | 1.5 | 0.8 | 1.1 | 1.7 | 2.3 |
| Total Savings Institutions | 20.9 | 23.7 | 22.4 | 25.6 | 29.1 | 32.4 | 32.4 | 32.9 | 34.3 |
| Commercial banks | 15.2 | 4.8 | 9.0 | 15.7 | 19.5 | 19.1 | 22.2 | 27.3 | 23.0 |
| Business corporations: | | | | | | | | | |
| Nonfinancial | 3.5 | 10.8 | −1.8 | 2.4 | 5.8 | 5.1 | 7.8 | 5.9 | 7.1 |
| Financial | −0.4 | 3.1 | 2.2 | 0.4 | 2.6 | 4.2 | 4.0 | 5.3 | 5.0 |
| Total Business Corporations | 3.1 | 13.9 | 0.4 | 2.8 | 8.4 | 9.3 | 11.7 | 11.2 | 12.1 |
| Other investor groups: | | | | | | | | | |
| Federal agencies | 0.4 | 2.3 | 1.8 | 0.8 | 0.8 | −0.8 | 0.4 | 1.2 | 2.1 |
| Brokers and dealers | 0.9 | — | −0.1 | 1.0 | −0.1 | 1.4 | −0.4 | 0.5 | — |
| Other consumer lenders | 0.1 | 0.4 | 0.4 | 0.4 | 0.5 | 0.6 | 0.6 | 0.7 | 0.7 |
| State and local governments* | 0.2 | 1.1 | 1.3 | 1.1 | 1.3 | 1.1 | 1.2 | 3.5 | 4.0 |
| Foreign investors | — | 4.6 | 1.8 | 0.6 | 2.0 | 0.8 | 0.8 | −0.7 | 0.2 |
| Total Other Investor Groups | 1.6 | 8.4 | 5.2 | 3.9 | 4.5 | 3.1 | 2.6 | 5.2 | 7.0 |
| Residual: Individuals and others† | −0.1 | 5.9 | 0.2 | −0.7 | −2.3 | −0.4 | 3.8 | 2.1 | 8.1 |
| Total Sources | 40.7 | 56.7 | 37.2 | 47.3 | 59.2 | 63.5 | 72.7 | 78.7 | 84.5 |

* Excluding retirement funds included with savings institutions above.
† Includes revaluation of book assets of some holders.
Note: Figures in this and in the following tables have been rounded and thus do not necessarily add to totals shown.
Source: Bankers Trust Co., *The Investment Outlook.*

## TABLE 2–2

## Summary of Sources and Uses of Short-Term Funds*

(In Billions of Dollars)

| | 1958 | 1959 | 1960 | 1961 | 1962 | 1963 | 1964 | 1965 (Est.) | 1966 (Proj.) |
|---|---|---|---|---|---|---|---|---|---|
| *Uses (funds raised)* | | | | | | | | | |
| Open market paper:† | | | | | | | | | |
| Commercial paper | .3 | −.3 | .7 | .4 | .4 | −.2 | .3 | −.3 | — |
| Finance company paper | −.2 | .6 | .6 | −.2 | .9 | .9 | 1.3 | 1.0 | .6 |
| Bankers' acceptances | −.1 | — | .9 | .7 | — | .2 | .5 | — | .1 |
| Total Open Market Paper | — | .3 | 2.2 | .8 | 1.3 | 1.0 | 2.1 | .7 | .7 |
| Other business credit: | | | | | | | | | |
| Bank short-term loans to business | .2 | 6.1 | 2.1 | 2.1 | 4.8 | 5.9 | 4.9 | 11.9 | 11.6 |
| Net trade credit of nonfinancial corporations | 2.5 | 2.2 | 3.0 | 2.5 | 3.9 | 3.3 | 6.9 | 5.6 | 6.0 |
| Finance company loans to business | −.1 | 1.2 | .7 | −.2 | .8 | 1.6 | 1.8 | 2.5 | 2.6 |
| Total Other Business Credit | 2.6 | 9.5 | 5.8 | 4.4 | 9.5 | 10.8 | 13.6 | 20.0 | 20.2 |
| Security credit: | | | | | | | | | |
| Bank loans | .4 | .2 | .2 | 1.1 | 1.1 | .6 | .5 | .2 | — |
| Other stock market credit‡ | 1.1 | −.2 | — | 1.1 | −.1 | 1.4 | −.5 | .9 | — |
| Total Security Credit | 1.5 | — | .2 | 2.2 | 1.0 | 2.0 | — | 1.1 | — |
| Consumer credit | .2 | 6.3 | 4.5 | 1.6 | 5.5 | 6.7 | 6.9 | 9.2 | 8.0 |
| Other bank loans | 1.6 | .8 | 1.2 | 1.5 | 1.5 | 1.2 | 4.3 | 1.5 | 1.6 |
| Policy loans | .3 | .4 | .6 | .5 | .5 | .4 | .5 | .5 | .8 |
| Total Uses | 6.2 | 17.3 | 14.5 | 11.0 | 19.3 | 22.1 | 27.4 | 33.0 | 31.3 |
| *Sources (funds supplied)* | | | | | | | | | |
| Life insurance companies | .2 | .4 | .8 | .4 | .7 | .5 | .4 | .8 | .9 |
| Credit unions | .2 | .6 | .6 | .4 | .6 | .7 | .8 | 1.1 | 1.2 |
| Total Savings Institutions | .5 | 1.0 | 1.5 | .8 | 1.2 | 1.2 | 1.2 | 1.9 | 2.1 |
| Commercial banks | 2.6 | 9.9 | 6.1 | 6.4 | 9.9 | 10.8 | 13.2 | 17.6 | 16.2 |
| Business corporations: | | | | | | | | | |
| Nonfinancial | 3.0 | 3.5 | 3.8 | 2.7 | 5.6 | 4.7 | 9.3 | 7.2 | 7.7 |
| Financial | −.9 | 2.9 | 2.2 | −.2 | 2.1 | 3.4 | 3.6 | 4.5 | 4.5 |
| Total Business Corporations | 2.1 | 6.4 | 6.0 | 2.5 | 7.7 | 8.1 | 12.8 | 11.7 | 12.2 |
| Other investor groups: | | | | | | | | | |
| Brokers and dealers (customer credit) | .9 | — | −.1 | 1.0 | −.1 | 1.4 | −.4 | .5 | — |
| Other consumer lenders | .1 | .4 | .4 | .4 | .5 | .6 | .6 | .7 | .7 |
| Foreign investors | −.1 | −.1 | .5 | — | — | — | .2 | — | .1 |
| Total Other Investor Groups | .9 | .3 | .8 | 1.4 | .4 | 2.0 | .4 | 1.2 | .8 |
| Residual: Individuals and others§ | .3 | −.2 | .1 | .1 | — | — | — | .6 | — |
| Total Sources | 6.2 | 17.3 | 14.5 | 11.0 | 19.3 | 22.1 | 27.4 | 33.0 | 31.3 |

* Excludes governmental securities and short-term funds included with investment funds.

† 1958–64, Federal Reserve.

‡ 1958–64, consists of customer credit (net debit balances with New York Stock Exchange firms) and broker and dealer credit (customers' net free credit balances), as reported by New York Stock Exchange.

§ Includes broker and dealer credit (customers' net free credit balances).

Source: Bankers Trust Co., *The Investment Outlook.*

banks, and therefore their capacity to lend, by engaging in open-market operations in U.S. government securities.[3]

In contrast, the capital market focuses on long-term funds. It is convenient to use the generally accepted demarcation line of one year or less maturity for the money market and over one year for the capital market. It is in the capital market that the demand for, and supply of, investment funds are brought together. Savings are converted into investments, as the summary of sources and uses of investment funds shown in Table 2–3 reveals. The major supply of funds for the capital market is channeled through specialized financial institutions such as insurance companies, pension and retirement funds, and savings institutions. At times dealings between borrowers and lenders may be direct, but often transfers are effected through intermediaries such as investment bankers, stockbrokers, and securities dealers. Instruments in the capital market include, of course, bonds, notes, mortgages, stock, and warrants.

Like the money market, the capital market has many faces. A large corporation borrowing directly from an insurance company is participating in the capital market even though the whole transaction may be arranged by phone. Another corporation borrowing through the facilities of an investment banker who in turn makes use of a selling organization that spans the country is also participating in the capital market. There is a market for corporate bonds, a market for longer-term U.S. government issues, a market for state and local bonds—"municipals," a market for corporate equities, and a mortgage market. There is an active primary or new issues market as well as large secondary markets. For mortgages, for example, the new issue market is significant and substantial, while the secondary market is negligible. For equities, on the other hand, the new issues market is relatively limited, but the secondary market is large and active. For bonds there is both a large and active new issues market and a substantial secondary market.

## Primary and Secondary Markets

Of total new corporate issues, in recent years, 70% to 85% consists of bonds. The percentage is even higher if U.S. government and state and municipal issues are included. The new issues market is therefore normally mainly a bond market. Securities in this market can be sold either through investment bankers or by private placements. Over 50% of all new bond issues over the past five years have been placed privately.[4] More and more of the largest firms with the best credit ratings have come to favor this quiet, unobserved method of financing. For large companies the method

---

[3] For further information see *Money-Market Investments: The Risk and the Return,* Morgan Guaranty Trust Co., New York, 1964.

[4] See "Direct Placement of Corporate Debt," *Economic Review,* Federal Reserve Bank of Cleveland, March, 1965.

## TABLE 2–3

## Summary of Sources and Uses of Investment Funds*

(In Billions of Dollars)

| | 1958 | 1959 | 1960 | 1961 | 1962 | 1963 | 1964 | 1965 (Est.) | 1966 (Proj.) |
|---|---|---|---|---|---|---|---|---|---|
| *Uses (funds raised)* | | | | | | | | | |
| Real estate mortgages | 13.5 | 17.1 | 14.2 | 16.9 | 21.3 | 24.7 | 25.6 | 25.3 | 24.7 |
| Corporate bonds | 5.8 | 4.1 | 5.0 | 5.2 | 4.9 | 5.6 | 6.6 | 8.2 | 11.2 |
| Corporate stocks | 2.1 | 2.4 | 1.7 | 2.7 | 0.7 | −0.2 | 1.4 | 0.3 | 1.0 |
| Total Corporate Securities | 8.0 | 6.4 | 6.7 | 7.8 | 5.6 | 5.3 | 8.1 | 8.5 | 12.2 |
| State and local government securities | 5.5 | 4.7 | 3.8 | 5.2 | 5.6 | 7.0 | 6.2 | 7.8 | 7.0 |
| Foreign securities | 1.4 | 0.8 | 0.6 | 0.8 | 1.0 | 1.0 | 0.7 | 0.9 | 0.8 |
| Bank term loans to U.S. business | −0.1 | −0.1 | 0.1 | −0.3 | 0.4 | 0.9 | 1.4 | 2.8 | 2.7 |
| Total Uses | 28.3 | 28.9 | 25.4 | 30.4 | 33.9 | 38.9 | 42.0 | 45.3 | 47.4 |
| *Sources (funds supplied)* | | | | | | | | | |
| Savings institutions: | | | | | | | | | |
| Life insurance companies | 4.8 | 5.1 | 5.0 | 5.6 | 5.7 | 6.5 | 7.2 | 7.8 | 8.2 |
| Corporate pension funds | 2.8 | 2.9 | 3.4 | 3.3 | 3.3 | 3.6 | 3.8 | 5.0 | 5.4 |
| State and local government retirement funds | 1.6 | 1.5 | 1.7 | 2.0 | 2.3 | 2.1 | 2.2 | 2.8 | 3.3 |
| Fire and casualty insurance companies | 0.8 | 1.2 | 1.2 | 1.2 | 1.0 | 1.1 | 1.0 | 0.9 | 1.1 |
| Contractual-type savings institutions | 10.0 | 10.7 | 11.3 | 12.1 | 12.3 | 13.3 | 14.2 | 16.5 | 18.0 |
| Savings and loan associations | 5.6 | 7.5 | 6.9 | 8.8 | 9.9 | 12.2 | 10.4 | 8.9 | 7.9 |
| Mutual savings banks | 2.8 | 1.7 | 2.1 | 2.1 | 3.0 | 3.7 | 4.2 | 4.1 | 3.9 |
| Credit unions | 0.1 | 0.1 | — | — | 0.1 | — | — | — | 0.1 |
| Deposit-type savings institutions | 8.5 | 9.3 | 9.0 | 10.9 | 13.0 | 15.9 | 14.6 | 13.0 | 11.9 |
| Investment companies | 1.4 | 1.2 | 1.0 | 1.4 | 1.1 | 0.8 | 1.1 | 1.6 | 2.5 |
| Total Savings Institutions | 19.9 | 21.2 | 21.3 | 24.4 | 26.4 | 30.0 | 29.9 | 31.1 | 32.4 |
| Commercial banks | 4.5 | 2.7 | 1.2 | 3.9 | 8.8 | 11.0 | 9.6 | 13.4 | 7.8 |
| Business corporations: | | | | | | | | | |
| Nonfinancial | 0.5 | 0.7 | −0.2 | — | — | — | — | — | — |
| Financial | 0.5 | 0.2 | — | 0.6 | 0.5 | 0.8 | 0.4 | 0.8 | 0.5 |
| Total Business Corporations | 1.0 | 0.9 | −0.2 | 0.6 | 0.5 | 0.8 | 0.4 | 0.8 | 0.5 |
| Other investor groups: | | | | | | | | | |
| Federal agencies | 0.4 | 2.3 | 1.8 | 0.8 | 0.8 | −0.8 | 0.4 | 1.2 | 2.1 |
| State and local governments† | 0.6 | −0.2 | 0.9 | 0.8 | 0.2 | 0.9 | 1.3 | 1.6 | 2.0 |
| Foreign investors | — | 0.4 | 0.3 | 0.2 | 0.1 | 0.2 | −0.2 | −0.5 | −0.4 |
| Total Other Investor Groups | 1.0 | 2.5 | 3.0 | 1.8 | 1.1 | 0.3 | 1.5 | 2.3 | 3.7 |
| Residual: Individuals and others‡ | 1.9 | 1.6 | 0.1 | −0.3 | −2.9 | −3.2 | 0.6 | −2.3 | 3.0 |
| Total Sources | 28.3 | 28.9 | 25.4 | 30.4 | 33.9 | 38.9 | 42.0 | 45.3 | 47.4 |

* Funds generally of a long-term nature; some short-term funds are unavoidably included because of the method of reporting.

† Excluding retirement funds included with savings institutions above.

‡ Includes revaluation of book assets of some holders.

Source: Bankers Trust Co., *The Investment Outlook.*

offers a variety of advantages, though investment bankers claim that the interest cost is somewhat higher than in a public offering. A private placement frees a borrower from the uncertainties of market conditions. Market fluctuations are avoided. For example, as IBM's computer program unfolded, it obtained a $500 million long-term credit from Prudential and drew down the funds from time to time as needed, without having to worry about changing conditions in the financial markets. Also, registration with the SEC was not necessary.

Investment bankers are, however, the traditional middlemen in the capital market. For the most part, they buy the new issue from the borrower at an agreed-upon price, assume a market risk, and hope to resell to the investing public at a higher price. In this respect, they differ from the stockbroker, who usually acts as an agent, earns a commission, and takes no risk. In the sale of certain issues, however, the investment banker may function more as a stockbroker. Instead of buying the issue he may take it on a "best efforts" basis, accepting a commission for what he is able to sell but not buying the issue himself. This type of arrangement occurs for the most part in cases that are poles apart. The seller may either be a small company whose securities are too unseasoned to warrant the investment banker's assuming the risk of purchase and redistribution. Or, on the other hand, the seller may be a very large corporation whose securities are so well known that it wants to pay the investment banker only for his sales effort and not for assuming the risks of distribution.

If an investment banker is used rather than a private placement, there is a further choice between a negotiated transaction and competitive bidding. Or there could be a rights offering with or without a standby underwriting. Market risk is greater in competitive bidding. The negotiated transaction can be more readily postponed if a sudden dip in the market should occur. On the other hand, competitive bidding may be less costly to the borrower. In the negotiated transaction, the borrowing company calls in the investment banking house with which it has had favorable previous dealings and probably a long-standing relationship. The investment banking house then works up the issue, develops all the relevant facts, assembles a buying group, sets a price, and arranges to buy the issue. It subsequently forms a selling syndicate to resell or redistribute the issue. In competitive bidding, on the other hand, the borrowing company invites investment bankers to form syndicates to bid for the issue. Certain types of securities, such as state and municipal issues and most public utility and railroad securities, must be sold at competitive bidding.

Prices set in the primary market when the new issue appears may thus be negotiated prices, or competitive auction prices, or privately agreed-upon prices, usually in all three taking into consideration prevailing prices for comparable or nearly comparable outstanding issues traded in secondary markets. Institutional investment managers are much more involved in prices and purchases in the primary market than are individual investors. While the value analysis of the individual investor is directed toward existing securities and secondary markets, institutional investment men must give substantial attention to new issue markets.

Secondary markets for securities—the organized exchanges and the over-the-counter markets—provide the trading forums, the liquidity, the familiarity with issues and companies, and the price and value determinations which encourage public interest in security investment and facilitate new financing. When an individual or an institutional investor buys a security, he buys a claim to assets or to future income, or to both, and faith in this claim is enhanced or diminished depending on the ease or difficulty of finding a ready market for the claim on short notice, if desired. No doubt many would hesitate to buy securities if they could not count on a ready market if needed. Clearly the development of the now elaborate machinery for trading in existing securities came about in response to a felt need.

The organized exchanges provide physical marketplaces where trading in existing securities occurs. They furnish facilities for the maintenance of a free, close, and continuous market for securities traded—free in that the trading price of any security, in the absence of now illegal manipulation, is governed by the forces of supply and demand; close in that the spread between the bid price for a security and the price at which it is offered for sale is normally relatively narrow; and continuous in that successive sales ordinarily are made at relatively small variations in price, thus providing a liquid market. Organized exchanges are competitive markets with prices set by thousands of buyers and sellers in numerous little auctions occurring daily on the floor of the exchange. The New York Stock Exchange is, of course, the most important, and accounts for about 85% of all trading on organized exchanges. The American Stock Exchange ranks next, with the Midwest and Pacific Coast exchanges of importance.

The over-the-counter market consists of a loose aggregation of brokers and dealers who make a market principally, though not exclusively, for securities not listed on organized exchanges. The term *over-the-counter market* itself is misleading. There are no counters and there is no market in the sense of a given place where buyers and sellers meet to dispose of wares. The over-the-counter market is rather a complex network of trading rooms all over the country, linked by telephone and teletype and telegraph, as well as by mail. The phrase is a carryover from the past, when shares were literally sold over the counter of private banking houses.

Securities transactions on the over-the-counter market run about 60% of the volume on all organized exchanges. Most federal, state, and municipal securities and many bank and insurance company stocks are traded over the counter. Because of the passage of the Security Acts Amendments of 1964, a number of larger unlisted companies, applied for listing on the major exchanges. There is, however, an apparently growing over-the-counter market in exchange-listed securities, the so-called third market. Over-the-counter securities are traded in a negotiated rather than an auction market like the organized exchanges. The price at which a given security can be purchased or sold on the over-the-counter market is determined by bargaining, with the broker-dealer acting as a principal in the transaction.

### The New York Stock Exchange

The New York Stock Exchange is almost as old as the country and about as new as modern automated communications equipment can make it. Established in 1792, it wasn't until 1863 that its name was changed to New York Stock Exchange. The exchange is a voluntary unincorporated private association consisting of 1,366 members who have bought "seats" (memberships) on the exchange. Only members of the exchange are permitted to trade on its "floor." A seat, or membership, has sold for as high as $625,000 (1929) and for as low as $17,000 (1942). The current price is around $200,000. In addition to the price of membership, the initiation fee is $7,500 and dues are $1,500 annually. The securities of more than 1,200 major companies are "listed" on the New York Stock Exchange, which means that they have been accepted for trading. Only those securities which have been accepted for listing may be traded on the exchange floor. Trading takes place between the hours of 10 A.M. and 3:30 P.M., New York time, Monday through Friday.

Located at the corner of Wall and Broad Streets, physically the exchange floor is almost the size of a football field. On the trading floor are 19 posts, at which over 1,600 listed stock issues are traded, and the "Bond Crowd," where almost 1,200 bond issues are bought and sold. On the floor last year were traded over 1.8 billion shares of stock in round and odd lots with a market value of over $73 billion and bonds with a market value of about $2.9 billion. Much more bond trading takes place in the over-the-counter market than on the floor of the New York Stock Exchange.

Under the floor are 40 miles of pneumatic tubes, connecting each post with telephone booths around the walls. Orders and reports, recorded on slips of paper, can be relayed through these tubes between the posts and booths. In the booths about 2,100 private telephone lines directly connect the floor of the exchange with member firm offices. The pneumatic tubes also link the "floor" with its "trading posts" with the ticker room upstairs.

On days of large volume in the past, the ticker, reporting transac-

FIGURE 2–1

Trading on the New York Stock Exchange

tions and prices, ran behind the market, but now with a new stock ticker capable of printing up to 900 characters per minute, the high-speed ticker is able to keep up with a 10-million-share day. A large computer center operates in the exchange building. One of its first uses was to improve the exchange's telephone quotation service. Formerly, a broker who wanted current market information for a customer would be connected with the exchange's manually operated quotation service. He would get the "bid" and "asked" quote. Now, a broker merely dials, on his private line telephone, a four-digit code to one of the 1,600 stocks listed on the exchange. He is answered almost instantly by an electronic voice identifying the stock, giving the current "quote" and last sales price. By dialing another sequence of numbers, the broker receives the opening price, range for the day, and up-to-the-minute volume. To provide market information in the form of speech, a voice-assembler unit in the computer center uses prerecorded words to translate computer language into spoken messages. This service is capable of handling 300 calls simultaneously, or up to 400,000 calls a day.

Under the new computer setup, a post reporter now simply marks the details of a trade on a preprinted card and drops it in an optical scanner. The optical scanner reads the card, flashes the data to the processing center, which continually checks for errors, compiles the data in time sequence, and stores it in memory drums. Data go onto the ticker and also to loudspeakers and to 20 specialized teletypewriters at trading posts. An important use for the machines is in the "stock-watching" program, the exchange's procedure for observing any unusual trading activity. The computer center is also utilized as a central accounting facility for member organizations. This new automated system cuts to a split second from minutes the interval between a trade being reported and its appearance on the ticker.

### Functions of Members

A member of the New York Stock Exchange may be a general partner or holder of voting stock in one of the brokerage concerns which, by virtue of his exchange membership, is known as a member firm or member corporation. There are 659 such member organizations—508 partnerships and 151 corporations. About half the members of the New York Stock Exchange are partners or officers in member organizations doing business with the public—so-called *commission houses.* These members execute customers' orders to buy and sell on the exchange, and their firms receive sliding-scale commissions on those transactions. Many commission brokerage houses, particularly the larger ones such as Merrill Lynch, Pierce, Fenner & Smith; Francis I. du Pont & Company; Bache & Company; and Goodbody & Company have more than one member.

About one fourth of all members of the exchange are *specialists,* so-called because they specialize in "making a market" for one or more stocks. To carry out this function of maintaining a fair and orderly market, insofar as it is reasonably practicable, the specialist is expected to risk his own capital by buying at a higher price or selling at a lower price than the public may be willing to pay or accept at that moment. For example, suppose the last sales of ZXY stock was at $55 a share; the lowest offer to sell is $55 a share and $54 is the highest bid. Depending on the conditions in the market the specialist might bid $54½ in order to narrow the temporary spread between supply and demand. In a rising market the specialist may be expected at times to sell stock for his own account at a lower price than that at which the public will sell.

The exchange sets specific requirements for specialists concerning market experience, their dealer function, and the amount of capital they must possess. The specialist is expected to subordinate his own interests in the market to the public's. The specialist, for example, cannot buy in the exchange market at any price for his own account until he has executed all public buy orders held by him at that price. The same rule also applies to sales by specialists. Specialists on the New York Stock Exchange must now be able to carry 1,200 shares of each stock handled, while on the American Stock Exchange, the specialist must either have a capital of $50,000 or be able to carry 1,000 shares of each stock, whichever is larger.[5]

The specialist's business is concentrated in one or more stocks at one trading post. He "keeps the book" in these stocks. He usually has an assistant, and one or the other is always at the post during trading hours. Thus he can also act for other brokers who cannot remain at one post until prices specified by their customers' buy and sell orders—either purchases below or sales above prevailing prices—are reached. The specialist must assume full responsibility for all orders turned over to him. Part of the commission the customer pays his own broker goes to the specialist when his services are used, and much of his earnings come from commissions on orders he executes for other brokers.[6]

A number of members of the New York Stock Exchange serve as *odd-lot dealers.* A round lot on the New York Stock Exchange is usually 100 shares. An odd-lot is usually less than 100 shares. The odd-lot member acts as a dealer, not as a broker. He buys odd lots of stock from, or sells odd lots of stock to, other members doing a public business, in this way serving investors who purchase or sell from one to 99 shares at a time, rather than the conventional 100-share round lot.[7]

Some members serve as *floor brokers,* assisting busy commission brokers to ensure swift execution of orders. Investors complain if their orders are not handled rapidly and efficiently. Commission brokerage houses are very sensitive to this. One large house advertises:

> Unsurpassed floor coverage for fast and efficient executions. Twelve brokers on the floor of the New York Stock Exchange, each with an intimate feel for

---

[5] See "Wall Street Can Live with the New Rules," *Business Week,* October 3, 1964.

[6] For more information see *Now, About the Specialist,* the New York Stock Exchange. For a free copy write to the Publications Division of the New York Stock Exchange, 11 Wall Street, New York, N.Y. 10005.

[7] In a few issues the round lot is 10 shares rather than 100 shares.

the market in the stocks he handles because he covers only two trading posts, an average of 125 stocks.

Smaller houses, which have only one member of the firm on the floor of the exchange, need help when orders flow in rapidly or in bunches. They can call upon the floor brokers to take over some of their volume and by this means secure quick execution of orders which might otherwise be delayed. The commission brokerage houses which utilize the services of floor brokers share commissions with them. Floor brokers are still popularly known as "$2 brokers," although the commission they receive for their services has long been above that amount.

There are some 30 members of the New York Stock Exchange, now known as *registered traders,* who use their privilege of being able to engage in transactions on the floor of the exchange, simply to buy and sell for their own accounts. Their transactions must meet certain exchange requirements and must contribute to the liquidity of the markets in the stocks in which they trade. Registered traders may also be called upon to help expedite the handling of blocks of stock bid for or offered on the exchange.

All members—whatever their function—in order to trade must own a "seat" on the exchange, a term that traces back to the earlier years when the brokers did remain seated while the president called the list of securities.

## Listing Requirements

To be listed on the New York Stock Exchange, a company is expected to meet certain qualifications and to be willing to keep the investing public informed on the progress of its affairs. In determining eligibility for listing, particular attention is given to such qualifications as: (*a*) whether the company is national or local in scope; (*b*) its relative position and standing in the industry; (*c*) whether it is engaged in an expanding industry, with prospects of at least maintaining its relative position.

While each application for *initial listing* is judged on its own merits, the exchange generally requires the following as a minimum:

(*a*) Demonstrated earning power under competitive conditions of $2 million annually before taxes.

(*b*) Net tangible assets of $10 million, but greater emphasis will be placed on the aggregate market value of the common stock, where $12 million or more applicable to publicly held shares at the time of listing is sought.

(*c*) One million shares outstanding, of which at least 700,000 common shares are publicly held among not less than 1,700 round-lot shareholders, and a total of 2,000 shareholders of record. The listing agreement between the company and the exchange is designed to provide timely disclosure to the public of earnings statements, dividend notices, and other information which may affect security values or influence investment decisions. The exchange requires actively operating companies to agree to solicit proxies for all meetings of stockholders. As a matter of general policy, the exchange has for many years refused to list nonvoting common stocks, and all listed common stocks have the right to vote.

There is no absolute right of *continued listing*. The exchange may at any time suspend or delist a security when it feels that continued trading is not advisable. For example, the exchange would normally give consideration to suspending or removing from the list a common stock of a company when there are:

(*a*) 700 round-lot holders or less, with 800 shareholders of record or less.

(*b*) 300,000 shares or less in public hands.

(*c*) $2.5 million or less aggregate market value of publicly held shares.

(*d*) $5 million or less in aggregate market value of all outstanding common stock or net tangible assets applicable thereto, combined with an earnings record of less than an average of $400,000 after taxes for the past three years.

While only 1,200 companies of the 1.3 million publicly and privately owned corporations that file reports with the U.S. Treasury are listed on the New York Stock Exchange, these include most of the larger, nationally known industrial companies. The total market value of all listed securities, stocks and bonds, is in excess of $600 billion.

### Types of Orders

Most generally used is the *market* order. When a customer places an order "at the market," it means that he is authorizing the commission broker to execute the order at the best possible price that can be obtained at the time the order reaches the post at which the stock is traded: in brief, at the then prevailing market price or close thereto. Probably about 75% to 85% of all orders are market orders. They can be executed very quickly and are used more by large traders, institutional investors, and professionals than by smaller investors. The latter often wish to specify the price at which they wish to buy or sell. Market orders are perhaps more common in sales than in purchases, since the seller is usually more anxious to obtain action than the buyer.

When the buyer or seller wishes to specify the price at which he wishes his order executed, he places a *limit order*. His broker is expected to execute it at the limit set or better. If it is a buy order, this means either at the price specified or lower, while if it is a sell order, at the price specified or higher. It may be that the order cannot, at the time given, be executed at the price specified. In that case the customer will have to wait until the market gets around to his price. Naturally the floor member of the commission brokerage house given the order to execute cannot wait at the trading post until the market moves to the specified price. This may take days, or weeks, or may never occur at all. Instead of waiting, he gives the order to the specialist in the stock. It is immediately entered in the specialist's book. If and when, minutes, or hours, or days, or weeks, or months later, the market price moves to the price specified in the limit order, and it is still in effect, the specialist will execute the order at the price specified and notify the commission broker, who in turn will notify the customer.

### How an Order Is Handled

Perhaps market operations will be clearer if we trace a typical order. Assume that Robert Wilton of New Orleans decides to buy a 100 shares of American Telephone and Telegraph Company. He asks the member firm's registered representative to find out for him what A.T.&T. shares are selling for on the exchange. Over a direct wire to his New York office, the representative asks for a "quote" on "Telephone." A clerk in the firm's New York office relays the question to the exchange's Quotation Service by dialing the four-digit code for A.T.&T. stock. Within seconds, the computer identifies the stock, locates the current "quote," assembles the response from a recording drum vocabulary, and sends it back to the inquirer. The clerk in the New York office immediately reports to New Orleans that "Telephone" is quoted "55 to a quarter, last at 55¼." This means that, at the moment, the highest bid to buy A.T.&T. stock is $55 a share, the lowest offer to sell is $55.25 a share, and the last transaction in that stock was at $55.25. Mr. Wilton is told that 100 shares will cost him approximately $5,500, plus a commission of about $41, and he decides to buy. The registered representative writes out an order to buy 100 shares of T "at the market." This is transmitted to the New York office at once and phoned from the firm's New York office to its clerk in a phone booth on the floor of the exchange. The clerk summons the firm's member partner and gives him the order. Each stock listed on the exchange is assigned a specific location at one of the trading posts, and all bids and offers must take place at that location. The floor partner hurries over to Post 15 where T is traded.

About the same time a Minneapolis grain merchant, Edward Hardy, decided he wants to sell his 100 shares of Telephone. He calls his broker, gets a "quote," tells his broker to sell. That order, too, is wired or phoned to the floor. Hardy's broker also hurries to Post 15. Just as he enters, the A.T.&T. "crowd," he hears Wilton's broker calling out, "How's Telephone?" Someone—usually the specialist—answers, "55 to a quarter."

Wilton's broker could, without further thought, buy the 100 shares offered at 55¼, and Hardy's broker could sell his 100 at 55. In that event, and if their customers had been looking over their shoulders, they probably would have said, "Why didn't you try to get a better price for us?" And they would have been right. Wilton's broker should reason: "I can't buy my 100 shares at 55. Someone has already bid 55, and no one will sell at that price. I could buy at 55¼ because someone has already offered to sell at that price but no one has come forward to buy. Guess I'd better try 55⅛." Hardy's broker reasons: "I can't sell my shares at 55¼ because someone has already tried and no one will buy them. I could sell at 55 but why don't I try 55⅛?" At that moment he hears Wilton's broker bid 55⅛ and instantly he shouts: "Sold 100 at 55⅛." They have agreed on a price and the transaction takes place.

The two brokers complete their verbal agreement by noting each other's firm name and reporting the transaction back to their phone clerks so that the respective customers can be notified. At the moment the transaction took place, an exchange reporter noted it on a card and placed the card in the optical card reader at the post. This transmitted the report of the transaction to the exchange's Computer Center and to the ticker. Automatically in a few seconds it appears as T 55⅛ on some 3,750 tickers all over the United States and Canada. In two or three minutes the buyer in New Orleans and the seller in Minneapolis are notified of the transaction. In a transaction on an organized exchange when you buy, you buy from another person. When you sell, you sell to another person. The exchange itself neither buys, nor sells, nor sets prices. It merely provides the marketplace, the physical setting, and the equipment. Prices are determined in "double auction," a number of prospective buyers and a number of prospective sellers bidding in an active market.

### The Odd-Lot Transaction

Suppose Mr. Wilton wanted to buy only 14 shares of A.T.&T. instead of 100. His commission broker's floor clerk would have sent the order to an odd-lot dealer at the post where Telephone is traded. The dealer would fill the order, out of his inventory, at a price based on the next round-lot transaction in A.T.&T. Assuming this next round-lot trade is made at 55⅛ a share, the odd-lot dealer would sell 14 shares at 55⅜. The additional one-quarter point, or 25 cents per share, included in the odd-lot price is known as a differential. On stocks selling at less than $55, it is 12½ cents a share above the round-lot price on purchases and below on sales. Much the same procedure would have been followed if Edward Hardy had only 20 or 53 or 87 shares to sell. His broker's clerk would have sent the sell order to an odd-lot dealer. If the next 100-share transaction in "Telephone" were at 55⅛ a share, the dealer would have bought Hardy's stock from him for 54⅞ a share. In every case, under present practice, odd-lot dealers stand ready to buy or sell. The customer never comes in contact, or even hears about the odd-lot dealer. He places the order with his commission broker, receives notice of execution through him, and is billed by him. The commission broker deals with the odd-lot house. About 99% of the business in odd lots on the New York Stock Exchange is handled by two large odd-lot firms, DeCoppet and Doremus and Carlisle and Jacquelin. On other exchanges odd lots are handled by the specialists.

### Special Types of Orders

Do you know what a W.O.W. order is? It is one of the numerous special types of orders, but you won't need to know about it until you buy your seat on the exchange. There are a few special types of orders, however, that are important.

*Stop orders* may be used in an effort to protect a paper profit or to try to limit a possible loss. There are stop orders to sell and stop orders to buy. They are essentially conditional market orders. They go into effect if something happens. For example, you bought Xerox at 31 and now it is 182. You want to continue to hold it as long as it keeps going up, but you want to protect your gain in case the market turns down. You place a stop order to sell at, say, 172, ten points below the current market. If the market turns down and goes to 172 or lower, your stock will be sold. Though you lose the last 10 points of your stock's climb, you preserve all the rest of the gain.

Or, to take another use, you note that General Motors is selling at 102. You think and hope it's going up farther and then split. But you're not sure, and 102 is a high price. You buy 100 shares at 102 but at the same time place a stop order to sell at 100. If your guess is incorrect and GM falls instead of rising, you will be out of it with a 2-point loss, plus commissions.

The stop order to buy is used in a short sale to limit losses. You sell Pennsylvania Railroad short at 60. You expect and hope that it will decline to 40. If it does, you will cover at that time and have a 20-point gain. But there is also the possibility that it may go up farther. To cut your possible loss, if it does, you place a stop order to buy at 65. Thus if the stock goes up contrary to your expectation, you will have bought back and covered at 65, and your loss will be held to 5 points.

The investor is not assured of getting the exact price designated by the stop order. If the market takes a sudden drop, the specialist sells the stock at whatever he can get; and that might be somewhat below the stop price. If you place a stop-loss order at 50, an accumulation of prior sell orders at this price, or a sharp drop in the market, may prevent the specialist from executing your order until the price is somewhere below 50. There is, however, a hybrid version called the *stop-limit order*. This enables the investor to stipulate the maximum or minimum price at which he is prepared to buy or sell. If the specialist cannot execute at that price or better, no transaction takes place.

At times the New York Stock Exchange has become worried about stop-loss orders in high-flying glamour stocks, because a downward dip in the market could set off a chain of stop orders and by enlarging sales cause a sharp break in the given stock or stocks. It has, therefore, from time to time, suspended the placement of stop orders in designated stocks to prevent undue market repercussions.[8]

Both stop-limit and stop-loss orders may be day, week, month, or "open" (GTC) orders. A market order is always a day order, good until the close of trading on the day it is written. When you give your broker a limit or stop order, you can specify that it is to be good for only one day—or for a week—or for a month. If the order is not executed during the period designated, it automatically expires. An open or GTC order is one that holds good indefinitely. The order holds until either the broker executes it or the customer cancels it.

A discretionary order is one which allows the broker to determine when to buy and when to sell, what to buy, what to sell, in what volume and when. This is a complete discretionary order. It must be given in writing by the customer and approved by a member of the firm. A limited discretionary order permits the broker to determine only the price and timing. Discretionary orders are used by those who are ill, aged, or off on a prolonged vacation. A long and close relationship with a reputable broker is a basic requirement for the use of such orders.

### Bull or Bear: Long or Short?

Where the expressions first arose we don't know, but a "bull" market is a rising market; a "bear" market is a falling market. A "bull" in Wall Street is an optimist, one who expects the market to go up. A "bear" is, of course, just the opposite, a pessimist who expects stock prices to decline. To take advantage of his forecast, a bull buys stock today in the hope of selling it later at a higher price. He goes "long." The bear, on the other hand, expecting the market to go down, "*sells short*"; that is he sells stock today in the hope of buying it back at a lower price, thus profiting from the decline.

Short selling in the securities market basically is selling shares you don't own and borrowing the same number of shares to deliver to the purchaser. When you buy the stock later to return to the lender, you hope to do so at a lower price, thus making a profit. How is it possible to sell something you don't own and buy it back later? In securities markets

---

[8] "Prohibiting Stop Orders," *Fortune*, December, 1965, pp. 236–38.

the short sale is possible as long as you can borrow the shares you have sold and deliver them to the buyer. Almost always you can do this, because your broker can borrow the stock either from some left in "Street names" with him, from some of his other customers, or from some other broker. Why are these people willing to lend? Because it is usually to their financial advantage. When you sell short and borrow a hundred shares, say of General Motors, to deliver to the purchaser, he, in turn, pays for the stock. You, the short seller, receive payment. If General Motors was selling at 100, you receive $10,000 (less costs). But you can't keep this $10,000.[9] You have to give it to the person or firm that loaned the 100 shares of General Motors. They hold it as collateral for the loan. When you return the shares, you get your funds back. Meanwhile they can use the money, lend it out at short-term and get 4% or 4½%, or use it to buy more stock, or for any other purpose. Since stock involved in a short sale now usually lends "flat," no fee attached, no charge, whereas the use of the cash turned over as collateral may bring a return, it is financially advantageous to lend stock, and that is why short sellers can function. The loan can be "called" at any time by either side. The borrower of the stock can ask for his funds back and return the shares, or the lender of the stock can ask for the shares back and return the funds, at any time.

If you are alert, several possible dilemmas may have suggested themselves. What, for example, if the lender of the stock wants his shares back, and you are not yet ready to close the short sale? Very simple. You borrow 100 shares of General Motors from someone else. Suppose General Motors rises to 110 and thus the stock is worth $11,000, but the money collateral given was only $10,000. The lender of the shares will call for more money collateral to support the loan. This is called "mark to the market." You, the short seller, will have to provide an additional $1,000, either from your own resources or by borrowing it. Conversely, if the stock price falls to $90 from the original $100—the short seller can and will ask for $1,000 of his cash collateral back. Both sides must "mark to the market."

Another problem may occur to you. Suppose a dividend is declared while the short sale is underway. Who is entitled to the dividend? It would seem as if two parties are, since seemingly two parties "own" the shares—the party to whom you sold the shares and the lender from whom you borrowed the shares you sold. Actually, both parties get the dividend. General Motors pays the dividend to the registered owner, and the short seller pays the dividend to the lender. Usually, this is not an extra cost to the short seller because when the stock goes "ex-dividend," the market

[9] The short seller must also provide the prevailing percentage margin. See p. 71.

price of the stock drops by an amount approximating the dividend and when the short seller covers later, he will do so at a lower price than if the stock had not gone ex-dividend.

In addition to short sales for speculative purposes, there are various technical types of short sales. One variety is known as a "sale against the box." This occurs when the short seller does actually own the stock, has it in his safe deposit box, but prefers to sell short "against the box." For example, an investor bought General Motors at $50, has watched it go to $100. He hears rumors that at a forthcoming directors meeting a week later the stock may be split. He reasons that if the stock is in fact split, it will continue to rise and he will want to hold it. If it is not split, he knows that a number of disappointed speculators will sell and the stock may decline. He wants to hold if the stock is split but avoid losing part of his profit if the stock is not split and declines. He sells General Motors short at $105, a point to which it has risen in anticipation of a split. The directors meet but do not vote a split. The stock declines to $95. Our seller against the box closes his short sale by delivering his own shares. He has gained time, bridged the directors meeting, and kept his gain from $50 to $105 intact, and now is out of the stock, as he wanted to be if there was no split, but at $105 instead of at $95.

A second use of a sale against the box is for tax purposes. A short sale can be used to carry over a capital gain from one year to the next. Mr. Astute bought Northwest Airlines at 65 and it's now 140. He has had a very good year—incomewise—and doesn't want to take his capital gain this year. He wants to carry it over to next year, which he estimates will not be as good for him or for the stock market as was the year just ending. Keeping his long position in Northwest, he sells short, against the box, at 140. At the end of the year he has two outstanding positions. He is both long and short Northwest. Neither transaction has been concluded, but by his short sale, he has ensured his gain in his long position. In January, he concludes his short sale. He covers by delivering the Northwest stock which he owns. He is out of Northwest, both long and short. He has his gain, and it has been taken in the year he preferred.

In a declining market, extensive short selling might cause a panic drop. Both the SEC and the exchange have been determined that short selling not be used to depress security prices artificially. There are rules to enforce this. No short sale of a stock is permitted except on a rising price. One can sell short at the price of the last sale providing that price was above the next preceding different price. For example, two sales of ZXY occur: the first at 44⅛, the second at 44. You cannot sell short at this point. You must wait for an uptick. The next transaction is at 44. You cannot sell short yet. The next price is 44⅛. Now you can sell short. The next transaction is also at 44⅛. You can sell short. As long as this price lasts, you can sell short, since the next preceding different price was lower. The market uses the terms "plus tick," "minus tick," and "zero plus tick," to indicate subsequent transactions. Dials at each post for each stock indicate the last sale and by + or −, whether a plus tick or minus tick. You can sell short on a plus tick. You cannot sell short on a minus tick. You can sell short on a zero plus tick. The prices 44, 44⅛, 44⅛ in succession provide an example of a zero plus tick.

Short selling is done mainly by professionals. The small investor, the odd-lot trader, seldom engage in short selling. The risk is very much greater than in a long transaction. If you buy 100 shares of a stock at 30, the worst that can happen, if the company goes bankrupt, is that you can lose $3,000. But if you sell short at 30 and sit mesmerized and watch the stock go up to 70, 80, 90, 100, etc., your potential loss is open-ended. It depends on your stubbornness and upon your financial resources. To engage in short selling, resources should and must be very ample and your temperament should include a quick capacity to admit a mistake.[10]

### Pay Cash or Buy on Margin?

Stock can be purchased for cash or on margin. When you buy on margin, you put up only part of the purchase price, and the broker lends you the remainder. What part you put up and what part you can borrow is not a matter for negotiation. It is determined by the Federal Reserve System, but the New York Stock Exchange also has its own requirements in addition. The Federal Reserve is involved because it is charged with control and regulation of the volume of credit. Under Regulation T, it controls the initial extension of credit to customers by members of national securities exchanges and by other brokers or dealers. Under Regulation U, the Federal Reserve regulates loans by banks for the purpose of purchasing and carrying stocks registered on national securities exchanges. Unregistered securities can only be purchased on a cash basis.

Since the Federal Reserve Board first set margin requirements in 1934, the amount of margin which a purchaser of listed securities has been required to deposit has ranged from 40% to 100% of the purchase price. Today the margin rate is 70%.

To understand margin fully you must know the difference between *initial* margin and *maintenance* margin, *debit balance* and *equity*, *undermargined* and *restricted* account. The Federal Reserve's present 70% requirement is an *initial* margin. It applies only to the day of purchase. The *maintenance* margin applies to the account after the day of the transaction. The New York Stock Exchange has both an initial and a maintenance margin. The former is very simple. There must be an initial equity of $2,000 in the account not to exceed the price of the shares

---

[10] For a more extensive discussion, see Mark Weaver, *The Technique of Short Selling* (rev. ed.; Palisades Park, N.J.: Investors Library, 1963).

purchased. The maintenance margin requirement is 25% of the current market value of the securities long in the account. When a customer buys securities on margin, puts up part of the purchase price and borrows the remainder from his broker, the securities bought become *collateral* for the loan and must be left with the broker. The collateral is normally carried in the broker's (Street) name but is the purchaser's property. He is entitled to receive dividends and to vote the stock.

By *debit balance* is meant the net amount owed to the broker. At the outset it is usually the amount of the loan. Interest is charged on the debit balance. *Equity* is the value of the collateral minus the debit balance. Margin then can be described as the equity expressed in dollars or as a percentage of the current market value of the securities. For example, if you purchase 100 shares at $100 per share, or a total of $10,000 worth of stock on margin, you put up $7,000 and you borrow $3,000 from the broker. Your margin is $7,000 or 70%. Your debit balance is $3,000 (ignoring commissions). Equity is the current market value ($10,000) minus the current debit balance ($3,000) which is $7,000. In percentage terms, then, margin can be expressed as:

$$\text{Margin} = \frac{\text{Value of collateral} - \text{debit balance}}{\text{Value of collateral}}$$

or

$$\text{Margin} = \frac{\text{Equity}}{\text{Value of collateral}}$$

Now, suppose the stock falls to 80. The value of the collateral is now $8,000 instead of $10,000; equity is $5,000 ($8,000 − $3,000); the margin has fallen to 62½%, the debit balance remaining at $3,000, of course. If the stock falls to 40, the value of the collateral becomes $4,000, the equity shrinks to $1,000, the margin falls to 25%, with the debit balance remaining at $3,000. Thus in this case the stock can drop 60% in market value before the New York Stock Exchange's maintenance margin is reached.

A simple method of determining the minimum security position in the account is 4/3rds of the debit balance.[11] This applies only to long positions. Thus:

$$\text{4/3rds of \$3,000} = \$4,000$$

On a market value of $15,000 and a debit balance of $4,500, the equity would be $10,500. Applying the 4/3rds method to $4,500, we get $6,000. This is the security value to which the account could fall without requiring additional equity. And 25% of the $6,000 security value is $1,500, which is the minimum maintenance margin.

---

[11] According to the New York Exchange staff.

An *undermargined* account is one which falls below the New York Stock Exchange's maintenance margin requirements. It results in a call for more margin. While brokerage practice varies, it is customary to call for an increase in the equity to about 35% of the then current market value of the collateral. An *unrestricted* account is one in which the equity equals or exceeds the Federal Reserve's initial margin requirement. The excess equity can be withdrawn in cash or in securities of equivalent loan value. To revert to our previous example. If the market price of the shares went from the initial purchase price of 100 to 120, the value of the collateral would be $12,000, the debit balance $3,000, the equity would thus be 9,000, or $600 more than 70% of $12,000. For the customer to make a withdrawal, the broker must refigure the account, and the 70% margin applies to the $12,000 market value to determine the excess margin for the purpose of making the withdrawal. Thus the customer could withdraw $600 in cash from his account or could use it as margin to buy an additional $857 worth of stock.

A *restricted* account is one that has less equity than the Federal Reserve's initial margin requirement demands. In our earlier case, where the price of shares dropped from 100 to 80, the margin at 80 was 62½%. Since this was less than the Federal Reserve's requirement, the account became restricted. The Federal Reserve has no objection to restricted accounts, but certain limitations on additional transactions are applied to them. The difference, then, between an undermargined account and a restricted account should be clear. The undermargined account is one that has fallen below the New York Stock Exchange's maintenance margin requirement. It results in a margin call. The restricted account, on the other hand, is one that has fallen below the Federal Reserve's initial margin requirement. It results in certain restrictions on subsequent transactions in the account.

Margin requirements also apply to short sales. The Federal Reserve's initial margin requirement applies to both long and short transactions. Under a 70% margin requirement, therefore, if you want to sell $8,000 worth of stock short, you must provide $5,600. Contrary to what happens in a long margin transaction, when the percentage margin decreases as the price of the stock falls, in short selling margins, as the price of the stock falls, the percentage margin increases. Thus, if you sold 100 shares short at 80 and put up $5,600 and the shares fall to 68, your margin rises to 100%. A formula has been developed which will help to explain this.[12]

$$\text{Margin} = \frac{\text{Net proceeds of sale} + \text{initial margin}}{\text{Current market value of stock}} - 1.00 \times 100$$

---

[12] See George L. Leffler and Loring C. Farwell, *The Stock Market* (3rd ed.; New York: Ronald Press Co., 1963), pp. 371–72.

Therefore, at a current market price of 68, the $5,600 deposited at the time of sale at 80, will bring your margin to 100%:

$$\text{Margin} = \left(\frac{8{,}000 + 5{,}600}{6{,}800} - 1\right) \times 100 = 100\%$$

Conversely, as the stock price rises, margin in a short sale falls percentage-wise. Thus, if the stock price goes up to 100, the margin drops to 36% as follows:

$$\text{Margin} = \left(\frac{8{,}000 + 5{,}600}{10{,}000} - 1\right) \times 100 = 36\%$$

Should the stock rise above 104, at which point the margin would have fallen to 30%, the New York Stock Exchange's maintenance margin requirements for short sales would come into play, resulting in a call for more margin. The New York Stock Exchange's maintenance margin requirement is 30% of the current market value of the borrowed securities, if their market value is $17 per share or over. Margin requirements are higher for lower priced shares, and it is possible, in the case of low-priced stock, for the maintenance margin requirement to be higher than the initial margin requirement.[13]

**TABLE 2–4**

**Relative Gain or Loss under Different Margin Requirements**

| *Requirement for Margin* | *Funds Advanced by Buyer* | *Amount of Credit Needed* | *Number of Shares Purchased at $50 Each* | *Per Share Change in Market Value* | *Profit (+) or Loss (−) Involved* |
|---|---|---|---|---|---|
| 10% | $1,000 | $9,000.00 | 200.00 | ±$5 | ±$1,000.00 |
| 20 | 1,000 | 4,000.00 | 100.00 | ± 5 | ± 500.00 |
| 50 | 1,000 | 1,000.00 | 40.00 | ± 5 | ± 200.00 |
| 75 | 1,000 | 333.33 | 26.67 | ± 5 | ± 133.33 |
| 100 | 1,000 | 0.00 | 20.00 | ± 5 | ± 100.00 |

The purpose of buying on margin, of course, is to stretch your funds. You can command more shares on margin with a given amount of funds than if you pay cash. If the stock rises in price, your profits are enhanced. On the other hand, if the stock goes down and you cannot put up more margin, assuming you are long, and you are forced to sell, or are sold out, you can lose more than you would if you had used the same amount of money to buy the stock for cash. With a 50% margin you can buy twice as many shares as in a cash transaction. With a 25% margin you

[13] When the stock has a market value below $5, the margin is 100% or $2.50 per share, whichever is greater. For stock with a market value of $5 per share or over, a minimum of $5 per share or 30% of the market value is required. At $17 the 30% becomes approximately equal to the $5-per-share minimum.

can buy four times as many. The principle of leverage comes into play. By operating with other people's money, the opportunity for profit or loss is magnified.[14] This may be seen in Table 2–4. Keep in mind, however, that if the chance for profit is increased two- or fourfold, the chance for loss also increases too.

### What It Costs to Buy Stock

Commissions charged by Stock Exchange members are said to average between 1% and 2% of the value of the transaction. Commissions are figured on the following basis for each 100 shares:

On a purchase or sale between $100 and $399.99, 2% plus $3. The minimum commission is $6.

On a purchase or sale from $400 to $2,399.99, 1% plus $7.

On a purchase or sale from $2,400 to $4,999.99, one half of 1% plus $19.

On a purchase or sale amounting to $5,000 or more, one tenth of 1% plus $39, provided that amount does not exceed $75 per 100-share transaction.

Thus, for stock transactions on the New York Stock Exchange involving $100 or more, the commission charge ranges between $6 and $75 per transaction, for 100 shares.[15]

On odd lots the commission is $2 lower per transaction, but in addition there is the odd-lot differential of ⅛ or ¼ per share.[16]

If you bought 100 shares at $40 per share, the commission would be $39 ($19 plus ½ of 1%). For an odd lot totaling the same $4,000, the commission would be $37 ($17 plus ½ of 1%), plus, of course, the odd-lot differential. For 100 shares at $100 per share, or $10,000 worth of stock, the commission would be $49 ($39 + 1⁄10 of 1%). For an odd lot amounting to $10,000, the commission would, of course, be $2 less, or $47 ($37 + 1⁄10 of 1%), plus the odd-lot differential. On, say, 99 shares, the extra 25 cents per share in the purchase price would add $24.75.

In addition, New York State levies a transfer tax of from 1¼ to 5 cents a share, based on the selling price of the stock. New York State transfer taxes are paid by the seller. Also, the SEC collects a transfer fee on all sales of securities on registered exchanges. It is paid by the seller and

---

[14] Leo Barnes has pointed out that many investors utilize margin irrationally. See his " 'Pseudo-Margin' and 'Pseudo-Leverage'—Grand Illusions of the Affluent Investor," *Financial Analysts Journal* July–August, 1964.

[15] If the money involved is less than $100, the commission is as mutually agreed upon between the customer and the broker.

[16] From 1951 to mid-1966, the "odd-lot" differential stood at 12.5 cents a share on stocks trading at less than $40 and 25 cents a share on those selling at $40 or more. Effective July 1, 1966, there was a change in the "break point." It was advanced from $40 a share to $55 a share, with the levy remaining at 12.5 cents a share below $55 and at 25 cents at and above $55 a share.

amounts to 1 cent per $500 value of the transaction (or portion thereof).

On a percentage basis, commissions on 100 shares purchased at $25 per share amount to 1.26% of the purchase price, while on an odd lot of 10 shares at $25 per share it would be 2.4%. These are, of course, one-way transactions. For a round trip—a purchase and a sale—the percentages would be about double. If we add the cost of the transfer tax and SEC fee to the brokerage fee, the total cost as a percentage of the value of the securities would be approximately 2.72% for the round lot, while for the odd lot, adding all costs, commission, tax, odd-lot differential and SEC fee, for the round trip, the percentage cost would be about 5.5%.

From a cost point of view alone, there is an advantage to trading in round lots rather than odd lots, and in higher priced shares rather than lower priced shares. This may be seen from the tabulation in Table 2–5.

**TABLE 2–5**

| | *Value of Stock* | *Total Trading Costs (In-and-Out)* | *Percent of Value of Stock* |
|---|---|---|---|
| *$200 Stock* | | | |
| 100 shares | $20,000 | $123.40 | 0.62% |
| 25 shares | 5,000 | 88.85 | 1.78 |
| 5 shares | 1,000 | 17.77 | 1.78 |
| *$100 Stock* | | | |
| 100 shares | $10,000 | $103.20 | 1.03% |
| 25 shares | 2,500 | 72.80 | 2.91 |
| 5 shares | 500 | 17.76 | 3.55 |
| *$50 Stock* | | | |
| 100 shares | $ 5,000 | $ 93.10 | 1.86% |
| 25 shares | 1,250 | 42.54 | 3.40 |
| 5 shares | 250 | 13.52 | 5.41 |
| *$10 Stock* | | | |
| 100 shares | $ 1,000 | $ 37.77 | 3.78% |
| 25 shares | 250 | 19.21 | 7.68 |
| 5 shares | 50 | 7.46 | 14.92 |
| *$3 Stock* | | | |
| 100 shares | $ 300 | $ 20.01 | 6.67% |
| 25 shares | 75 | 15.77 | 21.03 |
| 5 shares | 15 | 3.37 | 22.47 |

Source: George A. Chestnutt, Jr., *Stock Market Analysis,* 1966, p. 28.

This tabulation assumes a purchase and sale; it takes into consideration the brokerage commissions, the odd-lot fees, the SEC fee, and the tax involved.

## Institutional Investors and Large Blocks

On a May morning in 1963, a broker on the exchange floor received an order to sell 157,000 shares of Texaco. Within two and one-half hours—and with the help of the specialist—enough buyers were rounded up among other exchange member organizations to sell the entire block on the floor at just below the then going market price. In terms of market value—$10.3 million—the trade was the biggest ever to take place up to that time in the auction market during a single trading session. In April, 1964, a new market-value record was set when 191,811 shares of Gulf Oil—worth more than $10.5 million—were crossed on the floor at 55. The trade was successful largely because the Gulf specialist himself bought 141,811 shares for his own account at a cost of nearly $8 million.

Institutional investors have become a powerful factor in the market. Of the total value of all exchange-listed stock of about $550 billion, institutions are estimated to own approximately 21%. By far the most important buyers are the private noninsured pension funds. Their stockholdings at market value represented about 6% of the market value of all stock listed on the New York Stock Exchange. It is estimated that by 1980 they will own about 13%. With the great expansion in the scope of institutional investors has come a need to handle trading in the large blocks in which they customarily buy and sell. A variety of techniques for handling large blocks has been developed by the exchange, either meshing in with, or supplementing, the prevailing auction procedures.

The potential depth of the auction market is often greater than may appear on the surface. Through a member firm, an institutional investment manager can go beyond the "quote." This, after all, is simply a report of the highest bid to buy and the lowest offer to sell. It frequently is given in terms of a single round lot, or a few hundred shares. In the case of the Texaco transaction cited above, at the time the order was placed, the quoted market was rather thin—66¾ bid for 200 shares; 500 shares offered at 67 (the price of the last sale). The broker, knowing the full size of the order, was able to enlist the assistance of other commission brokers, floor traders, and, of course, the Texaco specialist. Despite the thin quote, within a few hours the selling team rounded up enough buy orders to take care of the entire block. With the last sale at 66½, most of the block was sold at 66. In the Gulf Oil transaction, the selling broker was able to develop offsetting buy orders for 7,000 shares within his own organization. Orders of the specialist's book ultimately accounted for another 15,000. The specialist not only provided information which led to orders for 28,000 shares among three commission brokers on the floor, but he bought 141,811 shares—nearly $8 million worth—for his own account.

There are a number of special methods for buying and selling large blocks on the NYSE. On the buy side, there is the specialist block sale, the exchange acquisition, and the special bid; on the sell side the specialist block purchase, an exchange distribution, a special offering, and a secondary distribution. The specialist block purchase or sale is simply a situation where a commission broker or a floor broker with a large block to buy or sell approaches the specialist in the stock to see if he wishes to, and is able

## FIGURE 2–2

### The Block That Almost Broke the Bank

***The New York Stock Exchange is based on a very simple principle: That for every buyer a seller can be found and for every seller a buyer. That principle faced—and passed—a very rough test early last month.***

AT AROUND 10:40 on Thursday morning, Oct. 6, a large crowd began to gather around Trading Post 16 on the floor of the New York Stock Exchange. What they came to see was the auction market being stopped dead in its tracks.

**Rude Awakening.** The specialist at Post 16, Robert Stott of Wagner, Stott & Co., arrived on the floor of the exchange that morning to face the kind of problem that gives specialists nightmares. Two brokerage firms, both representing institutional clients, came to him with orders to sell a huge block of 162,000 shares of Xerox Corp. Together these were worth almost $25 million at the previous day's closing price for Xerox. The Big Board's auction system is good and well-financed. . . . But $25 million at one fell swoop?

The firms, Donaldson, Lufkin & Jenrette Inc. with 96,000 shares to sell, and Dean Witter & Co. with 66,000 shares, had been unable to find buyers for the stock. So they turned to the auction market's helper, the specialist. Under normal circumstances the specialist would attempt to find buyers himself. If he couldn't buy it at all, he might buy some of it for his own firm's account. Specialists do this every day. Whatever they might lose on the trade at hand they hope to make up by selling the shares later in a more favorable market. But the situation that faced Stott on Oct. 6 made normal procedures impossible.

Xerox had been in a steady decline since late June, when it reached its high for the year of 267¾. On Wednesday, Oct. 5, the stock had been beaten down by 14 points to 150½ on a volume that ran just over 100,000 shares.

Stott's firm, which acts as specialist for 35 issues on the New York Stock Exchange, had from time to time taken positions of 25,000 and 30,000 shares of Xerox, but never anything like 162,000.

As the crowd gathered around Post 16, Stott called over Exchange Governors John J. Flanagan and John J. Anglim and requested permission to halt all trading in Xerox until some buyers could be located. They considered for a moment the panic that might result from such an action, which is something akin to a bank closing its doors in the face of a run on deposits. Then, after telling Stott to enter the 96,000-share DLJ order in his book to comply with Exchange regulations, Flanagan agreed to stop trading in Xerox.

While Stott, Flanagan and Anglim crossed their fingers, word went out around Wall Street and around the country that there was a lot of Xerox for sale and that the last quotation was 148. The stock had opened late that morning because of a pile-up of orders, then had sold down again as on the day before.

As the day wore on, instead of a panic-inspired flood of sell orders, buying strength picked up. Stott himself bought 30,000 shares. But matching up the orders was tricky. Most brokers are given limit prices, above and below which they may not buy or sell. DLJ's floor broker warned Flanagan during the day that Xerox had better not try to open below his price limit of 135, or he wouldn't sell. If that should happen, then DLJ's 96,000-share block would continue to hang over the market and nothing would be solved.

But Dean Witter cut its order during the day, eventually selling only 20,000 shares and coming back with the rest the next day. Finally, just before the 3:30 closing gong, enough buy orders had been rounded up to open Xerox at 143, $5 below the previous price and some $8 above DLJ's low limit. By the close of trading, 151,600 shares had changed hands, most of it in the closing moments. But the specialist's cool actions had averted potential disaster.

**Savor the Moment.** Many of the principals left the Exchange floor limp. But this relief could only be momentary. Still unresolved was what to do about handling other large blocks of stock from big institutional customers. There can be, and almost certainly will be, repeat crises of the type faced on Oct. 6. Institutions like mutual funds, pension funds and banks now own some 40% of all common and preferred stocks and they customarily trade in large blocks. Moreover, with the advent of the so-called "performance" mutual funds, heavy institutional trading should continue on the upswing. But on Oct. 6, the New York Stock Exchange came through a severe test with excellent marks.

**Source:** *Forbes,* **November 1, 1966.**

to, absorb the entire block, usually at a price very close to the market but with a slight concession to the specialist. The trade is made privately. There is no notice on the ticker, no announcement of any kind before or after, and no entry in the specialist's book.

For larger sized blocks the exchange distribution or acquisition may be used. It involves a large member firm (commission brokerage house) using its private communications system to generate buy or sell orders in sufficient volume to take up the block amount, with the block seller or buyer paying all brokerage costs. When sufficient orders have been accumulated, these are crossed with the block order on the floor, within the current auction market "bid-and-asked" range. Only after a "cross" has been executed does the ticker disclose that an acquisition or distribution has been accomplished. No prior public announcement of a forthcoming acquisition or distribution is made.

The special offering or bid involves appealing to the combined resources of the stock exchange community by announcing an attractive fixed, net price over the exchange's nationwide ticker system. The ticker message, appearing simultaneously across the country, sums up the terms of the special offering. An incentive commission is offered to induce brokerage interest. This is paid by the block seller or buyer. Customers responding to the special offer or bid pay no brokerage commission. Secondary distributions usually involve blocks exceedingly large in relation to the current market. The institutional investment manager agrees on a net price per share for his block, somewhat under the current auction market. A selling group is formed to handle the distribution. It offers the stock to buyers at a net price reflecting the current auction market level. Buyers are attracted by the fact that the price is net—that is, they pay no commission.

Sometimes when a block is very large and offsetting interest cannot readily be located either on the trading floor or among other institutions, the broker handling an institutional order may recommend the use of "*flow-in, flow-out*" trading, providing the institutional investment manager is willing and able to spread his purchases or sales over a longer period of time. The broker makes his bids or offers in such a way as to execute the order within a specified price range, with the least possible impact on the market and at the best possible average price for the institutional client. In one recent case, in one month's time 87,000 shares of a given stock were purchased for an insurance company at an average price of 39—less than the offer side of the market when the order was first placed. An estimated 250 sellers—institutions as well as individuals—had supplied the stock in 73 separate transactions. The specialist contacted the broker wherever selling interest appeared. In addition, the specialist, given specific limit orders by the broker, acquired more than 30,000 shares as the broker's agent.

Still another way a specialist can accommodate an institutional order is by "*stopping*" stock, as in the case of a recent bank order to sell 500 shares of a petroleum issue. The current market was 49¼ to 49½, 100 shares wanted, 1,000 offered. The bank's floor broker sold 100 shares at 49¼. The market became 49 bid (by the specialist), offered at 49½ (by the broker). The broker then asked if he could be "stopped" at 49, and the specialist agreed to "stop" the remaining 400 shares at that price. Thus, the broker was guaranteed at least 49 for the 400 shares and was assured that the specialist, now representing the order as a broker, would try to do better. As it turned out, a buyer appeared, and the specialist sold 200 shares at 49¼. Because sellers entered the market it became necessary for the specialist to buy the remaining 200 shares himself at 49. Even so, the "stop" had secured an extra ¼ point on 200 shares.

### Delivery and Clearance

After a transaction has taken place on the floor of the exchange, shares must be delivered from seller or buyer, and funds must pass the other way. The customary standard procedure in the absence of any agreement to the contrary is for delivery of certificates and cash to be made by noon of the fourth business day following the day of the transaction. Thus transactions occurring on Monday call for delivery by noon on Friday. Transactions on Tuesday require delivery by noon on the following Monday, since Saturday and Sunday are not counted as they are not business days. Holidays are not counted either.

In addition to *regular way* settlements, there are two other principal forms, *cash contracts* and *seller's option.* A *cash contract* calls for immediate delivery. A transaction for cash made before 2 P.M. on a given day requires delivery before 2:30 P.M. on the same day. If the transaction occurs after 2 P.M., delivery must be made within a half hour. There are a variety of special circumstances which dictate a cash contract, but three are recurrent. They involve expiration of tax years, rights, and conversion privileges. To establish a capital loss on December 30 or 31, a cash transaction is required, because a regular way contract would bring delivery and settlement into the following year. A cash contract is necessary to acquire rights on the last day of the period for which they run. When convertible securities are called for redemption, cash contracts are necessary the last three days the conversion feature is available. The cash contract must be specified at the time the transaction occurs and calls for same day settlement. *Seller's option* is a form of settlement contract which gives the seller, at his option, up to 60 days to deliver. Brokers clear through the Stock Clearing Corporation, a subsidiary of the NYSE. It involves a rather complex procedure, too detailed for elaboration here.

### The American and National Stock Exchanges

A satirical skit performed at the New York Financial Writers' "Follies" back in 1963 had a gangster, representing the Cosa Nostra, testifying before a congressional committee. He mentioned that the Cosa Nostra had plans to sell its stock to the public and then list it on an exchange. "The American Stock Exchange, no doubt," said one of the congressmen in the skit. "Oh, no, sir," the witness replied. "We wouldn't want that bad identification." The reference, of course, was to a long string of scandals that had plagued the American Stock Exchange (AMEX) during the 1950's and early 1960's, before the exchange administration was reorganized.[17]

AMEX, sometimes called the "Little Big Board," is located a few blocks away from the NYSE. Founded in the 1850's, it was known as the New York Curb Exchange until its name was changed in 1953. Its earlier name resulted from the fact it was an outdoor market from its origin until 1921, its members conducting trading along the curb on Broad and Wall Streets. Brokers' clerks sat or leaned out of second-story windows of office buildings lining the street and by the use of hand signals conveyed orders and messages to their brokers on the street down below. The brokers wore picturesque hats of various bright multicolored hues, so they could be distinguished from each other and recognized by their clerks in the second-story windows. Occasionally a clerk, in eagerness to attract the attention of his broker, gestured so vigorously that he lost his balance and fell out of a window, but the market went on, grew and prospered, and finally moved into its own building in 1921. One of the most colorful sights of old New York disappeared. Yet even today the hand signals survive, and a visitor to the American Stock Exchange can watch the rather esoteric hand signals between the telephone clerks in tiers around the floor of the exchange and brokers milling around the various trading posts.

Basically, procedures on the American Stock Exchange are much like those on the New York Stock Exchange. The listing requirements follow those of the NYSE but are not as stringent. While some stable old-line companies are listed on the AMEX, generally the companies listed are less mature and seasoned than those listed on the NYSE. Indeed, the AMEX has served as a kind of proving ground for newer companies, many of which, as they grow and expand, transfer their listing to the NYSE. Thus, for example, both Du Pont and General Motors were in their earlier days first traded on the AMEX. There is no dual listing of

[17] For an account of the change in administration at the American Stock Exchange, see T. A. Wise, "Young Ted Etherington's AMEX." *Fortune,* January, 1965.

companies on the NYSE and on the AMEX. No company at any given time may be listed on both exchanges. AMEX listing is terminated when a company moves to the Big Board. Many of the stocks on the AMEX are low priced (the average is about $15 per share versus approximately $55 on the Big Board), and many trade in round lots of 10, 20, and 50 shares, instead of the customary hundred. Unlike the New York Stock Exchange, the AMEX permits trading in some 200 unlisted companies. Specialists are granted the right by the American Stock Exchange to make a market in certain issues, even though the companies have not applied for listing privileges. There is also considerable trading in foreign securities on the AMEX. The AMEX, in fact, originated the ADR—American Depositary Receipts—by means of which American investors can trade in claims to foreign securities, the shares themselves being held by U.S. banks abroad. Many large commission brokerage houses hold membership on both the AMEX and the NYSE.

There is another small stock exchange in New York. It is the relatively new National Stock Exchange, founded in 1962. It has provision for some 400 members. Its listing requirements are even more relaxed than those of the American Stock Exchange. There is no duplication of trading or listing on the NYSE, the ASE, and the NSE. Stocks listed on one are not listed on another.

### The Regional Exchanges

At 2:24 P.M. on January 5, 1966, the biggest single dollar transaction ever made on any exchange chattered across the tape of the Midwest Stock Exchange—262,000 shares of Pennsylvania Railroad at $66.75 a share for a value of $17,488,500. The seller was one mutual fund, the buyers were two funds and a bank, and the trade—a "cross" in market jargon—was arranged by a young Chicago broker, Robert A. Jablonski of A. I. Jablonski & Company, which pocketed around $70,000 in commissions on the deal.[18]

The transaction illustrates the way the regional exchanges have been coming to life, partly as a result of the stringency of some NYSE rules. Most regional exchanges, but not the NYSE, allow members to split commissions with nonmember firms. This permits a mutual fund to give an order to an exchange member, then require that part of the commission go to nonmember firms as a reward for selling its shares. As a result more institutional business is going to regional exchanges. This has been especially true of the mutual funds business. As a means of trimming trading costs, two of the nation's largest mutual fund organizations purchased memberships on the Pacific Coast Stock Exchange.

---

[18] See "Big Blocks Make More of a Splash." *Business Week*. January 15, 1966.

The three principal regional exchanges are the Midwest Stock Exchange (MSE), the Pacific Coast Stock Exchange (PCSE), and the Philadelphia-Baltimore-Washington (PBWSE) exchange. There are, in all, 14 stock exchanges outside New York City. Ten are registered with the SEC while the remaining four are exempt because of their very small size and volume. In addition to the three principal regional exchanges, the other registered exchanges are in Boston, Cincinnati, Detroit, Pittsburgh, Salt Lake City, San Francisco, and Spokane. The last three are the so-called mining exchanges and differ in many respects from the others. The mining exchanges deal in mining and oil shares selling for under $1 per share. The four small exempt exchanges are located in Colorado Springs, Honolulu, Richmond, and Wheeling.

The Midwest Stock Exchange is the result of the consolidation of former exchanges in Chicago, Cleveland, St. Louis, and Minneapolis–St. Paul. Its trading floor and principal office are in Chicago, with branches in Cleveland and St. Louis, connected to Chicago by wire. Over a third of the member organizations of the MSE are also members of the NYSE, and over 80% of the issues traded on the MSE are also traded on either the NYSE or the AMEX.

The Pacific Coast Stock Exchange resulted from a consolidation in 1957 of the San Francisco and Los Angeles Stock Exchanges. It has two divisions, one in San Francisco and one in Los Angeles, each with its own trading floor, interconnected by an extensive communications system. The PCSE has the largest volume of shares traded of all regional exchanges. About one-third of the PCSE member firms are members of the NYSE, and over 90% of its stocks are those traded on either the NYSE or the AMEX. Because of the time differential, the PCSE provides trading facilities after the close of the NYSE and ASE.

Generally the larger regional exchanges list some 500 companies each, while the smaller ones list about 100 companies each. The companies listed are for the most part regional or local concerns, but there is extensive trading in securities listed on the NYSE or the AMEX. Such shares usually enjoy unlisted trading privileges on the regional exchanges. Odd lots are a larger part of total trading volume on regional exchanges than on the NYSE. For dually traded issues, transactions on the regional exchanges are based on the prices and quotations of the NYSE or the AMEX. The NYSE, AMEX, MSE, and PCSE account for 98% of the dollar volume and 97% of the share volume of securities traded on all exchanges.

### The Over-the-Counter Market

"The over-the-counter markets are large and important, they are heterogeneous and diffuse, they are still relatively obscure and even mysterious for most investors, and they are also comparatively unregulated." This is the way the *Report of the Special Study of the Securities Markets* characterized the over-the-counter market.[19]

Transactions in securities not taking place on an exchange are referred to as over-the-counter transactions. The over-the-counter market, unlike the exchanges, has no centralized place for trading. There are no listing requirements for issues traded, and all registered broker-dealers are entitled to participate. The broker-dealers vary in size, experience, and function; the securities differ in price, quality, and activity. Approximately 20,000 issues are traded over the counter in any given year compared to some 3,000 stock issues and 1,250 bond issues admitted to trading on exchanges.

The over-the-counter market encompasses all securities not traded on national securities exchanges. Securities traded over the counter are quite diverse in kind, price, quality, and activity, reflecting the free entry of securities into the over-the-counter market. Most of the trading in government and municipal bonds, bank and insurance company stocks, and common and preferred stocks in some seasoned industrial companies as well as in thousands of newer or smaller industrial companies, takes place in the over-the-counter market. The SEC Special Study estimated that $556 billion out of a total of $1,092 billion in securities outstanding in the United States were not listed on any national securities exchange. There is also an active over-the-counter market in exchange-listed securities.

The issues of corporate stocks traded over the counter vary considerably in asset size, number of shareholders, and shares outstanding. There are substantial numbers of over-the-counter companies that cannot be distinguished from companies with securities listed on exchanges. Many others, however, are small companies, often speculative ventures in the promotional stage which have recently obtained public financing.

The SEC Special Study sampled a large number of over-the-counter companies. It found that 31% had assets of $10 million or over, 47% had $5 million or over, and 77% had $1 million or over. (The NYSE requires a minimum of $10 million of net tangible assets, while the AMEX requires at least $1 million.) Approximately half of the companies in the study had 500 or more shareholders, and 16% had 2,000 or more. Seventeen percent had fewer than 100 shareholders. (Under the listing requirements of the NYSE, an issuer must have at least 1,700 shareholders; the AMEX requires 750 shareholders.) Approximately one half of the issuers in the sample had less than 200,000 shares of their principal issue outstanding. (The NYSE requires a minimum of 700,000 shares outstanding to

[19] See *Report of Special Study of the Securities Markets of the Securities and Exchange Commission*, Part 2, Chap. vii on Over-The-Counter Markets, p. 669, (88th Cong. 1st sess., House Document No. 95, Part. 2, [Washington, D.C.: U.S. Government Printing Office, 1963]).

qualify for listing, while the AMEX requires 200,000 shares.) Approximately 20% had shares outstanding with a total market value of $10 million or over and 60% had stock worth $1 million or over. (Under NYSE listing requirements, a company must have outstanding common stock with a minimum market value of $12 million. The AMEX requires a minimum market value of $2 million.) At the other end of the scale, the stock of 15% of the companies was valued at under $250,000 and that of 25% was under $500,000. Slightly over 50% of the securities in the sample were priced at less than $20 per share. The median price of the issues was $19.

Just as there is an unlimited right of entry of securities into the over-the-counter markets, there is also virtually free access of persons into the over-the-counter securities business. There are about 5,000 active broker-dealers registered with the SEC. By comparison, approximately 1,200 member firms participate in trading on the securities exchanges. There is a high concentration of over-the-counter business within a few large firms. Fifty-six broker-dealers, or less than 2% of the total number, accounted for half the dollar volume of over-the-counter sales.

Activity in the over-the-counter market breaks down into two general categories—wholesale and retail. The wholesale dealer "makes markets" by standing ready to buy or sell securities for his own account from or to professionals who act for themselves or for the public. There are about 1,100 broker-dealer firms who "make markets" in OTC securities. The retail firm, on the other hand, is engaged in selling securities to public customers and buying or finding buyers when its customers wish to sell. Sales efforts are extensive. The absence of a tape to report and publicize transactions in OTC securities and the fact that such securities are less widely known and distributed than exchange securities, tend to result in greater selling efforts.

In executing OTC transactions a firm may act either as principal or as agent for a public customer. If the firm owns the securities that the customer wishes to buy, it may sell then from its own account at a "net" price. The confirmation which the customer receives does *not* disclose the cost of the security to the firm, or its markup or profit.

If the broker-dealer does not own the security at the time of a customer's inquiry, it may buy the security from another broker-dealer (a wholesale dealer), place the security in its own account, and immediately resell it to the customer on a principal basis. Again the difference between the firm's cost (the price paid to the wholesale dealer) and the net price to the customer, known as the "markup," is *not* disclosed to the customer.

Alternatively, the transaction may be consummated on an agency basis. In this event the customer's firm buys the security from the wholesale dealer on behalf of its customer without placing the security in its own account. It charges a commission, which is disclosed to the customer in his confirmation. If the customer's broker-dealer uses the services of another firm to communicate with the wholesale dealer, or to "shop around," this second firm may also charge a fee for this service, in which case it is said to be "interpositioned." Although this fee may be passed on to the customer it is *not* disclosed.

Wholesale dealers, or market makers generally advertise their willingness to buy or sell through the facilities (known as the "sheets") offered by the National Daily Quotation Service, a private organization which publishes daily, for the use of professionals, the names of broker-dealers making markets in specified securities and their quoted prices. Prices quoted by wholesale dealers to other broker-dealers are known as "inside" or wholesale prices; those quoted to the public are "outside" or retail prices. If there are a number of competing wholesale dealers making markets in a given security, the customer's broker-dealer may shop around to determine which wholesale dealer is quoting the best price. The extent to which a retail firm will shop around for its customer may depend on a number of factors, including the number of firms with which it has wire connections, the sophistication of the customer, the size of the order, and the diligence and probity of the broker.

### The "Third" Market

The growth of institutional transactions in large blocks of securities and the rigidity of certain NYSE rules and rates have resulted in a rapid expansion of the so-called "third" market. This is the off-board market for exchange-listed securities. It is a negotiated market rather than an auction market; yet as a general rule the price of a stock on the third market rarely deviates from the price on the NYSE by more than the exchange commission. The larger the block traded, however, the more room for negotiation. The market appears to have developed to service the special needs of two groups: (*a*) institutional investors who have increasingly become large holders of, and traders in, common stock; and (*b*) broker-dealers, not members of an exchange and therefore without direct access to the trading of listed stocks.

The NYSE rate structure does not provide for volume discounts. Institutional investors dealing in large blocks of stock on the NYSE pay the same commission, computed on the dollar value of each round lot, as other public customers. They receive no adjustment or graduated discount for the number of round lots in multiple round-lot transactions. The commission charged on an order for 10,000 shares is 100 times that on an order for 100 shares at the same price. In specific terms, the commission on a single round-lot trade in a $40 stock is $39, and on a 10,000 share transaction it is $3,900. In contrast, institutions generally deal as principals on the third market and pay (or receive) a price net of commission fixed by a broker-dealer (nonmember of the NYSE) who can adjust his markup to shade the NYSE commission

The NYSE has forbidden its members and member firms to trade or execute orders in NYSE-listed issues off the NYSE floor, except on other organized exchanges or with special permission. It views the growth of the third market with alarm. Corporate bond trading, which was once centered on NYSE, is now conducted almost entirely over the counter. Indeed, NYSE has a special rule allowing member firms to trade over the counter in listed bonds whenever the transaction involves 10 bonds ($10,000) or more. A long list of high-grade preferred shares and rail stocks with guaranteed dividends, all fully listed on the NYSE, are also exempt from the usual requirement that a NYSE member firm must trade in listed securities on the floor. It does not want to be forced to exempt block transactions in common stock from trading on the floor, too.

Firms dealing in the third market operate in two ways. A number of large firms maintain continuous trading markets in a number of listed stocks—meaning that they inventory these stocks and stand ready to buy or sell them at a quoted price. They make markets in the same fashion as the wholesalers in the OTC market. Most often, there is no commission charged on such deals. The dealers' profit lies in the spread between the bid and offered prices. These firms also (along with some firms that don't maintain continuous trading markets) act as agents in bringing together buyers and sellers—almost always institutions—with big blocks to trade. They may aim for a profit on the spread but, more often, they charge a commission on such deals, usually less than the NYSE commission.[20] Where formerly off-board markets were made in listed utility stocks or others of comparable stability, today the market encompasses a wide variety of industrials and other equities.

The third market offers certain advantages. Institutions deal directly with market makers on the third market and do not need the services of a broker. Their market interest and trading receive no publicity. Their transactions, which tend to be large, are not likely to affect prices on the exchange in a way detrimental to the satisfactory completion of the remainder of a large-block transaction. The off-board market maker has considerable latitude in quoting prices to institutions net of commissions that are better than the combination of exchange price and commission. Depth of market, which is important to institutions in large transactions is easily and definitely ascertainable on the third market. The market makers, such as Weeden & Company, Blyth & Company, First Boston Corporation, American Securities Corporation, Chicago's H. S. Kipnis & Company, San Francisco–based J. S. Strauss & Company, etc., generally possess the capability of taking large positions.

[20] See "The Market That Serves the Pros," *Business Week*, September 19, 1964.

Comparison of the operations of the third market and the exchange market should not be construed as suggesting any equivalence in capacity to trade stocks. Though the off-board market has been growing, it is still small when compared with NYSE trading. Some 75% of block trading still takes place on the floor of the NYSE.

## SUGGESTED READINGS

"Big Blocks Make More of a Splash," *Business Week*, January 15, 1966.

Herbert E. Dougall. *Capital Markets and Institutions.* Englewood Cliffs, N.J.: Prentice-Hall, Inc., 1965.

Wilford J. Eiteman, Charles A. Dice, David K. Eiteman. *The Stock Market.* 4th ed. New York: McGraw-Hill Book Co., 1966.

Irwin Friend. *Investment Banking and The New Issues Market.* Philadelphia: Wharton School of Finance and Commerce, University of Pennsylvania, 1965.

John W. Hazard and Milton Christie. *The Investment Business.* New York: Harper & Row, Publishers, 1964.

George L. Leffler and Loring C. Farwell. *The Stock Market.* 3rd ed. New York: Ronald Press, 1963.

"The Market That Serves the Pros," *Business Week*, September 19, 1964.

*Report of the Special Study of the Securities Markets of the Securities and Exchange Commission*, Parts I and II: 88th Cong., 1st sess., House Document No. 95. Washington, D.C.: U.S. Government Printing Office, 1963.

Sidney M. Robbins. *The Securities Markets: Operations and Issues.* New York: Free Press of Glencoe, 1966.

Mark Weaver. *The Technique of Short Selling.* Rev. ed. Palisades Park, N.J.: Investors' Library, Inc., 1963.

# 3

# SOURCES OF INVESTMENT INFORMATION

"Investigate before you invest."
—Better Business Bureau

The "Bawl Street Journal" comes out once a year. In it many a true word is said in jest. "We sincerely hope the market catches up with our predictions before the SEC does," advertised one brokerage house specializing in growth stock recommendations. "Now that logical reasoning is no longer required in this crazy market we have more confidence in our recommendations," announced another large firm. "Let us review your holdings with an aim at increasing our commissions," announced another jokingly. "If you're looking for laughs come in and see us! Some of our offerings are hilarious," said a new issue house. "Get our research bulletin: Rarely do so many who know so little say so much," advertised another firm. Wall Street poking fun at itself but highlighting a real problem—which of many, many sources of information to rely upon? Where to go for unbiased, accurate information?

For the small, inexperienced investor, the vast outpouring of investment information, advice, alleged facts, and recommendations can be bewildering and confusing. Even the skilled analyst can be misled. For example, one large investment advisory service was sued by an irate investor who had lost a large sum in a land company, whose stock had been recommended by the advisory service. In pretrial discovery and examination it developed that the service had made its recommendation based, in part, on a forecast of earnings. To develop this forecast the securities analyst of the investment advisory service had made a trip to Florida, talked with company officials, including the president and financial vice president. The information they provided turned out to be incorrect, and changes they had made in accounting techniques gave an artificially favorable cast to current and prospective earnings. Instead of the expected and forecasted increase in earnings per share over the next two years, losses developed.

### The Individual Investor

No one invests in a vacuum. We act on some type of information, whether it be a tip from a friend, advice from a banker, a broker's recommendation, a newspaper report, or a magazine article. Not knowing which of the many sources of information to rely upon, one investor hit upon a simple expedient which yielded substantial returns in the 1961–65 bull market. He watched the most active list in the daily paper, and whenever a stock, which had not previously been on the list, appeared twice and each time showed an increase in price, he bought, held six months and a day, and then sold, regardless of where the stock was at that time. He was getting his investment advice and suggestions from the market itself, reasoning that whatever was being bought in large volume had many favorable judgments behind it, some carefully considered and reasoned, others possibly less well based, but all, on the whole, serving as a judgment and recommendation.

Individual investors have a difficult time. They don't usually have time to research a stock in depth before making their investment decision. They have a business life, a family life, a social life, and the time remaining from these pursuits, if any, is likely to be very limited. What they read, what they look into, must be most judiciously selected because it can't, by definition, be very extensive. For the small investor, investment selection may become almost a hit-and-run operation.

Ideally the intelligent investor should ask and obtain answers to at least four basic questions: (1) What is the state of business and the economy? In the light of such conditions is it a favorable time to invest? Where are we in the business cycle? Is the boom likely to top out shortly? Is a recession at hand? Questions in this area will vary with the stage of the business cycle. (2) What is the state of the market? Are we in the early stages of a bull market? Has the low point of a bear market about been reached? Is the bull market about to top out? Questions to be asked will vary with the state of the market. (3) If answers to the preceding two questions seem favorable, then there must be an investment selection. What industries are likely to grow most rapidly? Are there any special factors which favor a particular industry? (4) Which company or companies within the industry are likely to do best? Which companies are to be avoided because of poor prospects?

While the average small investor may not be able to devote the time to answer all these questions in depth, he must spend some time, with one or more sources of information, to come to an investment decision. Which source or sources should he choose? Reliance on a broker, on the financial press and on one or more investment services seem essential.

### The Financial Analyst and the Institutional Investor

The financial analyst and the institutional investment manager have both the time and the resources to dig deeper than the individual investor. Increasingly, they also have the capacity. Financial analysts, or securities analysts, organized in a national federation, have introduced a professional qualification examination leading to a CFA designation—Chartered Financial Analyst. A formal training program with three stages of examinations lead to this designation. It requires not only a thorough knowledge of accounting, balance sheet and income statement analysis, but also competence and maturity in investment management and securities analysis.[1]

Institutions are able to employ skilled economists, financial analysts, and investment managers. They are able to mesh economic forecasts with investment research.[2] They can study SEC filings and SEC Form 10–K's for detailed financial information about companies in which they have an interest.[3] They can purchase copies of registration statements and read them with understanding. Where published financial information is not clear or adequate, or where questions arise about the financial affairs of a company, or about its management or management policies, the institutional investment manager or his financial analyst can afford the time and expense of calling upon the company at its home office and putting the questions privately before making an investment decision or judgment. Not only is the initial investment commitment a considered one but there is usually continuous review and scrutiny of issues held. When and if conditions develop which are adverse, securities are eliminated from the portfolio on the basis of facts, research, and experienced evaluation. Many small investors tend to put securities away and forget about them. Institutional investors seldom do this. They can afford to purchase the talent to handle a portfolio and to provide their analysts with the documents, materials, reports, published services, etc., with which they can be assisted in arriving at intelligent investment decisions. The institutional investor thus has a great advantage over the average individual investor.

### Brokerage Houses

Brokerage houses with research departments provide a wealth of information for both individual and institutional investors. Most large brokerage houses maintain substantial research staffs. They publish market letters or market reviews. They provide individual company analyses and

---

[1] See C. Stewart Sheppard, "The 1965 C.F.A. Examinations," *Financial Analysts Journal*, November–December, 1965; see also his "The 1964 C.F.A. Examinations," *Financial Analysts Journal*, September–October, 1964.

[2] Daniel S. Ahearn, "Investment Management and Economic Research," *Financial Analysts Journal*, January–February, 1964.

[3] Carl W. Schneider, "SEC Filings—Their Use to the Professional," *Financial Analysts Journal*, January–February, 1965; see also his "SEC Filings—Their Content and Use," *Financial Analysts Journal*, March–April, 1965.

recommendations. They undertake portfolio reviews. They provide industry studies. If you tell them the approximate amount you wish to invest, they will provide a suggested portfolio in line with the investment objective you have indicated.

Leading brokerage houses with competent research departments include:

Abraham & Co.
Bache & Co.
Loeb, Rhoades & Co.
Bear, Stearns & Co.
Francis I. du Pont & Co.
Hayden Stone
Kidder, Peabody & Co.
Merrill Lynch, Pierce, Fenner & Smith
Dean Witter & Co.
Reynolds & Co.
Goodbody & Co.
Paine, Webber, Jackson & Curtis
Hornblower & Weeks—Hemphill Noyes
E. F. Hutton & Co.
Dreyfus & Co.
Smith, Barney & Co.
Walston & Co.
Hirsch & Co.
Hentz & Co.
McDonnell & Co.
Shearson Hammill & Co.
Eastman Dillon, Union Securities & Co.

The largest brokerage house, Merrill Lynch, Pierce, Fenner & Smith, has a huge research department, as might be expected. They have published general monographs and pamphlets[4] such as:

*How to Buy Stocks*
*How to Invest*
*How to Read a Financial Report*
*101 Growth Stocks*
*The Population Explosion*
*Rates of Return on Investments in Common Stock*

Industry reports have been issued on:

Airlines
Banks
Communications
Natural resources

[4] Free copies of any of these may be obtained by writing to Merrill Lynch, Pierce, Fenner & Smith, at 70 Pine Street, New York, N.Y. 10005

In addition, Merrill Lynch publishes a quarterly *Security and Industry Survey* organized largely on an industry-analysis basis. A page or two is devoted to each of the major industries. There is a statement of the position and outlook for the industry and a tabulation of the stocks of individual companies in the industry classified according to whether the stock is considered "investment type: growth," "investment type: stability," "liberal income," "good quality," or "speculative" (See Figure 3–1).

**FIGURE 3–1**

**Utility Stock Recommendations**

| UTILITIES | Fiscal Year Ends | Earnings—$ a Share | | Interim | | | Dividends—$ a Share | | | Price Range 1956-65 | | 1966 | | Approximate | |
|---|---|---|---|---|---|---|---|---|---|---|---|---|---|---|---|
| | | 1965 | 1964 | Period | 1966 | 1965 | Consec. Yrs. Pd. | Paid 1965 | Cur. or Indic. Annual Rate | High | Low | High | Low | Price 8-15-66 | Yield % |
| **INVESTMENT TYPE: GROWTH** | | | | | | | | | | | | | | | |
| *Amer. Elec. Pwr. | Dec. | 1.78[c] | 1.66[c] | 12 mo. 6-30 | 1.85 | 1.72 | 57 | 1.26 | 1.32 | 47¾ | 15 | 43½ | 34⅞ | 36 | 3.7 |
| Carolina Pwr. & Lt. | Dec. | 1.80 | 1.60 | 12 mo. 6-30 | 1.83 | 1.67 | 30 | 1.16 | 1.28 | 52¼ | 11⅛ | 49¾ | 41 | 45 | 2.8 |
| Mid. South Util. | Dec. | 1.11[c] | 1.00[c] | 12 mo. 6-30 | 1.07[c] | 1.09[c] | 18 | 0.62 | 0.68 | 27 | 6¾ | 26¾ | 21½ | 22 | 3.1 |
| Oklahoma Gas & Electric | Dec. | 1.30 | 1.16 | 12 mo. 6-30 | 1.34 | 1.19 | 59 | 0.83[q] | 0.92 | 34¼ | 7⅝ | 30⅜ | 26⅛ | 28 | 3.3 |
| *Pacific Gas & Elec. | Dec. | 2.08 | 1.83[n] | 12 mo. 6-30 | 2.17 | 1.99 | 48 | 1.17 | 1.30 | 40⅜ | 14⅝ | 36¾ | 30⅜ | 31 | 4.2 |
| Southern Co. | Dec. | 1.39 | 1.31 | 12 mo. 6-30 | 1.39 | 1.35 | 19 | 0.91 | 0.96 | 36⅛ | 9⅝ | 35 | 26⅞ | 27 | 3.6 |
| Virginia Elec. & Pwr. | Dec. | 1.95 | 1.72 | 12 mo. 6-30 | 1.98 | 1.83 | 42 | 1.18 | 1.28 | 53 | 12¾ | 49⅞ | 42⅛ | 43 | 3.0 |
| **INVESTMENT TYPE: STABILITY** | | | | | | | | | | | | | | | |
| ‡Amer. Tel. & Tel. | Dec. | 3.39 | 3.18 | 12 mo. 5-31 | 3.54[2] | 3.28[2] | 86 | 2.00 | 2.20 | 75 | 26¾ | 63½ | 52⅛ | 53 | 4.2 |
| Balt. Gas & Elec. | Dec. | 1.98 | 1.76 | 12 mo. 6-30 | 1.96 | 1.93 | 57 | 1.35 | 1.44 | 42¾ | 16 | 39⅜ | 32 | 32 | 4.5 |
| Boston Edison | Dec. | 2.35 | 2.22 | 12 mo. 6-30 | 2.43 | 2.24 | 77 | 1.60 | 1.76 | 51 | 18 | 46¾ | 37⅛ | 38 | 4.6 |
| ‡Commonwealth Edison | Dec. | 2.61 | 2.41 | 12 mo. 6-30 | 2.70 | 2.49 | 77 | 1.80 | 2.00 | 58¾ | 17¾ | 54¾ | 46 | 46 | 4.3 |
| *Consolidated Edison | Dec. | 2.42 | 2.21 | 12 mo. 6-30 | 2.27 | 2.42 | 82 | 1.80 | 1.80[x] | 49¼ | 20¼ | 43⅜ | 33⅝ | 34 | 5.3[x] |
| *Gen. Pub. Util. | Dec. | 1.95 | 1.85 | 12 mo. 6-30 | 2.00 | 1.92[3] | 21 | 1.37 | 1.40 | 40¾ | 16¾ | 37¾ | 28⅞ | 29 | 4.8 |
| *Pub. Svc. Elec. & G. | Dec. | 2.23 | 2.06 | 12 mo. 6-30 | 2.26 | 2.18 | 42 | 1.38 | 1.46 | 43⅝ | 14⅛ | 39¾ | 31⅛ | 32 | 4.6 |
| Union Electric | Dec. | 1.42 | 1.35 | 12 mo. 6-30 | 1.45 | 1.43 | 61 | 1.12 | 1.12[x] | 31½ | 12½ | 28⅜ | 24 | 24 | 4.7[x] |
| Wisconsin Elec. Power | Dec. | 1.96 | 1.64 | 12 mo. 6-30 | 1.98 | 1.87 | 28 | 1.12 | 1.24 | 34 | 14¼ | 31⅝ | 24⅝ | 25 | 5.0 |
| **LIBERAL INCOME** | | | | | | | | | | | | | | | |
| Duquesne Light | Dec. | 1.91 | 1.81 | 12 mo. 6-30 | 1.94 | 1.86 | 51 | 1.40 | 1.50[x] | 36½ | 15¼ | 33½ | 28½ | 30 | 5.0[x] |
| *Interstate Pwr. | Dec. | 1.44 | 1.43 | 12 mo. 6-30 | 1.51 | 1.39 | 18 | 1.15 | 1.20 | 32½ | 12 | 28⅛ | 23¾ | 24 | 5.0 |
| Montana Power | Dec. | 2.08 | 1.95 | 12 mo. 6-30 | 2.14 | 2.00 | 32 | 1.42 | 1.48 | 45⅜ | 12⅞ | 38⅝ | 30 | 30 | 4.9 |
| New Eng. Electric | Dec. | 1.60 | 1.50 | 12 mo. 6-30 | 1.67 | 1.53 | 20 | 1.20 | 1.28[x] | 30¼ | 14 | 29⅛ | 24½ | 25 | 5.1[x] |
| ‡Northn. States Pwr.(Minn.) | Dec. | 1.88 | 1.90 | 12 mo. 6-30 | 1.99 | 1.96 | 18[u] | 1.44 | 1.52 | 41¼ | 13½ | 35⅞ | 29⅞ | 31 | 4.9 |
| Penn. Power & Lt. | Dec. | 2.02 | 1.91 | 12 mo. 6-30 | 2.10 | 1.94 | 21 | 1.44 | 1.48 | 40 | 19¾ | 38½ | 31½ | 32 | 4.6 |
| United Illuminating | Dec. | 2.26 | 2.12 | 12 mo. 6-30 | 2.31 | 2.21 | 67 | 1.65 | 1.70 | 41⅜ | 22 | 39¼ | 33¾ | 35 | 4.9 |
| *Wash. Water Pwr. | Dec. | 1.39 | 1.34 | 12 mo. 6-30 | 1.46 | 1.37 | 68 | 1.08 | 1.16[x] | 27½ | 15 | 24¼ | 21⅝ | 22 | 5.3[x] |
| **GOOD QUALITY: WIDER PRICE MOVEMENT** | | | | | | | | | | | | | | | |
| Central Louisiana Elec. | Dec. | 1.00 | 0.91 | 12 mo. 6-30 | 1.04 | 0.94 | 32 | 0.66 | 0.72[x] | 26¼ | 7⅛ | 24⅝ | 21¼ | 24 | 3.0[x] |
| ‡Delmarva Pwr. & Lt. | Dec. | 1.33 | 1.20 | 12 mo. 6-30 | 1.43 | 1.25 | 23[a] | 0.84 | 0.90 | 32¼ | 9¼ | 30⅛ | 24 | 25 | 3.6 |
| ‡Florida Power | Dec. | 1.89 | 1.77 | 12 mo. 6-30 | 2.09 | 1.73 | 30 | 1.22 | 1.28 | 52½ | 14 | 48⅞ | 40 | 45 | 2.8 |
| *Gen. Tel. & Electron. | Dec. | 1.87 | 1.57 | 6 mo. 6-30 | 1.01[n] | 0.83[g] | 31 | 1.03 | 1.28 | 48⅞ | 12⅛ | 46⅜ | 39½ | 41 | 3.1 |
| Houston Lighting & Pwr. | Dec. | 1.99 | 1.70 | 12 mo. 6-30 | 2.02 | 1.85 | 45 | 0.92 | 1.00 | 57⅜ | 13¾ | 55½ | 44⅛ | 45 | 2.2 |
| Illinois Power | Dec. | 2.12 | 1.98 | 12 mo. 6-30 | 2.15 | 2.09 | 20 | 1.45 | 1.60 | 49¼ | 12½ | 45⅞ | 36¼ | 37 | 4.3 |
| Long Island Light. | Dec. | 1.56 | 1.45 | 12 mo. 6-30 | 1.61 | 1.51 | 17 | 0.98 | 1.08 | 38½ | 9¾ | 32⅝ | 26⅜ | 27 | 4.0 |
| Mid-Continent Tel. | Dec. | 0.98[g] | 0.88[g] | 12 mo. 6-30 | 1.07 | 0.90[g] | 6 | 0.65 | 0.76 | 29½[r] | 12[r] | 24¼ | 18¾ | 19 | 4.0 |
| Pub. Svc. Co. of Colo. | Dec. | 1.40 | 1.34 | 12 mo. 6-30 | 1.43 | 1.33 | 23 | 0.85 | 0.90 | 34½ | 12 | 28⅝ | 22¼ | 23 | 3.9 |
| Rochester Tel. | Dec. | 1.40 | 1.30 | 12 mo. 6-30 | 1.53 | 1.45 | 41 | 0.73 | 0.84 | 38⅞ | 8⅜ | 37½ | 25¼ | 27 | 3.1 |
| Tampa Electric | Dec. | 1.02 | 0.87 | 12 mo. 6-30 | 1.12 | 0.93 | 60 | 0.52 | 0.60 | 30 | 6⅛ | 29⅝ | 24½ | 27 | 2.2 |
| Toledo Edison | Dec. | 1.96 | 1.78 | 12 mo. 6-30 | 2.10 | 1.85 | 45 | 1.12 | 1.28 | 41¼ | 12 | 40¼ | 34 | 36 | 3.6 |
| ‡United Utilities | Dec. | 1.03[g] | 0.96[g] | 12 mo. 6-30 | 1.09[2] | 0.97[g,2] | 28 | 0.68 | 0.76 | 31⅝ | 4⅞ | 29 | 23⅜ | 24 | 3.2 |

[2]–Based on average shares outstanding. [3]–Restated.

Source: Merrill Lynch, Pierce, Fenner & Smith, *Security and Industry Survey.*

This survey is of real value in enabling an investor quickly to single out those industries with favorable prospects and to select companies within a given industry. A summary of recommendations is shown in Figure 3–2.

Individual company report sheets are also available. While most brokerage houses respond to an individual investor's request for information on a given company by sending one of the Standard & Poor's fact sheets, Merrill Lynch has its own analyses of most of the companies listed on the Big Board. The fact sheet on an individual company will generally contain a description of the firm's business, an evaluation of current

## FIGURE 3–2

### Summary of Recommendations

| ISSUE | Dividends–$ a Share: Current or Indicated Annual Rate | Approximate: Price 8-15-66 | Approximate: Yield % | ISSUE | Dividends–$ a Share: Current or Indicated Annual Rate | Approximate: Price 8-15-66 | Approximate: Yield % |
|---|---|---|---|---|---|---|---|
| **INVESTMENT TYPE: GROWTH** | | | | | | | |
| Amer. Elec. Power | 1.32 | 36 | 3.7 | Marathon Oil | 2.20 | 56 | 3.9 |
| American Natural Gas | 1.80 | 37 | 4.9 | Merck & Co. | 1.20[f] | 73 | 1.6[f] |
| FMC Corp. | 0.75 | 35 | 2.1 | ‡Minnesota Mining & Mfg. | 1.20 | 80 | 1.5 |
| Gulf Oil | 2.20 | 51 | 4.3 | Pacific Gas & Electric | 1.30 | 31 | 4.2 |
| Honeywell, Inc. | 1.10 | 74 | 1.5 | Phillips Petroleum | 2.20 | 50 | 4.4 |
| Int. Business Machines | 4.40 | 348 | 1.3 | Scott Paper | 1.00 | 27 | 3.7 |
| Kimberly-Clark | 2.00 | 50 | 4.0 | Standard Oil of California | 2.50 | 61 | 4.1 |
| Liberty National Life | 0.36 | 40 | 0.9 | | | | |
| **INVESTMENT TYPE: STABILITY** | | | | | | | |
| Consolidated Edison | 1.80[x] | 34 | 5.3[x] | Morgan Guaranty Trust | 4.00 | 80 | 5.0 |
| General Pub. Utilities | 1.40 | 29 | 4.8 | Public Service Elec. & Gas | 1.46 | 32 | 4.6 |
| Great Atlantic & Pacific Tea | 1.50[e,q] | 29 | 5.2[e,q] | Sherwin-Williams | 1.90 | 45 | 4.2 |
| **LIBERAL INCOME** | | | | | | | |
| Equitable Gas | 2.00 | 35 | 5.7 | Typical Aa 25 to 30 yr. Deferred Call Utility Bonds | — | — | 5.40-5.50[3] |
| Interstate Power | 1.20 | 24 | 5.0 | Typical Aa 25 to 30 yr. Callable Utility Bonds | — | — | 5.70-5.80[3] |
| Lone Star Gas | 1.12 | 21 | 5.3 | Typical A 25 to 30 yr. Callable Utility Bonds | — | — | 5.85-5.95[3] |
| National Fuel Gas | 1.60 | 29 | 5.5 | Typical A 20 yr. Municipal Bonds | — | — | 4.05-4.35[2] |
| North American Aviation | 2.80 | 47 | 6.0 | Typical A 10 yr. Municipal Bonds | — | — | 3.95-4.15[2] |
| Texas Eastern Transmission | 1.05 | 20 | 5.3 | Typical A 5 yr. Municipal Bonds | — | — | 3.90-4.05[2] |
| Washington Water Power | 1.16[x] | 22 | 5.3[x] | Typical Baa 20 yr. Municipal Bonds | — | — | 4.10-4.65[2] |
| **GOOD QUALITY: WIDER PRICE MOVEMENT** | | | | | | | |
| Amer. Smelting & Refining | 3.50[r] | 59 | 5.9[r] | ‡International Tel. & Tel. | 1.35 | 72 | 1.9 |
| Assoc. Dry Goods | 1.40 | 52 | 2.7 | Marshall Field | 2.00 | 49 | 4.1 |
| Bell & Howell | 0.50 | 46 | 1.1 | National Cash Register | 1.20[q] | 82 | 1.5[q] |
| Bendix Corp. # | 2.40 | 70 | 3.4 | Pittston Co. | 1.20 | 29 | 4.1 |
| California Packing | 1.00 | 25 | 4.0 | Radio Corp. of Amer. | 0.80 | 48 | 1.7 |
| Carrier Corp. | 1.60 | 67 | 2.4 | Revere Copper & Brass | 2.60 | 57 | 4.6 |
| Chesebrough-Pond's | 0.68 | 28 | 2.4 | Safeway Stores | 1.00 | 28 | 3.6 |
| Columbia Brdctg. | 1.20[q] | 61 | 2.0[q] | St. Regis Paper | 1.40[q] | 32 | 4.4[q] |
| Eaton Yale & Towne | 1.25 | 27 | 4.6 | Schering Corp. | 1.00 | 46 | 2.2 |
| Emhart Corp. | 1.20 | 29 | 4.1 | Sinclair Oil | 2.40 | 67 | 3.6 |
| Firestone Tire & Rubber | 1.30 | 48 | 2.7 | Stauffer Chemical | 1.60 | 42 | 3.8 |
| General Tel. & Electronics | 1.28 | 41 | 3.1 | TRW, Inc. | 1.40 | 48 | 2.9 |
| Genesco Inc. | 2.10 | 43 | 4.9 | United-Carr | 1.00 | 24 | 4.2 |
| Goodyear Tire & Rubber | 1.35 | 53 | 2.5 | Wurlitzer Co. | 0.80 | 20 | 4.0 |
| **SPECULATIVE** | | | | | | | |
| Burroughs Corp. | 1.00 | 84 | 1.2 | Gulf & Western Ind. | 0.25 | 27 | 0.9 |
| Cessna Aircraft | 1.40 | 42 | 3.3 | Mallory (P.R.) & Co. | 1.60 | 61 | 2.6 |
| General Dynamics | 1.00 | 45 | 2.2 | New York Central R.R. | 3.29[b,r] | 65 | 5.1[b,q] |
| General Tire & Rubber | 0.80 | 34 | 2.4 | Northrop Corp. | 1.00 | 25 | 4.0 |
| Grumman Aircraft | 1.00 | 42 | 2.4 | | | | |

[2]-Maturity yield; exempt from Federal income taxes. [3]-Maturity yield.

Source: Merrill Lynch, Pierce, Fenner & Smith, *Security and Industry Survey.*

operating results, a statement of earnings and dividends, and an estimation of outlook and prospects, as well as basic statistical data on capitalization, selected income account data, and selected balance sheet data.

Other large brokerage houses publish comparable material. Francis I. du Pont & Co., for example, publishes a monthly magazine, *Investornews.* The table of contents of a recent issue is shown in Figure 3–3. It also provides research reports on individual companies. These include an investment analysis and an evaluation. Walston & Co. issues a daily market letter and a weekly market letter based on technical analyses. Goodbody & Co. issues a weekly market letter, research bulletins on individual companies, and a monthly letter covering a given recommended industry, along with company selections within the industry. The January letter customarily contains "The Favorite Fourteen for 196x." Bache & Co.

FIGURE 3–3

FRANCIS I. duPONT & CO.

# Investornews

November 1966

and Loeb, Rhoades & Co. both issue "recommended" lists from time to time covering assorted companies in various industries.

Almost without exception the brokerage houses make their research bulletins and reports available to investors without charge. They will analyze and evaluate an existing portfolio, provide sample portfolio suggestions for given investment objectives such as growth, capital gains, income and stability, etc., or they will develop an individually tailored portfolio to meet age, amount, and investment objective requirements. Smaller brokerage houses which do not have research departments of their own sometimes buy their "research" from "wholesale" organizations like Argus Research or Data Digests, or else obtain it from large houses through which they clear.

### The Financial Press

The intelligent investor and the professional securities analyst generally browse through, read, or study a significant part of the financial press each week, ranging from the financial section of a large metropolitan daily newspaper, or *The Wall Street Journal* to the *Financial Analysts Journal* (published every two months) or the *Journal of Finance* (published quarterly). The financial section of a newspaper can range from the elaborate and informative pages of *The New York Times* to a mere listing of daily stock quotations.

*The Wall Street Journal* is a daily, published every weekday by Dow Jones & Co. in New York, Chicago, San Francisco, and Los Angeles. It provides full coverage of business and financial news, including special news of companies, corporate profits reports, new issues, bond financing, national and local over-the-counter quotations: and NYSE and ASE stock prices.

*The Wall Street Journal* each day contains the Dow-Jones Industrial stock price average, the most widely quoted and extensively used stock price average, though not the most accurate. The Dow-Jones Industrials consist of 30 blue chip stocks. There is also an average of 20 railroad stocks, 15 utility stocks, and a composite average of the 65. The DJI goes back a long way; originally it was published in 1897 based on 12 stocks. In 1916 it was broadened to 20, and in October, 1928, it was raised to 30. From time to time over the years, individual stocks have been dropped from the list and replaced by others. There have been some 30 such substitutions since October, 1928. The 30 at present are:

Allied Chemical, Aluminum Co. of America, American Can, A.T.&T., American Tobacco, Anaconda, Bethlehem Steel, Chrysler, du Pont, Eastman Kodak, General Electric, General Foods, General Motors, Goodyear Tire, International Harvester, International Nickel, International Paper, Johns-Manville, Owens-Illinois, Procter & Gamble, Sears, Roebuck, Standard Oil of California, Standard Oil of New Jersey, Swift & Co., Texaco, Union Carbide, United Aircraft, United States Steel, Westinghouse, Woolworth.

The only names in the above list that appeared in the original 12 are American Tobacco and General Electric.

The first computations were quite simple. The prices of the 12 stocks were added and the result divided by 12. That was the average. Complications developed when some stocks in the average split their shares. Some sort of compensation had to be made to avoid distorting the average. To cite an example given by Dow Jones & Co., take, for example, a three-stock average. One sells for $5, another for $10, a third for $15 a share. The average price is $10. Then the $15 stock is split three for one, automatically reducing the value of each share to $5. The day of the split the $5 stock advances to $6, the $10 stock to $11, and the split stock to $6—an average of $7.67 a share, down sharply from the preceding day's average of $10 a share despite the fact that the market actually advanced. To correct for this distortion, Dow Jones came up with a solution which has been in effect since 1928. They changed the divisor to reflect the split. Instead of dividing by 30, when a stock split they divided by a lesser divisor. Over the years each new split within the 30-stock group dropped the divisor lower. Thus today, when the Dow-Jones Industrial average is computed, the total of the 30 stock prices isn't divided by 30 but rather by 2.245. The arithmetical average of the 30 stocks making up the Dow-Jones Industrials at the close of the market on June 21, 1966, was $67; the average itself was 894.98.

There is, of course, a tremendous disparity, as a result of the way the average is derived, between DJI points and dollars and cents. This has led to some highly misleading descriptions of the market. The DJI advances 10 points, for example, and immediately there are reports that the market is soaring; the fact is that the stocks in the DJI have moved up an average of 75 cents a share. If the DJI declines 15 points, the market is said to have plunged; again the fact is that the stocks in the DJI have lost an average of $1.12 a share. With a divisor of 2.245, a 1-point change in the DJI equals about 7 cents in the arithmetical average of the stocks in the DJI. A 10-point decline is the equivalent of a dip of 75 cents per share in the dollar value. A 20-point decline represents $1.50 in dollar value. See Table 3–1.

In the light of the excitement about the DJI almost reaching 1000 early in 1966, it is interesting to note that but for one substitution, the DJI would have broken through the 1000 level in December, 1961. In 1939 IBM was removed from inclusion in the DJI 30 and A.T.&T. was substituted. Had IBM remained, the DJI would have reached a December 1961 high of 1017.39 instead of 734.91.

After the Dow-Jones Industrial average, probably the most widely known market barometer is the index prepared by Standard & Poor's Corporation based on 425 industrial stocks. It also has a 25-stock railroad index, a 50-stock utility index, and a 500-stock composite of the three, as well as other individual industry stock price indexes. Standard & Poor's, in

## TABLE 3–1

### HOW TO CONVERT DJIA POINTS TO DOLLARS AND CENTS PER SHARE

GENERAL PRINCIPLE. To convert from DJIA POINT changes to dollars and cents per share changes in the average price of the 30 components, multiply point change by the CURRENT DIVISOR (2.245 as of Nov. 1, 1965) and divide by 30.

CONVERSION TABLES. The following conversion tables give the dollars and cents equivalent of point changes up to 50 points.

TABLE I - FULL POINTS

| DJIA Points Change | Dollars & Cents PerShare | DJIA Points Change | Dollars & Cents PerShare | DJIA Points Change | Dollars & Cents PerShare | DJIA Points Change | Dollars & Cents PerShare | DJIA Points Change | Dollars & Cents PerShare |
|---|---|---|---|---|---|---|---|---|---|
| | | 10.00 | $ 0.75 | 20.00 | $ 1.50 | 30.00 | $ 2.24 | 40.00 | $ 2.99 |
| 1.00 | $ 0.07 | 11.00 | 0.82 | 21.00 | 1.57 | 31.00 | 2.32 | 41.00 | 3.07 |
| 2.00 | 0.15 | 12.00 | 0.90 | 22.00 | 1.65 | 32.00 | 2.39 | 42.00 | 3.14 |
| 3.00 | 0.22 | 13.00 | 0.97 | 23.00 | 1.72 | 33.00 | 2.47 | 43.00 | 3.22 |
| 4.00 | 0.30 | 14.00 | 1.05 | 24.00 | 1.80 | 34.00 | 2.54 | 44.00 | 3.29 |
| 5.00 | 0.37 | 15.00 | 1.12 | 25.00 | 1.87 | 35.00 | 2.62 | 45.00 | 3.37 |
| 6.00 | 0.45 | 16.00 | 1.20 | 26.00 | 1.94 | 36.00 | 2.69 | 46.00 | 3.44 |
| 7.00 | 0.52 | 17.00 | 1.27 | 27.00 | 2.02 | 37.00 | 2.77 | 47.00 | 3.52 |
| 8.00 | 0.60 | 18.00 | 1.35 | 28.00 | 2.09 | 38.00 | 2.84 | 48.00 | 3.59 |
| 9.00 | 0.67 | 19.00 | 1.42 | 29.00 | 2.17 | 39.00 | 2.92 | 49.00 | 3.67 |
| | | | | | | | | 50.00 | 3.74 |

TABLE II - FRACTIONS

| Points Change DJIA | Dollars and Cents (Per Share) | Points Change DJIA | Dollars and Cents (Per Share) |
|---|---|---|---|
| 0.01 to 0.06 | Less than 1 cent | 0.47 to 0.60 | $0.04 |
| 0.07 to 0.20 | $0.01 | 0.61 to 0.73 | 0.05 |
| 0.21 to 0.33 | 0.02 | 0.74 to 0.86 | 0.06 |
| 0.34 to 0.46 | 0.03 | 0.87 to 0.99 | 0.07 |

HOW TO USE THE TABLES. Read the whole number from Table I, and then adjust for the fraction by adding from Table II. For example, assuming a change of the DJIA by 15.71 points: from Table I, 15.00 converts into $1.12 per share. From Table II, point 0.71 converts into 5¢ (0.05) per share. Adding $1.12 and $0.05 totals $1.17 per share, the change in average price per share for the 30 stocks.

The New York Stock Exchange November, 1965

arriving at an index figure, doesn't just add up per-share prices and divide. It starts by multiplying the price of each share by the number of shares in that issue; for example, in the case of a stock selling at $10 a share with 10,000 shares outstanding, it would get $100,000. These market value figures are then added, giving the aggregate market value of the issues covered. This aggregate is expressed as a percentage of the average market value during the years 1941–43. Then, finally, this percentage figure is divided by 10. There is no need for a changing divisor. Adjustment for stock splits is made automatically—because each stock enters the index not as a per-share price but as a market value figure covering all the shares in the issue. Take the $10 stock with 10,000 shares outstanding and a consequent market value of $100,000. If that is split two for one, the result is 20,000 shares of $5 stock—still worth $100,000. It's the $100,000 not the $10 or the $5 that goes into the index.

The S & P 425 industrial stock price index is numerically far down the ladder from the DJI. At the time that the latter was about 900, the S & P index was about 90. This was not by accident. When a prior S & P industrial index was discontinued in 1957 and the present new index inaugurated, the old index was at around 370 on a 1935–39 equals 100 base. When the new index was launched on a 1941–43 base, it was made equal to 10 not to 100. This, in effect, divided the index by 10. The new Standard & Poor index started in 1957 at 47. That was almost precisely the same as the then average price of $45.23 for all common shares listed on the NYSE. The DJI 30 stocks represent about 32% of the market value of all NYSE listed stocks. Standard & Poor's index of 500 stocks accounts for about 85% of the market value of all listed shares.

In mid-1966 both the American and the New York Stock Exchanges developed and introduced their own stock price indexes. The AMEX average is computed by adding all of the plus net changes and minus net changes above or below previous closing prices. The sum is then divided by the number of issues listed and the result added to or subtracted from the previous close. For example, on a given day, the sum of all price changes was an increase of $170.94. Dividing by 952, the number of common stocks and warrants then listed, produced a result of $0.18, which, added to the closing value of the index on the previous day—$13.15—produced a price level index of $13.33.

Changes in the number of issues used as a divisor will be made when new stocks are listed or existing ones removed; adjustments in the previous day's closing index will be made in the case of stock splits, stock dividends, and cash dividends. Since the AMEX index considers net price changes only, no consideration is given to the importance of the relationship of the net change to its price. This means that a $1 move in a $5 stock receives the same weight as a $1 change in a $100 stock.[5]

The NYSE Common Stock Index is a composite index of all the equity issues listed on the Exchange. In addition the NYSE also publishes four separate indexes as follows:

---

[5] See William F. Balch, "Market Guides: Indexes of Stock Prices Lately Have Multiplied," *Barron's*, September 26, 1966, pp. 9 and 17. See also P. H. Cootner, "Stock Market Indexes—Fallacies and Illusions," *Commercial and Financial Chronicle*, September 29, 1966, and "Measuring the Market," *Financial Analysts Journal*, May–June, 1967, pp. 43–81.

*a*) The Finance Index includes 75 issues of closed-end investment companies, savings and loan holding companies, real estate holding and investment companies, and others in commercial and installment finance, banking, insurance, and related fields.

*b*) The Transportation Index is based on 76 issues representing railroads, airlines, shipping, motor transport, and other operating, leasing, and holding companies in the transportation field.

*c*) The Utility Index includes 136 issues of operating, holding, and transmission companies in gas, electric, power, and communications.

*d*) The Industrial Index comprises the nearly 1,000 NYSE-listed stocks not included in the other three subgroup indexes. These, of course, represent a wide variety of industrial corporations in many fields of manufacturing, merchandising, and service.

The Composite Index takes into consideration the total market value of every common stock traded on the exchange. Each transaction in every stock is reflected in the index. To compute the Common Stock Index, the market value of each common share is multiplied by the number of shares of that issue which are listed. The results are added to obtain total market value. The index is a number that expresses simply the relationship between total current market value and a base market value (as of December 31, 1965) after necessary adjustments have been made.

To establish a close relationship at the outset between the Common Stock Index and the actual average price of all listed common stocks, a figure of 50 as of December 31, 1965, was selected as the base for the index. The actual average price on that date was about $53. The subindexes are also based on 50 as of December 31, 1965. If the index gets too far away from the actual average price of listed stocks, the exchange plans to bring it back in line by changing the base date or splitting the index.

All the indexes are expressed in points. Point changes in the all-stock index are also converted into dollar-and-cent changes in the average price per share, which many investors may find more meaningful than points and easier to relate, in terms of actual market value, to the particular issue in which they may be interested.

Computers of the Stock Exchange's Market Data System calculate the new indexes throughout the trading day. Each half hour the exchange's international ticker network carries the Common Stock Index, with its net change in points from the previous day's close, and the net change in the average price of NYSE common stocks. The Industrial, Transportation, Utility, and Finance Indexes, with net changes, are reported hourly in points. Final results for the day are printed on the tape after the close of the market. The index, computed back to 1939, is shown in Figure 3–4. Statistical aspects of its computation are shown in Figure 3–5.

FIGURE 3–4

New York Stock Exchange Common Stock Index

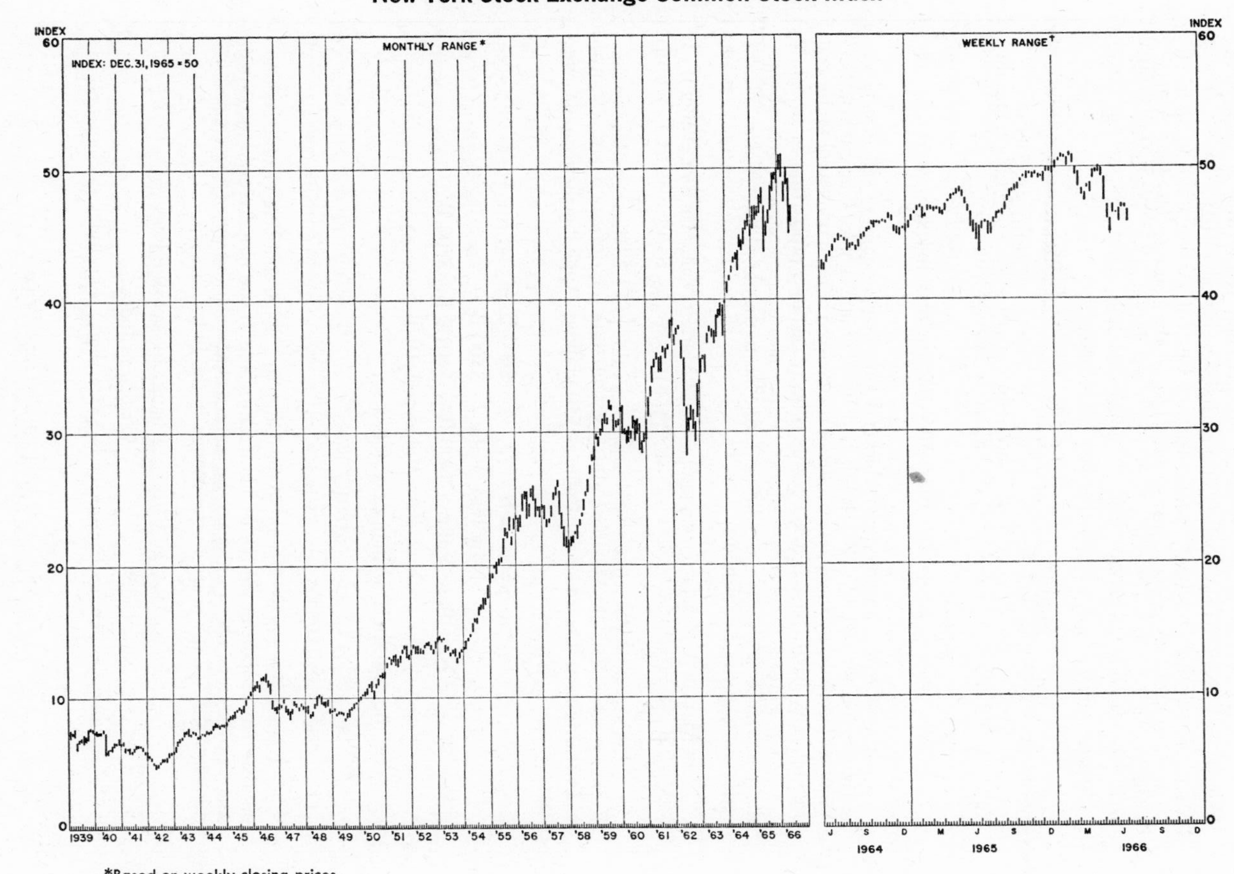


*Based on weekly closing prices.
†Based an daily closing prices.
Source: The Exchange.

**FIGURE 3–5**

**Computation of the NYSE Indexes**

For the benefit of the statistically minded, here is a capsule description of how the new New York Stock Exchange Indexes are calculated.

Assume that on January 10 this year the Current Market Value of all listed common stocks was $550 billion at the close of the market. The Base Market Value on the base date (December 31, 1965) was $500 billion. The Index on the base date, of course, is constant at 50. Then we have:

$$\frac{\$550\text{ B}}{\$500\text{ B}} = 1.1;\ 1.1 \times 50 = 55,\text{ the Index.}$$

If the Current Market Value should increase to, say, $600 billion and the Base Market Value remains at $500 billion, we would have:

$$\frac{\$600\text{ B}}{\$500\text{ B}} = 1.2;\ 1.2 \times 50 = 60,\text{ the new Index.}$$

In actual practice, the Base Market Value changes daily to reflect capitalization and other changes. If a stock is delisted, for example, Current Market Value is decreased by the market value of the delisted issue. To keep the Index on a comparable basis, Base Market Value is decreased by a proportionate amount.

The adjusted or new Base Market Value must bear the same relationship to the new Market Value as the old Base Value has to the old Market Value. These ratios are expressed as follows:

$$\frac{\text{New Market Value (after change)}}{\text{New Base Value}} = \frac{\text{Old Market Value (before change)}}{\text{Old Base Value}}$$

Let's assume a new issue with a market value of $1.2 billion is added to the Exchange's list. The old Market Value is $600 billion and the new Market Value is $601.2 billion. The old Base Value is $500 billion. Applying the formula, we have:

$$\frac{\$601.2\text{ B}}{\text{New Base Value}} = \frac{\$600\text{ B}}{\$500\text{ B}}$$

$$\text{New Base Value} \times \$600\text{ B} = \$601.2\text{ B} \times \$500\text{ B}$$

$$\text{New Base Value} = \$501\text{ B}$$

So the new Index is figured as follows:

$$\frac{\$601.2\text{ B}}{\$501\text{ B}} \times 50 = 60$$

Converting a point change in the Index to a dollar-and-cent change is done on a similar proportionate basis. The relationship of the new average price per share to the new Index must be the same as the relationship of the change in the average price per share to the change in the Index, or:

$$\frac{\text{New Average Price}}{\text{New Index}} = \frac{\text{Change in Average Price}}{\text{Change in Index}}$$

Assume the new average price is $55 a share. The Index declines .60 to 59.40, so:

$$\frac{\$55}{59.40} = \frac{\text{Change in Average Price}}{.60}$$

$$\text{Change in Average Price} \times 59.40 = \$55 \times .60$$

$$\text{Change} = 56\text{ cents a share}$$

Source: The Exchange.

There are other stock price averages or indexes—the New York Times Index and the Value Line Average of 1,100 stocks. From the viewpoint of investment analysis, the Standard & Poor's indexes with their 90-category industry breakdown would appear to be the most useful. These indexes are published weekly in *The Outlook*. See Figure 3–6.

Dow Jones & Co. publishes *Barron's National Business & Financial Weekly* as well as *The Wall Street Journal*. *Barron's* usually may be viewed as having three categories: leading articles in depth; departments such as The Trader, Up & Down Wall Street, News and Views of Investments, Capital Markets, etc.; and a substantial statistical section which includes "new highs and lows in stock," "mutual funds," "complete stock quotations," regional and foreign securities, over-the-counter market, bond quotations, "market laboratory," "pulse of trade and industry," and "secondary distributions."

The market laboratory section contains a wealth of basic figures on the Dow-Jones averages, price-earnings ratios, odd-lot trading, stock yields and bond yields, the 20 most active stocks of the week, and the widely followed Confidence Index. The Confidence Index is the ratio of the yield on *Barron's* high-grade bond (10) average to the yield on the broad Dow-Jones (40) bond average. The ratio generally ranges in the 80's and 90's. It is supposed to reflect the "smart money" judgment of institutional portfolio managers. As the Confidence Index moves down, some observers of the market believe that stock prices will reflect this "smart money" judgment and sentiment and turn downward from two to four months after the turn in the Confidence Index.[6] Those who follow the Confidence Index also believe that a rise in it will be reflected in a rise in stock prices two to four months later. The timing has varied substantially in the past, however.

*Forbes, Magazine of Business & Finance* is published twice monthly. It features articles on industry and company financial developments and trends. There are regular columns on "The Market Outlook," on "Stock Analysis," "Investment Pointers," "Market Comment," and "Technician's Perspective." The January 1 issue each year is devoted to rating companies within industries, comparing and contrasting profitability and performance. The August 15 issue each year contains the *Forbes* evaluation and rating of comparative mutual fund performance. It is one of the best tools available for mutual fund selection.

The *Commercial and Financial Chronicle* appears twice a week. The Monday issue is chiefly of interest to institutional investment managers. It contains summaries of SEC registrations; general corporation and investment news; detailed quotations for the previous week for the NYSE,

---

[6] Joseph E. Granville, *A Strategy for Daily Stock Market Timing for Maximum Profit* (1961), and *New Key to Stock Market Profits* (1963) (Englewood Cliffs, N.J.: Prentice-Hall, Inc.)

## FIGURE 3–6

### S & P Indexes of the Security Markets

Weekly Stock Price Indexes—1941–43 = 10

## S. & P. INDEXES OF THE SECURITY MARKETS

Weekly Stock Price Indexes—1941-43=10

| | Close Feb. 1 | Close Jan. 25 | % Change | Jan. Avgs. | 1966-67 Range High | 1966-67 Range Low |
|---|---|---|---|---|---|---|
| 500 Stocks, Combined | 86.43 | 85.85 | + 0.7 | 84.45 | 94.06 | 73.20 |
| 425 Industrials | 92.21 | 91.49 | + 0.8 | 89.88 | 100.60 | 77.89 |
| 20 Railroads | 45.96 | 45.77 | + 0.4 | 44.48 | 56.32 | 37.91 |
| 55 Utilities | 70.61 | 70.73 | — 0.2 | 70.63 | 75.37 | 59.03 |
| 128 Capital Goods | 85.28 | 84.39 | + 1.1 | 82.70 | 94.79 | 70.74 |
| 181 Consumer's Goods | 72.67 | 71.95 | + 1.0 | 69.97 | 84.95 | 65.35 |
| *25 High Grade Common | 77.15 | 76.13 | + 1.3 | 74.75 | 84.49 | 68.21 |
| *20 Low Price Common | 127.34 | 121.00 | + 5.2 | 115.25 | 136.81 | 97.28 |
| **INDUSTRIALS** | | | | | | |
| 9 Aerospace | 93.83 | 92.45 | + 1.5 | 90.43 | 108.45 | 70.06 |
| 5 Air Transport | 123.69 | 120.92 | + 2.3 | 118.52 | 145.43 | 84.93 |
| 4 Aluminum | 130.77 | 131.82 | — 0.8 | 123.52 | 149.56 | 99.24 |
| 4 Automobile | 93.28 | 92.75 | + 0.6 | 90.14 | 131.88 | 81.27 |
| Excl. Gen. Motors | 30.14 | 29.86 | + 0.9 | 28.84 | 41.77 | 25.26 |
| 9 Auto Parts & Accessories | 51.07 | 51.89 | — 1.6 | 49.11 | 62.15 | 44.45 |
| 5 Auto Trucks & Parts | 58.30 | 58.63 | — 0.6 | 55.92 | 70.16 | 50.44 |
| 3 Beverages: Brewers | 45.38 | 42.58 | + 6.6 | 41.61 | 57.95 | 36.85 |
| 5 Distillers | 106.42 | 105.82 | + 0.6 | 102.19 | 110.33 | 81.38 |
| 6 Soft Drinks | 60.17 | 60.71 | — 0.9 | 59.00 | 60.71 | 46.59 |
| Building Materials Composite | 44.05 | 42.13 | + 4.6 | 40.53 | 44.96 | 32.04 |
| ‡4 Air Conditioning | 24.38 | 22.67 | + 7.5 | 21.81 | 24.48 | 16.28 |
| 6 Cement | 26.40 | 25.49 | + 3.6 | 24.27 | 31.62 | 20.82 |
| 3 Heating, Plumbing | 30.86 | 30.38 | + 1.6 | 29.30 | 33.24 | 22.26 |
| 7 Roofing & Wallboard | 55.46 | 53.23 | + 4.2 | 51.29 | 55.90 | 39.75 |
| 12 Chemicals | 54.99 | 54.75 | + 0.4 | 53.38 | 75.38 | 49.82 |
| Excl. du Pont | 42.59 | 41.88 | + 1.7 | 40.59 | 54.00 | 37.14 |
| 5 Coal: Bituminous | 152.24 | 149.58 | + 1.8 | 144.78 | •152.24 | 113.70 |
| 2 Confectionery | 37.87 | 37.54 | + 1.0 | 36.74 | 41.15 | 33.08 |
| 5 Containers: Metal & Glass | 37.43 | 37.31 | + 0.3 | 36.55 | 42.02 | 35.44 |
| 6 Paper Containers | 107.97 | 105.53 | + 2.3 | 103.16 | 128.47 | 94.95 |
| 6 Copper | 44.63 | 43.83 | + 1.8 | 42.94 | 47.71 | 32.35 |
| §5 Cosmetics | 47.80 | 45.95 | + 4.0 | 46.31 | 49.00 | 40.26 |
| 12 Drugs | 110.19 | 109.60 | + 0.5 | 106.93 | •110.19 | 88.89 |
| 5 Electrical Equipment | 192.24 | 191.42 | + 0.4 | 185.49 | 217.20 | 157.01 |
| 5 Electronic—Major Cos. | 92.46 | 91.13 | + 1.5 | 90.50 | 110.41 | 80.06 |
| 3 Household Appl. | 125.77 | 126.57 | — 0.6 | 119.43 | 146.02 | 113.01 |
| 5 Electronics | 486.37 | 469.55 | + 3.6 | 440.58 | •486.37 | 352.22 |
| 5 Finance Companies | 52.27 | 51.99 | + 0.5 | 50.53 | 54.58 | 41.47 |
| 5 Small Loans | 111.41 | 109.60 | + 1.7 | 107.13 | 129.82 | 82.35 |
| Food Composite | 58.65 | 58.91 | — 0.4 | 58.43 | 68.90 | 50.41 |
| 2 Biscuit Bakers | 57.78 | 60.65 | — 4.7 | 58.80 | 64.16 | 49.31 |
| 4 Bread & Cake Bakers | 37.11 | 34.38 | + 7.9 | 33.73 | 39.28 | 28.34 |
| 5 Canned Foods | 68.78 | 68.34 | + 0.6 | 68.61 | 86.92 | 60.71 |
| 2 Corn Refiners | 57.75 | 56.75 | + 1.8 | 56.04 | 63.54 | 44.99 |
| 5 Dairy Products | 71.71 | 71.69 | 0 | 71.50 | 88.57 | 64.27 |
| 4 Meat Packing | 29.48 | 29.56 | — 0.3 | 29.20 | 35.21 | 22.70 |
| 6 Packaged Foods | 76.27 | 77.46 | — 1.5 | 76.70 | 88.89 | 66.68 |
| 3 Gold Mining | 28.54 | 29.41 | — 3.0 | 28.31 | 35.03 | 24.02 |
| 6 Home Furnishings | 23.57 | 22.16 | + 6.4 | 20.95 | 30.94 | 18.60 |
| 3 Lead and Zinc | 15.49 | 15.54 | — 0.3 | 15.08 | 19.37 | 13.70 |
| 5 Machine Tools | 43.70 | 42.58 | + 2.6 | 40.84 | 55.77 | 35.36 |
| 4 Machinery: Agricultural | 53.93 | 54.23 | — 0.6 | 54.85 | 68.56 | 46.42 |
| Machinery Composite | 82.18 | 80.05 | + 2.7 | 77.44 | 97.66 | 68.00 |
| 6 Constr. & Materials Hand. | 189.67 | 182.53 | + 3.9 | 179.62 | 236.22 | 163.19 |
| 9 Industrial | 77.69 | 75.55 | + 2.8 | 72.09 | 91.37 | 60.62 |
| 5 Oil Well | 105.66 | 103.27 | + 2.3 | 98.72 | 120.12 | 86.35 |
| 5 Specialty | 26.92 | 26.15 | + 2.9 | 24.75 | 33.41 | 22.41 |
| 3 Steam Generating | 159.42 | 163.47 | — 2.5 | 157.95 | 188.57 | 118.56 |

| | Close Feb. 1 | Close Jan. 25 | % Change | Jan. Avgs. | 1966-67 Range High | 1966-67 Range Low |
|---|---|---|---|---|---|---|
| 6 Metal Fabricating | 159.78 | 153.90 | + 3.8 | 143.39 | •159.78 | 101.95 |
| 5 Metals Misc. | 67.06 | 66.04 | + 1.5 | 64.92 | 76.90 | 54.41 |
| 6 Motion Pictures | 86.53 | 82.93 | + 4.3 | 80.82 | •86.53 | 58.14 |
| 8 Office and Business Equipt. | 736.21 | 733.80 | + 0.3 | 717.47 | •736.21 | 566.29 |
| Excl. I. B. M. | 238.68 | 230.67 | + 3.5 | 226.70 | 263.04 | 168.74 |
| Oil Composite | 117.10 | 116.27 | + 0.7 | 114.98 | 129.22 | 104.88 |
| 3 Crude Producers | 212.76 | 200.46 | + 6.1 | 192.28 | •212.76 | 165.51 |
| 9 Integrated: Domestic | 104.57 | 102.59 | + 1.9 | 100.76 | 105.41 | 90.57 |
| 6 : International | 119.06 | 119.02 | 0 | 118.16 | 139.76 | 108.20 |
| 9 Paper | 155.60 | 154.60 | + 0.6 | 150.38 | 187.59 | 134.62 |
| 8 Publishing | 329.02 | 326.74 | + 0.7 | 310.62 | •329.02 | 243.21 |
| 4 Radio-TV Broadcasters | 301.67 | 306.46 | — 1.6 | 301.66 | 314.07 | 221.40 |
| 5 Radio-TV Manufacturers | 243.41 | 229.58 | + 6.0 | 223.85 | 401.67 | 203.28 |
| 7 Railroad Equipment | 36.47 | 35.44 | + 2.9 | 33.86 | 45.78 | 30.95 |
| Retail Stores Composite | 70.20 | 68.45 | + 2.6 | 66.40 | 86.32 | 63.07 |
| 9 Department Stores | 108.77 | 105.82 | + 2.8 | 102.86 | 127.46 | 100.38 |
| §5 Discount Stores | 31.88 | 31.09 | + 2.5 | 29.78 | 42.41 | 26.03 |
| 10 Food Chains | 55.96 | 56.25 | — 0.5 | 55.23 | 69.11 | 49.54 |
| 3 Mail Ord. & Gen. Chains | 121.16 | 116.03 | + 4.4 | 112.34 | 154.80 | 107.55 |
| 6 Variety Stores | 25.22 | 25.61 | — 1.5 | 24.39 | 31.22 | 22.31 |
| ††5 Sav. & Loan Assns. Hld. Cos. | 12.58 | 11.15 | +12.8 | 10.68 | •12.58 | 5.49 |
| 3 Shipbuilding | 42.06 | 39.04 | + 7.7 | 37.96 | 53.27 | 33.66 |
| 3 Shipping | 68.32 | 67.72 | + 0.9 | 64.67 | 88.05 | 53.92 |
| 5 Shoes | 28.47 | 28.65 | — 0.6 | 26.92 | 30.98 | 22.80 |
| 4 Soaps | 82.27 | 80.75 | + 1.9 | 77.65 | •82.27 | 67.98 |
| 11 Steel | 55.47 | 54.68 | + 1.4 | 54.00 | 69.23 | 45.51 |
| Excl. U. S. Steel | 58.75 | 58.28 | + 0.8 | 57.33 | 73.42 | 48.18 |
| Sugar Composite | 32.04 | 31.29 | + 2.4 | 29.78 | 35.26 | 26.62 |
| 4 Beet Refiners | 23.08 | 22.55 | + 2.4 | 21.44 | 24.96 | 20.01 |
| 2 Cane Producers | 24.30 | 22.91 | + 6.1 | 21.24 | •24.30 | 15.47 |
| 3 Cane Refiners | 57.70 | 57.41 | + 0.5 | 55.49 | 71.68 | 49.72 |
| 3 Sulphur | 114.36 | 112.90 | + 1.3 | 108.69 | 117.78 | 76.96 |
| 7 Textiles: Apparel Mfrs. | 58.09 | 58.34 | — 0.3 | 57.10 | 77.94 | 52.09 |
| 3 Synthetic Fibers | 82.02 | 78.26 | + 4.8 | 75.04 | 122.43 | 64.32 |
| 6 Textile Products | 66.50 | 66.86 | — 0.3 | 63.57 | 107.15 | 57.19 |
| 4 Tires and Rubber Goods | 204.98 | 203.17 | + 0.9 | 201.43 | 230.69 | 183.51 |
| 5 Tobacco (Cigarette Mfrs.) | 33.80 | 31.80 | + 6.3 | 30.71 | 35.95 | 28.51 |
| 4 Cigar Mfrs. | 60.78 | 58.42 | + 4.0 | 56.48 | 103.19 | 49.30 |
| ¶10 Truckers | 25.76 | 25.23 | + 2.1 | 24.18 | 33.58 | 22.45 |
| 2 Vegetable Oil | 61.28 | 62.73 | — 2.3 | 61.38 | 70.51 | 49.30 |
| §6 Vending Machines | 33.14 | 33.21 | — 0.2 | 31.09 | 37.09 | 24.99 |
| **PUBLIC UTILITIES** | | | | | | |
| 35 Electric Companies | 53.90 | 54.08 | — 0.3 | 54.04 | 57.77 | 45.63 |
| 11 Nat. Gas Co's: Distributors. | 65.04 | 64.93 | + 0.2 | 64.44 | 74.95 | 59.72 |
| 7 Pipe Lines | 86.56 | 86.70 | — 0.2 | 86.42 | 94.66 | 74.43 |
| 3 Telephone | 27.93 | 28.30 | — 1.3 | 27.26 | 29.94 | 24.32 |
| Excl. A. T. & T. | 67.99 | 68.09 | — 0.1 | 65.96 | 68.09 | 55.37 |
| ***BANKS, INSURANCE, INVESTMENT COMPANIES** | | | | | | |
| 10 New York City Banks | 36.05 | 37.53 | — 3.9 | 37.08 | 38.00 | 27.95 |
| 16 Banks, Outside N. Y. C. | 67.18 | 70.25 | — 4.4 | 69.90 | 71.88 | 56.01 |
| 20 Fire-Casualty Insurance | 69.40 | 69.64 | — 0.3 | 70.03 | 71.46 | 58.63 |
| 11 Life Insurance | 252.58 | 255.52 | — 1.2 | 250.88 | 303.61 | 190.37 |
| 9 Investment Cos. (Closed-end) | 64.71 | 64.29 | + 0.7 | 63.05 | 68.56 | 56.08 |

### THE MARKETS LAST WEEK

Daily Stock Price Indexes (1941-43=10)

| | Feb. 3 | Feb. 2 | Feb. 1 | Jan. 31 | Jan. 30 | | Feb. 1 | Jan. Avgs. | 1966-67 High | 1966-67 Low | 1965 High | 1965 Low |
|---|---|---|---|---|---|---|---|---|---|---|---|---|
| **425 Industrials** | | | | | | | | | | | | |
| H.. | 93.97 | 93.18 | 92.84 | 93.30 | 93.14 | P/E Ratio. | 15.90 | 15.39 | 18.00 | 12.93 | 19.95 | 16.44 |
| L.. | 92.37 | 91.60 | 91.39 | 91.78 | 91.49 | Yield (%). | 3.30 | 3.42 | 2.81 | 2.93 | 3.05 | 2.81 |
| C.. | 93.31 | 92.57 | 92.21 | 92.35 | 92.38 | **Range of Price Index | | | 101.30 | 76.89 | 99.28 | 85.49 |
| **20 Rails** | | | | | | | | | | | | |
| H.. | 46.50 | 46.41 | 46.30 | 46.53 | 46.47 | P/E Ratio. | 10.12 | 9.68 | 15.88 | 8.79 | 14.52 | 12.26 |
| L.. | 45.75 | 45.67 | 45.86 | 45.97 | 45.80 | Yield (%). | 4.93 | 5.16 | 5.69 | 3.80 | 4.74 | 4.00 |
| C.. | 46.33 | 46.01 | 45.96 | 46.14 | 46.20 | **Range of Price Index | | | 56.87 | 37.47 | 51.89 | 40.80 |
| **55 Utilities** | | | | | | | | | | | | |
| H.. | 71.15 | 71.09 | 71.24 | 71.51 | 71.67 | P/E Ratio. | 15.90 | 15.86 | 18.03 | 14.75 | 21.34 | 17.99 |
| L.. | 70.22 | 70.18 | 70.05 | 70.42 | 70.65 | Yield (%). | 3.92 | 3.92 | 4.44 | 3.41 | 3.42 | 3.11 |
| C.. | 70.66 | 70.62 | 70.61 | 71.00 | 71.22 | **Range of Price Index | | | 75.80 | 58.32 | 78.62 | 71.21 |
| **500 Composite** | | | | | | | | | | | | |
| H.. | 87.97 | 87.31 | 87.04 | 87.46 | 87.35 | P/E Ratio. | 15.71 | 15.26 | 17.88 | 12.97 | 19.81 | 16.63 |
| L.. | 86.51 | 85.87 | 85.68 | 86.06 | 85.84 | Yield (%). | 3.40 | 3.51 | 3.89 | 3.01 | 3.11 | 2.88 |
| C.. | 87.36 | 86.73 | 86.43 | 86.61 | 86.66 | **Range of Price Index | | | 94.72 | 72.28 | 93.30 | 80.73 |

| Preferred Stocks | Close as of Feb. 1 | Jan. Avgs. | 1966-67 High | 1966-67 Low | 1965 High | 1965 Low |
|---|---|---|---|---|---|---|
| Price, Dollars per share | 141.0 | 138.3 | 155.6 | 131.2 | 168.7 | 155.2 |
| Yield, Percent | 4.96 | 5.07 | 5.34 | 4.50 | 4.51 | 4.15 |

Weekly Bond Yields (%)

| | Feb. 1 | Jan. Avgs. | 1966-67 High | 1966-67 Low | 1965 High | 1965 Low | Feb. 1 | Jan. Avgs. | 1966-67 High | 1966-67 Low | 1965 High | 1965 Low |
|---|---|---|---|---|---|---|---|---|---|---|---|---|
| **Composite** | | | | | | | **Industrials** | | | | | |
| AAA.. | 5.07 | 5.14 | 5.46 | 4.73 | 4.73 | 4.33 | 4.96 | 5.03 | 5.44 | 4.67 | 4.71 | 4.23 |
| AA.. | 5.22 | 5.31 | 5.58 | 4.83 | 4.83 | 4.43 | 5.00 | 5.07 | 5.56 | 4.75 | 4.75 | 4.28 |
| A.... | 5.32 | 5.41 | 5.66 | 4.89 | 4.90 | 4.53 | 5.13 | 5.21 | 5.63 | 4.83 | 4.82 | 4.46 |
| BBB.. | 5.78 | 5.89 | 6.25 | 5.06 | 5.09 | 4.70 | 5.78 | 5.75 | 6.02 | 4.94 | 5.07 | 4.60 |
| **Railroads** | | | | | | | **Utilities** | | | | | |
| AAA.. | 5.18 | 5.23 | 5.44 | 4.76 | 4.76 | 4.37 | 5.06 | 5.16 | 5.57 | 4.73 | 4.75 | 4.36 |
| AA.. | 5.57 | 5.64 | 5.74 | 4.94 | 4.95 | 4.56 | 5.08 | 5.21 | 5.64 | 4.77 | 4.81 | 4.39 |
| A.... | 5.66 | 5.73 | 5.79 | 4.99 | 5.00 | 4.65 | 5.19 | 5.30 | 5.79 | 4.85 | 4.92 | 4.43 |
| BBB.. | 6.00 | 6.18 | 6.61 | 5.24 | 5.28 | 4.87 | 5.56 | 5.73 | 6.28 | 4.95 | 5.00 | 4.59 |

| | Yields Feb. 1 | Yields Jan. Avgs. | Yields 1966-67 High | Yields 1966-67 Low | †Prices Feb. 1 | †Prices Jan. Avgs. | †Prices 1966-67 High | †Prices 1966-67 Low |
|---|---|---|---|---|---|---|---|---|
| CORP., AAA | 5.07 | 5.14 | 5.46 | 4.73 | 86.69 | 85.90 | 90.59 | 82.32 |
| Government: | | | | | | | | |
| Long Term | 4.40 | 4.43 | 4.90 | 4.38 | 84.75 | 84.51 | 84.95 | 79.98 |
| Intermediate | 4.57 | 4.61 | 5.53 | 4.55 | 90.13 | 89.88 | 90.25 | 84.64 |
| Short Term | 4.35 | 4.43 | 5.74 | 4.34 | 95.66 | 95.41 | 95.69 | 91.42 |
| Municipal | 3.45 | 3.58 | 4.26 | 3.43 | 107.9 | 106.0 | 108.2 | 96.52 |

Commodity Prices—Industrial Production

| | Latest Week | Week Ago | Year Ago | 1966-67 High | 1966-67 Low |
|---|---|---|---|---|---|
| ¹Indl. Raw Matl. Prices | 106.0 | 106.2 | 121.4 | 125.0 | 105.3 |
| ²Indl. Production, Weekly | 241.8 | 244.3 | 241.4 | 249.5 | 233.5 |

•Indicates a new high or low. Range for 500 stocks, 425 industrials, 20 rails, and 55 utilities is based on daily closing indexes. †Converted from average yield to maturity, assuming an appropriate coupon and maturity. *Not included in composite indexes. ¶1955=10; §1957=10; these special base indexes not included in composite indexes. ††1959=10. **Based on intraday high and low prices. ‡1957=10. ¹BLS Index (1957-59=100). ²S. & P. Sensitive (1947-49=100).

Source: Standard & Poor's, *The Outlook*, February 6, 1967, p. 941.

ASE, NSE, MSE, and Toronto Stock Exchange; extensive over-the-counter quotations; corporate and municipal financing ahead; state and city bond offerings; a record of dividends declared and payable;

redemption calls and sinking fund notices; and the course of bank clearings. Dividend payments records are available cumulatively in *Moody's* and in *S & P Dividend Record*.

The Thursday issue of the *Commercial and Financial Chronicle* contains articles and reproductions of addresses delivered in the field of finance and investments. A feature each week is "The Security I Like Best" written by security analysts from various brokerage and financial houses. This is a continuous forum in which each week one or two analysts give their reasons for favoring the securities they select. There is also usually a page listing broker-dealer literature and recommendations. It is a useful compendium of the vast outpouring of studies and reports suggesting specific stocks or industries. There are also regular columns on bank and insurance stocks, mutual funds, public utility securities, tax-exempt bonds, etc. Special supplements appear from time to time, such as the one covering the Investment Bankers Association Annual Convention, reproducing the speeches of the officers and the reports of the various committees. For example, the Public Utility Securities Committee published a report on "Public Utility Securities and Accounting Variations," while the Securities Studies Committee published an excellent study on "The Role of Pension Funds in the Capital Market."[7]

The *Financial World*, published weekly, and the *Magazine of Wall Street*, published biweekly, both feature articles on the trend of the market, industry evaluations, and individual company analyses. The *Financial World* has a monthly supplement in which common stocks are rated. Comparable data on preferred stocks and mutual funds are published quarterly. The publisher of the *Magazine of Wall Street* issues weekly a separate "Investment and Business Forecast." This is in the nature of an investment advisory report.

The *Financial Analysts Journal* is published every two months by the Financial Analysts Federation, an association devoted to the advancement of investment management and security analysis. Each issue features brief reviews of the economy, corporate profits, accounting and analysis, investment management, money market, and foreign developments. Articles cover all phases of investments ranging from industry studies, such as "Airline Earnings Perspective," to an analysis of major current problems in finance, such as "The U.S. Balance of Payments—Problems and Remedies." There are technical articles, such as "Per-Share Adjustments for Rights," and more esoteric efforts, such as that entitled "Shakespeare Revisited," which, written by a vice president of Lionel D. Edie & Co., was in fact a discourse on diversification and portfolio composition.

---

[7] See *Commercial and Financial Chronicle*, Vol. 203, No. 6546, Section 2 (January 27, 1966).

The *Journal of Finance* is published quarterly by the American Finance Association. It is much more academically and theoretically oriented than the *Financial Analysts Journal.* In recent years it has attempted to cover not only all phases of finance—banking, investments, international finance, real estate finance, corporate finance, but monetary and economic theory as well. The effort to cater to both applied and theoretic tastes in economics and finance tends to lessen its appeal somewhat to the practicing security analyst or portfolio manager.

### The Investment Advisory Services

A wealth of information is available in the publications of the investment advisory services. The major services are:

Moody's Investor Service, Inc. (owned by Dun & Bradstreet)
99 Church Street
New York, N.Y. 10007

Standard & Poor's Corporation (owned by McGraw-Hill)
345 Hudson Street
New York, N.Y. 10014

The Value Line Investment Survey (owned by Arnold Bernhard & Co.)
5 East 44th Street
New York, N.Y. 10017

A comprehensive and copious flow of bulletins and reports emerge daily, weekly, and monthly from these services. It is possible to subscribe to part or all of the publications. The annual cost of any of the services is a properly deducted expense from investors' income under the personal income tax regulations. A well-stocked college or university library will have one or more of these services, and the larger public libraries also make them available.

A basic part of both the Moody's and the Standard & Poor's services are the reference volumes: Moody's *Manuals* and Standard & Poor's *Corporation Records.* Moody's *Manuals* are big thick volumes issued each year and issued for various fields—industrials, public utilities, transportation, governments, and banks and finance. Each volume contains reports on thousands of corporations (or governmental bodies), giving the financial history and full investment data for a period of years. Standard & Poor's *Corporation Records* are continuous and alphabetical regardless of field. The volumes are kept up to date by current supplements—Standard & Poor's six-volume *Corporation Records* are augmented by a daily bulletin, while five Moody's *Manuals* are kept up to date by a semiweekly report. Most large brokerage offices will have one or the other of these basic services.

Standard & Poor's issues a weekly magazine, *The Outlook,* while Moody's issues a weekly *Stock Survey.* Both review market conditions and recommend investment choices in common stock. *The Outlook* generally contains an overall market forecast and policy recommendation, a list of the 10 best performing groups of the week, the 10 poorest performing groups, a monthly "Stock for Action" recommendation, stocks in the limelight, on-the-spot reports on individual companies, a report on business, and special articles, such as "Stocks with Tax Exemption on Dividends" and "Copper Stocks Have Speculative Appeal." A master list of recommended issues is maintained, classified into: "Group 1—Stocks Primarily for Stability"; "Group 2—Stocks Primarily for Capital Gain"; and "Group 3—High-Grade Bonds and Preferred Stocks for Income." The annual forecast issue of *The Outlook* features 10 stocks for action in the year ahead, 25 of the best low-priced stocks, 27 candidates for stock splits, 40 candidates for dividend increases, 9 stocks to outrun inflation, 8 S & P rapid growth stocks for long-term profits, etc.

The Standard & Poor's *Stock Guide* is a pocket-size condensed handbook, issued monthly, containing a thumbnail sketch of essential facts about some 5,000 common and preferred stocks. Two pages of one of these monthly guides are shown in Figure 3–7. Most of the 5,000 stocks are rated for earnings and dividend stability and growth. The S & P description of their stock ratings is given in Figure 3–8. Each month the *Stock Guide* also contains a list of "stocks for potential price appreciation" and another list of "recommended stocks primarily for stability." There are separate lists of "candidates for dividend increases," "candidates for stock splits," and "25 of the best low-priced stocks." At the back of the *Guide* each month are to be found "quality ratings of utility preferred stocks" and "industry classifications with stock ratings."

Both Moody's and Standard & Poor's publish compendiums on individual companies. *Moody's Handbook of Widely Held Common Stocks*, first published in 1964, is issued quarterly. It covers about 1,000 companies. For each one it has a chart, showing for the years 1950 to date, the DJI, the industry group stock price trend, and the company's stock price performance. Basic financial statistics for the past decade are given. The written analysis covers the company's financial background, recent financial developments, and prospects. An example of a typical page is shown in Figure 3–9. The Standard & Poor's compendium is called *Stock Market Encyclopedia*. It covers about 1,000 stocks. Full financial facts are given for each company. A chart shows the market performance of the stock, the average performance of stocks in its industry, and the performance of the stock market as a whole, in addition to showing the trading volume of the stock. Each report carries a Standard & Poor's evaluation and recommendation.

Both Standard & Poor's (see Figures 3–10 and 3–11) and Moody's publish weekly and monthly bond guides. Standard & Poor's issue a weekly "*Bond Outlook*," Moody's a weekly "*Bond Survey*." Each issue

# FIGURE 3–7

## Sample Pages from Standard & Poor's Stock Guide

| INDEX | Ticker Symbol | STOCKS NAME OF ISSUE (Call Price of Pfd. Stocks) Market | Earns & Div Ranking | Par Val. | ★ Inst. Hold Cos | Shs. (000) | STOCK CHARACTERISTICS Principal Business | PRICE RANGE 1936-64 High | 1936-64 Low | 1965 High | 1965 Low | 1966 High | 1966 Low | Nov. Sales in 100s | November, 1966 O-C Monthend High | Low | Last | % Div. Yield | P-E Ratio |
|---|---|---|---|---|---|---|---|---|---|---|---|---|---|---|---|---|---|---|---|
| 1 | GIS | General Mills, Inc...NYS, Bo, MW, PB, PC | A | 3 | 107 | 355 | Convenience foods, snack | 49⅝ | a5⅜ | 64 | 47¼ | 63⅞ | 52 | 784 | 66⅜ | 62 | 63¼ | 2.4 | 20 |
| 2 | Pr | $1.75 cm Cv Pref ([10]65) vtg........NYS | NR | No | ... | .... | products; specialty chems | .... | .... | .... | .... | 57 | 48 | 110 | 57 | 52¾ | 55½ | 3.2 | .. |
| 3 | GM | General Motors..........[2]NYS, De, MW | A | 1⅔ | 1253 | 10311 | Automobiles and commercial | 102⅝ | a4¼ | 113¾ | 91¼ | 108¼ | 66 | 12754 | 74⅜ | 66 | 66½ | †6.8 | 11 |
| 4 | Pr B | $5 cm Pfd (120)......NYS, MW, PB, PC | AAA | No | 204 | 361 | trucks; diesel engines; | 132 | 100⅜ | 118 | 110¼ | 111½ | 92¾ | 161 | 99⅜ | 94¾ | 95¼ | 5.2 | .. |
| 5 | Pr A | $3.75 cm Pfd (101 '71)..............NYS | AAA | No | 105 | 310 | electric appliances | 109 | 75¼ | 93¼ | 84½ | 85⅛ | 69 | 63 | 75 | 70 | 72⅛ | 5.2 | .. |
| 6 | GPY | General Plywood Corp..............ASE | C | 50¢ | ... | .... | Plywd flush doors; Microseal | 27¼ | 1⅜ | 11⅜ | 5¼ | 24½ | 9⅝ | 666 | 14¼ | 11⅜ | 14⅛ | ‡... | 29 |
| 7 | GPT | General Portland Cement.....NYS, MW | B+ | 1 | 41 | 341 | Low-cost cement producer | 43⅞ | a3¼ | 22 | 13⅝ | 15¼ | 9⅛ | 1085 | 10⅛ | 9⅛ | 9¼ | 8.6 | 10 |
| 8 | GPE | General Precision Equipment...NYS, Bo | B | 1 | 19 | 210 | Electronic systems, com- | 78 | 7¾ | 44⅞ | 24½ | 66½ | 39 | 3011 | 63½ | 51½ | 63½ | 2.4 | 14 |
| 9 |  | $4.75 cm Pfd ([8]103; SF 100) vtg....UNL | BB | No | 2 | 27 | ponents; simulators; data | 100 | 70½ | 95½ | 93 | 95½ | 94 | .... | .... | 95B | .... | 5.0 | .. |
| 10 | Pr | $1.60 cm Cv Pref (42) vtg.........NYS* | B | No | ... | .... | processing; indus'l controls | 52 | 27 | 40¾ | 34 | 44⅝ | 33½ | 71.1 | 42½ | 38 | 42 | 3.8 | .. |
| 11 | GPS | General Public Service......NYS, PB, PC | NR | 10¢ | 1 | 2 | Closed-end investment trust | 8 | ¼ | 7 | 5¾ | 6½ | 5½ | 582 | 6 | 5¾ | 6 | ‡3.0 | .. |
| 12 | GPU | General Public Utilities...........[3]NYS | A | 2½ | 254 | 2658 | Controls public utility cos | 39⅞ | a5½ | 40¾ | 34⅝ | 37¾ | 26⅛ | 1233 | 33¼ | 30⅛ | 30⅛ | 5.0 | 15 |
| 13 | GRX | General Refractories Co.........NYS, PB | B | 5 | 2 | 41 | Fire-brick for steel industry | 39¾ | a2¾ | 26⅜ | 14¼ | 27 | 12¾ | 294 | 13⅞ | 12¾ | 12¾ | 6.3 | 7 |
| 14 |  | General Reinsurance Corp..........UNL | NR | 10 | 32 | 99 | Reinsurance exclusively | 241 | a11⅜ | 252 | 164 | 300 | 205 | .... | .... | 281B | 286A | 0.7 | 27 |
| 15 |  | General Shale Products.............UNL | B+ | No | 2 | 2 | Face brick & concrete blocks | 25½ | 10¼ | 34½ | 21¼ | 32⅜ | 20 | .... | .... | 20B | 21A | †‡6.0 | 5 |
| 16 | GSX | General Signal Corp............NYS, PB | B+ | 6.67 | 8 | 52 | Electrical & electronic prods | 54¾ | a3 | 50¼ | 31¼ | 62¼ | 35⅞ | 271 | 40½ | 36¼ | 37¼ | 3.2 | 10 |
| 17. | GSI | General Steel Industries............NYS | B | 1 | 9 | 189 | Heavy duty castings; RR cars | 31½ | a2 | 31 | 22½ | 31¾ | 16 | 467 | 22½ | 19⅛ | 20½ | 5.9 | 10 |
| 18 | GSW | General Steel Wares, Ltd.........TS, MS | B− | No | ... | .... | Heating, plumbing, other eqp | 23 | 3 | 14⅞ | 10⅝ | 13⅛ | 8½ | 7 | 9¼ | 8½ | 8½ | .... | .. |
| 19 |  | General Stone & Materials..........UNL | NR | 5 | ... | .... | Terrazzo & quartz aggregates | 8⅝ | 6¾ | 8⅞ | 6½ | 10⅛ | 6 | .... | .... | 6⅜B | 6¾A | 5.9 | 7 |
| 20 | GSC | General Stores Corp.................ASE | NR | 1 | ... | .... | Subsids operate drug stores | a28½ | a⅜ | 2⅜ | 1⅛ | 3⅛ | 1⅝ | 144 | 1⅞ | 1⅝ | 1⅝ | .... | 15 |
| 21 |  | Gen. Tel. of Calif., 4½% Pfd (23½) vtg..UNL | A | 20 | 41 | 130 | Largest sub Gen Tel system | 28 | 15¼ | 19⅞ | 17½ | 19½ | 15¼ | .... | .... | 15⅜B | 15¾A | 5.7 | .. |
| 22 | GLF B | Gen. Tel. of Fla., [4]$1.30 cm B Pfd....NYS | A | 25 | 31 | 96 | Tel. service in Fla., Tampa | 28⅛ | 24 | 27¾ | 25¾ | 26½ | 21¼ | 25 | 23½ | 22⅞ | 23 | 5.7 | .. |
| 23 | Pr A | $1.25 cm Pfd (26½ '71)..............NYS | A | 25 | 31 | 214 | largest community served | 28 | 24¾ | 27¾ | 25 | 25⅝ | 21⅛ | 10 | 21¾ | 21½ | 21½ | 5.8 | .. |
| 24 | GEN | General Tel. & Electronics.......[2]NYS, Ci | A | 3⅓ | 424 | 7069 | 2d largest telephone system; | 38¾ | a1¼ | 48⅞ | 35⅝ | 46⅜ | 35⅝ | 4189 | 45½ | 43⅛ | 44½ | 2.9 | 21 |
| 25 |  | 5.28% cm Cv Pfd ([9]56) vtg........UNL | A | 50 | 4 | 2 | Sylvania radio & TV tubes, | 112 | 49 | 143 | 106⅞ | 139⅛ | 112 | .... | .... | 130B | 132A | 2.0 | .. |
| 26 |  | 4.36% cm Cv Pfd (53½) vtg.........UNL | A | 50 | 2 | 11 | electronics, lights | 84½ | 45 | 109 | 84 | 105¾ | 85¼ | .... | .... | 99½B | 100½A | 2.2 | .. |
| 27 | GLI | General Time Corp.............NYS, PB | B | 2½ | 3 | 27 | Clocks; time recording devices | 33⅛ | a2 | 21 | 12 | 24 | 11⅝ | 887 | 16⅜ | 13¼ | 14⅝ | 3.4 | 10 |
| 28 | GY | General Tire & Rubber.......[1]NYS, MW | A− | 30¢ | 58 | 1751 | Replacement and fleet tires; | a33¾ | a⅜ | 30 | 18⅜ | 37½ | 27½ | 1919 | 34½ | 30½ | 32¾ | 2.4 | 11 |
| 29 | Pr A | $5 cmPref(100½;SF100)vtg.....NYS, MW* | BBB | 100 | 2 | 4 | plastics; a leader in rockets | 103½ | 74½ | 103½ | 98¾ | 102 | 90¾ | 19.7 | 95⅞ | 95¼ | 95¼ | 5.2 | .. |
| 30 |  | Warrants (Pur 3.12 Com for $27.49)..UNL | NR | ..... | ... | .... | and propellants. | 74 | 5½ | 62 | 31½ | 84 | 60 | .... | .... | 70¾B | 72¾A | .... | .. |
| 31 |  | General Waterworks................UNL | NR | 1 | 3 | 76 | Waterworks system, tele cos; | 38½ | 6 | 43¾ | 35½ | 44½ | 31½ | .... | .... | 35¼B | 36A | ‡... | 11 |
| 32 |  | $2 cm Cv 2nd Pfd ([6]40) vtg.........UNL | NR | 1 | 4 | 7 | mfr subsids prov most rev | 55¾ | 37 | 64 | 54¼ | 63 | 46½ | .... | .... | 48½B | 50½A | 4.0 | .. |
| 33 | GCO | Genesco Inc.....................NYS, MW | A− | 1 | 19 | 471 | Shoe mfr, retailer; prestige | a31⅞ | a2⅞ | a40¼ | a29⅜ | a41¼ | 23 | 516 | 27¾ | 25¼ | 26¾ | 5.2 | .. |
| 34 | Pr | $4.50 cm Cv Pfd (104½)........NYS, MW | A | No | 51 | 99 | apparel stores; apparel mfr | 120½ | 99½ | 150 | 112½ | 152 | 95 | 3 | 104 | 100¼ | 101 | 4.5 | .. |
| 35 | GES | Genisco Technology.............ASE, PC | B− | 1 | ... | .... | Missile test eq; flight instr | 17 | 6⅜ | 15½ | 8¼ | 23 | 7½ | 211 | 9½ | 7¾ | 9½ | ‡3.2 | 11 |
| 36 |  | Genuine Parts Co...................UNL | B+ | 5 | 11 | 258 | Distri auto replacement parts | 35 | a1⅝ | 38 | 21¼ | 38½ | 21¼ | .... | .... | 21¼B | 22¼A | 4.0 | 11 |
| 37 | GNG | Genung's Incorporated..............ASE | B | 1 | ... | .... | Dept store chain; NY-Conn | 15⅜ | 7⅛ | 11½ | 8¼ | 9⅞ | 6½ | 70 | 7½ | 6½ | 7 | ‡7.1 | 5 |
| 38 |  | Georgia Intl. Life Insur..............UNL | NR | 1 | 1 | 45 | Life, annuities; accident | 40¼ | 4¼ | 34 | 15¾ | 24¼ | 9¼ | .... | .... | 11⅛B | 11⅝A | .... | d |
| 39 | GP | Georgia-Pacific Corp..............[1]NYS | A | 80¢ | 73 | 992 | Plywood products; paper; | a48¼ | a1 | a52½ | a41⅜ | a55⅛ | 30⅛ | 1753 | 37⅛ | 32¾ | 36⅜ | ‡2.7 | 14 |
| 40 | Pr | $1.64 cm Cv Pfd ([7] 43.05) vtg.......NYS | BB | No | 43 | 342 | gypsum products | .... | .... | 43⅝ | 37⅛ | 41¾ | 29½ | 450 | 32¼ | 30⅝ | 31 | 5.3 | .. |
| 41 | GOW A | Georgia Power, $5 cm Pfd (110) .....ASE* | A | No | 25 | 2 | Operates entirely in Ga.; | 111⅜ | 54¾ | 105 | 100 | 102½ | 83 | 0.1 | 88 | 88 | 88 | 5.7 | .. |
| 42 | Pr B | $4.60 cm Pfd (107 )..................ASE↓ | A | No | 70 | 161 | owned by Southern Co. | 111 | 85 | 101 | 90 | 94⅞ | 76 | 9 | 80 | 78½ | 80 | 5.8 | .. |

**Uniform Footnote Explanations—See Page 1.** Other: ‡Net invest income only. [1]Bo, Ds, PB, PC. [2]Bo, Ci, MS, PB, PC, Pi, TS. [3]Bo, De, MW, PB, PC [4]Callable at 26½. [5]As computed by Standard & Poor's. [6]From 1-1-70. [7]From 5-1-70. [8]To 6-15-70; then $102. [9]To 6-30-67; then $54½. [10]From Aug. '71. f—Δ$0.14, '64. q—Subsid. pfd stk. r—‡$0.34, '66; ‡$0.34, '65. s—Net gain from operations. t—Excl spec cr, $0.27, '62 & $2.64, '63; $1.13, '64; $0.80, '65. u—Aver shrs. v—Δ$0.30, '64; □$2.54, '65. w—Δ$0.09, '64.

# FIGURE 3–7 (Continued)

## Sample Pages from Standard & Poor's Stock Guide

| INDEX | Some Divs. Ea. Yr. Since | DIVIDENDS — Latest Payment — Per. $ | Date | Ex. Div. | —$— So Far 1966 | Total Ind. Rate | —$— Paid 1965 | FINANCIAL POSITION —Mil-$— Cash & Equiv. | Curr. Assets | Curr. Liabs. | Balance Sheet Date | CAPITALIZATION Long Term Debt Mil-$ | Shs. 000 Pfd. | Com. | Ended | $ Per Shr—EARNINGS—$ Per Shr Years ▼ 1962 | 1963 | 1964 | 1965 | 1966 | Last 12 Mos. | INTERIM EARNINGS OR REMARKS Period | $—Per Share—$ 1965 | 1966 | INDEX |
|---|---|---|---|---|---|---|---|---|---|---|---|---|---|---|---|---|---|---|---|---|---|---|---|---|---|
| 1 | 1898 | Q0.37½ | 11-1-66 | 10-5 | 1.45 | 1.50 | 1.40 | 46.7 | 130 | 60.3 | 5-29-66 | ‡90.4 | 1645 | 7604 | My | 1.25 | 1.90 | □2.11 | □2.65 | 3.07 | 3.19 | 3 Mo Aug | 0.65 | 0.77 | 1 |
| 2 | ...... | .... | .... | .... | .... | .... | .... | Each shr conv into 0.85 com. | | | | | 1645 | | My | .... | .... | .... | .... | .... | .... | | | | 2 |
| 3 | 1915 | 1.50 | 12-10-66 | 11-14 | †4.55 | 4.55 | †5.25 | 1138 | 5949 | 2637 | 9-30-66 | 247 | 2836 | 287403 | Dc | ▲5.09 | 5.55 | 6.04 | 7.40 | E6.15 | 6.35 | 9 Mo Sep | 5.36 | 4.31 | 3 |
| 4 | 1930 | Q1.25 | 2-1-67 | 1-4 | 5.00 | | 5.00 | | | | | | 1836 | | Dc | 514.6 | 561.4 | 611.8 | 749.6 | .... | .... | do | 542.61 | 437.18 | 4 |
| 5 | 1947 | Q0.93¾ | 2-1-67 | 1-4 | 3.75 | | 3.75 | | | | | | 1000 | | Dc | 514.6 | 561.4 | 611.8 | 749.6 | .... | .... | | | | 5 |
| 6 | ...... | 5% Stk | 6-1-66 | 4-27 | 5% Stk | Stk | .... | 0.19 | 3.27 | 3.10 | 10-31-65 | 0.26 | .... | 1234 | Oc | d0.15 | ■d0.52 | ■0.06 | 0.59 | .... | 0.49 | 9 Mo Jul | 0.40 | 0.30 | 6 |
| 7 | 1947 | Q0.20 | 12-9-66 | 11-22 | 0.80 | 0.80 | 1.00 | 8.60 | 25.8 | 5.84 | 12-31-65 | 9.49 | .... | 5216 | Dc | 1.47 | 1.50 | 1.33 | 1.24 | E0.90 | 1.01 | 9 Mo Sep | 0.97 | 0.74 | 7 |
| 8 | 1936 | Q0.37½ | 12-15-66 | 11-25 | 1.27½ | 1.50 | 1.20 | 9.29 | 117 | 47.6 | 12-31-65 | p30.0 | .391 | 2442 | Dc | 2.40 | 1.42 | □2.06 | 2.87 | E4.50 | 4.01 | 9 Mo Sep | 2.13 | 3.27 | 8 |
| 9 | 1955 | Q1.18¾ | 3-15-67 | 2-23 | 4.75 | | 4.75 | | | | | | 65 | | Dc | 63.53 | 40.13 | 57.10 | 78.41 | .... | .... | | | | 9 |
| 10 | 1956 | Q0.40 | 12-15-66 | 11-25 | 1.60 | | 1.60 | Each shr conv into ⅔ common | | | | | p326 | | Dc | 68.40 | 41.27 | 58.59 | 80.94 | .... | .... | | | | 10 |
| 11 | 1946 | 0.07 | 7-15-66 | 6-27 | r0.18 | ‡0.18 | r0.17 | Net Asset Val $6.29 | | | 9-30-66 | .... | .... | 14087 | Dc | #6.12 | #6.60 | #7.02 | #7.25 | .... | .... | | | | 11 |
| 12 | 1942 | Q0.37½ | 11-23-66 | 10-25 | 1.42½ | 1.50 | 1.37 | N/A | 58.6 | 45.8 | 9-30-66 | 736 | q78 | ‡24826 | Dc | 1.71 | 1.75 | 1.85 | 1.95 | E2.00 | 2.05 | 12 Mo Sep | 1.91 | 2.05 | 12 |
| 13 | 1939 | Q0.20 | 12-22-66 | 11-28 | 0.80 | 0.80 | 0.80 | 5.44 | 57.2 | 16.9 | 12-31-65 | ‡24.0 | .... | p3779 | Dc | 0.85 | 1.44 | 1.88 | 2.02 | E1.75 | 1.60 | 9 Mo Sep | 1.43 | 1.01 | 13 |
| 14 | 1934 | Q0.50 | 9-30-66 | 9-15 | 1.50 | 2.00 | 2.00 | Equity per sh $172.71 | | | [5]12-31-65 | .... | .... | 726 | Dc | X7.63 | X8.54 | X9.65 | X10.79 | .... | 10.79 | 9 Mo Sep | .... | X8.94 | 14 |
| 15 | 1951 | 5% Stk | 1-19-67 | 12-15 | †‡1.25 | 1.25 | †‡1.15 | 4.72 | 7.26 | 2.82 | 12-31-65 | 1.25 | .... | 574 | Dc | 2.06 | 2.81 | 3.24 | 3.72 | .... | 3.86 | 9 Mo Sep | 2.89 | 3.03 | 15 |
| 16 | 1940 | Q0.30 | 12-30-66 | 12-1 | 1.20 | 1.20 | 1.20 | 4.35 | 29.3 | 9.19 | 12-31-65 | 0.14 | q1.1 | 1514 | Dc | ■1.70 | 1.82 | f▵2.18 | 3.05 | E3.70 | 3.47 | 9 Mo Sep | 2.12 | 2.54 | 16 |
| 17 | 1952 | Q0.30 | 12-30-66 | 12-13 | 1.20 | 1.20 | 1.20 | 3.37 | 29.8 | 13.9 | 12-31-65 | 2.50 | .... | 2267 | Dc[15] | a1.79 | 2.43 | 2.26 | 1.61 | E2.00 | 1.86 | 9 Mo Sep | 1.19 | 1.44 | 17 |
| 18 | ...... | g0.05 | 12-30-61 | 12-15 | .... | Nil | .... | 0.03 | 19.3 | 11.5 | j12-31-65 | 3.71 | 35 | 629 | Dc | d2.69 | 1.12 | □1.22 | 0.04 | .... | 0.04 | | | | 18 |
| 19 | 1964 | Q0.10 | 12-16-66 | 11-29 | 0.40 | 0.40 | 0.30 | 0.34 | 3.55 | 0.82 | 6-30-66 | 1.51 | .... | 415 | Je | p0.50 | p▵1.17 | 0.87 | 1.02 | 1.08 | 0.94 | 3 Mo Sep | 0.34 | 0.20 | 19 |
| 20 | ...... | 0.10 | 10-24-47 | 10-6 | 0.90 | | 0.90 | 0.93 | 6.51 | 3.33 | 10-2-65 | 0.57 | .... | 2615 | Sp | d0.07 | ■d0.03 | ▵0.10 | □0.11 | .... | 0.11 | 24 Wk Mar | 0.05 | 0.05 | 20 |
| 21 | 1945 | Q0.22½ | 11-1-66 | 10-4 | 1.20 | 1.20 | 1.20 | 5.71 | 43.4 | 134 | 9-30-66 | ‡382 | +2499 | 9500 | Dc | 6.51 | 7.55 | 8.09 | 11.47 | .... | .... | 12 Mo Jun | 8.34 | 11.66 | 21 |
| 22 | 1959 | Q0.32½ | 2-15-67 | 1-20 | 1.30 | | 1.30 | 1.19 | 14.2 | 30.7 | 12-31-65 | ‡119 | +880 | ‡3320 | Dc | 5.68 | 6.99 | 10.67 | 10.84 | .... | .... | 12 Mo Sep | 11.70 | 12.71 | 22 |
| 23 | 1961 | Q0.31¼ | 2-15-67 | 1-20 | 1.25 | | 1.25 | | | | | | 400 | | Dc | 5.68 | 6.99 | 10.67 | 10.84 | .... | .... | | | | 23 |
| 24 | 1936 | Q0.32 | 1-1-67 | 11-15 | 1.16 | 1.28 | 1.03 | 61.1 | 772 | 769 | 9-30-66 | 1709 | 78 | 92965 | Dc | 1.14 | 1.35 | 1.57 | 1.87 | E2.15 | 2.13 | 9 Mo Sep | 1.31 | ▵1.57 | 24 |
| 25 | 1957 | Q0.66 | 1-1-67 | 11-15 | 2.64 | | 2.64 | Conv into 3 shrs of common | | | | | 14 | | Dc | 467.2 | 674.7 | 1839. | .... | .... | .... | | | | 25 |
| 26 | 1959 | Q0.54½ | 1-1-67 | 11-15 | 2.18 | | 2.18 | Conv into 2.28 shrs common | | | | | 32 | | Dc | 467.2 | 674.7 | 1839. | .... | .... | .... | | | | 26 |
| 27 | 1963 | Q0.12½ | 1-6-67 | 12-13 | 0.50 | 0.50 | 0.50 | 1.74 | 42.4 | 16.6 | 12-31-65 | 7.89 | .... | 2063 | Dc | 0.53 | 0.69 | w▵0.90 | 1.20 | E1.45 | 1.35 | 9 Mo Sep | 0.90 | 1.05 | 27 |
| 28 | 1937 | Q0.20 | 11-30-66 | 11-9 | 0.80 | 0.80 | 0.60 | 26.7 | 328 | 148 | 11-30-65 | 144 | 189 | 16927 | Nv[14] | 1.55 | 2.02 | 2.15 | 2.48 | E3.00 | 2.86 | 9 Mo Aug | 1.67 | 2.05 | 28 |
| 29 | 1956 | Q1.25 | 9-30-66 | 9-7 | 3.75 | | 5.00 | | | | | | 89 | | Nv | 143.3 | 190.7 | 213.1 | 224.8 | .... | .... | | | | 29 |
| 30 | ...... | .... | .... | .... | .... | | .... | Warrants expire 10-1-67 | | | | .... | .... | .... | Wrrt price equals $8.81 per com shr | | | | | | .... | | | | 30 |
| 31 | ...... | 3% Stk | 11-1-66 | 10-10 | 6% Stk | Stk | 6% Stk | 28.6 | 82.6 | 48.8 | 9-30-66 | 76.0 | 454 | 2061 | Dc | t1.27 | t1.60 | t1.74 | t▵2.25 | .... | 3.22 | 9 Mo Sep | ▵1.33 | ▵2.30 | 31 |
| 32 | 1959 | Q0.50 | 3-15-67 | 2-24 | 2.00 | | 2.00 | Cv into 1½ com thru 1-1-71 | | | | | 208 | | Dc | 7.56 | 9.44 | 13.42 | .... | .... | .... | | | | 32 |
| 33 | 1934 | Q0.35 | 1-31-67 | 1-16 | a1.25 | 1.40 | a1.16⅔ | 41.0 | 256 | 52.3 | 7-31-66 | 62.3 | p317 | 7902 | Jl[11] | a1.29 | a1.27 | a1.81 | a2.47 | 2.72 | 2.76 | 9 Mo Oct | a0.67 | 0.71 | 33 |
| 34 | 1963 | Q1.12½ | 10-31-66 | 10-10 | 4.50 | | 4.50 | Conv into com at $26.67 a shr | | | | | 202 | | Jl | .... | 30.85 | 51.46 | 81.00 | 110.9 | .... | | | | 34 |
| 35 | 1957 | Q0.07½ | 11-30-66 | 11-9 | ‡0.30 | 0.30 | ‡0.30 | 0.21 | 4.97 | 3.41 | 6-30-66 | 0.36 | .... | 437 | Sp | 0.82 | 0.48 | ▵0.77 | 1.01 | P0.86 | 0.86 | | | | 35 |
| 36 | ⊙'48 | Q0.22½ | 1-1-67 | 12-6 | 0.87½ | 0.90 | 0.77½ | 6.24 | 52.2 | 15.4 | 12-31-65 | 2.69 | 90 | 2845 | Dc[16] | 1.46 | 1.53 | 1.92 | 2.10 | .... | 2.10 | 9 Mo Sep | 1.24 | 1.24 | 36 |
| 37 | 1940 | 0.12½ | 1-3-67 | 12-13 | ‡0.50 | 0.50 | 0.65 | 1.39 | 17.1 | 7.71 | 1-29-66 | 5.85 | .... | 434 | Ja | 1.37 | 1.00 | v▵0.83 | v□1.07 | .... | 1.40 | 12 Mo Oct | ▵0.92 | □1.40 | 37 |
| 38 | ...... | None paid | | | .... | Nil | .... | Book Value $4.51 | | | 12-31-65 | .... | .... | 2355 | Dc | sd0.46 | sd0.29 | sd0.03 | sd0.03 | .... | d0.03 | | | | 38 |
| 39 | 1927 | ‡Q0.25 | 12-17-66 | 11-2 | a‡0.90 | 1.00a | ‡0.80 | 27.8 | 229 | 84.1 | 12-31-65 | 370 | 2386 | 1765 | Dc[12] | p1.64 | p1.94 | a2.31 | a2.42 | E2.65 | 2.59 | 9 Mo Sep | 1.89 | 2.06 | 39 |
| 40 | 1965 | Q0.41 | 1-1-67 | 12-19 | 1.64 | | 0.698 | Each shr conv into 0.709 com | | | | | 2286 | | Dc | .... | .... | 18.02 | 19.91 | .... | .... | | | | 40 |
| 41 | 1929 | Q1.25 | 1-1-67 | 12-8 | 5.00 | | 5.00 | 6.91 | 42.6 | 36.2 | 3-31-66 | ‡448 | ‡958 | 6397 | Dc | 35.53 | 36.91 | 39.03 | 39.17 | .... | .... | 12 Mo Oct | 38.78 | 37.96 | 41 |
| 42 | 1955 | Q1.15 | 1-1-67 | 12-8 | 4.60 | | 4.60 | | | | | | 434 | | Dc | 35.53 | 36.91 | 39.03 | 39.17 | .... | .... | | | | 42 |

▼**Stock Splits & Divs:** [11]3-for-2, '66. [12]25%, '64; 5-for-4, '66. [14]3-for-1, '62. [15]100%, '63. [16]200%, '62.

Source: Standard & Poor's, *Stock Guide.*

## FIGURE 3–8

## Description of S & P Stock Ratings

The relative "quality" of common stocks cannot be measured, as can that of bonds, which depends upon the degree of protection for interest and principal. However, there are differences in the nature of stocks and some of them are well worth measuring and comparing.

Standard & Poor's Rankings are designed to indicate by the use of symbols the relative stability and growth of earnings and the relative stability and growth of dividends. These measures of past records have a considerable bearing on relative quality, but do not pretend to reflect an examination of all other factors, tangible and intangible, that also bear on a stock's quality. *Under no circumstances should these rankings be regarded as a recommendation to buy or sell a security.*

### The Common Stock Formula

Standard & Poor's point of departure is a scoring system based upon earnings and dividend records. The first step is to examine the earnings record of the past eight years. In measuring earnings stability, a basic score is given for each year in which net per share equals or exceeds that of the preceding year. For any year in which earnings declined, the score is reduced by the percentage of that decline. The average of these eight annual scores, weighted for frequency of earnings declines, becomes our first "basic earnings index."

This stability index is then multiplied by a growth index, based on the square root of the percentage by which earnings increased between the base years period and the most recent three years. To prevent growth in extreme cases from dominating the rating, the growth factor is "topped" at 150%.

Scoring for dividend stability and growth is similar, with the principal exception that a longer period is used and results are weighted for recency. A dividend reduction fifteen years ago is obviously a less serious current investment consideration than one that was voted recently. A further weighting is applied for frequency of dividend reductions, because an erratic dividend policy is a matter affecting investment standing. The result is multiplied by a growth factor similar to that for earnings.

When this is completed, the two factors—earnings and dividends—are combined into a single numerical ranking. All the common stocks so graded are then grouped into seven classes. To these we have assigned an easy-to-understand code, as follows:

| | | |
|---|---|---|
| A+ Highest | B+ Average | C Lowest |
| A High | B Below Average | |
| A– Above Average | B– Low | |

These mathematically determined positions are modified in some instances by special considerations. Non-recurring costs, windfall profits, etc., must sometimes be allowed for. There are certain other exceptions. In the oil industry, for example, so-called "cash flow" is used rather than final net profit in order to avoid the distortions that might be caused by differences in accounting practices.

Since earnings and dividends of regulated public utilities characteristically are more stable than those of most non-regulated industries, numerous other factors must be considered. Among these are capital structure, amount of depreciation reserves, condition of properties, growth potentialities for individual service areas, the regulatory environment, and the rate of return.

These scorings are not to be confused with bond quality ratings, which are arrived at by a necessarily altogether different approach. Additionally, they must not be used as a substitute for market recommendations; a high graded stock may at times be so over-priced as to justify its sale, while a low score stock may be attractively priced for purchase. Rankings based upon earnings and dividend record are no substitute for analysis. Nor are they quality ratings in the complete sense of the term. They cannot take into account potential effects of management changes, internal company policies not yet fully reflected in the earnings and dividend record, public relations standing, recent competitive shifts, and a host of other factors that may be relevant to investment status.

N.R. signifies No Ranking possible, because of insufficient data, non-recurring factors, or some other reason.

* Preceding ranking denotes railroad guaranteed stock quality rating based on S&P bond rating scale.

### Preferred Stock Ratings

Quality ratings on preferred stock are expressed by symbols like those used in rating bonds. They are independent of Standard & Poor's bond ratings, however, in the sense that they are not necessarily graduated downward from the ranking accorded the issuing company's debt. They represent a considered judgment of the relative security of dividends, and—what is thereby implied—the prospective yield stability of the stock. These ratings are as follows:

| | | |
|---|---|---|
| AAA Prime | BBB Medium Grade | C Sub-Marginal |
| AA High Grade | BB Lower Grade | |
| A Sound | B Speculative | |

Source: Standard & Poor's, *Stock Guide*.

## FIGURE 3–9

## Sample Page from *Moody's Handbook*

### STANDARD OIL COMPANY OF CALIFORNIA

| LISTED | SYMBOL | INDICATED DIV. | RECENT PRICE | PRICE RANGE (1966) | YIELD |
|---|---|---|---|---|---|
| NYSE | SD | $2.50 | $58^3$ | $86 - 55^1$ | 4.3% |

THIS HIGH GRADE STOCK OFFERS A COMBINATION OF GROWTH AND INCOME RELIABILITY. ITS POSITION ON THE WEST COAST REMAINS DOMINANT, AND ACTIVITIES ARE BEING EXPANDED IN THE EAST.

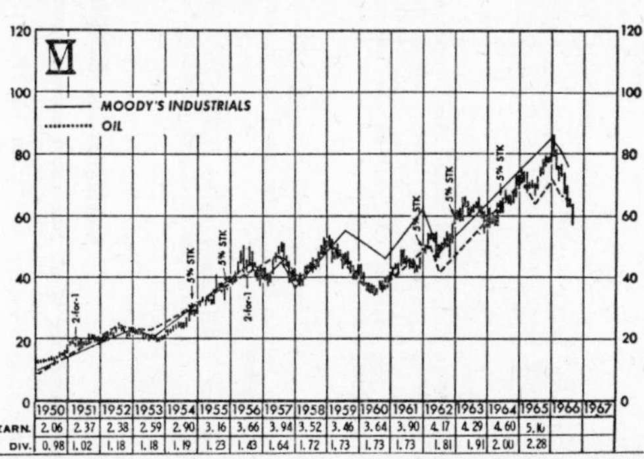


CAPITALIZATION: (12/31/65)

| | (000) | (%) |
|---|---|---|
| Debt | $ 216,334 | 6.2 |
| Minority int. | 1,146 | 0.0 |
| $3.30 pfd. c | 9,246 | 0.3 |
| Com. & Surp. | 3,270,979 | 93.5 |
| Total | $3,497,705 | 100.0% |

Shs. ($6.25)-(3/31/66)-75,561,109

INTERIM EARNINGS:

| Qu. | 1st | 2nd | 3rd | 4th |
|---|---|---|---|---|
| 63 | 1.09 | 1.05 | 1.12 | 1.03 |
| 64 | 1.18 | 1.10 | 1.11 | 1.21 |
| 65 | 1.21 | 1.38 | 1.23 | 1.28 |
| 66 | 1.32 | 1.46 | | |

| DIVIDENDS: | Record | Payable |
|---|---|---|
| 0.55Q | 8/10/65 | 9/10/65 |
| 0.625Q | 11/10 | 12/10 |
| 0.625Q | 2/10/66 | 3/10/66 |
| 0.625Q | 5/10 | 6/10 |
| 0.625Q | 8/10 | 9/9 |

BACKGROUND:

This is a large integrated oil company with worldwidc operations. Domestically, it is the dominant factor on the West Coast. Crude production in Calif. provides 37% of domestic output; in the Western Hemisphere company produced about 81% of its 1965 refinery requirements. Marketing covers the western half of the U.S., Alaska, the Northeast & the Southeast. Abroad it has a 50% interest in the Bahrein-Caltex group, 30% in Arabian American Oil and Trans-Arabian Pipe Line, and 7% in the Iranian Consortium...In 1965, Eastern Hemisphere operations supplied about 60% of total crude production, and 43% of net income. Standard Oil of Kentucky was merged in 1961 and a 100,000 barrel per day refinery in Mississippi was built to supply that company's outlets.

RECENT DEVELOPMENTS:

Western hemisphere gross production of crude oil and natural gas liquids rose 13% and refinery runs increased 5% in the first half. Chemical sales were up 14% and natural gas sales by volume was 17% above the year earlier level. As a result, first half revenues gained 9% and net income was up 5.5%. Exploration and development outlays will account for about 60% of total capital expenses budgeted at $575 million this year. The convertible preferred stock has been called for redemption on Oct. 1. As of July 27, there remained 618,388 shares outstanding.

PROSPECTS:

A good rate of profit improvement is anticipated for this company over the next few years, based upon improved marketing and increasing growth of petrochemicals, though serious price problems in the Eastern Hemisphere and international tensions could hamper progress. The company's 2 new refineries, in Mississippi and Alaska, and higher crude production will contribute to earnings. Increasing benefits from cost control efforts should offset a possible decline in dividend income, and permit earnings to reach an estimated $5.40 a share in 1966.

STATISTICS

| YEAR | GROSS REVS. ($ MILL.) | OPER. PROFIT MARGIN % | NET INCOME ($ 000) | WORK CAP. ($ MILL.) | SENIOR CAPITAL ($ MILL.) | NO. SHS. OUT. (000) | CASH FLOW PER SH. $ | EARN. PER SH. $ | DIV. PER SH. $ | DIV. PAY. % | PRICE RANGE | PRICE X EARN. | AVG. YIELD % |
|---|---|---|---|---|---|---|---|---|---|---|---|---|---|
| 55 | 1,277.8 | 15.1 | 231,139 | 283.2 | 78.6 | 73,190 | 5.57 | 3.16 | 1.23 | 39 | $40^5 - 30^1$ | 11.2 | 3.5 |
| 56 | 1,452.5 | 15.2 | 267,891 | 308.6 | 76.7 | 73,190 | 6.31 | 3.66 | 1.43 | 39 | $50^3 - 37^4$ | 12.0 | 3.2 |
| 57 | 1,650.8 | 14.6 | 288,230 | 297.2 | 82.3 | 73,190 | 6.73 | 3.94 | 1.64 | 42 | $51^5 - 37^3$ | 11.3 | 3.7 |
| 58 | 1,559.2 | 11.0 | 257,759 | 426.4 | 179.5 | 73,190 | 6.07 | 3.52 | 1.73 | 49 | $53^2 - 37^3$ | 12.9 | 3.8 |
| 59 | 1,564.8 | 11.1 | 253,599 | 416.5 | 175.6 | 73,190 | 6.07 | 3.46 | 1.73 | 50 | $53^6 - 39^3$ | 13.5 | 3.7 |
| 60 | 1,663.4 | 10.8 | 266,113 | 429.8 | 173.5 | 73,190 | 6.35 | 3.64 | 1.73 | 47 | $44^3 - 34^4$ | 10.8 | 4.4 |
| a61 | 2,046.5 | 9.5 | 294,405 | 426.0 | 192.6 | 73,190 | 6.96 | 3.90 | 1.73 | 44 | $49^2 - 40^4$ | 11.5 | 3.8 |
| 62 | 2,160.9 | 9.5 | 313,781 | 437.3 | 205.2 | 73,191 | 7.45 | 4.17 | 1.81 | 43 | $59^4 - 45^3$ | 12.6 | 3.5 |
| 63 | 2,202.5 | 8.2 | 322,068 | 465.7 | 203.6 | 73,191 | 7.67 | 4.29 | 1.91 | 44 | $66 - 54^3$ | 14.0 | 3.2 |
| 64 | 2,285.7 | 9.7 | 345,288 | 492.9 | 236.4 | 73,240 | 8.19 | 4.60 | 2.00 | 43 | $73^7 - 56^4$ | 14.2 | 3.1 |
| 65 | 2,442.5 | 11.5 | 391,225 | 417.6 | 225.6 | 75,247 | 8.87 | 5.10 | 2.28 | 45 | $79^7 - 66^3$ | 14.3 | 3.1 |

Note: Adj. for 2-for-1 stk. split 5/56; also 5% stk. divs. in 1955-62-63-64. a-Incl. Standard Oil of Ky. (merged 10/1/61) for entire year. c-Conv. into 1.45 common shs. for each pfd. sh.

INCORPORATED: January 27, 1926 - Del.

PRINCIPAL OFFICE: 225 Bush St. San Francisco, Calif.

ANNUAL MEETING: First Thurs. in May

NO. OF STOCKHOLDERS: 221,231

TRANSFER AGENT: Chase Manhattan Bk., N.Y. Montreal Tr. Co., Vancouver, B.C.

REGISTRAR: First Natl. City Bk., N.Y. Crocker Citizens Natl. Bk., San Francisco, Calif.

INSTIT. HOLDINGS: NO.: 346 SHS.: 5,223,427

OFFICERS:

CHAIRMAN: R.G. Follis

PRESIDENT: O.N. Miller

SECRETARY: H.L. Severance

TREASURER: H.D. Armstrong

852

Source: *Moody's Handbook of Widely Held Common Stocks, 1966.*

FIGURE 3–10

# STANDARD & POOR'S BOND RATINGS

In the Standard & Poor's bond quality ratings system, interest-paying bonds are graded into eight classifications ranging from AAA for the highest quality designation through AA, A, BBB, BB, B, CCC to CC for the lowest. Bonds on which no interest is being paid, either because of default or because of "income" characteristics, are given C, DDD, DD and D ratings. Rating symbols are the same for corporate and municipal bonds, and every effort has been made to keep the two systems on a comparable basis. United States Government bonds are not rated, but are considered as a yardstick against which to measure all other issues.

## BANK QUALITY BONDS

Under present commercial bank regulations bonds rated in the top four categories (AAA, AA, A, BBB or their equivalent) generally are regarded as eligible for bank investment.

**AAA** Bonds rated AAA are highest grade obligations. They possess the ultimate degree of protection as to principal and interest. Marketwise, they move with interest rates, and hence provide the maximum safety on all counts.

**AA** Bonds rated AA also qualify as high grade obligations, and in the majority of instances differ from AAA issues only in small degree. Here, too, prices move with the long term money market.

**A** Bonds rated A are regarded as upper medium grade. They have considerable investment strength but are not entirely free from adverse effects of changes in economic and trade conditions. Interest and principal are regarded as safe. They predominantly reflect money rates in their market behavior, but to some extent, also economic conditions.

**BBB** The BBB, or medium grade category is borderline between definitely sound obligations and those where the speculative element begins to predominate. These bonds have adequate asset coverage and normally are protected by satisfactory earnings. Their susceptibility to changing conditions, particularly to depressions, necessitates constant watching. Marketwise, the bonds are more responsive to business and trade conditions than to interest rates. This group is the lowest which qualifies for commercial bank investment.

## SUB-STANDARD BONDS

As we move down the rating scale, beginning with BB, investment characteristics weaken and the speculative elements become progressively stronger. The fortunes of the obligors change rapidly with economic and trade conditions and in adverse periods interest requirements may not be earned. Investment in bonds in this group must be under constant surveillance. Prices fluctuate widely with changing business conditions and with little regard for the money market.

**BB** Bonds given a BB rating are regarded as lower medium grade. They have only minor investment characteristics. In the case of utilities, interest is earned consistently but by narrow margins. In the case of other types of obligors, charges are earned on average by a fair margin, but in poor periods deficit operations are possible.

**B** Bonds rated as low as B are speculative. Payment of interest cannot be assured under difficult economic conditions.

**CCC-CC** Bonds rated CCC and CC are outright speculations, with the lower rating denoting the more speculative. Interest is paid, but continuation is questionable in periods of poor trade conditions. In the case of CC ratings the bonds may be on an income basis and the payment may be small.

**C** The rating of C is reserved for income bonds on which no interest is being paid.

**DDD-D** All bonds rated DDD, DD and D are in default, with the rating indicating the relative salvage value.

## CANADIAN BONDS

Canadian corporate bonds are rated on the same basis as American corporate issues. The ratings measure the intrinsic value of the bonds, but they do not take into account exchange and other uncertainties.

Source: Standard & Poor's, *Bond Guide*.

discusses new offerings in the corporate and municipal markets, opportunities in convertibles, changes in bond ratings, new issue ratings, bonds called for payment, etc. Both services issue one-page summaries of individual bond situations.

Both services now use computers in investment analysis, portfolio selection, and financial information retrieval. Standard & Poor's publishes as a monthly supplement to *The Outlook*, the *S & P 200 Rapid Growth Stocks*, screened and selected from nearly 6,000 stocks, by an electronic computer program. The Standard Statistics Company, Inc., a subsidiary of Standard & Poor's, provides the Compustat Service. Compustat, which is a computer magnetic tape data file, provides basic balance sheet and income account financial data. The Compustat tape contains 20 years of annual data for 1,000 companies with 65 financial items for each company for each year. Quarterly data are also available from 1962 to the present. The Compustat tapes can now be updated daily. A growing number of banks, brokerage houses, insurance companies, and mutual funds are utilizing the service to facilitate their security analysis work. By providing basic financial statistics on tape, comparative financial performance can be measured with speed, accuracy, and versatility by computers. With factual results made available quickly, security analysts are enabled to focus on investment decisions rather than on time-consuming statistical calculations.[8]

The Value Line Investment Survey covers 1,100 stocks in 60 industries. It is essentially a reference service. Each stock in the list is reviewed in detail once every three months. Interim reports are provided in weekly supplements on any new developments between the time of the regular quarterly reports. Each of the industries is reported upon quarterly. Each week the new edition of the Value Line Investment Survey covers three or four industries, on a rotating quarterly basis. Each industry report contains full-page reports on individual stocks. About 85 stocks are covered every week in the order of their industries. After all 1,100 stocks have been covered in 13 weeks, the cycle starts over again. There is also a weekly summary of advices and index, which includes the recent price, the current appraisal, and the estimated yield of each of the stocks under continuing study throughout the year.

Each week there are three or four parts to the Survey. Part I is the Weekly Summary of Advices and Index. It provides an average of estimated yields for the ensuing 12 months; the average appreciation potentiality of all 1,100 stocks in a hypothesized economic environment three to five years ahead; and a rank of industrial groups according to probable market performance over the next 12 months. Part II is the "Selection and

[8] For an extended discussion see Chapter 20. See also M. Kisor, Jr., "Automation for Investing," *Trusts & Estates*, July, 1965; also Dana L. Thomas, "Calculating Risks: Computers Are Winning Friends and Influencing Decisions on Wall Street," *Barron's*, June 28, 1965.

# FIGURE 3–11

## Sample Pages from Standard & Poor's Bond Guide

| INDEX | Exchange | BONDS Name and Description of Issue | Description, Interest Rate, Due | Interest Dates | S&P Quality Rating | Eligibility | Conn. | Me. | Mass. | N.H. | N.J. | N.J. tr | N.Y. | CALL PRICE For S.F. | CALL PRICE Regular | Ref. Start | PRICE RANGE 1960-64 High | 1960-64 Low | 1965 High | 1965 Low | 1966 High | 1966 Low | LAST SALE or Bid s=Sale | Yield to Mty. |
|---|---|---|---|---|---|---|---|---|---|---|---|---|---|---|---|---|---|---|---|---|---|---|---|---|
| 1 | • | New England Tel. & Tel. ....... | Deb 3s '74 | Ms15 | AAA | X | √ | √ | √ | √ | √ | √ | √ | .... | †100.70 | | 90 | 79 | 89¾ | 87½ | 88⅞ | 88¾ | 87½ | 4.81 |
| 2 | | do | Deb 3¼s '77 | jD15 | AAA | X | √ | √ | √ | √ | √ | √ | √ | .... | †102.07 | | 90½ | 78 | 89¾ | 86½ | 86⅝ | 84⅜ | 84⅜ | 5.00 |
| 3 | • | do | Deb 3s '82 | aO | AAA | X | √ | √ | √ | √ | √ | √ | √ | .... | †102.13 | | 85¼ | 72½ | 82⅝ | 76 | 76⅛ | 76⅛ | 76⅛ | 4.91 |
| 4 | | do | Deb 3⅛s '88 | jD15 | AAA | X | √ | √ | √ | √ | √ | √ | √ | .... | †103.76 | | 82½ | 74½ | 82 | 78 | 78 | 76⅞ | 76⅞ | 4.80 |
| 5 | | do | Deb 3¼s '91 | mN15 | AAA | X | √ | √ | √ | √ | √ | √ | √ | .... | †103.16 | | 84⅝ | 76 | 82½ | 78⅛ | 78¼ | 77⅛ | 77⅛ | 4.80 |
| 6 | | do | Deb 4s '93 | Ao | AAA | X | √ | √ | √ | √ | √ | √ | √ | .... | †106.32 | | 95¾ | 80¼ | 93⅞ | 88⅞ | 89 | 88 | 88 | 4.79 |
| 7 | | do | Deb 4⅝s '99 | Ao | AAA | X | √ | √ | √ | √ | √ | √ | √ | .... | 104 | '66 | 107¼ | 98¾ | 104 | 98⅜ | 98½ | 97½ | 97½ | 4.77 |
| 8 | | do | Deb 4½s 2002 | jJ | AAA | X | √ | √ | √ | √ | √ | √ | √ | .... | 104.43 | '67 | 104 | 98⅞ | 101⅞ | 96⅛ | 96¼ | 95¼ | 95¼ | 4.77 |
| 9 | | do | Deb 4⅝s 2005 | jJ | AAA | X | – | √ | √ | √ | √ | √ | – | .... | 104.32 | '70 | .... | .... | 100¾ | 98⅛ | 98¼ | 96¾ | 96¾ | 4.85 |
| 10 | | New Jersey Bell Telephone .... | Deb 3¼s '84 | Mn | AAA | X | √ | √ | √ | √ | √ | √ | √ | .... | †103.55 | | 86½ | 73 | 85⅜ | 82 | 82⅛ | 81¼ | 81¼ | 4.79 |
| 11 | • | do | Deb 3⅛s '88 | jJ15 | AAA | X | √ | √ | √ | √ | √ | √ | √ | .... | †103.56 | | 85 | 73¼ | 80½ | 79½ | 78½ | 78½ | 78½ | 4.78 |
| 12 | | do | Deb 3s '89 | Mn | AAA | X | √ | √ | √ | √ | √ | √ | √ | .... | †102.92 | | 81 | 72 | 79⅝ | 75¾ | 75⅞ | 74⅞ | 74⅞ | 4.78 |
| 13 | | do | Deb 2¾s '90 | Ms15 | AAA | X | √ | √ | √ | √ | √ | √ | √ | .... | †103.34 | | 86½ | 70 | 75⅝ | 71⅝ | 71¾ | 70⅞ | 70⅞ | 4.78 |
| 14 | | do | Deb 3⅞s '93 | Ao | AAA | X | √ | √ | √ | √ | √ | √ | √ | .... | †103.59 | | 93¼ | 85 | 92 | 87 | 87⅛ | 86⅛ | 86⅛ | 4.79 |
| 15 | | do | Deb 3⅜s '95 | jD | AAA | X | √ | √ | √ | √ | √ | √ | √ | .... | †103.22 | | 85⅛ | 75 | 83⅞ | 78½ | 78⅝ | 77¾ | 77¾ | 4.78 |
| 16 | | do | Deb 4⅞s 2000 | mN | AAA | X | √ | √ | √ | √ | √ | √ | √ | .... | †105.69 | | 108 | 101⅞ | 105 | 102 | 103 | 101⅝ | 101⅝ | 4.78 |
| 17 | | do | Deb 4⅝s 2005 | Jd | AAA | X | – | √ | √ | √ | √ | √ | | .... | 104⅞ | '70 | .... | .... | 101¾ | 98⅛ | 98¼ | 96¾ | 96¾ | 4.85 |
| 18 | • | New Jersey Junct. RR. .... | 1st Curr 4s '86 | Fa | BBB | X | – | – | – | – | – | – | – | .... | NC | | 78¼ | 69 | 74 | 74 | No Sale | | 75⅝ | 6.13 |
| 19 | • | New Jersey Power & Light ...... | 1st 3s '74 | Ms | AA | X | √ | √ | √ | √ | √ | √ | √ | .... | †102¾ | | 88¾ | 75⅛ | 88½ | 84¼ | No Sale | | 86 | 5.04 |
| 20 | | do | 1st 3s '78 | Jd | AA | X | √ | √ | √ | √ | √ | √ | √ | 101⅛ | †102¾ | | 87⅛ | 72 | 85⅞ | 82¾ | 82⅞ | 82½ | 82½ | 4.89 |
| 21 | | do | 1st 2⅞s '79 | Jd | AA | X | √ | √ | √ | √ | √ | √ | √ | †101.45 | †102.49 | | 84⅞ | 74½ | 83⅞ | 80½ | 80⅝ | 80¼ | 80¼ | 4.88 |
| 22 | | do | 1st 3⅛s '84 | fA | AA | X | √ | √ | √ | √ | √ | √ | √ | †100.94 | †102.95 | | 84¾ | 73 | 83½ | 78¾ | 78⅞ | 78⅝ | 78⅝ | 4.89 |
| 23 | | do | 1st 4⅛s '88 | Mn | AA | X | √ | √ | √ | √ | √ | √ | √ | †101.87 | †104.78 | | 98 | 91½ | 96 | 90 | 90⅛ | 89½ | 89½ | 4.90 |
| 24 | | do | 1st 4⅞s '90 | jJ | AA | X | √ | √ | √ | √ | √ | √ | √ | †101.09 | †105.02 | | 108 | 101⅛ | 104¾ | 100¼ | 100⅜ | 99⅝ | 99⅝ | 4.90 |
| 25 | | do | Deb 4¾s '89 | jJ | A | X | √ | – | – | √ | – | √ | √ | †102.52 | †107.25 | | 103½ | 101 | 102 | 97⅞ | 98 | 97¼ | 97¼ | 4.95 |
| 26 | | do | SF Deb 5s '90 | aO | A | X | √ | – | – | √ | – | √ | – | †101¼ | †106¼ | | .... | .... | 101½ | 100 | 101½ | 100¾ | 100¾ | 4.95 |
| 27 | | New Orleans Gr. Nor. Ry. . Inc | Deb 5s 2032 | jJ | B | Y | – | – | – | – | – | – | – | .... | 100 | | 86 | 53 | 90 | 78 | 78 | 77 | 77 | Flat |
| 28 | | New Orleans Public Service .... | 1st 3⅛s '74 | jJ | A | X | √ | √ | √ | √ | – | √ | √ | †101⅞ | †102 | | 90½ | 81½ | 90 | 87¾ | 87⅞ | 87½ | 87½ | 4.95 |
| 29 | | do | 1st 3¼s '78 | aO | A | X | √ | √ | √ | √ | – | √ | √ | †101.17 | †102.13 | | 89 | 82 | 87⅞ | 84¼ | 84⅜ | 83¾ | 83¾ | 4.95 |
| 30 | | do | 1st 4⅛s '83 | Ao | A | X | √ | √ | √ | √ | – | √ | √ | †102.20 | †103.52 | | 98 | 91 | 96¼ | 90⅞ | 91 | 90⅜ | 90⅜ | 4.95 |
| 31 | | do | 1st 3¼s '84 | jD | A | X | √ | √ | √ | √ | – | √ | √ | †102 | †103.53 | | 85¾ | 78 | 84½ | 79¾ | 79⅞ | 79¼ | 79¼ | 4.95 |
| 32 | | do | 1st 4½s '87 | Ao | A | X | √ | √ | √ | √ | – | √ | √ | †100.70 | †103.86 | | 102½ | 91½ | 100⅞ | 94¾ | 94⅞ | 94⅛ | 94⅛ | 4.95 |
| 33 | | do | 1st 5s '91 | Jd | A | X | √ | √ | √ | √ | – | √ | √ | †100.88 | †105.12 | | 105½ | 99⅞ | 105¼ | 101⅜ | 101½ | 100¼ | 100¼ | 4.98 |
| 34 | | do | 1st 4½s '92 | Ao | A | X | √ | √ | √ | √ | – | √ | √ | †100.95 | †104.94 | | 104 | 96½ | 100¾ | 94⅛ | 94¼ | 93⅜ | 93⅜ | 4.95 |
| 35 | • | New Orleans Terminal Co. ...... | 1st 3¾s '77 | mN | A | X | √ | √ | – | √ | – | √ | √ | 100⅛ | 101⅝ | | No Sale | | No Sale | | No Sale | | 86 | 5.35 |
| 36 | • | N.Y. Cent. & Hudson Riv. RR. ..... | 3½s '97 | jJ | BB | Y | – | – | – | – | – | – | √ | .... | NC | | 79 | 51½ | 76½ | 71 | 72½ | 72⅜ | s72½ | 5.30 |
| 37 | • | do Michigan Central | CT 3½s '98 | Fa | B | Y | – | – | – | – | – | – | – | .... | NC | | 68¾ | 47 | 73 | 67½ | 68⅝ | 68⅝ | 68⅝ | 5.63 |
| 38 | • | do Lake Shore | CT 3½s '98 | Fa | B | Y | – | – | – | – | – | – | – | .... | NC | | 66 | 47 | 69¾ | 64½ | 66 | 65 | s65½ | 5.92 |
| 39 | • | New York Central RR. ...... | Con A 4s '98 | Fa | B | Y | – | – | – | – | – | – | – | .... | NC | | 75⅝ | 42 | 79 | 72⅜ | 75¼ | 74 | s74⅛ | 5.79 |
| 40 | • | do | Ref & Imp A 4½s 2013 | aO | B | Y | – | – | – | – | – | – | – | .... | *110 | | 80 | 45¼ | 83⅝ | 77½ | 82¼ | 80½ | s80½ | 5.79 |
| 41 | • | do | Ref & Imp C 5s 2013 | aO | B | Y | – | – | – | – | – | – | – | .... | *105 | | 89 | 48½ | 92¼ | 84½ | 91¾ | 89⅜ | s91 | 5.54 |
| 42 | | do | CT 5¾s '80 | Jj | B | Y | – | – | – | – | – | – | – | †100¾ | †101½ | | 94 | 73 | 97 | 90½ | 97 | 97 | 97 | 6.05 |

**Uniform Footnote Explanations—See Page 4.** Other: [1]Preliminary Rating. [2]Incl $88.5 M adv fr parent co. [3]Incl $49.5 M adv from parent.

## FIGURE 3–11 (Continued)

## Sample Pages from Standard & Poor's Bond Guide



| INDEX | PRINCIPAL BUSINESS or General Information | UND'RWRIT'G Firm | UND'RWRIT'G Price | UND'RWRIT'G Year | OUTST'D'G Mil-$ This Issue | OUTST'D'G Long Term Debt | FINANCIAL POSITION Mil-$ Cash & Equiv. | Curr. Assets | Curr. Liabs. | Balance Sheet Date | Ratio Debt to Net Prop. | Yrs. End. | ANNUAL EARNINGS Times Int. & Misc. Charges Earned Common Share Earnings in Italics 1961 | 1962 | 1963 | 1964 | 1965 | INTERIM EARNINGS General Information Period | 1964 | 1965 | INDEX |
|---|---|---|---|---|---|---|---|---|---|---|---|---|---|---|---|---|---|---|---|---|---|
| 1 | Important subsid of Bell System, pro- | H6 | 100¾ | '49 | 35.0 | [2]404 | 7.69 | 88.8 | 95.4 | 12-31-64 | 33.9 | Dec | 6.15 | 6.44 | 6.10 | 7.00 | .... | 12 Mo Dec | 6.38 | 5.63 | 1 |
| 2 | vides telephone service in Me, Mass, | K12 | 101¾ | '52 | 20.0 | | | | | | | | | | | | | | | | 2 |
| 3 | NH, RI & Vt; about a third of phones | H6 | 101⅝ | '47 | 40.0 | | | | | | | | | | | | | | | | 3 |
| 4 | are in Boston & ¾ths of revenues | H6 | 102¼ | '54 | 30.0 | | | | | | | | | | | | | | | | 4 |
| 5 | from Mass. System is virtually all | H6 | 101 | '55 | 30.0 | | | | | | | | | | | | | | | | 5 |
| 6 | dial. Industry in area is widely di- | H6 | 102⅞ | '58 | 45.0 | | | | | | | | | | | | | | | | 6 |
| 7 | versified, including machine shops, | F3 | 101 | '61 | 45.0 | | | | | | | | | | | | | | | | 7 |
| 8 | foundries, chemicals, electronics | F3 | 101 | '62 | 50.0 | | | | | | | | | | | | | | | | 8 |
| 9 | | H6 | 100⅞ | '65 | 60.0 | *464 | | | | | | | | | | | | Dated July 1, 1965 | | | 9 |
| 10 | Operates virtually all the telephone | H6 | 102⅞ | '52 | 20.0 | [3]*280 | 5.42 | 65.8 | 89.9 | 12-31-64 | 34.5 | Dec | 10.17 | 10.32 | 10.06 | 11.62 | .... | 3 Mo Sep | 10.27 | 8.54 | 10 |
| 11 | stations in NJ. Property expendi- | H6 | 103⅛ | '48 | 55.0 | | | | | | | | | | | | | | | | 11 |
| 12 | tures have been heavy in recent yrs, | H6 | 101 | '54 | 25.0 | | | | | | | | | | | | | | | | 12 |
| 13 | incl large sums for modernization, | H6 | 102½ | '50 | 15.0 | | | | | | | | | | | | | | | | 13 |
| 14 | which, aided by rate increases, has | H6 | 101 | '58 | 30.0 | | | | | | | | | | | | | | | | 14 |
| 15 | widened operating margins. System | H6 | 101 | 55 | 25.0 | | | | | | | | | | | | | | | | 15 |
| 16 | is practically all dial operated | M25 | 102⅞ | '60 | 20.0 | | | | | | | | | | | | | | | | 16 |
| 17 | | W15 | 101⅜ | '65 | 40.0 | | | | | | | | | | | | | Dated June 1, 1965 | | | 17 |
| 18 | Gtd prin & int by N.Y. Central RR | .... | 103½ | '87 | 1.38 | .... | Assumed by N.Y. Central | | | | .... | | | | | | | | | | 18 |
| 19 | Electric to west & northwest NJ, a | M28 | 104⅝ | '44 | 9.00 | *50.5 | 1.16 | 5.00 | 5.30 | 9-30-65 | 51.4 | Dec | 3.51 | 3.83 | 3.40 | 3.39 | .... | 12 Mo Sep | 3.46 | 3.26 | 19 |
| 20 | well diversified area, having agri- | H6 | 101¾ | '48 | 6.00 | | | | | | | | | | | | | | | | 20 |
| 21 | culture (truck farm, dairy, poultry): | L19 | 101 | '49 | 3.50 | | | | | | | | | | | | | | | | 21 |
| 22 | manufacturing (machinery, paper, | K12 | 101¼ | '54 | 8.70 | | | | | | | | | | | | | | | | 22 |
| 23 | chemicals, textiles); iron & zinc | K12 | 102⅛ | '58 | 7.50 | | | | | | | | | | | | | | | | 23 |
| 24 | mining; & quarrying; Subsid. of | H6 | 101¼ | '60 | 5.00 | | | | | | | | | | | | | | | | 24 |
| 25 | General Public Utilities | H6 | 102½ | '64 | 5.88 | | | | | | .... | | | | | | | $120,000 called 8-1-65 | | | 25 |
| 26 | | D27 | 101¼ | '65 | 5.00 | | | | | | | | | | | | | Dated Oct. 1, 1965 | | | 26 |
| 27 | Road leased to Gulf, Mobile & Ohio | .... | Reorg | '33 | 4.12 | 10.2 | See Gulf, Mobile & Ohio | | | | .... | | | | | | | Paid full int since '61 | | | 27 |
| 28 | Electric, natural gas, transportation in | H6 | 103⅞ | '44 | 32.0 | 83.0 | 12.8 | 20.6 | 13.2 | 12-31-64 | 51.5 | Dec | 3.06 | 3.70 | 3.04 | 3.02 | .... | 12 Mo Nov | 3.07 | 2.91 | 28 |
| 29 | New Orleans, a major shipping point | L13 | 102⅛ | '48 | 10.0 | | | | | | | | | | | | | | | | 29 |
| 30 | & comm'l center for a large area & | E17 | 103 | '53 | 6.00 | | | | | | | | | | | | | | | | 30 |
| 31 | focal point for cotton. Area has | W15 | 102¾ | '54 | 6.00 | | | | | | | | | | | | | | | | 31 |
| 32 | small, diversified industries, indus- | H6 | 100⅞ | '57 | 6.00 | | | | | | | | | | | | | | | | 32 |
| 33 | trial load small. Generates all elec | E17 | 101 | '61 | 15.0 | | | | | | | | | | | | | | | | 33 |
| 34 | requirements, buys gas needs | S5 | 101 | '62 | 8.00 | | | | | | | | | | | | | | | | 34 |
| 35 | Gtd principal & int by Southern Ry | K7 | 99¼ | '52 | 5.69 | .... | See Southern Railway | | | | .... | | | | | | | | | | 35 |
| 36 | Pr lien important NY Central mileage | .... | 82¾ | '16 | 83.0 | .... | See N.Y. Central RR. | | | | .... | | | | | | | | | | 36 |
| 37 | 2nd lien important NY Cent mileage | .... | .... | '98 | 17.8 | | | | | | | | | | | | | | | | 37 |
| 38 | 2nd lien important NY Cent mileage | .... | .... | '98 | 17.3 | | | | | | | | | | | | | | | | 38 |
| 39 | System covers intensively highly in- | .... | 84¾ | '16 | 67.9 | 630 | 45.3 | 134 | 117 | 9-30-65 | 54.7 | Dec | c0.67 | c0.90 | c1.20 | c1.78 | .... | 9 Mo Sep | 1.68 | 1.82 | 39 |
| 40 | dustrialized terr between NYC & | .... | 95¾ | '14 | 96.0 | | | | | | | Dec | 0.84 | 1.10 | 1.49 | 2.14 | .... | | | | 40 |
| 41 | Chicago. However, earns relatively | .... | 94½ | '22 | 64.0 | | | | | | | | | | | | | | | | 41 |
| 42 | low & erratic & int cov-(see next pg) | .... | Exch | '55 | 0.50 | 630 | 56.7 | 140 | 132 | 12-31-64 | 53.2 | Dec | 0.67 | 0.90 | 1.20 | 1.78 | .... | | | | 42 |

Source: Standard & Poor's, *Bond Guide*.

Opinion" section. It covers topics such as "Buisness and The Stock Market," "Recommended Stock," "Inflation and Common Stocks," "Technical Background of The Market," "Local Service Airlines," etc. Part III, "Reports and Ratings," provides the industry and company analyses described above.

Value Line has developed statistical techniques designed, in each stock report, to answer five questions:

Question 1—How sound a stock is it?

Question 2—How well can it be expected to perform in the market during the next 12 months compared to other stocks?

Question 3—How attractive is it over a three-to-five-year pull relative to other stocks?

Question 4—How much will this stock yield over the next 12 months?

Question 5—How suitable is the stock for the individual investor in the light of his investment objectives?

To answer the first question Value Line provides a Quality Grade. This refers to the general safety of a stock and is derived by combining a Growth Index and a Stability Index, giving about three times as much weight to Stability as to Growth. The Quality Grades range from A+ down to C−, with the "safest" stock having the A+ Quality Grade. The average grade is B, the "riskiest" is C−. The Quality Grade is shown as Item 12 in Figures 3–12 and 3–13.

To answer the second question, a "Probable Market Performance Rank Next 12 Months" is provided. This is a relative measurement determined by combining a stock's cash earnings value, divided by its 52-week average price, with its nonparametric value position and with its earnings momentum. All 1,100 stocks under regular review are grouped into five categories according to their Probable Market Performance in The Next 12 Months, from Group I (Highest) down to Group V (Lowest). See Item 13 in Figures 3–12 and 3–13.

Question 3 is answered by the three-to-five-year Investment Desirability Rank, which is a relative measurement. It is determined by combining a stock's long-term potentiality with its risk. A stock's potentiality is measured, by Value Line, from the current price to the average price forecast for the whole three-year period, three to five years ahead. A stock's risk is a function of its price stability, its past five-year price performance and the yield of the general market, according to Value Line. All 1,100 stocks under regular review are grouped into five categories of 220 stocks each according to their three-to-five-year appreciation potentiality and risk, from Group I (Highest) down to Group V (Lowest). Appreciation potentiality is measured in terms of a hypothesized economic environment three to five years ahead. Item 14 in Figures 3–12 and 3–13 show the Desirability Rank.

Question 4 is answered by the "Estimated Yield next 12 months."

## FIGURE 3–12

### Sample Page from Value Line Survey

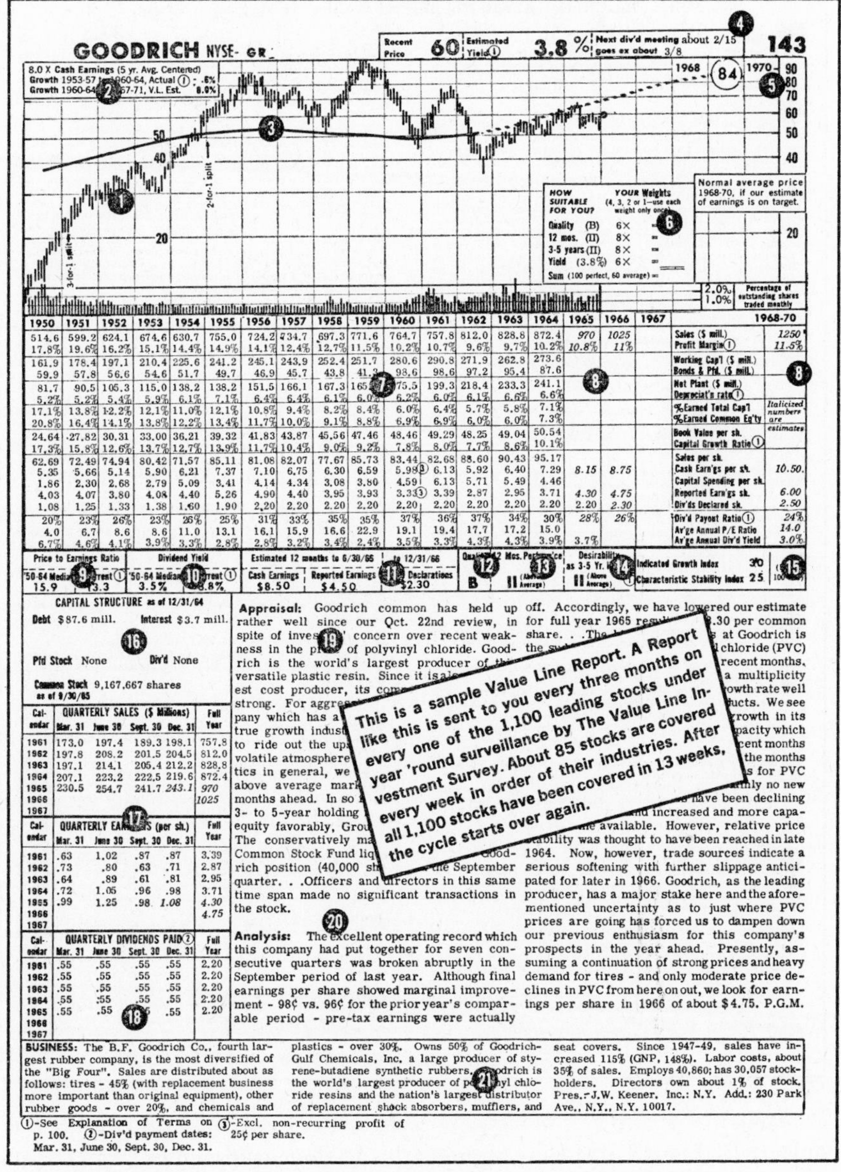



| | 1950 | 1951 | 1952 | 1953 | 1954 | 1955 | 1956 | 1957 | 1958 |
|---|---|---|---|---|---|---|---|---|---|
| Sales ($ mill.) | 514.6 | 599.2 | 624.1 | 674.6 | 630.7 | 755.0 | 724.2 | 734.7 | 697.3 |
| Profit Margin① | 17.8% | 19.6% | 16.2% | 15.1% | 14.4% | 14.9% | 14.1% | 12.4% | 12.7% |
| Working Cap'l ($ mill.) | 161.9 | 178.4 | 197.1 | 210.4 | 225.6 | 241.2 | 245.1 | 243.9 | 252.4 |
| Bonds & Pfd. ($ mill.) | 59.9 | 57.8 | 56.6 | 54.6 | 51.7 | 49.7 | 46.9 | 45.7 | 43.8 |
| Net Plant ($ mill.) | 81.7 | 90.5 | 105.3 | 115.0 | 138.2 | 138.2 | 151.5 | 166.1 | 167.3 |
| Depreciat'n rate① | 5.2% | 5.2% | 5.4% | 5.9% | 6.1% | 7.1% | 6.4% | 6.4% | 6.1% |
| %Earned Total Cap'l | 17.1% | 13.8% | 12.2% | 12.1% | 11.0% | 12.1% | 10.8% | 9.4% | 8.2% |
| %Earned Common Eq'ty | 20.8% | 16.4% | 14.1% | 13.8% | 12.2% | 13.4% | 11.7% | 10.0% | 9.1% |
| Book Value per sh. | 24.64 | 27.82 | 30.31 | 33.00 | 36.21 | 39.32 | 41.83 | 43.87 | 45.56 |
| Capital Growth Ratio① | 17.3% | 15.8% | 12.6% | 13.7% | 12.7% | 13.9% | 11.7% | 10.4% | 9.0% |
| Sales per sh. | 62.69 | 72.49 | 74.94 | 80.42 | 71.57 | 85.11 | 81.08 | 82.07 | 77.67 |
| Cash Earn'gs per sh. | 5.35 | 5.66 | 5.14 | 5.90 | 6.21 | 7.37 | 7.10 | 6.75 | 6.30 |
| Capital Spending per sh. | 1.86 | 2.30 | 2.68 | 2.79 | 5.09 | 3.41 | 4.14 | 4.34 | 3.08 |
| Reported Earn'gs sh. | 4.03 | 4.07 | 3.80 | 4.08 | 4.40 | 5.26 | 4.90 | 4.40 | 3.95 |
| Div'ds Declared sh. | 1.08 | 1.25 | 1.33 | 1.38 | 1.60 | 1.90 | 2.20 | 2.20 | 2.20 |
| Div'd Payout Ratio① | 20% | 23% | 26% | 23% | 26% | 25% | 31% | 33% | 35% |
| Av'ge Annual P/E Ratio | 4.0 | 6.7 | 8.6 | 8.6 | 11.0 | 13.1 | 16.1 | 15.9 | 16.6 |
| Av'ge Annual Div'd Yield | 6.7% | 4.6% | 4.1% | 3.9% | 3.3% | 2.8% | 2.8% | 3.2% | 3.4% |

| | 1959 | 1960 | 1961 | 1962 | 1963 | 1964 | 1965 | 1966 | 1967 | 1968-70 |
|---|---|---|---|---|---|---|---|---|---|---|
| Sales ($ mill.) | 771.6 | 764.7 | 757.8 | 812.0 | 828.8 | 872.4 | *970* | *1025* | | *1250* |
| Profit Margin① | 11.5% | 10.2% | 10.7% | 9.6% | 9.7% | 10.2% | *10.8%* | *11%* | | *11.5%* |
| Working Cap'l ($ mill.) | 251.7 | 280.6 | 290.8 | 271.9 | 262.8 | 273.6 | | | | |
| Bonds & Pfd. ($ mill.) | 41.3 | 98.6 | 98.6 | 97.2 | 95.4 | 87.6 | | | | |
| Net Plant ($ mill.) | 165.7 | 175.5 | 199.3 | 218.4 | 233.3 | 241.1 | | | | |
| Depreciat'n rate① | 6.0% | 6.2% | 6.0% | 6.1% | 6.6% | 6.6% | | | | |
| %Earned Total Cap'l | 8.4% | 6.0% | 6.4% | 5.7% | 5.8% | 7.1% | | | | |
| %Earned Common Eq'ty | 8.8% | 6.9% | 6.9% | 6.0% | 6.0% | 7.3% | | | | |
| Book Value per sh. | 47.46 | 48.46 | 49.29 | 48.25 | 49.04 | 50.54 | | | | |
| Capital Growth Ratio① | 9.2% | 7.8% | 8.0% | 7.7% | 8.6% | 10.1% | | | | |
| Sales per sh. | 85.73 | 83.44 | 82.68 | 88.60 | 90.43 | 95.17 | | | | |
| Cash Earn'gs per sh. | 6.59 | 5.98③ | 6.13 | 5.92 | 6.40 | 7.29 | *8.15* | *8.75* | | *10.50* |
| Capital Spending per sh. | 3.80 | 4.59 | 6.13 | 5.71 | 5.49 | 4.46 | | | | |
| Reported Earn'gs sh. | 3.93 | 3.33③ | 3.39 | 2.87 | 2.95 | 3.71 | *4.30* | *4.75* | | *6.00* |
| Div'ds Declared sh. | 2.20 | 2.20 | 2.20 | 2.20 | 2.20 | 2.20 | 2.20 | *2.30* | | *2.50* |
| Div'd Payout Ratio① | 35% | 37% | 36% | 37% | 34% | 30% | *28%* | *26%* | | *24%* |
| Av'ge Annual P/E Ratio | 22.9 | 19.1 | 19.4 | 17.7 | 17.2 | 15.0 | | | | *14.0* |
| Av'ge Annual Div'd Yield | 2.4% | 3.5% | 3.3% | 4.3% | 4.3% | 3.9% | 3.7% | | | *3.0%* |

*Italicized numbers are estimates*

| Price to Earnings Ratio | | Dividend Yield | | Estimated 12 months to 6/30/66 | | to 12/31/66 | Quality | 12 Mos. Perform'ce | Desirability as 3-5 Yr. Hold |
|---|---|---|---|---|---|---|---|---|---|
| '50-64 Median | Current① | '50-64 Median | Current① | Cash Earnings | Reported Earnings | Declarations | | | |
| 15.9 | 13.3 | 3.5% | 3.8% | $8.50 | $4.50 | $2.30 | B | II (Above Average) | II (Above Average) |

Indicated Growth Index 3'0
Characteristic Stability Index 25

**CAPITAL STRUCTURE as of 12/31/64**

Debt $87.6 mill. Interest $3.7 mill.

Pfd Stock None Div'd None

Common Stock 9,167,667 shares as of 9/30/65

| Calendar | QUARTERLY SALES ($ Millions) Mar. 31 | June 30 | Sept. 30 | Dec. 31 | Full Year |
|---|---|---|---|---|---|
| 1961 | 173.0 | 197.4 | 189.3 | 198.1 | 757.8 |
| 1962 | 197.8 | 208.2 | 201.5 | 204.5 | 812.0 |
| 1963 | 197.1 | 214.1 | 205.4 | 212.2 | 828.8 |
| 1964 | 207.1 | 223.2 | 222.5 | 219.6 | 872.4 |
| 1965 | 230.5 | 254.7 | 241.7 | *243.1* | *970* |
| 1966 | | | | | *1025* |
| 1967 | | | | | |

| Calendar | QUARTERLY EARNINGS (per sh.) Mar. 31 | June 30 | Sept. 30 | Dec. 31 | Full Year |
|---|---|---|---|---|---|
| 1961 | .63 | 1.02 | .87 | .87 | 3.39 |
| 1962 | .73 | .80 | .63 | .71 | 2.87 |
| 1963 | .64 | .89 | .61 | .81 | 2.95 |
| 1964 | .72 | 1.05 | .96 | .98 | 3.71 |
| 1965 | .99 | 1.25 | .98 | *1.08* | *4.30* |
| 1966 | | | | | *4.75* |
| 1967 | | | | | |

| Calendar | QUARTERLY DIVIDENDS PAID② Mar. 31 | June 30 | Sept. 30 | Dec. 31 | Full Year |
|---|---|---|---|---|---|
| 1961 | .55 | .55 | .55 | .55 | 2.20 |
| 1962 | .55 | .55 | .55 | .55 | 2.20 |
| 1963 | .55 | .55 | .55 | .55 | 2.20 |
| 1964 | .55 | .55 | .55 | .55 | 2.20 |
| 1965 | .55 | .55 | .55 | .55 | 2.20 |
| 1966 | | | | | |
| 1967 | | | | | |

**Appraisal:** Goodrich common has held up rather well since our Oct. 22nd review, in spite of inves[tors]' concern over recent weakness in the p[rice] of polyvinyl chloride. Goodrich is the world's largest producer of th[is] versatile plastic resin. Since it is al[so] ... est cost producer, its com[...] strong. For aggre[...] pany which has a [...] true growth indus[...] to ride out the up[...] volatile atmosphere [...] tics in general, we [...] above average mar[...] months ahead. In so [...] 3- to 5-year holding [...] equity favorably, Grou[...] The conservatively ma[...] Common Stock Fund liq[...] Goodrich position (40,000 sh[...] the September quarter. . .Officers and directors in this same time span made no significant transactions in the stock.

**Analysis:** The excellent operating record which this company had put together for seven consecutive quarters was broken abruptly in the September period of last year. Although final earnings per share showed marginal improvement - 98¢ vs. 96¢ for the prior year's comparable period - pre-tax earnings were actually off. Accordingly, we have lowered our estimate for full year 1965 resu[lts to $4].30 per common share. . .The [...] at Goodrich is the [...] chloride (PVC) [...] recent months, [...] a multiplicity [...] owth rate well [...] ucts. We see [...] rowth in its [...] pacity which [...] cent months [...] the months [...] s for PVC [...] ly no new [...] have been declining [...] increased and more capa[city ...] available. However, relative price stability was thought to have been reached in late 1964. Now, however, trade sources indicate a serious softening with further slippage anticipated for later in 1966. Goodrich, as the leading producer, has a major stake here and the aforementioned uncertainty as to just where PVC prices are going has forced us to dampen down our previous enthusiasm for this company's prospects in the year ahead. Presently, assuming a continuation of strong prices and heavy demand for tires - and only moderate price declines in PVC from here on out, we look for earnings per share in 1966 of about $4.75. P.G.M.

This is a sample Value Line Report. A Report like this is sent to you every three months on every one of the 1,100 leading stocks under year 'round surveillance by The Value Line Investment Survey. About 85 stocks are covered every week in order of their industries. After all 1,100 stocks have been covered in 13 weeks, the cycle starts over again.

**BUSINESS:** The B.F. Goodrich Co., fourth largest rubber company, is the most diversified of the "Big Four". Sales are distributed about as follows: tires - 45% (with replacement business more important than original equipment), other rubber goods - over 20%, and chemicals and plastics - over 30%. Owns 50% of Goodrich-Gulf Chemicals, Inc. a large producer of styrene-butadiene synthetic rubbers. Goodrich is the world's largest producer of polyvinyl chloride resins and the nation's largest distributor of replacement shock absorbers, mufflers, and seat covers. Since 1947-49, sales have increased 115% (GNP, 148%). Labor costs, about 35% of sales. Employs 40,860; has 30,057 stockholders. Directors own about 1% of stock. Pres.:-J.W. Keener. Inc.: N.Y. Add.: 230 Park Ave., N.Y., N.Y. 10017.

①-See Explanation of Terms on p. 100. ②-Div'd payment dates: Mar. 31, June 30, Sept. 30, Dec. 31. ③-Excl. non-recurring profit of 25¢ per share.

Source: Value Line Survey, © Arnold Bernhard & Co., Inc., January 21, 1966.

This is, of course, the estimated dividend income divided by recent price. At times a range is given. See Items 10 and 11 in Figures 3–12 and 3–13.

The fifth question is answered by combining the first four ratings, weighted in such a way as to give most consideration to your investment

FIGURE 3–13

**These Are the Questions Every Intelligent Investor Asks Himself When He Thinks About Holding or Selling or Buying a Stock.**

1. *What is the price range of the company's common stock?* The range between the highest price and the lowest price recorded for a transaction in the common shares during each month of the calendar year is plotted monthly from 1950 to the present.

2. *What is the growth rate of cash earnings?* The past actual percentage is the compounded annual growth rate from 1953-57 average cash earnings to 1960-64 average cash earnings. The estimated percentage is the compounded annual growth rate from 1960-64 average cash earnings to estimated 1967-71 average cash earnings.

3. *What is the cash earnings line?* The cash earnings line is a 5-year moving average (centered) of cash earnings, i.e., earnings per share before depreciation, depletion and amortization (adjusted for all splits and stock dividends), plotted at the multiple shown on the price chart in each full-page Report. The cash earnings line is plotted according to the median of the 1950-64 price to cash earnings ratios, with an adjustment for any persisting trend of these ratios relative to the trend of the general market's price to cash earnings ratio, giving due consideration to the range of price to cash earnings ratios of comparable stocks in the same industrial group.

4. *When is the next dividend meeting and when will the next dividend go ex?* The dates shown at the top of the Report page are approximate, based on the best information obtained from the company.

*What is normal average price 1968-70?* Normal average price 1968-70 is the potential value or the average price forecast for the whole three year period, 3- to 5-years ahead if our estimate of the average earnings and dividends for the period is on target.

6. *How good is this stock for me?* The suitability table indicates generally how good each stock is for your particular purposes in terms of four separate Value Line measurements — Quality, Probable 12 Months Performance, Desirability as a 3 to 5 Year Holding, Estimated Yield Next 12 Months (each defined elsewhere on this page). Your first preference as to these attributes is multiplied by 4, your second by 3, your third by 2, and your last by 1. You then get four numbers, the sum of which equals the suitability of the stock for your purposes, subject, of course, to your particular tax, estate, etc. considerations.

7. *What is the statistical background since 1950?* The pertinent income account and balance sheet figures are given. A definition of the terms is presented on pages 2 and 3.

8. *What will be the sales, earnings and dividends this year and in the period 3 to 5 years from now?* Estimates by the Value Line staff of sales, earnings per share and dividends per share as well as the estimated profit margin and dividend payout ratio based on earnings plus reserves for the current year and for the next 3 to 5 years are presented in italics.

9. *What is the current price to earnings ratio and what is the 1950-64 median price to earnings ratio?* To obtain the current price to earnings ratio, the recent price is divided by the earnings estimated for the 12 months to Dec. 31, 1965. The 1950-64 median price to earnings ratio is the eighth highest price to earnings ratio in the last 15 years.

10. *What is the estimated dividend yield and what is the 1950-64 median dividend yield?* To obtain the estimated dividend yield, the dividend declarations estimated for the 12 months to Dec. 31, 1966 are divided by the recent price. The 1950-64 median dividend yield is the eighth highest dividend yield in the last 15 years.

11. *What are the estimated 12 months cash earnings per share, reported earnings per share and dividends per share?* Estimates of cash earnings per share and reported earnings per share for the 12 months to June 30, 1966 and dividend declarations for the 12 months to Dec. 31, 1966 are presented. The current price to earnings ratio and dividend yield are based on these estimates of reported earnings and dividend declarations.

12. *What is the investment quality of the stock?* The Quality Grade refers to the general safety of a stock and is derived by combining the Indicated Growth Index and the Characteristic Stability Index giving about three times as much weight to Stability as to Growth. The Value Line Quality Grades range from A+ down to C—. The safest stock is one having an A+ Quality Grade. Average is B. The riskiest stock is one having a C— Quality Grade.

13. *What is the Probable Market Performance Rank?* The Probable Market Performance Rank, which is a relative measurement, is determined by combining a stock's earnings plus reserves value divided by its 52-week average price with its non-parametric value position, and with its earnings momentum. All 1,100 stocks under regular review are grouped into five categories according to their Probable Market Performance in the Next 12 Months, from Group I (Highest) down to Group V (Lowest). There are 100 stocks each in Groups I and V; 250 stocks each in Groups II and IV; 400 stocks in Group III. Stocks ranked in Groups I and II can be expected to perform better than the market, while stocks ranked in Groups IV and V can be expected to give a poorer-than-average market performance, regardless of the trend of the market.

14. *What is the 3- to 5-Year Investment Desirability Rank?* The 3- to 5-Year Investment Desirability Rank, which is a relative measurement, is determined by combining a stock's long term potentiality with its risk. A stock's potentiality is measured from the current price to the normal average price forecast for 1968-70 based on an economic environment in the next 3- to 5-years that is hypothesized by Value Line. A stock's risk is a function of its price stability, its past 5-year price performance and the yield of the general market. All 1,100 stocks under regular review are grouped into five categories of 220 stocks each according to their 3- to 5-year appreciation potentiality and risk, from Group I (Highest) down to Group V (Lowest). Stocks ranked in Groups I and II for 3- to 5-year Investment Desirability can be expected to prove more rewarding holdings over the long pull than stocks ranked in Groups IV and V.

15. *How do the stock's Past Growth and Past Stability compare with all other stocks?* Growth is measured in terms of the trend of cash earnings, seven years past and seven years into the future. Stability is based on the past price fluctuations and is measured in terms of the range of intra-year price changes since 1955. For both Growth and Stability, the Index range is from 100 down to 5. (The growth ratios and the stability ratios of all stocks under regular review are each arranged in order of magnitude into 20 equal groups at intervals of 5.)

16. *What is the Capital Structure of the company?* The Capital Structure box gives the long-term debt, the preferred issues outstanding, if any, and the number of shares of common stock.

*What are the quarterly sales and earnings?* In addition to the annual statistics, quarterly sales and earnings are shown back to 1961, if available—enabling you to study seasonal trends, and make quarter-to-quarter comparisons.

18. *What have been actual dividends paid on a quarterly basis?* This dividend payment record back to 1961 is particularly useful in computing your actual dividend income for income tax purposes. The latest quarterly dividend payment dates are also given. Please note dividends paid do not necessarily coincide with the annual statistics on dividends declared.

19. *What is Value Line's Appraisal of the stock?* Each Report contains a specific appraisal which, in effect, represents a summary of the analysis. It highlights the investment characteristics of the stock and weighs its suitability in terms of quality, performance, desirability and yield.

20. *What is Value Line's Analysis of the company?* The Analysis Comment provides you with a precise report and analysis of what is to take place in the company over both the near term (next 12 months) and the longer term (next 3 to 5 years).

21. *What is the company's business?* As part of the description of the company's business, you will find the sales growth vs. GNP, the labor costs as % of sales, the amount of common stock owned by management, the names of the principal officers, and the company's address.

Source: Value Line Survey.

objectives. How Value Line suggests this be done is shown in Figure 3–14. The result is called the Suitability Index. In addition to the Investment Survey, Value Line also has a Special Situation Service.[9]

There are many other investment services, some dealing with gen-

[9] See Chapter 12.

FIGURE 3–14

## Here is the key to how to use the Value Line Survey

First of all, decide which of the four universally desirable attributes you want most. Do you want Quality, Performance in the Next 12 Months, Potential with minimum risk over a 3- to 5-year Period, or Income? And in what order?

Each of 1100 leading stocks and 50 Special Situations is ranked by The Value Line Investment Survey according to four universally desirable attributes, as follows:

| I QUALITY | | II PERFORMANCE | | III DESIRABILITY | | IV YIELD | |
|---|---|---|---|---|---|---|---|
| Quality | Corresponding Index Number | Probable Market Performance next 12 months | Corresponding Index Number | Desirability as a holding next 3 to 5 years | Corresponding Index Number | Estimated Yield in next 12 months at current price | Corresponding Index Number |
| *from* | | *from* | | *from* | | *from* | |
| A+ and A (Highest) | 10 | I (Highest) | 10 | I (Highest) | 10 | 5.0% and up (Highest) | 10 |
| A– and B+ (Above Average) | 8 | II (Above Average) | 8 | II (Above Average) | 8 | 4.1% to 4.9% (Above Average) | 8 |
| B (Average) | 6 | III (Average) | 6 | III (Average) | 6 | 3.0% to 4.0% (Average) | 6 |
| B– and C+ (Below Average) | 4 | IV (Below Average) | 4 | IV (Below Average) | 4 | 2.1% to 2.9% (Below Average) | 4 |
| *down to* | | *down to* | | *down to* | | *down to* | |
| C and C– (Lowest) | 2 | V (Lowest) | 2 | V (Lowest) | 2 | .0% to 2.0% (Lowest) | 2 |

The foregoing ranks (except Quality) may change as prices or earnings change markedly during the year. (Quality seldom changes in the course of one year or even several.) All ranks are posted up to date for you on each stock every week in the Summary of Advices and Index.

### The Value Line Does This–

On the face of each Value Line Rating chart is a Table of Suitability. It applies specifically to that particular stock *and it applies currently.* This table translates the subject stock's ranks into index numbers for you. The ranks are equated to index numbers as follows:

| | |
|---|---|
| Rank I (Highest) | = 10 |
| Rank II (Above Average) | = 8 |
| Rank III (Average) | = 6 |
| Rank IV (Below Average) | = 4 |
| Rank V (Lowest) | = 2 |

The same goes for the five categories of Quality and Yield also.

Thus, Air Products & Chemicals as of October 22, 1965 had the following Suitability Table:

| | |
|---|---|
| Quality (B+) | 8 |
| Performance (Rank for 12 mos.-II) | 8 |
| Desirability (Potential 3-5 yrs.-I) | 10 |
| Yield (0.3%) | 2 |

### Then To Personalize The Suitability Index You Do This–

Multiply each index number by one of the following multiples, 4, 3, 2 *or* 1. The attribute that receives the greatest weight in your scheme of investing is multiplied by 4. The attribute that gets the next heaviest weight in your scheme is multiplied by 3. Next in order of importance to you is multiplied by 2. And the last attribute in *your* order of importance is multiplied by 1.

Of course, every investor wants the highest Quality, the strongest Market Performance in the next 12 months, the greatest Potential with minimum risk over the next 3 to 5 years and the largest Yield. If a stock were ranked in the top category in all four respects, it would have a total personal suitability score for you of 100% regardless of how your preferences were weighted. *For example:*

| | | |
|---|---|---|
| Quality | 10 x 4 = 40 | 10 x 1 = 10 |
| Performance (12 mos.) | 10 x 3 = 30 | 10 x 2 = 20 |
| Desirability (3-5 yrs.) | 10 x 2 = 20 | 10 x 3 = 30 |
| Yield (12 mos.) | 10 x 1 = 10 | 10 x 4 = 40 |
| | 100% | 100% |

But because no stock-not even Air Products -offers the best of everything at all times, you must decide on the attributes you wish to emphasize most. Suppose, for example, you were interested mainly in maximum safety (Quality), then in the largest available income, then in performance, and that growth received the least weight in your investment program. You would find that Air Products has a suitability score of 64 (out of a possible 100) for your purposes at this time.

*For example:*

| | |
|---|---|
| Quality | 8 x 4 = 32 |
| Performance (12 mos.) | 8 x 2 = 16 |
| Desirability (3-5 yrs.) | 10 x 1 = 10 |
| Yield (12 mos.) | 2 x 3 = 6 |
| | 64% |

However, if your main interest were growth, your next most important, performance, income and safety, in that order, the same stock, Air Products, would come out as follows:

| | |
|---|---|
| Quality | 8 x 1 = 8 |
| Performance (12 mos.) | 8 x 3 = 24 |
| Desirability (3-5 yrs.) | 10 x 4 = 40 |
| Yield (12 mos.) | 2 x 2 = 4 |
| | 76% |

Thus, you see that Air Products is not equally good for two investors whose objectives differ. By this method, you can figure out how well each stock in the Value Line Survey would fit your personal objectives at current market prices. All you have to do is to add your own weights to the index numbers in the Suitability Table and multiply. The sum would then give you the suitability score of the stock for your own purposes. (Note: A score of 60 would be average.)

Source: Published and copyrighted, 1965, by Arnold Bernhard & Co., Inc.

eral market conditions, some with specialized phases such as growth stocks, technical indicators, mutual funds, etc. Among these are:

*General*

*American Investors Corporation* (Larchmont, N.Y.). Stock Market Survey —a weekly report with market trends, buy and sell recommendations, and stocks ranked by percentage strength.

*Babson's Reports, Inc.* (Wellesley Hills, Mass.). Investment and Barometer Letter, stock market guidance based on fundamentals.

*United Business Service Co.* (Boston, Mass.). United Business and Investment

Reports—a weekly report on general business and stock market trends, including stock selections.

*Research Institute Investors Service* (New York, N.Y.). In depth studies of recommended issues as well as general market coverage and trends.

*Growth Stocks*

*Danforth-Epply Corporation* (Wellesley Hills, Mass.). The Growth Stock Letter, a weekly report on growth stocks, adding to and deleting from "The Growth Stock Portfolio."

*John S. Herold, Inc.* (Greenwich, Conn.). *America's Fastest Growing Companies*—a monthly report on growth companies and growth stocks.

*Technical Analysis*

*Indicator Digest, Inc.* (Palisades Park, N.J.). A monthly report on composite technical indicators as well as feature recommendations. Also *Technical Stock Reports* on market outlook and selected stock recommendations. *The Directory of Indicators* describes the composition and construction of various technical indicators.

*Dow Theory Letters, Inc.* (San Diego, Calif.). Publishes 40 letters a year on market trends as interpreted in accordance with the Dow Theory. *Basic Technical Theory* describes the various Dow Theory signals.

*Dow Theory Forecasts* (Hammond, Ind.). Provides a weekly commentary based on the Dow Theory, a digest of other advisers, overnight warning signals, and market portfolios.

*Drew Investment Associates, Inc.* (Boston, Mass.). A weekly letter interpreting the odd-lot indexes and ratios as a guide to market action.

*Convertibles*

*R. H. M. Associates* (New York, N.Y.). Publishes the weekly Convertible Survey, both charts and text analyzing investment opportunities in convertibles. They also issue the R.H.M. Weekly Warrant and Stock Survey.

*Kalb, Voorhis & Co.* (New York, N.Y.). A weekly computer processed statistical summary of convertible bonds, preferred stocks, and warrants, accompanied by explanatory text and recommendations.

*Mutual Funds*

*Vickers Associates, Inc.* (Huntington, N.Y.) publish *Vickers Guide to Investment Company Portfolios.* The Guide includes: Section 1, Directory of All Investment Companies; Section 2, Holdings of Securities; Section 3, Portfolio Holdings by Selected Funds; Section 4, Portfolio Changes by Securities (Issued monthly); Section 5, Portfolio Transactions by 75 Leading Investment Companies; Section 6, Favorite 50 (Quarterly). O-T-C Favorites (semiannually), and Industry Group Summary (monthly).

*Arthur Wiesenberger & Co.* (New York, N.Y.). In addition to *Investment Companies,* a basic compendium issued annually. Wiesenberger also issues a companion "Charts & Statistics," a quarterly *Investment Company Management Results,* a monthly Mutual Affairs advisory service, the Wiesenberger

*Investment Report*, and two expensive financial advisory services, *Findings and Forecasts* and the *Wiesenberger 333 Stock Service* ($12,000 per annum).

*Chart Services*

*M.C. Horsey & Co.* (New York, N.Y.) issues *The Stock Picture*, a book of over 1,600 charts, published every two months. Twice a year it also publishes *Selected Stocks*, which gives 25-year charts of some 200 stocks.

*Investors Intelligence and Chartcraft, Inc.* (Larchmont, N.Y.). *Chartcraft* is a book of over 1,750 point and figure charts on NYSE, ASE, and OTC stocks, and over 100 point and figure charts on market averages, group industries, and technical trend indicators. It is published monthly. *Investors Intelligence* is a semimonthly summary of both fundamental and technical analysis, and it provides a consensus of leading investment services. It utilizes point and figure charts extensively. A point and figure chart shows only one thing: price movement. It does not take into account volume of trading, or time. Unless the price of a stock changes by one point (or three points), no entry is made on the chart, even though days or even weeks may go by. X's are used to indicate price changes of the required magnitude or more when the price is going up and O's when the price is going down. When the stock changes price direction, a new column is started.

*Contrary Opinion*

*Fraser Publishing Company* (Wells, Vt.) issues the semimonthly *Neill Letter of Contrary Opinion*, and monthly *The Contrary Investor*, both designed to comment and warn on crowd approaches to the market.

## Investment Counseling Services

For the well-to-do investor who wants to avoid the burdensome and often time-consuming chore of digging up facts for himself, following industry and company trends, and judging the state of the economy and of the market, there is an easy and relatively inexpensive "out." He can use an investment counselor, or the investment counseling department of a bank, or of one of the large investment services. Under the Investment Advisers Act of 1940, independent (nonbank) investment counseling firms must be registered with the SEC. Busy professional people, active businessmen who have little or no time to do the digging involved in managing their own investments, or widows who have no knowledge whatsoever of finance and investments, make up the clientele, in general, of the professional money managers.

The usual annual fee charged by an investment counselor is ½ of 1% of the value of the portfolio being managed. For a $200,000 portfolio this means an annual fee of $1,000. Most of the larger investment counseling firms will not take accounts with portfolios of less than $100,000. The largest firms in the business—Scudder, Stevens & Clark; Loomis-Sayles; Lionel D. Edie; Calvin Bullock; Stein, Row & Farnham; Van Strum & Towne; Eaton & Howard, etc., maintain professional staffs of security analysts and portfolio managers to assist clients. They do the investment research and make recommendations to customers. The counselors prefer to have discretionary accounts in which they have the legal power to manage the client's funds. In almost all cases, of course, the client is informed of portfolio changes, proposed or accomplished. Many clients prefer to retain final authority for passing upon a proposed change. In some cases the investment counselors have custody of the client's securities, since this makes for more expeditious purchasing and selling; a number of clients prefer to retain possession of their own securities and turn them over to the investment counselor only to effectuate a transaction.

Some of the large investment counselors have their own mutual funds which they manage. Others advise corporate pension funds or college or university endowment funds. The mutual funds are for the investors whose assets are nowhere near the $100,000 minimum level. It is estimated that the investment counselors' clients' average portfolio is about $250,000.[10] Since investment counselors publish no records of performance, selecting a firm is usually an act of faith based on someone's recommendation or on the firm's general reputation.

Banks provide investment advisory services, sometimes on a formal, fee basis, sometimes on an informal customer-relations complimentary basis. A wealthy individual who wants investment help from his bank can usually obtain it without formally turning his funds over to the bank's trust department. An investment officer in the trust department, or in the investment advisory department if the bank has one, will serve as an investment counselor to those with portfolios of $100,000 and over. The investment officer ascertains the client's investment objectives and attempts to tailor his recommendations to meet the objectives. Again the account may be discretionary or nondiscretionary, custodial or the customer may retain possession of his securities. While the portfolio is reviewed regularly, the customer usually receives a quarterly report from the bank on his portfolio. The investment officer makes recommendations and in the case of the discretionary account arranges portfolio changes. For wealthier investors who wish to be free from money-management problems and are comfortable in conservative investment hands, this is a handy arrangement. In the discretionary account the owner does not surrender title to his own securities. The bank acts only as his agent.

Banks, of course, have more formal arrangements for the management of investors' funds. There are trust arrangements, either living trusts (*inter vivos*) set up during an individual's lifetime or testamentary trusts set up at death by will or other prior arrangement. There are individual trusts or common trust funds. The common trust fund, akin to a mutual

---

[10] See T. A. Wise, "How To Stay Rich," chap. xvii in *Fortune's Guide to Personal Investing* (New York: McGraw-Hill Book Co., 1963).

fund, is gaining in popularity and is designed to appeal to smaller investors, those with from $5,000 to $75,000 to invest, but some accounts go up to $100,000 and more. You set up a trust, name the bank as trustee, and the bank, in turn, mixes or pools your funds with other small individual trust accounts for investment in a common portfolio of securities. In a common trust fund, investments are spread far more widely than would be possible in an individual trust. Also, the cost is lower. At Chase Manhattan in New York, for example, the minimum yearly fee for a common trust fund is $250 for accounts up to $50,000, against $375 for an individual trust.

Banks offer several types of common trust funds. If you set up the trust without specifying the type of investment you want, the bank is required by law to put you into what is called a legal-investments fund. This is a conservative type, about 65% bonds and 35% stock. Since 1965, "legal" funds have been permitted to go up to 50% in common plus preferred stock. But if you give the bank discretion, you may be placed in one of four types of funds: the balanced fund, about 60% common stock, 40% bonds; the 100% common stock fund; the tax-exempt bond fund (a rapidly growing type); or finally a taxable corporate bond and preferred stock fund for income. When you establish the trust, you can name the type of fund you want. Thus banks have increasingly developed flexibility in serving investors.

The leading investment services, Moody's and Standard & Poor's, also provide investment counseling services. Moody's distinguishes between its "Investor's Advisory Service," which "was developed for the individual investor whose portfolio does not justify the more expensive Investment Counsel" and the latter service, which is for larger accounts. Charges are based on estimates of time required to service the account rather than on its size or the number of issues in the portfolio. Moody's also has a special investment counseling service for financial institutions—banks, trusts, and so forth.[11]

### Business Conditions and Corporate Profits

If the security analyst's starting point is an examination of business trends, including a forecast of the outlook for business, the economy, and corporate profits, it is not difficult to find material. Indeed, the real problem may be choosing from among the multiplicity of sources. A number of the leading banks publish monthly reports or surveys dealing with the business outlook and other topics. The First National City Bank of New York publishes a *Monthly Economic Letter*. The leading article is always on "General Business Conditions." The *Morgan Guaranty Survey* is published monthly by the Morgan Guaranty Trust Company of New

---

[11] For further information see H. C. Walter (ed.), *Investment Information and Advice: A Handbook and Directory* (Whittier, Calif.: FIR Publishing Co., 1964).

York. The first article always covers "Business and Financial Conditions." The Bank of New York issues *General Business Indicators* which is a statistical tabulation of selected economic indicators. It provides the bank's forecast of prospective gross national product, disposable personal income, index of industrial production, corporate profits, and earnings of the Dow-Jones Industrials, over the coming year. The Chase Manhattan Bank publishes *Business in Brief*, issued monthly by its Economic Research Division. The first article is usually devoted to an analysis of the business outlook.

The twelve Federal Reserve banks publish monthly bulletins devoted to banking, economic, and financial topics. The Federal Reserve Bank of New York, for example, publishes a *Monthly Review*, which always includes an article on "The Business Situation." The Federal Reserve Bank of Philadelphia publishes the *Business Review*, monthly. The Federal Reserve Banks of Chicago and of St. Louis also issue excellent monthly reviews. The Board of Governors of the Federal Reserve System in Washington publishes the *Federal Reserve Bulletin*, monthly. It contains a "National Summary of Business Conditions." This can be obtained as a separate release, monthly, as can "Business Indexes," a compilation of statistics on business trends. The Federal Reserve also publishes a *Chart Book on Business, Economic, and Financial Statistics*, monthly, as well as an annual *Historical Chart Book*.

The federal government provides a number of useful sources of information on developing business trends. The *Survey of Current Business* is published monthly by the U.S. Department of Commerce. It has two principal parts. The first deals with basic business trends and starts with an article on "The Business Situation" which reviews recent developments, pointing out underlying strengths or weaknesses. The second section is an elaborate compilation of basic statistical series on all phases of the economy. There is also a weekly supplement in which the indexes of business activity, prices, production, etc., appearing in the *Survey of Current Business* are kept up to date. The President's Council of Economic Advisors publishes the monthly *Economic Indicators* and the *Annual Economic Review*, which deal with the state of the economy and the outlook.

For economic forecasting purposes, perhaps the most useful publication of the government is *Business Cycle Developments*, issued monthly by the Bureau of the Census of the U.S. Department of Commerce. This report brings together many of the available economic indicators in convenient form for analysis and interpretation. The presentation and classification of the series follow the business indicator approach of the National Bureau of Economic Research (NBER). The classification of series and business cycle turning dates are those designated by NBER, which, in recent years, has been the leader in this field of investigation. About 90 principal indicators and over 300 components are included in the report. Among others there are 30 NBER leading indicators, 15 NBER roughly coincident indicators, 7 NBER lagging indicators, and 7 international comparisons. The movements of the series are shown against the background of the expansions and contractions of the general business cycle so that "leads" and "lags" can be readily detected and cyclical developments spotted. The report is divided into three parts. The first provides basic data, charts and tables on the leading, coincident, lagging indicators and on other economic series. The second part covers analytical measures such as diffusion indexes, direction of change indicators, and so forth. The third part is devoted to cyclical comparisons, showing current trends against expansions or contractions in earlier cycles and comparing current trends in selected economic series with earlier cyclical trends in these series. Appendixes provide historical data. See Figure 3–15.

A companion volume, published for the first time in 1966, is entitled *Long-Term Economic Growth*. This 250-page compendium contains just about every available statistical series bearing on the process of economic growth in the United States. The Bureau of the Census expects to publish *Long-Term Economic Growth* annually. Going back to 1890, it finds that the U.S. economy has grown at an annual rate of 3.3%, enough to double its size every 21 years.

A private source provides data on the NBER indicators weekly. This is the Statistical Indicator Associates of North Egremont, Massachusetts, directed by Leonard H. Lempert. These weekly reports include both current statistics and interpretive text. *Business Week*, in its "Business

**FIGURE 3–15**
**Key to Interpreting Business Cycle Series**

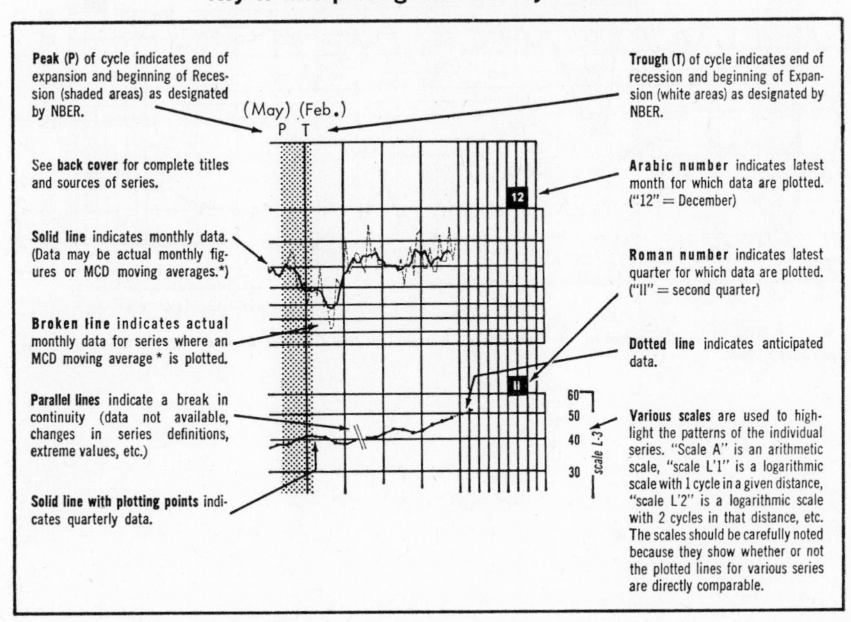

## FIGURE 3–15

### BASIC DATA: Business Cycle Series from 1948 to Present; NBER Leading Indicators

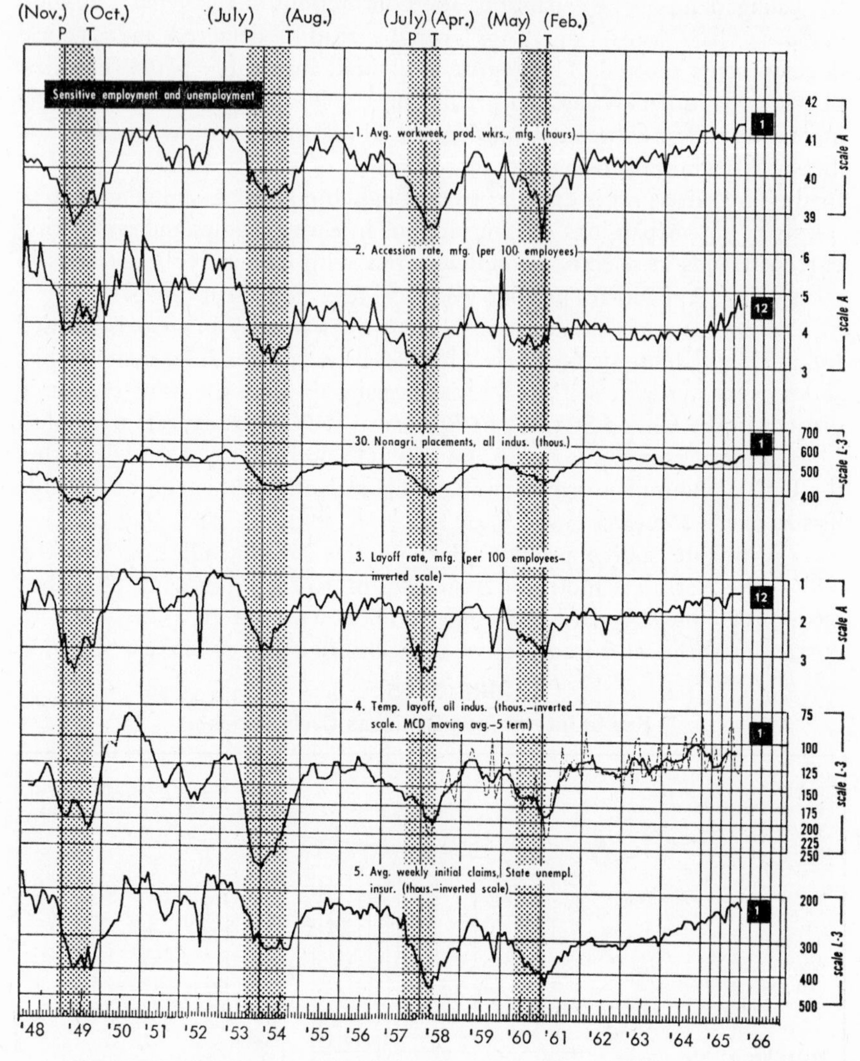


Source: U.S. Department of Commerce, Bureau of the Census, *Business Cycle Developments*, February, 1966.

FIGURE 3–15 (Continued)

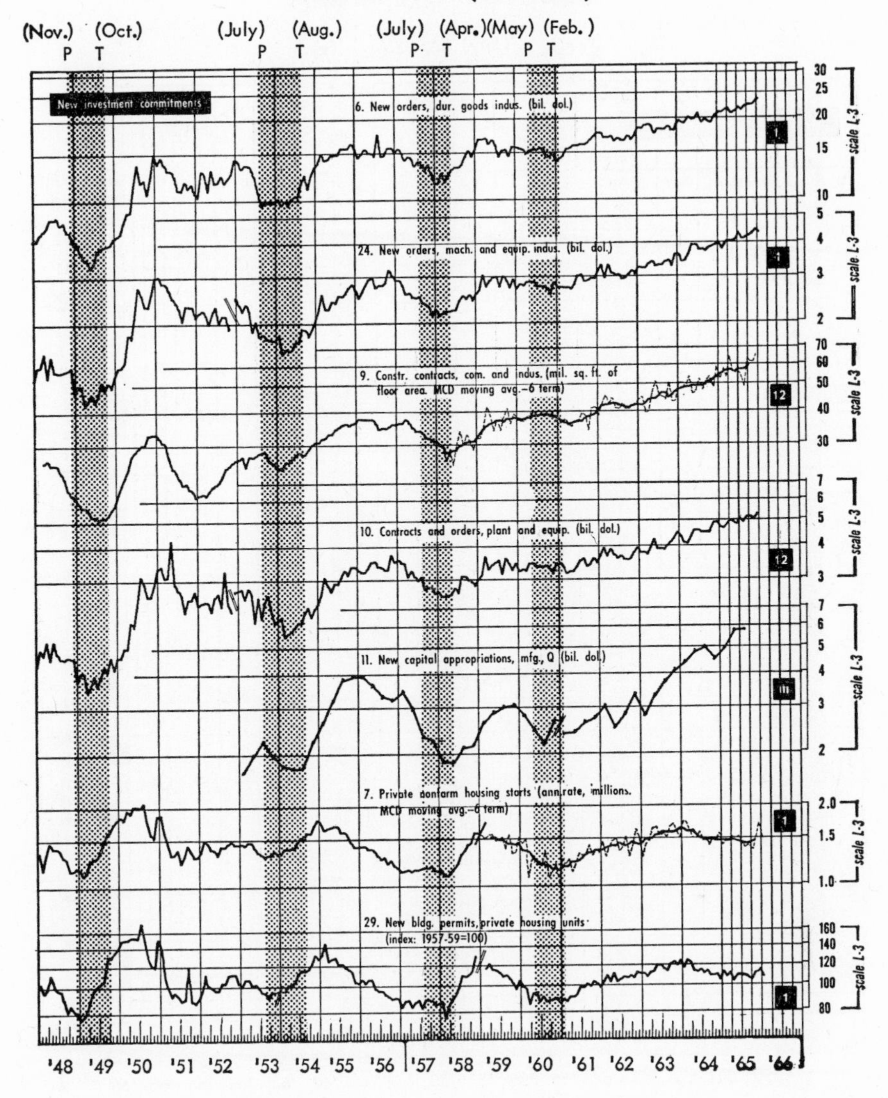

FIGURE 3–15 (Continued)

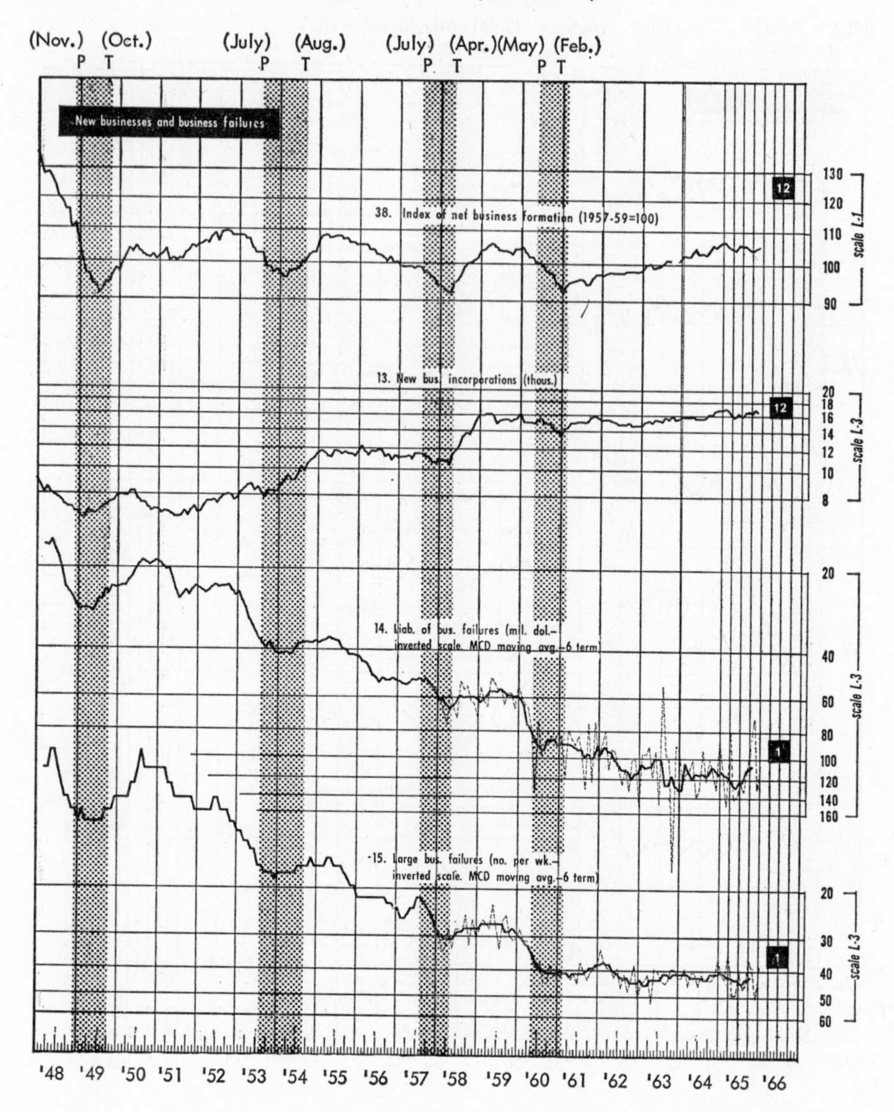


Outlook" section reviews the indicators from time to time and regularly provides an analytic review of changing business and economic developments. Published by McGraw-Hill, Inc., and written in a lively and interesting style, *Business Week*, provides coverage of major developments in many areas of business and finance. Two other journals which

**FIGURE 3–15 (Continued)**

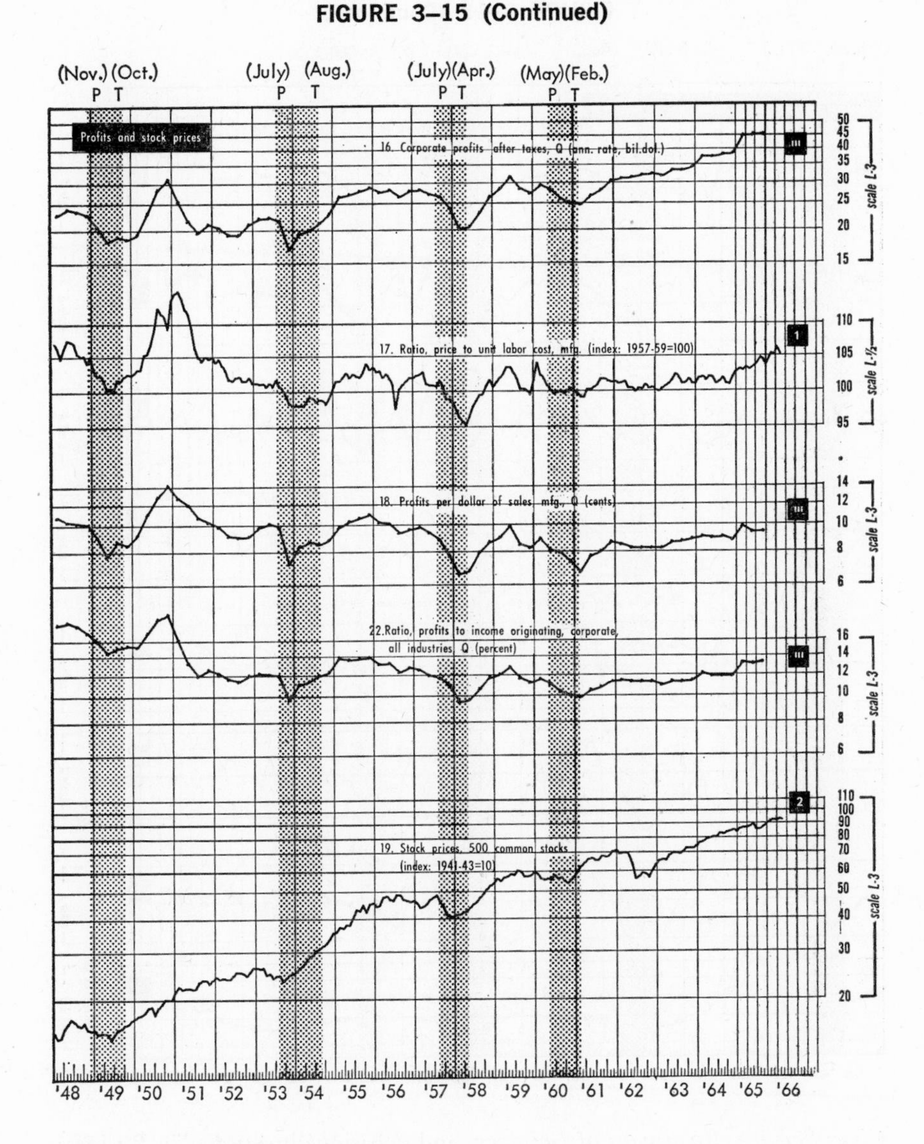


provide somewhat similar coverage are *Nation's Business* and *Dun's Review & Modern Industry*. *Fortune* magazine has a section each month entitled "Business Roundup." This is a monthly report on the economic outlook. The National Industrial Conference Board issues a monthly *Business Record*, a weekly *Desk Sheet of Business Indicators*, a weekly

FIGURE 3–15 (Continued)

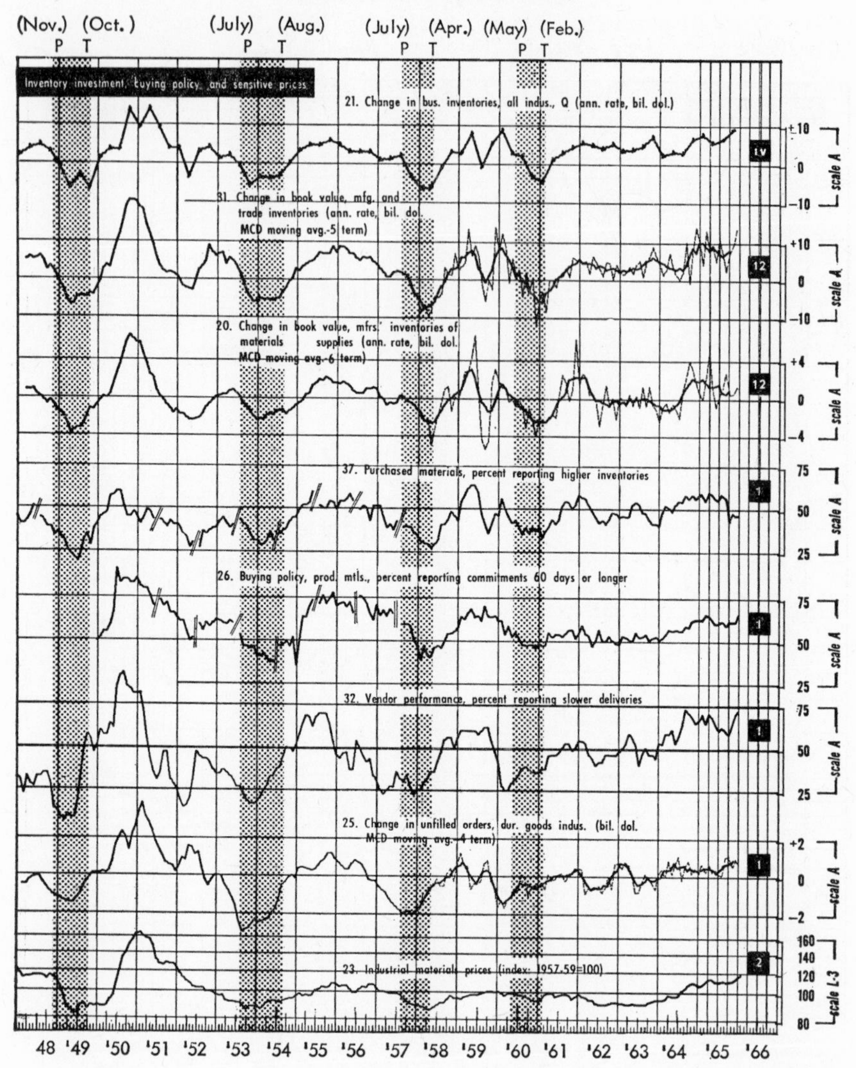


*Chart Service*, *Roadmaps of Industry*, and occasionally *Studies in Business Economics*. The "selected business indicators" section of the *Business Record*, and the weekly *Desk Sheet of Business Indicators*, are very useful in judging the trend of business and the economy.

On corporate profits, overall trends can be seen in the *Quarterly Financial Report for Manufacturing Corporations*, published jointly by the Federal Trade Commission and the Securities and Exchange Commission. The purpose of this survey is to produce, each calendar quarter, an income statement and balance sheet for all manufacturing corporations, classified by both industry and asset size. Profitability is reported in two ways—"profits per dollar of sales" and "annual rate of profit on stockholders' equity at end of period." The quarterly summaries may be used to measure efficiency and appraise costs by comparing a company's operating results with the average performance of companies of similar size or in the same line of business. See Figure 3–16.

Each year, in the April issue of its *Monthly Economic Letter*, the First National City Bank of New York publishes the results of its survey of the profits performance of almost 4,000 U.S. corporations, not only in manufacturing lines but also in trade, transportation, utilities, services, real estate, and banking. Profits are reported, for the two prior years, on two bases, as "percent return on net worth" and as "percent margin on sales."

**FIGURE 3–16**

**Profits per Dollar of Sales, by Industry**
(Cents)

| | *Before Federal Income Taxes* | | | | | *After Taxes* | | | | |
|---|---|---|---|---|---|---|---|---|---|---|
| *Industry* | *3Q 1964* | *4Q 1964* | *1Q 1965* | *2Q 1965* | *3Q 1965* | *3Q 1964* | *4Q 1964* | *1Q 1965* | *2Q 1965* | *3Q 1965* |
| All manufacturing corporations, except newspapers | 8.7 | 8.8 | 9.3 | 9.9 | 9.1 | 5.1 | 5.4 | 5.4 | 5.8 | 5.4 |
| Durable goods | 8.8 | 9.1 | 10.1 | 10.9 | 9.3 | 4.9 | 5.2 | 5.5 | 6.0 | 5.3 |
| Transportation equipment | 7.1 | 9.0 | 12.6 | 12.6 | 7.8 | 4.0 | 5.2 | 6.6 | 6.8 | 4.4 |
| Motor vehicles and equipment* | 8.0 | 11.1 | 15.4 | 15.2 | 8.4 | 4.7 | 6.4 | 8.1 | 8.2 | 4.8 |
| Aircraft and parts* | 5.3 | 4.9 | 5.1 | 5.9 | 6.7 | 2.9 | 2.7 | 2.7 | 3.1 | 3.6 |
| Electrical machinery, equipment, and supplies | 8.0 | 8.6 | 8.2 | 8.7 | 8.6 | 4.2 | 4.7 | 4.3 | 4.6 | 4.7 |
| Other machinery | 11.5 | 10.8 | 10.9 | 12.2 | 11.7 | 6.0 | 5.7 | 5.7 | 6.6 | 6.3 |
| Metalworking machinery and equipment* | 11.3 | 9.7 | 10.1 | 11.7 | 11.1 | 6.6 | 5.7 | 5.4 | 6.6 | 6.3 |
| Other fabricated metal products | 7.5 | 6.7 | 7.4 | 8.8 | 8.3 | 4.1 | 3.7 | 4.2 | 5.1 | 4.8 |
| Primary metal industries | 8.9 | 10.5 | 11.3 | 11.5 | 9.6 | 5.3 | 6.5 | 6.6 | 6.7 | 5.7 |
| Primary iron and steel* | 9.0 | 10.3 | 10.9 | 11.0 | 8.7 | 5.1 | 6.0 | 6.2 | 6.2 | 5.2 |
| Primary nonferrous metals* | 8.8 | 11.0 | 12.1 | 12.4 | 11.3 | 5.7 | 7.3 | 7.6 | 7.7 | 6.7 |
| Stone, clay, and glass products | 11.9 | 9.1 | 6.5 | 11.3 | 11.8 | 6.8 | 5.5 | 3.1 | 6.7 | 7.2 |
| Furniture and fixtures | 5.9 | 6.2 | 5.5 | 6.6 | 7.1 | 3.2 | 3.5 | 2.9 | 3.7 | 4.0 |
| Lumber and wood products, except furniture | 7.0 | 4.7 | 4.8 | 6.4 | 7.2 | 4.4 | 3.2 | 2.9 | 4.2 | 4.7 |
| Instruments and related products | 14.7 | 14.2 | 13.1 | 14.2 | 15.7 | 7.8 | 7.4 | 7.5 | 7.5 | 8.6 |
| Miscellaneous manufacturing and ordnance | 7.4 | 8.1 | 6.7 | 6.9 | 6.6 | 3.8 | 4.7 | 3.6 | 3.9 | 3.4 |
| Nondurable goods | 8.7 | 8.5 | 8.4 | 8.8 | 8.8 | 5.4 | 5.6 | 5.4 | 5.6 | 5.6 |
| Food and kindred products | 5.4 | 5.0 | 4.7 | 5.0 | 5.3 | 3.0 | 2.7 | 2.5 | 2.7 | 3.0 |
| Dairy products* | 4.6 | 4.0 | 4.0 | 4.6 | 4.6 | 2.6 | 2.2 | 2.2 | 2.6 | 2.6 |
| Bakery products* | 4.3 | 4.6 | 3.7 | 3.9 | 4.0 | 2.3 | 2.3 | 1.9 | 2.0 | 2.1 |
| Alcoholic beverages* | 8.4 | 7.2 | 6.4 | 7.6 | 7.7 | 4.7 | 3.9 | 3.1 | 4.0 | 4.3 |
| Tobacco manufactures | 11.6 | 11.6 | 10.5 | 11.2 | 11.9 | 6.0 | 6.2 | 5.5 | 6.0 | 6.1 |
| Textile mill products | 6.8 | 6.5 | 6.7 | 7.0 | 7.0 | 3.7 | 3.7 | 3.7 | 3.8 | 3.8 |
| Apparel and other finished products | 4.7 | 3.5 | 3.4 | 3.6 | 4.5 | 2.9 | 2.1 | 1.9 | 2.0 | 2.7 |
| Paper and allied products | 8.5 | 8.9 | 8.5 | 9.4 | 8.9 | 4.9 | 5.5 | 4.9 | 5.4 | 5.3 |
| Printing and publishing, except newspapers | 9.3 | 7.4 | 8.3 | 7.9 | 9.7 | 5.0 | 3.9 | 4.9 | 4.3 | 5.3 |
| Chemicals and allied products | 14.1 | 13.8 | 13.7 | 14.4 | 13.9 | 7.7 | 8.0 | 7.7 | 8.2 | 7.9 |
| Basic chemicals* | 14.4 | 14.6 | 14.4 | 16.0 | 13.9 | 8.0 | 8.8 | 8.3 | 9.1 | 8.0 |
| Drugs* | 21.4 | 19.8 | 21.0 | 18.9 | 21.7 | 11.3 | 10.7 | 11.3 | 10.4 | 11.7 |
| Petroleum refining and related industries | 11.6 | 13.1 | 12.3 | 12.7 | 12.8 | 10.2 | 11.8 | 10.7 | 10.8 | 10.7 |
| Petroleum refining* | 11.6 | 13.4 | 12.4 | 12.9 | 12.9 | 10.3 | 12.1 | 10.9 | 11.0 | 10.9 |
| Rubber and miscellaneous plastics products | 7.6 | 7.1 | 7.0 | 7.3 | 7.1 | 4.2 | 4.2 | 3.9 | 4.1 | 4.1 |
| Leather and leather products | 5.1 | 5.3 | 5.0 | 5.0 | 4.8 | 2.9 | 3.0 | 2.7 | 2.7 | 2.7 |

* Included in major industry above.

**FIGURE 3–16 (Continued)**

**Profits per Dollar of Sales, by Asset Size and Industry Group**
(Cents)

| Asset Size | *Before Federal Income Taxes* | | | | | *After Taxes* | | | | |
|---|---|---|---|---|---|---|---|---|---|---|
| | *3Q 1964* | *4Q 1964* | *1Q 1965* | *2Q 1965* | *3Q 1965* | *3Q 1964* | *4Q 1964* | *1Q 1965* | *2Q 1965* | *3Q 1965* |
| All manufacturing corporations, except newspapers | 8.7 | 8.8 | 9.3 | 9.9 | 9.1 | 5.1 | 5.4 | 5.4 | 5.8 | 5.4 |
| Under $1 million | 4.8 | 3.1 | 4.0 | 4.9 | 5.0 | 3.1 | 1.9 | 2.5 | 3.1 | 3.3 |
| $ 1 million to $ 5 million | 6.1 | 5.3 | 5.3 | 6.5 | 6.3 | 3.3 | 2.9 | 2.7 | 3.4 | 3.5 |
| $ 5 million to $ 10 million | 6.7 | 6.5 | 6.7 | 7.0 | 7.4 | 3.5 | 3.5 | 3.5 | 3.8 | 4.0 |
| $ 10 million to $ 25 million | 8.1 | 7.9 | 7.1 | 8.4 | 8.1 | 4.3 | 4.4 | 3.7 | 4.6 | 4.5 |
| $ 25 million to $ 50 million | 8.9 | 8.3 | 8.2 | 9.2 | 9.4 | 4.7 | 4.5 | 4.4 | 5.0 | 5.2 |
| $ 50 million to $ 100 million | 8.8 | 8.7 | 8.3 | 9.0 | 8.8 | 4.7 | 5.0 | 4.5 | 4.9 | 4.8 |
| $ 100 million to $ 250 million | 9.4 | 9.5 | 9.2 | 9.5 | 9.5 | 5.1 | 5.4 | 5.1 | 5.4 | 5.3 |
| $ 250 million to $1,000 million | 9.1 | 9.1 | 8.9 | 10.0 | 9.5 | 5.3 | 5.5 | 5.2 | 5.8 | 5.5 |
| $1,000 million and over | 2.0 | 13.7 | 15.0 | 14.9 | 12.5 | 7.9 | 9.1 | 9.3 | 9.2 | 8.2 |
| Durable goods | 8.8 | 9.1 | 10.1 | 10.9 | 9.3 | 4.9 | 5.2 | 5.5 | 6.0 | 5.3 |
| Under $5 million | 6.3 | 4.9 | 5.4 | 7.2 | 7.0 | 3.7 | 2.8 | 3.0 | 4.3 | 4.1 |
| $ 5 million to $ 10 million | 7.5 | 7.0 | 7.9 | 8.4 | 8.9 | 4.0 | 3.8 | 4.1 | 4.6 | 4.9 |
| $ 10 million to $ 25 million | 8.2 | 8.3 | 7.9 | 9.4 | 8.9 | 4.3 | 4.6 | 4.1 | 5.1 | 4.9 |
| $ 25 million to $ 50 million | 9.1 | 8.7 | 9.1 | 10.1 | 9.9 | 4.8 | 4.8 | 4.8 | 5.5 | 5.5 |
| $ 50 million to $ 100 million | 9.8 | 9.8 | 8.7 | 9.9 | 9.5 | 5.2 | 5.5 | 4.7 | 5.4 | 5.1 |
| $ 100 million to $ 250 million | 8.8 | 9.1 | 9.0 | 9.9 | 9.3 | 4.8 | 5.3 | 5.0 | 5.6 | 5.3 |
| $ 250 million to $1,000 million | 9.3 | 9.3 | 8.9 | 10.1 | 9.6 | 5.3 | 5.6 | 5.1 | 5.8 | 5.5 |
| $1,000 million and over | 10.6 | 12.7 | 15.7 | 15.4 | 11.2 | 5.8 | 7.1 | 8.3 | 8.3 | 6.3 |
| Nondurable goods | 8.7 | 8.5 | 8.4 | 8.8 | 8.8 | 5.4 | 5.6 | 5.4 | 5.6 | 5.6 |
| Under $5 million | 4.5 | 3.3 | 3.8 | 4.0 | 4.3 | 2.7 | 2.0 | 2.2 | 2.2 | 2.6 |
| $ 5 million to $ 10 million | 5.9 | 6.0 | 5.4 | 5.6 | 5.7 | 3.1 | 3.3 | 2.8 | 2.9 | 3.0 |
| $ 10 million to $ 25 million | 7.9 | 7.6 | 6.2 | 7.2 | 7.2 | 4.3 | 4.2 | 3.1 | 3.9 | 4.0 |
| $ 25 million to $ 50 million | 8.8 | 7.8 | 7.2 | 8.1 | 8.9 | 4.6 | 4.3 | 4.1 | 4.5 | 4.9 |
| $ 50 million to $ 100 million | 8.0 | 7.7 | 8.0 | 8.2 | 8.1 | 4.3 | 4.6 | 4.4 | 4.5 | 4.4 |
| $ 100 million to $ 250 million | 10.1 | 9.8 | 9.3 | 9.1 | 9.6 | 5.4 | 5.5 | 5.2 | 5.2 | 5.4 |
| $ 250 million to $1,000 million | 8.9 | 8.9 | 8.9 | 10.0 | 9.5 | 5.3 | 5.5 | 5.2 | 5.8 | 5.6 |
| $1,000 million and over | 13.9 | 15.2 | 14.1 | 14.2 | 14.2 | 10.5 | 12.0 | 10.8 | 10.7 | 10.6 |

The detailed industry classification and breakdown permits an investor or a securities analyst to compare a given company with the reported industry average. See Figure 3–17. The bank, at the time of its last annual survey, warned that comparing profits, both from year to year and between different companies, has become increasingly difficult. The growing complexity of business operations, changes in the tax laws, and lack of agreement on what constitutes "generally accepted accounting principles" have produced widespread variations in financial statements. Leonard Spacek, chairman of the accounting firm of Arthur Andersen & Co., declared in an address in 1965: "I would estimate that the profits reported for the year 1964 have a greater lack of comparability and are further removed from a reflection of the true facts than at any time in the last thirty years."[12]

The outlook for corporate profits is usually tied to a forecast of business conditions. While the securities analyst may occasionally undertake his own forecasts, the individual investor uually is not equipped, nor does he have the time, to make independent forecasts on his own. He must rely on one or more of the estimates of the business outlook described

[12] See Chapter 4, "Adjustment of Reported Net Income."

FIGURE 3–16 (Continued)

**Annual Rates of Profit on Stockholders' Equity, by Industry**
(Percent)

| Industry | Before Federal Income Taxes | | | | | After Taxes | | | | |
|---|---|---|---|---|---|---|---|---|---|---|
| | 3Q 1964 | 4Q 1964 | 1Q 1965 | 2Q 1965 | 3Q 1965 | 3Q 1964 | 4Q 1964 | 1Q 1965 | 2Q 1965 | 3Q 1965 |
| All manufacturing corporations, except newspapers | 19.0 | 20.2 | 20.8 | 23.4 | 20.6 | 11.2 | 12.4 | 12.1 | 13.8 | 12.3 |
| Durable goods | 19.4 | 21.6 | 23.8 | 27.5 | 21.8 | 10.8 | 12.2 | 12.9 | 15.3 | 12.3 |
| Transportation equipment | 17.4 | 25.8 | 39.2 | 40.3 | 20.0 | 9.9 | 14.8 | 20.6 | 21.8 | 11.3 |
| Motor vehicles and equipment* | 15.9 | 27.0 | 43.7 | 43.5 | 17.9 | 9.2 | 15.5 | 22.9 | 23.5 | 10.3 |
| Aircraft and parts* | 24.2 | 22.8 | 23.0 | 27.8 | 30.2 | 12.9 | 12.6 | 12.2 | 14.7 | 16.4 |
| Electrical machinery, equipment, and supplies | 21.0 | 24.6 | 22.2 | 24.5 | 24.1 | 11.0 | 13.3 | 11.7 | 13.1 | 13.2 |
| Other machinery | 24.7 | 23.2 | 23.0 | 29.2 | 26.6 | 12.9 | 12.3 | 12.0 | 15.8 | 14.4 |
| Metalworking machinery and equipment* | 25.4 | 22.2 | 22.4 | 28.6 | 26.8 | 14.9 | 12.9 | 12.1 | 16.0 | 15.2 |
| Other fabricated metal products | 20.9 | 19.2 | 20.1 | 26.0 | 24.7 | 11.4 | 10.7 | 11.3 | 15.0 | 14.1 |
| Primary metal industries | 13.7 | 17.1 | 19.3 | 20.7 | 15.7 | 8.2 | 10.5 | 11.3 | 12.1 | 9.3 |
| Primary iron and steel* | 14.1 | 17.2 | 19.5 | 20.3 | 14.5 | 8.0 | 10.1 | 11.0 | 11.5 | 8.6 |
| Primary nonferrous metals* | 12.9 | 16.8 | 18.9 | 21.4 | 17.6 | 8.4 | 11.2 | 11.8 | 13.3 | 10.4 |
| Stone, clay, and glass products | 21.7 | 15.0 | 9.6 | 20.2 | 22.2 | 12.5 | 9.2 | 4.6 | 12.1 | 13.5 |
| Furniture and fixtures | 21.3 | 22.3 | 18.4 | 23.0 | 25.6 | 11.5 | 12.8 | 9.8 | 13.0 | 14.5 |
| Lumber and wood products, except furniture | 18.4 | 11.3 | 11.0 | 16.6 | 19.3 | 11.7 | 7.9 | 6.7 | 10.7 | 12.7 |
| Instruments and related products | 29.2 | 31.1 | 25.4 | 29.1 | 31.7 | 15.6 | 16.3 | 14.5 | 15.4 | 17.3 |
| Miscellaneous manufacturing and ordnance | 19.8 | 23.7 | 16.0 | 18.6 | 18.2 | 10.3 | 13.9 | 8.7 | 10.5 | 9.4 |
| Nondurable goods | 18.6 | 19.0 | 17.8 | 19.4 | 19.5 | 11.7 | 12.5 | 11.4 | 12.3 | 12.4 |
| Food and kindred products | 20.8 | 19.6 | 17.6 | 19.1 | 20.7 | 11.5 | 10.8 | 9.5 | 10.4 | 11.6 |
| Dairy products* | 20.1 | 16.7 | 16.4 | 19.9 | 20.2 | 11.1 | 9.0 | 8.8 | 11.5 | 11.4 |
| Bakery products* | 18.2 | 19.3 | 15.6 | 17.2 | 17.9 | 10.0 | 9.8 | 7.8 | 8.8 | 9.5 |
| Alcoholic beverages* | 20.0 | 17.8 | 13.4 | 18.5 | 18.7 | 11.1 | 9.6 | 6.5 | 9.8 | 10.3 |
| Tobacco manufactures | 27.3 | 27.4 | 22.0 | 26.5 | 28.2 | 14.0 | 14.6 | 11.5 | 14.3 | 14.6 |
| Textile mill products | 18.6 | 18.7 | 18.1 | 19.3 | 19.9 | 10.2 | 10.6 | 9.9 | 10.5 | 10.9 |
| Apparel and other finished products | 27.6 | 20.6 | 17.0 | 19.5 | 25.5 | 17.2 | 12.4 | 9.5 | 10.8 | 15.3 |
| Paper and allied products | 15.5 | 16.9 | 15.4 | 17.5 | 16.8 | 8.8 | 10.5 | 8.8 | 10.1 | 9.9 |
| Printing and publishing, except newspapers | 27.0 | 22.1 | 23.4 | 22.6 | 28.3 | 14.5 | 11.8 | 13.8 | 12.4 | 15.6 |
| Chemicals and allied products | 25.7 | 26.0 | 25.6 | 28.7 | 26.3 | 14.0 | 15.1 | 14.5 | 16.4 | 15.0 |
| Basic chemicals* | 23.0 | 24.7 | 24.2 | 28.6 | 23.5 | 12.8 | 14.9 | 13.8 | 16.4 | 13.6 |
| Drugs* | 36.7 | 34.2 | 38.2 | 33.0 | 39.1 | 19.4 | 18.5 | 20.5 | 18.0 | 21.2 |
| Petroleum refining and related industries | 12.1 | 14.2 | 13.3 | 13.8 | 13.8 | 10.7 | 12.7 | 11.6 | 11.8 | 11.6 |
| Petroleum refining* | 11.8 | 14.2 | 13.3 | 13.7 | 13.5 | 10.5 | 12.8 | 11.6 | 11.8 | 11.5 |
| Rubber and miscellaneous plastics products | 19.3 | 19.2 | 18.2 | 20.5 | 19.3 | 10.7 | 11.4 | 10.2 | 11.7 | 11.1 |
| Leather and leather products | 20.7 | 22.3 | 19.8 | 19.5 | 19.6 | 12.0 | 12.6 | 10.9 | 10.5 | 11.2 |

* Included in major industry above.

previously. There are, of course, many sources in addition to those mentioned. The competent investor will absorb as much material as his time and energies permit. The wider his reading, the better equipped he will be to assess the outlook.

## The Securities Markets

The competent analyst must constantly make a judgment as to the trend and level of the market as a whole to provide the appropriate environmental setting for selection and timing of portfolio additions or deletions.

On an elementary level, one can keep abreast of the market by reading the financial section of a daily newspaper such as *The New York*

**FIGURE 3–16 (Concluded)**

**Annual Rates of Profit on Stockholders' Equity, by Asset Size and Industry Group**
(Percent)

| Asset Size | Before Federal Income Taxes | | | | | After Taxes | | | | |
|---|---|---|---|---|---|---|---|---|---|---|
| | 3Q 1964 | 4Q 1964 | 1Q 1965 | 2Q 1965 | 3Q 1965 | 3Q 1964 | 4Q 1964 | 1Q 1965 | 2Q 1965 | 3Q 1965 |
| All manufacturing corporations, except newspapers | 19.0 | 20.2 | 20.8 | 23.4 | 20.6 | 11.2 | 12.4 | 12.1 | 13.8 | 12.3 |
| Under $1 million | 24.0 | 16.1 | 19.0 | 24.8 | 25.8 | 15.5 | 10.0 | 11.8 | 16.0 | 16.8 |
| $ 1 million to $ 5 million | 21.2 | 18.9 | 18.3 | 23.4 | 23.0 | 11.4 | 10.3 | 9.3 | 12.4 | 12.5 |
| $ 5 million to $ 10 million | 19.2 | 19.5 | 18.3 | 21.1 | 22.2 | 10.1 | 10.6 | 9.6 | 11.4 | 12.0 |
| $ 10 million to $ 25 million | 20.4 | 20.2 | 17.7 | 22.7 | 21.9 | 10.7 | 11.2 | 9.2 | 12.4 | 12.1 |
| $ 25 million to $ 50 million | 20.5 | 19.5 | 18.1 | 22.0 | 22.4 | 10.9 | 10.7 | 9.8 | 12.0 | 12.3 |
| $ 50 million to $ 100 million | 20.0 | 20.4 | 19.1 | 22.3 | 21.1 | 10.7 | 11.7 | 10.3 | 12.1 | 11.5 |
| $ 100 million to $ 250 million | 20.8 | 21.4 | 20.1 | 22.1 | 22.3 | 11.3 | 12.2 | 11.1 | 12.5 | 12.6 |
| $ 250 million to $1,000 million | 18.8 | 19.4 | 18.9 | 22.6 | 20.8 | 10.8 | 11.7 | 11.0 | 13.1 | 12.0 |
| $1,000 million and over | 16.9 | 21.6 | 24.3 | 24.7 | 18.3 | 11.1 | 14.3 | 15.0 | 15.3 | 11.9 |
| Durable goods | 19.4 | 21.6 | 23.8 | 27.5 | 21.8 | 10.8 | 12.2 | 12.9 | 15.3 | 12.3 |
| Under $5 million | 23.0 | 18.4 | 19.2 | 28.2 | 26.6 | 13.4 | 10.5 | 10.6 | 16.8 | 15.8 |
| $ 5 million to $ 10 million | 19.3 | 18.4 | 19.6 | 22.9 | 23.7 | 10.3 | 9.9 | 10.3 | 12.5 | 13.1 |
| $ 10 million to $ 25 million | 18.6 | 19.2 | 18.4 | 24.2 | 22.5 | 9.6 | 10.5 | 9.7 | 13.1 | 12.3 |
| $ 25 million to $ 50 million | 19.3 | 19.2 | 18.6 | 22.5 | 21.3 | 10.3 | 10.5 | 9.8 | 12.1 | 11.7 |
| $ 50 million to $ 100 million | 19.6 | 20.3 | 18.4 | 23.0 | 21.1 | 10.3 | 11.3 | 9.8 | 12.5 | 11.4 |
| $ 100 million to $ 250 million | 19.2 | 20.1 | 19.1 | 22.6 | 21.1 | 10.6 | 11.8 | 10.5 | 12.7 | 11.9 |
| $ 250 million to $1,000 million | 19.0 | 19.3 | 18.8 | 23.0 | 20.9 | 10.7 | 11.6 | 10.8 | 13.1 | 11.9 |
| $1,000 million and over | 18.5 | 26.4 | 34.3 | 34.7 | 20.4 | 10.2 | 14.7 | 18.0 | 18.7 | 11.4 |
| Nondurable goods | 18.6 | 19.0 | 17.8 | 19.4 | 19.5 | 11.7 | 12.5 | 11.4 | 12.3 | 12.4 |
| Under $5 million | 21.9 | 16.6 | 17.9 | 19.0 | 21.4 | 13.2 | 9.8 | 10.3 | 10.7 | 12.9 |
| $ 5 million to $ 10 million | 19.0 | 20.9 | 16.7 | 18.9 | 20.0 | 9.9 | 11.5 | 8.5 | 9.9 | 10.4 |
| $ 10 million to $ 25 million | 22.8 | 21.7 | 16.7 | 20.7 | 21.2 | 12.3 | 12.0 | 8.5 | 11.4 | 11.8 |
| $ 25 million to $ 50 million | 21.9 | 19.8 | 17.5 | 21.3 | 23.7 | 11.6 | 10.8 | 9.9 | 11.9 | 13.2 |
| $ 50 million to $ 100 million | 20.4 | 20.4 | 19.8 | 21.4 | 21.1 | 11.1 | 12.0 | 10.9 | 11.7 | 11.4 |
| $ 100 million to $ 250 million | 22.5 | 22.7 | 21.1 | 21.6 | 23.4 | 12.1 | 12.7 | 11.7 | 12.3 | 13.2 |
| $ 250 million to $1,000 million | 18.5 | 19.4 | 18.9 | 22.2 | 20.6 | 10.9 | 11.9 | 11.1 | 13.0 | 12.1 |
| $1,000 million and over | 15.5 | 17.6 | 16.3 | 16.8 | 16.5 | 11.8 | 14.0 | 12.6 | 12.7 | 12.4 |

Source: Federal Trade Commission and Securities and Exchange Commission, Quarterly Financial Report for Manufacturing Corporations.

*Times* or *The Wall Street Journal.* See Figures 3–18 and 3–19. On a weekly basis, review of *Barron's*, Standard & Poor's, *The Outlook*, and the Sunday financial section of *The New York Times*, will provide basic data on stock market action and trends. See Figures 3–20, 3–21, and 3–22.[13] Looking daily at the *Times* market summary story and tabulation page and at *The Wall Street Journal* "Abreast of The Market" column and Dow-Jones index page, and weekly at *Barron's* "Study of Price Movement—Market Laboratory" page, and at *The Outlook's* "Forecast and Policy" page and at its "Indexes of the Security Markets" page, will build a continuing awareness of price trends.

On a more advanced level, fundamental and technical analysis may help to provide a perspective of where the market is and where it is likely to go. Fundamental market analysis involves the use of composite stock

---

[13] For elementary information on reading and understanding the financial section of a daily newspaper, see C. Norman Stabler, *How To Read The Financial News* (New York; Harper & Row, Publishers, 1965); also John G. Forest, *Financial News: How To Read And Interpret It*, New York Times, 1965.

## FIGURE 3–17

### Net Income of Leading Corporations for the Years 1964 and 1965

(Dollar Figures in Thousands)

| No. of Cos. | Industrial Groups | Reported Net Income After Taxes 1964 | Reported Net Income After Taxes 1965 | Per Cent Change | Net Worth-a Beginning of Year 1964 | Net Worth-a Beginning of Year 1965 | % Return on Net Worth 1964 | % Return on Net Worth 1965 | % Margin on Sales-b 1964 | % Margin on Sales-b 1965 |
|---|---|---|---|---|---|---|---|---|---|---|
| 17 | Baking | $ 75,446 | $ 76,564 | + 1 | $ 665,188 | $ 686,356 | 11.3 | 11.2 | 3.0 | 2.9 |
| 12 | Dairy products | 165,966 | 190,175 | +15 | 1,359,409 | 1,524,477 | 12.2 | 12.5 | 3.1 | 3.3 |
| 26 | Meat packing | 94,512 | 58,511 | −38 | 1,100,261 | 1,167,151 | 8.6 | 5.0 | 1.1 | 0.6 |
| 14 | Sugar | 43,766 | 51,996 | +19 | 537,960 | 558,633 | 8.1 | 9.3 | 3.1 | 3.7 |
| 81 | Other food products | 371,182 | 426,398 | +15 | 3,331,872 | 3,494,593 | 11.1 | 12.2 | 4.0 | 4.2 |
| 15 | Soft drinks | 87,967 | 100,201 | +14 | 438,255 | 490,634 | 20.1 | 20.4 | 6.6 | 6.8 |
| 14 | Brewing | 55,642 | 59,565 | + 7 | 554,048 | 586,760 | 10.0 | 10.2 | 4.7 | 4.4 |
| 15 | Distilling | 135,130 | 156,508 | +16 | 1,588,389 | 1,649,982 | 8.5 | 9.5 | 4.2 | 4.5 |
| 14 | Tobacco products | 297,125 | 310,805 | + 5 | 2,217,223 | 2,315,527 | 13.4 | 13.4 | 6.0 | 6.0 |
| 69 | Textile products | 223,359 | 308,390 | +38 | 2,506,982 | 2,650,342 | 8.9 | 11.6 | 3.4 | 4.2 |
| 91 | Clothing and apparel | 116,712 | 150,495 | +29 | 855,194 | 963,620 | 13.6 | 15.6 | 3.6 | 4.1 |
| 28 | Shoes, leather, etc. | 60,858 | 71,510 | +18 | 555,159 | 582,928 | 11.0 | 12.3 | 3.3 | 3.5 |
| 55 | Rubber and allied products | 333,240 | 376,823 | +13 | 2,920,299 | 3,146,191 | 11.4 | 12.0 | 4.3 | 4.5 |
| 29 | Lumber and wood products | 179,537 | 205,235 | +14 | 1,557,786 | 1,762,393 | 11.5 | 11.6 | 6.0 | 6.3 |
| 38 | Furniture and fixtures | 44,871 | 56,995 | +27 | 431,937 | 457,631 | 10.4 | 12.5 | 4.4 | 5.0 |
| 76 | Paper and allied products | 610,011 | 694,505 | +14 | 5,836,448 | 6,128,227 | 10.5 | 11.3 | 6.3 | 6.7 |
| 88 | Printing and publishing | 209,298 | 269,628 | +29 | 1,436,950 | 1,599,620 | 14.6 | 16.9 | 5.7 | 6.7 |
| 88 | Chemical products | 1,450,216 | 1,672,300 | +15 | 10,179,280 | 11,078,609 | 14.2 | 15.1 | 8.1 | 8.5 |
| 21 | Paint and allied products | 108,990 | 124,004 | +14 | 801,391 | 856,001 | 13.6 | 14.5 | 5.7 | 5.7 |
| 41 | Drugs and medicines | 524,509 | 620,106 | +18 | 2,649,583 | 2,811,447 | 19.8 | 22.1 | 10.8 | 11.2 |
| 27 | Soap, cosmetics | 275,983 | 297,344 | + 8 | 1,565,155 | 1,768,143 | 17.6 | 16.8 | 6.3 | 6.3 |
| 109 | Petroleum prod. and refining | 4,228,510 | 4,637,529 | +10 | 36,670,437 | 38,811,252 | 11.5 | 11.9 | 9.3 | 9.4 |
| 16 | Cement | 87,070 | 82,862 | − 5 | 885,812 | 913,088 | 9.8 | 9.1 | 10.4 | 9.1 |
| 14 | Glass products | 179,692 | 209,982 | +17 | 1,479,597 | 1,551,145 | 12.1 | 13.5 | 7.1 | 7.4 |
| 50 | Other stone, clay products | 230,284 | 229,472 | 0 | 2,195,415 | 2,308,803 | 10.5 | 9.9 | 7.1 | 6.7 |
| 77 | Iron and steel | 1,041,882 | 1,136,789 | + 9 | 11,534,037 | 11,971,108 | 9.0 | 9.5 | 5.9 | 5.9 |
| 59 | Nonferrous metals | 552,419 | 740,409 | +34 | 5,977,648 | 6,259,403 | 9.2 | 11.8 | 7.0 | 8.1 |
| 39 | Hardware and tools | 116,493 | 136,812 | +17 | 721,904 | 778,761 | 16.1 | 17.6 | 6.9 | 7.1 |
| 51 | Building, heat., plumb. equip. | 93,750 | 123,787 | +32 | 1,058,255 | 1,108,060 | 8.9 | 11.2 | 3.6 | 4.2 |
| 72 | Other metal products | 202,291 | 259,466 | +28 | 1,950,361 | 2,020,418 | 10.4 | 12.8 | 4.2 | 4.9 |
| 56 | Farm, constr., mat.-hdlg. equip. | 421,209 | 477,570 | +13 | 3,064,448 | 3,333,290 | 13.7 | 14.3 | 6.0 | 6.1 |
| 42 | Office, computing equipment | 521,974 | 586,157 | +12 | 2,908,751 | 3,316,607 | 17.9 | 17.7 | 9.3 | 9.2 |
| 218 | Other machinery | 559,971 | 699,444 | +25 | 4,565,829 | 4,878,815 | 12.3 | 14.3 | 5.4 | 5.8 |
| 308 | Electrical equip. & electronics | 904,433 | 1,245,533 | +38 | 8,140,663 | 8,537,073 | 11.1 | 14.6 | 3.9 | 4.7 |
| 19 | Household appliances | 147,708 | 167,135 | +13 | 1,047,043 | 1,127,011 | 14.1 | 14.8 | 5.4 | 5.5 |
| 14 | Autos and trucks | 2,510,881 | 3,102,324 | +24 | 12,640,341 | 13,630,519 | 19.9 | 22.8 | 7.4 | 10.2 |
| 49 | Automotive parts | 191,605 | 227,023 | +18 | 1,575,073 | 1,695,639 | 12.2 | 13.4 | 4.6 | 4.8 |
| 11 | Railway equipment | 89,946 | 108,181 | +20 | 806,203 | 857,045 | 11.2 | 12.6 | 5.2 | 5.4 |
| 50 | Aircraft and space | 414,458 | 533,821 | +29 | 3,157,344 | 3,451,039 | 13.1 | 15.5 | 2.7 | 3.3 |
| 97 | Instruments, photo goods, etc. | 423,893 | 549,241 | +30 | 2,546,652 | 2,784,790 | 16.6 | 19.7 | 8.1 | 9.0 |
| 88 | Misc. manufacturing | 181,934 | 221,641 | +22 | 1,476,834 | 1,572,708 | 12.3 | 14.1 | 5.3 | 5.9 |
| 2,298 | Total manufacturing | 18,564,723 | 21,753,236 | +17 | 147,491,416 | 157,185,839 | 12.6 | 13.8 | 6.1 | 6.6 |
| 19 | Metal mining-c | 48,276 | 56,487 | +17 | 457,792 | 480,931 | 10.5 | 11.7 | 11.2 | 12.7 |
| 17 | Coal mining-c | 92,229 | 104,559 | +13 | 941,565 | 971,843 | 9.8 | 10.8 | 8.2 | 8.9 |
| 11 | Other mining, quarrying-c | 61,758 | 80,618 | +31 | 545,443 | 585,634 | 11.3 | 13.8 | 13.3 | 14.6 |
| 47 | Total mining | 202,263 | 241,664 | +19 | 1,944,800 | 2,038,408 | 10.4 | 11.9 | 9.9 | 11.0 |
| 59 | Chain stores—food | 310,093 | 325,070 | + 5 | 2,472,777 | 2,610,605 | 12.5 | 12.5 | 1.3 | 1.3 |
| 79 | Chain stores—variety, etc. | 187,279 | 238,619 | +27 | 1,659,895 | 1,780,265 | 11.3 | 13.4 | 2.9 | 3.3 |
| 66 | Department and specialty | 330,521 | 393,483 | +19 | 2,649,213 | 2,945,648 | 12.5 | 13.4 | 2.8 | 3.0 |
| 9 | Mail order | 328,366 | 353,424 | + 8 | 2,527,567 | 2,697,061 | 13.0 | 13.1 | 4.3 | 4.2 |
| 191 | Wholesale and misc. | 230,203 | 296,514 | +29 | 2,025,266 | 2,208,113 | 11.4 | 13.4 | 2.1 | 2.4 |
| 404 | Total trade | 1,386,462 | 1,607,110 | +16 | 11,334,718 | 12,241,692 | 12.2 | 13.1 | 2.3 | 2.5 |
| 76 | Class I railroads-d | 693,591 | 814,887 | +17 | 17,840,552 | 17,622,350 | 3.9 | 4.6 | 7.1 | 8.0 |
| 33 | Common carrier trucking | 56,641 | 70,755 | +25 | 280,389 | 308,751 | 20.2 | 22.9 | 4.0 | 4.2 |
| 14 | Shipping | 55,765 | 48,227 | −14 | 723,776 | 770,614 | 7.7 | 6.3 | 6.9 | 6.8 |
| 29 | Air transport-d | 219,147 | 361,930 | +65 | 1,077,817 | 1,316,584 | 20.3 | 27.5 | 5.4 | 7.6 |
| 44 | Misc. transportation | 108,255 | 125,478 | +16 | 702,803 | 759,752 | 15.4 | 16.5 | 7.3 | 7.7 |
| 196 | Total transportation | 1,133,399 | 1,421,277 | +25 | 20,625,337 | 20,778,051 | 5.5 | 6.8 | 6.5 | 7.5 |
| 246 | Electric power, gas, etc.-d | 3,026,698 | 3,291,381 | + 9 | 27,575,792 | 28,832,942 | 11.0 | 11.4 | 13.7 | 14.0 |
| 30 | Telephone and telegraph-d | 1,909,792 | 2,093,775 | +10 | 18,592,190 | 21,026,082 | 10.3 | 10.0 | 14.4 | 14.5 |
| 276 | Total public utilities-d | 4,936,485 | 5,385,156 | + 9 | 46,167,982 | 49,859,024 | 10.7 | 10.8 | 13.9 | 14.2 |
| 49 | Amusements | 28,426 | 63,938 | +125 | 565,136 | 586,846 | 5.0 | 10.9 | 2.2 | 4.5 |
| 40 | Restaurants and hotels | 47,385 | 64,463 | +36 | 517,172 | 550,768 | 9.2 | 11.7 | 2.7 | 3.4 |
| 116 | Other business services | 184,545 | 225,006 | +22 | 1,000,162 | 1,142,739 | 18.5 | 19.7 | 5.6 | 5.9 |
| 29 | Construction | 67,180 | 78,042 | +16 | 681,905 | 698,959 | 9.9 | 11.2 | 4.8 | 5.0 |
| 234 | Total services | 327,536 | 431,449 | +32 | 2,764,375 | 2,979,312 | 11.8 | 14.5 | 4.2 | 5.0 |
| * | Commercial banks | 1,923,097 | 2,108,000 | +10 | 21,932,000 | 24,047,000 | 8.8 | 8.8 | ... | ... |
| 32 | Fire and casualty insurance | 124,188 | 101,857 | −18 | 3,187,532 | 3,588,583 | 3.9 | 2.8 | ... | ... |
| 219 | Investment trusts-e | 906,332 | 1,013,722 | +12 | 30,820,656 | 35,405,685 | 2.9 | 2.9 | ... | ... |
| 88 | Sales finance | 329,043 | 348,639 | + 6 | 2,669,182 | 2,876,883 | 12.3 | 12.1 | ... | ... |
| 68 | Real estate | 43,166 | 49,384 | +14 | 604,907 | 638,525 | 7.1 | 7.7 | ... | ... |
| 407 | Total finance | 3,325,826 | 3,621,602 | + 9 | 59,214,277 | 66,556,676 | 5.6 | 5.4 | ... | ... |
| 3,862 | Grand Total | 29,876,694 | 34,461,494 | +15 | 289,542,905 | 311,639,002 | 10.3 | 11.1 | 6.2 | 6.7 |

a—Net worth (listed previously as "Book net assets") is based upon the excess of total balance sheet assets over liabilities; the amounts at which assets are carried on the books may not represent present-day values. b-Profit margins are computed for all companies publishing sales or gross income figures, which represent 97 per cent of the total number of reporting companies, excluding the finance group; includes income from investments and other sources as well as from sales. c-Net income is reported before depletion charges in some cases. d-Due to the large proportion of capital investment in the form of funded debt, rate of return on total property investment would be lower than that shown on net worth only. e-Figures in most cases exclude capital gains or losses on investments. *-Federal Reserve Board tabulation of all member banks; number of banks (6,221) is not included in total number of companies; earnings include profits and losses on sale of securities; net worth figures are annual averages.

Source: First National City Bank of New York, April, 1966.

## FIGURE 3–18A

## New York Stock Exchange Transactions

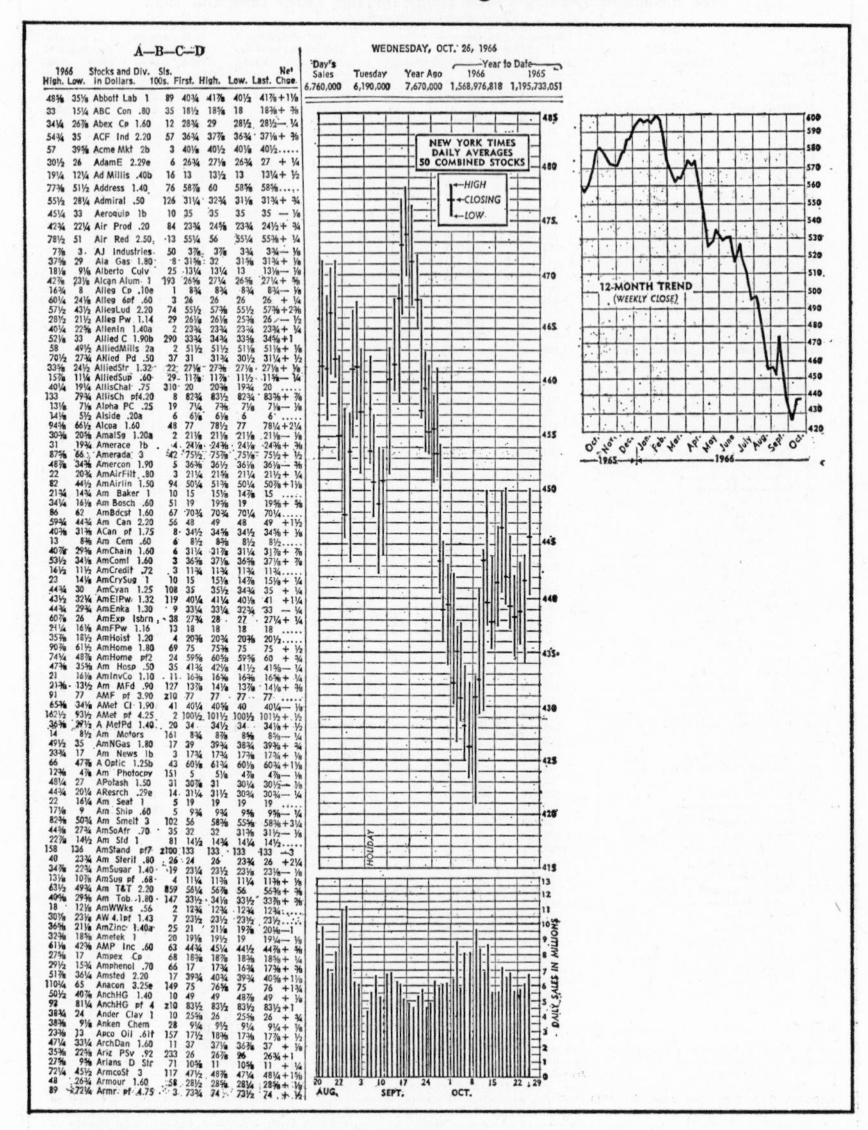

A—B—C—D

| 1966 High. | 1966 Low. | Stocks and Div. in Dollars. | Sls. 100s. | First. | High. | Low. | Last. | Net Chge. |
|---|---|---|---|---|---|---|---|---|
| 48⅝ | 35⅛ | Abbott Lab 1 | 89 | 40¾ | 41⅞ | 40½ | 41⅞ | +1⅛ |
| 33 | 15¼ | ABC Con .80 | 35 | 18½ | 18⅝ | 18 | 18⅜ | + ⅜ |
| 34¼ | 26⅞ | Abex Cp 1.60 | 12 | 28¾ | 29 | 28½ | 28½ | − ¼ |
| 54¾ | 35 | ACF Ind 2.20 | 57 | 36¾ | 37⅞ | 36¾ | 37⅛ | + ⅜ |
| 57 | 39⅝ | Acme Mkt 2b | 3 | 40⅛ | 40½ | 40⅛ | 40½ | ..... |
| 30½ | 26 | AdamE 2.29e | 6 | 26¾ | 27⅛ | 26¾ | 27 | + ¼ |
| 19¼ | 12¼ | Ad Millis .40b | 16 | 13 | 13½ | 13 | 13¼ | + ½ |
| 77⅜ | 51½ | Address 1.40 | 76 | 58⅞ | 60 | 58⅝ | 58⅝ | ..... |
| 55½ | 28¼ | Admiral .50 | 126 | 31¼ | 32¾ | 31⅛ | 31¾ | + ¾ |
| 45¼ | 33 | Aeroquip 1b | 10 | 35 | 35 | 35 | 35 | − ⅛ |
| 42¾ | 22¼ | Air Prod .20 | 84 | 23¾ | 24⅝ | 23¾ | 24½ | + ¾ |
| 78½ | 51 | Air Red 2.50 | 13 | 55¼ | 56 | 55¼ | 55⅜ | + ¼ |
| 7⅞ | 3 | AJ Industries | 50 | 3⅞ | 3⅞ | 3¾ | 3¾ | − ⅛ |
| 37⅝ | 29 | Ala Gas 1.80 | 8 | 31⅝ | 32 | 31⅝ | 31¾ | + ⅛ |
| 18⅛ | 9⅛ | Alberto Culv | 25 | 13¼ | 13¼ | 13 | 13⅛ | − ⅛ |
| 42⅞ | 23⅛ | Alcan Alum 1 | 193 | 26⅝ | 27¼ | 26⅝ | 27¼ | + ⅝ |
| 16¾ | 8 | Alleg Cp .10e | 1 | 8¾ | 8¾ | 8¾ | 8¾ | − ⅛ |
| 60¼ | 24⅛ | Alleg 6pf .60 | 3 | 26 | 26 | 26 | 26 | + ¼ |
| 57½ | 43½ | AllegLud 2.20 | 74 | 55½ | 57⅜ | 55½ | 57⅜ | +2⅜ |
| 28½ | 21½ | Alleg Pw 1.14 | 29 | 26⅛ | 26⅛ | 25⅜ | 26 | − ½ |
| 40¼ | 22⅝ | Allenin 1.40a | 2 | 23¾ | 23¾ | 23¾ | 23¾ | + ¼ |
| 52⅛ | 33 | Allied C 1.90b | 290 | 33¾ | 34¾ | 33⅝ | 34⅝ | +1 |
| 58 | 49½ | AlliedMills 2a | 2 | 51½ | 51½ | 51⅛ | 51⅛ | + ⅛ |
| 70½ | 27¾ | Allied Pd .50 | 37 | 31 | 31¾ | 30½ | 31¼ | + ½ |
| 33⅝ | 24½ | AlliedStr 1.32 | 22 | 27⅛ | 27⅜ | 27⅛ | 27⅛ | + ⅛ |
| 15⅞ | 11¼ | AlliedSup .60 | 29 | 11⅞ | 11⅞ | 11½ | 11⅝ | − ¼ |
| 40¼ | 19¼ | AllisChal .75 | 310 | 20 | 20⅜ | 19¾ | 20 | ..... |
| 133 | 79¾ | AllisCh pf4.20 | 8 | 82¾ | 83½ | 82¾ | 83⅜ | + ⅞ |
| 13⅛ | 7⅛ | Alpha PC .25 | 19 | 7¼ | 7⅜ | 7⅛ | 7⅛ | − ⅛ |
| 14⅛ | 5½ | Alside .20a | 6 | 6⅛ | 6⅛ | 6 | 6 | ..... |
| 94⅝ | 66½ | Alcoa 1.60 | 48 | 77 | 78½ | 77 | 78¼ | +2¼ |
| 30⅜ | 20⅝ | AmalSg 1.20a | 2 | 21⅛ | 21⅛ | 21⅛ | 21⅛ | − ⅛ |
| 31 | 19¾ | Amerace 1b | 4 | 24⅛ | 24⅜ | 24⅛ | 24⅜ | + ⅜ |
| 87⅝ | 66 | Amerada 3 | 42 | 75½ | 75⅞ | 75⅛ | 75½ | + ½ |
| 48⅞ | 34⅜ | Amercon 1.90 | 5 | 36⅜ | 36½ | 36⅛ | 36⅛ | − ⅜ |
| 22 | 20¾ | AmAirFilt .80 | 3 | 21¼ | 21⅝ | 21¼ | 21½ | + ¼ |
| 82 | 44½ | AmAirlin 1.50 | 94 | 50¼ | 51⅜ | 50¼ | 50⅞ | +1⅛ |
| 21¾ | 14¾ | Am Baker 1 | 10 | 15 | 15⅛ | 14⅞ | 15 | ..... |
| 34¼ | 16⅛ | Am Bosch .60 | 51 | 19 | 19⅝ | 19 | 19⅝ | + ⅝ |
| 86 | 62 | AmBdcst 1.60 | 67 | 70¾ | 70¾ | 70¼ | 70¼ | ..... |
| 59¾ | 44¾ | Am Can 2.20 | 56 | 48 | 49 | 48 | 49 | +1½ |
| 40⅜ | 31⅜ | ACan pf 1.75 | 8 | 34½ | 34⅝ | 34½ | 34⅝ | + ⅛ |
| 13 | 8⅜ | Am Cem .60 | 6 | 8½ | 8⅝ | 8½ | 8½ | ..... |
| 40⅞ | 29⅝ | AmChain 1.60 | 6 | 31¼ | 31⅞ | 31¼ | 31⅞ | + ⅞ |
| 53½ | 34⅛ | AmComl 1.60 | 3 | 36⅝ | 37⅛ | 36⅝ | 37⅛ | + ⅞ |
| 16½ | 11½ | AmCredit .72 | 3 | 11¾ | 11¾ | 11¾ | 11¾ | ..... |
| 23 | 14⅛ | AmCrySug 1 | 10 | 15 | 15⅛ | 14⅞ | 15⅛ | + ¼ |
| 44¾ | 30 | AmCyan 1.25 | 108 | 35 | 35½ | 34¾ | 35 | + ¼ |
| 43½ | 32¼ | AmElPw 1.32 | 119 | 40¼ | 41¼ | 40⅛ | 41 | +1¼ |
| 44¾ | 29¾ | AmEnka 1.30 | 9 | 33¼ | 33¼ | 32¾ | 33 | − ¼ |
| 60⅞ | 26 | AmExp Isbrn | 38 | 27¾ | 28 | 27 | 27¼ | + ¼ |
| 21¼ | 16⅛ | AmFPw 1.16 | 13 | 18 | 18 | 18 | 18 | ..... |
| 35⅞ | 18½ | AmHoist 1.20 | 4 | 20⅜ | 20¾ | 20⅜ | 20½ | ..... |
| 90⅞ | 61½ | AmHome 1.80 | 69 | 75 | 75⅜ | 75 | 75 | + ½ |
| 74¼ | 48⅞ | AmHome pf2 | 24 | 59⅝ | 60⅝ | 59⅝ | 60 | + ¾ |
| 47⅜ | 35⅝ | Am Hosp .50 | 35 | 41¾ | 42⅛ | 41½ | 41⅝ | − ¼ |
| 21 | 16⅛ | AmInvCo 1.10 | 11 | 16⅜ | 16⅝ | 16⅜ | 16⅝ | + ¼ |
| 21⅜ | 13½ | Am MFd .90 | 127 | 13⅞ | 14⅛ | 13⅞ | 14⅛ | + ⅜ |
| 91 | 77 | AMF pf 3.90 | z10 | 77 | 77 | 77 | 77 | ..... |
| 65⅜ | 34⅛ | AMet Cl 1.90 | 41 | 40¼ | 40⅝ | 40 | 40¼ | − ⅛ |
| 162½ | 93½ | AMet pf 4.25 | 2 | 100½ | 101½ | 100½ | 101½ | + ½ |
| 36⅜ | 29½ | A MetPd 1.40 | 20 | 34 | 34½ | 34 | 34⅛ | + ½ |
| 14 | 8½ | Am Motors | 161 | 8¾ | 8⅞ | 8⅝ | 8⅝ | − ¼ |
| 49½ | 35 | AmNGas 1.80 | 17 | 39 | 39¾ | 38¾ | 39⅜ | + ¾ |
| 23¾ | 17 | Am News 1b | 3 | 17¾ | 17¾ | 17⅜ | 17¾ | + ⅛ |
| 66 | 47⅜ | A Optic 1.25b | 43 | 60⅛ | 61¾ | 60⅛ | 60¾ | +1⅛ |
| 12⅜ | 4⅞ | Am Photocpy | 151 | 5 | 5⅛ | 4⅞ | 4⅞ | − ⅛ |
| 48¼ | 27 | APotash 1.50 | 31 | 30⅞ | 31 | 30¼ | 30½ | − ⅛ |
| 44¾ | 20¼ | AResrch .29e | 14 | 31¼ | 31½ | 30¾ | 30¾ | − ¼ |
| 22 | 16¼ | Am Seat 1 | 5 | 19 | 19 | 19 | 19 | ..... |
| 17⅛ | 9 | Am Ship .60 | 5 | 9¾ | 9¾ | 9⅝ | 9⅝ | − ¼ |
| 82⅜ | 50¾ | Am Smelt 3 | 102 | 56 | 58⅜ | 55⅝ | 58⅜ | +3¼ |
| 44⅝ | 27¾ | AmSoAfr .70 | 35 | 32 | 32 | 31⅜ | 31½ | − ⅛ |
| 22⅞ | 14½ | Am Std 1 | 81 | 14½ | 14¾ | 14¼ | 14½ | ..... |
| 158 | 136 | AmStand pf7 | z100 | 133 | 133 | 133 | 133 | −3 |
| 40 | 23¾ | Am Steril .80 | 26 | 24 | 26 | 23¾ | 26 | +2¼ |
| 34⅞ | 22¾ | AmSugar 1.40 | 19 | 23¼ | 23½ | 23⅛ | 23⅛ | − ⅛ |
| 13⅛ | 10⅞ | AmSug pf .68 | 4 | 11¼ | 11⅜ | 11¼ | 11⅜ | + ⅛ |
| 63½ | 49¾ | Am T&T 2.20 | 859 | 56¼ | 56⅞ | 56 | 56⅜ | + ⅜ |
| 40⅝ | 29⅝ | Am Tob 1.80 | 147 | 33½ | 34⅛ | 33½ | 33⅞ | + ⅜ |
| 18 | 12⅛ | AmWWks .56 | 2 | 12¾ | 12¾ | 12¾ | 12¾ | ..... |
| 30⅛ | 23⅛ | AW 4.1pf 1.43 | 7 | 23½ | 23½ | 23½ | 23½ | ..... |
| 36⅝ | 21⅛ | AmZinc 1.40a | 25 | 21 | 21⅛ | 19⅞ | 20⅛ | −1 |
| 32⅜ | 18⅝ | Ametek 1 | 20 | 19⅛ | 19½ | 19 | 19¼ | − ⅛ |
| 61⅛ | 42⅜ | AMP Inc .60 | 63 | 44¾ | 45¼ | 44½ | 44⅞ | + ⅝ |
| 27⅝ | 17 | Ampex Cp | 68 | 18⅜ | 18⅞ | 18⅜ | 18⅝ | + ¼ |
| 29½ | 15¾ | Amphenol .70 | 66 | 17 | 17¾ | 16¾ | 17⅜ | + ⅜ |
| 51⅞ | 36¼ | Amsted 2.20 | 17 | 39¾ | 40¾ | 39¾ | 40⅝ | +1⅛ |
| 110¼ | 65 | Anacon 3.25e | 149 | 75 | 76⅝ | 75 | 76 | +1¾ |
| 50½ | 40⅞ | AnchHG 1.40 | 10 | 49 | 49 | 48⅞ | 49 | + ⅛ |
| 92 | 81¼ | AnchHG pf 4 | z10 | 83½ | 83½ | 83½ | 83½ | +1 |
| 38¾ | 24 | Ander Clay 1 | 10 | 25⅝ | 26 | 25⅝ | 26 | + ¾ |
| 38⅜ | 9⅛ | Anken Chem | 28 | 9¼ | 9½ | 9¼ | 9¼ | + ⅛ |
| 23⅜ | 13 | Apco Oil .61t | 157 | 17½ | 18⅜ | 17⅜ | 17⅞ | + ½ |
| 47¼ | 33¼ | ArchDan 1.60 | 11 | 37 | 37⅛ | 36⅞ | 37 | + ⅛ |
| 35⅜ | 22⅝ | Ariz PSv .92 | 233 | 26 | 26⅞ | 26 | 26¾ | +1 |
| 27⅝ | 9⅝ | Arlans D Str | 71 | 10⅝ | 11 | 10⅝ | 11 | + ¼ |
| 72¼ | 45½ | ArmcoSt 3 | 117 | 47½ | 48⅞ | 47¼ | 48¼ | +1⅝ |
| 48 | 26¾ | Armour 1.60 | 58 | 28½ | 28⅝ | 28¼ | 28⅝ | + ⅛ |
| 89 | 72¼ | Armr pf 4.75 | 3 | 73¾ | 74 | 73½ | 74 | + ½ |

WEDNESDAY, OCT. 26, 1966

| Day's Sales | Tuesday | Year Ago | Year to Date 1966 | Year to Date 1965 |
|---|---|---|---|---|
| 6,760,000 | 6,190,000 | 7,670,000 | 1,568,976,818 | 1,195,733,051 |



Source: *The New York Times*, October 27, 1966.

**FIGURE 3–18B**

# *Market Place:* Defensive Issues Seen in Demand

**By ROBERT METZ**

RECENT stock market strength may not suggest that the bulls are back but rather that the smart money is searching for safe havens in the event of a recession.

This is the pitch of Indicater Digest, Inc., Palisades Park, N. J. The advisory service has analyzed the strong stocks in the Dow-Jones industrial average.

In its Oct. 25 letter, the Digest said that currently the 7 "bullish stocks" among the 30 in the index are considered to be in defensive industries—communications, food, soap, glass containers and oil. The stocks are American Telephone, General Foods, Procter & Gamble, Owens-Illinois, Standard Oil of California, Standard Oil (New Jersey) and Texaco.

On the other hand, the Digest says that every one of the index's 10 stocks showing a long-term bearish trend is in a cyclical industry. "The worst looking of the lot are du Pont, International Harvester, U. S. Steel and Chrysler," the Digest adds.

●

"This little X-ray of the internal cross currents inside the Dow-Jones industrial average tells us that a business recession is expected, while at the same time important money is flowing defensively into the type of stocks that are not customarily affected when business turns down," the article said.

"A month ago, we noted that only 4 of the top 15 [industry] groups were the type that depended on the business cycle. Now this has expanded into something we do not recall ever having seen before: Every one of the top 15 industry groups is a defensive one."

As of last weekend, the Digest notes, the industry groups ranked, in order: international oils, motion pictures, fire insurance, electric utilities, domestic oils, banks, cigarettes, soaps, telephone, life insurance, drugs, liquor, soft drinks, flour and natural gas utilities.

This confirms, the Digest said, that the stock market fears a business recession and that a significant shift of capital into recession-proof stocks of all varieties is taking place.

*

**Economic Dip Predicted**

Pierre A. Rinfret, head of the economic consulting firm of Lionel D. Edie & Co. who was once favorably mentioned by President Johnson, took issue yesterday with Washington's "politically inspired economic forecasts." Mr. Rinfret predicted a definite downturn in economic activity next year.

*

**Food Issues Perk Up**

Whether a recession threatens or not, it is clear that one leading group of defensive stocks—the food processors—has benefited from increased trader interest.

A new report on eight of these stocks by Charles A. Wetzel of Paine, Webber, Jackson & Curtis says that "top quality" stocks such as Borden, Corn Products and General Foods already have risen "15 per cent or more" from their 1966 lows.

The food processors are said to blend "strong basic demand, increasing diversification, aggressive marketing and new plant for increasing investor appeal."

Marian Sutta, food analyst for Blair & Co., will have a report in a few days on General Foods, Consolidated Foods and Pillsbury. Blair plans to analyze other food stocks in follow-up reports.

●

Food analysts say that the mild earnings improvements forecast for the food stocks are enough to draw investor interest now that many industrial stocks have palled and bond market yields are starting to drift lower. A year ago, investors tried to find industrial stocks that would show 50 per cent rises in earnings over a single year. Now the 5 to 10 per cent gains in profits anticipated for some food processors look attractive.

Here's Paine, Webber's list of eight food stocks. The brokerage house suggests Borden, General Foods and Corn Products for "top quality accounts." The others also "appear attractive for current purchase."

| | last price | 1966 range | 1965 earns | 1966* earns | '66P/E ratio |
|---|---|---|---|---|---|
| Borden | 33½ | 41-28 | $2.03 | $2.20 | 15 |
| Consol Fds. | 41⅛ | 49-39 | 2.46 | 2.80 | 15 |
| Cont Bak. | 42½ | 50-39 | 4.49 | 5.00 | 9 |
| Corn Food | 44¾ | 54-36 | 2.44 | 2.65 | 17 |
| Gen Fds. | 74½ | 83-63 | 3.73 | 4.00 | 19 |
| Green Giant. | 22 | 28-22 | 1.96 | 2.20 | 10 |
| Pepsi Co. | 67 | 87-55 | 3.21 | 3.60 | 19 |
| Pillsburg | 36 | 43-28 | 2.67 | 2.95 | |

Earnings for calendar years for all except Consolidated, whose fiscal year ends June 30; Gen. Foods, Mar. 31, and Pillsbury, May 31.
*Estimated.

The 1966 earnings estimates were taken from the report on the food stocks prepared by Paine, Webber.

*

**G.M.'s Dividend Outlook**

Now that General Motors has disappointed Wall Street with a 34-cents-a-share earnings report for the third quarter, observers are wondering if the industrial giant will drop the other brake shoe at the dividend meeting on Nov. 7.

The yearend dividend payment is traditionally G.M.'s largest. Hopes have been high that the payout this year would reach $4.50. G.M. has paid $3.05 so far this year, compared with $3 a share in the like period of 1965. The yearend payment of $2.25 last year brought shareholders a record $5.25 a share.

That was a 71 per cent payout on 1965's earnings of $7.41 a share, so 1966 dividends totaling $4.50 would be in line if the company earns the expected $6.25 a share.

The consensus seems to be that G.M. will pay a total of $4.50 even if 1966 earnings drop below $6.25 because G.M. has maintained a liberal dividend policy when earnings slipped in the past.

Meanwhile, the Capital Gains Research Bureau, Inc. of Larchmont, N. Y., said that initial reports showed that, in the third quarter, 10 funds sold 310,000 G.M. shares or about one-tenth of total Big Board volume in G.M. shares during the period.

Source: *The New York Times*, October 27, 1966.

**FIGURE 3–19A**

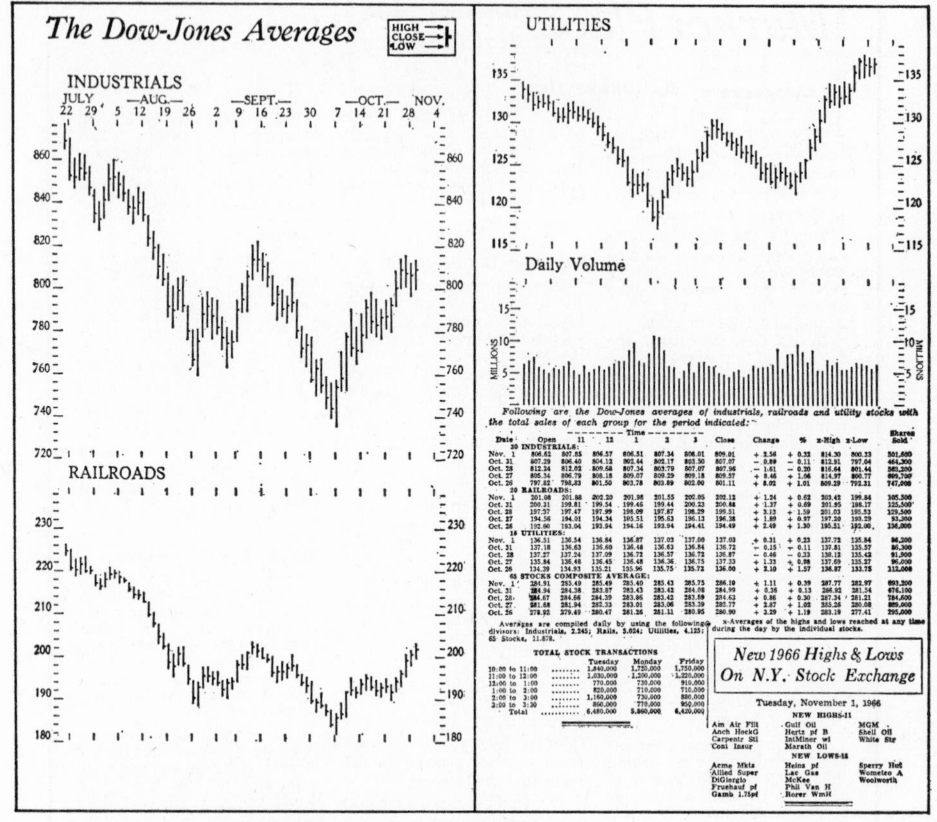


*Following are the Dow-Jones averages of industrials, railroads and utility stocks with the total sales of each group for the period indicated:*

| Date | Open | 11 | 12 | 1 | 2 | 3 | Close | Change | % | x-High | x-Low | Shares Sold |
|---|---|---|---|---|---|---|---|---|---|---|---|---|
| **30 INDUSTRIALS:** | | | | | | | | | | | | |
| Nov. 1 | 806.62 | 807.85 | 806.57 | 806.51 | 807.34 | 808.01 | 809.01 | + 2.56 | + 0.32 | 814.30 | 800.33 | 301,600 |
| Oct. 31 | 807.29 | 806.40 | 804.12 | 802.44 | 802.17 | 803.50 | 807.07 | – 0.89 | – 0.11 | 812.91 | 797.04 | 464,300 |
| Oct. 28 | 812.24 | 812.02 | 809.68 | 807.34 | 803.79 | 807.07 | 807.96 | – 1.61 | – 0.20 | 816.64 | 801.44 | 563,200 |
| Oct. 27 | 805.34 | 806.79 | 808.18 | 809.07 | 809.29 | 809.18 | 809.57 | + 8.46 | + 1.06 | 814.97 | 800.77 | 699,700 |
| Oct. 26 | 797.82 | 798.83 | 801.50 | 803.78 | 803.89 | 802.00 | 801.11 | + 8.02 | + 1.01 | 809.29 | 792.31 | 747,000 |
| **20 RAILROADS:** | | | | | | | | | | | | |
| Nov. 1 | 201.08 | 201.88 | 202.20 | 201.98 | 201.55 | 202.05 | 202.12 | + 1.24 | + 0.62 | 203.42 | 199.84 | 105,500 |
| Oct. 31 | 200.31 | 199.81 | 199.54 | 199.46 | 199.44 | 200.23 | 200.88 | + 1.37 | + 0.69 | 201.95 | 198.17 | 125,500 |
| Oct. 28 | 197.37 | 197.47 | 197.99 | 198.09 | 197.87 | 198.29 | 199.51 | + 3.13 | + 1.59 | 201.03 | 195.53 | 129,500 |
| Oct. 27 | 194.56 | 194.01 | 194.34 | 195.51 | 195.63 | 196.13 | 196.38 | + 1.89 | + 0.97 | 197.20 | 193.29 | 93,300 |
| Oct. 26 | 192.60 | 193.04 | 193.94 | 194.16 | 193.94 | 194.41 | 194.49 | + 2.49 | + 1.30 | 195.51 | 192.00 | 136,000 |
| **15 UTILITIES:** | | | | | | | | | | | | |
| Nov. 1 | 136.51 | 136.54 | 136.84 | 136.87 | 137.03 | 137.00 | 137.03 | + 0.31 | + 0.23 | 137.72 | 135.84 | 86,200 |
| Oct. 31 | 137.18 | 136.63 | 136.60 | 136.48 | 136.63 | 136.84 | 136.72 | – 0.15 | – 0.11 | 137.81 | 135.57 | 86,300 |
| Oct. 28 | 137.27 | 137.24 | 137.09 | 136.72 | 136.57 | 136.72 | 136.87 | – 0.46 | – 0.33 | 138.12 | 135.42 | 91,900 |
| Oct. 27 | 135.84 | 136.48 | 136.45 | 136.48 | 136.36 | 136.75 | 137.33 | + 1.33 | + 0.98 | 137.69 | 135.27 | 96,000 |
| Oct. 26 | 134.39 | 134.93 | 135.21 | 135.96 | 135.75 | 135.72 | 136.00 | + 2.10 | + 1.57 | 136.87 | 133.75 | 112,000 |
| **65 STOCKS COMPOSITE AVERAGE:** | | | | | | | | | | | | |
| Nov. 1 | 284.91 | 285.49 | 285.49 | 285.40 | 285.43 | 285.75 | 286.10 | + 1.11 | + 0.39 | 287.77 | 282.97 | 893,200 |
| Oct. 31 | 284.94 | 284.38 | 283.87 | 283.43 | 283.42 | 284.08 | 284.99 | + 0.36 | + 0.13 | 286.92 | 281.54 | 676,100 |
| Oct. 28 | 284.67 | 284.66 | 284.39 | 283.86 | 283.42 | 283.89 | 284.63 | + 0.86 | + 0.30 | 287.34 | 281.21 | 784,600 |
| Oct. 27 | 281.68 | 281.94 | 282.33 | 283.01 | 283.06 | 283.39 | 283.77 | + 2.87 | + 1.02 | 285.26 | 280.08 | 889,000 |
| Oct. 26 | 278.92 | 279.49 | 280.47 | 281.26 | 281.11 | 280.95 | 280.90 | + 3.29 | + 1.19 | 283.19 | 277.41 | 295,000 |

Averages are compiled daily by using the following divisors: Industrials, 2.245; Rails, 5.024; Utilities, 4.125; 65 Stocks, 11.878.

x-Averages of the highs and lows reached at any time during the day by the individual stocks.

**TOTAL STOCK TRANSACTIONS**

| | Tuesday | Monday | Friday |
|---|---|---|---|
| 10:00 to 11:00 | 1,840,000 | 1,720,000 | 1,750,000 |
| 11:00 to 12:00 | 1,030,000 | 1,200,000 | 1,220,000 |
| 12:00 to 1:00 | 770,000 | 730,000 | 910,000 |
| 1:00 to 2:00 | 820,000 | 710,000 | 710,000 |
| 2:00 to 3:00 | 1,160,000 | 730,000 | 880,000 |
| 3:00 to 3:30 | 860,000 | 770,000 | 950,000 |
| Total | 6,480,000 | 5,860,000 | 6,420,000 |

*New 1966 Highs & Lows On N.Y. Stock Exchange*

Tuesday, November 1, 1966

NEW HIGHS-11

Am Air Filt, Anch HockG, Carpentr Stl, Conl Insur, Gulf Oil, Hertz pf B, IntMiner wi, Marath Oil, MGM, Shell Oil, White Str

NEW LOWS-15

Acme Mkts, Allied Super, DiGiorgio, Fruehauf pf, Gamb 1.75pf, Heins pf, Lac Gas, McKee, Phil Van H, Rorer WmH, Sperry Hut, Wometco A, Woolworth

Source: *The Wall Street Journal*, November 2, 1966.

yields, composite price-earnings ratios, and the yield spread between stocks and bonds as market indicators. For example, the level of the market may be judged by yields on the Dow-Jones Industrials. At major bull market peaks in the past, the DJI and yields on its 30 stocks were as follows:

| Date | DJI | Yield |
|---|---|---|
| Sept. 3, 1929 | 381.17 | 3.33% |
| Mar. 10, 1937 | 194.40 | 3.76 |
| Nov. 12, 1938 | 158.41 | 3.56 |
| May 29, 1946 | 212.50 | 3.23 |
| Jan. 4, 1960 | 679.06 | 3.07 |
| Dec. 13, 1961 | 734.91 | 3.03 |
| Feb. 9, 1966 | 995.15 | 2.92 |

## FIGURE 3–19B

# Abreast of the Market

With glamor stocks in the lead, the stock market moved ahead yesterday afternoon across a fairly broad front. Trading picked up.

Airlines were particularly strong. The parade upward also included computer, housing, paper, rubber, steel and chemical stocks and some electronic and defense issues.

The Dow-Jones industrial average wavered during the morning and early afternoon between gains and losses of less than a point. At 2:30 p.m. it showed an advance of 1.00 and closed at 809.63, up 2.56, or 0.32%. The indicator was lowered 0.83 point by ex-dividends of Texaco, Union Carbide and U.S. Steel.

A greater percentage rise was registered by the railroad average, which closed at 202.12, up 1.24, or 0.62%. It was lowered yesterday 0.35 point by ex-dividends of Atlantic Coastline. The utility average gained 0.31, or 0.23%, to 137.03; an ex-dividend of Consolidated Edison lowered it 0.12 point.

Of the 1,400 stocks traded on the New York Stock Exchange, the gainers overshadowed the backsliders by a wide margin of 781 to 371.

Except for the second hour of the morning session, the Big Board trading pace yesterday topped Monday's level all day. The total was 6,480,000 shares, up from 5,860,000 the previous day.

Glamor stocks got a boost, brokers said, from news that the Dreyfus Fund, which had a large cash position a month ago, went heavily back into the market last month. Another factor in their rise, brokers added, is the large short position in many of these stocks. Many brokers regard big short positions—the amount of borrowed stock that has been sold and not yet replaced—as bullish since they regard it as potential demand for stock.

**Fear of Tax Rise Eases**

Analysts also said the fear of a tax increase next year is lessening. "We feel the jury is still out on a possible tax increase," commented one analyst. Another said, "There's an awareness any tax increase may not be as severe as had been expected earlier because of the perceptible slowdown in the economy."

The Big Board composite index rose 0.33 to 43.49. The American Stock Exchange indicator closed at $12.63, up nine cents.

Turnover on the American exchange also gained, to 1,520,000 shares from 1,230,000 Monday. More issues moved up than down.

Longer-term U.S. Government bonds and investment-quality corporates ended a quiet over-the-counter session mostly easier. State and city issues continued firm.

On the Big Board, 13 stocks touched lows for the year and 11 set highs.

Stocks that moved counter to the uptrend yesterday included some movie, retail and tobacco issues.

In the airline sector, Pan American World Airways headed the Big Board active list on turnover of 143,800 shares and climbed 2⅝ to 45⅝. It was helped by news that a White House emergency board recommended three 5% wage increases over an 18-month period for about 12,000 Pan Am mechanics, ground service workers and flight personnel; the recommendations of the board, appointed to avert a strike, are in line with wage increases won by the Transport Workers Union from American Airlines.

It was also announced yesterday that the State Department is expected to complete soon an agreement for direct flights between the U.S. and Russia.

In ninth place, United Air Lines gained 1¾ to 47. Also active, KLM Royal Dutch Airlines traded at 95¼ but ended at 103⅜, up 8¼; after the close the company reported its per-share earnings for the second quarter, ended Sept. 30, rose to $7.80 from $7.17 a year earlier. Eastern Air Lines, another active issue, jumped 4⅜ to 60⅞. Trans World advanced 3⅜ to 62⅛, National 3⅝ to 68½, Continental 4 to 57, American 2¼ to 53⅛, Delta 3⅜ to 100⅝ and Braniff 2¼ to 55¼.

**Aerospace Stocks Gain**

McDonnell Aircraft was second most active on turnover of 138,200 shares, most of which was a block of 129,600 shares at 25. The stock closed at 25¼, up ⅜. In sixth place, Boeing gained 2¾ to 51¼. On Monday the company reported third quarter profit per share slipped to 67 cents from $1.47 last year; brokers termed the report better than expected. Also the company was awarded a $235.8 million contract to develop and build the SRAM, an air-to-surface missile.

United Aircraft also was active on volume of 55,500 shares, of which 20,000 were a block at 64⅝. The stock closed at 64⅞, up 1½.

Among volatile stocks, Fairchild Camera was fourth most active and traded 97¼, but it ended at 102, up 3⅝. In seventh place, Itek touched 58⅝ and finished at 63⅝, up 4¾. Polaroid, an active issue, traded at 135 and closed at 139¾, up 5⅛. Xerox, another active issue, jumped 8¼ to 170¼. Sperry Rand, 10th most active, advanced 1⅜ to 24½. Texas Instruments rose 6⅛ to 102½, Motorola 8 to 106, Burroughs 4¾ to 66⅝ and SCM 3⅛ to 49½.

General Telephone gained ¾ to 45⅛. A block of 100,000 shares of the stock traded on the Pacific Coast Stock Exchange at 45 and another of the same size and at the same price traded on the Philadelphia-Baltimore-Washington Stock Exchange.

Gulf & Western Industries was in third place on turnover of 109,800 shares and rose 1⅝ to 25¼. The company recently completed the acquisition of Paramount Pictures. Metro-Goldwyn-Mayer hit a 1966 high of 35⅛ and finished at 34⅝, off ¼.

On the American exchange, Trans World Airlines warrants topped the active list on turnover of 67,600 and jumped 4 to 41¾.

Prentice-Hall gained 1¼ to 51¼ after climbing 3 on Monday. Directors yesterday boosted the dividend to 25 cents from 17 cents and declared a 2% stock dividend.

Audio Devices fell 2¾ to 18¼. The company yesterday declared a 2% stock dividend.

## Heard on the Street—

**Peabody Coal** and **Kennecott** have signed a letter of intent regarding the copper concern's previously announced plan to acquire the coal producer. A definitive contract is being developed, Peabody says. Since August Peabody has received orders for six million tons of coal to be supplied annually, bringing the total of new business thus far in 1966 to 12 million tons. . . . Third quarter sales of **Coleco Industries** (over the counter) were up about 150% from the like 1965 period to between $1,850,000 and $1,875,000, according to Leonard E. Greenberg, president of the manufacturer of recreational products and swimming pools. Net in the quarter rose more than 50% to between $70,000 and $75,000, or about 10 cents a share, from $48,590, or seven cents a share, he estimates. This would bring nine-month net up about 8% from the like 1965 period to around $1.05 a share on a rise in volume of about 35%. Both the third period and nine-month results were records, Mr. Greenberg says, and orders booked for 1967 spring and summer merchandise are running more than 25% ahead of the year-earlier high. . . . **Chrysler** has stopped building farmobils in Greece but isn't saying much about the step. It is believed the company is trying to get Greek government permission to build other vehicles at its Greek plant. Chrysler in 1963 bought the Greek company that builds the light-weight utility vehicle, hoping it would be a success in underdeveloped nations. . . . **Firestone Tire & Rubber**, symbol for which is FIR, and National Union Electric, identified by NUM, have been added to the Pacific Coast Stock Exchange list. . . . **Schlumberger**, with its symbol SLB, has been admitted to trading on the Boston Stock Exchange.

**MARKET DIARY**

| | Tues | Mon. | Fri. | Thur. | Wed. | Tues. |
|---|---|---|---|---|---|---|
| Issues traded | 1,400 | 1,420 | 1,426 | 1,433 | 1,430 | 1,421 |
| Advances | 781 | 583 | 702 | 809 | 890 | 596 |
| Declines | 371 | 568 | 489 | 410 | 310 | 549 |
| Unchanged | 248 | 269 | 235 | 214 | 230 | 276 |
| New highs, 1966 | 11 | 8 | 12 | 12 | 12 | 5 |
| New lows, 1966 | 13 | 15 | 32 | 22 | 23 | 54 |

**DOW-JONES CLOSING AVERAGES**

| | ----TUESDAY---- | | | |
|---|---|---|---|---|
| | 1966 | —Changes— | | 1965 |
| Industrials | 809.63 | +2.56 | +0.32% | Closed |
| Railroads | 202.12 | +1.24 | +0.62% | Closed |
| Utilities | 137.03 | +0.31 | +0.23% | Closed |
| Composite | 286.10 | +1.11 | +0.39% | Closed |

Ex-dividends of Texaco, Inc. 70 cents, Union Carbide Corp. 50 cents and United States Steel Corp. 60 cents lowered the Industrial Average by 0.83.

Ex-dividends of Atlantic Coastline Railroad Co. one dollar and seventy-five cents lowered the Rail Average by 0.35.

Ex-dividends of Consolidated Edison Co. of New York, Inc. 45 cents lowered the Utility Average by 0.12.

The above ex-dividends lowered the Composite Average by 0.35.

**OTHER MARKET INDICATORS**

| | 1966 | Change | 1965 |
|---|---|---|---|
| N. Y. S. E. Composite | 43.49 | +0.33 | Closed |
| Industrial | 42.94 | +0.37 | Closed |
| Utility | 45.53 | +0.04 | Closed |
| Transportation | 44.21 | +0.95 | Closed |
| Financial | 43.11 | +0.31 | Closed |
| Standard & Poor's Industrial | 85.84 | +0.69 | Closed |
| American Exchange Price Index | $12.63 | +$0.09 | Closed |
| N.Q.B. Over-Counter Industrial | 213.69 | −0.65 | Closed |

## Market Views—

OPINION: Leslie M. Pollack of Reynolds & Co. says, "The current market has turned around so swiftly that a pullback or consolidation area is badly needed at this time." . . . Aaron B. Feigen of Bregman, Cummings & Co. believes, "Once it becomes reasonably clear to the investor population at large that the sweeping emotional convulsions of the past six months have subsided, money again will begin to flow aggressively into sectors of the market according to merit. The trend will gather momentum over the next several weeks simply because the staying power of the rally will increasingly convince would-be investors who are now marking time on the sidelines that the stormy phase of the bear market cycle is behind." . . . Kenneth Ward of Hayden, Stone & Co. comments, "A policy of initiating strategic purchases of various issues that have declined to attractive technical and statistical levels, or succeeded in holding well during all recent selling squalls, seems a prudent one to follow at this point."

ANALYSIS: Piper, Jaffray & Hopwood, Minneapolis, has a report on **Donaldson** . . . Martin J. King of Auchincloss, Parker & Redpath on **Syntex** . . . Pennington, Colket & Co. on **Talon** . . . Loewi & Co., Milwaukee, on **Fabri-Tek** and **Time Insurance** . . . Hayden, Miller & Co., Cleveland, on **Mohawk Rubber** . . . Sincere & Co., Chicago, on **Zale** and brief comment on **Alloys Unlimited** and **Chicago Musical Instrument** . . . Aaron B. Feigen of Bregman, Cummings & Co. on **Lockheed** . . . C. S. McKee & Co., Pittsburgh, on **Pan American World Airways**

Source: *The Wall Street Journal*, November 2, 1966.

FIGURE 3–20

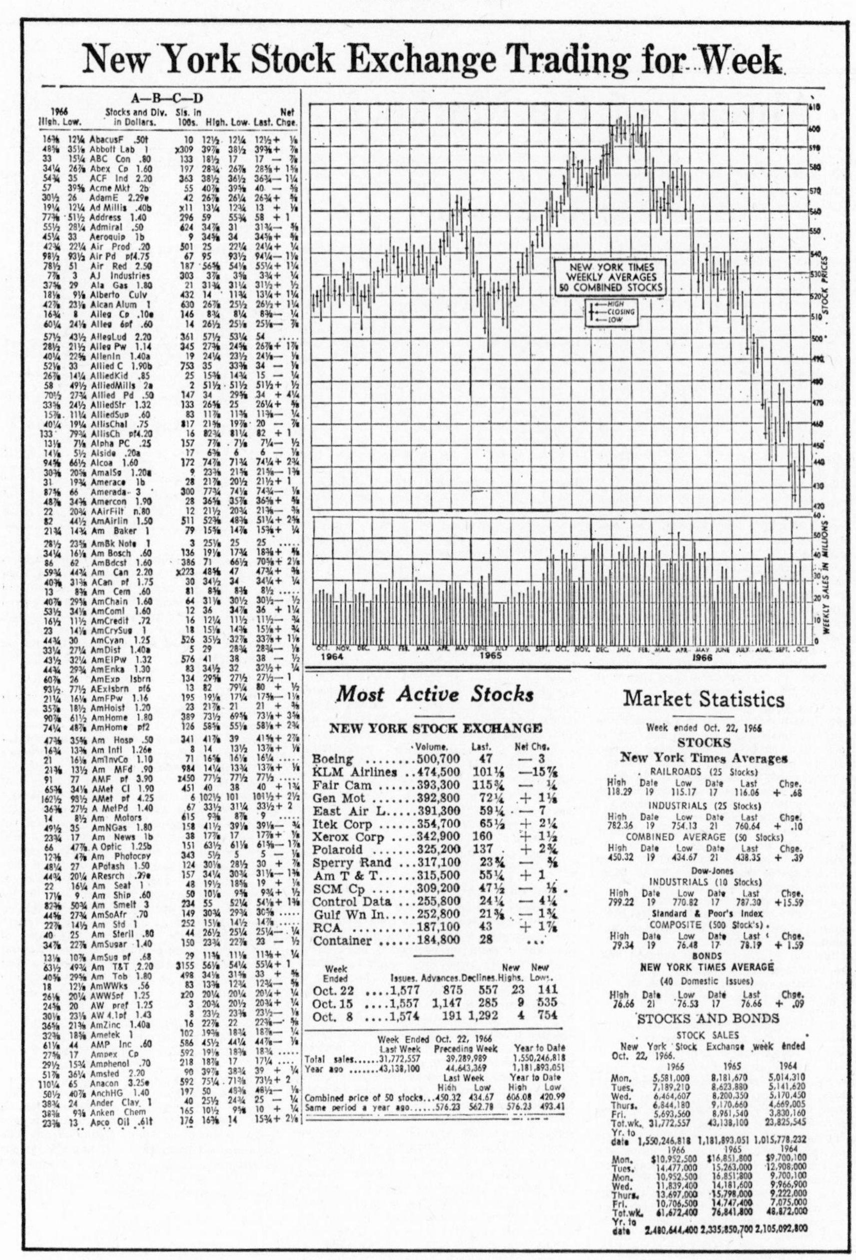


# New York Stock Exchange Trading for Week

## A—B—C—D

| 1966 High. | 1966 Low. | Stocks and Div. in Dollars. | Sls. in 100s. | High. | Low. | Last. | Net Chge. |
|---|---|---|---|---|---|---|---|
| 16⅜ | 12¼ | AbacusF .50t | 10 | 12½ | 12¼ | 12½ | + ⅛ |
| 48⅝ | 35⅛ | Abbott Lab 1 | x309 | 39⅞ | 38½ | 39⅜ | + ⅞ |
| 33 | 15¼ | ABC Con .80 | 133 | 18½ | 17 | 17 | — ⅞ |
| 34¼ | 26⅞ | Abex Cp 1.60 | 197 | 28¾ | 26⅞ | 28⅝ | + 1⅝ |
| 54¾ | 35 | ACF Ind 2.20 | 363 | 38½ | 36½ | 36¾ | — 1¼ |
| 57 | 39⅝ | Acme Mkt 2b | 55 | 40⅞ | 39⅝ | 40 | — ⅝ |
| 30½ | 26 | AdamE 2.29e | 42 | 26⅞ | 26¼ | 26¾ | + ⅝ |
| 19¼ | 12¼ | Ad Millis .40b | x11 | 13¼ | 12¾ | 13 | + ⅛ |
| 77⅜ | 51½ | Address 1.40 | 296 | 59 | 55¾ | 58 | + 1 |
| 55½ | 28¼ | Admiral .50 | 624 | 34⅞ | 31 | 31¾ | — ⅝ |
| 45¼ | 33 | Aeroquip 1b | 9 | 34⅝ | 34 | 34⅝ | + ⅝ |
| 42¾ | 22¼ | Air Prod .20 | 501 | 25 | 22¼ | 24¼ | + ¼ |
| 98½ | 93½ | Air Pd pf4.75 | 67 | 95 | 93½ | 94¼ | — 1⅛ |
| 78½ | 51 | Air Red 2.50 | 187 | 56⅝ | 54⅛ | 55¼ | + 1¼ |
| 7⅞ | 3 | AJ Industries | 303 | 3⅞ | 3⅝ | 3¾ | + ¼ |
| 37⅝ | 29 | Ala Gas 1.80 | 21 | 31¾ | 31¼ | 31½ | + ½ |
| 18⅛ | 9⅛ | Alberto Culv | 432 | 14 | 11¾ | 13¼ | + 1¼ |
| 42⅞ | 23⅛ | Alcan Alum 1 | 630 | 26⅞ | 25½ | 26½ | + 1¼ |
| 16¾ | 8 | Alleg Cp .10e | 146 | 8¾ | 8¼ | 8⅜ | — ¼ |
| 60¼ | 24⅛ | Alleg 6pf .60 | 14 | 26½ | 25⅛ | 25⅛ | — ⅞ |
| 57½ | 43½ | AllegLud 2.20 | 361 | 57½ | 53¼ | 54 | ..... |
| 28½ | 21½ | Alleg Pw 1.14 | 345 | 27⅜ | 24⅝ | 26⅞ | + 1⅞ |
| 40¼ | 22⅝ | AllenIn 1.40a | 19 | 24¼ | 23½ | 24⅛ | — ⅛ |
| 52⅛ | 33 | Allied C 1.90b | 753 | 35 | 33⅜ | 34 | — ⅛ |
| 26⅞ | 14¼ | AlliedKid .85 | 25 | 15⅜ | 14¾ | 15 | — ¼ |
| 58 | 49½ | AlliedMills 2a | 2 | 51½ | 51½ | 51½ | + ½ |
| 70½ | 27¾ | Allied Pd .50 | 147 | 34 | 29⅝ | 34 | + 4¼ |
| 33⅝ | 24½ | AlliedStr 1.32 | 133 | 26⅝ | 25 | 26¼ | + ⅝ |
| 15⅞ | 11¼ | AlliedSup .60 | 83 | 11⅞ | 11⅜ | 11⅜ | — ¼ |
| 40¼ | 19¼ | AllisChal .75 | 817 | 21⅝ | 19⅞ | 20 | — ⅞ |
| 133 | 79¾ | AllisCh pf4.20 | 16 | 82¾ | 81¼ | 82 | + 1 |
| 13⅛ | 7⅛ | Alpha PC .25 | 157 | 7⅞ | 7⅛ | 7¼ | — ½ |
| 14⅛ | 5½ | Alside .20a | 17 | 6⅜ | 6 | 6 | — ⅛ |
| 94⅝ | 66½ | Alcoa 1.60 | 172 | 74⅞ | 71¾ | 74¼ | + 2¾ |
| 30⅜ | 20⅝ | AmalSg 1.20a | 9 | 23⅜ | 21⅝ | 21⅝ | — 1⅜ |
| 31 | 19¾ | Amerace 1b | 28 | 21⅞ | 20½ | 21½ | + 1 |
| 87⅝ | 66 | Amerada 3 | 300 | 77¾ | 74⅛ | 74¾ | — ⅛ |
| 48⅞ | 34⅜ | Amercon 1.90 | 28 | 36⅝ | 35⅞ | 36⅝ | + ⅝ |
| 22 | 20¾ | AAirFilt n.80 | 12 | 21½ | 20¾ | 21⅜ | — ⅜ |
| 82 | 44½ | AmAirlin 1.50 | 511 | 52⅜ | 48⅜ | 51¼ | + 2⅝ |
| 21¾ | 14¾ | Am Baker 1 | 79 | 15⅝ | 14⅞ | 15⅜ | + ¼ |
| 28½ | 23⅝ | AmBk Note 1 | 3 | 25⅛ | 25 | 25 | ..... |
| 34¼ | 16⅛ | Am Bosch .60 | 136 | 19⅛ | 17¾ | 18⅜ | + ⅝ |
| 86 | 62 | AmBdcst 1.60 | 386 | 71 | 66½ | 70⅝ | + 2⅛ |
| 59¾ | 44¾ | Am Can 2.20 | x223 | 48⅝ | 47 | 47¾ | + ⅜ |
| 40⅜ | 31⅜ | ACan pf 1.75 | 30 | 34½ | 34 | 34¼ | + ¼ |
| 13 | 8⅜ | Am Cem .60 | 81 | 8⅝ | 8⅜ | 8½ | ..... |
| 40⅞ | 29⅝ | AmChain 1.60 | 64 | 31⅛ | 30½ | 30½ | — ½ |
| 53½ | 34⅛ | AmComl 1.60 | 12 | 36 | 34⅞ | 36 | + 1¼ |
| 16½ | 11½ | AmCredit .72 | 16 | 12¼ | 11½ | 11½ | — ¾ |
| 23 | 14⅛ | AmCrySug 1 | 18 | 15⅛ | 14⅜ | 15⅛ | + ¾ |
| 44¾ | 30 | AmCyan 1.25 | 526 | 35½ | 32⅞ | 33⅞ | + 1⅛ |
| 33¼ | 27¼ | AmDist 1.40a | 5 | 29 | 28¾ | 28¾ | — ⅛ |
| 43½ | 32¼ | AmElPw 1.32 | 576 | 41 | 38 | 38 | — ½ |
| 44¾ | 29¾ | AmEnka 1.30 | 83 | 34½ | 32 | 32½ | + ¼ |
| 60⅞ | 26 | AmExp Isbrn | 134 | 29⅝ | 27½ | 27½ | — 1 |
| 93½ | 77½ | AExIsbrn pf6 | 13 | 82 | 79¼ | 80 | + ½ |
| 21¼ | 16⅛ | AmFPw 1.16 | 195 | 19⅛ | 17¼ | 17⅝ | — 1⅛ |
| 35⅞ | 18½ | AmHoist 1.20 | 23 | 21⅞ | 21 | 21 | + ⅜ |
| 90⅞ | 61½ | AmHome 1.80 | 389 | 73½ | 69⅝ | 73⅛ | + 3⅝ |
| 74¼ | 48⅞ | AmHome pf2 | 126 | 58⅝ | 55⅛ | 58⅛ | + 2¾ |
| 47⅜ | 35⅝ | Am Hosp .50 | 341 | 41⅞ | 39 | 41⅝ | + 2⅞ |
| 16¾ | 13⅜ | Am Intl 1.26e | 8 | 14 | 13½ | 13⅞ | + ⅛ |
| 21 | 16⅛ | AmInvCo 1.10 | 71 | 16⅝ | 16⅛ | 16¼ | ..... |
| 21⅜ | 13½ | Am MFd .90 | 984 | 14¼ | 13¾ | 13⅞ | + ⅛ |
| 91 | 77 | AMF pf 3.90 | z450 | 77½ | 77½ | 77½ | ..... |
| 65⅜ | 34⅛ | AMet Cl 1.90 | 451 | 40 | 38 | 40 | + 1¾ |
| 162½ | 98½ | AMet pf 4.25 | 6 | 102½ | 101 | 101½ | + 2½ |
| 36⅜ | 27½ | A MetPd 1.40 | 67 | 33½ | 31¼ | 33½ | + 2 |
| 14 | 8½ | Am Motors | 615 | 9⅜ | 8⅞ | 9 | ..... |
| 49½ | 35 | AmNGas 1.80 | 158 | 41½ | 39⅛ | 39⅛ | — ¾ |
| 23¾ | 17 | Am News 1b | 38 | 17⅞ | 17 | 17⅞ | + ⅛ |
| 66 | 47⅞ | A Optic 1.25b | 151 | 63½ | 61⅛ | 61⅝ | — 1⅞ |
| 12⅜ | 4⅞ | Am Photocpy | 343 | 5½ | 5 | 5 | — ⅛ |
| 48¼ | 27 | APotash 1.50 | 124 | 30⅛ | 28½ | 30 | + ⅞ |
| 44¾ | 20¼ | AResrch .29e | 157 | 34¼ | 30¾ | 31⅛ | — 1⅜ |
| 22 | 16¼ | Am Seat 1 | 48 | 19½ | 18⅝ | 19 | + ⅛ |
| 17⅛ | 9 | Am Ship .60 | 50 | 10⅛ | 9⅝ | 9¾ | + ½ |
| 82⅜ | 50¾ | Am Smelt 3 | 234 | 55 | 52¼ | 54⅛ | + 1⅜ |
| 44⅝ | 27¾ | AmSoAfr .70 | 149 | 30¾ | 29¾ | 30⅝ | ..... |
| 22⅞ | 14½ | Am Std 1 | 252 | 15⅛ | 14½ | 14⅞ | ..... |
| 40 | 25 | Am Sterll .80 | 44 | 26½ | 25¼ | 25¼ | — ¼ |
| 34⅞ | 22⅞ | AmSugar 1.40 | 150 | 23¾ | 22⅞ | 23 | — ½ |
| 13⅛ | 10⅞ | AmSug pf .68 | 29 | 11⅜ | 11⅛ | 11⅜ | + ¼ |
| 63½ | 49¾ | Am T&T 2.20 | 3155 | 56⅛ | 54¼ | 55¼ | + 1 |
| 40⅝ | 29⅝ | Am Tob 1.80 | 498 | 34⅛ | 31⅝ | 33 | + ⅝ |
| 18 | 12⅛ | AmWWks .56 | 83 | 13⅜ | 12¾ | 12¾ | — ⅝ |
| 26⅛ | 20¼ | AWW5pf 1.25 | z20 | 20¼ | 20¼ | 20¼ | + ¼ |
| 24⅝ | 20 | AW pref 1.25 | 3 | 20¾ | 20½ | 20¾ | + ¼ |
| 30⅛ | 23⅛ | AW 4.1pf 1.43 | 8 | 23½ | 23⅜ | 23½ | — ⅛ |
| 36⅝ | 21⅜ | AmZinc 1.40a | 16 | 22⅞ | 22 | 22⅜ | — ⅝ |
| 32⅜ | 18⅝ | Ametek 1 | 102 | 19⅜ | 18¾ | 18⅞ | — ¼ |
| 61⅛ | 44 | AMP Inc .60 | 586 | 45½ | 44¼ | 44⅞ | — ⅛ |
| 27⅝ | 17 | Ampex Cp | 592 | 19⅛ | 18⅜ | 18¾ | ..... |
| 29½ | 15¾ | Amphenol .70 | 218 | 18⅞ | 17 | 17¼ | .... |
| 51⅞ | 36¼ | Amsted 2.20 | 90 | 39⅞ | 38¾ | 39 | + ¼ |
| 110¼ | 65 | Anacon 3.25e | 592 | 75¼ | 71⅜ | 73½ | + 2 |
| 50½ | 40⅞ | AnchHG 1.40 | 197 | 50 | 48⅜ | 48½ | — ⅛ |
| 38¾ | 24 | Ander Clay 1 | 40 | 25½ | 24¾ | 25 | — ¼ |
| 38⅜ | 9⅜ | Anken Chem | 165 | 10½ | 9⅝ | 10 | + ¼ |
| 23⅜ | 13 | Apco Oil .61t | 176 | 16⅜ | 14 | 15¾ | + 2⅛ |

## Most Active Stocks

**NEW YORK STOCK EXCHANGE**

| | Volume. | Last. | Net Chg. |
|---|---|---|---|
| Boeing | 500,700 | 47 | — 3 |
| KLM Airlines | 474,500 | 101¼ | —15⅞ |
| Fair Cam | 393,300 | 115¾ | — ¼ |
| Gen Mot | 392,800 | 72¾ | + 1⅛ |
| East Air L. | 391,300 | 59¼ | — 7 |
| Itek Corp | 354,700 | 65½ | + 2¼ |
| Xerox Corp | 342,900 | 160 | + 1½ |
| Polaroid | 325,200 | 137 | + 2¾ |
| Sperry Rand | 317,100 | 23¾ | — ⅝ |
| Am T & T | 315,500 | 55¼ | + 1 |
| SCM Cp | 309,200 | 47½ | — ⅛ |
| Control Data | 255,800 | 24¼ | — 4¼ |
| Gulf Wn In. | 252,800 | 21⅜ | — 1¾ |
| RCA | 187,100 | 43 | + 1⅞ |
| Container | 184,800 | 28 | ... |

| Week Ended | Issues. | Advances. | Declines. | New Highs. | New Lows. |
|---|---|---|---|---|---|
| Oct. 22 | 1,577 | 875 | 557 | 23 | 141 |
| Oct. 15 | 1,557 | 1,147 | 285 | 9 | 535 |
| Oct. 8 | 1,574 | 191 | 1,292 | 4 | 754 |

| | Week Ended Oct. 22, 1966 Last Week | | Preceding Week | | Year to Date | |
|---|---|---|---|---|---|---|
| Total sales | 31,772,557 | | 39,289,989 | | 1,550,246,818 | |
| Year ago | 43,138,100 | | 44,643,369 | | 1,181,893,051 | |
| | Last Week High | Last Week Low | | | Year to Date High | Year to Date Low |
| Combined price of 50 stocks | 450.32 | 434.67 | | | 606.08 | 420.99 |
| Same period a year ago | 576.23 | 562.78 | | | 576.23 | 493.41 |

## Market Statistics

Week ended Oct. 22, 1966

**STOCKS**

**New York Times Averages**

RAILROADS (25 Stocks)

| High | Date | Low | Date | Last | Chge. |
|---|---|---|---|---|---|
| 118.29 | 19 | 115.17 | 17 | 116.06 | + .68 |

INDUSTRIALS (25 Stocks)

| High | Date | Low | Date | Last | Chge. |
|---|---|---|---|---|---|
| 782.36 | 19 | 754.13 | 21 | 760.64 | + .10 |

COMBINED AVERAGE (50 Stocks)

| High | Date | Low | Date | Last | Chge. |
|---|---|---|---|---|---|
| 450.32 | 19 | 434.67 | 21 | 438.35 | + .39 |

Dow-Jones
INDUSTRIALS (10 Stocks)

| High | Date | Low | Date | Last | Chge. |
|---|---|---|---|---|---|
| 799.22 | 19 | 770.82 | 17 | 787.30 | +15.59 |

Standard & Poor's Index
COMPOSITE (500 Stock's)

| High | Date | Low | Date | Last | Chge. |
|---|---|---|---|---|---|
| 79.34 | 19 | 76.48 | 17 | 78.19 | + 1.59 |

**BONDS**

NEW YORK TIMES AVERAGE
(40 Domestic Issues)

| High | Date | Low | Date | Last | Chge. |
|---|---|---|---|---|---|
| 76.66 | 21 | 76.53 | 17 | 76.66 | + .09 |

**STOCKS AND BONDS**

STOCK SALES

New York Stock Exchange week ended Oct. 22, 1966.

| | 1966 | 1965 | 1964 |
|---|---|---|---|
| Mon. | 5,581,000 | 8,181,670 | 5,014,310 |
| Tues. | 7,189,210 | 8,623,880 | 5,141,620 |
| Wed. | 6,464,607 | 8,200,350 | 5,170,450 |
| Thurs. | 6,844,180 | 9,170,660 | 4,669,005 |
| Fri. | 5,693,560 | 8,961,540 | 3,830,160 |
| Tot.wk. | 31,772,557 | 43,138,100 | 23,825,545 |
| Yr. to date | 1,550,246,818 | 1,181,893,051 | 1,015,778,232 |

| | 1966 | 1965 | 1964 |
|---|---|---|---|
| Mon. | $10,952,500 | $16,851,800 | $9,700,100 |
| Tues. | 14,477,000 | 15,263,000 | 12,908,000 |
| Mon. | 10,952,500 | 16,851,800 | 9,700,100 |
| Wed. | 11,839,400 | 14,181,600 | 9,966,900 |
| Thurs. | 13,697,000 | 15,798,000 | 9,222,000 |
| Fri. | 10,706,500 | 14,747,400 | 7,075,000 |
| Tot.wk. | 61,672,400 | 76,841,800 | 48,872,000 |
| Yr. to date | 2,480,644,400 | 2,335,850,700 | 2,105,092,800 |

Source: *The New York Times*, Sunday, October 23, 1966.

FIGURE 3–21

# STUDY OF PRICE MOVEMENT • MARKET LABORATORY

## Dow-Jones Hourly Averages

30 Industrials

| Nov. | 14 | 15 | 16 | 17 | 18 |
|---|---|---|---|---|---|
| Opening | 819.26 | 812.58 | 818.26 | 821.77 | 813.58 |
| 11:00 | 817.20 | 812.52 | 820.71 | 820.76 | 811.30 |
| 12:00 | 813.68 | 812.63 | 820.26 | 816.98 | 810.74 |
| 1:00 | 812.30 | 813.58 | 819.20 | 812.19 | 811.63 |
| 2:00 | 812.08 | 813.47 | 819.87 | 814.42 | 810.96 |
| 3:00 | 812.19 | 815.36 | 821.93 | 816.20 | 810.46 |
| Close | 813.75 | 815.31 | 820.87 | 816.03 | 809.40 |
| High(h) | 823.10 | 819.48 | 827.33 | 825.61 | 817.81 |
| Low(h) | 808.29 | 808.12 | 812.69 | 808.90 | 804.95 |
| Change | —5.34 | +1.56 | +5.56 | —4.84 | —6.63 |

Wk's net chg. —9.69(h)High 827.33 Low 804.95

20 Railroads

| Nov. | 14 | 15 | 16 | 17 | 18 |
|---|---|---|---|---|---|
| Opening | 201.08 | 200.61 | 205.56 | 208.30 | 205.04 |
| 11:00 | 200.71 | 200.63 | 206.50 | 207.92 | 204.84 |
| 12:00 | 200.61 | 201.58 | 207.10 | 207.47 | 204.94 |
| 1:00 | 200.38 | 202.03 | 207.47 | 205.48 | 205.09 |
| 2:00 | 200.16 | 202.30 | 207.37 | 205.73 | 204.94 |
| 3:00 | 200.33 | 203.37 | 207.47 | 206.16 | 204.39 |
| Close | 200.56 | 204.14 | 208.79 | 205.73 | 202.77 |
| High(h) | 201.95 | 204.64 | 209.51 | 209.09 | 206.01 |
| Low(h) | 199.41 | 199.89 | 204.81 | 204.21 | 202.95 |
| Change | +0.03 | +3.58 | +4.65 | —3.06 | —1.96 |

Wk's net chg. —3.24(h)High 209.51 Low 199.41

15 Utilities

| Nov. | 14 | 15 | 16 | 17 | 18 |
|---|---|---|---|---|---|
| Opening | 137.75 | 136.90 | 137.42 | 137.57 | 137.15 |
| 11:00 | 137.81 | 136.93 | 137.84 | 137.45 | 137.24 |
| 12:00 | 137.21 | 137.15 | 137.90 | 137.27 | 137.03 |
| 1:00 | 137.48 | 137.09 | 137.90 | 136.96 | 136.90 |
| 2:00 | 137.39 | 137.12 | 137.87 | 137.15 | 136.84 |
| 3:00 | 137.33 | 137.24 | 137.81 | 137.30 | 136.90 |
| Close | 137.33 | 137.09 | 137.66 | 137.33 | 136.84 |
| High(h) | 138.63 | 137.96 | 138.78 | 138.27 | 138.06 |
| Low(h) | 136.39 | 136.24 | 136.54 | 136.42 | 136.06 |
| Change | —0.21 | —0.24 | +0.57 | —0.33 | —0.49 |

Wk's net chg. —0.70(h)High 138.78 Low 136.06

65 Stocks Composite Average

| Nov. | 14 | 15 | 16 | 17 | 18 |
|---|---|---|---|---|---|
| Opening | 287.73 | 285.98 | 289.32 | 291.20 | 288.12 |
| 11:00 | 287.21 | 285.99 | 290.33 | 290.81 | 287.64 |
| 12:00 | 286.29 | 286.48 | 290.52 | 289.84 | 287.50 |
| 1:00 | 286.03 | 286.83 | 290.48 | 287.99 | 287.69 |
| 2:00 | 285.89 | 286.93 | 290.55 | 288.57 | 287.48 |
| 3:00 | 285.93 | 287.79 | 290.96 | 289.14 | 287.18 |
| Close | 286.32 | 288.05 | 291.27 | 288.94 | 286.69 |
| High(h) | 289.13 | 289.35 | 293.18 | 292.50 | 289.65 |
| Low(h) | 284.48 | 284.60 | 287.65 | 286.64 | 285.23 |
| Change | —1.08 | +1.73 | +3.22 | —2.33 | —2.25 |

Wk's net chg. —0.71(h)High 293.18 Low 284.48

(h)-Averages of the highs and lows reached at any time during the day by the individual stocks.

### Shares Traded on N. Y. Exchange

Thous. shares

| | | | | | |
|---|---|---|---|---|---|
| 10-11 | 1,920 | 1,790 | 2,750 | 2,400 | 1,860 |
| 11-12 | 1,250 | 1,250 | 2,050 | 1,430 | 1,310 |
| 12-1 | 910 | 1,310 | 1,580 | 1,780 | 1,000 |
| 1-2 | 720 | 800 | 1,000 | 1,100 | 880 |
| 2-3 | 920 | 1,160 | 1,570 | 1,130 | 1,020 |
| 3-3:30 | 820 | 880 | 1,400 | 990 | 830 |
| Total | 6,540 | 7,190 | 10,350 | 8,900 | 6,900 |

Ratio of 10 Most Active Stocks to total trading, % of total.

| | | | | |
|---|---|---|---|---|
| 13.07 | 12.18 | 13.77 | 17.61 | 17.93 |

Average closings of 10 Most Active Stocks.

| | | | | |
|---|---|---|---|---|
| 42.81 | 50.19 | 44.31 | 52.95 | 60.49 |

By Groups-Thous. shares

| | | | | | |
|---|---|---|---|---|---|
| 30 Ind | 509.4 | 501.7 | 752.8 | 646.9 | 597.3 |
| 20 RR | 108.1 | 122.6 | 161.7 | 110.0 | 83.4 |
| 15 Util | 83.6 | 86.4 | 104.5 | 84.7 | 104.3 |
| 65 Stocks | 701.1 | [illegible]9.7 | 1,019.0 | 841.6 | 785.0 |

## Dow-Jones Weekly Averages

Stock Averages

| | First | High | Low | Last | Changes |
|---|---|---|---|---|---|
| Inds | 813.75 | 820.87 | 809.40 | 809.40 | — 9.69 |
| Rails | 200.56 | 208.79 | 200.56 | 203.77 | + 3.24 |
| Utils | 137.33 | 137.66 | 136.84 | 136.84 | — 0.70 |
| 65 Stks | 286.32 | 291.27 | 286.32 | 286.69 | — 0.71 |
| Bond Averages | | | | | |
| 40 Bonds | 80.84 | 80.84 | 80.48 | 80.48 | — 0.41 |
| 1st RRs | 72.63 | 72.63 | 72.20 | 72.20 | — 0.54 |
| 2nd RRs | 81.08 | 81.08 | 80.61 | 80.70 | — 0.24 |
| Utils | 82.55 | 82.55 | 82.15 | 82.21 | — 0.53 |
| Inds | 87.08 | 87.20 | 86.68 | 86.78 | — 0.36 |
| Inc RRs | 69.51 | 69.58 | 69.10 | 69.10 | — 0.48 |

### Dow-Jones Averages for 1966

| | Open | High | Low | Last | Chg. | % |
|---|---|---|---|---|---|---|
| 30 Inds | 967.87 | 995.15 | 744.32 | 809.40 | —159.86 | 16.49 |
| 20 RRs | 247.66 | 271.72 | 184.34 | 203.77 | — 43.71 | 17.66 |
| 15 Utils | 151.96 | 152.39 | 118.96 | 136.84 | — 15.79 | 10.34 |
| 65 Stks | 340.46 | 352.40 | 261.27 | 286.69 | — 54.19 | 15.90 |

### Other Market Indicators

| Nov. | 14 | 15 | 16 | 17 | 18 |
|---|---|---|---|---|---|
| N.Y.S.E. | | | | | |
| Comp. | 43.92 | 44.08 | 44.46 | 44.16 | 43.89 |
| Ind. | 43.47 | 43.62 | 44.03 | 43.73 | 43.46 |
| Util. | 45.52 | 45.48 | 45.67 | 45.44 | 46.07 |
| Tran. | 45.52 | 46.49 | 47.49 | 46.62 | 45.19 |
| Fin. | 43.22 | 43.28 | 43.57 | 43.59 | 43.46 |
| A.S.E. Index-$ | 13.01 | 13.10 | 13.25 | 13.18 | 13.16 |
| S&P 425 Ind. | 86.52 | 86.89 | 87.61 | 87.00 | 86.39 |
| 500 Comp. | 81.37 | 81.69 | 82.37 | 81.80 | 81.26 |
| N.Q.B. Ind. | 222.01 | 221.22 | 223.20 | 222.95 | 224.65 |
| Ins. | 76.43 | 76.51 | 76.70 | 76.68 | 76.03 |

### Dow-Jones Price-Earnings Ratio

| | Nov. 18 1966 | Oct. 18 1966 | Nov. 18 1965 | Nov. 18 1964 |
|---|---|---|---|---|
| Industrials | E-14.4 | E-14.1 | 18.7 | 20.1 |
| Railroads | 9.6 | 9.2 | 15.6 | 14.7 |
| Utilities | 15.6 | 15.2 | 19.4 | 21.4 |

Average per share earnings for 12 months ended June 30. E-Estimated.

### N. Y. Stock Exchange Volume Trends

| Date | Upside (Shares) | Downside (Shares) |
|---|---|---|
| November 14 | 2,040,000 | 3,570,000 |
| 15 | 4,310,000 | 2,260,000 |
| 16 | 7,760,000 | 1,640,000 |
| 17 | 1,800,000 | 5,980,000 |
| 18 | 2,300,000 | 3,940,000 |

Supplied by QUOTRON, Financial Information Service.

### N. Y. Exchange Monthly Figures

| | Latest period | Preceding period | Year ago |
|---|---|---|---|
| Stock vol, mil sh Oct. | 146.383 | 120.163 | 164.199 |
| Bond vol, mil $ Oct. | 286.548 | 232.942 | 290.837 |
| Security sales: | | | |
| All reg exch mil $ Aug. | 9,969 | 8,556 | 6,246 |
| Mem Lns mil $ (t) Sept. | 3,434 | 3,676 | 3,522 |
| Debit Bal mil $ Sept. | 5,355 | 5,610 | 4,994 |
| Credit bal. mil $ Sept. | 1,529 | 1,595 | 1,369 |
| Val listed stks, bil $ Oct. | 475.2 | 454.9 | 532.8 |
| Mkt lstd sls, mil $ Aug. | 7,805 | 6,655 | 4,937 |
| Short Int. th shs (d) Nov. | 14,135 | 12,604 | 9,883 |
| Ratio to d'ly vol (d) Nov. | 2.09 | 1.99 | 1.34 |
| NYSE seat sls th $ Nov. 18 | 200 | 200 | 220 |

(d)-For period Oct. 14 to Nov. 15. r-Revised. t-Excluding government bond loans.

## Week's Market Statistics

| Shares traded, thous: | Last week | Prev. week | Last year |
|---|---|---|---|
| Total sales NYSE | 39,915 | 30,113 | 39,717 |
| Total sales ASE | 10,169 | 7,810 | 15,831 |
| Dow-Jones groups: | | | |
| 65 Stks, th shs | 4,057 | 2,988 | 3,412 |
| 30 Ind, th shs | 3,008 | 2,272 | 2,621 |
| 20 RR, th shs | 586 | 337 | 352 |
| 15 Util, th shs | 463 | 379 | 439 |
| 20 Most Active Stocks: | | | |
| Average price | 56.01 | 53.68 | 40.86 |
| Ratio vol to tot vol, % | 18.84 | 17.75 | 21.00 |
| 20 Low Priced Stocks-v: | | | |
| Index | 194.0 | 191.5 | 207.3 |
| Volume, th shs | 551.0 | 350.4 | 742.7 |
| % of vol to D-J Ind vol | 19.06 | 14.92 | 26.70 |
| Odd-lot trading, week ended Oct. 28: | | | |
| Purchases, th shs | 2,132 | 2,175 | 2,481 |
| Purchases, th $ | 95,733 | 103,468 | 131,563 |
| Sales, th shs z | 1,791 | 1,713 | 2,654 |
| Sales, th $ z | 84,685 | 85,244 | 135,349 |
| Short sales, no shs | 100,727 | 114,527 | 32,517 |
| Member trading, week ended Oct. 28: | | | |
| % total | 24.36 | 24.02 | 22.81 |
| Purchases, th shs | 8,038.8 | 7,749.3 | 8,431.0 |
| Sales, th shs-z | 7,766.6 | 7,600.0 | 8,000.4 |
| Short sales, th shs | 2,055.6 | 2,107.0 | 1,804.2 |
| For week ended Friday: | | | |
| Bond vol, NYSE, th $ | 69,124 | 56,072 | 69,083 |
| Brokers' loans mil $-nw | 1,464 | 1,535 | 1,920 |
| Bond offerings, th $ | 370,110 | 32,750 | 371,605 |
| Stock offerings th $ | 10,703 | 34,750 | 73,670 |
| Bk clrgs, NYC, mil $-v | 26,987 | 25,942 | 30,135 |
| Barron's 10 Hi-Gr bond yields-v | 5.38 | 5.38 | 4.64 |
| Spread between yields for Barron's Hi-Gr Bonds & D-J Ind Stk Avg. | —1.64 | —1.65 | —1.61 |
| Ratio to D-J 40 Bonds (Confidence Index) | 92.9 | 93.6 | 96.5 |
| Prices and Yields (which include stock dividends) on Dow-Jones Averages: | | | |
| 30 Ind | 809.40 | 819.09 | 952.72 |
| 30 Ind, % | 3.74 | 3.73 | 3.03 |
| 30 Ind, % (cash only) | 3.68 | 3.68 | 2.97 |
| 20 RR | 203.77 | 200.53 | 237.08 |
| 20 RR,% | 5.60 | 5.69 | 4.28 |
| 15 Util | 136.84 | 137.54 | 156.81 |
| 15 Util, % | 4.08 | 4.06 | 3.27 |
| 40 Bonds, %-v | 5.79 | 5.75 | 4.81 |
| 10 Hi Gr, %-v | 5.63 | 5.61 | 4.86 |
| 10 2d Gr, %-v | 6.24 | 6.22 | 5.16 |
| 10 Ind, %-v | 5.61 | 5.54 | 4.55 |
| 10 Util, %-v | 5.67 | 5.62 | 4.67 |
| Municipal Bond, yield, % | 3.96 | 3.85 | 3.51 |

n-N. Y. City, excluding government bond loans. v-Week ended Thursday. w-Week ended Wednesday. z-Includes short sales.

### Foreign Stock Indexes

| | 1966 High | 1966 Low | Close Nov. 18 | Week's Change |
|---|---|---|---|---|
| Australia | 335.09 | 308.66 | 312.58 | — .77 |
| Austria | 2,278.00 | 1,978.00 | 1,978.00 | — 28.00 |
| Belgium | 128.70 | 99.00 | 100.40 | + .60 |
| Canada | 175.60 | 136.98 | 145.32 | — .02 |
| France | 112.10 | 84.00 | 87.60 | + .20 |
| Italy | 8,369.00 | 7,188.00 | 7,551.00 | — 82.00 |
| Japan | 1,588.73 | 1,410.43 | 1,427.23 | + 8.73 |
| Netherl. | 358.30 | 252.30 | 266.10 | — 4.30 |
| Switzer. | 216.50 | 167.70 | 168.90 | — .80 |
| U.K. | 374.20 | 286.70 | 295.50 | + 4.60 |
| U.K. Kaffirs | 66.50 | 50.10 | 50.10 | — .80 |
| West Ger. | 95.08 | 72.19 | 72.19 | — 1.14 |

## 20 Most Active Stocks

| 1966 High | 1966 Low | | Sales | High | Low | Close | Chg. |
|---|---|---|---|---|---|---|---|
| 36¼ | 18 | Gulf W In | 1,079,000 | 35 | 29⅛ | 33¼ | — 3¼ |
| 216¾ | 96⅞ | Fair Cam | 966,500 | 126½ | 100 | 102⅝ | —11⅝ |
| 100½ | 57⅞ | Itek Corp | 398,700 | 80½ | 71⅝ | 76 | + 3⅜ |
| 61⅜ | 31⅜ | Chrysler | 390,300 | 33⅛ | 31⅜ | 31½ | — 1½ |
| 27¾ | 16⅝ | Martin Mar | 388,000 | 21 | 18½ | 19¾ | + 1⅛ |
| 33⅝ | 17⅛ | Sperry Rand | 376,300 | 27⅛ | 26⅛ | 26⅛ | — ½ |
| 56¾ | 37⅝ | Magnavox | 347,500 | 45 | 41 | 41⅝ | — 3⅝ |
| 108¼ | 69¾ | Gen Mot | 335,700 | 72½ | 69¾ | 69¾ | — 3 |
| 155¾ | 75 | KLM Airlines | 307,300 | 99 | 89 | 94½ | + 4¼ |
| 82¼ | 44 | Boeing | 303,800 | 65¼ | 58⅛ | 63 | + 3 |
| 63½ | 49¾ | Am T&T | 300,000 | 57⅛ | 55½ | 55⅝ | — ½ |
| 85⅜ | 37⅝ | Collins Rad | 284,300 | 58 | 48¼ | 56 | + 6 |
| 21⅞ | 10⅛ | Transitron | 284,300 | 15⅛ | 13½ | 13⅝ | — ¾ |
| 73½ | 42⅜ | Tidewat Oil | 279,900 | 73½ | 63⅜ | 72⅞ | + 9½ |
| 139¾ | 88 | Texas Inst | 256,500 | 116½ | 97½ | 101½ | — 7¾ |
| 175 | 108⅛ | Polaroid | 263,200 | 159 | 148¾ | 152⅛ | — 1⅛ |
| 57½ | 40 | Ford Mot | 252,200 | 41⅜ | 40 | 40¼ | — 1 |
| 13¾ | 8¾ | Curtis Pub | 238,000 | 13⅜ | 11⅛ | 12⅞ | + 1⅜ |
| 32⅞ | 21¼ | Un Artist | 233,500 | 30⅜ | 27¼ | 28⅛ | — 1 |
| 33 | 20½ | McDonn | 224,800 | 29½ | 25¼ | 28¾ | + 2½ |

### Barron's 50-Stock Average

| | Nov. 17 1966 | Nov. 9 1966 | Nov. 1965 |
|---|---|---|---|
| Price | 318 | 315 | 375 |
| Projected quarterly earn | 6.25 | 6.25 | 7.44 |
| Projected annual earn | 25.00 | 25.00 | 29.76 |
| Ratio price to proj an earn | 12.7 | 12.6 | 12.6 |
| 5-year average earnings | 21.92 | 21.63 | 19.45 |
| Ratio price to 5-yr av earn | 14.5 | 14.6 | 19.3 |
| Earn for year just ended | 27.18 | 27.28 | 25.26 |
| Ratio price to yr end earn | 11.7 | 11.5 | 14.8 |
| Earn yield yr ended earn | 8.53 | 8.65 | 6.74 |
| Bond yields | 5.38 | 5.38 | 4.63 |
| Bond-stock ratio | .63 | .62 | .69 |
| Divs paid in year ended | 14.41 | 14.41 | 13.04 |
| Div yield in year ended | 4.54 | 4.58 | 3.48 |

### New York Stock Exchange Diary

| Nov. | 14 | 15 | 16 | 17 | 18 |
|---|---|---|---|---|---|
| Issues traded | 1,435 | 1,414 | 1,446 | 1,433 | 1,428 |
| Advances | 460 | 648 | 883 | 445 | 413 |
| Declines | 698 | 511 | 347 | 729 | 763 |
| Unchanged | 277 | 255 | 216 | 259 | 252 |
| New highs, 1966 | 9 | 11 | 23 | 11 | 11 |
| New lows, 1966 | 14 | 19 | 16 | 11 | 16 |

Weekly

| issues traded | Advances | Declines | Unchanged |
|---|---|---|---|
| 1,585 | 724 | 711 | 150 |

New 1966 highs last week 35; new lows 55.

### American Stock Exchange Diary

| | | | | | |
|---|---|---|---|---|---|
| Issues traded | 858 | 829 | 840 | 863 | 816 |
| Advances | 270 | 299 | 407 | 228 | 250 |
| Declines | 355 | 290 | 204 | 396 | 333 |
| Unchanged | 233 | 240 | 229 | 239 | 233 |
| New highs, 1966 | 5 | 5 | 13 | 9 | 2 |
| New lows, 1966 | 17 | 13 | 15 | 14 | 14 |
| Sales th shs | 1,860 | 2,190 | 2,480 | 2,200 | 1,840 |

New 1966 highs last week 19; new lows 59.

### Bond Averages and NYSE Bond Sales

| | | | | | |
|---|---|---|---|---|---|
| 40 Bonds | 80.84 | 80.75 | 80.68 | 80.58 | 80.48 |
| 10 Hi-Gr RR | 72.63 | 72.51 | 72.48 | 72.53 | 72.20 |
| 10 2d-Gr RR | 81.08 | 80.94 | 80.99 | 80.61 | 80.70 |
| 10 Util | 82.55 | 82.36 | 82.29 | 82.15 | 82.21 |
| 10 Ind | 87.08 | 87.20 | 86.95 | 86.68 | 86.78 |
| U.S. Govts. | 83.79 | 83.83 | 83.74 | 83.73 | 85.42 |
| Income RR | 69.51 | 69.51 | 69.58 | 69.54 | 69.10 |
| Sales, ths $ | 13,550 | 13,650 | 17,380 | 14,500 | 10,050 |

### Odd-Lot Trading

| Nov. | 11 | 14 | 15 | 16 | 17 |
|---|---|---|---|---|---|
| Purch, th shs | 404.5 | 460.8 | 414.2 | 582.1 | 568.2 |
| Sales, th shs | 357.5 | 456.4 | 428.1 | 551.0 | 482.8 |
| Short Sales, sh | 10,541 | 13,701 | 11,931 | 13,404 | 14,231 |

Source: *Barron's*, November 21, 1966.

It would appear that when the DJI yields approach the 3% level, at least in the past, major bull markets have tended to peak. The record at bear market lows is not as clear:

| *Date* | *DJI* | *Yield* |
|---|---|---|
| July 8, 1932 | 41.22 | 10.4 % |
| Apr. 28, 1942 | 92.92 | 7.58 |
| June 13, 1949 | 161.60 | 6.84 |
| Apr. 3, 1958 | 440.50 | 4.89 |
| Oct. 25, 1960 | 566.05 | 3.78 |
| June 26, 1962 | 535.76 | 4.32 |

FIGURE 3–22A

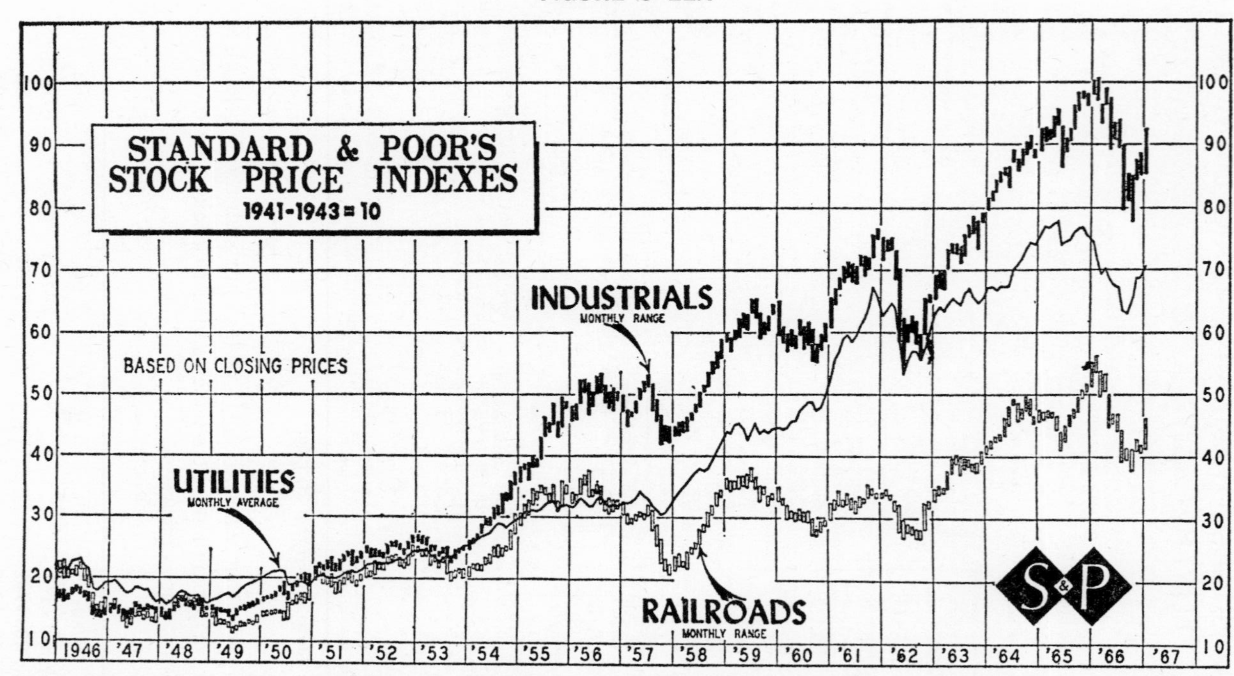


Hourly readings of the S. & P. 425 Industrials, 20 Rails, 55 Utilities and 500 Stock composite indexes are carried on the American Stock Exchange, Commodity News Service, Pacific Coast Stock Exchange tickers and PR Newswire Broker-Line as well as on many electric quotation boards. Investors in the New York City area are invited to telephone YUkon 9-0560 for the latest hourly index figures. The indexes are computed every five minutes on the Ultronics System.

Source: Standard & Poor's, *The Outlook*, February 6, 1967.

## FIGURE 3–22B

## Standard & Poor's Forecast and Policy

# *FURTHER ADVANCE INDICATED*

### FORECAST AND POLICY

The market's ability to absorb profit taking last week was encouraging. Monetary factors are still on the side of advance, and prospects for corporate earnings are assuming a somewhat better tone. We continue to advise a constructive approach.

• • •

THE stock market resumed its advance late last week after failing to make appreciable headway in the earlier sessions. The consolidation occasioned by profit taking on the part of short-term traders was thus rather short-lived, and the fact that the list did not give ground under this pressure apparently stimulated buying by investors who had been waiting for some price correction.

Although glamor stocks participated in the late advance, there were conspicuous weaker spots in the early trading. Some tempering of the exuberance in these volatile issues might be salutary if, in the rotation of interest in the market, proceeds from profit-taking in high fliers are attracted to the solid values available in investment issues.

These stocks, we believe, have yet to make anything like a full response to the dramatic easing of credit, though not too much should be expected too soon. Lower interest rates are attracting a good deal of bond financing that was deferred in the latter part of 1966. This could mean some temporary softness in the bond market, which already appears to have been anticipated by such "money-sensitive" groups as utilities and bank stocks. It is likely to be of moderate scope, however, and may result in no more than an extended period of hesitation for stocks, rather than a material price reaction.

• • •

Earnings reports for 1966 that are now beginning to appear have had little apparent effect on investor sentiment, even when disclosing fourth quarter weakness. While some further earnings contraction is to be expected in the current half, a number of considerations now emerging—tied chiefly to easier money conditions—suggest that a turn for the better will develop later in 1967, and that full-year declines may well be smaller than had earlier been anticipated. Our economists are now making some upward revisions of their 1967 projections, details on which will be published next week.

The cooling off of the economy, which in coming months will be featured by sluggishness in consumer durables, and probably by a sharp but temporary cutback in the rate of inventory accumulation, has in our opinion been pretty well discounted by the stock market. What has not been fully taken into account is the possibility of renewed effective demand later on for housing and allied durable goods, as well as a step-up in the tempo of business capital spending that should be supported by more attractive credit financing terms.

Notwithstanding the advance from the lows, many sound stocks are still attractively priced. Moreover, although institutional investors began to nibble at stocks in the final quarter of 1966 (see page 938) and stepped up their buying in January, the supply of funds on the sidelines is still unusually large. More of this money apparently has been moving into stocks recently. This remains one of the strongest potential supports for the market.

### MARKET MEASURES

| Feb. 1 | *Price Earns. Ratios | Yields |
|---|---|---|
| Industrials .. | 15.90 | 3.30% |
| Rails ....... | 10.12 | 4.93 |
| Utilities .... | 15.90 | 3.92 |
| 500 Stocks . | 15.71 | 3.40 |

INDUSTRIAL PRICE INDEXES (1941-43=10)

| Feb. | High | Low | Close |
|---|---|---|---|
| 3.. | 93.97 | 92.37 | 93.31 |
| 2.. | 93.18 | 91.60 | 92.57 |
| 1.. | 92.84 | 91.39 | 92.21 |
| Jan. | | | |
| 31.. | 93.30 | 91.78 | 92.35 |
| 30.. | 93.14 | 91.49 | 92.38 |
| 27.. | 92.48 | 90.93 | 91.82 |

*Based on 3rd quarter 1966 earnings seasonally adjusted to annual rate for industrials and utilities and a 12 months' moving total for the rails.

Industrials Rose 1.6% in The Week and Rails Climbed 0.8%, but Utilities Lost 0.5%

### BEST ACTING GROUPS

| | Chg. From Prev. Wk. |
|---|---|
| Savings & Loan .... | +12.8% |
| Bread & Cake ..... | + 7.9 |
| Shipbuilding ........ | + 7.7 |
| Air Conditioning .... | + 7.5 |
| Brewers ........... | + 6.6 |
| Home Furnishings ... | + 6.4 |
| Cigarettes .......... | + [illegible].3 |
| Cane Producers .... | + 6.1 |
| Crude Producers .... | + 6.1 |
| Radio-TV Mfrs. ...... | + 6.0 |

There Were 11 New 1966-67 Group Highs, the Largest Number Since Last April

### POOREST PERFORMERS

| | Chg. From Prev. Wk. |
|---|---|
| Packaged Foods ..... | — 1.5% |
| Variety Stores ...... | — 1.5 |
| Auto Parts ......... | — 1.6 |
| Radio-TV Bdcstrs. .... | — 1.6 |
| Vegetable Oil ...... | — 2.3 |
| Steam Gen. Mach. .. | — 2.5 |
| Gold Mining ........ | — 3.0 |
| N. Y. C. Banks ..... | — 3.9 |
| Banks Outside NYC .. | — 4.4 |
| Biscuit Bakers ..... | — 4.7 |

There Were No Group Lows for the Fourth Consecutive Week

Source: *The Outlook,* February 6, 1967.

The price-earnings ratio on the DJI has often, in the past, been used to judge the level of the market. At previous bull market highs, for example, the record was as follows:

| Date | DJI | Earnings | P/E Ratio |
|---|---|---|---|
| Sept. 3, 1929 | 381.17 | $19.94 | 19.1 |
| Mar. 10, 1937 | 194.40 | 11.12 | 17.5 |
| May 29, 1946 | 212.50 | 10.24 | 20.8 |
| Jan. 4, 1960 | 679.06 | 33.82 | 20.1 |
| Dec. 13, 1961 | 734.91 | 31.91 | 23.0 |
| Feb. 9, 1966 | 995.15 | 53.67 | 18.5 |

In the past, at least, one could say that when the DJI–p/e went above 19, bull markets tended to top out, but again the record at bear market lows is not as consistent, the p/e ratio at selected lows ranging from 7 to 18 approximately. Yet by looking at such fundamental indicators[14] and at the host of technical indicators,[15] it is possible to gain relative bearings in the market and thus make more intelligent judgments as to approximate values.

### Industry Analysis

Generally, after examining the state of business and corporate profits and the condition of the market, security analysts make industry-to-industry comparisons to select those industries whose growth and profitability outlook is most favorable. The importance of industry analysis may be seen from Figures 3–23A, 3–23B, and from the Appendixes to this chapter.

In the long bull market climb from 1961 through 1965, it made a very big difference whether you picked stocks in the air transport, sulphur, and textile industries or whether your selections ran to the cigarette, cement, or savings and loan industries. Over this period air transport composite stock prices rose 256%, sulphur stocks 211%, and textile products 190%, while savings and loan holding companies fell 63%, cement stocks dropped 40%, and cigarette stock prices declined 33%.

To secure data for industry studies and comparisons, the analyst may either research an industry in depth, using a variety of sources, or if he has less time available and wishes compact and concise information, he may turn to one of the investment services. Standard & Poor's issues an excellent series of *Industry Surveys,* covering 45 industries. In each case a *Basic Analysis* is issued, usually annually, followed by supplementary sections entitled *Current Analysis and Outlook,* issued at varying intervals, usually quarterly, during the year. The *Basic Analysis* contains a

[14] See Chapter 13.

[15] See Chapter 14.

FIGURE 3–23A

**Stock Price Changes by Industry Categories**

Percentage Change from December 13, 1961, to December 31, 1965

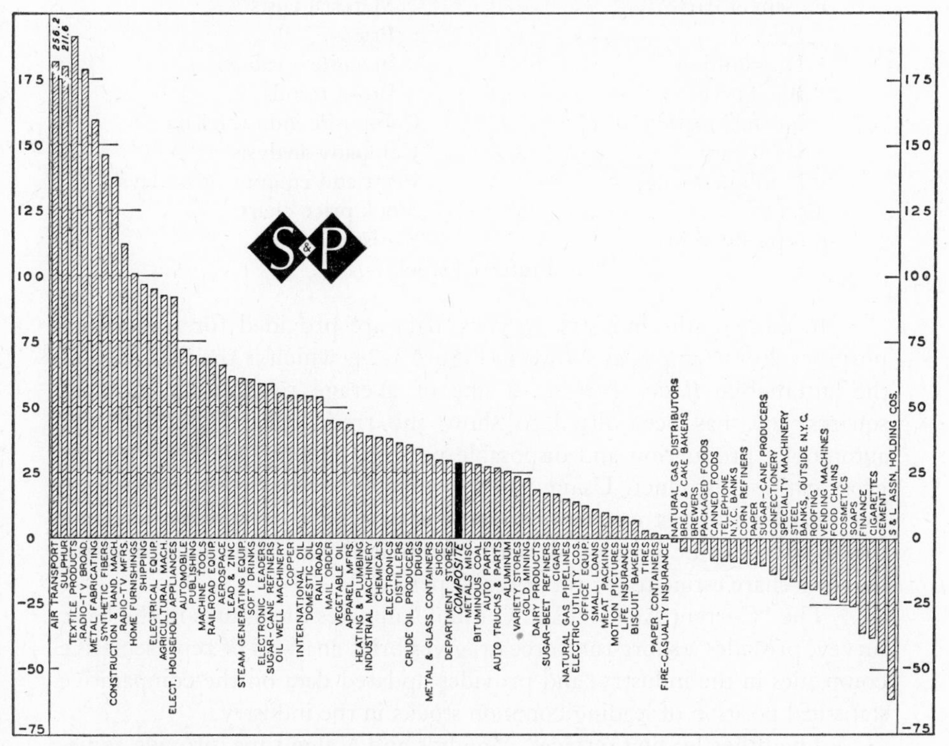


Source: Chart by Standard & Poor's Corp.

wealth of data, which would require an extensive expenditure of time by an individual analyst if he were to attempt to gather it himself. In the report on the aerospace industry, for example, the *Basic Analysis* includes:

| | |
|---|---|
| Government contracting | Helicopters |
| Military market | General aviation |
| Military aircraft | Export market |
| Missiles | Finances |
| Space | Composite industry data |
| Propulsion | Company analysis |
| Atomic energy | Plant and equipment outlays |
| Aircraft engines | Stock price chart |
| Research and development | Preferred stocks |
| Commercial transports | Statistical data |

Where the industry is more homogeneous, as in the case of automobiles, the content of the *Basic Analysis* will reflect more internal operational data. Thus the automobile industry survey contains:

In most of the industry surveys, data are provided for forecasting purposes. For example, as shown in Figure 3–24, which is the first page of the automobile *Basic Analysis*, a line of average relationship, or least squares line, has been fitted to show the trend relationship between automobile production and disposable personal income, a component of gross national product. Using a GNP and DPI estimate for the ensuing five years, a forecast can be obtained for passenger car production, and this in turn can be brought down to profitability to determine an earnings-per-share estimate for the forecast period.[16]

The "Current Analysis and Outlook" updates the figures in the basic survey, provides a short-run forecast, gives brief analyses of representative companies in the industry, and provides updated data on the comparative statistical position of leading common stocks in the industry.

The other leading services, Moody's and Value Line, provide somewhat similar industry data though perhaps not as conveniently assembled and packaged. Forbes publishes an "Annual Report on American Industry" at the beginning of each calendar year. It covers each of the major industries and within the industry makes comparisons of companies based on three yardsticks of performance: growth (6-year compounded rate for both sales and earnings); profitability (5-year average for return on equity, cash flow to equity, and operating profit margin); and trend (latest 12 months versus 3-year average earnings gain and pretax profit margin). See Figure 3–25 for an example covering the utility industry. Each industry covered is analyzed for both past and prospective performance.

For the analyst who wishes to do his own industry study in depth, a variety of sources are available. Various trade journals covering different industries include *Chemical Week*, *Drug and Cosmetic Industry*, *Modern Plastics*, *Oil, Paint, and Drug Reporter*, *Coal Age*, *The Coal Dealer*, *Coal Mining*, *Mining World*, *Electrical World*, *Electrical Equipment*, *Electri-*

[16] Such techniques will be considered in detail in Chapters 6–8.

## FIGURE 3–23B

### Group Performances

We publish below the record of group performances in 1966, showing only 15 groups with gains for the year, and 55 groups with losses exceeding the 13.4% decline of the S & P industrials. This contrasts sharply with the gains by 76 groups and declines by only 25 in 1965, but is similar to the 1962 record. In that year, only nine groups ended with gains and 56 groups sustained above-average losses.

To enable subscribers to THE OUTLOOK to cope with the particularly great selectivity we see ahead, we will publish later this month a comprehensive special report reassessing the investment prospects for each of the industry groups for coming months, and singling out some of the most promising issues in each category.

### *Stock Group Performances in 1966*

| *Rank | 1965 Dec. 31 | 1966 Dec. 30 | % Change | 1966 Range High | 1966 Range Low |
|---|---|---|---|---|---|
| 1 Radio-TV Broadcasters | 231.94 | 293.67 | + 26.6 | 303.39 | 221.40 |
| 2 Motion Pictures | 64.23 | 79.18 | + 23.3 | 81.36 | 58.14 |
| 3 Electronics | 353.55 | 417.55 | + 18.1 | 454.21 | 352.22 |
| 4 Sugar—Cane Producers | 16.13 | 18.60 | + 15.3 | 22.78 | 15.47 |
| 5 Coal: Bituminous | 124.52 | 143.02 | + 14.9 | 143.02 | 113.70 |
| 6 Sulphur | 89.94 | 103.07 | + 14.6 | 117.78 | 76.96 |
| 7 Cosmetics | 41.55 | 45.63 | + 9.8 | 49.00 | 40.26 |
| 8 Air Transport | 99.69 | 109.35 | + 9.7 | 145.43 | 84.93 |
| 9 Office Equipment | 626.39 | 679.70 | + 8.5 | 718.97 | 566.29 |
| 10 Metal Fabricating | 122.25 | 132.55 | + 8.4 | 147.95 | 101.95 |
| 11 Publishing | 277.09 | 289.81 | + 4.6 | 298.43 | 243.21 |
| 12 Gold Mining | 28.05 | 28.75 | + 2.5 | 35.03 | 24.02 |
| 13 Fire-Casualty Insurance | 68.31 | 69.93 | + 2.4 | 71.46 | 58.68 |
| 14 Aluminum | 115.37 | 116.15 | + 0.7 | 149.56 | 99.24 |
| 15 Oil: Integrated Domestic | 98.01 | 98.71 | + 0.7 | 105.41 | 90.57 |
| 16 Office Equip., Excl. I. B. M. | 206.90 | 205.74 | — 0.6 | 263.04 | 168.74 |
| 17 Vegetable Oil | 57.02 | 56.44 | — 1.0 | 70.51 | 49.30 |
| 18 Soft Drinks | 57.36 | 56.57 | — 1.4 | 58.19 | 46.59 |
| 19 Telephone, Excl. A. T. & T. | 65.64 | 64.47 | — 1.8 | 66.23 | 55.37 |
| 20 Drugs | 106.08 | 103.95 | — 2.0 | 108.79 | 88.89 |
| 21 Banks, Outside N. Y. C. | 69.08 | 67.59 | — 2.2 | 71.81 | 56.01 |
| 22 Tires & Rubber Goods | 201.98 | 195.57 | — 3.2 | 230.69 | 183.51 |
| 23 Banks—New York City | 37.09 | 35.60 | — 4.0 | 37.73 | 27.95 |
| 24 Oil: Crude Producers | 198.70 | 187.85 | — 5.5 | 210.97 | 165.51 |
| 25 Aerospace | 92.39 | 87.06 | — 5.8 | 108.45 | 70.06 |
| 26 Copper | 43.07 | 40.44 | — 6.1 | 47.71 | 32.35 |
| 27 Soaps | 80.74 | 75.62 | — 6.3 | 81.22 | 67.98 |
| 28 Metals Misc. | 68.15 | 63.77 | — 6.4 | 76.90 | 54.41 |
| 29 Natural Gas: Pipe Lines | 91.60 | 85.52 | — 6.6 | 94.66 | 74.43 |
| 30 Air Conditioning | 22.85 | 21.32 | — 6.7 | 24.48 | 16.28 |
| 31 Heating & Plumbing | 29.87 | 27.66 | — 7.4 | 33.24 | 22.26 |
| 32 Electric Companies | 58.05 | 53.49 | — 7.9 | 57.77 | 45.63 |
| **33 Utilities** | **75.51** | **69.35** | **— 8.2** | **75.37** | **59.03** |
| 34 Telephone | 29.07 | 26.59 | — 8.5 | 29.94 | 24.32 |
| 35 Biscuit Bakers | 63.12 | 57.32 | — 9.2 | 64.16 | 49.31 |
| 36 Confectionery | 39.26 | 35.52 | — 9.5 | 41.15 | 33.08 |
| 37 Investment Cos. (Closed-end) | 67.26 | 60.87 | — 9.5 | 68.56 | 56.08 |
| 38 Distillers | 107.11 | 96.84 | — 9.6 | 110.33 | 81.38 |
| 39 Shipping | 62.69 | 56.69 | — 9.6 | 88.05 | 53.92 |
| 40 Containers: Metal & Glass | 39.84 | 35.74 | — 10.3 | 42.02 | 35.48 |
| 41 Bread & Cake Bakers | 35.41 | 31.69 | — 10.5 | 39.28 | 28.34 |
| 42 Machinery: Agricultural | 57.26 | 51.24 | — 10.5 | 68.56 | 46.42 |
| 43 Oil Composite | 126.87 | 113.36 | — 10.6 | 129.22 | 104.88 |
| 44 Finance Companies | 53.65 | 46.98 | — 12.4 | 54.58 | 41.47 |
| 45 Corn Refiners | 63.98 | 55.88 | — 12.7 | 63.54 | 44.99 |
| 46 Oil Well Machinery | 105.89 | 92.37 | — 12.8 | 120.12 | 86.35 |
| **47 Composite, 500 Stocks** | **92.43** | **80.33** | **— 13.1** | **94.06** | **73.20** |
| 48 Sugar Composite | 31.39 | 27.26 | — 13.2 | 35.26 | 26.62 |
| **49 Industrials, 425 Stocks** | **98.47** | **85.24** | **— 13.4** | **100.60** | **77.89** |
| **50 Low Priced Stocks** | **121.17** | **104.51** | **— 13.7** | **136.81** | **97.28** |
| 51 Roofing & Wallboard | 53.94 | 46.47 | — 13.8 | 55.90 | 39.75 |
| **52 High Grade Common** | **84.57** | **72.58** | **— 14.2** | **84.49** | **68.21** |
| 53 Vending Machines | 33.42 | 28.67 | — 14.2 | 37.09 | 24.99 |
| 54 Building Materials Composite | 43.52 | 37.28 | — 14.3 | 44.96 | 32.04 |
| 55 Oil: Integrated Internatl. | 136.51 | 116.81 | — 14.4 | 139.76 | 108.20 |
| 56 Electrical Equipment | 210.69 | 178.64 | — 15.2 | 217.20 | 157.01 |
| 57 Sugar—Beet Refiners | 23.69 | 20.05 | — 15.4 | 24.96 | 20.04 |
| 58 Packaged Foods | 89.02 | 75.31 | — 15.4 | 88.89 | 66.68 |
| **59 Capital Goods** | **92.34** | **77.99** | **— 15.5** | **94.79** | **70.74** |
| 60 Shoes | 29.63 | 24.90 | — 16.0 | 30.98 | 22.80 |
| 61 Cigarette Mfgs. | 34.52 | 28.95 | — 16.1 | 35.95 | 28.51 |
| 62 Meat Packing | 32.79 | 27.39 | — 16.5 | 35.21 | 22.70 |
| 63 Electronic—Major Cos. | 105.74 | 88.08 | — 16.7 | 110.41 | 80.06 |
| 64 Food Composite | 68.57 | 57.03 | — 16.8 | 68.90 | 50.41 |
| 65 Household Appliances | 136.87 | 113.56 | — 17.0 | 146.02 | 113.01 |
| 66 Natural Gas Distributors | 74.16 | 61.49 | — 17.1 | 74.95 | 59.72 |
| 67 Steam Generating Mach. | 186.78 | 154.55 | — 17.3 | 188.57 | 118.56 |
| 68 Paper | 173.84 | 142.67 | — 17.9 | 187.59 | 134.62 |
| 69 Small Loans | 128.74 | 105.08 | — 18.4 | 129.82 | 82.35 |
| 70 Dairy Products | 86.45 | 70.41 | — 18.6 | 88.57 | 64.27 |
| 71 Cane Refiners | 63.06 | 50.40 | — 20.0 | 71.68 | 49.72 |
| **72 Railroads** | **51.28** | **41.04** | **— 20.0** | **56.32** | **37.91** |
| 73 Railroad Equipment | 39.59 | 31.20 | — 21.2 | 45.78 | 30.95 |
| 74 Containers—Paper | 120.69 | 94.95 | — 21.3 | 128.47 | 94.95 |
| **75 Consumer Goods** | **84.08** | **66.08** | **— 21.4** | **84.95** | **65.35** |
| 76 Textiles: Apparel Mfrs. | 70.70 | 55.60 | — 21.4 | 77.94 | 52.09 |
| 77 Department Stores | 128.45 | 100.47 | — 21.8 | 127.46 | 100.47 |
| 78 Auto Trucks & Parts | 65.90 | 51.30 | — 22.2 | 70.16 | 50.44 |
| 79 Lead & Zinc | 17.71 | 13.77 | — 22.2 | 19.37 | 13.70 |
| 80 Canned Foods | 85.64 | 65.53 | — 23.5 | 86.92 | 60.71 |
| 81 Life Insurance | 310.59 | 237.64 | — 23.5 | 303.61 | 190.37 |
| 82 Auto Parts & Accessories | 58.99 | 44.71 | — 24.2 | 62.15 | 44.45 |
| 83 Industrial Machinery | 90.04 | 67.95 | — 24.5 | 91.37 | 60.62 |
| 84 Machinery Composite | 96.42 | 72.79 | — 24.5 | 97.66 | 68.00 |
| 85 Food Chain Stores | 66.91 | 49.88 | — 25.5 | 69.11 | 49.54 |
| 86 Radio-TV Mfrs. | 273.42 | 203.28 | — 25.7 | 401.67 | 203.28 |
| 87 Machine Tools | 50.88 | 37.48 | — 26.3 | 55.77 | 35.36 |
| 88 Sav. & Loan Assn. Hld. Cos. | 11.83 | 8.64 | — 27.0 | 11.75 | 5.49 |
| 89 Variety Stores | 31.04 | 22.37 | — 27.9 | 31.22 | 22.37 |
| 90 Truckers | 31.73 | 22.79 | — 28.2 | 33.58 | 22.45 |
| 91 Retail Stores Composite | 88.10 | 63.07 | — 28.4 | 86.32 | 63.07 |
| 92 Specialty Machinery | 31.42 | 22.46 | — 28.5 | 33.41 | 22.41 |
| 93 Chemicals Excl. du Pont | 53.38 | 38.05 | — 28.7 | 54.00 | 37.14 |
| 94 Const. & Mat'l. Handl. Mch. | 236.89 | 168.70 | — 28.8 | 236.22 | 163.19 |
| 95 Home Furnishings | 27.20 | 19.23 | — 29.3 | 30.94 | 18.60 |
| 96 Steel | 66.83 | 47.13 | — 29.5 | 69.23 | 45.51 |
| 97 Steel, Excl. U. S. Steel | 71.23 | 50.21 | — 29.5 | 73.42 | 48.18 |
| 98 Beverages: Brewers | 53.93 | 37.82 | — 29.9 | 57.95 | 36.85 |
| 99 Cement | 30.49 | 20.82 | — 31.7 | 31.62 | 20.82 |
| 100 Shipbuilding | 52.87 | 35.69 | — 32.5 | 53.27 | 33.66 |
| 101 Mail Ord. & Gen. Chains | 160.17 | 107.69 | — 32.8 | 154.80 | 107.69 |
| 102 Chemicals | 74.93 | 49.82 | — 33.5 | 75.38 | 49.82 |
| 103 Autos, Excl. Gen. Motors | 38.83 | 25.26 | — 34.9 | 41.77 | 25.26 |
| 104 Discount Stores | 42.28 | 27.52 | — 34.9 | 42.41 | 26.03 |
| 105 Textile Products | 96.03 | 61.57 | — 35.9 | 107.15 | 57.19 |
| 106 Automobiles | 127.31 | 81.27 | — 36.2 | 131.88 | 81.27 |
| 107 Textiles: Synthetic Fibers | 115.55 | 67.94 | — 41.2 | 122.43 | 64.32 |
| 108 Cigar Mfrs. | 103.27 | 51.74 | — 49.9 | 103.19 | 49.30 |

*An alphabetical list of these group indexes, with rank numbers, is shown on page 989.

Source: Standard & Poor's, *The Outlook*, January 9, 1967, p. 982.

*cal Manufacturing*, *Electronics*, *Food Industries*, *The Timberman*, *Iron Age*, *Paper Trade Journal*, *Oil and Gas Journal*, *Petroleum World*, *The Rubber Age*, *Tires*, *The Tire Age*, *Rock Products*, *Boot and Shoe Recorder*, *Textile World*, *Automotive Industries*, *Leather and Shoes*, *Paper Trade Journal*, etc. The *Business Periodicals Index* and the *Science and Technology Index* list articles in all trade journals. In addition, each

## FIGURE 3–24



# Further Long-Term Growth Indicated

DESPITE continuing wide year-to-year fluctuations, the automotive industry should grow at least in line with the national economy over the coming decade.

Chart 1 and Table 2 on this page show the relationship between disposable income and the passenger car business. In the 1920-29 decade, factory value of domestic passenger car production averaged 2.9% of disposable income. The average in the 1930s fell to 2.3%. The average for the postwar years 1946-49 was 2.4%. In the 1950-59 decade, the average rose to 3.4%.

In 1964, 1963, 1962, 1961, and 1960, factory sales of new cars amounted to 3.4%, 3.6%, 3.4%, 2.8%, and 3.5%, respectively, of consumer disposable income, compared with a high of 4.5% in 1955 and a low of 1.3% in 1932. Automobiles should capture a greater share of disposable income in 1965, since car production should be up more than 10% while the year-to-year advance in disposable income is estimated at 5%-6%.

### Longer-Term Outlook

Abnormal factors prevailed in some postwar years; a ceiling was placed on production in 1946-48 by the availability of materials, labor, and plant facilities; the Korean crisis provided a sharp stimulus to demand in 1950; car production was curbed by the Government under the defense program in 1951-52; the outstanding 1955 showing reflected a combination of favorable demand factors and a build-up of dealer inventories. Growth in the truck field and expanded non-automotive activities enhance future industry prospects.

Passenger car sales will be determined primarily by general business conditions, as evidenced in disposable income. Moreover, fluctuations will be accentuated by the fact that the proportion of income spent for cars contracts in poor times and expands in good times. Other factors which will influence car demand are trends in population and the number of households, the growth in the number of multi-car families, prices in relation to all consumer prices, the average age at which cars are scrapped, the availability of credit, the state of the used car market and its effect on trade-in allowances, and style and engineering changes which would hasten obsolescence of existing units.

A relatively new consideration is the encroachment of foreign cars in both domestic and export markets, and the extent to which this can be stemmed or capitalized upon through the output of U.S.-built compact cars and production in other countries. The former sharp growth in foreign car sales has been halted. After rising more than six-fold to about 615,000 units from 1956 to 1959, domestic sales of

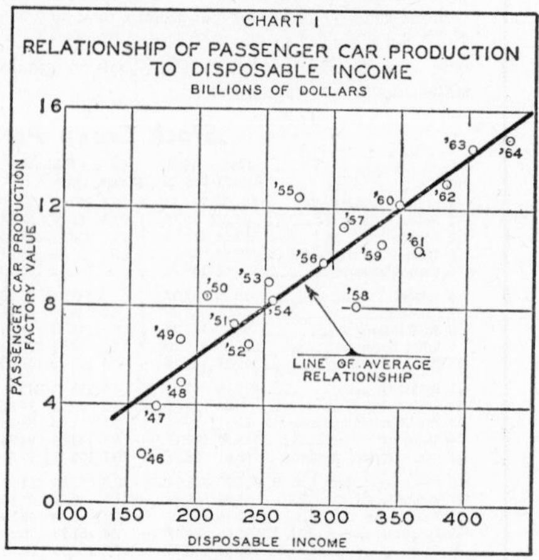


**Table 2**

**U. S. MOTOR VEHICLE FACTORY SALES AND DISPOSABLE INCOME**

| | Disposable Income (Bil. $) | Passenger Cars Number | Passenger Cars Value (Bil. $) | % of Dispos. Inc. | Trucks and Buses Number | Trucks and Buses Value (Bil. $) | Total Vehicles Number | Total Vehicles Value (Bil. $) |
|---|---|---|---|---|---|---|---|---|
| 1964 | 431.8 | 7,751,822 | 14.86 | 3.4 | 1,540,453 | 3.10 | 9,292,275 | 17.96 |
| 1963 | 402.5 | 7,637,728 | 14.43 | 3.6 | 1,462,708 | 3.09 | 9,100,436 | 17.52 |
| 1962 | 384.6 | 6,933,240 | 13.08 | 3.4 | 1,240,168 | 2.58 | 8,173,408 | 15.65 |
| 1961 | 364.7 | 5,542,707 | 10.29 | 2.8 | 1,133,804 | 2.15 | 6,676,511 | 12.44 |
| 1960 | 349.9 | 6,674,796 | 12.16 | 3.5 | 1,194,475 | 2.35 | 7,869,271 | 14.51 |
| 1959 | 337.1 | 5,591,243 | 10.53 | 3.1 | 1,137,386 | 2.34 | 6,728,629 | 12.87 |
| 1958 | 317.9 | 4,257,812 | 8.01 | 2.5 | 877,294 | 1.73 | 5,135,106 | 9.74 |
| 1957 | 308.2 | 6,113,344 | 11.20 | 3.6 | 1,107,176 | 2.08 | 7,220,520 | 13.28 |
| 1956 | 292.9 | 5,816,109 | 9.75 | 3.3 | 1,104,481 | 2.08 | 6,920,590 | 11.83 |
| 1955 | 274.4 | 7,920,186 | 12.45 | 4.5 | 1,249,090 | 2.02 | 9,169,276 | 14.47 |
| 1954 | 256.9 | 5,558,897 | 8.22 | 3.2 | 1,042,174 | 1.66 | 6,601,071 | 9.88 |

Source: Automobile Manufacturers Association.

**Table 1**

**PROJECTIONS OF THE POPULATION OF THE U.S.**

**By Age Groups**

| Age | 1963 Number (thous.) | 1963 % of Tot. | 1970 Number (thous.) | 1970 % of Tot. | 1975 Number (thous.) | 1975 % of Tot. | 1980 Number (thous.) | 1980 % of Tot. | 1985 Number (thous.) | 1985 % of Tot. |
|---|---|---|---|---|---|---|---|---|---|---|
| Under 5 years | 20,722 | 10.9 | 21,277 | 10.3 | 24,028 | 10.7 | 26,823 | 11.1 | 28,682 | 11.0 |
| 5 to 9 years | 20,012 | 10.6 | 20,667 | 9.9 | 21,314 | 9.5 | 24,055 | 10.1 | 26,842 | 10.3 |
| 10 to 14 years | 18,000 | 9.5 | 20,469 | 9.8 | 20,716 | 9.3 | 21,362 | 8.8 | 24,098 | 9.2 |
| 15 to 19 years | 15,536 | 8.2 | 18,941 | 9.2 | 20,516 | 9.2 | 20,762 | 8.6 | 21,407 | 8.2 |
| 20 to 24 years | 12,600 | 6.7 | 17.104 | 8.2 | 19,057 | 8.5 | 20,624 | 8.5 | 20,868 | 8.0 |
| 25 to 29 years | 10,971 | 5.8 | 13,795 | 6.6 | 17,254 | 7.7 | 19,195 | 7.9 | 20,753 | 8.0 |
| 30 to 34 years | 11,385 | 6.0 | 11,415 | 5.5 | 13,885 | 6.2 | 17,322 | 7.2 | 19.252 | 7.4 |
| 35 to 39 years | 12,343 | 6.5 | 11,079 | 5.3 | 11,448 | 5.1 | 13,889 | 5.7 | 17,299 | 6.6 |
| 40 to 44 years | 12,261 | 6.5 | 11,917 | 5.7 | 11,010 | 4.9 | 11,378 | 4.7 | 13,790 | 5.3 |
| 45 to 49 years | 11,234 | 5.9 | 12,239 | 5.9 | 11,715 | 5.2 | 10,833 | 4.5 | 11,200 | 4.3 |
| 50 to 54 years | 10,255 | 5.4 | 11,121 | 5.3 | 11,859 | 5.3 | 11,361 | 4.7 | 10,518 | 5.0 |
| 55 to 59 years | 8,866 | 4.7 | 10,046 | 4.8 | 10,567 | 4.7 | 11,279 | 4.7 | 10,816 | 4.1 |
| 60 to 64 years | 7,528 | 4.0 | 8,454 | 4.1 | 9,278 | 4.2 | 9,777 | 4.0 | 10,450 | 4.0 |
| 65 to 69 years | 6,242 | 3.3 | 6,982 | 3.3 | 7,484 | 3.3 | 8,231 | 3.4 | 8,694 | 3.3 |
| 70 to 74 years | 5,093 | 2.7 | 5,239 | 2.5 | 5,743 | 2.6 | 6,258 | 2.6 | 6,906 | 2.7 |
| 70 yrs. & over | 6,232 | 3.3 | 7,440 | 3.6 | 7,945 | 3.6 | 8,597 | 3.5 | 9,407 | 3.6 |
| All ages | *189,375 | | 208,105 | | 223,818 | | 241,746 | | 260,978 | |

*Revised estimate of total population for July 1, 1963.

Note: Data include Armed Forces overseas.

Source: U. S. Department of Commerce, Bureau of the Census.

Source: Standard & Poor's *Industry Survey on Autos*, June, 1965.

FIGURE 3–25

# *Utilities*

***Threatened by higher costs, affected by the economy's problems and a few all their own, the electric companies are counterattacking with massive spending for massive new plants, many of them nuclear. They realize they must keep up with the economy's burgeoning energy demands—or else.***

ONLY ONCE in a blue moon will the earnings of an electric company decline. Ordinarily, population growth plus more efficient power generation and transmission offset any downward pressure on earnings. But New York's Consolidated Edison Co. seems likely to report slightly lower earnings for 1966 than its $2.42 a share of 1965 when the final figures are in. Since Con Ed is not alone among the utilities in its disappointing record, it is probably a good example of the problems the industry faced last year.

Con Ed was hit hardest by the great blackout of Nov. 9, 1965, not only by the power interruption (as long as 14 hours) but also by costly damage to equipment. For example, the lack of power to run the lubrication pumps burned out 50 bearings in Con Ed's generators. Total blackout costs, Con Ed reported, were over $2 million.

This does *not* include about $7.5 million to give the system more protection, in the form of two 15,000-kilowatt gas turbines for its Ravenswood and Astoria plants and 28 diesel-powered generators for other plants. These quick-starting engines will insure safe shutdown of generators in the event of a power failure, will speed up their start afterward.

**Never Again?**

Preventing blackouts, however, requires good switching equipment, line capacity protective devices and, most important, "spinning reserve"—that is, generating capacity that can produce electricity almost instantly should other power sources suddenly fail.

The best such plants are hydroelectric, like the Cornwall pumped-storage plant Con Ed has long wanted to build north of New York City. It would use off-peak nighttime power from other generators to pump water into a mountain-top reservoir; during peak daytime demand periods the water would be released, driving generators. Generation can begin within one minute after the water valves are opened. Therefore, said Con Ed President John V. Cleary, "The project will minimize the possibility of our being affected by a major regional electric disturbance such as triggered the blackout here."

The catch: Conservationists say the project will mar the Hudson River's scenic beauties, even though the plant will be underground and the reservoir will look like a natural lake. As a result of a conservationist suit, a U.S. appeals court ordered new Federal Power Commission hearings on the project, which began Nov. 14 and will probably not be ended for months.

Con Ed's earnings were also affected by New York City's 12-day subway strike last January; and last July the city upped Con Ed's tax bill by $13 million a year. All of which led one investment service to comment that while an electric utility equity was normally not considered a risk security, Con Ed's shares threatened to "earn" the distinction. Yet there are some people who think that running a utility is a dull job.

While Con Ed, the second-largest

## YARDSTICKS OF PERFORMANCE: Utilities

(Companies are listed in each group in order of their performance.)

**GROWTH**
(7-year compounded rate)

| | Sales | Earnings | Group Ranking |
|---|---|---|---|
| *Flow-through* | | | |
| So. Calif. Edison | 9.5% | 8.8% | 1 |
| Public Service E&G | 6.3 | 10.6 | 2 |
| Virginia Electric | 7.1 | 8.7 | 3 |
| Pacific G&E | 6.7 | 8.0 | 4 |
| Ohio Edison | 5.8 | 8.4 | 5 |
| Amer. El. Power | 5.8 | 7.5 | 6 |
| Union Electric | 6.4 | 6.2 | 7 |
| Niagara Mohawk | 5.3 | 6.5 | 8 |
| Gen. Pub. Util. | 5.6 | 5.2 | 9 |
| Con Edison | 5.4 | 3.9 | 10 |
| Philadelphia Elec. | 4.6 | 4.8 | 10 |
| *Normalized & Standard* | | | |
| Commonwealth Edison | 5.3 | 8.5 | 1 |
| Texas Utilities | 8.0 | 7.7 | 1 |
| Middle South | 6.4 | 7.9 | 2 |
| Consumers Power | 8.4 | 6.9 | 3 |
| Central & SW | 6.8 | 7.1 | 4 |
| Detroit Edison | 5.2 | 7.7 | 5 |
| Southern Co. | 7.2 | 6.4 | 6 |
| New Eng. Elec. | 5.2 | 3.6 | 7 |
| INDUSTRY MEDIAN | 6.3 | 7.5 | |

**PROFITABILITY**
(5-year average)

| | Return on Equity | Cash Flow to Equity | Oper. Profit Margin† | Group Ranking |
|---|---|---|---|---|
| Union Electric | 12.3% | 21.7% | 23.9% | 1 |
| Virginia Elec. | 12.3 | 19.8 | 25.9 | 1 |
| Ohio Edison | 12.1 | 20.5 | 25.3 | 2 |
| Amer. El. Power | 11.5 | 20.9 | 24.6 | 3 |
| Gen. Pub. Util. | 11.4 | 19.0 | 27.2 | 4 |
| Pub. Ser. E&G | 12.1 | 21.4 | 20.7 | 4 |
| Phila. Elec. | 11.0 | 19.2 | 22.5 | 5 |
| Niagara Mohawk | 10.7 | 19.4 | 18.0 | 6 |
| So. Calif. Edison | 10.0 | 17.8 | 24.0 | 6 |
| Pacific G&E | 10.1 | 18.2 | 20.9 | 7 |
| Con Edison | 8.4 | 16.7 | 18.9 | 8 |
| Texas Utilities | 14.2 | 21.8 | 28.0 | 1 |
| Central & SW | 11.8 | 19.5 | 25.0 | 2 |
| Common. Edison | 11.1 | 18.9 | 21.6 | 3 |
| Southern Co. | 9.8 | 19.0 | 23.8 | 3 |
| Con. Power | 10.0 | 17.6 | 18.4 | 4 |
| Middle South | 9.4 | 18.4 | 19.1 | 5 |
| Detroit Edison | 9.7 | 16.0 | 19.4 | 6 |
| New Eng. Elec. | 8.6 | 16.1 | 17.2 | 7 |
| INDUSTRY MED. | 11.0 | 19.0 | 22.5 | |

**TREND**
(latest 12 months vs. 2-year average)

| | Earnings Gain | Net Profit Margin* | Group Ranking |
|---|---|---|---|
| Philadelphia Elec. | 13.2% | 0.9 | 1 |
| Virginia Elec. | 12.8 | 0.1 | 2 |
| Amer. El. Power | 12.2 | ** | 3 |
| Ohio Edison | 10.0 | 0.6 | 3 |
| Pacific G&E | 10.9 | 0.3 | 3 |
| So. Calif. Edison | 11.2 | 0.1 | 3 |
| Public Service E&G | 9.1 | ** | 4 |
| Niagara Mohawk | 2.7 | 0.1 | 5 |
| Gen. Pub. Util. | 7.9 | —0.2 | 6 |
| Union Electric | 6.9 | —0.1 | 6 |
| Con Edison | —1.9 | —0.5 | 7 |
| Middle South | 11.8 | 0.9 | 1 |
| Consumers Power | 14.6 | 0.4 | 2 |
| Common. Edison | 10.8 | 0.5 | 3 |
| New Eng. Elec. | 10.0 | 0.6 | 3 |
| Central & SW | 9.2 | 0.2 | 4 |
| Detroit Edison | 9.5 | ** | 4 |
| Texas Utilities | 8.0 | ** | 5 |
| Southern Co. | 6.3 | —0.7 | 6 |
| INDUSTRY MED. | 10.0 | 0.1 | |

*Gain or loss in percentage points. †After depreciation & taxes. **No change.

Source: *Forbes*, January 1, 1967, p. 70.

industry has one or more trade associations with specialized libraries and books, bulletins and monographs on industry developments.[17] The U.S. Department of Commerce publishes a number of industry reports such as *Chemical and Rubber*, *Containers and Packaging*, *Copper*, *Motor Truck Production*, *Pulp, Paper and Board*, etc., some monthly, some quarterly. Department of Commerce industry reports include a full series entitled *Facts for Industry*. Also the Commerce Department's Business and Defense Services Administration issues an annual volume (*U.S. Industrial Outlook, 1966*) with forecasts for many specific industries. *The Construction Review*, also published by the Business and Defense Services Administration has an annual forecast issue. Many of the trade associations issue annual reports or compilations. For example, in one field, the American Iron and Steel Institute issues an *Annual Statistical Report*. The American Metal Market, Inc., issues an annual *Metal Statistics*. The American Bureau of Metal Statistics issues a *Yearbook*. The U.S. Bureau of Mines releases the *Minerals Yearbook*, and McGraw-Hill publishes *The Mineral Industry*, an annual. The deeper the analyst digs into a given industry, the more likely he is to find a superabundance of information, rather than a paucity. Selecting, organizing, and analyzing the information may become a major task. The economy and usefulness of the financial services will become apparent in the course of the process.

### Company Analysis

After industry analysis comes company selection within the chosen industry or industries. The most obvious source of information about a company is its own annual reports, including balance sheets and income accounts. Frequently these are not as informative as they might be, and the analyst may wish to look at the SEC Form 10–K which listed, and certain larger unlisted, companies must file annually with the SEC and the exchange on which shares are listed and traded. This is a detailed annual financial report which must be prepared in accordance with the accounting specifications of the SEC and is therefore somewhat more detailed and informative than the regularly published annual balance sheet and income account.[18]

---

[17] For an extensive listing see Edwin T. Coman, Jr., *Sources of Business Information* (rev. ed.; Berkeley, Calif.: University of California Press, 1964). See also *Encyclopedia of American Associations* (Detroit: Gale Research Corp., 1961). Also *Guide to Special Issues and Indexes of Publications* (New York: Special Libraries Association).

[18] For those who are not fully acquainted with balance sheet, income account, and financial ratio analysis, the following are recommended: "How to Read A Financial Report," Merrill Lynch, Pierce, Fenner & Smith, New York, current; "Understanding Financial Statements," New York Stock Exchange, September, 1965; Benjamin Graham and Charles McGolrick, *The Interpretation of Financial Statements* (rev. ed.; New York: Harper & Row, Publishers, 1964).

In addition, the various investment services publish individual company reports. Standard & Poor's covers both listed and unlisted companies. An example of both sides of an S & P individual company report is shown in Figure 3–26 and 3–27. These reports provide, in capsule form, much of the relevant information the analyst seeks. They provide data on sales, operating revenues, common share earnings, recent developments, fundamental position, dividend data, prospects, finances, capitalization, and pertinent balance sheet and income account statistics for the prior 10 years. In addition, the investment service recommendation is given. The individual company reports are dated and are revised every three or four months or more often as developments require. S & P has consolidated all of its individual company reports in a large *Stock Market Encyclopedia.*

Extensive sources of company data and information are to be found in the registration statements, prospectuses, proxy statements, and other reports resulting from SEC, ICC, FPC, FCC, CAB, NYSE "full disclosure" philosophy. SEC filings, for example, contain much essential information that is generally omitted from voluntary reports. To be specific, the following are subjects about which there is important information commonly found in SEC filings but not in voluntary reports or the principal manuals—detail which may not interest a casual unsophisticated investor but which may be highly significant to a professional security analyst—expenses (rentals, maintenance, repairs, royalties, interest, etc.), receivables, inventories (classification, method of valuation, etc.), source and application of funds, depreciation, depletion, amortization, tax accounting (accounting for the investment credit, information on loss carryovers, deferred taxes, etc.), employment costs (pensions, etc.), backlogs, information on significant unconsolidated subsidiaries, additions and retirements of fixed assets, treatment of nonrecurring "special items," commitments (for capital expenditures, guarantees, long-term leases, etc.), investments in subsidiaries, reserves, management (direct and indirect compensation, options, bonuses, pensions, etc.), and wasting assets. These subjects relate principally to financial statement disclosures. Of course, there is a great deal of other material in SEC filings, not found in any other source. For example, the filings may be the exclusive source of information on control, background of management, and stockholdings of, and transactions with, insiders.[19]

The registration statement is the basic disclosure document in connection with a public distribution of securities registered under the Securities Act. It is made up of two parts. The prospectus, the first section, is the only part which is generally distributed to the public. Part II of the registration statement contains information of a more technical nature

---

[19] See Carl W. Schneider, "SEC Filings—Their Use to the Professional," *Financial Analysts Journal,* January–February, 1965, pp. 33–37.

FIGURE 3–26

T[1] **American Tel. & Tel.** 182

| Stock— | | Approx. Price | Dividend | Yield |
|---|---|---|---|---|
| CAPITAL | .............................. | 60⅛ | [2]$2.20 | [2]3.7% |

**RECOMMENDATION: The company has a dominant position in the communications field, not only through its telephone subsidiaries but also through Western Electric, Bell Telephone Laboratories, and the numerous wire services provided. The forthcoming FCC rate investigation is likely to put a damper on the stock for some time ahead, but considering the inherent growth potentialities, long-term holdings need not be disturbed.**

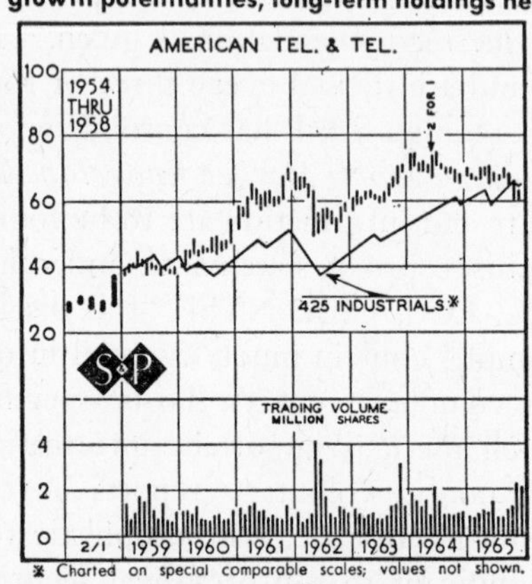


✱ Charted on special comparable scales; values not shown.

[3]OPERATING REVENUES (Million $)

| Quarter: | 1965 | 1964 | 1963 | 1962 | 1961 |
|---|---|---|---|---|---|
| Feb. ....... | 2,661 | 2,475 | 2,295 | 2,174 | 2,029 |
| May ....... | 2,725 | 2,540 | 2,378 | 2,242 | 2,083 |
| Aug. ....... | 2,772 | 2,584 | 2,401 | 2,256 | 2,106 |
| Nov. ....... | 2,839 | 2,627 | 2,432 | 2,269 | 2,150 |

For the 12 months ended November 30, 1965, total operating revenues exceeded those of a year before by 7.5%. A sharper rise in expenses was cushioned by an increase of only 2.2% in taxes, and the operating ratio dipped to 82.3%, from 82.5%. As a result, the gain in operating income was extended to 8.9%. After lower other income and 3.8% higher interest charges, net income was up 8.6%. The lesser rise in earnings to $3.40 a share, from $3.24, reflected the larger average number of shares outstanding.

Revenues and operating income for the three months ended November 30, 1965, gained 8.1% and 9.9% respectively, year to year. After a moderate rise in other income and 6.5% larger deductions, net income also was up 9.9%.

[3,4]CAPITAL SHARE EARNINGS ($)

| Quarter: | 1965 | 1964 | 1963 | 1962 | 1961 |
|---|---|---|---|---|---|
| Feb. ....... | 0.81 | 0.79 | 0.71 | 0.71 | 0.68 |
| May ....... | 0.83 | 0.81 | 0.75 | 0.74 | 0.69 |
| Aug. ....... | 0.86 | 0.81 | 0.78 | 0.74 | 0.68 |
| Nov. ....... | 0.89 | 0.83 | 0.78 | 0.72 | 0.70 |

PROSPECTS

Near Term—Earnings for 1966 are expected to exceed the estimated minimum of $3.40 an average share of 1965. However, the anticipated gain may be held to moderate proportions by recent and prospective wage increases. Dividends were raised to $0.55 quarterly, from $0.50, with the January 3, 1966, payment.

Long Term—The outlook for continued growth in all phases of operations is highly promising. The conversion to electronic switching over the next 35 years, involving an additional $12 billion of investment in plant facilities, will make possible many unique services heretofore unavailable.

RECENT DEVELOPMENTS

The FCC has decided to proceed with its full-scale investigation of AT&T's rates for interstate and foreign services. The order for the inquiry, issued on October 27, 1965, followed an FCC staff report which suggested that AT&T's profitable telephone operations may be subsidizing unreasonably low rates for services that compete with those offered by Western Union. The report also recommended the sale by AT&T of its TWX teletypewriter network to Western Union.

The investigation will be divided into two phases, the first of which will deal with the rate-making principles for interstate and foreign operations of the entire Bell System. Upon conclusion of that phase, interim rate changes will be considered. The second phase will deal with other matters, such as the reasonableness of prices paid by Bell System companies for equipment purchased from Western Electric, AT&T's manufacturing arm. The inquiry could lead to important revisions in AT&T's charges; however, a final determination of issues may be several years away, and may ultimately show the company's rates to be justified.

DIVIDEND DATA

Dividends in the past 12 months were:

| Amt. of Divd. $ | Date Decl. | Ex-divd. Date | Stock of Record | Payment Date |
|---|---|---|---|---|
| 0.50... | Feb. 17 | Feb. 24 | Mar. 1 | Apr. 1'65 |
| 0.50... | May 19 | May 26 | Jun. 1 | Jul. 1'65 |
| 0.50... | Aug. 18 | Aug. 27 | Sep. 1 | Oct. 1'65 |
| 0.55... | Nov. 17 | Nov. 26 | Dec. 1 | Jan. 3'66 |

[1]Listed N.Y.S.E., Boston, Phila.-Balt.-Wash., Midwest, and Pacific Coast S.Es. and Paris Bourse; also traded Cincinnati, Detroit, and Pitts. S.Es. [2]Indicated rate. [3]Consol. [4]Based on average shares outstanding; adj. for 2-for-1 split in 1964.

Source: *Standard Listed Stock Reports,* © 1966 by Standard & Poor's Corp., Vol. 33, No. 22 (February 1, 1966).

## FIGURE 3–26 (Continued)

# 182 AMERICAN TELEPHONE & TELEGRAPH COMPANY

### [1] INCOME STATISTICS (Million $) AND PER SHARE ($) DATA

| Year Ended Dec. 31 | Revenues Local | Revenues Toll | [3]Gross | % of Gr. Revs. Dep. & Maint. | % of Gr. Revs. Taxes | [2]Oper. Ratio | Fxd. Chgs. Tms. Earn. | Net Inc. | [5]Capital Share ($) Data [4]Earns. | Divs. Paid | Price Range | Price-Earns. Ratios HI LO |
|---|---|---|---|---|---|---|---|---|---|---|---|---|
| 1966— | ——— | ——— | ——— | ——— | ——— | ——— | ——— | ——— | ——— | 0.55 | ——— | ——— |
| 1965— | ——— | ——— | ——— | ——— | ——— | ——— | ——— | ——— | ——— | 2.00 | 70½ –60⅛ | ——— |
| 1964— | 5,633.7 | 4,205.5 | 10,306.0 | 31.6 | 23.1 | 82.5 | 6.47 | 1,658.6 | 3.24 | 1.95 | 75 –65⅜ | 23–20 |
| 1963— | 5,389.7 | 3,737.1 | 9,569.0 | 31.0 | 23.5 | 82.7 | 6.00 | 1,479.5 | 3.03 | 1.80 | 70⅝ –57¼ | 23–19 |
| 1962— | 5,088.5 | 3,471.8 | 8,980.2 | 30.6 | 23.4 | 82.5 | 6.15 | 1,388.2 | 2.90 | 1.80 | 68⅛ –49 | 24–17 |
| 1961— | 4,797.5 | 3,217.3 | 8,414.4 | 30.1 | 23.4 | 83.0 | 6.18 | 1,284.6 | 2.76 | 1.73 | 69⅞ –51½ | 25–19 |
| 1960— | 4,547.4 | 2,996.4 | 7,920.5 | 30.1 | 23.3 | 83.4 | 6.34 | 1,213.0 | 2.77 | 1.65 | 54¼ –39⅞ | 20–14 |
| 1959— | 4,250.8 | 2,786.1 | 7,393.0 | 30.0 | 22.9 | 83.4 | 6.69 | 1,113.2 | 2.61 | 1.58 | 44½ –37⅜ | 17–14 |
| 1958— | 3,944.4 | 2,490.6 | 6,771.4 | 30.4 | 21.9 | 84.4 | 6.28 | 952.3 | 2.34 | 1.50 | 37¾ –27⅞ | 16–12 |
| 1957— | 3,647.6 | 2,357.7 | 6,313.8 | 31.2 | 20.1 | 86.1 | 7.00 | 829.8 | 2.17 | 1.50 | 29⅞ –26⅝ | 14–12 |
| 1956— | 3,368.6 | 2,176.2 | 5,825.3 | 30.5 | 19.8 | 86.4 | 7.31 | 755.9 | 2.20 | 1.50 | 31⅛ –27½ | 14–13 |
| 1955— | 3,086.5 | 1,959.7 | 5,297.0 | 30.0 | 19.7 | 86.4 | 6.74 | 664.2 | 2.19 | 1.50 | 31¼ –28¾ | 14–13 |

### [1] PERTINENT BALANCE SHEET STATISTICS (Million $)

| Dec. 31 | Gross Prop. | Capital Expend. | % Depr. of Gross Prop. | [6]% Earn on Net Prop. | Funded Debt | % Funded Debt of Net Prop. | % Funded Debt of Gross Rev. | % Funded Debt of Invest. Cap. | Total Invest. Cap. | [6]% Earn. on Inv. Cap | Net Inc. per Tel. | [5]($) Book Val. Cap. Sh. |
|---|---|---|---|---|---|---|---|---|---|---|---|---|
| 1964— | 32,544 | 3,519 | 21.4 | 7.0 | 8,725 | 34.1 | 84.6 | 31.0 | 28,136 | 7.2 | 23.03 | 35.39 |
| 1963— | 30,064 | 3,136 | 21.3 | 7.2 | 8,579 | 36.2 | 89.7 | 33.5 | 25,612 | 7.2 | 21.54 | 32.87 |
| 1962— | 27,914 | 2,976 | 21.3 | 7.2 | 8,224 | 37.5 | 91.6 | 34.0 | 24,221 | 7.1 | 21.04 | 31.42 |
| 1961— | 25,893 | 2,696 | 21.6 | 7.0 | 7,271 | 35.8 | 86.4 | 32.6 | 22,299 | 7.1 | 20.33 | 29.91 |
| 1960— | 24,072 | 2,658 | 21.8 | 7.0 | 7,232 | 38.4 | 91.3 | 35.4 | 20,452 | 7.3 | 19.97 | 28.25 |
| 1959— | 22,205 | 2,249 | 22.2 | 7.1 | 6,432 | 37.3 | 87.0 | 34.2 | 18,832 | 7.2 | 19.20 | 27.24 |
| 1958— | 20,646 | 2,186 | 22.4 | 6.6 | 6,042 | 37.7 | 89.2 | 34.2 | 17,651 | 6.6 | 17.41 | 26.29 |
| 1957— | 19,117 | 2,566 | 22.8 | 6.0 | 5,688 | 38.6 | 90.1 | 35.7 | 15,945 | 6.2 | 15.88 | 25.62 |
| 1956— | 17,074 | 2,249 | 24.1 | 6.1 | 4,618 | 35.6 | 79.3 | 31.9 | 14,487 | 6.2 | 15.29 | 24.94 |
| 1955— | 15,344 | 1,643 | 25.4 | 6.3 | 4,376 | 38.2 | 82.6 | 34.1 | 12,844 | 6.2 | 14.37 | 25.07 |

[1]Consol. [2]After depr. & taxes. [3]Aft. deduct. uncollectible revs. [4]Based on aver. shs. outstg. [5]Adj. for 3-for-1 split in 1959 & 2-for-1 split in 1964. [6]Based on bk. value; may differ from return on rate base.

#### Fundamental Position

A holding and operating company, American Telephone & Telegraph, through its telephone subsidiaries comprising the Bell System, controls around 75,900,000 telephones, about 81% of the country's total. Non-controlling stock interests are held in other telephone operating companies which are not now considered part of the Bell System. Approximately 55% of system revenues is derived from local service, and 41% from toll operations. The parent company directly operates long-distance lines connecting regional units and independent systems.

Equipment is purchased largely from the Western Electric Company, 99.8% owned, which has been a substantial contributor to earnings in recent years. Research work is conducted for the company and Western Electric on a non-profit basis by Bell Telephone Laboratories, a wholly owned subsidiary.

Auxiliary services of the company include teletypewriter exchange service, private line telephone and teletypewriter services, and facilities for transmission of television and radio programs. Overseas service is provided by means of cable and radio circuits, and interconnections are maintained between telephone systems in the United States and those in 186 countries and territories. To supplement the maximum 520-channel capacity of existing transatlantic cables (including the link completed in September, 1965), the company has applied for 100 channels in Communications Satellite Corp.'s Early Bird unit. Through its ownership of 2,895,750 shares ($57.9 million) of the latter's common stock, AT&T will play an important part in Comsat's future.

The company does not use accelerated depreciation. Savings from the 3% investment credit are amortized over the life of the property giving rise to the credit.

The $100 million cut in interstate tariffs ordered by the FCC in November, 1964, was effected in February and April of 1965. The FCC lowered the company's rate of return on its long-distance business to 7%, from 7.9%, but at the time indicated that it did not consider the lower rate a ceiling for future interstate earnings.

Dividends have been paid each year since 1885. The increase in 1959 was the first since 1922.

Employees: 761,611. Shareholders: About 2,800,000.

#### Finances

Capital expenditures in 1966 are expected to be in the vicinity of the $3.9 billion spent in the preceding year. The company intends to sell $250 million of debentures through competitive bidding in March, 1966. During 1965, the system raised more than $1 billion of new funds, primarily through six debt issues by subsidiaries and employee stock purchases. No common stock rights offering is expected in 1966.

#### CAPITALIZATION

FUNDED DEBT: Parent...... $3,490,000,000
Subs. .......... $5,235,000,000
SUBSIDIARY PFD. STOCKS: $17,904,300
MINORITY INTEREST....... $579,292,000
CAPITAL STOCK: 529,752,199 shares ($16-2/3 par).

**Incorporated** in N.Y. in 1885. **Office**—195 Broadway, NYC 10007. **Pres**—H. I. Romnes. **VP-Secy**—C. E. Wampler. **VP-Treas**—J. J. Scanlon. **Dirs**—F. R. Kappel (Chrmn), W. M. Batten, L. D. Brace, J. E. Dingman, E. B. Hanify, H. T. Heald, J. V. Herd, W. A. Hewitt, J. R. Killian, Jr., J. J. McCloy, E. J. McNeely, J. I. Miller, W. B. Murphy, T. F. Patton, M. J. Rathbone, H. I. Romnes, G. F. Smith, J. Taylor, W. White. **Transfer Agents**—Company's offices; 195 Broadway, NYC 7; New England Tel. & Tel. Co., Boston; Illinois Bell Telephone Co., Chicago; Pacific Tel. & Tel., San Francisco. **Registrars**—Bankers Trust Co., NYC; Old Colony Trust Co., Boston; First National Bank, Chicago; Wells Fargo Bank, San Francisco.

FIGURE 3–27

GM[1]

# General Motors

978

| Stock— | Approx. Price | Dividend | Yield |
|---|---|---|---|
| COMMON | 105¼ | [2]$5.55 | [2]5.3% |
| $5 PREFERRED | 108 | 5.00 | 4.6 |
| $3.75 PREFERRED | 82 | 3.75 | 4.6 |

**RECOMMENDATION: Considering GM's entrenched competitive position, strong finances, and favorable earnings prospects for the longer term, its COMMON stock, a logical split candidate, deserves consideration for any well-rounded investment portfolio. The PREFERREDS are high-grade income issues.**

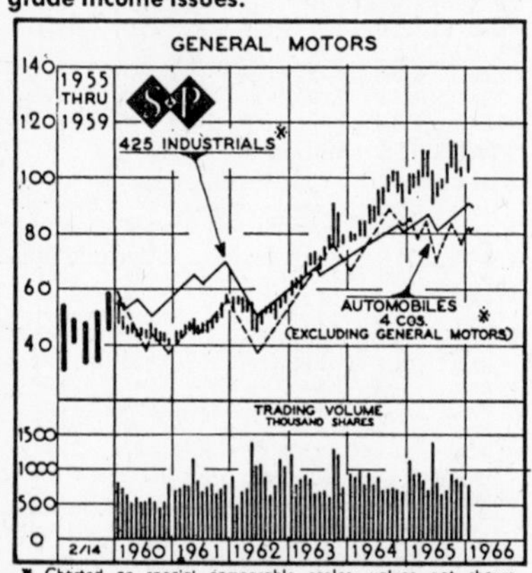


* Charted on special comparable scales; values not shown.

**SALES (Million $)**

| Quarter: | 1965 | 1964 | 1963 | 1962 | 1961 |
|---|---|---|---|---|---|
| March | 5,558 | 4,786 | 4,147 | 3,665 | 2,724 |
| June | 5,657 | 5,082 | 4,517 | 4,026 | 3,088 |
| Sept. | 3,743 | 3,291 | 3,017 | 2,760 | 1,968 |
| Dec. | [5]5,742 | 3,838 | 4,814 | 4,149 | 3,616 |

Based on the preliminary report, sales in 1965 advanced 22% from those of 1964 to a new peak on a 19% increase in world-wide factory shipments of cars and trucks. Output at U. S. plants gained 24% on higher industry-wide retail demand for motor vehicles, the strike-caused deferment of production from late 1964, and a slightly higher GM share of the total domestic passenger car market. Foreign shipments of automobiles and trucks were up 3%. Despite heavier pension, overtime, and tooling amortization expenses, results benefited from the higher unit volume and the absence of year-earlier strike expenses. Pretax profits increased 25%. After higher taxes at 48.0%, compared with 47.2%, net income rose 23% to the highest level in the company's history.

**[4]COMMON SHARE EARNINGS ($)**

| Quarter: | 1965 | 1964 | 1963 | [3]1962 | 1961 |
|---|---|---|---|---|---|
| March | 2.22 | 1.87 | 1.45 | 1.31 | 0.65 |
| June | 2.23 | 2.11 | 1.62 | 1.41 | 0.88 |
| Sept. | 0.91 | 0.77 | 0.72 | 0.64 | 0.30 |
| Dec. | [5]2.05 | 1.30 | 1.77 | 1.74 | 1.28 |

**PROSPECTS**

**Near Term**—Sales for 1966 may approach the record $20.7 billion of 1965. Although total domestic passenger car registrations are expected to continue at an excellent level, GM's automobile production will not benefit as in 1965 from the need to rebuild dealer inventories of new cars which were depleted during the strike of late 1964. No sizable change in the company's share of the total U. S. automobile market appears likely. Growth in foreign motor vehicle volume is anticipated, demand for trucks should rise moderately, and deliveries of non-automotive products should increase.

Despite higher wage rates, materials costs, and depreciation charges, results would be boosted by efficiency gains, prospective reduced overtime payments, a probable more favorable product mix, and an improved contribution from foreign operations. Profits for 1966 may come close to the peak $7.41 a share (preliminary) of 1965. An $0.85 dividend is being paid for the first quarter of 1966, compared with $0.75 a year earlier.

**Long Term**—Allowing for interim fluctuations, an outstanding automotive trade position and diversification point to growth.

**RECENT DEVELOPMENTS**

World-wide capital expenditures of about $2.6 billion are planned for 1965-66, about half in each year. Roughly $1.9 billion should be spent in the U. S., $150 million in Canada, and $550 million overseas.

In January, 1965, duPont made the last of three distributions of GM shares in compliance with the Supreme Court's ruling.

**DIVIDEND DATA**

Payments in the past 12 months were:

| Amt. of Divd. $ | Date Decl. | Ex-divd. Date | Stock of Record | Payment Date |
|---|---|---|---|---|
| 0.75... | May 3 | May 10 | May 13 | Jun. 10'65 |
| 0.75spl. | May 3 | May 10 | May 13 | Jun. 10'65 |
| 0.75... | Aug. 2 | Aug. 9 | Aug. 12 | Sep. 10'65 |
| 2.25y.e. | Nov. 1 | Nov. 5 | Nov. 10 | Dec. 10'65 |
| 0.85... | Feb. 7 | Feb. 14 | Feb. 17 | Mar. 10'66 |

[1]Listed N.Y.S.E.; com. & $5 pfd. also listed Midwest, Phila.-Balt.-Wash. & Pacific Coast S.Es.; com. listed Detroit, Toronto & Montreal S.Es. & Paris Bourse, & traded Cincinnati, Pittsburgh & Boston S.Es. [2]Estimated rate, incl. extras as paid in 1965. [3]Incl. $0.27 non-rec. inc. [4]Based on avge. shs. [5]Preliminary.

Source: *Standard Listed Stock Reports,* © 1966 by Standard & Poor's Corp., Vol. 33, No. 31 (February 14, 1966).

## FIGURE 3–27 (Continued)

# 978 GENERAL MOTORS CORPORATION

### [1]INCOME STATISTICS (Million $) AND PER SHARE ($) DATA

| Year Ended Dec. 31 | Net Sales | [3]% Op. Inc. of Sales | Amort. Depr. & Depl. | Equity Earns. Unconsol. Subs. | Net Bef. Taxes | [4]Net Inc. | Common Share ($) Data: [4]Earns. | *Cash Generated | Divs. Paid | Price Range | Price-Earns. Ratios HI LO |
|---|---|---|---|---|---|---|---|---|---|---|---|
| 1966-- | ----- | --- | ---- | --- | ----- | ------ | --- | --- | 0.85 | ---------- | ---- |
| 1965-- | [6]20,700 | --- | ---- | --- | [6]4,092.0 | [6]2,126.00 | [6]7.41 | --- | 5.25 | 113¾-91¼ | 15-12 |
| 1964-- | 16,997 | 21.3 | 494.8 | 45.0 | 3,283.7 | 1,734.78 | 6.05 | 7.88 | 4.45 | 102⅝-77¼ | 17-13 |
| 1963-- | 16,495 | 22.4 | 475.2 | 47.5 | 3,353.9 | 1,591.82 | 5.56 | 7.37 | 4.00 | 91⅜-57⅞ | 16-10 |
| 1962-- | 14,640 | 21.7 | 444.6 | 50.6 | 2,934.5 | 1,459.08 | 5.10 | 6.72 | 3.00 | 59⅝-44½ | 12- 9 |
| 1961-- | 11,396 | 18.1 | 408.5 | 58.1 | 1,768.0 | 892.82 | 3.11 | 4.54 | 2.50 | 58 -40⅝ | 19-13 |
| 1960-- | 12,736 | 18.0 | 388.5 | 56.0 | 2,037.5 | 959.04 | 3.35 | 4.72 | 2.00 | 55⅞-40¼ | 17-12 |
| 1959-- | 11,233 | 18.6 | 413.7 | 51.2 | 1,792.2 | 873.10 | 3.06 | 4.52 | 2.00 | 58⅞-45 | 19-15 |
| 1958-- | 9,522 | 15.2 | 420.2 | 61.2 | 1,115.4 | 633.63 | 2.22 | 3.71 | 2.00 | 52 -33¾ | 23-15 |
| 1957-- | 10,990 | 17.8 | 414.9 | 51.3 | 1,648.7 | 843.59 | 2.99 | 4.47 | 2.00 | 47½-33⅛ | 16-11 |
| 1956-- | 10,796 | 18.4 | 347.2 | 57.2 | 1,741.4 | 847.40 | 3.02 | 4.26 | 2.00 | 49¼-40¼ | 16-13 |
| 1955-- | 12,443 | 22.2 | 293.8 | 45.6 | 2,542.8 | 1,189.48 | 4.30 | 5.32 | 2.17 | 54 -29⅞ | 13- 7 |

### [1]PERTINENT BALANCE SHEET STATISTICS (Million $)

| Dec. 31 | Gross Prop. | [2]Capital Expend. | Cash Items | Inven-tories | Receiv-ables | Current Assets | Current Liabs. | Net Workg. Cap. | Cur. Ratio Assets to Liabs. | Long Term Debt | ($) Book Val. Com. Sh. |
|---|---|---|---|---|---|---|---|---|---|---|---|
| [5]1965----- | 9,731 | ---- | 1,818.9 | 3,184.3 | 1,095.0 | 6,098.2 | 2,206.7 | 3,891.5 | 2.8-1 | 238.50 | 27.27 |
| 1964----- | 8,865 | 929.6 | 1,390.5 | 2,677.8 | 1,387.2 | 5,455.5 | 1,804.5 | 3,651.0 | 3.0-1 | 231.98 | 25.22 |
| 1963----- | 7,967 | 647.2 | 1,890.7 | 2,221.2 | 1,250.6 | 5,362.6 | 1,635.2 | 3,727.4 | 3.3-1 | 260.46 | 23.53 |
| 1962----- | 7,510 | 645.1 | 2,082.8 | 2,006.5 | 1,069.6 | 5,158.9 | 1,630.8 | 3,528.0 | 3.2-1 | 344.18 | 21.87 |
| 1961----- | 7,005 | 503.2 | 1,696.1 | 1,800.1 | 987.3 | 4,483.5 | 1,424.9 | 3,058.6 | 3.1-1 | 365.32 | 19.69 |
| 1960----- | 6,667 | 526.0 | 1,637.5 | 1,811.0 | 608.6 | 4,057.0 | 1,257.7 | 2,799.3 | 3.2-1 | 305.37 | 19.02 |
| 1959----- | 6,186 | 319.9 | 1,261.8 | 1,799.8 | 643.2 | 3,704.8 | 1,138.7 | 2,566.2 | 3.3-1 | 308.30 | 17.55 |
| 1958----- | 5,954 | 269.4 | 1,123.3 | 1,529.5 | 585.5 | 3,238.2 | 1,139.5 | 2,098.7 | 2.8-1 | 329.92 | 16.39 |
| 1957----- | 5,765 | 472.9 | 733.4 | 1,730.8 | 553.4 | 3,017.6 | 1,156.2 | 1,861.4 | 2.6-1 | 342.20 | 16.04 |
| 1956----- | 5,272 | 890.5 | 672.2 | 1,719.6 | 570.7 | 2,962.5 | 1,216.5 | 1,746.0 | 2.4-1 | 341.78 | 14.94 |
| 1955----- | 4,354 | 608.1 | 1,201.5 | 1,601.7 | 580.4 | 3,392.6 | 1,334.3 | 2,058.3 | 2.5-1 | 300.00 | 13.92 |

[1]Consol.; incl. all subs. engaged in mfg. or wholesale marketing opers.; does not incl. G.M. Acceptance Corp. & Yellow Mfg. Acceptance or their subs. [2]Excl. additions for spec. tools. [3]Bef. depr., but aft. amort. of special tools & employee bonus. [4]Based on avge. shs. outstanding; incl. non-recurring inc. of $0.27 a sh. in 1962. [5]As of Sept. 30. [6]Preliminary.
*As computed by Standard & Poor's.

### Fundamental Position

General Motors derives approximately 89% of total sales from automotive products, including cars, trucks, buses, parts and accessories. The Frigidaire and Delco appliance divisions, and the Allison, Diesel Electro-Motive, and Euclid divisions contribute most of the remainder. Defense work represented 2.5% of 1964 sales.

Chevrolet (including the Corvette, Chevelle, Corvair, and Chevy II), Buick (including the Special and Riviera), Cadillac, Oldsmobile (including the F-85), and Pontiac (including the Tempest) accounted for 49.1% of total new domestic registrations (including foreign-built cars) in 1964, compared with 51.0% in 1963 and 51.9% in 1962. Comparable figures for Chevrolet and GMC trucks are 42.8%, 41.3%, and 41.8%. There are about 16,000 U. S. and Canadian car and truck dealers. World-wide factory sales of cars and trucks in 1965 were 7,278,000 units, compared with 6,114,000 in 1964 and 5,974,000 in 1963. Domestic production in these years was 5,706,000, 4,591,000, and 4,662,000, respectively.

The company operates as a decentralized organization, with about 124 plants in 19 states, five plants in Canada, and assembly, manufacturing, and warehousing operations in 22 other countries. About 13% of consolidated net income in 1964 resulted from participation in markets outside of the U. S. and Canada, compared with 8% in 1963 and 7% in 1962. Investments in non-consolidated subsidiaries, including General Motors Acceptance Corp. and Yellow Mfg. Acceptance Corp., totaled $473 million at the 1964 year-end. The interest in Ethyl Corp. was sold in Nov., 1962.

Dividends, paid since 1915, averaged 71% of available earnings in the five years through 1965. Employees (world-wide): 734,000. Shareholders (common and preferred): 1,296,000.

### Finances

Growth has been financed primarily from retained earnings, but this source has been supplemented since the end of World War II by $98 million of preferred stock sold in 1946, $300 million of debentures in 1953, and $325 million of common stock sold in 1955, plus borrowings by foreign subsidiaries. Finances are impressive, with a current ratio of at least three to one in 1959-64 and with cash items substantial.

### CAPITALIZATION

LONG TERM DEBT: $238,504,000, divided $70,804,000 3¼% debs. due 1979 and $167,700,000 foreign subsidiary notes to 1977.
$5 CUM. PREFERRED STOCK: 1,835,644 shares (no par); redeemable at $120.
$3.75 CUM. PFD. STOCK: 1,000,000 shs. (no par); red. at $102 through Nov. 1, 1966, then less.
COMMON STOCK: 285,068,784 shares ($1.66-2/3 par).

**Incorporated** in Del. in 1916. **Office**—3044 W. Grand Blvd., Detroit 2. **Chairman & Chief Exec Officer**—F. G. Donner. **Pres**—J. M. Roche. **Secy**—E. B. Wallace. **Dirs**—H. C. Alexander, E. N. Beesley, L. D. Brace, A. Bradley, H. Branch, Jr., L. D. Clay, E. N. Cole, F. G. Donner, E. F. Fisher, L. C. Goad, J. F. Gordon, O. E. Hunt, J. R. Killian, Jr., S. E. Knudsen, R. M. Kyes, J. W. McAfee, R. S. McLaughlin, R. K. Mellon, H. J. Morgens, C. S. Mott, T. L. Perkins, J. L. Pratt, J. M. Roche, E. D. Rollert, G. Russell, G. F. Towers, W. K. Whiteford. **Transfer Offices**—Company's office, 1775 Broadway, NYC; Wilmington Trust Co., Wilmington, Del.; Continental Illinois Natl. Bank & Trust Co., Chicago; National Bank of Detroit; Bank of America, N.T. & S.A.; San Francisco; National Trust Co., Toronto and Montreal; (Pfd.), National Bank of Detroit. **Registrars**—Chase Manhattan Bank, NYC; Bank of Delaware, Wilmington, Del.; Northern Trust Co., Chicago; Wells Fargo Bank, San Francisco; Royal Trust Co., Montreal and Toronto (Pfd.) Detroit Trust Co., Detroit.

dealing wth such matters as marketing arrangements, the expenses of the distribution, relationships between the registrant and certain experts, sales of securities to special parties, recent sales of unregistered securities, a list of subsidiaries, treatment of proceeds from stock being registered, etc. In addition, Part II contains signatures, financial schedules, and historical financial information not required in the prospectus. Filed with the registration statement are exhibits such as contracts relating to the underwriting; the charter and bylaws of the registrant, specimen copies of securities; instruments relating to long-term debt, option agreements, pension plans, retirement plans, and deferred compensation plans; an opinion of counsel; material foreign patents; and certain material contracts not made in the ordinary course of business.

The Exchange Act has four types of disclosure requirements relating to registration, periodic reporting, proxy solicitation, and insider trading. Listed and OTC-registered companies are required to file certain periodic reports. The three most important of these reports are Forms 8–K, 9–K, and 10–K. Form 8–K is a current report which is filed for each calendar month during which an event occurs which requires reporting. The report is due by the 10th day of the following month. The various events to be reported on Form 8–K include the following: (*a*) changes in control of registrant; (*b*) acquisition or disposition of assets; (*c*) interest of management and others in certain transactions; (*d*) legal proceedings; (*e*) changes in securities; (*f*) changes in security (i.e., collateral) for registered securities; (*g*) defaults upon senior securities; (*h*) increase in the amount of securities outstanding; (*i*) issuance of debt securities by subsidiaries; (*j*) decrease in the amount of securities outstanding; (*k*) options to purchase securities; (*l*) revaluation of assets or restatement of capital share account; (*m*) submission of matters to a vote of security holders; (*n*) newly enacted requirements affecting registrant's business; (*o*) other materially important events; and (*p*) financial statements and exhibits. When a business of significant size is acquired, the registrant is required to file financial statements of the acquired business.

Form 9–K includes certain unaudited financial information for the first six months of each fiscal year. It is due within 45 days after the end of the period covered and contains key figures on gross sales, operating revenues, extraordinary items, income or loss before federal income taxes, taxes, net income or loss after taxes, special items, and earned surplus items.

Form 10–K is an annual report which is due 120 days after the end of each fiscal year. The SEC's Regulation S–X governs the form and content of most of the financial statements, including 10–K, required to be filed with the Commission. Financial statements prepared in compliance with Regulation S–X, and particularly the notes to the statements, often give substantially more information than other financial statements distributed by companies. For instance, Regulation S–X requires the notes to contain certain details on long-term leases, funded debt, management stock options, classification of inventories, and basis for computing depreciation which often do not appear in other financial statements. Regulation S–X also requires supplemental schedules to complete the financial statements. The information in these schedules almost never appears in financial statements generally distributed to the public. The Form 10–K report contains certified financial statements, including a balance sheet, a profit and loss statement for the fiscal year covered by the report, an analysis of surplus and supporting schedules.[20]

Forms, publications and reports may be consulted at the Commission's main and regional offices.[21] All officially filed forms may be consulted and photocopied. In similar fashion, official filings of certain types of companies may be consulted at the offices of the Interstate Commerce Commission (railroads and trucking companies), Federal Communications Commission (telephone, TV broadcasting, etc., companies), Federal Power Commission (electric and gas utilities), Comptroller of the Currency, and Federal Deposit Insurance Corporation (commercial banks). A vast array of data on individual companies can be found in official filings with governmental agencies. Increasingly these data are being made available to the public in accordance with the SEC's "full disclosure" concept. They are, of course, of great value to the professional securities analyst.

The careful securities analyst may wish to know more about the company's competitive position, about its financial condition and profitability, about its operating efficiency and management, about its outlook and prospects, than published data and statistics provide. It has been routine procedure for analysts to invite company officials to address meetings of analysts at which an opportunity is afforded to ask questions and receive company replies.

While most analysts attend as many of these luncheon and dinner meetings as possible, a source is fortunately available which reproduces the proceedings at such meetings. This is *The Wall Street Transcript.* It is a tabloid-sized weekly newspaper specializing in the full texts of analysts' studies of leading corporations and full texts of executives' talks before securities analysts meetings. It sells on a subscription basis for $180 a year or $5 an individual issue.

It has also become standard procedure for an analyst doing a report in depth to visit the company's plant or main office and talk with top management. Homework needs to be done carefully prior to such visits. All available published data about the company should have been reviewed,

[20] See Carl W. Schneider, "SEC Filings—Their Content and Use," *Financial Analysts Journal*, March–April, 1965, pp. 42–47.

[21] Regional offices (and branches of regional offices) are maintained in New York City, Boston, Atlanta (Miami), Chicago (Cleveland, Detroit, St. Paul, St. Louis), Fort Worth (Houston), Denver (Salt Lake City), San Francisco (Los Angeles), Seattle, and Washington, D.C. (at a separate location from the main office).

an initial analysis undertaken, and a list of questions for management prepared. The competent analyst will approach his visit and interviews as thoroughly prepared as he can be from external sources. Complete security analysis usually requires discussion with top management and involves much more than mere financial ratio analysis, a somewhat mechanical technique largely carried over from the old days when corporations regarded their financial and industrial position and prospects as closely guarded company secrets unavailable to the public.

## SUGGESTED READINGS

Edwin T. Coman, Jr. *Sources of Business Information.* Rev. ed. Berkeley, Calif.: University of California Press, 1964.

Maurice L. Farrell (ed.). *The Dow Jones Investor's Handbook.* Princeton, N.J.: Dow-Jones Books, 1967.

Benjamin Graham and Charles McGolrick. *The Interpretation of Financial Statements.* Rev. ed. New York: Harper & Row, Publishers, 1964.

Merrill Lynch, Pierce, Fenner, and Smith. *How To Read A Financial Report.* Latest ed. A free copy can be obtained by writing to this firm at 70 Pine Street, New York, N.Y. 10005.

Moody's Investor's Service. *Moody's Handbook of Widely-Held Common Stocks.* Latest edition. New York.

*Moody's Stock Survey,* published weekly by Moody's Investor's Service, 99 Church Street, New York, N.Y. 10007. A free sample copy will be sent on request.

New York Stock Exchange. *How To Understand Financial Statements.* A free copy may be obtained from the Publications Division, New York Stock Exchange, 11 Wall Street, New York, N.Y. 10005.

*The Outlook,* published weekly by Standard & Poor's, Inc., 345 Hudson Street, New York, N.Y. 10014. A free sample copy will be sent on request.

*Security and Industry Survey,* issued quarterly by Merrill Lynch, Pierce, Fenner, and Smith. A free copy may be obtained by writing to 70 Pine Street, New York, N.Y. 10005.

Standard & Poor's, Inc. *Industry Surveys.* Latest issue. New York.

Standard & Poor's *Stock Market Encyclopedia.* 7th ed. New York, 1966.

H. C. Walter (ed.), *Investment Information and Advice: A Handbook and Directory.* Whittier, Calif.: FIR Publishing Co., 1964.

## FIRST APPENDIX TO CHAPTER 3

The importance of industry analysis may be seen in the following charts, one for each of the years 1946–66 inclusive. These are reproduced with the kind permission of George A. Chestnutt, Jr. They are to be found in *Stock Market Analysis: Facts and Principles* by George A. Chestnutt, Jr., copyright by the Chestnutt Corporation, 88 Field Point Road, Greenwich, Connecticut 06830, 1967.

## FIRST APPENDIX TO CHAPTER 3

## Industry Group Performance Charts, 1946–66

### 1946

1946 was a bear market year in the averages, The American Investors Service Composite Geometric Average declined 16%. Despite this general decline, 8 out of 42 industry group averages advanced during the year.

The chart on this page shows the percentage advance or decline for each of 42 industry groups. The Dow-Jones and American Investors Composite Averages are also shown for comparison.

Even though 1946 was a bear market year, an investment in the average Baking or Gas stock appreciated 11% in value. At the other extreme, an investment in the average Airline stock shrank 55% and an investment in the average Communication stock shrank 45%.

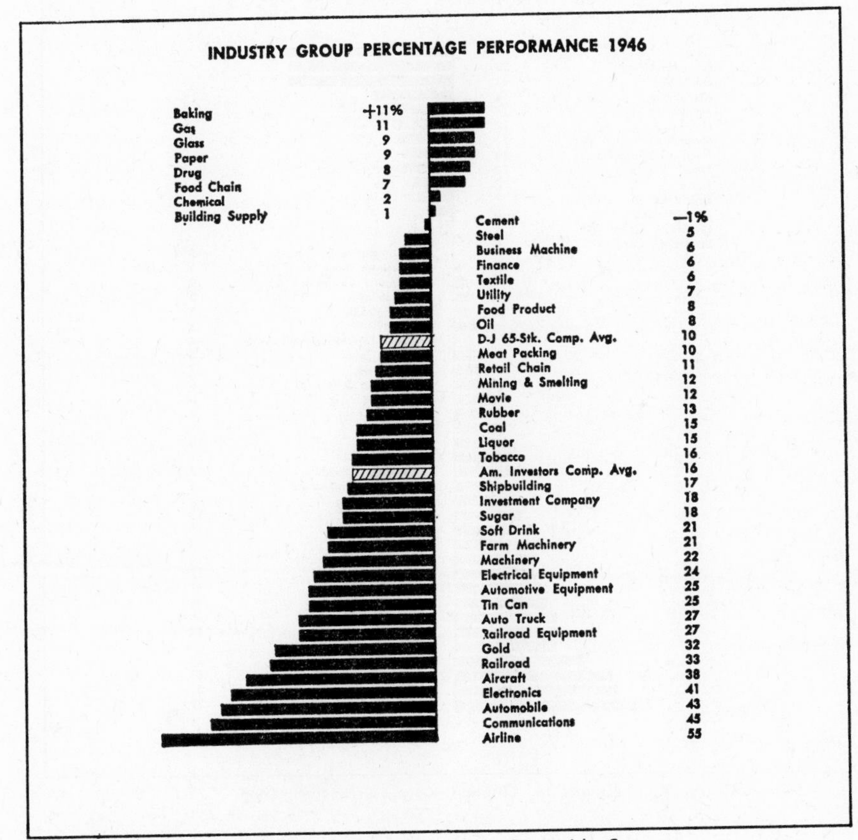


Source: George A. Chestnutt, Jr., Chestnutt Corp., Greenwich, Conn.

## FIRST APPENDIX TO CHAPTER 3 (Continued)

### 1947

The general market decline which began in June 1946 ended about a year later, in May 1947. The Dow-Jones 65-Stock Average ended the year 1947 about 1% higher than it began. However, only 13 out of 44 industry groups advanced while 31 groups declined. The more representative Composite Geometric Average declined 4%.

Coal Mining, Farm Machinery and Oil stocks were the star performers in 1947. Movie, Airline and Drug stocks were very weak.

As in the preceding chart, the bars on this chart show percentagewise gains and losses for each industry group and two general market averages.

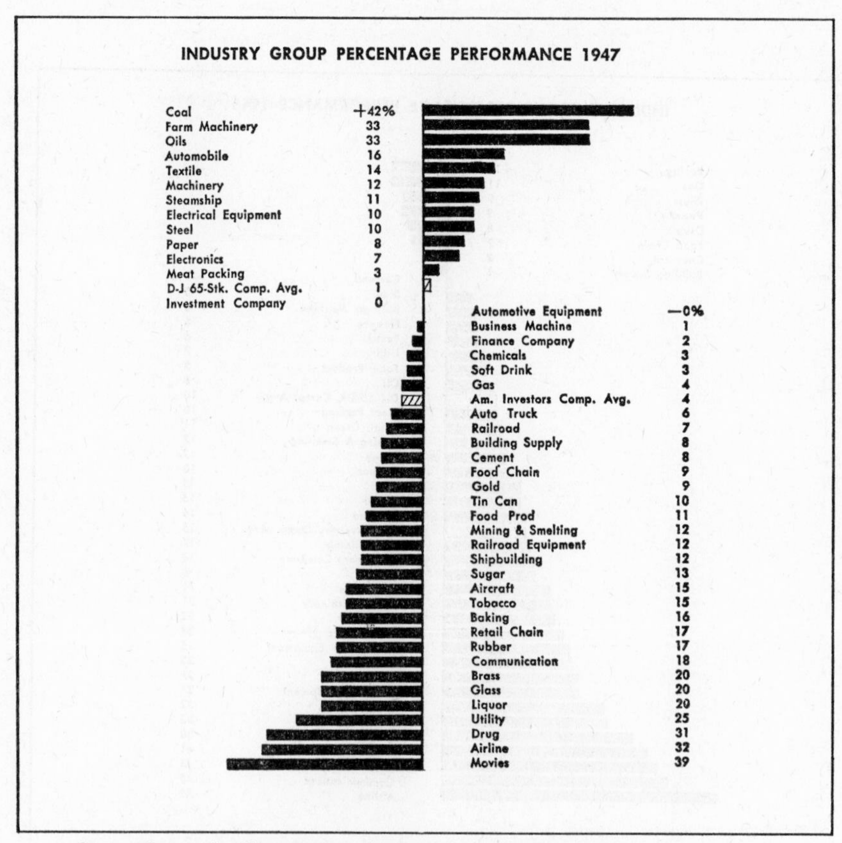


Source: George A. Chestnutt, Jr., Chestnutt Corp., Greenwich, Conn.

## FIRST APPENDIX TO CHAPTER 3 (Continued)

### 1948

As you will see from this chart of group performance in 1948, the 1% decline in the Dow-Jones Composite average was misleading. Only 9 out of 44 groups advanced; 35 groups declined. The much broader Composite Geometric Average shows that the "average stock" actually declined 9% in 1948.

Except for the outstanding performance of the Electronics Group, which advanced 51%, the group performance chart shows that 1948 was almost as poor a year as 1946 for the average investor who diversified his holdings across-the-board.

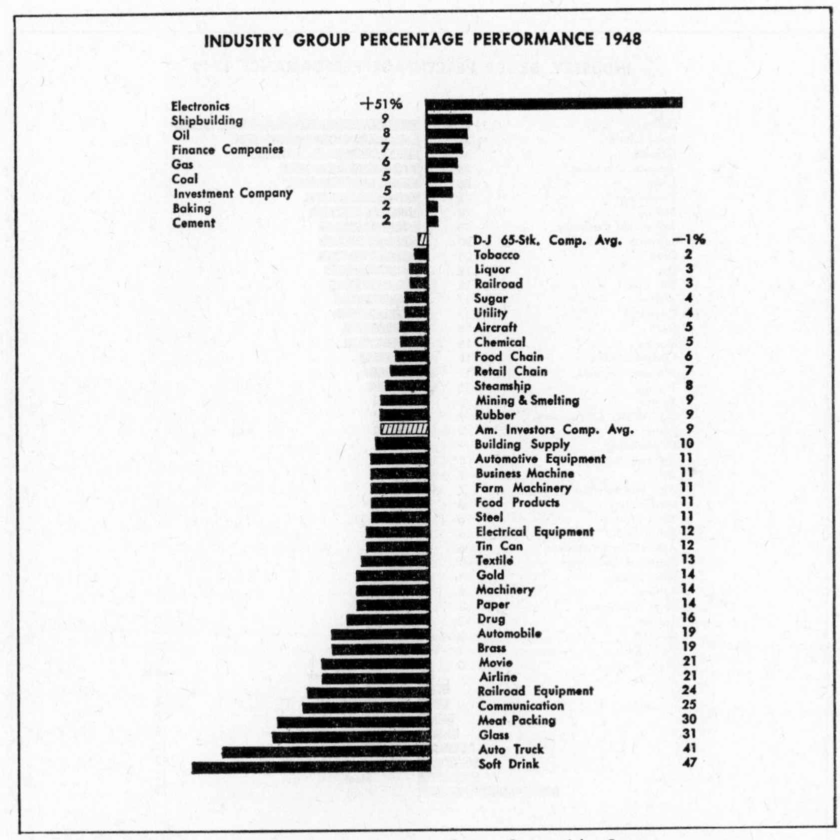


Source: George A. Chestnutt, Jr., Chestnutt Corp., Greenwich, Conn.

## FIRST APPENDIX TO CHAPTER 3 (Continued)

### 1949

The long bear market decline in the general market averages, that began in 1946, ended in June 1949. However, the groups that went up the most in 1949, such as Utility, Food Chain, Cement and Finance Company, had already made their bottoms prior to the beginning of 1949. They maintained steady uptrends throughout the year. Make a note of these groups. They belong to the defensive quality-yield classification along with such others as Tobacco, Food Products, Baking, Drug, Gas, Glass and Tin Can. You'll find them strongly represented in the early phases of every Bull Market. Note the similarity of group leadership in 1949, 1953 and 1957. These were years in which important General Market bottoms occurred and new Bull Markets were just beginning.

Only 9 groups finished 1949 in the minus column, but 8 other groups gained only 3% or less. Thus, even in this first year of the new bull market, it was very important to know which groups to avoid and which groups to select for better-than-average capital appreciation.

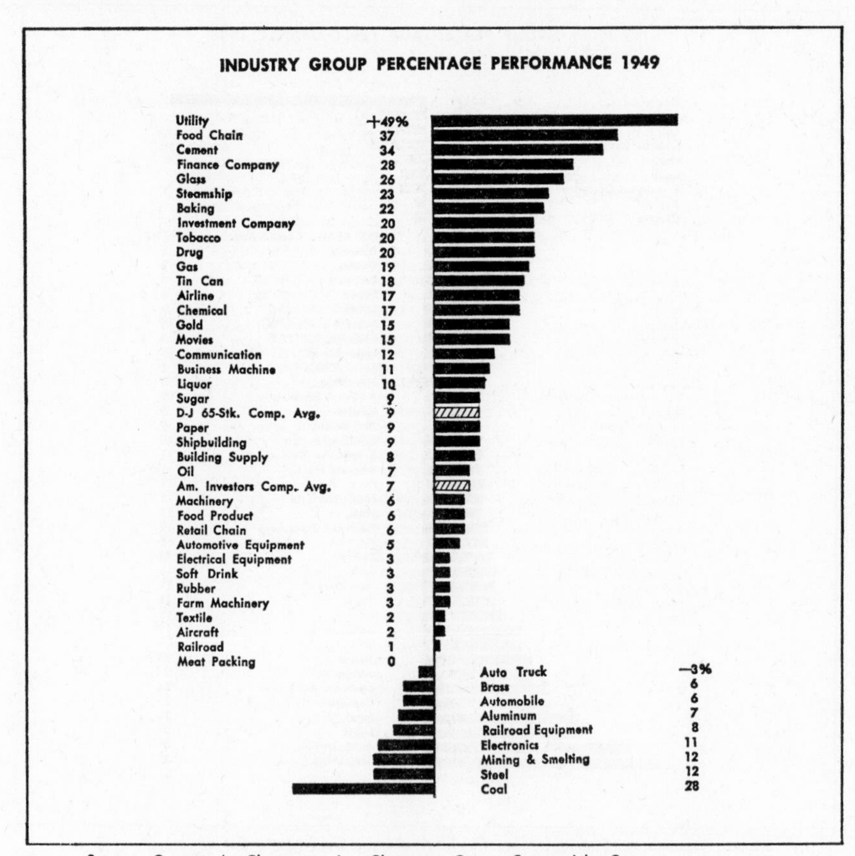


Source: George A. Chestnutt, Jr., Chestnutt Corp., Greenwich, Conn.

## FIRST APPENDIX TO CHAPTER 3 (Continued)

### 1950

The year 1950 was dominated by the outbreak of war in Korea. 'War babies' and inflation beneficiaries went up the most. Defensive or 'deflation hedge' stocks were prominent among the losers.

Even though 1950 was the strongest bull market year in the interim between 1945 and 1954, there still were 9 industry groups out of 45 that had to be avoided in order to prevent actual shrinkage of capital in your investment holdings. Notice that the four strongest years from 1946 to date, 1950, 1954, 1958 and 1965 were the only ones in which the blue-chip-dominated Dow-Jones 65-Stock Average performed substantially worse than average, compared with the market as a whole.

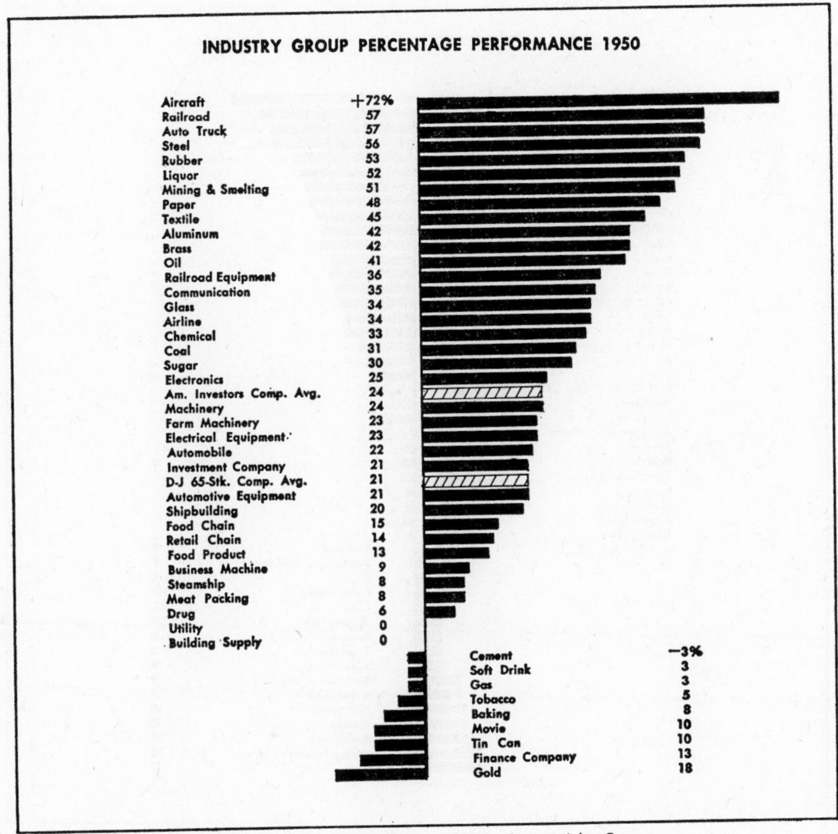


Source: George A. Chestnutt, Jr., Chestnutt Corp., Greenwich, Conn.

## FIRST APPENDIX TO CHAPTER 3 (Continued)

### 1951

1951 was another bull market year for the averages, but a long-term investor had to be careful and stay out of the weakest third of the market if losses were to be avoided.

$1,000 invested in the average Rubber stock grew to $1,370; $1,000 in the average Chemical stock grew to $1,310. On the opposite end of the scale, $1,000 invested in the average Truck stock shrank to $830; and $1,000 in the average Meat Packing Stock shrank to $870.

Notice that, if you had refused to buy Rubbers and Chemicals at the beginning of 1951 simply because they had already advanced 53% and 33% respectively in 1950, you would have missed the two best groups.

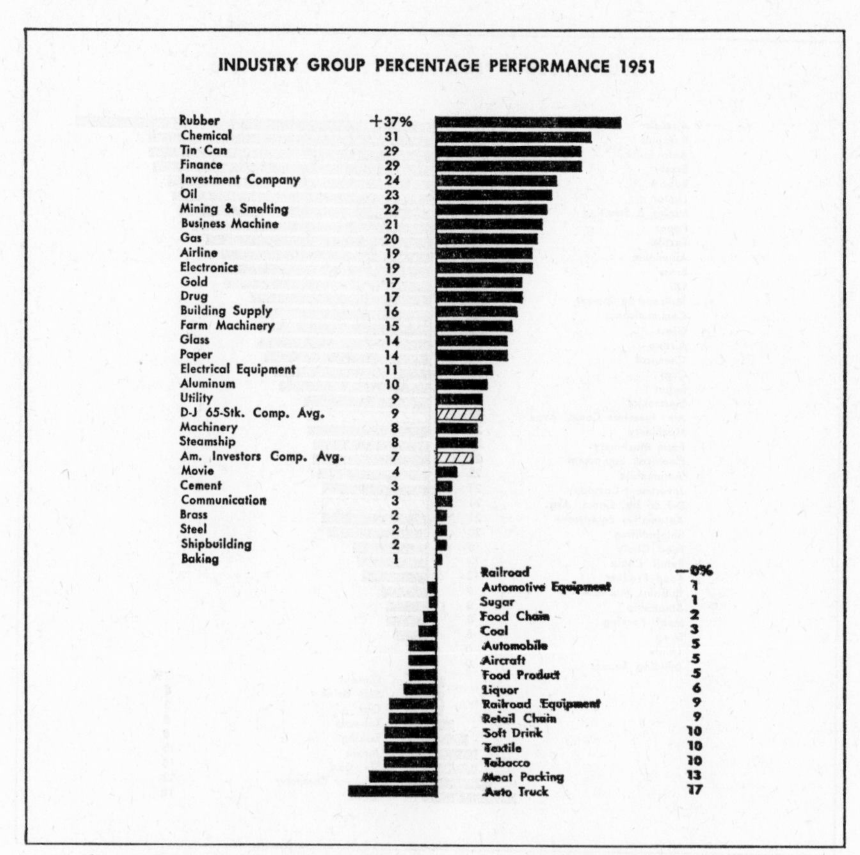


Source: George A. Chestnutt, Jr., Chestnutt Corp., Greenwich, Conn.

## FIRST APPENDIX TO CHAPTER 3 (Continued)

### 1952

1952 was a year of uncertainty. Although the average stock was down most of the year, it ended on a strong note following the Eisenhower victory in November.

But there was a bull market going on all year in the better-grade or blue-chip stocks. Notice that only 5 industry groups out of a total of 45 were able to advance more than the Dow-Jones 65-Stock Composite Average!

What happened was that most high-priced stocks went up while most low-priced stocks went down. Since the Dow-Jones Averages weight each stock in proportion to its price, the blue chips carried this average higher. The American Investors Service Composite Geometric Average, which weights all stocks equally regardless of price, is found near the middle of the group tabulation, as it always must be, because it is mathematically constructed to reflect *the average performance of all stocks.*

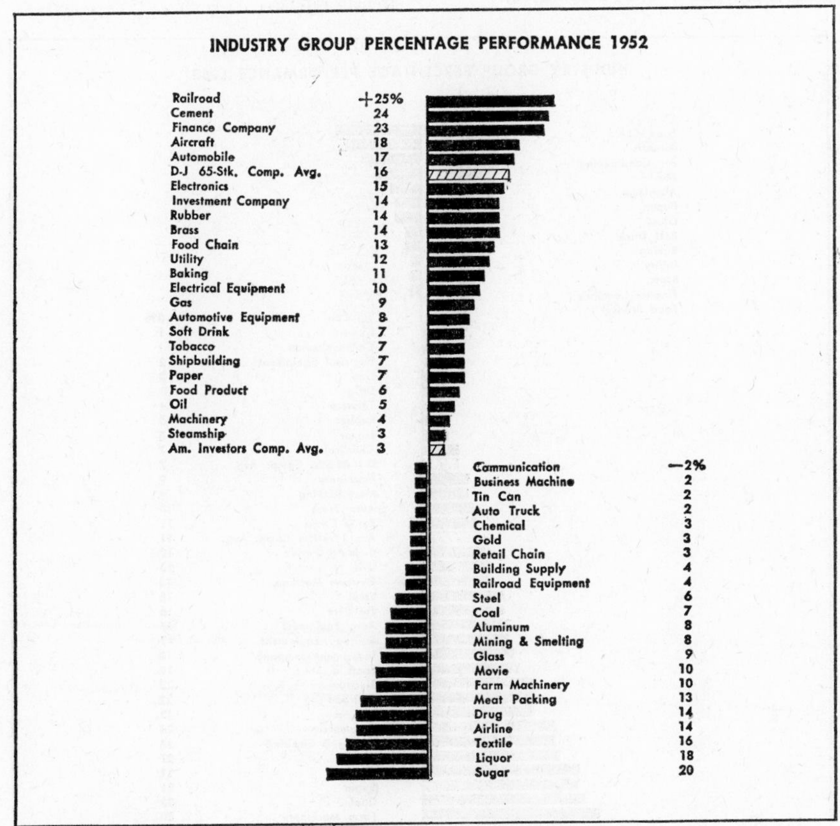


Source: George A. Chestnutt, Jr., Chestnutt Corp., Greenwich, Conn.

## FIRST APPENDIX TO CHAPTER 3 (Continued)

### 1953

When you compare the 1953 group performance chart on this page with those on the preceding pages, you will see that 1953 was generally a bear market year. The 1953 performance chart looks like those for 1946, 1948, 1957 and 1962.

Only 13 industry group averages out of 46 ended the year in the plus column. The 'average stock,' as indicated by the Composite Geometric Average, declined 11%.

For those who held Food Chain and Aircraft stocks, 1953 provided a fine bull market; for those who held Farm Machinery and Coal stocks it provided a severe bear market.

$1,000 invested in the average Food Chain stock in 1953 increased to $1,170; in the average Aircraft stock $1,000 increased to $1,150. On the other hand $1,000 in the average Farm Machinery stock would have shrunk to $650; in the average Coal stock $1,000 would have shrunk to $680.

American Investors Service Industry Group Ranking and Stock Selection methods enabled subscribers to stay out of Farm Machinery and Coal stocks, and at the same time to hold Food Chain and Aircraft stocks in 1953. The guiding principles through which this result was accomplished are the basis of percentage-strength ratings.

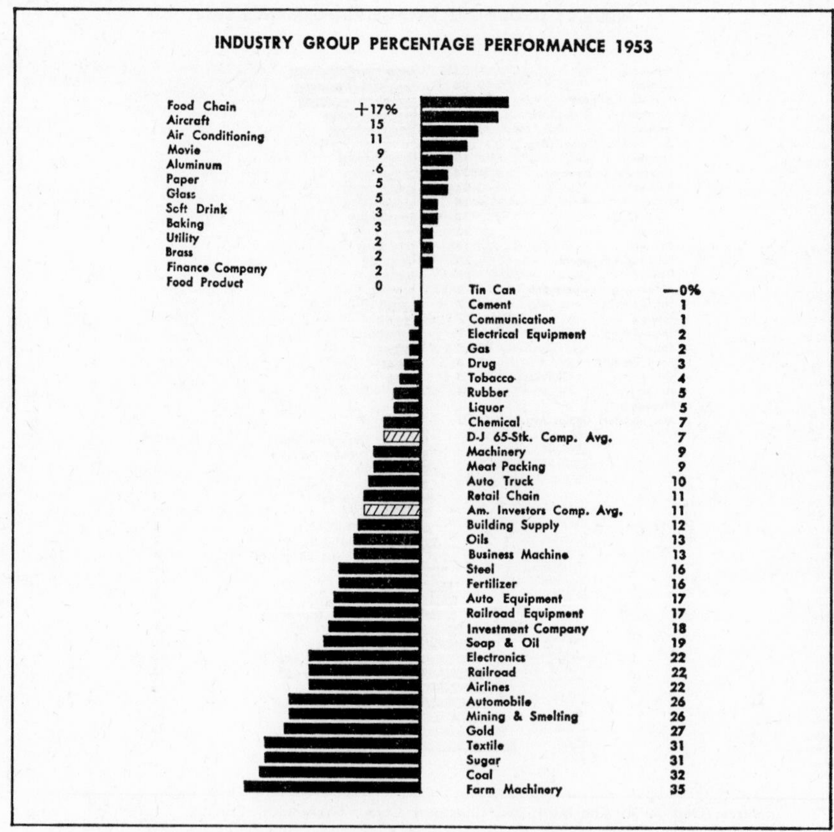


Source: George A. Chestnutt, Jr., Chestnutt Corp., Greenwich, Conn.

## FIRST APPENDIX TO CHAPTER 3 (Continued)

### 1954

As shown by the group performance table below, nearly all stocks went up in 1954. Aircrafts and Airlines were the leaders with advances of more than 100%.

$1,000 in the average Aircraft stock increased to $2,190. In the average Airline $1,000 increased to $2,150.

But what a difference if you had your money invested in Automobile or Tobacco stocks! $1,000 in the average Automobile stock increased to only $1,050. And in the average Tobacco stock $1,000 increased to only $1,040.

Investors making use of the industry group rankings and stock ratings made available by American Investors Service held Aircraft, Cement and Aluminum stocks throughout the year 1954. On the other hand, no positions were held in the Automobile and Tobacco groups, which occupied below-average ranking positions throughout 1954.

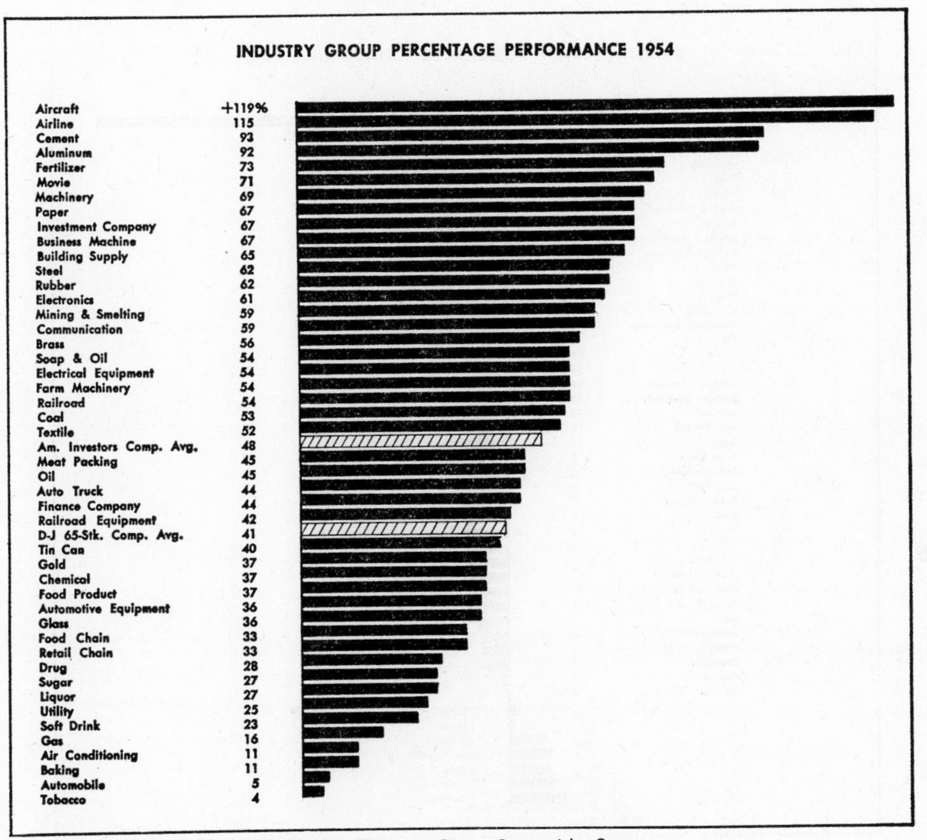


Source: George A. Chestnutt, Jr., Chestnutt Corp., Greenwich, Conn.

## FIRST APPENDIX TO CHAPTER 3 (Continued)

## 1955

With an advance of 81% in 1955 the Aluminum Group did almost twice as well as its nearest competitor the Coal Group. It is highly significant and there is a good lesson to be learned from the fact that the Aluminum Group made that 81% advance on top of a 92% advance in 1954. Two other groups that were among the top four in 1954, Aircraft and Cement, are also found among the top six in 1955! Thus, if you had arbitrarily refused to buy for 1955 the four groups that went up the most in 1954, you would have automatically eliminated three of the six best performers in 1955.

At the other end of the scale, two of 1954's poorest performers, Air Conditioning and Baking, were among 1955's five worst performers.

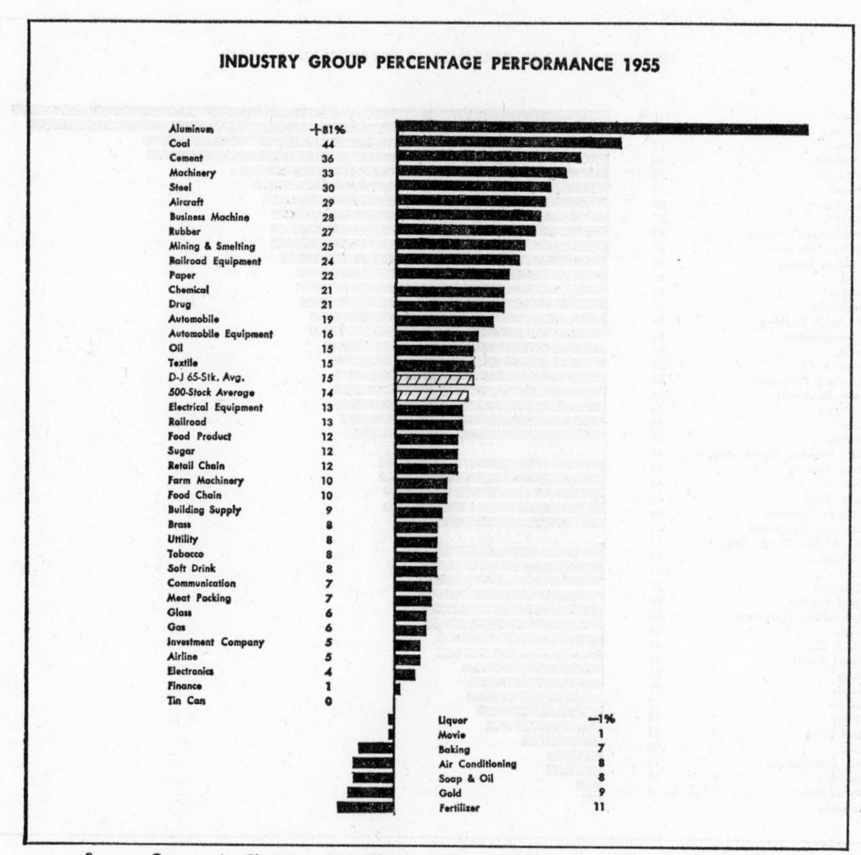


Source: George A. Chestnutt, Jr., Chestnutt Corp., Greenwich, Conn.

## FIRST APPENDIX TO CHAPTER 3 (Continued)

### 1956

The market, as represented by the averages, ended 1956 about where it began. The American Investors 500-Stock Composite Geometric Average gained 1.56%; the Dow-Jones 65-Stock Average gained 0.68%. Your stock selection *had to be good* if you were to make money in 1956.

As usual, the groups that had gone up the most in the preceding year were among this year's best performers. Machinery and Steel, which gained most in 1956, had been 1955's 4th and 5th best performers. Aluminum and Coal, which had been 1st and 2nd best in 1955, were 8th best and 5th best, respectively, in 1956.

Nine out of 1955's ten poorest performers ended 1956 in the loss column; the only exception, Air Conditioning, was 4th best in 1956.

The point of these observations is that it pays to stay with the strong ones. Don't shop for "bargains" among the weak ones just because they may appear to be "undervalued."

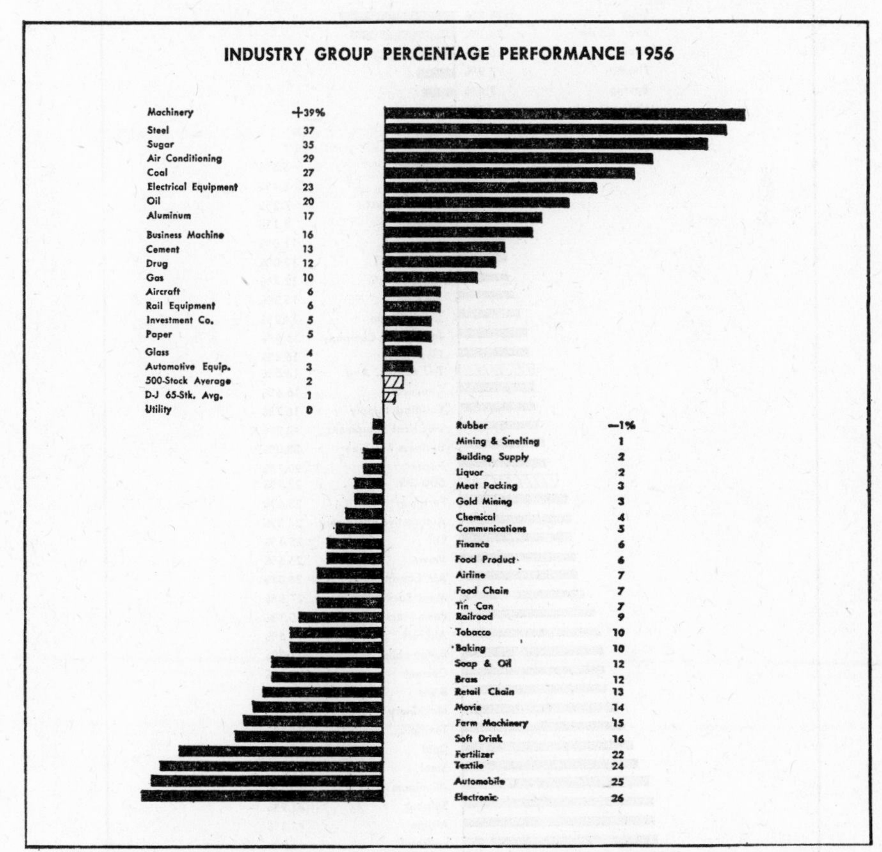


Source: George A. Chestnutt, Jr., Chestnutt Corp., Greenwich, Conn.

## FIRST APPENDIX TO CHAPTER 3 (Continued)

### 1957

Studies of previous years in which the market averages declined severely, or in which important bear market bottoms were made, reveal that the industry groups most likely to go up, or go down the least, are the low-volatility, quality-yield groups: *Baking, Food Chain, Finance, Tobacco, Utility* and *Gas.* Other groups which often do well in a downtrend market are *Food Products, Glass, Paper, Drug, Cement, Soap, Soft Drink* and *Sugar.*

For the year 1957 the "average stock", as represented by the A.I.S. 500-Stk. Composite Geometric Avg., declined 22.3%. The D-J 65-Stk. Avg. declined 16.5%. From the performance chart below you will see that 1957 followed very closely the industry group performance pattern of previous bear market years.

You should see this situation reversed within a year after a bear market bottom. 1950 and 1954 are good examples of strong bull market years. Note that the volatile-cyclical groups generally did much better than average in those years.

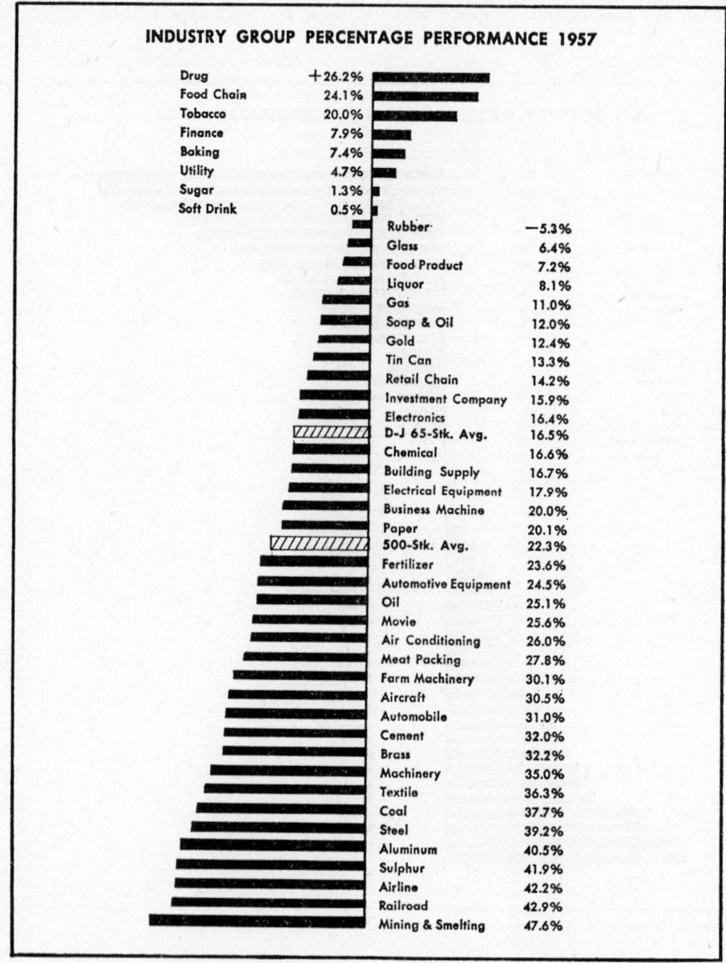


Source: George A. Chestnutt, Jr., Chestnutt Corp., Greenwich, Conn.

## FIRST APPENDIX TO CHAPTER 3 (Continued)

### 1958

Marketwise, the year 1958 bore a striking resemblance to 1954. The 500-Stk. Avg. advanced 49.4% in 1958 vs. 48% in 1954!

As in 1954, all industry groups advanced —a situation that is normal in the *first year of a bull market,* but almost never would occur otherwise.

As always we find the 500-Stk. Composite Geometric Avg. where a true average should be — in the middle of the tabulation. As in 1954, the D-J 65-Stk. Avg. lagged behind the market, outperforming in 1958 only 10 out of 44 groups.

The outstanding industry group was Electronics. Several members of this group tripled in value in 1958, including Raytheon and Zenith which were repeatedly recommended by American Investors Service throughout the year.

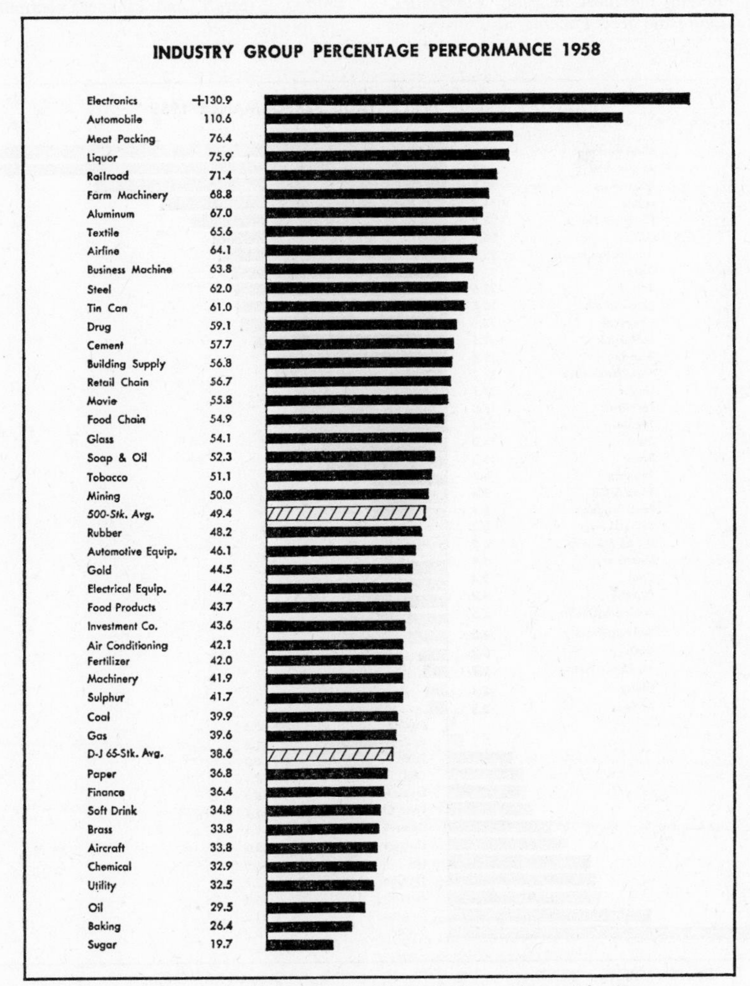


Source: George A. Chestnutt, Jr., Chestnutt Corp., Greenwich, Conn.

## FIRST APPENDIX TO CHAPTER 3 (Continued)

### 1959

In 1959 the market became much more selective than in 1958 with the 500 Stock Average advancing only a modest 8.2%. It was important to have held the strongest issues at this phase of the advance.

Probably one of the most striking points illustrated by these charts concerns the fact that one year's star performers often star again the next year. 1959 was certainly no exception in this respect! The three groups that went up the most in 1958, *Electronics, Automobile* and *Meat Packing*, also turned out to be the three top performers for 1959! Two of these groups, Electronics and Automobile, had more than doubled in 1958.

The fact that a stock has already doubled in price is perhaps the worst possible reason for selling it short. On the contrary, the stocks most likely to double during the coming year are those that doubled in price the preceding year.

As we forecast, the 1958 laggards, Sugar, Baking, Aircraft, and Finance, continued to lag during 1959.

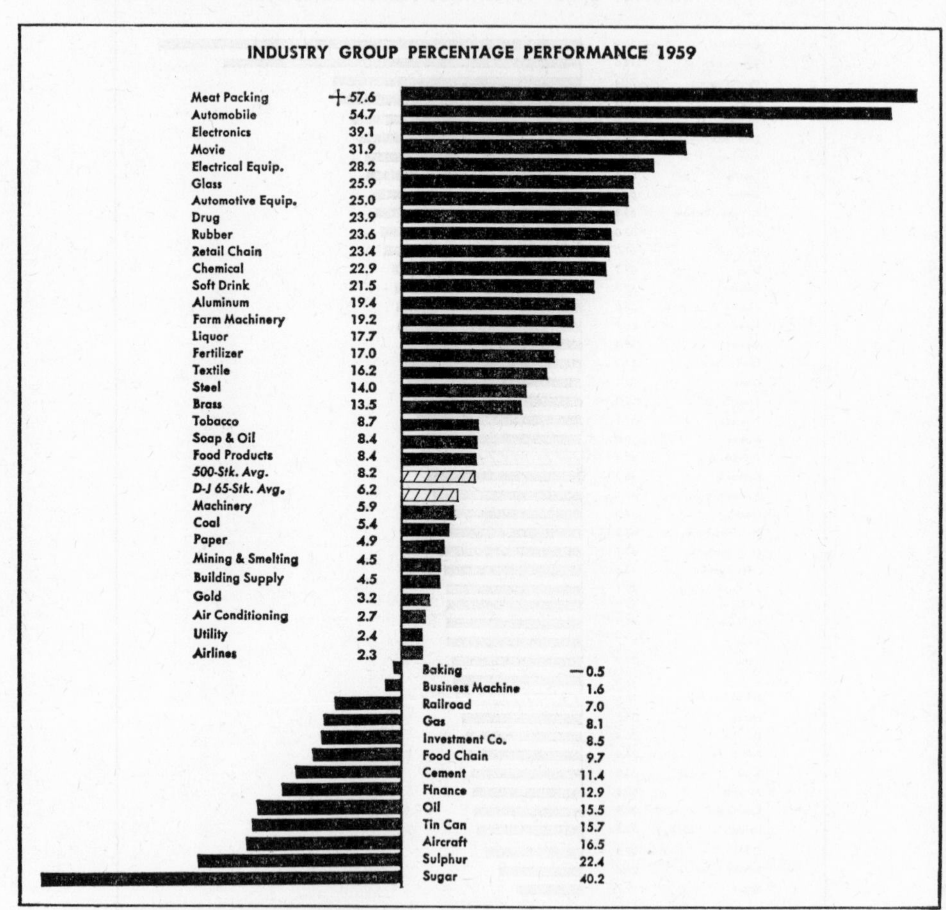


Source: George A. Chestnutt, Jr., Chestnutt Corp., Greenwich, Conn.

## FIRST APPENDIX TO CHAPTER 3 (Continued)

### 1960

Although 1960 was generally classified by economists as a year of either high plateau or mild business recession, the stock market treated it as a typical bear market year. With the exception of the Vending Machines and Financial Savings & Loan Groups, the strongest groups were the same ones that are normally stronger than average during a general bear market: *Soft Drink, Food Products, Tobacco, Utility, Finance Companies, Gas,* etc.—the defensive quality-yield investments. The cyclical industries suffered severe declines ranging from 21% for *Railroad* to 40% for *Automobiles.*

The top two performance spots were occupied by the *Vending Machines* and the *Financial Savings & Loan Groups,* two industry classifications newly added to the American Investors Service group coverage during the year 1960. Gaining over 70% during 1960, these two groups reflected a growing recognition of their own independently strong growth trends. This situation, in which the two strongest groups gained over twice as much as their nearest competitors, reminds one of the 1948 performance of the then budding *Electronics Group.*

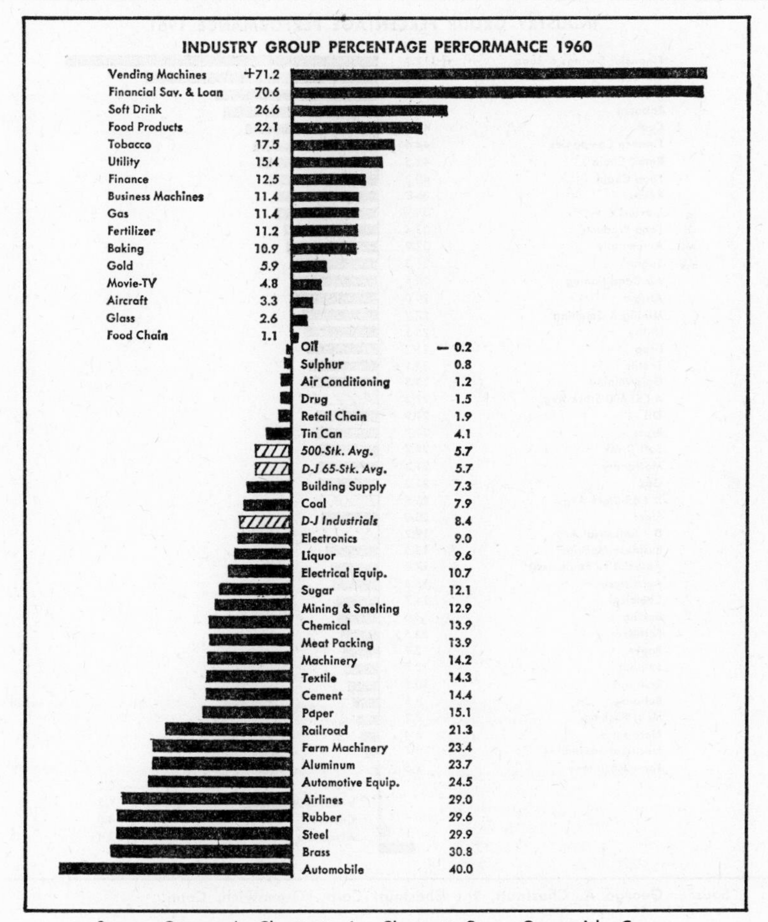


Source: George A. Chestnutt, Jr., Chestnutt Corp., Greenwich, Conn.

## FIRST APPENDIX TO CHAPTER 3 (Continued)

### 1961

The near unanimity of upside group action was somewhat typical of the first year of a bull market. However, the major part of the advance occurred between October 1960 and May 1961, so that the last half of the year included much selective and mixed performance. Strength in the quality-yield section carried over from 1960, with the growth leader of that section, Financial Savings and Loan, gaining the top spot after being second in 1960. Industrial stocks were generally below average, topping out early. Quality-yield stocks began to fail around year-end, responding to their competitive disadvantage vis-a-vis higher rates on savings deposits. It was a difficult year for anyone without adequate industry group timing information, but very profitable with it.

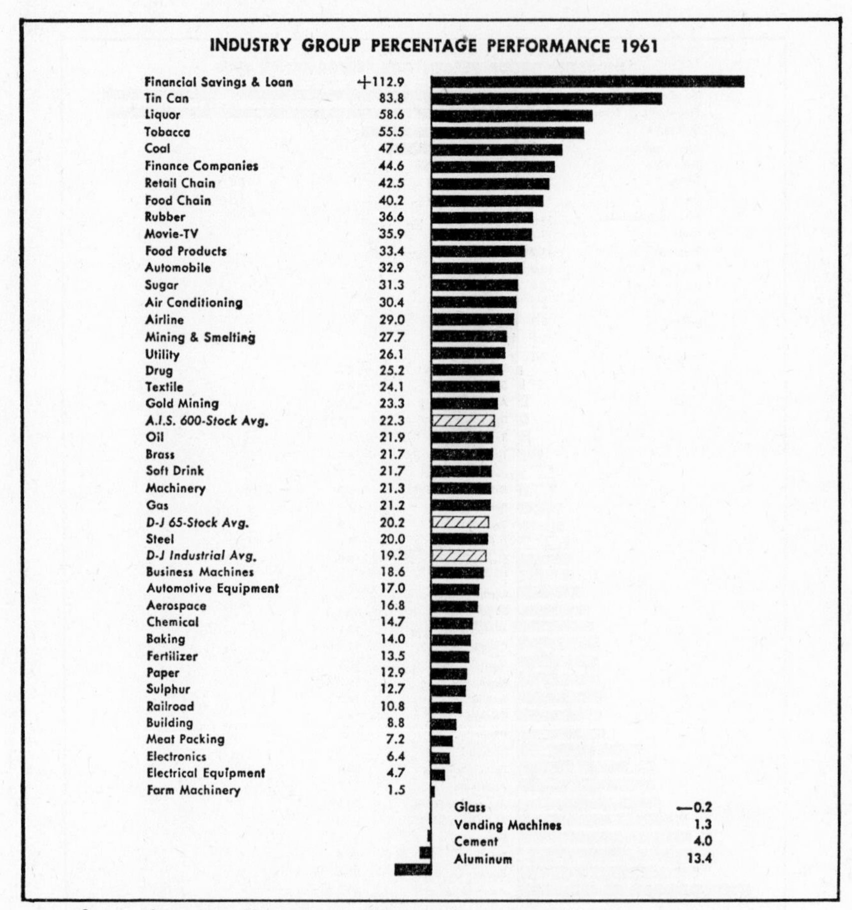


Source: George A. Chestnutt, Jr., Chestnutt Corp., Greenwich, Conn.

## FIRST APPENDIX TO CHAPTER 3 (Continued)

### 1962

During 1962, our coverage was increased from 600 to 800 stocks. Not shown in the table are 11 new industry groups that exerted an influence on the AIS Geometric Average during most of 1962. As usual in bear market years, the Dow-Jones Averages declined a great deal less than the average stock. In 1962 only 5 out of 51 industry groups outperformed the Dow-Jones 65-Stock Average and only 12 groups outperformed the Dow-Jones Industrial Average. The Financial Savings & Loan Group, which was an outstanding performer in both 1960 and in 1961, was one of the worst performers in 1962. We foresaw this change and recommended selling the last of our holdings in this Group on January 18, 1962 after favoring them strongly during the preceding two years. During 1962 the majority of our recommendations were in the Oil, Airline, Utility, Sugar, Aerospace and Automobile Groups.

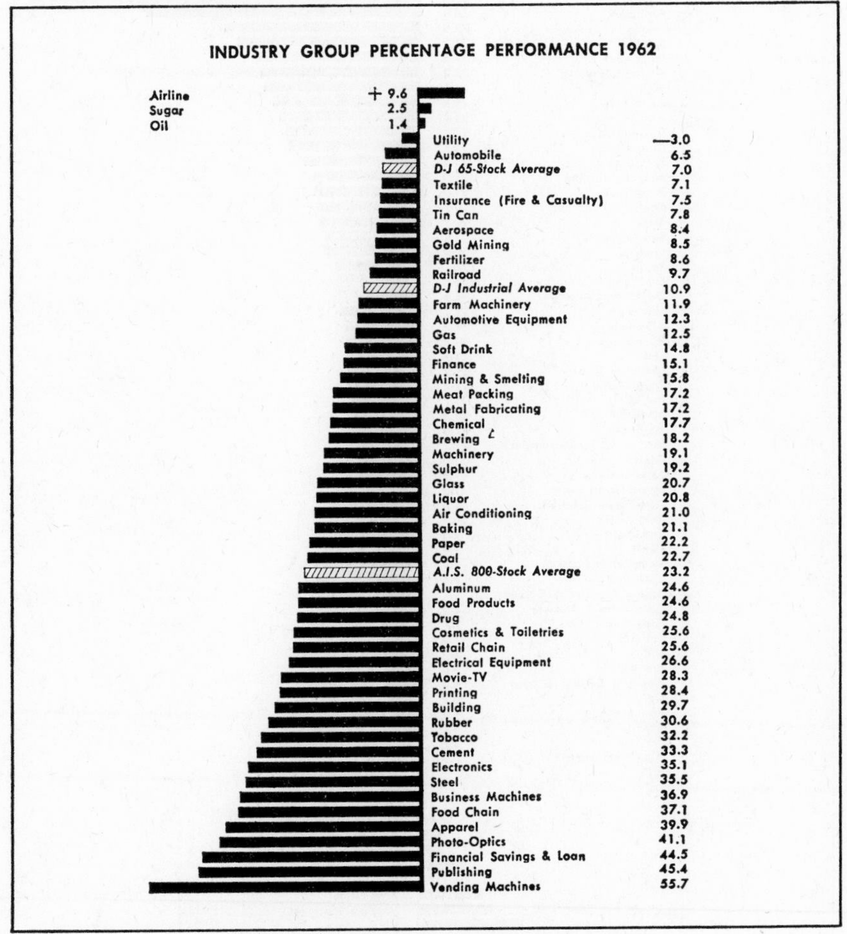


Source: George A. Chestnutt, Jr., Chestnutt Corp., Greenwich, Conn.

## FIRST APPENDIX TO CHAPTER 3 (Continued)

### 1963

During 1963, the two Dow-Jones Averages outperformed the general market by a considerable margin. The Airline Group, the top-ranking industry group at the beginning of the year, outperformed all others. The Bowling Group, bottom-ranking group at the beginning of the year, went down more than any other. The odds against this happening by pure chance are of the order of several thousand to one.

A vast majority of the other groups that were ranked near the bottom of the Table at the beginning of the year performed far below average and the vast majority of other groups that began the year in high-ranking positions performed well above average—proof of the high degree of reliability of Percentage-Strength Rating.

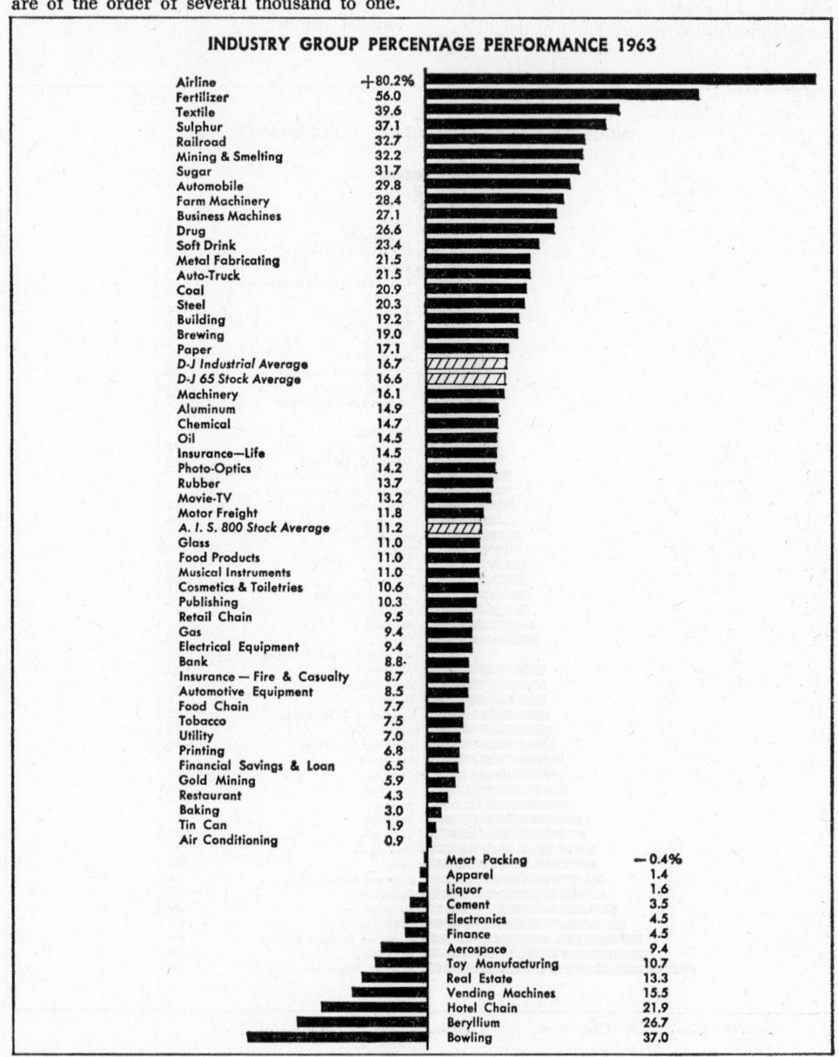


Source: George A. Chestnutt, Jr., Chestnutt Corp., Greenwich, Conn.

## FIRST APPENDIX TO CHAPTER 3 (Continued)

### 1964

At the beginning of 1964, based on IBM calculations as of December 30, 1963, Airline was the top-ranking industry group with a Percentage-Strength Rating of 96, while Bowling was the lowest-ranking industry group with a Percentage-Strength Rating of 1. The following tabulation of the 1964 industry group performance shows the Airline Group the fourth best performer and the Bowling Group the worst. The two outstanding performers for 1964, Sulphur and Fertilizer, had ranked seventh and fifth respectively at the beginning of 1964 with industry group Percentage-Strength Ratings of 78 and 88. Thus, we see that even though industry group Percentage-Strength Ratings are not specifically designed to forecast a full year in advance, the record shows a remarkable degree of reliability in this respect.

The average gain for 1964, as shown by the 800-Stock Geometric Average was only 9.3%. The bluechip-dominated Dow-Jones Industrial Average gained 14.6% making it a hard average to beat in 1964. Under these circumstances the public did not become overenthusiastic, since the average man's holdings were not keeping up to what he assumed was the general market.

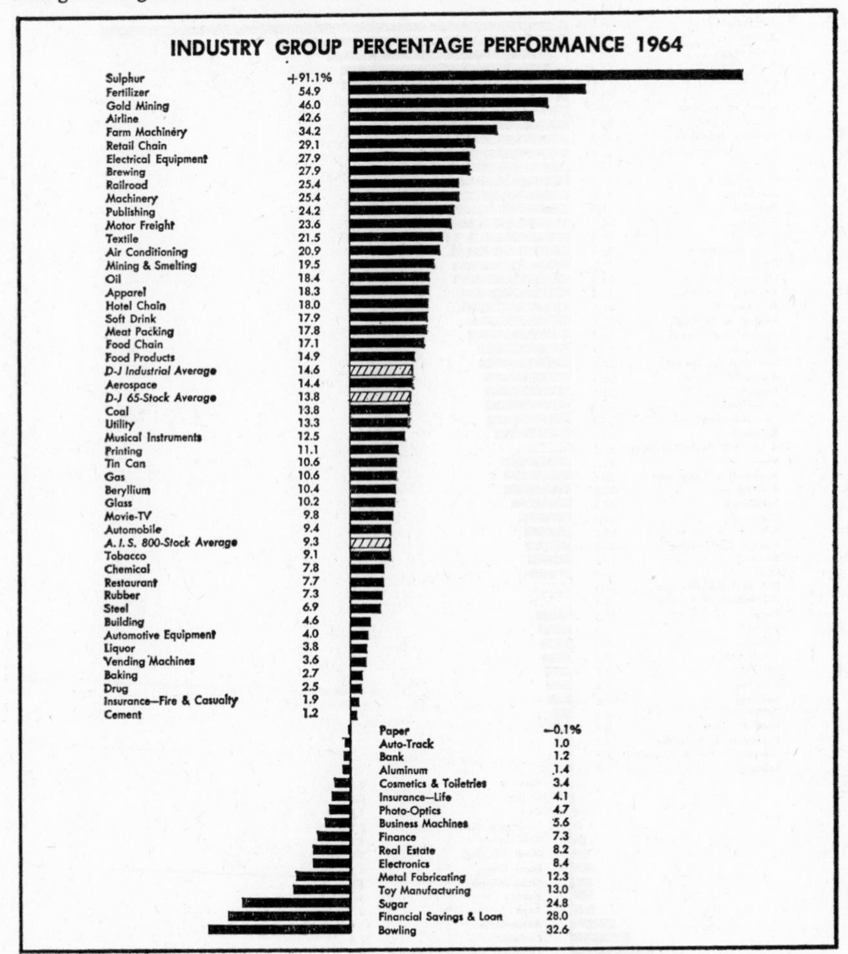


Source: George A. Chestnutt, Jr., Chestnutt Corp., Greenwich, Conn.

## FIRST APPENDIX TO CHAPTER 3 (Continued)

### 1965

Although the Dow-Jones Industrial Average outperformed the market in 1963 and 1964, making it a hard average to beat, almost everybody succeeded in beating the Dow in 1965. The average stock as represented by the A.I.S. 800 Stk. Avg. went up 21.9%, or twice the Dow's 10.9% gain.

The Airline Group, top performer in 1962 and 1963, and 4th best in 1964, took 2nd place honors in 1965 with a further gain of 89.8%. The closely related Air Freight Group stole top honors with its 144.8% gain.

While it pays to follow new leaders when they appear and become well established, it also pays to stay with former market leaders until they have been clearly dislodged by new leaders. That is the lesson of market history.

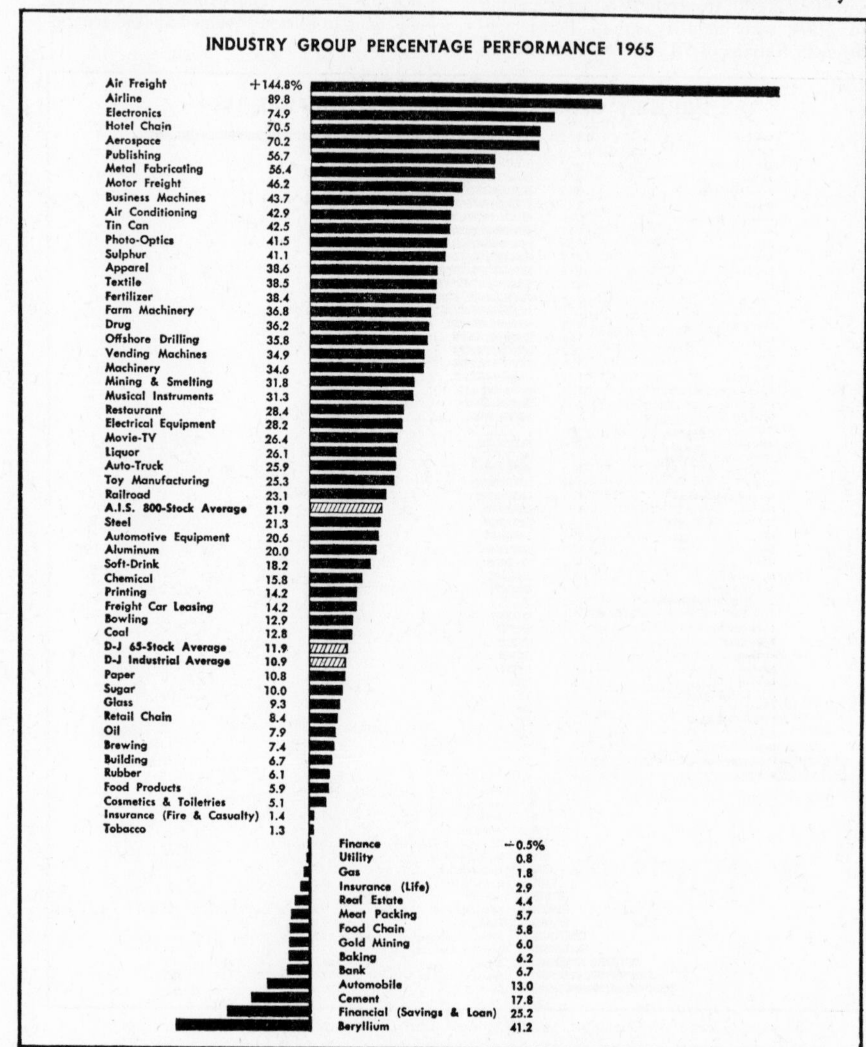


Source: George A. Chestnutt, Jr., Chestnutt Corp., Greenwich, Conn.

## FIRST APPENDIX TO CHAPTER 3 (Concluded)

**PROGRESS OF INDUSTRY GROUPS — PERCENTAGE PERFORMANCE**

**December 27, 1965 to December 29, 1966**

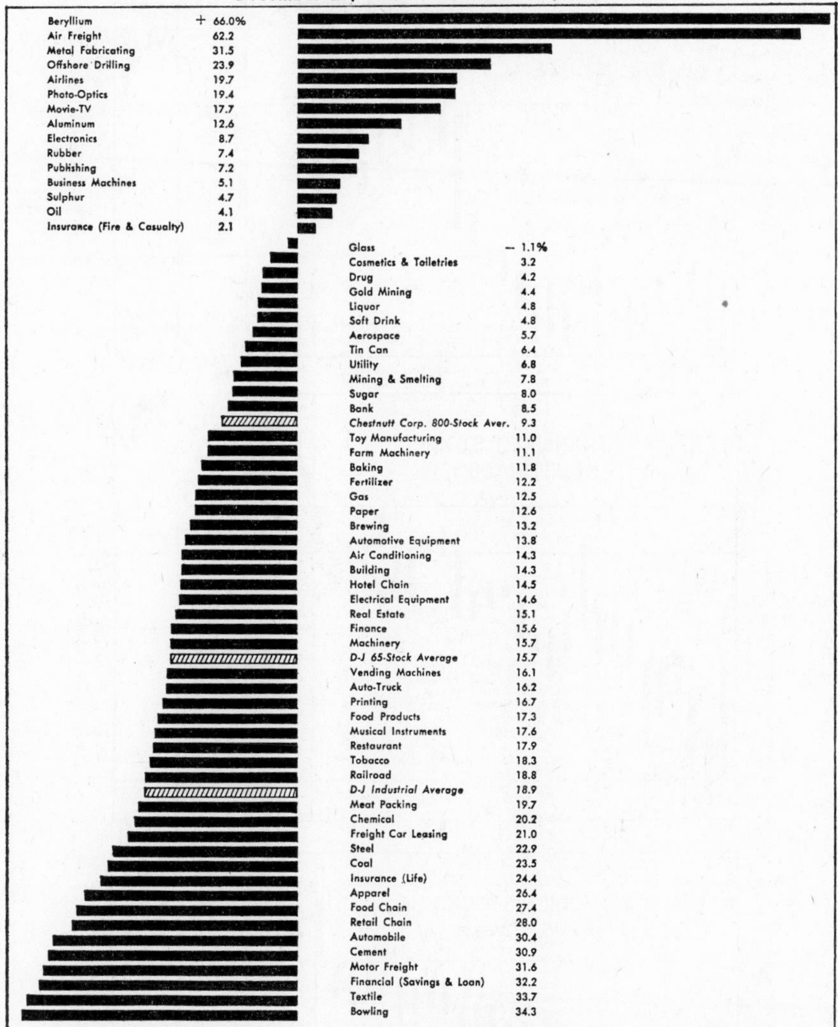


Source: George A. Chestnutt, Jr., Chestnutt Corp., Greenwich, Conn.

## SECOND APPENDIX TO CHAPTER 3

The importance of industry analysis may also be seen from the following charts showing "Barron's Group Stock Averages." These are reproduced from *The Dow Jones Investor's Handbook*, 1967 edition, with the kind permission of Dow Jones & Co., Inc., New York, N.Y.

## SECOND APPENDIX TO CHAPTER 3

### Barron's Group Stock Averages

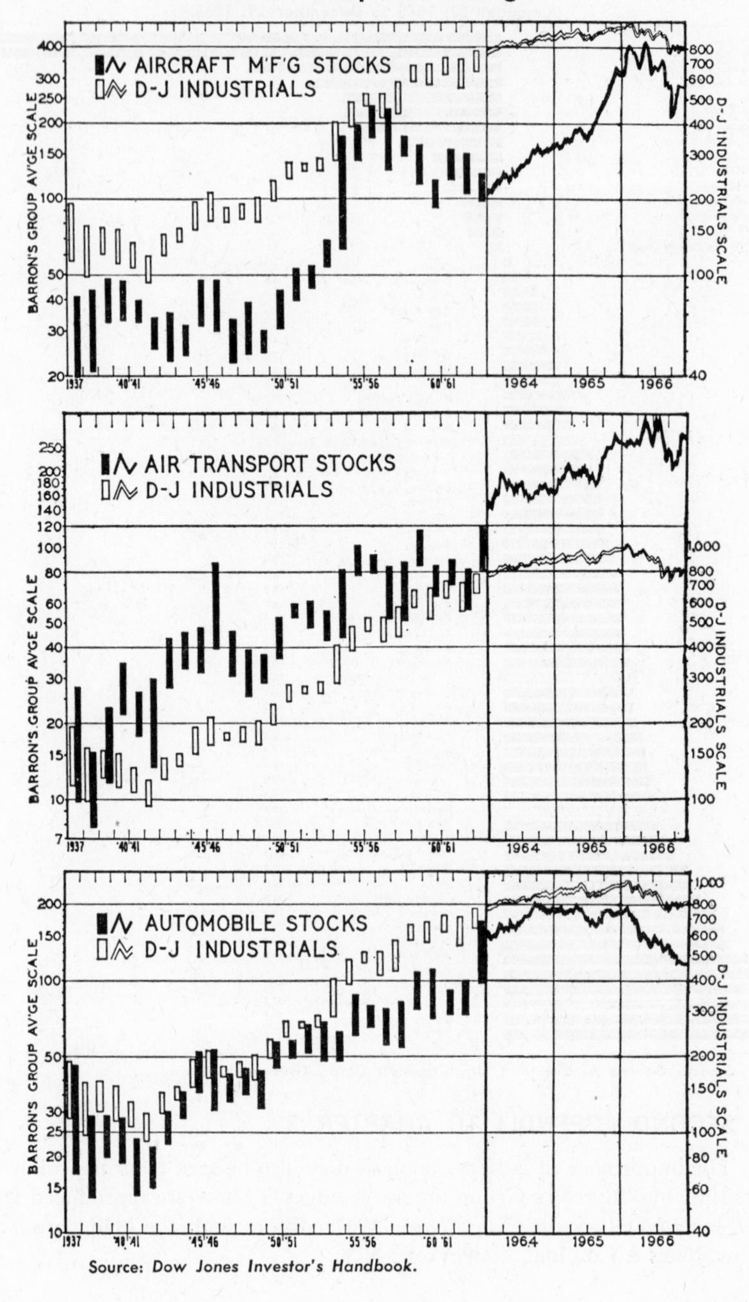


Source: *Dow Jones Investor's Handbook.*

## SECOND APPENDIX TO CHAPTER 3 (Continued)

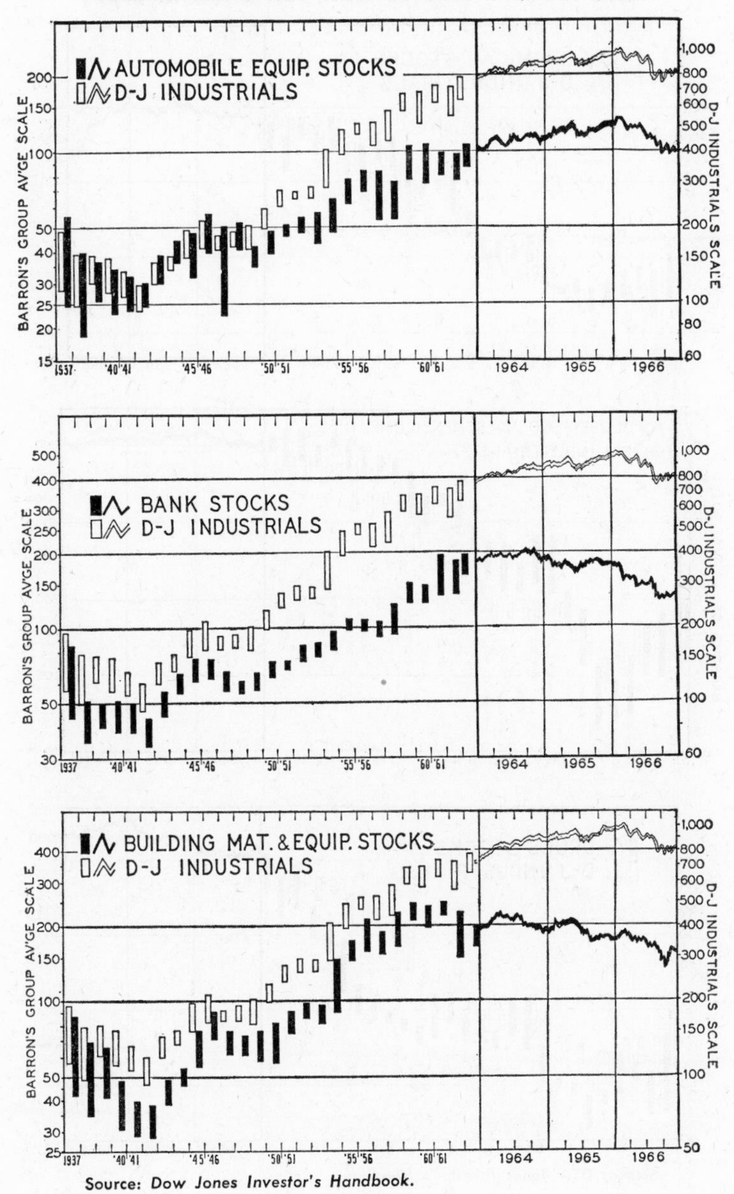


Source: *Dow Jones Investor's Handbook.*

## SECOND APPENDIX TO CHAPTER 3 (Continued)

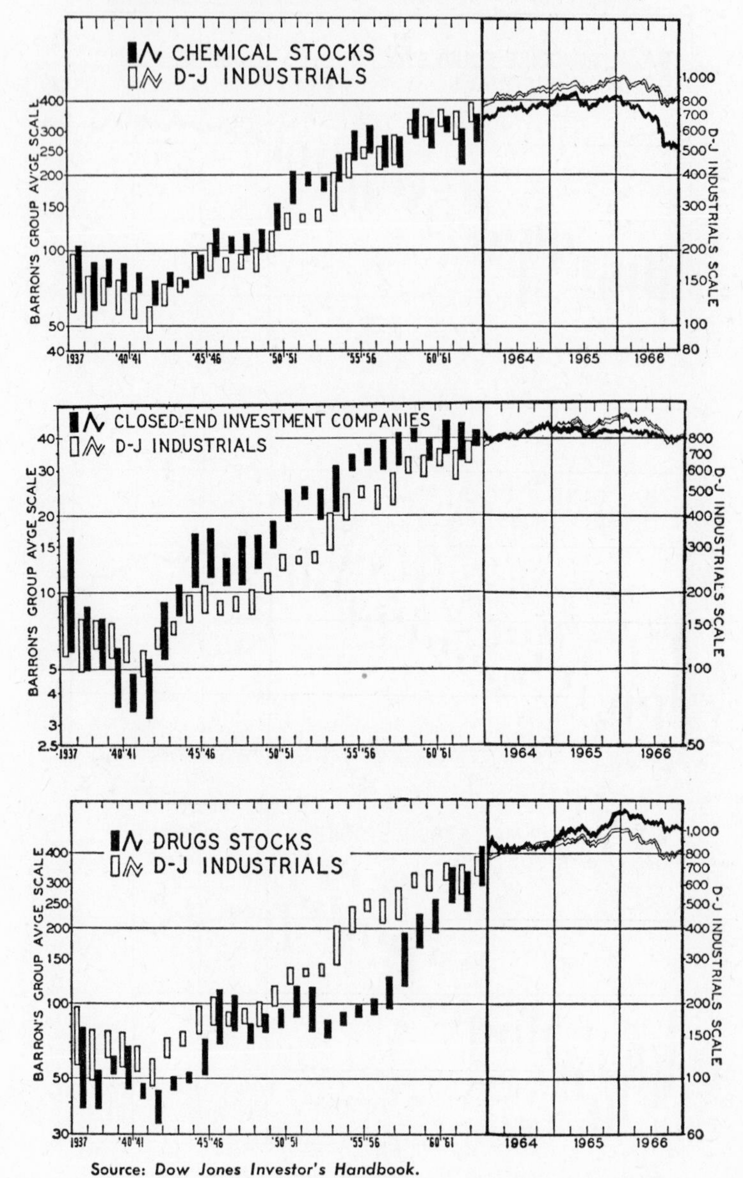


Source: *Dow Jones Investor's Handbook.*

## SECOND APPENDIX TO CHAPTER 3 (Continued)

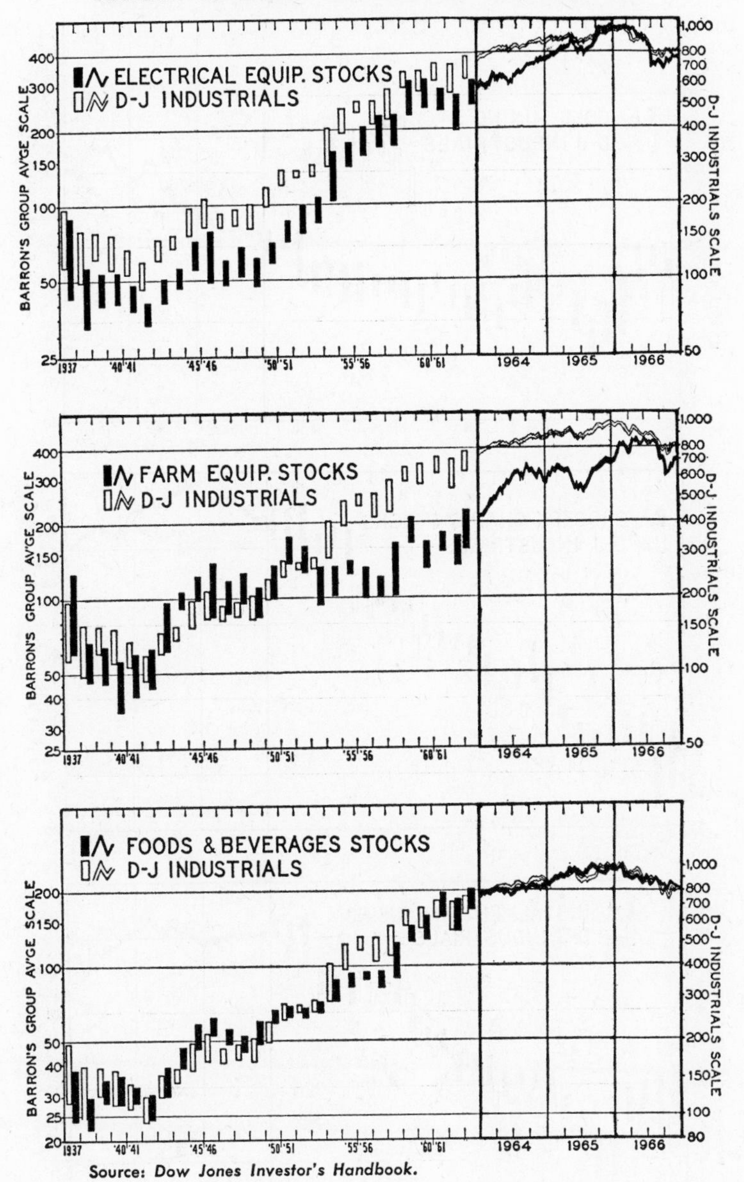


Source: *Dow Jones Investor's Handbook.*

## SECOND APPENDIX TO CHAPTER 3 (Continued)

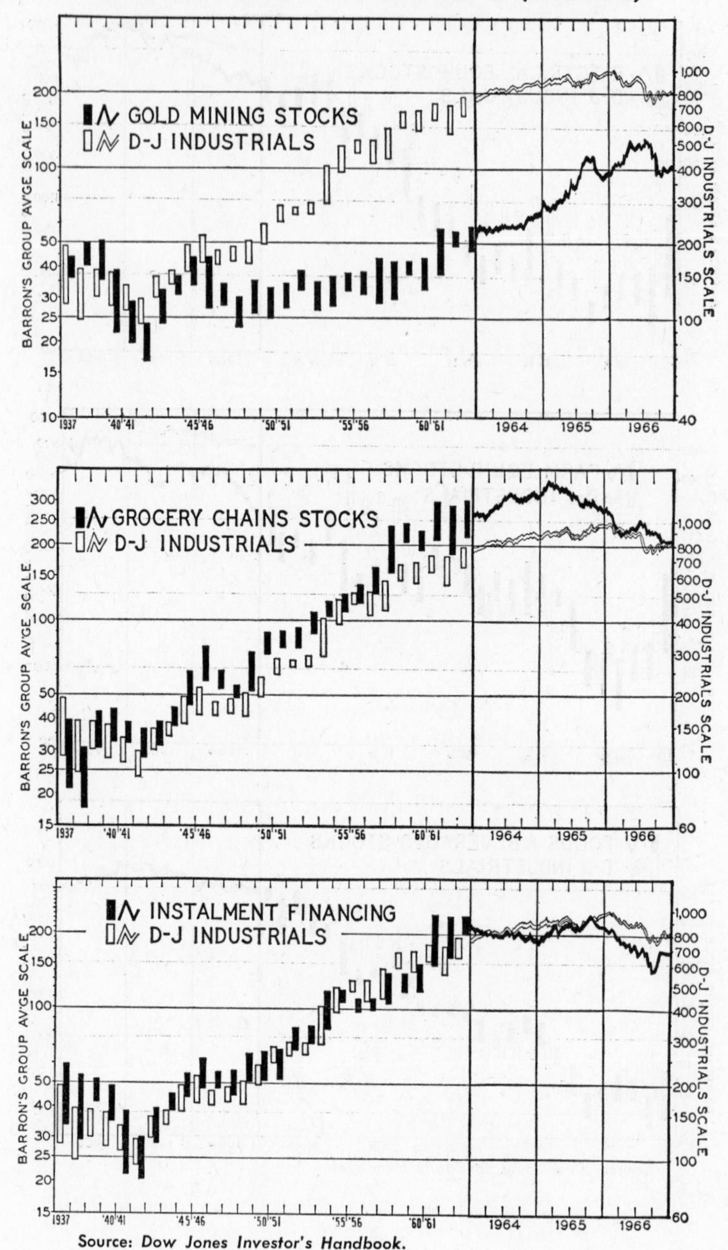


Source: *Dow Jones Investor's Handbook.*

## SECOND APPENDIX TO CHAPTER 3 (Continued)

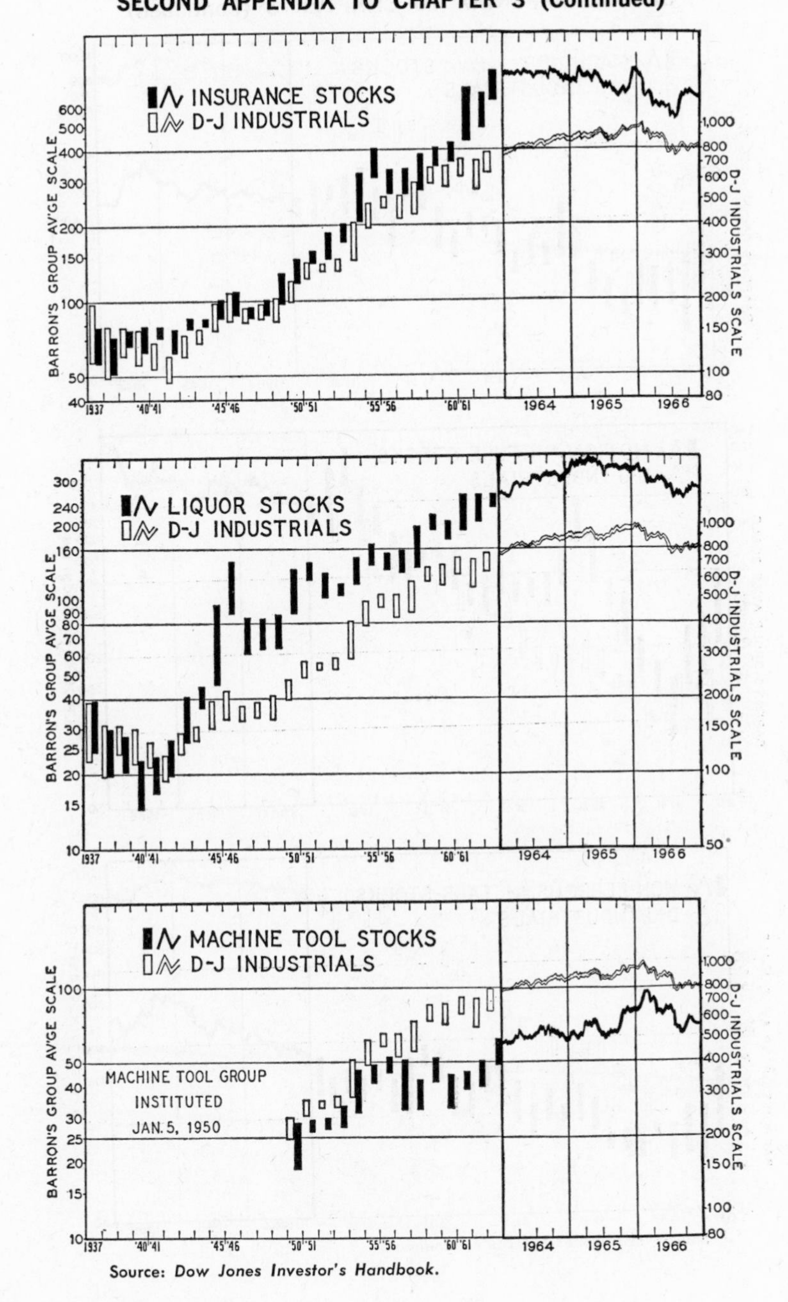


Source: *Dow Jones Investor's Handbook.*

SECOND APPENDIX TO CHAPTER 3 (Continued)

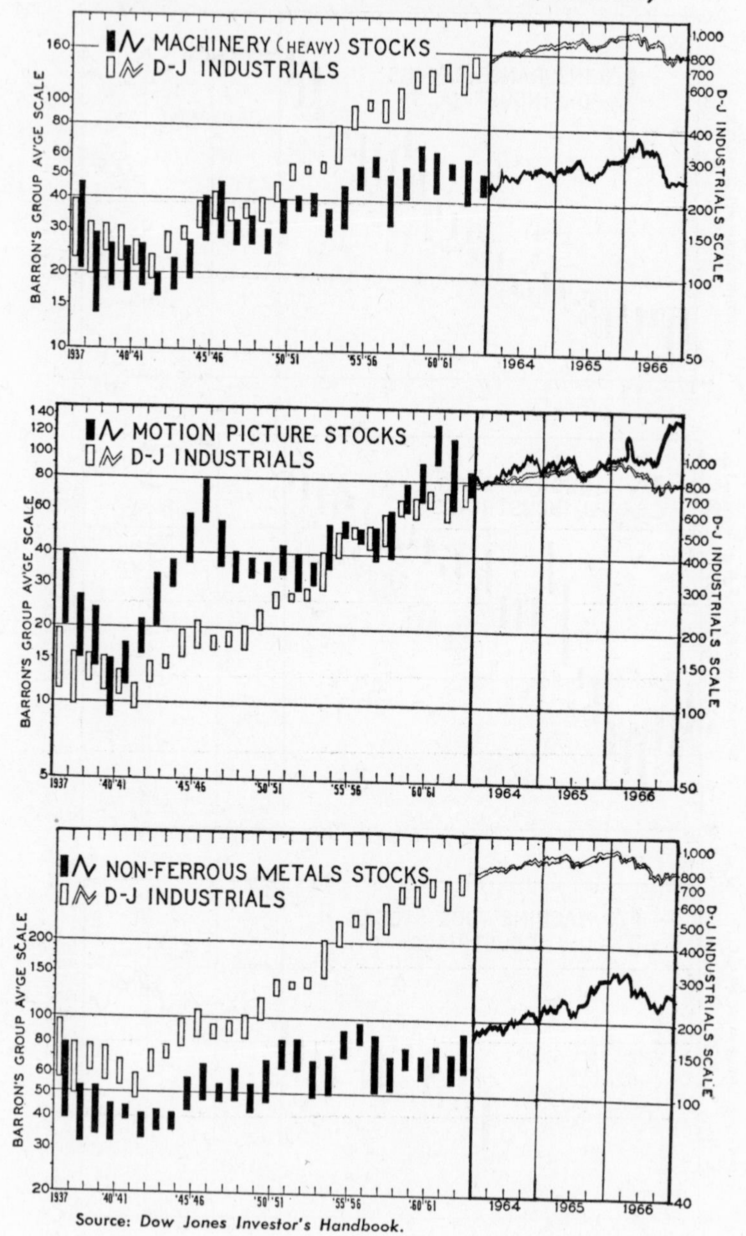


Source: *Dow Jones Investor's Handbook.*

## SECOND APPENDIX TO CHAPTER 3 (Continued)

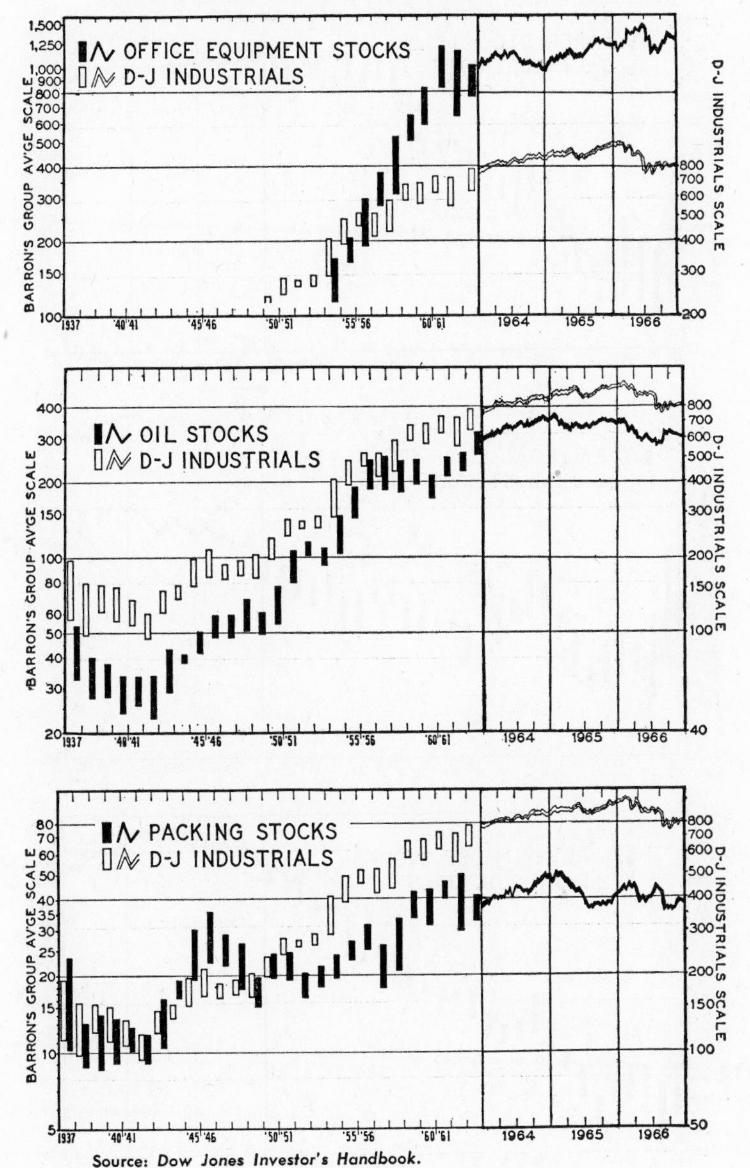


Source: *Dow Jones Investor's Handbook.*

## SECOND APPENDIX TO CHAPTER 3 (Continued)

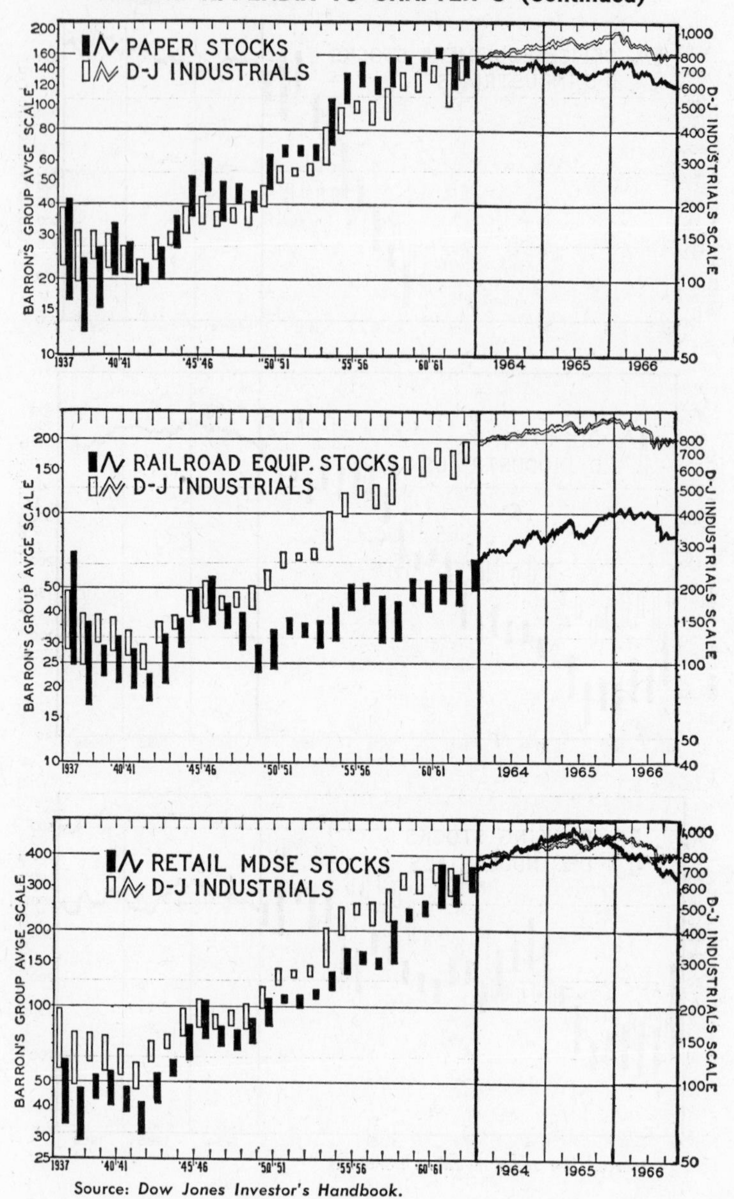


Source: *Dow Jones Investor's Handbook.*

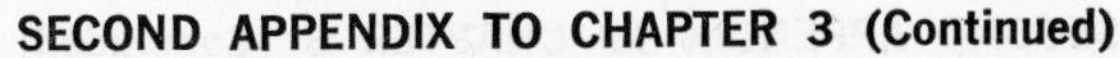

## SECOND APPENDIX TO CHAPTER 3 (Continued)

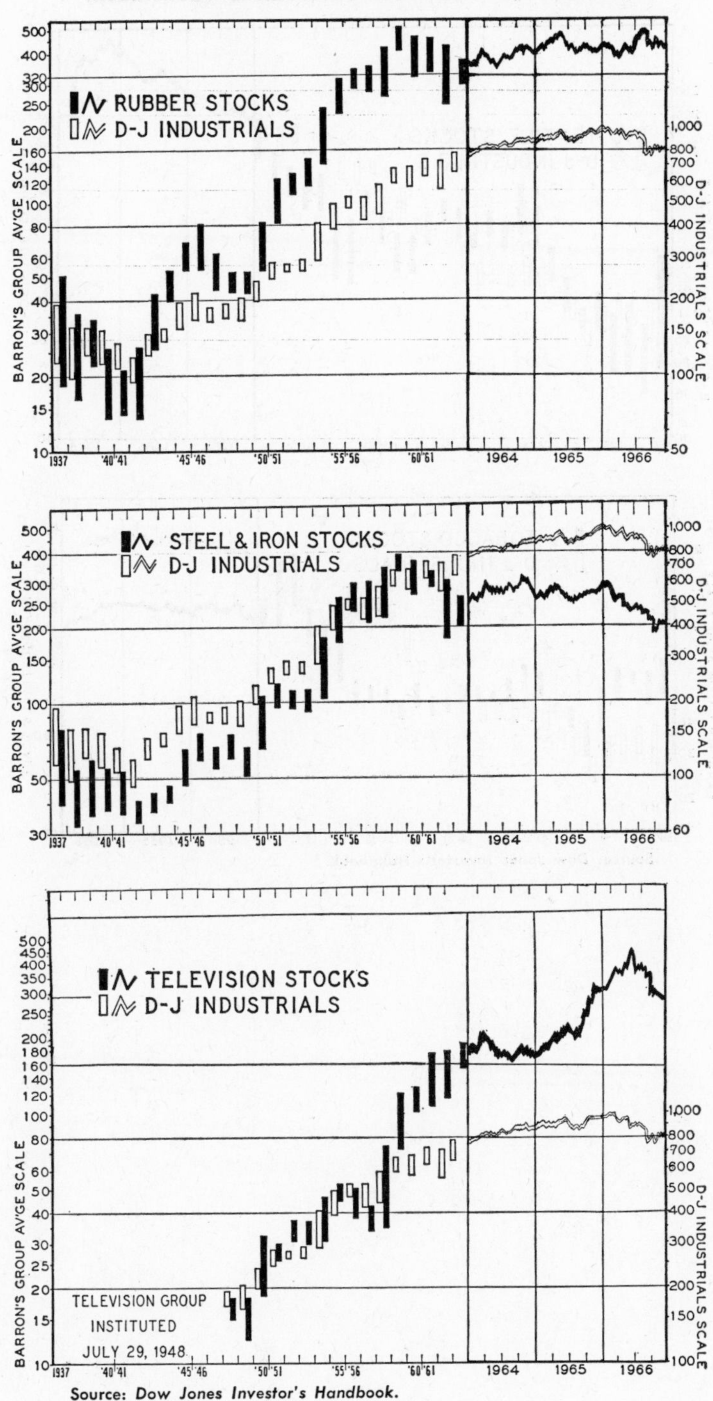


Source: *Dow Jones Investor's Handbook.*

**SECOND APPENDIX TO CHAPTER 3 (Concluded)**

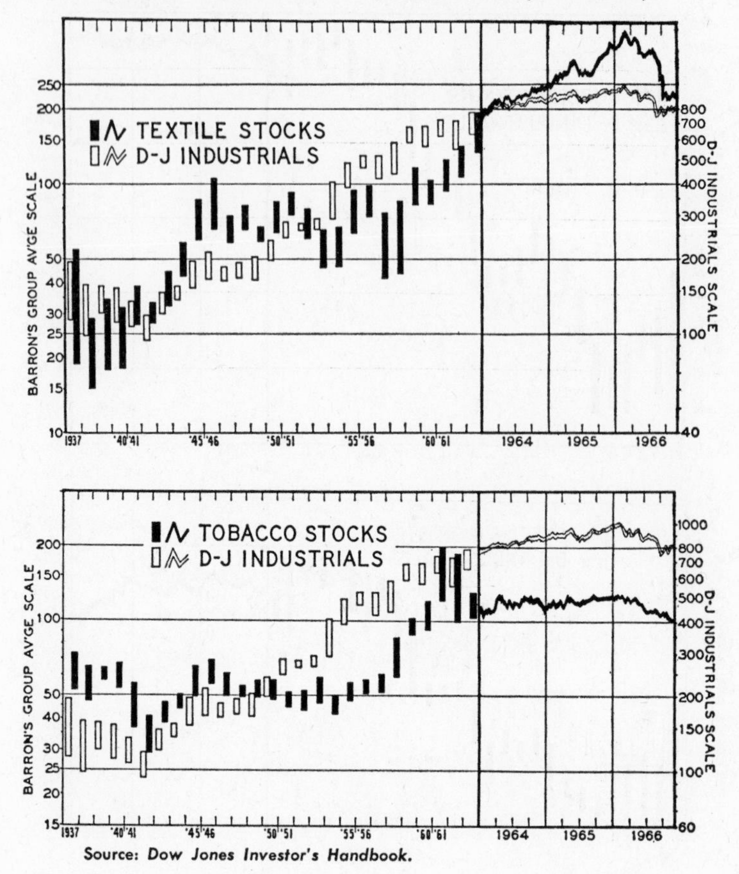


Source: *Dow Jones Investor's Handbook.*

# Part II

# SECURITY VALUATION

# 4

# ADJUSTMENT OF REPORTED NET INCOME

We can easily represent things as we wish them to be.

—Aesop

In its 1965 annual report, the General Electric Company introduced a new method of reporting its financial results. For the first time, the giant electrical equipment producer incorporated the operating results of its overseas subsidiaries with the results of its American and Canadian operations. Under the new system of reporting, earnings per share of GE stock amounted to a record high of $3.90. If the old system had been retained, however, per-share earnings would have been 28 cents per share higher, or $4.18. According to the company's president, currency devaluations and unsettled economic conditions in several foreign lands produced an adverse impact on earnings.

## The Problem

The announcement of GE's 1965 earnings also indicated that 1964 earnings on a comparable basis were $3.24 per share. But a look at the company's 1964 annual report reveals earnings of $2.62. Does this mean that the inclusion of foreign earnings would have added 62 cents per share in 1964 ($3.24 minus $2.62) whereas they caused a reduction of 28 cents in 1965?

The answer is no! For in 1964, GE charged earnings with 82 cents per share to reflect amounts paid to various electric utility customers in settlement of damage claims arising in connection with an antitrust suit. If General Electric had followed the accounting practices of its major codefendant in the suit, Westinghouse, it would have charged the loss directly to surplus instead of earnings and would have reported earnings of $3.44 per share in 1964. Since the company now claims that 1964 earnings per share would have been $3.24 on an accounting basis comparable to 1965, when foreign operations were included but when there were no antitrust charges, the difference between $3.44 and $3.24 presumably represents the impact of foreign subsidiary operations. So foreign subsidiaries apparently caused a 20 cents per share reduction of earnings in 1964 and 28 cents per share in 1965.

At this point, the investor has a legitimate reason to feel a bit like Alice in Wonderland. Was the *true level* of earnings in 1964 $2.62 per share, or $3.24, or $3.44? In 1965, was it $3.90 or $4.18? Obviously, earnings in 1965 were at a record high, but what was the *true percentage gain* over 1964? And how can one determine the *real trend* of GE earnings during the past decade, if those earnings did not reflect free-market prices or the operating results of the entire worldwide complex of GE activities?

Of all the sources of investment information discussed in the previous chapter, a company's income statement is one of the most vital. It is an indispensable ingredient of any effort to determine the value of a corporate stock or bond. It is the reference we turn to for information on the level and trend of a company's earnings. But as we see from the GE example, it leaves much to be desired.

Many years ago, security analysts had to guard against the possibility that corporate income statements might be fraudulent. Today, however, regulations of the Securities and Exchange Commission, the New York and American Stock Exchanges, and the American Institute of Certified Public Accountants have all but eliminated this problem except in the case of small, closely owned corporations. Nevertheless, a security analyst cannot accept at face value the figure designated by a company as net income. Although the figure may have been calculated in accordance with "accepted accounting principles," these principles are neither unambiguous, nor uniformly interpreted and applied, nor most useful from an *investment* point of view. The purpose of this chapter is to provide the student of investments with some guides to help him through the income statement maze.[1]

## Income Statement Format

For purposes of security analysis, it is convenient to adopt as an income statement format something similar to the following:

| | |
|---|---|
| | Sales |
| *minus:* | Cost of Goods Sold |
| | Selling and Administrative Expenses |
| | Depreciation and Depletion |

[1] We shall consider balance sheet problems in Chapter 10, which deals with bond evaluation.

| | |
|---|---|
| *equals:* | Net Operating Income[2] |
| *plus:* | Nonoperating Income |
| *minus:* | Nonoperating Expenses |
| | Interest on Loans |
| *equals:* | Net Income before Taxes |
| *minus:* | Federal and State Income Taxes |
| *equals:* | Net Income |
| *minus:* | Dividends on Preferred Stock |
| *equals:* | Net Income on Common Stock Equity |
| *minus:* | Dividends on Common Stock |
| *equals:* | Net Income Transferred to Surplus (Retained Earnings) |

Problems of interpretation are involved in almost every item of this sample income statement. Among the most common problems are the following, which we shall examine in detail:

1. Cost of goods sold is affected by the company's method of evaluating ("costing") inventories. Different companies use different methods.

2. Depreciation and depletion charges are subject to a great deal of managerial discretion and are further affected by legislative changes.

3. Inclusion in the net income figure of such nonoperating items as capital gains or losses on sales of corporate assets often divert attention from the basic profitability of the firm's essential activities—manufacturing, wholesaling, retailing, and the like. Decisions regarding the inclusion or exclusion of subsidiary company activities can likewise create an unrealistic picture of the company's profitability.

4. Many companies report to the Internal Revenue Service one way and to stockholders another way, especially when tax regulations are changed frequently.[3]

## Cost of Goods Sold

Accountants calculate cost of goods sold in an indirect manner. At the beginning of an accounting period, the value of the firm's inventories on hand is ascertained. The sum of this value plus the value of goods subsequently acquired for sale equals the cost of all goods *available* for sale during the period. By subtracting from this sum the value of invento-

---

[2] The term "net operating income" is often defined in other ways. Some analysts define it, less inclusively, as sales minus operating expenses *other than* depreciation. Others define it more inclusively, deducting federal income taxes also.

[3] This enumeration of common problem areas in the analysis of income statements should not be taken to infer that other income and expense items are necessarily trouble-free. Indeed, even so apparently simple an item as "sales" can cause difficulty. For example, if a company enters into an installment sales contract, questions may arise as to *when* the various installments should be recorded as revenue.

ries on hand at the *end* of the period, a determination is made of the cost of what was actually sold. For wholesale and retail firms, this is simply the value of merchandise which they bought from others. For manufacturing firms, cost of goods sold includes not only merchandise—i.e., raw material—costs, but also wage and other costs directly associated with the manufacturing process.

If prices were unchanging, the method of determining cost of goods sold would involve no problems. It would merely be a matter of counting the *number of units* in inventory at the start of the period, adding the number purchased or produced during the period, and subtracting the number on hand at the end of the period. But the fact is that prices do change. And this means that the number of units is only one variable in determining cost. To illustrate, suppose a retailing firm begins the year with no inventory, and during the year buys three lots of 1,000 units of an item at successive prices of 15, 16, and 17 dollars per unit. Its purchases, then, will be:

| | |
|---|---|
| 1,000 units @ 15 = | $15,000 |
| 1,000 " " 16 = | 16,000 |
| 1,000 " " 17 = | 17,000 |
| Total Purchases | 48,000 |

Assume now that during this same year the firm sold 2,500 of the 3,000 units purchased. This being the case, it will end the year with 500 units of inventory. A key question is how to value these 500 units. The traditional rule is "lower of cost or market," which usually means cost in a period of rising prices. But what is the "cost" of the 500 units on the shelves?

*LIFO versus FIFO.* On the one hand, the firm can assume that units were sold in the same order as they were purchased. This is the so-called first-in–first-out method of inventory accounting, referred to in brief as FIFO. Using FIFO accounting, final inventory will have a unit cost equal to the most recent price—17—and will be worth $8,500. On the other hand, the firm can apply the "coal-bin analogy." When coal is delivered, it is poured into the cellar to form a pile. And when the furnace has to be stoked, coal is shoveled off the top of the pile first. Application of this analogy to inventory accounting is known as last-in–first-out, or LIFO accounting. Under this method, the unit cost of the final inventory would be the earliest price—15—and the total inventory value would be $7,500.[4]

[4] Actually, while the coal-bin analogy is helpful in exposition, a more important reason for using LIFO is that since some inventory must always be on hand in a going concern, it makes sense to maintain a reasonably stable value for this asset, much like any other fixed asset. LIFO accounting produces a more stable carrying price of inventory than FIFO. An even more practical consideration is the tax saving that results from reporting higher costs and lower profits during an inflationary period.

Thus, both accepted accounting procedures produce different inventory "costs"—$8,500 and $7,500.[5] When final inventory is subtracted from the $48,000 of purchases, cost of goods sold becomes either $39,500 or $40,500. But the value of *sales* during the period was what it was, regardless of the method of inventory accounting. Therefore, the *gross profit* on these sales will be highest under FIFO accounting (sales minus $39,500), and lowest under LIFO accounting (sales minus $40,500). This occurs during a period of rising prices. During a period of falling prices, FIFO would produce the lowest profits and LIFO the highest.

In other words, FIFO accounting causes reported profits to move in the direction of price changes as compared with LIFO accounting. Stated another way, FIFO accounting incorporates inventory profits and losses while LIFO accounting does not.

Since FIFO incorporates inventory gains and losses, it usually causes profits to be more volatile during the course of the business cycle than LIFO. During prosperous periods, when profits are normally rising, prices also frequently rise, and FIFO accounting causes inventory profits to be recorded on top of regular operating profits. LIFO does not. The opposite often occurs during recessions, when normal operating profit declines are augmented by inventory losses under FIFO but not under LIFO.

It is seldom pointed out, however, that FIFO accounting *need not necessarily* cause profits to be more volatile than LIFO accounting. Indeed, FIFO can, under some circumstances, be the more stabilizing factor. For example, meat-packing companies' selling prices to wholesalers and food chains tend to be less flexible than their raw materials prices (i.e., the prices of freshly slaughtered animals). Therefore, when meat prices in general are falling, total packing company costs often fall far more than dollar sales, and as a result profits rise. The contrary often occurs when meat prices are rising; costs tend to rise faster than sales, and profits fall. In this type of environment, FIFO accounting can be a stabilizer and LIFO a destabilizer. For under FIFO accounting, inventory losses during downward price cycles would tend to offset rising operating profits, and inventory gains during upward price cycles would tend to offset falling operating profits. Under LIFO accounting, on the other hand, there would be no inventory gains and losses to smooth out total net profits.

In studying many companies, the security analyst does not have to be very concerned about differences in inventory accounting systems because inventories do not bulk large in the total operation. But in some industries—not only meat packing but also retailing, tobacco, shoes, and other food processing—fluctuations of inventory values are very significant, and it is vital that the analyst be familiar with the impact on profits of different accounting procedures. Unfortunately, accountants' footnotes

---

[5] Other inventory valuation methods are possible but are not in general use.

to income statements usually do not facilitate a dollars-and-cents determination of what the cost of goods sold would have been had alternative procedures been used. Often it is difficult even to find out what system is in present use. But a careful reading of the footnotes in several years' annual reports may give the security analyst a better grasp of the situation than if he simply accepts cost of goods sold as reported. It will usually be time particularly well spent when he is comparing two companies, in the same industry, which use different inventory accounting systems, or is analyzing a company that has changed its inventory accounting system during the period under review.

*Overhead Costing.* In years to come, security analysts may be confronted with yet another problem stemming from inventory accounting, namely, the problem of "direct" versus "absorption" costing. Without getting into the accounting complexities,[6] the issue revolves around the method of reflecting in the income statement certain manufacturing *overhead* items such as depreciation and executive salaries. Under one view, direct costing, these expenses should be charged against income in their entirety regardless of the level of production during a period. Under the other view, absorption costing, these expenses should be allocated to the number of units produced. Thus, if in a given period production exceeds sales, and inventories rise, part of the overhead will be "absorbed" in rising inventory valuation, and reported profits for the period will be higher than under direct costing. The reverse would be true when inventories decline during a period.

To date, absorption costing has been the general rule in reports to stockholders and on income tax returns. However, an increasing number of companies have been using direct costing for internal control purposes, and pressure is building up for more widespread acceptance of direct costing. The day may be near when security analysts will have to scrutinize income statement footnotes not only for evidence on the LIFO–FIFO question but also on the direct versus absorption cost question.

### Depreciation and Depletion

When a company acquires a plant or machinery, or other fixed asset, it obviously expects to use the asset for many years. Consequently, it would not be appropriate to charge the full cost of the asset against the income of the year in which it was acquired. Instead, the asset is recorded on the balance sheet at cost (which is what is meant by "capitalizing an expense"), and each year thereafter, for the duration of the asset's estimated life, a portion of the cost is charged against income. At the same

[6] A good technical discussion may be found in W. Wright and F. P. Kollaritsch, "The Concept of Direct Costing," *The Controller* (now *The Financial Executive*), July, 1962.

time, the balance sheet value of the asset is lowered by the amount of the depreciation charge.

Thus, one function of depreciation charges is gradually to write off the cost of a fixed asset as its economic value shrinks due to wear and tear and obsolescence. The term "amortization" refers to essentially the same procedure, except that it involves the charging off of the cost of an *intangible* asset such as a patent. Hereafter, when we use the term depreciation, we mean amortization as well. Finally, the term "depletion" refers to the literal physical exhaustion of an asset, such as a mine or oil well, during the process of conducting the business.

*The Rate of Charge-off.* In connection with the expense–charge-off function of depreciation and depletion, a problem of interpretation arises for security analysts. This results from the fact that management has considerable leeway in the *rate* at which it depreciates assets. There are many acceptable accounting techniques, and the Internal Revenue Service sanctions several of them. For example, under "straight-line" depreciation the charge-off occurs in equal annual installments. But under other methods, a greater proportion of an asset's cost is charged off in the earlier years of its life. And the specific proportion varies with the method—"double declining balance," "sum of the years' digits," and so forth. Moreover, different companies may depreciate the identical type of asset over a different number of years. Further complicating things is the fact that Congress and the Internal Revenue Service change the depreciation rules every so often.[7] As a result, depreciation charges are difficult to compare not only among companies at any instant of time but also for a single company over a span of many years.

Depletion is an even more complex matter. As with depreciation, differences arise among companies because of managerial judgment. But, in addition, depletion has become a political football. Under the guise of encouraging certain lines of mineral exploration, Congress has legislated different depletion bases and rates for different mineral industries. Indeed, in some industries, the original cost of obtaining a raw material may be recovered many times before the resource is exhausted.

Interyear and intercompany variations in depreciation and depletion accounting can severely distort profit comparisons. Many differences are more apparent than real. Ideally, the security analyst should restate all income accounts, putting them on a consistent depreciation basis. For example, all depreciation might be stated on a straight-line basis (with an appropriate adjustment of the income tax liability). In practice, however, available data are not usually adequate to make such adjustments. The

[7] For example, in an anti-inflation action certain methods of accelerated depreciation, as applied to structures, were temporarily suspended in late 1966 and early 1967. This was in addition to temporary suspension of the 7% investment credit.

analyst knows little about the true economic life of various types of assets or about the age composition of a particular company's assets at a given time. Frequently, as with inventory, he does not even know what depreciation-depletion accounting procedures are actually being followed by a company, nor whether these have been changed recently—although he should read the footnotes of the income statements carefully to see if he can find out. The really diligent analyst will examine a copy of the

**FIGURE 4–1**

**Reported Net Income versus Cash Flow, U.S. Steel Corporation**

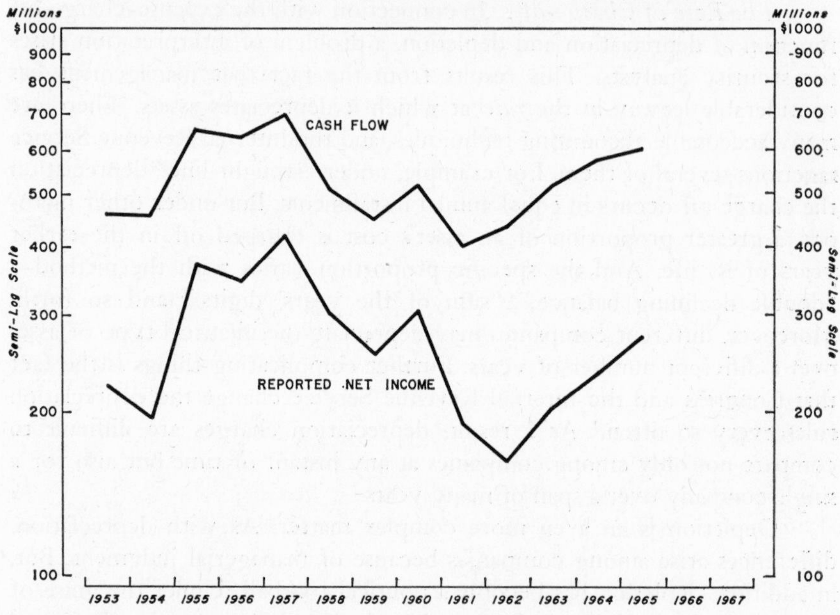


company's 10–K report to the SEC in his efforts to unravel the mysteries of its depreciation practices.[8]

*Cash Flow.* During recent years, many security analysts have been trying to cope with these problems by, in effect, ignoring depreciation and depletion altogether. Against the advice of the accounting profession[9] and many of their own colleagues, they have been using a concept known widely as "cash flow"—defined as net income plus depreciation and deple-

[8] A recent study of publicly available information on the depreciation practices of 110 large companies revealed that "in only 16 of the 110 annual reports to stockholders was it possible to determine the depreciation method." On the other hand, most of the 10–K reports contained fairly detailed information on the subject. See J. H. Myers, "Depreciation Disclosure," *Journal of Accountancy*, November, 1965.

[9] P. Mason, *"Cash Flow" Analysis and the Funds Statement* (New York: American Institute of Certified Public Accountants, 1961).

tion. In other words, it is the difference between sales and all expenses (including taxes) *other than* depreciation and depletion. Figure 4–1, for example, compares the reported net income with the "cash flow" of a company (U.S. Steel) that has been greatly affected by various revisions of the depreciation sections of the tax code. Some rather striking differences in the movement of the two series will be noted.

Security analysts who use the cash flow concept, if they are intelligent, do not consider cash flow to be a measure of the *level* of profits. For they recognize that depreciation and depletion should be deducted from revenues in determining profits. What they do argue, however, is that differences in depreciation-depletion accounting procedures can so distort reported net income that if the analyst hasn't the data with which to restate the account, cash flow often is more useful than reported net income in comparing the *trends* of profitability among companies and over time. We are in substantial agreement with this view,[10] although we must in all frankness acknowledge that some analysts have shifted from net income to cash flow simply to make "price-earnings ratios" appear lower, thus "justifying" their purchase recommendations.

To be sure, we are not wholly satisfied with the practice of simply adding depreciation to net income after taxes. A company's income tax liability is greatly affected by its depreciation policies. Other things being equal, the higher the depreciation the lower the income tax. By adding depreciation back to net income after taxes, to derive "cash flow," the problem of depreciation noncomparability is not completely sidestepped, because net income reflects the tax liability which, in turn, reflects depreciation policies. If it is truly desired to put all companies on a comparable predepreciation basis, it might be better to add only half of depreciation (and depletion) to net income, assuming a 50% tax rate for simplicity. Another alternative would be to use "*pretax* cash flow"—i.e., net income before deducting either federal income taxes or depreciation.

Furthermore, we recognize that "cash flow" is a poor descriptive phrase for the sum of net income plus depreciation and depletion. For it infers that this sum is a correct representation of the amount of *cash* generated by operations during the accounting period. That is, depreciation does not involve a cash outlay; it is a noncash expense. So, by adding it back to net income, the inference is that the resulting figure equals the difference between cash income and cash outlays. But this is not true at all.

There are many transactions which increase or reduce cash but do not affect reported net income. For example, when a company makes

[10] The view also is supported by a recent study of corporate dividend practices, which shows that dividends are more closely related to cash flow than to net income. See J. A. Brittain, *Corporate Dividend Policy* (Washington, D.C.: Brookings Institution, 1966).

sinking-fund payments on its bonds, cash is reduced but income is not. On the other hand, when the company sells new bonds, the proceeds increase cash but not net income. And there are many transactions which increase or reduce net income without causing cash to increase or decline. For example, when a company sells goods or services it builds up income. But its customers may not pay all the bills in the current accounting period. As a result, accounts receivable rise, rather than cash, to the extent of the uncollected income. The reverse holds true in the case of purchases unpaid for. The purchases are a charge against income, but accounts payable rise and cash does not decline.

Thus, a distinction should be made between cash flow as an attempt to determine the true *trend* of profits, and cash flow as a sources and uses of funds network. An example of the latter is shown in Figure 4–2. Despite all of its shortcomings, however, the addition of net income plus depreciation and depletion in a profit analysis is, in our opinion, a simple and useful procedure.

*Expensing versus Capitalizing.* Another aspect of intercompany differences in depreciation policies concerns "intermediate-term expenses." Some items purchased by a company are so obviously short-lived that they are almost invariably charged against income during the year in which they are acquired. Examples of such items are pencils, pads, drill bits, light bulbs, etc. Other items are so obviously long-lived that they are capitalized (set up on the balance sheet as assets) and charged off gradually —for example, buildings, lathes, office furniture, etc. But many companies incur expenses which cannot be clearly labeled as short or long term in nature. Some of these companies follow a policy of "expensing" such items immediately, while others capitalize them and charge them off over several years.

Examples of intermediate-term expenses are numerous. Automobile companies, for example, spend huge sums for dies when they make basic style changes in their cars. These dies are usually used on a few years' models thereafter, but it is not too long before a major restyling is underway again. Should these dies be expensed or capitalized? Oil companies are constantly exploring for new wells. Should the drilling expenses of each year be attributed to that year's operations, or should such expenses be considered in the nature of longer term capital outlays? Should a distinction be made between expenses incurred in actually bringing in wells versus drilling "dry holes"? A similar question may apply to research and development expenses. And what about the costs of producing a motion picture? If a movie is good, it may run for two or three years, and it may be rerun several years later, or sold to television. Should the production costs be charged to the year in which incurred or spread over a period of several years?

There are no right or wrong answers to these questions. They are

### FIGURE 4–2

**One Form of Cash Flow Statement**

(In Millions of Dollars)

| | | |
|---|---|---|
| In 1960, sales and other revenue amounted to | | $150.6 |
| Whereas cost of goods sold and operating "cash" expenses (exclusive of $7.2 "noncash" depreciation) was | | 118.9 |
| So that pretax net income before noncash charge for depreciation was | | $ 31.7 |
| And there would have been a net inflow of cash of this amount, if collections from customers had been the same as sales and if the company had bought and paid exactly the cost of the goods it shipped. BUT these conditions did not prevail, for: | | |
| A. The company collected less than it billed | ($14.1) | |
| B. The company bought and manufactured more than the cost of the goods it shipped | ( 2.9) | |
| C. The company paid out less cash than the costs it incurred | .8 | |
| The net effect of the three items being | | ( 16.2) |
| So that activities related to buying, manufacturing, selling, and collecting brought in cash of | | $ 15.5 |
| Outgo of cash for income tax paid was | | 9.9 |
| With the result that inflow of cash "internally generated" was | | $ 5.6 |
| There were inflows from: | | |
| Sale of Common stock | $12.6 | |
| Increase in short-term loans | 5.0 | |
| Increase in long-term debt | 2.4 | 20.0 |
| | | $ 25.6 |
| Outgo of cash was required for: | | |
| Dividends | $ 3.0 | |
| Property, plant, and equipment acquired in excess of dispositions | 30.8 | |
| Purchase of preferred stock | .3 | |
| Increase in investment and other assets | 1.7 | $ 35.8 |
| With the effect on the company's cash (and cash equivalent in the form of marketable securities), as between the beginning and end of 1960, being a decrease of | | ($ 10.2) |

Source: Almand R. Coleman, "Funds Statements and Cash Flow," *The Controller* (now *The Financial Executive*), December, 1961.

entirely matters of managerial discretion. For the security analyst, however, they create a problem in comparing the level and trends of profitability among companies.

Moreover, the use of "cash flow" does not overcome the problem. In fact, it aggravates it. When one company is fully expensing a cost, and another is amortizing it gradually, cash flow does not let *any* of the expense show up for the latter company, while continuing to allow the full expense to be reflected for the former.

*Replacement of Assets.* In addition to posing an analytical problem because of *differences* in accounting treatment, depreciation also causes a problem because of one outstanding similarity of treatment. Regardless of the rate of depreciation, accepted accounting practice and tax regulations allow only the original cost of the asset to be written off during its useful life.[11] The reason this is significant to security analysts is that there is a second function of depreciation. The first function, as we have seen, is to allocate the cost of a capital asset over its useful life. But a second, indirect, function is to provide a fund for the replacement of the assets after they have worn out, either physically or technologically. Of course, depreciation per se does not provide a company with cash. It is an expense. Cash is generated primarily by making sales. But by deducting depreciation from sales revenues in computing net income, the company withholds cash which might otherwise be paid out in the form of higher wages, dividends, and taxes.

The function of depreciation as an (indirect) source of funds for asset replacement has created analytical problems during inflationary periods such as we have witnessed since World War II. For having charged off the original cost of assets, companies have found that the costs thus recovered are inadequate, because replacement cost has risen far above original cost. Most companies have allowed for this depreciation deficiency by paying out a smaller percentage of earnings as dividends to common stockholders than they otherwise would have paid. Therefore, security analysts should compare the dividend payout ratios (dividends as a percentage of earnings) of competing companies. If a company's ratio seems unusually high for a period of several years, there is a possibility that sufficient funds have not been retained internally for replacement of plant and equipment. Heavy resort to the capital markets in such cases may impair the earning power behind the existing stockholders' equity.

High payout ratios, on the other hand, may merely indicate that the company has already completed its plant modernization while its competitors have not. If subsequent replacement costs are expected to remain fairly stable, a high-dividend policy would be warranted for the company. Furthermore, a management may consciously decide to finance replacement by selling bonds rather than by retaining earnings. If its existing debt is low, and if it can raise money at a modest interest rate, the stockholders could benefit from such a policy, particularly stockholders in a fairly low income tax bracket to whom dividends are almost as desirable as capital gains. Clues to the significance of unusually high or low dividend payout ratios may be found in the text of annual reports, in speeches by company executives to financial analysts' societies, and by direct interrogation of the management.

---

[11] As noted previously, this is not true of depletion.

## Nonoperating Income and Expense

One of the main reasons for studying corporate income statements in security analysis is to estimate the "normal" earning power of the companies being studied, as to both level and trend. To the extent that reported net income reflects debits and credits attributable to transactions which are not part of a company's everyday operations, *normal* earning power may be obscured. There are three principal problem areas: nonrecurring items, contingency "reserves," and accounting for subsidiary company activities.

*Nonrecurring Items.* As is indicated by the name, nonrecurring income and expense items make only occasional appearances on the income statement. For example, if a manufacturing company sells one of its plants and makes a capital gain by doing so, the accountant may include[12] this capital gain, after deducting the appropriate capital gains tax (usually 25%), in the net income for the year. But from the security analyst's point of view, the capital gain does not reflect the normal earning power of the company. It may very well recur, but the timing and amount of the recurrence simply cannot be estimated. Therefore, it should usually be omitted from net income for security analysis purposes. Likewise, nonrecurring expenses—for example, an uninsured flood loss—should usually be added back to net income. (On the other hand, a case can be made for excluding nonrecurring items from net income in a year-to-year analysis but including them in an overall calculation of average income for a period of many years.)

Some nonoperating items, however, may be recurring in nature. For example, royalties earned by a manufacturing company from the licensing of a patent to other companies would usually be classified as nonoperating income. But the royalties are a regular feature of the income statement and should be considered part of the company's normal earning power. Likewise, dividends received on a long-term stock investment in another company—such as Du Pont's holding of General Motors stock prior to the court order that it be sold—are nonoperating income items but are recurring in nature.

There is one type of nonrecurring item which has caused much confusion, namely tax credits arising from the loss carry-back and carry-forward provisions of the Internal Revenue Code. The law provides that when a company operates at a net loss it can, in effect, merge the losses with years of profits in order to determine its tax liability on

[12] The word "may" is used because accountants differ as to the degree of inclusiveness which is appropriate in the calculation of net income. For an extended discussion of this point, see Douglas H. Bellemore, *Investments* (2nd ed.; New York: Simmons-Boardman Publishing Corp., 1960), pp. 570–79.

profits. For example, a $10 million loss in, say, the recession year of 1960 can offset a total of $10 million of profits earned in the years 1957 through 1965, because the loss can be "carried back" three years and "carried forward" five years. This means that in, say, 1961 and 1962 the company may have had two very profitable years yet paid little or no income tax. (Indeed, the tax-loss factor has been an important reason for many mergers during recent years. Within limits established by the Internal Revenue Service, profitable companies can buy unprofitable ones and thereby reduce their income taxes.)

The question thus arises whether the security analyst should consider the "true" net income of 1961 and 1962 to have been the very high amounts actually reported. This would be the most liberal treatment of the tax credit, but it would greatly distort the trend of true profits. A more appropriate treatment would be to assume that net income for 1961 and 1962 was half of reported pretax profit (assuming an effective tax rate of 50% for simplicity[13]) and to reduce the 1960 loss by the amount of the tax credits taken as a result of that loss.[14] In other words, tax credits should be *reallocated* to the years to which they apply.

Reallocation is also an effective way of handling problems arising from defense contract renegotiation proceedings. Renegotiation of the terms of defense contracts often takes place several years after work has been completed and paid for. It may result in the supplying company owing the government money, or vice versa. The company will report the assessment or refund in the year of the renegotiation settlement. But the security analyst should properly reallocate the settlement amount to the year in which the work was originally reflected in the income statement. Similar considerations apply to the increasing use by the Defense Department of incentive bonuses and penalties for speedy or slow performance on contracts.

Finally, mention might be made of a type of transaction that is neither fish nor fowl. Many companies give their customers the option to lease or buy the product offered. During most years, the mix between outright sales and lease arrangements is usually fairly stable. Occasionally, however, an extremely large outright sale may be made which distorts the year-to-year revenue trend. For example, in 1964 the federal government made a decision to buy rather than lease the bulk of its electronic computers. For IBM, the government's largest supplier, this decision meant a sharp rise in 1964 revenues and earnings, but it was not likely to be

---

[13] Where depletion allowances, etc., make the usual effective tax rate significantly lower, that rate should be applied.

[14] Ordinarily this would be about half the loss, but in some cases a part of the tax credit might go unused because there are not sufficient profits against which to offset the entire credit. The security analyst should always keep track of unused, but still available, tax credits.

repeated in subsequent years. Clearly, such a transaction is part of the company's "normal" operations and cannot be omitted from the analyst's calculations. Yet it is equally clear that the transaction has the characteristics of a nonrecurring item. Perhaps the best advice that can be offered is that the analyst be aware of the possible distortions in the situation and that he concentrate on *average* sales and earnings for a period of a few years, while deemphasizing year-to-year changes.

*Contingency "Reserves."* It is common practice to make advance provision for possible future losses. The accounting procedure is to deduct an amount from the income of a given year and establish a balance sheet liability in that amount.[15] Then, in a later year, if the anticipated loss actually occurs, it is charged directly against the balance sheet liability rather than against income.

When advance provisions are made for frequent types of losses—for example uncollectible accounts receivable—they should be accepted by the security analyst as given, unless he has some reason to believe that they are unrealistic. Indeed, they are permissible deductions on a company's federal income tax return. Occasionally, however, the analyst will come across provisions for losses which are quite uncertain in amount or which may well not even occur. For example, companies doing a large volume of international business may provide for losses on foreign currencies due to devaluations (Firestone Tire is one such company).

The Internal Revenue Service does not allow most provisions for contingencies to be deducted from taxable income. They are deductible only when they occur. Likewise, the security analyst usually should exclude them from his net income computations for several reasons. First, since the existence, timing, and amount of the losses are usually very uncertain, the amount and timing of the advance provisions are likely to be quite arbitrary. Second, management may use contingency provisions as a means of bolstering the reported profits of poor years by holding down the reported profits of good years. Although it may seem desirable to smooth out reported earnings, the effect may be to conceal an otherwise significant trend.[16] Finally, even where the loss seems quite likely to occur and its amount seems reasonably predictable—for example, the company may be involved in litigation in which counsel expects to make an out-of-court settlement—the *actual* loss would usually be treated as a nonrecurring item and excluded anyhow. If it would be excluded when it actually occurred, it should certainly not be included before it occurs.

---

[15] The liability item may be labeled "reserve for . . . ," but accounting practice frowns on this designation unless a specific cash fund has been set aside, which is not usually the case. "Provision for" or "liability for" are preferable terms.

[16] In the "old days" contingency reserves were frequently used deliberately to *destabilize* reported earnings, in the hope that stock prices would rise more on good profit reports than they would fall on poor reports.

There is one type of provision for future expenses which has been too often neglected by accountants and security analysts but which is extremely important. Most large corporations, and many smaller ones, have pension plans for their employees. Pension expenses are by no means uncertain contingencies. Competent actuaries can calculate with a fair degree of accuracy how much money will have to be paid in pension benefits, and when. But this does not mean that accounting for these pension liabilities is clear-cut; far from it.

A company's pension liabilities are divisible into two major segments. One part, the "past service liability," stems from the fact that when a company adopts a pension plan it has a large number of old hands among its employees. Thus, if a worker with, say, 25 years of service is 50 years old when the plan is adopted, the company will have to begin paying him a pension in 15 years. But the amount of his pension will be based on as much as 40 years of service. Therefore, the company starts right out with a "past service liability" to which is added the "current service liability" for service rendered after the adoption of the plan. Past service liabilities are also incurred when benefits under an existing plan are improved.

A company can provide for these liabilities in a large number of ways. These can be briefly outlined.[17] At one extreme, a company can adopt a so-called "pay-as-you-go" system. Here there is no advance recognition of the liabilities. The company simply pays pension benefits as they come due, out of the general corporate funds, charging the income account at that time. Public Service Electric & Gas Co. is an example of a large company which is on a pay-as-you-go system.

On the other hand, there are various income tax and personnel relations benefits in putting money aside in advance, usually with a commercial bank or life insurance company. This is known as "funding," and most large corporations follow the practice. But the rate at which the pension liabilities are funded, and reflected in current net income, is a matter of managerial discretion, thus giving rise to a problem quite similar to that presented to the security analyst by differing depreciation practices. Current service liabilities are usually funded as they accrue each year; but past service liabilities may be funded over a period of 10 to 30 or more years (the tax code sets 10 years as a minimum)—or, indeed, not at all.

Some companies, moreover, have manipulated their pension funding in much the same way as noted in the previous discussion of contingency reserves. U.S. Steel, for example, has often been criticized for artificially smoothing reported earnings by increasing pension fund contributions in good years and reducing them in poor years. Controversy is further stimulated by the increasing tendency of pension fund trustees to invest the funds in common stocks. For a question arises regarding the method

---

[17] See Chapter 19, pp. 715 ff., for additional details.

of taking into account unrealized capital appreciation in determining a company's unfunded pension liabilities.

Pension liabilities are often huge relative to total income and assets. The manner of providing for them can profoundly affect reported earnings. Yet only a careful reading of income statement footnotes will reveal the magnitude of the problem in any given case, and frequently not even then. Of 600 annual reports of large corporations recently surveyed by the American Institute of Certified Public Accountants, one third did not make any mention at all of pension plans and one sixth mentioned the subject but did not indicate the annual costs or the ultimate liabilities.[18] Accountants and professional security analysts have yet to come to grips with the problem satisfactorily.[19]

*Subsidiaries and Affiliates.* When a company owns more than 50% of the common stock of another company, a parent-subsidiary relationship is said to exist (although the most typical ownership percentage in such cases is 100% or close to it). If the ownership proportion is substantial, but less than 50%, the owned company is referred to as an affiliate.

Dividends received on the stock of affiliates are treated by accountants as nonoperating (but recurring) income, and this is usually acceptable for security analysis purposes. However, problems of interpretation often arise in the treatment of dividends received on the stock of subsidiaries. When a subsidiary exists, the parent, by definition, controls it and could compel it to pay out 100% of its earnings as dividends. Since the parent could compel full payment, it is usually more realistic to "consolidate" the income statements, and also the balance sheets,[20] of the parent and subsidiary, rather than merely include the subsidiary's dividend payments in the parent's income statement. (As a matter of fact, a consolidated statement might be more realistic even when accounting for affiliates. Although the stock ownership may be under 50%, effective control may, nevertheless, exist.)

---

[18] Cited by T. A. Wise in "Those Uncertain Actuaries: Part II," *Fortune*, January, 1966, p. 184.

[19] The most comprehensive analysis to date of the financial statement aspect of pension plans is E. L. Hicks, *Accounting for the Cost of Pension Plans* (New York: American Institute of Certified Public Accountants, 1965). In late 1966, the Accounting Principles Board published several opinions which call for more uniform systems of accounting for pension liabilities, nonrecurring items, and related matters. Time did not permit the inclusion of these developments in the body of this text. While such efforts by the AICPA will be of great benefit to financial analysts in interpreting future income statements, analysts will still be confronted with the problem of reconciling past data to the new reporting systems in order to interpret *trends* properly.

[20] It is often argued that finance company subsidiaries of manufacturing and retailing companies are best consolidated only in the income statement, but not in the balance sheet, because of their disproportionately large liabilities to banks and bondholders. But this approach can delude the analyst of the parent company's finances. See V. L. Andrews, "Captive Finance Companies," *Harvard Business Review*, July–August, 1964.

In a consolidated statement, the parent and subsidiary are looked upon as one big company, with the subsidiary being treated as a division of the parent. All sales and all expenses are added together, except that transactions *between* the parent and subsidiary are netted out. If a minority interest in the subsidiary is held by other parties, the minority percentage of the subsidiary's net income is deducted in computing the consolidated net income.

Most parent companies report on a consolidated basis, but in many cases one or more subsidiaries may not be consolidated. First, counsel may advise nonconsolidation as evidence of "arm's-length dealing" in the event of, say, antitrust action against the parent or bankruptcy of the subsidiary. Second, many companies choose to keep foreign subsidiaries unconsolidated. Finally, consolidation on tax returns is permissible only where 80% ownership exists, directly or indirectly, and there may be various other tax considerations in the choice of whether to consolidate.

The footnotes to the income statement contain a description of the extent of consolidation. If any subsidiaries are not consolidated, there will usually appear a footnote item called "equity in undistributed earnings of unconsolidated subsidiaries." In general, it is best for the security analyst to add this amount to reported net income, thus producing the net income figure which would have been reported in a fully consolidated statement. This fully consolidated net income is more representative of the true earning power of the enterprise, with one major exception. When there is some question about the ability of a subsidiary to remit its earnings to its parent, consolidation is inadvisable. Prominent in this category are subsidiaries located in foreign lands which maintain foreign exchange controls, or which are very unstable politically, making uncompensated nationalization a serious threat.

An example will help clarify the difference between consolidated and unconsolidated income statements. Assume the following facts for two companies, one of which is 90% owned by the other:

| | *Parent Company* | *90%-Owned Subsidiary* |
|---|---|---|
| Sales | $100 million | $20 million |
| Total expenses and taxes | 80 | 16 |
| Net income | 20 | 4 |
| Dividends paid | | 3 |

If the parent company were to prepare an unconsolidated income statement, it would appear as follows:

| | |
|---|---|
| Sales | $100.0 million |
| Expenses and taxes* | 80.0 |
| Dividend income* | 2.7 |
| Net income | 22.7 |

* We ignore, for illustrative purposes, the fact that corporate income tax must be paid on 15% of the dividends received from unconsolidated subsidiaries.

The $2.7 million nonoperating dividend income represents the parent's 90% share of the subsidiary's $3 million dividend payment. A footnote to the statement will point out that the subsidiary's accounts are not consolidated with those of the parent and will indicate that the parent has an $0.9 million equity in the undistributed earnings of the unconsolidated subsidiary. This $0.9 million is derived by taking 90% of undistributed earnings of $1 million ($4 million net income minus $3 million distributed as dividends leaves $1 million undistributed).

A consolidated income statement would appear as follows, assuming no transactions took place between the two companies:

| | |
|---|---|
| Sales | $120.0 million |
| Expenses and taxes | 96.0 |
| Minority interest | 0.4 |
| Net income | 23.6 |

The minority interest of $0.4 million represents 10% of the subsidiary's $4 million net income. Note that the consolidated statement does not distinguish between distributed and undistributed earnings of the subsidiary. Note also that the security analyst who is presented with the unconsolidated statement can indirectly determine consolidated net income (23.6) by adding unconsolidated net income (22.7) and equity in undistributed subsidiary earnings (0.9).

The security analyst must be particularly careful to avoid being misled by the fact that many companies—for example, in the office equipment industry—have recently been consolidating subsidiaries which previously were unconsolidated. Obviously, this introduces a discontinuity in the reported net income of recent years as compared with previous years. The discontinuity can be overcome by following the indirect method described above—that is, adding back equity in undistributed earnings of unconsolidated subsidiaries during those earlier years. The trouble is that the analyst may not realize that a discontinuity exists if he merely looks at the footnotes of the most recent income statement. For these will tell him the current basis of consolidation but will not necessarily alert him to the fact that the current basis is different from that of earlier years. In other words, the analyst should read the footnotes to the statements of *each* year covered in his analysis.

*Mergers.* Along somewhat similar lines, a severe discontinuity is introduced when one company merges with another. What must be done is to try to create hypothetical merged income statements for the pre-merger years, thus eliminating the discontinuity. An income statement which shows the situation that would have existed in the past had current conditions (in this case a merger) prevailed at that time, is known as a "pro forma" statement.

The analyst can usually obtain pro forma statements for at least a few years back when the merger proceedings involve the solicitation of proxies from shareholders or the sale of new securities. Under such circumstances, the official proxy statements, prospectuses, or registration statements will usually contain some pro forma financial accounts. And when the merger partners are both publicly held companies, the analyst can extend the pro forma record back even further in time by combining the individual published statements of each of the companies. When the company being merged is small or privately owned, however, the task of compiling a consistent earnings record becomes exceedingly complicated, and sometimes impossible.[21]

Part of the problem created by mergers is caused by the fact that when shares are exchanged by the acquiring company for those of the acquired company they are not usually equal in book value. Differences should be adjusted in the surplus accounts of the acquiring company but often are not. Where the acquiring company's shares are worth more, a "goodwill" asset in the amount of the difference may be established, and subsequently amortized and charged against net income. The distortion of the trend of true earning power in such a situation (Revlon is an example) should be obvious to the reader. Equally distorting is the situation where the acquiring company's shares are worth less than those of the acquired company. The book value "profit" achieved by the acquiring company would be treated best as an addition to capital surplus. But some companies on occasion—for example, Litton Industries—have added the profit directly to the year's reported net income.

### Income Tax Reconciliation

A simple test can be very rewarding in security analysis. It is to compare reported net income with the reported federal income tax deduction. Since most publicly owned corporations now pay a 48% tax on regular income, their reported net income and income tax should be roughly equal in amount. If they are not, it is for one of three major reasons, each of which may call for some adjustment of reported net income on the part of the security analyst.

1. A significant portion of the company's income may not have been taxable at regular income rates, for example, capital gains, dividends from affiliates, etc. Both of these examples have been discussed under the headings "nonrecurring items" and "subsidiaries and affiliates."

2. The company may have been the beneficiary of a significant tax credit, either as a result of the loss carry-back and carry-forward provisions of the law, or because of a government contract renegotiation, or because its capital spending program entitled it to a 7% tax credit under

---

[21] Conversion of all dollar data, sales as well as earnings, into per-share terms is absolutely essential when pro forma statements cannot be obtained. See section below on per-share calculation.

the provisions of the 1962 law. The potential distorting effect on "true net income" of tax credits has also been discussed previously.[22]

3. The company may have reported different income and expense items to stockholders than it reported to the Internal Revenue Service. Prominent in this connection is the reporting of depreciation. Many companies, particularly public utilities, have followed a practice in recent years of charging depreciation at the most rapid rate possible on their income tax returns, but at a traditional straight-line rate on their stockholder reports. This creates a lower pretax profit on the tax return than on the stockholder report, and therefore the income tax actually paid is a good deal less than 48% of the pretax profit reported to stockholders.[23]

If the tax saving from accelerated depreciation is allowed to "flow through" to net income reported to stockholders, the security analyst can be misled. For the tax saving may be only temporary. Since the tax-reported assets will become fully depreciated faster than under a straight-line basis, the tax bill will ultimately be higher than 48% of stockholder-reported pretax profit, unless new capital spending keeps filling the void. Conservative managements and security analysts, therefore, might present a more realistic statement of profits if they charged income with a "deferred tax liability" when stockholder-reported depreciation is at a slower rate than tax-reported depreciation.[24]

A similar observation may be made with regard to companies that sell on an installment payment basis. If they report the full amount of sales and related expenses in their stockholder reports during the years in which shipments are actually made, but report to the Internal Revenue only as payments are received, there obviously will be discrepancies between taxes actually paid and taxes which normally would be expected. Again, the establishment of deferred tax liabilities would provide a more realistic picture of results.

A study of 70 large corporations in 12 different industries, for the year 1958, revealed that pretax profit reported to stockholders in annual

---

[22] The accounting profession is of divided opinion as to whether the entire 7% investment credit should be reported to stockholders in the year in which taken, or whether it should be spread over the lifetime of the capital assets whose purchase generated the credit.

[23] Indeed, the dividends of many utility companies are partially tax-exempt because they exceed the net income reported to the government and are thus considered partial returns of capital. For example, in recent years two thirds or more of Consolidated Edison's dividends have been tax-free. This is because the company has charged accelerated depreciation on its tax returns and thus reported lower net income than the amount it actually has paid in cash dividends—the amount of the dividends having been based on stockholder-reported profits of a much higher amount than tax-reported profits.

[24] Public utility commissions, on the other hand, may insist on "flow-through accounting" because higher reported profits mean less pressure for rate increases during inflationary periods.

reports was almost 50% higher than reported on income tax returns.[25] In each of the 12 industries, stockholder reports showed profits at least 10% higher than tax reports. In two industries, petroleum and nonferrous metals, stockholder reports showed profits of more than double (almost triple in the case of petroleum) the level reported to the IRS. Undoubtedly, depletion allowances account for much of the discrepancy in these two industries.

Clearly, a lack of rough equivalence between the amount of reported net income and the amount of federal income tax should put a security analyst on notice that he has a sleuthing job to do. For this reason, it is a good idea to make the test right at the outset of the analysis. Income tax complications, particularly during periods of rapidly changing legislation and administrative rulings, also suggest that security analysts may be well advised to pay at least as much attention to pretax profit as to after-tax profit. Indeed, *pretax cash flow* often is the best way to get a realistic impression of trends in profitability.

Pretax cash flow is defined conventionally as net income before deducting depreciation or income taxes. As noted earlier, in the discussion of the use of after-tax cash flow, such a measure should not purport to reflect the *level* of corporate earning power. However, with tax and depreciation policy assuming growing roles as tools for achieving national goals, there is need for a measure of profit *trends* which is undistorted by frequent changes in tax and depreciation laws and regulations.

### Conclusion

Two final observations are in order before concluding our discussion of adjustments to reported net income. First, financial authorities often suggest that it probably does not pay to go to the trouble of adjusting reported profits unless the adjustments amount to more than 5%–10% of the reported amount.[26] In our view, this suggestion is beguiling. It sounds fine, but how does one know whether the adjustments will be substantial without doing the analysis? And once the analysis is done, why not make the adjustments even if they are relatively small?

The second observation is a note of optimism. While the accounting profession is virtually split over the question of whether to make income

---

[25] Edmund A. Mennis, "Different Measures of Profits," *1961 Proceedings* of the Business and Economic Statistics Section, American Statistical Association. Also see W. D. Williams, "A Look Behind Reported Earnings," *Financial Analysts Journal*, January–February, 1966. A discussion of the subject from an accounting point of view is contained in H. A. Black, "Interperiod Allocation of Corporate Income Taxes," *Journal of Accountancy*, July, 1966.

[26] See B. Graham, D. L. Dodd, and S. Cottle, *Security Analysis*. (4th ed.; New York: McGraw-Hill Book Co., 1962), p. 112.

statements and balance sheets uniform,[27] there is growing agreement on the need for more adequate disclosure. Accordingly, a rule was adopted by the AICPA, as of January 1, 1965, that corporate financial statements must disclose the *dollar effect* of any important departures from the preferred methods of handling various transactions, as expounded in published form by the Accounting Principles Board. Furthermore, in May, 1964, the SEC ruled that any material difference between the methods of reporting to the SEC and of reporting to stockholders must be noted in the annual report, together with an indication of how the differences can be reconciled. Thus, the security analyst's need to adjust reported net income will remain, but he will have an improved information base for making the necessary adjustments.

### Calculation of Earnings per Share

It is a standard analytical procedure to convert total dollar earnings into dollars and cents *per share*. To make clear why this conversion is made, let us take an example. Suppose that in 1963 Company X had 1 million shares of common stock outstanding and had net income available to common (i.e., net income minus preferred dividends) of $2 million. In 1964 Company X decided to expand its business by acquiring another company. To consummate the deal, Company X issued 250,000 shares of its stock in exchange for the other company's stock. Thus, Company X now had 1¼ million shares of stock outstanding.

Suppose that the acquisition raised 1964 earnings on common stock to $2½ million from the $2 million earned in 1963. From the point of view of the individual stockholder, earnings did not rise at all. The 25% increase of total dollar earnings was accompanied by a 25% increase in capital stock *held by others*. From the individual investor's point of view, progress means higher earnings on *his* share interest so that he can look forward to higher dividend payments or to a higher market value on his stock.

In our example the dividend potential of the individual shareholding did not increase at all. This can be shown by dividing each year's net income (after deducting any preferred stock dividend obligations) by the number of shares outstanding *that year*. Thus 1963's earnings of $2 million, divided by the 1 million shares outstanding in 1963, produces earnings per share of $2. And 1964's earnings of $2½ million, divided by that year's 1¼ million shares outstanding, also produces per share earnings of $2. No progress is indicated for the individual investor.

The use of 1¼ million shares in the 1964 calculation assumes that the

---

[27] "Uniformity in Financial Accounting" (a symposium), *Law and Contemporary Problems* (Durham, N.C.: Duke University, Autumn, 1965).

entire earnings of the merged company for 1964 were included in the surviving company's earnings that year. But sometimes earnings are included only from the date of the merger. Where this is the case, an accurate per-share calculation results only if the number of shares used in the divisor is a *weighted* total of the number outstanding during the year.

For example, suppose the merger took place October 1, 1964, and only an extra $125,000 of earnings was included in the report of the merged company—i.e., total earnings of $2,125,000 were reported. It also is true, however, that the extra 250,000 shares were outstanding for only three months. The weighted number of shares in 1964, therefore, would be 1,000,000 plus ¼ of 250,000, or 1,062,500. Dividing $2,125,000 by 1,062,500 produces earnings per share of $2, whereas the use of the full 1,250,000 shares in the divisor would have produced a misleading $1.70 earnings per share.

Similarly, a weighted total number of shares is useful when new shares are sold for cash during a year, since the company does not have use of the cash for the full year. In lieu of a strictly weighted total, many analysts use the average of beginning and ending number of shares, thus implicitly assuming that the additional shares were issued gradually during the year or, alternatively, that they were issued on June 30.

*Stock Splits and Stock Dividends.* In the above example, the 25% increase in outstanding shares reflected new capital invested in the business. Many times, however, the number of shares rises because of stock splits and stock dividends. The holders of a corporation's stock are often given additional stock certificates to represent their ownership interest. Technically, there is a difference between a stock split and a stock dividend. In the case of a split, the capital account is maintained at a constant amount and the par or stated value per share is reduced. In the case of a stock dividend, the par value per share is maintained and a transfer is made from the earned surplus account to the capital account. For purposes of the present discussion, these accounting differences are unimportant. Both a 100% stock dividend and a two-for-one split cause the owner of 100 shares to end up with 200. Both a 20% stock dividend and a six-for-five split cause the owner of 100 shares to end up with 120.

Companies have various reasons for splitting their stock or paying stock dividends. The principal reason for large percentage increases in number of shares (say 20% or more) is to broaden the market for the stock. Most small investors have an aversion to very high-priced stocks, notwithstanding their apparent willingness to buy a few shares of IBM or Polaroid or Du Pont at prices above $100 a share. Thus, a two-for-one split of, say, an $80 stock cuts its price to $40, other things being equal, and makes it more attractive to a wider group of investors.

Managements like to foster broader markets for many reasons. If the company produces consumer goods, for example, more stockholders may mean more customers. Public utilities benefit from large stockholder bodies, since stock ownership probably reduces public resistance to rate increases. Broad stock ownership may also result in less public support of antibusiness legislation, particularly antitrust actions by the government. Improved marketability also may tend to raise the price of a stock.[28] And, not least, management has less fear of proxy fights if ownership is widely diffused.

The reasoning behind *small* stock dividends is not at all as clear. The public seems to like stock dividends, according to various surveys which have been taken. Some of this attitude is probably due to the fact that stock prices seem to respond favorably when stock dividends are declared. On the other hand, there is considerable statistical evidence to suggest that the favorable price response is not due to the stock dividend per se, but rather to the fact that the *cash* dividend per share is usually maintained on the greater number of shares, so that the stock dividend really means an effective increase in the cash dividend.[29]

The effective increase in the cash dividend also raises questions about another alleged reason for small stock dividends, namely the desire to conserve cash. The argument is that if a company wants to retain cash in the business, payment of periodic small stock dividends enables it to do so, but at the same time gives the recipient of the stock dividend the opportunity to realize cash by selling his extra shares. Certainly, proponents argue, periodic stock dividends are more efficient than paying large cash dividends, on the one hand, but then taking the cash back by selling new stock to existing stockholders in a "rights offering."[30] The rebuttal to the cash-retention argument is that (*a*) the total cash dividend may really be increased, as noted above; (*b*) the company could retain earnings without paying a stock dividend; (*c*) stock dividends involve the company in a large clerical expense; (*d*) stockholders have to pay odd-lot commissions to sell their shares; (*e*) if stockholders want cash they can always sell off a part of their original holdings; and (*f*) uninformed stockholders are deluded into thinking that they're getting something for nothing.

---

[28] It is noteworthy, however, that most of the price improvement that occurs takes place several months *before* the actual announcement of the split, as the market begins to anticipate the possibility of a split. See R. C. Rieke, "Selling on the News," *Barron's*, Nov. 30, 1964. Furthermore, a recent study by the brokerage firm of Hardy & Co. suggests that price performance in split stocks is not very closely related to the number of additional shareholders resulting from the split. The study is cited in the November–December, 1965, *Financial Analysts Journal*, pp. 156–57.

[29] Price may rise in response to a dividend increase either because the original dividend payout rate was less than optimum or because the market takes the increase as a sign that earning power has significantly improved.

[30] In addition to the company's extra work in paying cash and then selling new stock, the stockholder has to pay an income tax on the cash dividend. If he sells a stock dividend, he merely pays a capital gains tax on the difference between the selling price and his adjusted cost price.

Whatever the reason, let's assume that Company X, in our example, split its stock two for one in 1966, at a time when earnings had risen to $5 million. That is, total dollar earnings had doubled without any additional capital being raised. But since there were 2½ million shares outstanding, instead of 1¼ million, earnings per share remained at $2. Thus, no progress is indicated in the per-share data when, in fact, there was great progress. The dividend potential of each individual investor's holdings had doubled. He had twice as many shares, and earnings on each share remained constant.

In order to make the series of per-share earnings meaningful, we must go back and adjust all the *presplit* data. What we want to do is put the presplit data at the level they would have been had the stock always been split. Thus, in 1963, when earnings were $2 million on 1 million shares, per-share earnings on a split basis were $2 million divided by *two* million shares, or $1 per share instead of $2. And in 1964, $2½ million of earnings should be divided by 2½ million shares instead of 1¼ million, for per-share earnings of $1 instead of $2. Accordingly, per-share earnings for 1963, 1964, and 1966, on an adjusted basis, would be $1, $1, and $2, respectively. No progress would be shown from 1963 to 1964, as before, but a doubling would be shown from 1964 to 1966.

A simpler method of adjusting presplit per-share data is to apply the following formula: Divide presplit per-share data by 100% plus the percentage stock dividend or split. Thus, with a two-for-one stock split, divide presplit data by 100% + 100%. Dividing by 200% is the same as dividing by $2/1$, which is the same as multiplying by ½. So $2 presplit, times ½, equals $1 adjusted.

Likewise, with a 20% stock dividend we would divide presplit data by 100% + 20%. Dividing by 120% is the same as dividing by $6/5$, which is the same as multiplying by $5/6$. Conversion to fractions, however, is inconvenient for small stock dividends. Therefore, with a 2% stock dividend we would divide presplit data by 100% + 2%, or 1.02.

Although we have been discussing *earnings* per share, the same comments apply to dividends per share, price per share, and any other per-share calculation which the analyst may desire to make, such as sales per share in the case of mergers when no pro forma data on total dollar sales are available.

*Potential Dilution on Conversions.* During recent years the use of convertible debentures and convertible preferred stocks has been increasing. When a company under analysis has a large convertible issue outstanding, and there is a considerable possibility that the issue will actually be converted into common stock in the near future,[31] the analyst should calculate an alternative series of per-share earnings. This alternative series

---

[31] See Chapter 12 for a discussion of when this might happen.

would show earnings per share on the assumption that the company had always had common stock rather than convertibles outstanding. The procedure is to add back to total dollar net income the amount of the annual preferred dividend, in the case of convertible preferreds, or one half the amount of the annual interest, in the case of convertible debentures.[32] Then divide the resulting earnings by the number of shares actually outstanding *plus* the additional number which would be issued on full conversion.[33]

*Published Per-Share Data.* Many novices take the subject of per-share calculation very lightly, on the theory that the data published by the investor services—Moody's, Standard & Poor's, etc.—are adequate. Unfortunately, this assumption often is far from correct. For one thing, the earnings shown by the services usually are simply those reported by the company. Little or no attempt is made to derive "true" net income in the light of the various accounting complexities which have been discussed in this chapter. For example, a Standard & Poor's Listed Stock Report for Consolidated Edison (dated February 7, 1966) indicates that earnings per share "includes tax savings from rapid depreciation and other items," and lets it go at that without trying to quantify the significance of these items. Furthermore, the investor services rarely reproduce the detailed footnotes which appear in the original company statements and which may provide the analyst with clues to necessary adjustments.

Another common shortcoming of published per-share data is that the services frequently adjust for stock dividends only where the dividend is fairly large, say 10% or greater. This is not too bad if a company has only an occasional 2% or 5% stock dividend. But it can result in severely distorted data where a company pays a whole series of small stock dividends. For example, an S & P Listed Stock Report for Bush Terminal Company (dated February 15, 1966) points out that there were stock dividends of 3% in 1953–54, 4% in 1955–57, 6% in 1958–60, 10% in 1961, 8% in 1962–64, 10% in 1965 and 2% in 1966. But the prices, earnings, and dividends per share shown in the report are not adjusted for these stock dividends.

Care also must be taken in using published stock price data. For example, the Moody's Manuals contain a section showing a 10-year record of the annual high and low prices of hundreds of issues. But these price ranges are not adjusted for stock dividends. Thus, a high-low range of 60–30 may be shown. But if the high of 60 occurred before a 20% stock

---

[32] This assumes a 50% tax rate. At other rates add back: interest × (100% − tax rate). The reason for the difference in treatment between preferred dividends and interest is that interest costs had been reduced by the fact that they were tax deductible, whereas preferred dividend costs hadn't.

[33] Where the conversion terms change periodically, the terms at the time of the analysis are the pertinent ones.

dividend, while the low occurred afterward, the true price range is really 50–30 on an adjusted basis, not 60–30 ($5/6 \times 60 = 50$).

Despite their many inadequacies, however, the per-share data published by the investor services can be used to gain an initial impression of an investment situation. Obviously, one cannot do a full-scale analysis of each and every situation that comes to one's attention. The published data provide a means of quickly scanning the basic facts in order to determine whether a more thorough investigation is warranted.

## SUGGESTED READINGS

Corliss D. Anderson. *Corporate Reporting for the Professional Investor.* Financial Analysts Federation, 1962.

Douglas H. Bellemore. *Investments.* 2nd ed. New York: Simmons-Boardman Publishing Corp., 1960, chaps. xxii–xxv.

Paul Grady. *Inventory of Generally Accepted Accounting Principles for Business Enterprises.* New York: American Institute of Certified Public Accountants, 1965.

Benjamin Graham, David L. Dodd, and Sidney Cottle. *Security Analysis.* 4th ed. New York: McGraw-Hill Book Co., 1962, chaps. ix–xv, xxxvi.

The Institute of Chartered Financial Analysts. *C.F.A. Readings in Financial Analysis,* Part II. Homewood, Ill.: Richard D. Irwin, Inc., 1966.

Leonard E. Morrissey. *Contemporary Accounting Problems: Text and Cases.* New York: Prentice-Hall, Inc., 1963.

M. Richard Sussman. *The Stock Dividend.* Ann Arbor: University of Michigan Bureau of Business Research, 1962.

"Uniformity in Financial Accounting" (a symposium). *Law and Contemporary Problems.* Durham, N.C.: Duke University, Autumn, 1965.

William D. Williams. "A Look Behind Reported Earnings," *Financial Analysts Journal,* January–February, 1966.

# 5

# VALUATION OF COMMON STOCKS: A FRAMEWORK

The greatest of all gifts is the power to estimate things at their true worth.

—LA ROCHEFOUCAULD

THE object of common stock evaluation is to obtain standards against which prevailing prices of stocks may be judged. It is assumed that investors as a whole are essentially rational over the long run (although their actions occasionally seem to border on the insane), and that rational individuals attempt to measure the economic, or "going-concern" values of the corporations whose stock they buy and sell. Since there are millions of investors, there will exist vastly different ideas about the value of any given stock at any given time, and purchases and sales of the stock will be made in accordance with this multitude of ideas. Therefore, over an extended period of time, prices will fluctuate in a wide range, *but they will tend to fluctuate around some concensus of value.*

## The Rationale

The normal tendency of the marketplace, it is assumed, is to drive prices to extremes. When optimism is dominant, conceptions of value are liberalized, and prices rise steadily. Ultimately, it is recognized that the optimism was excessive, and prices react downward. As prices fall, caution turns to fear, and the price decline snowballs until it is finally recognized that the pessimism was overdone. At this point a price reversal occurs once again. The successful evaluator of common stocks, therefore, will try to avoid becoming overly optimistic or overly pessimistic. He will attempt to determine the approximate level around which the price tides will swell and ebb.

The evaluation process can be described graphically, as follows:

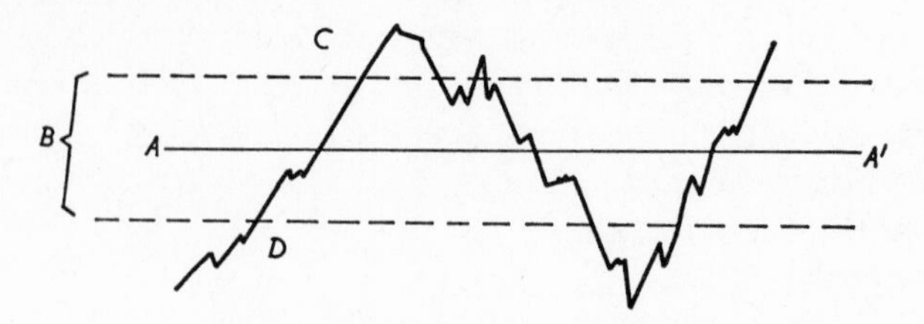


Where: $AA'$ is an objectively determined value line; $B$ is a range allowed for errors which may have been made in the determination of $AA'$; $C$ represents an area where prices would be considered too dear; and $D$ represents an area where prices would be considered bargains. With regard to $AA'$, we do not mean to imply that an evaluation must necessarily cover an extended span of time. The analyst may be content to make an estimate of any *point* on the line, near or distant.

### The Sources of Common Stock Value

If the reader ponders the problem for a while, he will realize that a common stock has value for only three possible reasons. First, the ownership of common stock confers a claim to a corporation's net income. This claim bears fruit when the corporation's board of directors declares dividends. Second, if the corporation enjoys growing success, earnings and dividends will rise, and the price of its stock may rise also. The third, and least significant, source of common stock value is that if a corporation is liquidated, the common stock owner has a pro rata claim to any asset value that may remain after all creditors and preferred stockholders have been paid. This claim, therefore, may give the common stock some value. But it is not a very important source of value as a rule, because an efficiently operating corporation is not usually liquidated. And if it is liquidated because it is not operating efficiently, the asset value is not likely to be high enough to leave much of a residual for the stockholders.[1]

The juxtaposition above of earnings and dividends in the context of common stock value gives rise to an interesting question on both a

---

[1] Nevertheless, asset values can, in some cases, be of significance. A corporation may have net *current assets* per share (cash, receivables, and inventories minus all liabilities and preferred divided by number of common shares) in excess of the market price of its stock. It will thus be "worth more dead than alive," for which reason another corporation or syndicate of investors may be willing to pay a sizable premium over the current market price of the shares in order to acquire control.

In addition to this "special situation" (see Chapter 12) reason why asset values may influence stock values, some corporations have as their principal earning asset money or other liquid resources. For such corporations—banks, insurance companies, investment companies, etc.—stock prices are frequently closely geared to asset values. In actuality, however, to say that the prices are geared to asset values is a bit of a semantic trick. What we are really saying is that the assets provide the basis for *earnings*, and in fact it is earning power which causes assets to have a value that can be transmitted to stock prices.

practical and a philosophical plane. Often the argument will be heard that dividends are distinctly subordinate to earnings as a determinant of stock values. The evidence offered in support of this argument is the activity of thousands, perhaps millions, of investors whose dominant objective in buying common stock is to sell it to someone else at a higher price rather than to collect dividends.

It is, of course, true that many individual stockholders do not intend to hold their stocks for dividends, hoping instead to sell the stocks to others at capital gains. But to conclude from this observation that "dividends don't count" would be quite mistaken. In the first place, it can be demonstrated by statistical analysis that stock price changes are often more closely related to dividend changes than to changes in reported earnings.[2] One possible explanation for this fact is that since reported earnings do not necessarily represent "true" earnings (see Chapter 4), investors look to dividends for an indication of what management really thinks earnings are.

On a more theoretical plane, the significance of dividends has sometimes been illustrated by hypothesizing the existence of a corporation which has written into its bylaws a perpetual prohibition of dividend payments or of return of capital to stockholders via sale of assets or by any other means. With these bylaws, no rational investor should be willing to purchase the corporation's stock, no matter how high its earnings or how low the asking price. (We exclude from consideration purchasing the stock in order to become an operating officer and thus receive a salary, or purchasing the stock in the hope of changing the bylaws.) Of course, people sometimes become irrational. For example, in the tulip mania in Europe a few centuries ago, people bought and sold tulip bulbs at fantastic prices without the vaguest intention of actually planting the bulbs to get flowers.[3] But such bubbles must inevitably burst. Our hypothetical corporation's stock might trade for a while, but people must eventually recognize that they are buying and selling a mere piece of paper, without any *value* in the absence of an ability to pay dividends or liquidate.[4]

Thus, while much of a stock's value to an investor undoubtedly lies

---

[2] The results of an extensive (unpublished) cross-sectional multiple regression analysis with which the authors are familiar indicates that in 11 of the 15 years, 1949–63, dividend change was significantly related to price change, whereas earnings change was significant in only 7 of the 15 years.

[3] For a fine account of this and other speculative manias see Charles Mackay, *Extraordinary Popular Delusions and The Madness of Crowds*. Originally published in 1841; reprinted by Investors Library, Inc., Palisades Park, N.J.

[4] Prior to the securities legislation of the 1930's, there was a good deal of outright *manipulation* of stock prices. Stocks often were, indeed, mere pieces of paper being bought and sold without regard to "intrinsic values." While it cannot be denied that manipulative practices still exist, particularly in the new issues market, such practices seem to be relatively rare.

in the prospect of price appreciation, prices cannot be divorced from dividend prospects any more than they can be divorced from prospective earning power. It is no accident that during the past half century the growth rates of prices, earnings, and dividends on a broad index of the stock market such as Standard & Poor's 425 Industrials have all been within about ½ of 1% of each other.[5]

### The Concept of Present Value of Future Dividends

If the reader will accept the significance of dividends as a determinant of stock values, he can understand the reasoning behind a widely accepted tenet of investment theory. The tenet is that a common stock is "worth" the *present value* of all future dividends.

The concept of present value is really quite simple and can be prosaically illustrated. Assume that Mr. A wants to borrow money from Mr. B, repayable at a future date. Mr. B is willing to make the loan, but feels that, considering the risks involved, he is entitled to a 10% annual rate of return. This being the case, how much money will B advance to A on A's I O U for $10 payable one year hence? The answer is $9.09, because the $10 paid next year provides 91 cents interest, which is 10% of a $9.09 loan. Thus, $9.09 is the "present value" of $10 payable one year hence at a "discount rate" of 10%.

Likewise, if A offers a $10 I O U payable *two* years hence, how much will B be willing to lend? Answer: $8.26. Ten percent of $8.26 is 83 cents (first year's interest); $8.26 plus $0.83 = $9.09. Ten percent of $9.09 is 91 cents (second year's interest); $9.09 plus $0.91 = $10. The present value of $10 payable two years hence is $8.26 at a discount rate of 10%.

Table 5–1 shows the present values of $1 payable in 1 to 50 years, at discount rates of 5% to 10%. More detailed tables are available in published form.[6] Note that $1 payable 50 years hence is worth only 9¢ at a 5% discount rate and only 1¢ at a 10% discount rate. Obviously, the higher the discount rate the lower the present value.

Returning to the matter of future dividends on common stock, suppose we estimate that dividends on Standard & Poor's Industrial Stock Price Index will grow at a rate of 5% per annum for as far into the future an anyone can imagine. Suppose we also estimate that "the market"—not any individual investor but all investors as a group—will always demand an 8% rate of return in order to undertake the risks of common stock

[5] An interesting theoretical discussion of the dividends versus capital gains controversy is contained in W. S. Bauman, "The Investment Value of Common Stock Earnings and Dividends," *Financial Analysts Journal*, November–December, 1965. A stimulating analysis of the subject of investor rationality is presented by W. J. Baumol in *The Stock Market and Economic Efficiency* (New York: Fordham University Press, 1965), chap. iii.

[6] For example, *Financial Compound Interest and Annuity Tables* (3rd ed.; Boston: Financial Publishing Co., 1961).

## TABLE 5–1
## Present Value of $1

| Payable in: | Discount Rate 5% | 6% | 7% | 8% | 9% | 10% |
|---|---|---|---|---|---|---|
| 1 year | .952 | .943 | .935 | .926 | .917 | .909 |
| 2 | .907 | .890 | .873 | .857 | .842 | .826 |
| 3 | .864 | .840 | .816 | .794 | .772 | .751 |
| 4 | .823 | .792 | .763 | .735 | .708 | .683 |
| 5 | .784 | .747 | .713 | .681 | .650 | .621 |
| 6 | .746 | .705 | .666 | .630 | .596 | .564 |
| 7 | .711 | .665 | .623 | .583 | .547 | .513 |
| 8 | .677 | .627 | .582 | .540 | .502 | .467 |
| 9 | .645 | .592 | .544 | .500 | .460 | .424 |
| 10 | .614 | .558 | .508 | .463 | .422 | .386 |
| 11 | .585 | .527 | .475 | .429 | .388 | .350 |
| 12 | .557 | .497 | .444 | .397 | .356 | .319 |
| 13 | .530 | .469 | .415 | .368 | .326 | .290 |
| 14 | .505 | .442 | .388 | .340 | .299 | .263 |
| 15 | .481 | .417 | .362 | .315 | .275 | .239 |
| 16 | .458 | .394 | .339 | .292 | .252 | .218 |
| 17 | .436 | .371 | .317 | .270 | .231 | .198 |
| 18 | .416 | .350 | .296 | .250 | .212 | .180 |
| 19 | .396 | .331 | .277 | .232 | .194 | .164 |
| 20 | .377 | .312 | .258 | .215 | .178 | .149 |
| 21 | .359 | .294 | .242 | .199 | .164 | .135 |
| 22 | .342 | .278 | .226 | .184 | .150 | .123 |
| 23 | .326 | .262 | .211 | .170 | .138 | .112 |
| 24 | .310 | .247 | .197 | .158 | .126 | .102 |
| 25 | .295 | .233 | .184 | .146 | .116 | .092 |
| 26 | .281 | .220 | .172 | .135 | .106 | .084 |
| 27 | .268 | .207 | .161 | .125 | .098 | .076 |
| 28 | .255 | .196 | .150 | .116 | .090 | .069 |
| 29 | .243 | .185 | .141 | .107 | .082 | .063 |
| 30 | .231 | .174 | .131 | .099 | .075 | .057 |
| 31 | .220 | .164 | .123 | .092 | .069 | .052 |
| 32 | .210 | .155 | .115 | .085 | .063 | .047 |
| 33 | .200 | .146 | .107 | .079 | .058 | .043 |
| 34 | .190 | .138 | .100 | .073 | .053 | .039 |
| 35 | .181 | .130 | .094 | .068 | .049 | .036 |
| 36 | .173 | .123 | .088 | .063 | .045 | .032 |
| 37 | .164 | .116 | .082 | .058 | .041 | .029 |
| 38 | .157 | .109 | .076 | .054 | .038 | .027 |
| 39 | .149 | .103 | .071 | .050 | .035 | .024 |
| 40 | .142 | .097 | .067 | .046 | .032 | .022 |
| 41 | .133 | .092 | .062 | .043 | .029 | .020 |
| 42 | .129 | .087 | .058 | .039 | .027 | .018 |
| 43 | .123 | .082 | .055 | .037 | .025 | .017 |
| 44 | .117 | .077 | .051 | .034 | .023 | .015 |
| 45 | .111 | .073 | .048 | .031 | .021 | .014 |
| 46 | .106 | .069 | .044 | .029 | .019 | .012 |
| 47 | .101 | .065 | .042 | .027 | .017 | .011 |
| 48 | .096 | .061 | .039 | .025 | .016 | .010 |
| 49 | .092 | .058 | .036 | .023 | .015 | .009 |
| 50 | .087 | .054 | .034 | .021 | .013 | .009 |

investment. What is the value of the S & P Index today, per dollar of current dividends, unaer these assumptions?

Actually, there is a simple formula for calculating the present value of perpetual growth, at any given discount rate. The formula is:

$$\text{Present value} = \frac{1}{[(1 + \text{discount rate})/(1 + \text{growth rate})] - 1}$$

Under our assumptions, this works out as:

$$\frac{1}{[(1.08)/(1.05)] - 1} = \frac{1}{1.02857 - 1} = \frac{1}{.02857} = 35$$

In other words, given a perpetual 5% growth rate and a perpetual 8% discount rate, the S & P Index is today worth 35 dollars for every $1 of current dividends. But does this mean that today's investors have to actually estimate dividend growth and discount rates *to perpetuity* in order to utilize the theoretical concept of present value of future dividends? Not really, as we shall now demonstrate.

Starting with a dividend base of $1, the following tabulation (Table 5–2) shows the annual stream of dividends that will be produced at a 5% growth rate over the next 50 years.

**TABLE 5–2**

**Growth of $1 at 5% Compound Interest**

(Rounded to Nearest 1 Cent)

| *1st Decade* | *2nd Decade* | *3rd Decade* | *4th Decade* | *5th Decade* |
|---|---|---|---|---|
| 1.00 | 1.63 | 2.65 | 4.32 | 7.04 |
| 1.05 | 1.71 | 2.79 | 4.54 | 7.39 |
| 1.10 | 1.80 | 2.93 | 4.76 | 7.76 |
| 1.16 | 1.89 | 3.07 | 5.00 | 8.15 |
| 1.22 | 1.98 | 3.23 | 5.25 | 8.56 |
| 1.28 | 2.08 | 3.39 | 5.52 | 8.99 |
| 1.34 | 2.18 | 3.56 | 5.79 | 9.43 |
| 1.41 | 2.29 | 3.73 | 6.08 | 9.91 |
| 1.48 | 2.41 | 3.92 | 6.39 | 10.40 |
| 1.55 | 2.53 | 4.12 | 6.70 | 10.92 |

The next tabulation shows the present value of each of these dividends at an 8% discount rate. (Note that the present value of any given year's dividend is equal to the product of that dividend multiplied by the present value of $1 for the given number of years, as shown in Table 5–1 under the 8% discount rate column.) At the bottom of the tabulation are shown the 10-year sums of present values, and the percentage of the total $35 "value" represented by these sums.

It will be seen from Table 5–3 that the proportion of the total value to perpetuity represented by distant years' dividends diminishes rapidly. Almost 60% of the total "value" is accounted for in the first 30 years, 80% in the first 50. And this would be true of most growth and discount assumptions that might be used by a security analyst.[7] Accordingly, the

**TABLE 5–3**

**Present Value, at 8% Discount Rate, of Dividend Stream Shown in Table 5–2**

| | *1st Decade* | *2nd Decade* | *3rd Decade* | *4th Decade* | *5th Decade* |
|---|---|---|---|---|---|
| | 1.00 | 0.75 | 0.57 | 0.43 | 0.32 |
| | 0.97 | 0.73 | 0.56 | 0.42 | 0.32 |
| | 0.94 | 0.71 | 0.54 | 0.40 | 0.30 |
| | 0.92 | 0.70 | 0.52 | 0.40 | 0.30 |
| | 0.90 | 0.67 | 0.51 | 0.38 | 0.29 |
| | 0.87 | 0.66 | 0.49 | 0.38 | 0.28 |
| | 0.84 | 0.64 | 0.48 | 0.36 | 0.27 |
| | 0.82 | 0.62 | 0.47 | 0.35 | 0.27 |
| | 0.80 | 0.60 | 0.45 | 0.35 | 0.26 |
| | 0.78 | 0.59 | 0.44 | 0.34 | 0.25 |
| Sum of each decade's present values: | 8.84 | 6.67 | 5.03 | 3.81 | 2.86 |
| Percent each decade's sum represents of $35 total value to perpetuity: | 25.3% | 19.1% | 14.4% | 10.9% | 8.2% |

necessity for reasonable accuracy in one's estimates diminishes rapidly beyond a horizon of several decades.

Of course, 30–50 years is by no means a short period for estimating either growth rates or discount rates. Indeed, most security analysts consider themselves fortunate if their growth rate estimates for the companies they follow hold good for *five* years.[8] On the other hand, while very long-term estimates are highly uncertain for individual stocks, the potential errors are not nearly as great when considering all stocks in aggregate, as we shall demonstrate next.

## ESTIMATING THE VALUE OF "THE MARKET"

### Dividend Growth Prospects for Stocks in Aggregate

As economists, the authors have a proclivity to relate most economic variables to gross national product, which they feel can be forecast more

[7] The only situations in which the first 30–50 years would represent substantially lower proportions of total value would be where the discount rate is quite close to the growth rate. Speaking realistically, however, such situations would be rare, for as the discount rate approaches the growth rate, "value" approaches infinity.

[8] The relevance of forecasting difficulties to the application of present-value theory has been the subject of a lively exchange between R. A. Bing and N. Molodovsky in the pages of the *Financial Analysts Journal*. See their articles in the May–June, 1964, and July–August, 1964, issues of that journal.

accurately than most other variables. The question of aggregate dividend growth, therefore, is broken into three parts. First, what rate of GNP growth can be expected in the years ahead; second, will earnings per share of common stock keep pace with GNP; and third, will dividend growth keep pace with earnings growth?

*GNP Growth.* The growth of gross national product can be conveniently divided into four variables for analytical purposes: the growth of the employed labor force, the trend of average hours worked per week, the trend of output per hour worked ("productivity"), and the rate of change in the price level. By combining forecasts of the first three of these variables, a forecast of growth of so-called *real* GNP is derived—that is, growth of physical output of goods and services excluding the effects of price changes.

The three determinants of real GNP have had a stable enough history during the past century to enable us to make some long-term estimates with a fair degree of confidence. Without going into detail, our estimates are: approximately 1½% per annum growth in the empolyed labor force; ½ of 1% per annum decline in hours worked per week; and 2½%–3% per annum growth of output per manhour. These elements combine to produce a 3½%–4% range of real GNP growth possibilities. To put this range in historical perspective, consider these past growth rates of real GNP: 1909–65: 3%; 1923–29 (the last previous period of general peacetime prosperity): 3½%; 1947–65: 3½%.[9]

To the 3½%–4% physical growth rate, we expect price increases to add about 1½%–2% per annum.[10] There is little room for doubt that our economy has a moderate inflationary bias. During the past half century, price growth has been at a rate of 2% per annum. True, part of this "inflation" was probably more apparent than real, being a result of inadequate statistical adjustment for *quality* improvements in the products and services being priced (for example, color TV versus black and white, today's auto versus the Model-T Ford). Nevertheless, the upward pres-

---

[9] Three and one half percent is the 1947–65 growth rate derived by fitting a least squares line to logarithms of the annual data. The rate is 3.8% if only the initial and terminal years are included in the calculation. For an excellent discussion of growth prospects in the American economy, see E. F. Denison, *The Sources of Economic Growth in the United States and the Alternatives before Us* (Supplementary Paper No. 13 [New York: Committee for Economic Development, 1962]). A more optimistic projection than Denison's will be found in A. T. Sommers, "The Economy in the Next Decade," *Conference Board Record*, December, 1965. A summary of reasons why major depressions are unlikely to occur is contained in Borden Helmer, "Economic Perspectives for Planning," *Financial Analysts Journal*, July–August, 1964. A comprehensive volume of background data is U.S. Bureau of the Census, *Long-Term Economic Growth*, 1966.

[10] All price references in this paragraph are in terms of the implicit price index of the GNP accounts.

sures on prices, as traditionally measured, have been pronounced.[11] Even during the years 1957–61, when the economy was relatively sluggish, prices rose at a rate of about 1¾% per annum.

Using the official price indexes published by the government, and recognizing that part of what looks like a price increase is a "real" increase, a 1½%–2% estimated rate of price growth seems realistic. Combining the estimates of real GNP and price growth, we foresee overall GNP growth in current dollars at a long-term rate of 5%–6% per annum.

FIGURE 5–1

**Ratio of After-Tax Earnings (S & P Industrials) to Current Dollar GNP**

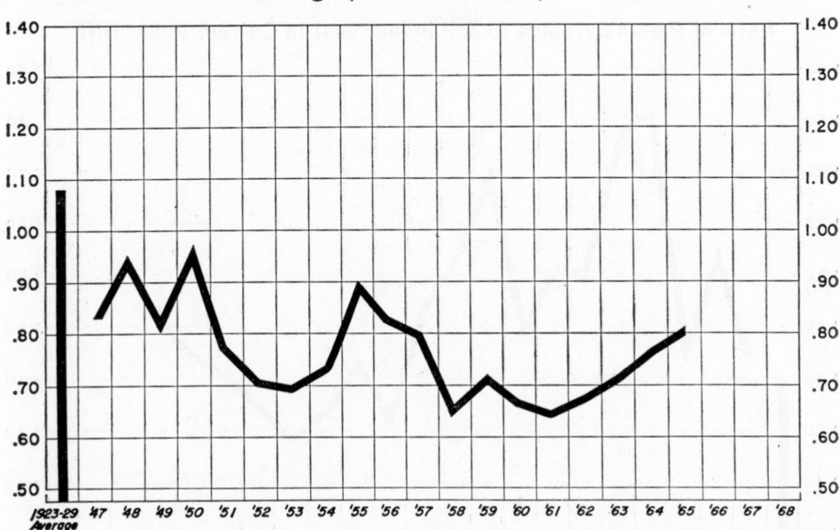


*Earnings per Share Relative to GNP.* Turning to the question whether earnings per share will keep pace with GNP, a look at the past is again in order. Figure 5–1 shows the ratio of earnings on the Standard & Poor's Industrials to GNP for the post–World War II period. For comparison purposes, the average ratio for 1923–29 is also shown.[12] The chart

[11] A comprehensive survey of various theories of inflation is contained in Joseph W. Conard, "The Causes and Consequences of Inflation," in *Inflation, Growth and Employment* (Staff Papers prepared for the Commission on Money and Credit [New York: Prentice Hall, Inc., 1964]). Also see G. L. Perry, *Unemployment, Money Wage Rates and Inflation* (Cambridge, Mass.: M.I.T. Press, 1966).

[12] This chart, and several others which follow, have also been used in a paper by one of our colleagues. See W. C. Freund, "Price Relationship of Equities to Profit and Fiscal Outlook," *Commercial and Financial Chronicle,* March 25, 1965. Postwar data are as published by Standard & Poor's; prewar data are derived from Alfred Cowles, 3rd., *Common Stock Indexes* (2nd ed.; Principia Press, 1939) and also reflect certain estimates by the present authors and by Mr. Kerwin Stallings, assistant vice president, Morgan Guaranty Trust Company of New York.

indicates that over the past several decades earnings per share have *not* kept pace with GNP. Before coming to overly pessimistic conclusions, however, two other factors must be considered:

1. Since the 1920's, corporate income tax rates have more than tripled. But future corporate income taxes are not likely to undergo another major increase. Therefore, for our purpose, which is to examine the past as a guide to the future, the trend of *pretax* profits relative to GNP may be more relevant than the after-tax ratio. This relationship is presented in Figure 5–2, where a quite different picture emerges. Instead

**FIGURE 5–2**

**Ratio of Pretax Earnings (S & P Industrials) to Current Dollar GNP**

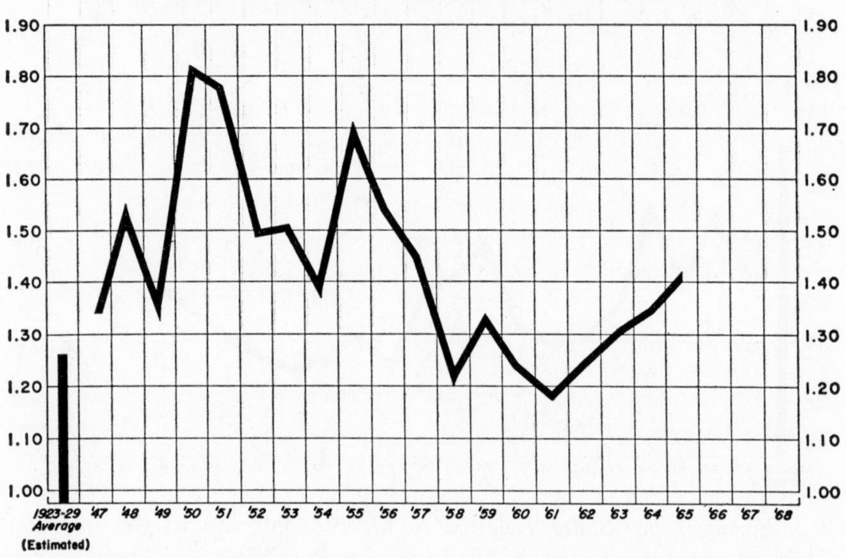


of a downtrend running from the 1920's to date, the ratios for recent years compare favorably with those of the 1920's. The peak ratios of 1950 and 1955 were the abnormal ones!

Admittedly, it can be argued that the corporate income tax is not really a reduction of corporate profits but is passed on to consumers—that is, in the form of higher prices. According to this view, after-tax profits are not fundamentally altered by changing corporate tax rates and are, therefore, more relevant than pretax profits in interpreting trends. The literature on the subject is voluminous[13] but inconclusive. Perhaps the

---

[13] For a summary see M. Krzyzaniak and R. A. Musgrave, *The Shifting of The Corporation Income Tax* (Baltimore: John Hopkins Press, 1963); also see C. A. Hall, Jr., "Direct Shifting of the Corporation Income Tax in Manufacturing," *American Economic Review*, May, 1964, and R. Goode, *Rates of Return, Income Shares, and Corporate Tax Incidence*" (Washington, D.C.: Brookings Institution, 1966).

most reasonable argument is that part of the tax is passed on and part is not. If this is true, one can conclude that there is probably some long-run tendency for per-share profits to decline relative to GNP, but that the tendency is much less pronounced than indicated in Figure 5–1.

A nagging question remains, however. Whatever the long-range trends, the ratio of profits to GNP—before or after tax—did trend downward from 1950 to 1961 and did not regain its earlier level even after the downtrend was halted in 1961. This brings us to the second factor which must enter our interpretation of the historical record.

2. The single most important factor in the downtrend of profits relative to GNP since the end of World War II has been rising depreciation charges. Numerous studies, including our own, all suggest quite clearly that depreciation charges from 1947 through 1954 or 1955 were too low for an inflationary economy. They were based on the original cost of assets acquired many years earlier at much lower prices. These low depreciation charges were made against sales revenues which reflected the inflated postwar price level. As a result, reported profits until the mid-1950's were exaggerated from an economic point of view. True, accepted accounting procedure and, possibly more important, the rules of the Internal Revenue Service, did not permit any other kind of profit reporting. But our job as analysts is to try to separate the apparent from the real, and much of the so-called "profit squeeze" of the 1950's was more apparent than real.

One way to correct the distortion of profits caused by inadequate depreciation is to restate the reported depreciation of earlier years. Lacking adequate data to do this,[14] however, we can relate "cash flow per share" to GNP. Figure 5–3 presents the cash flow/GNP relationship, defining cash flow in the traditional manner—after-tax profits plus depreciation. Here it will be seen that, except for cyclical fluctuations, there has been no apparent "profit squeeze" since the end of World War II. If, as suggested in Chapter 4, cash flow were defined as after-tax profits plus *one half* of depreciation, or if the concept of pretax cash flow were employed (i.e., after-tax profits plus depreciation plus federal income taxes), the ratio to GNP would show a slight downtrend in the postwar period.

In view of the evidence presented regarding after-tax profits, pretax profits, and cash flow per share, all in relation to GNP, we conclude that it is reasonable to expect corporate earning power to grow at approximately the same rate as aggregate economic activity, or perhaps to grow slightly less rapidly. Given a GNP growth estimate of 5%–6%, we would put the growth of earning power at 4½%–5½%.

---

[14] For an attempt to restate corporate depreciation in the national income accounts, see M. Brown, "Depreciation and Corporate Profits," *Survey of Current Business*, October, 1963. Brown's findings tend to confirm the conclusions reached in this and the following paragraph.

**FIGURE 5–3**

**Ratio of Cash Flow* (S & P Industrials) to Current Dollar GNP**

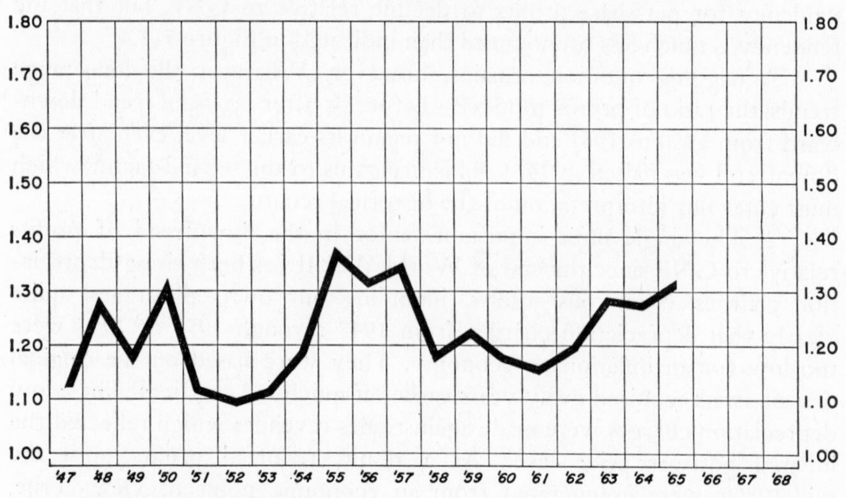


* Reported profit plus depreciation.

*Dividends Relative to Earnings.* Except during periods of depression, when dividend payout ratios have risen sharply because managements try to maintain payments to stockholders even in the face of declining earnings, dividends on the S & P Industrials have averaged about 55% of reported earnings for several decades. This central tendency has been so pronounced and persistent that we think it quite safe to assume its continuation. Therefore, if earnings grow at a rate of between 4½% and 5½% per annum, dividends should grow correspondingly.

The 4½%–5½% growth rate estimate is supported by an alternative approach to the problem. As will be discussed in detail in Chapter 8, the long-term earnings growth of industrial corporations reflects primarily the profits earned on the plowback of earnings into enterprises. Available statistics suggest that the "typical" rate of return on stockholders' investment in such corporations in recent years has been approximately 11%–12% after taxes.[15] As noted in the previous paragraph, dividend payout ratios on the S & P Industrials have averaged about 55%, which means that 45 cents of every dollar earned usually is plowed back by the corporations represented in the index. If the rate earned on these plowed-back funds continues to average about 11%–12%—a reasonable probability—earnings growth will average 11.5% of 45 cents or somewhat more than 5 cents per dollar of earnings. In other words, looked at from

[15] See annual earnings compilations prepared by First National City Bank of New York, or earnings and book value data for the S & P Industrials published by Standard & Poor's. Frequency distributions for large cross sections of individual corporations confirm these data.

this point of view, expectable average earnings growth is about 5% per annum.

Thus, we conclude that long-term dividend growth for stocks in aggregate will be between 4½% and 5½% per annum. Obviously, this will not be the growth rate in every single year. In some years, dividends will doubtless increase 10% or more. In other years, dividends will actually be reduced. But the trend is likely to be stable enough to be introduced realistically into a present-value calculation.

### Choosing an Appropriate Discount Rate

If we are to discount future dividends on the S & P Industrials, we must have some idea of the rate of return that investors demand in order to take the risks of common stock investment. Bear in mind that we are speaking of investors in aggregate, not any single investor, and that we are considering all stocks in aggregate, not any specific stock.

We cannot go out and ask millions of investors what their yield demands are. Even if it were physically possible to do so (for example, using a sampling technique), it is doubtful that we would get very reliable answers. But there are at least three independent items of indirect evidence which seem pertinent:

1. As noted above, the annual return on stockholders' equity in American industry has typically been about 11%–12%.[16] But *stockholders* should not expect this whole rate to be passed on to them. The marketability and diversification potential inherent in share ownership justifies a somewhat lower rate of return than that earned by corporations directly —say 8%–9% per annum.[17]

2. While the first item of evidence comes from industry's operating record, the second item of evidence comes from the bond market. The rate of return on the *safest* kinds of fixed income investments—long-term government bonds, Aaa corporate bonds, and savings accounts in insured banks and savings and loan associations—have typically ranged between 4% and 5% in recent years. Clearly, the added risk of owning common stocks justifies a higher rate of return. How much higher is difficult to say, but a rule of thumb of double the yield on highest grade fixed income securities seems reasonable. Such a rule of thumb suggests an overall yield requirement on common stocks of between 8% and 10% per annum.

3. The final item of evidence comes from the stock market's own

---

[16] McGraw-Hill's *17th Annual Survey of Business Plans for New Plants and Equipment* (1964) disclosed that the average rate of return required by manufacturers to justify capital expansion was about 11% after taxes.

[17] In other words, when investors purchase the earning power of a business via marketable shares, they purchase an investment medium which gives them more flexibility than direct ownership of the business. This extra "utility" is probably worth a substantial amount, even though it entails turning operating control over to others.

history. During the past half century, the average annual dividend yield on Standard & Poor's 425 Industrial Stock Price Index was about 4½%, excluding a few years of high yields near 6½%–7%. The compound annual growth rate of the price index during this same period was also about 4½%. Thus, if today's stockholders expected an overall return of approximately 9% (before taxes), their expectations would be in line with historical precedent.[18]

These three items of evidence all tend to "zero in" on 8%–9% as being reasonable estimates of the discount rate that should be applied to the 4½%–5½% dividend growth rate previously estimated.

### Estimated Value of the S & P Industrials

It will be recalled that the theoretical formula for calculating the value per dollar of dividends at a given point in time is equal to:

$$\frac{1}{[(1 + \text{discount rate})/(1 + \text{growth rate})] - 1}$$

This formula can now be applied to the outer limits of our growth and discount estimates, namely 4½% growth–9% discount and 5½% growth–8% discount. The calculations produce a value range of between $23 and $42 of stock value per dollar of dividends at any point in time, with a mean (geometric mean) of $31 of stock value per dollar of dividends. Actually, since our growth estimates are *trend* values, the calculated dividend multiples should be applied to the trend values of dividends rather than to the actual current dividend amounts, which may be cyclically high or low.

Figure 5–4 superimposes a value range on the monthly movements of Standard & Poor's Industrial Stock Price Index during the past decade. The value range is derived as follows: (1) Define dividend trend value each year as the average dividend of that year plus the immediately preceding and succeeding years (i.e., a three-year "moving average").[19] (2) Center the dividend trend values on June 30 and multiply by 23, 31, and 42. (3) Connect the June 30 values with freehand curves. The chart is drawn on semilogarithmic graph paper, which is scaled to make equal vertical distances represent equal percentage changes.[20]

It will be observed from the chart that prices have stayed within the "band of value" during the past 10 years, but have moved from the lower limits of the range toward the upper limits. Prior to 1956, prices were

---

[18] A study of all common stocks listed on the New York Stock Exchange since 1926 confirms the 9% figure. See L. Fisher and J. H. Lorie, "Rates of Return on Investments in Common Stocks," *Journal of Business*, January, 1964.

[19] Except for retrospective calculations, this procedure requires the analyst to *estimate* dividends for the current and succeeding years.

[20] The use of this type of graph in growth analysis is described in detail in an appendix to Chapter 6.

FIGURE 5–4

**Stock Prices* and Stock Values†**

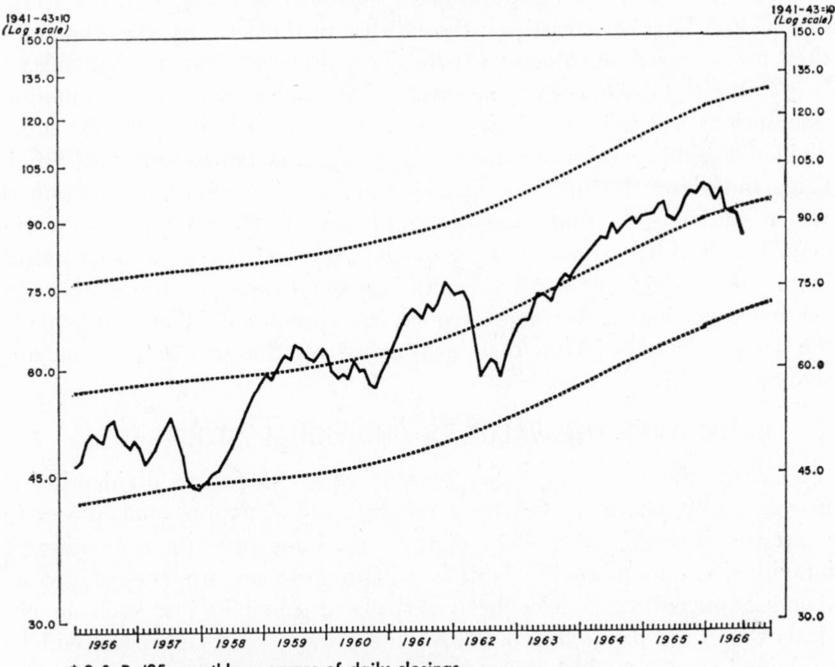


* S & P 425, monthly averages of daily closings.
† Based on 4½%–5½% growth rate and 8%–9% discount rate.

almost continuously below a backward projection of the band. Since 1959, however, prices have tended to oscillate about the mean value.

It also will be noted that a sharp upturn in the slope of the value band occurs near the end of the period. This reflects a major improvement in corporate profits and dividends, stimulated to a large extent by a massive tax cut in 1964. If our assumptions regarding long-term growth potentials are at all valid, the change in slope should prove to be temporary, and the value band should resume a more moderate rate of growth.

### Recapitulation

It will be helpful to pause at this point for a brief review of the discussion thus far. A widely accepted investment theory is that the value of a common stock is equivalent to the *present value* of all future dividends. To calculate the value of a stock on the basis of this theory, it is necessary to estimate the growth rate of the stock's dividend stream and to discount the estimated dividends at a rate which is felt to be appropriate.

It has been shown that the present-value theory can be applied with practical results to an appraisal of a general index of common stock prices such as Standard & Poor's Industrials. Specifically, reasons have been given why dividends on a broad cross section of common stocks can be expected to exhibit a long-term growth rate of 4½%–5½%. In addition, a case has been made for discounting an aggregate dividend series at a rate of 8%–9%. Finally, it has been shown that mathematically these assumptions produce a mean value of $31 for every dollar of current dividends.

No one can be so presumptuous as to claim that a set of economic assumptions will remain valid forever. Thus, it is not claimed that 31 times dividends will be the mean value of the Standard & Poor's Industrial Stock Price Index for all time to come. However, a chart has been presented which illustrates the usefulness in recent years of the assumptions herein described, and it is hoped that the assumptions will continue to be useful in appraising the level of stock prices in general for many more years. In any event, an analytical framework has been presented which can provide the basis for any revisions that seem called for due to changed circumstances.

## ESTIMATING THE VALUE OF INDIVIDUAL STOCKS

Since the concept of the present value of future dividends has proven to be useful in estimating the value of common stock prices in aggregate, it is reasonable to try to apply the concept to the evaluation of individual common stocks. And, as a matter of fact, students of investments in recent years have been actively engaged in just such an endeavor.[21] In the pages which follow, the present-value approach will be examined for its applicability to individual stock appraisal, and a supplementary—more pragmatic—approach will be outlined as well.

### Estimation Problems

In several respects, the present-value concept is more difficult to apply to individual common stocks than to stocks in the aggregate. First, it is much more difficult to project the growth rate of an individual company than it is to project total corporate growth. Second, it is much more difficult to select an appropriate discount rate for an individual company's estimated dividend stream than it is to select a rate for all corporations combined. Finally, the discounting approach has been framed in terms of dividends rather than earnings, making it difficult to deal with companies which do not pay cash dividends. These problem areas are considered further in the paragraphs which follow.

---

[21] For example: (1) R. M. Soldofsky and J. T. Murphy, *Growth Yields on Common Stock: Theory and Tables* (Rev. ed.; Ames, Iowa: State University of Iowa, Bureau of Business and Economic Research, 1963). (2) N. Molodovsky, C. May, and S. Chottiner, "Common Stock Valuation: Principles, Tables, and Application," *Financial Analysts Journal*, March–April, 1965. (3) P. F. Wendt, "Current Growth Stock Valuation Methods," *Financial Analysts Journal*, March–April, 1965. (4) D. Eiteman, "A Graphic Framework for Growth Stock Selection," *California Management Review*, Winter, 1965.

*Extraordinary Growth.* Theoretically, a corporation cannot grow indefinitely at a faster rate than companies generally, because it would ultimately swallow up the entire economy. But there are many companies which have managed for a decade or longer to outperform the average company by a wide margin. International Business Machines Corporation is probably the foremost example of such a company. Its earnings and dividends have been growing at a rate of 15%–20% per annum for many years. If we try to derive a value for IBM by discounting its annual dividend growth potential during the next 30 to 50 years, we know that an ultimate slowdown in its growth rate must be assumed. But the specific pattern of this projected slowdown will have a great impact on the calculated value.

Some proponents of the discounting technique of evaluation have attempted to avoid making long-term dividend growth estimates by assuming a selling price some years in the near future and discounting it in lieu of a stream of dividends. For example, they may project dividend growth for 10 years and assume some price-dividend multiple at that date.[22] Then, to calculate present value, they discount the 10 dividend payments and the assumed ultimate selling price. In reality, however, this procedure merely disguises the problem without overcoming it. For the assumed future price-dividend multiple must explicitly or implicitly incorporate an estimate of dividend growth beyond that point.

*Uncertainty.* An estimate of the growth potential of a company should be considered in light of the probability of its being accurate. Clearly, one is likely to feel more confident of an estimate of the future growth of stocks in the aggregate than of a single company's growth. An estimate of the future behavior of a broad aggregate contains a built-in protection against error—the protection of diversification. An estimate of the future behavior of a single component of the aggregate does not have this hedge and is less likely to be correct, particularly if the estimate is that the component will grow more or less rapidly than the aggregate. Furthermore, the projected growth of a company whose past earnings have fluctuated violently usually contains a greater element of uncertainty than the projected growth of a company with a history of stability.

Present-value theory adjusts for uncertainty via the discount rate. The more uncertain the growth projection, the higher the discount rate should be.[23] But the appropriate relationship between uncertainty and

---

[22] An alternative is to project earnings, assuming a constant dividend payout ratio, and hypothesize an ultimate price-earnings multiple. Some analysts project earnings and also allow for changes in dividend payout ratios.

[23] Of course, it might be assumed that some investors prefer uncertainty—placing a higher value on the chance of doing very well than they deduct for the chance of doing very poorly. But most theoreticians believe that investors, in general, are "risk averters."

discount rate is not at all apparent. Thus there are grave difficulties posed by the need to select different discount rates for different stocks—and even to select different discount rates for different time periods in the growth cycle of any individual stock. In the case of IBM, for example, we would be more certain about an above-average growth rate projected for, say, the next 5 years than for an above-average growth rate projected for, say, the 10 years thereafter. This means that we might select two, three, or even more different discount rates in evaluating IBM stock by the method of discounting future dividends.[24]

*Non-Dividend Payers.* Many rapidly growing companies, especially young ones, plow all of their earnings back into the business, paying no cash dividends to their common stockholders. Ultimately, of course, a dividend-paying policy will be instituted. But if the company's stock is to be valued by discounting its future dividends, a rather precise estimate must be made of when the policy will commence—quite a difficult task when there is no history of management's attitude toward dividends.

### Illustration of Present-Value Analysis Applied to an Individual Stock

To illustrate the application of present-value theory to the evaluation of an individual stock, let us use the case of IBM, since we have had occasion to refer to that company so frequently. In May, 1966, IBM split its stock three for two and established a cash dividend rate of $4.40 per share. The price of the newly split stock at the time was approximately $375. This price represented the high point of the 1965–66 range, up to that date, of about $275–$375.

Let us hypothesize that the company's dividend rate can be expected to grow at an above-average rate for 25 years beyond 1966, but that the growth rate will slow down gradually during that period due to competition and product obsolescence. Specifically, assume that the pattern of dividend growth will be as follows:[25]

| | |
|---|---|
| 1966–71 | 15% per annum |
| 1971–76 | 12 |
| 1976–86 | 10 |
| 1986–91 | 8 |
| 1991 and beyond | Average growth of about 5% per annum |

[24] If interest rates are expected to fluctuate sharply during the forecast period, different discount rates technically should be used for different time periods to reflect this expectation (to the extent it can be quantified). Such adjustments of the discount rate should be made for evaluations of the market as a whole as well as for evaluations of individual issues.

[25] The hypothesized dividend growth rates may well be higher than the company's earnings growth, since a rising dividend payout ratio is likely to coincide with a lessening of profitable plowback opportunities.

As for the discount rate to be applied to this growing stream of dividends, assume that the market demands a 10% per annum rate of return as long as the company's growth rate is above average. Once the growth rate becomes average, however, assume that the discount rate drops to the 8%–9% range which has been used in our analysis of the present value of the S & P Industrials.

Admittedly, these are heroic assumptions, but the present value technique requires that assumptions of this character be made. Indeed, the very fact that the assumptions are so heroic illustrates the difficulty of applying the present-value technique to individual stock appraisal. The effort is worthwhile, but it is not easy. In any event, given the stated assumptions the following calculations can be made:

**TABLE 5–4**

**Present Value of Dividend Stream of IBM Common Stock, 1966–91**

(Based on Assumptions Outlined in Text)

| *Year* | *Dividends* | *Discounted Value of Dividends in 1966 at 10% Discount Rate* |
|---|---|---|
| 1966 | $ 4.40 | $ 4.40 |
| 1967 | 5.06 | 4.60 |
| 1968 | 5.82 | 4.81 |
| 1969 | 6.69 | 5.02 |
| 1970 | 7.70 | 5.26 |
| 1971 | 8.85 | 5.50 |
| 1972 | 9.91 | 5.59 |
| 1973 | 11.10 | 5.69 |
| 1974 | 12.43 | 5.80 |
| 1975 | 13.93 | 5.91 |
| 1976 | 15.60 | 6.02 |
| 1977 | 17.16 | 6.01 |
| 1978 | 18.88 | 6.01 |
| 1979 | 20.76 | 6.01 |
| 1980 | 22.84 | 6.01 |
| 1981 | 25.12 | 6.01 |
| 1982 | 27.64 | 6.01 |
| 1983 | 30.40 | 6.01 |
| 1984 | 33.44 | 6.01 |
| 1985 | 36.78 | 6.01 |
| 1986 | 40.46 | 6.01 |
| 1987 | 43.70 | 5.90 |
| 1988 | 47.19 | 5.80 |
| 1989 | 50.97 | 5.71 |
| 1990 | 55.05 | 5.62 |
| 1991 | 59.45 | 5.47 |
| | Sum | $147.20 |

The table indicates that by 1991 IBM's dividends will have grown from the $4.40 rate of mid-1966 to about $59. Growth beyond 1991 is assumed to approximate that of corporations in aggregate. Since it is hypothesized that an 8%–9% discount rate for aggregate dividends will be as appropriate in 1991 as it appears to be today, and since it is hypothesized that aggregate dividend growth beyond 1991 will be similar to long-term dividend projections made today—4½%–5½% is the range we have estimated—then an appropriate multiple of the $59 of IBM dividends in 1991 will be 31. Thirty-one, it will be recalled, is the multiple which has been derived for the S & P Industrials, assuming 4½%–5½% dividend growth and an 8%–9% discount rate.

Multiplying $59 of dividends by a value of $31 per dollar of dividends produces an estimated value of about $1,830 for IBM's common stock in the year 1991. The present value (in 1966) of this $1,830 value, at a 10% discount rate, is about $168. In addition, the sum of the present values of dividends through 1991 is shown in Table 5–4 to be $147.20. The total of the discounted values of all future dividends, then, is $168 plus $147, or about $315. This calculated value is almost precisely in the middle of IBM's price range from 1965 to mid-1966 of $275–$375. In other words, if the various assumptions about growth and discount rates are realistic, IBM's stock was fully priced at the high point of the range which prevailed at the time of the split.[26]

The analyst should not stop at this point, however. He should recalculate IBM's value under different assumptions about growth and discount rates. For other sets of fairly reasonable assumptions surely will occur to him. One of the most fruitful steps he might take would be to determine what sets of assumptions would produce a value of more than $375, and then to consider whether these assumptions are at all reasonable. In other words, he can approach the problem backwards. Instead of saying, "These are my assumptions; what value do they produce?" He can say, "This is the value currently placed on the stock by the market; what assumptions must be made to justify it?"

### A More Pragmatic Approach—The Price-Earnings Ratio

As discussed above, the application of the concept of present value of future dividends to individual stock evaluation requires many assump-

[26] It must be recognized, of course, that no evaluation procedure should be used without building a margin for error around the value estimate. This point was illustrated in the diagram presented on the second page of this chapter. A common margin for error is plus-or-minus 20%. However, if a particular stock issue has a history of great price volatility, a larger margin for error probably is advisable; if its price tends to be quite stable, a smaller margin usually can be used. Furthermore, if a particular *investor* has a very limited risk-taking ability, he would be wise to use a nonsymmetrical margin of error. For example, instead of plus-or-minus 20%, he might use +20% and −40%, in which case he would be attracted to a stock only when an outstanding bargain appears to be offered.

tions about developments in the quite distant future. In addition to the difficulties posed by the need for such assumptions, there is the further problem that some companies follow a policy of paying little or no dividends as long as highly profitable reinvestment opportunities are plentiful. Practicing security analysts generally overcome the latter problem by evaluating stocks in terms of price-earnings multiples rather than price-dividend multiples. The former problem usually is attacked by devising various rules of thumb for selecting an appropriate price-earnings ratio which can be applied to a company's existing level of earnings per share. The basis for these rules of thumb may range from the purely intuitive to elaborate statistical analysis.

*"The Market's" Price-Earnings Ratio.* Most security analysts begin their attempt to select an appropriate price-earnings ratio (often referred to simply as p/e) for an individual stock with a judgment regarding the appropriate price-earnings ratio for the market as a whole—i.e., for one of the popular stock price indexes. Many analysts assume that an appropriate market p/e is the average actual p/e of, say, the last 10 years or the last 3 to 5 years. Table 5–5, for example, indicates the high and low price-earnings ratios on the Standard & Poor's Industrial, Railroad, and Utility Stock Price Indexes during the 10 years, 1956–65. From this table, it can be calculated that the 10-year average of p/e ratios on the Industrials has been about 17, and has ranged from 12 to 23. The corresponding figures for the Rails are an average of 11, and a range of 7 to 16. For Utilities the average p/e has been 18, with a range of 13 to 24.

**TABLE 5–5**
**Price-Earnings Ratios on Standard & Poor's Stock Price Indexes, 1956–65**

| | *Industrials* | | *Rails* | | *Utilities* | |
|---|---|---|---|---|---|---|
| | *High* | *Low* | *High* | *Low* | *High* | *Low* |
| 1956 | 15.1 | 13.0 | 9.4 | 7.6 | 15.3 | 14.0 |
| 1957 | 15.2 | 12.0 | 10.1 | 6.5 | 15.2 | 12.9 |
| 1958 | 20.0 | 14.6 | 11.9 | 7.5 | 18.3 | 13.6 |
| 1959 | 18.5 | 16.2 | 12.5 | 10.5 | 19.1 | 17.6 |
| 1960 | 19.3 | 16.8 | 14.3 | 11.1 | 19.2 | 16.3 |
| 1961 | 22.8 | 18.1 | 16.4 | 13.8 | 24.4 | 18.4 |
| 1962 | 19.4 | 14.2 | 11.9 | 9.2 | 21.3 | 16.4 |
| 1963 | 18.7 | 15.4 | 12.8 | 10.3 | 21.1 | 19.0 |
| 1964 | 18.9 | 16.5 | 14.0 | 11.4 | 21.4 | 19.0 |
| 1965 | 17.9 | 15.7 | 13.0 | 10.3 | 20.2 | 18.6 |

Note: Data based on range of closing prices during each year divided by earnings per index share for year.
Source: Standard & Poor's Corp.

While many analysts use a simple average of actual price-earnings ratios as their estimate of an appropriate earnings multiplier, others use some variant of the present-value approach. For example, the use of present-value theory in preceding sections resulted in an estimate that the Standard & Poor's Industrials are worth between 23 and 42 times "normalized" current dividends. The term "normalized" refers to a dividend level which would prevail if earnings were neither cyclically depressed nor cyclically inflated. The average price-dividend multiple (geometric mean) was calculated as 31. It also has been indicated that the companies in this stock price index typically distribute 55 cents of dividends, on average, for every dollar earned.

Given this information, a simple algebraic transformation can be made. Letting $D$ equal dividends and $E$ equal earnings:

$$\begin{aligned} 31D &= 31(0.55E) = 17E \\ 23D &= 23(0.55E) = 13E \\ 42D &= 42(0.55E) = 23E \end{aligned}$$

In other words, 31 times normalized dividends on the S & P index is equivalent to 17 times normalized earnings. The equivalent *range* of price-earnings ratios is 13 to 23. It is interesting that these data are almost identical to the actual p/e ratios of the index cited above. A major difference, however, is that the actual ratios were computed by dividing each year's actual annual earnings rather than "normalized" earnings into price. This difference is significant conceptually. For if actual annual rather than normalized earnings are used as the divisor, p/e can be very high or very low not because price is very high or low but rather because earnings are cyclically depressed or inflated. This shows up clearly in Figure 5–5, which portrays the movement of quarterly prices, earnings, and price-earnings ratios on the Dow-Jones Industrial Average. Note that price-earnings ratios rose in 1957 and 1960 not because prices rose—actually they were in a downtrend—but because earnings fell more than prices. Likewise, in 1964–65, price-earnings ratios declined even though prices rose moderately. The reason was that earnings soared. Thus, price-earnings ratios based on normalized earnings often are more meaningful for evaluation purposes than p/e ratios based on actual earnings. On the other hand, actual earnings usually are *easier* to work with because the definition of normalized earnings involves a large element of subjective judgment.

*The Stock's Price-Earnings Ratio.* Whatever method is used for determining an appropriate price-earnings ratio for "the averages," the analyst's next step is to make a judgment as to whether the particular stock under study should sell at an equivalent, a higher, or a lower p/e than that of the averages. This judgment is frequently a mere seat-of-the-pants estimate based on the analyst's experience. More often, intui-

FIGURE 5–5

Dow-Jones Industrials—Prices, Earnings, and P/E Ratios

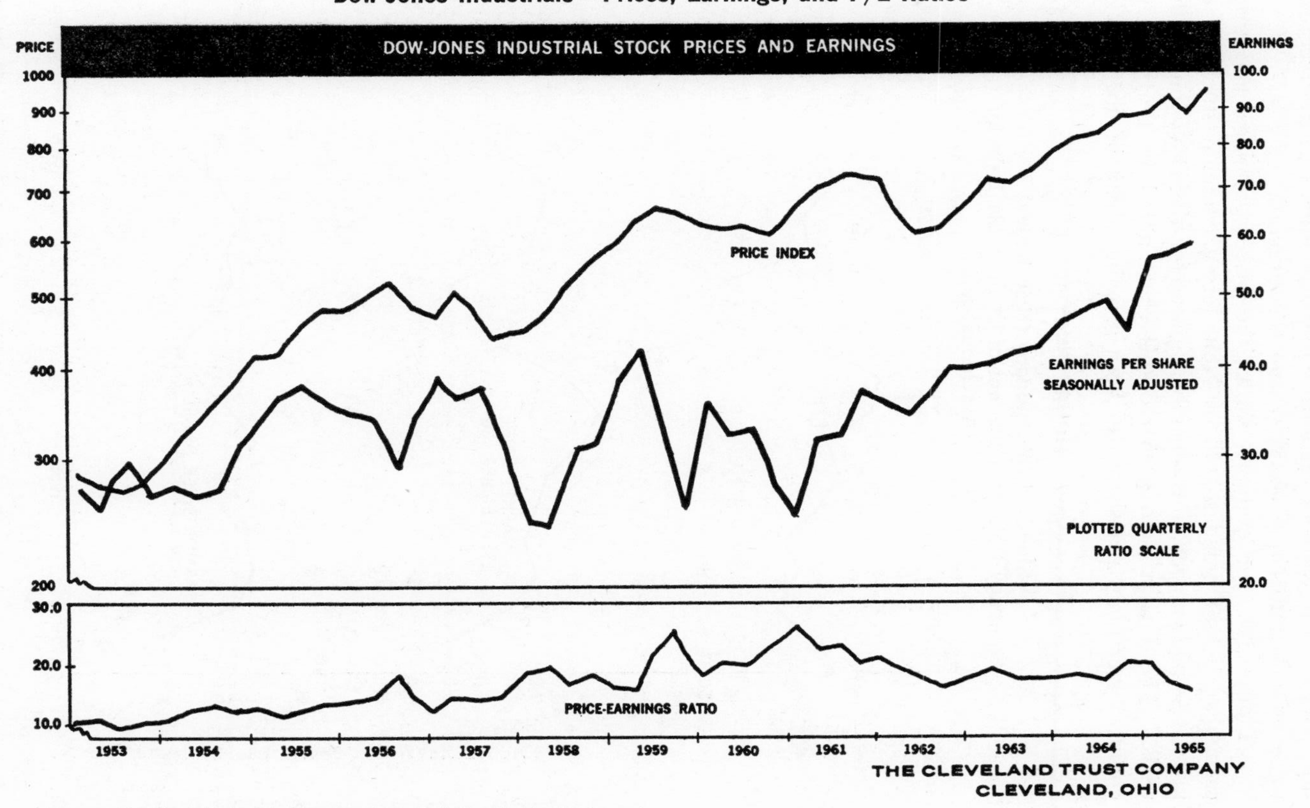


Source: Cleveland Trust Company, *Business Bulletin*, March, 1966, p. 4.

tion is combined with an examination of the stock's actual record of price-earnings ratios in relation to the market's record.

Figure 5–6, for example, shows the prices, earnings, and price-earnings ratios of Standard Oil of New Jersey common stock, all expressed as percentages of comparable figures for the Dow-Jones Industrials.[27] The analyst who prepared this chart noted in 1961 that the company's earnings per share had been growing about in line with the

**FIGURE 5–6**

**Standard Oil Company (New Jersey)**
**Company Data as a Percent of Comparable Data for Dow-Jones Industrials**

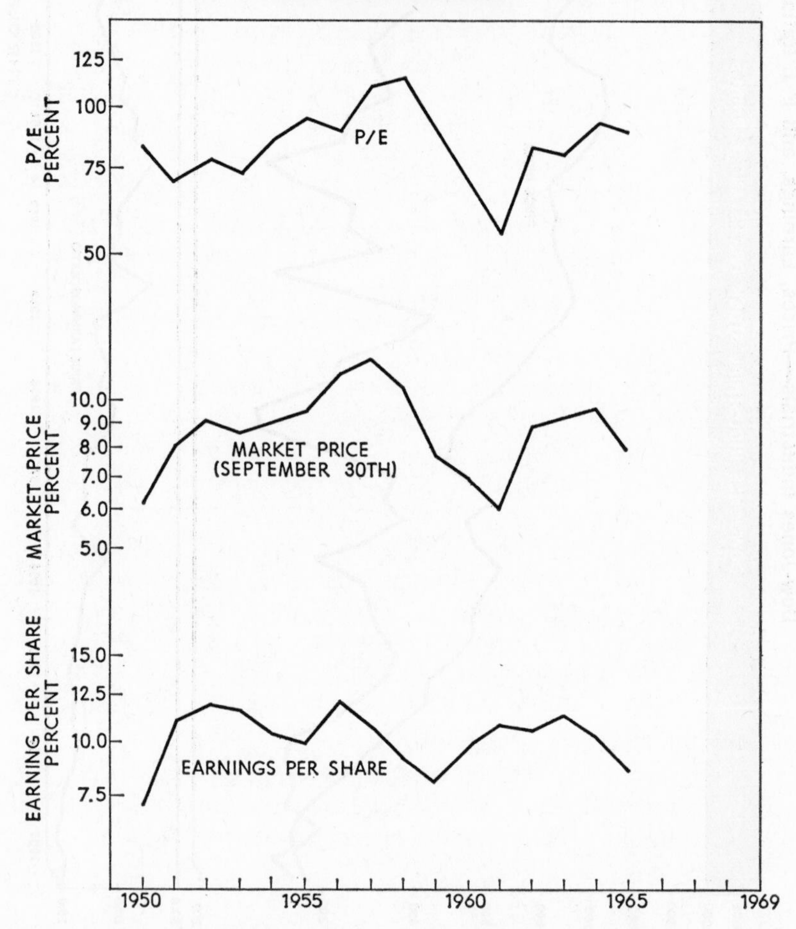


[27] The price and price-earnings data on this particular chart are as of September 30. Earnings are for the full calendar year, with the analyst estimating the latest year's earnings. The lines are plotted on semilogarithmic scales so that equal vertical distances represent equal percentage changes.

combined earnings of all the stocks in the Dow-Jones Industrials, but that the stock's price-earnings ratio relative to that of the DJI was at its lowest point in many years. His estimate of the company's future earnings growth did not seem to warrant such a low relative price-earnings ratio, and he recommended that the stock be purchased. This recommendation turned out well. As the chart shows, Standard Oil of New Jersey's stock rose in price relative to the market for the next three years. Late in 1964, however, the analyst observed that relative earnings growth was turning downward, and his forecast for the following year suggested a continuation of this relative earnings downtrend. Yet the stock's price-earnings ratio had risen almost to parity with that of the DJI, and above its long-term average relationship to the DJI. He recommended that the stock be sold promptly—another good recommendation in view of the relatively poor price performance of the stock in 1965.

Table 5–6 presents the p/e ratios during 1961–65 of 50 well-known companies—two companies in each of 25 different industry groupings. The p/e ratios represent annual averages of high and low prices divided by actual annual earnings. The companies and industry groups were selected to illustrate certain aspects of the subject of p/e ratios. First, it will be noted that the market typically has valued the earnings of some industries (for example, aluminum) more highly than the earnings of others (for example, copper). Second, it can be seen that different companies in the same industry group frequently carry quite different price-earnings ratios. For example, the Aluminum Company of America typically has carried a higher p/e than its close competitor, Reynolds Metals. Third, even over a period as brief as five years, relative price-earnings ratios can change significantly. For example, Johns-Manville's p/e was four points higher than that of National Gypsum in both 1961 and 1962, but this premium disappeared in the years which followed. Finally, the p/e of 34 of Chrysler Corporation in 1961 illustrates clearly the distortions that sometimes can be introduced by using actual annual earnings rather than normalized earnings in computing p/e ratios. The ratio was not 34 because the market was valuing Chrysler so highly, but rather it was attributable to the company's very low earnings that year in comparison with what was anticipated for subsequent years.

Interindustry and intercompany differences in price-earnings ratios may reflect many differences in the basic characteristics of various industries and companies. Probably the most important characteristic is the expected growth rate of earning power. But other characteristics also may be important—for example, the *past* growth and volatility of sales and earnings; dividend policies; capital structures; and the ephemeral, but nevertheless vital, "corporate image." Finally, some differences in price-earnings ratios exist for no readily identifiable reason.

Increasingly in recent years, investment institutions have been mov-

**TABLE 5–6**

**Price-Earnings Ratios of Selected Companies, 1961–65**

| *Industry* | *Company* | *1961* | *1962* | *1963* | *1964* | *1965* |
|---|---|---|---|---|---|---|
| Airlines | American | 15 | 19 | 12 | 11 | 13 |
| | Pan American | 15 | 9 | 7 | 13 | 13 |
| Automobiles | Chrysler | 34 | 8 | 8 | 9 | 10 |
| | General Motors | 16 | 10 | 13 | 15 | 14 |
| Building materials | Johns-Manville | 20 | 17 | 14 | 15 | 14 |
| | National Gypsum | 16 | 13 | 13 | 15 | 15 |
| Cement | Lone Star | 15 | 11 | 12 | 13 | 10 |
| | Marquette | 17 | 13 | 12 | 13 | 15 |
| Cigarettes | American Tobacco | 17 | 15 | 12 | 12 | 12 |
| | Liggett & Myers | 14 | 13 | 12 | 13 | 14 |
| Copper | Anaconda | 12 | 10 | 11 | 9 | 10 |
| | Kennecott | 14 | 12 | 13 | 14 | 12 |
| Industrial machinery | Caterpillar Tractor | 18 | 16 | 15 | 15 | 16 |
| | Clark Equipment | 20 | 12 | 12 | 12 | 13 |
| Domestic petroleum | Shell | 17 | 13 | 14 | 16 | 16 |
| | Sinclair | 14 | 11 | 10 | 13 | 12 |
| International petroleum | Standard Oil of Calif. | 12 | 13 | 14 | 14 | 14 |
| | Standard Oil of N.J. | 13 | 13 | 14 | 17 | 17 |
| Steel | Bethlehem | 17 | 15 | 15 | 12 | 12 |
| | U.S. Steel | 20 | 16 | 15 | 15 | 11 |
| Tires | Goodyear | 18 | 16 | 16 | 16 | 16 |
| | U.S. Rubber | 12 | 12 | 13 | 12 | 12 |
| Chemical | Commercial Solvents | 16 | 13 | 13 | 15 | 18 |
| | Du Pont | 25 | 21 | 23 | 23 | 28 |
| Containers | American Can | 16 | 15 | 16 | 17 | 14 |
| | Owens-Illinois Glass | 20 | 19 | 19 | 18 | 18 |

ing away from simply observing and averaging past price-earnings ratios, in trying to decide what multipliers are appropriate for evaluation purposes, and have turned toward sophisticated statistical analyses. Several financial institutions, for instance, are applying the technique of multiple regression to cross sections of stocks at given points in time. For example, the price-earnings ratios of a sample of stocks in, say, June, 1966, may be related to the expectations of professional security analysts, at that time, regarding the earnings growth potential, dividend payout policy, and sales stability of each company in the sample. Growth expectations in such research usually cover a period of about five years and may be based on

**TABLE 5–6 (Continued)**

| Industry | Company | 1961 | 1962 | 1963 | 1964 | 1965 |
|---|---|---|---|---|---|---|
| Dairy products | Borden | 24 | 18 | 19 | 20 | 22 |
| | National Dairy | 20 | 17 | 17 | 17 | 18 |
| Department stores | Associated Dry Goods | 17 | 19 | 17 | 16 | 16 |
| | Federated | 22 | 21 | 20 | 21 | 21 |
| Lumber | Georgia Pacific | 28 | 17 | 17 | 18 | 19 |
| | Weyerhaeuser | 23 | 21 | 20 | 17 | 16 |
| Publishing | McGraw-Hill | 34 | 22 | 21 | 22 | 26 |
| | Time | 20 | 15 | 12 | 12 | 17 |
| Aluminum | Aluminum Co. of America | 33 | 22 | 27 | 26 | 20 |
| | Reynolds Metals | 28 | 23 | 21 | 19 | 14 |
| Drugs | Merck | 32 | 29 | 28 | 31 | 34 |
| | Parke, Davis | 20 | 18 | 20 | 18 | 14 |
| Electrical equipment | General Electric | 26 | 22 | 26 | 30 | 27 |
| | Honeywell | 39 | 27 | 24 | 23 | 27 |
| Mail-order chains | Montgomery Ward | 20 | 20 | 23 | 23 | 20 |
| | Sears, Roebuck | 26 | 24 | 26 | 29 | 33 |
| Office equipment | Burroughs | 23 | 27 | 20 | 18 | 16 |
| | International Business Machines | 54 | 40 | 34 | 37 | 36 |
| Packaged foods | Kellogg | 27 | 23 | 23 | 26 | 25 |
| | Standard Brands | 26 | 21 | 22 | 22 | 21 |
| Paper | International | 18 | 18 | 20 | 18 | 16 |
| | Scott | 32 | 27 | 26 | 25 | 22 |
| Soft drinks | Coca-Cola | 30 | 26 | 27 | 27 | 30 |
| | Pepsi-Cola | 24 | 19 | 21 | 20 | 22 |

whatever evidence the analysts consider to be pertinent—usually the past trends of reported net income, "cash flow," dollar sales, unit output, etc., plus an evaluation of factors which may cause past trends to change. Stability and payout estimates usually assume a continuation of past experience, unless there is some very significant new factor at work. The same usually is true of any other variables which may be introduced into the analysis.

*An Illustration.* Details regarding the results of the type of research described above are usually kept confidential, particularly since most of the findings have not yet withstood the test of time. However, the broad outlines of the results of one such research program can be described here.

We believe that even this sketchy outline may prove useful to the reader.[28]

The tentative findings of this research suggest that a company's price-earnings ratio has tended during recent years to be higher or lower than the price-earnings ratio of "the averages" under the following conditions:

1. P/e is about one point higher (or lower) than the averages for every 1% by which a company's expected five-year growth of earning power exceeds (or falls short of) the corresponding expected growth of the averages.

2. P/e is about three fourths of a point higher (or lower) for every 10% by which a company's normal dividend payout ratio exceeds (or falls short of) the payout ratio of the averages.

3. P/e is one to two points higher (or lower) if a company's sales stability is substantially higher (or lower) than average. (The average mean absolute percentage deviation of sales from a 10-year trend line is about 5%. The higher the percentage for any given company, of course, the lower its indicated stability.)

4. Price-earnings ratio seems to rise if a large number of financial institutions own a stock—perhaps one point of extra p/e for every 400 institutional owners. The number of institutions owning a stock probably reflects some potpourri of factors that we can lump together under the general heading "quality." These factors may include size, nature of trading market, depth of management, product reputation, etc. Data gathered from Standard & Poor's *Stock Guide* indicate that the average number of institutional owners of the 425 companies included in the S & P Industrials is about 100.

5. Price-earnings ratio tends to vary inversely with financial leverage, other things held constant. P/e is one to two points lower (or higher) than average if a company's financial leverage is substantially higher (or lower) than the average 20% ratio of long-term debt plus preferred stock to total book value of capital.[29]

As an illustration of how these relationships might be applied to investment decisions, we have again chosen the stock of International

---

[28] At least one brokerage house—Dominick & Dominick—offers a monthly common stock valuation service to clients based on the multiple regression approach to p/e ratios. Probably the most well-known published work is that of V. S. Whitbeck and M. Kisor, Jr., "A New Tool in Investment Decision Making," *Financial Analysts Journal*, May–June, 1963.

[29] There are some interesting implications for corporate financial management in these findings. Companies which are able to earn very high rates of return on capital may be able to improve their price-earnings ratios by restricting dividends and employing above-average financial leverage, since the p/e premium for extra earnings growth may offset the p/e discount for low dividends and high leverage. On the other hand, companies with subnormal rates of return on capital might be better off with high dividend payouts and conservative financial structures.

Business Machines Corporation. For 1966, IBM's earnings amounted to $9.66 per share, adjusted for the May split and with all subsidiaries consolidated. Suppose we assume that a round figure of $9.75 is normal for the period—i.e., neither significantly exaggerated nor depressed by cyclical or nonrecurring factors. Suppose we further assume that a thorough analysis of the company, and of the office equipment industry, produces an expectation of earning power growth at a rate of 15% per annum for the next five years. In addition, let us assume a dividend payout ratio of 40%–45% (the company's traditional ratio has been about 30%–40%; in 1965 it was 44%), better-than-average sales stability, somewhat below average leverage (13% in 1965), and continued heavy institutional ownership (the stock was owned by over 1,000 financial institutions at the end of 1965).

Given the above assumptions, a 1966 "value" for IBM can be estimated on the basis of the rules of thumb suggested by the multiple regression analysis.

*a*) Earning power growth of all corporations is estimated at about 5% per annum, so IBM's growth will be about 10% above average. This is worth an extra 10 in its price-earnings ratio (1 × 10).

*b*) IBM's dividend payout ratio is expected to be about 10%–15% below the 55% normal payout of the Standard & Poor's Industrials. Therefore, deduct 1 from the price-earnings ratio (¾ for each 10% differential).

*c*) Add 2 for IBM's above-average sales stability.

*d*) Add 2½ for its large institutional ownership.

*e*) Add ½ for its below-average leverage.

*f*) The sum of items (*a*) through (*e*) indicates that IBM's price-earnings ratio should be about 14 higher than whatever p/e is considered appropriate for the broad stock price averages.

*g*) If a figure of 17 is accepted as being an appropriate p/e for the averages, then IBM is worth about 17 + 14, or 31 times normalized earnings.

*h*) Using a figure of $9.75 per share to represent normalized earnings of IBM in 1966, the indicated value of the stock in that year was about $300, plus or minus an appropriate margin for error.

It is interesting to note that the value of IBM resulting from this highly pragmatic approach is almost identical to that obtained earlier by discounting an estimated long-term dividend stream ($315).[30] Such close

[30] It may be noted that the pragmatic approach can be used to determine "relative" as well as "absolute" values. For example, in evaluating IBM we have assumed a normal price-earnings ratio for "the market" of 17. But suppose the actual p/e of the averages at a given point of time is 20 and a particular analyst says: "I do not know what the market in general is worth, but I would like to value IBM in relation to the market." In such a situation, he could substitute 20 for 17 in step (*g*) and derive a p/e of 34.

correspondence of results under the two methods, which are quite different in concept, is the exception rather than the rule. Generally, the analyst who uses both methods will have the task of reconciling differences which may be fairly sizable. But the very process of reconciling differences in the results usually will produce greater insights into the appropriate evaluation.

## SUGGESTED READINGS

David Eiteman. "A Graphic Framework for Growth Stock Selection," *California Management Review*, Winter, 1965.

E. Bruce Fredrikson (ed.). *Frontiers of Investment Analysis*, esp. Parts II and IV. Scranton, Pa.: International Textbook Co. 1965.

Myron J. Gordon. *The Investment, Financing, and Valuation of the Corporation.* Homewood, Ill.: Richard D. Irwin, Inc., 1962.

Benjamin Graham, *et. al. Security Analysis*, Part IV. 4th ed. New York: McGraw-Hill Book Co., 1962.

The Institute of Chartered Financial Analysts. *C.F.A. Readings in Financial Analysis*, Part IV, "Financial Analysis." Homewood, Ill.: Richard D. Irwin, Inc., 1966.

Eugene M. Lerner and Willard T. Carleton. *A Theory of Financial Analysis.* New York: Harcourt, Brace & World, Inc. 1966.

Daniel Seligman. "Why the Stock Market Acts That Way," *Fortune*, November, 1966.

Robert M. Soldofsky and James T. Murphy. *Growth Yields on Common Stock: Theory and Tables.* Rev. ed. Ames, Iowa: State University of Iowa, Bureau of Business and Economic Research, 1963.

Paul F. Wendt. "Current Growth Stock Valuation Methods," *Financial Analysts Journal*, March–April, 1965.

John B. Williams. *The Theory of Investment Value.* Cambridge, Mass: Harvard University Press, 1938.

# 6

# ANALYSIS OF GROWTH—I: SOME BASIC CONCEPTS

Good order is the foundation of all things.
—EDMUND BURKE

VIRTUALLY any logical approach to the evaluation of a corporation's common stock requires as primary information an estimate of the corporation's probable growth in earning power—either in absolute terms or relative to the growth of all corporations in aggregate. So important is the estimate of earning power that four full chapters, of which this is the first, will be devoted to a survey of techniques that can assist the analyst in making such estimates.

## Introduction

Experience indicates clearly that the best way to begin to estimate future developments is to examine what has happened in the past. The analyst first becomes familiar with the historical data—with the actual record of sales growth, earnings growth, and related matters. He then tries to learn *why* the past record was what it was. For example, if sales growth had been exceptionally rapid relative to the sales of competitors, the analyst might want to find out the extent to which exclusive patent rights accounted for the competitive advantage.

As he begins to understand the conditions that created the past trends, the analyst questions whether these conditions are likely to persist in the future. Continuing the above illustration, the analyst would investigate whether any basic patents were nearing expiration or whether any other companies had developed some improvements that would render the existing product technologically obsolete. If the conditions that created the past trends seem likely to persist in the future, the analyst can simply project the past trends forward. But if, as is more likely, the analyst believes that certain past conditions will probably be altered in form, or disappear entirely, he will try to estimate the impact of the changes and make allowance for them in his projection of the past record. In either event, however, the key to the future lies in an understanding of the past.

If possible, the analyst should try to gather data for a period which encompasses a variety of economic conditions. In this way he has an opportunity to observe the impact of changing conditions on the company's sales, prices, labor costs, raw material supplies, and other profit determinants. He also can examine management's response to change more adequately than if he has only a few years of data available.

The period since about 1952 is a good one for purposes of analyzing a company's growth pattern. It includes the recessions of 1953–54, 1957–58, and 1960–61. It includes two capital goods booms—in 1955–57 and 1963–66. Prices during this period were sometimes stable and sometimes under considerable upward pressure. Fiscal and monetary policies were sometimes expansive and sometimes restrictive. A period of this length also enables the analyst to observe the impact of changes in the world economic and political scene. Companies had to respond to alternations between cold war and hot war; and they had to adapt themselves to the growing competition of foreign enterprises.

The analyst should try to include an estimate of the current year's results as part of his compilation of the historical record. This will not be easy at the beginning of the year and in such cases may be deferred to a later stage of the analysis. But if data for the first two quarters already are available at the time of analysis, an estimate for the full year usually can be made quite readily. It ordinarily will be apparent that the last half of the current year will be higher or lower than the last half of the previous year, although the *magnitude* of the difference may not be so apparent. By making a "guesstimate" of the difference, and adding the difference to or subtracting it from the known results of the previous year's last half, an estimate of the current year's last half can be derived. This is then added to the first-half data for a full-year estimate.[1]

The analyst who is familiar with statistical procedures often will find it very helpful to "seasonally adjust" the reported quarterly data in his effort to estimate near-term results. When a company's operations are heavily influenced by seasonal factors, the use of unadjusted data may result in a distorted impression of current trends. The Appendix at the end of this chapter contains a further discussion of the subject of seasonal adjustment.

### The Industrial Life Cycle

An analysis of the growth record and growth prospects of an industry or a company frequently can be conducted within the frame-

[1] The analyst should be aware, however, that accounting practices in interim financial statements frequently differ from accounting practices in annual statements.

work of the so-called "industrial life cycle." Many students of economic history have argued that industries, like people, go through a few fairly well-defined stages of development. In the early part of their lives they grow at a very rapid rate. After a time the growth rate slows down; they continue to expand, but at a more moderate pace. Finally, they stop growing and either live a relatively stable existence for a long time—or die. The "industrial life cycle," visualized from an investment perspective, is illustrated in Figure 6–1.

**FIGURE 6–1**

**The Industrial Life Cycle**

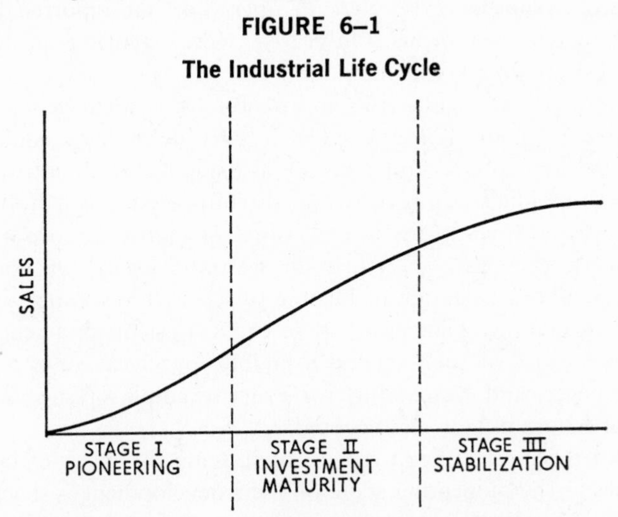


*Pioneering Stage.* One of the foremost exponents of the industrial life cycle concept, the late Professor Julius Grodinsky of the Wharton School of Finance and Commerce has written[2]:

> Every industry has a life cycle. In its early stage, demand expands rapidly. Opportunities for large profits are numerous. Venture capital enters the field. Competition normally, though not always, is rife. As a rule, business mortality is high, surviving corporations lay the foundations for success.

Thus the phase of an industry's development that is labeled on the graph as the "pioneering stage" is characterized by rapid expansion in the market for the industry's product or service. But a concomitant of rapidly expanding demand in a young industry is usually widespread competition and high risk of bankruptcy. The automobile industry provides a dramatic example of this phenomenon. Between 1900 and 1908, more than 500 automobile companies were organized. Of these, about 300 quickly went out of business, either voluntarily or involuntarily. By 1917, 76 companies were active in the industry, but 10 produced three-quarters of the total output.[3] More recent examples of rampant competition in new

[2] Julius Grodinsky, *Investments* (New York: Ronald Press Co., 1953), p. 64.

[3] Herman E. Krooss, *American Economic Development* (New York: Prentice-Hall, Inc., 1955), pp. 357–69.

fields include room air conditioners, television and electronic components.

Some recent statistics compiled by the Securities and Exchange Commission are suggestive of the risks involved during the pioneering stage of the industrial life cycle. A sample was gathered of 504 small, newly organized companies which sold shares publicly during the period 1952–62. The post-offering performance of each company was then traced. As of the end of 1962, fully 55% of the companies either could not be located or were inactive, liquidated, dissolved, or in receivership or reorganization. Another 25% were in operation but reported losses on their latest income statements. Only 20% were operating profitably or had merged with other companies.[4]

Further evidence of the risks an investor faces when he tries to "get in on the ground floor" is contained in a study of the new issues market which has been conducted under the sponsorship of the Investment Bankers Association.[5] The study reveals a persistent tendency for the aggregate rates of return on investments in new issues of industrial corporations to be lower than the rates of return on seasoned issues. Of course, the investor who is astute enough to be able to select those companies which manage to survive the pioneering stage can reap a magnificient reward. Recent illustrations of such successes include purchases of the stock of Polaroid, Syntex, and Xerox. But for every example of success, several examples of failure usually can be cited.

One of the most difficult aspects of judging the merit of companies or industries in the pioneering stage of their development is sheer lack of information. The discussion in the previous section concerned companies with fairly extensive histories. But in the case of pioneering companies, the investment analyst frequently is confronted with so little data that no meaningful historical analysis is really possible. His estimate of future prospects, therefore, cannot be cast in terms of an analysis of the factors which contributed to the past results.

With no past record to use as a bench mark, the analyst is like a navigator in uncharted waters. Like the navigator, therefore, he may refer to his previous experiences with similar situations. While some new products or processes are so unique that nothing currently in existence is at all comparable with it, most new fields are amenable to "reasoning by analogy." Consider, for example, the three companies mentioned above—Polaroid, Syntex, and Xerox. It is true that instant photographic processing, birth control drugs, and electrostatic reproduction of documents were all unique developments. But they were not totally unrelated to other developments in home photography, "miracle" drugs, or office

---

[4] *Report of the Special Study of Securities Markets of the Securities and Exchange Commission* (House Document No. 95, Part I, 1963), p. 551.

[5] Irwin Friend, *Investment Banking and the New Issues Market, Summary Volume* (Philadelphia: University of Pennsylvania Press, 1965), pp. 78–85.

equipment. Some idea of potential markets and potential profits could be gained by examining the histories of producers of these other products.

Some investment authorities recommend that the best way to participate in the pioneering phase of the industrial life cycle is to buy the stocks of several competing companies. By thus spreading his risks, the investor takes the position that even if only one of the several companies survives, the profits on that one will more than make up for the losses on the others.

*Investment Maturity and Stabilization Stages.* Most of the discussion in the balance of this chapter, and in the three chapters which follow, will focus on the phases of growth that follow the pioneering stage. The second stage of growth is labeled "investment maturity" on Figure 6–1. It refers to the fact that after some years, through consolidations and internal expansion, a relatively few companies usually take over a fairly large percentage of a young industry's total volume of business. They broaden the market by improving the quality and reducing the price of the product or service. They establish a strong financial position and a record of dividend payments—even if the dividends are quite modest. Growth of the industry's market continues to be quite rapid. It is not as rapid as in the pioneering stage, but neither are the risks as great.

The "scatter diagrams" in Figure 6–2 illustrate the growth of three industries which have been in the investment maturity stage during the past decade and which are expected to continue to be in this stage for many years longer. The captions under each panel reflect the 1965 views of a large investment advisory organization regarding the outlook for these industries. The outlook is quantified in terms of a 1970 projection for each industry.[6]

Gradually, however, even this second stage of growth begins to slow down. Technological advances become fewer and occur after longer time lags. Unit costs become more difficult to reduce, and the ability to broaden markets through reduced prices is thereby restricted. The market itself tends to become saturated, a process which is aggravated by the inroads of newer products and services.

But the theory of the industry life cycle departs from a strict anthropomorphic analogy at this point. Although the industry may, in fact, die, it is not argued that an aging industry necessarily must ultimately die. Indeed, in absolute terms its sales may continue to grow. But the growth may be below average. The industry's sales may expand less rapidly than the economy during periods of general prosperity, and they may decline more rapidly during recessions. This stage in the evolution of an industry is labeled "stabilization" on Figure 6–1.

---

[6] Scatter diagrams, and the related technique of regression analysis, are described in detail in the statistical appendix to this chapter.

## FIGURE 6–2

### Industries in the Investment Maturity Stage

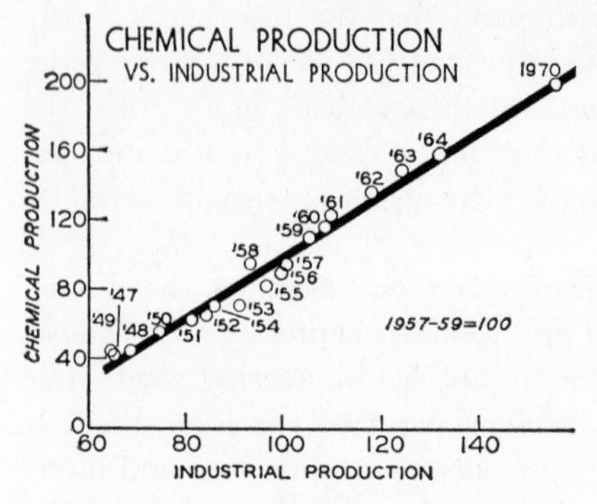


**Resultful research is the catalyst for continuing record growth in sales and earnings in the CHEMICALS industry in 1965 and for the foreseeable future, with a firming price structure underlining its immediate bright prospects.**

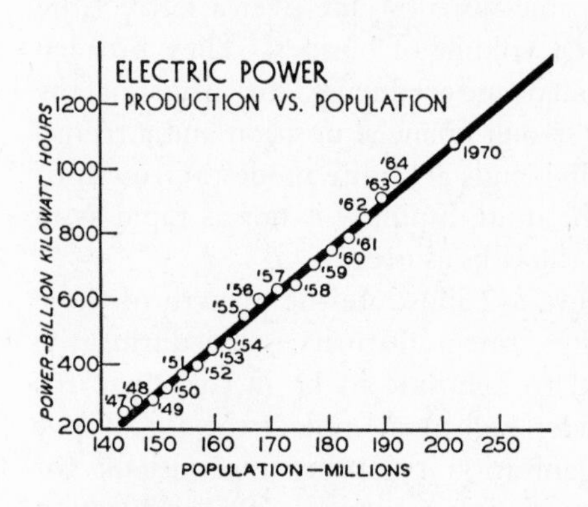


**Continued growth with vast potentials face the ELECTRIC POWER AND LIGHT industry. Earnings and profits are heading upward.**

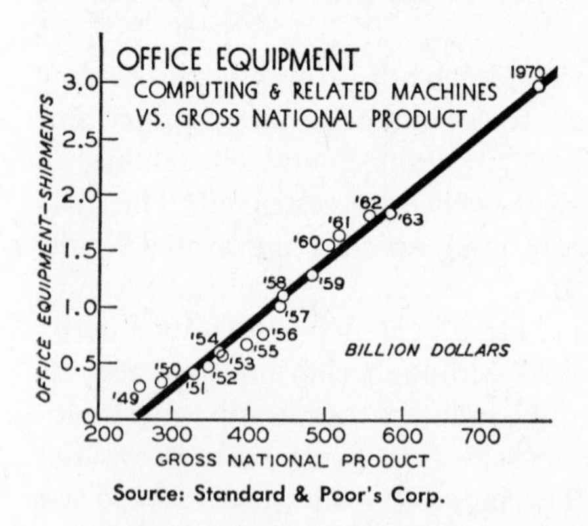


Source: Standard & Poor's Corp.

**Dynamic growth potentials for the OFFICE EQUIPMENT industry arise out of world-wide efforts to cope with a crushing burden of paper work and ever growing clerical costs. We see virtually unlimited growth ahead.**

To many proponents of the industrial life cycle concept, the investment implications of the stabilization stage are quite bleak. In their view, the investor should dispose of his stockholdings in the industry *before* stabilization takes hold. If he waits until it is common knowledge that the industry is leveling off, it may be too late. Stock prices may decline, and opportunities for a good rate of return may disappear. According to this approach, investment success will be achieved by (*a*) detecting growth industries that are about to emerge from the pioneering phase; (*b*) investing in the stocks of the dominant companies in those industries; and (*c*) selling the stocks just before the industries enter the stabilization phase.

*Critique.* In many respects, the life cycle approach offers a convenient method of classifying the growth patterns of different companies. For example, the recent histories of five major corporations fit quite neatly into the life cycle framework. Table 6–1 shows the history of net sales since 1955 of American Airlines; International Paper; Texas Instruments; Time, Inc.; and U.S. Steel. These data suggest that Texas Instruments, a producer of transistors and other electronic components, was in a pioneering phase of growth from 1955 to 1959 but moved into the second stage of

**TABLE 6–1**

**Sales Growth of Five Selected Companies, 1955–65**

(In Millions of Dollars)

| Year | *American Airlines* | *International Paper* | *Texas Instruments* | *Time Inc.* | *U.S. Steel* |
|---|---|---|---|---|---|
| 1955 | 261 | 796 | 29 | 200 | 4,080 |
| 1956 | 292 | 970 | 46 | 229 | 4,199 |
| 1957 | 306 | 940 | 67 | 254 | 4,378 |
| 1958 | 317 | 915 | 92 | 245 | 3,439 |
| 1959 | 378 | 1,030 | 193 | 271 | 3,598 |
| 1960 | 429 | 1,013 | 233 | 287 | 3,649 |
| 1961 | 421 | 1,045 | 233 | 302 | 3,302 |
| 1962 | 463 | 1,096 | 241 | 326 | 3,469 |
| 1963 | 488 | 1,145 | 277 | 357 | 3,599 |
| 1964 | 544 | 1,246 | 328 | 413 | 4,078 |
| 1965 | 612 | 1,304 | 436 | 453 | 4,400 |

growth thereafter. American Airlines and Time, Inc., appeared to be in the second stage throughout the period. International Paper probably can be characterized as having been in the latter part of the second stage, while U.S. Steel was apparently in stage three.

But while the industrial life cycle concept is useful in many ways, several criticisms can be leveled at the concept and at its investment implications. First, it is not necessarily true that a new industry is pioneered by large numbers of small companies which kill each other off in a bitter competitive struggle. The synthetic fiber industry, for example, was largely pioneered by a single giant company—Du Pont—and vigorous competition did not emerge until many years *after* the original introduction of nylon.

Furthermore, the latter years of an industry's life are not necessarily characterized by permanent stagnation. Many industries go through a long period of oscillation between prosperity and recession. This type of oscillation may be noted in the cement industry, for example, as portrayed in Figure 6–3. The point also is brought out in a recent Department of Commerce study of the growth patterns of 339 products.[7] Ninety of the products had a negative growth rate during the years 1948–57. Of these

**FIGURE 6–3**

**Portland Cement Production in the United States**

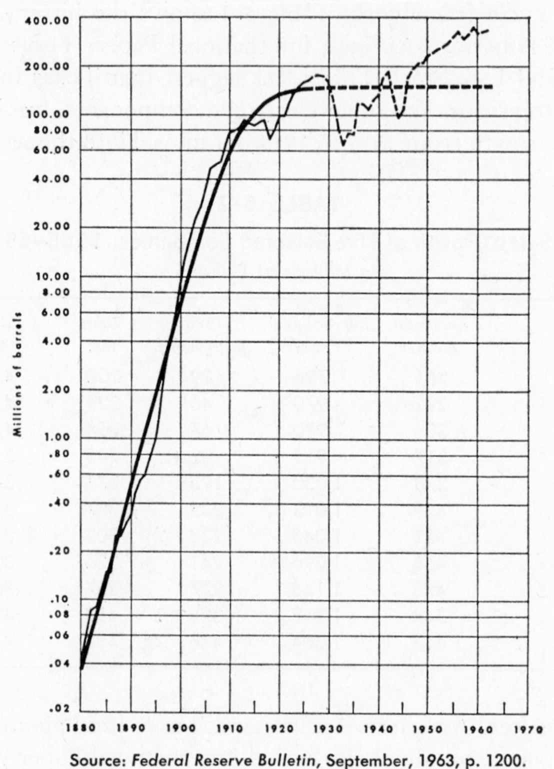


Source: *Federal Reserve Bulletin*, September, 1963, p. 1200.

90, 36 had positive growth rates from 1957 to 1963, with a few even shifting into the "rapid-growth" category in the later period.

Still another illustration of the inability of the life cycle analogy to encompass all patterns of industrial growth is offered by the field of

[7] F. L. Hirt, "Patterns of Output Growth," *Survey of Current Business*, September, 1964. Further details of this study are discussed in the chapter on sales growth which follows. In an article in the November–December, 1965, issue of the *Harvard Business Review*, entitled "Exploit the Product Life Cycle," T. Levitt discusses various marketing strategies which may delay the onset of the stabilization phase. The diversity of long-term growth patterns among different industries is illustrated clearly in J. F. Gaston, *Growth Patterns in Industry: A Reexamination* (New York: National Industrial Conference Board, 1961).

"cryogenics." Cryogenics is the science of liquifying gasses, such as oxygen, nitrogen, and hydrogen, under conditions of extreme cold. For many years, the production of oxygen for industrial uses was not particularly dynamic. But in the late 1950's, major new developments in the art of steelmaking gave rise to an enormous demand for oxygen. Suddenly, cryogenics became a rapid-growth industry. Figure 6–4 portrays these developments and indicates clearly that the growth of this industry has not been characterized by a typical life cycle curve.

Finally, the most important criticism of the life cycle approach to investment analysis is that to equate automatically each growth stage with a different degree of investment attractiveness is to overlook the factor of security *prices* and *values*. A major premise of this text is that it is possible to pay too much for growth and that at the right price even a no-growth situation can be attractive.

**FIGURE 6–4**

**United States Oxygen Production—High Purity**

*(1941–1964)*

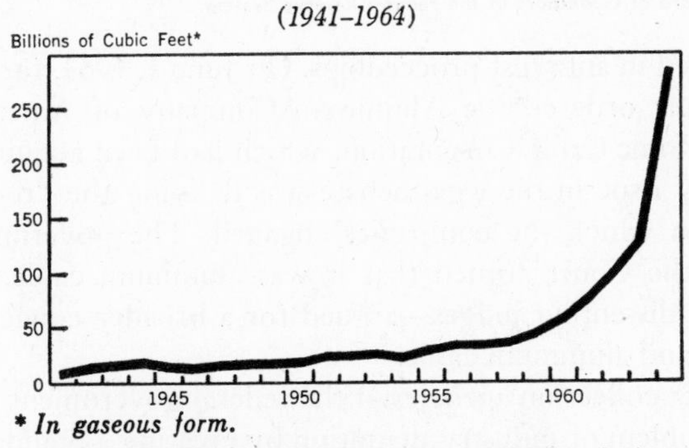


* *In gaseous form.*

Source: Federal Reserve Bank of Philadelphia, *Business Review*, March, 1966, p. 6.

## What Is an Industry?

Frequently, one of the most confusing aspects of a growth analysis is the fact that many companies operate in more than one industry and that the term "industry" is itself often difficult to define. Take the "chemical" industry, for example. Most people have a fairly clear mental picture of the industry—test tubes, bunsen burners, bubbling cauldrons. But a moment's reflection will reveal that the industry consists of many disparate elements. Are not *drugs* chemicals? And plastics? And synthetic fibers? Figure 6–5 illustrates the many facets of the "chemical industry." Yet shall we consider all of these products part of a single industry—chemicals—or is it more realistic to look upon them as separate industries? If the latter, where shall we draw the line?

The problem of industry definition has been perhaps most dramati-

FIGURE 6–5

**The "Chemicals and Products" Component of the Federal Reserve Board Index of Industrial Production**

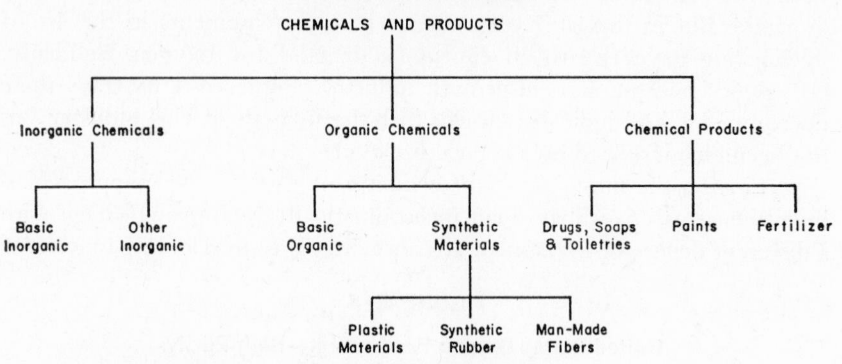


Source: Board of Governors of the Federal Reserve System.

cally illustrated in antitrust proceedings. On June 1, 1963, for example, the Supreme Court ordered the Aluminum Company of America to divest itself of the Rome Cable Corporation, which had been acquired five years earlier. A key issue in the legal debate was defining the "relevant line of commerce" in which the companies engaged. The government and the majority of the Court argued that it was aluminum cable, whereas Alcoa—and the dissenting judges—argued for a broader concept, including both copper and aluminum cable.

The data collection agencies of the federal government have tried to tackle the problem of industry definition by creating a Standard Industrial Classification code. This code is a four-digit system wherein the first two digits represent a "Major Group" (01 through 89). The third digit represents the most important subdivisions of the major group, and the fourth digit represents specific product lines within each subdivision. Continuing with the "chemical industry" as an example, the code number 28 refers to Chemicals and Allied Products. Under number 28 there are subdivisions 281 through 287, representing, respectively, industrial inorganic and organic chemicals; plastic and synthetic materials; drugs; soaps and cosmetics; paints and allied products; gum and wood chemicals; and agricultural chemicals. There is also a "miscellaneous" subdivision, 289.[8] Taking subdivision 281 for an example of the four-digit breakdown, we find alkalies and chlorine (2812), industrial gases (2813), coal tar crudes (2814), dyes (2815), inorganic pigments (2816), miscellaneous industrial organic (2818), and miscellaneous industrial inorganic (2819).[9]

[8] There is no subdivision 288. Miscellaneous subdivisions normally end with the number 9.

[9] Details are given in a bound volume published by the Bureau of the Budget, entitled *Standard Industrial Classification Manual.* The volume is revised from time to time, the latest edition being 1957.

The Standard Industrial Classification does not, of course, solve the problem of defining an "industry" meaningfully for purposes of security analysis. It merely puts the problem in better perspective. But even if it offered a solution, a massive problem would remain, because modern enterprises tend to be highly complex operations. Most large oil companies, for example, produce a good deal more than automobile gasoline. The fact is that petroleum is an important raw material in the production of chemicals (hence the term "petrochemicals"). Moreover, natural gas usually is found side by side with petroleum, so an oil company usually is a natural gas producer as well. And natural gas also is an important raw material in the production of chemicals and related products. The wide variety of products derived from petroleum and natural gas include the following:

| | | |
|---|---|---|
| Aerosols | Explosives | Rubber substitutes |
| Adhesives | Fertilizers | Solvents |
| Antifreeze | Insecticides | Synthetic fibers |
| Coatings | Polyethylene plastic | Vinyl plastic |
| Detergents | Refrigerants | Weed killers |
| Dyes | | |

Some oil companies stick to the oil business; their involvement with chemicals consists of selling raw materials to chemical producers. But many oil companies are directly engaged in the production of chemicals. While they are oil companies in the sense that the bulk of their business consists of producing and refining petroleum, they are in a very significant sense chemical companies as well.

Multi-industry participation is a widespread feature of modern corporate life. A recent study of 111 large American manufacturing companies revealed that, on average, each company operated separate establishments in 10 different four-digit industries. While a four-digit classification system probably represents more a breakdown by product than by "industry," the average of 10 per company is quite high. Classifying the companies according to their primary occupation, it was found that petroleum and tobacco concerns were the least diversified, operating in four different four-digit industries on average. At the other end of the scale, the electrical machinery companies under study operated in an average of 22 different four-digit industries. Detailed findings are presented in Table 6–2.

There is no simple solution to the analytical dilemma posed by multi-industry companies. A competent researcher will try to determine the proportion of total sales and earnings accounted for by each of the industries in which such a company operates.[10] This will enable him to

[10] In addition to trying to determine the breakdown of sales and earnings by major product line, it has become important, in recent years, for the analyst to try to determine the proportions attributable to foreign operations.

TABLE 6–2

Industry Diversification of 111 Large Enterprises, 1954

| *Primary Industry of Company* | *Number of Companies Studied* | *Total Number of Four-Digit Industries in Which Separate Establishments Were Maintained* | *Average Number of Industries per Company* |
|---|---|---|---|
| Food products | 12 | 132 | 11.0 |
| Tobacco manufactures | 5 | 22 | 4.4 |
| Textile mill products | 4 | 30 | 7.5 |
| Paper products | 8 | 68 | 8.5 |
| Chemicals | 14 | 173 | 12.4 |
| Petroleum | 10 | 39 | 3.9 |
| Rubber products | 5 | 62 | 12.4 |
| Stone, clay, and glass products | 7 | 61 | 8.7 |
| Primary metals | 10 | 110 | 11.0 |
| Fabricated metal products | 5 | 55 | 11.0 |
| Machinery | 13 | 89 | 6.8 |
| Electrical machinery | 5 | 111 | 22.2 |
| Transportation equipment | 13 | 121 | 9.3 |
| Total | 111 | 1,073 | 9.7 |

Source: Michael Gort, *Diversification and Integration in American Industry* (Princeton, N.J.: Princeton University Press, 1962), p. 36.

give appropriate weights to his separate appraisals of the prospects for each major product line. To derive such information, he will read company reports, especially prospectuses, with diligence. He will attend annual meetings and question the management. He will sit in at meetings of financial analysts' societies when the corporation is "telling its story." But for all his efforts he is likely to find that most companies are reluctant to disclose their sales breakdown, and are even more reluctant to disclose the distribution of earnings by product lines. Their unwillingness to do so stems from two principal fears: (1) that they will invite competition in their most profitable lines and (2) that they may unwittingly provide antitrust investigators with ammunition to be used against them.[11]

It should be recognized, however, that half a loaf is often better than none. For example, suppose a company's sales can be broken down by product line, but not its earnings. Yet it may be possible to approximate

[11] In this connection, the Federal Trade Commission recently sought unsuccessfully to get congressional approval of a questionnaire that would ask each of the nation's 1,000 largest industrial corporations to disclose the sales volume of each of its major products. Each company also would have to list the sales breakdown of each affiliated company in which it had a share interest of more than 5%. The SEC has been studying similar proposals (see *The Wall Street Journal*, April 1, 1966, p. 7).

A recent departure from the tradition of nondisclosure of operations by product line was the 1965 annual report of the Martin-Marietta Corporation, which shows divisional sales *and profits*. Several other companies have since done likewise.

earnings for each line by applying to each sales component the profit margins of some other companies which are heavily concentrated in that particular product. The derived profits by product line can then be summed up and the sum compared with actual reported profits. If the two do not reconcile, the analyst then can try to discover which of the various lines is being produced less or more efficiently by the subject company than by its competitors.

## Focal Points of a Growth Analysis

In some situations a paucity of information is the security analyst's chief problem in attempting to understand the sources of a company's growth and its prospects for the future. In other situations precisely the reverse is true—he literally is inundated with information, and his chief problem is to separate the relevant from the irrelevant. Either situation, however, requires that he develop a systematic approach to his task. Whether he has too much information or too little, he must know what kind of information he really wants, and what to do with it once he gets it. In the remaining pages of this chapter, an effort is made to indicate some of the most important questions that have to be answered by the security analyst when he tries to estimate a company's growth prospects. The three chapters which follow elaborate upon the various issues raised here.

*The Sales Record.* A useful way to begin a growth analysis of any particular company is to seek answers to two basic questions about sales: (1) What has been the sales pattern of the industry (or industries) of which the company is a part, relative to the sales of other industries which serve similar markets, and relative to general economic activity? (2) What has been the sales pattern of the company relative to competing companies?

The "sales pattern" referred to has several dimensions. It includes (*a*) the rate of growth over the entire time span for which data have been gathered; (*b*) the persistence of this growth rate—i.e., whether it has proceeded in fairly steady fashion or come in fits and starts; (*c*) the growth rate of the most recent years in comparison with the longer term rate; and (*d*) the vulnerability of sales to general economic recessions. Some practical statistical techniques for measuring growth rates, and for comparing the growth patterns of different industries and companies, are outlined in an appendix to this chapter.

The term "sales" itself has two dimensions—unit volume and price per unit. One can derive very misleading impressions of a company's or an industry's sales pattern by analyzing only total dollar sales without separately studying the volume and price components of dollar sales. In a generally inflationary environment, many stagnant companies are likely to report rising dollar sales. But analysis will reveal that this does not reflect growth in the underlying demand for the company's output. On the other hand, a truly rapid-growth company may report only modest gains in dollar sales. But analysis will reveal that it is reducing prices in order to broaden the market for its output and is thus paving the road for long-run growth.

*Sales Determinants.* Once the nature of the sales record has been established, the major determinants of that record must be ascertained. Useful insight into an industry's sales record can be gained by examining the nature of the various markets for the industry's products or services. Have the markets themselves been growing or declining? Have the markets been allocating a larger or smaller share of their resources to the subject industry's products? If a larger share, is it because the industry's products have been superior to potential competing products in either technology or price? Adequate answers to these questions usually will suggest some answers to the ultimate question: Will the sales patterns of the past persist in the future?

Similar questions must be asked regarding the relative market share of the particular company under study, but the questions tend to be more qualitative. For example, in what way is the company's product line differentiated from the lines of competing companies? Are its marketing policies in any way unique? Has it done much to capitalize on foreign demand for American goods, services, and know-how?

*The Profit Record and Profit Determinants.* In parallel with his examination of sales, the analyst must explore the record and outlook for an industry's and a company's profit picture. For profits and dividends, after all, are the ultimate determinants of security values. In Chapter 8, a method is suggested for systematically isolating the critical profit variables. This method may be outlined briefly here.

The method begins with a recognition that the most prevalent source of profit growth for most industrial corporations is the plowback of earnings into the business and the reinvestment of these retained earnings at an attractive rate of return. With this as a framework, attention is focused on the rate of return. Rate of return on stockholders' equity is expressed as a function of two interacting factors: (1) the ability to translate a dollar of sales into some number of pennies of earnings, and (2) the number of dollars of sales which can be generated for each dollar of equity capital. These two factors are then subdivided into component parts. An understanding of changes in the ratio of profits to sales, or profit margin, requires an analysis of (*a*) operating income and expenses, (*b*) nonoperating income and expenses, and (*c*) corporate income tax rates. The ratio of sales to equity, or turnover ratio, is expressed as a function of two other ratios—sales to operating assets and operating assets to equity. The latter ratio gives recognition to the role of leverage—i.e., the relationship of debt to equity—as a profit determinant. As he studies the history of each of these ratios, the security analyst gains the insight necessary to make estimates of their probable future level. By combining these estimates he ultimately derives a forecast of earnings growth which he can compare for consistency with his forecast of sales growth.

*Internal Strengths and Weaknesses.* By utilizing these methods of probing behind sales and profit trends, the analyst is enabled to bring to bear all manner of quantitative and qualitative information about the company or industry. Growth analysis, both of sales and profits, requires a constant interaction of quantitative and qualitative approaches. The quantitative approach, of course, is easier to comprehend and easier to convey to others. But the qualitative approach is no less vital. Indeed, the qualitative approach deals with an aspect of growth analysis that is considered by many people to be the more crucial. It concerns the extent to which growth stems from the internal efforts of companies, as opposed to growth which merely reflects various favorable external developments.

For example, companies which manufacture clothing for children and teen-agers have been the beneficiaries in recent years of a change in the age distribution of the population. Since the percentages of young and old people in the total population have risen while the percentage of those in the middle years has fallen, companies which cater to the young and old have tended to prosper. Such companies, of course, have no reason to be embarrassed because they have benefited from a favorable demographic trend. But a company can be truly proud if it has been more than a passive beneficiary of the trend and has done something positive to capitalize on it. Thus, a key question that needs to be asked by the analyst is whether an observed growth pattern has been significantly different, as a result of a company's efforts, from what it would have been if the company had simply "ridden the growth curve" of the economic sector in which it operated.

Some of the things that a company can do to influence directly its pattern of growth have been noted earlier. Foremost is an effort to develop new products and production processes and in any other way to differentiate its product from those of its competitors. Product differentiation may be technologically oriented or psychologically oriented. That is, a product may be truly different from competing products because of unique construction, styling, or performance characteristics; or it may be similar physically but lower in price because the company has developed methods of producing it more cheaply; or it may be similar both physically and in price but may appear to be different as a result of creative merchandising strategies. Consequently, a company's research and development abilities and its marketing abilities hold important clues to its future progress—clues to its potential for increasing the penetration of existing markets, as well as clues to its potential for creating brand new markets.

The security analyst cannot stop with an examination of the forces a company has brought to bear on its marketing potential. He must consider carefully the physical facilities which have been created to meet the market's demands and to translate sales into profits. Is plant and equipment adequate in both quantity and technology? Is the degree of vertical integration adequate—i.e., the linkages among the sources of raw materials, the productive facilities, and the marketing outlets? Is the company well located in relation to its raw material sources, its labor supply, and its markets? Are labor-management relations amicable?

The last question posed above introduces still another dimension to the qualitative picture of a company's internal strengths and weaknesses. It is the human element—the management team. Analysis of a company's past record may not necessarily reveal the management's capacity to cope with changing conditions. Yet we know that change is inevitable. No product, no matter how good, is invulnerable to competition. Competition in the modern world probably is more dynamic than ever before in history, requiring ever increasing flexibility on the part of the managers of a company. Therefore, the analyst must make a judgment as to management's drive, its willingness to take risks, its conception of the market, its ability and willingness to train younger men to take over in the future. The analyst, in short, must be an appraiser of men as well as an appraiser of companies and industries.

## APPENDIX TO CHAPTER 6: SOME USEFUL STATISTICAL TECHNIQUES FOR ANALYSIS OF GROWTH

Most readers of this text have had a formal course in elementary statistics. For those who have not had such a course, or who have had one but have forgotten much of its content, this appendix is designed to outline some *mechanical* techniques for measuring and analyzing growth trends. Readers desiring greater detail than can be provided in the space available here should consult one of the statistics textbooks recommended at the end of the chapter.

### Semilogarithmic Charts

There is an old saying that "one picture is worth a thousand words." This saying has a counterpart in statistical analysis. A well-drawn *chart* usually leads to far greater understanding than the *tabulation* on which the chart is based. A well-drawn chart reveals at a glance important trends, cyclical swings, and relationships among different series of data (if all are drawn on the same chart). A table of data *can* reveal the same facts, but usually only with a good deal of further processing by the analyst (for example, via calculation of percentage changes).

To be most useful in studying growth over a span of years, a chart usually should be drawn on semilogarithmic rather than arithmetic graph paper. On arithmetically ruled paper, equal distances represent *equal absolute quantities*. For example, if from 1953 to 1963 Company A's sales grew from $10 million to $20 million, while B's grew from $50 million to $60 million, and C's from $90 million to $100 million, an arithmetic chart of these three companies' sales would show three parallel lines. This is illustrated in Figure 6–1A.

But for growth analysis, Figure 6–1A presents a most deceiving picture. For the three companies have in fact had quite different *rates* of progress. Company A's sales have doubled during the period, while B's have increased only 20% and C's only 11%. Semilogarithmic graph paper is designed to show comparative growth more meaningfully.

The horizontal scale of semilogarithmic graph paper is also ruled arithmetically. In our example, each heavily shaded line represents one year. The vertical scale, however, is ruled so that equal distances represent not equal *amounts* of change but equal *percentage* changes. This is the same type of scale utilized on a slide rule.[12] Each ruling of 1 through 10 is known as a "cycle." Thus, any increase of tenfold or less can be graphed on one-cycle paper. Two-cycle paper has two banks of 1–10 rulings, and thus covers a hundredfold increase (1–10; 10–100). Likewise, three-cycle paper covers a thousandfold increase (1–10; 10–100; 100–1,000).

Figure 6–2A portrays the sales growth of Companies A, B, and C on semilogarithmic scaling. The improvement it renders in an ability to make visual comparisons is obvious. Moreover, by imaginative handling of the scales, even greater visual comparability can be achieved. Two of the possible variations will be described.

Although a cycle on semilog paper represents a change from 1 to 10, the starting point need not be 1 or 10 or 100. It can be *any* number—other than zero or a negative value.[13] In fact, it can be several numbers simultaneously, with each number applying to a different line to be drawn on the graph. This fact permits a very useful type of presentation, as exhibited in Figure 6–3A. Here the sales of the three companies are all brought together at the initial year, using a different numerical scaling for each company. By allowing the lines to fan out from a common starting point, differences in growth rate can be dramatically illustrated.

Figure 6–3A, in effect, is a graphic counterpart of the "index number" technique. Index numbers are constructed by choosing some year(s) as a "base period" and making each value of the original data series equal to a percentage of the base period value. Returning to our three compa-

---

[12] The scale is called "logarithmic" because when two pairs of figures have the same percentage relationship, the differences between the logarithms of each pair are equal. A logarithmic scale is often referred to as a "ratio scale." The paper is called "semilogarithmic" because only one of the two scales is logarithmic.

[13] The inability to plot negatives can be a handicap in portraying an earnings record—i.e., if there are years of deficits.

FIGURE 6–1A

Sales Growth of Three Companies—
Arithmetic Chart

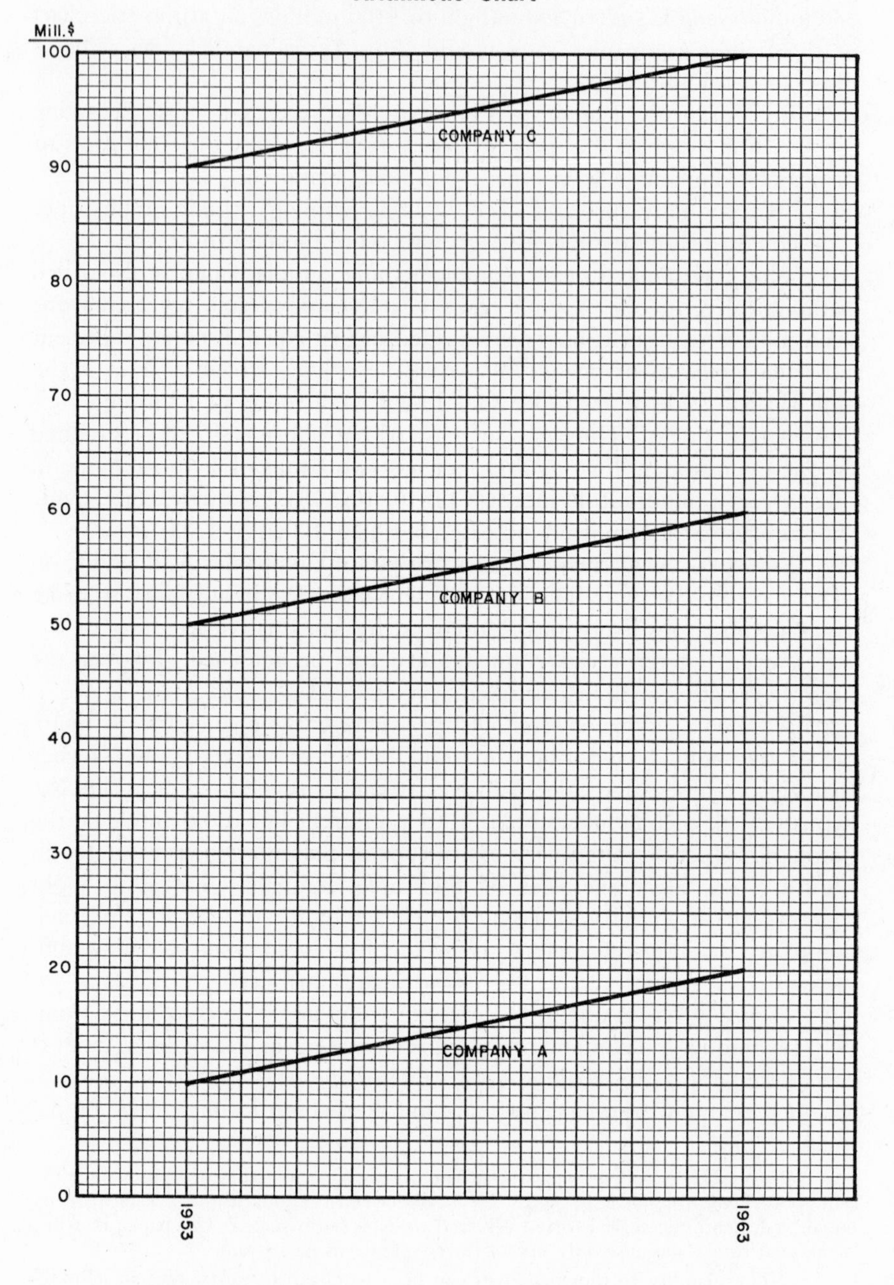

FIGURE 6–2A

Sales Growth of Three Companies—
Semilogarithmic Chart, Single Scale

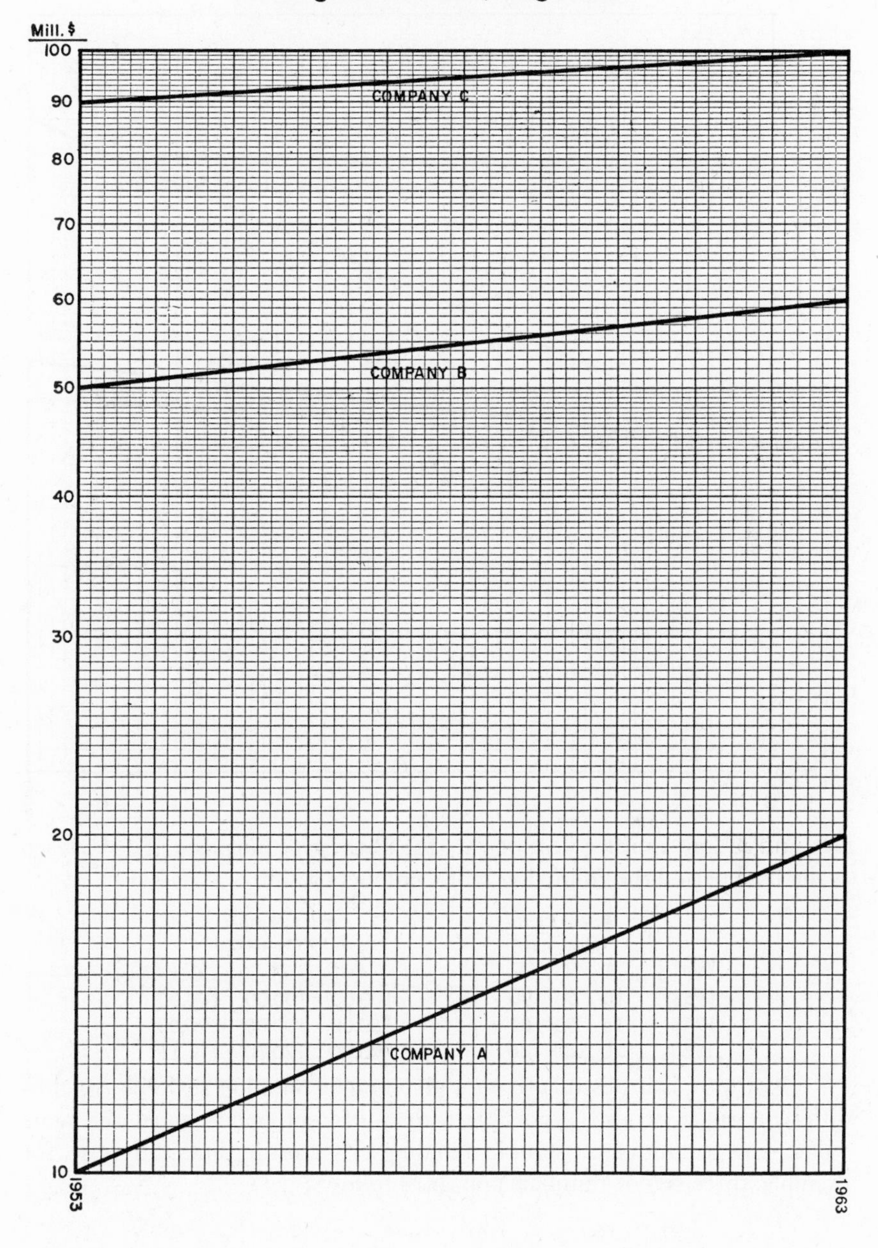

FIGURE 6–3A

Sales Growth of Three Companies—
Semilogarithmic Chart with Common Starting Point

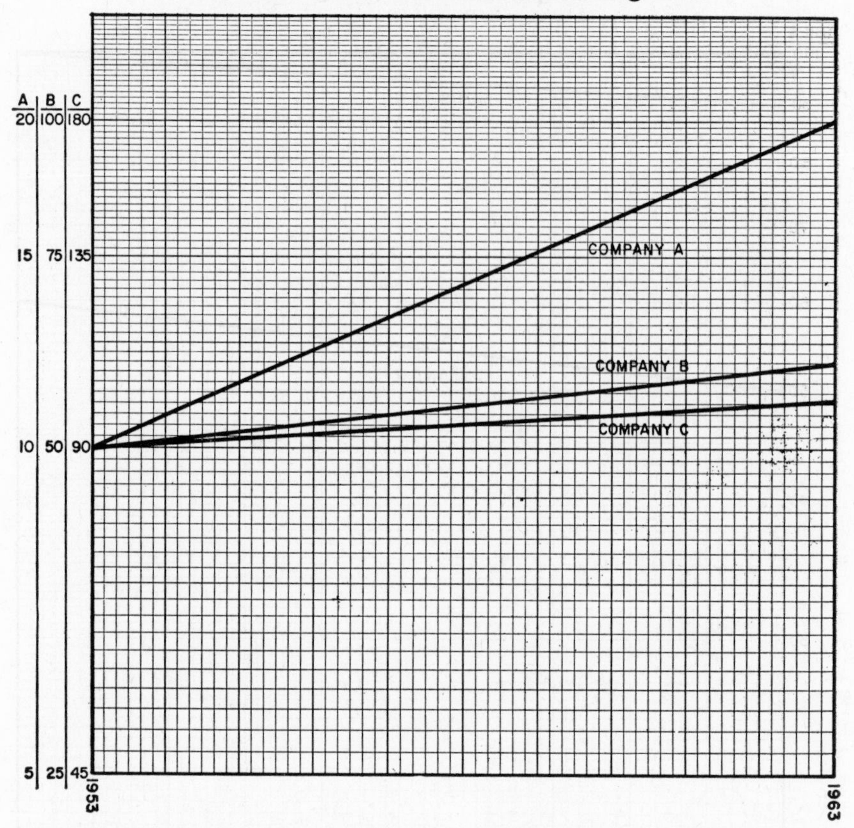


nies, and adding another year of data for illustrative purposes, if 1953 is set as the base period the following index numbers result:

| | Actual Data (Million $) | | | Index Numbers (1953 = 100) | | |
|---|---|---|---|---|---|---|
| Year | A | B | C | A | B | C |
| 1953 | 10 | 50 | 90 | 100.00 | 100.00 | 100.00 |
| 1958 | 15 | 50 | 81 | 150.00 | 100.00 | 90.00 |
| 1963 | 20 | 60 | 100 | 200.00 | 120.00 | 111.11 |

Not only is it possible to let a given point on a log scale be equal to different values, it also is possible to let different points equal the same value. This technique is useful in avoiding crisscrossing lines. Suppose, for example, three sets of numbers appear as follows:

| Year | A | B | C |
|---|---|---|---|
| 1953 | 20 | 20 | 10 |
| 1958 | 40 | 30 | 50 |
| 1963 | 60 | 80 | 75 |

FIGURE 6–4A

Semilogarithmic Chart with Crossing Lines

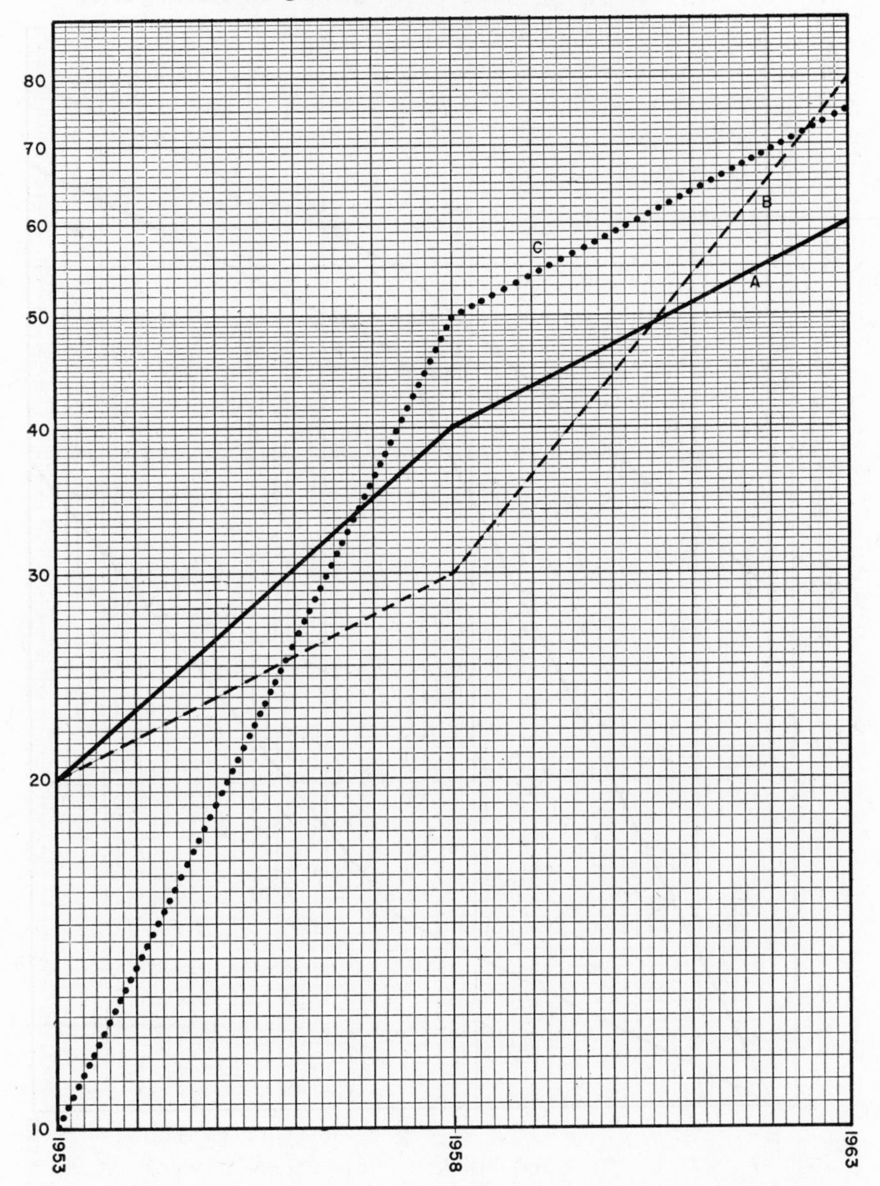


In Figure 6–4A these data are plotted on a single scale of 10 to 100. Note the confusing crisscrossing of lines, a problem only partially overcome by the use of different type faces, colors, etc. In Figure 6–5A, on the other hand, flexible scaling produces a picture that is far easier to interpret.

FIGURE 6–5A

Semilogarithmic Chart with Scales Arranged to Avoid Crossing Lines

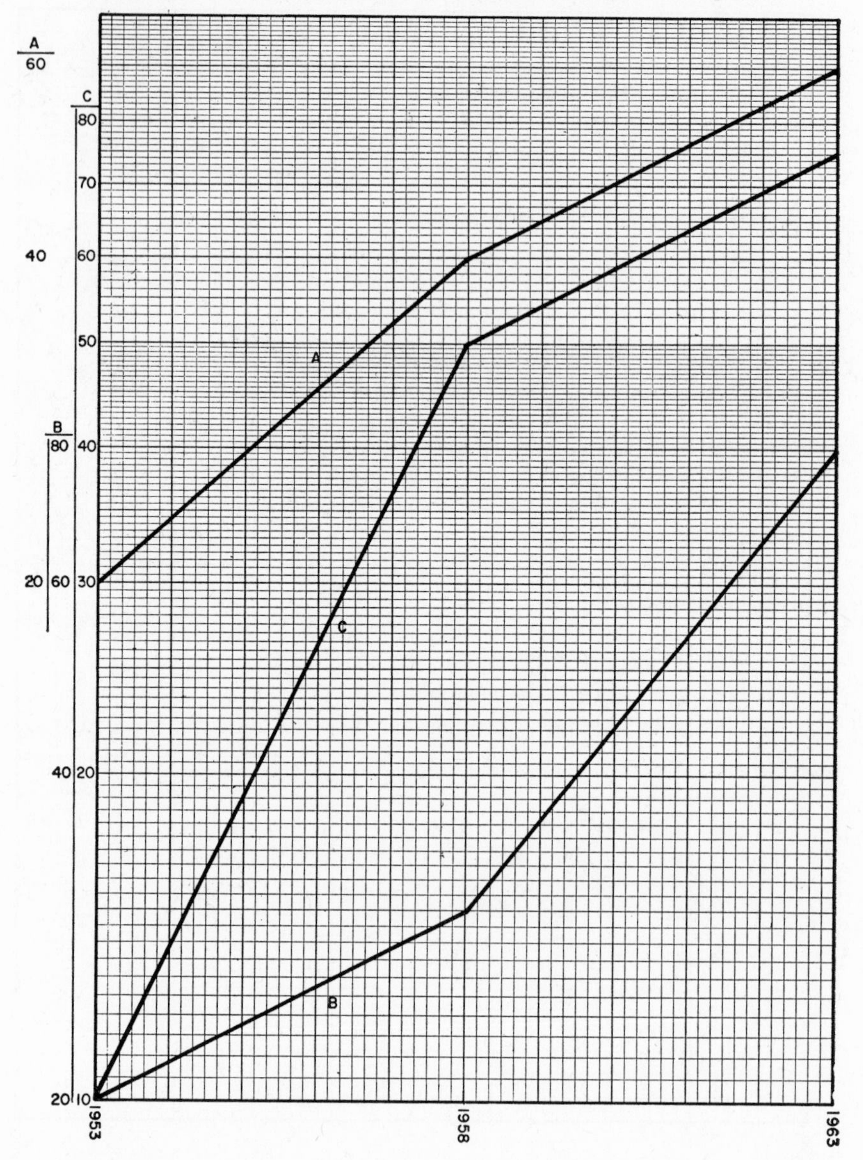


While semilogarithmic charts usually are superior to arithmetic charts in growth analysis, it should be pointed out that it is not always crystal clear that the one is superior to the other. An excellent illustration of the occasional ambiguity that arises is contained in Figure 6–6A. Here is shown the Israeli balance of trade in two perspectives, semilogarithmic

FIGURE 6–6A

The Israeli Balance of Trade in Two Perspectives 1949–61

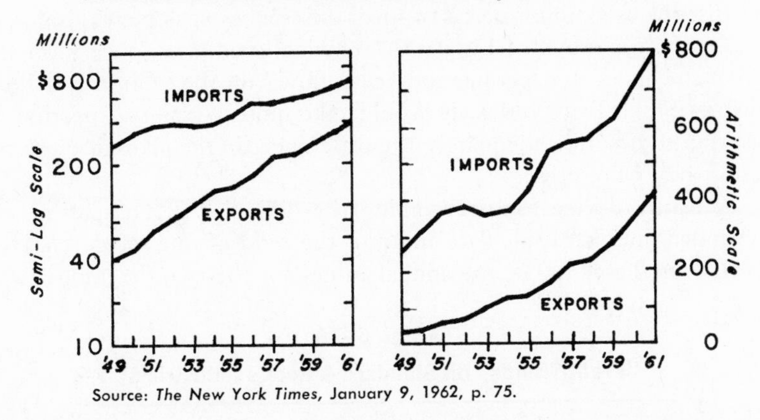


Source: *The New York Times*, January 9, 1962, p. 75.

and arithmetic. Although each chart shows identical data, the semilog chart at the left conveys the impression that the situation improved steadily during the period covered; the deficit became a steadily smaller percentage of total trading volume. The arithmetic chart, on the other hand, shows a worsening of the situation; the absolute amount of the deficit grew from about $200 million to almost $400 million.

## Relative Growth Ratios

When differences in growth rates are quite pronounced, as in the illustrations used thus far, a semilogarithmic chart with one line for each series of numbers portrays those differences quite clearly. Lines with equal slopes—parallel lines—have equal growth rates.[14] Where the slope of one line is steeper than the slope of another line, a more rapid growth rate is indicated. Where the slope is shallower, a slower rate is indicated. Moreover, the *curvature* of a line indicates whether its growth rate is accelerating or decelerating. Thus:

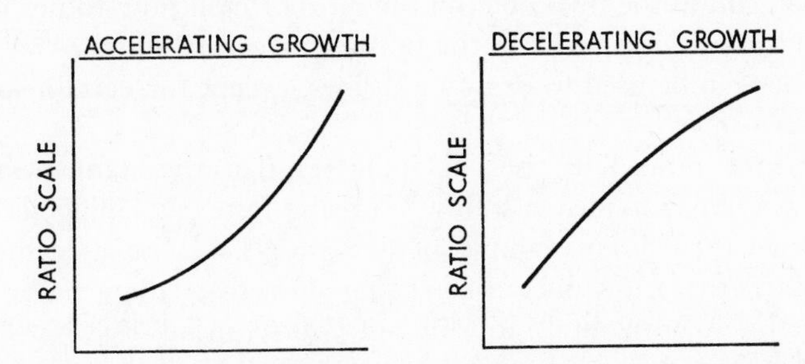


[14] It might be noted that although equal slopes imply equal percentage changes, a given vertical distance in an *upward* direction represents a greater percentage change than the same vertical distance in a *downward* direction. Thus, an increase from 4 to 5 is a change of +25% but a decrease from 5 to 4 is a change of −20%.

However, when differences in growth rates are not pronounced, semilog charting of each series may be inadequate for visual analysis. This is because the eye cannot perceive small differences in slope. Consider, for example, the top panel of Figure 6–7A, which compares on a ratio scale the movements of net income and "cash flow" on the Standard & Poor's Industrial Stock Price Index. It would take quite a bit of inspection and measuring to describe adequately the differences in the growth characteristics of these two series.

A handy device for overcoming the difficulty of comparing similarly sloped lines is to calculate and plot the *ratio* of one series relative to the other. In Table 6–1A, the annual values for the two "earnings" series

**TABLE 6–1A**
**"Profit Trends" on Standard & Poor's Industrials**

| | Per Index Share | | |
|---|---|---|---|
| *Year* | *Net Income* | *Cash Flow* | *Ratio: Cash Flow/ Net Income* |
| 1952 | 2.45 | 3.79 | 1.55 |
| 1953 | 2.57 | 4.10 | 1.60 |
| 1954 | 2.69 | 4.35 | 1.62 |
| 1955 | 3.58 | 5.50 | 1.54 |
| 1956 | 3.50 | 5.54 | 1.58 |
| 1957 | 3.53 | 5.94 | 1.68 |
| 1958 | 2.95 | 5.33 | 1.81 |
| 1959 | 3.47 | 5.94 | 1.71 |
| 1960 | 3.40 | 5.96 | 1.75 |
| 1961 | 3.37 | 6.03 | 1.79 |
| 1962 | 3.83 | 6.72 | 1.75 |
| 1963 | 4.24 | 7.64 | 1.80 |
| 1964 | 4.85 | 8.09 | 1.66 |
| 1965 | 5.50 | 9.02 | 1.64 |

are shown, and in the final column the ratio of cash flow to net income is shown. This ratio is plotted in the bottom panel of Figure 6–7A. (Arithmetic scales can be used to draw ratio lines, except for certain specialized purposes.)

When a ratio line rises, it indicates that the numerator of the fraction (in our example, cash flow) is rising faster or falling slower than the denominator (in our example, net income). Likewise, a declining ratio line indicates that the numerator is rising slower or falling faster than the denominator. A horizontal ratio line, of course, means that both numerator and denominator are changing at equal rates. Note that the numerator and denominator do *not* have to be expressed in similar units to make the ratio calculation meaningful. Tons of one commodity, for example, can be compared with pounds—or even bushels—of another.

FIGURE 6–7A

"Profit Trends" on Standard & Poor's Industrials

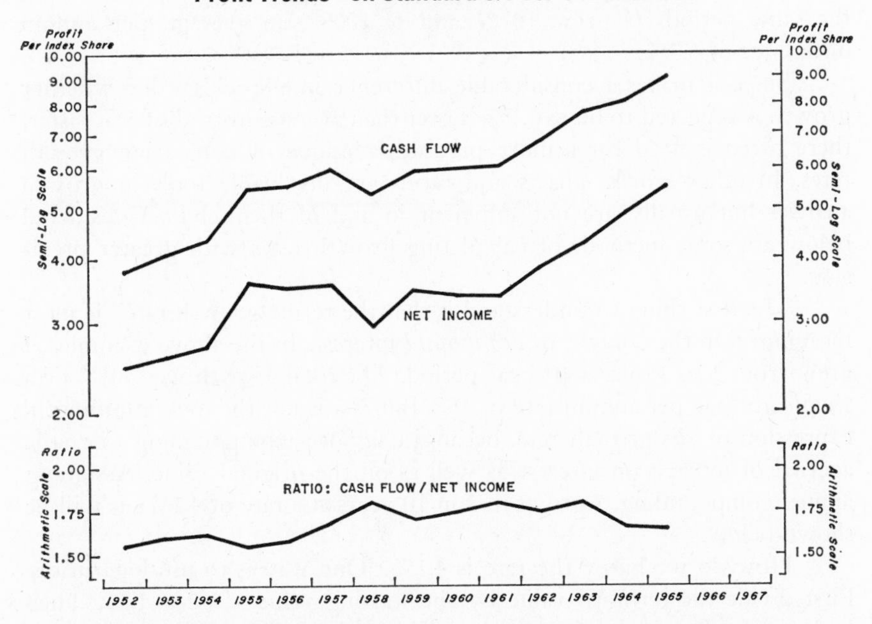


Turning to the bottom panel of the chart, then, it quickly can be determined that: (*a*) over the full period covered, cash flow grew more rapidly than net income; (*b*) however, this relative growth occurred in two distinct phases. From 1952 to 1958, cash flow substantially outpaced net income; but from 1959 to 1965, they both grew at about the same rate.

## Growth Rate Calculations

Suppose, now, that more than simply a quick visual image of differences in growth is desired. After all, a ratio line merely indicates that the numerator of the ratio has grown faster or slower than the denominator. It indicates nothing about *how much* faster or slower. Take the following data, for example:

| Year | A | B | Ratio: B/A | C | D | Ratio: D/C |
|---|---|---|---|---|---|---|
| 1953 | 2 | 6 | 3.0 | 4 | 12 | 3.0 |
| 1963 | 3 | 12 | 4.0 | 8 | 32 | 4.0 |
| Percent increase | 50% | 100% | | 100% | 167% | |
| Difference in percent increase | | +50% | | | +67% | |

The ratios $B/A$ are identical to $D/C$—both pairs rise from 3.0 to 4.0. Yet the percentage change data show that $D$ grew more rapidly relative to $C$ than $B$ grew relative to $A$. During the 10-year period, $B$ grew 100% and

*A* 50%—a difference of 50%, or an average difference of 5% per annum. (Compounding is ignored at this point for simplicity of exposition.) In the same period, *D* grew 167% and *C* 100%, an average per annum difference of 6.7%.

Since it makes a considerable difference in a stock's value whether growth is expected to be, say, 7% faster than average instead of 5% faster, there often is need for a more precise technique of comparing growth rates. In other words, charts and ratios are invaluable tools in growth analysis but usually are not sufficient in and of themselves. Considered below are some methods of calculating growth rates with greater precision.

The first thing to understand is that the term "growth rate" is most meaningful in the context of *compound* interest. In the above example, *A* grew from 2 to 3 over a 10-year period. The total growth was 50%, or a *simple average* per annum rate of 5%. But 5% is not the most meaningful expression of *A*'s growth rate, because it ignores compounding—i.e., the accrual of interest on interest as well as on the original value. Assuming annual compounding, 2 grows to 3 in 10 years at a rate of 4.1%, as will be shown below.

How do we know the rate is 4.1%? One way is to use logarithms. First divide the terminal value by the starting value: $(3/2 = 1.5)$. Then look up the logarithm of the ratio: $(\log 1.5 = 0.17609)$. Then divide the logarithm by the number of years involved: $(0.17609/10 = .017609)$. Look up the antilog of this value: $(\text{antilog } .017609 = 1.0414)$. Subtract 1.00, and we have the answer: .0414, or 4.1% per annum.

In the same manner, "negative growth rates," or rates of *decline*, can be calculated. For example, if 4 falls to 2 in five years: (1) ratio $2/4 = 0.5$ (2) $\log 0.5 = 9.69897 - 10$ (3) $9.69897 - 10/5 = 1.93979 - 2$ (4) antilog $1.93979 - 2 = .8705$ (5) $.8705 - 1.00 = -.1295$, or a rate of decline of 13.0% per annum.

If the reader is confused by the use of logarithms, or if he will be satisfied with an approximate answer, Table 6–2A should prove useful. It covers periods from 1 through 15 years, and growth rates from −15% through +25%. To use the table, divide the terminal value by the starting value, as before (e.g., $3/2 = 1.5$). Then locate the column that covers the number of years involved (e.g., 10). Search down the column for the ratio that is closest to the ratio just calculated (it is 1.48 in the table), and run your finger to the far left column to find the growth rate (4%).

Users of the "terminal/initial method" of calculating growth rates must be wary of a serious potential distorting factor. If either the initial or terminal values are atypical—unusually high or unusually low—the resulting growth rate will not truly reflect developments during the period. For example, if the initial year happens to be one of recession and the terminal year one of boom, the indicated growth rate will be unrealistically high.

## TABLE 6–2A

### Growth Rates Indicated by Ratio of Terminal to Initial Value

| Growth Rate % | Number of Years | | | | | | | | | | | | | | |
|---|---|---|---|---|---|---|---|---|---|---|---|---|---|---|---|
| | 1 | 2 | 3 | 4 | 5 | 6 | 7 | 8 | 9 | 10 | 11 | 12 | 13 | 14 | 15 |
| −15 | 0.85 | 0.72 | 0.61 | 0.52 | 0.44 | 0.38 | 0.32 | 0.27 | 0.23 | 0.20 | 0.17 | 0.14 | 0.12 | 0.10 | 0.09 |
| 14 | 0.86 | 0.74 | 0.64 | 0.55 | 0.47 | 0.40 | 0.35 | 0.30 | 0.26 | 0.22 | 0.19 | 0.16 | 0.14 | 0.12 | 0.10 |
| 13 | 0.87 | 0.76 | 0.66 | 0.57 | 0.50 | 0.43 | 0.38 | 0.33 | 0.29 | 0.25 | 0.22 | 0.19 | 0.17 | 0.15 | 0.13 |
| 12 | 0.88 | 0.77 | 0.68 | 0.60 | 0.53 | 0.46 | 0.41 | 0.36 | 0.32 | 0.28 | 0.25 | 0.22 | 0.19 | 0.17 | 0.15 |
| 11 | 0.89 | 0.79 | 0.70 | 0.63 | 0.56 | 0.50 | 0.44 | 0.39 | 0.35 | 0.31 | 0.28 | 0.25 | 0.22 | 0.20 | 0.17 |
| −10 | 0.90 | 0.81 | 0.73 | 0.66 | 0.59 | 0.53 | 0.48 | 0.43 | 0.39 | 0.35 | 0.31 | 0.28 | 0.25 | 0.23 | 0.21 |
| 9 | 0.91 | 0.83 | 0.75 | 0.69 | 0.62 | 0.57 | 0.52 | 0.47 | 0.43 | 0.39 | 0.35 | 0.32 | 0.29 | 0.27 | 0.24 |
| 8 | 0.92 | 0.85 | 0.78 | 0.72 | 0.66 | 0.61 | 0.56 | 0.51 | 0.47 | 0.43 | 0.40 | 0.37 | 0.34 | 0.31 | 0.29 |
| 7 | 0.93 | 0.86 | 0.80 | 0.75 | 0.70 | 0.65 | 0.60 | 0.56 | 0.52 | 0.48 | 0.45 | 0.42 | 0.39 | 0.36 | 0.34 |
| 6 | 0.94 | 0.88 | 0.83 | 0.78 | 0.73 | 0.69 | 0.65 | 0.61 | 0.57 | 0.54 | 0.51 | 0.48 | 0.45 | 0.42 | 0.40 |
| − 5 | 0.95 | 0.90 | 0.86 | 0.81 | 0.77 | 0.74 | 0.70 | 0.66 | 0.63 | 0.60 | 0.57 | 0.54 | 0.51 | 0.49 | 0.46 |
| 4 | 0.96 | 0.92 | 0.88 | 0.85 | 0.82 | 0.78 | 0.75 | 0.72 | 0.69 | 0.66 | 0.64 | 0.61 | 0.59 | 0.56 | 0.54 |
| 3 | 0.97 | 0.94 | 0.91 | 0.89 | 0.86 | 0.83 | 0.81 | 0.78 | 0.76 | 0.74 | 0.72 | 0.69 | 0.67 | 0.65 | 0.63 |
| 2 | 0.98 | 0.96 | 0.94 | 0.92 | 0.90 | 0.89 | 0.87 | 0.85 | 0.83 | 0.82 | 0.80 | 0.78 | 0.77 | 0.76 | 0.74 |
| 1 | 0.99 | 0.98 | 0.97 | 0.96 | 0.95 | 0.94 | 0.93 | 0.92 | 0.91 | 0.90 | 0.89 | 0.88 | 0.87 | 0.86 | 0.85 |
| + 1 | 1.01 | 1.02 | 1.03 | 1.04 | 1.05 | 1.06 | 1.07 | 1.08 | 1.09 | 1.10 | 1.12 | 1.13 | 1.14 | 1.15 | 1.16 |
| 2 | 1.02 | 1.04 | 1.06 | 1.08 | 1.10 | 1.13 | 1.15 | 1.17 | 1.20 | 1.22 | 1.24 | 1.27 | 1.29 | 1.32 | 1.35 |
| 3 | 1.03 | 1.06 | 1.09 | 1.13 | 1.16 | 1.19 | 1.23 | 1.27 | 1.30 | 1.34 | 1.38 | 1.43 | 1.47 | 1.51 | 1.56 |
| 4 | 1.04 | 1.08 | 1.12 | 1.17 | 1.22 | 1.27 | 1.32 | 1.37 | 1.42 | 1.48 | 1.54 | 1.60 | 1.67 | 1.73 | 1.80 |
| 5 | 1.05 | 1.10 | 1.16 | 1.22 | 1.28 | 1.34 | 1.41 | 1.48 | 1.55 | 1.63 | 1.71 | 1.80 | 1.89 | 1.98 | 2.08 |
| + 6 | 1.06 | 1.12 | 1.19 | 1.26 | 1.34 | 1.42 | 1.50 | 1.59 | 1.69 | 1.79 | 1.90 | 2.01 | 2.13 | 2.26 | 2.40 |
| 7 | 1.07 | 1.14 | 1.23 | 1.31 | 1.40 | 1.50 | 1.61 | 1.72 | 1.84 | 1.97 | 2.10 | 2.25 | 2.41 | 2.58 | 2.76 |
| 8 | 1.08 | 1.17 | 1.26 | 1.36 | 1.47 | 1.59 | 1.71 | 1.85 | 2.00 | 2.16 | 2.33 | 2.52 | 2.72 | 2.94 | 3.17 |
| 9 | 1.09 | 1.19 | 1.30 | 1.41 | 1.54 | 1.68 | 1.83 | 1.99 | 2.17 | 2.37 | 2.58 | 2.81 | 3.07 | 3.34 | 3.64 |
| 10 | 1.10 | 1.21 | 1.33 | 1.46 | 1.61 | 1.77 | 1.95 | 2.14 | 2.36 | 2.59 | 2.85 | 3.14 | 3.45 | 3.80 | 4.18 |
| +11 | 1.11 | 1.23 | 1.37 | 1.52 | 1.69 | 1.87 | 2.08 | 2.30 | 2.56 | 2.84 | 3.15 | 3.50 | 3.88 | 4.31 | 4.78 |
| 12 | 1.12 | 1.25 | 1.40 | 1.57 | 1.76 | 1.97 | 2.21 | 2.48 | 2.77 | 3.11 | 3.48 | 3.90 | 4.36 | 4.89 | 5.47 |
| 13 | 1.13 | 1.28 | 1.44 | 1.63 | 1.84 | 2.08 | 2.35 | 2.66 | 3.00 | 3.39 | 3.84 | 4.33 | 4.90 | 5.53 | 6.25 |
| 14 | 1.14 | 1.30 | 1.48 | 1.69 | 1.93 | 2.19 | 2.50 | 2.85 | 3.25 | 3.71 | 4.23 | 4.82 | 5.49 | 6.26 | 7.14 |
| 15 | 1.15 | 1.32 | 1.52 | 1.75 | 2.01 | 2.31 | 2.66 | 3.06 | 3.52 | 4.05 | 4.65 | 5.35 | 6.15 | 7.08 | 8.14 |
| +20 | 1.20 | 1.44 | 1.73 | 2.07 | 2.49 | 2.99 | 3.58 | 4.30 | 5.16 | 6.19 | 7.43 | 8.92 | 10.70 | 12.84 | 15.41 |
| 25 | 1.25 | 1.56 | 1.95 | 2.44 | 3.05 | 3.82 | 4.77 | 5.96 | 7.45 | 9.31 | 11.64 | 14.55 | 18.19 | 22.74 | 28.42 |

Distortion can be avoided in one of two ways: (1) Choose initial and terminal years that have similar economic characteristics. (2) Do not use single years' data, but rather the *averages* of the first few (e.g., three) and last few years' data. Actually, the second method seems preferable because it involves less subjective judgment. Table 6–3A applies the method to earnings on the Standard & Poor's Industrials. Note especially the effect of the averaging procedure on the number of years used in the final calculation.

A more sophisticated method of calculating a growth rate is to fit a "least squares line" to the logarithms of all the data in the series. A description of this method can be found in most standard statistics texts. However, while the method is more precise, especially in that it includes *each* observation of the period rather than merely the initial and terminal values, our experience suggests that unless the growth rate is quite high the additional precision is not worth the considerable extra calculation effort.[15] In a recent study, we had occasion to calculate growth rates by

[15] The calculation effort can be reduced, however, by the use of Glover's *Tables*. See J. W. Glover, *Tables of Applied Mathematics. . . .* (Ann Arbor, Mich.: George Wahr Publishing Co., 1951).

**TABLE 6–3A**

**Illustration of Growth Rate Calculation**

| *Year* | *S & P Earnings* | |
|---|---|---|
| 1952 | 2.45 | |
| 1953 | 2.57 | Average earnings: 1952–54 = 2.57 |
| 1954 | 2.69 | 1962–64 = 4.31 |
| 1955 | 3.58 | |
| 1956 | 3.50 | Ratio: 1962–64/1952–54 = 1.68 |
| 1957 | 3.53 | |
| 1958 | 2.95 | Number of years = 10 (The 1952–54 average is |
| 1959 | 3.47 | equivalent to 1953. The 1962–64 average is |
| 1960 | 3.40 | equivalent to 1963. 1953 to 1963 is 10 years.) |
| 1961 | 3.37 | |
| 1962 | 3.83 | Logarithm of ratio/10 = .225309/10 = .022531 |
| 1963 | 4.24 | Antilog = 1.053 |
| 1964 | 4.85 | Growth rate = 5.3% |

each method for 1,200 different sets of earnings data. For growth rates up to 10%, the two methods typically produced answers within 1% of each other. For growth rates over 10%, substantial differences appeared.

### Scatter Diagrams

Suppose it is desired to examine the relationship between the sales of General Motors Corporation and the gross national product. Several ways to compare the growth rates of the two series already have been discussed.

**FIGURE 6–8A**

**Scatter Diagram, GM Sales versus GNP, 1953–65**

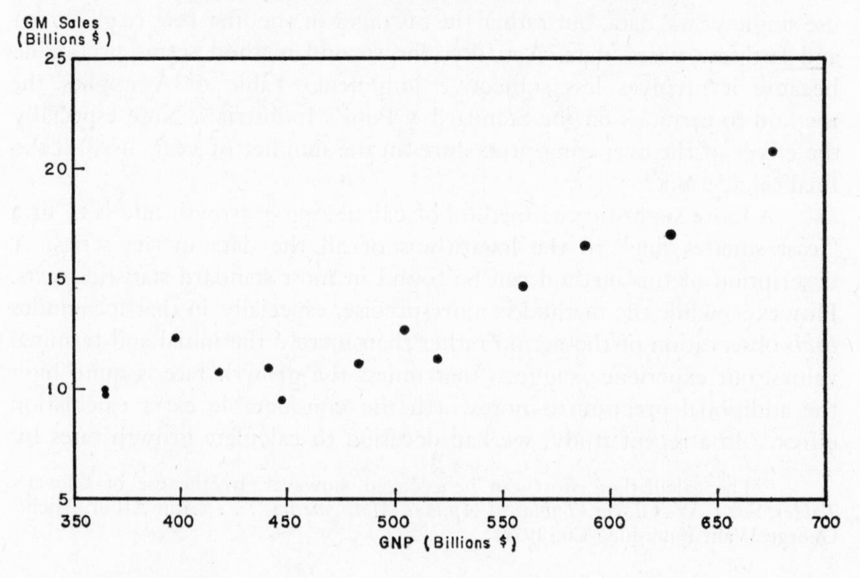

FIGURE 6–9A

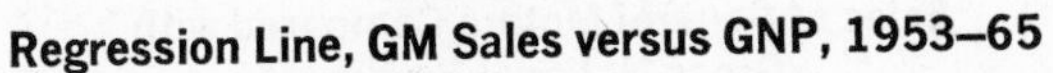


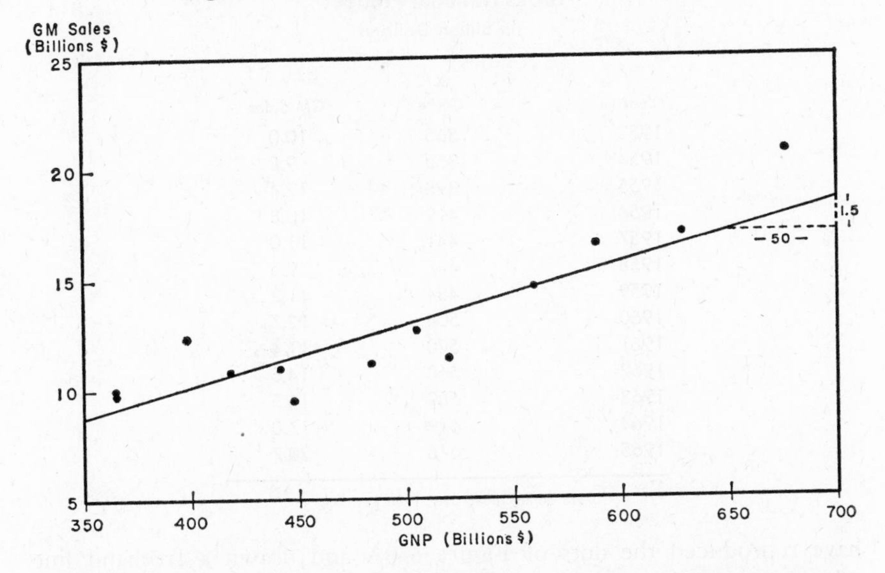


Still another analytical approach is to draw a "scatter diagram." Scatter diagrams are a component of the statistical technique known as correlation, or regression analysis.

Table 6–4A shows the two columns of data with which we are dealing. Column *X* contains the GNP figures, and column *Y* General Motors' sales. The scatter diagram, Figure 6–8A, is a series of dots, with each dot representing a pair of *X* and *Y* data for a specific year. For example, to plot the 1953 data ($X = 365$; $Y = 10.0$), run your finger along the horizontal *X*-axis to 365, then move vertically until you are alongside 10.0 on the vertical *Y*-axis. Place a dot at that point. (The "independent" or "causal" variable is always plotted on the horizontal *X*-axis of a scatter diagram, while the "dependent" variable is plotted on the vertical *Y*-axis. Although it is not always clear which variable is cause and which effect, we may assume that it is more correct to think of GM's sales as being dependent on the state of the economy rather than vice versa. It is often worthwhile, though not necessary, to indicate on the scatter diagram the year represented by each dot.)

If GM's sales increased (or declined) by some constant dollar amount each time GNP increased (or declined) by some constant amount, the dots would fall in a straight line. This is known as "perfect linear correlation." If the dots all fell on a smooth *curved* line, we would have a case of "perfect curvilinear correlation." Perfect correlation is, of course, rare, and our example is no exception. But Figure 6–9A indicates that the relationship, while not perfect, is fairly close. In Figure 6–9A we

TABLE 6–4A

**Sales of General Motors Compared with Gross National Product**

(In Billion Dollars)

| Year | X GNP* | Y GM Sales |
|---|---|---|
| 1953 | 365 | 10.0 |
| 1954 | 365 | 9.8 |
| 1955 | 398 | 12.4 |
| 1956 | 419 | 10.8 |
| 1957 | 441 | 11.0 |
| 1958 | 447 | 9.5 |
| 1959 | 484 | 11.2 |
| 1960 | 504 | 12.7 |
| 1961 | 520 | 11.4 |
| 1962 | 560 | 14.6 |
| 1963 | 589 | 16.5 |
| 1964 | 629 | 17.0 |
| 1965 | 676 | 20.7 |

* Data do not reflect July, 1966, revisions.

have reproduced the dots of Figure 6–8A and drawn a freehand line which seems to best describe the path of the dots. This is known as the "line of regression."

The dashed right triangle drawn on the chart indicates the "slope" of the regression line. It shows that, on average, a change of $1½ billion in GM sales has been associated with a $50 billion change of GNP. It also will be noted that the GM sales level associated by the regression line with a $700 billion level of GNP is about $18½ billion. This compares with *actual* GM sales of almost $21 billion in 1965, when GNP approached the $700 billion level. The discrepancy provides a good starting point for further analysis.

Although freehand "fitting" of regression lines frequently produces acceptable results, mathematical techniques exist for obtaining more precise fits. In addition to greater precision, the mathematical techniques provide a specific measure of the "goodness of fit" and a measure of the range of variation of the dots around the line of regression. The calculations involved are relatively simple, and one technique will be outlined briefly.[16]

First, a work sheet is set up in which column 1 is the independent variable ($X$), column 2 is the dependent variable ($Y$), column 3 is the

[16] For a discussion of the theory of regression analysis, together with illustrations of other computational techniques, see one of the statistical texts cited at the end of this chapter—in particular, Ezekiel and Fox. These texts also show how regressions can be calculated where more than two variables are involved. This is known as multiple regression.

TABLE 6–5A

**Work Sheet 1 for Simple Regression Analysis**
(Data in Billion Dollars)

| Year | X (GNP) | Y (GM Sales) | XY | $X^2$ |
|---|---|---|---|---|
| 1953 | 365 | 10.0 | 3,650.0 | 133,225 |
| 1954 | 365 | 9.8 | 3,577.0 | 133,225 |
| 1955 | 398 | 12.4 | 4,935.2 | 158,404 |
| 1956 | 419 | 10.8 | 4,525.2 | 175,561 |
| 1957 | 441 | 11.0 | 4,851.0 | 194,481 |
| 1958 | 447 | 9.5 | 4,246.5 | 199,809 |
| 1959 | 484 | 11.2 | 5,420.8 | 234,256 |
| 1960 | 504 | 12.7 | 6,400.8 | 254,016 |
| 1961 | 520 | 11.4 | 5,928.0 | 270,400 |
| 1962 | 560 | 14.6 | 8,176.0 | 313,600 |
| 1963 | 589 | 16.5 | 9,718.5 | 346,921 |
| 1964 | 629 | 17.0 | 10,693.0 | 395,641 |
| 1965 | 676 | 20.7 | 13,993.2 | 456,976 |
| Sum | 6,397 | 167.6 | 86,115.2 | 3,266,515 |

product of multiplying each pair of $X$, $Y$ data, and column 4 is the square of each X observation. At the bottom of each column, the sum of the data in that column is entered. These steps are shown in Table 6–5A.

Two equations are then constructed from the data. Letting $N$ equal the number of pairs of observations (i.e., the number of years in our example), and letting $a$ and $b$ be "unknowns," the two equations are:

$$\begin{aligned}(1)\ \text{Sum } Y &= (N)a + (\text{Sum } X)b \\ (2)\ \text{Sum } XY &= (\text{Sum } X)a + (\text{Sum } X^2)b\end{aligned}$$

Substituting the values obtained in Table 6–5A, the equations may be written as follows:

$$\begin{aligned}(1)\quad 167.6 &= 13a + 6{,}397b \\ (2)\quad 86{,}115.2 &= 6{,}397a + 3{,}266{,}515b\end{aligned}$$

The equations are solved by multiplying one or the other by a factor which causes either the $a$'s or the $b$'s to be equal. Thus if equation (1) is multiplied by 492.1, the two equations become:

$$\begin{aligned}(1)\quad 82{,}476 &= 6{,}397a + 3{,}147{,}964b \\ (2)\quad 86{,}115 &= 6{,}397a + 3{,}266{,}515b\end{aligned}$$

Equation (1) is then subtracted from equation (2), which gives:

$$\begin{aligned}3{,}639 &= 118{,}551b \\ b\text{, therefore, } &= .0307\end{aligned}$$

Substituting .0307 for $b$ in equation (1) gives:

$$\begin{aligned}167.6 &= 13a + 6{,}397\ (.0307) \\ 167.6 &= 13a + 196.4 \\ -28.8 &= 13a \\ a\text{, therefore } &= -2.2\end{aligned}$$

The mathematically computed line of regression has the form: $Y = a + bX$. In our example, this means GM sales $= a + b$ (GNP). Substituting the computed values of $a$ and $b$, the regression line is:

$$\text{GM sales} = -2.2 + .0307\ (\text{GNP})$$

The $b$-value represents the "slope" of the regression line. As noted above, the slope indicates how much change in $Y$ is associated with a change in X. Since the slope is .0307, GM sales typically change by $31 million for every $1 billion change in GNP, or by $1.55 billion for every $50 billion change in GNP. This answer is virtually identical to that obtained by the freehand method.

**TABLE 6–6A**

**Work Sheet 2 for Simple Regression Analysis**

| *Year* | *X (GNP)* | *bX (.0307 × GNP)* | *Regression Values of Y (bX − 2.2)* | *Actual Values of Y (GM Sales)* | *Difference: Actual minus Regression Values* |
|---|---|---|---|---|---|
| 1953 | 365 | 11.2 | 9.0 | 10.0 | +1.0 |
| 1954 | 365 | 11.2 | 9.0 | 9.8 | +0.8 |
| 1955 | 398 | 12.2 | 10.0 | 12.4 | +2.4 |
| 1956 | 419 | 12.9 | 10.7 | 10.8 | +0.1 |
| 1957 | 441 | 13.5 | 11.3 | 11.0 | −0.3 |
| 1958 | 447 | 13.7 | 11.5 | 9.5 | −2.0 |
| 1959 | 484 | 14.9 | 12.7 | 11.2 | −1.5 |
| 1960 | 504 | 15.5 | 13.3 | 12.7 | −0.6 |
| 1961 | 520 | 16.0 | 13.8 | 11.4 | −2.4 |
| 1962 | 560 | 17.2 | 15.0 | 14.6 | −0.4 |
| 1963 | 589 | 18.1 | 15.9 | 16.5 | +0.6 |
| 1964 | 629 | 19.3 | 17.1 | 17.0 | −0.1 |
| 1965 | 676 | 20.8 | 18.6 | 20.7 | +2.1 |

Once the regression equation has been developed, the regression values of GM sales for each year can be computed readily. Table 6–6A shows the regression values and the differences between the actual and the regression values.

A further sequence of calculations produces some very useful additional information about the nature of the relationship between the dependent and independent variables. The steps are as follows:

(1) Square each difference between the actual and the regression values of $Y$.

(2) Sum the squared differences. (In our example, the sum is 24.81.)

(3) Divide this sum by $N$. (24.81 divided by 13 = 1.91.)

(4) Take the square root of the number obtained in the previous step. (The square root of 1.91 is 1.38). This number is referred to as the "standard error of estimate." Generally, about two thirds of the actual values of

$Y$ will fall within the range of the regression value plus-or-minus one standard error. Ninety-five percent of the actual values usually will fall within the range of the regression value plus-or-minus two standard errors.

(5) Compute the "variance" of the actual values of $Y$. This is done by calculating the arithmetic average of $Y$; calculating the difference between each individual value and the average; squaring the differences; summing the squared differences; and dividing the sum by $N$. (In our example, the variance of $Y$ is 10.5.)

(6) Divide the number obtained in step (3)—i.e., the square of the standard error—by that obtained in step (5)—i.e., the variance—and subtract this percentage from 100%. (1.91 divided by 10.5 = 18%, which, subtracted from (100% = 82%.) This number is referred to as the "coefficient of determination." It is a direct measure of how closely $X$ and $Y$ are associated. With most economic data, a coefficient of 80% or more (it cannot exceed 100%) can be considered very high, 60% to 80% fairly high, and 40% to 60% moderate.

The higher the coefficient of determination, the more confidence one can have in using the line of regression for *forecasting* purposes. In the present example, the relationship is close enough to be quite useful in forecasting. Thus, if GNP rises, as can be expected, to about $900 billion by 1970, the regression value of GM sales would be about $25 billion (.0307 × 900 − 2.2 = 25.4). This amount plus-or-minus two standard errors (2 × 1.38 = 2.76), produces a forecast of GM sales in 1970 within a range of approximately $23–28 billion. On the other hand, if a regression line were fitted to only the data of, say, 1958–65, a sharper upward slope would be indicated and a higher sales range for 1970 would be suggested.

### Seasonal Adjustment

Most companies report sales and earnings quarterly, and monthly sales data are available in many industries. The security analyst studies these interim data for an indication of recent trends and as a basis for estimating full-year data. Most analysts recognize that it may be misleading to compare directly the results of any given month or quarter with the results of the previous month or quarter. This is because many companies are influenced by a recurring seasonal pattern in the demand for their products or in their mode of production. Two traditional solutions to the problem of seasonality have been (1) to compare the results of any given month or quarter with the results during the *same period of the previous year*, or (2) to examine 12-month or 4-quarter moving totals instead of individual monthly or quarterly data.

Economic statisticians are in widespread agreement, however, that both of these "solutions" can themselves produce distorted impressions of current trends. This is particularly likely to happen when a cyclical turning point is taking place after an extended period of upward or downward movement. A far better resolution of the problem is the statistical technique of seasonal adjustment, whereby mathematical manipulations produce a series of factors which can be used to adjust the raw data. The "seasonally adjusted" data purport to represent the probable pattern of movement of the data if no seasonal influences were present.

Seasonal adjustment techniques range from very simple calculations which can be performed with pencil and paper, to more complex methods requiring electric calculators, to extremely sophisticated procedures requiring electronic computers. Even the crudest techniques, however, ordinarily produce more meaningful data than the raw unadjusted data which most security analysts persist in using. Space does not permit an elaboration of the mathematics of seasonal adjustment in this appendix, but perusal of one of the texts included in the bibliography is strongly recommended.

The automobile industry's sales offer an excellent illustration of the value of seasonal adjustments. The top panel of Figure 6–10A shows the monthly movement of auto sales in 1962–65. Sharp July–September declines are typical of this industry. The next panel of the chart shows the percentage change of sales each month from sales in the same month of the previous year, with the figures smoothed by a lagged three-month

**FIGURE 6–10A**

**Sales of Domestic New Cars**

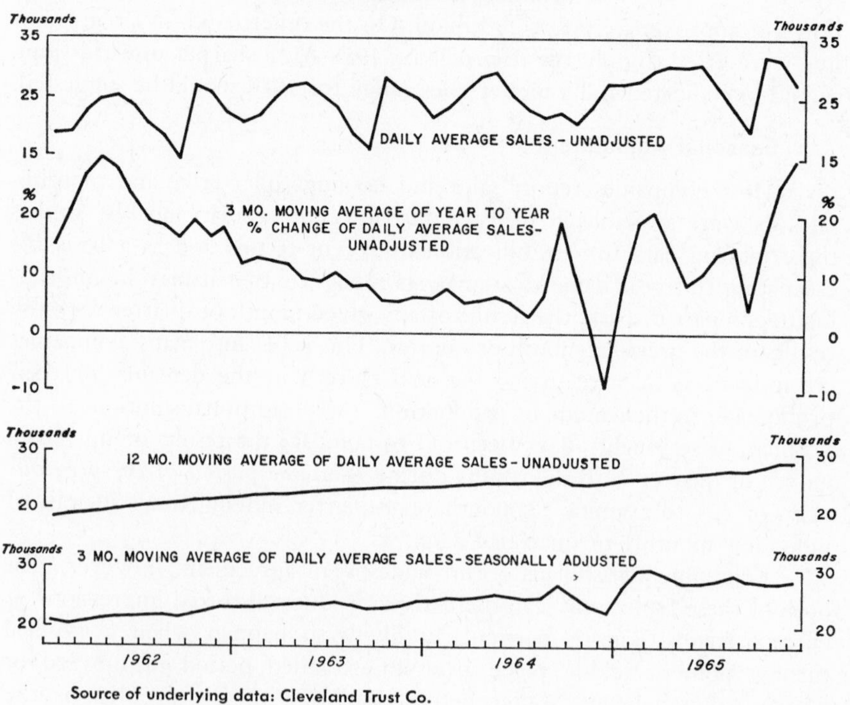


Source of underlying data: Cleveland Trust Co.

moving average. ("Lagged" means plotted on the third month.) The third panel shows a lagged 12-month moving average of the data in the top panel. Finally, the bottom panel presents the monthly sales data, *after seasonal adjustment* and smoothed by a lagged three-month moving average. For purposes of studying *changes as they are unfolding*, the bottom panel gives the most useful picture.

## SUGGESTED READINGS


Herbert Arkin and Raymond R. Colton. *An Outline of Statistical Methods.* 5th ed. New York: Barnes & Noble, Inc., 1966.

Peter L. Bernstein. "Growth Companies vs. Growth Stocks," *Harvard Business Review*, September–October, 1956.

Ya-Lun Chou. *Applied Business and Economic Statistics*, chaps. xiv–xix. New York: Holt, Rinehart & Winston, 1963.

Frederick E. Croxton and Dudley Cowden, Jr. *Practical Business Statistics.* 3rd ed. Englewood Cliffs, N.J.: Prentice-Hall, Inc., 1964.

Mordecai Ezekiel and Karl A. Fox. *Methods of Correlation and Regression Analysis.* 3rd ed. New York: John Wiley & Sons Inc., 1959.

J. Frank Gaston. *Growth Patterns in Industry: A Reexamination.* New York: National Industrial Conference Board, 1961.

Douglas A. Hayes. *Investments: Analysis and Management*, Part II. 2nd ed. New York: Macmillan Co., 1966.

Paul F. Wendt. "Current Growth Stock Valuation Methods," *Financial Analysts Journal*, March–April, 1965.

# 7

# ANALYSIS OF GROWTH—II: SALES GROWTH

Observe always that everything is the result of a change.

—MARCUS AURELIUS

SINCE the mid-1920's, when common stocks first attained a degree of respectability as a sound investment vehicle,[1] security analysts have stressed growth of demand for a company's products as a keystone of investment success. Why the emphasis on growing demand? On growing sales? Probably the main reason is that overhead has been a factor of steadily increasing importance in American industry. Except during depressions, the U.S. economy has always had a shortage of skilled labor. Pressure has therefore constantly been in the direction of increasing utilization of laborsaving plant and equipment. But capital equipment carries a heavy fixed overhead in the form of interest on debt incurred to buy it, depreciation, maintenance, insurance, taxes, supervisory salaries, etc. This raises the "break-even point" of companies—that is, the number of units which must be produced and sold in order to cover costs. In order for a company to operate profitably under conditions of increasing mechanization and skilled-labor shortage (with consequent high wages), it is essential that its market expand so that its plants can operate at a high percentage of capacity.

Not that expanding production and sales *guarantee* rising *profits*, which in the final analysis is what investors are after. But rising demand does, at least, give a company an *opportunity* to earn a rising profit. In many cases, rising demand can even absorb losses from managerial errors that must be expected to occur from time to time. Indeed, without the

[1] A thin volume by Edgar L. Smith, *Common Stocks as Long-Term Investments* (2nd ed.; New York: Macmillan Co., 1928), is widely regarded as a prime mover in gaining respectability for common stocks.

cushion of rising demand, management may be loathe to take risks, and without risk taking, little should be expected in the way of rising profits.

### Life Cycle Perspective

The theme of the preceding chapter was that the best way to begin an appraisal of the future is with an examination of the past. To illustrate some of the procedures that can be employed in the analysis of sales growth, the Aluminum Company of America has been chosen as an example. First, the past and potential growth of the aluminum industry as a whole will be considered. This will be followed by a review of Alcoa's position within the industry.

The history of the American aluminum industry is a long one. Aluminum production was begun in 1888 by the Pittsburgh Reduction Company, a predecessor of the Aluminum Company of America. For many years the one company represented the bulk of the industry's output. During the past 25 years, however, other companies have entered the field, encouraged particularly by the federal government during World War II and the Korean War, when emergency demands for the metal were intense.

In a study of the long-term growth patterns of 30 different industries, J. F. Gaston fitted a mathematical growth curve (known as a Gompertz curve) to primary aluminum production from 1890 to 1960. This growth curve is shown in Figure 7–1. A life cycle proponent probably would suggest that the industry was in its pioneering phase from 1890 to about 1910 and has been in the investment maturity phase since then. A question clearly emerging from this view is whether the stabilization phase was approaching as the decade of the 1950's came to an end. Closer examination of aluminum sales since the early 1950's is necessary to answer this question.

### Relative Growth in Recent Years

An adequate study of an industry's sales growth contains four parts:

1. A comparison of the dollar sales of the industry with the dollar sales of industries serving similar markets—particularly industries in direct competition with the one under study.[2]

2. A comparison of the dollar sales of the industry with one or more broad economic measures such as gross national product, personal consumption expenditures, or gross private domestic investment.

3 and 4. Conversion of comparisons 1 and 2 from dollar terms into physical units—pounds, tons, ton-miles, etc.

The aluminum industry will now be examined from these four viewpoints.

---

[2] If large proportions of a company's sales are the products of more than one major industry, each of the principal areas of activity should be examined separately.

*The Data.* Columns (1), (2), and (3) of Table 7–1 show annual dollar sales since 1953 for the leading companies in the U.S. aluminum industry and its two major competing industries, copper and steel. It must be admitted that a summation of leading companies' sales usually is not equivalent to aggregate U.S. industry sales, because (*a*) there are other firms in each industry[3] and (*b*) the sales of most large companies are not

**FIGURE 7–1**

**The Growth of Primary Aluminum Production in the United States**

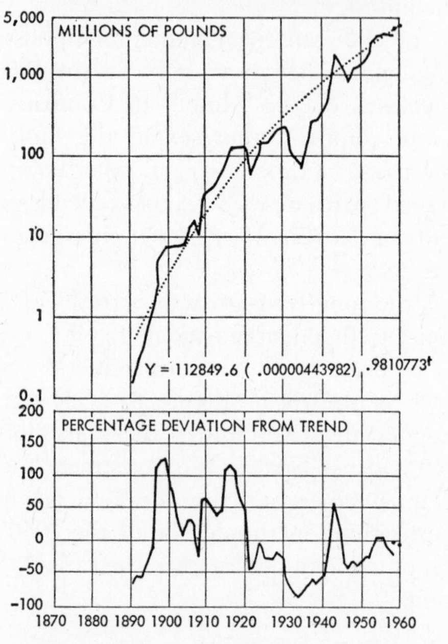


Source: J. Frank Gaston, *Growth Patterns in Industry: A Reexamination* (Studies in Economics No. 75 [New York: National Industrial Conference Board, 1961]), p. 40.

exclusively concentrated in the products of a single industry and often include foreign operations. However, up-to-date aggregate industry data, in dollar amounts, usually are available only for broader categories than we are interested in—for example, all nonferrous metals—and summations

---

[3] For example, in addition to the "big four" aluminum companies included in the tabulation, a sizable proportion of primary aluminum is produced by: Ormet (a joint venture of Olin Mathieson and Revere); Intalco (joint venture of American Metal Climax, Howmet, and Pechiney); Harvey; Anaconda; and Consolidated. There are also about 70 producers of secondary aluminum from scrap. The names of the leading companies in most major industries can be obtained from the relevant Standard & Poor's *Industry Survey*, among other sources.

of leading companies' sales generally serve as a convenient and useful substitute.[4]

In addition to interindustry comparisons, it has been suggested that sales of the subject industry be compared with one or more national economic aggregates. Accordingly, columns (4) and (5) of the first table present two relevant measures—gross national product, and the portion of GNP represented by final sales of durable goods. (Final sales exclude inventory accumulation.)

**TABLE 7–1**

**Dollar Sales of Aluminum versus Competition**

(In Billion Dollars)

| Year | *Sales of Leading U.S. Companies* Aluminum* (1) | Copper† (2) | Steel‡ (3) | *Gross National Product§* (4) | *Final Sales of Durable Goods§* (5) |
|---|---|---|---|---|---|
| 1953 | 1.568 | 1.271 | 10.741 | 365 | 78 |
| 1954 | 1.622 | 1.221 | 8.813 | 365 | 75 |
| 1955 | 1.973 | 1.628 | 11.397 | 398 | 83 |
| 1956 | 2.116 | 1.858 | 12.204 | 419 | 88 |
| 1957 | 2.169 | 1.436 | 12.732 | 441 | 93 |
| 1958 | 2.044 | 1.305 | 10.252 | 447 | 86 |
| 1959 | 2.253 | 1.470 | 11.275 | 484 | 93 |
| 1960 | 2.217 | 1.531 | 11.301 | 504 | 97 |
| 1961 | 2.251 | 1.577 | 10.479 | 520 | 97 |
| 1962 | 2.439 | 1.663 | 11.089 | 560 | 106 |
| 1963 | 2.595 | 1.790 | 11.554 | 589 | 113 |
| 1964 | 2.851 | 2.002 | 12.919 | 629 | 123 |
| 1965 | 3.310 | 2.323 | 14.193 | 676 | 134 |

* Alcoa, Alcan Aluminium Ltd., Kaiser, and Reynolds. Although Alcan is not a U.S. company, it is a major competitor of the three leading U.S. companies.

† Anaconda, Copper Range, Inspiration, Kennecott, Magma, Phelps Dodge.

‡ Armco, Bethlehem, Colorado Fuel & Iron, Crucible, Inland, Jones & Laughlin, National, Republic, United States Steel, Wheeling, Youngstown.

§ Data do not reflect July, 1966 revisions.

Sole reliance on *dollar* sales data is inadvisable. Dollar sales are equal to the number of *units* sold multiplied by the sales price per unit. But as is well known, the prices of different commodities, such as aluminum, copper and steel, do not change uniformly. Differences in price movement exist both in timing and in magnitude. Thus it is quite possible to conceive of the following situation. Industry A expands its unit sales faster than competing Industry B. In order to accomplish this, Industry A has grad-

[4] For current sales data on broad manufacturing industry groupings see the FTC–SEC's *Quarterly Survey of Manufacturing Corporations*. Narrower groupings are presented in the *Census of Manufactures*, and *Census of Mineral Industries*, but there is a considerable time lag in the availability of these data. Various trade journals and trade associations also make sales tabulations which may be useful.

ually reduced its prices relative to those of Industry B. As a result, the *dollar* sales of A have expanded less rapidly than those of B.

The analyst who concerns himself solely with *dollar* sales comparisons in this example would miss an opportunity to gain real insight into the competitive forces at work. If he projects future sales relationships on the basis of the past without recognizing that the past record reflects sharply contrasting price-volume patterns, his projection probably will turn out to be quite inaccurate. For it is most unlikely that the past price-volume patterns will remain unchanged. Accordingly, it is strongly recommended that interindustry and industry-economy sales comparisons be carried out in terms of volume in addition to dollars.

**TABLE 7–2**

**Volume of Primary Aluminum Production versus Competition**

| | *Production (Thousand Short Tons)** | | | *(In Billions of 1958 Dollars)* | |
|---|---|---|---|---|---|
| | *Aluminum* | *Copper* | *Steel* | *Gross National Product†* | *Final Sales of Durable Goods†* |
| *Year* | *(1)* | *(2)* | *(3)* | *(4)* | *(5)* |
| 1953 | 1,252 | 1,395 | 111,610 | 413 | 90 |
| 1954 | 1,461 | 1,311 | 88,312 | 407 | 85 |
| 1955 | 1,566 | 1,467 | 117,036 | 438 | 93 |
| 1956 | 1,679 | 1,580 | 115,216 | 446 | 94 |
| 1957 | 1,648 | 1,617 | 112,715 | 452 | 95 |
| 1958 | 1,566 | 1,447 | 85,255 | 447 | 86 |
| 1959 | 1,954 | 1,222 | 93,446 | 476 | 92 |
| 1960 | 2,014 | 1,675 | 99,282 | 488 | 96 |
| 1961 | 1,904 | 1,679 | 98,014 | 497 | 95 |
| 1962 | 2,118 | 1,772 | 98,328 | 530 | 104 |
| 1963 | 2,313 | 1,727 | 109,261 | 550 | 111 |
| 1964 | 2,553 | 1,794 | 127,076 | 578 | 120 |
| 1965 | 2,755 | 1,849 | 131,185 | 610 | 130 |

* Data from National Industrial Conference Board, *Economic Almanac.*
† Data do not reflect July, 1966 revisions.

Columns (1), (2), and (3) of Table 7–2 show the physical volume of production of the domestic aluminum, copper, and steel industries. Interestingly, volume data are often available for industry aggregates while they may be unavailable for individual companies. The situation is quite the opposite from that of dollar sales. Sources of industry volume statistics may be readily obtained from the *Statistical Abstract of the United States*, together with summary data for selected years. The National Industrial Conference Board and trade journals are other excellent sources of statistics. In addition, one of the several dozen industry subgroups of the Federal Reserve Board Index of Industrial Production may be used. Many of these subindexes are published monthly in the *Federal Reserve Bulletin*, and additional details are contained in monthly releases by the Board, which are kept on file at most business libraries.

(The fact that these are index numbers rather than actual volume data makes no difference for our present purposes.)

Of course, production volume is not synonymous with sales volume—the difference being inventory accumulation or liquidation.[5] However, while the short-term movements of production can differ markedly in amplitude from sales movements, over a period of several years the trends of the two series usually will be quite similar.

If physical volume data are not available from any of the above-indicated sources, an approximation can often be calculated by the analyst. Since dollar sales are equal to volume multiplied by price, it follows that volume equals sales *divided by* price. Thus, if the analyst has a series of dollar sales for his industry, or for the leading companies in the industry, he can try to obtain a statistical series which reflects reasonably accurately the price history of the industry. Then, by dividing each year's dollar sales by the corresponding prices, he can obtain a reasonable estimate of annual volume.[6]

Where can price data for an industry be obtained? Probably the most convenient source is the Bureau of Labor Statistics' Wholesale Price Index (or Consumer Price Index if the industry is one of the relatively few that deal directly with the public). Like the Industrial Production Index, the Wholesale Price Index is broken down into a large number of product group subindexes. These subindexes are published in the *Monthly Labor Review* and similar government periodicals, with greater detail being presented in monthly releases sent to libraries all over the country. Recently, the Bureau of Labor Statistics has been developing improved industry composites of the individual commodity price indexes, and these should prove very helpful in the type of research under discussion.[7]

To illustrate the procedure of approximating volume data—a procedure known as "deflating"—consider the processed foods industry. The companies in this industry produce cans of peas, boxes of corn flakes, packages of bacon, bottles of mayonnaise, containers of milk, and thousands of other items with no common unit denominator. Yet there *is* a wholesale price index component labeled "processed foods." The 1955

---

[5] In the case of metal industries, moreover, production of primary metals can be supplemented with secondary production—i.e., the reprocessing of scrap.

[6] In many instances this indirect measure of volume may, in fact, be more satisfactory than actual unit data because of the possibility of changes in the nature of the unit. For example, a million cars means something quite different when a large percentage are compacts from when most are full size or when they are equipped with air conditioners, power steering, and other expensive accessories. In other words, when the quality of the product-mix changes significantly, unit measures can become obsolete.

[7] For a description see B. R. Moss, "Industry and Sector Price Indexes," *Monthly Labor Review*, August, 1965. The BLS intends to compile price indexes not only of industry sales but also of industry purchases. This will permit both sales and cost of goods sold to be studied in physical volume terms.

value of this index was 94, and in 1964 it was 101 (1957–59 = 100). A representative cross section of companies in this industry, studied by the authors, reported dollar sales of $1.25 billion in 1955 and $1.90 billion in 1964. Dividing these dollar sales figures by the corresponding price indexes we get, respectively, 1.33 and 1.88 "billions of 1957–59 dollars," otherwise referred to as "billions of dollars of constant purchasing power," or simply as "constant dollars" or "real dollars." Regardless of the label attached to the data, they can be used just like any actual physical volume data in measuring growth patterns. The percentage changes are significant, not the terminology employed. Thus, the growth of "current dollar" sales of these companies during the decade was 52% (1.90/1.25), but the growth of "constant dollar" sales—or volume—was only 41% (1.88/1.33).

This method of approximating volume data by deflating "current dollar" data with price indexes is precisely the method employed by the Department of Commerce to convert the national income statistics into "constant dollar" terms. Thus, columns (4) and (5) of Table 7–2 present gross national product and final sales of durable goods in "billions of 1958 dollars." The price indexes used to do the deflating are known as "implicit price indexes" and are published together with the national income data.

*Ratio Analysis of the Data.* Once the relevant sales data have been assembled, they must be put in a form that facilitates interpretation. Some methods of doing this were outlined in an appendix to the preceding chapter. For present purposes it is appropriate to cast the data into ratio form and chart the ratios. Table 7–3 contains the ratios of aluminum

**TABLE 7–3**

**Ratios: Aluminum Sales and Production Relative to Competition**

| | Dollar Sales: Aluminum ÷ | | | | Production: Aluminum (Tons) ÷ | | | |
|---|---|---|---|---|---|---|---|---|
| Year | Copper | Steel | GNP | Final Sales of Durables | Copper (Tons) | Steel (Tons) | GNP (Constant Dollars) | Final Sales of Durables (Constant Dollars) |
| 1953 | 1.234 | 0.146 | 0.0043 | 0.0201 | 0.897 | 0.011 | 3.031 | 13.911 |
| 1954 | 1.328 | .184 | .0044 | .0216 | 1.114 | .017 | 3.590 | 17.188 |
| 1955 | 1.212 | .173 | .0050 | .0238 | 1.067 | .013 | 3.575 | 16.839 |
| 1956 | 1.139 | .173 | .0051 | .0240 | 1.063 | .015 | 3.765 | 17.862 |
| 1957 | 1.510 | .170 | .0049 | .0233 | 1.019 | .015 | 3.646 | 17.347 |
| 1958 | 1.566 | .199 | .0046 | .0238 | 1.082 | .018 | 3.503 | 18.209 |
| 1959 | 1.533 | .200 | .0047 | .0242 | 1.599 | .021 | 4.105 | 21.239 |
| 1960 | 1.448 | .196 | .0044 | .0229 | 1.202 | .020 | 4.127 | 20.979 |
| 1961 | 1.427 | .215 | .0043 | .0232 | 1.134 | .019 | 3.831 | 20.042 |
| 1962 | 1.467 | .220 | .0044 | .0230 | 1.195 | .022 | 3.996 | 20.365 |
| 1963 | 1.450 | .225 | .0044 | .0230 | 1.339 | .021 | 4.205 | 20.838 |
| 1964 | 1.424 | .221 | .0045 | .0232 | 1.423 | .020 | 4.417 | 21.275 |
| 1965 | 1.425 | .233 | .0049 | .0247 | 1.490 | .021 | 4.516 | 21.192 |

industry sales, in dollar and unit terms, to copper and steel sales, and to the broad economic measures[8] which have been discussed. These ratios are all, in turn, presented graphically in Figures 7–2 and 7–3.

FIGURE 7–2

**Dollar Sales of Aluminum Relative to Sales of Competing Industries**

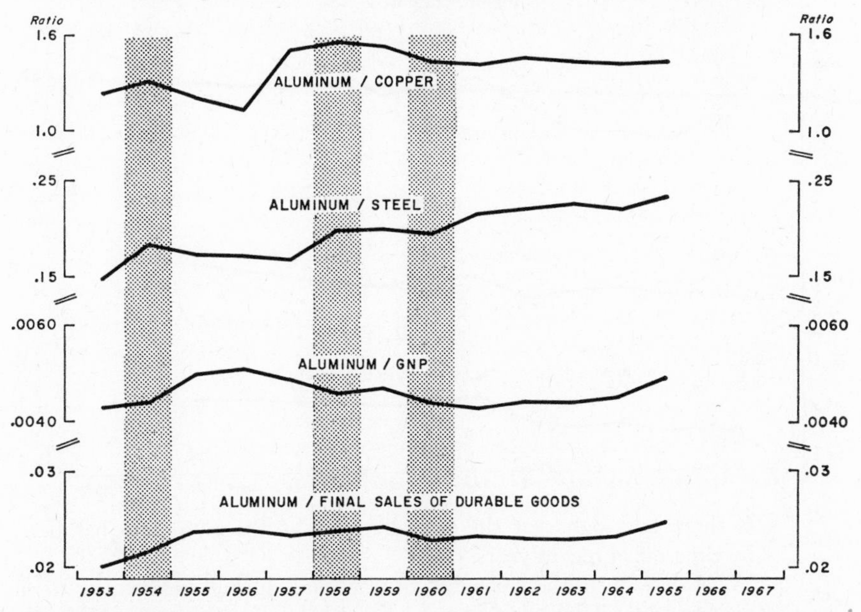


In examining each ratio line, answers should be sought to four questions:

1. Is the numerator of the ratio growing more or less rapidly than the denominator over the whole length of the period—i.e., from initial to terminal years?
2. Has the relative growth (or relative decline) of the numerator been fairly uniform or has it occurred in fits and starts? The less the variability around trend, the more confidence one can have in using the past trend as the starting point of an analysis. Indeed, if the variability is slight it may be possible to use some type of *mechanical* projection technique.[9] (It also will be recalled that sales stability is an important component of the price-earnings ratio "formula" outlined in Chapter 5.)

---

[8] As noted in the Appendix to Chapter 6, two series of data need not be expressed in similar units to make a ratio calculation useful. Tons of one product can be compared with bushels, or quarts, or, as in our example, with "constant dollars." The absolute amounts of the ratios are not significant; the *changes* in the ratios are.

[9] For a discussion of such techniques, see H. D. Wolfe, *Business Forecasting Methods*. (New York: Holt, Rinehart & Winston, Inc., 1966). Also see *Forecasting Sales* (Studies in Business Policy No. 106 [New York: National Industrial Conference Board, 1963]).

FIGURE 7–3

**Production of Aluminum Relative to Production of Competing Industries**

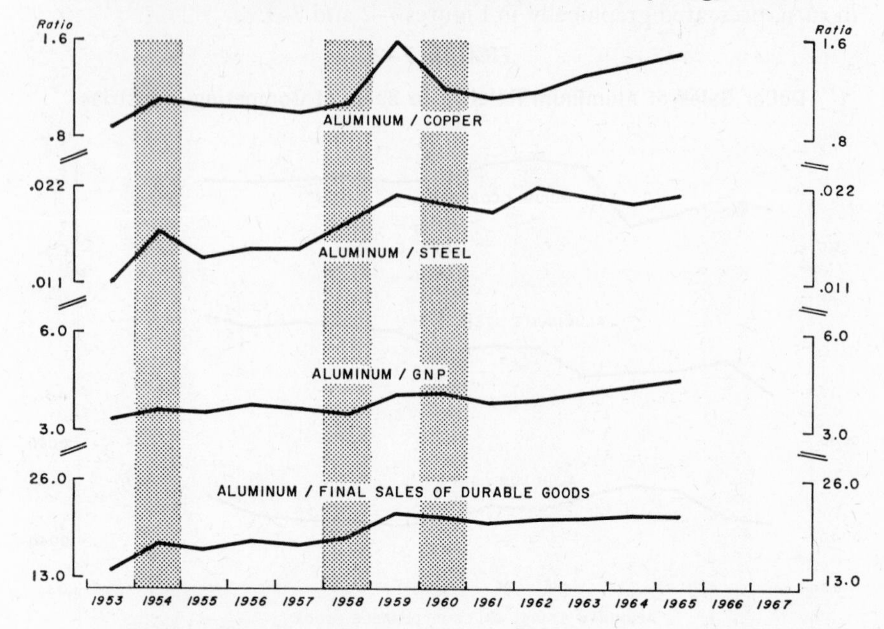


3. Is there any sign that the overall trend of the ratio line has been leveling off in recent years?
4. What has been the behavior of the line during years of general economic recession? Has the numerator been more or less vulnerable to economic adversity than the denominator? To facilitate this comparison it is convenient to shade in the years of recession, as indicated on the charts for the years 1954, 1958, and 1960. (See Chapter 13 for a detailed chronology of modern business cycles.) It is even more helpful to examine the data on a quarterly or monthly basis. Figure 7–4, for example, compares the Federal Reserve Board index of aluminum production with the aggregate industrial production index.

When these questions are applied to the charts at hand, some interesting observations emerge. The physical production of aluminum has risen much more rapidly than either total economic output, total durable goods output, or copper and steel production. This relative growth of aluminum, however, has not proceeded steadily from year to year but has been quite volatile. The industry's performance in recessions also has been erratic but in general shows up fairly well when related to other types of production.

When *dollar* sales of aluminum are compared with sales of other products, aluminum's growth advantage is less pronounced than when physical output alone is considered. In other words, aluminum prices have fallen in relation to other products. Dollar sales of the leading alu-

FIGURE 7–4

**Aluminum Production Compared with Total Industrial Production (Raw Data Smoothed with Centered 12-Month Moving Average)**

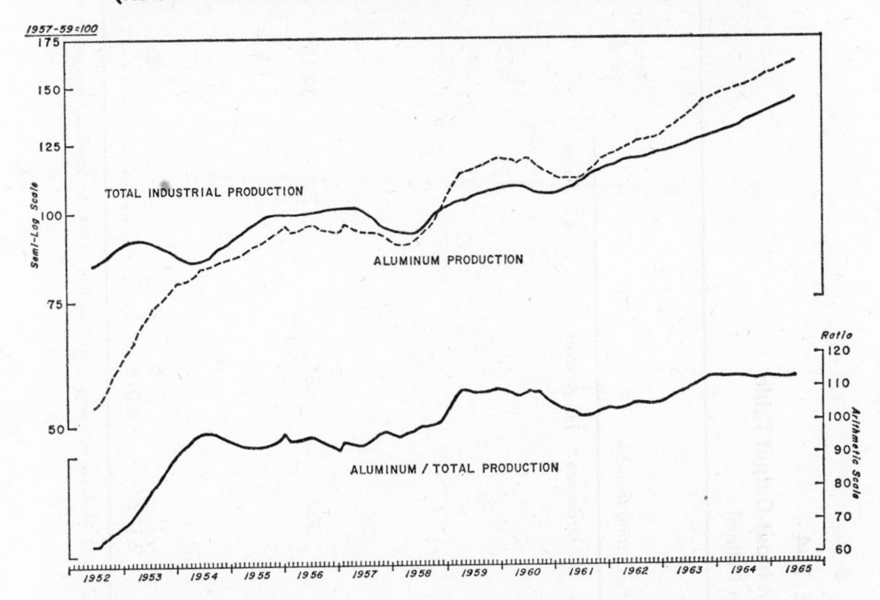


minum companies have grown at about the same rate as gross national product, although at a faster rate than durable goods sales or sales of copper and steel companies.

Having established these basic historical facts about aluminum sales, the next task is to gain insight into the most important *reasons* for their presence. If this can be done, the analyst will be in a much better position to venture an estimate of what the future holds in store. One of the most fruitful ways of approaching such a task is to examine the end uses of the industry's output.

## End-Use Analysis

An industry can grow at an above-average rate in three ways: (1) by supplying a stable share of a rapidly growing end use; (2) by supplying a growing share of an end use having only average growth; and (3) most dynamically, by supplying a growing share of a rapidly growing end use. The study of end uses has been facilitated by the development and improvement of a social accounting system known as input-output analysis. This accounting system, which is still in the process of evolution and expansion, currently divides the economy into over 80 industrial groupings. The sales volume of each of these industries to each of the other industries—several thousand purchase and sale entries—is shown in the input-output tabulations, and an effort is made to tie the whole

**TABLE 7–4**

**Excerpt from a Recent Input-Output Table**

(In Million Dollars)

| *Selling Industry* | *Purchasing Industry* | | | | | | | *Total Sales* | *Final Sales of Industry That Enter GNP Accounts* |
|---|---|---|---|---|---|---|---|---|---|
| | 1. *Leather Products* | 2. . . . . | 9. *Special Machinery* | 10. *Ordnance* | 11. *Aircraft* | . . . . | 81. *Scrap* | | |
| 1. Leather products | 345 | | | | | | 1 | 4,133 | 3,583 |
| 2. | | | | | | | | | |
| 3. | | | | | | | | | |
| . | | | | | | | | | |
| . | | | | | | | | | |
| . | | | | | | | | | |
| . | | | | | | | | | |
| 36. Primary nonferrous Metal Manufacturing | 2 | | 151 | 302 | 481 | | 70 | 12,189 | 786 |
| . | | | | | | | | | |
| . | | | | | | | | | |
| . | | | | | | | | | |
| . | | | | | | | | | |
| . | | | | | | | | | |
| 81. Scrap | | | 5 | | 8 | | | 961 | −758 |
| Value added by purchasing industry | 1,822 | | 1,499 | 2,172 | 8,018 | . . . . . . . . . . . . . . . . . . . . . . . . . . . . | | | 600,000 |

Source: W. W. Leontief, "The Structure of the U.S. Economy," *Scientific American*, April, 1965, pp. 31–32. Reprinted with permission. 

network of data to the gross national product figures. An excerpt from a recent input-output table is presented in Table 7–4.[10]

In a penetrating recent article, a General Electric sales analyst (working without the benefit of detailed official input-output tables) compared the use of the three major metals in each of five types of end product: construction materials; motor vehicles; containers and packaging; other producer durables; and other consumer durables.[11] Figure 7–5 is an updated composite of several of his charts. It shows that high-growth areas for aluminum have been construction, motor vehicles, and packaging. Electrical uses, not shown separately on the chart, have been another very rapid-growth sector. Table 7–5 shows that the first two of these

**TABLE 7–5**

**Estimated Distribution of Aluminum Shipments by End Use, 1960–65 Totals**

| End Use | Shipments (Millions of Pounds) | % of Total Shipments |
|---|---|---|
| Construction | 8,800 | 24 |
| Transportation | 8,300 | 22 |
| Electrical wire, cable, etc. | 4,300 | 12 |
| Household appliances | 4,100 | 11 |
| Packaging | 2,800 | 8 |
| Industrial machinery and equipment | 2,700 | 7 |
| Other uses and exports | 6,000 | 16 |
| Total | 37,000 | 100 |

Source: Aluminum Association, *Annual Statistical Reviews.*

major growth areas also have absorbed the largest absolute quantities of aluminum. (Motor vehicles account for about one half of the transportation sector's use of aluminum.)

Having determined the major end uses which have accounted for aluminum's *past* growth, the next questions are: What are the growth *prospects* of these end-uses? What is the likelihood that the use of aluminum in each of these products will rise?

Figure 7–6 is a scatter diagram of the postwar relationship between

---

[10] For further elaboration of the system see W. Leontief, *Input-Output Economics* (New York: Oxford University Press, Inc., 1966); also M. R. Goldman, M. L. Marimont, and B. N. Vaccara, "The Interindustry Structure of the United States," *Survey of Current Business*, November, 1964. Interesting discussions of the way input-output tables can be utilized by market analysts are contained in J. M. Gould, "Using Input-Output Studies in Sales Forecasting," *Commercial and Financial Chronicle*, May 13, 1965, and D. A. Hodes, "Input-Output Analysis: An Illustrative Example," *Business Economics*, Summer, 1965.

[11] G. W. Marsh, "Forecasting Industry Growth," *Financial Executive*, March, 1964.

## FIGURE 7–5

**Metal Consumption, Classified by End Use**
(Equivalent Steel Weight)

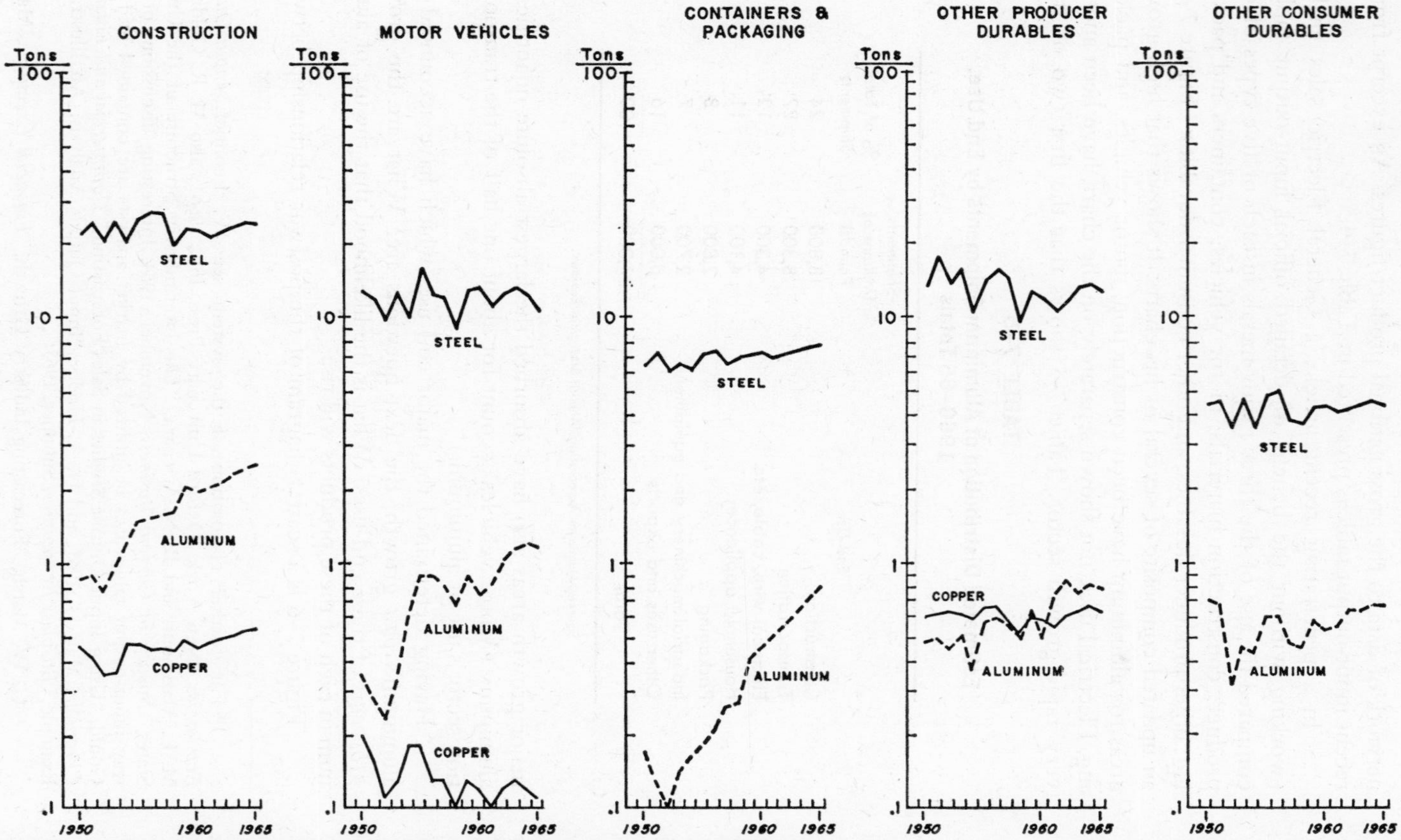

FIGURE 7–6

Construction versus Total Economic Activity

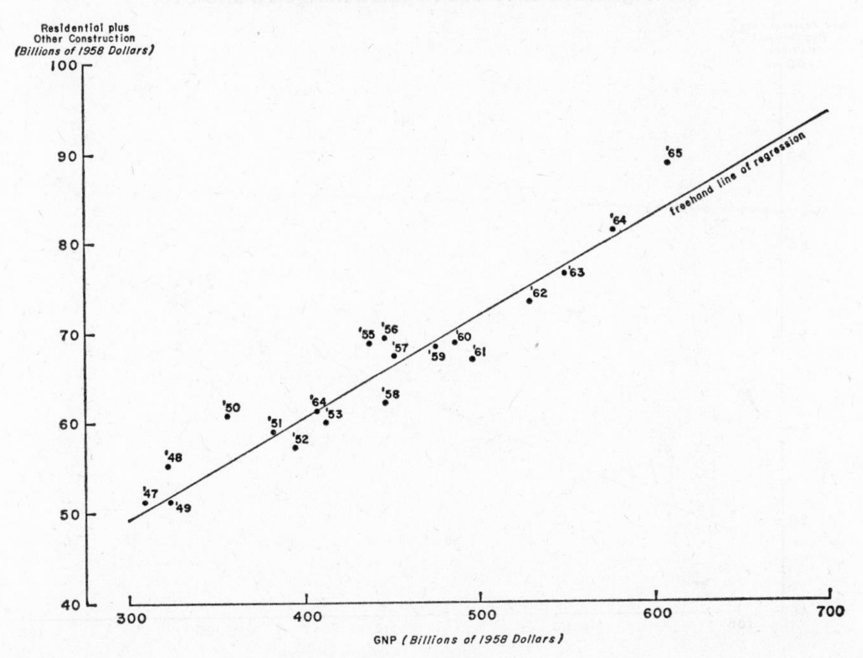


construction (residential, commercial, and industrial) and gross national product, expressing both in constant dollar terms. The line of relationship drawn through the scatter suggests that the growth of total construction has followed rather closely the growth of total economic activity.[12] There are no impelling reasons to expect any dramatic change in this relationship during the years ahead, although prospective increases in household formation should tend to stimulate residential construction.

Figure 7–7 illustrates the relationship of new automobile registrations and the population of auto-driving age. It will be noted that the slope of the relationship was much steeper from 1961 to 1965 than the longer term line of relationship. This reflects the growth of multicar families in an increasingly prosperous and suburbanized United States. There is much debate over the possibilities of a further growth of multicar families, but it can be assumed for present purposes that some further growth will occur for several years longer. The outlook for the growth of truck, trailer, and freight car production also appears somewhat better than average.

Other major growth areas for aluminum have been packaging—particularly cans and foil wrapping—and electrical wire and cable. Most

---

[12] Actually, the slope of the regression line suggests a somewhat slower growth rate of construction than of GNP.

FIGURE 7–7

**Auto Registrations versus Population Age 18 and Over**

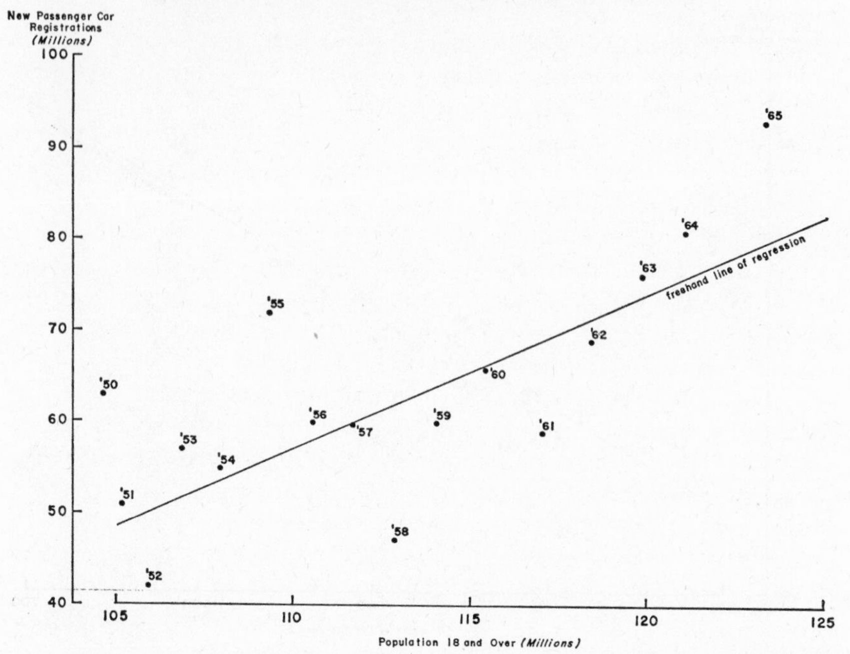


observers are agreed that packaging and electrical transmission will continue to be rapid-growth sectors of the economy, as they have been during the postwar years. Combining packaging, electrical transmission, transportation, and construction, it can be concluded that the past growth markets for aluminum will grow somewhat more rapidly than total economic activity in the foreseeable future. Aluminum's other principal domestic markets—household appliances and machinery—can be assumed to have a combined prospective growth rate about equal to aggregate economic growth.

The potential growth of foreign markets for aluminum is quite high. While per capita consumption of aluminum in the United States is almost 40 pounds annually, it is only half as much in Great Britain, one third as much in France, and one fifth as much in Japan. In most of Africa, and in other underdeveloped areas, per capita consumption of aluminum is negligible. Imaginative managements can tap these markets. For example, in a recent article the head of the Singer Company envisions the growth of "transnational" enterprises—joint ventures of American and foreign companies operating all over the globe.[13]

[13] D. B. Kircher, "Now The Transnational Enterprise," *Harvard Business Review,* March–April, 1964. Also see J. C. Tanner, "Overseas Partners," *The Wall Street Journal,* March 30, 1965, p. 1.

The subject of per capita consumption of aluminum turns us from the question of the growth prospects of aluminum's end uses to the question of the intensity of aluminum's use in those end products. In residential construction, for example, the quantity of aluminum used to build a house has more than tripled during the past decade. Aluminum's corrosion-resistant qualities make it ideal for roofing, siding, windows, doors, and ornamental uses. But most of the obvious applications of the metal have now been exploited. While the use of aluminum in construction probably will continue for many more years to grow more rapidly than the construction industry itself, further increases in the penetration of the construction market by aluminum seem likely to be far less pronounced than in the recent past. It must be admitted, however, that the possibility exists of large-volume aluminum use in prefabricated homes and in aluminum curtain walls in multistory buildings.

The amount of aluminum used in the average American passenger car also has increased sharply during the past decade, the increase being well over 100%. Most of the aluminum used in automobiles has gone into castings for the engine and power train areas, replacing cast iron and steel, which are heavy and costly to machine to close tolerances. But the use of aluminum for these purposes is now widespread, and a decline in the growth rate of aluminum use per car has been evident since 1963. Nevertheless, some significant potentials remain, if aluminum producers can find ways of reducing costs. Areas in which aluminum probably would be technologically superior to steel include the braking system, engine block, and radiator. Differences of opinion exist on the relative merits of aluminum versus stainless steel for external trimming and bumper material.

On balance, it seems safe to assume that aluminum will make further inroads into the automotive market. In the nonautomotive segment of the transportation market, increased use of aluminum for railroad freight cars can be expected. On the other hand, the relative use of aluminum in the aircraft industry has declined in the past decade due to the Defense Department's growing emphasis on missiles, which require much less aluminum than manned fighters and bombers.[14] In other markets for aluminum, further penetration is a distinct possibility in packaging and electrical products. With regard to electrical markets, violent copper price fluctuations in the past decade have encouraged many copper wire and cable users to shift to aluminum.[15]

Yet, further market penetrations by aluminum cannot be taken for granted. While aluminum has obvious advantages over other metals, its competition is not inherently limited to other metals. Since World War

---

[14] The Vietnam conflict caused a temporary surge in aircraft consumption of aluminum.

[15] This also has been true in other traditional copper markets. See C. B. Camp, "Down With Copper," *The Wall Street Journal*, August 24, 1966, p. 1.

II, plastic technology has progressed by leaps and bounds. Plastics are being used for pipes, walls, auto parts, containers, and countless other products formerly made of metals. In the packaging field, aluminum has benefited mightily from the inventiveness of housewives and package designers in finding uses for aluminum foil and thin sheet. But plastic and paper producers have not lacked for inventiveness themselves. Goods are being packaged in plastic film, squeeze bottles, rigid containers, and semi-rigid coated paper containers. In addition, the steel industry itself is counterattacking with such products as "thin tin" and vapor-coated aluminum steel for canneries. And the glass industry is countering with inexpensive throwaway bottles.

In short, steel, copper, aluminum, wood, and glass are not clearly defined materials with clearly defined markets. They must face the competition of substitute materials and of refined versions of the old standbys.[16] Steel has been combined with concrete, and the resulting reinforced concrete is challenging the original challengers of raw steel. Glass is being stretched into fiber form and woven into textile products. Some fiberglass producers have hopes of one day taking over the entire market for automobile tire cord. As one expert has aptly put it: "Until recent years, manufacturers were forced to tailor their products to the properties provided by the relatively few existing materials. But now the desired performance of a structure can be established first and then the materials with the right combination of properties can be obtained."[17]

The competition of substitute products is dramatically illustrated by a recent Department of Commerce study of the growth patterns of 339 different products.[18] During the years 1948–63, 20% of the products grew much more rapidly than general economic activity (7½% per annum or faster); 21% grew at an annual rate of 3½% to 7½%; 34% at a 0%–3½% rate; and 25% declined. The 70 products in the fastest growing group averaged 15% per annum growth. But the newer products in the group grew at a 20% rate versus 10% for the older items. Most of the so-called "new" products were, in fact, substitutes for previously existing items. Practically all of the products in the middle two groups were long-established lines, and a large proportion of the declining products were established items which had been confronted during the period by the competition of substitutes.

Rapid growth rates, moreover, did not prove to be long-lived. For example, during the first nine years of the period (1948–57) 24% of the products were in the fastest growing group. Of these, far less than half

---

[16] Indeed, producers of primary aluminum may have to face increasing competition from scrap reprocessors as the flow of scrapped aluminum products increases.

[17] Cited in "The Battle of the Materials," *Forbes*, March 1, 1964.

[18] F. L. Hirt, "Patterns of Output Growth," *Survey of Current Business*, September, 1964.

remained in the fastest growing group in the next six years (1957–63), and almost one third had fallen into the lowest two categories. Indeed, relatively few products that were "new" in the 1948–57 period, and showed rapid growth at that time, continued to show very high growth rates in the 1957–63 period. Most had either saturated their markets or been confronted with still newer, still better products. In the context of the previous chapter's discussion of the "industrial life cycle," it might be argued that the pioneering and investment maturity stages of industries have been shortened by technological advances.

Analysis of end uses leads to a reasonable basis for estimating the growth in physical volume of aluminum sales during the next 5 to 10 years. The sum total of the markets which use aluminum seems likely to grow at a rate moderately above that of aggregate economic activity. Within these markets, the penetration of aluminum seems likely to grow, but one's confidence in this judgment must be tempered by a recognition of the dramatic changes that are taking place in the materials field.[19] Assuming that "real" gross national product grows at a 3½%–4% per annum rate, as suggested in Chapter 5, a 6% growth rate of sales volume of the major aluminum companies can be used as a working hypothesis. This growth rate would be approximately 1% per annum lower than that of the period since 1953. As for cyclical sensitivity, several of the industry's principal markets—residential construction, packaging, electric utilities—tend to be fairly resistant to recessions. Therefore, aluminum sales volume can be expected to continue its past record of relative resistance to business cycle downturns. (See Chapter 13 for a discussion of techniques of business cycle forecasting.)

### Prices

Earlier in this chapter it was noted that dollar sales comparisons are considerably less favorable to the aluminum industry than physical volume comparisons, because aluminum prices have fallen in relation to other products. Here, two factors have been at work which should be distinguished because they have different implications for the future. One is the natural secular price decline of a growth product; the other is the erratic price movement of an industry whose productive capacity has periodically spurted far ahead of immediate sales potential.

Think of an industry which has been growing rapidly in sales volume for the past 10 or 20 years, and then think of what has happened to its selling prices relative to the general price level. Almost invariably,

[19] In May, 1966, General Electric announced the development of a process for die-casting ferrous metals. If the process could be perfected for large-scale production, it could reduce the cost of steel parts for, say, automobiles below the cost of similar aluminum and zinc parts. At the time of the announcement, an Alcoa official was quoted as saying: "If die-casting of ferrous metals comes about, it would open up all sorts of competitive nightmares." See *Business Week*, May 14, 1966, p. 176.

the selling price of a growing product has shown a secular downtrend—either in absolute terms or at least relative to other prices. Aluminum is one example; nylon, the miracle drugs, television, transistors, and air transport are others.

Where the basic demand for a product is strong, managements try to tap and expand the market by reducing cost and improving quality. Productivity gains are used, in part, to lower selling prices. On the other hand, in nongrowth industries, like steel and railroad passenger transport, selling prices tend to be raised whenever possible, instead of lowered to broaden markets. When prices do get cut in nongrowth industries, it usually takes the form of price warfare rather than secular price reduction. Price warfare refers to intraindustry price cutting in an attempt to capture a larger share of a relatively fixed market. But secular price reduction is designed to enlarge the total effective demand for a product or service.

Frequently, however, situations are encountered where an industry exhibits the price characteristics of a stagnant market and yet demand for the industry's product is, in fact, growing at an above-average rate. Typically, the cause of this peculiar behavior is excess capacity. Although demand for the product is rising, productive capacity may be rising much more rapidly.[20] As a result, the companies in the industry engage in extremely vigorous price competition in order to build up their sales relative to capacity. Then, when a better sales-capacity balance is achieved, they attempt to restore their previous prices. Perhaps as good an example as any of this pattern has been the aluminum industry in recent years.

Figure 7–8 illustrates the overcapacity of primary aluminum ingot which plagued the industry from 1957 to 1963, and its depressing impact on price. Moreover, in the fabricating end of the aluminum business (the major aluminum companies fabricate the bulk of their ingot output into finished or semifinished products), the overcapacity problem was even more severe. By 1964–65 (not shown on the chart), the industry once again was operating at or near ingot capacity, and at a fairly high level of fabricating capacity, and many analysts were predicting confidently the return of a stable price structure. That is, they envisioned that aluminum prices probably would decline secularly relative to other prices, in line with the industry's expansion of markets, but without the cyclical price warfare which recently has characterized the industry.

This type of forecast may well be too sanguine, however. It is true that aluminum producers have recently exhibited great moderation in their plant expansion programs, emphasizing improvements in existing

---

[20] Capacity can rise sharply not only through the deliberate construction of new facilities but also through the chance discovery of new sources and through the development of major new productive processes which substantially increase output per dollar of cost.

FIGURE 7–8

Capacity Utilization versus Price: Aluminum Industry

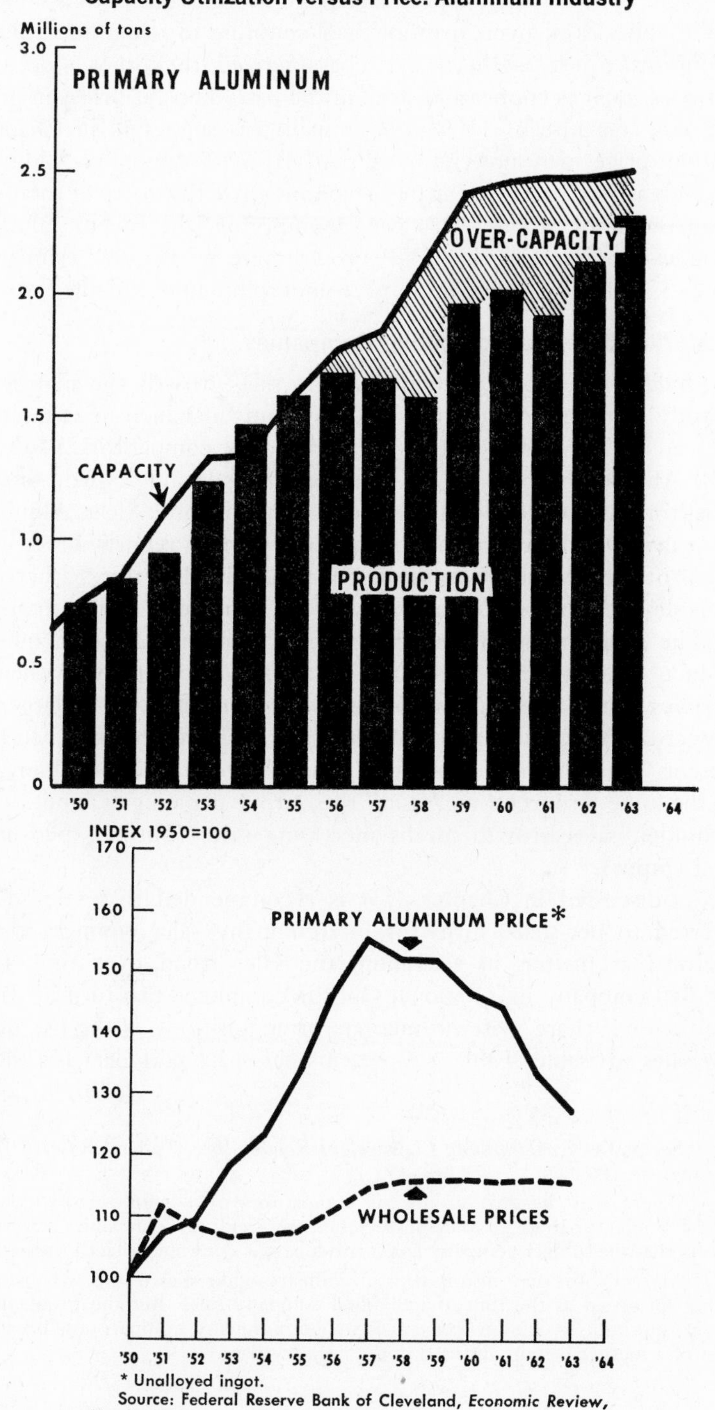


* Unalloyed ingot.

Source: Federal Reserve Bank of Cleveland, *Economic Review*, March, 1964.

facilities rather than placing huge blocks of new capacity on the market all at once.[21] But it would appear safer, and more realistic, to assume that periodic episodes of overexpansion will continue to occur in the aluminum industry, just as they have characterized the other older metal "industries, such as copper and steel, in the past. Thus, if prices in general are to rise at a rate of 1½%–2% annually, as suggested in Chapter 5, aluminum prices may not rise more than ½%–1% annually. Adding this price increase to the 6% estimate of volume growth produces total dollar sales growth of about 7% per annum for the major aluminum companies—better than the GNP growth rate of 5%–6% estimated in Chapter 5, and with a more impressive underpinning of volume growth.

### Market Share of Competing Companies

Once an estimate is made of industry sales growth, the analyst turns to a study of the sales growth of the company in which he is interested, compared with the sales pattern of its principal competitors.[22] Sales data for the Aluminum Company of America and its leading North American competitors—Reynolds Metals, Kaiser Aluminum, and Alcan Aluminium, Ltd.—can be gathered readily from their annual reports or from the manuals of the investment services. But while the data thus gathered will be reliable, they may not be appropriate for comparative growth analysis.

The problem that frequently arises is that mergers or acquisitions introduce discontinuities into sales totals for a company. When two companies merge, the sales of the surviving company will be larger than they were before the merger. But this sales increase does not necessarily represent "growth" in a meaningful sense. "Growth" means doing more with the same resources; increasing the output per unit of input. To the shareholder, sales growth means increasing sales (output) per unit of capital (input).[23]

As discussed in Chapter 4, it is recommended that sales data be converted to per-share form for intercompany sales comparisons (and also, for that matter, in examining the sales trend over time for an individual company in isolation). Only if complete "pro forma" data are available, or if there were no mergers or acquisitions, is the use of total dollar sales advisable. Table 7–6 presents per-share sales data for the four

---

[21] See Y. Levy, *Aluminum: Lightweight Rebounding* (Federal Reserve Bank of San Francisco, 1966).

[22] There may be two groups of competitors: (1) companies which make products similar to those of the subject company, and (2) companies which make products that the subject company *could* produce but does not in fact produce.

[23] Mergers also may distort data on industry-wide sales trends, when industry sales are measured as the sum of individual company sales. But the problem is less acute in interindustry comparisons than in intercompany comparisons, because the impact of a merger is more diffused in the industry data.

TABLE 7–6

**Sales per Share—Four Major Aluminum Companies**

| Year | Alcan Aluminium Ltd. | Aluminum Co. of America | Kaiser Aluminum & Chemical | Reynolds Metals |
|---|---|---|---|---|
| 1953 | 12.75 | 35.94 | 19.96 | 18.94 |
| 1954 | 12.51 | 35.22 | 19.30 | 20.00 |
| 1955 | 13.78 | 41.46 | 22.50 | 25.03 |
| 1956 | 16.74 | 42.06 | 23.38 | 26.35 |
| 1957 | 15.28 | 42.19 | 26.64 | 26.62 |
| 1958 | 14.41 | 36.48 | 27.79 | 26.55 |
| 1959 | 15.49 | 40.81 | 29.01 | 28.86 |
| 1960 | 16.71 | 40.41 | 27.08 | 25.75 |
| 1961 | 16.17 | 39.99 | 27.75 | 28.96 |
| 1962 | 16.88 | 43.93 | 29.07 | 32.53 |
| 1963 | 19.97 | 45.45 | 28.58 | 34.25 |
| 1964 | 21.82 | 48.42 | 33.12 | 37.53 |
| 1965 | 26.63 | 54.41 | 36.96 | 44.50 |

major aluminum companies. The data are fully adjusted for all stock splits and stock dividends.[24]

Generally speaking, there is little point in gathering physical volume data when comparing different companies in the same industry. This is because their price movements usually will be quite similar. Of course, where the *product mix* varies considerably from company to company, even though they are in the same "industry," it would be quite informative to have comparative volume data. But companies that handle a broad product line usually do not publish volume data, and rarely can the analyst obtain price indexes that adequately enough reflect the differences in product mix to permit a meaningful approximation of the different companies' volumes.[25] Obviously, if the same price index is used for each company, the deflated figures will bear the same relationship to each other as the actual dollar amounts.

Table 7–7 relates per-share sales of Alcoa to the sales of the other three companies. These ratios are presented graphically in Figure 7–9.

The chart reveals that Alcoa's sales per share have declined markedly relative to the sales of the three other major aluminum producers. To some extent this is merely a reflection of the fact that Alcoa was a giant when the others were just being born In this light, a decline in Alcoa's

[24] Some analysts supplement sales per-share data with sales per dollar of *total capital,* thus washing out the influence of changing debt-equity ratios in the capital structure.

[25] A prominent exception is General Electric, which publishes a composite price index for its products in each annual report.

TABLE 7–7

**Ratios: Alcoa's Sales per Share to Competition**

| Year | Alcoa/Alcan | Alcoa/Kaiser | Alcoa/Reynolds |
|---|---|---|---|
| 1953 | 2.8 | 1.8 | 1.9 |
| 1954 | 2.8 | 1.8 | 1.8 |
| 1955 | 3.0 | 1.8 | 1.7 |
| 1956 | 2.5 | 1.8 | 1.6 |
| 1957 | 2.8 | 1.6 | 1.6 |
| 1958 | 2.5 | 1.3 | 1.4 |
| 1959 | 2.6 | 1.4 | 1.4 |
| 1960 | 2.4 | 1.5 | 1.6 |
| 1961 | 2.5 | 1.4 | 1.4 |
| 1962 | 2.6 | 1.5 | 1.4 |
| 1963 | 2.3 | 1.6 | 1.3 |
| 1964 | 2.2 | 1.5 | 1.3 |
| 1965 | 2.0 | 1.5 | 1.2 |

market share was inevitable. But there also has been some evidence over the years of a lack of competitive vigor on the company's part.[26]

Since the general subject of marketing philosophy and strategy is discussed in detail in Chapter 9 (although not with specific reference to

FIGURE 7–9

**Alcoa's Sales per Share Relative to Sales of Other Aluminum Companies**

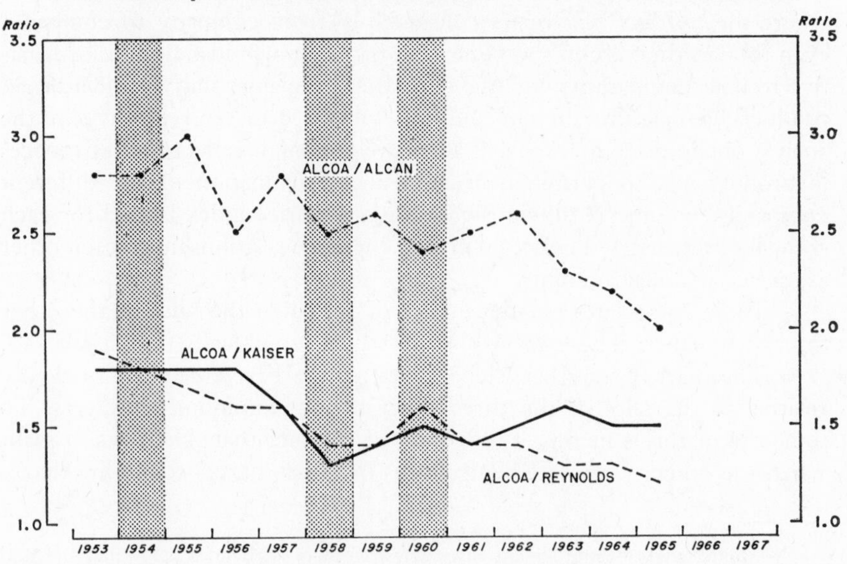


[26] One possible reason for the company's lack of aggressiveness may have been a fear of antitrust litigation, since the company has had several serious encounters with the government on this subject.

Alcoa), we will not elaborate here. It may be noted, however, that Alcoa's marketing policies recently have become more aggressive. Furthermore, the company has done a much more extensive job of "vertical integration" than its competitors. Alcoa presently fabricates about 85% of its ingot production, considerably higher than most of its competitors. Although a weak price structure has prevented this fabricating capacity from being profitable per se, this capacity will aid the company in its fight to maintain and expand its market share, and it provides the basis for the profitable production of primary ingot. Thus, there would appear to be a fairly good chance that the erosion of Alcoa's market share is at or is nearing an end. It seems reasonable to assume for the company the same 7% growth rate of dollar sales that has been assumed for the entire aluminum industry.

## SUGGESTED READINGS

Clopper Almon, Jr., *The American Economy to 1975.* New York: Harper & Row, Publishers, 1966.

Howard B. Bonham, Jr. "Input-Output in Common Stock Analysis," *Financial Analysts Journal,* January–February, 1967.

William F. Butler and Robert A. Kavesh (eds.). *How Business Economists Forecast.* New York: Prentice-Hall, Inc., 1966.

James E. Fanning. "How to Improve Investment Decisions," *Harvard Business Review,*" January–February, 1966.

Morris R. Goldman *et al.* "The Interindustry Structure of the United States," *Survey of Current Business,* November, 1964.

Hans H. Landsberg *et al. Resources in America's Future.* Baltimore: Johns Hopkins Press, 1963.

National Industrial Conference Board. *Forecasting Sales.* Studies in Business Policy, No. 106. New York, 1963.

Harry D. Wolfe. *Business Forecasting Methods.* New York: Holt, Rinehart & Winston, Inc., 1966.

8

# ANALYSIS OF GROWTH—III: EARNINGS GROWTH

Shallow men believe in luck, wise and strong men in cause and effect.

—RALPH WALDO EMERSON

SINCE stock values ultimately are dependent upon prospective earnings and dividends, the analysis of sales growth is merely the starting point of a broader investigation. Some analysts do not go very much further than this starting point, however. After making an estimate of a company's sales growth, they examine the record of profit margins—i.e., net profits as a percentage of sales. If the record suggests that profit margins will hold steady, they estimate earnings growth at the same rate as sales growth. If profit margins are weakening or strengthening, they project a slower or more rapid growth rate of profits than of sales.

This approach to the analysis of earnings growth is too simplistic. It fails to recognize the interdependence of sales and earnings over extended periods of time. For example, if earnings do not grow at a rate considered satisfactory by the stockholders and the management, there will be a diminished incentive to expand the company's productive facilities in its traditional lines. And if these facilities are not expanded, sales growth itself will be restrained. On the other hand, if profits seem likely to grow at a much more rapid rate than projected sales, one of two consequences may result. The high growth of earnings may spur the company to make even greater efforts to broaden the market for its products or to capture a larger share of the existing market. Alternatively, the high growth of earnings may encourage a larger number of competitors to enter the field. In either case, both sales growth and profit growth projections may have to be revised.

In a very real sense, therefore, a sales projection for a company, such as that made for Alcoa in the previous chapter, should be considered a *potential* rather than a *forecast*. It is a potential that will be realized only if it is possible to foresee a balanced relationship between sales growth and earnings growth. Likewise, a projection of earnings growth in isolation from a consistent projection of sales growth could not be accepted with much confidence.

## Earnings Growth Record of Aluminum Companies

Tables 8–1 to 8–3 illustrate the growth, since 1953, of aluminum company earnings from several points of view. First, the net income of the four major aluminum companies combined is compared with the net income of all 425 companies in the Standard & Poor's Industrial Stock Price Index. Second, a comparison is made of the aluminum companies and the 425 industrials in terms of "pretax cash flow"—i.e., net income before deducting depreciation and income taxes. Finally, each of the four companies is compared with its competitors. (In this discussion, and that which follows, references to net income should be taken to mean income "available to common stockholders"—i.e., after deducting preferred dividends, if any. For simplicity of exposition, income is taken essentially as reported by the companies, with adjustments only for obvious nonrecurring items. In practice, of course, more sophisticated adjustments may have to be made.[1])

**TABLE 8–1**

**Earnings per Index Share—**
**S & P Aluminum Group versus 425 Industrial Composite**

| | *Earnings per Index Share* | | |
|---|---|---|---|
| *Year* | *Four Aluminum Companies* | *425 Industrials* | *Ratio: Aluminums/ Industrials* |
| 1953 | 4.34 | 2.57 | 1.69 |
| 1954 | 4.31 | 2.69 | 1.60 |
| 1955 | 6.06 | 3.58 | 1.69 |
| 1956 | 6.64 | 3.50 | 1.90 |
| 1957 | 5.17 | 3.53 | 1.46 |
| 1958 | 3.63 | 2.95 | 1.23 |
| 1959 | 3.99 | 3.47 | 1.15 |
| 1960 | 3.36 | 3.40 | 0.99 |
| 1961 | 3.21 | 3.37 | 0.95 |
| 1962 | 4.01 | 3.83 | 1.05 |
| 1963 | 3.47 | 4.24 | 0.82 |
| 1964 | 4.59 | 4.85 | 0.95 |
| 1965 | 6.06 | 5.50 | 1.10 |

Source: Standard & Poor's Corp., *Analysts Handbook*, 1966 edition.

[1] In general, Alcoa's accounting policies have been more conservative than those of its competitors—for example, with regard to inventory, depreciation, and pension accounting.

## TABLE 8–2

### "Pretax Cash Flow" per Index Share*— S & P Aluminum Group versus 425 Industrial Composite

| Year | Pretax Cash Flow per Index Share: Four Aluminum Companies | Pretax Cash Flow per Index Share: 425 Industrials | Ratio: Aluminums/ Industrials |
|---|---|---|---|
| 1953 | 11.61 | 7.05 | 1.65 |
| 1954 | 11.53 | 6.64 | 1.74 |
| 1955 | 15.54 | 8.73 | 1.78 |
| 1956 | 16.85 | 8.50 | 1.98 |
| 1957 | 14.00 | 8.81 | 1.59 |
| 1958 | 11.56 | 7.73 | 1.50 |
| 1959 | 12.76 | 8.93 | 1.43 |
| 1960 | 11.27 | 8.83 | 1.28 |
| 1961 | 11.40 | 8.83 | 1.29 |
| 1962 | 12.52 | 9.88 | 1.27 |
| 1963 | 11.87 | 11.15 | 1.06 |
| 1964 | 14.05 | 11.79 | 1.19 |
| 1965 | 17.00 | 13.16 | 1.29 |

* Net income plus depreciation plus Federal income taxes.
Source: Standard & Poor's Corp., *Analysts Handbook*, 1966 edition.

Figure 8–1 shows that the aluminum industry's reported earnings compared favorably with the earnings of all industrial corporations through 1956, but deteriorated thereafter until 1963, when relative earnings again began to rise. Aluminum company earnings have exhibited considerable year-to-year volatility and have tended to decline more sharply than aggregate industrial corporate earnings during periods of general economic recession.

## TABLE 8–3

### Comparison of Earnings per Share of Four Major Aluminum Companies

| | Earnings per Share | | | | Index of Earnings per Share (1953-100) | | | |
|---|---|---|---|---|---|---|---|---|
| Year | Alcan | Alcoa | Kaiser | Reynolds | Alcan | Alcoa | Kaiser | Reynolds |
| 1953 | 1.45 | 2.95 | 1.12 | 1.20 | 100 | 100 | 100 | 100 |
| 1954 | 1.34 | 2.95 | 1.95 | 1.32 | 92 | 100 | 174 | 110 |
| 1955 | 1.61 | 4.18 | 2.69 | 2.23 | 111 | 142 | 240 | 186 |
| 1956 | 1.93 | 4.24 | 2.39 | 2.57 | 133 | 144 | 213 | 214 |
| 1957 | 1.39 | 3.55 | 1.54 | 2.14 | 96 | 120 | 137 | 178 |
| 1958 | 0.76 | 1.96 | 1.43 | 2.24 | 52 | 66 | 128 | 187 |
| 1959 | 0.83 | 2.52 | 1.17 | 2.39 | 57 | 85 | 104 | 199 |
| 1960 | 1.28 | 1.76 | 1.20 | 1.26 | 88 | 60 | 107 | 105 |
| 1961 | 0.96 | 1.90 | 1.27 | 1.26 | 66 | 64 | 113 | 105 |
| 1962 | 1.14 | 2.53 | 1.74 | 1.35 | 79 | 86 | 155 | 112 |
| 1963 | 0.94 | 2.27 | 1.23 | 1.42 | 65 | 77 | 110 | 118 |
| 1964 | 1.42 | 2.72 | 1.55 | 1.96 | 98 | 92 | 138 | 163 |
| 1965 | 1.79 | 3.41 | 2.10 | 2.92 | 123 | 116 | 187 | 243 |

When depreciation and income taxes are added back to reported earnings, as in Figure 8–2, the same overall trends appear as when reported earnings alone are considered. However, the relative downtrend of the aluminum industry is somewhat less pronounced, suggesting that depreciation has taken a bigger bite out of aluminum company earnings than out of aggregate corporate earnings. To a large extent this is attributable to accelerated depreciation of heavy capital investments made during the Korean War.

FIGURE 8–1

**Earnings per Index Share—S & P Aluminum Group versus 425 Industrial Composite**

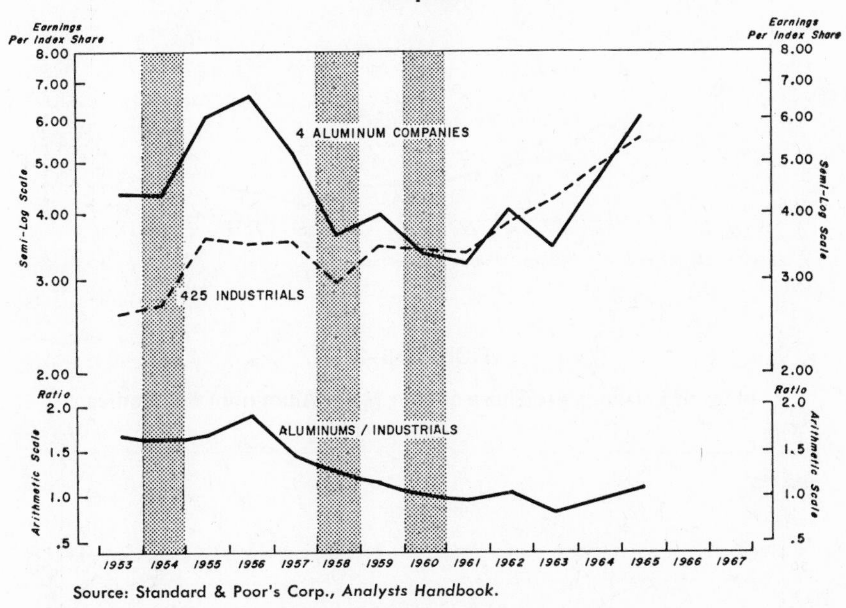


Source: Standard & Poor's Corp., *Analysts Handbook.*

Figure 8–3 reveals very substantial variations in the earnings trends of different aluminum companies. For example, over the entire period, Reynolds Metals turned in the best performance of the four companies. In the early 1960's, however, Reynolds showed the poorest results. Alcoa and Alcan have exhibited fairly parallel earnings trends, while Kaiser Aluminum's earnings have been the most volatile of the group.

An overview of aluminum company earnings thus casts the industry in a less favorable light than did the overview of aluminum sales in the previous chapter. To understand the forces at work, it is helpful to break down the past earnings growth record into several key component parts. It is the objective of the balance of this chapter to illustrate the analysis of earnings by component parts.

FIGURE 8–2

"Pretax Cash Flow" per Index Share—S & P Aluminum Group versus 425 Industrial Composite

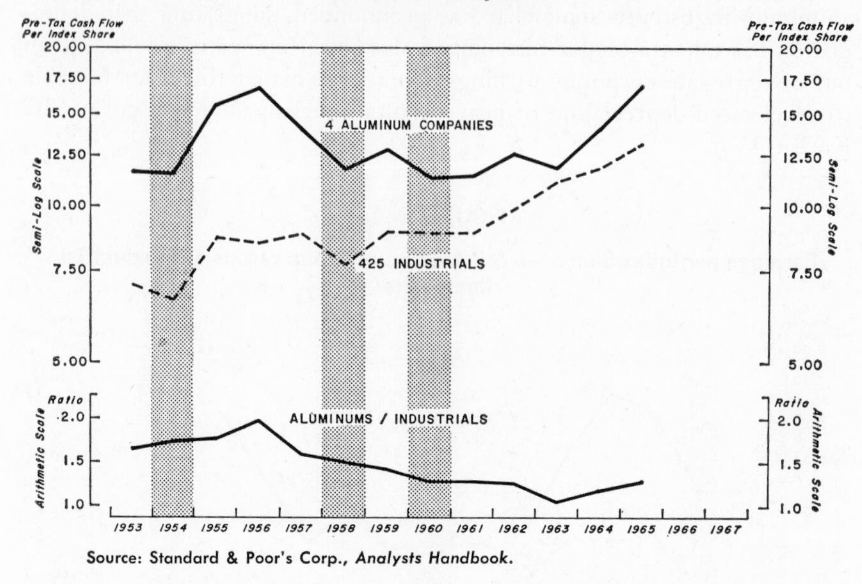


Source: Standard & Poor's Corp., *Analysts Handbook.*

FIGURE 8–3

Index of Earnings per Share of Four Major Aluminum Companies

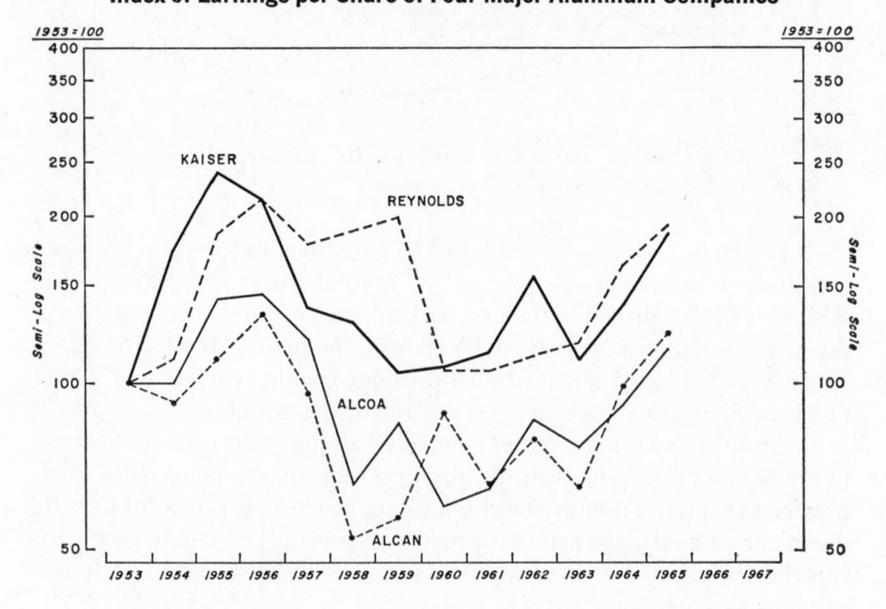

## The Sources of Earnings Growth

Net income per share of common stock is equal to the rate of return on stockholders' equity multiplied by the per share value of stockholders' equity. This can be shown algebraically, as follows:

$$\text{Net income per share} = \frac{\text{Net income}}{\text{Stockholders' equity}} \times \frac{\text{Stockholders' equity}}{\text{Number of common shares}}$$

Note that stockholders' equity appears in the denominator of one fraction and in the numerator of the other, thus canceling out and leaving Net income/Number of common shares, or net income per share. Stockholders' equity, also referred to as book value, equals the balance sheet value of common stock plus surplus items. Alternatively, it can be defined as total assets minus liabilities and preferred stock.[2]

It follows from this relationship that *growth* of net income per share can stem from either an increase in stockholders' equity per share, or from an increase in return on stockholders' equity,[3] or from some combination of the two. (Actually, a sufficient increase in one can offset a reduction in the other.)

Growth of stockholders' equity per share has two principal sources. First, and foremost, is the plowback of earnings into the business—i.e., paying out only a portion of net income in cash dividends to common stockholders and retaining and reinvesting the balance. The contribution of earnings retention to growth of net income per share can be illustrated by a numerical example. Assume that a company is earning 10% on stockholders' equity—that is, $1 of net income per common share for every $10 of stockholders' equity per share. And assume, further, that the company has a dividend payout ratio of 60%—that is, it pays dividends of $0.60 per share for every $1 of available earnings. Its "retention rate," then, is 40%—$0.40 plowed back into the business out of every $1 earned.

Now, if the company continues to earn 10% on the old capital and, in addition, is able to put the new, plowed-back funds to work at a 10%

---

[2] If any intangible assets appear on the balance sheet, they usually are deducted from stockholders' equity.

[3] We wish to make it clear at the outset of this discussion that by defining "rate of return" simply as each year's net income divided by the same year's capital investment we are not using the term in its modern capital budgeting theory context. In modern capital theory, which we accept as valid, "rate of return" refers to the discount rate that equates all future cash flows from an investment with the original cost of the investment. Our only reason for not defining rate of return in this way is that the *external* analyst rarely, if ever, has available the information necessary to make the calculation.

return, its earnings per share will grow by 4%. This may be shown as follows:

10% × $10.00 previous stockholders' equity per share ("old capital")
= $1.00 earned per share
Plus 10% × $0.40 retained earnings per share ("new capital")
= 0.04 earned per share
Equals new level of earnings............................$1.04 earned per share
Growth rate of earnings per share = 1.04/1.00 = 4%

It should be noted that the 4% growth rate is equal to the rate of return on stockholders' equity (10%) multiplied by the retention rate (40%). That is, 40% × 10% = 4%. This algebraic function is of great significance in security analysis.

In the preceding illustration it was assumed that the growth of stockholders' equity per share came from earnings retention. But stockholders' equity per share also can grow in another way—by the company selling additional shares of common stock at a price per share which is higher than the existing book value per share. For example, if book value is $100 million and 10 million shares are outstanding, book value per share is $10. If 1 million additional shares are sold at 2 times book value, or $20 a share, total book value rises to $120 million and total shares outstanding to 11 million. Book value per share thus is raised to 120/11, or $10.91 per share. This provides a basis for growth in earnings per share if the rate of return on stockholders' equity can be maintained.

Sale of common stock at a "premium over book value" is an important source of growth for public utility companies.[4] These companies typically pay out in dividends a relatively high proportion of each year's earnings—about ⅔ payout and ⅓ retention, compared with about 55% and 45%, respectively, for large industrial corporations—and raise additional common equity by selling new stock. Most industrial corporations, however, do relatively little new common stock financing, so that earnings retention is the major source of growth of stockholders' equity per share.[5]

---

[4] One writer has demonstrated that when the premium over book value is high enough, sale of new common stock can raise per-share earnings even more than the introduction of leverage. See L. K. Richardson, "Misconceptions About Earnings Dilution in Electric Utility Analysis," *Financial Analysts Journal*, September–October, 1964. A critique of this deemphasis of leverage will be found in W. T. Hyde, Jr., "Are Utilities Financing Too Extravagantly?" (mimeographed, F. S. Smithers & Co., December 3, 1964.)

[5] In recent years, much of the common stock financing which has been done by industrial corporations has been done indirectly, through the medium of convertible debentures. Such financing initially has its impact on earnings growth through the leverage influence on return on equity—to be discussed below—rather than through

To summarize, growth of net income per common share can be looked upon as stemming from two sources: growth of stockholders' equity per share and/or improvement in the rate of return on stockholders' equity. Since the former source of growth is primarily a reflection of earnings retention, it may be stated as a generalization that the growth rate of earnings per share is a function of the product of the rate of return on stockholders' equity multiplied by the retention rate. Algebraically, this can be expressed as:

$$\frac{\text{Net income}}{\text{Stockholders' equity}} \times \frac{\text{Net income} - \text{dividends}}{\text{Net income}}$$

It should be noted that in applying this expression, general practice is to use the average of beginning-of-the-year and end-of-the-year stockholders' equity, to allow for the gradual plowback of earnings during the year and for any new common stock financing that may have been done during the year.[6]

It is instructive to multiply these two growth factors for industrial stocks as a group, using data on the S & P 425 Industrials. The S & P Industrials have earned an average of 11%–12% on stockholders' equity in recent years, and have retained about 45% of earnings (paying out 55%). The product 11%–12% × 45% is equal to an indicated earnings growth rate of 5.0%–5.4%,[7] which is in line with the long-term growth estimate made in Chapter 5 based on a projection of gross national product.

The accompanying table and charts show the rates of return on equity and the retention rates of the four major aluminum companies. Note that:

1. All of the companies have suffered a severe decline in return on equity, especially between 1956 and 1963. During the four years, 1960–63,

---

growth of equity per share. Only in later years, if and when conversion takes place, is equity per share affected, unless some unusual accounting procedures are followed. On the other hand, it should be noted that *mergers* often result in a rise in book value per share of the surviving corporation. This comes about when the acquiring corporation exchanges its shares for those of the acquired corporation and the book value of the acquired shares is greater than the book value of the shares given in exchange. The problem for security analysts is that such increases in book value, while important, cannot be forecasted.

[6] It will be observed that the expression reduces to Retained earnings/Stockholders' equity, which is equivalent to the growth rate of stockholders' equity if no new stock is sold (or if stock is sold at a price equal to prevailing book value). In other words, if no new stock is sold, and if there are no accounting adjustments made to book value of equity, growth rate of earnings per share and growth rate of book value per share will be equal. In actuality, of course, the two growth rates rarely are identical. Mergers are one important source of adjustments in book value (see footnote 5 on preceding page).

[7] 11% × 45% = 4.95%; 12% × 45% = 5.40%.

return on equity averaged a substandard 7% compared with an average of 19% during the years 1953 through 1956. Alcan's decline was least severe, not because its rate of return held up but rather because it began at a substantially lower level (14%) than its competitors. Alcoa's rate of return dropped from an average of 17% in 1953–56 to an average of 6% in 1960–63 and 8% in 1964–65.

2. Dividend payout policies have differed significantly from company to company. Alcan typically has paid out about half of its earnings and retained half. Alcoa apparently has shifted from a policy of 25%

**TABLE 8–4**
**Return on Equity and Retention Rates of Four Major Aluminum Companies**

| | *Rate of Return on Mean Stockholders' Equity* | | | | *Retention Rate* | | | |
|---|---|---|---|---|---|---|---|---|
| *Year* | *Alcan* | *Alcoa* | *Kaiser* | *Reynolds* | *Alcan* | *Alcoa* | *Kaiser* | *Reynolds* |
| 1953 | 14.3% | 17.4% | 18.4% | 18.5% | 54% | 73% | 61% | 90% |
| 1954 | 12.1 | 15.5 | 27.9 | 17.4 | 50 | 73 | 74 | 86 |
| 1955 | 14.2 | 18.9 | 28.3 | 24.3 | 55 | 77 | 71 | 87 |
| 1956 | 14.6 | 16.8 | 21.5 | 22.9 | 59 | 72 | 64 | 83 |
| 1957 | 9.9 | 12.7 | 13.0 | 16.3 | 37 | 66 | 42 | 80 |
| 1958 | 5.3 | 6.6 | 11.5 | 13.9 | 01 | 39 | 37 | 81 |
| 1959 | 5.6 | 8.3 | 9.3 | 13.3 | 34 | 52 | 23 | 80 |
| 1960 | 8.5 | 5.5 | 9.1 | 6.5 | 45 | 32 | 25 | 60 |
| 1961 | 6.6 | 5.8 | 9.3 | 6.1 | 37 | 37 | 29 | 60 |
| 1962 | 8.1 | 7.5 | 12.0 | 6.2 | 47 | 53 | 48 | 63 |
| 1963 | 6.6 | 6.4 | 8.1 | 6.3 | 36 | 47 | 27 | 65 |
| 1964 | 9.4 | 7.5 | 9.9 | 8.3 | 54 | 56 | 42 | 74 |
| 1965 | 11.1 | 8.9 | 12.5 | 11.4 | 54 | 59 | 57 | 75 |

payout–75% retention to a significantly lower rate of retention. Kaiser's pattern has been quite erratic. Reynolds has followed the most aggressive plowback policy of the four companies. In no year during the past decade have its dividends exceeded 40% of earnings, and its average payout has been about 25%.

### Analysis of Return on Equity

Additional insight into the factors underlying a company's record of earnings growth can be gained by examining the components of its rate of return on common stock equity. By examining the trends in each component, the analyst can isolate the principal causes of a decline or rise in return on equity, which gives him a sounder basis for determining whether past rates of return will persist or change during the years ahead.

One way of viewing return on common stock equity (although the reader should understand that it is not the only way) is as the product of the "profit margin" on every dollar of sales multiplied by the "equity turnover," or number of dollars of sales per dollar of stockholders' equity. This can be expressed algebraically as follows:

FIGURE 8–4

Return on Equity—Four Major Aluminum Companies

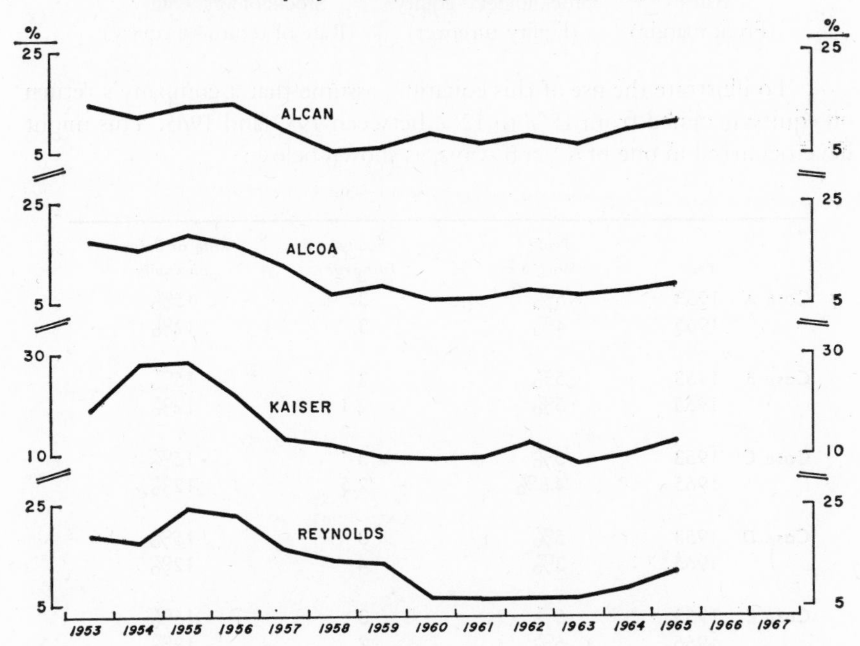


FIGURE 8–5

Retention Rate—Four Major Aluminum Companies

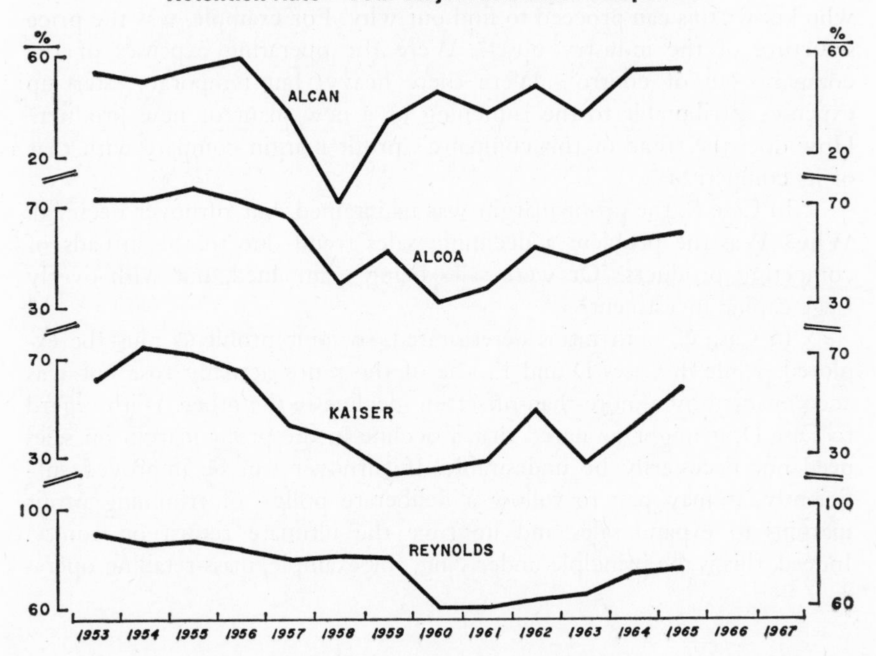

$$\frac{\text{Net income}}{\text{Sales}} \times \frac{\text{Sales}}{\text{Stockholders' equity}} = \frac{\text{Net income}}{\text{Stockholders' equity}}$$

(Profit margin) (Equity turnover) (Rate of return on equity)

To illustrate the use of this equation, assume that a company's return on equity declined from 15% to 12% between 1953 and 1965. This might have occurred in one of several ways, as shown below:

| | Year | *Profit Margin* | × | *Equity Turnover* | = | *Rate of Return on Equity* |
|---|---|---|---|---|---|---|
| **Case A** | 1953 | 5% | | 3 | | 15% |
| | 1965 | 4% | | 3 | | 12% |
| **Case B** | 1953 | 5% | | 3 | | 15% |
| | 1965 | 5% | | 2.4 | | 12% |
| **Case C** | 1953 | 5% | | 3 | | 15% |
| | 1965 | 4.8% | | 2.5 | | 12% |
| **Case D** | 1953 | 5% | | 3 | | 15% |
| | 1965 | 3% | | 4 | | 12% |
| **Case E** | 1953 | 5% | | 3 | | 15% |
| | 1965 | 6% | | 2 | | 12% |

In Case A, the problem was a reduced profit margin, and the analyst who knows this can proceed to find out why. For example, was the price structure of the industry upset? Were the operating expenses of the company out of control? Were there heavy, but temporary, start-up expenses attributable to the launching of a new plant or new product? How does the trend of this company's profit margin compare with that of its competitors?

In Case B, the profit margin was maintained, but turnover declined. Why? Was the problem a declining sales trend due to the inroads of competing products? Or were sales being maintained, but with overly large capital investment?

In Case C, both ratios deteriorated, so joint problems must be explored, while in Cases D and E, one of the ratios actually rose but was accompanied by a more-than-offsetting decline in the other. With regard to Case D, it might be noted that a decline in the profit margin on sales need not necessarily be undesirable. If turnover can be improved sufficiently, it may pay to follow a deliberate policy of trimming profit margins to expand sales and improve the ultimate return on equity. Indeed, this is the principle underlying, for example, mass-retailing operations such as food chains or discount department stores. Of course, in Case D the rise in turnover was not adequate to offset the profit margin decline.

Turning to the aluminum companies again, Table 8–5 and Figures 8–6 and 8–7 provide some interesting insights into the operating trends of the four firms. Alcan's profit margin on sales has declined from an average

**TABLE 8–5**

**Profit Margins and Equity Turnover of Four Major Aluminum Companies**

| | *Net Income/Sales* | | | | *Sales/Mean Stockholders' Equity* | | | |
|---|---|---|---|---|---|---|---|---|
| *Year* | *Alcan* | *Alcoa* | *Kaiser* | *Reynolds* | *Alcan* | *Alcoa* | *Kaiser* | *Reynolds* |
| 1953 | 11.4% | 8.3% | 5.6% | 6.4% | 126% | 212% | 328% | 291% |
| 1954 | 10.7 | 8.4 | 10.1 | 6.6 | 113 | 185 | 276 | 263 |
| 1955 | 11.7 | 10.1 | 12.0 | 8.9 | 121 | 187 | 237 | 273 |
| 1956 | 11.5 | 10.1 | 10.2 | 9.8 | 127 | 167 | 210 | 236 |
| 1957 | 9.1 | 8.4 | 5.9 | 8.1 | 108 | 151 | 225 | 202 |
| 1958 | 5.3 | 5.4 | 5.2 | 8.4 | 100 | 124 | 223 | 165 |
| 1959 | 5.4 | 6.2 | 4.1 | 8.3 | 105 | 134 | 228 | 161 |
| 1960 | 7.7 | 4.3 | 4.4 | 4.9 | 111 | 127 | 206 | 133 |
| 1961 | 5.9 | 4.7 | 4.6 | 4.3 | 111 | 122 | 204 | 139 |
| 1962 | 6.8 | 5.7 | 6.0 | 4.1 | 119 | 130 | 201 | 150 |
| 1963 | 4.7 | 5.0 | 4.3 | 4.1 | 139 | 129 | 189 | 152 |
| 1964 | 6.5 | 5.7 | 4.7 | 5.2 | 145 | 133 | 212 | 158 |
| 1965 | 6.7 | 6.3 | 5.7 | 6.6 | 165 | 142 | 219 | 174 |

of about 11% in 1953–56 to an average of 6% in 1961–65, with equity turnover holding fairly constant until very recently, but at the lowest level of the four companies. Alcoa's margin dropped from about 9% to 5½% over the same period, together with a moderate decrease in turnover. Kaiser's profit margin was cut more sharply than Alcoa's, but its turnover held up somewhat better. Finally, Reynolds Metals was hit by both reduced margins on sales and by the most pronounced decline in turnover.

*Profit Margin.* The usefulness of the profit margin–equity turnover dichotomy can be further enhanced by subdividing each of these two ratios into component parts. For example, net income has three key components—net operating income before taxes, net nonoperating income before taxes and after interest expense, and the effective rate of income tax—each of which is worthy of separate analysis. Thus, the ratio of net income to sales can be viewed as equal to:

$$\left(\frac{\text{Pretax net operating income}}{\text{Sales}} + \frac{\text{Pretax net nonoperating income}}{\text{Sales}}\right) \times \left(1.00 - \frac{\text{Income taxes}}{\text{Net before taxes}}\right)$$

FIGURE 8–6

Profit Margin—Four Major Aluminum Companies

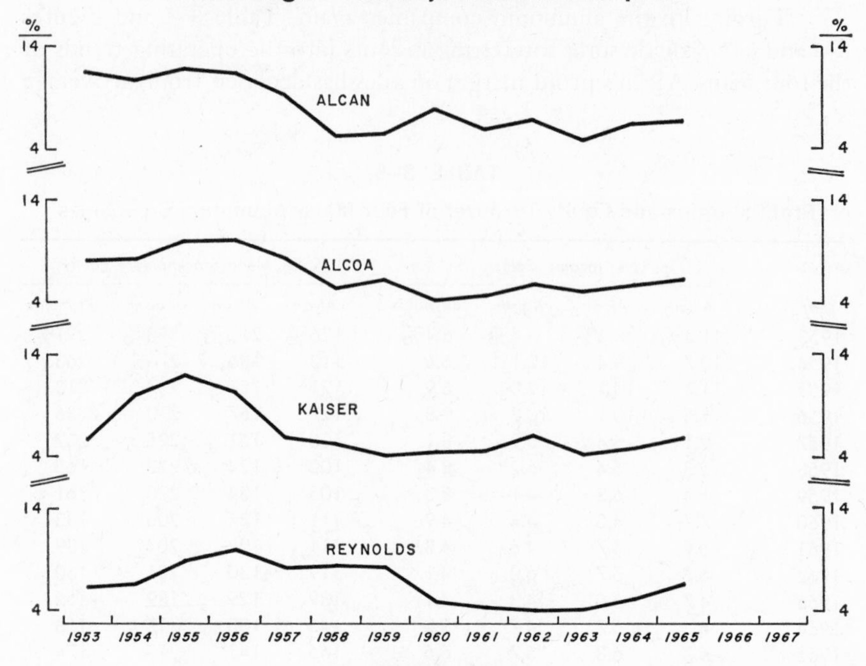


FIGURE 8–7

Equity Turnover—Four Major Aluminum Companies

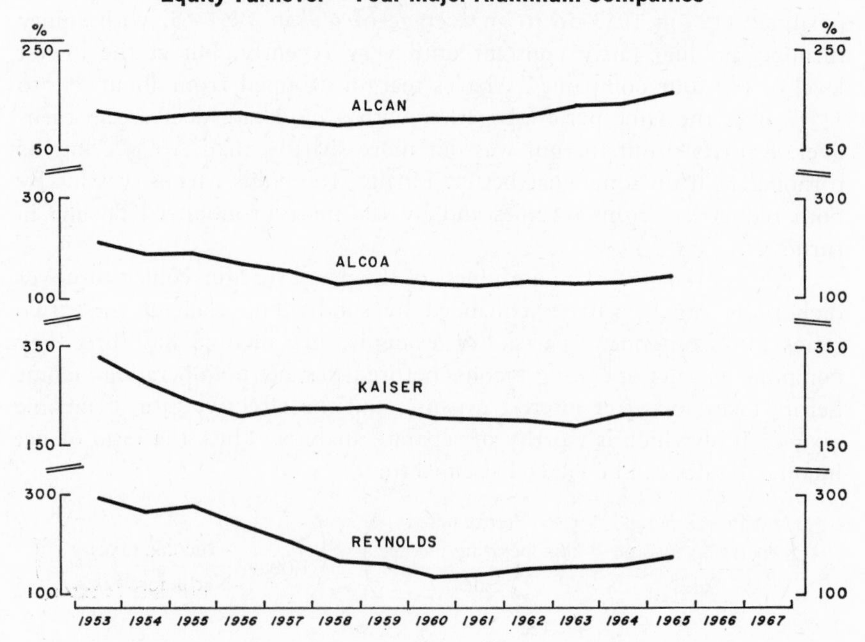

Table 8–6 presents the data for applying this type of profit analysis to the Aluminum Company of America. The table shows clearly that the deterioration of Alcoa's profit margin stems directly from its aluminum operations rather than from any external factors. The ratio of net non-operating income to sales has been steady at the negative amount of about −1½%. That is, fixed charges, preferred stock dividends, and other net nonoperating items[8] have reduced earnings to the extent of about 1½% of sales. Income taxes actually have been a supporting factor for the company, with the effective tax rate declining markedly. Thus, the deterioration of profit margins is due exclusively to a falling ratio of operating income (after depreciation) to sales.

**TABLE 8–6**

**Profit Margin Analysis, Aluminum Company of America**

| *Year* | *Pretax Net Operating Income as Percent of Sales* | *Pretax Net Nonoperating Income* as Percent of Sales* | *Effective Rate of Income Tax* |
|---|---|---|---|
| 1953 | 19.1% | −1.3% | 53% |
| 1954 | 17.9 | −1.4 | 48 |
| 1955 | 21.7 | −1.1 | 50 |
| 1956 | 20.7 | −0.8 | 49 |
| 1957 | 17.6 | −1.3 | 48 |
| 1958 | 11.6 | −2.0 | 42 |
| 1959 | 11.8 | −1.5 | 39 |
| 1960 | 6.4 | −1.2 | 15 |
| 1961 | 8.5 | −1.5 | 31 |
| 1962 | 9.3 | −0.7 | 32 |
| 1963 | 9.3 | −1.0 | 38 |
| 1964 | 10.4 | −1.3 | 37 |
| 1965 | 11.8 | −1.7 | 37 |

* After deducting fixed charges and preferred stock dividends.

Space does not permit a thorough analysis of the causes of the declining ratio of pretax net operating income to sales. Essentially, it reflects a classical "cost-price squeeze." Selling prices of aluminum ingot and fabricated aluminum (sheet, wire, rods, etc.) have been depressed relative to rising costs of labor, distribution, research, and depreciation. It would appear, however, that the squeeze has eased since 1960, and a 13%–14% average ratio of pretax net operating income to sales seems a reasonable expectation for the years ahead. Deducting 1% rather than

[8] Alcoa's principal nonoperating activity in recent years has been in the real estate field. The company has participated in the construction of aluminum-clad high-rise buildings for two reasons: (1) to demonstrate the versatility of aluminum for this purpose, and (2) to hold the properties and eventually realize a profit on their sale. To the company's chagrin, its real estate operation has been a losing proposition of late.

1½% for nonoperating items, on the assumption that the company's real estate endeavors soon will become profitable,[9] and assuming an average effective tax rate of about 40%,[10] produces an estimated profit margin on sales of about 7½%—higher than the 5½% average of 1961–65, but well under the margins of the early and middle 1950's.

*Equity Turnover.* Just as profit margins can be divided into component parts to improve the analyst's insight, so too can equity turnover, which is the ratio of sales to stockholders' equity. A useful procedure is to separate this ratio into (*a*) the relationship between sales and operating assets, and (*b*) the relationship between operating assets and stockholders' equity. Algebraically this is expressed as follows:

$$\frac{\text{Sales}}{\text{Operating assets}} \times \frac{\text{Operating assets}}{\text{Stockholders' equity}} = \frac{\text{Sales}}{\text{Stockholders' equity}}$$

Operating assets can be defined as net plant plus cash, receivables, and inventories (average of beginning- and end-of-year data). Thus, the ratio of sales to operating assets, or "asset turnover," is a measure of the intensity of utilization of assets. The ratio of operating assets to stockholders' equity is a measure of a firm's "leverage" position—i.e., the degree to which it is financing its expansion with debt and preferred stock as opposed to common stock and retained earnings.[11] Since both of these concepts are probably less familiar to the reader than the components of profit margins, some extended discussion of their significance is in order before proceeding to examine the data for Alcoa.

In order to exploit effectively a growing demand for a company's output, the company must expand its productive assets and working capital so as to keep it in a balanced relationship with demand. If demand rises much faster than productive capacity, or than the company's willingness to finance larger receivables or larger inventories, the company may find itself in the position of being unable to satisfy its customers to the full extent of their demands. If this results in the customers turning elsewhere

---

[9] With regard to real estate losses, the company's September, 1966, prospectus notes (p. 11) that the losses have been "more than offset by reduction in the income tax liability of the Company resulting from inclusion of these real estate developments in consolidated tax returns, and by unrecorded appreciation in land values."

[10] The relatively low effective tax rate primarily reflects depletion charges and low-taxed earnings from bauxite mining operations in Central and South America.

[11] When measured in this fashion, leverage refers to financing via both long-term *and short-term* debt, the latter including accounts payable and short-term bank loans. A more traditional measure of leverage relates only to long-term debt, and can be expressed as either:

$$\frac{\text{Funded debt plus preferred stock}}{\text{Stockholders' equity}} \text{ or } \frac{\text{Funded debt plus preferred stock}}{\text{Total capital}}$$

for supplies, it may represent a permanent loss of markets. Thus, a steadily rising ratio of sales to operating assets may be a sign of unbalanced growth. On the other hand, it may reflect the fact that some newly acquired plant and equipment is technologically more advanced than older facilities and is capable of carrying a higher sales load.

While a steadily rising sales/operating assets ratio may be a warning of trouble ahead, so too may a steadily falling ratio. If expansion of productive facilities is rapidly outpacing the expansion of sales, the usual result is a weakening in the product's price structure until a better balance is achieved. The aluminum and paper industries, among others, have been characterized by this type of imbalance between sales and capacity in recent years.

A few caveats are in order regarding the interpretation of changing ratios of sales to operating assets.[12] In the first place, capital is a "lumpy factor of production," in economists' jargon. New plants usually cannot be built in installments. Consequently, when a company expands its facilities, some time usually elapses before sales rise sufficiently to use the full new capacity. In the meantime the sales/operating assets ratio is likely to fall. But the falling ratio, in such cases, should not be interpreted pessimistically unless there is reason to doubt that sales will shortly justify the expansion.

A second source of difficulty relates to rising sales/operating assets ratios, and is caused by a change in company "lease versus buy" policies. A company which has been buying most of its physical facilities may begin increasingly to lease them. Leased facilities do not show up in the company's property accounts, but they do result in sales. Thus, a rising sales/operating assets ratio will result, and the rise may be interpreted favorably by the analyst when, in fact, if the leased facilities were taken into account the inference might be quite the opposite. A similar problem may be caused if a company sets up an unconsolidated subsidiary to finance its receivables. Sales will rise relative to the indicated working capital of the parent company, but the rise will be more apparent than real.

---

[12] Most analysts also keep track of the relationship of *unit* sales to plant capacity if the data are available. Problems of data nonavailability are least existent in the raw materials and public utilities industries, where capacity data—in tons, barrels, kilowatts, etc., are published frequently in company annual reports and, on an industry-wide basis, by trade associations and government agencies. It should be recognized, however, that although the data *look* precise, the concept of capacity is inherently imprecise. Most capacity measures are based on existing technology and customary methods of operation. But these are both subject to changes that can have a significant impact on the potential output of existing facilities—for example, adding a third shift of workers, or using oxygen in blast furnaces, or thermal recovery methods in oil pumping.

Making allowance for these caveats, it can be concluded that the most desirable trend for the sales/operating assets ratio is for it to be stable at a high level. The high level tends to assure optimum efficiency of operation,[13] and the stability tends to assure that the market will neither be unsatisfied nor glutted. For greater insight, the analyst can examine separately the ratio of sales to each individual component of operating assets—net plant, cash, receivables, and inventories. In addition, since depreciation accounting practices can cause severe distortions in intercompany and intertemporal comparisons, it pays to look at the trends of sales/gross plant and depreciation/gross plant ratios in connection with asset turnover analysis.[14]

Turning from the concept of "asset turnover" to the concept of "leverage," while it is true that common equity is the principal source of long-term capital for most firms, another important source is funded debt—bonds and other long-term loans. In addition, some industries, such as public utilities, use preferred stock as a financing vehicle. In 1965 only some 10% of the 425 companies in Standard & Poor's Industrial Stock Price Index had capital structures consisting of common equity only.

Notwithstanding the frequent comments one encounters regarding the virtues of a "clean balance sheet"—i.e., one where common stock is the only source of long-term capital—the judicious use of leverage can be very advantageous to the common stockholder. For if a corporation sells bonds on which it pays an interest rate of, say, 5% (which is really an effective after-tax rate of only 2½%),[15] and if it can earn, say, 12% after taxes on the funds so secured, the differential accrues to the benefit of the stockholders. This is often referred to as "trading on the equity." Moreover, if the rate of return on total funds used in the business rises, the rate earned on stockholders' equity alone will rise at an even faster rate, because the charges on the senior issues remain fixed.

These observations can be illustrated with a hypothetical example. Let us assume two companies, each with $50 million of capital in 1960 and $60 million in 1965. However, assume that one of these companies (Company "A") has all of its capital in common stock, and one (Company

---

[13] *Too* high a level, however, can be inefficient because obsolete facilities have to be brought into use. McGraw-Hill's *19th Annual Survey of Business Plans for New Plants and Equipment* reveals that manufacturers prefer to operate, on average, at a rate of about 93% of physical capacity.

[14] In some industries, trends of operating assets per se, in addition to asset *turnover*, are of interest. For example, in setting electric utility rates, public regulatory commissions seek to allow utility companies to earn a "fair" rate of return on investment. The investment, or "rate base," to which this "fair return" is applied, is largely a function of the book value of the plant. For a good concise discussion see Benjamin Graham *et al.*, *Security Analysis* (4th ed.; New York: McGraw-Hill Book Co., 1962), chap. xx.

[15] Preferred stock dividends are not tax-deductible expenses, hence the paucity of new preferred stock issues in recent years.

"B"), has four fifths in common and one fifth in 5% bonds. Let us also assume that both companies have annual sales of $200 million in 1960 and $250 million in 1965 and that net income before taxes and before interest expense equaled 3% of sales in 1960 and 4% in 1965. The income statements of these two companies would appear as follows (in million dollars):

| | Company A | | Company B | |
|---|---|---|---|---|
| | *1960* | *1965* | *1960* | *1965* |
| Sales | 200 | 250 | 200 | 250 |
| Net before taxes and interest (3% of sales in 1960 and 4% in 1965) | 6 | 10 | 6 | 10 |
| Interest (5% on Company B's $10 million of bonds in 1960 and $12 million in 1965) | — | — | 0.5 | 0.6 |
| Net before taxes | 6 | 10 | 5.5 | 9.4 |
| Income taxes (at 50% rate) | 3 | 5 | 2.75 | 4.7 |
| Net income available to common | 3 | 5 | 2.75 | 4.7 |
| Stockholders' equity | 50 | 60 | 40 | 48 |
| Rate of return on stockholders' equity | 6% | 8.3% | 6.9% | 9.8% |

Note that the leveraged company's rate of return on stockholders' equity was higher than that of the unleveraged company in both years,[16] and also that it increased by almost 3 percentage points between 1960 and 1965, compared with a gain of less than 2½ percentage points for the unleveraged company. The railroad industry is a prime example of the impact of leverage on stockholders' earnings. As can be seen from the scatter diagram in Figure 8–8, stockholder profits (pretax in the chart) are estimated to have the potential of rising 100% (from $1 billion to $2 billion) on a revenue increase of only 20% (from $10 billion to $12 billion). This is because so much of the railroad industry's expenses are fixed charges on funded debt that substantially higher revenue will generate a much smaller increase in total costs.[17]

---

[16] It may be noted, as an aside, that the advantage of leverage might appear to be even greater if "cash flow" were being used rather than net income. This is because the entire depreciation allowance is attributed to stockholders' equity rather than allocated between equity and debt. Despite our generally favorable disposition toward the use of cash flow, we must admit that this is a valid criticism. There is no theoretical justification for attributing all depreciation to equity investment.

[17] In addition to heavy fixed interest charges, there also are heavy fixed charges related to the large capital investment—for example, depreciation and maintenance expenses. The latter give rise to what is known as "operating leverage," while the

FIGURE 8–8

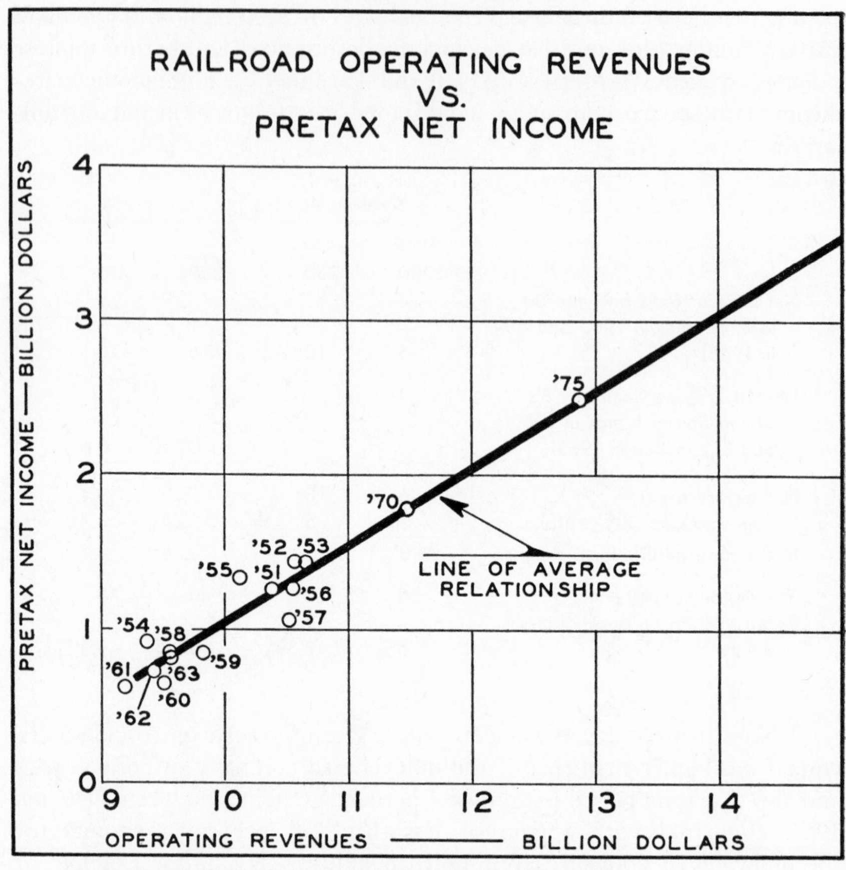


Source: Standard & Poor's Corp., *The Outlook*, June 1, 1964, p. 784.

Of course, as the past history of the railroads suggests, stockholder profits are also made more *vulnerable* by leverage. For in a period of poor business the existence of heavy fixed charges causes the return on equity to fall faster than the rate on total capital. Clearly, what is necessary from the stockholder's point of view is a sensible balancing of debt and equity in relation to the risks of the specific business at its particular stage of development.

The usefulness of separating equity turnover into asset turnover and leverage components should now be clear. Accordingly, data on these two

---

former relate to "financial leverage." "Break-even" analysis is used to study operating leverage. But the data needed for a good break-even analysis seldom are available to the external analyst. The subject is discussed in detail in textbooks on managerial economics.

components of Alcoa's equity turnover can be introduced. Table 8–7 presents the figures. Included in the tabulation are annual sales per share and the ratio of long-term debt plus preferred stock to total capitalization.

The first two columns of the table show that when dollar sales have been in a rising trend, as in the period 1953–56, asset turnover has maintained a level of about 80%–85%. When dollar sales have been in the doldrums, on the other hand, as in 1957–61, asset turnover has fallen to a

**TABLE 8–7**

**Equity Turnover Analysis, Aluminum Company of America**

(Based on Average of Beginning- and End-of-Year Assets and Capital)

| Year | Sales per Share (1) | Sales as Percent of Operating Assets (2) | Long-Term Debt Plus Preferred Stock as Percent of Total Capitalization (3) | Operating Assets as Percent of Stockholders' Equity (4) |
|---|---|---|---|---|
| 1953 | $36 | 86% | 53% | 246% |
| 1954 | 35 | 79 | 50 | 235 |
| 1955 | 41 | 88 | 46 | 212 |
| 1956 | 42 | 83 | 41 | 201 |
| 1957 | 42 | 73 | 40 | 206 |
| 1958 | 36 | 60 | 44 | 208 |
| 1959 | 41 | 67 | 45 | 200 |
| 1960 | 40 | 67 | 42 | 190 |
| 1961 | 40 | 66 | 40 | 184 |
| 1962 | 44 | 74 | 38 | 175 |
| 1963 | 45 | 77 | 37 | 167 |
| 1964 | 48 | 77 | 39 | 172 |
| 1965 | 54 | 80 | 41 | 178 |

level of about 60%–70%. In other words, a dollar of assets can support a quite flexible sales load. In view of the favorable sales forecast offered in the previous chapter, therefore, asset turnover can be projected at the higher end of the historical range. An estimate of 85% seems reasonable.

Columns (3) and (4) of the table show that Alcoa has a fairly heavy financial leverage position,[18] but one which has gradually been reduced.

[18] The sales/operating assets data in column (2) show that in addition to heavy *financial* leverage, Alcoa, like other aluminum companies, has heavy *operating* leverage. *Forbes* magazine recently noted that the four largest steel companies, usually thought of as capital-intensive companies, "required an average $1.01 in capital to get $1 in sales, while aluminum's Big Four required $1.63." *Forbes* also noted that aluminum companies' fixed costs are intensified by long-term contracts for electric power. Thus, high break-even costs put pressure on the companies to try to operate at near capacity levels (which explains much of the price cutting that has characterized the industry) and make profit margins greatly dependent upon strong sales performance. See "Golden (Sometimes) Leverage," *Forbes*, August 15, 1966, p. 15.

Long-term debt and preferred stock have been reduced from approximately one half of capital to about 40%. The ratio of operating assets to stockholders' equity has been reduced from more than 200% to around 170%–180%. Indications are that the management of the company intends to stabilize its leverage position at about current levels. An average operating asset/equity ratio of about 180% seems a reasonable estimate, therefore. Multiplying this estimate by the 85% estimate of asset turnover produces an equity turnover ratio of about 150%, a better level than generally has prevailed since the mid-1950's, although it is still considerably lower than the level of the early 1950's (see Table 8–5).

*Earnings Growth Forecast.* It has been estimated in this chapter that Alcoa's profit margin on sales will average about 7½% in the foreseeable future and that equity turnover will average about 150%. The multiplication of these two factors produces an estimate of rate of return on stockholders' equity. It is somewhat more than 11%, which is only an average rate for an industrial company, although it is higher than Alcoa's typical rate of recent years.

As demonstrated at the outset of this chapter, growth in earnings per share can be estimated by multiplying the rate of return on stockholders' equity by the proportion of earnings retained in the business. Studies of corporate dividend and retention policies suggest that many interacting factors are at work in any given situation. Among these factors, the following may be listed, although not necessarily in order of importance: (1) an effort to project systematically future financial requirements, rates of return, and costs of alternative sources of funds; (2) subjective attitudes of the executives toward debt; (3) a weighing of the desires and tax status of the principal stockholders against the desires and tax status of the "typical" stockholders; (4) the policies of competing companies; and (5) a reluctance to set dividends at a rate that may later have to be cut back. In general, the result of all these crosscurrents is a relative stability of dividend payout ratios. While payout ratios vary considerably from company to company (the modal range is about 50%–60%, but 40% and 70% ratios are also quite common), any one corporation's average dividend payout ratio tends to remain fairly stable for extended periods of time. On a year-to-year basis, of course, payout and retention ratios may fluctuate considerably because dividends—the numerator of the dividend payout ratio—tend to be kept relatively stable while earnings—the denominator—fluctuate cyclically. Therefore, reference must be made to *average* payout ratios.

In Alcoa's case, Table 8–4 suggests that management appears to be aiming at a policy of approximately 40% payout and 60% retention. If this interpretation is correct, the company's growth rate of earnings per share will be 60% of the estimated 11+% rate of return on stockholders' equity, or slightly under 7% per annum. This rate of earnings growth would be approximately equal to the estimate of 7% in dollar sales growth which was made in the previous chapter. Thus, a fairly balanced growth of sales and earnings appears to be in prospect for Alcoa. This is in marked contrast to the "profitless prosperity" period which the company encountered in the late 1950's and early 1960's, when unit sales were in an uptrend but dollar sales were level and profits declined. Nevertheless, it may be noted that while an earnings growth rate of almost 7% is attractive, it is not dramatically higher than the expected range of earnings growth of "the averages" (4½%–5½%), and entails a subnormal dividend payout ratio and above-average financial leverage. Yet Alcoa's price-earnings ratio typically has been considerably above that of the averages—usually well in excess of 20 times earnings. If our estimates are correct, this would appear to be too liberal an appraisal of the company's prospects.[19]

### Further Observations on Rate of Return Calculations

*Return on Total Capital.* Another popular method of analyzing the impact of leverage is to compare the return on stockholders' equity with the return on total capital. Total capital is equal to the sum of common stock plus surplus items plus preferred stock plus funded debt. The income earned on total capital is equal to the sum of net income available to common plus preferred dividends plus one half of interest on funded debt.[20] Therefore, parallel to the equation for return on stockholders' equity we can write:

$$\frac{\text{Earnings on total capital}}{\text{Sales}} \times \frac{\text{Sales}}{\text{Average Total capital}} = \begin{array}{l}\text{Rate of return}\\ \text{on total capital}\end{array}$$

---

[19] *Normalized 1966* earnings for Alcoa were approximately $4.50 per share. (This compares with actual 1965 earnings of $3.41 and with actual 1966 earnings of $4.83 per share.) Given the company's longer term growth prospects, as described in this chapter and the previous chapter, and making allowance for its sales stability characteristics (about average), its dividend payout policy (below average), its institutional ownership (moderately above average), and its leverage (well above average), a reasonable price-earnings ratio would appear to be about 17–18 based upon the results of the multiple regression analysis described in Chapter 5. Applying this ratio to the $4.50 estimate of normalized earnings produces a 1966 value of about $80 per share. The actual price range of the stock in 1966 was $66–$95.

[20] Since interest is a tax-deductible expense, the government pays about half the interest expense. Thus, net income available for common is, in effect, after deducting one half of interest. Therefore, to derive after-tax earnings on *total capital* we add back only one half of interest to net income after taxes. For companies with low effective tax rates, add back interest × (1.00 minus tax rate).

Actually, the definitions used in this section should be expanded to reflect the "disguised leverage" of long-term leases. In this connection, see the discussion of leases on pp. 374–377 of Chapter 10. For further algebraic manipulations introducing the leverage factor, see M. Kisor, Jr., "The Financial Aspects of Growth," *Financial Analysts Journal*, March–April, 1964; also M. J. Gordon, *The Investment, Financing, and Valuation of the Corporation* (Homewood, Ill.: Richard D. Irwin, Inc., 1962).

If this equation is applied to the hypothetical example given on page 325, the following calculations can be made:

| Company A | Company B |
| --- | --- |
| *1960* | *1960* |
| $\frac{3}{200} \times \frac{200}{50} = 6\%$ | $\frac{2\frac{3}{4} + \frac{1}{4}}{200} \times \frac{200}{40 + 10} = 6\%$ |
| *1965* | *1965* |
| $\frac{5}{250} \times \frac{250}{60} = 8.3\%$ | $\frac{4.7 + 0.3}{250} \times \frac{250}{48 + 12} = 8.3\%$ |

It will be seen that both companies have the same rates of return on *total capital.* The presence of leverage, however, causes Company B to have a higher rate of return on *stockholders' equity,* as demonstrated previously. Given a constant rate of return on total capital, the greater the leverage the higher the rate of return on stockholders' equity.

*Marginal Analysis.* The fact that return on capital increased between 1960 and 1965 in the preceding example brings up another aspect of the subject. Readers who have studied economics will be acquainted with the concept of marginal rate of return, in contrast to *average* rate of return. Let us hypothesize a company whose total capital, from all sources, increased by 5% from 1960 to 1961, and by 10%, 0%, 20%, and 5% in each of the following four years, respectively. Assume also that the company's rate of return on total capital is 10½%, 10%, 10½%, 10%, 11%, and 11% in each of the six years, 1960–65, respectively. The average rate of return in this series is 10½%, and the individual figures are so close to the average that most analysts would be willing to assume it as a "normal" rate of return on *increments* of capital in trying to estimate the company's growth potential. But further analysis would reveal that the return on increments of capital—the "marginal" rate of return—has been considerably higher than 10½%. The following tabulation, which is not strict marginal analysis but yet is simple and useful,[21] suggests that the increments to capital have actually been invested at a rate of about 12%.

| Year | (1) *Total Capital (1960 = 100)* | (2) *Earnings on Total Capital* |
| --- | --- | --- |
| 1960 | 100 | 10.5 (10½% of column 1) |
| 1961 | 105 (+5%) | 10.5 (10% " " ) |
| 1962 | 115.5 (+10%) | 12.1 (10½% " " ) |
| 1963 | 115.5 (no increase) | 11.6 (10% " " ) |
| 1964 | 138.6 (+20%) | 15.3 (11% " " ) |
| 1965 | 145.5 (+5%) | 16.0 (11% " " ) |

5-Year increment......45.5 (145.5 minus 100) 5.5 (16.0 minus 10.5)
Incremental return..............5.5/45.5 = 12.1%

[21] The method is suggested by Professor Douglas A. Hayes in "Some Reflections on Techniques for Appraising Growth Rates," *Financial Analysts Journal,* July–August, 1964.

Thus, the really incisive analyst has reason to suspect that the company's potential earnings growth rate may be greater than surface data indicate. Before jumping to that conclusion, however, he should try to determine why the marginal return on capital has been significantly different from the average return. Among the possibilities are: introduction of new and more efficient equipment; a new product line; or a particularly advantageous merger. Once he isolates the major reason, he must make a judgment whether its effects are likely to persist and whether the event itself is likely to be repeated in the future. He will usually find it of assistance in this connection to examine marginal returns over *successive* three-year or five-year periods instead of just a single period. Care should be taken that the initial and terminal years of each period are not too dissimilar in economic characteristics.

## SUGGESTED READINGS

William M. Bennett. "Capital Turnover versus Profit Margins," *Financial Analysts Journal*, March–April, 1966.

John A. Brittain. *Corporate Dividend Policy*. Washington, D.C.: Brookings Institution, 1966.

Jerome B. Cohen and Sidney M. Robbins. *The Financial Manager*. New York: Harper & Row, Publishers, 1966.

Myron J. Gordon. *The Investment, Financing, and Valuation of the Corporation*. Homewood, Ill.: Richard D. Irwin, Inc., 1962.

Manown Kisor, Jr. "The Financial Aspects of Growth," *Financial Analysts Journal*, March–April, 1964.

Milton H. Spencer and Louis Siegelman. *Managerial Economics*. Rev. ed. Homewood, Ill: Richard D. Irwin, Inc., 1964.

James E. Walter. "Dividend Policy: Its Influence on the Value of the Enterprise," *Journal of Finance*, May 1963.

The Institute of Chartered Financial Analysts. *C.F.A. Readings in Financial Analysis*. Homewood, Ill.: Richard D. Irwin, Inc., 1966.

# 9

# ANALYSIS OF GROWTH—IV: MANAGEMENT AS AN INDEPENDENT FACTOR

The wise man does no wrong in changing
his habits with the times.

—Cato

In the August, 1964, issue of its monthly business bulletin, the First National City Bank of New York presented the following tabulation:

**100 Largest Manufacturing Corporations by Year of First Appearance**

| | *1926* | *1935* | *1948* | *1963* |
|---|---|---|---|---|
| Newcomers | 22 | 23 | 26 | 20 |
| Survivors from 1919 list | 78 | 65 | 57 | 49 |
| Survivors from 1926 list | | 12 | 8 | 6 |
| Survivors from 1935 list | | | 9 | 8 |
| Survivors from 1948 list | | | | 17 |
| Total | 100 | 100 | 100 | 100 |

The table shows that of the 100 largest manufacturing corporations in 1919, only 78 were still among the 100 largest seven years later, in 1926. By 1963 only 49 remained on the list of 100 largest. Of the 22 new additions to the list in 1926, only 12 remained on by 1935, and only 6 by 1963. A similar tale is told for the 1935 and 1948 additions to the list.

### The Quality of Management

One obvious reason why so many companies "fall from grace" is that the growth of the industries of which they are members slows down relative to the growth of other industries. This is a natural concomitant of a healthy and growing competitive economy. But interindustry competition is far from a complete explanation, although it is an important factor. Intraindustry competition is also crucial. For example, 21 oil companies were on the list in 1919 and 20 in 1963. But only 12 of the original 21 were among the 1963 leaders. Nine oil companies had dropped off the list, to be replaced by eight others.[1]

Why do some companies in the same industry have better growth records than others? Sometimes it is because they possess an unduplicatable characteristic such as a unique geographic location or a patented production process. More often, however, it is because they are *better managed*. For example, the difference between the stagnant Underwood Corporation (taken over by Olivetti) and the dynamic International Business Machines Corporation—both in the office equipment industry—is largely traceable to differences in the caliber of their managements.

Differences in management ability also can explain why the same company may have a better relative growth record within its industry in one period than in another. For example, one might contrast the Chrysler Corporation under the old Colbert-Newberg regime with the drastically different, and improved, Chrysler under Messrs. Love and Townsend.[2] Moreover, examples can be cited of companies whose executives recognized the onset of industrial stagnation and shifted part or all of their operations into completely new lines, while the heads of similarly situated companies rested on their laurels. Thus, two major textile companies, Celanese and J. P. Stevens, were among the top 100 manufacturing firms in 1948. But in 1963, Stevens was still a textile company and was off the list, while Celanese had become an important chemical company in addition to being a textile company, and it remained on the list.[3] Adroit management also can often develop above-average growth in essentially stagnant industries.

The caliber of management, however, is not very amenable to quantification. To a certain extent it is true that management can be judged by its statistical record—the growth of sales and earnings which it was capable of generating. But frequently it is impossible to separate the causes of the growth record into specific managerial decisions, on the one hand, and external factors over which management had little or no control, on the other. Moreover, the statistical record does not necessarily reveal very well management's capacity for coping with change. And if anything is certain about the future of most companies, it is that changes will occur with increasing rapidity. Thus, a thorough analysis of a company's growth prospects must go beyond the quantitative approach which has

---

[1] One of the nine had been merged into one of the eight.

[2] See R. Sheehan, "The Price of Success at Chrysler," *Fortune*, November, 1965.

[3] See "And Then There Was One," *Forbes*, January 15, 1966.

been discussed in the previous chapters. It must take into account the *quality* of management.

Modern management science teaches that good managers will be effective in almost any company. This is because they are masters, not of a particular business, but rather of the critical *managerial functions:* setting objectives, formulating plans to achieve these objectives, organizing and inspiring subordinates to carry out the plans, and innovating when previous methods seem outmoded. Thus, the present chapter is concerned with the way men—management men—do their work.

It is recognized, of course, that an outsider is at a great disadvantage in trying to assess the caliber of a company's managers, for he usually does not have an opportunity to observe them in their day-to-day work. The disadvantage is particularly pronounced for the small, individual investor. A professional security analyst, however, can gain some understanding of a company by personally visiting both its corporate headquarters and its outlying plants. These trips afford the analyst a chance to speak with the company's managers face-to-face, to speak with the managers' subordinates, and to wander about the company's plants (preferably unescorted) and observe the attitudes of the workers, the condition of the equipment, the smoothness of the work flow, and similar clues to management's efficiency. Over and above these surface indications of the quality of management, however, the analyst should search for more subtle clues.

### Management's Motivation

One thing the analyst should try to ascertain is whether the senior officers of the company have a strong desire, perhaps passion is an even better word, to make their company grow. Without the presence of such ambition among the key personnel, "competence" usually will not suffice.[4]

In business, at least, it is a fairly valid generalization that a firm must either grow or lose its market share. A firm whose essential philosophy is to preserve the status quo soon becomes unable to attract or retain capable young personnel, for whom the death or retirement of existing officers is the only route to promotion. Preservation of the status quo tends to be an unattainable goal because the firm's products become displaced by the newer and better products of expansion-minded competitors. A policy of nonexpansion incurs grave risks of loss of markets through technological obsolescence and consumer withdrawal.

It is true, of course, that growth-oriented managers may pose another risk for investors in their enterprises. For they may seek growth at the expense of *profit*. This risk, however, appears less serious than the

---

[4] An interesting series of vignettes on the subject of management motivation, written by W. Guzzardi, Jr., appeared in the June, July, September, and October, 1964, issues of *Fortune*. They have been put into book form under the title, *The Young Executive* (New York: New American Library, 1966).

risks posed by managers of opposite temperament. Penrose has observed: "There is no need to deny that other 'objectives' are often important—power, prestige, public approval, or the mere love of the game—it need only be recognized that the attainment of these ends more often than not is associated directly with the ability to make profits."[5]

## Management's "Grand Design"

*Conception of the Market.* History suggests that if managers are to bring their desires for growth to fruition, they should have a rather broad conception of their company's "natural" product line. Few successful companies have continued to produce the same type of product throughout their lifetime. Successful companies are usually market oriented rather than product oriented, and the type of product demanded by the *relevant market* tends to undergo radical changes as time passes. Unless a company's product mix is restructured to meet the market's changing demands, growth is impeded, if not prevented.

Consider the contrast between IBM and Underwood prior to the Olivetti takeover of the latter. Here is a classic example of the difference between a well-conceived and an ill-conceived product line. For almost 50 years, until World War II, Underwood was the premier business machine company in the nation. During this period, the word "business machine" was virtually synonymous with "standard manual typewriter," and Underwood was the typewriter king.

But a new business machine technology was developed during and after the war. For one thing, manual typewriters were increasingly displaced by electric typewriters. While Underwood failed completely to make the shift, IBM virtually took over the market. Furthermore, typewriters became only a small segment of a much broader office equipment market, which included electric calculators, punched card equipment, electronic computers, and duplicating devices. Underwood waited until 1956 to move into electronic computers—long after its competitors—and was hopelessly outclassed. IBM, on the other hand, maintained a consistent technological lead in punched card equipment and computers, and more recently, perhaps tardily, has begun to move into the duplicating machine field.

Significantly, IBM itself might not have made the move into electronic computers if the elder Mr. Watson had not turned the company's leadership over to his son. This points up all the more strongly the dangers of a management resting on its laurels, continuing to do that which it has always done best but overlooking newer aspects of the relevant market.

Theodore Levitt has gone so far as to say that "there is no such thing as a growth industry; there are only companies organized and operated to

[5] E. T. Penrose, *The Theory of the Growth of the Firm* (New York: John Wiley & Sons, Inc., 1959), p. 30.

create and capitalize on growth opportunities."[6] To his mind, management's conception of its market is crucial. For example, he argues that the failure of most railroad companies to grow after World War II was not attributable to a reduced need for passenger and freight transportation. Obviously, transportation requirements grew strongly. The trouble was that most railroad companies considered themselves to be in the railroad business rather than in the transportation business. Accordingly, they let automobiles, trucks, and airplanes take away transportation customers. In rebuttal it might be noted that the ability of public utility companies to adapt to changes is greatly limited by the fact that (*a*) their assets are long-lived and highly specialized, and (*b*) regulatory commissions impede exit from receding markets and entry into newer markets.[7] Nevertheless, there is doubtless much merit in Levitt's argument.

If it be claimed, moreover, that Levitt's analysis of the railroads' stagnation is pure hindsight, he ventures some observations about the future of another great industry, petroleum. He points out that significant technological breakthroughs are occurring in automobile fuel systems. These developments, including chemical fuel cells, advanced electric storage batteries, and solar energy conversion systems, have the potential for eliminating the demand for gasoline—something the average driver would dearly love. Yet the pioneers in these developments are largely non-petroleum companies,[8] posing the risk for the latter that they may become "companies without an industry." What is called for, Levitt says, is a reorientation by these companies of their conception of their market. For their own self-preservation they have to look upon themselves not as being in the business of finding, refining, and selling oil and oil derivatives, but rather in the business of servicing the transportation market. Thus, railroads and oil companies, in Levitt's view, are far more related than is conventionally presumed.[9]

*Plan of Action.* Even a broad conception of the market is not a sufficient precondition for rapid growth. The security analyst should inquire whether management has specific objectives, and specific plans and timetables for achieving those objectives. "We're keeping a watchful eye on things" is not very convincing evidence that management is doing its job.

---

[6] T. Levitt, "Marketing Myopia," *Harvard Business Review*, July–August, 1960, p. 47.

[7] For an elaboration of this viewpoint, see B. A. Kolb, "The Rise and Fall of Public Utilities—An Appraisal of Risk," *Journal of Business*, October, 1964.

[8] A few years subsequent to Levitt's article, however, Esso Research & Engineering Company announced some significant breakthroughs in chemical fuel cell technology.

[9] Some recent combinations of coal companies with oil companies suggest that the reorientation of the industry's conception of its market, called for by Levitt, is taking place, but not along the lines suggested by him. Instead of servicing the "transportation market," the focus seems to be on the broader "energy market."

Plans obviously will go astray, no matter how well thought out. But it is far better to have specific plans which are altered as circumstances change than to have no plans at all. In this connection, Professor John Mee has stressed the importance of what he calls "causative thinking." Some managers, he says, simply react, however skillfully, to changes in the external environment as they occur. Others go one step further; they try to forecast changes and plan their reactions in advance. But there is still a higher plane of managerial thought. Mee writes:

If a business administrator can imagine a situation which has not yet taken place, he can also creatively fashion a series of prior events that can fulfill his desired purpose and satisfy his objectives. By thinking backwards from such imagined future situations, an enterprising individual may conceive of a series of related events by which a present situation can be converted into the desired future situation. . . . Administrators . . . can do more than plan for future results. They can follow courses of action, with each action making a change in the existing environment according to the previously conceived series of events, until the desired result becomes a reality."[10]

Mee uses the Apollo moonlanding project as an illustration of causative thinking, but less exotic examples can be cited. For instance, consider the case of Henry Ford the elder. Theodore Levitt points out in the article previously referred to that we habitually praise Ford for the wrong reason—his genius in inventing mass production, which led to lower automobile prices and a vastly expanded auto market. Actually, Ford was more a marketing genius. His writings show clearly that he created the assembly line *because* he had concluded that at lower prices he could sell millions of automobiles. Mass production was the result, not the cause, of low automobile prices.[11]

Here was "causative thinking" at its finest. Objective: sell millions of cars. How to sell so many cars: lower prices. How to lower prices: produce cars more cheaply. How to produce cars more cheaply: make them on an assembly line.

*Product Differentiation and Marketing Strategy.* The Ford example illustrates the important role of price reductions in the effort to broaden markets. But in our modern economy, product differentiation, often called "quality competition," has become at least as important as price competition. Quality competition refers to the attempt to attract customers by changing the design of a product, or the materials from which it is made, or the ancillary services offered to the customer, or the packaging and advertising of the product. Management's creativeness in differentiating its product from competing products should be an important area of inquiry for the security analyst.

[10] J. F. Mee, "Haruspices, Happenings, and Horizons," *Advanced Management Journal*, July, 1964, p. 12.

[11] Levitt, *op. cit.*, p. 51. Paradoxically, Levitt notes, Ford made a terrible marketing error by producing only black cars.

Zenith Corporation, for example, enjoys a reputation for soundness of construction that is unmatched by most other producers of radios, television sets, or related products. As a result, many people are willing to buy Zenith products at somewhat higher cost than competitors' lines. As for customer servicing, ask any user of electronic computing equipment which producer offers the broadest variety and highest quality of accompanying services and the answer almost invariably will be IBM. There is no doubt that IBM's fantastic success is as much, if not more, attributable to the excellence of it's service as to the excellence of its product.

The development of ingenious distribution methods offers another clue to management's market orientation. Avon Products' door-to-door selling technique, for example, has enabled that company to grow much faster than many other producers of quite similar toiletry items.[12]

Actually, selection of the proper distribution channel is sometimes a more critical decision than what product to sell. As an illustration of this thesis, Peter Drucker, the famed management consultant, has cited the case of one of the largest producers of packaged foods (not named by Drucker) which brought out a line of gourmet foods some years back. In Drucker's words:

> Whereas all its other products were distributed through mass-retailers of food, especially the supermarkets, the company decided to distribute the gourmet foods through specialty stores only. The line failed. Yet similar lines, offered a little later by much less well-known companies through the supermarkets, did well. The idea behind the gourmet foods was to offer the housewife the opportunity to produce without any cooking skill an unusual dinner once in a while. But for most housewives the food specialty store is not an available distributive channel; they hardly know of its existence and certainly do not shop there. For those few who go in for elaborate cooking and shop in the specialty stores, processed and packaged food made by a mass-producer of staples is the wrong product, no matter what it is called.[13]

Nor is the selection of a distribution channel a once-and-for-all-proposition. What is appropriate at one stage of a market's development is not necessarily appropriate at the next stage. "Indeed," says Drucker, "I have never seen a decision with respect to distributive channels that was not obsolescent five years later, and badly in need of new thinking and fundamental change."[14]

In many industries the success of the marketing effort is a function of the skill and imaginativeness of the advertising and promotion personnel.

---

[12] See S. Freedgood, "Avon: The Sweet Smell of Success," *Fortune*, December, 1964.

[13] P. F. Drucker, *Managing For Results*, (New York: Harper & Row, Publishers, 1964), pp. 20–21.

[14] *Ibid.*, p. 24.

Companies do not stop at the creation of new products or of product differences. They attempt to impress upon the buying public the name of the product and the nature of its differences from other products. This effort often costs as much as 10 times what was spent in developing the product improvement in the first place.[15]

Procter and Gamble has spent more on advertising and sales promotion in recent years than any other corporation. The company makes it a practice of "pouring in ad money disproportionately to sales until a new product gets to the point where it brings home the duck to dinner."[16] And although it is difficult to measure the success of a sales promotion campaign in isolation from all the other factors affecting sales, not the least of which is the quality of the product itself, P&G clearly is convinced that its technique works. In the fall of 1963, for example, the company introduced a new hair shampoo and spent $12 million in the next several months to promote it. Within a year it had captured one quarter of the market.

## Research and Development[17]

Nowhere, perhaps, is the innovative spirit of a company's managers more discernible than in the conduct of its research and development activities. "R.&D." has become of such critical importance to modern security analysts that the subject warrants some extended discussion.

Corporate growth is greatly dependent on the development of new products and the improvement of existing products and processes of production. Product and process development and improvement, in turn, can be shown to be directly related to the scale of a company's R.&D. expenditures. The first column of Table 9–1, for example, lists in ranked order the ratio of R.&D. spending to sales for 13 different industries in 1958. These data are representative of the scale of research in these industries during the middle and late 1950's. The second column shows the extent to which new products accounted for sales volume in these industries in the early 1960's. Note that, with some exceptions, the industries in which R.&D. spending was highest relative to sales also had the highest proportion of new products in succeeding years.

But while it is clear that the magnitude of research outlays is related to successful product development and improvement, it is not crystal clear that there is a direct connection of R.&D. with *profitability*. Some

---

[15] W. Smith Greig, "Quality Competition and Product Development," *Business Topics* (Michigan State University), Spring, 1964, p. 77.

[16] *Time*, September 11, 1964, p. 98.

[17] This section is based on E. D. Zinbarg, "Research and Development—The Stockholder's View," *Financial Executive*, July, 1965.

TABLE 9–1

**Comparison of Research Outlays and New Products Marketed**

| Industry | (1) 1958 R.&D. Expenditures as Percent of Sales* | (2) Percent of 1962 Sales Accounted for by Products Not in Existence in 1952 |
|---|---|---|
| Aircraft, ships, and railroad equipment | 18.7% | 60 |
| Electrical machinery (including communication) | 12.9 | 49 |
| Machinery | 4.4 | 38 |
| Chemicals | 4.3 | 31 |
| Motor vehicles and parts | 4.2 | 38 |
| Fabricated metals and instruments | 3.5 | 30 |
| Rubber | 2.0 | 4 |
| Petroleum and coal products | 0.9 | 4 |
| Nonferrous metals | 0.9 | 18 |
| Paper | 0.7 | 31 |
| Iron and steel | 0.6 | 18 |
| Food and beverages | 0.3 | 11 |
| Textiles | 0.2 | 22 |
| All Manufacturing | 4.0 | 25 |

* For companies performing R.&D.

Sources: Column (1)—N. E. Terleckyj, *Research & Development: Its Growth and Composition* (New York: National Industrial Conference Board, 1963), p. 56.

Column (2)—McGraw-Hill, *16th Annual Survey of Business Plans for New Plants and Equipment*, 1963, p. 11.

studies do suggest that there is a connection; other studies suggest that the connection is tenuous at best.[18]

For the security analyst the problem is not so much to determine whether or not a firm is actively engaged in research. Almost every

---

[18] The studies referred to include the following:

G. Lazarcik, "Scientific Research and Its Relation to Earnings and Stock Prices," *Financial Analysts Journal*, January–February, 1962.

E. F. Renshaw, "Does Research and Development Pay Off?" 6th ed. of a privately circulated investor service—*Market Perspective*—dated February, 1962.

J. Minasian, "The Economics of Research and Development," in *The Rate and Direction of Inventive Activity: Economic and Social Factors* (Princeton, N.J.: Princeton University Press, 1962).

D. Hamberg, "Invention in the Industrial Research Laboratory," *Journal of Political Economy*, April, 1963.

A. C. Cooper, "R&D Is More Efficient in Small Companies," *Harvard Business Review*, May–June, 1964.

E. Mansfield, "Industrial Research and Development Expenditures," *Journal of Political Economy*, August, 1964.

E. Mansfield, "Rates of Return from Industrial Research and Development," *American Economic Review*, May 1965.

F. M. Scherer, "Firm Size, Market Structure, Opportunity and the Output of Patented Inventions," *American Economic Review*, December, 1965.

modern firm is as a matter of survival.[19] What the security analyst really has to do is distinguish between the sheer *volume* of research and the *quality* of research.

Most investment analysts think of R.&D. in the sense of genuine technological innovation. They do not, and should not, include in this context outlays for market research and routine product testing. To be sure, market research and product testing are important aspects of a company's product development efforts. Market research, for example, can discover consumer wants that are not being satisfied and can pass this information along to scientific personnel for technological development. It also plays a vital role in assuring that the output of the laboratories can and will be sold to the company's customers, and in determining the appropriate pricing strategy for new products. Indeed, poor integration of research and marketing activities is a major inadequacy of many industrial R.&D. programs.[20] But investors do not have market research in mind when they think of R.&D. Yet with increasing public awareness of R.&D. as a determinant of corporate growth, many managements have been tempted to include these types of activities in their financial statements under the heading "research and development," where previously they were included under the catchall heading of "selling and administrative expenses."

At the other extreme, many managements still refuse to report any research outlays at all as a separate item in their financial statements to stockholders, although they may be more diligent in their 10–K reports to the SEC. At either extreme, however, it is clear that a major sleuthing task facing the modern security analyst is to determine the level and trend of a company's scientific and engineering research as distinct from other types of "research" outlays.

Another distinction which should be made by the intelligent analyst is between company-sponsored and "contract" research, the latter usually being government sponsored. During the past decade, a period of enormous growth in the total magnitude of R.&D. spending, the relative extent of government sponsorship has increased markedly, particularly in the aerospace and other defense-related industries. There is no doubt that defense-oriented research has contributed importantly to the introduction and improvement of products for civilian use. Notable examples are jet aircraft, electronic computers, and antibiotics. Moreover, defense research has added significantly to the general know-how of the companies conducting the research, even where no specific civilian applications of the research can be cited. But while it may be granted that defense-oriented

---

[19] A recent survey of 180 manufacturing companies revealed that more than 50% expect their ratio of R.&D. expenditures to sales to rise over the next five years. See "Company R&D: Status and Outlook," *Conference Board Record*, February, 1966.

[20] A good illustration of brilliant scientific achievement coupled with several major marketing blunders is the case of Control Data Corp. See T. A. Wise, "Control Data's Magnificent Fumble," *Fortune*, April, 1966.

research spills over into civilian technology, it is doubtful whether security analysts should equate a dollar of federally sponsored research with a dollar of company-sponsored research. For the former results principally in an improved capability to supply the defense establishment. There is also considerable question about whether such contracted research entitles a private company to any patents or royalties on inventions produced by the research. In this context, recent discussion of tax rebates or other governmental subsidies for consumer-oriented research is particularly intriguing.[21]

Hand in hand with the decidedly "practical" distinction that should be made between defense-oriented and civilian-oriented research, it often seems that both business executives and security analysts give far too little weight to that most "impractical" aspect of R.&D., *basic research.* Basic research has no specific commercial objective. It seeks knowledge for knowledge's sake. As such, it has been pretty well confined to universities and nonprofit research foundations. Only some 4% of industrial R.&D. spending in recent years has been labeled "basic" by the National Science Foundation.[22] Yet some of the most dramatic commercial innovations in such fields as communications, energy production, and chemicals can be traced directly to the research findings of "pure scientists" who did not initially envision specific commercial applications of their work.

Admittedly, the "payoff period" is longer for basic than for applied research. McGraw-Hill's 1964 capital spending survey revealed that most executives expect a 6- to 10-year lag between basic research and commercial production, but only a 3- to 5-year lag between applied research and commercial production. But there can be no doubt that the mental cross-fertilization of pure and applied scientists working side by side in an industrial research laboratory—even one of modest size—can produce eminently practical, and profitable, results.

In probing the quality of a company's research effort, the analyst also must make sure that the management envisions research as a continuing program. If a company expects to make continuing profits from innovation, it must continually innovate. Otherwise, its profit potential will be exhausted when the market for a particular product becomes exhausted. Too often research is treated as a variable, rather than a fixed, cost. Thus, when business is good, research outlays are expanded, only to be cut back when hard times hit. Such programs are likely to fail, if only because capable research personnel will not stay with the company.

---

[21] R. F. Janssen, "Industrial Subsidies," *The Wall Street Journal,* November 9, 1964, p. 1; and J. Spivak, "New Curbs are Sought on Patents Stemming from U.S. Research," *The Wall Street Journal,* June, 1965, p. 11.

[22] At least one writer, however, has argued that industry engages in far more basic research than this figure suggests. See V. Tanzi, "The Impact of Basic Research on Inventions," *Challenge,* December, 1964.

A further clue to the quality of research lies in the actual record of product and process developments and improvements, and the number and significance of ideas on the drawing boards or in pilot plants. In examining the record, the analyst should recognize that a steady stream of new ideas, each of which makes only a modest contribution to the company's total activities, is probably more symptomatic of high-quality research than a single "blockbuster" invention that transforms the entire character of the company. Of course, foreknowledge of the latter can be enormously profitable to the investment sleuth who ferrets out the information. We are not disparaging such inventions but are merely noting their relevance to an analysis of research quality. They are often largely accidental and not reflective of the long-term capability of a research organization.

Finally, the analyst should be aware that whereas history is replete with examples of scientists who underestimated the true significance of their discoveries, investors usually make quite the opposite mistake. They seem rather oblivious of the fact that some 90% of new products are not commercial successes.[23] This tendency to exaggerate the importance of discoveries is probably furthered by the secrecy that surrounds such things. But in order to keep a proper perspective, investors should try to assure themselves, if possible, that a new product or process is really a significant improvement over what now exists; that it has a broad enough market to warrant the expense of bringing it out; that it offers good value per dollar expended by the buyer; and that it has promise of leading to still other new products or processes in the future.

### Management's Willingness to Take Large Risks

Few companies will grow at an above-average rate if their managers are not willing to eliminate obsolete product lines, add completely new lines, make large commitments to research and to the marketing of research output, go into debt, or slash prices to broaden markets or meet competition. Each such action carries the possibility of serious, even catastrophic, mistakes, and the growth-oriented manager must be prepared to risk making serious mistakes.

*Fortune* magazine recently reviewed the history of Sears, Roebuck & Co., one of America's great growth companies. The article cited a number of strategic decisions during the past 40 years which shaped that compa-

[23] See "How Do You Pick the Next Winner?" *Business Week*, May 16, 1964, pp. 81–82. This percentage refers to all new products discovered. For major new products actually marketed, the failure ratio is lower, but still high. In a survey article entitled, "Why New Products Fail," B. Cochran and G. C. Thompson report that "three out of ten major new products marketed in the past five years failed in some important respect to come up to expectations, and one of the three was considered so disappointing that it was withdrawn from the market." (*Conference Board Record*, October, 1964.)

ny's growth path. Those decisions will be outlined here, because they are illustrative of a management which had the courage to take the risks involved in radically altering a company's character:[24]

1. In the mid-1920's, retail stores were added to Sears' original mail-order business. Farmers, the backbone of the mail-order business, now had cars and wanted to drive into town to shop. Sears obliged.

2. But a large chain of retail stores posed new problems of managerial control. Sears responded by centralizing buying and promotional functions in Chicago, while actual store operations were decentralized territorially. Moreover, contrary to traditional retailing practice, it was decided that the bulk of Sears' merchandise would be manufactured to its own specifications. In addition, Sears invested heavily in the stock of its supplier corporations, which both strengthened supply channels and paved the way for large capital gains.

3. After World War II an aggressive store expansion program was launched, while Sears' chief competitor, Montgomery Ward, decided to wait for the "typical" postwar economic depression. Sears moved with its customers westward and into the suburbs, preempting the best store locations.

4. Beginning in the mid-1950's the image of the company's stores was drastically changed from hardware-oriented to full-line department stores. Style and fashion were emphasized along with economy.

5. Operations also were diversified during the 40-year period into insurance and other financial services. In 1931 the company decided to sell low-cost auto insurance by mail, and in 1934 insurance sales were moved into Sears' stores as well. Both moves were startling innovations in the staid insurance industry. Today, through its Allstate subsidiary, Sears is the largest stockholder-owned auto insurance company in the nation, is one of the top five fire and casualty insurance companies, is growing rapidly in life insurance, and has plans to enter the mutual fund field. The company also operates a motor club, a tourist agency, and two savings and loan associations, and is actively considering the small loan, credit card, auto leasing, and mortgage financing businesses. Sears, Roebuck Acceptance Corporation is a giant installment finance company; and Sears operates a fleet of several thousand service and installation trucks to back up its durable goods sales.

6. The company also has been an innovator in personnel relations. It has instituted college training programs for young employees, established a practice of promoting from within the organization, and set up a generous profit-sharing plan which has been invested in Sears' own stock,

---

[24] J. McDonald, "Sears Makes It Look Easy," *Fortune*, May, 1964. See also S. Furst and M. Sherman (ed.), *Business Decisions that Changed Our Lives* (Random House, 1964), for more information about some of Sears' decisions, and also those of other key companies.

thus giving its employees over 25% ownership of the company by the end of 1964.

Are the managers of all large companies willing to take large risks? No, they are not. A long-entrenched management frequently becomes so personally committed to doing things a given way that it is unwilling to risk doing them any other way. It even may be literally unable to see the possibility of doing things differently. How common it is to see a new management take over a company and, within a short period of time, dramatically improve profits by slashing unnecessary costs and enabling the company to compete more effectively.

Consider, as as example of risk aversion, the steel industry in the 1950's and early 1960's. Facing the competition of substantial imports of steel and steel products, at lower than domestic prices, the large, integrated steel companies preferred in many instances to abandon whole product lines rather than figure out how to sell in a market where their tidy price structure had been upset.[25] Furthermore, in the area of technological improvement, it was chiefly the small companies rather than the giants that paved the road which the larger firms only recently have begun to travel. Only recently have the managers of the top steel companies begun to be oriented toward growth rather than maintenance of status in setting their research, production, and marketing policies.[26]

Additional evidence of deliberate risk avoidance is contained in the frequent comment by chief executives of large corporations that the ideal financial structure for a nonutility company is virtually all common stock with as little debt as possible. In interviews with executives of 20 fairly sizable corporations in five different industries, Gordon Donaldson found a widespread reluctance to issue long-term bonds despite the executives' awareness of the "theoretical" advantages of leverage.[27] There was a common tendency to "see what other companies' policies are" rather than make independent judgements. Frequently, reference was made to the dangers of debt if another depression should strike, although upon further questioning it usually was admitted that a major depression is an extremely unlikely event. So entrenched was this fear of debt (and of external financing generally) that in many instances managements would consider new investment opportunities only to the extent that internal funds were available to finance the undertakings—regardless of prospective rates of return. A related finding, also indicative of risk avoidance, was that management standards for investment "favored the established

---

[25] W. Adams and J. B. Dirlam, "Steel Imports and Vertical Oligopoly Power," *American Economic Review*, September, 1964. Also *Comments* and *Reply* in the March, 1966, issue of the same journal.

[26] J. McDonald, "Steel Is Rebuilding for a New Era," *Fortune*, October, 1966.

[27] G. Donaldson, *Corporate Debt Capacity* (Boston: Harvard Graduate School of Business, 1961) chap. iv.

and familiar investment areas over new and unfamiliar opportunities, even to the point of having no minimum earnings standard for the established areas and a prohibitive one for the new opportunity.[28]

### How Effectively Have Mergers Been Accomplished?

Since so many companies have been involved in one or more mergers during the postwar years, the security analyst usually has available a virtual laboratory situation for studying the capacity of a given management team to cope with many of the problems that growth entails. One of those problems focuses on the word "team."

A successful company's management is more than a group of individuals, each carrying out his assigned function. It is a group of individuals who have developed an effective working relationship. And when a new group of individuals is introduced via a merger, a whole new set of relationships has to be developed.

Thus, when the security analyst is examining a company which has a merger in its history, he would do well to inquire whether the inevitable changes in the relationships among the managers, and between management and labor, have been accomplished smoothly. Human relationships cannot be mandated by drawing up organization charts and job descriptions. They must evolve, usually with the persuasive guidance of the chief executive. If the analyst detects a continuing residual of ill will stemming from a merger that took place several years earlier, he may have reason to wonder whether the managers of the company are emotionally equipped to cope with the strains of growth.

By considering the degree of planning that went into a merger, the security analyst can gain further insight into management's abilities. A recent study by the Stanford Research Institute revealed a distressing tendency of firms to "buy into growth industries" just when obsolescence was about to set in—largely as a result of failure to plan for the future.[29] Another study also concluded that many acquiring firms "set no real operating objectives at all; they concern themselves only with the financial arrangements and dismiss operating matters with the assumption that the acquired company will keep on operating the way it did in the past."[30] This, of course, is a delusion. As has just been noted, the introduction of a new firm into a business causes all sorts of personality problems. It also raises questions about the integration of the new product line and new operating facilities with the existing enterprise.

The security analyst should inquire as to the *raison d'être* of the

---

[28] *Ibid.*, p. 67. Also see R. O. Swalm, "Utility Theory—Insights Into Risk Taking," *Harvard Business Review*, November–December, 1966.

[29] P. J. Lovewell and R. B. Young, *Corporate Strategy*, Stanford Research Institute, 1962.

[30] B. McLagan, "Why Mergers Go Wrong," *Dun's Review & Modern Industry*, November, 1964.

merger itself. There are many valid reasons for negotiating a merger. For example, a company may be underutilizing its plant capacity, and a merger may provide a convenient way of adding product lines that can be produced by the idle plant. Frequently, the new and existing products have complementary seasonal patterns. Similarly, the products added by a merger may be sold through the same channels as a company's existing product, thus making for more efficient use of marketing facilities. Another reason may be that the products of the merged company serve as raw materials for the products of the merging company (backward integration) or as end products which utilize the products of the merging company (forward integration). Or, as suggested earlier, the market for a company's existing product line may be decaying, and merger may seem to offer quick entry to a more rapidly growing market.

All of the reasons for merger just cited have a common denominator. They involve some sort of product diversification. However, the *degree* of diversification can offer a clue to managerial competence. It seems rather clear that although most of the successful growth companies of our era have had a broad conception of their relevant market, they have been careful not to stray too far too quickly from their existing lines of endeavor. This is because their managers recognize the possibility of losing control of events by spreading themselves too thin. A recent study reached the following conclusion: "Diversification moves have been most frequently successful when the company drew heavily on *both* its marketing and production or technological capabilities. About 70% of such ventures have returned average or above average profits while only 40% of the moves into fields relatively unrelated to company experience have done so."[31]

Numerous examples can be cited of corporations which have gotten into serious difficulty because diversification was permitted to run rampant. Twelve years ago, for instance, Olin Industries and Mathieson Chemical Corporation merged to form the giant Olin Mathieson Chemical Corporation. The product lines of the new firm were among the broadest in American industry. They included industrial chemicals, agricultural chemicals, brass, aluminum, cellophane, batteries, firearms, lumber, tools, fuels, and drugs.[32] After 12 years, it still is not clear whether this multitude of parts has been coordinated into an efficient whole. Similar problems have plagued the General Dynamics Corporation and Sperry Rand Corporation.[33]

---

[31] R. R. Larson and E. M. Brandes, *Success Characteristics in Diversification*, Stanford Research Institute, 1964, p. 1. See also S. Miller, *The Management Problems of Diversification* (New York: John Wiley & Sons, Inc., 1963).

[32] R. A. Smith, "Olin Mathieson's Goat-Feathers," *Fortune*, September, 1958.

[33] See R. A. Smith, "How a Great Corporation Got Out of Control," *Fortune*, January and February, 1962; and "At Sperry Rand a Conglomerate Finally Works to One Purpose," *Business Week*, March 19, 1966.

It must be admitted, however, that the executives of several rapidly expanding "conglomerate enterprises" have managed to keep good control of events. Recent examples include Litton Industries and International Telephone & Telegraph.[34] By sound application of the principles of decentralization, the chairman and president of a corporation can run the enterprise without being expert in every field of its operation. Indeed, highly centralized management usually is quite unlikely to be able to cope with the problems of growth. We turn, therefore, to a more detailed consideration of organization and control.

### Management's Delegation of Authority and Responsibility

*Decentralization.* In most modern large enterprises, the "one-man show" has given way to some form of decentralized operation. On paper, a decentralized organization typically has the following characteristics: Each major product line, or each major geographic area, of a company is headed by a different vice president and is run as if it were a separate company. That is, the vice president of the "division" has under him a number of functional officers—production, marketing, finance, research, etc.—and this team makes the decisions for that division. These decisions, however, are made within a broad framework of corporate policy established by the highest echelon of management—the chairman, president, and one or more executive vice presidents—acting in concert with both the divisional vice presidents and a group of vice presidents in the "corporate home office" who have *functional* rather than divisional responsibilities. For example, there will usually be a vice president–marketing at the corporate level, and a number of lower echelon marketing managers at the divisional level. The marketing managers are responsible to their respective divisional vice presidents, but the decisions of the latter are made within an overall corporate sales policy framework which is strongly influenced by the vice president–marketing. In addition, at the corporate home office level there usually will be a group of vice presidents and "staff" personnel whose authority and responsibilities cut across divisional lines—for example, in the financial and legal areas.

Thus, most large firms nowadays are decentralized, *at least on paper*. What the security analyst must be concerned with, however, is whether the paper surface is truly reflective of the underlying substance. All too frequently it is not. What occurs in some cases is that the divisional vice presidents' authority is severely limited by the "home office" superstructure, with corporate people interfering with, instead of supporting, divisional activities. When this condition is present, there is a grave danger

---

[34] "What Puts the Whiz in Litton's Fast Growth?" *Business Week*, April 16, 1966; and J. B. Weiner, "ITT: Can Profits Be Programmed?" *Dun's Review & Modern Industry*, November, 1965.

that the vitality of the entire organization will eventually be sapped—if it is not already—and the security analyst must be on guard.

To understand the seriousness of the problem, it is necessary to understand the presumed benefits of truly effective decentralization—which is really just an extension of the age-old concept of delegation of authority and responsibility. Simply stated, the idea is that the best efforts of people are forthcoming when they are given wide latitude to exercise their own discretion and are then rewarded or punished on the basis of their performance. Pride of accomplishment comes to the fore, "buck-passing" is minimized, innovation is encouraged, and executive development takes place in the best possible atmosphere. Moreover, members of top management are freed from most of the day-to-day chores involved in running a business and can concentrate on planning for the future.

The innovation aspect of decentralization is particularly significant. When power and decision making are too centralized, lower echelon people become "yes men" and creative thoughts are stifled. Decentralization, on the other hand, is conducive to innovation—innovation which results not only through the attempt to solve specific problems but innovation which occurs by the process of "serendipity."

Horace Walpole, reflecting on the role of chance in the development of new ideas, is said to have told the story of three princes of Serendip who took a trip in search of some particular object. They did not find the object they were looking for, but during the course of their journey found many new things simply because they were looking for *something*. Walpole called this kind of discovery "Serendipity," in honor of the princes. Serendipity refers to the chance discoveries of prepared minds functioning within an environment that is conducive to discovery. Polyethylene offers a modern example of serendipity. It was a substance found to be clogging the pipes in a study of the behavior of gases under very high pressures.

In a business organization context, decentralization is an environment more conducive to serendipity than centralization. For in a highly centralized atmosphere, potentially creative minds are discouraged from looking, from asking questions, from challenging the established order—and thus the probabilities of innovative inspiration occurring are severely reduced.

To be sure, decentralization is not entirely free from criticism. For example, in the early 1960's U.S. Steel Corporation found it necessary to drastically reorganize because its decentralization had gotten completely out of hand. Multiple layers of supervisory personnel had evolved, and too many independent production divisions and overlapping sales, accounting, and engineering offices were operating with inadequate policy guidelines. The most vivid way of illustrating the extent of this corporate sprawl is to cite some of the changes that were made during the five-year period, 1960–64:

1. About 3,000 management-level people—more than 10% of all the managers—were released or retired.
2. Seven production divisions were consolidated with larger units.
3. All research, development, and facility planning operations were coordinated under the direction of a single executive vice president.
4. Twenty-five district sales offices were closed and more than 50 others were consolidated. New area sales vice presidencies were established to direct and coordinate the activities of the district sales offices.

Thus, it is possible for decentralization to run rampant and for top management to lose control—much the same as in an improperly executed merger program. The numerous executives "in the field" lack a sense of overall corporate purpose and are unwilling to sacrifice their own immediate goals, on occasion, to the overriding long-term goals of the entire enterprise. Furthermore, recent technological breakthroughs in the areas of automated information retrieval and data processing have led some management experts to call for a movement back toward centralization.

Machines have been developed, and are now being improved and brought down in cost, which "read" printed characters, "understand" human speech, and "simulate" human thought processes. Therefore, within the next 10 years or so, something like the following may well be feasible for a large corporation: (1) Vast quantities of information regarding current operations in hundreds or thousands of scattered plants and offices are fed into a home office computer installation. (2) This information is rapidly processed to prepare reports for management which indicate the current status of operations, alternative courses of action, and the probable results of these alternative actions. (3) Management then makes its decisions—i.e., chooses among the alternatives—and immediately transmits instructions to the field. (4) Soon after these decisions have been implemented, the rapid information retrieval system enables management to learn whether its decisions are having the expected results (known as "feedback"). If not, modifications are instituted before errors begin to accumulate.

All of this is not science fiction. For example, it has been estimated by responsible authorities that as early as the mid-1970's telephone lines will be used more for data transmission than for voice communications. Many serious students of management processes believe that the logical result of such developments will be "that large industrial organizations will recentralize, that top managers will take on an even larger proportion of the innovating, planning, and other 'creative' functions than they have now."[35]

[35] H. J. Leavitt and T. L. Whisler, "Management in the 1980's," *Harvard Business Review*, November–December, 1958, p. 41.

Other, equally serious, students of management processes, however, take issue with this line of reasoning. In the first place, they believe that it tends to exaggerate the potential role of computers in decision making. For unless an operation is repetitive, the cost of computerization can become prohibitive. And the most critical, the most "creative," management decisions are precisely in nonrepetitive areas.[36] In the second place, they believe that skilled "middle management" will become more, rather than less, valuable in the age of automation. As one writer has put it, "because of heightened concern with problem identification, decision implementation, and new opportunities to find solutions, middle managers will be top managers in miniature."[37]

It does seem true that improved information technology will expand the "span of control" of top management. But today's and tomorrow's top managers are the middle managers of yesterday and today. And if middle managers are to be trained for the role of top managers, what better training ground than an effectively decentralized operation, with all of the flexibility, local autonomy, and encouragement of creativity that the term connotes? If our vital concern is management *ability*, as it is in this chapter, a parallel concern must be management *development.*

*Executive Development.* A Washington regulatory official recently paid the American Telephone & Telegraph Company a backhanded compliment when he said: "If the entire Bell top management were snapped off the earth, the system would continue operating without a detectable tremor."[38] In more positive fashion, the head of the American Management Institute has said: "If I were allowed only one question by which to evaluate an executive, this one would suffice: *Has he developed an adequate replacement for his own job?*"[39] Perhaps this question can serve as a useful guideline to the security analyst seeking to appraise the quality of a company's management team.

Frequently, a company's compensation system can serve as evidence of its policies regarding executive development. The analyst should be wary of an organization whose chief executive earns several times as much as his three or four closest subordinates, or whose junior officials have impressive titles but unimpressive material rewards. High salaries and fringe benefits for the whole spectrum of managers are necessary if the participants in the executive training program are to remain with the

---

[36] For an excellent elaboration of this point of view, see J. Dearden, "Can Management Information be Automated?" *Harvard Business Review,* March–April, 1964. See also the same author's "Computers: No Impact on Divisional Control," *Harvard Business Review,* January–February, 1967.

[37] M. Anshen, "The Manager and the Black Box," *Harvard Business Review,* November–December, 1960, p. 92.

[38] Cited in R. Sheehan, "A.T.&T.: A Study in 'Federalism' " *Fortune,* February, 1965, p. 200.

[39] J. Martindell, *The Appraisal of Management* (New York: Harper & Row, Publishers, 1962), p. 125.

company. At the same time, capable, high-spirited, hard-working executives are not retained by a policy of guaranteed job security. Junior executives should be challenged to make decisions which will be backed up by company funds, and they should be held accountable for those decisions.

### Is the Board of Directors Being Used Wisely?[40]

It is sometimes said that the function of a company's board of directors is to set basic policies, which management is then charged with executing. This is an overly idealized conception. Actually, management both sets and executes policy in most companies, and the principal function of the board is to review and appraise management's decisions. If the appraisal is favorable, the board ratifies the decisions. If the appraisal is unfavorable, the board suggests that management try a different course, or, in a crisis, replaces the management. Generally, the only time the board is the prime policymaker is when there is a conflict among the managers themselves, in which case the board serves as a superior court of appeal.

In carrying out its functions of review, appraisal, and appeal, a board of directors can be independent and objective or a mere rubber stamp. It can be a truly valuable and useful corporate asset, or a mere public relations showpiece. Since a security analyst is not usually privy to the inner workings of a company's board, he must judge it on the basis of indirect evidence.

Foremost among the pieces of evidence is whether or not a majority of the board members are drawn from outside the management. Although it is acknowledged that some companies have done very well with "inside" boards, it would seem that they have done well *in spite* of the system rather than because of it. For an inside board—even if composed of full-time directors in the manner pioneered by Standard Oil Company of New Jersey—tends to be too parochial in perspective and too much under the thumb of the chief executive. On the other hand, outside board members can provide the operating managers with new insights based upon their diversified experience and knowledge.[41]

---

[40] This section draws heavily on Chapter 7 of Martindell, *op. cit.* Another good source is *The Corporate Director and the Investing Public*, New York Stock Exchange, 1965.

[41] It is worth noting, however, that there is at least one serious study which casts "inside boards" in a more favorable light than outside boards. See S. C. Vance, *Boards of Directors: Structure and Performance* (Eugene: University of Oregon Press, 1964). Furthermore, legislative proposals have recently been made which might severely limit the rights of companies to employ outside directors. For a discussion of these proposals, see A. R. Towl, "Outside Directors under Attack," *Harvard Business Review*, September–October, 1965. On the other hand, it is noteworthy that in February, 1966, Standard Oil of New Jersey announced that for the first time in its history, outsiders would be elected to its board.

A second area of evidence, therefore, is the record of the board members' accomplishments in other capacities in other enterprises. The analyst will find it helpful, in this connection, to refer to *Poor's Directory of Directors*, *Who's Who in America*, *Who's Who in Commerce and Industry*, and other Who's Who–type publications.

The typical board of directors of a large company ranges in size from 9 to 15. There is no ideal, however, and many excellent companies have smaller or larger boards. However, the security analyst should be wary of companies which make frequent *changes* in the size of their boards. This may be evidence of managerial dissension.

## SUGGESTED READINGS

William A. Alberts and Joel E. Segall. *The Corporate Merger*. Chicago: University of Chicago Press, 1966.

Ernest Dale. *Management: Theory and Practice*. New York: McGraw-Hill Book Co., 1965.

Peter F. Drucker. *Managing For Results*. New York: Harper & Row, Publishers, 1964.

Townsend Hoopes, "Appraising Management," in The Institute of Chartered Financial Analysts, *C.F.A. Readings in Financial Analysis*. Homewood, Ill.: Richard D. Irwin, Inc., 1966.

Warren C. Lothrop. *Management Uses of Research and Development*. New York: Harper & Row, Publishers, 1964.

Jackson Martindell. *The Appraisal of Management*. New York: Harper & Row, Publishers, 1962.

Elizabeth Marting. (ed.). *New Products/New Profits*. New York: American Management Association, 1964.

William H. Newman. *Administrative Action*. 2nd ed. New York: Prentice-Hall, Inc., 1963.

Edith T. Penrose. *The Theory of The Growth of The Firm*. New York: John Wiley & Sons, Inc., 1959.

Nestor E. Terleckyj. *Research and Development: Its Growth and Composition*. New York: National Industrial Conference Board, 1963.

# SUMMARY OF CHAPTERS 5–9: EVALUATION OF COMMON STOCKS

The modern approach to common stock evaluation revolves around a two-part question: What is the potential growth of earnings and dividends of a company whose stock is being analyzed? What is a reasonable price to pay for that potential? Chapter 5 dealt with the growth potential of all corporations combined, and with various methods of determining the appropriate price to pay for growth—both in terms of stocks in the aggregate and in terms of individual stocks. Chapters 6 through 9 considered some of the problems and techniques involved in estimating the growth potential of individual companies and industries.

The approach to growth analysis that has been presented in these chapters proceeds from the general to the specific, and from the retrospective to the prospective. First, an appraisal of total economic activity and total corporate profits is undertaken. Next, the role of the industry within the economy is examined; and, finally, attention is focused on the position of the company within its industry. In each of these steps, an analysis is made of the factors responsible for the past record of growth. This provides the basis for an estimate of probable future developments. Although heavy emphasis is placed upon the marketing aspects of growth, sales are not equated automatically with profits, as is all too frequently the case among common stock analysts. Rather, a method is presented for appraising in depth the growth of profits in relation to the growth of sales.

The determination of a reasonable stock price, given an estimate of growth prospects, can take several forms. A relatively abstract and theoretical—but nonetheless useful—approach is to discount the projected income stream from a stock to a present-value basis, at a discount rate which seems appropriate in relation to the risks involved and in relation to yields available on alternative investments. More pragmatic approaches are based upon analyses of current and past price-earnings ratios. The method of analyzing price-earnings ratios may vary from simple calculations of average p/e ratios in recent years to elaborate multiple regression studies. Chapter 5 suggests that the most desirable approach is an eclectic one in which the results of different procedures are compared and inconsistencies are resolved.

Although specific analytical procedures are presented in these chapters, it would be a serious error for the reader to come away with the impression that the process of common stock evaluation is somewhat analogous to a recipe for baking a cake. One cannot simply mix together a number of statistical ingredients in accordance with a fixed formula and produce an acceptable result. For example, Chapter 9 stressed the importance of appraising the *quality* of a company's management as distinct from the company's statistical record. And Chapter 4, which is relevant both for common stock and bond evaluation, indicated that even the statistical record cannot be accepted at face value—that what is reported as net income by a company may be a far cry from its "true" earnings.

Thus, a good securities analyst must combine a firm grasp of technical skills with a large element of imagination, creativity, and intuition. Without a spark of ingenuity, statistical techniques are likely to prove sterile.

# 10

# EVALUATION OF BONDS AND PREFERRED STOCKS—I: TRADITIONAL APPROACHES TO QUALITY ANALYSIS

It's better to be safe than sorry.
—LESLIE FORD

STUDENTS often have a tendency to view the subject of bond and preferred stock analysis as highly academic and, quite frankly, rather a waste of time. This attitude stems from their overriding concern with common stocks as a personal investment medium. But the analysis of fixed income securities is a subject about which they should become informed.

### Principles

In the first place, individual investors are important factors in the market for certain types of fixed income securities, particularly tax-exempt bonds of states and municipalities and *convertible* bonds and preferred stocks. Second, many students go to work for banks, insurance companies, and investment bankers. Frequently, part of the training program in these institutions involves bond and preferred stock analysis. Some students may even make their careers in the field. Finally, a knowledge of corporate bonds and preferreds is very useful even to an investor whose interest is exclusively in common stocks. A company with a high credit standing can finance growth more readily and more efficiently than a company whose senior securities are held in low esteem. Therefore, in evaluating the common stock of a company which has senior securities outstanding, it is usually well worthwhile to examine the merits of the latter. Similarly, it is worthwhile to examine the *potential* credit standing of a company which does not currently have senior securities outstanding.

Except in the case of convertible securities and certain other investment outlets, which will be discussed at length in Chapter 12,[1] investors in bonds and preferred stocks sacrifice most of the benefits that may ensue from a company's future growth.[2] In exchange for this sacrifice, bondholders get a promise by the company to pay a fixed amount of interest on specified dates, and to repay the principal at a specified time. Investors in preferred stocks do not get a promise, but they do get a *prior claim* on income and assets ahead of the common stock.

Since a bond or preferred stock investor foregoes the benefits of growth, he must try to assure himself that the issuer will be able to fulfill his obligations. Analytical procedures must be more concerned with the issuer's probable financial condition under adverse circumstances than under favorable circumstances. Asset values will be of more significance than to a common stock investor, although we shall see why such values should not be overemphasized. In addition, more weight must be given to the possibility of a bear market for fixed income securities (i.e., a rise in interest rates[3]) than of a bull market (falling interest rates)—not because a bear market is more likely, but because risks should be more emphasized than opportunities in this area of investment.[4]

A logical approach to bond and preferred stock evaluation would proceed along the following lines:

1. Establish standards of quality which will not be compromised readily.
2. Determine whether the outlook for interest rates militates against the purchase of fixed income securities generally. That is, determine whether an extended uptrend of interest rates is in prospect.
3. Compile a list of securities meeting the quality standards, and choose the most attractive securities on the list. Frequently this means the highest yielding securities on the list, but not necessarily, as will be shown.

## QUALITY STANDARDS

By establishing quality standards we hope to be able to sift through all available fixed income issues and eliminate those which carry too much *credit risk*. "Too much risk," of course is a relative rather than an absolute

---

[1] For example, bonds of bankrupt companies undergoing reorganization.

[2] Some benefit may accrue if the growth raises the senior security's credit standing, thereby lowering its yield in the market and raising its price.

[3] Rising interest rates mean declining prices of fixed income securities. If you buy a 5% coupon bond at par, and two years later newly issued bonds of the same quality carry a higher coupon, no one will pay you par for your bonds. The price you can get will decline until the yield is competitive with new issues. At a later point, yield calculations are discussed more precisely.

[4] *Falling* interest rates also can pose a risk for investors in fixed income securities. Although the market prices of such securities tend to rise when interest rates fall, unless their terms include nonrefunding clauses they may be called by their issuers, thus confronting investors with the problem of reinvesting at lower interest rates than originally anticipated. If the "call premiums" are inadequate to compensate for the lower reinvestment rates, significant losses may be suffered. The subject of callability will be considered at greater length in Chapter 11.

phrase. The primary investment objective of bond and preferred stock buyers (except in the case of convertibles, etc.) is a steady flow of income. But it may be far more important to Mr. Jones than to Mr. Smith that this flow not be interrupted due to an adverse turn in the issuer's ability to pay. Therefore, Jones's quality standards must be higher than Smith's.

It might be that Mr. Jones cannot afford any risk of default whatsoever. The only bonds eligible for his portfolio, then, would be U.S. government securities. Only issues of the federal government carry no risk of default, because Congress has the power to issue money to pay its debts.[5] Corporate bonds, however, and even bonds of state and local governments, do carry varying degrees of risk of default. To these securities, tests of quality must be applied.

### The Rating Agencies[6]

One way of judging the quality of a bond is to examine the unbiased opinions of informed and experienced professionals. Bond rating agencies, such as Moody's, and Standard & Poor's,[7] provide the investment community with an up-to-date record of their opinions on the quality of most large, publicly held corporate and governmental bond issues. These rating organizations are not in the business of selling bonds. Moreover, their ratings are made by committees rather than by single individuals. Thus, there is a minimal possibility that ulterior motives will cause one bond to be more highly rated than another. Indeed, agency ratings are held in such high regard that official regulatory commissions utilize them in evaluating the safety of the securities held by banks and insurance companies. The ratings and descriptions of the rated bonds are made available in a variety of publications which are sold on a subscription basis. In addition, the indexes at the front of Moody's Manuals indicate Moody's ratings of the bonds of the indexed corporations or governments.

Bond ratings are designed essentially to rank issues in order of the probability of default—that is, inability to meet interest or sinking-fund payments or repayment of principal.[8] Thus, "triple-A" bonds (Aaa using Moody's designation, AAA using S & P's) are those judged to have a

---

[5] As noted in Chapter 1, however, government bonds do entail a risk of loss of purchasing power, and marketable government bonds entail an "interest-rate risk"—i.e., risk of capital loss due to rising interest rates.

[6] This section is based on E. D. Zinbarg, "What's in a Rating?" *Barron's*, May 4, 1964.

[7] Although Moody's and Standard & Poor's are the principal rating agencies, two other organizations publish bond ratings. One is Fitch, now a subsidiary of S & P, and the other is Dun & Bradstreet, of which Moody's is now a subsidiary. D & B specializes in municipal bond ratings.

[8] The word "essentially" is used in this sentence because the ratings also give weight to marketability factors in addition to default risk per se.

TABLE 10–1

**Industry Distribution of Moody-Rated Corporate Bonds, by Rating**

(Percent of Par Value Outstanding, December 31, 1964)

| | *Aaa* | *Aa* | *A* | *Baa* | *Ba & Lower* | *Total* |
|---|---|---|---|---|---|---|
| Industrials | 10 | 16 | 30 | 26 | 36 | 21 |
| Railroads | 4 | 9 | 8 | 31 | 50 | 16 |
| Utilities | 86 | 75 | 62 | 43 | 14 | 63 |
| | 100 | 100 | 100 | 100 | 100 | 100 |

Source: Computed from unpublished data provided by Moody's Investor's Service.

negligible risk of default and therefore to be of highest quality. "Double-A" bonds are of high quality also but are judged not to be quite as free of default risk as triple-A. Bonds rated A and Baa (BBB is S & P's designation) are generally referred to as medium-quality obligations, with the latter possessing a higher risk of default than the former. Bonds not falling within the first four rating categories are believed to contain a considerable "speculative" element.

*Rating Statistics.* At the end of 1964, there were 2,400 corporate bond issues outstanding which had Moody's ratings. The par value of these bonds was $57 billion—about half the value of all publicly and privately held corporate bonds outstanding at the time. Tables 10–1 and 10–2 show the distribution of these bonds by broad industrial grouping and by rating. The final column of Table 10–1 indicates that almost 65% of the bonds were issued by public utility companies, 20% by industrial companies, and 15% by railroads. Table 10–2 shows that only about 10% of the utility bonds were of Baa quality or lower. Of the industrial bonds, on the other hand, about 60% by number, and 30% by amount, were Baa or lower. The percentages of lower quality bonds were even higher for the railroads.

TABLE 10–2

**Rating Distribution of Moody-Rated Corporate Bonds, by Industry**

(Percent of Number and Par Value Outstanding, December 31, 1964)

| | *Industrials* | | *Railroads* | | *Utilities* | | *Total* | |
|---|---|---|---|---|---|---|---|---|
| | *No.* | *Value* | *No.* | *Value* | *No.* | *Value* | *No.* | *Value* |
| Aaa | 3 | 12 | 2 | 6 | 15 | 34 | 11 | 25 |
| Aa | 13 | 26 | 12 | 18 | 41 | 39 | 30 | 33 |
| A | 24 | 32 | 23 | 24 | 31 | 18 | 29 | 22 |
| Baa | 16 | 13 | 23 | 20 | 10 | 7 | 13 | 10 |
| Ba & Lower | 44 | 17 | 40 | 32 | 3 | 2 | 17 | 10 |
| | 100 | 100 | 100 | 100 | 100 | 100 | 100 | 100 |

Source: Computed from unpublished data provided by Moody's Investor's Service.

Data on bonds rated by other agencies would show a quality distribution similar to that of Moody's. Of the bonds rated by several agencies, perhaps half are rated identically. Where differences exist, they usually are not in excess of one rating category. That is, a bond rated, say, Aa by Moody's is most unlikely to be rated BBB by Standard & Poor's. While cynics may suspect collusion from the fact that such similarity exists, a more reasonable conclusion is that bond quality evaluation has become a rather precise art.[9] This will become clearer as we examine the factors that the rating agencies take into consideration.

Statistics on ratings of state and local government bonds are not available in as fine detail as corporate bond data. From what is available, however, it appears that about 80%–85% of the value of rated bonds of such governments are in the top three rating categories. In terms of *number* of issues, however, only some 60%–70% are in these categories. Furthermore, there are a vast number of relatively small issues (around $1 million to $5 million in value) that are unrated, even though publicly held.

*Default Record.* A strong argument for the use of agency ratings as a guide to bond quality is their excellent record of correlation with actual default experience. The National Bureau of Economic Research has made an exhaustive analysis of investor experience with corporate bonds sold during the period 1900–1943. Among the data compiled were the following, which show the percentage of bonds in each rating category at the time of offering which subsequently defaulted.[10]

| *Rating Category (Composite of Ratings of Various Agencies)* | *Default Rate (% of par value)* |
|---|---|
| 1 | 6 |
| 2 | 6 |
| 3 | 13 |
| 4 | 19 |
| 5–9 | 42 |

Thus, during the more than 40 years covered, including the greatest depression in history, only 6% of the par value of bonds originally rated in the top two categories subsequently defaulted. Twice as high a percentage of third-category bonds defaulted, and three times as high a

[9] On the other hand, common stock quality evaluation remains far from a precise art. Indeed, there is not even a commonly accepted conception of "quality," such as absence of default risk in the case of bonds. Therefore, we do not recommend that investors pay much heed to the common stock quality ratings of various investment advisory organizations. Advice on the gain or loss potential of a stock is one thing; assignment of a quality rating is something quite different. It may be recalled, in this context, that in Chapter 5 we used the number of institutional investors in a stock as a sort of proxy measure of quality.

[10] W. Braddock Hickman, *Corporate Bond Quality and Investor Experience* (New York: National Bureau of Economic Research, 1958), p. 10. These data cover "regular issues" only, excluding bonds issued as part of a reorganization.

percentage of fourth category. Over 40% of the bonds classified as speculative subsequently defaulted.

Since these default percentages reflect the impact of the Great Depression, they should not be considered representative of conditions during the years ahead. But while the specific default rates may be unrepresentative, the agencies' accuracy in *ranking* issues by probability of default was so impressive that it is justifiable to assume a continuation of such accuracy.

*Inadequacies of Ratings.* Although agency ratings should be held in high regard, investors in fixed income securities should go beyond mere examination of ratings in evaluating the quality of various issues. Agency ratings should be used primarily as a tool for quickly eliminating obviously unsuitable issues from consideration. For example, the investor may say: "Any issues rated less than Baa (10% of the par value of all Moody-rated corporate bonds) are probably too risky for me. Maybe a few *would* be suitable, but the effort involved in ferreting them out is very great, and I'll always have doubts. It's just not worth it to me."

But having said this much, the investor is still left with an enormous range of issues from which to choose. And four rating categories is not a very detailed classification system for 90% of all rated bonds. Every Aaa bond is not necessarily of equal quality; and it may well be that a given investor may think that a particular Aa bond is really as good as many Aaa issues. For example, a corporation's debentures will almost automatically be rated one category lower than its mortgage bonds. Yet the quality of the debentures may be so high that for practical purposes they can be considered as good as the mortgage bonds. Similarly, many professional investors deny that middle-rated municipal bonds are really as risky as, say, middle-rated railroad bonds. Moreover, even the rating agencies often differ in evaluation by one rating category.

Nor are these the only reasons why it is important to go beyond the ratings. *Privately* placed bonds, about half of all corporate bond issues in recent years, are rated only at the specific request of the institutional buyers—for a fee, of course. Preferred stocks and small bond issues are also unrated.[11] Finally, there are the frequently voiced criticisms that ratings are not comparable over time—that Baa, for example, does not connote the same risk today as it did 20 years ago—and that the agencies do not *change* their ratings quickly enough when underlying conditions change. This latter comment warrants more extended discussion at this point.

Ask a member of an agency rating committee what factors go into making the rating. His answer will surely be: "Everything we know about the company and the issue. There is no set formula."[12] This is

---

[11] Standard & Poor's *Stock Guide*, and other investment services, contain ratings for preferred stocks which appear similar to bond ratings. In fact, however, preferred stocks are not rated on a basis consistent with bond ratings.

certainly true. There is no formula. Nevertheless, certain of the more important yardsticks are well known because they are in common use by all bond analysts. In the next section some of these yardsticks will be examined. But for the subject at hand, the significant point is that these yardsticks are very heavily weighted by past developments.

The agencies are engaged in a continuous process of reviewing and reconsidering their ratings on each issue, and ratings are changed when the circumstances warrant. The National Bureau study shows (see Table 10–3) that 43% of the value of bonds which were highest rated at the time of issue were subsequently downgraded. Forty-four percent of the second-category issues later had their ratings raised or lowered, as did

**TABLE 10–3**

**Revisions of Agency Ratings of Corporate Bonds, 1900–1943**

| Rating Category at Time of Issue | Rating Category at Time of Extinguishment | | | | | | |
|---|---|---|---|---|---|---|---|
| | 1 | 2 | 3 | 4 | 5–9 | Unrated | Total |
| 1 | **57%** | 21% | 7% | 6% | 9% | | 100% |
| 2 | 9 | **56** | 13 | 7 | 13 | 2 | 100 |
| 3 | 2 | 12 | **45** | 18 | 21 | 2 | 100 |
| 4 | 1 | 2 | 15 | **43** | 35 | 4 | 100 |
| 5–9 | 1 | 1 | 3 | 14 | **75** | 6 | 100 |

Source: W. Braddock Hickman, *Corporate Bond Quality and Investor Experience* (New York: National Bureau of Economic Research, 1958), p. 158. Ratings are a composite of the ratings of various agencies.

55% of the third-category, and 57% of the fourth-category issues. Clearly, ratings are not frozen once made. Neverthless, they are revised only when the agencies feel confident that changes in the factors which influence them are not just temporary aberrations. Since these factors are largely *historical* balance sheet and income ratios, it usually takes some time before changes can be viewed as nontransitory.

While it is perfectly sound analytical procedure to wait for proof before revising a rating, the investor who can detect fundamental changes (as opposed to purely cyclical changes) before they are conclusively proven can gain an advantage over other investors. If for no other reason than this, an understanding of the important yardsticks of bond quality is essential.

### Protective Provisions of the Issue

The rights of bond and preferred stock owners are spelled out in detailed legal instruments—bond indentures and preferred stock contracts.

[12] See, for example, correspondence by a member of Standard & Poor's rating committee, cited in F. J. Calkins, *Cases and Problems in Investments* (New York: Prentice-Hall, Inc., 1955), pp. 172–78. Also, D. Day, "Determinants that Shape Moody's Railroad Bond Rating," *Commercial and Financial Chronicle,* February 13, 1964.

The specifics of these instruments are important ingredients of quality estimates although, as will be stressed below, continuance of the issuer's earning power is more significant than the contractual provisions of the issue.

With regard to contractual provisions, there is, first, the question of collateral. A corporate *mortgage bond* provides that in the event of bankruptcy the bondholders have first claim on the value of specified corporate assets. Other creditors' claims on the assets are thus "subordinated" to the claims of the mortgage bondholders. Where a bond is not secured by a mortgage on specified corporate assets, it is referred to as a *debenture*. Debentures are like accounts payable; they are general liabilities of the corporation. Debenture owners, therefore, have a claim on the value of corporate assets, in the event of bankruptcy, which precedes the claim of preferred and common stock owners but comes after the claim of mortgage bondholders, corporate employees (for unpaid wages), the government (for unpaid taxes), and other claims to which the bankruptcy statutes give priority.[13] The claim of preferred stockholders may be exercised after the general creditors have been satisfied and before the common stockholders receive anything.

Various clauses may be inserted into the indenture of a bond to protect its priority position vis-à-vis other creditors. For example, an *equal-and-ratable-security* clause specifies that if a prior lien subsequently is placed on corporate assets, the bond in question will have an equal and pro rata share in the lien. *Open-end* mortgage clauses provide that additional bonds may be issued with an equivalent lien, but only if the additional debt does not cause the total to exceed a specified percentage of the mortgaged assets. Another limitation on the issuance of additional debt may be that earnings have to bear a minimum relationship to the amount of debt or to the amount of interest charges.[14] *After-acquired-property* clauses state that if property is acquired after the issuance of a first-mortgage bond, it automatically will fall under the lien of that mortgage unless waived by the existing mortgage bond owners. In the case of preferred stock contracts, it usually is provided that subsequent issues of secured debt or stock with a priority over the preferred are not permitted unless approved by the holders of a certain percentage of the preferred stock outstanding.[15]

*Collateral De-emphasized.* The collateral provisions of bonds used to be very heavily stressed by investment analysts. They are much less emphasized today. Not that they are ignored—indeed, as noted above, the

---

[13] *Convertible* debentures usually are subordinated to the claims of all other creditors.

[14] In the case of municipal bonds, the level of indebtedness usually is restricted by statute.

[15] These provisions may not be too strict with regard to unsecured debt, however.

rating agencies usually grade a corporation's debentures one notch lower than the same corporation's first-mortgage bonds—but merely less emphasized.

The reasons for the de-emphasis of collateral are quite clear. Property value is a function of the earnings which the property can produce. Most property which serves as bond collateral is in the form of specialized plant and equipment—for example, a steel mill. When the economics of the issuing company deteriorate to the point of bankruptcy, the likelihood is that its property is incapable of earning a decent rate of return and is therefore not worth very much.

In some cases, the property may be convertible into some other use, or may be made more profitable by more efficient managers. Such property can have an intrinsic worth sufficient to meet the claims of secured creditors. But in bankruptcy cases involving truly valuable property, the courts have been extremely reluctant to allow secured creditors to exercise their lien and sell the property to meet their claims. Typically, reorganization proceedings are ordered, the end result of which is to liquidate existing claims by issuing new securities to the claimants. The trouble is that the more valuable the property, the more strenuously the junior claimants will fight to keep from being left out of the reorganized company.

Under the Supreme Court's "doctrine of absolute priority," each rank of securities must be compensated for the full amount of its claim before anything can be alloted to a junior claim. However, determination of the value of the assets of the bankrupt company, and of the manner in which the claims are to be satisfied, are subject to debate and interpretation.[16] Court proceedings can last for years. A classic example of the extremes to which debate can be carried is that of the Missouri Pacific Railroad. Trustees in bankruptcy were appointed in 1933, and reorganization was not achieved until 1956—23 years later. In the end, even if the senior creditors emerge without a loss of principal, they may well have lost a substantial amount of interest payments, and they may have been locked into their investment for an extended period of time, because the market value of even first-mortgage bonds usually is very depressed during reorganization proceedings.

*The Preferred Stock's Priority.* While investors often have given too much weight to the collateral features of bond contracts, they often have paid too *little* heed to the nature of preferred stock contracts. Preferred stock is classified legally as equity, but investors traditionally have looked upon preferreds as almost the same thing as bonds. The reasoning has been as follows.

---

[16] For a discussion of reorganization procedures see J. B. Cohen and S. M. Robbins, *The Financial Manager* (New York: Harper & Row, Publishers, 1966), chap. xxvi.

The major legal difference between a bond and a preferred stock lies in the nature of the holder's claim. The bondholder gets a legally enforceable claim while the preferred stockholder does not. Legally, he gets only a priority above the common stockholder. Failure to pay bond interest is an act of bankruptcy; failure to pay a preferred stock dividend is not. But practically speaking, when a corporation is operating profitably, the claims of both bond and preferred stock owners will be met without any hitches. And when a corporation is in serious trouble, it isn't too much comfort that you're a bondholder rather than a preferred stockholder; you're in trouble either way. This very practical observation has led many investors to believe that a preferred stock is, by its nature, just about as good as a bond.

The conclusion that preferred stocks are inherently as investment worthy as bonds is faulty, however. It omits consideration of the great number of corporations which are neither so consistently profitable that there is no question of omitting interest or preferred dividend payments, nor in such dreadfully poor condition that the bankruptcy courts loom ahead. Such corporations will make every possible effort to meet their bond obligations as they come due but often will not be nearly as diligent in paying preferred stock dividends. Numerous instances can be cited of companies whose earnings were high enough to pay preferred dividends but whose directors chose to keep the money in the business to build up future earning power. True, the inclusion of a cumulative dividend feature in most preferred stock issues acts as a deterrant to the promiscuous passing of dividends. (An unpaid dividend on a cumulative preferred stock is carried as an "arrearage" which must be cleared before common stock dividends can be paid.) Nevertheless, when management thinks it is to the company's long-term advantage to pass preferred dividends, it will do so. Unfortunately for the preferred stockholders, even if management is right about the long-term merits of its action, passing a dividend invariably depresses the market price of the preferred stock considerably.

*Municipals.* The bonds of states, municipalities, and other local subdivisions are all classified under the broad heading, "municipals." This broad heading, in turn, is broken into two groupings—general obligations (also known as G.O.'s or full-faith and credit bonds), and revenue bonds (or assessment bonds). The former are backed by the total taxing power of the issuer, while the latter are backed only by specific revenues, usually those derived from the facilities which are constructed with the proceeds of the bonds, such as turnpikes, dormitories, sewers, etc. With municipal bonds, even more than with corporates, the bondholder's security lies in the *income* potential of the community or facility rather than in *asset* values. For courts certainly will not allow vital public facilities to be seized by creditors.

*An Ounce of Prevention.* It should be clear by this point that the modern tendency in the analysis of fixed income securities is to stress *avoidance* of trouble rather than protection in the event of trouble. For this reason, it is as important to examine the bond or preferred stock contract for the presence of what have been called "rules of good financial housekeeping" as it is to examine such things as collateral, promises, priorities, and form. For example, a useful provision from the bondholder's point of view is that if the working capital of a debtor corporation falls below a specified level, common stock dividends must be suspended. Preferred stock contracts may provide for the transfer of some or all of the common stock's voting power to the preferred stock if various financial tests cannot be passed by the corporation. While the voting privilege per se might be of limited value to preferred stockholders, the possibility of such a transfer of control should encourage management to keep the company's financial condition sound.

Usually it is required that an annual "sinking-fund" payment must be made by a corporate issuer for the purpose of gradually retiring the issue. The specific bonds or preferred stock certificates to be retired at any given time may be selected at random and "called" at a specified price,[17] or they may be bought in the open market if a sufficient supply is available at below the call price. In some cases, the annual sinking-fund payments may be left in an escrow account (usually earning interest) for eventual retirement of the entire issue at once. With municipals, serial maturity provisions are generally used in place of sinking funds. Under this procedure, a portion of the issue actually matures each year, so the holder knows precisely when his bonds will be retired.[18]

Sinking funds are disadvantageous to the investor in one significant respect. After he has gone to all the trouble of evaluating and purchasing a security at what he considers to be an attractive rate of return, the investor may find the security snatched away from him by a sinking-fund call. And at that time interest rates may be considerably lower than when he purchased the issue, so that reinvestment in an equally attractive issue may not be possible. But there are several advantages of sinking funds to the investor, and these outweigh the disadvantage:

1. Sinking funds for bonds, like amortization provisions in home mortgages, give the lender greater assurance that the principal amount of the debt will be repaid by the maturity date. Chances of the borrower being embarrassed are much greater when a huge principal balance suddenly comes due. If the original proceeds of the issue had been used to

[17] The sinking fund call price is usually par, or a very small premium above par, unlike an "optional" call price, which is usually par plus one or more years' coupon. Optional call privileges are strictly devices to protect the corporation—mostly to enable it to refinance its debt in a period of low interest rates. For this reason, the investor gets a sizable premium. The subject will be treated in greater detail in the next chapter.

[18] Different maturity dates usually carry different interest rates.

acquire plant and equipment, as is likely, payments into a sinking fund as the property depreciates help maintain a healthy balance between fixed assets and long-term liabilities.

2. With preferred stocks, a sinking fund compensates for the fact that such securities have no maturity dates as bonds do. This can be particularly important in a period of persistently rising interest rates and resulting declining prices of fixed income investments. The owner of a preferred stock which has no sinking fund is doomed to a capital loss, whereas the owner of an issue which has a sinking fund knows that eventually he will get back the par value.[19]

3. If the company's earnings hold steady, the retirement of a portion of its bonds or preferred stocks leaves the remaining investors better protected.

4. If the price of the bonds or preferreds falls below par, the company will use the sinking fund to buy up securities in the open market rather than call them at par, or par plus a premium. This provides some price support for the issue, although it by no means constitutes a floor. Of course, the other side of the coin must also be recognized, namely that call price tends to set a ceiling on market price. Since an investor who pays more than the call price will suffer a loss if his holding is called, he is reluctant to pay the high price.[20]

### Ratio Analysis of Corporate Securities: 1—Earnings Coverage

Every analyst of fixed income securities has favorite ratios to which he gives heavy weight in reaching his decisions about quality. A few measures, however, are very widely utilized. The first is earnings coverage, also referred to as "times charges earned."

The concept involved in earnings coverage is quite simple to grasp, for it is analogous to a measure used by banks and finance companies in judging applications for *consumer* credit. The lending officer considering the application will examine the relationship between the applicant's normal monthly or annual income and the size of the required monthly debt payments. The higher the income relative to debt service liabilities, the safer it is to extend credit, other things remaining equal. It is precisely the same with a bond or preferred stock.

*Earnings Available—Bonds.* To calculate the coverage ratio on a corporate bond, it is necessary first to determine the amount of earnings available for payment of the charges. The best working definition is: net income before taxes and before loan interest. In this context, net income refers to "true" net income, as described in Chapter 4—that is, after any

---

[19] This is not to suggest that he should necessarily sit and wait for his stock to be called. It may well pay him to sell at a loss and reinvest in something else.

[20] The situation is somewhat different in the case of *convertible* bonds and preferreds. See Chapter 12, pp. 426–28.

necessary analytical adjustments. We recommend the use of pretax earnings in preference to after-tax earnings even though many analysts and investment services use the latter. Since interest is a tax-deductible expense, it is logical to compare it with net *before* taxes. Earnings are taken before deduction of interest, since we want to know how much is available for payment of interest.

*Charges—Bonds.* After determining earnings available for the payment of bond charges, it is necessary to determine the amount of charges to be covered. In corporate bond analysis, charges are usually equal to the item "interest on loans," which appears on the income statement. Typically, the bulk of this item equals the par value of outstanding funded debt times the coupon rate.[21] If a corporation has more than one class of bonds outstanding—say first-mortgage bonds and debentures—the pertinent figure is usually the sum of the annual interest charges on *all* of the debt. This is because all the bonds are legally enforceable claims; a default on any one of them can put the company into bankruptcy, thus jeopardizing the holders of the other issues as well. Therefore, we do not usually speak of coverage of mortgage bond charges and coverage of debenture charges, but rather coverage of total debt charges. However, there may be some justification for evaluating senior mortgage bonds separately. Senior mortgage bondholders generally receive better treatment in reorganization than other bondholders. For example, in the event of bankruptcy the courts may allow a well-secured issue to continue to receive interest payments even though payments on other issues are suspended.[22]

Sinking-fund requirements—i.e., amortization of principal—usually are not included in the definition of fixed charges when analyzing corporate bonds, although they are included in appraising consumer credit and municipal revenue bonds (often they also are included in railroad bond analysis). There are two main reasons for the omission: (1) Although sinking fund default is an act of bankruptcy, creditors usually are willing to waive payments for a year or two if the company is temporarily embarrassed. (2) Sinking-fund payments are presumed to be covered by depreciation charges. If it is desired to include sinking-fund requirements in fixed charges, earnings available for payment should be defined as *predepreciation* pretax earnings.

*Coverage Ratio—Bonds.* After calculating (*a*) earnings available for payment of bond charges, and (*b*) the amount of bond charges, the earnings coverage ratio is calculated by dividing (*a*) by (*b*). An example

---

[21] There also may be interest on short-term bank loans, and amortization of debt discount or premium.

[22] An interesting question arises with regard to the definition of fixed charges when analyzing commercial bank debentures. Should the analyst calculate coverage of bond interest only, or of bond interest *plus interest on savings deposits,* which have a prior claim? For a discussion of this question, see E. W. Lambert, Jr., "Bank Debt Securities: The Investor's Viewpoint," *Financial Analysts Journal,* May–June, 1966.

will clarify the procedure. Suppose a corporation's income account shows net income before taxes equal to $30 million. And suppose its balance sheet shows $25 million of 4% First Mortgage Bonds, $10 million of 5% Second Mortgage Bonds, and $10 million of 5% Debentures. Therefore, interest payments on the First Mortgage Bonds would be 4% × $25 million, or $1 million; interest on the Second Mortgage Bonds would be 5% × $10 million, or $0.5 million; and interest on the Debentures would be 5% × $10 million, or $0.5 million. Earnings coverage would be calculated as follows.

If the so-called *Overall Method* were being utilized—i.e., if the analyst took the usual view that a default on junior bond issues is just as serious as a default on senior mortgage bonds—then a single coverage ratio for all three classes of bonds would be computed. Earnings available for payment of charges would be equal to net income before taxes ($30 million), plus bond interest ($2 million), or $32 million. Bond charges would be equal to $2 million; and the coverage ratio would be 32/2, or 16.

As noted earlier, however, there may be some justification for evaluating the First Mortgage Bonds and the junior issues separately. In this case, three coverage ratios would be calculated, using the so-called *Cumulative Deductions Method.* Earnings available for paying interest on the First Mortgage Bonds would be the full $32 million of net income before taxes and before interest; but charges would be only $1 million, and the coverage ratio would be 32. To calculate coverage on the junior issues, earnings available for all interest charges ($32 million) is divided successively by interest charges on each junior issue *plus* interest charges on issues senior to it. Thus, the coverage ratio of the Second Mortgage Bonds would be 32/1.5, or 21⅓. The coverage ratio of the Debentures would be 32/2, or 16.

Although the Overall Method of calculating earnings coverage ratios generally is preferable to the Cumulative Deductions Method, in no case should the so-called *Prior Deductions Method* be utilized! Under this method, earnings available for payment of charges on each particular bond being analyzed is determined by deducting prior interest charges from total earnings available for all interest charges. This amount, in turn, is divided by only the charges on that particular bond. Thus, the coverage ratio of the First Mortgage Bonds under this method would be $32 million divided by $1 million, or 32, while the coverage ratio of the Second Mortgage Bonds would be $32 million, minus $1 million, divided by $0.5 million, or 62 (31/0.5 = 62). But this is patently absurd. The Second Mortgage Bonds cannot be safer—better covered by earnings—than the First Mortgage Bonds.

In spite of its obvious inadequacy, a version of the Prior Deductions Method frequently is encountered in connection with preferred stock analysis. Many investment services calculate "earnings per preferred share" by dividing net income (after bond interest as well as other expenses) by the number of preferred shares outstanding. When this figure is divided by the dividend rate on the preferred stock, a coverage ratio results which is analogous to coverage calculated by the misleading Prior Deductions Method. In the following section, a more meaningful approach to coverage of preferred stock dividends is presented.

*Coverage Ratio—Preferred Stock.* In earnings coverage analysis of preferred stocks, the Overall and Cumulative Deductions methods are identical. Preferred dividend requirements are added to interest charges, if any, in calculating charges to be covered, and this sum is divided into total "available earnings."

The preferred stock dividend requirement is equal to the par value of the outstanding preferred times the percentage dividend rate, or the number of preferred shares times the dollar dividend rate. But a complication arises. We cannot simply add preferred dividends to interest charges because the latter are tax deductible whereas the former are not. At a tax rate of almost 50%, a corporation has to earn $2 before taxes to pay $1 of preferred dividends, but need earn only $1 before taxes to pay $1 of interest.[23]

In order to equate preferred dividends and interest charges when comparing them with earnings available for payment of charges, the preferred dividends ought to be doubled at a 50% tax rate. As a generalized formula, to take account of other tax rates, preferred dividends should be divided by 100% minus the tax rate. For example, assume a tax rate of 48% and preferred dividend obligations of $1 million. Dividing $1 million by 0.52 (1.00 − 0.48 = 0.52) produces adjusted preferred dividends of $1,923,000. That is, at a 48% tax rate a company has to earn $1,923,000 before taxes to pay $1 million of preferred dividends.

Once preferred stock dividends have been adjusted for the tax factor, earnings available for payment of *interest charges plus preferred dividends* can be defined identically to earnings available for payment of interest charges alone—i.e., net income before taxes and before interest. Note that preferred dividends are not added back to net income before taxes, as are interest charges, because they were not deducted in calculating net before taxes whereas interest was.

---

[23] Indeed, for this reason new preferred stock issues have been quite low relative to bond issues, and many corporations which issued preferreds years ago are retiring them and substituting debentures. Some writers have even urged the substitution of *income bonds* for preferred stocks, but the financial community remains suspicious of income bonds. See S. M. Robbins, "A Bigger Role for Income Bonds," *Harvard Business Review*, November–December, 1955; also, F. A. Halford, "Income Bonds," *Financial Analysts Journal*, January–February, 1964.

To illustrate the coverage calculations, assume that a company's net income before taxes amounts to $33 million. And assume that its balance sheet shows:

| | |
|---|---|
| 4% First Mortgage Bonds | $25,000,000 |
| 5% Debentures | 20,000,000 |
| 5% Preferred Stock | 30,000,000 |

Total charges to be covered, adjusted for the preferred stock tax factor (assuming a 50% tax rate for simplicity), are as follows:

| | | |
|---|---|---|
| Preferred dividends: | 5% × $30,000,000 = | $1,500,000 |
| × Adjustment factor | | ×2 |
| = Adjusted preferred dividends | | $3,000,000 |
| + Interest on bonds: | 4% × $25,000,000 = | 1,000,000 |
| | 5% × $20,000,000 = | 1,000,000 |
| = Total charges, adjusted | | $5,000,000 |

Earnings available for payment of the $5 million of charges equal net income before taxes ($33 million), plus bond interest ($2 million), or $35 million. The coverage ratio of the preferred stock, therefore, is 35/5, or 7. On the other hand, the overall coverage of the two bond issues is 35/2, or 17½. Note that where a company has both bonds and preferred stock in its capital structure, the coverage of the preferred always will be lower than the coverage of the bonds. Thus it is entirely possible that the bonds will be of acceptable quality whereas the preferred stock will not.

*Standards.* The next logical question is whether 7 times charges or 17½ times charges should be considered high or low, good or bad. It is impossible to be dogmatic in answering this question. Different investors have different safety standards. However, we would suggest the following guidelines:

1. Compute a coverage ratio whose numerator is *average* earnings available for the payment of charges during at least the past 5 years, and perferably the past 10. This would include years of recession as well as prosperity. It often is misleading to use recent earnings only, since a bond's quality can appear high during prosperity and low during recession. What is desired is a conception of quality which holds good over extended periods of time.

2. The denominator of the coverage ratio should be the amount of charges at the time the analysis is being made. Average charges of the past 5 or 10 years usually should not be used because they may reflect past capitalization changes, and it is desired to see whether the company has a demonstrated ability to earn enough to cover today's charges not yesterday's. Only in the case of very rapidly growing companies should an

average of past charges be used. In such cases, earnings and indebtedness usually grow together, and it would be unreasonable to expect yesterday's earnings to be adequate relative to today's interest charges.[24]

3. In evaluating the coverage ratio which results from dividing (1) by (2), a distinction should be made between companies whose earnings are very vulnerable to economic recessions (for example, steel), and companies which are more stable (for example, retailing or utilities). A better historical coverage record of the former should be demanded than of the latter. By demanding a higher average coverage for cyclical companies, the investor is better protected against an unusually severe recession.

4. The National Bureau of Economic Research study of bond default experience, referred to earlier in this chapter, revealed a sharp difference between the default rates of bonds with coverage ratios of less than 4, as defined above,[25] and bonds with higher coverage ratios. Bonds with coverage ratios of 6 and over proved particularly safe. Based on these statistics, and upon the standards we have observed among large institutional investors, it is suggested that coverage ratios of fixed income securities, whether bonds or preferred stocks,[26] may be graded in accordance with the following standards, in conjunction with all of the other quality tests discussed in this chapter.

---

[24] A somewhat related aspect of this subject has to do with the timing of a corporation's borrowing. It often develops *quite fortuitously* that one corporation borrows at a time when interest rates are fairly high while another similar corporation borrows when rates are low. Other things being equal, this causes the coverage ratio of the former company's bonds to be lower than the coverage ratio of the latter's bonds. Recognizing this possibility, some bond analysts relate earnings to the principal amount of debt rather than to the interest charges.

[25] The NBER study defined earnings coverage as average annual income *after taxes*, but before interest charges, over the five-year period preceding the offering date, divided by fixed charges for the first full year following offering. Since the coverage ratio recommended in this chapter is based on *pretax* earnings, the NBER ratios should be approximately doubled for comparability. The default rates referred to were as follows for large new offerings during 1900–1943 (from Hickman, *op. cit.*, p. 413).

| | *Coverage Ratio, After Taxes* | | | | |
|---|---|---|---|---|---|
| | *Under 1.0* | *1.0–1.4* | *1.5–1.9* | *2.0–2.9* | *3.0 and over* |
| All industries | 35.0% | 34.1% | 17.9% | 4.0% | 2.1% |
| Railroads | 55.2 | 49.9 | 28.0 | 15.1 | 5.5 |
| Public utilities | 41.8 | 11.5 | 9.3 | 0.1 | 0.2 |
| Industrials | 9.7 | 16.0 | 16.5 | 7.4 | 4.0 |

[26] Since we have suggested that coverage ratios of preferred stocks be adjusted to a tax basis comparable with bonds, there is no need to establish separate sets of standards for the two types of fixed income securities.

| Coverage Ratio | Characteristic of Company | Relative* Quality of Issue |
|---|---|---|
| 6 and Over | Cyclical | Very high |
| 4 and Over | Stable | Very high |
| 3–6 | Cyclical | Medium to high |
| 2–4 | Stable | Medium to high |
| Under 3 | Cyclical | Low |
| Under 2 | Stable | Low |

* A distinction between relative quality and absolute quality will be drawn in Chapter 11.

*Illustration.* Since the Aluminum Company of America was used to illustrate methods of analyzing sales and earnings growth, it is instructive to carry the example over into our analysis of bond quality. At the end of 1965, Alcoa had $491 million of long-term debt obligations in the form of unsecured notes and debentures with various coupon rates, and $66 million of 3¾% preferred stock. During the year, interest payments totaled almost $24 million, of which a significant, but not dominant, proportion represented interest on short-term bank loans.[27] Preferred stock dividends amounted to $2.5 million.

Earnings available for payment of fixed charges and preferred dividends amounted to $143 million in 1965, and averaged $121 million in the 5 years 1961–65 and $113 million in the 10 years 1956–65. Thus, the earnings coverage of 1965's $24 million of bond interest was 5 times based on 5- and 10-year average earnings, and 6 times based on 1965 earnings. Coverage of interest plus adjusted preferred dividends ($24 million plus 2 times $2.5 million[28] = $29 million) was 4 times based on 5- and 10-year average earnings, and 5 times based on 1965 earnings. It should be noted, however, that the 1965 interest expense of $24 million was quite high relative to the company's previous experience. In 1964 the figure was $19 million, and from 1957 to 1963 interest expense was in the $15 to $17 million range. A large part of this rise in interest expense was due to a major long-term loan in 1964 at a significantly higher interest rate than prevailed on previous borrowings. The loan, made for expansion purposes, increased long-term debt by more than 25%. Therefore, the comparison of 1965 interest expense with average 5- and 10-year earnings is a conserv-

[27] Notes payable to banks amounted to $82 million, and "long-term debt due within one year" amounted to $15 million. In September, 1966, the company sold $125 million of convertible subordinated debentures for the purpose of repaying an equal amount of long-term debt due to commercial banks. Calculations in this, and subsequent, sections do not reflect the new financing.

[28] Since Alcoa's effective tax rate is closer to 40% than 50%, a more accurate adjustment of the preferred dividend would be $2.5 million divided by (1.00 − 0.40), or $4.2 million.

ative calculation, since the use of the proceeds of the new loan is not reflected in the earnings of most of those years.

Applying the standards suggested above for cyclical companies to Alcoa's coverage ratios, and without giving reflection to other measures of quality, it may be concluded that the company's bonds can be classified as of fairly high quality and its preferred stock slightly lower. On the Moody's and Standard & Poor's rating scale, the quality probably would be either "A" or "double-A" for the bonds and "A" for the preferred. The agencies actually rate the bonds "double-A" (preferred stock is not rated by the agencies on a basis consistent with bond ratings).

### Ratio Analysis of Corporate Securities: II—Capitalization Ratio

Another quality measure which almost all bond analysts stress is the proportion of total capitalization represented by equity. As was noted in the section on profit trends, in Chapter 8, leverage can be very advantageous to the common stockholder. For if a corporation can earn a higher rate on funds secured by selling senior securities than the rate of interest (or preferred dividends) it pays for these funds, the differential accrues to the benefit of the stockholders. It also was noted, of course, that leverage makes stockholder profits more vulnerable in a period of poor business, especially if carried to an extreme. The significant point, however, is that whatever benefits leverage confers are conferred upon the common stockholders. The individual bond or preferred stock owner would be best off if his certificate were the only senior security outstanding, because earnings coverage then would be at a maximum (assuming that the corporation could raise elsewhere the funds necessary to operate a prosperous business).

Thus, to the bondholder or preferred stockholder, the greater the junior capital as a percent of total capitalization the better. An analysis of the corporation's capital structure is, therefore, a sort of "asset coverage" measure which supplements the earnings coverage measure previously discussed. It is true that asset protection is de-emphasized in modern security analysis. It is also true that in most cases earnings coverage and asset coverage will be highly correlated. Nevertheless, capital structure analysis provides useful insight into the quality of a company's securities.

Unfortunately, just as the income statement of accountants is not necessarily most useful from a security analysis point of view, so too the capital structure as reported on the balance sheet is not in its most useful form.

*Leases.* The corporation's funded debt (bonds and long-term bank loans) may be taken at par from the balance sheet. But it does not portray the full picture in many cases. A large number of companies rent most of their buildings, and many are now renting equipment as well. But other companies borrow money and build or buy their own facilities. The "lease versus buy" controversy is one of the most torrid in modern corporation finance.[29] Significant to security analysts is the fact that two companies may be working with the same amount of fixed assets and producing the same profits, but one company may show significantly lower debt and interest charges on its financial statements because its policy is to lease rather than buy. Earnings and asset coverage of its outstanding senior securities, therefore, will appear more adequate. But is it really?

The company which rents fixed assets usually signs a long-term lease agreement to assure itself of the continued availability of the assets. Its monthly (or annual) rental payments, therefore, are very similar to the other company's bond interest obligations. However, the *full* rental payment is not analogous to interest. A so called "net" lease covers the landlord's own interest expense and profit margin, plus depreciation of the property. A "gross" lease covers these expenses plus taxes, insurance, repairs, etc., which, under a net lease, are the lessee's independent responsibility. Under either type of lease, only the landlord's interest and profit are analogous to bond interest since the portion of rent that represents taxes, insurance, depreciation, repairs, etc., would have to be paid even if the property were owned rather than rented.

Although the accounting and security analysis professions have been reviewing the problem for several years,[30] there has as yet been no widespread acceptance of adequate lease disclosure standards. Many financial statements have footnotes appended which state the company's obligations under long-term leases. But some do not.[31] Even more important, those statements that show rental obligations usually provide little or no basis for judging the portion which represents interest payments. This figure is the minimal necessary information if one is to determine the equivalent amount of debt represented by long-term leases. What is really

---

[29] Over the years the *Harvard Business Review* has contained many articles which elucidate the details of the controversy. The writings of Richard F. Vancil are particularly useful. See his "Lease or Borrow—New Method of Analysis," and "Lease or Borrow—Steps in Negotiation," in the September–October, 1961, and November–December, 1961, issues of the *Harvard Business Review*. Also see his *Leasing of Industrial Equipment* (New York: McGraw-Hill Book Co., 1963).

[30] The literature includes R. F. Vancil and R. N. Anthony, "The Financial Community Looks at Leasing," *Harvard Business Review*, November–December, 1959; J. H. Myers, *Reporting of Leases in Financial Statements* (New York: American Institute of Certified Public Accountants, 1962); A. T. Nelson, *The Impact of Leases on Financial Analysis* (East Lansing: Michigan State University, 1963); and Accounting Principles Board, AICPA, Opinion No. 5, *Reporting of Leases in Financial Statements of Lessee*, September, 1964.

[31] Form 10-K reports filed with the SEC are more detailed than reports to stockholders with respect to lease disclosure.

required is, in one scholar's words, "(1) the determination of the part of the rentals which constitutes payment for property rights, and (2) the discounting of those rentals at an appropriate rate of interest."[32] But, as the same writer points out, the determination of "the existence of property rights and obligations for those rights. . . . is easy only near the extremes,"[33] although the choice of the "appropriate rate of interest" should not be too difficult.[34]

One rule of thumb which might be used to cope with the leasing problem for the time being is as follows. If annual rental obligations under a company's long-term leases can be determined, together with some indication as to whether most of the leases are net or gross, assume that one fourth of rentals under predominantly gross leases, and one half under predominantly net leases, represent interest payments. Assume also that most companies can borrow at an interest rate of between 5% and 6%, depending on their "quality." This would mean that the equivalent amount of debt represented by the long-term leases is equal to 25%–50% of annual rentals "capitalized" at (i.e., divided by) 5%–6%.

For example, suppose a company makes annual rental payments of $2 million under long-term leases which are predominantly net. And suppose its quality status suggests that it could borrow at around 5½% if it wanted to build instead of lease the properties on which it is paying rent.[35] The equivalent amount of debt represented by the leases, under the suggested rule of thumb, would be:

$$\frac{50\% \times \$2 \text{ million}}{.055} = \frac{\$1{,}000{,}000}{.055} = \$18{,}181{,}000$$

In other words, it would be assumed that if the company borrowed and built its own property, instead of leasing it, its annual interest charges would be $1 million higher than actually shown on the income statement, and its long-term debt would be about $18 million higher than shown on the balance sheet. Under these assumptions, earnings coverage ratios should be recomputed, with both fixed charges and earnings available for payment of charges raised $1 million. And in analyzing the company's

---

[32] Myers, *op. cit.*, p. 5. It may be noted, however, that the Accounting Principles Board believes that the existence of "property rights" is less significant than whether or not the lease is "in substance a purchase of the property" (Opinion No. 5, *op. cit.*, p. 29).

[33] *Ibid.*, p. 44.

[34] *Ibid.*, pp. 46–47.

[35] In a very real sense, this statement contains circular reasoning by referring to the company's assumed quality status, since the purpose of capitalizing the rentals is to assist in the determination of quality. However, the historical record of the company's borrowing rates relative to the rates paid by other companies can be used as a guide, together with quality measures exclusive of lease influences.

capital structure, which is the subject of the present section, recognition should be given to the implied $18 million long-term debt.[36]

*Preferred Stock Par Value.* Whereas the balance sheet statement of debt frequently is in need of adjustment when one is analyzing a company's capital structure, the analyst usually is safe in accepting the par value of preferred stock as it is shown on the balance sheet. Occasionally, however, there is no par value or it is merely a nominal amount, such as $1 per share, whereas the liquidating value in the event of corporate dissolution is, say, $100 per share. In such cases, the analyst must use the liquidating value as the amount of preferred stock in the capital structure, deducting the added amount from the surplus accounts.[37]

For example, suppose a corporate balance sheet shows:

| | |
|---|---|
| 100,000 shares no par preferred stock | $ 100,000 |
| 1,000,000 shares no par common stock | 1,000,000 |
| Capital surplus | 13,000,000 |
| Retained earnings | 50,000,000 |
| Total | $64,100,000 |

If the 100,000 shares of preferred stock are determined to have a liquidating value of $100 per share, or $10 million, the $100,000 stated value on the balance sheet is deficient by $9,900,000. The analyst should, therefore, revise the data as follows:

| | |
|---|---|
| Preferred stock | $10,000,000 |
| Common stock | 1,000,000 |
| Capital surplus | 3,100,000 |
| Retained earnings | 50,000,000 |
| Total | $64,100,000 |

*Common Stock Book Value.* Common stock and surplus accounts shown on the balance sheet represent the difference between the book value of all the assets and the sum of all liabilities plus preferred stock. But plant and equipment is carried on the books at original cost less depreciation, and this may or may not be realistic in view of current reproduction costs or earning power. Moreover, there may be questions regarding the value of inventories, patents, subsidiary assets, "goodwill," and other intangibles. Furthermore, various "reserve" accounts may or may not represent real liabilities. Consequently, the balance sheet summation of

[36] The legally inclined may argue that leases and debts are fundamentally different because lessors' rights in bankruptcy are not nearly as great as those of bondholders. While this is true, in our opinion the security analyst is less likely to go astray by treating the two obligations as essentially similar.

[37] No reduction of surplus need be made when capitalizing rentals, because an offsetting amount must be assumed to exist on the asset side of the balance sheet.

common stock plus surplus accounts does not necessarily reflect the true asset value of the common equity.

Although it would be nice to send out teams of industrialists, engineers, and real estate appraisers to evaluate corporate assets, this usually is not feasible. Accordingly, the practice has developed among security analysts of using two measures of common stock equity: (1) the book value as shown on the balance sheet,[38] and (2) the market value, derived by multiplying the number of shares outstanding by current market price, or by an average of recent high and low market prices. Where the two measures produce quite different results, the analyst must use his judgment as to which is more representative of realistic asset values.

*Illustration.* The following information was derived from the 1965 year-end balance sheet of the Aluminum Company of America (rounded to nearest million dollars):

| | |
|---|---|
| Long-term debt (ex. due in 1 year) | $ 491 |
| Preferred stock ($100 par) | 66 |
| Common stock (21,423,722 shares no par) | 21 |
| Capital surplus | 47 |
| Retained earnings | 776 |
| Intangibles (net of amortization) | (1) |
| Total Long-Term Capital | $1,400 |

The capital structure of Alcoa, at 1965 book value, thus can be stated as:[39]

| | | |
|---|---|---|
| Long-term debt | 35% | (491/1400) |
| Preferred stock | 5 | ( 66/1400) |
| Common stock and surplus | 60 | (843/1400) |
| Total | 100% | |

During 1965, the high-low price range of Alcoa's common stock was 61–80. If the mean of this range, 70, is taken as a reasonable approximation of the market's appraisal of Alcoa's stock value, the total market value of the common equity works out to $70 × 21.4 million shares, or $1.5 billion. Thus, the 1965 capital structure, with common equity at market value is as follows:

---

[38] Intangibles are almost invariably deducted from book value, however, even if the other balance sheet values are taken as shown.

[39] At the end of 1965, the company had a $106 million "reserve for future taxes on income," attributable to tax savings from accelerated amortization. Some analysts include this type of reserve in common equity. If it were so included in our computations, total long-term capital would be $1,506 million, comprised of 33% debt, 4% preferred stock, and 63% common equity.

| | Million $ | % of Total |
|---|---|---|
| Long-term debt | 491 | 24 |
| Preferred stock | 66 | 3 |
| Common equity | 1,500 | 73 |
| Total | 2,057 | 100 |

If the company's bonds were being analyzed, the relevant "capitalization ratio" would be the percentage of total capital represented by securities junior in priority to the bonds—i.e., the sum of preferred stock and common equity. This ratio would be 65% or 76%, depending on whether book or market value of common stock were being used. If the company's preferred stock were the focus of interest, the relevant ratio would be common equity relative to total capital—60% or 73%.

*Standards.* Again the question arises: Are these ratios high or low? Again, one cannot be dogmatic, especially since the NBER study of bond default experience, which provides some objective data on earnings coverage ratios, does not provide similar data on capitalization ratios. Some guidelines may be offered, however, on the basis of general observation. They are indicated below. By these standards, both Alcoa's bonds and preferred stock deserve a very high rating—probably "double A."

| | *Minimum Percent of Junior Capital to Total Capital for Security Quality to be Classified as:* | | |
|---|---|---|---|
| *Company Characteristic* | *Very High* | *Medium to High* | *Low* |
| Cyclical | 60% | 50% | 40% |
| Stable | 50 | 40 | 30 |
| Public utility* | 40–50 | 25–40 | 25 |

*Separate standards are given for public utility companies, as distinct from stable companies generally, and are given as a *range*, because the subject of optimal leverage is even more controversial for public utility companies than for corporations in aggregate. See, for example, W. T. Hyde, Jr., "Are Utilities Financing Too Extravagantly?" (mimeographed, F. S. Smithers & Co., December 3, 1964).

## Ratio Analysis of Corporate Securities: III—Working Capital

Some companies may have satisfactory earnings and capital yet be "cash poor." That is, their earnings are high relative to obligations and they are not overly leveraged, yet they frequently are operating from hand to mouth as far as working capital is concerned. The bondholder or preferred stockholder must not only be sure that earnings will be sufficient to pay his claims but also that enough cash will be on hand to do so. Accordingly, other tests of quality are the current ratio (current assets divided by current liabilities), or the acid-test ratio[40] (current assets

[40] The acid-test ratio also is known as the quick assets ratio.

exclusive of inventories, which are not as readily convertible into cash as are receivables, divided by current liabilities), or the cash ratio (bank deposits plus liquid securities owned,[41] divided by current liabilities).[42]

For the Aluminum Company of America, at the end of 1965, the following calculations could be made.

| | *Million $* |
|---|---|
| Cash | 44 |
| Accounts and notes receivable | 193 |
| Inventories | 283 |
| Prepaid expenses | 4 |
| Total Current Assets | 524 |
| Total Current Liabilities | 220 |

Current ratio = 524/220.......................... = 2.4
Acid-test ratio = (524−283)/220 = 241/220......... = 1.1
Cash ratio = 44/220.......................... = 0.2

It is even more difficult to generalize about what constitutes high or low working capital than it is to generalize about earnings coverage or capitalization ratios. Although a current ratio of at least 2 to 1 often is set as a standard (1 to 1 for the acid test), liquidity requirements are very much a function of the nature of a company's business. For example, a telephone company can operate with a very low current ratio because there is a relatively short time lag between the provision of services to subscribers, the billing, and the receipt of payment. On the other hand, a machinery company faces a long time span between the acquisition of raw materials, the construction and shipment of machines, and the receipt of payment. This is particularly true if the machine is leased rather than sold. Consequently, the best procedure probably is to compare the working capital ratios of the company under analysis with the ratios of other similarly-situated companies, although there is an obvious element of circular reasoning in an approach where everyone looks at what someone else is doing. Referring to our case illustration, Alcoa's 1965 working capital ratios were relatively low in comparison with those of its leading competitors, as can be seen in the following data.

---

[41] Many companies invest income tax reserves in short-term government securities. If the balance sheet shows these securities as an offset to taxes payable, they should be transferred to cash assets by the analyst, with a corresponding increase in current liabilities.

[42] Some analysts believe that a better measure of cash adequacy relates liquid assets to *cash operating expenses* rather than to current liabilities. See S. Davidson, G. H. Sorter, and H. Kalle, "Measuring the Defensive Position of a Firm," *Financial Analysts Journal,* January–February, 1964.

| | *Current Ratio* | *Acid Test Ratio* | *Cash Ratio* |
|---|---|---|---|
| Alcoa | 2.4 | 1.1 | 0.2 |
| Alcan Aluminium | 2.6 | 1.0 | 0.2 |
| Kaiser | 2.7 | 1.4 | 0.3 |
| Reynolds | 3.2 | 1.7 | 0.6 |

In judging working capital adequacy, the analyst should examine not only the most recent data, but also the data for a period of at least five years, preferably including at least one year of recession. This will give him a better "feel" of the company's working capital policies. For example, although Alcoa's current ratio was 2.4 at the end of 1965, at the end of the previous five years it was 3.2, 2.9, 3.5, 3.2, and 3.6, respectively. Thus, the 1965 level was not really representative. The average of the six annual figures was 3.1. This compares with the following averages for Alcoa's competitors: Alcan, 2.6; Kaiser, 3.0; Reynolds, 3.4.

If possible, the analyst also should obtain working capital data at quarterly intervals rather than at year-ends only, since many companies follow a policy of "window dressing"—paying off their short-term bank loans at year-end and then borrowing again after the turn of the year. Even though debt repayment depletes current assets by an amount equal to the reduction of current liabilities, the current ratio will be improved. For example, suppose current assets are $5 million and current liabilities $2 million, for a current ratio of 2½ to 1. The simultaneous reduction of both the numerator and denominator of the ratio by, say, $1 million—to $4 million and $1 million—increases the current ratio to 4 to 1.[43]

An additional aspect of working capital analysis is to see whether rising sales of a company are being accompanied by a proportionately larger buildup of accounts receivable. If so, it is important to investigate whether the company's customers are creditworthy, and whether adequate bad-debt reserves are being built up. Admittedly, it is extremely difficult for an outsider to get information on these matters, but an effort should be made.

### Ratio Analysis of Municipal Bonds

Since the focus of this text is on corporate securities, we will not dwell at length on the ratios employed in analyzing the bonds of states, municipalities, and other local subdivisions. For "full faith and credit" bonds, three ratios are most widely used:[44]

---

[43] As long as the ratio is higher than 1 to 1, offsetting reductions of the numerator and denominator will improve it. The procedure will worsen the ratio, however, when it is less than 1 to 1.

[44] Good sources of statistical data are the Municipal Credit Report service of Dun and Bradstreet, and Moody's *Governments* manual.

1. Principal amount of tax-dependent debt as a percent of the assessed valuation of taxable real estate. This measure is used because property taxes are the key revenue-raising devices of most local governments, and property values are a good indirect measure of the wealth and income of a community. In comparing the level of this ratio among different communities, allowance must be made for differences in assessment methods. For example, one community may assess property at, say, 70% of estimated market value, while another may assess at full value. Another complication stems from the existence of overlapping debt, which occurs when the same piece of property is taxed by different governmental units.

After making allowance for these analytical problems, a ratio of 8% of debt to property values for smaller governments, and 10% for larger ones, generally is considered a practical maximum in order for their bonds to be considered high quality. Thus, Dun & Bradstreet rates the bonds of New York City only "better medium grade." The City's ratio of debt to assessed value was 12% in 1965, and debt to "estimated full value" was 9%. In contrast to New York City's 9% ratio of debt to estimated full value, Dun & Bradstreet data showed a median ratio of 3%–4% for other large cities.[45]

2. Debt per capita. Small cities with good credit ratings generally do not have more than $100 principal amount of debt per resident. For larger cities the figure may run to $150–$200, and giant cities may reach as high as $300–$400 before their bonds get accorded less-than-highest ratings. New York City's per capita debt in 1965 was close to $500. Obviously debt per capita must be analyzed in conjunction with the ratio previously discussed, since the number of residents is not necessarily representative of the taxpaying potential of a community. But debt per capita is a highly significant measure of municipal bond quality.

3. Debt service (annual interest and debt retirement obligations) as a percent of the community's budgeted operating expenses. If debt service begins to approach 25% of the budget, a clear warning signal usually can be inferred. New York City's debt service was well below this level in 1965. Annual debt service was about $500 million versus a total budget in excess of $3 billion (and about $4½ billion two years later).

In addition to these ratios, municipal bond analysts also place heavy emphasis on the amount of debt maturing within five years, on the prospective capital expenditures of the governmental unit, and on the unit's ability to avoid persistent deficit financing.

Revenue bonds are very much like the bonds of business corporations. Their quality depends largely on the "profitablity" of the facilities

---

[45] It may be noted, however, that the well-publicized downgrading of New York City's bonds by Dun & Bradstreet in 1965, was not due so much to the City's high debt *level* as to its increasingly strained liquidity position.

whose revenues are pledged to support the bonds. Therefore, the key ratio in revenue bond analysis is earnings coverage. Since civic facilities are not profit-making operations in the business sense—fees are usually designed to meet only operating expenses and debt service, with a small addition for contingencies—coverage ratios are not expected to be as substantial as for corporate bonds. Ratios of 1½ to 2 times charges are common for good quality obligations.

### Other Traditional Quality Considerations

When the rating agencies say that they consider everything they know about the company and the issue, they mean it. For example, while most of the quantitative analysis which stands behind a bond rating is concerned with *historical* data, much thought must be given to the question of whether the past is truly reflective of probable future conditions. In this connection, traditional bond analysis places heavy emphasis on the nature of the industry, the size and trade position of the issuer, and the trend as well as the level of earnings available for the payment of fixed charges.

Bond analysts usually are inclined to look most favorably upon companies which are in industries that are considered "indispensable." While it should be recognized that modern technology causes all industries to have a substantial degree of latent obsolescence, clearly some industries can be considered more basic than others. For example, most analysts would consider the bonds of a company which produces primary aluminum ingot less risky than the bonds of a company which only fabricates aluminum products for some end use such as construction—other things being equal.[46]

Similarly, large corporations which represent a substantial share of their industries' output are believed to involve less risk to creditors than smaller corporations with less entrenched trade positions. Small corporations (or small municipalities for that matter) are inherently more vulnerable than larger issuers because they usually lack strong banking connections, are not too well-financed, and often lack qualified administrative talent. Of course, *some* small issuers may be even safer than larger issuers, but on the average the risks usually are greater. The National Bureau study, to which frequent reference has been made in this chapter, contains clear evidence of a correlation between size and default rate.[47] One of the major justifications for rating Alcoa's bonds "double-A" rather than "A"

---

[46] Of course, other things are not necessarily equal, and it is easy to believe that an industry which has been indispensable until now will continue to be indispensable—and profitable. Classic examples of the danger of such a viewpoint are the railroad and streetcar industries.

[47] Hickman, *op. cit.*, chap. viii.

would be the large size of the company and its entrenched position within its industry. A pertinent observation with regard to size and trade position is that of Dun & Bradstreet in a review of New York City's bonds:

> While no easy or speedy rehabilitation of the city's credit appears likely, the facts remain that the economic resources are extraordinary in quality and extent, that great cities die but very slowly, and that the legal protection of the city's bonded debt is of unique strength.[48]

Finally, it must be recognized that while earnings coverage, or any other financial ratios, may be adequate in retrospect and on average, it is possible for average ratios to conceal incipient weaknesses. Therefore, bond analysts must pay careful attention to recent trends and to developments which may cause the future earning power of a corporation to deteriorate. In this sense, the bond analyst must adopt some of the forward-looking point of view of the common stock analyst.

## SUGGESTED READINGS

*Annual Review of the Bond Market.* Salomon Brothers & Hutzler, 60 Wall Street, New York.

Gordon L. Calvert (ed.). *Fundamentals of Municipal Bonds.* 4th ed. Washington, D.C.: Investment Bankers Association of America, 1965.

John F. Childs. *Long-Term Financing.* New York: Prentice-Hall, Inc., 1961.

Jerome B. Cohen and Sidney M. Robbins. *The Financial Manager.* New York: Harper & Row, Publishers, 1966.

First Boston Corporation. *Handbook of Securities of the United States Government.* New York, issued biennially.

Benjamin Graham, *et al. Security Analysis,* Part III. 4th ed. New York: McGraw-Hill Book Co., 1962.

W. Braddock Hickman. *Corporate Bond Quality and Investor Experience.* New York: National Bureau of Economic Research, 1958.

---

[48] Dun & Bradstreet, Inc., Municipal Credit Report, *City of New York,* January 24, 1966, p. 1.

# 11

# EVALUATION OF BONDS AND PREFERRED STOCKS—II: NEWER TECHNIQUES OF QUALITY ANALYSIS, AND SELECTION AMONG QUALIFYING ISSUES

Be not the first by whom the new are tried,
Nor yet the last to lay the old aside.

—ALEXANDER POPE

THE various rule-of-thumb quality ratios we have discussed provide a reasonable basis for ranking fixed income securities in order of default probability. And in this sense, traditional approaches to bond evaluation constitute a rather precise art. They do enable the analyst to identify *relative* risks. On the other hand, they do not provide much, if any, information on *absolute* risks. Surely an earnings coverage of, say, three times, or a Baa rating, does not infer the same probability of default today as it did 30 years ago, because investors today attach a lower probability than they did then to the occurrence of a major depression. Professor Gordon Donaldson has put the risk problem into clear focus, as follows:

> The basic questions in the appraisal of the magnitude of risk associated with long-term debt can be stated with deceptive simplicity: What are the chances of the business running out of cash in the foreseeable future? How are these chances changed by the addition of X thousands of dollars of annual interest and sinking fund payments? . . . .
>
> There are, of course, a variety of possible circumstances under which a company might have its cash reserves drained off. However, considering the problem from the point of view of mature, normally profitable, and reasonably

well-managed companies, it is fair to say that the primary concern with debt is with what might happen during a general or industry recession when sales and profits are depressed by factors beyond the immediate control of management. . . .[1]

### Absolute versus Relative Quality

*Principles.* Thus, Donaldson and other recent critics of traditional ratio calculations argue that what is needed is a thoroughgoing cash flow analysis. "Cash flow analysis," in this context, is more than merely a comparison of fixed charges plus sinking-fund obligations with net income plus depreciation. It is a complete sources and uses of funds network. For, in Donaldson's words, "it is somewhat artificial to think in terms of 'the cash available for debt servicing,' as the earnings-coverage standard does, as if it were an identifiable hoard when a number of needs equally as urgent are competing for a limited cash reserve."[2]

Cash flow advocates admit that detailed probability analyses are difficult for investors to make, since they usually lack much of the relevant data. The approach is more applicable to "internal" analysts—the corporate financial managers who must decide how much leverage to undertake. Nevertheless, the principles are applicable to "external" analysts as well, and in particular to institutional investors with trained staffs and access to detailed corporate records.

Table 11–1 outlines the major components of cash flow.[3] Those components which are derived from the income statement are so labeled and may be familiar to the reader. On the other hand, the components labeled as being derived from the balance sheet are probably less familiar. Generally speaking, decreases in assets and increases in liabilities represent cash inflows, while increases in assets and decreases in liabilities represent cash outflows.

For convenience of analysis and exposition, Table 11–2 condenses the cash flow items, and also shows how the net cash flow reconciles the beginning and ending cash balance (including "cash equivalents" such as Treasury bills). Taxes are kept as a separate category, instead of being lumped together with the other expense items, for several reasons. First, the basis for calculating income taxes has changed frequently for most companies during recent years (for example, because of changes in inven-

---

[1] G. Donaldson, "New Framework for Corporate Debt Policy," *Harvard Business Review*, March–April, 1962, pp. 123–24. This article is an abbreviated version of Part 2 of Donaldson's excellent book, *Corporate Debt Capacity* (Boston: Harvard Graduate School of Business, 1961). The approach is also discussed at length in J. E. Walter, *The Investment Process—As Characterized by Leading Life Insurance Companies* (Boston: Harvard Graduate School of Business, 1962), chap. xi.

[2] *Ibid.*

[3] Another version will be found in Chapter 4, p. 201.

tory, depreciation, and depletion accounting methods). Second, the tax *rate* has changed frequently and may well change further in the years to come. Finally, the gradual movement toward a pay-as-you-go corporate income tax system has caused distortions in the interaction between taxes incurred and taxes actually paid in any given year.

The issuance or voluntary retirement of long-term debt or equity capital, the payment of cash dividends on common stock, and capital expenditures are combined in a category labeled "discretionary transac-

**TABLE 11–1**

**Major Components of Cash Flow**

| | SOURCE OF DATA |
|---|---|
| *Major Cash Inflows (Sources of Funds)* | |
| 1. Net sales | Income statement |
| 2. Other cash income (e.g., dividends from subsidiaries) | " |
| 3. Increase in current liabilities (ex. taxes payable)* | Balance sheet |
| 4. Issuance of funded debt, preferred stock, or common stock*† | " |
| *Major Cash Outflows (Uses of Funds)* | |
| 5. Cost of goods sold (ex. depreciation) | Income statement |
| 6. Selling and administrative expenses | " |
| 7. Interest and preferred dividends | " |
| 8. Common stock dividends (paid in cash) | " |
| 9. Taxes incurred on year's operations minus increase in taxes payable‡ | Balance sheet |
| 10. Increase in current assets (ex. cash)§ | " |
| 11. Increase in gross fixed assets and other investments§ | " (*a*) |
| 12. Retirement of funded debt and preferred stock via sinking fund | " |

Notes: * Outflow if a decrease.
† Excluding changes due to conversions of bonds or preferred stock into common stock.
‡ Plus if a decrease.
§ Inflow if a decrease.
(*a*) While increase in gross plant, as shown on the balance sheet, is a commonly-used measure of capital expenditures, property disposals frequently make it a less useful measure than change in *net* plant, plus depreciation—in other words, a combination of income and balance sheet items.

tions." Admittedly, such transactions are not discretionary in the long run, except perhaps for the first. In order to keep a company economically viable, capital expenditures must be made and dividends must be paid. But in a period of emergency—and, after all, in the analysis of fixed income securities our focus is on emergencies—they can be suspended if the cash drain to which they give rise is intolerable. Donaldson has distinguished between the internal analyst, who is concerned with the probabilities of cash "inadequacy," and the external analyst, who is concerned with "insolvency." Thus, cash flow may be inadequate, from management's point of view, if it is insufficient to build new plants; yet, from the bondholder's point of view, this condition may be tolerable for many years.

The first step in the cash flow approach is to compile a historical record, on a pro forma basis if possible, of each major cash flow component for the company being analyzed, and to examine the percentage changes in each during years of adversity. In particular, it is important to note the degree of interrelationship among the components. For example, when sales decline do expenses tend to decline in proportion, more than proportionately, or less than proportionately? The method used to discover interrelationships can vary from a simple comparison of percentage changes to sophisticated correlation analysis and "model building."[4] It is also quite important, in studying the sales history, to distinguish between changes in the physical volume of sales and changes in selling prices (see Chapter 7 for an elaboration of this point).

**TABLE 11–2**

**Summary Reconciliation of Cash Balance**

| | | *Line of Table 11–1* |
|---|---|---|
| | A. Sales | 1 |
| *plus* | B. Nonoperating income | 2 |
| *minus* | C. Expenses (other than taxes) and sinking fund | 5, 6, 7, 12 |
| *minus* | D. Taxes | 9 |
| *plus or minus* | E. Change in net working capital, ex. cash | 3, 10 |
| *plus or minus* | F. Discretionary transactions | 4, 8, 11 |
| *equals* | G. Net cash inflow or outflow | |
| *plus* | H. Beginning cash balance | |
| *plus or minus* | I. Errors and omissions (e.g., nonrecurring expenses) | |
| *equals* | J. Final cash balance | |

The next step, and by far the more complicated one, especially for the external analyst, is to estimate the probability that in a future recession sales will decline $X\%$, the probability that they will decline $Y\%$, and the probability that they will decline $Z\%$.[5] More than three possible percentage declines can, of course, be considered, but as will be seen in a moment, the number of calculations increases with frightening speed each time an addition is made to the range of possibilities. Concurrent with estimating the "probability distribution" of sales declines, probability estimates must be made for the other cash flow components—which is a very practical reason for condensing the components into subgroupings.

Once these estimates have been made, they can be combined mathematically to produce a range of possible recessionary changes in cash flow,

[4] See, for example, J. R. Ferrari, "Quantitative Decision-Making for Life Insurance Company Investments: Possibilities and Limitations" (unpublished Ph.D. dissertation, University of Pennsylvania, 1964), chap. vi.

[5] A recession of course, is not the only possible sales depressant. For example, a company's product may become technologically obsolete, or its principle customer may turn elsewhere for supplies. This kind of risk was discussed at length in Chapter 7.

with a probability attached to each. This, in turn, provides the basis for an estimate of the probability of exhausting cash during a period of adversity. In other words, in analyzing Company A it may be concluded that the chances of insolvency during a recession are, say, 1 in 10, whereas for Company B the chances are 1 in 30. Such a conclusion enables us not only to *rank* the bonds of the two companies in order of their relative risk of default; it also gives us a measure of their *absolute* risk—although the measure will obviously be only as good as the assumptions that went into it.

*Example.* Suppose that a thorough analysis of a company's record and mode of operations suggests that the following assumptions are reasonable:

1. There is a 1-in-10 chance (probability .1) that a rather serious recession will reduce sales (category "A" of Table 11–2) by 40%.

2. There is a 3-in-10 chance (probability .3) of a sales decline of between 10% and 30%—the midpoint being 20%.

3. There is a 6-in-10 chance (probability .6) of a 10% sales decline.

4. Expenses, other than taxes, plus sinking-fund requirements (category "C" of Table 11–2) vary closely with sales, but usually decline somewhat more than sales during recessions due to extra-vigorous cost-control efforts. As a rule, the percentage decline in expenses is about 1.1 times the percentage decline in sales, and we can use this relationship in our estimates with a probability of .8. However, there is a .2 probability that this item will decline less than sales—say 0.9 times the percentage decline in sales.

5. Other income (category "B" of Table 11–2) has fluctuated between $0.5 million and $1.5 million, with a modest upward trend. Probabilities in a future recession are: $1 million (.6); $.05 million (.4).

6. During recession, the interaction of current assets and current liabilities (category "E" of Table 11–2) has usually drained cash, sometimes violently. Probabilities: −$5 million (.2); −$3 million (.6); −$1 million (.2).[6]

In addition to making assumptions regarding cash flow *changes*, it is necessary to make assumptions regarding the *initial conditions* from which these changes start. In general, it is more reasonable to assume that a recession begins at a cyclically high level of activity than at a cyclical low, or even at a normal, level. But there is no compelling reason why the analyst should not test the results under all three sets of possibilities. In any event, let us assume in the present example that the recession begins at a time when sales are $50 million and nontax expenses plus sinking fund

[6] It should not be assumed that recessions necessarily drain a company's cash through "current account" transactions. Some companies do become net creditors of other companies—i.e., accounts receivable rise more than accounts payable, either voluntarily or involuntarily. But other companies are consistently net recipients of trade credit—i.e., their payables rise more than receivables in recession, thereby adding cash rather than depleting it.

payments are $45 million. We leave the initial cash balance assumption for a later point.

If the initial sales level is $50 million, and the probable declines during recession are as given above, we can make the following calculations (all dollar data in millions):

| *A sales decline of:* | *Will result in sales of:* | *With a probability of:* |
|---|---|---|
| (a) 40% | 60% × $50 = $30 | .1 |
| (b) 20 | 80 × 50 = 40 | .3 |
| (c) 10 | 90 × 50 = 45 | .6 |
| | | 1.0 |

We have also assumed a .8 probability that "expenses" will decline by a percentage equal to 1.1 times the percentage sales decline, and a .2 probability that the relationship will be 0.9. Thus:

| *A sales decline of:* | *Will result in an "expense" decline of:* | *Therefore, "expenses" will be:* | *With a probability of:* |
|---|---|---|---|
| (a) 40% | (a) 1.1 × 40% = 44% | 56% × $45 = $25.2 | .1 × .8 = .08 |
| (a) 40 | (b) 0.9 × 40 = 36 | 64 × 45 = 28.8 | .1 × .2 = .02 |
| (b) 20 | (a) 1.1 × 20 = 22 | 78 × 45 = 35.1 | .3 × .8 = .24 |
| (b) 20 | (b) 0.9 × 20 = 18 | 82 × 45 = 36.9 | .3 × .2 = .06 |
| (c) 10 | (a) 1.1 × 10 = 11 | 89 × 45 = 40.1 | .6 × .8 = .48 |
| (c) 10 | (b) 0.9 × 10 = 9 | 91 × 45 = 41.0 | .6 × .2 = .12 |
| | | | 1.00 |

(Note: This and the following tabulations are sometimes presented graphically in the form of a so-called "probability tree," in which each "branch" of the tree represents a successive multiplication of individual probabilities.)

Subtracting "expenses" from sales we have:

| | *Sales Minus "Expenses"* | *Probability (Same as Above)* |
|---|---|---|
| (a)(a) | $30 − $25.2 = $4.8 | .08 |
| (a)(b) | 30 − 28.8 = 1.2 | .02 |
| (b)(a) | 40 − 35.1 = 4.9 | .24 |
| (b)(b) | 40 − 36.9 = 3.1 | .06 |
| (c)(a) | 45 − 40.1 = 4.9 | .48 |
| (c)(b) | 45 − 41.0 = 4.0 | .12 |
| | | 1.00 |

These 6 combinations expand to 12 when we take into account the two assumptions for other income as shown in the table at the top of p. 391.

At this point a deduction must be made for income taxes. The complications involved have already been alluded to, and there is no need to belabor the point. Some simplifying assumption is called for, at least for illustrative purposes.

| *Assuming combination:* | *Other income is* | *With a probability of:* | *Therefore, sales plus other income minus "expenses" is:* | *With a probability of:* |
|---|---|---|---|---|
| (a)(a)(a) | $1 | .6 | $5.8 | .08 × .6 = .048 |
| (a)(a)(b) | 0.5 | .4 | 5.3 | .08 × .4 = .032 |
| (a)(b)(a) | 1 | .6 | 2.2 | .02 × .6 = .012 |
| (a)(b)(b) | 0.5 | .4 | 1.7 | .02 × .4 = .008 |
| (b)(a)(a) | 1 | .6 | 5.9 | .24 × .6 = .144 |
| (b)(a)(b) | 0.5 | .4 | 5.4 | .24 × .4 = .096 |
| (b)(b)(a) | 1 | .6 | 4.1 | .06 × .6 = .036 |
| (b)(b)(b) | 0.5 | .4 | 3.6 | .06 × .4 = .024 |
| (c)(a)(a) | 1 | .6 | 5.9 | .48 × .6 = .288 |
| (c)(a)(b) | 0.5 | .4 | 5.4 | .48 × .4 = .192 |
| (c)(b)(a) | 1 | .6 | 5.0 | .12 × .6 = .072 |
| (c)(b)(b) | 0.5 | .4 | 4.5 | .12 × .4 = .048 |
| | | | | 1.000 |

The figures just calculated—sales plus other income minus "expenses"—include sinking-fund payments and exclude depreciation and other noncash expenses. Taxable income is just the reverse; debt retirement is not a tax-deductible outlay, whereas depreciation and similar items are deductible even though no cash is expended. (The cash, of course, was expended at the time the depreciable assets were purchased.) Suppose we assume, for purposes of this illustration, that depreciation exceeds sinking-fund payments by $0.5 million, that income taxes are paid as accrued, and that the company in question has an effective tax rate of 45%—lower than the normal 48% because other income is low-taxed dividends from common stock owned in affiliated corporations.

Under these assumptions, income tax is equal to 45% of the previously calculated data reduced by $0.5 million. A negative result would represent a tax refund. Continuing the calculations on this basis, we have:

| *Combination* | *Tax Base* | *Tax @ 45% (Rounded)* | *Sales Plus Other Income minus "Expenses" and Taxes* | *Probability (Same as Above)* |
|---|---|---|---|---|
| (a)(a)(a) | $5.3 | $2.4 | $3.4 | .048 |
| (a)(a)(b) | 4.8 | 2.2 | 3.1 | .032 |
| (a)(b)(a) | 1.7 | 0.8 | 1.4 | .012 |
| (a)(b)(b) | 1.2 | 0.5 | 1.2 | .008 |
| (b)(a)(a) | 5.4 | 2.4 | 3.5 | .144 |
| (b)(a)(b) | 4.9 | 2.2 | 3.2 | .096 |
| (b)(b)(a) | 3.6 | 1.6 | 2.5 | .036 |
| (b)(b)(b) | 3.1 | 1.4 | 2.2 | .024 |
| (c)(a)(a) | 5.4 | 2.4 | 3.5 | .288 |
| (c)(a)(b) | 4.9 | 2.2 | 3.2 | .192 |
| (c)(b)(a) | 4.5 | 2.0 | 3.0 | .072 |
| (c)(b)(b) | 4.0 | 1.8 | 2.7 | .048 |

Finally, we must reflect the impact on cash flow of changes in current assets and current liabilities. It will be recalled that our probability estimates were:

(*a*) – $5 million (.2 probability)
(*b*) – 3 (.6 " )
(*c*) – 1 (.2 " )

Combining these probabilities with the calculations above, we have 36 possible recessionary cash flow changes, as follows:

| *Combination* | *Cash Flow Change* | *Probability* |
|---|---|---|
| (a)(a)(a)(a) | $−1.6 | .048 × .2 = .0096 |
| (a)(a)(a)(b) | 0.4 | .048 × .6 = .0288 |
| (a)(a)(a)(c) | 2.4 | .048 × .2 = .0096 |
| (a)(a)(b)(a) | −1.9 | .032 × .2 = .0064 |
| (a)(a)(b)(b) | 0.1 | .032 × .6 = .0192 |
| (a)(a)(b)(c) | 2.1 | .032 × .2 = .0064 |
| (a)(b)(a)(a) | −3.6 | .012 × .2 = .0024 |
| (a)(b)(a)(b) | −1.6 | .012 × .6 = .0072 |
| (a)(b)(a)(c) | 0.4 | .012 × .2 = .0024 |
| (a)(b)(b)(a) | −3.8 | .008 × .2 = .0016 |
| (a)(b)(b)(b) | −1.8 | .008 × .6 = .0048 |
| (a)(b)(b)(c) | 0.2 | .008 × .2 = .0016 |
| (b)(a)(a)(a) | −1.5 | .144 × .2 = .0288 |
| (b)(a)(a)(b) | 0.5 | .144 × .6 = .0864 |
| (b)(a)(a)(c) | 2.5 | .144 × .2 = .0288 |
| (b)(a)(b)(a) | −1.8 | .096 × .2 = .0192 |
| (b)(a)(b)(b) | 0.2 | .096 × .6 = .0576 |
| (b)(a)(b)(c) | 2.2 | .096 × .2 = .0192 |
| (b)(b)(a)(a) | −2.5 | .036 × .2 = .0072 |
| (b)(b)(a)(b) | −0.5 | .036 × .6 = .0216 |
| (b)(b)(a)(c) | 1.5 | .036 × .2 = .0072 |
| (b)(b)(b)(a) | −2.8 | .024 × .2 = .0048 |
| (b)(b)(b)(b) | −0.8 | .024 × .6 = .0144 |
| (b)(b)(b)(c) | 1.2 | .024 × .2 = .0048 |
| (c)(a)(a)(a) | −1.5 | .288 × .2 = .0576 |
| (c)(a)(a)(b) | 0.5 | .288 × .6 = .1728 |
| (c)(a)(a)(c) | 2.5 | .288 × .2 = .0576 |
| (c)(a)(b)(a) | −1.8 | .192 × .2 = .0384 |
| (c)(a)(b)(b) | 0.2 | .192 × .6 = .1152 |
| (c)(a)(b)(c) | 2.2 | .192 × .2 = .0384 |
| (c)(b)(a)(a) | −2.0 | .072 × .2 = .0144 |
| (c)(b)(a)(b) | 0.0 | .072 × .6 = .0432 |
| (c)(b)(a)(c) | 2.0 | .072 × .2 = .0144 |
| (c)(b)(b)(a) | −2.3 | .048 × .2 = .0096 |
| (c)(b)(b)(b) | −0.3 | .048 × .6 = .0288 |
| (c)(b)(b)(c) | 1.7 | .048 × .2 = .0096 |
| | | 1.0000 |

We now rank these in order from most adverse to least adverse, indicating the probability of each and also the *cumulative* probability distribution:

| Cash Flow Change | Combination | Probability | Cumulative Probability |
|---|---|---|---|
| −$3.8 | (a)(b)(b)(a) | .0016 | .0016 |
| −3.6 | (a)(b)(a)(a) | .0024 | .0040 |
| −2.8 | (b)(b)(b)(a) | .0048 | .0088 |
| −2.5 | (b)(b)(a)(a) | .0072 | .0160 |
| −2.3 | (c)(b)(b)(a) | .0096 | .0256 |
| −2.0 | (c)(b)(a)(a) | .0144 | .0400 |
| −1.9 | (a)(a)(b)(a) | .0064 | .0464 |
| −1.8 | (a)(b)(b)(b) | .0048 | .0512 |
| −1.8 | (b)(a)(b)(a) | .0192 | .0704 |
| −1.8 | (c)(a)(b)(a) | .0384 | .1088 |
| −1.6 | (a)(a)(a)(a) | .0096 | .1184 |
| −1.6 | (a)(b)(a)(b) | .0072 | .1256 |
| −1.5 | (b)(a)(a)(a) | .0288 | .1544 |
| −1.5 | (c)(a)(a)(a) | .0576 | .2120 |
| −0.8 | (b)(b)(b)(b) | .0144 | .2480 |
| −0.5 | (b)(b)(a)(b) | .0216 | .2264 |
| −0.3 | (c)(b)(b)(b) | .0288 | .2768 |
| 0.0 | (c)(b)(a)(b) | .0432 | .3200 |
| 0.1 | (a)(a)(b)(b) | .0192 | .3392 |
| 0.2 | (a)(b)(b)(c) | .0016 | .3408 |
| 0.2 | (b)(a)(b)(b) | .0576 | .3984 |
| 0.2 | (c)(a)(b)(b) | .1152 | .5136 |
| 0.4 | (a)(a)(a)(b) | .0288 | .5424 |
| 0.4 | (a)(b)(a)(c) | .0024 | .5448 |
| 0.5 | (b)(a)(a)(b) | .0864 | .6312 |
| 0.5 | (c)(a)(a)(b) | .1728 | .8040 |
| 1.2 | (b)(b)(b)(c) | .0048 | .8088 |
| 1.5 | (b)(b)(a)(c) | .0072 | .8160 |
| 1.7 | (c)(b)(b)(c) | .0096 | .8256 |
| 2.0 | (c)(b)(a)(c) | .0144 | .8400 |
| 2.1 | (a)(a)(b)(c) | .0064 | .8464 |
| 2.2 | (b)(a)(b)(c) | .0192 | .8656 |
| 2.2 | (c)(a)(b)(c) | .0384 | .9040 |
| 2.4 | (a)(a)(a)(c) | .0096 | .9136 |
| 2.5 | (b)(a)(a)(c) | .0288 | .9424 |
| 2.5 | (c)(a)(a)(c) | .0576 | 1.0000 |

The cumulative probability column of the preceding tabulation indicates that the chance of a negative cash flow in a year of recession is 28% (.2768), or about one chance in four. But this probability does not measure the chance of the corporation becoming insolvent because, presumably, there was some initial cash balance to begin with. Suppose, for example, that cash has never dropped below $2.5 million in recent years and that we assume this as an initial starting position. The tabulation shows that the probability of a negative cash flow equaling or exceeding $2.5 million is less than 2% (.0160). Thus, even under the most adverse hypothesized circumstances, the probability of insolvency in a year of recession is extremely small.[7]

On the other hand, the chances of "cash inadequacy" may not be nearly as slight for the company in this example. Suppose it has to spend $2 million annually for several years in order to replace worn-out and obsolete plant and equipment and thus remain an efficient producer. Suppose further that it has been paying common stock dividends of $1.5 million and that a cut of more than 50% would shatter the price of its stock, leading to additional adversity (for example, an inability to attract the best personnel). In other words, suppose the company needs at least $2.75 million more than we have taken into account—$2 million for capital spending and $0.75 million for dividends. If an initial cash position of $2.5 million is assumed, cash inadequacy would result even if there were a net cash *inflow* of $0.2 million. As the tabulation shows, there is a 34% chance that cash inflow will be less than $0.2 million in a recession year.

Furthermore, we have considered only a single year of recession in this example. Conceivably, a company might suffer two or more years of adversity back-to-back. Even though the general economy has not gone through such an experience since the 1930's, many individual companies have. The same type of probabilistic approach as we have just outlined can be applied to this situation. What must be done is to specify a set of probabilities for the second, third, etc., years of recession, and to work out the results, using as initial conditions the various possibilities emerging from the first-year calculations. (The probabilities for subsequent years may be treated either as independent of, or highly dependent on, the assumed initial conditions.) Obviously, the number of computations involved in such a complex "sequential analysis" problem can become very large, and such computations are not usually feasible unless the services of an electronic computer are available.[8]

### Recapitulation

It was noted at the outset of Chapter 10 that the fixed income investor generally should be more concerned with the possibilities of adverse conditions than with the possibilities of favorable conditions. As a

---

[7] One study we are familiar with (unpublished) undertook a similar cash flow analysis of 21 fairly large corporations whose bonds carried Moody's ratings ranging from Aaa to B. Of the 21 companies studied, only one—whose subordinated debentures were rated B at the time of the analysis—showed a substantial probability of insolvency in a single year of serious economic adversity.

[8] See Chapter 20. For a discussion of sequential analysis as applied to the bond quality problem see Walter, *op. cit.*, Appendix 11–A. A more general discussion of the mathematics of sequential analysis is contained in R. Schlaifer, *Probability and Statistics for Business Decisions* (New York: McGraw-Hill Book Co., 1959).

result, before he begins to select specific issues for purchase it is essential that he establish minimum quality standards which a bond or preferred stock must meet if it is to be eligible for his portfolio. Chapter 10 and the first section of this chapter indicate various methods of measuring bond and preferred stock quality.

The quality ratings assigned to different bonds by the well-known rating agencies are designed to rank bonds in order of their *relative probabilities* of default. The major factors considered by the agencies in assigning the ratings include the contractual features of the issues, the earnings record of the issuers relative to the required interest payments, the issuers' capital structure and working capital position, and any similar information which sheds light on the relative creditworthiness of different companies. These measures of relative quality should be understood by bond investors so that they are better able to appraise the usefulness of the agency ratings for their own investment activities and so that they may be in a position to make independent quality judgments.

A recently developed approach to the analysis of bond and preferred stock quality seeks to go beyond measures of relative probabilities of default and to make a judgment about *absolute probabilities*. This approach views the problem in a broader perspective than the traditional ratio analysis approach. It is concerned with the ability of the company to meet all of its obligations, not just its financial ones. And it requires the analyst to make specific estimates of the range of possible future cash inflows and cash outflows. To date, this approach, which might be referred to as "cash flow simulation," has won few adherents among professional investors, but it appears to be worthy of serious consideration.

## The Interest Rate Risk

Although it is crucial for the fixed income investor to appraise the risk that an issuer of a bond or preferred stock may not be able to meet its obligations, the investor's risks extend beyond this possibility. One additional risk concerns the possibility of an inflation which may seriously reduce the purchasing power of fixed income and fixed principal. This risk will be discussed in Part IV of this text, which deals with portfolio management. Another major risk, however, must be considered here. It is the so-called "interest rate risk," which refers to the fact that if the general level of interest rates rises subsequent to the time an investment commitment is made in a fixed income security, the market price of that security will decline until its "yield" becomes competitive with new, higher interest rate securities. A corresponding opportunity for capital gain lies in the possibility of a decline in interest rates subsequent to making a bond or preferred stock investment.

The inverse relationship between market prices of bonds and the movement of interest rates is illustrated in Figure 11-1, which traces the month-end prices and "yield to maturity" of the U.S. government "3's of '95" (i.e., 3% coupon rate; 1995 maturity date) since they were first issued.[9] To better understand the nature of the inverse relationship between price and yield, it is necessary to know something about the arithmetic of yield calculations.

*Yield to Maturity.* The yield of a bond is equal to its coupon rate only when the bond's price is par. At any other price, yield must be calculated according to one of two definitions. The first definition, "cur-

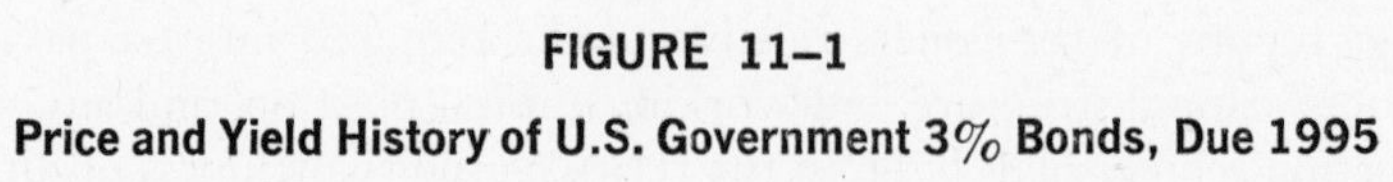

**FIGURE 11–1**

**Price and Yield History of U.S. Government 3% Bonds, Due 1995**

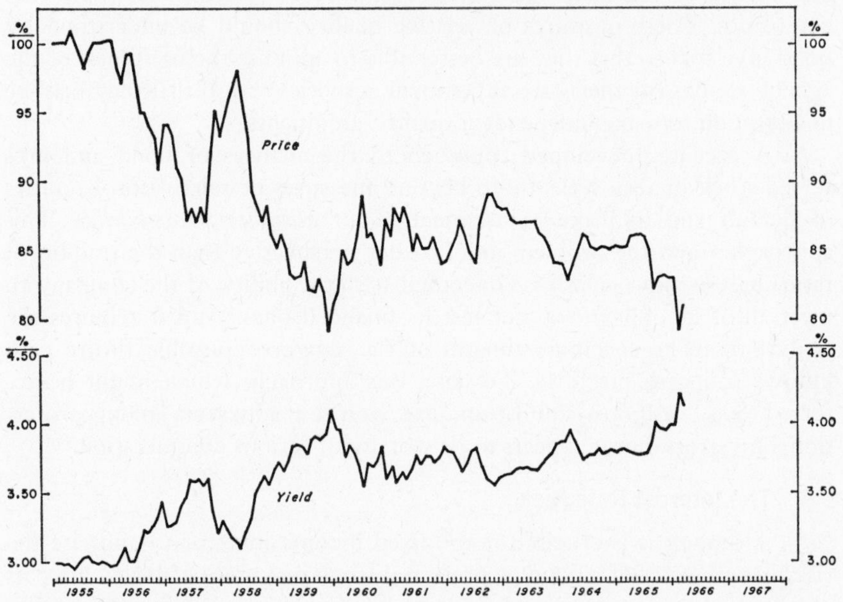


rent yield," is simply the coupon rate expressed in dollars, divided by the price. Thus, a 4½% coupon bond selling at 90 (i.e., $900 per $1,000 bond) has a current yield of 45/900, or 5%. This is the same type of calculation used in determining the yield on a common stock—dividend divided by price—and is applicable to preferred stocks as well.

For most purposes, however, current yield is an inadequate measure of a bond's rate of return. It fails to reflect the fact that unless the issuer defaults, the holder will receive the par value at maturity. (In a subse-

[9] This issue of bonds is one of several which are applicable at par toward the payment of federal estate taxes, even if they were purchased at a discount (they also must be included at par in evaluating the estate). Thus they are particularly attractive investments for wealthy people, and therefore usually sell at a higher price than would prevail if they did not possess the tax advantage.

quent section we discuss the possibility of the issue being "called" before maturity.) In addition to annual coupon payments, therefore, allowance must be made for the ultimate appreciation in value of bonds purchased at a "discount" (below par), or the ultimate depreciation of bonds purchased at a "premium" (above par). Even if the individual investor has no intention of holding the bond to maturity, it ultimately will be sold to a party who does so intend. And more important than the personal predilections of investors is the need for a common denominator in expressing the yields on different bonds of varying maturity. Obviously, a discount of, say, $100 per $1,000 bond is worth more if the bond will mature in 5 years than if it will mature in 20 (assuming that it will, in fact, be paid off at maturity). For these reasons, the concept of "yield to maturity" is the accepted common denominator in the financial community.

A simple analogy should make the yield-to-maturity concept clear. Assume you are examining a 4½% coupon bond, with 10 years remaining to maturity, selling at a price of 90. The yield to maturity in this situation is equivalent to the rate of interest, compounded semiannually, which a savings bank would have to guarantee to enable you to deposit $900 today, withdraw $22.50 every half year (bond interest usually is paid semiannually), and have $1,000 in your passbook 10 years hence. In more technical terms, it is that discount rate which will cause the present values of (*a*) $1,000 ten years hence plus (*b*) a 10-year semiannual annuity of $22.50, to total $900.

Those conversant with mathematics will realize that yield to maturity cannot be precisely derived algebraically. It would have to be found by trial and error. In practice, however, there are published tables which can be used to find the answer, or, lacking tables, an approximation formula is available which can be applied.

*Yield Tables.* Table 11–3 is excerpted from a book of bond value tables. It is a relatively simple matter to find one's way through such a book, despite its forbidding appearance. In the upper right- or left-hand corner of each page a percentage figure appears—in our example 4½%. This represents the coupon rate of the bond under study. Having turned to the appropriate page, move to the column which corresponds to the number of years (and months) remaining to maturity, as indicated by the column heading—10 years in our example. Then scan the column for the price closest to the price of the bond under consideration. Seldom will the precise price appear.[10] In our example, the price of 90 lies between 89.89 and 90.24. The first column at the left shows the yield to maturity

---

[10] This is because bond tables are compiled by beginning with a known yield and computing present value, rather than beginning with present value and computing yield. Only the former approach lends itself to precise algebraic formulation.

at the given prices. Thus, our bond has a yield to maturity of between 5.80% and 5.85%.

If a more precise yield is desired, a simple interpolation can be performed. In this case, a price spread of 0.35 (90.24 minus 89.89) produces a yield spread of 0.05% or 5 "basis points" (each 0.01% yield is known as a basis point; 100 basis points equals 1 percent). The price of 90 is 0.11 higher than 89.89. At the latter price, the yield is 5.85%. Therefore, the yield at 90 would be 5.85% *minus* (11/35 × 0.05), or 5.83%.

**TABLE 11–3**
**Excerpt From Bond Value Table**

| | 4½% | |
|---|---|---|
| | *Years to Maturity* | |
| *Yield (%)* | *10* | *20* |
| 3.00 | 112.88 | 122.44 |
| 3.30 | 110.15 | 117.47 |
| 3.35 | 109.70 | 116.66 |
| 3.75 | 106.21 | 110.49 |
| 3.80 | 105.78 | 109.74 |
| 5.00 | 96.10 | 93.72 |
| 5.30 | 93.85 | 90.21 |
| 5.35 | 93.48 | 89.64 |
| 5.80 | 90.24 | 84.73 |
| 5.85 | 89.89 | 84.21 |

Source: *Investors Bond Values Table* (Boston: Financial Publishing Co., 1962), pp. 1738–39, 1756–57.

*Yield Formula.* When yield tables are not handy, an approximation formula can produce satisfactory results. The formula is:

$$\frac{\text{Annual coupon interest plus (Discount/number years to maturity)} \text{ or } \text{minus (Premium/number years to maturity)}}{\text{(Current price + Par value)/2}}$$

The reasoning behind this formula will be explained in a moment, but as applied to our example it would produce this result:

$$\frac{45 + 100/10}{(900 + 1000)/2} = \frac{45 + 10}{950} = \frac{55}{950} = 5.79\%$$

Our answer would thus be only 0.04% away from the correct yield. Now suppose the same bond were selling for 110 instead of 90. Applying the formula, we would get:

$$\frac{45 - 100/10}{(1100 + 1000)/2} = \frac{45 - 10}{1050} = \frac{35}{1050} = 3.33\%$$

Turning back to Table 11–3, it will be noted that 110 falls between the entries 110.15 and 109.70. The correct yield is, therefore, between 3.30% and 3.35%, and interpolating produces a result of 3.32%. Our estimate is off by only one basis point.

The same formula can be used in reverse. Instead of calculating the approximate yield based on a known purchase price, we can calculate the approximate purchase price which would produce a desired yield. Continuing the previous example, suppose we want to find the price necessary to provide a yield to maturity of 5%. Since the coupon rate is 4½%, we know that the bond must sell at a discount to produce 5% yield. Therefore, letting $X$ = purchase price and $1{,}000 - X$ = discount, we have the following:

$$0.05 = \frac{45 + (1{,}000 - X)/10}{(X + 1{,}000)/2}$$

This reduces to:

$$0.05 = \frac{45 + 100 - .1X}{.5X + 500}$$

Cross-multiplying, we get: $0.05(.5X + 500) = 145 - .1X$, or

$$.025X + 25 = 145 - .1X$$

Transposing, we have:

$$.125X = 120, \text{ thus}$$

$$X = 120/.125, \text{ or}$$

$X = \$960$ (Actual price from bond table is 96.10, or \$961)

In the same way, if we wanted to find the price that produces a 3% yield, we know that a premium bond is involved. Let $X$ = purchase price, $X - 1{,}000$ = premium. Therefore:

$$0.03 = \frac{45 - (X - 1{,}000)/10}{(X + 1{,}000)/2}$$

$$0.03 = \frac{45 - .1X + 100}{.5X + 500}$$

$$0.015X + 15 = 145 - .1X$$

$$0.115X = 130$$

$X = \$1{,}130$ (Actual price from bond table is 112.88, or \$1,128.80)

Regarding the derivation of the formula, the numerator assumes that each year from the date of purchase the bondholder will receive: (a) \$45 of coupon interest, plus (or minus) (b) a pro rata portion of the appreciation (or depreciation) attributable to the purchase at a discount (or premium) of a bond which will be paid off at par at maturity. Obviously, the appreciation or depreciation will not be *realized* until maturity, but an annual amortization of the amount makes good sense.

The denominator of the formula represents the average "true" investment during the period to maturity. On an amortized basis, a bond purchased at a discount or premium appreciates or depreciates in value each year. It would, therefore, be unrealistic to assume that the investor has a constant commitment throughout the life of the bond, equal to his purchase price. What he really has committed is the average of each year's amortized value. This average is approximated by the expression ½ (purchase price + par value). It is, in effect, the amortized value in the middle year of the bond's remaining lifetime.

*Maturity and Risk.* A comparison of the 10- and 20-year maturity columns of Table 11–3 brings out another very significant fact to bond investors. Note that when the yield rises ½ of 1% from 3.30 to 3.80, the 10-year bond falls in price from 110.15 to 105.78, a decline of 4.37 points or approximately 4%. The same ½ of 1% yield rise, however, causes the 20-year bond to decline 7.73 points from 117.47 to 109.74, or a 6½% drop. It is virtually axiomatic that fluctuations in the general level of interest rates cause long-term bonds to fluctuate more in price than shorter term bonds. When interest rates rise, long-term bonds fall more sharply in price than shorter term bonds; when interest rates fall, long-terms rise faster in price. Reference to the yield approximation formula will demonstrate more clearly why this is so.

Let us assume the existence of three bonds of identical quality and identical coupon rate—say 3%. All are selling at par. The only difference among the bonds is maturity. Bond A has a 1-year maturity; Bond B has a 20-year maturity; and Bond C has a 40-year maturity. Let us next suppose that a rise in the general level of interest rates causes all three bonds to go to a 3½% yield basis. To what price will each fall? The following tabulation shows the approximate answers:

| Calculation Step | Bond A (1 year) | Bond B (20 years) |
|---|---|---|
| (1) | $0.035 = \frac{30 + (1{,}000 - X)/1}{(X + 1{,}000)/2}$ | $0.035 = \frac{30 + (1{,}000 - X)/20}{(X + 1{,}000)/2}$ |
| (2) | $0.035 = \frac{30 + 1{,}000 - X}{.5X + 500}$ | $0.035 = \frac{30 + 50 - 0.05X}{.5X + 500}$ |
| (3) | $0.0175X + 17.50 = 1030 - X$ | $0.0175X + 17.50 = 80 - 0.05X$ |
| (4) | $1.0175X = 1{,}012.50$ | $0.0675X = 62.50$ |
| (5) | $X = 995$ | $X = 926$ |

| Calculation Step | Bond C (40 years) |
|---|---|
| (1) | $0.035 = \dfrac{30 + (1{,}000 - X)/40}{(X + 1{,}000)/2}$ |
| (2) | $0.035 = \dfrac{30 + 25 - 0.025X}{.5X + 500}$ |
| (3) | $0.0175X + 17.50 = 55 - .025X$ |
| (4) | $0.0425X = 37.50$ |
| (5) | $X = 882$ |

Thus, with the same ½ of 1% yield increase, the 1-year issue drops 0.5% in price ($5 per $1,000), the 20-year issue drops 7.4% and the 40-year issue drops 11.8%. The reason may be inferred directly from the formula. The additional ½ of 1% yield to maturity must be derived from the discount since, as will be seen in calculation step (1), every other value in the formula is identical. But as maturity increases, the discount is being amortized over an increasing number of years. Therefore, in order for the discount to produce an extra ½ of 1% *per annum*, it must be progressively larger in dollar amount as maturity increases.

Even if account is taken of the fact that *yields* on short-term securities typically fluctuate more violently than on long-term securities (see Chapter 13), it remains true that *price* typically fluctuates more on long-term issues. For example, suppose the 1-year security in our example rose in yield, not to 3½%, but to 5%. Solving for price, we have:

$$0.05 = \frac{30 + (1{,}000 - X)/1}{(X + 1{,}000)/2}$$

$$0.05 = \frac{30 + 1{,}000 - X}{0.5X + 500}$$

$$0.025X + 25 = 1{,}030 - X$$
$$1.025X = 1{,}005$$
$$X = 980$$

A yield increase of a full two percentage points from a 3% level causes the price of the 1-year issue to fall only 2%, compared with 7% and 12% price declines on 20- and 40-year issues, respectively, when yield rises ½ of 1% from a 3% level. Clearly, then, bond risk is in large part a function of maturity. Indeed, long maturity increases risk not only because of the interest rate factor but also because it increases the time available for unexpected occurrences, such as obsolescence of the borrower's product line, general economic dislocations, or severe depreciation in the value of the dollar.[11]

[11] A recent unpublished doctoral dissertation considered the nature of this risk more explicitly. It concluded that for corporate bonds carrying the three highest agency ratings, losses from default or credit impairment have indeed been greater the

*Interest Rate Changes.* We have seen that it is essential for the fixed income investor to consider the major factors which tend to shape the direction of interest rates, because the market value of his investments will change as interest rates change. Figure 11–2 portrays the movement of yields on corporate bonds of highest quality since 1900. Three features of the data stand out:

1. There was no overall trend in bond yields during this period.[12]
2. Although there was no overall trend, bond yields have moved in "long cycles." Thus they rose from 1900 to 1920, declined from 1920 to 1946, and climbed steadily back to the level of the 1920's during the post–World War II years.
3. Superimposed on the long cycles have been cycles of shorter duration. For example, during the long post-World War II rise, interest rates eased in periods of economic slack such as 1949, 1954, 1958, and 1960.

While it may sound trite to say that the level of interest rates is determined by the relative strength of supply and demand for loanable funds, it is true. When lenders have more funds and are more anxious to lend than borrowers need or want to borrow, interest rates fall. When the tables are turned, interest rates rise.[13]

The demand for funds has two major components: demands from private borrowers—businesses and consumers—and demands from government—federal, state, and local. The supply of funds likewise has two major components—individuals' savings and, at least in the shorter run, extension of credit by the commercial banking system.

Private demands for funds are largely a function of the actual and expected level and growth rate of economic activity. Government demands are determined by the socioeconomic philosophy of the electorate and its chosen representatives. Over the long run, a remarkably steady percentage of disposable personal income has been saved by the private sector of the economy. But short-run cyclical changes in the savings-to-income ratio are common. Commercial bank credit extension also is cyclically volatile, hinging largely on Federal Reserve policy, which, in

---

longer the original term to maturity. But for bonds of fourth quality, credit losses have not been a function of term to maturity, and for bonds of less than fourth quality, shorter term issues actually resulted in greater losses than longer maturity issues. See R. E. Johnson, "Relationships of Financial Risk to the Term Structures of Corporate Bond Yields" (Ph.D. dissertation, University of Wisconsin, 1966).

[12] There has been a secular downtrend in interest rates over a period of several centuries, however, in nations for which data are available. For evidence see Sidney Homer, *A History of Interest Rates* (New Brunswick, N.J.: Rutgers University Press, 1963).

[13] Strictly speaking, it is not completely realistic to view interest rates as being *caused* by the supply of and demand for funds, because changes in interest rates also *affect* supply and demand by affecting saving and capital investment. In a complex economy, all variables interact simultaneously. Nevertheless, some factors, such as interest rates, do seem to be more effect than cause.

turn, is geared to the outlook for business activity and prices, and, more recently, to the danger of international capital outflows.

Thus, the level and trend of economic activity (including prices) is a common denominator on both the supply and demand sides of the interest rate equation.[14] Governmental fiscal philosophy is a second major factor, and international economic relationships a third. These subject will be discussed at length in Chapter 13.

FIGURE 11–2

High-Grade Corporate Bond Yields

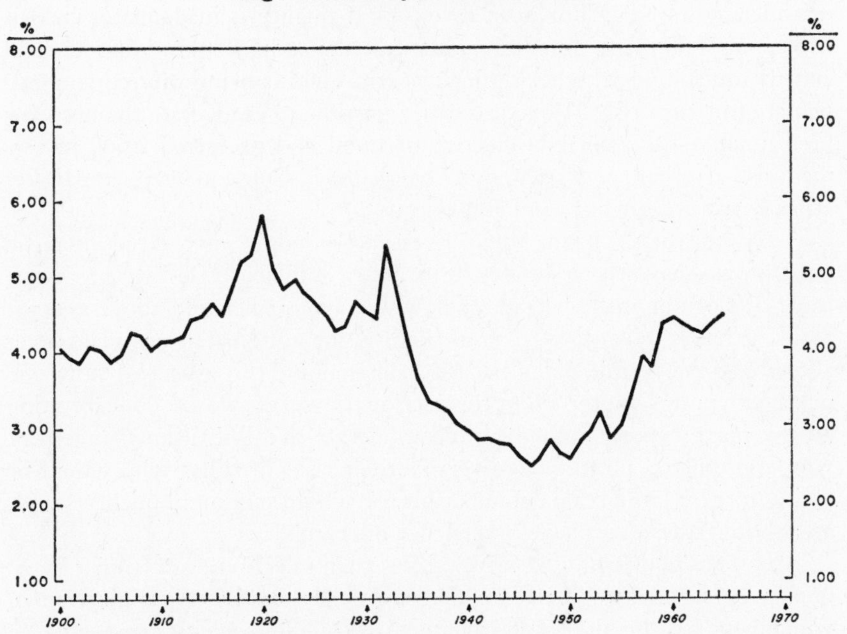


Source: Board of Governors of the Federal Reserve System.

## Selecting among Qualifying Issues

At this point, let us assume that the investor has decided that neither the interest rate outlook nor any other portfolio considerations militate against the purchase of fixed income securities and that he wishes to buy some bonds.[15] Let us also assume that he has a clear conception of the

[14] Again the student should be aware of the simultaneity of economic phenomena. The level of economic activity affects the levels of saving and investing; but the levels of saving and investing also affect the level of economic activity. Furthermore, investment affects income, which affects saving; and saving is the reverse side of consumption, which affects the incentive to invest. Thus savings and investment affect each other. No wonder a famous physicist is said to have given up the study of economics because he considered it too difficult.

[15] Many large institutional investors may find themselves forced to buy bonds even when they anticipate extended rises of interest rates. These problems are discussed in Chapters 18 and 19.

minimum bond quality which is acceptable to him and that he has compiled a list of issues meeting his quality standards. For example, such a list may include all long-term U.S. government bonds, all corporate and municipal bonds carrying agency ratings of "triple A" or "double A," and several lower rated bonds which pass various ratio tests established by the investor.[16] He must now choose from among the issues on the list, and therefore a consideration of relative yields *finally* is in order.

*Safety First.* The word "finally" is stressed in the previous sentence because we believe strongly that for most investors the proper order of investigation is to consider the quality of a bond or preferred stock before considering its yield. For most investors, if quality is inadequate, yield is irrelevant. Too many bond buyers reverse the order, looking first at yield and then deciding whether sufficient extra yield is being offered to compensate for extra risk. While it is easily possible to exaggerate the need for high quality, the primary objective of bond and preferred stock investment is, after all, a *steady flow of income.* Consequently, a cavalier attitude toward quality can be disastrous.

On the other hand, *some* investors—notably very large financial institutions—have the resources to diversify sufficiently so that aggressive trade-offs can be made between below-average quality and above-average yield. What is most significant to them is the anticipated net yield after allowing for probable defaults. We shall examine this aspect of portfolio management in Chapter 19. In this section, however, we are concentrating on the more typical individual and moderate-size institutional investors, who are not in a position to diversify their risks broadly, who would be badly hurt by large-scale defaults, and for whom minimum quality standards should, therefore, have precedence over yield.

If one's philosophy is "safety first," then selection even from a list of qualifying issues should not be dictated solely by the determination of which issue has the highest relative yield. While high yield is undoubtedly a plus factor, one should ask the question, even among qualifying issues: Is the yield *enough* higher relative to other qualifying issues to justify any extra credit risk that may be present? Even though one is prepared to assume the risks inherent in, say, "A" quality, if the yield on such issues at a particular time is not substantially higher than, say, "Aaa" yields, one might be better off buying the higher quality issues.

Consider Figure 11–3 for a moment. During the past 15 years, the average "spread" between Moody's Aaa and A corporate bond yields has been about 25 basis points. That is, the yield to maturity on corporate bonds of A quality has usually been about ¼ of 1% higher than yields on Aaa corporates. This has been the market's evaluation, perhaps correctly, perhaps not, of the extra risk involved. But note that in 1955 and 1965 the

[16] Such a list might be unduly large, and the investor might decide to draw up a list from only those issues discussed in, say, *Moody's Bond Survey* during the latest 12 months.

spread was unusually narrow, only 18 basis points and 9 basis points, respectively. A conservative investor during those years might well have reasoned that a sacrifice of less than 20 basis points was a rather cheap insurance premium to pay for the protection of Aaa quality in comparison with A.

*Preferred Stock Yields.* Figure 11–3 also illustrates another interesting yield spread. In the early 1950's, high-grade preferred stocks yielded (current yield basis) 1%–1¼% more than highest quality corporate bonds (yield to maturity basis). That spread steadily narrowed, and in

**FIGURE 11–3**

**Selected Bond and Preferred Stock Yields**

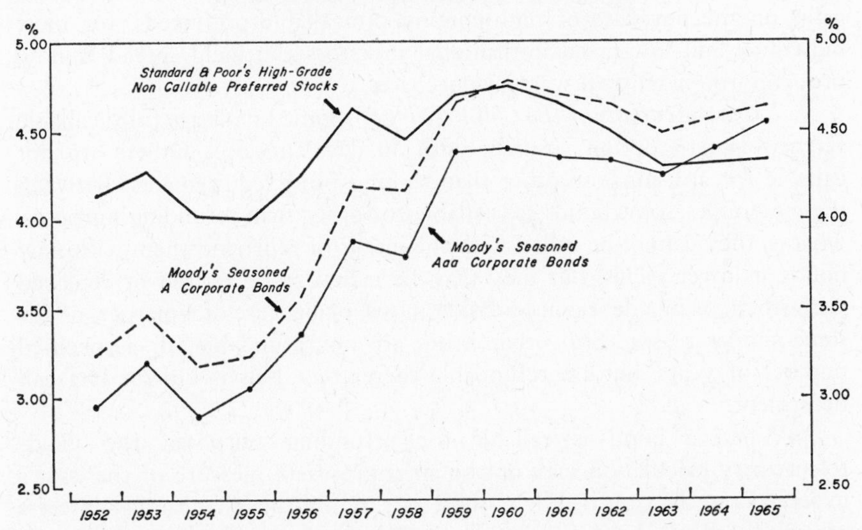


1964 and 1965 the spread was negative—high-grade preferreds were yielding less than Aaa corporate bonds. Three main factors have been responsible for this narrowing:

1. *Corporate* investors have a tax advantage in buying preferred stocks rather than bonds. Interest income is taxed in full whereas only 15% of dividend income is taxed. Consequently, after-tax yields on preferred stocks have been extremely attractive relative to bond yields for such institutional investors as fire and casualty insurance companies, and the demand for preferreds has been at a high and rising level.

2. In the face of high investment demand, the supply of new preferred stock issues has been small. Since bond interest is a tax-deductible expense to the issuer, whereas preferred dividends are not, high federal corporate income tax rates discourage managements from financing via preferred stock. They rely heavily on bonds.

3. Not only have corporations refrained from issuing new preferred stocks, they also have contracted the amount of already outstanding issues

by exercising their call privileges and refunding high-coupon preferreds with bonds. Moreover, in cases where *noncallable* preferreds had been issued at high yields many years ago, the issuing corporations have made generous exchange offers to the owners of such issues. This has introduced a capital gains element into the demand for preferred stocks. Buyers of noncallable preferreds stand a chance of benefiting from corporate exchange offers (for example, for every $100 of 6% preferreds, a corporation might offer $150 of 5% debentures).

The steady alteration of the prewar supply and demand curves has caused preferred stock yields to drop below Aaa corporate bond yields. Granted that highly taxed corporate investors will continue to find preferreds attractive, and granted that there is a chance of making capital gains on the purchase of high-coupon noncallable preferreds, for most individual and low-taxed institutional investors the yield spread is now probably too narrow to warrant purchases.

*Taking Account of the Call Privilege.* Some bonds are fully callable at their issuer's option (usually with 30 days' notice). Others are not callable for any purpose other than sinking-fund requirements. Between these extremes, some bonds are callable for other than refunding purposes. That is, they cannot be called with the intent of replacing them with new bonds at lower yields, but they may be called to be retired or replaced with stock, or in a debt consolidation move, or because of a merger, or for some similar reason. Still other issues are nonrefundable for a specified number of years, but are refundable thereafter. This is known as a call deferment.

When a bond is callable for refunding purposes, the yield-to-maturity calculation may not be an appropriate measure of the issue's expected rate of return. For if there is a significant chance that interest rates will fall to a level which makes refunding attractive to the issuer, he may exercise his call privilege. If he does, the investor will be faced with the necessity of reinvesting his money—presumably at lower interest rates if he does not reduce quality. In addition to reinvesting at lower rates, he will incur the expense and bother of making a new search for an acceptable issue. An offset against this expense will be the "call premium" which the issuer is required to pay in order to exercise his call privilege. The end result of all these factors may be a realized yield that is substantially different from the originally calculated yield to maturity.

Bond investors have typically been unduly lax in taking call features into account when calculating yields.[17] Occasionally reference will be made to the "yield to first call date." This calculation is usually made on high-coupon bonds selling at a premium during a period of low interest rates. In terms of the yield formula described above, instead of amortizing

---

[17] See A. P. Hess, Jr., and W. J. Winn, *The Value of the Call Privilege* (Philadelphia: University of Pennsylvania Press, 1962).

the premium over the number of years remaining to maturity, the number of years to the earliest date at which the bonds may be called for refunding is used in the numerator. In the denominator, the call price is substituted for the par value. An analogous calculation may be made to reflect the possibility of sinking-fund calls, if the investor owns a large block of a given bond issue. For example, suppose a bond issue has 20 years left to maturity when a major financial institution buys a large amount at a discount. If the bond has a regular annual sinking-fund requirement, the actual "average life" of this institution's block is likely to be closer to 10 than to 20 years. Accordingly, in calculating yield the discount may be amortized over a shorter number of years.

But this is a faulty method of taking the call feature into account when calculating the expected yield from a bond. For it gives no weight to the *probability* of call, nor, more important, does it take into account the yield on the resulting *reinvestment.* Moreover the yield to first call date is usually calculated only after interest rates have already fallen.

To illustrate with a simple example what an investor ought to do, suppose a 20-year bond with 5½% coupon is being considered for purchase at par, and assume the bond is refundable at any time at 105 (i.e., a 5% premium[18]). The first step should be to estimate the amount of interest rate decline which would persuade the issuer to call and refund. Bearing in mind that refunding costs him a premium and may involve him in substantial underwriting expenses on a new issue, suppose we decide that rates would have to fall 1% to make refunding attractive. Also assume that if he refunded at that lower level of rates, the investor would reinvest for the balance of the period at that level—i.e., in 4½% coupon issues—and would incur credit investigation and brokerage expenses of 1%.

Next, an estimate should be made of the probability that interest rates will, in fact, fall 1% sometime during the next 20 years. Suppose historical evidence suggests a 50% chance that they will and a 50% chance that they will not. Taking the midpoint of the 20-year period as the probable time of call in the case where call is assumed to occur, the following calculation can be made:

(1) Interest received for first 10 years = 5½% × $1,000 = $55 per year
(2) Interest received for last 10 years = 4½% × $1,040 = $46.80 per year
(3) Final principal value of investment = $1,040
(Note the $1,040 results from the 5% call premium minus the 1% reinvestment expense.)
(4) Discount rate equating $1,000 today with 10 years of income at $55 per year, 10 years at $46.80 per year, and a final value of $1,040 is approximately 5¼% (arrived at by a trial and error procedure).

[18] The fact that call premiums are so frequently equal to about one years' coupon, regardless of maturity or level of rates at time of offering, is prima-facie evidence that the market is not doing much sharp-penciled calculation.

Thus, there is a 50% chance of a 5¼% realized yield and a 50% chance that it will be 5½%. The "probability-weighted yield," therefore, is 5⅜%. In a more sophisticated analysis, of course, the number of possibilities would not be limited to two in a 50–50 ratio.[19]

An illustration of the importance of taking more careful account of the call features of bonds can be drawn from the period of very high interest rates in late 1959 and early 1960.[20] At that time, investors demanded a yield of about ¼ of 1% more on callable prime new public utility issues than on similar quality new issues with call deferment features. But in the period of easier money which followed, many of the callable issues were redeemed, and the investors in those issues had to reinvest at much lower rates of return. As a result, even allowing for the call premiums, the investors in the callable bonds received a substantially *lower* rate of return than the investors in the deferred-call bonds. In other words, the original ¼ of 1% yield premium was quite inadequate as an offset to the added risks represented by the call feature.

*Tax Factors.* In comparing the yield of a tax-exempt security with the yield of a fully taxable issue, allowance should be made for the investor's tax bracket. For example, if a man in the 50% tax bracket buys a 3½% coupon tax-exempt issue *at par,* he is getting the same after-tax return as a 7% coupon taxable bond *bought at par.* The formula for calculating "taxable equivalent yields" is: tax-exempt yield divided by 100% minus the tax rate. Note that this is akin to the formula used to adjust preferred stock dividends for tax factors in calculating earnings coverage.

Stress is placed on purchase at par value in the preceding paragraph, because yield to maturity of a bond purchased at a discount or premium includes not only regular income but also a capital gain or loss component. Gains and losses are taxed differently from regular income. Suppose the same 3½% municipal bond is purchased by the same 50%–bracket individual, but at a discount to yield 3¾% to maturity. As a rule of thumb, the following calculation can be made:

| | *Pretax Yield* | *Tax Rate* | *After-Tax Yield* |
|---|---|---|---|
| Coupon income | 3.50% | 0 | 3.50 % |
| Capital gain | 0.25 | 25%* | 0.1875 |
| Total | 3.75% | | 3.6875% |

* The regular rate on one half the gain, but not more than 25%.

[19] Appendix A of Hess and Winn, *op. cit.,* contains an extensive discussion of the mathematics of evaluating call privileges. The principles expounded are applicable to the calculation of yields given the terms and costs of callability.

[20] This illustration has been published by Salomon Bros. & Hutzler, in its April 1, 1966, *Bond Market Review,* p. 8.

If a 3½% coupon *taxable* bond were available at a discount to yield 5¾% to maturity, the calculation for the same individual would be:

| | Pretax Yield | Tax Rate | After-Tax Yield |
|---|---|---|---|
| Coupon income | 3.50% | 50% | 1.75 % |
| Capital gain | 2.25 | 25 | 1.6875 |
| Total | 5.75% | | 3.4375% |

Thus, although the taxable bond's yield to maturity (5¾%) is nowhere near double that of the tax-exempt issue (3¾%), when the differences between coupon and capital gains, and the related taxes, are considered, the taxable bond's net yield to the 50%-bracket investor is only ¼% lower than the tax-exempt issue.

*Capital Gains Possibilities.* It should be recognized that capital gains on fixed income securities do not stem only from purchasing bonds at a discount and holding them to maturity. If bonds or preferred stocks are purchased prior to a sharp decline in interest rates, and are sold at or near the trough of the interest rate cycle, substantial capital appreciation can result. For example, it may be noted on Figure 11–1 that if an investor had purchased the U.S. government 3's of '95 late in the summer of 1957, as a recession commenced, and sold six to nine months later, his selling price would have been 10% or more higher than his purchase price. Likewise, purchases in the winter of 1959–60 produced gains of 5%–10% in just a few months' time. Of course, the capital loss possibilities from *improper timing* are also quite evident on the chart.[21]

Capital-gains-minded students of the bond market are particularly on the lookout for abnormally wide yield spreads during a period of high interest rates. For example, as was noted earlier, it often is wise to avoid lower quality, higher yielding, securities when yield spreads are too narrow to warrant the extra risk. However, if the yield spreads on securities of different quality become abnormally wide during a period of generally high interest rates, the purchase of lower quality issues may not only produce greater *current* income than higher quality issues, but also may provide greater capital gains during a subsequent recession. At that time, when interest rates in general are declining, the yield decline (price rise) of the lower quality issues may be greater than the yield decline of the higher quality issues.

It must be admitted that such opportunities are relatively infrequent because yield spreads on issues of different quality usually narrow rather

[21] Venturesome investors can enhance their capital gains potential (but also their loss potential) by purchasing bonds on margin. Government bonds, in particular, can be bought with relatively low cash down payments. Thus, if bonds are bought on 10% margin, a 5% price rise produces a 50% profit on the investor's funds.

than widen during periods of high rates and vice versa during periods of low rates (see Chapter 13). Moreover, while the yield spreads may be attractive, the lower quality issues may be *too low* in quality to be considered investment-worthy, even for purposes of short-term holding. This possibility is particularly significant since bond price rises would be expected to come in a period of recession, when lower quality companies are most vulnerable economically. But the fact remains that such opportunities do arise, even in the high-quality sector of the bond market. Figure 11–4, for example, shows that as interest rates climbed during the

**FIGURE 11–4**

**Yield Spread of Callable Aa Utility Bonds versus Long-Term Governments**

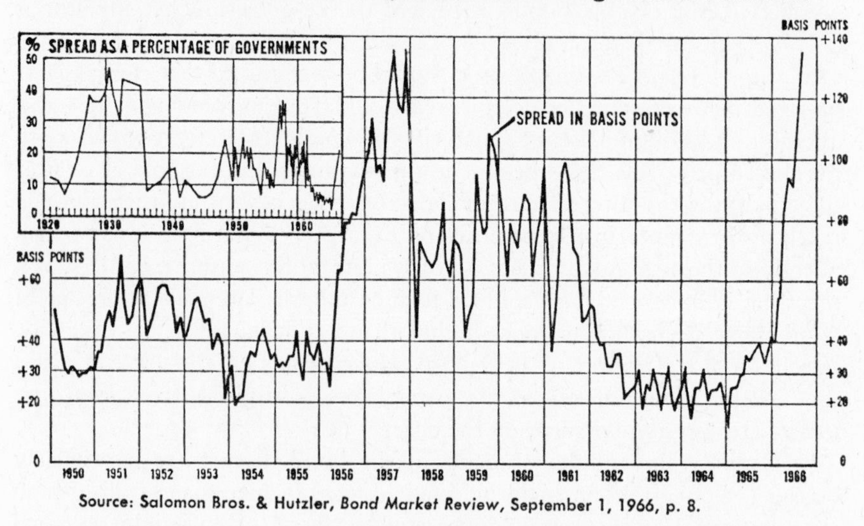


Source: Salomon Bros. & Hutzler, *Bond Market Review*, September 1, 1966, p. 8.

period of very heavy corporate financing in the spring and summer of 1966, yields on new issues of high-quality utility bonds rose dramatically relative to yields on long-term U.S. government bonds.

Capital gains opportunities also arise among issues of identical quality. Mr. Sidney Homer, partner of the investment firm of Salomon Bros. & Hutzler, made this point vivid in a speech a few years ago.[22] Homer introduced the subject with an incisive, and amusing, analogy:

> The man who first said that all Chinamen look alike (and to the Occidental eye many do) was merely confessing his lack of familiarity. In the same vein, many of us have received such instructions as this: "Next week buy us $100,000 of good corporate bonds, in four blocks of $25,000 each, rated Aa or better, not over twenty-five years maturity." The implication is that of the

[22] S. Homer, *Guides to Profitable Bond Selection*, Salomon Bros. & Hutzler, October 16, 1962.

hundreds of issues which meet these requirements, all are more or less alike and the first four to come along will do about as well as any other assortment.

To "illustrate the wastefulness of this grabbag technique of bond buying," Homer cited the following example, among others. He chose three bonds of American Telephone & Telegraph, all of approximately the same maturity but with different coupon rates. By picking bonds of the same company, the problem of quality differences was completely eliminated. For each of these three bonds, Homer showed the price and yield to maturity at the low point of the bond price cycle (the high point of interest rates) in 1957. The data were:

| *Issue* | *Price* | *Yield to Maturity* |
|---|---|---|
| 3¼s of 1984 | 81 | 4.47% |
| 4⅜s of 1985 | 94½ | 4.73 |
| 5s of 1983 | 101½ | 4.90 |

The casual bond buyer would probably have purchased the 5% coupon bonds, with a yield of 4.90%. But only six months later the interest rate cycle had moved sharply downward. Prices of all three issues were up—but by decidedly different amounts. Indeed, the price increases were inversely related to coupon and to the yield six months earlier:

| *Issue* | *Price* | *Price Rise* |
|---|---|---|
| 3¼s | 96½ | 19% |
| 4⅜s | 106½ | 13 |
| 5s | 112 | 10 |

What happened was that the threat of call became paramount to potential buyers, and the bonds most subject to the call threat were the higher coupon bonds. Therefore, call price tended to place an upper limit on the extent of the price rise of these issues. Indeed, the only reason the 5s managed to get up as high as 12% over par was the fact that they had a nonrefundable clause which did not permit call until *1962*. But the 3¼s were so unlikely to be called, and so far away from call price to begin with, that they could respond fully in price to the interest rate cycle.

The astute investor would have recognized something else about the relative yields of the three issues in 1957, namely that *after-tax* yields to tax-paying investors were almost identical. (This point was not made by Homer since his audience was a group of tax-free pension fund managers.) Consider these calculations for an investor in the 50% tax bracket, assuming that in the case of capital loss the loss can be used to offset capital gains elsewhere in the portfolio:

| (a) Yield to Maturity | (b) Coupon Portion of Yield | (c) After-Tax Yield on Coupon Portion | (d) Capital Gains Portion of Yield | (e) After-Tax Yield on Capital Gains Portion | (f) Total After-Tax Yield (c) & (e) |
|---|---|---|---|---|---|
| 4.47% | 3.25% | 1.625% | 1.22% | 0.915% | 2.54% |
| 4.73 | 4.375 | 2.188 | 0.355 | 0.265 | 2.45 |
| 4.90 | 5.00 | 2.500 | (0.10) | (0.08) | 2.42 |

For an investor in the 30% tax bracket, column (*f*) would read, from top to bottom, 3.32; 3.36; 3.41. Thus, even if the general level of interest rates had not fallen and created capital gains, taxpaying investors would not have suffered any significant income diminution by purchasing the issue with the *apparently lowest* yield.[23]

*Marketability and Expenses.* Two final factors in the investor's interpretation of any given yield spread should be the relative marketability of the two issues and the relative expenses of acquiring and maintaining them. For example, government-insured mortgages—which are of unimpeachable quality because of their insurance feature—have traditionally traded in the marketplace at substantially higher yields than a sample of corporate bonds which most objective observers would probably rate lower in quality. There are two major reasons for this seeming paradox. (1) The costs of acquiring (for example, brokerage commissions) and "servicing" (for example, collecting interest and periodically reevaluating the investment to make sure its quality is being maintained) mortgages are many times higher than the corresponding costs for bonds. (2) In general, bonds have broader markets and therefore are easier to dispose of promptly than mortgages. To most investors—individual and institutional—the ability to dispose of investments promptly is quite important, and they are willing to sacrifice some yield for this feature. On the other hand, some investors, such as a few large life insurance companies, have developed methods of holding down the costs of mortgage investing and also have little need for marketability (see Chapter 19[24]). It should be clear, therefore, that different investors will have quite different ideas regarding the opportunities presented by any particular yield spread.

---

[23] It may be noted, however, that tax-exempt municipal bonds generally have yielded still more than discount corporate bonds to high-tax-bracket investors. Therefore, none of the three bonds may have been an attractive purchase for such investors.

[24] In Chapter 19, a third reason is given for the large yield advantage which mortgages have traditionally commanded over bonds. It is the fact that many investors are simply ignorant of the characteristics of mortgages.

## SUGGESTED READINGS

Gordon Donaldson. *Corporate Debt Capacity*. Boston: Harvard Graduate School of Business Administration, 1961.

Benjamin Graham *et al. Security Analysis,* Part III. 4th ed. New York: McGraw-Hill Book Co., 1962.

Arleigh P. Hess and Willis J. Winn. *The Value of the Call Privilege*. Philadelphia: University of Pennsylvania Press, 1962.

Sidney Homer. *A History of Interest Rates*. New Brunswick, N.J.: Rutgers University Press, 1963.

Frank C. Jen and James E. Wert. "Imputed Yields of a Sinking Fund Bond and the Term Structure of Interest Rates," *Journal of Finance*, December, 1966.

Carol J. Loomis. "You May Be Missing A Bet In Bonds," in *Fortune's Guide to Personal Investing,* by the editors of *Fortune*. New York: McGraw-Hill Book Co., 1963.

James E. Walter. *The Investment Process*. Boston: Harvard Graduate School of Business Administration, 1962.

# 12

# CONVERTIBLE SECURITIES AND SPECIAL SITUATIONS

One cannot eat one's cake and have it too.
—T. H. HUXLEY

## CONVERTIBLE SECURITIES

### What They Are and Why They Are Issued

THE term "convertible security" usually implies a preferred stock or a debenture which may be exchanged for common stock at the owner's discretion on specified terms.[1] Prior to World War II, the convertible feature was used to make offerings of senior securities more attractive than they would be as "straight" (i.e., nonconvertible) issues. In other words, the issuing corporation wanted to float debt or preferred securities, but its credit standing was rather poor and it had to add a "sweetener" in order to sell the issue at a reasonable interest or dividend rate. Since World War II, however, convertible securities have been issued by companies of the highest credit standing as well as by companies with lesser credit ratings. This is because convertible securities have become primarily a tool for acquiring common stock capital rather than senior capital.

There are several reasons why corporations may issue convertible securities rather than sell common stock directly. Since this is not a text in corporation finance, it is not our intention to present an exhaustive list of these reasons. Instead, we shall concentrate on what appears to be the typical situation. An understanding of the issuer's principal motives sheds light on the analysis of convertibles from the investor's point of view.

[1] A bond or preferred stock with warrants attached is not a convertible in this sense because the exercise of the warrants does not extinguish the issues to which they were attached. Nevertheless, much of the following discussion on analysis of convertibles applies implicitly to issues bearing warrants, where the warrants have not been detached.

Suppose Company X is earning $50 million a year and has 10 million shares of common stock outstanding. Thus it is earning $5 per share. Suppose further that the stock is selling at 15 times earnings, or $75 a share. The market value of the company's common stock, therefore, is $750 million.

At this point, the management decides to expand productive capacity by building a major new facility which will cost $75 million. This $75 million, moreover, will have to be raised externally. That is, retained cash flow is adequate to replace obsolete existing facilities but is not deemed adequate to expand capacity. Furthermore, it is management's opinion that the company's capitalization is already top-heavy with debt and preferred stock and that the $75 million of new capital should be in the form of common stock.

The problems in this plan are these. A $75 million common stock offering represents 10% of the company's total common stock market value. An offering of such magnitude could not possibly be put across at $75 per share, the present price of the stock. Let us say the stock would have to be offered at $70 (net to the company). Thus, the company would have to sell almost 1,100,000 shares, raising outstanding stock to 11.1 million shares. But even after the company has raised the money by selling its stock at a discount from the going price, it will take a long time—say a year or more—before the new facility is constructed, equipped, and running efficiently. In the meantime, per-share earnings will have declined from $5 to about $4.50—the same $50 million of earnings divided by the new number of shares, 11.1 million. (Actually this is probably an overstatement, since the overhead of a partly completed plant would tend to reduce profits; but there is no need to complicate the example.) Assuming the price-earnings ratio remains at 15, the market price of the shares will fall to about $68. Under these circumstances, the original stockholders may well be annoyed at management's "dilution" of their equity.

A convertible issue may be a convenient alternative for management in this example. Suppose the company sold $75 million of 5% subordinated debentures,[2] convertible "at 75." In other words, each $1,000 bond could be converted by the holder into 13⅓ shares of the company's common stock.[3] Interest payments on the debenture would amount to 5%

---

[2] Convertible debentures usually are subordinated to other debt of the corporation.

[3] The conversion terms may be expressed as a ratio (i.e., 13⅓ shares per $1,000 of face value) or as a price (i.e., convertible at 75). Occasionally the investor may have to put up additional cash when converting (for example, the American Telephone & Telegraph issues).

The conversion price may be set at, or higher than, the going price of the stock at the time of issue. The investor should be sure that the issue has an "antidilution"

of $75 million annually, or $3.75 million. After tax, this would come to about $2 million, cutting net income to $48 million before the new facility was contributing to profits (again assuming no further reduction due to uncovered new overhead). But there still would be only 10 million shares of common outstanding, so earnings would fall to only $4.80 instead of $4.50.

After the new facility comes into operation, earnings and dividends should rise, and the market price of the stock should do likewise. When dividends on 13⅓ shares exceed $50 annually (the interest per $1,000 bond), original purchasers of the debenture will be encouraged to convert. But they may prefer to stay with their bonds, feeling that the greater safety is worth a somewhat lower income as long as the value of the bonds is rising in line with the price of the stock (a point which will be discussed at greater length below). In this event, management can "call" the bonds at a price which will have been specified in the bond indenture, say 105.

If the market value of the company's stock at the time of call is $80 or higher, the value of the shares which can be obtained on conversion (13⅓ × $80 = $1,067) will be significantly higher than the call price ($1,050). This being the case, the bondholders will convert, albeit involuntarily.[4] But whether conversion takes place voluntarily or involuntarily, management will have achieved its goal of financing the new facility with common stock. And the stock will, in effect, have been sold at 75—a better price than could have been obtained on a direct offering at the outset. Furthermore, the original stockholders are likely to have been much more satisfied by the introduction of new stock *after* the company had built up its earning power.

There are a few other important reasons why corporations sell convertible securities, two of which may be briefly noted at this point:

1. Many institutional investors, such as banks and life insurance companies, either are prohibited legally from buying common stock or are severely restricted in the amounts which they may buy. However, they have greater leeway in buying convertible securities. Commercial banks cannot buy preferreds, straight or convertible, but can buy convertible bonds of reasonably high quality if their yields aprroximate those

---

clause which proportionately lowers the conversion price if a stock split or stock dividend is subsequently declared.

Conversion may be permitted immediately, or not until some stated period of time has elapsed. Also, there may be a cutoff date after which the conversion privilege expires. Or there may be a series of dates on which the conversion price gradually increases (i.e., fewer shares can be obtained by converting after each date passes). Managements try to tailor the terms of the issue in line with their expectations of future conditions. For a description of an unusual "Convertible Preference" stock, which is convertible into an *increasing* number of common shares as time passes, and whose dividend is geared to that of the common stock, see *Financial Analysts Journal*, July-August, 1966, pp. 122–24. The issuer is Litton Industries.

[4] The main reason for inserting a "sliding scale" conversion price—i.e., one which rises over time—is to encourage *voluntary* conversions.

on nonconvertibles of similar quality. Life insurance companies can buy either convertible preferreds or convertible bonds of good quality.

2. Convertible preferred stocks have become an important medium for financing corporate mergers. For example, Company A wants to acquire Company B by purchasing B's outstanding stock. If stockholders of B take cash or notes for their stock, they incur an immediate capital gains tax liability, assuming they receive an amount in excess of their original investment. But if they exchange their stock for Company A's common or preferred stock, the transaction is regarded as a tax-free exchange of assets. Only when the newly acquired shares ultimately are sold is any capital gains tax payable, again assuming that the proceeds of the sale exceed the original cost of the Company B shares.

This being the case, Company A can make a very tempting offer to Company B's stockholders. Company A can offer convertible preferred stock in exchange for shares of B. If the dividend rate on the convertible is set at least as high as the rate on B's common, the selling stockholders will have a more *secure* income than they had formerly. And if the conversion price is close to the current market price of A's shares, they also will be able to participate in the future growth of the merged company via the conversion privilege. This attractive package may encourage B's holders to ratify the merger, and may enable A to consummate the merger with a minimum dilution of its own equity, since on a straight common for common exchange it might have had to offer a good deal more stock than it is offering via conversion.

### Convertibles from the Investor's Viewpoint

Many investors see in convertible securities "the best of all possible worlds." As debentures or preferreds, they offer stable income as opposed to the variable income of common stock. This stable income appears to make them relatively less vulnerable to price decline during a stock market downturn. At the same time, the conversion privilege appears to offer most of the prospects for capital gain which are offered by common stocks. Moreover, persons desiring to buy on margin can finance a much larger proportion of a convertible's purchase price than of a common stock's. At least 75% usually can be legitimately borrowed from a bank on a convertible, and sometimes as much as 85%–90%, whereas the Federal Reserve's variable margin requirements on common stock usually limit the borrowed portion to 50% or less.[5] It would seem that nothing could be

[5] Strictly speaking, it is necessary to distinguish among loans from brokers, from banks, and from other moneylenders. The Federal Reserve has no control over the percent loaned on securities by others than stockbrokers or banks. Stockbrokers can lend on listed securities only, and the "margin requirement" is the same for both bonds and stocks. Banks can lend on listed stocks the same percentage of market value that stockbrokers are permitted to lend; but on bonds and unlisted stocks they have greater leeway. There have been reports recently that the Federal Reserve is considering stricter limitations on the financing of investments in convertibles.

FIGURE 12–1

**Illustration of the Profit Potential of a Convertible Bond**

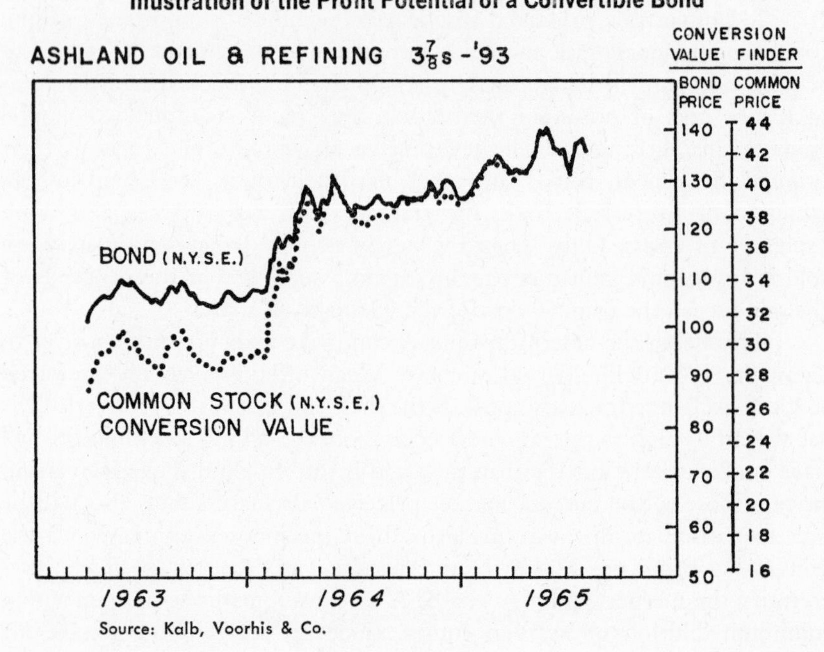


Source: Kalb, Voorhis & Co.

better than a security which provides stable income, capital gains potential, and a hedge against stock market declines[6]—and which can be heavily margined if necessary. Figures 12–1 and 12–2 illustrate these features of convertibles. Figure 12–1[7] shows the price of a convertible bond benefit-

[6] The term "hedge" often is used in a more specific context in connection with convertibles. A "convertible hedge" refers to a transaction in which a bearish investor buys a convertible and simultaneously sells short the common stock into which it may be converted. If the stock declines in price, as he anticipates, the price of the convertible declines less than proportionately (he hopes). He then sells the convertible at a loss, buys common at the depressed price, and covers his short sale at a greater profit than the loss on the convertible. If he is wrong about the market, and a rise in the stock's price confronts him with a potential loss on the covering of the short sale, he has two alternatives. If the price of the convertible has risen, he can sell it at a profit which offsets the short-sale loss in whole or in part. Indeed, the price rise of the convertible may exceed that of the stock, resulting in a net profit. At the very worst, if the price of the convertible has not risen, he can exercise his conversion privilege and use the shares received to cover the short sale. His maximum loss will be the difference between the cost of the convertible and the proceeds of the short sale, namely the "premium" which he paid over conversion value. Thus, the main purpose of a "convertible hedge" is to profit from a declining stock market at a predeterminable risk.

[7] In this chart, and the others which follow, the price scale for the bond is a constant multiple of the price scale of the stock, the multiple being the number of shares into which the bond is convertible. Therefore, the spread between the line representing the bond (solid) and that representing the stock(broken) indicates the "premium," if any, at which the bond is selling over its "conversion value" at any given time.

ing from a rise in the price of the common stock into which it is convertible. Figure 12–2 shows the lesser percentage price decline of a convertible bond in the 1962 bear market than the price decline of the related common stock.

Actually, things are not so black and white. In the first place, analysis of the investment merits of convertibles is quite complex. Since the issuer has to consider a large number of factors in deciding what terms to place on the issue—coupon rate, conversion price, time span of conversion privilege, call price, etc.—the investor also has to consider this large

FIGURE 12–2

**Illustration of the Defensive Properties of a Convertible Bond**

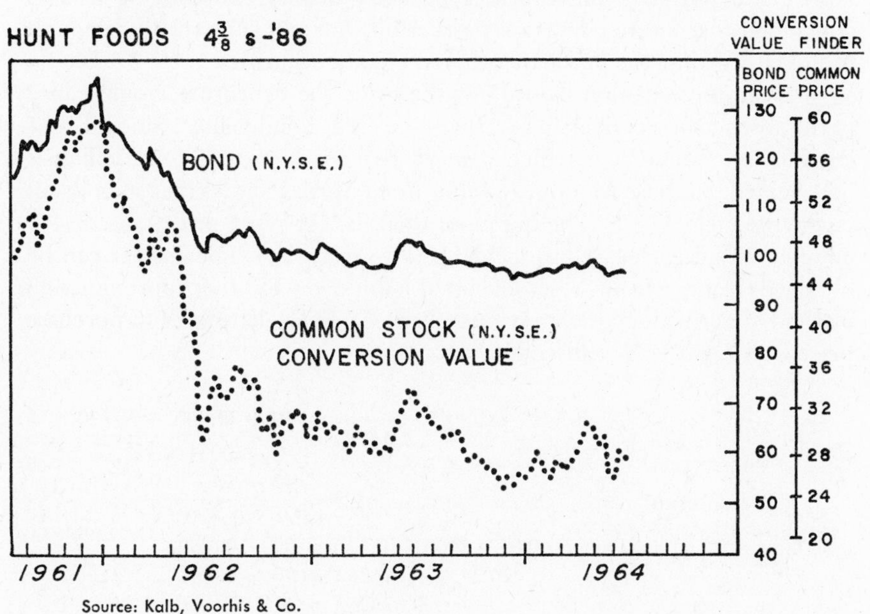


Source: Kalb, Voorhis & Co.

number of variables. Second, since the form of convertibles is inherently attractive to investors, one should not expect to find them generally selling at bargain prices. Indeed, in 1965, prices of convertibles were bid up so high that in 1966, when both the stock and bond markets declined, many convertible issues declined even more than the stocks into which they were convertible. Thus, the analysis of convertibles must be fairly precise if their theoretical advantages are to be realized.

## Analytical Procedures

The following hypothetical example can be used to illustrate the method of evaluating a convertible security. A 4% coupon debenture, with 20 years remaining to maturity, is convertible at any time into common stock at $50. It is currently selling at 90 (i.e., $900 for a $1,000 debenture),[8] and the stock into which it is convertible currently is selling at $42.

The first phase of the analysis is to evaluate the issue as if it were a "straight" (i.e., nonconvertible) debenture. As indicated in the earlier discussion of bond and preferred stock analysis, this involves a determination of quality of the issue, a decision as to whether the quality is satisfactory, and a judgment as to whether the time is propitious for buying fixed income securities in general. Suppose it is concluded that the issue is of medium quality, that this estimate is confirmed by the rating agencies (assume Moody's rates it Baa),[9] and that the investor's standards permit the purchase of securities of such quality. Suppose it also is concluded that interest rates may rise a bit, but not substantially enough to militate against the purchase of fixed income securities.

Next, a calculation is made of the price the debenture would carry in the absence of a conversion feature—i.e., it's "bond value." Since it is of Baa quality, the yield at which *straight* Baa issues currently are selling is determined. Suppose Moody's weekly *Bond Survey* shows that such issues currently yield 5¼%. The question, then, is: At what price must a 4% coupon, 20-year issue, sell to yield 5¼% to maturity? The answer can be obtained readily from a set of bond tables, or by the approximation method described in the previous chapter. Thus, letting $X$ = purchase price, and 1,000 − $X$ = discount:

$$0.0525 = \frac{40 + (1{,}000 - X)/20}{500 + 0.5X}$$

This reduces to:

$$.0525 = \frac{40 + 50 - 0.05X}{500 + 0.5X}$$

Cross-multiplying, we get:

$$0.0525\ (500 + 0.5X) = 90 - 0.05X$$
$$26.25 + 0.02625X = 90 - 0.05X$$
$$0.07625X = 63.75$$
$$X = 836$$

[8] In this example, and those that follow, we assume that the investor is evaluating a convertible issue which has been outstanding for some time and which has a market price above or below par. The principles discussed, however, are equally applicable to the evaluation of a new issue being offered at par.

[9] A representative cross section of convertible debentures at any given time is likely to include 25%–50% with ratings of Baa or better and at least 50% with lower ratings. For data on ratings and other characteristics of postwar issues, see Keith L. Broman, "The Use of Convertible Subordinated Debentures by Industrial Firms 1949–59," *Quarterly Review of Economics and Business*, Spring, 1963. In considering ratings of convertible debentures, it should be borne in mind that the agencies almost automatically downgrade subordinated issues by one rating category. Therefore, the proportion of truly lower grade issues is probably considerably less than indicated by the data.

In other words, the debenture would have to fall in price from $900 to $836 to yield 5¼%.[10] But some allowance also must be made for the fact that a moderate rise in interest rates is believed to be possible. Suppose it is thought that Baa issues can rise ¼% to a 5½% yield basis. If this were to occur, the debenture could decline in price to $806, derived as follows:

$$0.055 = \frac{40 + (1000 - X)/20}{500 + 0.5X}$$

$$27.50 + 0.0275X = 90 - 0.05X$$

$$0.0775X = 62.50$$

$$X = 806$$

The conclusion of the first phase of the analysis, therefore, is that purchase of the convertible debenture entails a *maximum risk*, based on its straight bond value, of about $100 per $900 invested ($900 purchase price less $806 minimum price), or 11%. The second phase of the analysis is designed to determine how much an investor stands to *gain* from the conversion privilege.

The first concept to be understood is that of the "conversion parity price" of the common stock. The debenture is convertible into common stock "at 50." This means that each $1,000 of par value can be exchanged for 20 shares of common stock (1000/50 = 20). By paying $900 for the bond, therefore, the investor can be viewed as in effect buying the company's stock at $45 per share (900/20 = 45). This price is the conversion parity price of the stock.[11]

The conversion parity price, then, is different for different investors, depending on the price paid for the convertible security. Conversion parity price is equal to the purchase price of the convertible security divided by the number of common shares into which it is convertible. This price is highly significant analytically. For, as will be demonstrated, once the actual market price of the stock rises to the investor's conversion parity price, any further rise is certain to increase the value of his convertible security at least as rapidly percentagewise.

The minimum price of a convertible security, regardless of the level of interest rates or any other considerations, is equal to the current price of the common stock multiplied by the number of shares into which it can be converted. In our example, the current price of the stock is $42 and the debenture is convertible into 20 shares of common. Therefore, the mini-

---

[10] At $900 its yield to maturity is:

$$\frac{40 + \frac{1}{20}(1000 - 900)}{500 + \frac{1}{2}(900)} = \frac{45}{950} = 4.7\%$$

[11] Fifty is the "conversion price," and 45 is the "conversion parity price." The two terms are equivalent in value only for an investor who buys the issue at par.

mum price of the debenture is $42 times 20, or $840. Any lower price would have to be temporary, because it would give rise to "arbitrage" transactions which would restore the balance. For example, if the debenture sold at, say, $800 when the stock's price was $42, a guaranteed profit could be made as follows. Buy the debenture for $800. Simultaneously sell short 20 shares of common for $840. Then convert the debenture into 20 shares with which to cover the short sale, and make a $40 profit, less brokerage commissions, transfer taxes, etc. The existence of the profit guarantee would cause enough such transactions to drive the debenture price up to $840.[12]

If the logic presented above is understood, the significance of the "conversion parity price" of the common should begin coming into focus. If the stock in our example rose from its present price of $42 to its conversion parity price of $45, the minimum price of the debenture would be 20 × $45, or $900, which is the purchase price. Every additional $1 rise in the stock would increase the debenture's price by at least $20. The actual price of the debenture might well rise more than proportionately if buyers became enthusiastic enough. Indeed, in strong markets, convertible issues often sell at high and rising premiums over conversion value.

Thus, the conversion parity price can be viewed as a break-even point. Once the common stock attains that value, the investor is assured of at least getting his money back; and any further rise in the price of the common guarantees him at least a proportionate profit. In our example, the $45 conversion parity price is only $3, or 7%, away from the current $42 price of the common.

Having considered the relationship of the conversion parity price to the current price of the common stock, the next step of the analysis is to consider the *potential price* of the common stock. To make such a determination, of course, the investor would have to apply all of the evaluation techniques which were discussed in earlier chapters. Suppose he decides that the stock is worth $65.

If the stock were to go to $65, the convertible debenture would be worth at least 20 × $65, or $1,300. Thus, there exists a potential gain, based on the debenture's conversion feature, of $400 per $900 invested, or 44%.

All of these facts now can be brought together in a simple summary statement. The convertible security under analysis offers a potential gain of 44% at a maximum risk of 11%. If a mistake has been made regarding the value of the stock, and its price declines sharply, the bond value of the

---

[12] It need not go to precisely $840 for two reasons. First, brokerage commissions would have to be allowed for; and second, the short selling could depress the price of the common to below $42.

security should prevent the loss from exceeding 11%.[13] But the investor does not have to be completely right about the stock to earn a profit. A price advance of only 7%, to $45, will assure him of breaking even, because the minimum price of the convertible would then be 20 × $45, equal to the $900 purchase price. A further advance in the price of the stock will produce a profit. Furthermore, while waiting for the capital gain he will be earning a *current* yield on the bond of 40/900, or almost 4½%. This may well be as good as, or better than, the dividend yield on the stock.

Thus, our example represents an ideal convertible situation—significant profit potential with small loss possibility and high probability of at least breaking even. It is useful to state formally the characteristics of an attractive convertible. Ideally, six tests must be passed:

1. The issue must meet the investor's minimum quality standards.
2. The long-range outlook for interest rates should be fairly stable or down.
3. The minimum value of the issue as a straight bond or preferred stock must not be too far below the current selling price (not more than, say, 15% below), taking into account any expected rise in the level of interest rates.
4. The current price of the common stock must not be too far below conversion parity (say a maximum of 20%).
5. The potential price of the common stock must be well above conversion parity (say 25% or more).
6. The *current* yield on the bond or preferred stock should compare favorably with the dividend yield on the common stock.

## Illustrative Applications of the Tests

We now set forth a number of cases, both real and hypothetical, which are typical of the convertibles usually available. That is, most fall short of the ideal by at least one of the tests. Brief analysis of each case should make clear the practical application of the procedures which have been discussed.

In each of the cases, it will be assumed that the quality level of the convertible issue is satisfactory. It also will be assumed in each case that straight issues of comparable quality are likely to yield a maximum of 5%.

CASE 1. A 4%, 20-year debenture, convertible at $50, is selling at

---

[13] However, the stock's decline may be due to circumstances which also have the effect of lowering the bond's quality from Baa to, say, Ba. In that case, the maximum loss would be a function of yields on straight bonds of this lower quality, say 6% instead of 5½%. To yield 6%, the bond would have to drop in price to $750, a loss of $150 per $900 invested, or 17% instead of 11%. On the other hand, if the stock's price declines because of a general economic recession, falling interest rates actually may cause the price of the bond to rise.

$1,500. The common stock is selling at $70 and is likely to rise substantially.

ANALYSIS. The bond is yielding 1.2% to maturity and could fall more than 40% in price if the stock declined sharply and the bond had to sell strictly on its merits as a bond. The conversion parity price of the common is $75, which is $5 above the going price of $70. Since it is assumed that the stock has much further to go, the investor should, if anything, buy the stock directly rather than the convertible debenture. By selling at so high a premium above its *bond* value, the convertible provides no hedge against a decline in the stock market. Suppose the stock drops 20% to $56. The debenture easily could drop an equal 20%, to $1,200, and it still would be yielding only 2.7% to maturity. Therefore, if the stock is believed to be very attractive, why pay $75 for it in effect, when it can be bought at $70? Indeed, the *dividend yield* of the stock might well be higher than the bond's current yield of 2⅔% (40/1,500), so the investor not only would be getting the stock at a lower price but might get higher current income as well.

**FIGURE 12–3**

**Illustration of a Convertible with Negligible Defensive Properties**

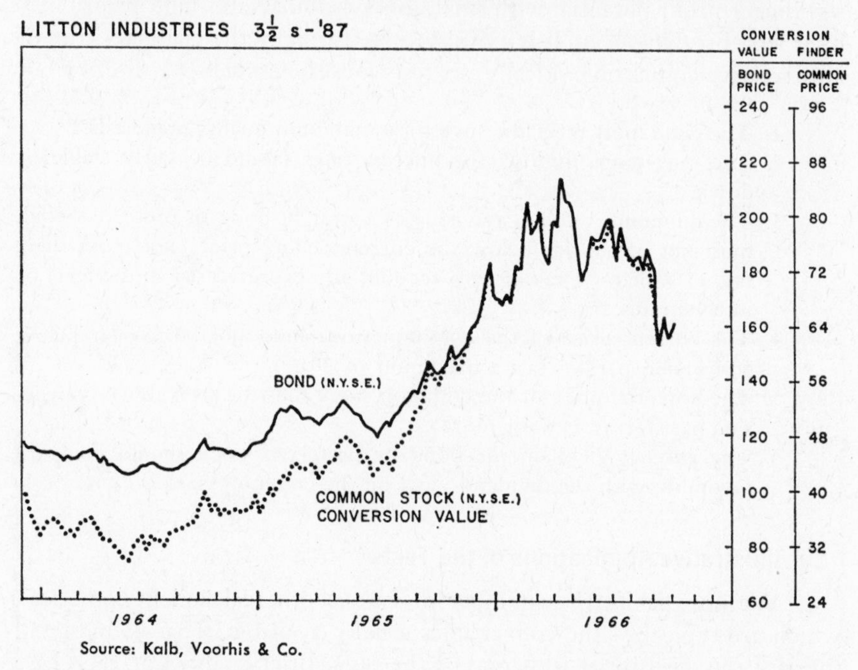


Source: Kalb, Voorhis & Co.

Figure 12–3 illustrates a convertible bond with negligible downside protection. It is the 3½% convertible of Litton Industries, which sold as high as $2,100 in early 1966 compared with a bond value of about one third that amount at the time. It was completely vulnerable to the ensuing decline in the price of the stock.

CASE 2. A 4½%, 20-year debenture, convertible at $50, is selling at par. The common stock is selling at $25 and is likely to rise substantially.

ANALYSIS. The bond is yielding 4½%. To yield 5%, it would have to sell at $930, a maximum downside risk of only 7%. But the conversion parity price of the common stock is $50, which is double the present market price. Although a substantial rise in the stock's price can be expected, conversion parity is so far away that most of the stock price rise would not have a counterpart in the bond. It would be wiser to buy the stock directly, since the debenture provides no hedge. It is selling almost as if it were a straight bond and is quite lacking in appreciation potential from its common stock element. (In Case 1 the debenture was selling as if it were strictly a stock. It lacked price protection from its bond element.) Figure 12–4 illustrates such a convertible. It is the Automatic Canteen 4¾% bond, which in 1963–64 sold at par when its value if converted into

**FIGURE 12–4**

**Illustration of a Convertible with Minor Profit Potential**

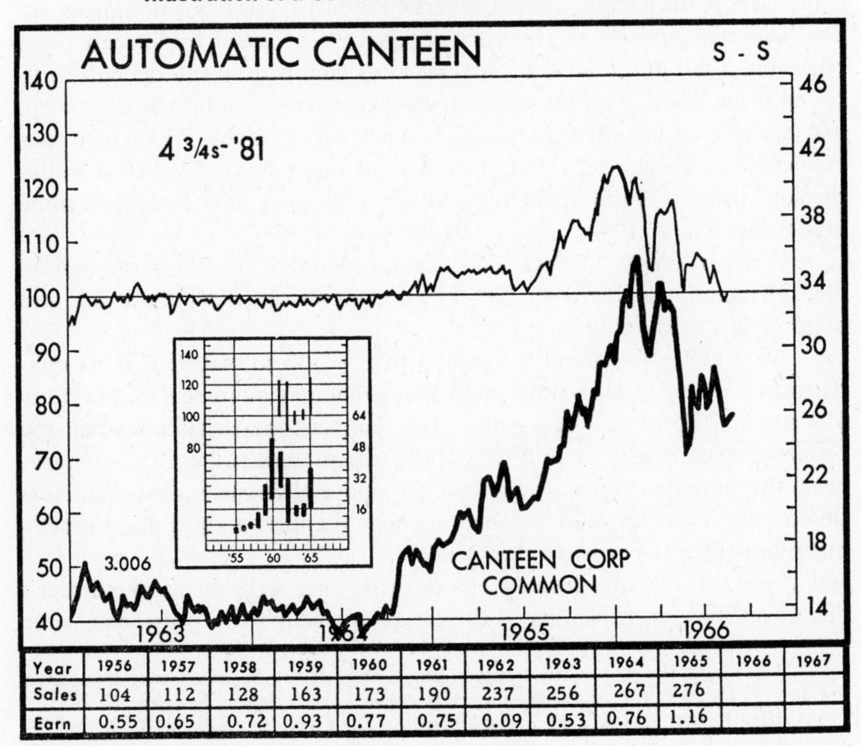


| Year | 1956 | 1957 | 1958 | 1959 | 1960 | 1961 | 1962 | 1963 | 1964 | 1965 | 1966 | 1967 |
|---|---|---|---|---|---|---|---|---|---|---|---|---|
| Sales | 104 | 112 | 128 | 163 | 173 | 190 | 237 | 256 | 267 | 276 | | |
| Earn | 0.55 | 0.65 | 0.72 | 0.93 | 0.77 | 0.75 | 0.09 | 0.53 | 0.76 | 1.16 | | |

Source: R.H.M. Associates, *The R.H.M. Convertible Survey*.

stock was less than half that amount. In 1965, when the stock price more than doubled, the bond rose only 25%. Commercial banks are probably the only investors for whom this type of investment might have attraction. Although the appreciation potential of the bond may be remote, something is better than nothing if close to full bond value also is obtained, since commercial banks are not permitted to buy stocks directly.[14]

CASE 3. A 4½%, 20-year debenture, convertible at 50, is selling at a discount price of $980. The common stock is selling at $45, but already has risen sharply above a normal value range, and seems to be settling at this new plateau.

ANALYSIS. As in Case 2, the bond feature provides a limited price risk ($50 on $980, or 5%). In addition, the conversion parity price of the common stock ($49) is less than 10% above the present market price ($45), which is an attractive spread. But the potential price of the stock is quite limited.

A purist would not buy this convertible bond. It provides a good hedge against a stock market decline but little appreciation potential. On the other hand, a reasonably good argument can be made for buying the issue. The estimate of the stock's value may be overly conservative. A modest further price rise would provide a profit on the convertible debenture, while a stock market reversal might have little or no impact on the debenture. Indeed, if a market reversal were caused by an economic recession, a fall in the level of interest rates could cause the debenture to rise in price. Moreover, the current yield of over 4½% on the debenture may well be higher than the dividend yield on the stock into which it is convertible and may be above that of most other stocks as well. Finally, the low margin requirement may be an additional plus factor to some investors.

CASE 4. A 6%, 20-year debenture, issued five years ago, is convertible at $25 and is selling at $1,200. The common stock is selling at $28 and might easily rise to $40.

ANALYSIS. The bond is yielding over 4½% to maturity at its current price. At $1,130 it would yield 5%, so its maximum risk as a bond is $70 on $1,200, or less than 6%. The conversion parity price of the common stock is $30, or only 7% above the present price of $28. Moreover, the potential price of the stock is more than 30% above conversion parity. This convertible debenture would appear to be a good investment, but there is a possible drawback.

Most, if not all, convertible securities are callable at the issuer's discretion. Indeed, callability is the means by which the issuer can force

---

[14] Actually, the Automatic Canteen bond, rated Ba by Moody's, may have been too low in quality for active commercial bank consideration. See W. S. Skelly, *Convertible Bonds: A Study of Their Suitability for Commercial Bank Bond Portfolios* (Salomon Bros. & Hutzler, 1959).

conversion when circumstances warrant. Suppose the debenture in our example is callable at 106 (one year's interest is a common call premium). If the bond were called, what would happen?

With the stock selling at $28, the bond has a conversion value of 40 times $28, or $1,120. Thus, as long as the stock's price stays at $28, a bondholder would be better off converting into stock (or selling to someone else who will convert) than turning the bond in for $1,060. Those investors who bought the bond at par at original issue, five years earlier, would have a 12% profit. But those who bought at $1,200 would have a loss of $80, or 7%. And if the call announcement depressed the price of the stock because of the imminent addition to the number of outstanding shares, the loss would be greater.[15]

The moral of this example is that even when a convertible security meets all of our rules, if it is selling above call price there is a risk present. The risk is that the security will be called before the stock's price rises to conversion parity (once it reaches conversion parity, the investor will at least break even).[16] Therefore, the investor has to consider the situation from the corporation's point of view as well as from his own.

In this particular example, it seems most unlikely that the company would call the bonds for the purpose of forcing conversion. In the first place, it would have created a large number of rather dissatisfied investors—those people who bought *at original issue* and who are having their investment taken away after five years with an average of only 2½% per annum profit, just at the time when a substantial advance in the price of the stock appears to be at hand.[17] Second, a call at this time might easily boomerang. Suppose the call announcement depressed the price of the stock to $26. At this price, the debenture would have a conversion value of only $1,040. People would not convert but would turn the bonds in for $1,060 in cash. But this is not what the company wanted. It wanted more common stock in the business, and instead, would be faced with a huge

---

[15] It may be noted that the announcement of the call is made in the financial press several weeks before the actual call date. Since the decision to sell the issue, or to convert it, must be made within this short time period, it is imperative that the investor be aware of the call announcement. He can keep track of such announcements by reading the newspaper carefully or by regularly perusing one of several published financial services which report corporate developments of this type.

[16] Since nonconvertibles give no such opportunity to get out even, the call price tends to set a ceiling on the market price of straight bonds in a period of falling interest rates. For example, if a 20-year bond were issued with a 5% coupon and interest rates on similar quality bonds fell to 4% shortly thereafter, the 5% bond might be expected to rise in price to about 114, at which point its yield would also be 4%. But if the bond were callable at, say, 105, it is not likely that investors would be willing to pay much more than 105 for it because, if they did so, a subsequent call would cause them to suffer a capital loss.

[17] Actually, they probably shouldn't be too dissatisfied. After all, they've gotten 6% per annum in current income and 2½% a year in capital gain—a good overall rate of return by most standards.

depletion of cash and capital.[18] Thus, a call for the purpose of forcing conversion is unlikely, given the set of facts in this case, and purchase of the debenture is probably a wise move.

On the other hand, suppose the company has found a merger partner. And suppose this partner has ample equity capital and can borrow at 5%. In this situation, a 6% *convertible* debenture has less place in the merged company's capital structure than, say, a 5% straight debenture. A call might well be at hand, and purchase of the debenture would be quite risky.

### Sources of Information

Several investment service organizations publish data on convertible securities in a tabular or graphic form which is convenient for quick screening preliminary to an in-depth analysis. Among these are Kalb, Voorhis & Co.'s weekly *Convertible Fact Finder* and the same firm's *Convertible Bond Chart Book*, the R.H.M. Associates' *Convertible Survey*, and the convertible bond section of Standard & Poor's *Bond Reports*. A copy of the front sheet of the latter service is reproduced in Figure 12–5. The columns show:

(1) Name of issuer, coupon rate, maturity date, and market in which the bond is traded.

(2) Standard & Poor's rating of the bond's quality.

(3) Amount of the issue currently outstanding.

(4) Conversion price.

(5) Number of common shares into which the bond is convertible.

(6) Expiration date of the conversion privilege.

(7) Percentage increase in outstanding common stock which would result if all convertibles were, in fact, converted—i.e., the potential "dilution" of earnings per share.

(8) Earnings per share of common stock in latest three years.

(9) Indicated dividend rate of common stock.

(10) Dividend rate multiplied by number of shares into which the bond is convertible—i.e., dividend income which would be received if the bond were converted.

(11) Latest price of the common stock, and market in which it is traded.

(12) Price range of the common stock in the year to date.

(13) Conversion parity price of the common stock—i.e., the current price of the bond divided by the number of shares into which it is convertible.

---

[18] A number of companies have hedged against this risk by entering into an underwriting agreement when calling convertible issues. Under such an agreement, an investment banker, for a fee, agrees to buy any unconverted securities and to convert them. Thus, the underwriter rather than the company takes the risk of a sharp decline in the stock's price during the call period. See B. S. Williams and M. Letwat, "Underwritten Calls of Industrial Convertible Securities, 1950–61," *Quarterly Review of Economics and Business*, Winter, 1963.

FIGURE 12–5

Page from Standard & Poor's Bond Reports

**Standard & Poor's Bond Reports** | **Convertible Bonds** | **Statistical Analysis**

Vol. 32, No. 115 — October 25, 1965 — Section 18

| Issue | S & P Rating | Outstg. (Million $) | Conversion Price $ | Shares per $1,000 bond | Conversion Good Until | *% Dilution | ‡Earnings Per Share E1965 | 1964 | 1963 | Dividend Per Share $ | †Dividend Inc. Per $1,000 Bd. | Stock Price | 1965 Price Range | Conver. Value □Conv. Parity | Conver. Value per $100 | #Invest. Worth | Bond Price | Current Return |
|---|---|---|---|---|---|---|---|---|---|---|---|---|---|---|---|---|---|---|
| ✣Air Reduction 3⅞s, 1987 | BBB | 45.00 | 62.50 | 16 | 1987 | 17.2 | 4.75 | 3.68 | 3.33 | 2.50 | 40.00 | ✣ 68⅜ | 68⅝-53¾ | 78½ | 109⅜ | 87 | 125 | 3.10 |
| ∇Alaska Airlines 6½s, 1979 | CC | 3.33 | 6.50 | 153.85 | §1979 | 76.8 | ---- | d1.78 | d0.01 | Nil | ---- | ∇ 5⅝ | 6¼- 4⅛ | 6¾ | 86½ | -- | 101½ | 6.40 |
| ✣Allegheny-Ludlum Steel 4s, 1981 | BBB | 16.19 | 55 | 18.18 | 1981 | 8.7 | 4.65 | 4.02 | 2.75 | 2.00 | 36.36 | ✣ 49⅝ | 50⅜-39¾ | 62⅛ | 90¼ | 90½ | 113 | 3.54 |
| ✣Allied Stores 4½s, 1981 | BBB | 26.99 | 70 | 14.29 | 1981 | 18.4 | [1]A5.84 | [1]4.66 | [1]4.10 | 3.00 | 42.87 | ✣ 88⅛ | 89⅞-68⅝ | 91¼ | 125⅞ | 95 | 130½ | 3.45 |
| ★✣American Airlines 4s, 1990 | BB | 53.17 | 61.50 | 16.26 | 1977 | 26.2 | 5.25 | [14]3.93 | [14]2.93 | 1.25 | 20.33 | ✣ 60½ | 61½-44⅛ | 75 | 98⅜ | 82 | 122 | 3.28 |
| American Biltrite Rubber 4¾s, 1983 | BB | 5.00 | 13.50 | 74.07 | 1983 | 14.5 | ---- | 1.47 | 1.22 | 0.50 | 37.04 | ∇ 17 | 17⅞-13¼ | 17 | 125⅞ | 92 | 125⅞ | 3.77 |
| ✣American Distilling 4⅜s, 1986 | BBB | 9.55 | 43.18 | 23.16 | 1971 | 21.5 | [9]2.90 | [9]2.74 | [9]2.63 | 1.20 | 27.79 | ✣ 32⅞ | 34½-29¼ | 42⅞ | 76⅛ | 92 | 99¼ | 4.41 |
| Amer. Fletcher Natl. Bk. 3⅝s, 1990 | N.R. | 12.00 | 70 | 14.29 | 1990 | 19.0 | ---- | 4.05 | 3.75 | 2.00 | 28.58 | ■ 68 | 68 -56½ | 72⅜ | 97⅛ | -- | 103½ | 3.50 |
| ★American Greetings 4⅜s, 1983 | BBB | 7.50 | 37.02 | 27.01 | 1983 | 11.8 | [8]A2.23 | 1.91 | 1.80 | [39]0.80 | 21.61 | ■ 43⅜ | 43⅜-32⅛ | 45⅛ | 117⅛ | 92 | 122 | 3.59 |
| ✣American Machine & Fdry. 4¼s, 1981 | BB | 39.91 | 57.68 | 17.34 | §1981 | 5.8 | 1.15 | 1.06 | 1.09 | 0.90 | 15.61 | ✣ 19 | 20⅜-16⅛ | 52½ | 33 | 84 | 91 | 4.67 |
| ★✣American Optical 4.40s, 1980 | BBB | 7.70 | 27.83 | 35.93 | §1980 | 17.8 | 3.25 | 2.55 | 1.98 | 1.25 | 44.91 | ✣ 53⅛ | 55 -38 | 55⅛ | 190⅞ | 96 | 198 | 2.22 |
| American Pipe & Construction 4¾s, 1977 | BBB | 6.00 | 23 | 43.48 | §1977 | 14.7 | [11]--- | [11]1.00 | [11]0.95 | 0.50 | 21.74 | ■ 11⅛ | 12 - 9⅝ | 21⅜ | 48⅜ | 93 | 93 | 5.11 |
| American Petrofina 5½s, 1973 | B | 6.95 | 15 | 66.67 | §1973 | 9.7 | --- | 0.22 | 0.64 | 0.15 | 10.00 | ∇ 8¼ | 8¼- 5¾ | 14¼ | 55 | -- | 95½ | 5.76 |
| American St. Gobain 5½s, 1983 | CCC | 11.17 | 24.71 | 40.47 | §1971 | 60.5 | ---- | d0.15 | d3.99 | Nil | ---- | ■ 7⅝ | 12½- 6¼ | 23⅛ | 30⅞ | -- | 93½ | 5.88 |
| ★Arlan's Depart. Strs. 4½s, 1982 | BB | 3.00 | 16 | 62.5 | 1982 | 11.8 | [1]A1.82 | [1]1.21 | [1]0.81 | Nil | ---- | ✣ 22⅛ | 28⅜-21 | 22⅛ | 138¼ | 91½ | 138¼ | 3.25 |
| ★✣Armour & Co. 4½s, 1983 | BB | 32.65 | 51.14 | 19.55 | 1983 | [2]12.3 | [10]3.15 | [10]3.77 | [10]2.73 | 1.60 | 31.28 | ✣ 39⅜ | 53⅛-35¼ | 56⅞ | 77 | 90 | 111¼ | 4.04 |
| ★✣Ashland Oil & Refining 3⅞s, 1993 | BBB | 33.04 | 31 | 32.26 | 1993 | 14.8 | [9]3.90 | [9]3.06 | [9]2.33 | 1.60 | 51.62 | ✣ 49⅜ | 49½-38 | 49⅜ | 159¼ | 85 | 159¼ | 2.43 |
| ∇Associated Oil & Gas 6s, 1975 | CCC | 7.60 | 5.50 | 181.82 | §1976 | 26.5 | --- | 0.41 | [13]0.09 | Nil | ---- | ∇ 4¾ | 8 - 4¼ | 5¾ | 86⅜ | -- | 105 | 5.71 |
| ∇Associated Oil & Gas 6s, 1977 | CCC | 6.50 | 5.25 | 190.48 | §1977 | 48.0 | ---- | 0.41 | [13]0.09 | Nil | ---- | ∇ 4¾ | 8 - 4¼ | 56¾ | 90½ | -- | 108 | 5.56 |
| Astrodata Inc. 5s, 1980 | B | 4.00 | 42 | 23.81 | §1980 | 20.5 | [6]A1.50 | [6]1.10 | [6]0.63 | Nil | ---- | ∇ 38⅞ | 39⅜-28 | 47½ | 92⅝ | -- | 113 | 4.42 |
| ✣Automatic Canteen of Am. 4¾s, 1981 | B | 19.78 | 33.26 | 30.07 | 1981 | 12.9 | [9]1.20 | [9]0.75 | [9]0.53 | 0.80 | 24.06 | ✣ 26¼ | 27¼-16⅛ | 37¼ | 79 | -- | 111⅞ | 4.25 |
| ✣Avco 5s, 1979 | BBB | 4.31 | 11.50 | 86.96 | 1979 | 4.6 | [11]1.75 | [11]2.08 | [11]1.99 | 1.00 | 86.96 | ✣ 21¾ | 26⅜-19 | 22¼ | 189⅛ | 99 | 194 | 2.58 |
| ∇Baldwin-Montrose Chemical 5½s, 1980 | B | 4.14 | 15.50 | 64.52 | 1980 | 98.8 | --- | 2.08 | 1.02 | Nil | ---- | ∇ 9 | 17¼- 8¾ | 15¼ | 58 | -- | 98½ | 5.58 |
| ✣Baltimore Gas Elec. 4¼s, 1974 | AA | 4.69 | 24 | 41.66 | 1974 | 1.3 | 1.95 | 1.76 | 1.63 | 1.44 | 59.99 | ✣ 39½ | 41⅜-36 | 39½ | 164⅝ | 97¾ | 164⅝ | 2.58 |
| [20]Barium Steel 5½s, 1969 | CCC | 5.23 | 16.67 | 60 | 1969 | 28.9 | 2.50 | [13]1.01 | [13]d1.27 | Nil | ---- | ∇ 18⅞ | 18⅞-11½ | 18⅞ | 113¼ | -- | 113¼ | 4.86 |
| ★Bausch & Lomb 4½s, 1979 | BBB | 6.76 | 36 | 27.78 | 1979 | 35.7 | 4.00 | 3.05 | 1.87 | 1.20 | 33.34 | ✣ 58⅜ | 59⅞-41 | 59⅜ | 164⅞ | 97½ | 165 | 2.73 |
| Bausch & Lomb 4¾s, 1980 | BBB | 7.04 | 56 | 17.86 | 1980 | 35.7 | 4.00 | 3.05 | 1.87 | 1.20 | 21.43 | ✣ 59⅜ | 59⅞-41 | 66⅝ | 106 | 100 | 119 | 3.99 |
| ✣Baxter Laboratories 4s, 1982 | BBB | 10.00 | 38 | 26.32 | 1982 | 13.5 | 1.40 | 1.08 | 1.03 | 0.40 | 10.53 | ✣ 39⅝ | 40¼-27 | 46¾ | 104¼ | 90 | 123⅛ | 3.25 |
| ★✣Beaunit Corp. 4¼s, 1990 | BB | 25.00 | 48 | 20.83 | 1990 | 28.1 | [3]A3.16 | [3]2.66 | [3]2.02 | 1.40 | 29.16 | ✣ 42⅝ | 45½-34⅝ | 54¾ | 88¾ | 86 | 114 | 3.82 |
| Belco Petroleum 6s, 1974 | BB | 3.77 | 13 | 76.92 | 1974 | 13.0 | 1.05 | 0.90 | 0.81 | 0.50 | 38.46 | ✣ 22⅛ | 23¾-14½ | 22¼ | 170¼ | 105 | 171 | 3.50 |
| Belco Petroleum 5s, 1977 | BB | 7.50 | 21 | 47.62 | 1977 | 13.0 | 1.05 | 0.90 | 0.81 | 0.50 | 23.81 | ✣ 22⅛ | 23¾-14½ | 23¾ | 105⅜ | 96½ | 113 | 4.42 |
| ✣Berman Leasing 5½s, 1983 | B | 5.44 | 19.23 | 52.00 | 1983 | 30.7 | [6]A0.28 | [6]0.40 | [6]1.32 | Nil | ---- | ✣ 9⅛ | 11 - 7⅛ | 17½ | 47½ | -- | 91 | 6.04 |
| ✣Boeing 4½s, 1980 | BB | 30.51 | 50 | 20 | 1980 | 8.7 | 8.25 | 5.64 | [15]2.71 | 2.00 | 40.00 | ✣104⅜ | 108½-60⅜ | 105½ | 208¾ | 89½ | 211 | 2.13 |
| Bonanza Air Lines 5¼s, 1979 | B | 3.20 | 11.11 | 90 | §1979 | 27.2 | --- | [13]0.60 | 0.88 | Nil | ---- | ∇ 9⅞ | 12 - 8½ | 11⅛ | 88⅞ | -- | 100 | 5.25 |
| ✣Brunswick Corp. 4½s, 1981 | B | 25.62 | 50.66 | 19.74 | 1981 | 6.1 | --- | 0.03 | [15]0.27 | Nil | ---- | ✣ 8¼ | 11½- 7⅛ | 40¼ | 16¾ | -- | 79½ | 5.66 |
| ✣Bulova Watch 4½s, 1984 | BB | 8.08 | 24.75 | 40.40 | 1984 | 18.6 | [3]A1.44 | [3]1.26 | [3]0.79 | [36]0.60 | 24.24 | ✣ 20¾ | 24¾-17 | 27⅛ | 83⅞ | 90 | 109½ | 4.11 |
| ★✣Burroughs Corp. 4½s, 1981 | BB | 29.87 | 37.42 | 26.72 | 1981 | 11.4 | 2.10 | 1.38 | [14]1.15 | 1.00 | 26.72 | ✣ 44¼ | 45½-24⅞ | 49⅜ | 118¼ | 94½ | 132 | 3.41 |
| Canada Dry 4¾s, 1981 | BBB | 7.10 | 29 | 34.48 | 1981 | 10.4 | [8 13]A2.10 | [3]1.88 | [3]1.50 | 1.00 | 34.48 | ✣ 32¼ | 40 -28⅜ | 33⅞ | 111¼ | 99 | 117 | 4.06 |
| ★Carrier Corp. 4⅛s, 1982 | BBB | 15.84 | 40.49 | 24.7 | 1967 | 24.3 | [10]4.60 | [10]3.23 | [10]2.40 | 1.30 | 32.11 | ✣ 73⅝ | 74 -36 | 73⅝ | 181⅞ | 91½ | 102 | 2.27 |
| Cascade Nat'l Gas 5¼s, 1970 | BB | 5.82 | 14.29 | 69.98 | 1970 | 58.2 | --- | 0.94 | 1.17 | 0.50 | 34.99 | ■ 16⅞ | 19½-16⅞ | 17½ | 118⅛ | 101 | 122 | 4.30 |
| ★✣Celanese Corp. 4s, 1990 | BB | 78.86 | 100 | 10 | 1990 | 7.2 | 5.15 | 4.25 | 3.42 | 2.00 | 20.00 | ✣ 85¾ | 92 -72¾ | 111¼ | 85¾ | 82 | 111¼ | 3.60 |
| ★Cenco Instruments 4½s, 1980 | BB | 5.00 | 27¾ | 36.04 | 1980 | 9.6 | [4]A1.19 | [4]1.12 | [4]0.87 | 0.30 | 10.81 | ✣ 35¼ | 36 -27½ | 35¼ | 127 | 92 | 127 | 3.54 |
| ★✣Cerro 5½s, 1979 | BB | 22.31 | 26.34 | 37.97 | 1968 | 18.2 | 5.00 | 4.68 | 2.50 | 1.60 | 60.75 | ✣ 35¾ | 42⅝-31¼ | 38⅞ | 135¾ | 101½ | 147½ | 3.73 |
| ✣Chadbourn Gotham 5.90s, 1971 | CCC | 2.48 | 5½ | 181.82 | 1971 | 48.5 | ---- | [7]d0.15 | [7]d0.15 | Nil | ---- | ✣ 4⅜ | 5⅛- 3¼ | 5⅝ | 79½ | -- | 97⅞ | 6.03 |
| ✣Chadbourn Gotham 6s, 1974 | CCC | 2.17 | 5½ | 181.82 | 1974 | 48.5 | ---- | [7]d0.15 | [7]d0.15 | Nil | ---- | ✣ 4⅜ | 5⅛- 3¼ | 5½ | 79½ | -- | 99 | 6.06 |
| ★✣Champion Paper 4½s, 1984 | BBB | 20.03 | 46.08 | 21.70 | 1984 | 11.1 | 2.80 | 2.60 | 2.36 | 1.20 | 26.04 | ✣ 38⅞ | 42 -31⅛ | 50¾ | 84¾ | 95½ | 110 | 4.09 |
| Chance (A. B.) Company 5s, 1985 | BB | 3.00 | 22 | 45.45 | 1985 | 12.5 | ---- | 1.72 | 1.01 | 0.72 | 32.72 | ■ 20 | 25 -16 | 26 | 90⅞ | 95½ | 118 | 4.24 |
| ✣Chicago & Eastern Illinois 6s, 1997 | CCC | 11.64 | 22.68 | 44.09 | 1997 | 109.2 | 2.70 | 1.55 | 4.42 | Nil | ---- | ✣ 28⅛ | 28⅞-17⅛ | 29⅝ | 124 | -- | 130½ | 3.83 |
| ✣Chicago & North Western 4½s, 1999 | CCC | 67.51 | 66.67 | 15 | 1999 | 225.3 | [8]18.60 | 2.74 | 5.24 | 3.00 | 45.00 | ✣119¾ | 122½-52⅝ | 120⅝ | 179⅝ | -- | 181 | 2.49 |
| ✣Chock Full O' Nuts 4⅛s, 1981 | BB | 6.39 | 28.50 | 35.09 | 1981 | 8.6 | [7]A0.65 | [7]0.62 | [7]0.59 | 0.40 | 14.04 | ✣ 11⅛ | 13⅝-10⅛ | 26 | 40⅝ | 87 | 91⅜ | 4.92 |
| ✣City Products 5s, 1982 | B | 14.90 | 31.32 | 31.93 | 1982 | 24.0 |  | 3.24 | 2.53 | 1.60 | 51.09 | ✣ 54⅝ | 56¼-39⅞ | 54⅜ | 173⅝ | -- | 173⅝ | 2.88 |
| ✣Cluett Peabody 4¼s, 1984 | BB | 12.60 | 62 | 16.13 | 1984 | 17.4 | 5.15 | 4.13 | 3.55 | 2.00 | 32.26 | ✣ 80¼ | 80⅞-59⅞ | 85⅜ | 129⅝ | 87½ | 137⅞ | 3.09 |
| ∇Coburn Credit 5½s, 1978 | B | 2.25 | 12½ | 80 | §1978 | 39.3 | [2]A0.58 | [2]0.42 | [2]0.48 | 0.30 | 24.00 | ∇ 11¼ | 11⅛- 8⅜ | 13⅛ | 90 |  | 105 | 5.24 |
| Cole National 4¾s, 1984 | B | 6.00 | 23.50 | 42.55 | 1984 | 36.5 | [10]---- | [10]1.74 | [4]11.00 | 0.60 | 25.53 | ■ 15⅜ | 21 -13¼ | 21⅝ | 65½ |  | 92 | 5.16 |
| ✣Collins Radio 4⅜s, 1980 | BB | 12.00 | 61.54 | 16.25 | 1980 | 31.8 | [7]A2.04 | [7]1.08 | [7]1.65 | 0.50 | 8.13 | ✣ 47⅜ | 47½-19⅝ | 62¼ | 77 | 88 | 101¼ | 4.69 |
| ✣Collins Radio 4¾s, 1983 | BB | 12.50 | 27.50 | 36.36 | 1983 | 31.8 | [7]A2.04 | [7]1.08 | [7]1.65 | 0.50 | 18.18 | ✣ 47⅜ | 47½-19⅝ | 47⅜ | 172¼ | 86½ | 172¼ | 2.76 |
| ✣Colorado Fuel & Iron 4⅞s, 1977 | B | 16.27 | 27 | 37.04 | §1977 | 15.5 | 4.00 | 1.47 | 0.83 | Nil | ---- | ✣ 20¼ | 21⅛-10¼ | 28⅞ | 75 | -- | 106⅝ | 4.57 |

★Recommended for Current Purchases ✣N.Y.S.E. ∇A.S.E. See page 4 for all other footnotes.

Source: Standard & Poor's Corp.

(14) Conversion value of the bond—i.e., the current price of the stock multiplied by the number of shares into which the bond is convertible (expressed relative to each $100 of bond par value).

(15) Standard & Poor's estimate of what the bond would be worth if it were not convertible.

(16) Current price of the bond. (This price divided by items 14 and 15 represents the premium of the bond over its value as a straight stock and straight bond, respectively.)

(17) Current yield of the bond—i.e., coupon rate divided by purchase price.

## SPECIAL SITUATIONS

For the sophisticated investor special situations offer considerable attraction. They afford the opportunity for capital gains because of some special development either within the company or in the external environment affecting the company. The development, if it occurs, will ensure the gain regardless of the general trend of the market. Narrowly defined, the true special situation has a mathematically predictable gain, like buying a $10 bill for only $7.50. More broadly and more usually, a special situation may work out to a calculable gain if certain developments come to pass. It also includes calculation of downside risk if the developments anticipated do not materialize.

### True Special Situations

In the more limited sense of the term, special situations may arise from:

*Liquidations* (In a complete liquidation the company disposes of its assets and distributes the proceeds to its shareholders.)

*Residual Stubs* (These are certificates of participation representing a residual interest in a company. They usually arise out of liquidations.)

*Tenders* (An offer by a corporation to buy back its own shares. Or an offer by an outsider, interested in acquiring control, to buy up shares, usually at a price above the market.)

*Spin-Offs* (A corporate divestiture of a division or a subsidiary by distributing shares in the new corporate entity to existing shareholders of the divesting company.)

*Appraisals* (Court determination of the fair value of a dissenting shareholder's stock which he refuses to exchange in a merger or acquisition.)

*Oversubscriptions* (These arise in rights offerings when shareholders who have exercised their rights are additionally offered an opportunity to buy remaining unsubscribed shares.)

*Mergers and Acquisitions* (A merger usually involves an exchange of shares and a pooling of interests.)

*Hedges and Arbitrages* (Out of mergers and acquisitions frequently arises the opportunity to profit by arbitrage and to minimize losses by hedging.)

*Reorganizations* (When a company undergoes reorganization certain of its securities bought at panic prices may subsequently emerge from the reorganization at higher values.)

*Recapitalizations* (Administrative changes in the capital structure of a corporation may involve a realignment of relationships among the company's securities with attendant profit possibilities.)

True special situations have three distinguishing characteristics:

1. Some unique development is occurring which makes this particular security attractive apart from general industry, economic, or security market conditions.
2. This development is usually noncontinuing in nature. If not seized upon when it appears, the specific opportunity may be lost. The security may continue to be a worthwhile purchase but not as a "special situation."
3. The situation is usually amenable to measurement of expected gains and calculation of probable risks.

### The Broader Special Situation

In the broader sense of the concept of special situations as used by investment advisory services and stock brokerage houses, the following also may be included:

Undervalued or Sold-Out Situations
Hidden Earnings
Court Orders and Litigation
New Technological Developments
Changing Government Regulations or Tax Rulings
New Management
Comeback Situations
New Markets

In this broader sense the special situation may often depend upon events and developments external to the corporation and look to future growth rather than fortuitous developments for the clue to capital gains.

Several investment advisory firms have special situation services. This is true of Forbes, Arnold Bernhard & Co., Spear & Staff, etc. In the view of Arnold Bernhard "a special situation refers to some security in which an extraordinary, non-recurring corporate development is taking place—a development which can reasonably be expected to enhance the value of the security in question irrespective of the trend of the market as a whole."

In the prospectus governing the offering of shares of the Value Line Special Situations Fund, the following explanation of a "special situation" appears:

. . . The term "special situation" is intended to refer to a security of a company as to which a development applying particularly to that company has happened or is expected to happen, which in the opinion of the fund's manager will, for reasons unrelated to general business conditions cause the security within an estimated period of time to attain market recognition according the security a higher value, regardless of the movement of the market as a whole. The particular development (actual or prospective) may be one or more of many different things; for example: a reorganization; a recapitalization or other development involving a security exchange or conversion; a merger, liquidation or distribution of cash, securities or other assets; a break up or workout of a holding or other company; payment of dividend or other arrears; litigation which, if resolved favorably, will improve the value of the company's stock; a technological improvement or important discovery or acquisition which, if the expectations for it materialize, will effect a substantial change in the company's business; new or changed management or material changes in management policies. The fact, if it exists, that an increase in the company's earnings, dividends or business is expected, or that a given security is undervalued, is not in itself sufficient to make a security a "special situation."

The Forbes Special Situation Survey states:

As the name implies, a Special Situation is a condition in a security in which a particular development, or a set of internal circumstances, could within a reasonable period of time produce a substantial upward movement in the price of the security relative to the market as a whole. The primary characteristic of the Special Situation is that it offers exceptional profit potentials for reasons which have little or nothing to do with the general level of the stock market or the direction of the economy—factors which are unknown or unappreciated by the general investing public.

### Some Examples

In its true form the special situation has a gain potential which can be calculated in advance. For example, two simple illustrations cited by *Business Week* are as follows:

1. LIQUIDATION
   Hidden Value Corporation was preparing to sell all its assets.

| | |
|---|---|
| The sales price per share would yield | $10.00 |
| On liquidation, it could claim a tax refund of | 4.40 |
| Making a total sure value of | $14.40 |
| But the stock was then selling for | 11.00 |
| So the buyer could count on a net profit of | $ 3.40 |

2. MERGER
   Attractive Company was about to merge with High-Powered Company.

| | |
|---|---|
| Shareholders of Attractive were due to get one share of High-Powered common worth | $26.00 |
| Plus 4/50 of a share of High-Powered 4½% preferred (selling at $44 a share) | 3.50 |
| Making a total sum value of | $29.50 |
| Attractive Co. stock was selling for | 25.75 |
| So the buyer could make a profit of | $ 3.75 |

*Business Week* added:

In its narrowest sense the special situation is best examined in simple arbitraging—where a stock, say, can be bought in one place for one price and sold immediately for a higher price. The profit potential is clear, and it is pocketed immediately. There is a whole body of special situations revolving around arbitraging—such as buying one stock on a merger announcement and selling the other. . . .

But in the broad sense special situations are long-term ventures. They spring mostly from reorganizations, liquidations, mergers, litigations, and spin-offs—and these often take time to work out. But in each, the condition that could make the stock rise lies in the particular company, not in the market.[19]

## Mergers and Acquisitions

A merger usually involves a chance to buy the shares of one of the companies involved and sell short the shares of the other company. Usually, the shareholders of the company to be absorbed are offered shares of the acquiring company in exchange for their holdings. In its eagerness to consummate the merger, the acquiring company may offer more (in value) of its own shares than the then market price of the shares of the company to be acquired. When this occurs it may be possible to buy the shares of the company to be acquired and simultaneously sell short the shares of the acquiring company. Then when the merger is consummated, the short sale is covered, closed out, by delivery of the shares received in the exchange.

Two examples may be cited from a study by a leading authority on special situations.[20] In the first example, Federated Department Stores absorbed Bullocks, Inc. The merger terms provided for the exchange of 1.4 shares of Federated for each Bullock share. Based on the price of 61¾ for Federated at the time the merger terms were publicly announced, each share of Bullocks, then selling at 80, would be exchanged for Federated stock worth 1.4 times $61.75, or $86.45. The appropriate special situation action would have been as follows:

| | |
|---|---|
| Buy 100 Bullocks at $80 per share | $8,000 |
| Sell short 140 FDS at 61¾ per share | 8,645 |
| Gross Profit | $ 645 |

From the gross profit, of course, would have to be deducted the cost of brokerage commissions and any dividends paid on FDS stock while the short sale was open.

The second example cited by Schiller involved the absorption of

[19] "How to Profit for Sure," *Business Week*, June 14, 1958, p. 115.

[20] See Maurece Schiller, "Special Situations in Securities," chap. xliii in *Encyclopedia of Stock Market Techniques* (rev. 2nd ed.; Larchmont, N.Y.: Investors Intelligence, Inc., 1965), p. 769.

Hanson–Van Winkle by American Can Company. Terms called for 0.465 shares of American Can to be exchanged for each Hanson–Van Winkle share. Since American Can was priced at 44, the value of Hanson–Van Winkle shares would amount to $20.46 as compared to the market price of $17.75 a share. The appropriate special situation action would have been as follows:

| | |
|---|---|
| Buy 100 shares of Hanson–Van Winkle at 17.75 | $1,775 |
| Sell short 46½ shares of American Can at $44 | 2,046 |
| Gross Profit | $ 271 |

Some merger-acquisitions involve a very minimum downside risk. Two examples may be cited. Rollins Broadcasting, Inc., absorbed Orkin Extermination Company. At the time, Rollins chief interest was in 10 radio and television stations and an outdoor advertising agency. Orkin, of Atlanta, Georgia, ranked as the nation's largest pest control concern. It was also far larger than Rollins. Orkin's sales of over $37 million compared with revenues of just under $8 million for Rollins. Rollins swung the deal for $62.4 million. The bulk of the funds was borrowed—$15.5 million coming from Equitable Life Assurance and Chase Manhattan Bank and $40 million from Prudential Insurance Company. From a 1964 low of 4¾, Rollins shares zoomed to 51¾ in 1965. At 1964 preacquisition levels, Rollins stock had a very minimum of downside risk.[21]

In June, 1965, Storer Broadcasting purchased 87% of the stock of Northeast Airlines. Northeast had been in the red since 1956 and among other things brought Storer a tax-loss carry-forward of $50 million, equal to over $12 per Storer share. At the time of the acquisition, Storer shares were selling on a 4% yield basis and appeared statistically undervalued when compared with the shares of other TV broadcasters. If the acquisition fell through, Storer—at worst—would probably incur a nonrecurring write-off of its option money. At best, it would acquire Northeast and add a substantial turnaround profit possibility to its operation, particularly if Northeast, with new financing via Storer, could retain the New York to Miami run. The downside risk in Storer's stock at the time appeared minimal, the profit possibility unusual.

Not all merger situations, of course, present such possibilities. There must exist a chance to purchase shares of the company to be acquired at a discount from their ultimate exchange value in terms of the acquiring company's stock to be received. Even where the desired discount is to be found, it may quickly be narrowed or wiped out by market action. Thus, as in all investments, timing is an important factor in the merger-acquisition special situation.

---

[21] See Joseph Rosenberg, "Minnow and Whale: Leverage Is the Key to Some Unusual Corporate Couplings," *Barron's*, January 24, 1966, p. 5.

## Liquidations

A classic example of the special situation is the liquidation, where a company decides to dispose of its assets and distribute the proceeds to its stockholders. In some cases the liquidating value is considerably in excess of the market price of the company's stock. Hunters of special situations are always on the lookout for "companies worth more dead than alive." Cuban Atlantic Sugar was one example of a profitable liquidation. String puller behind the deal was John L. Loeb of Loeb, Rhoades & Co. He and his associates managed to buy up 50% of the company's 2 million shares outstanding at about $16 per share for a stock with a book value of about $24 per share. They then sold off one part of the company's properties for $24.5 million, which meant $12 per share to the stockholders. They then spun off another property as a separate company with common which then sold for $12 per share. Meanwhile the original company's stock rose from $16 to $25. Thus Loeb's group benefited not only from the $9 per share appreciation but also from the proceeds of the sale of property and the spin-off.

At a time when Delhi Taylor Oil Company's stock was priced at $16, liquidation rumors began to circulate. In due course, stockholders received the equivalent of $28.50 a share. Universal Oil Company was absorbed by Gulf Oil Corporation. When Universal Oil shares were selling at $64 a share, a Gulf Oil subsidiary offered to, and did, buy them at $68 a share, liquidating the company.

## Acquisition-Liquidation Deals

An acquisition-liquidation deal in which a mutual fund concentrating on special situations, Mutual Shares Corporation, achieved a substantial capital gain, was the purchase of the operating assets of Republic Aviation Corporation by Fairchild Hiller.[22] The way it worked was as follows:

| | *Fund's Position* | |
|---|---|---|
| | *Debit* | *Credit* |
| September, 1965—Republic Aviation Corp. (RAC) stockholders approve sale of assets to Fairchild. Mutual Shares buys 2,000 shares of RAC at $20 a share. Estimates book value at $23. | $40,000 | |
| November, 1965—RAC stockholders approve liquidation of their company. Plan calls for liquidating dividends of about $14.50 a share plus ½ share of Fairchild for each 1 share of RAC held. Mutual Shares sells short 1,000 shares of Fairchild at $20 a share. Fund does not enter gain from sale until it receives its Fairchild stock in March. | | |
| December, 1965—Mutual Shares receives liquidation dividends of $12.25 a share. More to come. | | $24,500 |

[22] "Thriving on Rewards of Patience," *Business Week*, August 6, 1966, p. 134.

| | | |
|---|---|---|
| March, 1966—Mutual Shares receives 1,000 shares of Fairchild stock. Covers short position and now enters gain from sale. | | $20,000 |
| May, 1966—RAC stock is delisted from NYSE. Now trading over the counter | | |
| August, 1966—Current value of RAC stock is $2.25 equal to balance of liquidating dividend expected. If Mutual Shares now sells its 2,000 shares of RAC, its profit on the entire transaction would be 22%. | | $ 4,500 |
| | $40,000 | $49,000 |

The reason for the short sale is to protect the anticipated profit from the vagaries of the market. In the RAC–Fairchild Hiller situation this was important. Mutual Shares sold short 1,000 shares of Fairchild Hiller in November at $20 and delivered in March. Had it waited until March to sell, it would have realized only $14 a share from its holdings in Fairchild Hiller.

### Merger-Hedges

In a study of merger-hedges, Dr. John Shelton points out that the hedging operation is not devoid of risk. He points to two risks in merger-arbitrages: (1) the merger may never be completed; and (2) the merger may be completed only after such a long delay that the profit represents an unsatisfactory return for the length of time the money was held in the hedge.[23] Of 402 merger or buy-out proposals studied, occurring during the five-year period 1958–62, only 41 were deemed suitable for the arbitrage procedure. Of the 41, eight were not completed and a ninth resulted in a loss because the company on the short side of the hedge paid large dividends during the pendency period.

Dr. Shelton concluded:

> Merger-hedges, if properly screened, appear to offer a satisfactory rate of return in view of the limited risk associated with them. They may not appeal to many investors either because the actual profit spread (typically about 3% to 4% after transaction costs) may seem too small to justify the effort if consideration is not given to the rather fast turnover of the capital, or because the operation requires fairly close scrutiny of the securities markets. This study indicates that the professional would have to sift through about ten potential mergers to find one that is suitable for hedging. . . . Finally, the merger-hedge appears to be a special situation that offers moderately good rewards for moderately low risk.

### Reorganizations

Reorganizations are also traditional special situations. In the case of a company facing reorganization, the old securities will be greatly de-

[23] John P. Shelton, "An Evaluation of Merger-Hedges," *Financial Analysts Journal,* March-April, 1965, p. 49.

pressed in value. Through careful financial analysis, workout values can be approximated for some classes of securities. Two trading procedures can then be utilized. Either the selected depressed securities can be purchased and held and in due course exchanged for new securities issued under the plan of reorganization, or a hedge operation can be undertaken. This is accomplished by buying the old securities and then subsequently selling on a "when, as, and if issued" basis, the new securities to be received in exchange. This is predicated, of course, on the assumption that the market value of the new securities to be received in the exchange will be greater than the cost of the old securities purchased at very depressed prices. This occurs often in reorganizations but not inevitably or invariably, and thus careful financial evaluation of pro forma balance sheets and income accounts in reorganization plans is essential. It is not an area for amateurs. Schiller[24] provides an example of a situation which arose during the course of the reorganization of the Denver & Rio Grande Western Railroad Company. Under the ICC plan of reorganization approved by the Federal District Court, senior bonds were to be exchanged for a package of assorted securities in the reorganized company. The special situation arbitrage which could have been worked out was as follows:

| | | |
|---|---|---|
| *BUY* | $10,000 Denver Rio Grande 4's/1936 at $53 | $5,300.00 |
| | Approximate commissions and taxes on completed arbitrage operation | 65.00 |
| | Total Cost | $5,365.00 |
| Later *SELL* | "When-issued" new securities authorized by Reorganization Plan | |
| A. | $3,189.20 DRG 1st Mtge. 3–4s 1933 at 87¾ | $2,798.52 |
| B. | $2,170.80 DRG Income 4½s 2018 at 56½ | 1,226.50 |
| C. | 32.16 shares DRG Pfd. at 41¼ | 1,326.60 |
| D. | 48.24 shares DRG Common at 18¾ | 904.50 |
| | Accrued interest on above 1st Mtge. bonds (estimated) | 191.35 |
| | Proceeds | $6,447.47 |
| | Cost | 5,365.00 |
| | Net Spread | $1,082.47 |

Source: Maurece Schiller, "Special Situations in Securities," chap. xliii in *Encyclopedia of Stock Market Techniques* (rev. 2nd ed.; Larchmont, N.Y.: Investors Intelligence, Inc., 1965), p. 775.

## The Spin-Off

Another traditional special situation is the spin-off. This occurs when a company distributes the stock of one or more of its subsidiaries to the shareholders of the parent company. Since the shareholders of the parent company in effect own the subsidiaries controlled by the parent, the shares of the subsidiaries are usually not sold but rather distributed

[24] Schiller, *op. cit.*, p. 775.

free of any additional charge. They are "spun off." In a spin-off special situation one and one do not add up to two—but to more. That is, the sum of the parts is equal to more than the whole. Matson Navigation was primarily in the steamship business. But at a time when Matson stock was selling at $40 a share, discerning analysts noted that it held other assets besides steamships. Matson's stake in Honolulu Oil alone had a then current market value of approximately $21 a share. This was about one half of the market price of Matson stock. Buried in another part of its balance sheet was Matson's investment in Pacific National Life Assurance Company, a profitable operation worth another $10 per share. For other properties on Oahu, Matson was offered $18 million, equivalent to $12 a share on Matson stock. In anticipation of a management decision to spin off some of its holdings, Matson stock rose from 40 to 65 in 11 months' time, at the end of which the spin-off was announced.

Sometimes a spin-off results from a court decision or from the ruling of a regulatory authority. Some years ago, under the Public Utility Holding Company Act, the SEC ruled that the Electric Bond & Share Company had to divest itself of a number of companies which it controlled. For each 100 shares held in Electric Bond & Share, stockholders received 1.6 shares of Carolina Power & Light, 2.85 shares of Middle South Utilities, 3.75 shares of Texas Utilities, 2.2 shares of Florida Power & Light, 2.2 shares of Montana Power, 2 shares of Washington Water Power, and 21.6 shares of United Gas. Twenty years later, the market value of this distribution was $3,004—to say nothing of the $1,930 increase in the value of 100 shares of Electric Bond & Share.

### Hidden Assets

Another type of special situation is the discernment of undervalued or hidden assets. The net worth of institutions such as banks, insurance companies, etc., can largely be measured in dollars and cents, rather than in fixed assets like plant and equipment. Where the market has been restrictive in its evaluation of the underlying assets of a financial institution, a special situation may develop. At one time, for example, it was possible to buy the common stock of the First National Bank of Jersey City for under $100 per share. This represented a discount of better than 50% from the bank's reported book value of $215. Largely responsible for this discount was a rather unimpressive earnings record in the previous several years. However, analysis revealed that First National should experience a profits rebound, and in the following year, earnings on the common rose to $18.18 compared with $7.80 in the previous year. The common rose to $150 per share, a profit of some 50% in one year's time.

Another example of hidden assets was found in the case of General Tire and Rubber. In 1958 the stock was selling at $27 with a very low price-earnings ratio. Careful analysis indicated that the market valuation was low relative to General's basic business. The downside risk was minimal. In addition, General Tire controlled Aerojet, then a fledgling but burgeoning rocket company. By buying General Tire, an investor got Aerojet free. During 1959, investors began to recognize rocket stocks, and General Tire was very profitably revalued. It rose to more than three times its 1958 level. Aerojet-General went on to become a major contributor to General Tire's earnings. In 1965 the 84% owned subsidiary provided 53% of consolidated sales.[25] Aerojet's sales went from $2.5 million to over $700 million annually, and the value of General Tire's investment in Aerojet rose from an original $1.2 million to more than $150 million.[26]

Each year *Forbes* magazine publishes a tabulation entitled "Loaded Laggards." See Figure 12-6. It is a list of companies whose shares are either selling below net working capital or at a substantial discount from book value. A recent classic example was Admiral Corporation. In 1964 Admiral sold as low as 15, a discount of 45% from its book value of $27.68 a share. During 1966, with color-TV shares in high favor, Admiral sold as high as 120—a premium of 300% over book value. Careful scrutiny of "loaded laggards" sometimes yields interesting special situations.

**FIGURE 12–6**

**Loaded Laggards: 1966**

RECENT GRADUATES: These companies were on the 1965 Loaded Laggard List but are off this year.

| | 1965 Price | 1966 Price | 1965* Book Value | 1966* Book Value |
|---|---|---|---|---|
| Allied Mills | 41 | 51½ | $57.33 | $ 59.25E |
| Allis-Chalmers | 24½ | 38¾ | 32.55 | 33.44 |
| Anaconda | 65 | 97½ | 97.54 | 101.25 |
| Baldwin-Lima-Hamilton | Acquired by Armour & Co. | | | |
| Bell Intercontinental | 9⅝ | 12⅜ | 16.37 | 15.29 |
| Continental Motors | 11¾ | 16¾ | 16.38 | 16.91 |
| Crane | 30⅝ | 54½ | 53.10 | 58.26 |
| Cudahy Co. | 7½ | 8⅝ | 13.12 | 0.29 |
| Curtiss-Wright | 18⅞ | 25½ | 23.81 | 23.99 |
| Foster Wheeler | 34¾ | 63⅜ | 58.17 | 60.54 |
| Gar Wood Industries | 5 | 10 | 6.97 | 7.46 |
| General Baking | 9 | 20½ | 15.99 | 13.41 |
| Hamilton Watch | 15 | 28⅛ | 21.07 | 23.37 |
| Kelsey-Hayes | 42 | 55 | 56.72 | 59.36 |
| Leonard Refineries | 11¾ | 14⅞ | 16.42 | 17.00E |
| Loew's Theatres | 20 | 37½ | 31.49 | 38.59 |
| Merritt, Chapman & Scott | 18⅛ | 28 | 30.01 | 33.38 |
| Mueller Brass | Acquired by U.S. Smelting & Refining Co. | | | |
| National Sugar Ref. | 18 | 22⅛ | 29.62 | 21.61 |
| Nautec | Delisted | | | |
| Oxford Paper | 14¾ | 22½ | 19.73 | 20.80 |
| Pacific Amer. Corp. | Delisted | | | |
| Pittsburgh Coke & Chemical | 20¼ | 53¾ | 35.19 | 37.18 |
| Stand. Pressed Steel | 14⅝ | 17⅞ | 19.44 | 20.39 |
| United Biscuit | 27⅜ | 34¾ | 43.55 | 40.78 |
| United Fruit | 21⅛ | 29⅝ | 32.71 | 34.37 |
| Vanadium Corp. of America | 23 | 31⅜ | 31.13 | 33.95 |

E-Estimate. *Beginning of fiscal year.

[25] See Arnold M. Glanz, "Finding Special Situations in Any Market Level," *Commercial and Financial Chronicle*, June 30, 1966, p. 18.

[26] See "The Family Affairs of General Tire & Rubber," *Forbes*, October 1, 1966, pp. 32–34.

## FIGURE 12–6 (Continued)

***These companies sell near or below net working capital per share***

| Company | Main Business | Recent Price | Book Value* | Discount From Book Value Per Share | Net Working Capital† | Latest 12 Month Earnings | Indicated 1966 Dividend | 1965-66 Price Range |
|---|---|---|---|---|---|---|---|---|
| Bath Iron Works | shipbuilder | 48½ | $68.11 | 29% | **$48.65** | $2.24 | 1.40 | 55 —31¾ |
| Bayuk Cigars | cigar manufacturer | 11¼ | 16.33 | 31 | **11.24** | 0.51 | 0.50 | 16¾—10⅞ |
| Bond Stores‡ | apparel stores, clothing mfg. | 25½ | 33.65 | 24 | **24.23** | 1.99 | 1.00 | 29½—20¼ |
| Endicott Johnson | shoe mfg. | 25½ | 52.64 | 52 | **30.64** | 1.01 | none | 33⅜—22 |
| Fenestra | building & auto products | 18⅜ | 25.30 | 27 | **17.77** | 0.87 | 0.25†† | 20⅛—15⅝ |
| Hat Corp. | hat making | 10 | 14.73 | 32 | **10.35** | 0.99 | 0.40 | 13⅝— 7 |
| Howard Stores | clothing mfg. & outlets | 11½ | 25.22 | 55 | **19.12** | 0.10 | stock | 14½— 9⅜ |
| McQuay-Norris | auto parts | 21 | 29.80 | 30 | **22.69** | 1.35 | 1.10 | 26⅞—19¼ |
| Neisner Brothers | variety stores | 11⅞ | 27.97 | 58 | **12.89** | 1.08 | none | 14¾— 7¼ |
| Publicker Industries | industrial alcohol & chemicals | 8 | 17.84 | 55 | **10.13** | d0.47 | none | 10½— 7 |
| Schick Electric | electric shavers | 8½ | 10.32 | 18 | **8.15** | 0.46 | none | 10½— 6⅞ |
| Wyandotte Worsted | woolen fabrics | 14⅝ | 20.98 | 30 | **15.77** | 0.88 | 0.10†† | 18⅜— 9⅝ |

***These companies sell at a discount of 20% or more from book value***

| Company | Main Business | Recent Price | Book Value* | Discount From Book Value Per Share | Net Working Capital† | Latest 12 Month Earnings | Indicated 1966 Dividend | 1965-66 Price Range |
|---|---|---|---|---|---|---|---|---|
| Acme Markets | food store chain | 45¾ | **58.00E** | 21 | NA | 4.10 | 2.00** | 73½—43¼ |
| Alpha Portland Cement | cement producer | 12⅜ | **25.97** | 52 | d7.11 | 0.36 | 0.125†† | 15⅛—10⅞ |
| American Cement | regional cement producer | 11⅛ | **16.63** | 33 | d5.59 | 1.14 | 0.60 | 13⅜—10½ |
| American Consumer Industries | cold storage, ice, fuel | 18¼ | **25.40** | 28 | d28.96 | 0.25 | 0.50†† | 22⅜—16 |
| American Crystal Sugar | beet sugar producer | 18¾ | **34.00E** | 45 | NA | 1.36 | 1.00 | 23 —16½ |
| American Export Isbrandtsen | shipping; holding co. | 51 | **79.47** | 36 | d10.11 | 4.95 | 1.50 | 60⅞—23⅝ |
| American Motors | autos & appliances | 10¼ | **13.50E** | 24 | NA | d0.01 | none | 15⅛— 7¼ |
| Anderson Clayton | commodity merchandiser | 34¼ | **56.00E** | 39 | NA | 3.23 | 1.00 | 38¾—26⅛ |
| Archer-Daniels-Midland | agric. & chem. processor | 46 | **60.25E** | 24 | NA | 3.01 | 1.60 | 47¼—30 |
| Associated Brewing‡ | brewer | 16¾ | **22.02** | 24 | d1.37 | 0.46 | 0.40 | 18 — 9⅝ |
| Belding Hemingway | fabrics, threads & chemicals | 18¾ | **24.15** | 22 | 15.03 | 0.93 | 0.70 | 22⅜—16½ |
| Budd Co. | auto bodies, rail cars | 18⅞ | **32.72** | 43 | 8.06 | 2.01 | 0.80 | 23¼—13¾ |
| Central Foundry | cast iron pipes & fittings | 13 | **19.00E** | 32 | NA | 0.43 | 0.15†† | 19¼—11⅝ |
| Checker Motors | auto assembler | 16¾ | **24.62** | 32 | 4.79 | d0.68 | none | 27⅞—14½ |
| City Stores | department & specialty stores | 17 | **22.00E** | 23 | NA | 1.50 | none | 16⅞—10⅛ |
| Colorado Fuel & Iron | rail & wire products | 16⅞ | **32.19** | 48 | 5.18 | 3.23 | none | 21⅛—10¼ |
| Cone Mills | cotton textile mfgr. | 28¾ | **36.11** | 20 | 14.88 | 2.71 | 1.20 | 32 —20¾ |
| Cuneo Press | printer | 10⅞ | **24.75E** | 56 | NA | 0.25 | 0.40†† | 14 —10 |
| Detroit Steel | rolled sheet & strip steel | 17 | **23.96** | 29 | d1.23 | 1.19 | 0.60 | 18⅞—13 |
| DWG Cigar | cigar maker | 14 | **19.05** | 27 | 11.38 | d2.14 | none | 21⅝—12⅜ |
| First National Stores | regional food chain | 33½ | **60.50E** | 45 | NA | 2.47 | 1.50†† | 51¼—33 |
| Franklin Stores | women's apparel shops | 13⅛ | **17.00E** | 23 | NA | 1.25 | 0.40 | 14⅜— 8⅞ |
| Granite City Steel | steel products | 24¾ | **32.23** | 23 | 10.26 | 1.99 | 1.40 | 27½—23 |
| Hazeltine | patent licenser; electronic equip | 9½ | **13.53** | 30 | 8.24 | 0.37 | none | 15⅝— 6¼ |
| Hilton Hotels | hotel operations | 19⅛ | **30.67** | 38 | d29.76 | 1.91 | 0.60 | 19⅞—11⅛ |
| Holly Sugar | beet sugar producer | 38¾ | **61.00** | 37 | NA | 5.96 | 1.80 | 42¼—33⅝ |
| Intn'l. Packers | meat packer | 12⅛ | **18.31** | 34 | 2.31 | d2.62 | none | 16⅜— 9¾ |
| Jones & Laughlin | steel products | 63⅝ | **80.19** | 21 | 7.31 | 6.55 | 2.70 | 74¼—58 |
| Keystone Steel & Wire | wire products | 35½ | **47.00E** | 25 | NA | 3.95 | 2.00 | 41¾—35¼ |
| Lehigh Portland Cement | cement producer | 16¼ | **27.46** | 41 | d5.75 | 1.37 | 1.00 | 20½—14⅞ |
| Libby, McNeill & Libby‡ | canning & frozen food | 12⅝ | **18.91** | 33 | 6.48 | 0.52 | stock | 15¾—11⅞ |
| Lowenstein, M. | textile manufacturer | 23 | **35.85** | 36 | 16.67 | 2.23 | 0.60 | 27 —16 |
| Lykes Bros. | freight & passenger carrier | 24⅞ | **60.08** | 59 | 6.54 | 2.45 | 0.80 | 28½—18¼ |
| Marquette Cement | cement producer | 18¾ | **30.48** | 39 | d5.42 | 1.76 | 1.00 | 33⅜—18¾ |
| McLouth Steel | steel producer | 32⅛ | **44.19** | 27 | 2.49 | 2.82 | 1.55 | 46¾—31¾ |
| Montgomery Ward | mdser. & mail-order | 34⅝ | **51.92** | 33 | 23.66 | 1.83 | 1.00 | 39¾—30½ |
| Moore & McCormack | int'l. shipper | 28⅜ | **43.33** | 35 | d1.97 | 1.12 | 0.60 | 31¼—16½ |
| Morrell, John | meat packer | 30 | **42.52** | 30 | 18.55 | d0.28 | 0.25†† | 32½—21⅛ |
| Natco Corp. | building tile | 14 | **18.23** | 23 | 10.18 | 0.53 | 0.30 | 14⅞— 8 |
| Newberry, J.J. | variety stores | 21¾ | **36.00E** | 40 | NA | 2.14 | stock | 24⅞—18½ |
| Penn-Dixie Cement | cement producer | 12¼ | **23.04** | 47 | 3.36 | 1.03 | 0.60 | 18 —11½ |
| Penn Fruit‡ | supermarket chain | 8 | **11.86** | 33 | 3.23 | 0.29 | none | 10⅜— 7¼ |
| Pittsburgh Steel | steel products | 15 | **33.13** | 55 | d6.96 | 0.43 | none | 17½—12½ |
| Republic Steel | steel products | 41⅝ | **56.86** | 27 | 2.70 | 4.58 | 2.00 | 46¼—38½ |
| Sharon Steel | strip & sheet steel | 28 | **67.07** | 58 | d10.11 | 3.22 | 0.60 | 33½—18⅞ |
| Shattuck, Frank G. | restaurant chain; candy | 15¾ | **24.49** | 36 | 4.66 | J.82 | 0.50 | 20½—13 |
| Smith, A.O. | pipes & car frames | 38½ | **50.16** | 23 | 21.44 | 4.22 | 1.15** | 42½—27⅛ |
| Swift & Co. | meat packer; dairy products | 53⅛ | **72.01** | 26 | 25.28 | 2.70 | 2.00 | 65 —44⅜ |
| U.S. Lines | steamship lines | 42¼ | **67.45** | 37 | d17.05 | 2.20 | 2.00** | 42⅝—32 |
| U.S. Pipe & Foundry | cast iron pipe producer | 23 | **29.92** | 23 | 12.25 | 2.06 | 1.20 | 24 —19¾ |
| U.S. Steel | steel & cement producer | 47¾ | **62.94** | 24 | d3.23 | 4.62 | 2.00 | 55⅞—46 |
| Wheeling Steel | steel products | 30¼ | **84.19** | 64 | d40.55 | d2.94 | none | 36 —23⅛ |
| Woolworth, F.W. | variety chains | 25⅞ | **37.61** | 31 | 3.51 | 2.51 | 1.00 | 33⅜—25⅝ |
| Youngstown Sheet & Tube | steel producer | 38⅛ | **53.50E** | 29 | NA | 4.85 | 1.80 | 47¼—37½ |

*Includes deferred income taxes arising from depreciation charges. †After prior obligations, i.e. long-term debt, minority interest and preferred stock. **Plus stock. ††Paid so far. d-Deficit. ‡Company balance sheet data prior to 9/30/65; losses in such companies can significantly reduce equity. E-Estimate. NA-Not available.

Source: *Forbes*, May 1, 1966.

### Management Changes

Turning to the broader concept of special situations, a resurgence in earnings may result from a change in management or from some technological innovation or from a change in regulatory climate. At times a top-management change signals dynamic and constructive changes in the direction of a company. Such shifts may lead to improved earnings results being achieved by already successful companies or to a "turnaround" of problem companies.

In the last half of 1961, a new president and a new chairman of the board took over the direction of the Chrysler Corporation. At the time, Chrysler was wracked by adverse publicity concerning its previous top management, and earnings were faltering badly. The new management installed effective cost controls, began rebuilding a shaky dealer system, initiated new styling programs, and took numerous other steps to put this ailing giant on the road to recovery. Less than a year and a half later, earnings turned sharply upward, and the stock price by year-end 1962 nearly doubled the levels which prevailed at the time of the change. By year-end 1963, another doubling of the market price took place in concert with a further sharp earnings increase. Adjusted for stock splits and stock dividends, Chrysler stock rose from 9 in 1961 to 66 in 1964.

### Technological Innovation

This is the era of the research breakthrough and of the birth of whole new markets or the rapid expansion of older ones as a result of industry's continuing vast investment in technological developments. For example, in March, 1960, Xerox Corporation introduced the 914 Copier. This new machine revolutionized and expanded what has now come to be recognized as a growth industry. At the time the new machine was first offered in commercial markets, that company had sales in the neighborhood of $35 million a year and the stock was valued at around $5 per share (adjusted for subsequent stock splits through 1964). By the end of 1964, the company's volume was $268 million and the stock was valued at nearly $100—and subsequently rose to $190 during 1965 and to $267 during 1966.

### The Regulatory Environment

Changes in the regulatory environment produce special situations, in the broader sense, from time to time. For example, in 1958, shares of Schenley Industries rose from $15 to $41 mainly due to the extension of the tax-free period on bonded liquor. In 1960 the Real Estate Investment Trust of America rose more than 50% in price as a result of a law eliminating the corporate tax on real estate investment companies that meet stated requirements. More recently, a change in the regulatory climate affecting local service airlines by the Civil Aeronautics Board enhanced the profitability of these carriers. The lines were permitted to drop some unprofitable routes, were fully reimbursed for the cost of serving other locations, and were allowed to develop the profit potential of their more lucrative routes. Recommended as special situations by Value Line in February, 1961, a number of these lines appreciated substantially in price as may be seen in the accompanying tabulation:

| *Airline* | *Recommended Price** | *Recent Price†* | *% Appreciation* |
|---|---|---|---|
| Allegheny | $3¾ | $20⅛ | 437% |
| Bonanza | 2⅜ | 19 | 700 |
| Central | 1 | 10¾ | 975 |
| Frontier | 2⅜ | 28 | 1,079 |
| Lake Central | 5½ | 14¼ | 159 |
| Mohawk | 3¾ | 20⅝ | 450 |
| North Central | 1¾ | 5¾ | 229 |
| Ozark | 3⅞ | 13¾ | 255 |
| Pacific | 1⅞ | 15 | 700 |
| Piedmont | 2 | 18⅝ | 831 |
| Southern | 3.07 | 19⅝ | 539 |
| West Coast | 3⅝ | 15½ | 328 |

* February 6, 1961.
† July 14, 1966.
Source: Value Line.

## Conclusion

Examples of past special situations could be multiplied. To spot and capitalize on a true special situation requires professional skill in financial analysis and meticulous attention to the details of investment happenings. Numerous situations must be examined and explored before one promising one is located. Then its details must be analyzed painstakingly and all probable and possible outcomes evaluated. There is no easy road or shortcut to finding true special situations. In the broader, more popular sense of the term, several of the services, Value Line, Forbes, Spear & Staff, etc., provide special situation recommendations. Value Line has a Special Situation Fund and Mutual Shares Corporation seeks capital gains by concentrating on special situations.

## SUGGESTED READINGS

Ashby Bladen. *Techniques for Investing in Convertible Bonds.* Salomon Bros. & Hutzler, 1966.

Eugene F. Brigham. "An Analysis of Convertible Debentures: Theory and Some Empirical Evidence," *Journal of Finance*, March, 1966.

Keith L. Broman. "The Use of Convertible Subordinated Debentures by Industrial Firms, 1949–59," *Quarterly Review of Economics and Business*, Spring, 1963.

*Business Week*, "How to Profit For Sure," June 14, 1958.

———. "Thriving on Rewards of Patience," August 6, 1966.

Lin Tso, *Techniques for Discovering Hidden-Value Stocks.* New York: Frederick Fell, Inc., 1965.

Maurece Schiller. *Fortunes in Special Situations in the Stock Market.* American Research Council, 1961.

———. "Special Situations In Securities," chap. xliii in *Encyclopedia of Stock Market Techniques.* Rev. 2nd ed. Larchmont, N.Y.: Investors Intelligence, Inc., 1965.

John P. Shelton. "An Evaluation of Merger-Hedges," *Financial Analysts Journal,* March–April, 1965.

William S. Skelly. *Convertible Bonds: A Study of Their Suitability for Commercial Bank Bond Portfolios.* Salomon Bros. & Hutzler, 1959.

## APPENDIX TO CHAPTER 12—"THE A.B.C. OF PUTS & CALLS"*

### Puts & Calls

Puts, Calls and other forms of Stock Options have been widely used in the securities markets ever since these markets were organized.

In New York, the brokers and dealers who transact the buying and selling of options for the public are members of the Put and Call Brokers and Dealers Association, Inc. This group was formed in 1932 to foster and maintain the highest standards of integrity in all the business activities of its members.

### The Use of Option Contracts

Over the years, the vast majority of investors have not purchased (or sold) stock options . . . simply because they have never thoroughly understood how these buy or sell options may be used profitably. Some even feel that Put and Call Options are purely speculative, rather than a stock market tool.

Although options can be used speculatively to enter the market with a small cash investment, this is only one of their functions. Puts and Calls have a far greater use in protecting paper profits that have not been realized or to take a position in a specific stock with a limited pre-determined risk. Thus, Puts and Calls can be more accurately described as anti-speculative, since the majority of option contracts are purchased to reduce or limit risk.

### General Description of Contracts

Let us describe the various kinds of Put and Call option contracts available, so that we can have a better basic knowledge of the 'working tools' of the trade.

PUT OPTION—a contract that entitles the holder to SELL to the endorser (a New York Stock Exchange Member Firm) a definite amount of a specific stock at a predetermined price within the life of the contract.

---

* Reproduced with permission of Godnick & Son, Inc., New York, N.Y. and Beverly Hills, Calif.

The life of the contract can be for any length of time, but it usually runs 30, 60, 90 days or 6 months or even longer. (Stock Exchange rules prohibit the endorsement of options for less than 21 days.) As with any other option, the life of the option is a matter of negotiation between buyer and seller. The option buyer pays a fee for the privilege of having time to consider his purchase or sale. The bulk of the fee goes to the writer (seller) of the contract and a small amount to the dealer who brought the two parties together.

The cost of the option varies with the terms of the contract. ie: the price at which you can PUT (sell) the stock and the duration of the option. This cost is a matter of negotiation. But, as in any open market, competition serves to maintain a fair and realistic price. Several firms advertise regularly in New York papers. They quote specific rates on selected options they have to offer. . . . Let us see how the terms of the PUT contract dictate the price. The more favorable the terms for the buyer, the higher the price. If the terms favor the seller, the price of the PUT option contract is lower.

*Example: 100 shares of XYZ Today's Market Price $50.* If the negotiated terms are for a short term contract (30 days) and the buyer is entitled to PUT (sell) the stock to the seller of the option at 48 or 2 points below the market, the terms are not very favorable to the buyer and the PUT contract would probably be quoted at the lowest rate—$137.50.

The price obviously is higher if the buyer asks for more favorable terms. If the contract entitles the buyer to PUT (sell) the stock at the current price of 50, instead of at the concession price of 48 and the duration of the contract is extended to 60 or 90 days or 6 months, then the price of the option might be $275, $350 or any other negotiated figure.

When you buy a PUT contract, you are guaranteed that you can SELL stock at a specific price any time during the life of the contract. You have purchased protection against a decline in the price of the stock. A CALL contract is the opposite of the PUT. A CALL option entitles the holder to BUY from the endorser a definite number of shares of a specific stock at a predetermined price within the life of the contract. And, as in the case of the PUT, the time or length of the option period can vary and the price that the buyer pays depends upon the number of advantages purchased.

CALL OPTIONS are quoted at the negotiated price plus tax. Currently, the maximum tax is $12 per 100 shares. ($4 State and $8 Federal.) Example: Let us take the same XYZ stock. Current market price 50.

If you purchase a call on XYZ at 52 for 30 days (this gives you the right to purchase XYZ stock anytime for the next 30 days at a price of 52—no matter how high the price rises). Of course, if the price of the stock should decline, you would not exercise your option. The cost of this option would probably be $137.50 plus tax. Since the terms favor the seller, the cost is minimal. However, if you want the privilege to purchase XYZ at 50 for a period of 60 or 90 days or 6 months, you would have to pay more for that privilege.

### The Straddle

A relatively simple combination . . . it's just as you would expect . . . the buyer is straddling a particular stock. He buys a PUT and a CALL on the same stock, at the same price, on the same number of shares, for the same period of time. A STRADDLE is two IDENTICAL options . . . one a PUT and the other a CALL. You can execute one and not the other. In a widely fluctuating market, the holder could benefit both ways. He would execute the CALL on an upward movement and the PUT on the decline.

### The Spread

Here again, this term is almost self-explanatory. We are taking two positions on the same stock and like the STRADDLE it is a PUT and a CALL on the same stock for the same length of time. However, there is this DIFFERENCE—the PUT price is below the current market and the CALL price is above the current market. Example: XYZ stock, current price 50.

In the case of a STRADDLE, both PUT and CALL option would be at 50. Now, in the case of a SPREAD, the PUT might permit the holder to SELL at 48 and the CALL to BUY at 53. Since the SPREAD does not grant the same advantages as the STRADDLE, a SPREAD on XYZ would be purchased at a concession in price.

### Strips and Straps

These terms are not as self-descriptive as the others. STRIPS and STRAPS are founded on STRADDLES, and you will remember that a STRADDLE is a PUT and a CALL with identical terms. When these options are used in combination, we assign the following terms:

STRIP—2 PUTS and 1 CALL
(STRADDLE plus a PUT)
STRAP—1 PUT and 2 CALLS
(STRADDLE plus a CALL)

### Risk is Limited

These basic explanations of PUTS and CALLS and other combinations of options, point out that in every case the total risk to the buyer cannot exceed the price of the contract. The buyer executes his option if it is profitable to do so—or permits it to expire if the stock does not act in his favor during the life of the contract. The cost of the option, if it is not executed, is a tax deductible item. It is either a short or long-term capital loss depending upon the length of time the option was held.

### Dividend Treatment

A PUT or a CALL option is entitled to any and all dividends, rights, splits or other benefits that are issued to the stock during the life of the contract. If the stock sells 'ex' one of these benefits' . . . then the holder who exercises his CALL gets the benefits or if he exercises his PUT must in turn give the benefit.

Thus, suppose during a 90 day contract, XYZ, selling at 50, goes ex a $1 dividend. This dollar belongs to the stock. When the holder of the CALL exercises his privilege, he does so at $49, even though the figure specified on the CALL option is 50, because this is how he receives the benefit of the $1 dividend.

On the other hand, selling a PUT on XYZ at 50, in the same example, entitles the option seller to the dividend. Therefore, when the option is exercised, a point is given up. If the holder exercises the PUT, he must PUT (sell) the stock at 49 and not 50. The same principles apply to whatever benefits are issued to the stock during the contract period.

### Examples: Who Writes the Options

No matter what the nature of a contract; real estate, business, Puts or Calls, a contract must have at least two parties. In most cases, a broker negotiates the transaction and receives compensation for his services.

Most investors who use the option market are on the buying side. For a relatively small amount of money they can buy protection and seek to make a profit. Who then is on the other side (the seller's side)? Why is it that, for a comparatively small amount of money, another party will guarantee to buy from you or sell to you a quantity of stock at a specific price within a certain time limit?

The answer lies in our basic American business system. Each party, in any kind of contract expects to enjoy a profit and is fully aware of the risk factors. Option contracts are no different. Each party looks for a potential gain. In the case of Puts and Calls, the writer (seller) of the contract, the one who binds himself, is usually an individual (or a corporation) with a large position in a security and who is perfectly willing to add to or subtract from his portfolio at a price. Experience indicates that these writers of contracts have increased their annual profits considerably with the added fees they have earned. EXAMPLE: Smith has 1,000 shares of XYZ Corporation. He likes the stock, keeps in touch with conditions affecting the company and is accustomed to trading in and out of its shares. Smith has accumulated his present 1,000 shares at various prices and the stock is currently quoted at 50. He thinks 50 is a fair price and is willing to sell some of his stock a little above 50 or to buy, and add to his holdings, a little below 50. Instead of buying or selling, however, he permits a member of the Put and Call Brokers and Dealers Association to sell options for him. Let us assume that the dealer sells a PUT, good for 90 days at a price of 50. Smith therefore contracts to buy 100 shares at the price of 50. For this he receives $300. If the Put is exercised, Smith has to buy an additional 100 shares, which means an investment of $5,000. But since he receives $300 when he issued the contract, the actual price to him amounts to 47 instead of 50. If the Put is not exercised, he still has the $300, which is profit, and he is free to write another Put.

Let us suppose that Smith permitted his dealer to sell a Call on 100 shares for $350. Again, if the Call is not exercised, he has gained $350. But if the market advances, he must sell the purchaser of the option 100 shares at 50. That doesn't bother him for he too has benefited from the advance in the market. He has an additional paper profit on the 900 shares he still holds, and has received 53½ (50 plus $350) for the 100 shares sold.

A long-term investor in a stock is able to make a high rate of return on his investment with a continuous program of option writing. By writing a straddle instead of just a Call or Put, Smith in effect doubles his chances. If the price of XYZ remains about the same, he has earned $650 cash; if it goes one way or the other, he still has the $650 to compensate for his services.

Big portfolio investors, individuals or funds that maintain long-term investments in securities, are the main source of Put and Call options.

### What are the Margin Requirements?

If you are long a stock and sell a Call on it, or if you are short a stock and sell a Put on it, there is no additional margin requirement since you already have the proper amount on deposit.

If on the other hand, you have no long or short position, but sell an option, the minimum margin required is 30% of the market value of the stock involved. However, most Stock Exchange firms require a minimum of 50% overall on your total account.

### Use of Options

How can the ordinary individual make use of this fascinating market tool, either as a speculative device or as protection for paper profits already on their books? Suppose you like to trade in XYZ. To buy 100 shares will require an investment of $5,000. Perhaps you do not wish to tie up this amount of cash. You can get a quotation on a Call and find that for $375 you can secure the right to buy 100 shares of XYZ at 50 within 90 days. If it sells at 60 within that time limit, you may exercise your Call at 50. If the price declines to 40, there is no further obligation. You have lost the $375 you paid for the protection, the same as you might in the case of any other option.

The same applies to the Put contract. You think the price of 50 is too high, but to sell it short would again require a deposit of $5,000 to your brokerage account. You risk the $325 and buy a Put option contract.

If you were right, and the price declines to 40, you instruct your regular broker to Put (sell) the stock to the endorser of the option at 50. If you guessed wrong and the price advances, your liability is limited to only $325 and you have no further obligation.

This may be considered speculation by some, although it is no different than the use of options in other phases of our economy.

### Protection of Profits

Let us assume that you bought XYZ at 40 and you see it now at 50. You think it will go higher, but you are concerned. You have three possible courses of action. You can sell it and take your 10 point profit. In that event, you make $1,000 minus commissions and taxes.

You can instruct your broker to enter a stop order, say at 46, which means that should the price sink to 46, then he is to sell you out at the market. Suppose he gets 46 for it, or possibly 45⅞. You have made $600, or thereabouts, minus commission and taxes.

Or, you can buy a Put for $325, good for 90 days, entitling you to sell the 100 shares at 50 during that period.

If XYZ continues to rise, you ignore the Put, and your cost for protection has been $325, but you still own the stock and have added something more than the $1,000 to your paper profit. If the market breaks, you can collect the $5,000 by exercising the Put, and your profit, even though XYZ may have dropped to 35 or 30, is $1,000 minus the $325 cost of the Put and the commission and taxes. It protects the major part of a paper profit, for a minimal cost. (For the tax effect on the purchase of a Put refer to page 450.) Reverse the above description for the case of the individual who is short of a stock and wishes to protect part of his profit through the purchase of a Call. He had sold XYZ at, let us say, 60. It is now at 50. He buys a Call at 50 for 90 days and pays $375. He immediately knows he has guaranteed himself the 10 points profit, for at least 90 days at a cost of $375. If XYZ declines to 40, he forgets about the Call and doesn't exercise it. If on the other hand, the market firms and XYZ goes back to 60, where he sold it short, he calls on the endorser of the option and covers his short position. He received $6,000 when he sold it short, so he is able to close out that transaction with his broker, earning $1,000, minus the $375 paid for the Call and commissions.

It is cases such as the above that have brought the Put and Call option market more into public favor in the last year or two, rather than cases where such options are used for straight speculation.

### Are there Options on Over-the-Counter Securities?

There are, in a limited number of cases. It all depends on the security itself. If the company has a sufficient number of shares outstanding in the hands of the public to permit active trading, it can be optioned as well as a listed security.

### Who Fixes the Price of an Option?

The price is fixed by supply and demand, which is another way of saying it is subject to negotiation, the same as the price of a stock, a bond, or a used car. Many factors are weighed by the man who makes the bid and the one who makes the offer.

Dominant factors considered by both include the quality of the stock to be optioned, the length of time of the contract, the market history of the stock, its price level and the demand from others for similar Puts and Calls. As a general rule, the better the quality of the stock, the less the percentage cost to the buyer. Lower-priced securities, and those of poorer quality, usually involve a higher percentage cost to the purchaser. The best market, and therefore the market where closest prices are available to both buyer and seller, is in medium or higher priced quality securities.

### Volatile Stocks Preferred

As dealers in options, we do not attempt to select particular stocks for our clients. It is sound advice, however, to recommend that option trading be directed to the more active stocks on the list. In any market, the most advantageous sales can normally be made where there is the greatest demand.

There is always an active demand for options on top quality stocks, and dealers make close markets in these issues. Examples of stocks in which option dealing has been very active are Chrysler, Pan-American, Ford, U.S. Steel and N.Y. Central, to mention a few. There are others which may be relatively quiet for short or long periods of time, but when news or other developments cause them to shake off their lethargy, they too develop an option demand.

### Can My Broker Get Me Quotations on Puts & Calls?

He can. Ask him to phone us and we can give him a quotation on almost any active stock. These will be prices at which options are offered for sale.

Prices at which you can sell are more subject to negotiation, especially in less active issues.

### Why Are Puts Cheaper than Calls?

This difference in price reflects the spirit of optimism that is characteristic of a people who are convinced of the long-term potential growth of our country. One of the familiar sayings of the late Charles M. Schwab was, "Never sell America short." Few do so. There are several million times as many investors owning stocks as there are those short of stocks. Thus, there is more demand for Calls than for Puts, and the price of the former is therefore somewhat higher. Most investors look forward to buying their favorite stock at a price low enough to justify taking the risk; there is less appeal for the contract that entitles him to Put (sell) the same block of shares to someone else, at a specified figure.

### Options and Taxes

Treasury decisions and rulings handed down from time to time clarify provisions of the 1954 Internal Revenue Code under which individual and corporate taxpayers file their returns. These provisions will apply until the law is amended. Certain provisions of the 1954 Act, and subsequent rulings, have made it possible for the astute investor to utilize Puts and Calls to his advantage and thus lessen the drain on his personal income and his estate. Sound business practice dictates that the investor should know these provisions and adapt them to his individual situation.

Sydney Smith, early nineteenth century English author voiced the common complaint of all taxpayers of every era in his "Sketches of Moral Philosophy."

"The schoolboy whips his taxed top," he wrote, "the beardless youth manages his taxed horse with a taxed bridle on a taxed road; and the dying Englishman, pouring his medicine, which has paid seven per cent, into a spoon that has paid fifteen per cent, flings himself back upon his chintz bed which has paid twenty-two per cent and expires in the arms of an apothecary who has paid a license of a hundred pounds for the privilege of putting him to death."

There are situations in which the trader in securities, however, can lighten his tax burden if he understands the uses of options.

It is the purpose of this section to call attention to these, and by explanation and the use of examples from actual trades, to make them available to all investors.

### The Tax Effects

Keeping in mind that options can be used to reduce risk, and to that extent minimize the hazards of speculation, it may be well to review briefly their tax effect. If a Call is exercised, its cost is added to the cost of the stock purchased. If a Put is exercised, its cost is deducted from the amount received for the stock.

The option seller adds the premium received to the selling price of the stock when a Call is exercised. He reduces the purchase price of the stock when a Put is exercised.

If either expires without having been exercised, the cost to the option buyer is a capital loss, sustained on the date of its expiration. It is either a short-term or long-term capital loss depending upon whether it was held for less than six months or for more than six months. For the option seller, the premium received for unexercised options becomes ordinary income.

The 1954 Internal Revenue Code (Sec. 1233) (b) regards the purchase of a Put as a short sale under ordinary conditions and it considers that the date of the short sale is the day the Put is acquired.

There is a way, however, to avoid having the Put regarded as a short sale by the Internal Revenue Service. It involves the purchase of stock and Put on the same day. In such cases, the trader adds the cost of the Put to the cost of his stock, to fix the purchase price for tax purposes.

### How Does It Work?

Some may question why anyone who likes a stock well enough to buy it, would at the same time risk additional money on the chance it may go down. The reason is that he wants protection. He expects a rise, but should there be a general decline in the market, his Put has given him protection against a severe loss. If he can Put the stock to the seller of the option, at the contract price, his risk is limited to the cost of the option.

If the stock advances, here is an example of how it would work. We'll assume he bought 100 shares of ABC at 60 and simultaneously bought a Put of "over six months" also at 60 for $425. His cost was $6,000 plus $425, or $6,425. At the expiration of six months and one day, the transaction is considered long-term by the Internal Revenue Service, and thus any gain that may result is a long-term capital gain and given preferential treatment in compiling the trader's income tax statement. If he sells ABC at 87 at this time he has a long-term capital gain of $2,275 ($8,700 less than $6,425). In other words, the price of the Put was part of his cost price, and did not create a short sale.

It was not essential for him to buy an "over six months" option in this case. A shorter-term Put, say ninety days, would have protected him for only half as long, but if purchased when he bought the stock for about $325 it would be added to his cost price.

In such a case the trader's price would be entered on his records as 63¼ (60 for the stock and $325 for the option). If we assume ABC has advanced to 87 in ninety days and his Put expires, he has about 23 points protection on the downside before he faces a loss. Normally this would appear to be adequate enough to warrant maintaining his long position for an additional three months, so as to qualify his profit as a long-term capital gain.

### Is It the Same with Calls?

The bookeeping is quite similar in the case of Call options but there are two important differences which must be emphasized. Both relate to securing the advantage that goes with long-term gains as against those made in less than six months.

Applying the Call option to the above example, an "over six months" Call costs about $550, covering 100 shares. With ABC at 60, the total cost of the investment to the trader, on the exercise of the option would be 65½ (60 for the stock plus $550 for the Call), or $6,550.

If ABC advances to 87 within the life of the option, the trader can liquidate and take approximately a 21½ point profit. Here is an important point, however. While he held the Call over six months, he did not own the shares during that time, therefore the profit would be a short-term capital gain, subject to the full force of taxation in his particular bracket. To qualify for a long-term capital gain he must have owned the shares for a minimum of six months and a day.

Instead of calling the stock, and then selling it, the Call itself is sold, the profit constitutes a long-term gain, since the buyer owned the option for more than six months.

There is another point to be watched, in the event that the stock declines during the period of the Call option. In order to secure the advantage of writing off the cost of the Call as a short-term loss, it must be sold before six months elapse. The same procedure applies to a Put.

As an example, we will assume that while ABC was selling for 60 at the time the option was purchased, it had declined to 50 as the time neared for the option to expire. The option should be sold. We as dealers will buy it for a nominal price. Obviously, the price will be small, as there is little value in an option that is about to expire and which is far out of line with the market.

It is a bonafide transaction, however, and is recognized by the tax authorities as constituting a short-term capital loss. If the six months' period is completed before this sale is made, then the original cost is also deductible, but as a long-term loss and thus it is less desirable. If we buy your Call and the market changes suddenly, to a point where the Call would yield some proceeds, the profits accrue to us.

In any market transactions it is well to keep in mind that profits are more valuable if they are long-term, and losses can be used to better advantage if they are short-term. In this connection, and closely identified with the above discussion on Calls, there is another factor relating to Puts, that should be kept in mind.

If the buyer bought stock and purchased a Put, as protection, in the event of a decline, and the market does decline considerably, under Sec. 1233(c) the buyer must Put the stock before the expiration of the six months' period in order to qualify the transaction as a short-term capital loss.

### Help for the Upper Echelon

Facts and figures on short and long term capital gains and losses are of special interest to investors in the upper income brackets. Options can play an important role by giving the trader a good run for his money while saddling him with relatively small risks.

Let's take an example to demonstrate this. We'll assume a trader in the 50 per cent tax bracket has a short-term capital gain of $5,000. His tax liability, under these conditions, will be $2,500, leaving him the remaining $2,500 which is all he could count as net profit.

If he cares to risk the $5,000 (which is only $2,500 to him) there are opportunities in the option market which could increase his profit, and the gains would be long-term, and thus more advantageous to favorable tax treatment. Here is how it could work.

For $5,000, he could buy various Calls, say one on 1,000 shares of United

States Steel, or on 3,000 shares of Studebaker, or any other stock that strikes his fancy. He should limit himself to the "over six months" Calls. A profit of $25,000 is not unusual in such a transaction. If he has purchased such a Call and held it for at least six months and a day before selling it, the profit would be a long term gain. In this case, he would not call the stock, as that would require retaining the shares an additional six months in order to qualify as a long term transaction. He would sell the Calls.

Thus he gets a gross profit of $25,000 and the capital gains tax will be $6,250, bringing him a profit, net after income tax, of $18,750. Although the Call cost $5,000, his risk was only $2,500, since the first $2,500 would have gone to the tax collector anyway.

In the event the stock did not advance to the point where he could show a gross profit of $25,000, or, in fact, if it showed him no profit, the entire cost of the Call, $5,000 is balanced out against his former short-term capital gain of that amount. He ends up with neither a capital gain nor a capital loss. He is even, but the risk of $5,000 which was made available to him through the Put and Call Market, involved an actual risk on his part of only $2,500.

In this connection, it is well to keep in mind that an excess of capital losses over capital gains may be applied as a deduction against ordinary income to the extent of $1,000 a year. A capital loss in one year can be used to reduce a capital gain in succeeding years, in the amount of $1,000 each year.

To illustrate this, we will assume that a salaried executive receives $30,000 a year and is in the 50 per cent bracket. There is a use of options which may well interest an executive of this type, who earns a good salary but whose capital is limited to the point where he hesitates to trade in a fast moving stock that could give him a quick loss of $2,000 or more.

It is not unusual to see ten, fifteen or twenty points advance or decline in a six months period in active pivotal issues. The man with limited capital might well hesitate to take a position in 300 shares of such stocks.

Yet he can trade in these volatile stocks, with limited risk, through the purchase of options. His risk is limited to the price he pays for the option since he doesn't have to exercise a Put or a Call unless it is to his advantage. To get the same potential in the higher priced issues, he would have to invest a much greater amount of capital if he purchased them outright.

To illustrate this, we will take an extreme case and assume an individual in the 70 per cent income tax bracket has a short-term capital gain of $25,000. His tax liability is $17,500, leaving him a net gain of only $7,500.

If he should invest $25,000 in options and they all went against him, and became valueless, he could write this loss off against his short-term profit of $25,000 and the net loss to him therefore would amount to only $7,500. Thus, all he actually risked was $7,500.

If, on the other hand, the options were more fortunately chosen, it is well within the realm of possibility that he could achieve a long-term capital gain of $125,000. A gain of this nature would incur a tax liability of approximately $31,000. He would therefore emerge with a profit after taxes of approximately $94,000; and all he would have risked was $7,500.*

---

* From "The A.B.C. of Puts & Calls" by Godnick & Son, Inc., New York, N.Y. and Beverly Hills, Calif.

# Part III

## INVESTMENT TIMING

# INTRODUCTION TO PART III

INVESTMENT decisions usually are classified under two broad headings, "selection" and "timing." Selection deals with the question: *What* to buy—bonds or stocks; which bonds; which stocks? Timing deals with the question: *When* to buy—now or wait? As a practical matter, of course, these two categories are not mutually exclusive. The question of what to buy is not made in a time vacuum. The real question is: *What* to do with my capital *now?* Granting the interlocking nature of selection and timing, however, it is useful to differentiate between them conceptually.

The traditional textbook approach to both the selection and timing aspects of investment has been that of "security analysis," or "evaluation." In Chapter 5 of this text, for example, it was shown that the goal of common stock evaluation is to determine the approximate trend line around which actual stock prices can be expected to fluctuate. At any given time, according to this approach, the common stock analyst should have a reasonably clear idea whether stocks generally, and individual stocks in particular, seem underpriced or overpriced. This enables him to come to grips with both the what and when questions. For example, he may seek to buy issues which are relatively most underpriced, at a time when the market in general seems underpriced.

Value analysts assume that underpriced and overpriced situations ultimately will come into better balance. But they typically make little or no effort to predict when the corrective price movement will occur. Their reasons for ignoring efforts to predict are several. First, they argue that it is not possible to make predictions about turning points of prices with a better-than-chance probability of being accurate. Second, they point out that investors confront "a market of stocks rather than a stock market." By this they mean that efforts to predict the turning points of, say, the Dow-Jones Industrial Average are rather futile, since an average can go up or down, but there is great disparity in the price movement of the individual component stocks of the average. Furthermore, they note with regard to attempts to predict the averages, most downturns during the postwar period have amounted to only some 10%–20%. Certainly one cannot expect to be prescient enough to sell at the very peaks and buy back at the troughs. Assuming that even a good forecaster will make his sales at least 3%–5% below the peaks, and that repurchases will be made 3%–5% above the troughs, and making allowance for brokerage commissions and taxes of several percent on combined sale-repurchase transactions, the average price decline of 10%–20% doesn't leave much, if anything, for profit. Moreover, there are very real dangers of being "whip-sawed" by selling in anticipation of a price decline which fails to occur.

So strong is the antipathy of many value analysts toward price prediction efforts outside of the value context that it seems important to comment on the logic of their position. In the first place, it is hoped that the following two chapters will demonstrate that predictive tools are available which can produce better-than-chance results. It will not be argued that these tools are perfect or that they can be employed with little effort. But neither are the tools of security valuation perfect or easy to utilize.

The claim that the stock market is "selective"—i.e., that individual stock prices do not all move in tandem—is quite correct. But improper implications seem to have been drawn from this observation. Major upward and downward swings of "the averages" usually do reflect the overall tone of the market rather well, as is shown in the accompanying tabulation. The tabulation indicates that when the averages fall, stocks in most industries fall also. Likewise, when the averages rise, the majority of stock groups rise also.

"Selectivity" means that in a bull market different stocks rise by very different percentage amounts, and in a bear market they fall by very different amounts. Nor do all stocks make their highs and lows at the same time. Therefore, the investor's attention should not be focused exclusively on the averages. But neither should the averages be ignored. For once a major trend in the averages gets underway, it is extremely difficult to select the issues that will resist the trend. The true significance of the existence of disparate price movements among different stocks would seem to be that value analysis and price forecasting approaches should be considered powerful allies rather than opposing philosophies.

The argument that the mildness of postwar bear markets reduces the importance of timing also has some flaws. First, as the value analysts themselves admit, "selectivity" means that some stocks may have quite severe downturns even when the averages decline only moderately. Second, venturesome investors can enhance the rewards of correct forecasts of downturns by *short* selling over and above their sales of existing holdings. Third, although the postwar period has brought forth no price decline in the averages comparable in depth to some declines of previous years (for example, 40% in 1920–21 and again in 1937, to say nothing of the 80% Great Crash of 1929–32), there is no guarantee that far more severe declines will not occur in the years ahead. Admittedly, the chance does not seem great. But the difficulty is that if it should happen, the early

**Industry Group Price Changes during Bull and Bear Markets**

| | Bear Market Dates | | | | |
|---|---|---|---|---|---|
| Peak Month | 6/48 | 1/53 | 7/56 | 7/59 | 12/61 |
| Trough Month | 6/49 | 9/53 | 12/57 | 10/60 | 6/62 |
| % Change S & P 500 | −17 | −11 | −17 | −10 | −23 |
| % Change S & P 425 | −18 | −12 | −17 | −11 | −23 |
| No. of groups with price changes of: | | | | | |
| +10.1% and over | 2 | 1 | 8 | 18 | 0 |
| + .1 to +10.0% | 4 | 6 | 9 | 13 | 0 |
| 0 to −10.0 | 20 | 37 | 13 | 12 | 8 |
| −10.1 to −20.0 | 18 | 29 | 24 | 12 | 23 |
| −20.1 and over | 39 | 10 | 31 | 33 | 57 |
| | *Bull Market Dates* | | | | |
| Trough Month | 6/49 | 9/53 | 12/57 | 10/60 | 6/62 |
| Peak Month | 1/53 | 7/56 | 7/59 | 12/61 | 1/66 |
| % Change S & P 500 | +87 | +110 | +48 | +34 | +68 |
| % Change S & P 425 | +93 | +125 | +48 | +33 | +70 |
| No. of groups with price changes of: | | | | | |
| +100.1% and over | 21 | 29 | 11 | 4 | 24 |
| + 50.1 to +100.0% | 26 | 20 | 38 | 21 | 29 |
| + 25.1 to + 50.0 | 20 | 21 | 29 | 32 | 19 |
| 0 to + 25.0 | 14 | 12 | 8 | 27 | 12 |
| − .1 to − 10.0 | 2 | 1 | 1 | 4 | 0 |
| − 10.1 to − 20.0 | 0 | 1 | 0 | 0 | 1 |
| − 20.0 and over | 0 | 0 | 0 | 0 | 2 |

NOTES: (1) The industry groups covered in the analysis are as classified by Standard & Poor's. Excluded are various "composites"—for example, Food Composite, Machinery Composite—and also various redundant groupings—for example, Autos, ex. G.M. The number of groups has changed over the years. (2) The peak and trough dates are based on monthly average prices of the S & P 425 and 500 stock price indexes. Daily highs and lows may not have taken place in precisely those months. For example, the 1966 daily high occurred in February, although the high month was January.

warning signals probably will not be much different from the warning signals prior to moderate downturns. In other words, it can be argued that it pays to sell (or at least to stop buying) even in anticipation of a moderate downturn, as insurance against the possibility that the downturn will be very sharp.

Even when price-value divergences are short-lived and mild, the position that only "in-and-out traders" should attempt to forecast these swings and act accordingly is unconvincing. Merely consider the impact of an extra 1% per annum rate of return on the results of a lifetime investment program. If a man of 35 invests $1,000 a year in a cross section of common stocks which produce an annual rate of return of, say, 8% in dividends plus capital appreciation, he will have a portfolio worth $122,000 when he retires at age 65. If, through more appropriate timing of his investments, he can raise his annual rate of return from 8% to 9%, he will retire with a portfolio worth $148,000, a 20% advantage.

Moreover, it may well be that the impact on investment yield of improved timing will be greater in the years ahead than has been the case during much of the post–World War II period. If the analysis of the value of the broad stock price averages which was presented in Chapter 5 is correct, a great, sweeping stock price uptrend, such as occurred in the 1950's, probably should not be expected to recur once the market has recovered from its 1966 setback. The past growth stemmed from two factors. First, there was a growth in corporate earnings and dividends. This can be expected to continue. But second, and far more important, a great upturn took place in the price investors were willing to pay for a dollar of earnings. Ten to fifteen times earnings used to be considered normal. Now, 15 to 20 times earnings is a more accepted norm. But the chances of price-earnings ratios increasing another 50% seem slim. If it is true that the overall rate of return on buying and holding common stocks in the years ahead will be closer to 8%–9% than to the 12%–15% earned in much of the postwar period, then a more substantial proportion can be added to one's overall rate of return in the future by accurately anticipating turning points.

Finally, a psychological observation is in order. Focusing on long-term value is supposed to enable the investor to weather the cyclical storms of the capital markets—to enable him to avoid being overwhelmed emotionally by cyclical swings. Unfortunately, human beings are not as strong-willed as they should be for their own good. Even institutional investors, who are professionally trained and in an eminent position to take a long-term view of things, have a tendency to get carried away by the market's gyrations. It is only too common for members of bank and insurance company investment committees to change their minds about "values" because of the incessant pronouncements of the ticker-tape. Would they not have a better frame of reference if they understood the causes of divergences from value, as well as the causes of value itself?

In the first two chapters of the three which follow, two approaches to the problem of forecasting turning points of security prices are examined. One approach relates security prices to general business cycle developments; another focuses attention exclusively on internal developments within the stock market itself. The final chapter of Part III deals with so-called "formula plans," which represent an effort to improve investment timing while keeping the need for forecasting to a minimum.

# 13

# BUSINESS CYCLE ANALYSIS

Better is one fore thought than two after.

—ERASMUS

THIS chapter is divided into two sections. The first section surveys the impact on stock prices and interest rates of the broad movements of economic activity which are referred to as the business cycle. It demonstrates that certain relationships between the capital markets and overall business activity have been sufficiently stable in the past to expect them to recur frequently. From this demonstration it will be clear that an ability to foresee business cycle turning points a few months in advance can be extremely helpful to the investor.

The second section of the chapter follows logically from the first. If economic forecasting can be helpful to the investor, how should the investor go about making or using such forecasts? Obviously, in a single section of a single chapter we cannot present all there is to know about the subject of economic forecasting. But we can encourage familiarity with some of the most useful tools of the forecaster.

## CAPITAL MARKET IMPACTS OF BUSINESS CYCLES

### Impact on Stock Prices

Figure 13–1 compares Standard and Poor's Industrial Stock Price Index with the Federal Reserve Board Index of Industrial Production. Examination of the chart reveals that:

1. Both series have been in uptrends during the postwar years, with stock prices rising more steeply than production.

2. From 1947 through 1965, there were five extended reversals in the stock price uptrend. In 1948–49, prices declined 18%; in 1953, they declined 12%; in 1956–57, 17%; in 1959–60, 11%; and in 1962, 23%. (All percentages are based on *monthly average* prices at the beginning and end of the reversal periods. See Table 13–1 for the monthly dates used.)

**FIGURE 13–1**

**Stock Prices and Industrial Production**

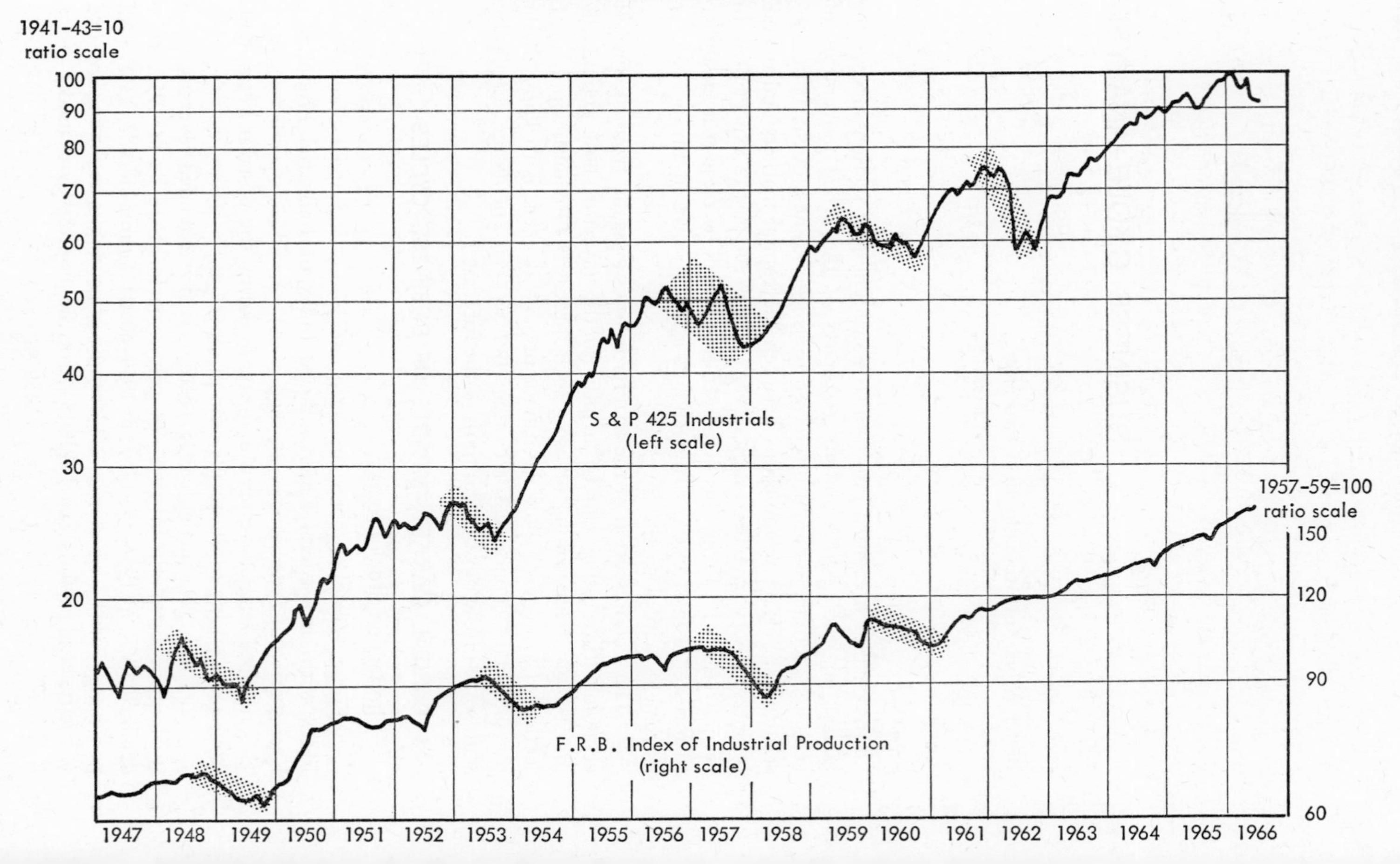

3. Four of these five stock price reversals began several months prior to extended periods of decline in industrial production, and ended shortly before the start of renewed advances in production. The 1962 stock price decline did not precede an actual slump in industrial production, but rather a seven-month period of no growth. The end of the stock price decline occurred a few months prior to a strong resumption of growth.

This evidence suggests strongly that an ability to foresee business cycle turning points several months in advance should improve one's ability to foresee major turning points in the general level of stock prices. The evidence does not imply that a bear market cannot take place unless an economic recession is in the offing, or that a bear market necessarily foreshadows a recession. What the evidence does indicate, however, is that if a recession appears to lie ahead, the investor should consider the odds to be high that it will be preceded by a significant stock market downturn.

It is essential to stress the fact that stock price peaks and troughs typically have *preceded* turning points of general business activity. Untutored investors invariably are surprised when, in the midst of rather dreary business news, stock prices rise, and in the midst of prosperity, stock prices fall. But such is the nature of the stock market.

Several hypotheses have been offered to explain the stock market's apparent forecasting ability. One is that investors in aggregate have good foresight, and that they act on the basis of what they think is *going to happen* to business activity rather than on the basis of what they currently see happening. Another argument is that investors act on the basis of current rather than anticipated future developments, but that the chief current indicators they watch—corporate profits and profit margins—tend to turn in advance of general business activity. Therefore, profit-oriented investors coincidentally bid stock prices up and drive them down in advance of general business activity. Yet a third theory is that stock price reversals help *cause* subsequent economic reversals by affecting consumer and business confidence and spending decisions. Finally, various monetary explanations for the stock price lead have been offered, as will be noted in our subsequent discussion of stock-bond yield spreads and of the rate of change in the money supply. Perhaps the truth lies closest to a combination of all these hypotheses.

Since an ability to foresee business cycle turning points normally would improve one's ability to foresee major turning points in the stock market as a whole, would it also improve one's ability to select the particular stocks to be most affected by the change in overall trend? The answer to this question is "sometimes yes, sometimes no." The relative price changes of individual stocks over short periods of time reflect many factors. These factors include relative changes in company sales, earnings, and dividends, but they also include the degree to which different stocks had been overpriced or underpriced prior to the turning point of the general market. To the extent that accurate economic forecasts improve the investor's ability to forecast relative changes in the sales, earnings, and dividends of different corporations, his ability to forecast relative price changes among different stocks is improved. For example, companies in heavy goods industries typically fare worse in recessions than companies in consumer goods industries. Corresponding to these economic relationships, the stocks of heavy goods producers traditionally have been more vulnerable to bear markets than the stocks of consumer-oriented companies. This pattern is illustrated in Table 13–1, which shows the percentage

**TABLE 13–1**
**Performance of Six Industry Group Price Indexes during Major Stock Market Downturns***

| | *June '48– June '49* | *Jan. '53– Sept. '53* | *July '56– Dec. '57* | *July '59– Oct. '60* | *Dec. '61– June '62* |
|---|---|---|---|---|---|
| Vulnerable Industries | | | | | |
| Automobiles | −19% | −20% | −27% | −23% | −17% |
| Machinery | −23 | −11 | −25 | −27 | −24 |
| Steel | −27 | −16 | −18 | −29 | −34 |
| Average | −23 | −16 | −23 | −26 | −25 |
| "Defensive" Industries | | | | | |
| Electric power | − 5% | − 2% | 0% | + 9% | −18% |
| Food | −10 | − 1 | − 6 | +19 | −26 |
| Retail | −10 | − 4 | −16 | − 3 | −26 |
| Average | − 8 | − 2 | − 7 | + 8 | −23 |
| S & P Industrials | −18 | −12 | −17 | −11 | −23 |

* Downturns are measured by monthly average highs and lows of the Standard & Poor's composite stock price indexes.

declines (based on monthly average S & P data) of a half-dozen selected industry price indexes during the same months in which the composite industrial stock price index had major downturns. The average decline of the traditionally vulnerable groups was 23%, while the average decline of the traditionally "defensive" groups was 6%.

However, it will be noted that in 1962 two of the defensive groups—food and retail—suffered worse declines than two of the vulnerable groups—automobile and machinery. This probably reflects the fact that during the preceding market upswing, food and retailing stocks had been bid up to extremely high levels and thus became as vulnerable in price as the stocks of heavy goods producers. Thus, it should be emphasized again that *value* analysis must never be ignored by intelligent investors, regardless of what other tools of analysis they choose to employ.

### Impact on the Level of Bond Yields

Figure 13–2 compares the movements since 1952 of yields on long-term U.S. government bonds and Moody's Aaa corporate bonds with the

**FIGURE 13–2**

**Bond Yields and Industrial Production**

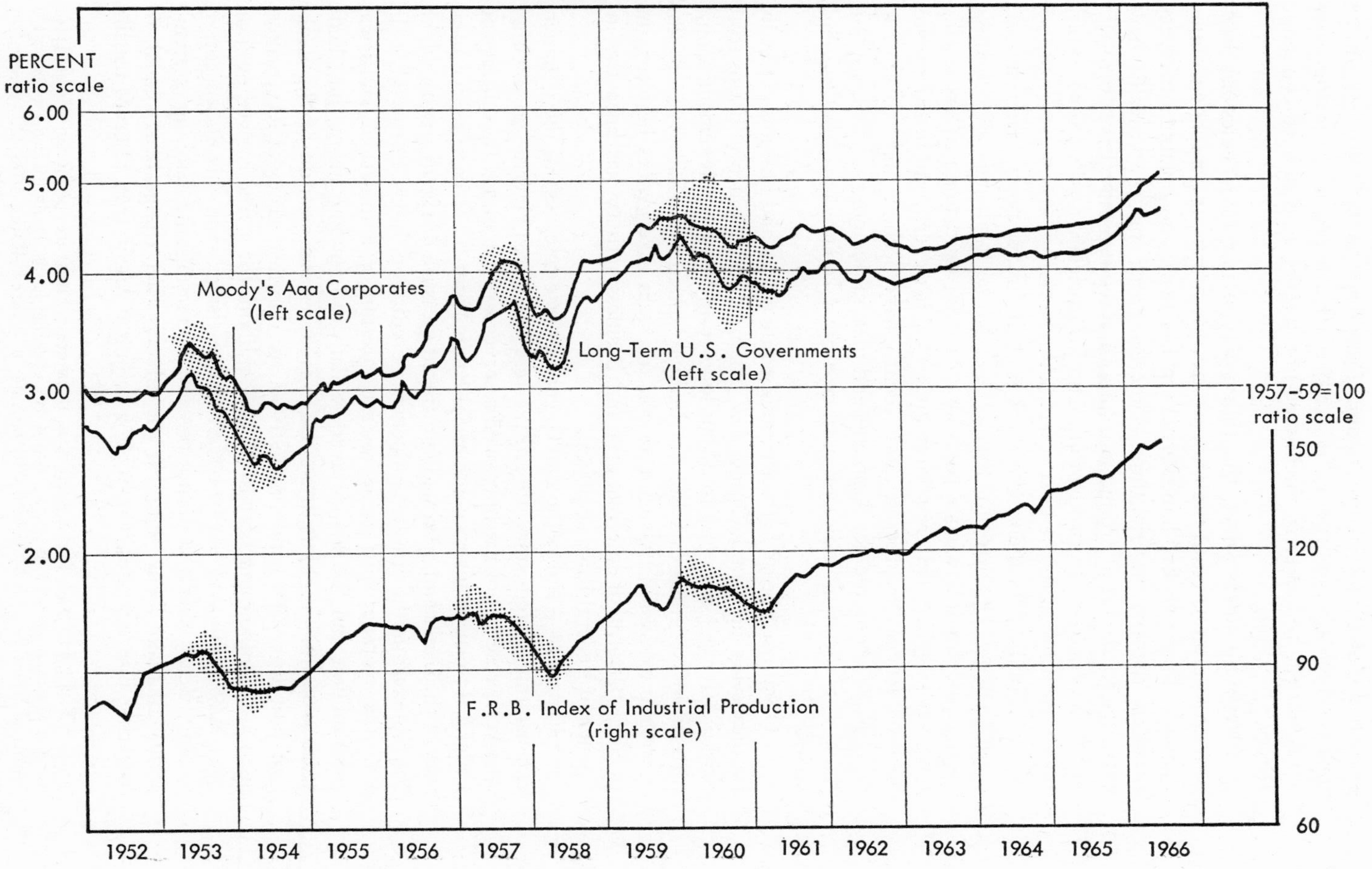

FRB Index of Industrial Production. Data prior to 1952 are not shown because the bond market was "pegged" by the monetary authorities until spring, 1951, and interest rates were not freely responsive to economic forces.

As with stock prices, the timing of interest rate cycles has been rather closely related to the upturns and downturns of general economic activity. Traditionally, however, there has been one notable difference between the two relationships. Whereas stock prices typically have turned well ahead of production, interest rates typically have turned at about the same time as production. Thus, historically the best time to buy bonds has been when the peak of economic activity has been reached, not before. Bond prices then have been at their lowest point (interest rates were highest). The best time to sell bonds has been when a new economic advance begins following a recession. At such time, bond prices usually have been highest (interest rates lowest). However, some bond market analysts believe that interest rates recently have become more sensitive to *anticipated* economic developments and may in due course become classifiable as a "leading indicator" rather than a "coincident" or "lagging" series.[1]

Of course, the tie between interest rate cycles and business cycles by no means has been undeviating. For example, industrial production rose briskly after the spring of 1961, but long-term bond yields remained on a plateau for several years before finally responding in late 1965 to the economic expansion. A major reason for such divergences between the cyclical patterns of interest rates and business activity has been the influence of Federal Reserve policy.

Figure 13–3 shows the movement of "free reserves" of the commercial banking system since 1952. Free reserves, often referred to as either net excess reserves or net borrowed reserves, are calculated by subtracting Federal Reserve loans to commercial banks from the excess reserve position of the banks and are a widely utilized measure of the degree to which the monetary authorities are influencing credit conditions. For example, in 1959 the average daily excess reserve position of commercial banks was $482 million and the banks' average daily borrowings from the "Fed" were $906 million. Thus, the average free reserve position of the banks that year was −$424 million. In 1960, by contrast, excess reserves averaged $756 million and borrowings $87 million, for a free reserve position of +$669 million. When free reserves are rising, as in this illustration, it usually means that the authorities are increasing the banking system's ability to make loans. This has the effect, other things being equal, of lowering interest rates. Likewise, a falling level of free reserves usually

---

[1] T. E. Holland has argued that if interest rates are properly adjusted for normal seasonal variations they would be classifiable as leading series even on a historical basis. See his "Cyclical Movements of Interest Rates, 1948–61," *Journal of Business*, October, 1964.

FIGURE 13–3

Free Reserves and Industrial Production

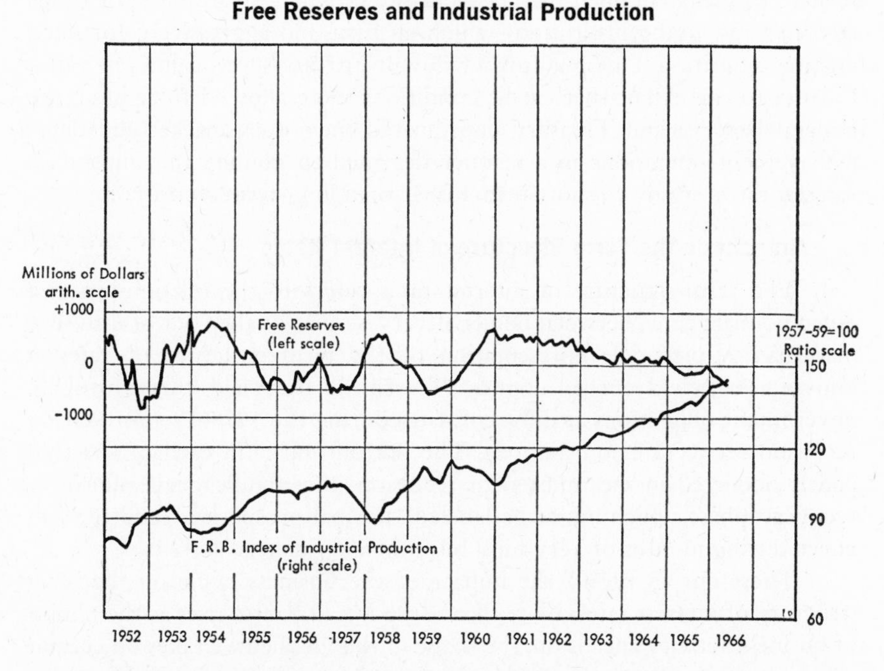


means that the authorities are retarding loan expansion, thus putting upward pressure on interest rates.[2]

Since one of the major goals of monetary policy is to help smooth out business cycles, the Fed typically has increased free reserves during recessions (thus stimulating debt-financed expenditures) and reduced them thereafter. When the movement of free reserves is compared with industrial production (Figure 13–3), it is clear that the response of monetary policy to economic recovery was much slower (i.e., free reserves were not as quickly and sharply reduced) following the 1960–61 recession than following the 1953–54 or 1957–58 recessions. This was because the level of unemployment stubbornly remained at a 5% or higher level for several years after 1961, with little of the inflationary pressure of the previous recoveries being present until 1965—when monetary policy shifted toward greater restrictiveness.

Thus, a relatively easy credit policy from 1961 through early 1965 kept bond yields from rising as they usually do during periods of expand-

---

[2] The novice must be careful not to give undue significance to a brief change in the direction of free reserve movement. Only when there is a *consistent* pattern in evidence is an inference warranted that Federal Reserve policy is changing. Moreover, the focus of attention should be on the magnitude of change in, rather than the absolute level of, free reserves. Finally, the rate of change in *total* reserves, in the money supply, and in bank loans and investments should be examined for confirmation of the implications of free reserve movements (see pp. 481–484 below).

ing business activity.[3] In addition, increases in rates paid on time deposits relative to yields on open-market securities caused a great inflow of funds to banks and saving institutions which, in turn, bid aggressively for fixed income securities. This put further downward pressure on interest rates. Finally, to the extent that credit conditions were allowed to tighten, the Federal Reserve and Treasury coordinated their open-market and debt-management operations in a manner designed to confine the impact on interest rates largely to short-term rather than long-term securities.[4]

### Impact on the Term Structure of Interest Rates

The term structure of interest rates refers to the relationship at a given point in time, between bonds of very similar quality but of different maturity. A pictorial representation of the term structure of rates is known as a "yield curve." Figure 13–4 shows the yield curves of U.S. government obligations at different dates during the 1958–59 and 1960–66 recession-recovery-boom periods. The bottom curve in each of the two panels occurred in the midst of a recession, the middle curve during a recovery phase which might be labeled "normal prosperity," and the top curve during months of very high business and financial activity.

These curves typify the impact of the business cycle on the term structure of interest rates. Note that as the *level* of rates rises as the tempo of business activity speeds up, the shape of the yield curve takes on certain characteristics. These characteristics can be outlined as follows:[5]

1. Up to maturities of about three years—the "short end" of the yield curve—longer term securities tend to have higher yields than shorter term securities whether the level of the yield curve is high or low. Although the short end of the yield curve typically is "upward sloping," this slope is more shallow when the level of rates is high than when it is low.

2. Beyond maturities of about 20–25 years, yield usually does not change significantly as maturity is extended. That is, the "long end" of the yield curve typically is rather "flat" regardless of level.

---

[3] Of course, one might not have expected bond yields to rise as sharply as in 1954–57 or 1958–59 even if monetary policy had been restrictive. In those earlier years, interest rates still were recovering from their artificially depressed levels of the "peg" period as well as responding to cyclical influences. But Figure 13–3 does indicate that when the rise in interest rates finally took place in 1965–66, it was quite pronounced. Many observers believe, however, that the increase would have been much more moderate if the administration had been more willing to increase taxes and/or reduce government spending instead of relying almost exclusively on monetary policy to check inflationary pressures.

[4] These actions will be discussed at greater length later.

[5] There are many theories purporting to explain the shape of the yield curve. For a summary and analysis of several theories see R. A. Kessel, *The Cyclical Behavior of the Term Structure of Interest Rates* (New York: National Bureau of Economic Research, 1965), and B. G. Malkiel, *The Term Structure of Interest Rates; Expectations and Behavior Patterns* (Princeton University Press, 1966). Also, F. M. Struble, "Current Debate on the Term Structure of Interest Rates," *Monthly Review* of the Federal Reserve Bank of Kansas City, January–February, 1966.

FIGURE 13–4

**Yield Curves of U.S. Government Securities in Successive Business Cycles**

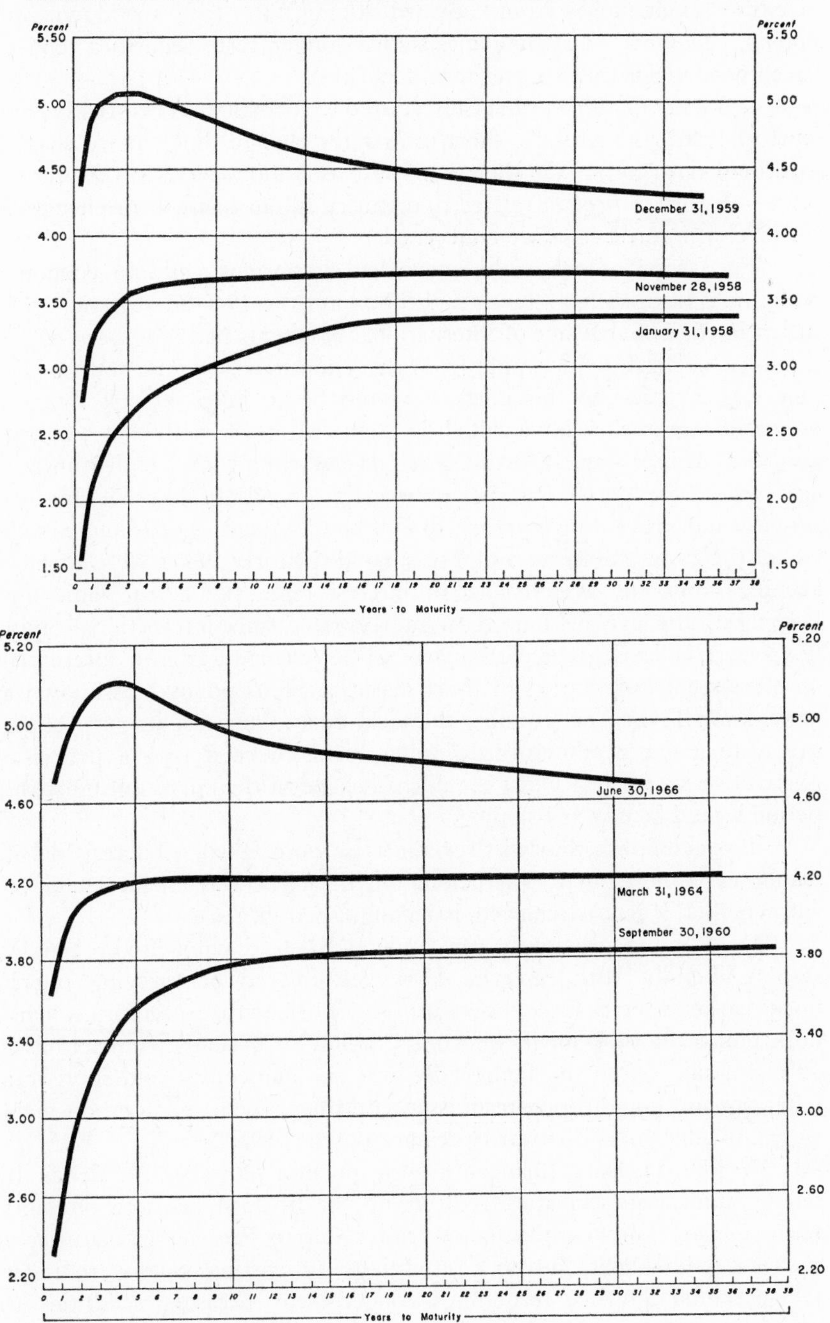


Source: *Treasury Bulletin.*

3. In between the boundaries of relatively short-term and relatively long-term securities, the yield curve gradually changes shape as the level of rates rises. It moves from "upward sloping," to "flat," to "downward sloping." Downward sloping means that longer term securities tend to have lower yields than shorter term securities.

4. Yield volatility is inversely related to maturity. When the general level of rates rises or falls, short-term rates change much more sharply than long-term rates. (On the other hand, as demonstrated in Chapter 11, *price* volatility is *directly* related to maturity so far as effects of changes in the level of interest rates are concerned.)

The shape of the yield curve had important national economic policy implications for a few years following the 1960–61 recession. The deficit in the U.S. balance of international payments had long been aggravated by an outflow of capital from this country to Europe and Canada. One way to dampen this outflow would be to keep interest rates on domestic securities relatively high in comparison with rates on securities abroad, thus reducing the profitability of exporting funds. Unfortunately, high rates here posed the risk of overly restricting domestic business activity and preventing a return to full employment. Accordingly, policies of the Federal Reserve and Treasury in the early 1960's were aimed at keeping down the overall level of interest rates, but at the same time keeping up the level of short-term interest rates, since international capital flows were believed to be particularly sensitive to interest rate differentials on investment instruments of short maturity. This policy was known as "Operation Twist," or "twisting the yield curve," because its purpose was to create a flat or downward-sloping yield curve during a period of relatively easy money, when the normal shape of the curve during such a period would be upward sloping.

To accomplish the twist several steps were taken. (There is debate among economists as to whether or not the twist was, in fact, achieved and whether, if it was achieved, it accomplished its goals.)

1. As noted previously, the Federal Reserve supplied the banking system liberally with reserves. However, instead of carrying out its open-market operations exclusively in the short-maturity sector, as it had done under the traditional "bills-only" policy, it executed transactions in all maturities. Often the Federal Reserve simultaneously sold short-term securities and bought long-term issues, putting upward pressure on yields of the former and downward pressure on the latter.

2. The Treasury financed a large portion of its sizable deficit by selling short-term securities, reinforcing the upward pressure on short-term yields. To prevent this policy from reducing the average maturity of the total federal debt, "advance refundings" of existing issues were undertaken. Under advance refundings, longer term Treasury securities are offered as exchanges for the short-maturity holdings of existing investors.

This is believed to cause less upward pressure on yields of long-maturity issues than regular new sales of such securities.

3. Downward pressure on long-term yields was reinforced by amending "Regulation Q" to permit commercial banks to increase rates paid on savings accounts and certificates of deposit. This stimulated an increase in such deposits, which the banks then used to bid aggressively for tax-exempt bonds and for real estate mortgages.[6]

4. The export of long-term capital was restrained by means other than raising the level of domestic long-term interest rates. An "Interest Equalization Tax" was enacted, which penalized lending by Americans to industrially developed foreign nations, and President Johnson appealed directly to American businessmen to curtail voluntarily their new investments abroad.

### Impact on Yield Spreads

The business cycle has a significant effect on the interrelationships of yields on securities of different types and quality as well as on securities of different maturity. Figure 13–5 illustrates the yield spreads since 1952 between (1) Aaa corporate bonds and long-term U.S. government bonds; (2) Baa corporates and Aaa corporates; and (3) conventional mortgages and Baa corporates. Business cycle movements are represented by the FRB Index of Industrial Production.

The chart indicates that there is a general tendency for yield spreads on different types of long-term fixed income investments to narrow during the major portion of prosperity periods and to widen as the prosperity reaches a peak and the economy turns down. As an economic advance progresses, investor confidence in the nation's ability to avoid a severe recession is bolstered. They are, therefore, increasingly reluctant to pay relatively high prices (low yields) for high-quality securities, and increasingly willing to raise their bid prices for lower quality issues relative to high-quality issues. Interest rates on both types of securities rise, but those of highest quality and lowest yield have the most rapid increases, and yield spreads therefore narrow. Conversely, as the boom ends and turns into recession, investor confidence tends to wane and high quality becomes more important to them. Fixed income securities of most quality grades are characterized by declining interest rates, but those of highest quality decline most rapidly in yield, and yield spreads widen.

Care must be taken, however, not to make an interpretation of changing yield spreads too demand oriented. While shifts in investor confidence have a powerful effect on yield spreads, changes in supply conditions also are important and may work in an opposite direction. For

---

[6] Many people doubt, however, that the Federal Reserve actually foresaw this effect when it amended Regulation Q.

FIGURE 13–5

Yield Spreads on Fixed Income Investments

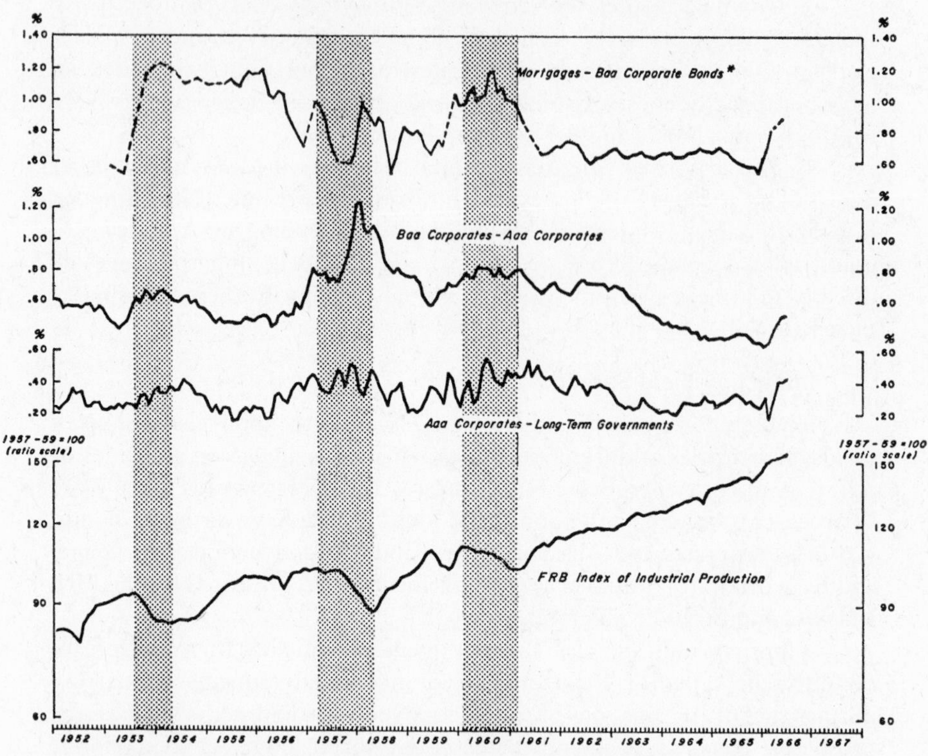


Note: Dashed lines represent periods for which no monthly data are available.
Sources: Federal Reserve Board; Moody's; Prudential Insurance Co.

example, a major reason for a widening rather than a continued narrowing of yield spreads between corporate bonds and government bonds as a boom period nears a peak is the very heavy volume of corporate bond flotations which usually occurs at such times to finance plant and equipment expenditures. This heavy corporate financing usually occurs when Treasury financing diminishes due to favorable budgetary conditions, so corporate bond yields tend to rise faster than governments and the yield spread widens.

Perhaps the most dramatic illustration of a supply-caused shift of yield spreads is the experience of the 1930's, when the spread between yields on government bonds and yields on corporate bonds narrowed instead of widened. That is, corporate bond yields fell more sharply than government bond yields despite the fact that investors' desires for safety would normally have led them to bid more strenuously for governments than for corporates. An important reason for this departure from expected patterns was the fact that the supply of new government bonds was expanding rapidly to finance the federal deficit, while new corporate offerings all but dried up. Thus, corporates acquired a "scarcity value" not possessed by governments. Indeed, one might argue that the yield data on corporates are really quite artificial for that period. (Another influence was a gradual change in the tax status of governments, from partially tax-exempt toward fully taxable. This reduced their relative attractiveness to investors.)

Yield spreads between corporate bonds and residential mortgages also are affected greatly by changes in supply conditions in addition to changes in demand conditions. During postwar recessions, for example, consumer demand for new housing usually has been stronger than corporate demand for new plant and equipment. Therefore, mortgage financing is relatively stronger than corporate bond financing, and mortgage yields tend to hold firmer than bond yields. Both decline, but the latter decline further, and spreads widen.

A cyclical yield spread pattern is observable not only in comparisons of yields on different types of fixed income investments, but also shows up very strongly in comparisons of common stock dividend yields with bond yields. As has been shown, stock prices usually rise during most of the prosperity phase of the business cycle. At the same time, dividend payments usually rise also, but at a slower rate. Consequently, dividend yields on stocks fall rather steadily during prosperity. Accompanying the declining trend of dividend yields, typically, is a rising trend of bond yields.

The changing spread between stock and bond yields as the economic advance progresses—stock yields falling and bond yields rising—gradually begins to draw income-minded investors away from stocks and into bonds. In addition, capital-gains-minded investors begin selling stocks as corporate profit margins narrow and economic recession begins to threaten. The proceeds of these sales either are put into the bank or into fixed income securities. The shifting of funds out of the stock market weakens stock prices prior to the peak of business activity, but dividends are still high or rising. Therefore, stock yields begin to reverse their downward movement prior to the business peak.

Eventually the economy reaches a peak and turns down. Interest rates likewise move down. Dividends reach a plateau or decline, but stock prices decline faster, and stock yields therefore rise. The yield spread thus becomes gradually less favorable to bond investment. Income seekers begin switching back into stocks, and bargain hunters do likewise in anticipation of eventual recovery. The expansion process begins anew shortly thereafter.

In the foregoing discussion of stock-bond yield spreads, no mention was made of the magnitude of the spread as it changes during the business cycle. This omission stems from the fact that any compilation of historical data on the spread is greatly affected by: (1) the time period chosen for analysis, and (2) the bond yield series chosen for comparison with stock yields.

For well over 20 years, from 1930 through the mid-1950's, bond yields were below, and common stock dividend yields were above, any level which might be considered normal. Realistically, therefore, the only recent years relevant to our present discussion of stock-bond yield spreads are those since about 1955. (The period of the 1920's also is relevant, but many readers probably would put little store in the relationships of 40 years ago.)

The choice of a bond yield series likewise is crucial. One could logically use U.S. government bond yields, high-grade corporate bond yields, or medium-quality corporate bond yields. At the extremes, these series are as much as 2% apart. Depending on which one is used, the spread between stock and bond yields can be positive or negative, wide or narrow.[7]

With these qualifications noted, attention may be directed to Figure 13–6, which relates yields on long-term U.S. government bonds to dividend yields on the Standard & Poor's Industrial Stock Price Index. The data are quarterly averages and cover the period since 1955. The bottom line of the chart shows the stock-bond yield spread, thus defined. Two aspects of the chart are of particular interest:

1. Stock yields averaged 1% higher than government bond yields in 1955, but the yield spread became negative in 1958 and has remained negative since then. This negative spread sometimes has been referred to as the "reverse yield gap," with the implication that it is an abnormal situation. But a negative spread should be considered quite normal in the present economic environment.

Those who look upon a negative stock-bond yield spread as being abnormal argue that common stock investment is riskier than bond investment and that the greater risk should be compensated for by a higher yield expectation—particularly if the bonds under consideration are of highest quality. This argument is perfectly valid. Indeed, it is a major premise underlying the approach to common stock evaluation presented in Chapter 5. But a meaningful comparison of stock and bond yields must take account of the fact that the yield available on stocks includes more than the current dividend yield. Over a period of many years, dividends are likely to grow and to be augmented by price appreciation. And if a growth rate of several percent per annum is added to the current dividend yield, the expected *overall yield* on stocks becomes significantly higher than bond yields. It would appear that "the market" in recent years has built a growth factor into its stock yield expectation, and that it will continue to do so, with justification. Accordingly, cyclical variations in

---

[7] A good article on the subject is Nicholas Molodovsky, "The Many Aspects of Yields," *Financial Analysts Journal*, March-April, 1962.

FIGURE 13–6

Stock Yields versus Bond Yields

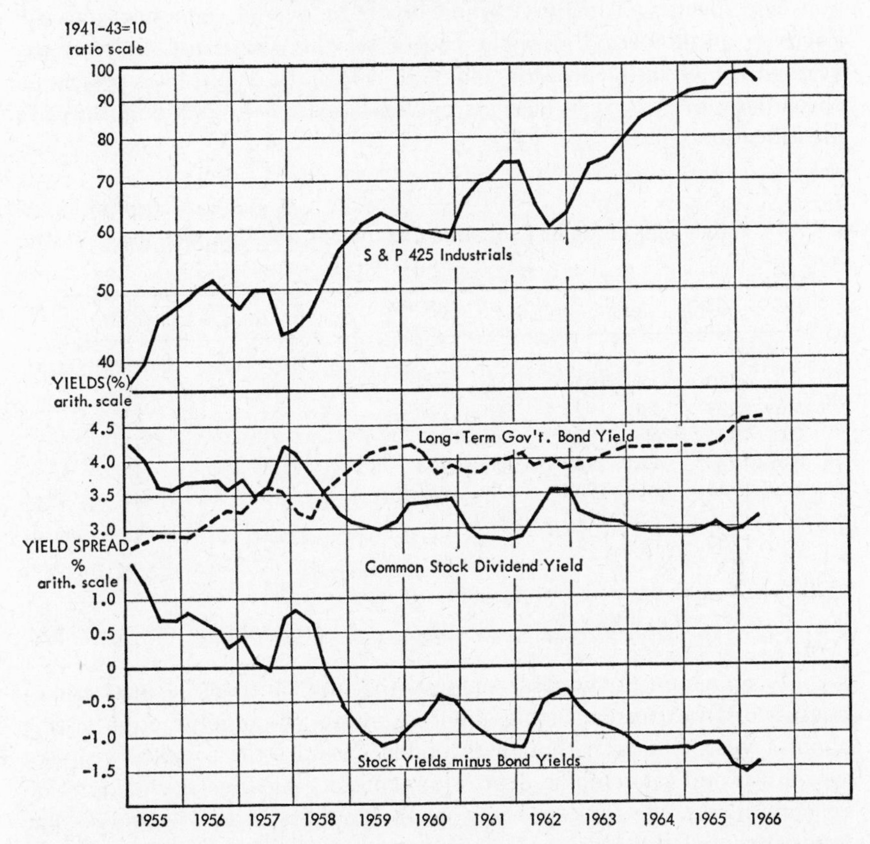


the spread between bond yields and *dividend* yields should be expected to continue to occur within a negative plane.

2. The second very interesting aspect of Figure 13–6 is that when the negative yield spread substantially exceeded 1% in 1959 and 1961, stock prices dropped shortly thereafter. A bear market did not occur in 1964 or 1965, when the negative spread again reached, and even exceeded, the 1959 and 1961 extremes. But it did occur in 1966. While there is no theoretical reason for any particular spread to be an outer limit, investors probably would do well to regard stock prices as being increasingly vulnerable when the negative spread reaches the 1¼% level during the course of a business cycle upswing.

## BUSINESS CYCLE FORECASTING

### A Business Cycle Chronology

During the past several decades, the National Bureau of Economic Research, a private nonprofit organization, has sponsored the research efforts of America's leading students of the business cycle. Among the products of their efforts are techniques for measuring economic fluctuations and identifying major turning points of overall economic activity. Focusing on the period since the end of World War I, and omitting the years of the Great Depression and World War II, Table 13–2 presents a chronology of American business cycles, based on the National Bureau's identification system.

**TABLE 13–2**
**A Calendar of Major Economic Expansions and Contractions, 1920–29, 1946–66**

| *Dates of Turning Points* | | | *Duration, in Months, of:* | |
|---|---|---|---|---|
| *Peak* | *Trough* | *Peak* | *Contractions* | *Expansions* |
| Jan., 1920 | July, 1921 | May, 1923 | 18 | 22 |
| May, 1923 | July, 1924 | Oct., 1926 | 14 | 27 |
| Oct., 1926 | Nov., 1927 | Aug., 1929 | 13 | 21 |
| Nov., 1948 | Oct., 1949 | July, 1953 | 11 | 45 |
| July, 1953 | Aug., 1954 | July, 1957 | 13 | 35 |
| July, 1957 | Apr., 1958 | May, 1960 | 9 | 25 |
| May, 1960 | Feb., 1961 | * | 9 | * |
| | | | Average: 12 | 29 |

* No peak as of end of 1966.
Source: Bureau of the Census, *Business Cycle Developments*, Appendix Table A.

Examination of the table suggests that the "average business cycle" consists of an expansion lasting about 2½ years and a contraction lasting about a year. But even though the table excludes the atypical years of world war and catastrophic depression, considerable diversity of duration remains. The range for expansions up to 1960 was 21 to 45 months. The latter included the Korean War effects, but the range still would be considerable—21 to 35 months—if it were excluded. The range for contractions was 9 to 18 months.

These findings clearly suggest that the timing of American business cycles has not been consistent enough to warrant calendar-oriented judgments as to the probability of a peak or trough occurring at any given time. For example, in the fall of 1962 the expansion phase of the most recent business cycle was more than 1½ years old, industrial production had been leveling out for several months, and the stock market had been declining since the spring. On the basis of historical precedent, a general economic downturn should have been approaching. But the economy shortly surged upward, advancing steadily for several years thereafter, and breaking the all-time duration record for an American peacetime prosperity.[8]

[8] In view of the Viet Nam conflict, one might quarrel with the appellation "peacetime" prosperity, but this would not negate the point that calendar-oriented forecasting is unwise.

The extreme length of the latest business expansion, and also the gradual shortening of the duration of contractions which can be observed in Table 13–2, have tempted some people to believe that recessions are now only of historical interest—that the worst which is to be expected is a slowdown in the rate of growth. To hold such an opinion, however, one must believe either that (*a*) no important imbalances can occur between production and consumption or between saving and investment, or that (*b*) when such imbalances begin to develop, the government will recognize them quickly and act promptly to offset them. Neither of these beliefs can be held with much confidence, however.

It is true that many things have happened in our modern economic system to foster stability. For example, businessmen try to maintain closer control of their inventories and plan their capital expenditures further in advance than previously. Also, the government's knowledge of economic processes has improved, and stabilizing measures are more likely to be implemented. But to assume that these and similar developments have made recessions extinct seems quite naïve. While recessions cannot be forecast by reference to the calendar, they are likely to recur, and efforts to foresee them are very worthwhile.

### Leading Economic Indicators

It is a common observation that no two business cycles are exactly alike. Indeed, most modern business economists have become increasingly impressed with the almost endless variety of the cyclical fluctuations they are trying to forecast. Nevertheless, the unique aspects of each individual cycle usually fit into a common framework which has been referred to as "the cumulative process" or "the self-generating cycle." The essential characteristics of this framework can be described briefly.

If we break into a cycle as revival is beginning, we find business sales and inventories at a depressed level and considerable excess plant capacity. As sales begin to rise and profit expectations improve, businessmen start planning for production increases. They expand working hours, and gradually rehire previously laid-off workers. This increases employee incomes and stimulates personal consumption expenditures. With sales and profits rising, the managers begin to expand and modernize production facilities. These purchases from the capital goods industries create still more jobs and incomes and more consumption by workers in those industries. And so the expansion *cumulates*.

Men, machines, and materials eventually are being utilized at capacity, and demand exerts upward pressure on prices and wages. Businessmen go increasingly into debt to finance expanding inventories, receivables, and fixed assets. Interest rates rise. Soon costs are rising faster than prices, and profit margins deteriorate. This coincides with the gradual realization that productive capacity has outstripped potential sales. Businessmen become uneasy and pull in their reins. They reduce their orders for heavy equipment, cut back on the rate of inventory accumulation, repay loans, lay off marginal personnel, and even sell some of their personal common stock holdings. Caution spreads as incomes are reduced. Consumers postpone purchases of durable goods, businessmen slash inventories sharply, and the cumulative process is at work in a downward direction.

As the downturn continues, credit terms ease and interest rates fall. The monetary authorities usually reinforce the ease. Housing construction often picks up as reduced mortgage rates, lowered downpayments, and extended maturities bring monthly carrying charges to a level which buyers are willing to undertake despite the recessionary atmosphere. Government spending acts as a strong prop to the economy. The stock market, after a sizable shake-out, stabilizes and begins to move up. Soon consumers realize that the worst is over and begin to unloosen their purse strings. A new revival is in the making.

It should be clear from this brief "physiology of a business cycle" that fluctuations of the whole of economic activity reflect fluctuations of the economy's many parts. These parts, moreover, do not move in unison but rather in sequence. One part changes direction and pushes another part, which pushes still another. It is logical, therefore, that if we wish to predict turning points of the whole economy, we should try to isolate and study those parts which usually turn *before* the whole.

*Characteristics of Leading Indicators.* The search for "leading indicators" of general economic activity has been one of the major projects of the National Bureau of Economic Research. Its work in this direction has been given great impetus by the economic policymaking requirements of the federal government. The most recent impetus came during the years 1956–60, when large-scale application of electronic computing equipment to National Bureau methods was begun at the request of the President's Council of Economic Advisers.[9]

Building on the pioneering research of the NBER's founder, Wesley C. Mitchell, his co-worker Arthur F. Burns, and a group of distinguished scholars such as Geoffrey H. Moore, the Bureau of the Census has made available to the public a monthly summary of key economic statistics, among which are a large number of leading indicators. The data are presented in seasonally adjusted form[10] and are conveniently charted in the monthly publication, *Business Cycle Developments.*[11]

---

[9] J. Shiskin, *Signals of Recession and Recovery* (New York: National Bureau of Economic Research, 1961).

[10] Most economic data are greatly influenced by seasonal factors—summer vacations, holidays, etc. For purposes of cyclical analysis, it is necessary to eliminate these seasonal influences—i.e., to estimate what the numbers would have been in the absence of the seasonal impact. Highly sophisticated mathematical adjustments are performed in a matter of minutes on modern electronic computers, thus achieving a degree of accuracy unattainable until very recently.

[11] As an aid in the use of the material in this publication, see J. Shiskin, *The Current Expansion in Historical Perspective* (BCD Technical Paper No. 6, Bureau of

FIGURE 13–7

**Selected Leading Economic Indicators**

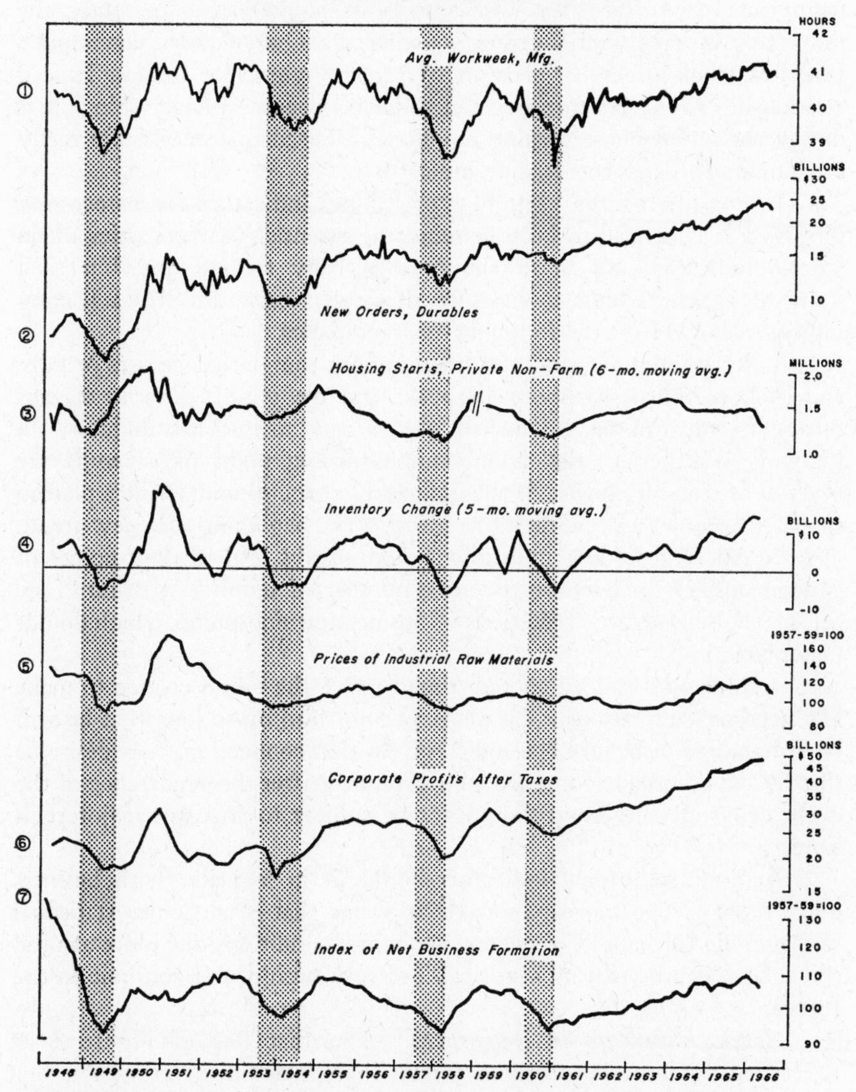


NOTE: All data seasonally adjusted, except ⑤. Scales ②, ③, ⑤, ⑥, ⑦, logarithmic; ①, ④, arithmetic. Shaded areas are periods of recession, using National Bureau dates.

Source: Bureau of the Census, *Business Cycle Developments.*

Figure 13–7 shows the movement of seven widely studied leading indicators. Many others are contained in *Business Cycle Developments*,[12]

---

the Census, 1965). Also, by the same author, *Business Cycle Indicators: The Known and The Unknown* (Bureau of the Census, 1963).

[12] There are currently 30 leading indicators charted in *Business Cycle Developments*. Chapter 3 contains reproductions of some of these. See Figure 3–15.

and each economist has his own group of favorites. No experienced economist relies on only one or two indicators, however, because individual series very often give false signals. It is preferable to study the movement of a substantial group of indicators. One of every economist's favorites, stock prices, has been omitted from Figure 13–7 because its lead relationship to the business cycle already has been examined. (Since it is one of the series whose turning points it is desired to forecast, we really are looking for leads to a leading indicator.)

In considering the usefulness of leading indicators for forecasting purposes, it is helpful to keep in mind the essential characteristics of an "ideal" indicator—not in the hope of actually finding one, but as a standard against which to measure those that exist. Ideally, a leading indicator should have the following characteristics.

1. It should move smoothly from month to month as it rises or falls, and it should turn sharply at its peaks and troughs. If a series zigzags during its upward or downward swings, the analyst has difficulty in knowing whether a "zig" is a genuine turning point or a *temporary* reversal of trend. Likewise, if the indicator's turning points have a plateau shape, it becomes more difficult to identify the beginning of a new trend.

2. An ideal leading indicator should always lead turning points of general business activity by the same number of months, with no "false leads." (False leads are predictions of business turning points which do not materialize.)

3. It should lead by enough time to give the user a chance to make any necessary alterations in his plans, but not lead by so long that he will be tempted to disbelieve the indicator. In this connection, it is desirable that the data should become available promptly after the occurrence of the event being measured and should not be subject to frequent major revisions.

4. An ideal leading indicator should fit in logically with business cycle theory. The more reasonable it seems that a particular statistical series *should* turn ahead of general economic conditions, the more assured the analyst can be that its historical lead relationship will continue in the future.

*Seven Indicators in Retrospect.* The first line of Figure 13–7 reflects manufacturers' decisions to run their factories overtime (or undertime). Consistently during the postwar period, the turning points of this series have preceded general economic turning points. But it will be noted that the lead times have been far from uniform, and the month-to-month movements have been quite jagged.

The second line reflects what has been one of the most useful of all business barometers. It represents new orders placed on the books of manufacturers of durable goods, probably the most volatile sector of the whole economy. The lead time of the new orders series has been about 6 to 12 months at the peaks, with the notable exception of 1951. At that time, the Korean War buildup caused orders to rise sharply to a level which could not be sustained, even though prosperity continued for more than two years longer. At the troughs, new orders for durables usually have turned up a few months before the end of recessions. This series, moreover, generally has moved smoothly enough to make turning points rather quickly identifiable. Data revisions, however, sometimes have caused problems of interpretation.

Residential construction accounts directly for about 4% of the nation's total output of goods and services, and its importance to the economy is even greater than indicated by that figure. When houses are built, ancillary demands arise for furniture, appliances, repairmen's services, highways, utilities, etc. Housing starts, the third line of the chart, represent construction work *begun,* thus preceding the ultimate expenditures. Historically, housing starts have turned down quite early during the prosperity phase of the business cycle and have risen well before the end of recessions. (Indeed, some observers have argued that the housing starts series should be inverted and classified as a *lagging* indicator.)

In presenting the theory of the "cumulative process," the key role of inventory accumulation and liquidation (line 4 on the chart) was stressed. Unfortunately for forecasters, reliable data on inventory change do not become available until several months after the event. Furthermore, the extreme volatility of the data makes interpretation difficult.

Demands for basic raw materials are highly sensitive to underlying changes in the economic environment. Therefore, prices of such goods (line 5 on the chart) long have been regarded as an indicator of things to come. Unfortunately, many commodities—for example, copper, lead, zinc, and aluminum—often have been in excessive supply for years on end. When this occurs, prices are less responsive to changes in user demand and thus are less reliable as a leading indicator than when supply is more closely in gear with demand.

Corporate profits (line 6), like inventories, played a crucial role in the description of the "typical" business cycle. Profit data are extremely useful for forecasting purposes. Rising profits produce business optimism; falling profits produce gloom. As with inventories, however, there are long delays in profit reporting and frequent revisions. Furthermore, the lead time has been quite variable from cycle to cycle.

The seventh line, index of net business formation, (representing business starts minus failures), has performed fairly well as an economic barometer during most of the postwar period. In addition to the empirical justification for using this series as a lead indicator, its use is *logically* defensible. The behavior of business starts and failures can be made an integral part of almost any reasonable business cycle theory.

In judging the various leading indicators against the ideal standards

**FIGURE 13–8**

**Stock Prices and Diffusion of Leading Economic Indicators**

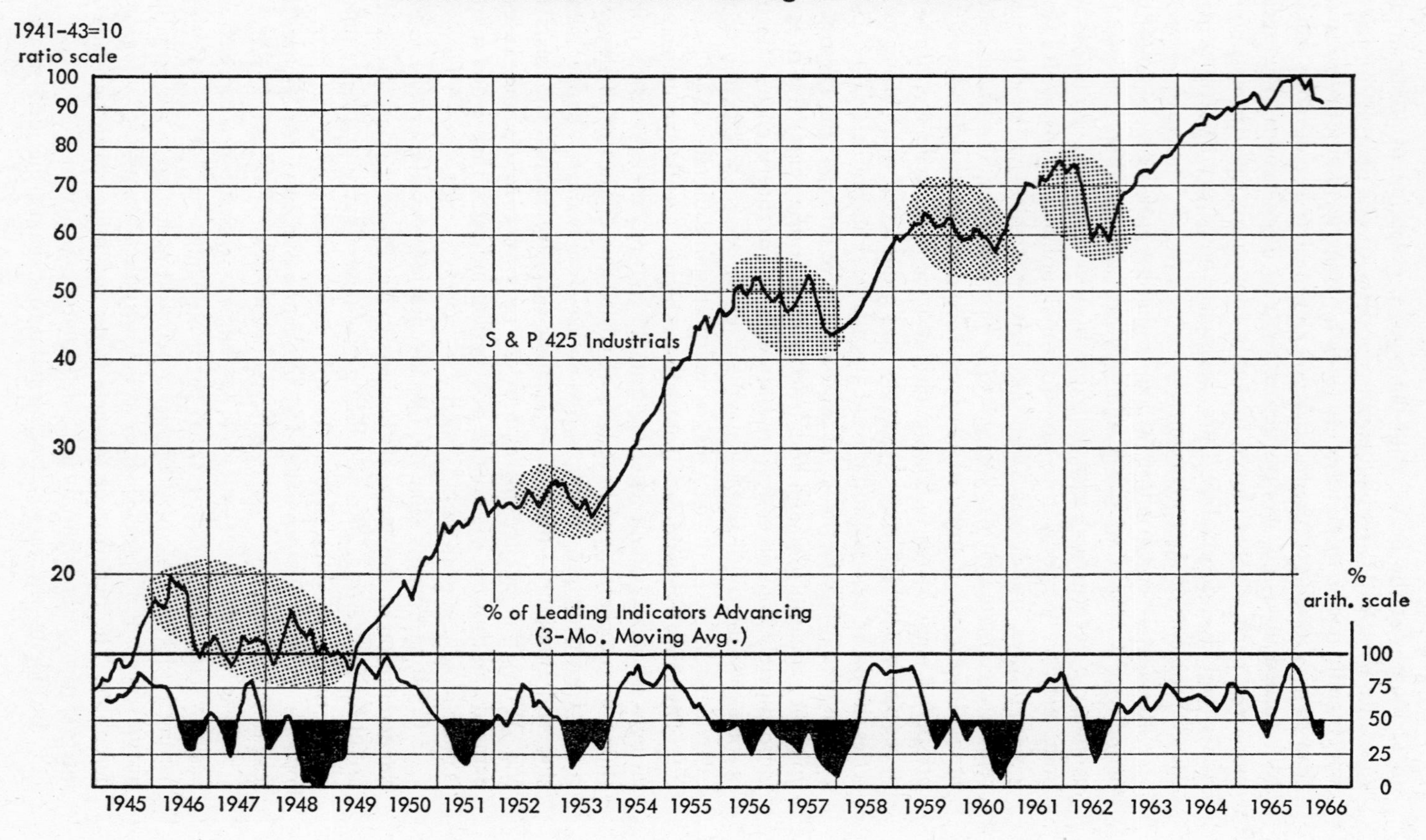

noted earlier, one must conclude that they are far from ideal. Without the background information possessed by a professional economist, most investors doubtless will feel lost among a mass of charts and data such as have been discussed. There is need for a summary measure of some kind. Fortunately, such a summary is available. It is known as a "diffusion index."

*Diffusion Indexes.* A diffusion index, as its name implies, is a measure of how widespread (diffused) a phenomenon is. Thus, in analyzing the leading indicators, we can create a diffusion index of economic strength by counting the number of indicators which rise each month and expressing that number as a percent of the total number of indicators. For example, the NBER has focused attention upon 12 leading indicators which seem particularly worthy of study.[13] If six of these should rise during a given month, the diffusion index for that month would be 50%. If in the following month eight rise (not necessarily including all of the six which rose the previous month), the index for that month is 67%. More complex types of diffusion indexes also can be constructed.[14]

Figure 13–8 compares the Standard & Poor's Industrial Stock Price Index with a diffusion index of the NBER's selected leading indicators. As can be seen from an examination of the shaded areas on the chart, stock prices usually have not fallen sharply unless the diffusion index was in a depressed state.

## Monetary Indicators

A notable omission from the NBER's selected list of leading indicators is a series which is at the center of a good deal of dispute among economists. That series is the rate of change in the nation's active money supply—demand deposits plus currency. Some economists view money as a prime mover of the economy, as a causal factor of business cycles. Others see money as a sort of lubricating oil—a good supply is necessary

---

[13] The 12 indicators are: average workweek (mfg.); accession rate (mfg.); lay-off rate (mfg.); new orders (durable mfg.); housing starts (private nonfarm); construction contract awards (comm'l and ind.); net change in operating businesses; current liabilities of business failures; corporate net income; common stock prices; change in business inventories; industrial materials prices. For greater detail see Geoffrey H. Moore (ed.), *Business Cycle Indicators,* (New York: National Bureau of Economic Research, 1961), Vol. I. The basic data necessary to keep the diffusion index up to date are available monthly in *Business Cycle Developments* (Bureau of the Census). As this text went to press the NBER announced some revisions in its list of key indicators. See G. H. Moore and J. Shiskin, *Indicators of Business Expansions and Contractions,* New York, NBER, Occasional Paper #103, 1967.

[14] See, for example, Leo B. Shohan, "New Diffusion Indexes," *Conference Board Business Management Record,* September, 1963. The NBER currently is experimenting with two differently composed indexes, one to be used to detect peaks and the other to detect troughs. Statistical Indicator Associates, a private organization, offers a weekly service on a subscription basis which reviews the individual indicators and interprets the movement of diffusion indexes of these series.

to keep the economic engine running, but it doesn't cause any moving by itself.

This is not the place to join the controversy over theory,[15] but it is appropriate to note money supply's empirical relationship to business and stock market cycles. Figure 13–9 shows that the rate of change in the money supply usually peaks in advance of major stock market downturns (and therefore in advance of business recessions).[16] At the troughs, the rate of change in money supply tends to coincide with the stock market (and thus precede business cycle troughs). Of course, the timing relationships are by no means uniform, and the money supply series falls far short of the criteria for an ideal leading indicator. Nevertheless, the data deserve serious study by investors.[17]

Change in the money supply is but one aspect of a whole series of data on the monetary system which have forecasting value. Demand deposits, the major component of money, rise as a result of the lending and investing activities of commercial banks. But a rise of deposits due to lending has more bullish connotations than a rise due to investing. Loans are made at the borrowers' initiative. Rising loans mean that the banks' customers are optimistic about the future and have rising expenditure plans. Investments, on the other hand, usually are made at the banks' initiative and suggest a shortage of borrowers. Many analysts, therefore, use the ratio of commercial bank loans to investments as a forecasting tool.

Other monetary indicators which are widely followed are the rates of change in total bank reserves (not just "free" reserves), in total "bank credit" (the sum of loans plus investments), and in total liquid assets of the public. (Included are savings accounts at banks and savings and loan associations in addition to demand deposits and currency.[18] Under some definitions, U.S. Savings bonds and short-term marketable securities also are included.) Many analysts also watch the debit/loan ratio and the "velocity" of demand deposits (debits/deposits). Bank debits are charges

---

[15] For an excellent compendium of papers on the subject, the interested reader is referred to *The State of Monetary Economics*, A Conference of the Universities–National Bureau Committee for Economic Research, published as a supplement to *The Review of Economics and Statistics*, February, 1963. In addition, the staff papers prepared for the Commission on Money and Credit, published in eight volumes by Prentice-Hall in 1963, are an excellent source of empirical and theoretical insight into the role of money in business cycles. Also see M. Friedman and A. J. Schwartz, *A Monetary History of the United States* (Princeton, N.J.: Princeton University Press, 1963).

[16] The 1966 stock market decline was an exception to this as well as to other historical precedents. However, while money supply per se did not provide a lead to the stock price decline, severe strains in the money and capital markets were taking place as the decline got under way.

[17] See B. W. Sprinkel, *Money and Stock Prices* (Homewood, Ill.: Richard D. Irwin, Inc., 1964).

[18] See L. E. Gramley and S. B. Chase, Jr., "Time Deposits in Monetary Analysis," *Federal Reserve Bulletin*, October, 1965.

FIGURE 13–9

Stock Prices and Changes in the Money Supply

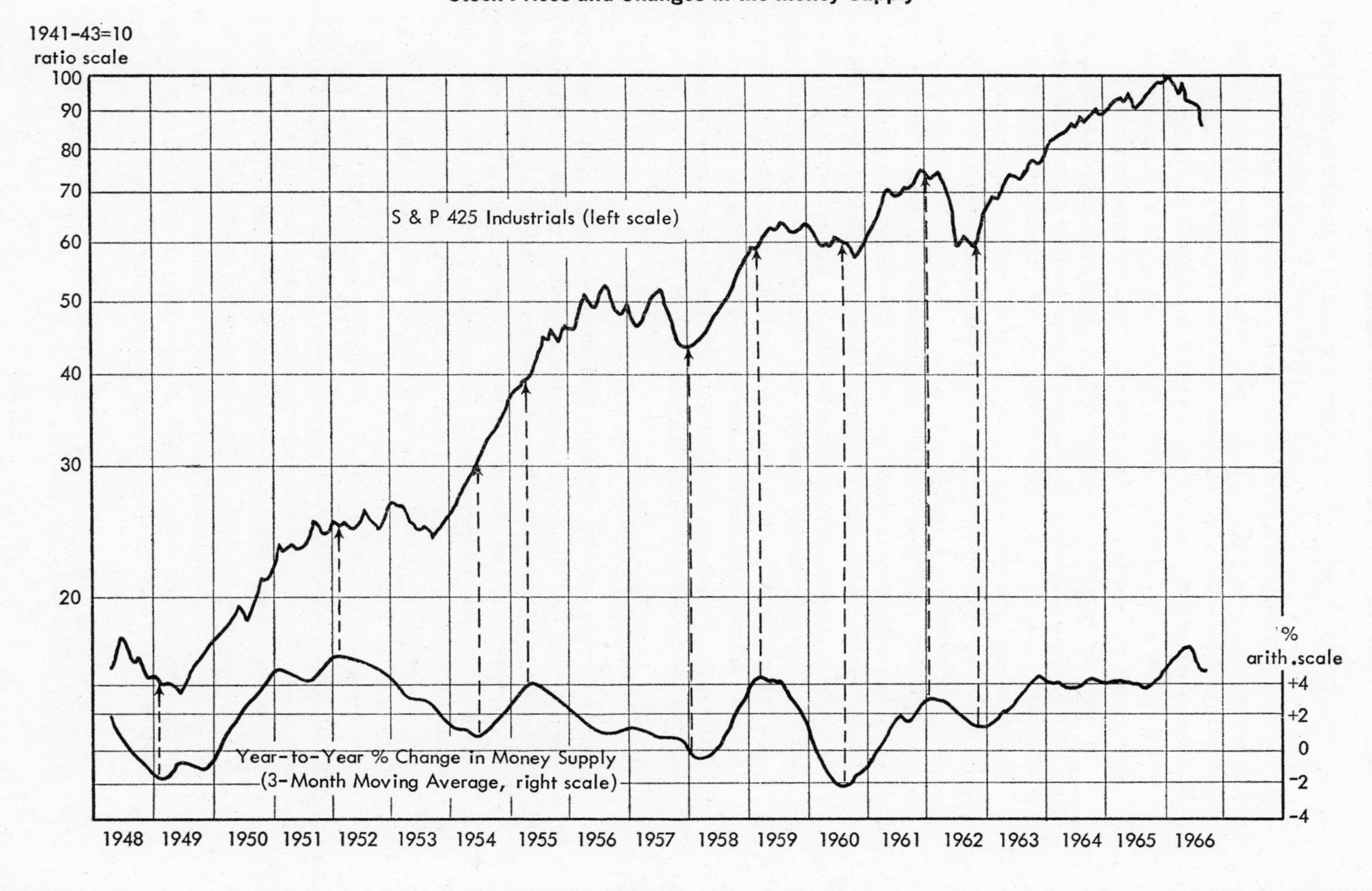

against deposit accounts in commercial banks. They arise when people make payments by check, and are a measure of the total volume of economic and financial activity in the nation. Ratios of debits to loans and debits to deposits, therefore, indicate whether private indebtedness (loans) is increasing or falling relative to the volume of business activity (debits), and whether the money supply (deposits) is becoming more or less adequate to finance the activity. By keeping track of the movement of these ratios, analysts hope to improve their "feel" of the economy.

One well-known brokerage firm has developed what it calls the "Three-Steps-and-Stumble Rule." The rule states that when three successive rises occur in any of the three rates set by the Federal Reserve Board—margin requirements, member bank reserve requirements, and discount rate—the stock market is likely to decline significantly after a time lag of about six months.[19]

Investors who wish to study current trends in money supply and related financial statistics would do well to have their names placed on the mailing lists for several monthly publications of the Federal Reserve Bank of St. Louis. Among these publications are the *Review* and one entitled *Rates of Change in Bank Reserves and Money*. A statistical tabulation from a recent issue of the latter publication is reproduced here (Table 13–3) to indicate the scope of the material covered. A noted private organization, Bolton-Tremblay, offers an investor-oriented review of banking and monetary developments on a subscription basis.

### Anticipations Surveys

The economic and monetary indicators discussed thus far all are measures of what might be called accomplished facts—orders *placed*, hours *worked*, prices of *transactions*, houses *started*, changes in *existing* money supply, etc. In addition to these accomplished facts, economists have available for analysis a group of surveys of spending *intentions* of businessmen and consumers. These surveys are conducted by various governmental and private organizations, and the student should be familiar with at least some of them.

Probably the most widely used group of surveys are those relating to business spending for plant and equipment. In October each year, the economists of McGraw-Hill Publishing Company conduct a survey of business capital expenditure plans for the year ahead. The results are published in *Business Week* magazine during the month of November. In December, the Department of Commerce and the Securities and Exchange Commission jointly publish (in the *Survey of Current Business* and elsewhere) an estimate of capital spending in the first quarter of the

---

[19] E. Gould, "Three Steps and Stumble?" *Barron's*, December 27, 1965. The firm is Arthur Wiesenberger & Co.

TABLE 13–3

**Compounded Annual Rates of Change of Reserves and Money, Seasonally Adjusted, to *September, 1966,* from Base Period Indicated**

| | Base Period | Total Reserves[1] | Reserves Available for Private Demand Deposits[2] | Demand Deposits | Money Supply | Time Deposits | Money Supply Plus Time Deposits |
|---|---|---|---|---|---|---|---|
| 1966 | Aug. | +10.7% | +12.9% | +8.5% | +7.3% | + 2.3% | +4.9% |
| | July | − 7.6 | − 2.1 | +2.8 | +2.9 | + 6.8 | +4.7 |
| | June | − 2.1 | − 3.3 | −3.3 | −1.4 | + 8.9 | +3.4 |
| | May | − 1.6 | − 3.3 | −0.7 | +0.5 | + 8.1 | +4.1 |
| | Apr. | − 2.0 | − 6.2 | −2.0 | −0.6 | + 9.1 | +3.9 |
| | Mar. | + 1.3 | − 0.9 | +0.5 | +1.4 | +10.3 | +5.5 |
| | Feb. | + 1.6 | − 0.1 | +1.6 | +2.4 | +10.0 | +5.9 |
| | Jan. | + 2.0 | + 0.2 | +1.4 | +2.2 | + 9.5 | +5.6 |
| 1965 | Dec. | + 2.4 | + 0.7 | +1.7 | +2.6 | + 9.3 | +5.7 |
| | Nov. | + 4.1 | + 2.0 | +2.9 | +3.6 | + 9.6 | +6.4 |
| | Oct. | + 3.5 | + 2.3 | +2.8 | +3.5 | +10.1 | +6.6 |
| | Sept. | + 3.4 | + 2.6 | +3.2 | +3.9 | +10.9 | +7.1 |
| | Aug. | + 3.2 | + 2.4 | +3.7 | +4.2 | +11.2 | +7.4 |
| 1964 | Sept. | + 3.6 | + 2.0 | +3.3 | +3.8 | +13.4 | +8.1 |
| 1963 | Sept. | + 4.1 | + 2.2 | +3.5 | +4.0 | +13.1 | +8.0 |
| Averages for selected periods | | | | | | | |
| 1957–65 | | + 3.0 | + 1.1 | +2.0 | +2.2 | +12.1 | +5.8 |
| 1951–65 | | + 2.6 | + 1.4 | +2.2 | +2.2 | + 9.8 | +4.8 |

Note: Daily average figures. September preliminary.

[1] Figures have been adjusted to take account of reserve requirement changes.

[2] Deposits of member banks included in the usual definition of the money supply. Seasonal adjustment computed by this bank.

Source: Prepared by Federal Reserve Bank of St. Louis, October 10, 1966.

coming year based on a survey conducted through government auspices. By March, Commerce–SEC have run another survey, this time covering expectations for the first and second quarters and for the full year. In April, McGraw-Hill publishes the results of a follow-up to their October survey, and in June and September, Commerce–SEC provide estimates for the current and succeeding quarters based on still more surveys. In addition to this abundance of data, the National Industrial Conference Board compiles a quarterly record of budgetary appropriations for future capital spending by the boards of directors of America's largest corporations. These findings are discussed and interpreted in the Conference Board's monthly publication, the *Record.*

Since capital spending plays such an important role in our economy (many economists believe it is the single most important generating factor in the business cycle), a successful forecast of such spending obviously is desirable. While the surveys do not have a perfect record, use of the data usually results in a correct forecast of the direction of capital spending, although not necessarily in a correct forecast of magnitude.

Closely related to surveys of capital spending intentions are surveys of inventory stockpiling expectations. Several organizations conduct periodic inventory surveys of sizable samples of business corporations. The Department of Commerce has been doing it since the fall of 1957, and private organizations such as Dun & Bradstreet, *Fortune* Magazine, and the National Association of Purchasing Agents have an even longer experience. To provide maximum analytical insight, the surveyors ask questions about related topics such as employment, price, and profit expectations. The surveys generally are for a shorter forecast period than the capital spending surveys, since it is recognized that businessmen do not plan inventory buildups or liquidations very far in advance.

The nature of business processes is such that inventory plans are less likely to materialize than capital spending plans. Whereas the latter are essentially decisions based on long-term considerations and taken after much deliberation, the former are more or less short-term adjustments to changing patterns of sales and new orders. But while less reliable than capital spending surveys, inventory surveys have produced results sufficiently useful to warrant the attention of serious students of business forecasting.[20]

During recent years, consumers have joined businessmen as objects of economic surveyors' attentions. While no one claims that consumers "plan" their future spending in the same sense as businessmen do, it seems reasonable to hypothesize that families "talk things over" some time prior to purchasing major items such as automobiles, houses, home furnishings and appliances, and perhaps even some nondurables such as clothing. Surely "impulse buying" cannot be the only driving force behind consumer spending, particularly on expensive durable goods. Although consumer spending intentions are subject to swift revisions due to unexpected changes in employment conditions, fluctuations in purchases of consumer durables are such a key element in the business cycle that all available evidence should be brought to the fore in an attempt to forecast these fluctuations.

Since 1952, the Survey Research Center of the University of Michigan has conducted several nationwide surveys each year in an attempt to determine changes in consumer attitudes and in their intentions to purchase durable goods. The findings are made public via books and press conferences. Other organizations, notably the Bureau of the Census, have built upon the work of the Survey Research Center but have taken issue with the Center's emphasis on attitudes as distinguished from intentions. A much-debated question among economists is whether attitude data really

---

[20] The interested reader is referred to progress reports on the Department of Commerce efforts in the August, 1961, *Survey of Current Business* and in subsequent issues of that publication.

add significantly to the forecasting potential of intentions data, and vice versa.[21]

Finally, mention should be made of statistical series which are in the nature of anticipations data but which are not developed by survey techniques. For example, applications for FHA home insurance reflect intentions to buy houses. As another example, the federal budget is an expression of the administration's spending intentions. Of course, the President doesn't always get what he wants from Congress, and he may also change his mind during the year. Nevertheless, perusal of the January budget message, the "midyear" budget review (in August or September), and the course of legislation can enable the astute economist to forecast federal spending reasonably well at least six months in advance.

It may seem as if there is no efficient way to utilize this mass of survey material on capital spending, inventory spending, consumer spending, and government spending. These data are such that they cannot be summarized conveniently in a diffusion index. But some kind of summary is needed. Economists attack the problem by utilizing what is known as a "GNP model."

### The GNP Model

The word "model" in the context of economic forecasting often refers to a complex set of mathematical equations.[22] But it also may be used simply to convey an impression of *structure*. The gross national product (GNP) is a framework within which economic information may be arranged in an orderly fashion. Each analyst can bring to bear whatever amount of mathematics he desires in his attempt to gain insight from this information.

Gross national product, simply defined, is the market value of the nation's output of goods and services. Its measurement can be approached from either of two directions: (*a*) by adding up the incomes generated by the economy—wages, salaries, profits, interest, and rent; or (*b*) by adding up the expenditures of consumers, businesses, and governments (plus net exports). For short-term forecasting purposes, the expenditure approach is more useful than the income approach. What one does is to forecast each major expenditure component of GNP, add up the component forecasts, and thus forecast the movement of aggregate economic activity

---

[21] See, for example, F. G. Adams, "Consumer Attitudes, Buying Plans, and Purchases of Durable Goods," *Review of Economics and Statistics*, November, 1964.

[22] See, for example, M. Liebenberg, A. A. Hirsch, and J. Popkin, "A Quarterly Econometric Model of the United States: A Progress Report," *Survey of Current Business*, May, 1966. Also D. B. Suits, "Forecasting and Analysis with an Econometric Model," *American Economic Review*, March, 1962. A far more technical reference is J. Duesenberry, G. Fromm, L. Klein, and E. Kuh, *The Brookings Quarterly Econometric Model of the United States* (Skokie, Ill.: Rand McNally & Co., 1965).

as measured by GNP. This is why GNP model building is often referred to as "sector analysis."

GNP data are compiled by the Department of Commerce every quarter (on a seasonally adjusted annual rate basis), and are published in most complete detail in the *Survey of Current Business*. The data are revised frequently as new information becomes available, and the analyst must be careful that he is working with the most up-to-date statistics. Extensive revisions usually are published in each July issue of the *Survey*, and historical data running back to 1939 on a quarterly basis and to 1929

**TABLE 13–4**

**Major Components of Gross National Product, 1965**

(In Billions of Dollars)

| | | |
|---|---|---|
| *Personal Consumption Expenditures* | | |
| Durable goods | 66.1 | |
| Nondurable goods and services | 365.4 | |
| Total | | 431.5 |
| *Gross Private Domestic Investment* | | |
| Residential construction (inc. farm) | 27.8 | |
| Business capital spending | 69.7 | |
| Business inventory accumulation | 9.1 | |
| Total | | 106.6 |
| *Government Purchases of Goods and Services* | | |
| Federal | 66.8 | |
| State and local | 69.4 | |
| Total | | 136.2 |
| *Net Exports of Goods and Services* | | 7.0 |
| GROSS NATIONAL PRODUCT | | 681.2 |

Source: *Survey of Current Business*, July, 1966, p. 8. Details may not add to totals due to rounding.

on an annual basis have been published in a supplement entitled *The National Income and Product Accounts of the United States, 1929–1965: Statistical Tables*. Detailed descriptive material on the conceptual underpinnings of national income accounting have been published in supplementary volumes entitled *National Income* and *U.S. Income and Output*. An analytically convenient statement of the United States GNP accounts is shown in Table 13–4.

As noted previously, the economic forecaster's task is to enter the numbers he believes are most realistic for each calendar quarter of the period he is forecasting. To do this, he makes use of any and every piece of evidence he thinks is pertinent. The latter point should be stressed. Sector analysis permits a maximum degree of analytical flexibility and ingenuity. As one analyst has put it, a GNP model has "a ravenous appetite for any data, evidence or insight concerning the current situation and outlook."[23]

Space does not permit an extended discussion of the problems and pitfalls of sector analysis. It should be helpful, however, to present a series of charts showing the recent movement of the major sectors listed on the GNP statement above and to note briefly some of the data which should be considered in forecasting each.

*Personal Consumption Expenditures.* Figure 13–10 shows the two

**FIGURE 13–10**

**Personal Consumption Expenditures**

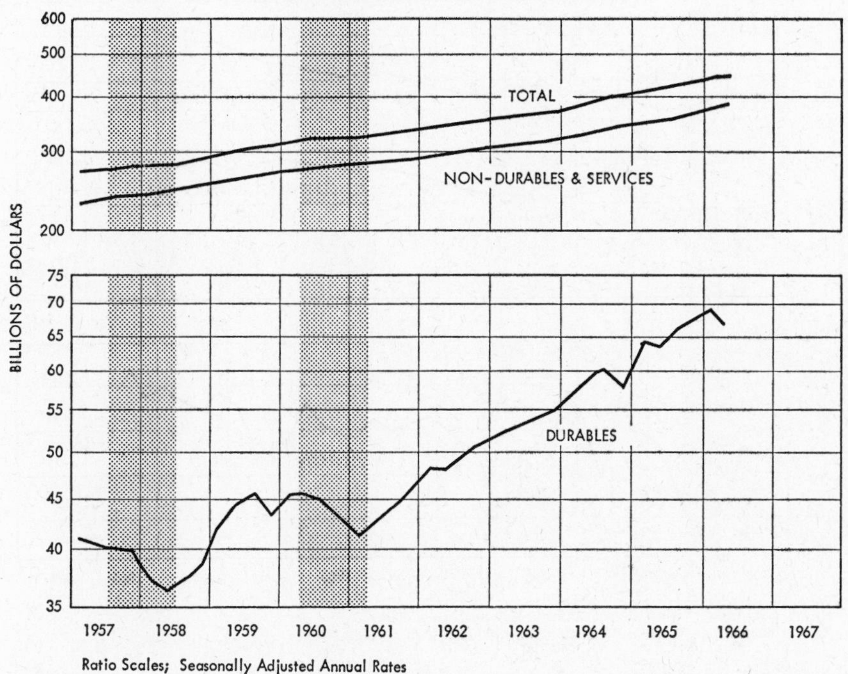


major components of consumer spending. It can be seen that nondurable goods and services have risen almost continuously. The only reflection of recessions (denoted by shaded vertical areas, using NBER dating) is some tapering off of the rate of growth. The forecaster, therefore, is reasonably safe, at least as a first approximation, if he bases his forecast on the rate of change of the past few quarters. If nondurables and services have been changing rather slowly, the forecaster can assume a somewhat more rapid

---

[23] John P. Lewis, "Indicators That Tell the Whole Story," *Challenge*, February, 1962, p. 27.

change for the coming quarters. On the other hand, if this sector has been rising rapidly, a slower rate of change can be projected.

Consumer expenditures for durable goods contrast sharply in volatility with expenditures for nondurables and services. Surveys of buying intentions are useful forecasting tools in this area. Also useful is an analysis of consumer credit. Purchases of consumer durable goods, especially automobiles, are heavily dependent on installment financing. Typically,

**FIGURE 13–11**

**Components of Gross Private Domestic Investment**

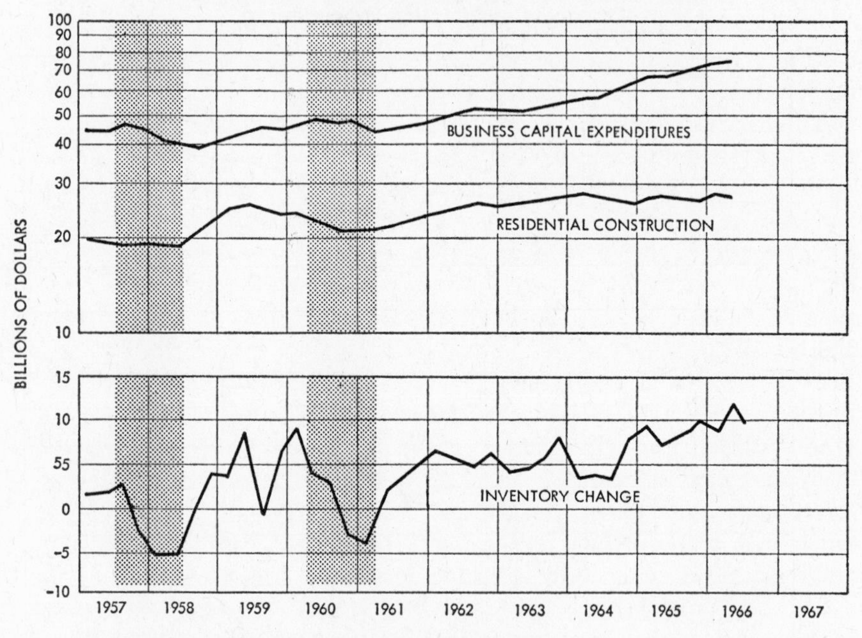


Top Panel, Ratio Scale; Seasonally Adjusted Annual Rates
Bottom Panel, Arithmetic Scale; Seasonally Adjusted Annual Rates

the rate of change in outstanding installment credit (published monthly in the *Federal Reserve Bulletin*) turns in advance of peaks and troughs of consumer durables expenditures.

*Housing, Capital Goods, and Inventories.* Figure 13–11 illustrates the cyclical behavior of three GNP components which are commonly grouped under the heading "Gross Private Domestic Investment." It can be seen that all three components are quite volatile. As a result, the accuracy of one's forecast hinges largely on correct analysis of this sector.

Residential construction, as noted in the discussion of leading indicators, often has tended to move countercyclically—that is, to remain stable or rise when most other things are declining, and vice versa. A principal reason for this behavior is the crucial role of credit conditions in the housing market. Low down payments, low interest rates on mortgages, and long mortgage maturities encourage potential buyers to enter the market.[24] Such conditions are far more prevalent when the economy is depressed than when it is booming. Consequently, the forecaster must put great emphasis on credit conditions in considering the housing outlook. Other useful information includes surveys of home-buying intentions, the rate of new marriages and household formation, vacancy rates, applications for FHA insurance, and issuance of building permits. The government publication, *Construction Review*, is a good statistical source and, in addition, presents annual forecasts of construction activity.

Surveys of capital expenditure plans and capital appropriations provide a good starting point for the forecaster of the business capital component of GNP. The reasonableness of stated intentions to expand and modernize plant and equipment can be checked by referring to recent trends in backlogs of unfilled orders relative to sales, and in the level of manufacturing capacity utilization. When ratios of unfilled orders to sales and of sales to capacity are high and rising, business capital expenditures can be expected to rise. Data on unfilled orders and sales can be found in the *Survey of Current Business*, and various estimates of capacity utilization are available from the Federal Reserve Board, McGraw-Hill, *Fortune*, and the Wharton School of Finance and Commerce of the University of Pennsylvania. Other data which should be brought to bear on the problem of forecasting capital spending are: current and anticipated profit margins (the business letter of the First National City Bank of New York, especially the April issue, is an excellent source of profit margin data and interpretation); the trend of retained earnings plus depreciation ("retained cash flow"), which is closely related to capital spending decisions; and the availability of credit for plant expansion purposes.

There is no GNP sector for which a simple projection of recent trends will produce poorer results than inventory accumulation and liquidation. Generally speaking, inventory accumulation will be heavy when businessmen's sales expectations are optimistic and/or supply problems are anticipated (for example, when suppliers are operating near capacity or strikes are threatened). Inventory liquidation will be heavy when the opposite conditions prevail. Here again, economists can make use of survey findings. Interrelationships among data on new orders, current sales, unfilled order backlogs, and existing inventory stocks also provide insight.

---

[24] Changing credit conditions have been said to affect the housing cycle even more importantly through their impact on the profit potential of builders than through their impact on the willingness of buyers to enter the market. See Sherman J. Maisel, "A Theory of Fluctuations in Residential Construction Starts," *American Economic Review*, June, 1963.

*Government Spending.* The two government components of gross national product appear in Figure 13–12. The outlook for federal spending is best approached by studying the administration's budget reports and trends in congressional appropriations. It usually is wise to separate defense spending from other spending in making a forecast of federal government purchases of goods and services because the basic factors at work can be brought into clearer focus. Unfortunately for the forecaster,

**FIGURE 13–12**

**Government Spending**

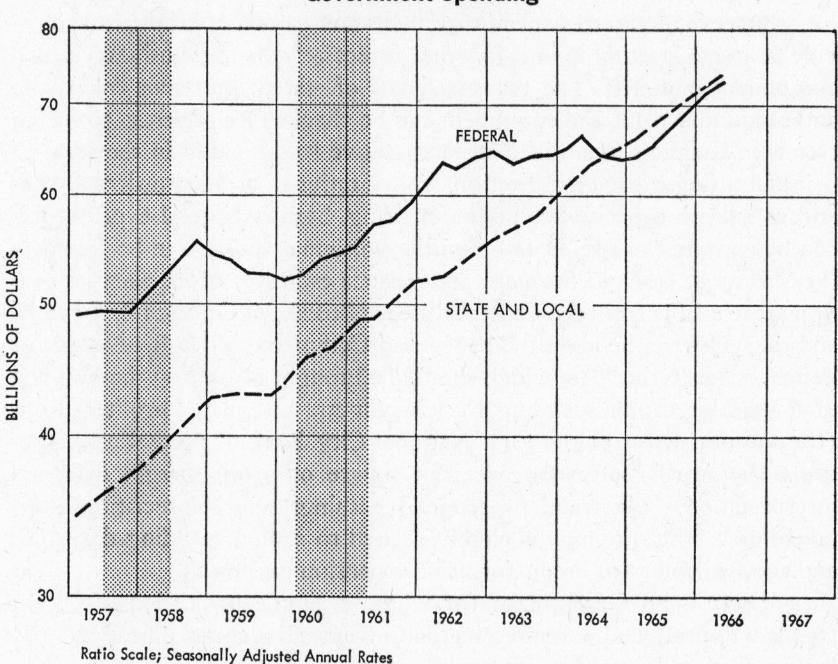


the dollar level of federal expenditures as shown in the executive budget is quite different from federal purchases of goods and services as shown in the national income accounts. This is due to definitional distinctions which cause the inclusion in the former, but not in the latter, of certain items such as interest on the public debt and various types of subsidies. Even the year-to-year *changes* in expenditures revealed by the budget data cannot always be carried over to the GNP model. Furthermore, the budget is cast in fiscal year terms whereas the forecaster is generally more interested in calendar year data.

A good clue to the probable relationship between budgeted federal expenditures and expenditures which will be included in GNP can be obtained by carefully reading the Annual Report of the President's Council of Economic Advisers.[25] This Report appears each January, about a week after the Budget Message. As a matter of fact, the CEA has begun to publish its own economic forecast in considerable detail as part of its Annual Report. Accordingly, the Report should be considered "must reading" regardless of which GNP sector is being analyzed.

The forecasting of state and local government spending may appear to involve procedures similar to forecasting federal spending. However, no consolidated budget statement exists for the thousands of state and local spending units. On the other hand, a glance at the chart reveals that non-federal government spending has moved upward so steadily that a simple extension of recent trends usually is satisfactory.

*Foreign Trade.* American exports and imports of goods and services, looked at individually, are very sizable—$39 billion and $32 billion, respectively, in 1965. However, foreign trade enters the GNP accounts as a net figure and as such is not a critical forecasting variable. Of course, foreign trade has significant indirect effects upon GNP, for example by influencing monetary policies, but this need not concern us at the moment. The most practical way of forecasting net exports is to project it slightly upward when business activity in foreign nations is advancing more rapidly than in this country and slightly downward when the opposite is true. For current information on foreign economies and foreign trade generally, the monthly review published by the Federal Reserve Bank of New York is recommended.

*Achieving Internal Consistency in a Forecast.* Since investment timing depends far more on a proper forecast of the *direction* than of the *magnitude* of economic change, it may seem unnecessary to attempt quantitative forecasts of the GNP sectors. Quantification is necessary, however. In the first place, without quantification the significance of each component of the economic outlook cannot be assessed properly. For example, a decline in defense spending may be foreseen and a rise in residential construction may be foreseen. But without an estimate of the magnitude of the change in each sector, the analyst cannot determine direction of change of the two sectors *combined.*

Furthermore, the various GNP sectors are interrelated. Consumer spending for goods and services is related to purchases of homes; these expenditures affect saving; saving affects business investment; business investment affects consumer incomes, thereby affecting consumer spending. The circles go on and on. Since the major economic sectors are so fundamentally interrelated, an overall forecast based on a summation of individual sector forecasts must be internally consistent. The sectors must

[25] In December, 1966, the Federal Reserve Bank of St. Louis instituted a new quarterly publication, entitled *Federal Budget Trends,* which can be quite helpful in the analysis of the government sector of GNP.

be in reasonable proportion to the whole and to each other—reasonable in the sense of conforming to the analyst's theory of business cycles and reasonable in the light of past empirical relationships. The only way to achieve internal consistency is to quantify.

With regard to internal consistency, it also must be recognized that the entire discussion thus far has been in terms of the expenditure, or demand, components of gross national product. No forecaster can rest easy, however, until he compares his estimate of national spending with some measures of *supply* potential—that is, with some measures of national productive capacity. He must try to determine what his projection of gross national product implies for the rate of employment, for example. Can the projected demand for goods and services in fact be supplied by the available labor force? Or will the need for labor become so intense that production bottlenecks will result? On the other hand, does the projected demand fall far short of the productive capacity of the economy, leaving a high degree of slack in labor utilization? Similarly, what are the implications for plant and equipment adequacy?

If the forecast's implied rate of utilization of physical and human resources is very high, the forecaster may consider either scaling down his projections or maintaining his projections but adding a substantial price increase factor. The preceding discussion of the various GNP sectors was in terms of current dollar values rather than in "real," or "constant dollar" terms. For almost 10 years prior to 1966, no serious forecasting errors were likely to result from simply assuming that price increases, as measured by the GNP "implicit price deflator," would represent about 1½–2 percentage points of any annual percentage change in gross national product and that the balance would represent the change in actual output of goods and services. But in 1966, the forecaster was confronted by the tightest supply-demand balance in a decade. Under such circumstances, price pressures became intense, and the forecaster then had to analyze each economic sector in constant prices and make explicit forecasts of price changes. This involved an investigation into the relationships in different industries between wages and productivity and between sales and capacity. It also involved a careful estimate of the impact of price increases on the nation's balance of international payments. These considerations, in turn, led to an appraisal of the probable course that would be followed by the fiscal and monetary authorities in an effort to combat inflation.

Suppose, however, that a preliminary forecast indicates that gross national product will be far below the economy's productive capacity. In this case, the forecaster must consider the possibility of federal government measures designed to take up the slack. The "Keynesian revolution" in economic thinking, which began in the mid-1930's, focused attention on the role of fiscal policy as a tool to supplement monetary policy in the attempt to smooth out sharp peaks and valleys of business activity. It gradually became generally accepted that the federal government should play an active role in the effort to counter recessions. But until the early 1960's, a rather pronounced distinction was made between short-term cyclical fluctuations and long-term economic growth. While an active role for the government was accepted in relation to short-term cycles, there was little acknowledgement that it could, or should, do anything to influence long-term growth.

This restricted view of fiscal policy's sphere of influence changed drastically as a result of the tax reduction measures incorporated in the Revenue Acts of 1962 and 1964. For the first time in the nation's history, federal taxes were reduced while expenditures were maintained, thus deliberately increasing the government deficit, not for the purpose of combating a recession (which had come to an end early in 1961), but in order to accelerate the rate of economic growth and help raise the level of national income to its full potential. The theory was that if this stimulation of the economy succeeded in its goal of raising national income, sufficient additional tax revenues would be generated to minimize the deficit.

The general concensus of economic observers has been that the tax reduction policy was successful,[26] and as a result forecasters must now *continuously* take into account the likely fiscal strategy of the administration—not merely when a sharp reduction in the pace of business activity is anticipated. The task of incorporating fiscal policy into a GNP model is complicated, however, by the fact that a concensus does not exist regarding the appropriate forms of federal fiscal action under different circumstances. While it generally is agreed that the 1962 and 1964 tax cuts "worked," many observers believe that another cut should be concentrated in the lower income brackets rather than in upper income individual and business brackets. Still other observers argue that the next step in the evolution of policy should be on the expenditure rather than the revenue side of the budget. These people distinguish between the quantity and the "quality" of federal intervention in the economy. Clearly, then, the forecaster must become concerned with political and social as well as essentially economic considerations.

*The Industrial Production Index.* A valuable by-product of the effort to achieve internal consistency in a GNP forecast, and to recognize the influence of price changes, is a forecast of the Federal Reserve Board Index of Industrial Production. In the first part of this chapter, stock prices and interest rates were compared with the FRB index. This is a

[26] Some of these observers, however, may give excessive credit to the tax reduction policy. It must be recognized that, along with tax cuts, an aggressive policy of monetary expansion was followed. And this policy should receive some of the credit for the economic boom of the period.

## FIGURE 13–13

### FRB Index Compared with Real GNP

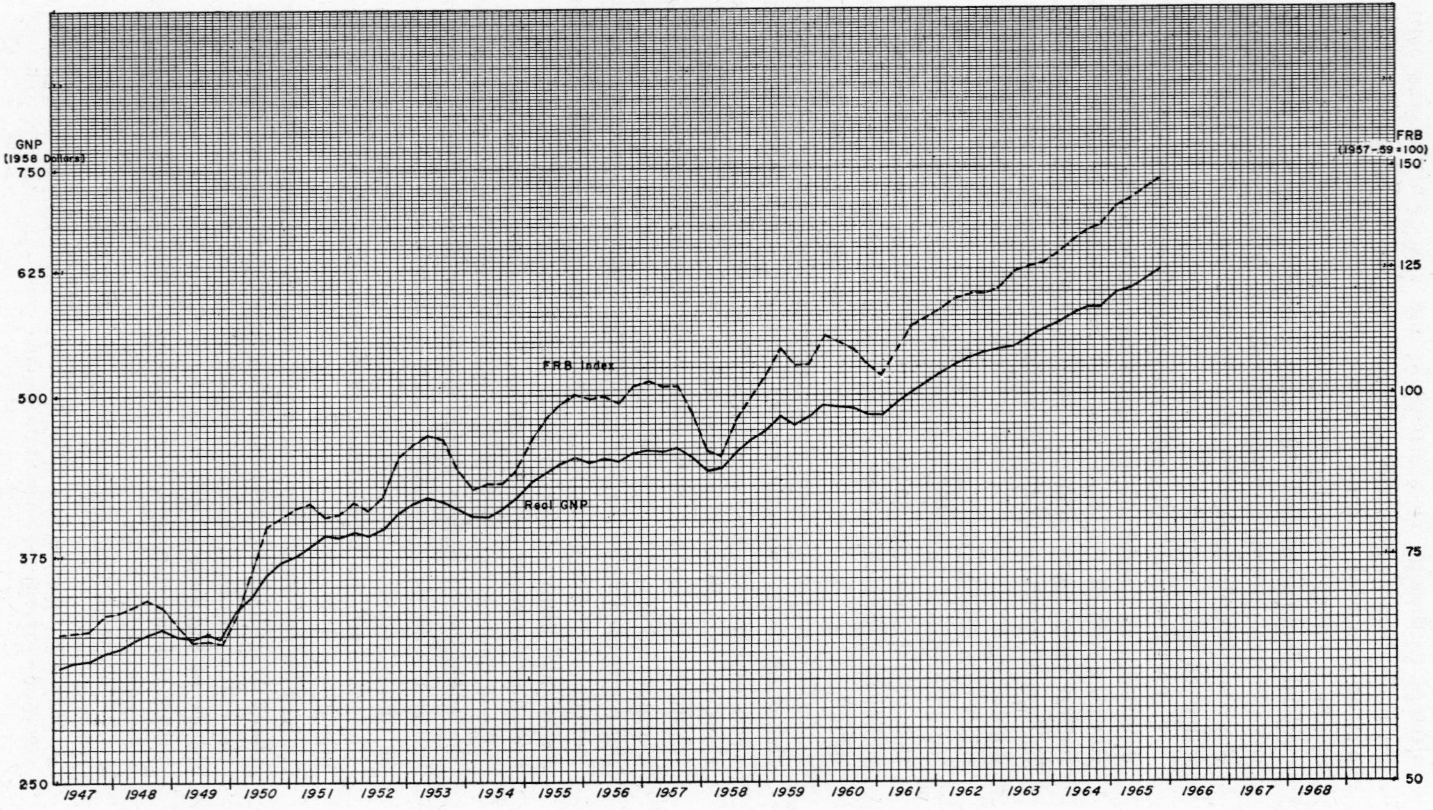

monthly rather than a quarterly series, is based upon physical output rather than current dollar data, and is highly sensitive to the supply and demand forces which have a strong influence on capital market conditions.

Most economists forecast the FRB index two ways and then reconcile the two forecasts. First, they build up a forecast of the aggregate FRB index by forecasting the individual components—manufactured durables, manufactured nondurables, mining, and utility output. The factors entering these forecasts are similar to those entering the forecast of the individual GNP sectors. Second, they translate their forecast of *real* GNP into a forecast of the FRB index. Figure 13–13 shows that the postwar relationship between real GNP and quarterly averages of the monthly FRB index has been quite close, but that the FRB index has tended to be somewhat more volatile.

### Sources and Uses of Funds Model

Closely allied to the GNP model is an analytical structure which is widely used in interest rate forecasting. It is known as sources and uses of funds analysis. The object of sources and uses of funds analysis is to quantify the individual supply and demand forces at work in the money and capital markets, and thereby to determine whether the balance of forces lies in the direction of higher or lower interest rates. For example, Table 13–5 shows the major components of 1965 sources and uses of investment funds, based on data contained in Federal Reserve Flow-of-Funds tabulations. These tabulations are updated quarterly in the *Federal Reserve Bulletin.* Other organizations also publish similar tabulations. although with somewhat different definitions and usually on an annual rather than a quarterly basis. Perhaps most prominent among these is *The Investment Outlook*, published in February of each year by Bankers Trust Company and containing a detailed analysis of recent developments together with an estimate of trends in the coming year. Several tabulations from the Bankers Trust study were reproduced in Chapter 2 (Tables 2–1, 2–2, and 2–3).

Since, by definition, sources and uses of funds must always balance, it may be wondered how such tabulations can be useful in forecasting interest rates. After all, changes in interest rates, like changes in any prices, come about because of *imbalances* in supply and demand. Unsatisfied demands for funds pull interest rates upward, and pressures of excess supplies push them down.

Admittedly, it would be very helpful to have statistics on ex ante sources and uses of funds, which would reveal such imbalances. But even a balanced ex post framework can be useful. In the first place, as the analyst attempts to forecast the various components of the sources and uses statement—as he tries to strike a balance between the forecast supplies and

**TABLE 13–5**

**Sources and Uses of Investment Funds, 1965**

(In Billions of Dollars)

| | | |
|---|---|---|
| *Net Uses (demand for funds)* | | |
| Federal government and agency obligations (net of trust fund purchases) | | 4.1 |
| State and local government obligations | | 7.4 |
| Corporate and foreign bonds | | 9.3 |
| Corporate stocks (ex. net new mutual fund shares) | | 0.0 |
| 1–4 family mortgages | | 15.4 |
| Other mortgages | | 10.1 |
| Consumer credit | | 9.1 |
| Bank loans to business, commercial paper, etc. | | 20.2 |
| Total | | 75.6 |
| *Net Sources (supply of funds)* | | |
| Institutional sources—contractual and savings: | | 34.6 |
| Savings banks, savings and loan associations, and credit unions | 14.8 | |
| Life insurance and fire and casualty insurance | 8.8 | |
| Noninsured corporate and state-local pension funds | 9.0 | |
| Investment companies | 2.0 | |
| Institutional sources—commercial banks and monetary authorities | | 32.1 |
| "Noninstitutional" sources: | | 8.9 |
| Nonfinancial businesses | 0.1 | |
| Nonbank financial businesses | 4.2 | |
| Federal, state, and local governments (ex. pension) | 4.1 | |
| Foreigners | −0.3 | |
| Direct individual investment and omissions | 0.8 | |
| Total | | 75.6 |

Source: Federal Reserve Flow-of-Funds Accounts, Tables 1 and 4, credit market instruments sections, excluding direct federal loans. *Federal Reserve Bulletin*, April, 1966.

demands—he develops a "feel" for the ex ante gap between supply and demand. To quote a recent article on the subject:[27]

In the first forecast of the sources and uses of funds, the investigator is unlikely to come up with a balance between the two sides of the statement, since his estimates of the components are prepared independently. He may find, for example, that the total demand for funds, based on a forecast of business, far outstrips the supply and that the statement can be balanced only by assuming a contraction of demand brought about by tightening conditions in the financial markets. It is thus in the process of closing the gap between demand and supply that the forecaster gains some insight into the likely direction of rates.

Another clue to the probable direction of interest rate changes is the

[27] W. C. Freund and E. D. Zinbarg, "Application of Flow of Funds to Interest Rate Forecasting," *Journal of Finance*, May, 1963, p. 237.

magnitude of "noninstitutional sources of funds"[28] which the forecaster envisions in estimating forthcoming sources and uses of investment funds. In Table 13–5, sources of funds are divided into two broad components—institutional and noninstitutional. The institutional sector, in turn, is divided into two components: (1) contractual- and savings-type institutions, and (2) commercial banks and monetary authorities. The former normally exhibit relatively stable growth over time,[29] and the latter fluctuate widely in response to changes in national monetary policy.

Institutional investors are under considerable pressure to commit their funds whether interest rates are high or low. Therefore, when demands for funds are low relative to the available institutional supply, interest rates usually are depressed. But when demands rise rapidly relative to institutional supply, they cannot be met unless funds are forthcoming from other sources, such as individuals, foreigners, nonfinancial businesses, etc. In order to entice these noninstitutional funds into the capital markets, higher interest rates must be offered. Figure 13–14 shows a definite

**FIGURE 13–14**

**Interest Rates and Noninstitutional Sources of Funds, Quarterly**

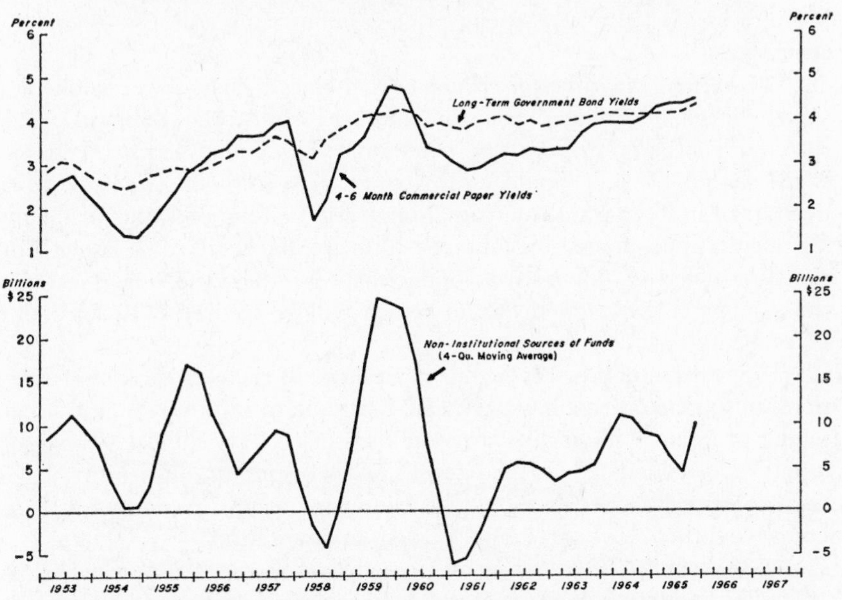


[28] This component of the sources and uses statement also is frequently referred to as "residual sources." For an extensive discussion of the subject, see W. C. Freund, and E. D. Zinbarg, "Forecasting Interest Rates," in M. E. Polakoff (ed.), *Financial Institutions and Markets* (Boston: Houghton Mifflin Co., forthcoming).

[29] During the past few years, however, savings institutions have been a far less stable source than formerly, due to increasingly vigorous interest rate competition between these institutions and commercial banks.

relationship between interest rate fluctuations and changes in noninstitutional sources of funds. Accordingly, a correct forecast of the demand for investment funds and the component sources of supply can be quite useful in attempting to forecast interest rate changes.

### Summary and Critique

Historical precedent, as outlined in the first part of this chapter, suggests various investment strategies which may be employed profitably if the investor develops an ability to forecast major economic turning points about four to six months in advance—or if he relies on the counsel of others who have such an ability. The precise implementation of these strategies depends on how aggressive, self-confident, *and flexible* the investor is. For example, large institutional investors are much less flexible than individual investors, as will be described in Chapters 18 and 19. Nevertheless, the general nature of the strategies may be indicated.

1. If the investor suspects that the prosperity phase of the business cycle is coming to an end but is not yet firmly convinced of the fact, he probably would be wise to continue buying common stocks but to confine purchases to companies whose sales are likely to be least vulnerable to recession and whose stocks' price-earnings ratios still seem relatively attractive.

2. When the investor becomes convinced that a recession lies shortly ahead, even though the stock market is still strong, he should have the courage to stop making new common stock commitments. Investable funds should be kept liquid at this stage, however—i.e., in bank time deposits or in short-term securities. Long-term bond investments probably are not yet appropriate, since interest rates are likely still to be rising. But the typical flat or downward-sloping shape of the yield curve at such times suggests that a good rate of return will be secured even on liquid investments.

3. When stock prices begin to weaken, in their classical lead relationship to general economic activity, it is time to institute quickly a net selling program with regard to common stocks. In particular, stocks of highly cyclical companies and stocks whose price-earnings ratios have risen to unrealistic levels should be eliminated from the portfolio. Proceeds from these sales still should be kept in liquid form.

4. When the recession seems immediately at hand, and stock prices are falling rapidly, interest rates are likely to be at a peak, and liquid funds should be shifted into high-quality bonds of long maturity. These are likely to appreciate most in value when the cyclical decline in interest rates takes place.

5. In the midst of the recession, yield spreads between high-quality and lower quality bonds, and between bonds and mortgages, are likely to become relatively wide. Income-oriented investors often find it worth-

while to shift funds from high-quality bonds to these higher yielding investments at such times.

6. When the investor perceives the forthcoming end of the recession, a renewed stock buying program is in order—particularly the stocks of cyclical and "glamour-growth" companies which probably were severely depressed during the bear market. Profits on long-maturity bonds should be realized through sales, and the proceeds of the sales should be invested once again in common stocks.[30]

This outline of investment strategies is based on the assumption that the investor or his counselors, using the techniques described in the second part of this chapter, can forecast economic turning points with a fair degree of accuracy. But how successful have these techniques in fact been in enabling their users to make accurate forecasts?

A study conducted by the National Bureau of Economic Research sheds some light on the question posed.[31] It reveals that forecasts of conditions a year or more ahead actually have produced only slightly better than chance results. But it also reveals that three- and six-month forecasts have been a good deal better. And investment timing, after all, usually does not require much more than a good six-month forecast. Furthermore, the NBER's study suggests that as economic statistics improve, so that the forecaster has more knowledge of what is currently happening at the time he is making his forecast, the accuracy of the forecasts also will improve. Finally, the study indicates that, as in any other activity, some forecasters are better than others. While some have a mediocre record, at best, others have done quite well.

It must be recognized, however, that the "business cycle approach" to investment timing has faults as well as virtues. First, if many full-time professional economists have only mediocre forecasting records, the investor who is not an economist cannot be expected to do very well in forecasting on his own—or in evaluating the forecasts of professionals. Second, even a consistent record of perfect six-month forecasts is unlikely to result in consistently correct investment timing. For although the timing relationships among stock price, interest rate, and business cycle turning points have been reasonably stable, they have not been, and doubtless will not in the future be, unchanging.

In the following chapter, another approach to common stock timing is presented. The approach is known as "technical analysis." It is offered not as a substitute for, but as a supplement to, business cycle analysis. Both

---

[30] All of these investment operations, of course, should take place within an overall policy framework regarding the appropriate percentages of total assets to be allocated to stocks versus fixed income investments. This latter aspect of investment policy is discussed in Part IV of the text.

[31] See Victor Zarnowitz, *Appraisal of Short-Term Economic Forecasts*, New York: NBER, Occasional Paper 104, 1967.

of these analytical approaches, in turn, are offered as supplements to, rather than as substitutes for, value analysis.

## SUGGESTED READINGS


Elmer C. Bratt. *Business Cycles and Forecasting.* 5th ed. Homewood, Ill.: Richard D. Irwin, Inc., 1961.

William F. Butler and Robert A. Kavesh (eds.). *How Business Economists Forecast.* New York: Prentice-Hall, Inc., 1966.

Joseph W. Conard. *The Behavior of Interest Rates: A Progress Report.* New York: National Bureau of Economic Research, 1966.

*Economic Report of the President.* Washington, D.C.: U.S. Government Printing Office, annually.

Robert A. Gordon. *Business Fluctuations.* 2nd ed. New York: Harper & Row Publishers, 1961.

Paul M. Horvitz. *Monetary Policy and the Financial System.* New York: Prentice-Hall, Inc., 1963.

Thor Hultgren. *Costs, Prices, and Profits: Their Cyclical Relations.* New York: National Bureau of Economic Research, 1965.

The Institute of Chartered Financial Analysts. *C.F.A. Readings in Financial Analysis*, Part III. Homewood, Ill.: Richard D. Irwin, Inc., 1966.

John P. Lewis and R. C. Turner. *Business Conditions Analysis.* 2nd ed. New York: McGraw-Hill Book Co., 1967.

Geoffrey H. Moore (ed.). *Business Cycle Indicators, Vol. I.* New York: National Bureau of Economic Research, 1961.

Geoffrey H. Moore and Julius Shiskin, *Indicators of Business Expansions and Contractions*, Occasional Paper No. 103, New York, National Bureau of Economic Research, 1967.

Organization for Economic Cooperation and Development, *Techniques of Economic Forecasting*, 1965.

Julius Shiskin. *Signals of Recession and Recovery.* Occasional Paper No. 77. New York: National Bureau of Economic Research, 1961.

Victor Zarnowitz, *Appraisal of Short-Term Economic Forecasts*, Occasional Paper No. 104, National Bureau of Economic Research, New York, 1967.

# 14

# TECHNICAL ANALYSIS OF THE STOCK MARKET

There is nothing so disastrous as a rational investment policy in an irrational world.

—John Maynard Keynes

The business cycle approach to common stock timing deals with factors outside the stock market itself—for example, industrial production and interest rates. The technical approach, on the other hand, seeks to improve the basis of timing decisions by studying phenomena which are an integral part of the market mechanism—for example, prices and volume of trading. For this reason, technical analysis is often referred to as internal analysis or market analysis.

Technical analysts study internal stock market data in an attempt to gain insight into what economists call the "supply and demand schedules" for a stock or for the stock market as a whole. They do this by looking for recurring patterns of price movement or recurring interrelationships between stock price movements and other market data. Since price movements reflect the opinions of millions of different people about everything having a bearing on stocks, it is unlikely that "technicians" can know in all cases *why* the discovered patterns occur. They may try to learn why—including in this effort an examination of relevant external information in addition to internal data—but the probability remains that many patterns and relationships will be unexplainable. Nevertheless, if the patterns are known to recur consistently, it seems sensible to take advantage of this knowledge even though the explanations remain unknown. After all, physicians do not know why aspirin works as well as it does, but they prescribe it nonetheless.

Technical analysts who are intellectually honest will be quick to admit that they have no hope of discovering foolproof methods of forecasting stock prices. Mistakes are bound to be made, often severe mistakes.

But they also will argue that as long as their methods improve the *probabilities* of investment success, as long as they reduce the margin of error, they are worthy of serious consideration.

The purpose of this chapter is to examine the validity of the technicians' claims that they have methods which "work." Obviously, each and every technical tool cannot be examined, just as all of the methods of analyzing the business cycle could not be covered in the previous chapter. But the reader will be exposed to some of the most widely used technical tools. We shall try to point out the basic strengths and weaknesses of each tool and in doing so to note whether it is applicable to an analysis of the market as a whole, of individual securities, or of both.

### Breadth of Market

Breadth-of-market analysis is used to study major turning points of the market as a whole. It is based on a theory of the nature of stock market cycles. Bull markets are viewed as being long-drawn-out affairs during which individual stocks reach peaks gradually, with the number of individual peaks accelerating as the market averages (for example, the Dow-Jones Industrials) rise toward a turning point. Bear markets, on the other hand, are viewed as concentrated collapses of a large number of stocks in a short period of time. Accordingly, to detect a condition of internal market weakness before it is generally recognized that a bull market tide has turned, evidence is sought to determine whether large numbers of stocks are falling while the averages rise. And to detect the approaching end of a bear market, technical analysts consider how widespread the selling pressure is. In short, what is being examined is the dispersion of a general price rise or decline; thus the phrase "breadth of market."

There are many ways of measuring breadth of market. The easiest to apply, and probably the most widely used, is a daily cumulation of the net number of advancing or declining issues on the New York Stock Exchange. The daily newspapers publish a table showing the number of issues traded on the previous day, the number which advanced in price, the number which declined, and the number which were unchanged. If the declines are subtracted from the advances, a net positive or negative figure results (described as net advances or net declines). For example, a week's market activity might produce the following data.

| | Number of Issues Traded | Advances | Declines | Unchanged | Net Advances or Declines |
|---|---|---|---|---|---|
| Monday | 1,301 | 530 | 535 | 236 | − 5 |
| Tuesday | 1,310 | 464 | 597 | 249 | −133 |
| Wednesday | 1,323 | 303 | 739 | 281 | −436 |
| Thursday | 1,295 | 607 | 453 | 235 | +154 |
| Friday | 1,308 | 807 | 241 | 260 | +566 |

The next step is to cumulate the net advances and net declines, thus constructing a measure of a breadth. Cumulation simply means the successive addition of a series of numbers. In the above example, cumulation of the final column of data would produce the following:

| | Breadth of Market |
|---|---|
| Monday | − 5 |
| Tuesday | −138 |
| Wednesday | −574 |
| Thursday | −420 |
| Friday | +146 |

The cumulation is continued ad infinitum. Obviously, over a period of many years of generally rising stock prices the absolute *level* of the breadth measure can become very high. Moreover, if different analysts begin their cumulations on different days, the levels of their breadth series will differ. However, breadth analysis focuses on *change* rather than on level, and the change during any given time period will be the same no matter what the original starting date of the cumulation.

Having measured breadth, the next step is to chart it in conjunction with one of the market averages, such as the Dow-Jones Industrials. Normally, breadth and the DJI will move in tandem. What the analyst must be wary of during a bull market is an extended divergence of the two lines—that is, a breadth line which declines to successive new lows while the DJI makes new highs. Such a divergence indicates that an increasing number of issues are turning down while the "blue chips," which weigh heavily in the DJI and in most other market averages, continue to rise. According to the theory underlying breadth analysis, this suggests an approaching peak in the averages and a major downturn of stock prices generally.[1]

Evidence that this theory has considerable validity is contained in Figure 14–1, which shows that price-breadth divergences preceded the major market downturns of 1956–57, 1960, and 1962. A divergence also occurred prior to the 1948–49 downturn, which is not shown on the chart. On the other hand, the 1953 stock price decline (not shown) was not preceded by a price-breadth divergence. Moreover, the chart indicates that there often may be room for differing interpretations of the movement in breadth. For example, some observers claim that the 1966

[1] It should be stressed that this theory of the nature of bull markets suggests that they usually end "not with a bang but a whimper." It is a contradiction of the thesis that bull markets typically end with a "speculative blowoff." According to breadth theory, the prices of low-quality and speculative stocks, together with volume of trading, reach a blowoff stage before the market averages hit a peak, and then settle down while better quality stocks move up somewhat further in price. Finally, when the better quality stocks turn down, the whole price structure deteriorates.

**FIGURE 14–1**

**Stock Prices and Breadth of Market**

(Last Day of Each Week)

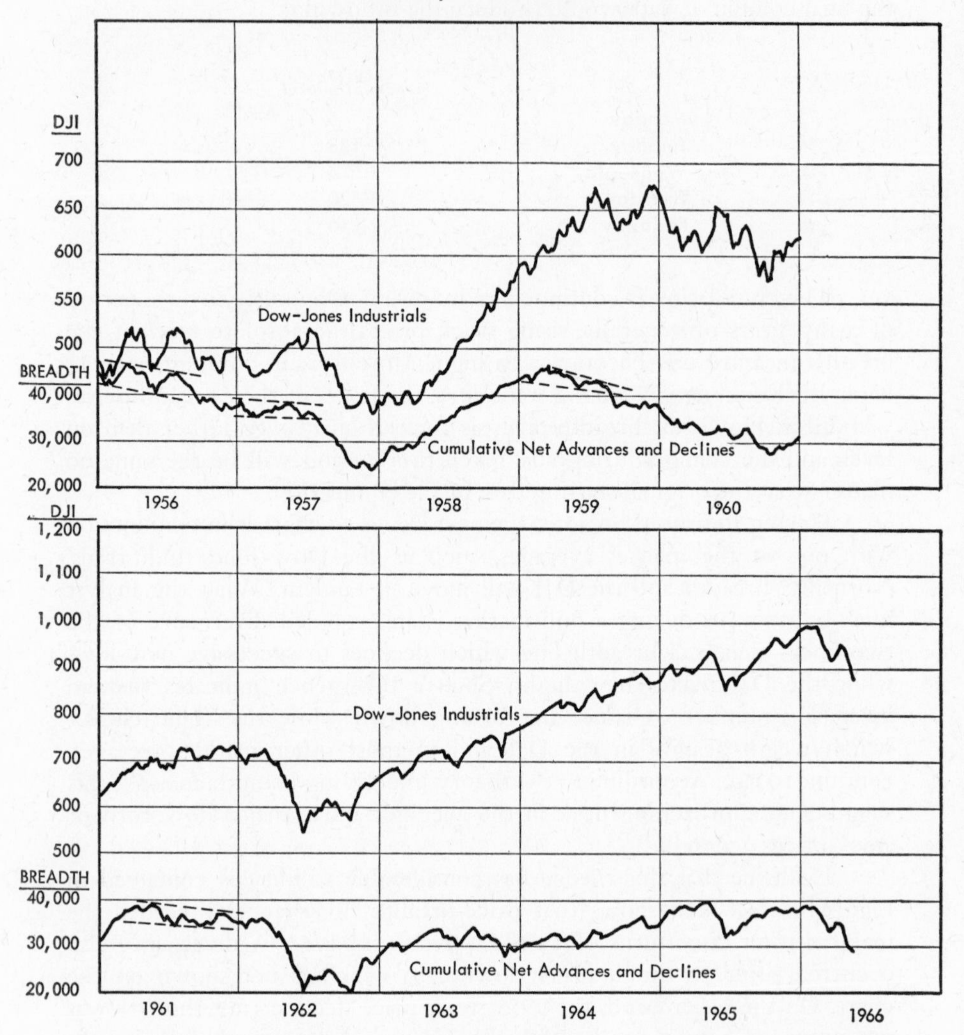


stock market downturn was preceded by a pronounced price-breadth divergence. However, others counter that although breadth was lower in January, 1966, than in May, 1965, while the DJI was higher, breadth did not make *new lows* during the intervening months and, therefore, a true divergence did not occur. This evidence suggests that breadth of market may be a useful advance indicator of major stock price declines but that, like any other indicator, it is by no means infallible.

Once the market has entered its declining phase, breadth also can be useful in detecting an impending recovery. It will be recalled that a major premise of breadth analysis is that large numbers of stocks tumble in price in a short period of time during bear markets. Therefore, the end of a bear market is likely to be near when all anxious and panicky investors rush to sell out at once. Evidence of a so-called "selling climax" may be obtained by examining the movement of breadth in conjunction with prices and the volume of trading. Typically, for a number of weeks during the latter stages of a bear market the cumulative net advance-decline line will fall by several thousand, the Dow-Jones Industrials will fall several percent, and trading volume will be substantially higher than in previous weeks. Prices will not necessarily begin rising immediately after such a selling climax—indeed, they typically bump along the bottom for a few months—but the worst is usually over.[2]

An interesting side aspect of Figure 14–1 is an apparent *long-term* divergence of breadth from the averages—the former tending to move horizontally or even decline in the face of a strong uptrend in the latter. This can be traced partly to declining preferred stock prices (which are included in the advance-decline data), reflecting rising interest rates.[3] But the long-term divergence more importantly illustrates how difficult it has been in recent years to "beat the averages."

### Volume of Trading

Volume of trading data can be helpful in detecting the end of a general market decline, since volume rises sharply during selling climaxes. In addition to being useful at market troughs, volume also is a useful indicator of the end of a *bull* market. It has a tendency to fall in advance of major declines in the stock price averages, as shown in Figure 14–2.

A third application of volume data is in the study of individual stocks. Prices obviously do not move steadily in the same direction every day. Even if a stock's price is in a major uptrend, it frequently will decline. It does not move up like an arrow, but zigzags up. Many technical analysts believe that if the volume of trading in a stock rises on the days when its price rises during the course of this zigzag movement, and then falls off when price recedes temporarily, the overall pattern is bullish. On the other hand, if volume rises when price falls, and falls when price rises, the overall pattern is believed to have bearish connotations (unless the volume rise and price decline are of such magnitude as to suggest a selling climax).

---

[2] Professional stock traders frequently wait until the second big "bump" before they resume buying. This second bump often occurs on relatively light volume.

[3] The inclusion of preferred stocks in the advance-decline statistics reinforces the tendency of breadth to decline prior to the stock price averages. Since interest rates usually rise during the course of a bull market, preferred stock prices decline and put downward pressure on the advance-decline line prior to the peak of common stock prices.

**FIGURE 14–2**

**Stock Prices and Volume of Trading**

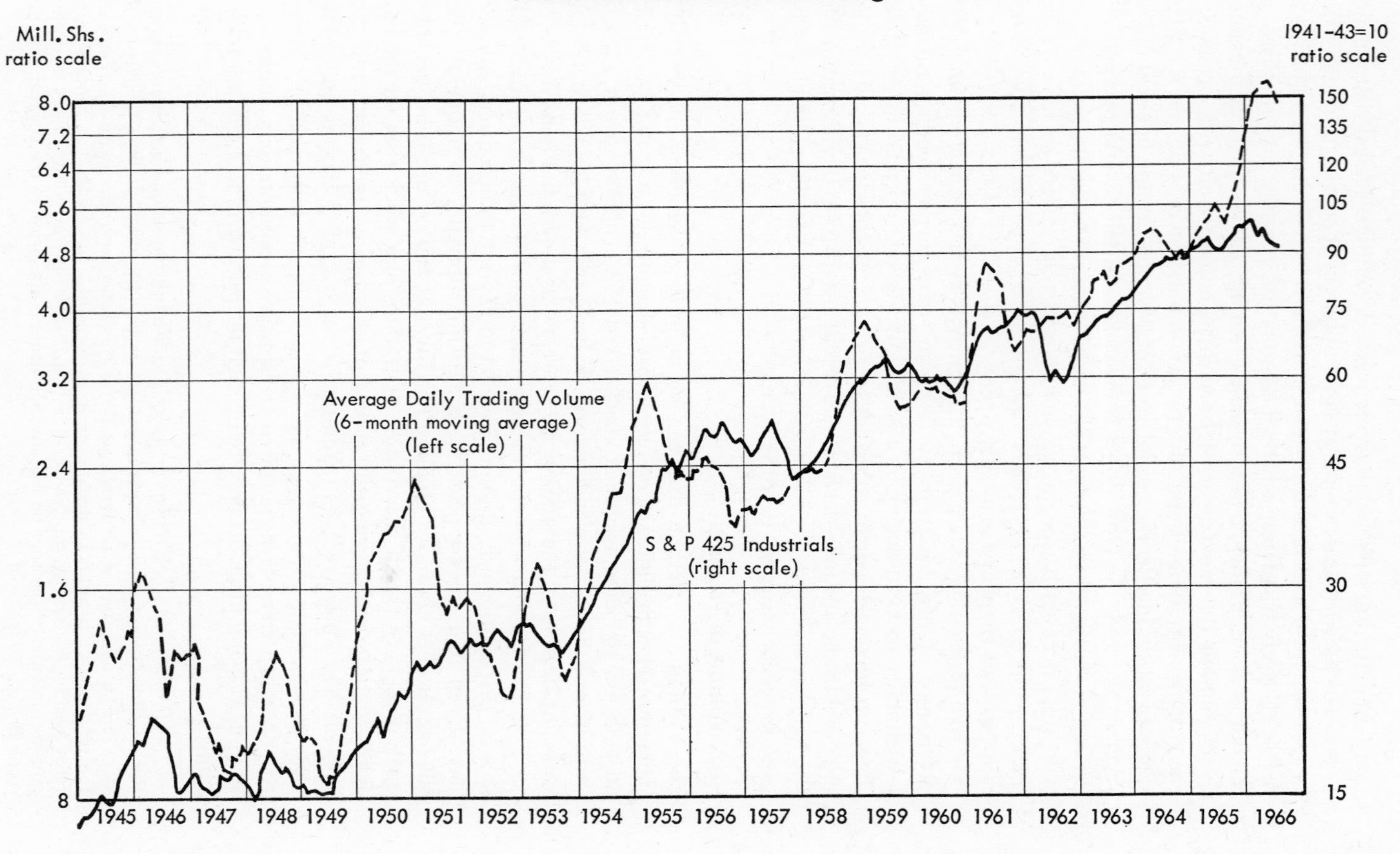

The idea behind this application of volume data to the analysis of individual stocks is that volume of trading varies directly with the intensity of emotion on the part of stock buyers and sellers. When anxious buyers outnumber anxious sellers, they bid aggressively and push prices up on heavy volume. When anxious sellers come to dominate events, they offer stock in increasing volume at markdowns in price. Volume therefore becomes a clue to shifts in the supply and demand schedules for a stock. This theory has not been subject to much formal testing,[4] but our general impression is that it is essentially correct.

### Short Selling

Short sales are made by people who expect stock prices to decline. From the technical analyst's point of view, it makes no difference whether short sellers are right or wrong. The fact is that most short sales eventually must be covered by purchases.[5] Therefore, an increase in the outstanding (meaning uncovered) short interest generally means an increased potential demand for stock. A reduction in the short interest generally means a reduced potential demand. Thus, when trying to judge whether the time is ripe to purchase or sell a stock, it may be helpful to record its short interest outstanding each month relative to the average daily trading volume for the month.[6] When this ratio rises steadily, it implies that a larger and larger percentage of future trading activity is likely to be represented by anxious buyers, the short coverers. A steady decline in the ratio implies that the price cushion to be had from the short sellers is deflating. Of course, a high short interest should lead the investor to double-check the underlying value of the stock. He should try to ascertain whether the short sellers have discovered some critical condition which makes the stock fundamentally unattractive at existing prices.

The data needed to calculate short-interest ratios are readily available. The New York and American Stock Exchanges make public, around

---

[4] M. F. M. Osborne has done some statistical analysis of the theory and finds that it has a good deal of validity. His findings were presented in a paper entitled "Some Quantitative Tests for Stock Price Generating Models and Trading Folklore," *Journal of the American Statistical Association*, June, 1967.

[5] Short sales "against the box," or in "arbitrage" operations, need not be covered by subsequent purchases. Short sales against the box are made by people who already own the stock. In the usual case, they have capital gains or losses which they want to realize immediately, but they do not wish to record the gain or loss on the current tax return. By selling short, they can realize the gain or loss now, but transfer it to a following year for taxation. Arbitrage short sales are made by people who own bonds or warrants convertible into the stock sold short. If prices rise after the short sale, they can cover by converting their bonds or warrants instead of buying stock in the open market.

[6] A contrary view of the usefulness of short-interest data is presented by B. M. Biggs in "The Short Interest—A False Proverb," *Financial Analysts Journal*, July-August, 1966.

**FIGURE 14–3**

**Stock Prices and Short Selling**

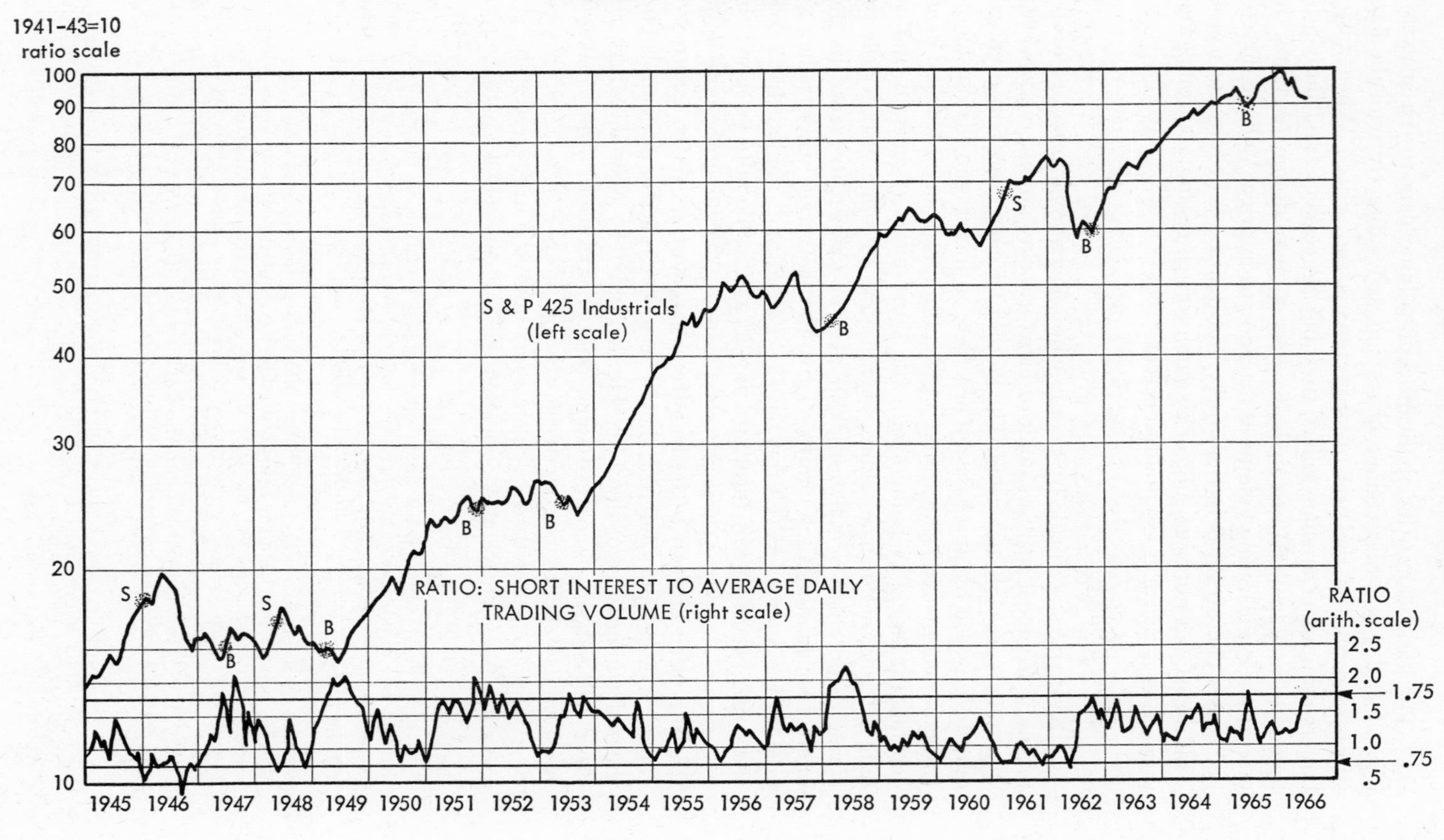

the 20th of each month, a detailed list of all issues in which a sizable short interest existed as of the middle of the month or which showed a sizable increase in short interest from the previous month. These data are published in whole or part by the financial press. Volume of trading data, of course, are published daily, and can be averaged by the analyst.

In addition to giving the short interest of individual stocks, the monthly releases indicate the total short interest in all stocks. The ratio of total short interest on the New York Stock Exchange to average daily trading volume on that exchange is useful in appraising general market conditions. Figure 14–3 compares the movement of this ratio with the Standard & Poor's Industrial Stock Price Index. Horizontal lines are drawn through the levels 0.75 and 1.75 on the short-interest ratio. Penetrations of this band by the monthly ratio are designated sell and buy signals. Note that most, though not all, of the indicated signals were justified by subsequent market price movements.[7]

### Odd-Lot Trading

The use of odd-lot trading statistics as a guide to the stock market's future falls into a general category of technical methods which has been referred to as the "theory of contrary opinion." The approach is, essentially, to develop methods of measuring the state of popular opinion regarding the trend of stock prices, to determine when popular opinion is becoming "too uniform," and, at that time, to take the opposite position in the market. Odd-lot trading (transactions involving less than 100 shares) is engaged in primarily by the proverbial "man in the street." It is assumed that by examining odd-lot trading data in conjunction with the stock price averages a useful composite picture of popular opinion can be obtained.

Odd-lot trading data are published in the newspapers on a daily and weekly basis. Until recently, these data covered only total transactions in all NYSE-listed issues. Since early 1965, the SEC has made available weekly odd-lot statistics on 75 selected individual stocks. But because there are no earlier data on individual stocks available, the discussion which follows refers only to the use of odd-lot data in analyzing the market as a whole. It is not yet known whether the conclusions are applicable also to individual issues.[8]

---

[7] Successive buy signals are indicated in 1949, 1951, 1953, 1958, and 1965, despite the fact that there were no intervening sell signals, because they occurred so far apart in time. The reader must be careful not to infer that the 0.75 to 1.75 band is useful for individual stocks as well as for the total market. Each individual stock tends to develop its own unique short interest pattern.

[8] In an article entitled "Lambs in the Street" (*Barron's*, January 31, 1966), J. Slatter argues, on the basis of the small amount of odd-lot data available on individual issues, that "odd-lotters are no better at picking stocks than at calling turns."

Most analysts of odd-lot data place primary emphasis upon the ratio of odd-lot selling volume to odd-lot buying volume. Usually volume is expressed in number of shares rather than dollar amounts, although dollar amounts are published in the monthly SEC *Statistical Bulletin* and are used by some analysts. Some analysts also use ratios of odd-lot short sales to total odd-lot sales, and total odd-lot volume (purchases plus sales) to round-lot volume on the New York Stock Exchange. But these latter ratios are used chiefly as devices to confirm the indications of the sales-to-purchases ratio, rather than as indicators in their own right.

Examination of the odd-lot sales-to-purchases ratio over an extended period of time reveals clearly that the odd-lot public tries to do the right thing most of the time. Throughout most of an advancing market the sales-to-purchases ratio rises—that is, odd-lot sales rise faster or fall slower than odd-lot purchases. Likewise, during most of a market decline the ratio falls—sales rise slower or fall faster than purchases. Most of the time, therefore, the odd-lotters are following a correct timing policy. They step up their buying as prices fall, and step up their selling as prices rise (see the following chapter for a discussion of ratio-type formula plans, which incorporate this policy).

But while odd-lot investors try to do the right thing most of the time, the historical record suggests that they usually do the wrong thing *at turning points.* Thus, although they are conspicuous sellers as the market advances,[9] right near the peak they tend to get carried away by the prevailing enthusiasm. A rising sales-to-purchases ratio turns into a declining ratio. Likewise, as the market falls they are usually conspicuous buyers. But right near the trough, a declining ratio turns into a rising ratio as the odd-lotters suddenly panic—too late. Figure 14–4 shows the weekly action of the ratio versus the S & P Industrials at major postwar turning points of the market. The perverse timing of the odd-lotters can be seen in many of the panels of the chart, where the sales-to-purchases ratio usually diverges in direction from the market just as the latter is reaching a peak or trough.

Overreliance on the odd-lot sales-to-purchases ratio as a timing indicator would not be wise, however. There are two reasons for recommending caution in its use. First, on several occasions the sales-to-purchases ratio either did not change direction near the peak or trough of the market, or changed so little that the divergence is probably more apparent with hindsight than it was at the time it took place. For example, there was no divergence at the peak or trough of 1960 or the peak of 1961.

---

[9] This is not to say that sales necessarily exceed purchases. They often do, but more typically purchases exceed sales. What we are concerned with is not the *level* of the ratio but the *direction*.

Also, the divergence at the 1953 trough was extremely shallow.[10] (On the other hand, interpretation sometimes can be facilitated by the use of supplementary measures of man-in-the-street participation in the stock market. Such measures include the price action of low-priced stocks relative to the market generally; activity on the American Stock Exchange relative to that on the New York Stock Exchange; and the volume of mutual fund sales of new shares relative to redemptions of outstanding shares.)

**FIGURE 14–4**

**Stock Prices and Odd-Lot Index**

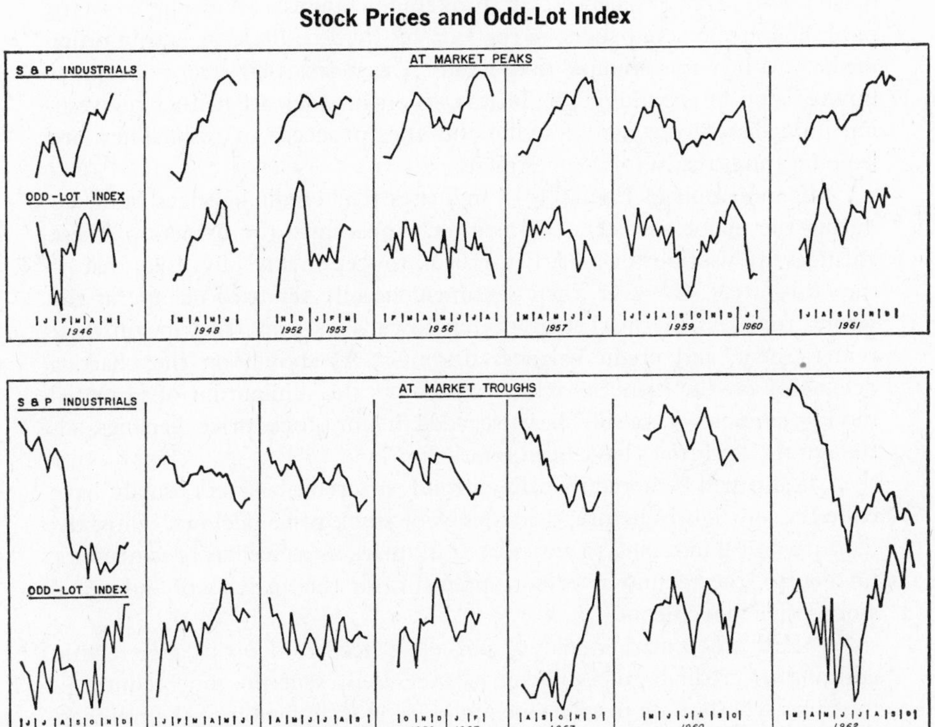


A second, and more important, reason for using odd-lot data with caution is that the sales-to-purchases ratio often has given "false signals." That is, it often has diverged in direction from the market averages *without* a subsequent turning point taking place in the market. Although many of these signals may have been disregarded in the light of other evidence, one cannot ignore the fact that they occurred.

---

[10] There was a fairly pronounced divergence for several months prior to the 1966 stock price peak, which is not shown on the chart.

### Credit Balances in Brokerage Accounts

When an investor sells stock without concurrently purchasing an equal dollar amount of some other stock, he has one of two options regarding the proceeds of the sale. If he intends to reinvest the funds in the foreseeable future, he is likely to leave the funds with the broker, who credits his account with an appropriate sum. But since he receives no interest on credit balances, he will withdraw the proceeds in cash if he does not foresee a reinvestment opportunity.

Each month, the New York Stock Exchange reports the amount of outstanding credit balances at brokerage houses. (The figures are published in the newspapers, in the *Federal Reserve Bulletin*, and in other media.) When this amount rises steadily, it means that strong potential buying support is building up. That is, sellers of stock are neither reinvesting immediately nor withdrawing the sales proceeds in cash. They are keeping funds ready for reinvestment.

Examination of Figure 14–5 indicates that credit balances build up during the major part of a bull market. Apparently the owners of these balances are waiting for a market setback to step in any buy. Like that of the odd-lotters, however, their sentiment usually tends to change at the wrong time. As the market moves up toward its peak, they begin their reinvestment, and credit balances decline.[11] As shown on the chart, a decline of credit balances—which represents the diminution of potential buying support—typically has preceded major stock price declines, although the lead times have been erratic.[12]

It also will be noted that downtrends of credit balances usually have ended at, or slightly before, the troughs of stock price declines. Thus, the data are useful in trying to anticipate bull markets as well as bear markets. Of course, the technique is not applicable to the analysis of individual stock price movements.

Many stock market analysts pay close heed to *debit* balance data in addition to credit balances. Debit balances represent the indebtedness of investors who buy on margin—i.e., who borrow a portion of the purchase price from their brokerage houses. (Borrowing from banks or from other private lenders is not reflected in the debit balance statistics.) As such, the data often provide insight into the activities of "professional traders," who are believed to be the heaviest users of borrowed funds. There is some evidence that debit balances peak and trough in advance of major stock

[11] The decline of credit balances might also reflect transfers of funds to bank accounts, as the owners of the balances get tired of waiting for an opportunity to reinvest. However, the fact that the market keeps rising suggests that most of the balances are actually being reinvested.

[12] In 1966, however, credit balances did not peak until several months *after* stock prices peaked.

**FIGURE 14–5**

**Stock Prices and Credit Balances in Brokerage Accounts**

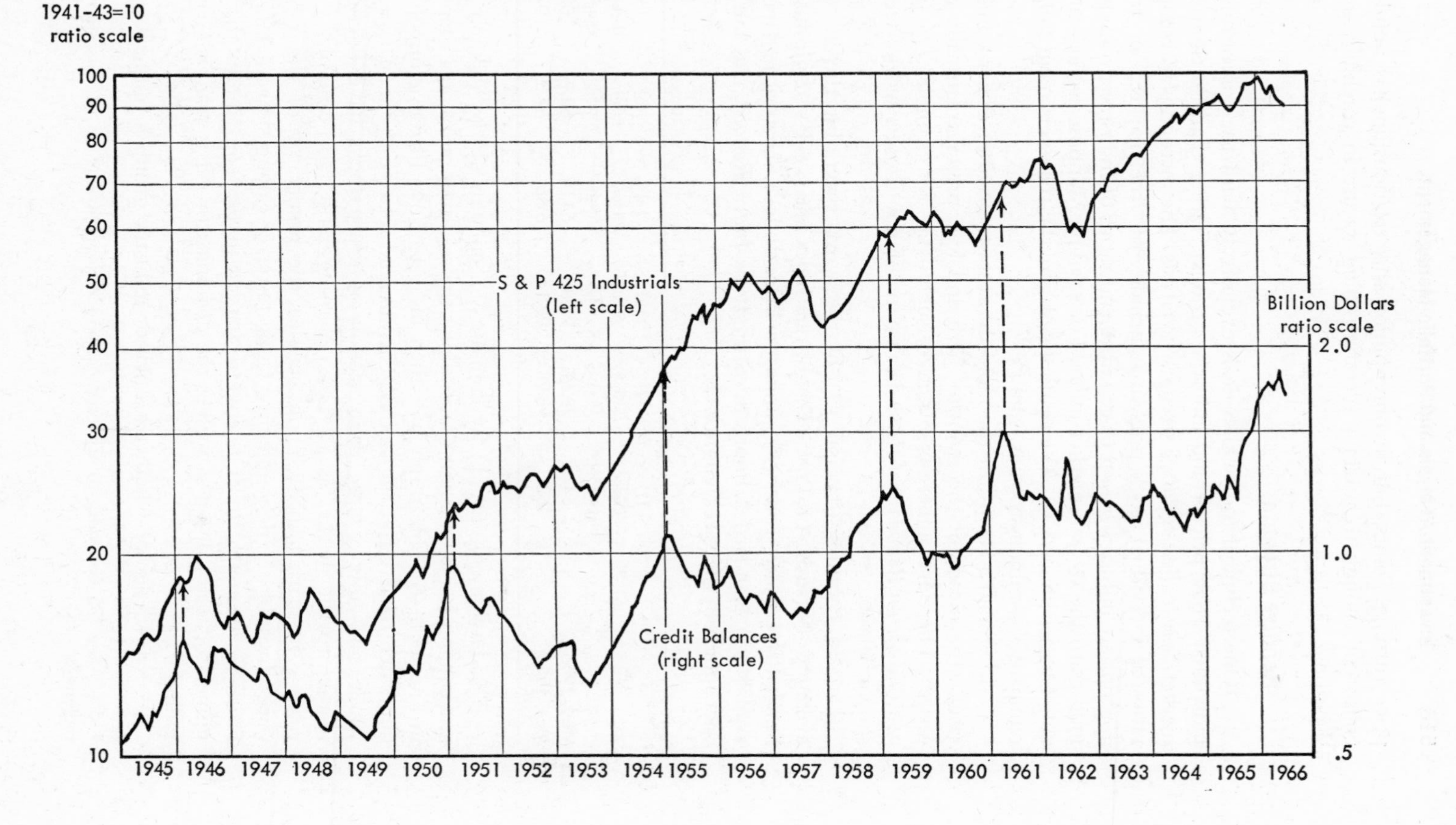

price turning points, but in our opinion this relationship has not been consistent enough to warrant recommending its use in reaching timing decisions.

### Relative Strength

One technical tool which deals exclusively with the forecasting of individual stock prices (and industry groups), rather than the aggregate market, is so-called "relative strength" analysis. The method is to compute ratios of individual stock prices to an index of "the market," or to an appropriate industry group price index, and ratios of industry group price indexes to the overall market index. For example, suppose we are analyzing Charles Pfizer & Co. We could investigate the relative strength of the company's common stock as follows:

1. Obtain a record of the monthly average price of Pfizer common stock (the means of the monthly high and low prices are usually adequate). There are numerous sources of such data—for example, *The Bank and Quotation Record*. Set these data up in column (1) of a work sheet, as shown below.

2. In columns (2) and (3) of the work sheet, list the monthly averages of Standard & Poor's Drug Price Index and S & P's 425 Industrial Stock Price Index (or 500 Composite Price Index). Historical data are available in Standard & Poor's *Security Price Index Record*, and current data appear in the weekly *Outlook*.

| | (1) Pfizer Hi-Lo Mean | (2) S & P Drugs | (3) S & P 425 | (4) Pfizer/ Drugs | (5) Pfizer/ Market | (6) Drugs/ Market |
|---|---|---|---|---|---|---|
| May, 1966 | 64 | 98.69 | 92.85 | 64.8 | 68.9 | 106.3 |
| June, 1966 | 62 | 98.98 | 92.14 | 62.6 | 67.3 | 107.4 |

3. Divide column (1) by column (2), column (1) by column (3), and column (2) by column (3), and plot the resulting ratios on a graph, as in Figure 14–6. The graph will then indicate how Pfizer common has fluctuated relative to drug stocks generally and relative to the market as a whole, and how a large cross section of drug stocks have fluctuated relative to the market as a whole. A rising ratio (for example, Pfizer relative to market in 1965) means that the numerator of the ratio is outperforming the denominator—rising faster or falling slower. A falling ratio (for example, Pfizer relative to market in 1963–64) means that the numerator is not doing as well as the denominator—it is rising slower or falling faster.[13]

Knowledge of whether a stock or industry group is outperforming

[13] See the appendix to Chapter 6 for additional discussion of this statistical technique.

FIGURE 14–6

Relative Price Behavior—Charles Pfizer & Co.

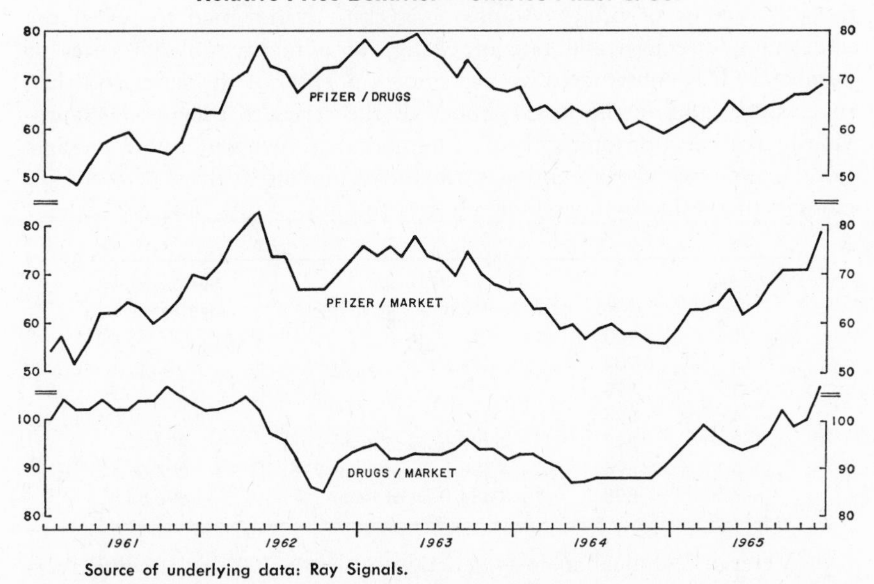


Source of underlying data: Ray Signals.

or doing worse than the market has forecasting value. Our research (unpublished) indicates that when the market is in a bull or bear trend, stocks which outperformed the market during the first half of the period usually continue to do so in the second half, while stocks which did worse continue to do worse. But when the market reverses direction, stocks which had been consistently outperforming the market begin to do worse, and stocks which had been consistently doing worse begin to do better. Of course, we are only claiming these to be general tendencies, not invariable rules. However, the tendencies are strong enough to suggest that by coupling relative strength analysis to techniques for analyzing overall market trends and turning points, the investor should be able significantly to improve his results.[14]

## Rate-of-Change Analysis

Many technical analysts believe that a reversal in a major uptrend of the price of an individual stock, or of the market in general, can be

[14] Relative strength analysis is frequently coupled to "fundamental" analysis by showing for each company, on a single chart, a relative price line, a relative earnings line, and a relative price-earnings ratio line. An effort is then made to detect disparities between relative price and relative earnings performance. For empirical evidence of the improvement in investment results which can flow from relative strength analysis, see R. A. Levy, "An Evaluation of Selected Applications of Stock Market Timing Techniques, Trading Tactics and Trend Analysis" (unpublished Ph.D. dissertation, American University, 1966).

detected in advance, or at least confirmed shortly after its occurrence, by studying the movement of current prices in relation to a long-term moving average of prices. A moving average is designed to reveal the underlying direction and rate of change of a highly volatile series of numbers.[15] It is constructed by averaging a portion of the series and then successively adding the next number of the series to the numbers previously averaged, dropping the first number, and securing a new average. For example, we could construct a five-day moving average of the daily closings of the Dow-Jones Industrials as follows:

| *Trading day* | *DJI* | *Five-Day Moving total* | *Five-Day Moving Average* |
|---|---|---|---|
| 1 | 900 | | |
| 2 | 902 | | |
| 3 | 899 | | |
| 4 | 894 | | |
| 5 | 897 | 4,492 (sum of items 1–5) | 898.4 |
| 6 | 896 | 4,488 (sum of items 2–6) | 897.6 |
| 7 | 898 | 4,484 (sum of items 3–7) | 896.8 |

Veteran technical analysts generally utilize a 200-day moving average of daily closing prices in their work. Frankly, we have been unable to discover any evidence that a 200-day average—covering about 40 weeks of trading—produces any better results than some other long-term average, say 250 days (covering a year of trading). Since our illustration of this technique will utilize monthly price data instead of daily data, we have used a 12-month moving average for convenience.[16]

Figure 14–7 shows the postwar movements of the Standard & Poor's 425 Industrials, of a 12-month moving average of that series, and of the ratio of actual to average price each month. Note first that the ratio of actual to average price reaches a high point well before the peak of actual prices. Second, observe the tendency of the moving average to begin to flatten some time after the ratio's turning point. This reflects the *gradual* ending of bull markets, as hypothesized by breadth-of-market analysis. Finally, note the fact that when actual price penetrates the moving average after the latter has flattened, it often has a considerable further decline or at least does not resume its previous uptrend for many months.

There are obvious dangers in interpreting all such penetrations as sell signals. When a bear market is shallow, as often has been the case with the

[15] Rates of change can also be analyzed by other procedures, ranging all the way from simple year-to-year percentage changes to sophisticated methods involving calculus.

[16] One investment advisory service—Electronic Stock Evaluator, Inc.—utilizes both 10-week and 30-week moving averages, weighted by volume of trading and with current data given more weight than past data.

FIGURE 14–7

Rate of Change—Standard & Poor's Industrials

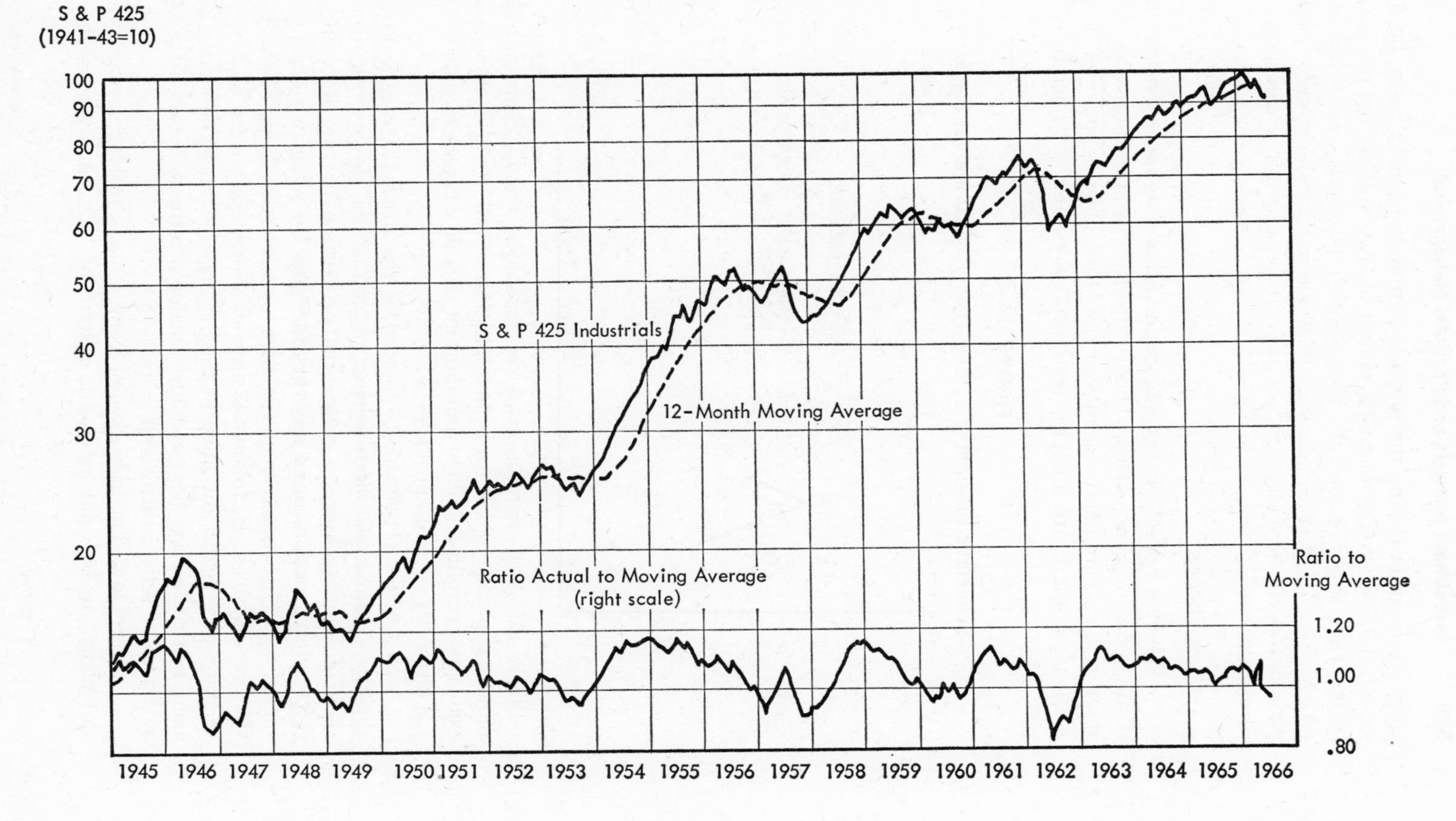

aggregate market during the postwar period, one might easily be whipsawed. That is, stocks might be sold at a lower price than the price at which they are subsequently repurchased. However, individual stocks usually have deeper bear markets than the averages, and sales based on penetrations of moving averages may have a better chance of being profitable.

### Dow Theory

Whereas rate-of-change analysis involves a significant risk of being whipsawed, the famous Dow Theory probably is even more risky in this respect. There are many versions of the Dow Theory—perhaps as many versions as there are analysts who profess to use it. Therefore, it is

FIGURE 14–8

**Schematic Diagram of a "Dow Theory" Bear Market Signal**

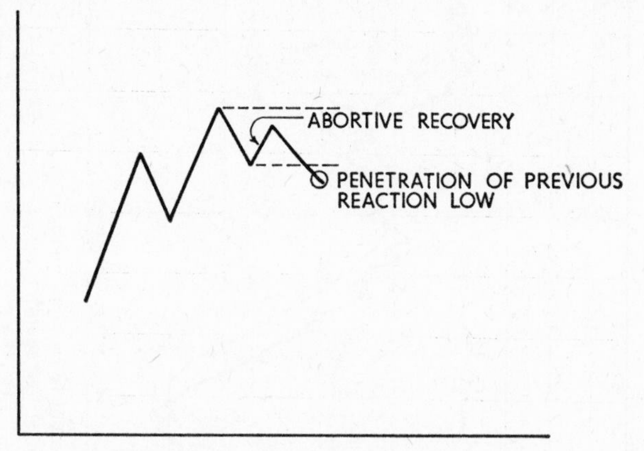


unlikely that any description of the technique would command unanimous acceptance of what it *is*, much less how well it works. Nevertheless, aside from certain relatively unimportant details, what seem to be its essential characteristics can be outlined briefly.

As a major ("primary") uptrend of the market averages proceeds, there are numerous intermediate ("secondary") downward reactions, each of which retraces a substantial proportion of the preceding rise. After each reaction, price recovers and goes on to surpass the previous high. Dow Theorists keep on the alert for a recovery which falls short of the previous high. If, following such an abortive recovery, a downward reaction pierces the low point of the last previous reaction, evidence is at hand that the market has gone into a major ("primary") downtrend. This is illustrated schematically in Figure 14–8.

Most Dow Theorists do not consider a signal of a new primary downtrend to be valid unless the pattern of "descending tops and bottoms" just described occurs in both the Industrial and the Railroad averages.[17] Since the Industrials and Rails usually will not form the pattern simultaneously, the market may have a very sizable decline before a confirmed sell signal is given. Herein lies the principal failing of the technique. In shallow bear markets such as have been experienced during the postwar years, the signal usually comes shortly before the downtrend is about to reverse itself. Even this would not be too bad if the Dow Theory promptly called the bottom of the market. A few percent saved is better than nothing. But to get a signal of a renewed uptrend the whole pattern previously described must repeat itself in reverse. That is, the Industrials and the Rails must each trace out a pattern of *ascending* bottoms and tops. By the time they do, the investor who has acted upon the signals is likely to have been whipsawed.

### Price Chart Patterns

The Dow Theory deals with the market as a whole. But the underlying principle of ascending and descending tops and bottoms as symptoms of primary trend reversals also is applied to individual securities. Technical analysts keep hundreds of price charts on stocks in which they have an interest.

Since individual stocks have much more extensive cyclical swings in price than the market averages, it might be that a Dow-type approach produces generally favorable results. The trouble is that we simply have no statistically significant method of appraising the method. For in addition to ascending and descending tops and bottoms, which are often referred to as "channels" and which are amenable to reasonably precise definitions, technicians refer to "heads and shoulders" formations, "triangles," "rectangles," "flags and pennants," and a host of other configurations with equally exotic names but with quite imprecise definitions. A half-dozen analysts looking at the same chart will rarely give anything near a unanimous interpretation, as shown in Figure 14–9 which is reproduced from a recent *Business Week* article on the subject. We therefore end up testing the performance of the *man* rather than the *method*.

Of course, somewhat the same comments can be made with regard to intrinsic value analysis. Given the same "fundamental" information, numerous evaluations are possible. But the lack of clarity seems particularly troublesome in price chart reading.

---

[17] This insistence on the "confirmation" of a signal by both the Industrial and Railroad averages originally was based on the idea that the Industrials reflect productive processes and the Railroads distributive processes. To have a healthy economy, both types of activities have to be sound. In recent times, the declining importance of railroads in the economy has caused many critics to question the significance of railroad stock prices as a barometer. Some technicians have argued that railroad stock prices, if not a barometer of economic affairs, are at least a barometer of *speculation* in the stock market and therefore are of legitimate interest.

FIGURE 14–9

**The chart that the chartists use . . . . . . and what they say about it**

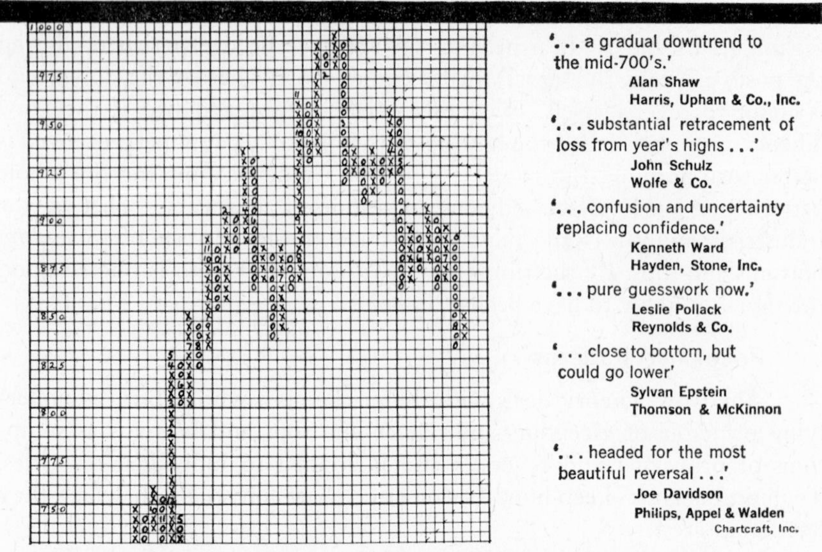


Source: Reprinted from August 13, 1966, issue of *Business Week* by special permission. Copyright © 1966 by McGraw-Hill, Inc.

## Point-and-Figure Charting

Figure 14–9 is an illustration of a "point-and-figure" chart. Of all the techniques described thus far in this chapter, not one attempts to forecast how far a price swing will carry. They all have sought to answer such questions as: Are we in a major uptrend or downtrend? Is the trend about to reverse itself? Point-and-figure analysts ask these questions and one more: What price is likely to be achieved by a particular stock or by the market averages?

There are three basic types of price charts utilized by technical analysts: line charts, bar charts, and point-and-figure charts. On both line and bar charts the horizontal axis represents time—days, weeks, or months—and the vertical axis represents price. On a line chart, which is the type of chart that has been used in this chapter until now, the closing prices of successive time periods are connected by straight lines. On a bar chart, vertical lines are drawn at each time period, with the top and bottom of each bar plotted at the high and low prices for the period. A small horizontal line is drawn across the bar at the closing price level. Bar charts of various market averages are published regularly in the financial sections of the newspapers. Most such charts include a vertical scale at the bottom of the chart against which are drawn bars representing the volume of trading during each time period. Figure 14–10 contains several exam-

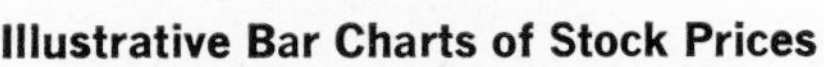

**FIGURE 14–10**

**Illustrative Bar Charts of Stock Prices**

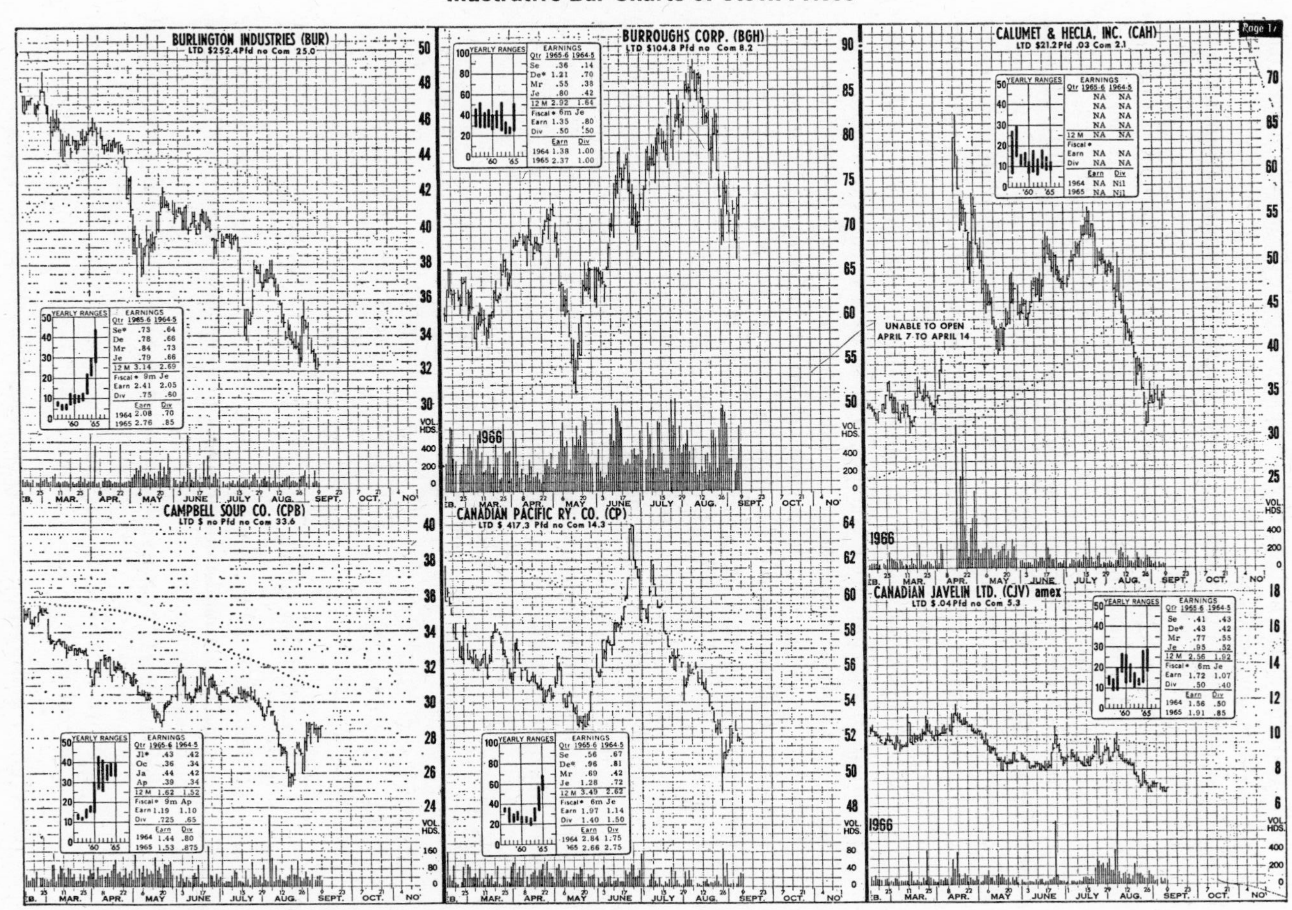


Source: Trendline Corp., *Daily Basis Stock Charts.*

ples of this type of chart, each of which also shows a 200-day moving average of the daily closing price of the stock together with summary data on earnings, dividends, and capital structure.

A point-and-figure chart is quite different in concept from a line or bar chart. First, there is no time scale on such a chart—only a vertical price scale. Second, plots are made on the chart only when price moves up or down by a predetermined amount—typically 1 or 2 points in the case of medium-priced stocks, ½ point in the case of low-priced stocks, and 3 or 5 points for high-priced stocks. In addition to these differences, a point-and-figure chart provides no volume data unless the analyst works out some intricate scheme of his own, such as making his plots in different colors to represent different volumes. Most point-and-figure chartists take volume into account only indirectly.

The purpose of point-and-figure charting is to show a compressed picture of *significant* price changes. The analyst decides in advance that he will consider all movements of, say, ⅞ of a point or less as irrelevant. Thus, if price changes by ½ during a given day, no entry will be made on the chart. On the other hand, if price changes by 3 points in one day, three entries will be made on a 1-point chart. If his time and facilities are limited, the analyst may work only with closing prices, but most serious chartists work with intraday prices as revealed by the ticker tape.

To illustrate the point-and-figure method of charting prices, let us assume that we are constructing a 1-point chart of a particular stock on the basis of the following closing prices (ignoring, for the sake of simplicity, any other intraday price changes):

December 30, 1966—45
January 3, 1967—46⅛
" 4, " —45¾
" 5, " —48⅛
" 6, " —46½
" 9, " —45⅞
" 10, " —47⅛

There are a few simple rules to follow:

1. Put an *X* in the appropriate box each time the price rises to or through a round number, and a *O* each time it falls to or through a round number.
2. Do not allow gaps. If successive closing prices, are, say, 45 and 47, make entries for 45, *46* and 47.
3. Move to a new column each time the *direction* of price *reverses*, except if there is only one entry in a column at the time of reversal.

The resulting point-and-figure chart for these data appears below. The first entry of a new month (46 for January 3, in this example) is designated by a number (1 through 12) instead of by an *X* or *O*, in order to give some idea of time for future reference. The new year also is indicated for this reason. There is no entry for January 4, because price did not change by a sufficient amount. Two entries (47 and 48) are made for January 5, as price went through two round numbers beyond the previous entry. The January 6 entry (47) calls for a new column because the direction of price reversed by more than a point from the previous entry (48)—and so forth.

**FIGURE 14–11**
**Illustration of Point-and-Figure Method of Charting**

| | | | | | | |
|---|---|---|---|---|---|---|
| 50 | | | | | | |
| 49 | | | | | | |
| 48 | X | | | | | |
| 47 | X | 0 | X | | | |
| 46 | 1 | 0 | | | | |
| 45 | X | | | | | |

1967

The point-and-figure analyst examines his charts to discover areas of "congestion," also called "upside resistance areas," "downside support areas," "tops," "bases," "lateral trends," etc. Essentially these are extended narrow horizontal bands of price fluctuation, indicating a standoff between relative supply and demand pressures. Point-and-figure charting technique, by condensing many months of price fluctuation within a limited space, is uniquely designed to reveal such congestion areas. Since a breakout of price from a congestion area very often seems to be symptomatic of a new trend, point-and-figure technique can be said to have merit in making detection easy. Figures 14–12 and 14–13 illustrate upside and downside breakouts from congestion areas. But at this stage the point-and-figure chartist broadens his scope and thereby calls into question the value of his technique.

Having detected what appears to be a new trend, the point-and-figure chartist measures the width of the band of congestion by counting horizontally the number of columns covered. If the price breakout has indicated an uptrend, the "horizontal count" is added to the price level of the congestion area, and the resulting price is said to be the level

## FIGURE 14–12

### Point-and-Figure Upside Breakouts

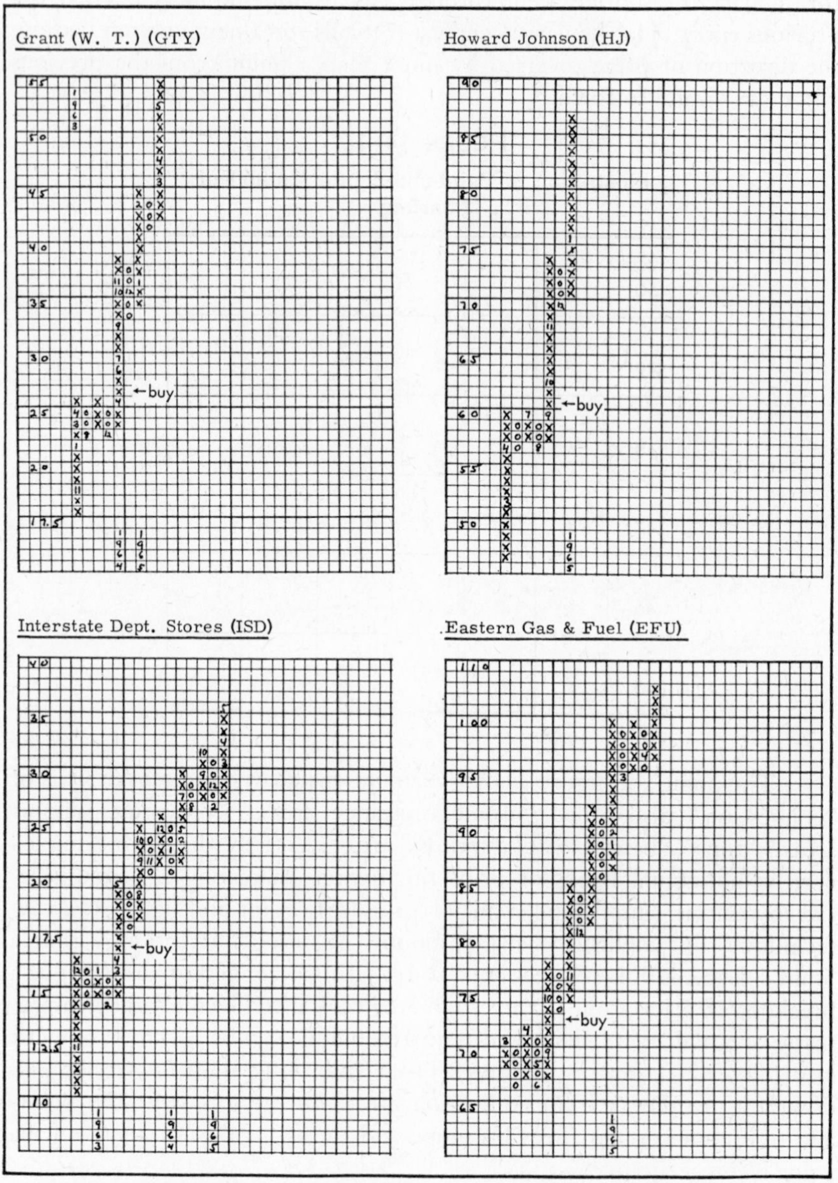

Grant (W. T.) (GTY)

←buy

Howard Johnson (HJ)

←buy

Interstate Dept. Stores (ISD)

←buy

Eastern Gas & Fuel (EFU)

←buy

Source: Chartcraft, Inc.

FIGURE 14–13

Point-and-Figure Downside Breakouts

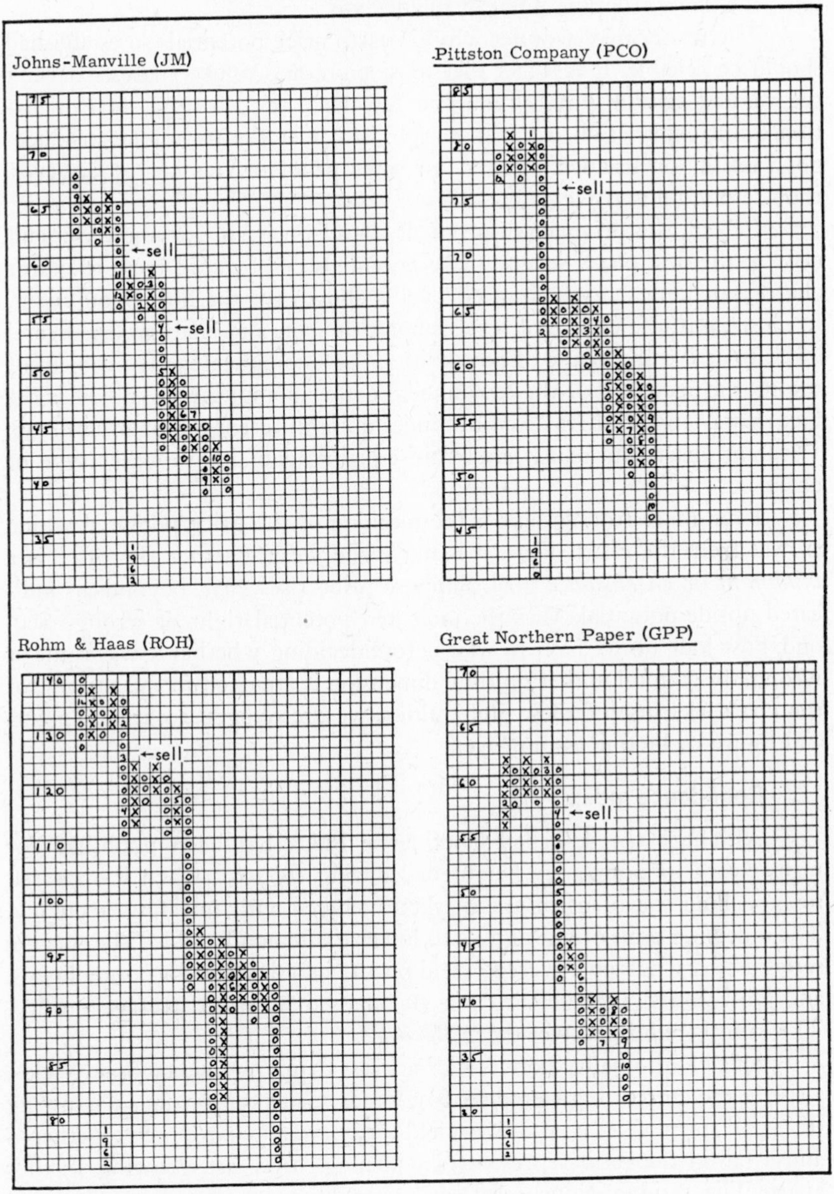

Source: Chartcraft, Inc.

toward which the new uptrend is heading. In a downtrend, the horizontal count is subtracted from the price level of the congestion area to determine the likely stopping point of the decline.

The reader may wonder why on earth price potentials so established should be reliable. It is a fact that most point-and-figure analysts haven't the vaguest notion why, although a few have tried to give an explanation.[18] But explanation or no, they all claim that the technique produces good results on balance. Pressed for some proof of this claim, however, they respond unsatisfactorily.

Indeed, the proof or disproof of the claim is an extremely difficult task. In the first place, several price potentials can be read from the same chart, depending on which price level is chosen for the horizontal count. In most cases, the choice of level is not clear-cut, and analysts use several levels to arrive at a range of possibilities. This complicates the problem of testing the accuracy of the technique. Further complicating testing is the fact that a 1-point chart often produces quite different target prices from a 3-point chart, and many stocks are equally adaptable to either type of chart.

Even more troublesome is the meaning of the price potential which is read from the chart. First, it is not made clear whether the price is a *minimum* or an *absolute* goal. Suppose price rises 50% beyond an indicated upside potential. Was the indicated potential right or wrong? Second, how long do we have to wait before deciding whether it was right or wrong? Bear in mind that no time dimension is attached to the reading of the chart. Because of these ambiguities, we are obliged to regard point-and-figure technique as unproven.

### Confidence Index

Although the so-called Confidence Index has been published for many years, its popularity heightened during 1960–61, when it appeared to be calling the turns of the market averages with uncanny accuracy. The index is a ratio of high-grade to lower grade bond yields. The specific series used are Barron's average yield on 10 highest grade corporate bonds, and Dow-Jones' average yield on 40 bonds of a lower average quality. The ratio is published weekly in *Barron's*.

Since high-quality bond yields are less than low-quality bond yields, a rise in the *ratio* of high-grade to low-grade yields represents a narrowing of "yield spreads"—i.e., the two yield series are coming closer together—and a fall in the ratio represents a widening—they are growing further apart. The ratio obviously has an upper limit of 1.0, or 100%, since high-grade yields should never be expected to exceed low-grade yields. As indicated in Chapter 13, yield spreads on issues of different quality typi-

[18] For example, see J. W. Schulz, *The Intelligent Chartist* (WRSM Financial Service Corp., 1962).

cally widen in periods of economic recession, when investors attach growing importance to safety, and narrow during prosperous periods, when investors become more willing to undertake risks. Therefore, the Confidence Index can be expected to fall during recession and rise during boom times.

Users of the Confidence Index reason that the investors whose actions cause bond yield spreads to change represent so-called "smart money."[19] They are the pros of the investment game, the investment managers in the banks and insurance companies. Since they are so smart, the reasoning continues, they try to anticipate recessions and recoveries rather than wait until economic turns are actually at hand. Therefore, yield spreads should begin to change direction *before* the economy does.

Going further, Confidence Index proponents argue that when smart investors become cautious and shift their relative preference away from lower grade bonds, they shift away from common stocks also. Before long, therefore, their wisdom should be borne out, and common stock prices can be expected to decline. Likewise, when smart investors shift toward lower grade bonds, they also are supposed to shift toward common stocks. And before long, common stock prices will rise. Thus, it is claimed that the Confidence Index can be used as a leading indicator of both the economy and the stock market. Joseph Granville, the foremost exponent of the Confidence Index theory, estimates that the typical lead time of the Index over the stock market is two to four months.

The line of reasoning just outlined seems to us to have several weaknesses. In the first place, while relative demands for high- versus low-quality bonds are doubtless influenced by changing business cycle expectations, the principal buyers of corporate bonds are also very much influenced by considerations of long-term portfolio balance. Therefore, their actions should not be expected to be perfectly attuned to the state of the business cycle. Second, the reasoning makes bond yield spreads seem completely demand determined. It does not allow for any impact on yield spreads of shifts in the relative *supply* of bonds of varying quality. Third, if the reasoning is essentially sound, other ratios of high-quality to lower quality bond yields should move parallel to the Confidence Index. But a comparison of the Confidence Index with a ratio of, say, Moody's Aaa to Baa corporate bond yields reveals many periods of divergent movement.

When all is said and done, of course, "the proof of the pudding is in the eating." If the Confidence Index really has *worked* fairly consistently as a stock market barometer, theory can stand aside or be modified. Figure 14–14 presents a 20-year record of the Confidence Index, in terms of monthly averages of weekly data, compared with the movement of Standard & Poor's 425 Industrials.

---

[19] See J. E. Granville, *A Strategy of Daily Stock Market Timing for Maximum Profit* (New York: Prentice-Hall, Inc., 1960), chap. iii.

## FIGURE 14–14

**Stock Prices and Confidence Index**

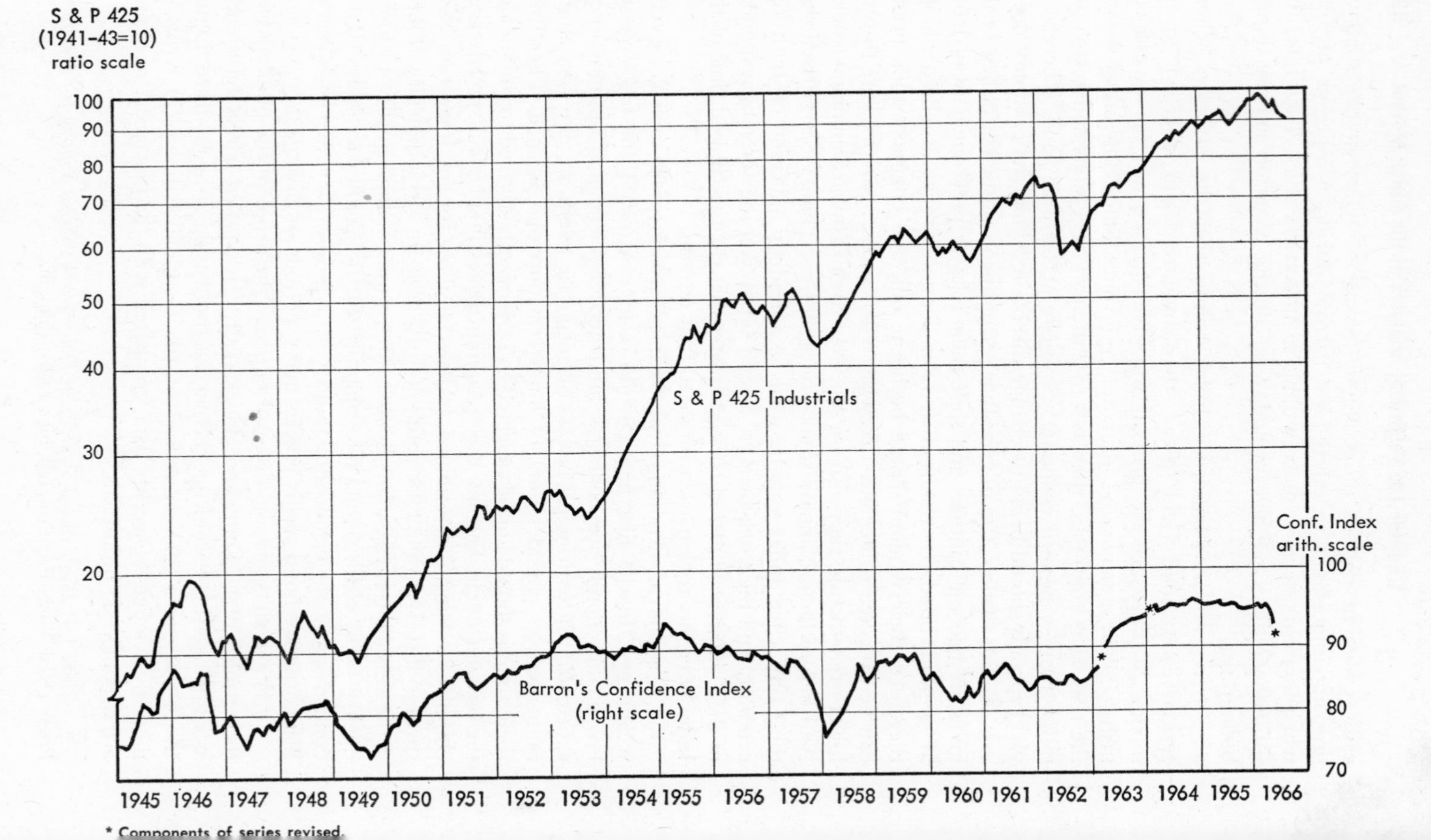


* Components of series revised.

A tally of the hits and misses of the Confidence Index shows that it was a notably good lead indicator of stock prices only at the peaks of 1946 and 1961, and at the trough of 1960. At most other major stock market turning points, the Confidence Index either had a long and erratic lead time over the market or was a coincident or even lagging indicator. Trading on the basis of this indicator certainly would have whipsawed the investor on numerous occasions.[20]

## CRITIQUE AND CONCLUSIONS

Readers of investments texts usually are led to think of stock market technicians in much the same way as scientists think of astrologers. To be perfectly candid, there are some understandable grounds for this attitude. The field of technical analysis has attracted large numbers of self-styled "professionals" who might be better classified as crackpots, or even charlatans.

Even some of the more serious and sophisticated technical analysts sometimes give objective observers cause to be suspicious by making exaggerated claims. Some of them seem to adopt the following line of reasoning: Stock price, volume, and other trading data reflect everyone's knowledge and opinions about everything. Therefore, an independent understanding of investment "fundamentals" is not necessary for intelligent investment decision making. As a matter of fact, a knowledge of the fundamentals tends to impede objective technical analysis. The ideal procedure for a technician is to lock himself in a room with only his charts and market statistics, preferably unidentified as to company or industry to prevent the interference of preconceived notions about prospects for sales, earnings, and dividends.

Thus, we can understand the characterization of technical analysis as "crystal-ball gazing." But we consider this characterization to be rather unfortunate, for it casts aside the good with the bad. The more scholarly and sophisticated technical analyst uses his tools with a proper sense of proportion. Typically, he uses technical analysis as a guide to further study. If a stock looks attractive to him on technical grounds he probes into its "fundamentals." While his decisions may be more heavily influenced by technical considerations, he is certainly not unmindful of earnings growth, of "values," or of the impact of business cycles.

The honest technical analyst knows that his approach will not solve all investment problems. But he also knows that no other single approach will either. He believes his tools can reduce the margin of error.

---

[20] In a recent article ("Bull vs. Bear," *Barron's*, September 12, 1966), Granville appears to have adopted the position that one should not look at the Confidence Index per se but should try to appraise *the reasons* for its movement at any given time in order to interpret its signals. This position seems far more reasonable than the mechanical approach espoused in his earlier writings.

We have examined this belief and found it to be basically correct. We are not enthusiastic about all technical methods, but we do appreciate the merit of some. Moreover, while no single technical indicator can be expected to "work" every time, a useful picture can be expected to emerge when one follows several indicators which appear to be reasonably reliable, particularly in conjunction with the various economic indicators which have been discussed. Indeed, just as a diffusion index of a large number of economic indicators can be created, so too can a composite index of many technical indicators be constructed. There are several commercial investment services which publish such a composite index on a subscription basis. Figure 14–15 shows the "buy and sell signals" that would have been given since 1958 by a composite of 11 technical indicators, weighted as shown. While we do not necessarily endorse the particular choice of indicators on which the chart is based, or the assigned weights,[21] the results are quite intriguing. The only important error

**FIGURE 14–15**

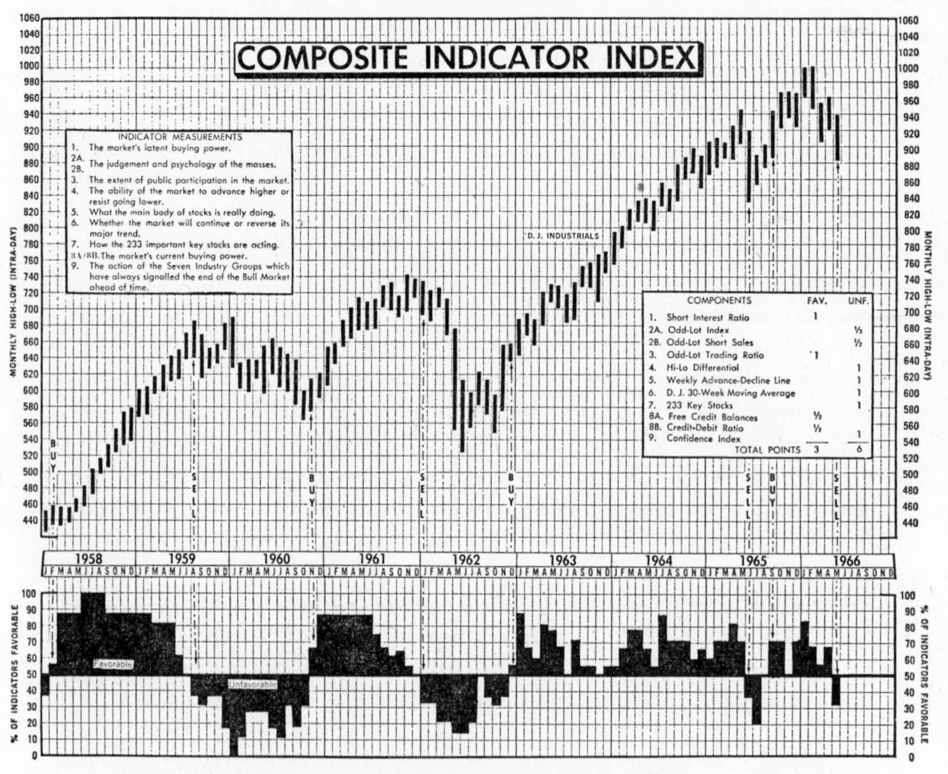


Source: *Indicator Digest*, May 10, 1966. The service began in 1961.

[21] Since the interpretation of whether any particular component of the composite is favorable or unfavorable involves subjective judgments, the method is not as "scientific" as it appears at first glance.

evident in retrospect was the June, 1965, sell signal, because it was shortly followed by a buy signal at a higher price level. The May, 1966, sell signal was followed by a buy signal in January, 1967, at a slightly lower price level.

Furthermore, technical analysis may be on the threshold of new discoveries. Economic statisticians are becoming increasingly interested in the subject of price fluctuations in the stock market. They have been investigating the so-called "random-walk hypothesis." The hypothesis is that stock prices respond quickly to new information as it becomes available and that new items of information enter the marketplace in random fashion. Therefore prices also move in random fashion. Specifically, periodic changes in price—hourly, daily, weekly, or monthly—are independent of the price changes during equivalent preceding periods.

The random-walk hypothesis does not deny the possibility of forecasting stock prices. It accepts the principle that investment analysts who can forecast company earnings and dividends accurately should do a fairly good job of forecasting stock prices.[22] What it denies is that the analysis of *past data*, particularly past market price data, can produce better-than-chance price forecasts.

Most of the statistical investigations of the random-walk hypothesis confirm the belief that successive price changes are generally statistically independent.[23] In our opinion, however, this fact does not necessarily warrant a conclusion that technical analyses of the type which have been described in this chapter are useless as methods of predicting future price movements. Several additional avenues of research appear to be called for. Among them are the following:

1. While successive changes in *absolute* prices may be independent, successive changes in *relative* price may not be. For example, if a particular stock's price shows the sequence 50, 49½, 49, 49½, the direction of change is down, down, up. But suppose that at the same time the S & P Industrial Stock Price Index moves as follows: 90, 90.5, 91, 92.5. *Relative to the market*, the stock's price action is down, down, down, a different sequence from that revealed by absolute price data. Since the concept of relative strength plays so important a role in technical analysis, as indi-

---

[22] In other words, random-walk proponents see stock prices as moving randomly around an earning-power–related trend line. Forecast the earnings *level* and you can forecast the price *level*, they believe; but you cannot forecast the timing of the *swings* around that level by analyzing past data. It is worth noting that from an *economic* point of view a random walk of stock prices around an earnings-related trend line is highly desirable. Such movement implies that rational processes are basically determining stock prices, thus improving the chances that capital is allocated "efficiently." For a discussion of this subject see S. Robbins, *The Securities Markets*. (New York: Free Press of Glencoe, 1966), chap. ii.

[23] See P. H. Cootner (ed.), *The Random Character of Stock Market Prices* (Cambridge, M.I.T. Press, 1964). Also, E. F. Fama, "The Behavior of Stock Market Prices," *Journal of Business*, January, 1965.

cated earlier in this chapter, it would be helpful if students of the random-walk hypothesis would apply some of their tests (serial correlation, analysis of runs, spectral analysis, etc.) to relative price behavior.[24]

2. Price patterns may become significant when interpreted *in conjunction with* other technical phenomena such as volume of trading, short selling, etc.[25] Furthermore, it may be that a statistical combination of technical and "fundamental" data will produce better clues to the future than either one used independently. Some recent work done by Standard & Poor's Corporation[26] suggests that past rates of change of profits offer good clues to subsequent stock price changes. This implies that there is a significant time lag between the market's receipt of fundamental information and the ultimate price response to that information. If so, statistical investigations of the interaction of technical and fundamental data may prove to be very fruitful.

3. Specific technical theories should be tested directly, as a supplement to the indirect approach which has characterized most of the research to date. Essentially, this involves (*a*) establishing trading decision rules which incorporate the premises of a technical theory, (*b*) simulating investment transactions based on these decision rules, and (*c*) observing whether these transactions produce better results, on average, than some sort of random investment policy. Such investigations may well prove that, say, the search for patterns of ascending or descending price tops or bottoms is a waste of time if the analyst is trying to predict future prices. But a proof obtained in this manner probably would be more convincing to investment practitioners than a demonstration that any given period's price change is statistically independent of an equivalent previous period's price change.

We would conclude this chapter by suggesting that the key impediment to investment success is inflexibility of approach. There is no method which is appropriate under all situations. Thus let the intelligent investor discard unjustified biases and consider the possibility of using any and all methods from which there is a theoretical or empirical reason to expect assistance.

## SUGGESTED READINGS

Leo Barnes. *Your Investments*, chap. xxxii. Rye, N.Y.: American Research Council, 1967.

---

[24] For evidence of nonrandom behavior of relative prices, see the dissertation by Levy, *op. cit.*

[25] Evidence of nonrandom price behavior when volume is taken into account has been offered by M. F. M. Osborne in "Some Quantitative Tests for Stock Price Generating Models and Trading Folklore," *op. cit.*

[26] M. Kisor Jr., "Quantitative Approaches to Common Stock Selection," *Business Economics*, Spring, 1966.

George W. Bishop, Jr. *Charles H. Dow and the Dow Theory.* New York: Appleton-Century-Crofts, 1960.

Paul H. Cootner (ed.). *The Random Character of Stock Market Prices.* Cambridge, Mass.: M.I.T. Press, 1964.

Garfield A. Drew. *New Methods for Profit in the Stock Market.* 4th ed. Wells, Vt.: Fraser Publishing Co., 1966.

R. D. Edwards and John Magee, Jr. *Technical Analysis of Stock Trends.* 4th ed. Springfield, Mass.: Stock Trend Service, 1958.

Joseph E. Granville. *A Strategy of Daily Stock Market Timing for Maximum Profit.* Englewood Cliffs, N.J.: Prentice-Hall, 1960.

———. *New Key to Stock Market Profits.* Englewood Cliffs, N.J.: Prentice-Hall, Inc., 1963.

Hsiu-Kwang Wu and Alan Z. Zakon. "Short Term Price Movements and Forecasting," *Elements of Investments: Selected Readings,* Part V. New York: Holt, Rinehart & Winston, Inc., 1965.

Investors Intelligence, Inc. *Encyclopedia of Stock Market Techniques,* Sec. I, "Technical Patterns and Indicators." 2nd rev. ed. Larchmont, N.Y., 1965.

William L. Jiler. *How Charts Can Help You in the Stock Market.* New York: Commodity Research Publications Corp., 1962.

John W. Schulz. *The Intelligent Chartist.* New York: WRSM Financial Service Corp., 1962.

Daniel Seligman. "Playing the Market with Charts" and "The Mystique of Point-and-Figure," *Fortune,* February and March, 1962.

Alexander H. Wheelan. *Study Helps in Point and Figure Technique.* Morgan, Rogers & Roberts, Inc., 1957.

# 15

# FORMULA PLANS

Who shall decide when doctors disagree?
—ALEXANDER POPE

ALTHOUGH the advantages of improved timing are obvious, some investors may feel unable to cope with the business cycle and technical analyses outlined in Chapters 13 and 14. Formula plans are designed to assist such investors. By introducing an element of automaticity into investment programs, formula plans attempt to protect investors from the risks of (*a*) commiting all available funds at peak prices, and (*b*) being frightened out of making commitments when prices are depressed. It should be stressed, however, that the *selection* problem is in no way overcome by a formula plan. Formula plans attempt only to cope with the timing problem. This chapter deals with formula plans which are designed to assist common stock investors. Automatic bond investment programs are discussed in Chapter 18, in connection with commercial bank portfolio management.

## STRICT DOLLAR AVERAGING

Dollar averaging (sometimes referred to as dollar-cost averaging) frequently is described as the simplest type of formula plan. In its purest form, the investor selects a stock or group of stocks and then buys equal dollar amounts per stock at equal time intervals, regardless of the level of the market. Since most stocks move up and down cyclically, usually revolving around a long-term upward trend, the investor will be buying at all points of the cycle—high, "normal," and low. By investing the same amount each time, he will buy more shares when prices are low than when prices are high. This is in contrast to the more typical practice of buying the same number of shares (e.g., 100) each time—or the perhaps even more typical practice of concentrating most purchases in the high phase of a stock price cycle.

The principles underlying dollar averaging can be illustrated by three hypothetical examples, which are deliberately made extreme to highlight the key points. The examples are presented in outline form below, and the section which follows draws conclusions from the examples.

### Examples

*Example 1—Low Volatility, No Growth.* Suppose the investor puts away $500 every six months in a single stock which moves up and down within a narrow horizontal band. Assume his first five purchases are made at prices of 80, 75, 80, 85, 80. His records will appear as follows. (In this example and the two which follow, dividends, brokerage commissions, and taxes are ignored to simplify the exposition. It also is assumed that fractional shares can be purchased.)

| Period | (1) Market Price of Stock | (2) No. Shares Bought with $500 | (3) Total No. Shares Owned | (4) Total Investment | (5) Value of Shares Held (Col. 3 × 1) | (6) Unrealized Profit or Loss (Col. 5 − 4) | (7) Average Cost per Share (Col. 4 ÷ 3) | (8) Average Market Price (Cum. Avg. of Col. 1) |
|---|---|---|---|---|---|---|---|---|
| 1 | $80 | 6.25 | 6.25 | $ 500 | $ 500 | $ 0 | $80.00 | $80.00 |
| 2 | 75 | 6.67 | 12.92 | 1,000 | 969 | − 31 | 77.40 | 77.50 |
| 3 | 80 | 6.25 | 19.17 | 1,500 | 1,534 | + 34 | 78.25 | 78.33 |
| 4 | 85 | 5.88 | 25.05 | 2,000 | 2,129 | +129 | 79.84 | 80.00 |
| 5 | 80 | 6.26 | 31.31 | 2,500 | 2,505 | + 5 | 79.85 | 80.00 |

*Example 2—High Volatility, No Growth.* In this second case, the stock's price falls sharply and then rebounds. The $500 inputs are made at prices of 80, 60, 40, 60, 80. At no point does price exceed the starting level.

| | | | | | | | | |
|---|---|---|---|---|---|---|---|---|
| 1 | 80 | 6.25 | 6.25 | 500 | 500 | 0 | 80.00 | 80.00 |
| 2 | 60 | 8.33 | 14.58 | 1,000 | 875 | −125 | 68.59 | 70.00 |
| 3 | 40 | 12.50 | 27.08 | 1,500 | 1,083 | −417 | 55.39 | 60.00 |
| 4 | 60 | 8.33 | 35.41 | 2,000 | 2,125 | +125 | 56.48 | 60.00 |
| 5 | 80 | 6.25 | 41.66 | 2,500 | 3,333 | +833 | 60.01 | 64.00 |

*Example 3—Low Downside Volatility, Strong Growth.* Finally, assume a situation where the stock has only minor downturns around a strong upward trend: 80, 75, 90, 85, 100.

| | | | | | | | | |
|---|---|---|---|---|---|---|---|---|
| 1 | 80 | 6.25 | 6.25 | 500 | 500 | 0 | 80.00 | 80.00 |
| 2 | 75 | 6.67 | 12.92 | 1,000 | 969 | − 31 | 77.40 | 77.50 |
| 3 | 90 | 5.56 | 18.48 | 1,500 | 1,663 | +163 | 81.17 | 81.67 |
| 4 | 85 | 5.88 | 24.36 | 2,000 | 2,071 | + 71 | 82.10 | 82.50 |
| 5 | 100 | 5.00 | 29.36 | 2,500 | 2,936 | +436 | 85.15 | 86.00 |

## Conclusions from Hypothetical Examples

A mathematical property of all dollar averaging programs is illustrated by the final two columns of each tabulation. At any time after the starting date, the average *cost* per unit of stock purchased is less than the average of the stock's *market prices* on all transaction dates up to that time. This is because more shares are purchased when prices are low than when prices are high, so that more than half the shares are purchased at below-average prices.[1] It follows, therefore, that prices do not necessarily have to be in an uptrend for dollar averaging to produce a profit. This will be made clearer by examining the potential profits or losses under each of the three hypothetical situations, as summarized in the accompanying tabulation.

| | Example 1 Low Volatility—No Growth | | Example 2 High Volatility—No Growth | | Example 3 Low Downside Volatility—Strong Growth | |
|---|---|---|---|---|---|---|
| Period | Price | Profit or Loss | Price | Profit or Loss | Price | Profit or Loss |
| 1 | 80 | 0 | 80 | 0 | 80 | 0 |
| 2 | 75 | − 31 | 60 | −125 | 75 | − 31 |
| 3 | 80 | + 34 | 40 | −417 | 90 | +163 |
| 4 | 85 | +129 | 60 | +125 | 85 | + 71 |
| 5 | 80 | + 5 | 80 | +833 | 100 | +436 |

As would be expected, the first situation produces neither significant gains nor significant losses. The second and third cases, however, present an interesting comparison. In the second case, losses run as high as $417 on an investment of $1,500. But if the investor can weather the storm, he is in the black by period 4, even though the stock's price is still 25% below the starting point. By the time the price is back to where it started, he is ahead $833 on a $2,500 investment.

When prices follow a healthy uptrend, with only occasional modest declines, as in example 3, the dollar averaging investor is far less exposed to risk than in example 2. But his gains are more limited. Furthermore, a weaker growth trend would have produced an even poorer comparison.

Thus, high volatility is a desirable characteristic for stocks to have in a dollar averaging program. Volatility plus growth is an ideal combination.[2] Having illustrated the principles of dollar averaging, we can turn

[1] For the statistically inclined reader, the average *cost* is the harmonic mean of market prices (the reciprocal of the arithmetic mean of the reciprocals of the market prices). A harmonic mean always is lower than an arithmetic mean.

[2] If a choice must be made between 1% greater volatility and 1% greater growth, the choice should be for greater growth. A statistical demonstration of this proposition is contained in J. J. Harrington, Jr., "The Effect of Growth Rates and

now to an examination of more realistic situations than have been considered thus far.

### Results of Dollar Averaging in "The Market"

Assume that $1,000 is invested each year in the stocks comprising the Standard & Poor's 425 Industrial Stock Price Index. (At a later point the impracticality of investing a small sum in a large number of issues will be considered.) To simplify matters, assume the money is invested at midyear at average prices for the year, and that dividends are reinvested at average prices for the year in which received. Finally, assume that brokerage commissions and taxes are paid from other funds.

If such a plan had been started in 1946, the fund could have been liquidated at the end of 1965 at a value of $110,000 (before capital gains taxes). This would represent an annual compounding of the twenty $1,000 inputs at a rate of almost 15%.

**TABLE 15–1**

**Median Results of Dollar Averaging Plans, 1918–65**

| | 5–Year (44 Plans) | 10-Year (39 Plans) | 15–Year (34 Plans) | 20–Year (29 Plans) | 25–Year (24 Plans) | 30–Year (19 Plans) |
|---|---|---|---|---|---|---|
| Median value | $6,900 | $18,700 | $37,600 | $73,000 | $144,000 | $274,000 |
| Implied rate of return | 13% | 12% | 11% | 12% | 12% | 12% |

The reader may wonder what would have happened if the fund were not cashed in at a high point of the market, such as the end of 1965, but at a much lower level, such as the end of 1962. The answer is that it would have been worth $65,000, representing an annual rate of almost 14% on the 17 inputs of $1,000 each.[3]

Of course, these are selected examples. To provide better perspective, results have been calculated for all possible 5-, 10-, 15-, 20-, 25-, and 30-year plans since 1918. For example, plans running from 1918 through 1922, 1919–23, 1920–24, . . . 1961–65 represent all possible five-year plans during the period under study. There are 44 such plans. Likewise, there are 39 possible 10-year plans, 34 15-year plans, etc. Table 15–1 shows the median liquidating values of each type of plan, and the compounded annual rates of return (in round numbers) necessary to build up such values on inputs of $1,000 at the middle[4] of each year.

Cyclical Variability on the Results of Dollar Averaging Programs," *1963 Proceedings* of the Business and Economic Statistics Section of the American Statistical Association.

[3] Note that 15% for 20 years produced $45,000 more than 14% for 17 years. Such is the "magic" of compound interest.

[4] Since inputs are made at midyears, a "five-year plan" is really a four-and-one-half-year plan, etc.

TABLE 15–2

**Dispersion of Results of Dollar Averaging Plans, 1918–65**

| Compound Annual Rate | 5-Year Plans | 10-Year Plans | 15-Year Plans | 20-Year Plans | 25-Year Plans | 30-Year Plans |
|---|---|---|---|---|---|---|
| *Loss Plans:* | | | | | | |
| 10% and up | 2 | 1 | 0 | 0 | 0 | 0 |
| 5.00%–9.99% | 1 | 1 | 0 | 0 | 0 | 0 |
| 0.00 –4.99 | 2 | 0 | 1 | 0 | 0 | 0 |
| *Profit Plans:* | | | | | | |
| 0.01%– 4.99% | 4 | 5 | 6 | 2 | 0 | 0 |
| 5.00 – 9.99 | 10 | 8 | 8 | 11 | 9 | 7 |
| 10.00 –14.99 | 13 | 13 | 12 | 10 | 15 | 12 |
| 15% and up | 12 | 11 | 7 | 6 | 0 | 0 |
| *Total Plans:* | 44 | 39 | 34 | 29 | 24 | 19 |

On an average basis, the results certainly are intriguing. But averages never tell a complete story. It also is necessary to consider the range of deviation around the averages. Table 15–2 shows the distribution of rates of return on the 189 plans covered in the study.

Of the 189 plans, 8 produced losses and 17 produced positive returns of under 5% per annum. Every one of these 25 plans, however, was a plan liquidated during the major bear markets of the early 1930's, 1937, and the early 1940's. The remaining plans—over 85% of all the plans studied—produced results that would be considered good by almost any standards.[5]

## Conclusions Regarding Dollar Averaging

It is not likely that most future programs of "dollar averaging in the averages" will produce quite as good results as most of the hypothetical plans cited above. It is difficult to believe that the years ahead will witness stock market booms similar to those of the 1920's and 1950's, or opportunities to purchase stocks as cheaply as in the 1930's or late 1940's. But while a return of 11%–12% per annum is unlikely, a rate of 7%–9% (including dividends) is not. And at this rate money doubles every 8–10 years. Furthermore, the results herein described were achieved with no security analysis whatsoever—simply investing in the averages. If better-than-average stocks can be selected, the results will be improved.

[5] Other studies demonstrate that the good results of dollar averaging in a broad cross section of companies cannot be attributed simply to remarkably good performances by a small minority of companies. The large majority of companies produced high rates of return. See, for example, W. J. Eiteman and F. P. Smith, *Common Stock Values and Yields* (Ann Arbor: University of Michigan, 1953); and a follow-up, under the same title, by W. S. Eiteman and D. S. Eiteman ( Ann Arbor: University of Michigan, 1962). More recently, a definitive study of rates of return on individual securities has been made by L. Fisher. See his "Outcomes for 'Random' Investments in Common Stocks Listed on the New York Stock Exchange," *Journal of Business*, April, 1965.

Thus, good results can be expected from a dollar averaging program—provided that the following requirements are met:

1. The prices of the stocks purchased should be reasonably volatile, and trending upward.
2. Investments must be made in bad times as well as good—*particularly in bad times*, when stocks are cheap.
3. There must be a minimal risk—economic or psychological—of having to liquidate in a bear market.[6]
4. The contemplated time span of the program should be at least 10–15 years, to allow several market cycles to run their course. This produces a low average cost in relation to potential selling price, even if the plan is started at a time when prices are quite high.
5. The interval between investments should not be too long—at most a year and preferably a good deal less. This avoids the possibility of missing purchase opportunities in bear markets, which are typically of shorter duration than bull markets.

To give a concrete example of what the fulfillment of these conditions might mean to an investor, a hypothetical case can be constructed. A man age 35 begins a program of dollar averaging $500 a year ($10 a week) in a diversified list of common stocks, paying brokerage commissions from other funds. The stocks produce an average dividend yield of 2.4% per annum *after taxes* (3% minus an assumed effective tax rate of 20%), and an average capital gain of 5% per annum. All dividends, after taxes, are reinvested.

If such a program is continued for 30 years, until the man retires at age 65, the value of his accumulated stock portfolio will be $55,000. The components of this value are $15,000 of original principal (the 30 inputs of $500 each), $13,000 of after-tax dividends, and $27,000 of untaxed capital gains. The tax on these gains probably will be about $3,000–$6,000, depending on the effective tax rate of the man at the time he sells the stock and realizes the gains. Thus, the net retirement fund will be about $50,000—from a $10-per-week investment.

Of course, it must be admitted that a man cannot buy a diversified list of stocks for a few hundred or even a thousand dollars a year. But this is not an overwhelming problem. In the first place, if his selection skills are reasonably good, he does not need too much diversification. For example, Table 15–3 shows that the stocks of seven well-known companies can provide an investor with a participation in 25 different industries. Second, even if he does need substantial diversification, the investor can obtain it indirectly by purchasing investment company shares. These are discussed in Chapter 17.

---

[6] Indeed, it probably is most desirable to liquidate a fund *gradually*, thus minimizing the possibility of selling the bulk of one's holdings at low prices.

TABLE 15–3

**Industry Diversification of Seven Well-Known Companies**

*Key to Companies*

1 *General Electric*
2 *Minn. Mining & Mfg.*
3 *Intl. Tel. & Tel.*
4 *Celanese*
5 *Shell Oil*
6 *Union Carbide*
7 *Textron*

| | 1 | 2 | 3 | 4 | 5 | 6 | 7 |
|---|---|---|---|---|---|---|---|
| Aerospace | 1 | 2 | 3 | .. | .. | 6 | 7 |
| Atomic energy | 1 | .. | .. | .. | .. | 6 | .. |
| Auto parts | .. | 2 | .. | .. | .. | .. | 7 |
| Building materials & equip. | 1 | 2 | .. | 4 | .. | 6 | 7 |
| Chemicals | 1 | 2 | .. | 4 | 5 | 6 | 7 |
| Drugs & cosmetics | .. | .. | .. | .. | .. | 6 | .. |
| Electrical equip. & products | 1 | 2 | 3 | .. | .. | .. | .. |
| Electronics | 1 | .. | 3 | .. | .. | 6 | 7 |
| Fertilizers | .. | .. | .. | .. | 5 | .. | .. |
| Finance | 1 | .. | 3 | .. | .. | .. | .. |
| Home furnishings | .. | 2 | .. | .. | .. | 6 | 7 |
| Insurance | .. | .. | 3 | .. | .. | .. | .. |
| Machinery | 1 | .. | .. | .. | .. | .. | 7 |
| Metals | .. | .. | .. | .. | .. | 6 | 7 |
| Natural gas | .. | .. | .. | 4 | 5 | .. | .. |
| Office equipment | 1 | 2 | .. | .. | .. | .. | .. |
| Oil | .. | .. | .. | 4 | 5 | .. | .. |
| Paper | .. | 2 | .. | 4 | .. | .. | .. |
| Plastics | .. | 2 | .. | .. | 5 | 6 | .. |
| Radio–TV | 1 | .. | 3 | .. | .. | .. | .. |
| Rail equipment | 1 | .. | .. | .. | .. | .. | .. |
| Soaps | .. | .. | .. | .. | .. | 6 | .. |
| Steel & iron | .. | .. | .. | .. | .. | 6 | 7 |
| Synthetic fibers | .. | .. | .. | 4 | .. | 6 | .. |
| Tires & rubber | .. | .. | .. | .. | 5 | 6 | .. |

Source: Standard & Poor's Corp., *The Outlook*, October 3, 1966.

## MODIFIED DOLLAR AVERAGING

Strictly speaking, a dollar averaging investor should put equal amounts of money into each of a fixed list of stocks at the same time each year. For example, every January and July a man might purchase $500 worth of each of five different issues, for a total annual investment of $5,000. However, several lines of departure from so straightforward an approach may be considered.

1. The man might invest a constant $2,500 semiannually, but continuously vary the issues purchased. The five purchased one year may be different from those purchased previously. Indeed, at any particular time he might put the whole $2,500 into only one issue. Or he might even *sell* some overpriced stocks and replace them (reinvesting any capital gains) with more attractive issues. This type of modification of strict dollar averaging is designed to take advantage of any ability he may have to determine the *relative* values of different stocks, while at the same time

refraining from making any judgments about the state of *the market as a whole.*[7]

2. The man might buy the same issues each time he invests but vary the timing of the investments during the year. For example, a decision may be made to invest $5,000 each year. But *within* the year purchases may be geared to the current level of the market relative to an estimate of what the average level will be for the full year. If any portion of the year's allocation remains uninvested at year-end, it automatically would be invested at that time.

3. Variations (1) and (2) can be combined.

4. Even greater flexibility can be built into variation (2) by allowing the total annual common stock investment to vary on the basis of a relatively long-term evaluation of the market. Thus, a broad commitment can be made to invest an *average annual amount* of $5,000 for a period of 20 years. But the pace at which the investments are made can be accelerated or decelerated as the market fluctuates above and below an estimated trend line. In considering this type of modification of dollar averaging, an understanding of ratio-type formula plans is essential.

## RATIO FORMULAS

While dollar averaging calls for continuous purchases of stocks, ratio-type formula plans call for an alternation of investments between stocks and bonds (or other "defensive" holdings). They are designed to force the investor to act counter to prevailing market psychology—to switch from stocks into "bonds" when others anxiously are buying stocks, and to switch back into stocks when others anxiously are selling them. Advocates of these plans think it improbable that the average investor—or even the professional—will recognize the market's peaks and troughs at the time they are occurring. Accordingly, stock sales are made gradually as prices rise, and purchases are made as prices fall. Or purchases can be made constantly, but at a slower rate as prices rise and at a faster rate as prices fall. The "formula" specifies in advance the *rules* by which the timing and amounts of transactions *automatically* will be carried out. The essential difference between one plan and another lies in the varying characteristics of the rules.

As with dollar averaging, the investor should contemplate a long-term program encompassing several price cycles. Again, the stocks purchased should be reasonably volatile and should be in a secular uptrend. The question arises, however, as to the form in which funds should be kept at times when they have been shifted out of stocks.

Most writers suggest that the defensive portion of the portfolio

[7] For an interesting discussion see George E. Rejda, "The Role of Dollar Averaging in the Common Stock Investment Operations of Life Insurance Companies," *Journal of Insurance*, December, 1962.

should be in high-grade bonds, for two reasons. First, such securities provide a good, and safe, current income. Second, bond prices are likely to be falling (interest rates rising) during periods of prosperity, at which time stock prices are likely to be rising. The reverse is likely to be true during recessions—bond prices usually rise while stock prices fall. Thus, bonds will tend to be bought at falling prices as stocks are sold at rising prices; and bonds will tend to be sold at rising prices as stocks are bought at falling prices—an ideal transaction pattern within the framework of a formula plan.

**FIGURE 15–1**
**Stock Prices and Interest Rates**

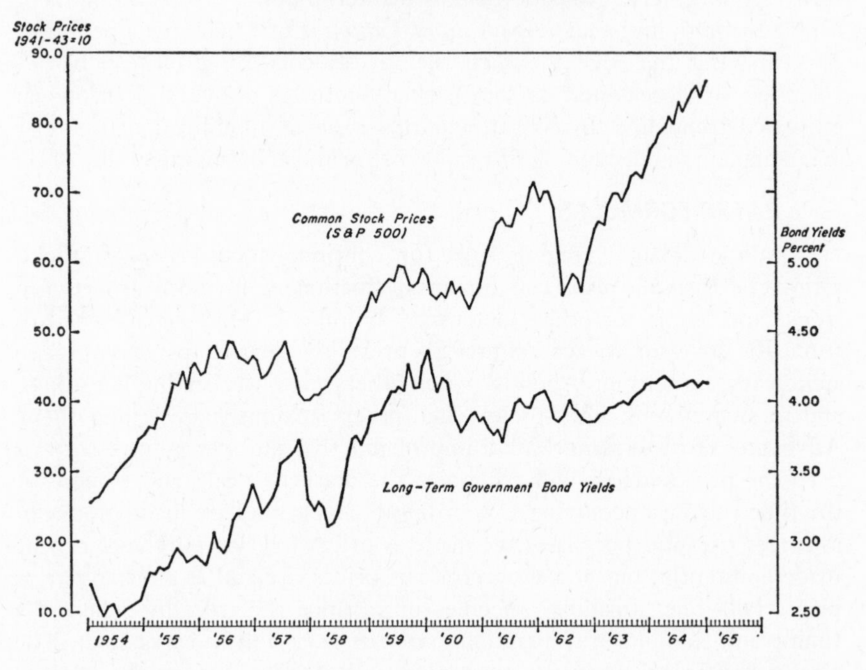


Frequently, however, this complementarity of stock and bond prices is present more in theory than in fact. For stock price cycles are by no means perfectly integrated with interest rate, or bond price, cycles. As shown in Chapter 13, turning points of interest rates tend to lag behind turning points of stock prices. Thus, shifts between stocks and bonds occasionally may result in losses being taken on the bond transactions. Figure 15–1 shows, for example, that the 1956–57 stock price decline occurred while interest rates were rising strongly—i.e., bond prices were falling. The same thing happened again in 1966 (not shown on the chart). Accordingly, it may be advisable for a small investor to keep the defensive portion of his portfolio in a bank savings account. Certainly it would be a lot easier.[8]

Turning to an examination of the rules characterizing various ratio-type formula plans, there are two broad categories of plans—constant ratio and variable ratio. It frequently is implied that such plans are useful only in the management of an existing fund of money and not for the gradual accumulation of a fund. This is not correct. However, comprehension of the principles underlying the two categories of ratio plans is facilitated by discussing their application to *existing* funds. Therefore, in the first two of the following sections it will be assumed that no additions to principal are made once a plan is started. In a later section, this assumption will be dropped.

## Constant Ratio Plans

*Principles.* Constant ratio plans are the simplest of the ratio-type formula plans. The investor decides to keep a fixed percentage relationship between the stock and defensive components of his portfolio. When stock prices rise, causing the stock proportion to get larger than the established norm, stocks are sold and "bonds" are purchased in sufficient amounts to restore the desired proportions. Likewise, when stock prices fall, "bonds" are sold and stocks are purchased until the proportions are restored.

A constant ratio plan is particularly suited to an investor who hesitates to make any market forecasts other than that his stocks will trend upward and will fluctuate in price. However, an additional bit of forecasting is necessary at the outset of even this simple type of plan, when a specific stock percentage must be chosen as the norm. If the price uptrend is expected to be steep, or if the plan is started at what is believed to be a low point of a market cycle, the investor probably will choose a higher stock percentage than if he expects a more shallow trend or if he is starting the plan at a high point of the cycle. Other considerations involved in the choice of a stock percentage are the investor's need for current income as opposed to capital gain and the degree of risk that he is able to undertake.

Having decided what distribution to keep between stocks and defensive holdings, a rule must be set as to when transactions will be made to restore these percentages. After all, the stock market fluctuates constantly, and each fluctuation throws the portfolio out of balance. Yet it would be unduly time-consuming and wasteful of brokerage commissions to reshuffle the portfolio continuously.

If a shallow trend seems likely, one can restore the desired ratio

---

[8] For a more extensive discussion of the effects of alternative methods of investing the defensive portion, see R. R. Dince, "Portfolio Income: A Test of a Formula Plan," *Journal of Financial and Quantitative Analysis*, September, 1966.

every time prices rise or fall by, say, 5%. Or, if a sharper uptrend seems more likely, the ratio might be restored each time prices rise by 10% or fall by 5%.

A word is in order about the meaning of the phrase "each time prices rise or fall." If the stocks held in the portfolio are so diversified that they move like the market averages, it makes no difference whether the signal for a transaction is given by a movement of a market average or of the value of the portfolio itself. But if the holdings do not move closely with the averages, a decision has to be made as to which set of prices will give the transaction signals.

*Examples.* To illustrate the results that might be achieved with a constant ratio plan, two hypothetical plans have been constructed. One was started in January, 1946, and one in January, 1956. Each began with $10,000. A 75% stock proportion was set as the constant ratio target, to be invested in the Standard & Poor's Industrial Stock Price Index. The balance of the portfolio was assumed to be kept in a savings account (hereafter referred to as "cash").

The 75%–25% stock-cash distribution was restored each time the monthly average of the S & P Index rose 10% or fell 5% from the price which triggered the previous transaction. (This rule produced an average of two transactions a year.) All stock transactions were assumed to take place at the average index value of the month following the signal. No brokerage commissions, dividends, or taxes were taken into account.

To provide some basis for evaluating the performance of these constant ratio plans, two comparison portfolios were constructed. These were assumed to begin on the same dates as the constant ratio plans, with the same $10,000 divided the same way—$7,500 in the S & P Industrials and $2,500 in cash. But no further transactions were assumed to take place thereafter. The cash portion of the portfolio remained a constant $2,500, and the value of the $7,500 stock investment fluctuated up and down in direct proportion to the S & P index. These comparison portfolios can be labeled "buy-and-hold plans."

Figure 15–2 is designed to portray the most relevant aspects of the portfolio comparisons.[9] In the left-hand panel, the results of the 1946 plan are shown through 1955. In the right-hand panel, the 1956 plan is shown through 1964. At the top of each panel are shown the monthly average values of the stock portions of the constant ratio (solid line) and buy-hold (dashed line) plans. In the middle of each panel are the monthly cash holdings of each type of plan. The stock and cash values are then summed up, and at the bottom of each panel the total value of the constant ratio

---

[9] To prevent the chart from becoming unduly complex, one aspect of performance is omitted—comparative current income from dividends and interest. Inclusion of this aspect would not have altered significantly the overall conclusions.

**FIGURE 15–2**

**Comparisons of Hypothetical 75%–25% Constant Ratio Plans with Buy-and-Hold Plans**

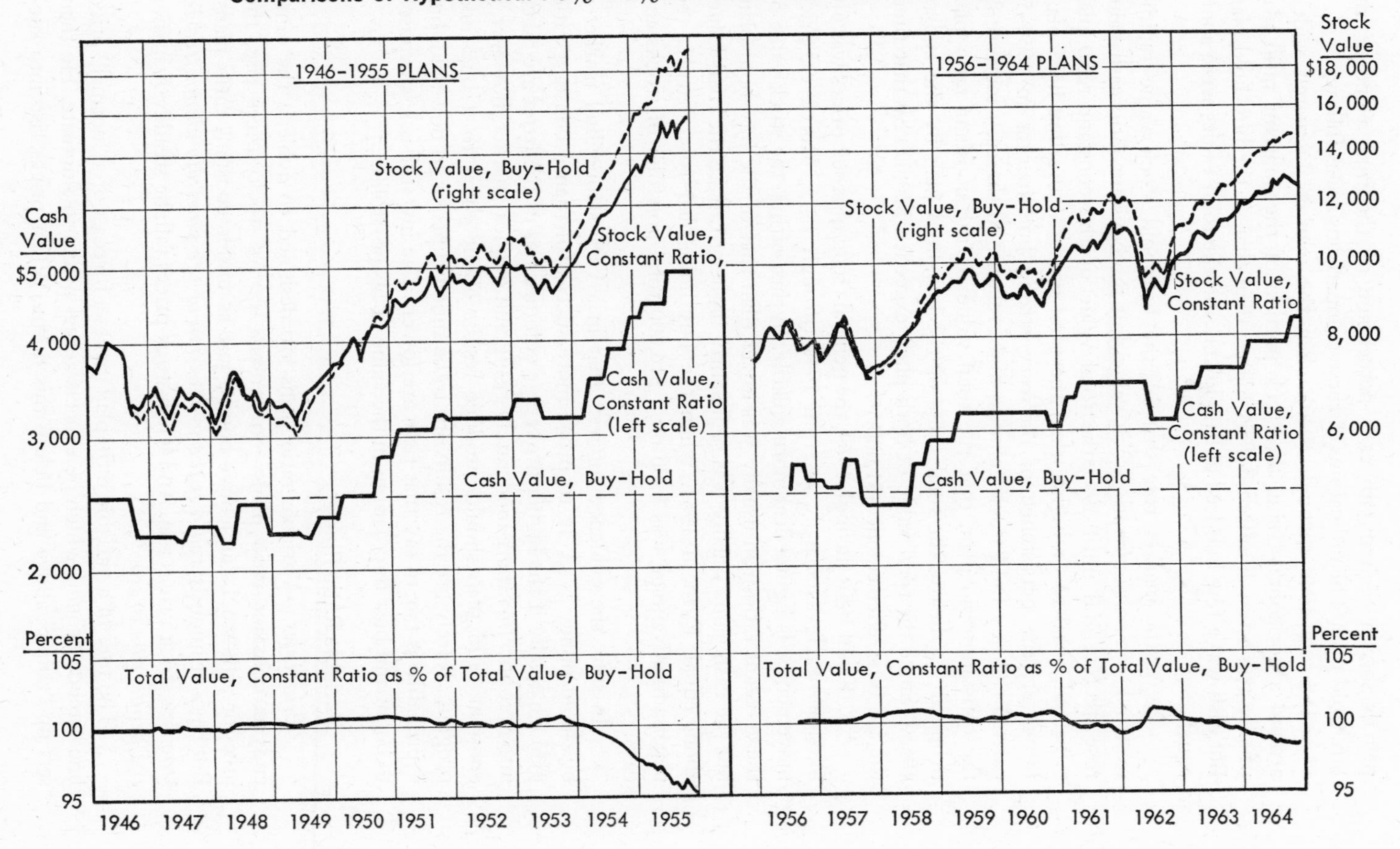

plan is shown each month as a percentage of the total value of the buy-hold plan. The indications of these comparisons are as follows:

1. From 1946 through 1949, when the market fluctuated widely around a horizontal trend, the stock portion of the constant ratio plan usually was a few hundred dollars higher than that of the buy-hold plan. But cash was a few hundred dollars lower, and the total values were about equal.

2. As the market rose sharply, the buy-hold stock value rapidly overtook the constant ratio stock value. But the constant ratio cash value rose steeply, and until 1953 the total value of the constant ratio plan remained equal to or higher than the total value of the buy-hold plan. However, the persistence of the very strong bull market in 1954–55 carried the buy-hold stock value so high, relative to the cash increase of the constant ratio plan, that the total value of the constant ratio plan dropped 5% below the total value of the buy-hold plan by the end of 1955. (Since the total value of both plans exceeded $20,000 by that time, the 5% difference equaled $1,000.)

3. From 1956 through 1964, the general trend of stock prices was up, but not nearly as sharply as from 1949 through 1955. Moreover, price movement was a good deal more volatile. In this setting, the stock value of the constant ratio plan usually was lower than that of the buy-hold plan, but the cash value usually was sufficiently higher to make the total values about equal. Even in 1964, when the buy-hold plan rose sharply, the maximum advantage was $300 on a $16,000 total portfolio of stocks and cash.

In sum, the evidence suggests that in a very strong bull market a buy-hold policy is likely to prove more successful than a constant ratio plan, especially if the higher brokerage commissions of the latter are taken into account. In a more moderately rising and cyclical market, however, a constant ratio plan should produce results about equal to a buy-hold program. Rarely are the results apt to be much superior to buy-hold, but it probably is fair to say that risks are lower. The investor is less exposed to boom and bust fluctuations in the value of his portfolio.

### Variable Ratio Plans

*Principles.* Variable ratio plans are designed to achieve the same ends as constant ratio plans—only more so. As stock prices rise, the investor sells stocks and buys bonds, just as under constant ratio plans. But he continuously *reduces the proportion of the portfolio committed to stocks* as stock prices rise. And when stock prices fall, he steadily *increases the proportion in stocks.*

The user of a variable ratio plan makes a forecast of a "normal" price line (trend) around which he expects actual prices to fluctuate. He then sets up "zones" above and below this norm. When prices rise into successively higher zones, he progressively reduces the stock proportion of his fund to predetermined amounts. Likewise, he increases the proportion as prices fall into successively lower zones. For example, when prices are normal—i.e., right on the estimated trend line—a 50% stock percentage may be required under the plan. Price zones 1, 2, 3, etc., above normal may call for stock percentages of 40, 30, 20, etc., respectively. And zones 1, 2, 3, etc., below normal may call for stock percentages of 60, 70, 80, etc.

It also is customary to employ a so-called "halfway rule," which does not permit any stock purchases above the trend line nor sales below the trend. Using the preceding example, suppose prices have risen to zone 3 above trend and the investor has sold enough stock to reduce his stock proportion to 20%. Now suppose that prices fall back to zone 2 above trend, which is supposed to have 30% in stocks. Under the halfway rule, stocks will *not* be purchased to bring the proportion up to 30%. They will not be purchased, in fact, until prices have fallen to zone 1 *below* trend, and at that time sufficient purchases will be made to bring the porportion up to 60%.

Employment of the halfway rule has two purposes. First, it prevents overtrading in narrowly fluctuating markets when prices jiggle up and down between only two zones. (Further rules may be employed to prevent overtrading if prices keep fluctuating between the two zones immediately above and below trend.) Second, the halfway rule is designed to take advantage of the market's usual momentum. If the trend line has been estimated properly, once a downswing of prices begins from a high zone the odds are in favor of it continuing down with only minor reversals. By delaying transactions in the manner described, the investor should be able to improve his results.[10]

Variable ratio plans obviously involve far more long-term forecasting than constant ratio plans. One must have a clear idea of what price level is normal at any given time, and a clear idea of the probable range of fluctuation around normal. Without reasonable estimates of these data it is not possible to establish a useful schedule for varying the stock proportions. If the trend line or variations about trend are estimated improperly, the result may be too rapid a buildup of stocks to a 100% position or too rapid a liquidation to zero. There also might be long periods of total inactivity during which the investor might be tempted to abandon the plan entirely. These possibilities are in marked contrast to a constant ratio plan, which never puts the investor into an all-or-nothing stock position and which rarely immobilizes the portfolio for long periods. In other words, a constant ratio plan protects the investor against the consequences

---

[10] On the other hand, if the zones are made too wide—for example, each zone representing a 10% price change—the halfway rule usually will do more harm than good. This is so because most bear markets are relatively shallow, and the account will be immobilized in all except the more drastic price swings.

of an erroneous trend forecast, while a variable ratio plan produces greater profits from a correct forecast.[11]

*Trend Estimation.* Many approaches have been applied to the problem of forecasting a normal stock price trend. The simplest is to fit a line to historical data, either by inspection or by a statistical procedure,[12] and then to project this past trend into the future. The simplicity of this approach is apparent. The fault is, perhaps, less apparent. It revolves around the fact that stock prices swing both in short cycles of approximately the length of a business cycle and in long cycles of as much as a decade or more. This means that the growth rate of a fitted trend line will be largely a function of which past years are chosen for the fitting. For example, a logarithmic trend fitted to the Standard & Poor's Industrials for the years 1909–65 has a growth rate of about 5%. The years 1947–65, on the other hand, exhibited a growth rate of 11%. And the growth rate in 1957–65 was 8%. If a historical trend projection is employed at about the time a new long cycle is beginning, the formula will be hopelessly improper. This is exactly what happened to many formula plans started in the early 1950's. They were based on the experience of the previous 25 years or so and called for liquidation of stocks in 1954 or 1955 because prices seemed much too high.

A practical way of improving the results of the trend-fitting procedure is to utilize as a trend line a moving average of prices. Normal price in any year is made equal to an average of prices in the past *X* years. Each year the average is recalculated, adding the price of the year just passed and dropping the price of the first year of the period. If the price of the past year is higher than the price of the first year, the average will rise. Thus a moving average will change as prices change,[13] and its employment avoids the possibility of the formula losing touch with present market realities.

The trouble with a moving average is that if the time period on

---

[11] We have not discussed one version of a variable ratio plan which requires little forecasting. It is a "constant dollar" plan. Under this scheme the investor decides to keep a specified *number of dollars* in stocks at all times, with the balance of the fund in defensive form. As prices rise (or fall) he sells (or buys) enough stocks to reduce (or raise) the dollar value to the specified amount. The similarity to the constant ratio type plan is apparent. The difference is that as stocks are sold during the price rise the constant dollar *amount* of stocks becomes a progressively smaller *percentage* of the total portfolio, and vice versa as stock prices fall. There are two drawbacks to constant dollar plans: (1) Where the program involves periodic additions to the fund (see p. 551 below), the constant dollar target is in need of continuous revision. (2) Although the percentage of the portfolio represented by stocks properly falls as prices rise and rises as prices fall, the actual percentage achieved is more a matter of chance than of predetermination by the investor.

[12] For example, fitting a least squares line to logarithms of the price data.

[13] See p. 518 of Chapter 14 for an example of moving average calculation procedures.

which it is based is too long, it will be little better than the long-term trends described above. On the other hand, if it is too short, it merely will trace the short-term price cycle and will not be a very adequate "norm."

Many authorities prefer a less mechanical method of estimating trend and utilize instead an "intrinsic value" calculation. For example, one can estimate a normal price-earnings ratio for the market averages, or a normal dividend yield, or normal ratio of price to book value. Our preferred approach to stock price evaluation was presented in detail in Chapter 5.[14] Zones of fluctuation can be built around the trend line which results from such a procedure. Of course, a formula plan based on a calculation of the market's value entails the risk that one's ideas about value, even if sound, may depart quite sharply from general opinion for a period of many years. In such case, the portfolio will be immobilized much of the time.

With regard to estimating the range of fluctuation around trend, the obvious beginning point would be an examination of the historical record. But the record must be interpreted and adapted in light of the probable depth and duration of future economic recessions and in the light of the likely state of public psychology.

### Application of Ratio Plans when a Fund Is Being Accumulated

It was noted earlier that people frequently imply incorrectly that ratio plans are pertinent only to the management of an existing fund and not to the gradual accumulation of a fund. As a matter of fact, the foremost experimenters with such plans during the early 1950's were college endowment fund trustees. These investors obviously anticipate cash inflows and outflows during the life of a plan.

There is no reason why the same set of ratios that are used to manage an existing fund cannot be used for an accumulating fund as well. For example, suppose the desired stock percentage at a given level of prices is 60% while the actual percentage is 50%. Instead of liquidating defensive holdings to buy stocks, one can invest *new money* in both stocks and bonds in such proportions as will produce an overall 60–40 split.

Of course, if additions to and deletions from the original amount of investment are contemplated during the life of a ratio plan, the likely timing of the cash flow should be considered in setting the target stock percentages. For example, if additions are just as likely to be made at low points of market cycles as at high points, the same percentages can be used as if no additions are contemplated. But if it seems more realistic to assume that additions will be made most often during bull markets when, as is

[14] For a formula plan based on the relation of stock prices to gross national product, see R. R. Dince, "Another View of Formula Planning," *Journal of Finance*, December, 1964.

often the case, the investor's income rises, it might be wiser to set lower stock percentages.

The *dollar averaging* investor also can build a formula into his program, designed to have him hold back some of his investable funds at high points of the market and accelerate his purchases at low points. While it may be anomalous to describe as dollar averaging anything other than the investment of a constant dollar amount at constant intervals, the concept is clear enough. (It was described above in the section entitled "Modified Dollar Averaging.") In operation it might take something like the following form.

Suppose the investor decides that he can put $500 into stocks twice a year and, if the market drops sharply, that he can draw down his bank account to put in up to $1,000 more. Once having drawn down his account by that much, however, he must at some point replace the withdrawal. Given these conditions, he might build a formula around the "band of value" which was developed in Chapter 5. This band of value is reproduced here as Figure 15–3, together with the superimposition of

**FIGURE 15–3**

**A Modified Dollar Averaging Program**

(Based on a Value Analysis of S & P 425 Industrials)

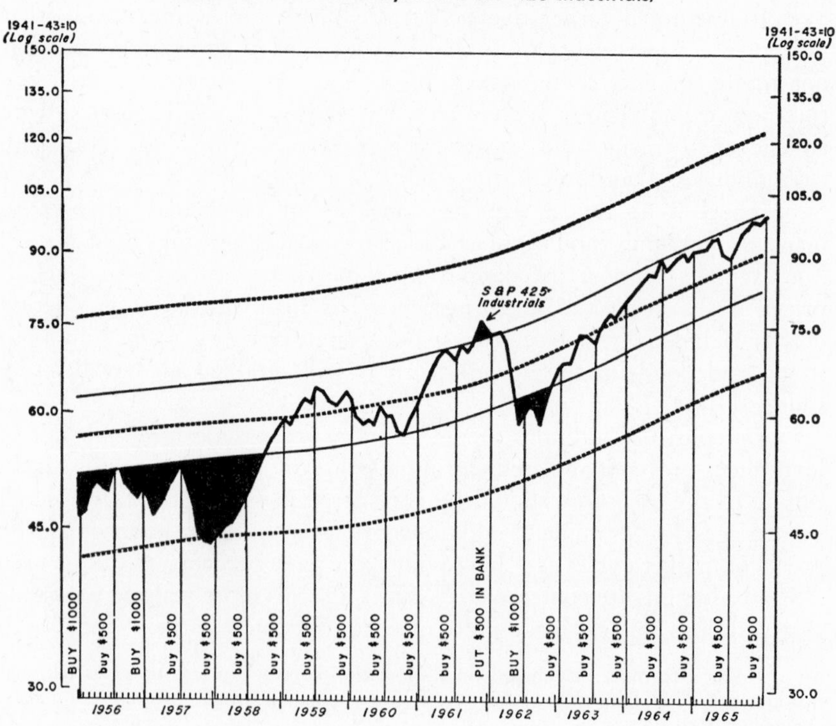

another band representing a 10% swing above and below the mean value.

The formula could be that every January and July a $500 stock purchase will be made, *provided that the S & P Index is within the inner band of value* at the time. If, at any January or July, the price index is below the value band, he will invest the regular $500 *plus* an additional $500 taken from the bank. (But this extra investment only can be made twice unless a replacement of funds is made during an intervening period.) On the other hand, if at any January or July the price index is above the value band, he will invest nothing in stocks but will, instead, put that period's $500 into his bank account. This either will replace previously withdrawn funds or provide the basis for additional accelerated investments at a low point of prices. The amounts of the periodic investments under such a formula, for the years 1956–65, are shown on the chart.

## CONCLUSIONS

In a sharply rising stock market with infrequent and shallow downward movements, such as the market of 1949–55, the investor with an existing accumulation of capital probably would be best off buying a diversified list of reasonably valued stocks and just holding on. The investor in the process of accumulating a fund, in such a market, probably would be best off with a strict dollar averaging approach or with a modification allowing flexibility in choice of issues.

It may well be, however, that the stock market of the years ahead will not resemble that of 1949–55, when a situation of gross undervaluation was being corrected. The subsequent pattern of a more moderate growth rate punctuated by frequent and pronounced declines may be a better precursor of the future. If such a pattern occurs, cyclical timing will be crucial to the investor, and formula plans other than strict dollar averaging offer one solution to the problem.

To be sure, at the outset of this chapter we hypothesized an investor who feels unable to undertake the business cycle and technical analyses necessary for sound, unemotional timing decisions. If he is, indeed, thus unqualified, he very well may be unable to make the decisions that must underlie a successful ratio-type formula plan or a complex version of dollar averaging. Such plans, after all, do require an initial forecast of the long-term trend of stock prices and the probable amplitude of shorter-term fluctuations around trend. They also require the investor to set target stock-bond proportions that are consistent with his overall market forecast and with his personal needs for income, safety, etc. While it is hoped that satisfactory guidelines have been provided in this text for the initial forecast, and while it should be recognized that the adaptation of portfolio policy to personal needs is a problem which must be faced in any event, still it would seem that a straightforward dollar averaging approach may be best for some investors.

What about ratio-type formula plans or complex versions of dollar averaging for highly skilled, even professional, investors? Most students of the subject agree that if an investor is skillful enough to construct a very successful formula plan, he does not need a plan to begin with. The essence of a formula plan, it is stressed, is to commit oneself to a predetermined course of action in an environment that constantly is subject to change. In a changing environment, should not the skillful investor maintain a high degree of flexibility? To cap the argument, it is noted that most of the early pioneers in formula planning eventually scrapped the idea because their initial assumptions about stock prices proved to be too conservative and the resulting formulas required that the stock portion of their portfolios be reduced far too early in the bull market.

Perhaps a more appropriate position is somewhere between the all-out advocates and the all-out critics of formula plans for skilled investors. One can adopt a formula plan but maintain flexibility by periodically reviewing the assumptions and altering the plan if necessary. Indeed, the plan may have to be altered occasionally for reasons other than a change in the underlying assumptions. For example, tax considerations might make profit taking inappropriate at certain times.

In our opinion, formula planning does have some singular advantages. First, it forces the investor to spell out his assumptions and to translate the assumptions into policy. Far too many so-called "flexible" investors in reality operate with no policy at all. Their investments are not flexible but haphazard.

When assumptions and policies are spelled out, moreover, an objective evaluation of the investor's performance is facilitated. Success can be judged best by comparing performance against goals. And with a clear statement of policies and an objective evaluation of performance, the investor is in a better position to learn from his own mistakes and to take action to correct the mistakes.

Furthermore, formula plans reduce the danger of inaction due to an inability to make up one's mind, and also the opposite danger of acting too hastily on the basis of the temporary emotionalism of the times. Even professional investors are exposed to these dangers, with the first being particularly present where decisions are in the hands of a committee rather than a single individual. With regard to the avoidance of hasty action, the periodic review procedure that we advocate should not be more frequent than once a year unless there is overwhelming evidence that some fundamental change is occurring unexpectedly.

In short, if a formula plan is used as a general policy framework rather than a set of rules to be either enforced rigidly or scrapped entirely, it may be quite beneficial to even the most skilled investor.

## SUGGESTED READINGS

Leon B. Allen. *A Method For Stock Profits Without Price Forecasting.* Garden City, N.Y.: Doubleday & Co., Inc., 1962.

C. Sidney Cottle and W. Tate Whitman. *Investment Timing—The Formula Plan Approach.* New York: McGraw-Hill Book Co., 1953.

Robert R. Dince. "Another View of Formula Planning," *Journal of Finance,* December, 1964.

———. "Portfolio Income: A Test of a Formula Plan," *Journal of Financial and Quantitative Analysis,* September, 1966.

Sherman F. Feyler. *Income Growth with Security.* New York: Macmillan Co., 1958.

Edgar S. Genstein. *Stock Market Profit Without Forecasting.* Rev. ed. American Research Council, 1961.

Lucile Tomlinson. *Practical Formulas for Successful Investing.* New York: Wilfred Funk, Inc., 1953.

# Part IV

# THE ULTIMATE DECISIONS

# 16

# PERSONAL PORTFOLIO MANAGEMENT

We should all be concerned about the future because we will have to spend the rest of our lives there.

—Charles Kettering

Making personal investment decisions is very difficult. "Jam yesterday," said Alice of *Alice in Wonderland*, "and jam tomorrow—but never jam *today*." It is easy to see how you could have made a good investment decision yesterday. Hindsight, as someone once said, always has 20–20 vision. It may even seem easy to make a good investment decision tomorrow.

But today, no. Too many uncertainties. So there is a strong temptation either to put off making a decision—or else to decide on whim or blind impulse.

There are so many choices. Whether you have $500 or $5,000, or $50,000 or $500,000 to place, the alternatives are so many and the decisions so onerous that personal investment may become a nerve-racking process. Is the time to invest now or should you wait? Should you act on the tip you got yesterday, or should you try to check it out, or should you forget it? Is this the time to buy stocks, or bonds, or nothing? Is real estate a better hedge against inflation than common stock? Will you become locked in? Should you use analytic techniques to select and buy common stock directly or should you buy mutual fund shares and let the professional managers worry about investment selection and timing. But if it's to be mutual funds, then which one? There are now more than 500. How do you find the limited number of effective ones among the many mediocre ones? Or, to be sure of preserving principal, should you play it safe and put your money in U.S. Savings Bonds, or in a savings account? Should the savings account be in a commercial bank, in a savings bank, or in a savings and loan association? Or perhaps you should increase your life insurance or buy an annuity? But these are fixed dollar investments. What about inflation? What about the variable annuity? Perhaps this *is* the time to buy common stock, but what kind and in what industry and in what company? What really are your investment objectives? Are you timid or aggressive; conservative or a speculator? Do you want safety of principal or appreciation of capital or both? Should you choose blue chips or speculative special situations? Income stocks or growth stocks? Cyclical issues or defensive issues? Should you invest in airline stocks, in electronics, in color-TV manufacturers, in aluminum, in copper, in electrical machinery manufacturers, in foods, or chain stores, or tobacco, or utilities? And when you decide upon the industry, then which company? If it's aluminum, then should it be ALCOA, or Alcan Aluminium, or Kaiser, or Reynolds Metals?

In view of the complexity of the personal investment decision, it's amazing that there are now over 20 million shareowners in the United States.[1] This is triple the number who owned stock 15 years earlier. The more than 20 million individual shareholders hold stock worth over $400 billion. While women shareholders slightly outnumber the men, the incidence of ownership among men is somewhat higher. One out of 6 American adults own shares in a publicly held business, compared with 1 out of 16 in 1952. Almost 6 out of every 10 Americans who completed college own stock. One out of 35 shareowners is a student. New shareholders account for 1 out of 16. The average American shareowner now holds from three to four different stock issues.

The median household income of America's 20,120,000 individual shareowners reached a new high of $9,500 in 1965. This compared with $8,600 in 1962, $7,000 in 1959, and $6,200 in 1956. The largest single increase in share ownership came in the $10,000-to-$15,000 category, where the number of American shareholders rose by nearly 2 million from 3.3 million to 5.2 million, or some 60%. At the same time, the number of shareowners with annual incomes of less than $7,500 actually declined. Despite the upward shift in income distribution, more than half—almost 11 million—of all U.S. investors have household incomes of less than $10,000. See Table 16–1. These individuals account for 55% of all shareholders.

Most shareowners appear to look on stock as only part of their total personal financial programs. This is evident from other Census data which show that:

88% have savings accounts
88% have life insurance
79% own their homes
56% have pension plans
53% have U.S. Savings Bonds
12% own other U.S. government, corporate, or municipal bonds

[1] New York Stock Exchange, *1965 Census of Shareowners.*

TABLE 16–1

Total Shareowners of Public Corporations by Income

| Reported Household Income* | Individual Shareowners, 1965 Number | Percent of Total | Estimated Total U.S. Population by Income | Percent of Each Income Group Who Are Shareowners, 1965 |
|---|---|---|---|---|
| Under $3,000 | 1,087,000 | 5.5% | 36,574,000 | 3.0% |
| $3,000–$5,000 | 2,096,000 | 10.6 | 32,193,000 | 6.5 |
| $5,000–$7,500 | 3,223,000 | 16.3 | 51,051,000 | 6.3 |
| $7,500–$10,000 | 4,369,000 | 22.1 | 32,573,000 | 13.4 |
| $10,000–$15,000 | 5,199,000 | 26.3 | 27,430,000 | 19.0 |
| $15,000–$25,000 | 2,649,000 | 13.4 | 8,762,000 | 30.2 |
| $25,000 and Over | 1,147,000 | 5.8 | 1,905,000 | 60.2 |
| Subtotal | 19,770,000 | 100.0% | 190,488,000 | 10.4 |
| Not classified by income | 350,000 | | 7,012,000 | |
| Total | 20,120,000 | | 197,500,000 | |

* "Household Income" is the total combined income before taxes of all members of the household. If, for example, a shareowner had $8,000 income and a nonshareowner member of the same household had $4,000, the shareowner's household income is $12,000. On the other hand, if both are shareowners, each is considered to have $12,000 household income.

Source: New York Stock Exchange, *1965 Census of Shareowners.*

The financial programs and investment policies of individuals will vary according to a variety of factors, including age, background and education, income level, financial resources, temperament, and personality. Financial programs and investment portfolios must be tailored to meet individual needs and requirements. Never are two identical and seldom are they alike. While generalizations are therefore not easy, let us take a family at three different illustrative stages of development and consider its financial requirements and investment programs. First, the family where the head is aged 25–30—the young family.

## The Young Family

"Thrift is a wonderful virtue, especially in an ancestor," someone once said. Naturally, a young family which has inherited a substantial amount has no financial problem. It has merely an investment problem. But for the average family, Mark Twain's quip holds true: "The first half of life consists of the capacity to enjoy without the chance; the last half consists of the chance without the capacity." The head of the average family between 25 and 30 years of age is married and has one child. Income ranges from $5,000 to $10,000 per annum. Of take-home pay (after tax and pension and social security deductions) the nationwide pattern of expenditures is as follows:

| | |
|---|---|
| Housing | 27%–30% |
| Food | 19%–25% |
| Transportation | 14%–17% |
| Clothing | 9%–13% |
| Medical care | 6%– 7% |
| Recreation | 5%– 6% |
| Personal Care | 2%– 3% |
| Tobacco and alcoholic beverages | 3%– 4% |
| Education | 1%– 3% |
| Miscellaneous | 3%– 6% |

The largest single expenditure for the young American family is on housing. For many families it may be the largest single purchase and the biggest investment of a lifetime. The average price of new homes bought with conventional mortgages (not insured by FHA or VA) is now about $25,800, while the average resale price on existing homes has risen to $20,300. How much to pay for a house and how to finance the house are likely to be the first major investment problems for the young family. Generally, experts suggest that one should not pay more than 2½ times take-home pay for a house. Thus, if take-home pay is $8,000 a year, the head of the household can afford a $20,000 house. Another useful concept for quick calculation is the "1 percent" rule. Total monthly operating costs will approximate 1 percent of the purchase price of the house. Thus a $30,000 home will absorb and require a $300-a-month housing expense. *Changing Times* puts it in slightly different fashion:

For every $1,000 increase in the price of a new house, you can expect to spend about $10 more a month for mortgage payments, bond insurance, real estate taxes, heating and utilities. The margin is usually larger on older homes.

And that $10 a month more is only part of the extra cost of a large home. You will need more furniture, carpets, curtains. You may have to put up a few extra storm windows. There are more walls to paint or paper, more plumbing and heating lines to maintain. You may want another phone extension. Little by little, your costs mount to a permanently higher level.[2]

The major costs of living—housing, food, transportation, clothing—account for over 75% of the average family's expenses. Most young families go into debt to finance a house, a car, furniture, trees and shrubs, etc. But even these families manage to accumulate some assets—the equity in paying off the mortgage, contributions to a retirement system or pension plan, the cash surrender value of life insurance. While debts usually exceed assets at first, in time, with financial progress, this position tends to reverse, with assets exceeding debts. Some young families are, however, able to accumulate small surpluses from the outset. When this is the case they should be utilized in the following order of priority:

---

[2] "Where the Family Money Goes," *Changing Times, The Kiplinger Magazine*, August, 1966, p. 8.

*a*) Savings account
*b*) Life insurance
*c*) Investments

Every young family needs an emergency fund, cash in the bank, to fall back upon in the event of trouble such as loss of job or serious illness in the family. A good rule of thumb to follow is that the emergency fund, the savings account, should be built up until it amounts to at least three months take-home pay. It should then be maintained at least at this level as a cushion of caution, serving to protect against possible disaster.

After this requirement has been met, family protection via life insurance is next in order. The quickest way for the young family to build an estate is via life insurance. It need not and should not be the more costly forms of life insurance such as life paid-up at 65, 20-payment life, retirement income at 65, or 20-year endowment. It should be lower cost types such as renewable and convertible term or straight life insurance.

There are only three basic types of policies: (*a*) *term,* which is temporary protection, (*b*) *whole life*, which is lifetime protection with savings values, (*c*) *endowment*, which is mostly savings with protection until the endowment matures. Whole life may be purchased as limited payment life or straight life insurance. Every other type of policy is a variation or combination of the three basic types. Think of them in order from maximum protection to maximum savings, keeping in mind that for your insurance dollar, the policy that provides the most protection provides little or no savings, while policies that maximize savings give you relatively less insurance protection for your money. The initial need for the young family is, of course, for maximum protection at minimum cost.

This is provided by term insurance. Term insurance provides temporary protection for a given period of time. It pays off only if you die within the given period, which may be 1 year, 5 years, 10 years, etc. Term insurance is the lowest premium life insurance because it provides only temporary protection. It may not require a payment by the insurance company and does not as a rule build any cash value.

Term policies may be convertible, or nonconvertible. In the case of the former, the policy may be exchanged later on, when the young head of family can better afford it, for a higher premium lifetime policy, without taking a medical examination. Term policies are also renewable or nonrenewable. In the former case, the company agrees to extend the policy in the same amount for a similar period (at a higher premium) when the present one expires, without requiring a medical examination. The renewable privilege usually does not extend beyond a certain age—either 55 or 60.

As the following tabulation indicates, the premium cost of term insurance is very much less than on other types of insurance:

**What Various Policies Cost**

(Approximate Annual Premium for $10,000 of Insurance)*

| *Type of Policy* | *Cost†* |
|---|---|
| Five-year Term‡ | $ 61.00 |
| Ten-year Term‡ | 73.00 |
| Straight life | 161.00 |
| Life paid-up at 65 | 187.00 |
| 20-payment life | 283.00 |
| Retirement income at 65 | 301.00 |
| 20-year endowment | 472.00 |

* At age 25.
† Per annum.
‡ Renewable and convertible.

When the term policy is renewed, however, the premium for the next term goes up. At age 20, for example, you pay $56.50 for a five-year term policy for $10,000 of insurance; at age 25, if you renew it, you pay $61; at age 30 it becomes $67.50; at age 35 it will be $81. Thereafter it rises sharply until at 55, if you can qualify to buy it, the cost will be $265 per annum.

The rising cost in contrast to the level premiums of lifetime insurance is one of the main disadvantages of term insurance. There are others, as for example, the fact that there is no savings feature which can be taken in a lump sum or converted to living benefits upon retirement. You cannot borrow against a term policy, nor does it carry the very useful other nonforfeiture provisions of the lifetime policies. But for young families when budgets are tight and costs are important, when the first child comes along and the wife can no longer work, with the resultant decrease of family income, term insurance provides maximum protection at minimum cost. This may be seen in the following tabulation showing what an expenditure of $100 a year will provide in the way of insurance protection:

**What $100 a Year Will Buy in Life Insurance***

| *Type of Policy* | *Amount of Insurance $100 a Year Will Buy†* | *Cash Value at Age 65 per $100 Annual Premium* |
|---|---|---|
| Five-year term‡ | $19,500 | None |
| Ten-year term§ | 19,300 | None |
| Straight life | 7,000 | 4,200 |
| Life paid-up at 65 | 6,250 | 4,475 |
| Modified life (5 years) | 6,000 | 3,510 |
| Family income (20 years) | 5,600 | 3,360 |
| Endowment at 65 | 5,400 | 5,400 |
| 20-payment life | 4,100 | 2,935 |
| Retirement income at 65 | 3,960 | 6,555 |
| 20-year endowment | 2,200 | Matured age 42 |

* Approximate amounts for male age 22.
† Most policies are issued in $1,000 units or in multiples of $500.
‡ Convertible and renewable.
§ Convertible and nonrenewable.

Thus, by the expenditure of about $125 a year, a young head of family can build an immediate estate of $25,000 for the protection of his wife and child. Assuming that there are any additional funds that can be eked out of the tight annual budget, the young man will be able to turn to the possibility of investment, having first met his financial needs for housing, savings, and insurance.

If the young man can achieve an additional surplus of, say, $500 for investment, what are his alternatives, what are his risks, and what are his requirements? He can invest in common stock directly, purchasing either odd lots or round lots. He can invest in common stock via the Monthly Investment Plan (MIP). He can buy mutual fund shares. Bonds and real estate can be omitted from consideration since his resources are limited. At his stage in life he is building for the future. He can look forward to 40 to 50 years of ability to earn income, accumulate surpluses, and invest them. If the past is any indicator of the future, the purchasing power of the dollar will continue to decline, and prices will, over the long run, continue to rise. Any investment he makes has time to grow, and it should over time be both a hedge against inflation and provide a substantial return, combining dividend accumulation and capital gain. Over the long pull any investment he makes will also face both a business risk (possible decline in earnings) and a financial risk (possible decline of the securities market as a whole). Since he is new at investment, he should not be involved in undue speculative risk as a result of which he might have to face the loss of a significant share of his hard-earned initial accumulation.

He will probably be building his portfolio one stock at a time, slowly at first, possibly more rapidly as his earnings rise later. Most portfolios are built one stock at a time, slowly over a period of years. It is usually only the hypothetical textbook example which provides a $100,000 or $500,000 fund, inherited, to invest *de novo*, all at once. He ought to be able to buy his one stock at the least possible cost, minimizing commissions, if possible. The relative costs of the alternatives open to him would suggest direct investment in a round lot as the least expensive in commission, odd lots and MIP next, and mutual funds with their 8½% loading charge as the most expensive.[3] This would suggest buying stock directly rather than through a mutual fund. It would also suggest that he build his savings account until he has accumulated the cost of a round lot of the stock of his selection. While it is accumulating he will earn 4% to 5% on it, and the accumulation period will give him time to consider his first choice carefully.

On the other hand, to avoid buying at the wrong time, he may find it worthwhile to use the NYSE Monthly Investment Plan to take advantage of dollar-cost averaging. If he invests a modest sum monthly or quarterly, on a continuing basis he will automatically be buying more

[3] See Chapter 17 for a discussion of mutual funds.

shares when prices are low and fewer when they are high. Or he can combine the savings account and dollar-cost averaging by depositing a given sum each month and then quarterly or semiannually buying as many shares as his accumulation permits. He will be earning interest on his money while it is awaiting stock investment.

Clearly, the first selection should be a quality growth stock so that his first investment experience will be both rewarding and encouraging. Over time there will, of course, be modest setbacks, but a good-quality growth stock should repeatedly surpass previous levels. For example, some years ago, two professors at the University of Michigan Graduate School of Business made hypothetical periodic investments in randomly chosen NYSE common stocks for a 14-year period. They found that the stocks, with reinvested dividends, grew at an annual rate of 12.2% compounded. Later the study was extended to 25 years, and the rate rose to 14%. A similar study by two professors at the University of Chicago Graduate School of Business showed that an investment in *all* NYSE stocks in 1926, with dividends reinvested, held until 1960, would have shown an average growth of 9% a year compounded.

### The Growth Portfolio

For years "growth" was the hottest word in Wall Street. A growth company, of course, is one whose sales and earnings per share are increasing at a rate faster than the growth of the nation's gross national product and usually faster also than the average of the industry of which the company is a part. It has become customary to attempt to distinguish between quality growth stocks and speculative growth stocks, between conservative growth stocks and aggressive growth stocks. Mature companies with excellent long-standing records of expanding sales and earnings, with stable and highly competent management, with large interest in research and development, and with long-unbroken dividend payment records, include companies such as Bristol-Myers, Eastman Kodak, General Electric, International Business Machines, and Zenith. Newer companies, with less maturity and more dependence on specialized interests, have at times been characterized by the terms "aggressive" or "speculative growth" companies. Some examples include Litton Industries, Fairchild Camera, Polaroid, Xerox, SCM, etc.

The young investor who seeks suggestions for a growth-stock portfolio or selection will find them in abundance in the publications of brokerage houses and investment services. The recommendations are so numerous that the problem for the average investor, as contrasted to the professional security analyst, is how to narrow the lists. One technique is to gather a number of lists over a short period of time—one month or one quarter—and tabulate the frequency of selection. Then take the 5 or 10 more frequently recommended—those recurring on most lists—and choose 1 or 2 of these, either by reading individual company reports (for example, Standard & Poor's Fact Sheets), or by applying various tests suggested in Chapters 5 through 9.

In his stimulating annual compilation *Your Investments*, Professor Leo Barnes provides three sample growth-stock portfolios. These are shown in Table 16–2. He notes that five annual sample growth portfolios showed the following appreciation records from September 1, 1961, to September 1, 1966; Sample Portfolio D—57%; Sample Portfolio E—41.5%; and Sample Portfolio F—121.2%. During the same period, the Standard & Poor's 500 stock index advanced only 13.2%.

In an issue of *The Outlook*, Standard & Poor's provided a master list of growth stocks chosen from among its computer-selected 200 Rapid Growth Stocks. This Master List is shown as Table 16–3. Average annual growth rates for earnings per share were given for the latest five years. Yields, as is common for growth stocks and as was therefore to be expected, were low on a current dividend basis, without factoring in capital gains accretions over time. Price-earnings ratios, as is to be expected for growth stocks, were for the most part higher than the then prevailing average for the Dow-Jones 30 Industrials, or for the Standard & Poor's 425 Industrials.

In its *Investment Review and Outlook*, Eastman Dillon, Union Securities & Co.[4] classified common stocks recommended for purchase under the following five categories:

Group I: *Above-Average Current Income and Moderate Growth.* For the income-oriented investor. Stocks offering a yield of not less than 4.8%, a proven earnings growth rate of at least 3% and a combined return of at least 8%.

Group II: *Above-Average Growth with Moderate Current Income.* For the "conservative-growth" investor. Stocks having a potential for no less than 5½% average annual earnings growth with a combined return of at least 9%.

Group III: *High Quality, Exceptional Growth.* For the investor primarily concerned with growth. Stocks that offer a growth rate of not less than 10% and in most cases closer to 15%.

Group IV: *Favorably Situated Cyclicals.* For the investor who wants the potentially dramatic rewards that come from investing in areas that respond strongly to swings of an economic or industrial cycle.

Group V: *Specialty Capital Gains Vehicles.* For the aggressive investor seeking more enterprising means to achieve maximum growth. Revitalized and unrecognized growth situations.

---

[4] Fall, 1966, edition.

TABLE 16–2

**Sample Portfolio D**
(Conservative Issues for Long-Term Growth)

| | |
|---|---|
| Bristol-Myers | Mobil Oil |
| Caterpillar Tractor | Pepsi Co. |
| Continental Assurance | Sprague Electric |
| First National City Bank | Tampax |
| General Telephone & Electronics | Texaco |
| International Business Machines | Texas Utilities |
| Interstate Department Stores | Time, Inc. |
| Lincoln National Life Insurance | Union Oil |
| McGraw-Hill | Valley National Bank |
| Merck | Westinghouse Electric |

**Sample Portfolio E**
(Aggressive Issues for Long-Term Growth)

| | |
|---|---|
| Carrier | General Cable |
| Cincinnati Milling Machine | Gulf & Western Ind. |
| Coastal States Gas | International Silver |
| Coca-Cola Bottling Co. of L.A. | Litton Industries |
| Continental Telephone | Longs Drug Stores |
| Delta Air Lines | National Can |
| Dr. Pepper | Royal Crown Cola |
| Donaldson | Russ Togs |
| Dover Corp. | Texas Oil & Gas |
| Emhart | Time, Inc. |

**Sample Portfolio F**
(More Speculative Issues for Long-Term Growth)

| | |
|---|---|
| Alexander & Baldwin | National Chemsearch |
| Ampco Metal | Northwest Airlines |
| Barden | Parkview-Gem |
| Barnes-Hind Pharm. | Pettibone Mulliken |
| Capital Cities Broadcasting | Smith Industries Intl. |
| Cutter Labs | Swank |
| Diversified Metals | Tektronic |
| Eckerd Drugs of Fla. | Tidewater Marine Service |
| Giddings & Lewis Mach. | Tremco Mfg. |
| Grumman | UTD Corp. |

Source: Leo Barnes, *Your Investments* (Rye, N.Y.: American Research Council, 1967).

We are here concerned with Groups II and III. Group II included Abbott Laboratories, Anheuser-Busch, Colgate-Palmolive, Deere & Co., First National City Bank of New York, Kansas City Power & Light, Mobil Oil, Pepsi, Standard Oil of California, Standard Oil of Ohio, and Sterling Drug. Eastman Dillon divided recommended growth stocks in Group III into two categories. Stocks in the first category, "established industry leaders," play a dominant or a relatively broad role in their industries, or both. Stocks in this category usually appeal to the more conservative among growth-oriented investors who are willing to pay a

## TABLE 16–3

### Master List of Growth Stocks

(From 200 Rapid Growth Stocks)

| | Earnings Per Share ($) | | | | | *Growth Rate % | | 1965-66 | Approx. | | §P/E | % |
|---|---|---|---|---|---|---|---|---|---|---|---|---|
| | 1962 | 1963 | 1964 | 1965 | E1966 | 5-Yr. Trend | Latest Year | Price Range | Price | Div. | Ratio | Yield |
| **Fundamental Growth— | | | | | | | | | | | | |
| American Electric Pwr. | 1.42 | 1.54 | 1.66 | 1.78 | 1.90 | 9 | 7 | 47⅝- 35⅞ | 40 | 1.32 | 21.1 | 3.3 |
| Beech-Nut Life Savers | 1.76 | 1.94 | 2.22 | 2.44 | 2.70 | 12 | 10 | 63½- 51 | 59 | 1.30 | 21.9 | 2.2 |
| Black & Decker | [2]1.38 | [2]1.54 | [2]1.92 | [2]2.37 | [2]2.90 | 15 | 23 | 68¾- 37⅜ | 63 | 1.40 | 21.7 | 2.2 |
| Bristol-Myers | 1.53 | 1.81 | 2.18 | 2.64 | 3.10 | 21 | 18 | 109½- 67¼ | 105 | †1.35 | 33.9 | 1.3 |
| Celanese Corp. | 3.00 | 3.42 | 4.25 | 5.10 | 5.25 | 21 | 20 | 92 - 69 | 82 | 2.00 | 15.6 | 2.4 |
| Coca-Cola | 1.69 | 1.92 | 2.30 | 2.66 | 3.00 | 14 | 16 | 90¾- 69¼ | 80 | 1.90 | 26.7 | 2.4 |
| Int'l. Tel. & Tel. | 2.36 | 2.73 | 3.16 | 3.58 | 4.00 | 13 | 15 | 77½- 48¾ | 76 | 1.35 | 19.0 | 1.8 |
| Texaco, Inc. | 3.60 | 4.04 | 4.27 | 4.71 | 5.10 | 10 | 10 | 87½- 72 | 78 | ‡2.55 | 15.3 | 3.3 |
| Texas Utilities | 1.84 | 2.05 | 2.17 | 2.31 | 2.50 | 9 | 6 | 68⅜- 53⅝ | 60 | 1.44 | 24.0 | 2.4 |
| Warner-Lambert | 1.15 | 1.24 | 1.41 | 1.60 | 1.80 | 9 | 13 | 43¾- 32⅝ | 40 | 0.90 | 22.2 | 2.3 |
| **Fast-Growing Companies | | | | | | | | | | | | |
| American Enka | 1.62 | 1.76 | 2.56 | 2.91 | 3.40 | 68 | 14 | 48⅜- 33 | 43 | †1.32½ | 12.6 | 3.1 |
| Automatic Retailers | [2]1.35 | [2]1.48 | [2]1.73 | [2]2.01 | [2]2.25 | 27 | 16 | 54½- 36⅛ | 50 | 0.50 | 22.2 | 1.0 |
| Chicago Musical Instr. | [3]1.39 | [3]1.52 | [3]1.62 | [3]2.10 | [3]2.50 | 16 | 30 | 38 - 24⅛ | 36 | 0.80 | 14.4 | 2.2 |
| E. G. & G. Inc. | 0.68 | 0.81 | 0.90 | 1.02 | 1.15 | 38 | 13 | 32¼- 18⅞ | 25 | 0.20 | 21.7 | 0.8 |
| Emery Air Freight | 0.64 | 0.74 | 1.01 | 1.49 | 1.90 | 28 | 48 | 89 - 34½ | 83 | 1.00 | 43.7 | 1.2 |
| Litton Industries | [4]0.76 | [4]1.06 | [4]4.33 | [4]1.68 | [4]2.15 | 35 | 28 | 86½- 36⅜ | 79 | [5]Stk. | 36.7 | -- |
| National Can | 1.07 | 1.23 | 1.56 | 2.03 | 2.45 | 25 | 30 | 32⅞- 17 | 31 | ‡0.50 | 12.7 | 1.6 |
| Perkin-Elmer | [4]0.75 | [4]0.82 | [4]1.00 | [4]1.23 | [4]1.55 | 18 | 24 | 53½- 23½ | 48 | Nil | 31.0 | -- |
| Plough, Inc. | 1.31 | 1.48 | 1.72 | 2.15 | 2.40 | 12 | 25 | 53½- 34⅞ | 52 | 0.80 | 21.7 | 1.5 |

*Adjusted for all stock dividends and based on earnings through 1965. **Listed on New York Stock Exchange. †Incl. extra. ‡Plus stock. §Based on estimated 1966 earnings. [2]Years ended Sept. 30. [3]Years ended June 30. [4]Years ended July 31. [5]2½% in stock paid November, 1965. E—Estimated. P—Preliminary.

Source: Standard & Poor's, *The Outlook*, May 2, 1966, p. 821.

premium for relatively assured performance. Recommended "established industry leaders" included General Telephone & Electronics, International Business Machines, Polaroid, Xerox.

Companies in the second category of Group III, were termed "emerging high-growth enterprises." They generally have not attained the same degree of dominance in their fields or breadth of activities as those in the first category. As a result, their well-above-average past records and future potential have not attracted the same amount of investor attention. This is reflected in a level of price-earnings multiples more moderate, with a few exceptions, than that accorded the premium issues. The "emerging high-growth enterprises" recommended were Capital Cities Broadcasting, Combined Insurance Company, Famous Artists Schools, Grumman Aircraft Engineering, Magnavox, Marion Laboratories, Schering, Syntex, and Western Power & Gas. It is not on this category but rather on the previous one, "established industry leaders," that the young head of family's attention should be focused.

Merrill Lynch, Pierce, Fenner & Smith, Inc., has made numerous

## TABLE 16–4

### How Growth Stocks Grow

The table shows how a $1,000 cash investment in any of 20 different stocks regarded as growth stocks in 1953 would have grown since mid-1953.

Full adjustment has been made in this tabulation for splits and stock dividends. But no account has been taken of cash dividends or rights offerings, and no allowance has been made for brokerage fees.

| | *Mid-1953* | *Mid-1963* | *End 1965* | *End 1966* |
|---|---|---|---|---|
| American Cyanamid | $1,000 | $ 2,615 | $ 3,866 | $ 2,726 |
| Bristol-Myers | 1,000 | 15,671 | 30,308 | 34,727 |
| Caterpillar Tractor | 1,000 | 5,356 | 12,358 | 8,694 |
| Corning Glass Works | 1,000 | 5,548 | 7,419 | 10,033 |
| Factor (Max) | 1,000 | 23,484 | 26,182 | 30,188 |
| General Electric | 1,000 | 3,320 | 4,960 | 3,720 |
| Grumman Aircraft | 1,000 | 2,540 | 5,053 | 5,619 |
| Gulf Life Insurance | 1,000 | 4,336 | 3,875 | 2,695 |
| International Business Machines | 1,000 | 14,557 | 20,822 | 23,256 |
| Magnavox | 1,000 | 18,556 | 36,085 | 32,458 |
| Minneapolis-Honeywell | 1,000 | 3,500 | 5,228 | 4,658 |
| Minnesota Mining & Manufacturing | 1,000 | 7,235 | 8,612 | 9,879 |
| Pacific Gas & Electric | 1,000 | 2,601 | 2,990 | 2,929 |
| Pitney-Bowes | 1,000 | 7,557 | 7,461 | 7,442 |
| Polaroid | 1,000 | 33,777 | 101,168 | 137,700 |
| Procter & Gamble | 1,000 | 5,071 | 4,644 | 4,887 |
| Radio Corporation of America | 1,000 | 3,106 | 7,028 | 6,478 |
| Safeway Stores | 1,000 | 4,857 | 5,245 | 4,070 |
| Texaco | 1,000 | 5,646 | 6,759 | 6,012 |
| Union Bank (Los Angeles) | 1,000 | 8,681 | 5,639 | 3,573 |

Source: Merrill Lynch, Pierce, Fenner & Smith, Inc.

growth-stock portfolio suggestions in recent years. Two are shown in Tables 16–4 and 16–5. Table 16–4 is interesting because it shows relative performance of some leading growth stocks over a 14-year period. Over this time Polroid, Magnavox, Bristol-Myers, and Max Factor outperformed International Business Machines. Selected Issues (Table 16–5) has several categories of recommended types. The first category entitled "Investment Type: Growth" is a conservative growth group.

## TABLE 16–5
## Portfolio Suggestions

| ISSUE | Dividends-$ a Share | Approximate | | ISSUE | Dividends-$ a Share | Approximate | |
|---|---|---|---|---|---|---|---|
| | Current or Indicated Annual Rate | Price 11-14-66 | Yield % | | Current or Indicated Annual Rate | Price 11-14-66 | Yield % |
| **INVESTMENT TYPE: GROWTH** | | | | | | | |
| Amer. Elec. Power | 1.44[q] | 40 | 3.6[q] | Liberty National Life | 0.36 | 40 | 0.9 |
| American Natural Gas | 1.80 | 40 | 4.5 | Marathon Oil | 2.40 | 58 | 4.1 |
| FMC Corp. | 0.75 | 34 | 2.2 | Merck & Co. | 1.20[f] | 78 | 1.5[f] |
| Gulf Oil | 2.20 | 59 | 3.7 | Minnesota Mining & Mfg. | 1.20 | 80 | 1.5 |
| Honeywell, Inc. | 1.10 | 57 | 1.9 | Pacific Gas & Electric‡ | 1.30 | 35 | 3.7 |
| Int. Business Machines | 4.40 | 349 | 1.3 | Scott Paper | 1.00 | 26 | 3.8 |
| Kimberly-Clark | 2.00 | 53 | 3.8 | Standard Oil of California | 2.50 | 64 | 3.9 |
| **INVESTMENT TYPE: STABILITY** | | | | | | | |
| Consolidated Edison | 1.80[x] | 33 | 5.5[x] | Morgan Guaranty Trust | 4.00 | 84 | 4.8 |
| General Pub. Utilities‡ | 1.50 | 33 | 4.5 | Public Service Elec. & Gas | 1.46 | 37 | 3.9 |
| Great Atlantic & Pacific Tea | 1.50[e,q] | 27 | 5.6[e,q] | Sherwin-Williams | 2.00 | 42 | 4.8 |
| **LIBERAL INCOME** | | | | | | | |
| Equitable Gas | 2.00 | 34 | 5.9 | Typical Aa 25 to 30 yr. Deferred Call Corp. Bonds | — | — | 5.80[3] |
| Interstate Power | 1.20 | 25 | 4.8 | Typical Aa 25 to 30 yr. Callable Corp. Bonds | — | — | 6.00[3] |
| Lone Star Gas | 1.12 | 20 | 5.6 | Typical A 25 to 30 yr. Callable Corp. Bonds | — | — | 6.23[3] |
| National Fuel Gas | 1.60 | 29 | 5.5 | Typical A 20 yr. Municipal Bonds | — | — | 3.75-3.80[2] |
| North American Aviation | 2.80 | 48 | 5.8 | Typical A 10 yr. Municipal Bonds | — | — | 3.70-3.75[2] |
| Texas Eastern Transmission | 1.05 | 19 | 5.5 | Typical A 5 yr. Municipal Bonds | — | — | 3.65-3.70[2] |
| Washington Water Power | 1.16[x] | 22 | 5.3[x] | Typical Baa 20 yr. Municipal Bonds | — | — | 4.10-4.25[2] |
| **GOOD QUALITY: WIDER PRICE MOVEMENT** | | | | | | | |
| Amer. Smelting & Refining | 3.50[e] | 59 | 5.9[e] | Ins. Co. of N. Amer. | 2.00 | 87 | 2.3 |
| Bell & Howell | 0.50 | 47 | 1.1 | International Tel. & Tel. | 1.35 | 70 | 1.9 |
| Bendix Corp. | 1.40 | 32 | 4.4 | National Cash Register | 1.20 | 66 | 1.8 |
| California Packing | 1.00 | 24 | 4.2 | Pittston Co. | 1.20 | 27 | 4.4 |
| Carrier Corp. | 1.80[e] | 66 | 2.7[e] | Radio Corp. of Amer. | 0.80 | 47 | 1.7 |
| Chesebrough-Pond's | 0.68 | 25 | 2.7 | Revere Copper & Brass | 3.10[e] | 52 | 6.0[e] |
| Columbia Brdctg. | 1.40[q] | 55 | 2.5[q] | Safeway Stores | 1.00 | 26 | 3.8 |
| Eaton Yale & Towne | 1.25 | 25 | 5.0 | Schering Corp. | 1.00 | 52 | 1.9 |
| Emhart Corp. | 1.20 | 25 | 4.8 | Sinclair Oil | 2.40 | 65 | 3.7 |
| Firestone Tire & Rubber | 1.30 | 48 | 2.7 | Stauffer Chemical | 1.60 | 41 | 3.9 |
| General Tel. & Electronics | 1.28 | 44 | 2.9 | TRW, Inc. | 1.40 | 47 | 3.0 |
| Genesco Inc. | 1.40 | 27 | 5.2 | Wurlitzer Co. | 0.80 | 16 | 5.0 |
| Goodyear Tire & Rubber | 1.35 | 48 | 2.8 | | | | |
| **SPECULATIVE** | | | | | | | |
| Burroughs Corp. | 1.00 | 76 | 1.3 | Grumman Aircraft | 1.00 | 49 | 2.0 |
| General Dynamics | 1.00 | 47 | 2.1 | New York Central R.R. | 3.42[e] | 64 | 5.3[e] |
| General Tire & Rubber | 0.80 | 32 | 2.5 | | | | |

[2]–Maturity yield; exempt from Federal income taxes. [3] Maturity yield.

Source: Merrill Lynch, Pierce, Fenner & Smith, Inc.

Examples could be extended. The record is fairly clear. Building a portfolio of quality growth stocks is a suitable and wise objective for the young family. While it may not yield the spectacular profits from trading in either more speculative, newer growth stocks, or in the transitory market leaders, there is less risk, more stability, and less pain. The lesson of the past speaks clearly. Some of the leading growth companies of the first half of the 20th century and their percentage appreciation were as follows:

| | |
|---|---|
| National Biscuit | + 4,145% |
| Sears, Roebuck | +15,854% |
| General Electric | + 8,830% |
| National Lead | +24,130% |
| Eastman Kodak | + 8,973% |
| Du Pont | + 4,798% |
| Woolworth | + 2,224% |
| United Fruit | + 1,436% |
| Otis Elevator | + 5,963% |

Just how a young investor (or any investor) would have fared over a more recent decade had he invested systematically in some leading conservative growth stocks, may be seen in Tables 16–6 and 16–7. Table 16–6 shows how an investor would have stood on July 1, 1965, if he had invested $100 each month in any of the 20 stocks most popular with Merrill Lynch's MIP investors at the end of the decade. Assuming dividend reinvestment, the $12,000 total invested would have grown to

**TABLE 16–6**

THE MONTHLY INVESTMENT PLAN IN RETROSPECT
July 1955 - July 1965

JULY 21, 1965

How an investor would have stood on July 1, 1965, if he had invested $100 each month in any of the 20 stocks presently most popular with Merrill Lynch's MIP investors. Starting in July 1955, and continuing through June 30, 1965, the performance of the present 20 most popular stocks is shown below.

These stocks are not necessarily all presently suggested for purchase. Those stocks that Merrill Lynch, Pierce, Fenner & Smith does suggest for long-term investment are listed in the latest issue of "20 Stocks for Long-Term Growth."

| Stock | ---Without Reinvestment of Dividends--- Total Invested | Shares Owned | Market Value | Total Dividends Received | -With Dividends Reinvested- Total Invested | Shares Owned | Market Value |
|---|---|---|---|---|---|---|---|
| American Telephone & Telegraph | $12,000 | 276.88 | $18,048 | $3,369 | $15,964 | 338.79 | $22,826 |
| Dow Chemical | 12,000 | 179.74 | 12,694 | 1,327 | 13,418 | 200.74 | 14,177 |
| Eastman Kodak | 12,000 | 320.44 | 25,555 | 2,217 | 14,421 | 366.17 | 29,202 |
| General Electric | 12,000 | 159.27 | 15,270 | 1,720 | 13,884 | 182.57 | 18,504 |
| General Motors | 12,000 | 220.98 | 21,131 | 3,957 | 16,721 | 290.03 | 27,734 |
| General Telephone & Electronics | 12,000 | 550.42 | 21,810 | 2,619 | 14,960 | 659.28 | 26,124 |
| Gulf Oil | 12,000 | 315.16 | 17,294 | 2,286 | 14,538 | 371.40 | 20,380 |
| International Business Machines | 12,000 | 70.28 | 32,188 | 1,326 | 13,383 | 74.82 | 34,268 |
| International Harvester | 12,000 | 498.81 | 18,207 | 3,319 | 15,923 | 637.56 | 23,271 |
| Minnesota Mining & Manufacturing | 12,000 | 297.09 | 17,120 | 1,362 | 13,435 | 322.82 | 18,602 |
| Monsanto Company | 12,000 | 272.73 | 23,864 | 1,625 | 13,757 | 305.50 | 26,732 |
| Pacific Gas & Electric | 12,000 | 502.64 | 18,095 | 2,792 | 15,203 | 614.88 | 22,136 |
| Pfizer (Charles) | 12,000 | 407.45 | 21,544 | 2,387 | 14,636 | 472.44 | 24,980 |
| Phillips Petroleum | 12,000 | 235.11 | 12,255 | 2,372 | 14,682 | 285.53 | 14,883 |
| Radio Corporation of America | 12,000 | 754.30 | 25,740 | 1,785 | 13,949 | 852.89 | 29,105 |
| Safeway | 12,000 | 667.39 | 23,609 | 3,163 | 15,539 | 801.81 | 28,364 |
| Sears Roebuck | 12,000 | 481.42 | 32,797 | 2,432 | 14,695 | 556.06 | 37,882 |
| Standard Oil of California | 12,000 | 239.58 | 16,351 | 2,413 | 14,733 | 288.79 | 19,710 |
| Standard Oil of New Jersey | 12,000 | 204.85 | 16,029 | 2,813 | 15,259 | 255.90 | 22,024 |
| Tri-Continental | 12,000 | 305.74 | 13,988 | 2,731 | 15,176 | 379.30 | 17,353 |

The above table shows for each stock the number of shares an investor would have owned at June 30, 1965 and the market price of such shares on that day (1) if dividends had not been reinvested and (2) if dividends had been reinvested. Dividends received and dividends reinvested are before deduction for income taxes. Brokerage commissions on all purchases have been deducted.

The table illustrates how an investment through MIP can work out over a period of years. It is, of course, no indication as to future performance of any of the 20 stocks or of any other stock which might be purchased under MIP. Accordingly, the investor should take into account his financial ability to continue purchases through periods of low price levels. An investor should understand that he will incur a loss if he discontinues his purchases or sells when the market price of his shares is less than his average cost and that the MIP does not protect against loss in value in declining markets. The Monthly Investment Plan is designed to take advantage of temporary fluctuations in the market price and its advantages depend upon continuous, regular investment.

Source: Merrill Lynch, Pierce, Fenner & Smith, Inc.

TABLE 16–7

A SPECIAL INVESTOR'S ACCOUNT IN RETROSPECT
July 1955 - July 1965

JULY 21, 1965

How an investor would have stood on July 1, 1965 if he had invested $1,000 in any of the 20 stocks presently most popular with Merrill Lynch's MIP investors. The investment figures below show what would have happened if an investor had either had his dividends paid out to him, or had his dividends reinvested in the particular stock shown.

These stocks are not necessarily all presently recommended for purchase. Those stocks that Merrill Lynch, Pierce, Fenner & Smith does recommend for long-term investment are listed in the latest issue of "20 Stocks for Long-Term Growth."

| | ---Without Reinvestment of Dividends--- | | | | With Reinvestment of Dividends | | |
|---|---|---|---|---|---|---|---|
| Stock | Total Invested | Shares Owned | Market Value | Total Dividends Received | Total Invested | Shares Owned | Market Value |
| American Telephone & Telegraph | $1,000 | 32.6347 | $2,199 | $684 | $1,898 | 51.3456 | $3,459 |
| Dow Chemical | 1,000 | 19.6772 | 1,390 | 254 | 1,279 | 23.7756 | 1,679 |
| Eastman Kodak | 1,000 | 54.1104 | 4,315 | 526 | 1,601 | 67.3926 | 5,375 |
| General Electric | 1,000 | 18.4942 | 1,773 | 364 | 1,419 | 23.9929 | 2,300 |
| General Motors | 1,000 | 27.4600 | 2,626 | 761 | 1,995 | 43.4628 | 4,156 |
| General Telephone & Electronics | 1,000 | 79.5003 | 3,150 | 596 | 1,270 | 109.5539 | 4,341 |
| Gulf Oil | 1,000 | 44.2418 | 2,428 | 489 | 1,568 | 57.8604 | 3,175 |
| International Business Machines | 1,000 | 18.0491 | 8,266 | 426 | 1,454 | 19.9013 | 9,115 |
| International Harvester | 1,000 | 50.6220 | 1,848 | 563 | 1,727 | 78.8321 | 2,877 |
| Minnesota Mining & Manufacturing | 1,000 | 53.5714 | 3,087 | 335 | 1,361 | 60.9933 | 3,515 |
| Monsanto Company | 1,000 | 24.5988 | 2,152 | 241 | 1,272 | 30.3461 | 2,655 |
| Pacific Gas & Electric | 1,000 | 60.2827 | 2,170 | 547 | 1,675 | 86.6938 | 3,721 |
| Pfizer (Charles) | 1,000 | 63.6857 | 3,367 | 540 | 1,632 | 82.1536 | 4,344 |
| Phillips Petroleum | 1,000 | 26.2796 | 1,370 | 488 | 1,588 | 37.6366 | 1,962 |
| Radio Corporation of America | 1,000 | 67.9720 | 2,320 | 281 | 1,328 | 87.9595 | 3,002 |
| Safeway | 1,000 | 135.7655 | 4,803 | 916 | 2,088 | 182.1549 | 6,444 |
| Sears Roebuck | 1,000 | 65.4159 | 4,456 | 474 | 1,557 | 84.1582 | 5,733 |
| Standard Oil of California | 1,000 | 28.0232 | 1,913 | 488 | 1,588 | 39.3349 | 2,685 |
| Standard Oil of New Jersey | 1,000 | 23.0991 | 1,808 | 559 | 1,695 | 34.5418 | 2,703 |
| Tri-Continental | 1,000 | 36.0595 | 1,650 | 602 | 1,679 | 55.6884 | 2,548 |

The above table shows for each stock the number of shares an investor would have owned at July 1, 1965 and the market price of such shares on that day (1) if dividends had not been reinvested and (2) if dividends had been reinvested. Dividends received and dividends reinvested are before deduction for income taxes. Brokerage commissions on all purchases have been deducted.

The table illustrates how an investment can work out over a period of years. It is, of course, no indication as to future performance of any of the 20 stocks or of any other stock which might be purchased. An investor should understand that he will incur a loss if he sells when the market price of his shares is less than his cost and that a Special Investors Account does not protect against loss in value in declining markets.

Source: Merrill Lynch, Pierce, Fenner & Smith, Inc.

$37,882 in Sears, Roebuck stock, to $34,268 in IBM stock, and to $29,202 in Eastman Kodak shares. These were the three best performances. Table 16–7 shows how an investor would have stood on July 1, 1965, if he had invested $1,000 in any of the 20 stocks most popular with Merrill Lynch's MIP investors at the end of the decade. With dividend reinvestment his $1,000 would have risen to $9,115 in IBM stock, to $6,444 in Safeway shares, and to $5,733 in Sears, Roebuck stock. This was, of course, over a decade of rising stock prices. Whether prices of leading conservative growth stocks will be higher in July, 1975, than they were in July, 1965, remains to be seen, but this is the implicit assumption a common stock investor makes when he invests for the long pull. Over most of the decades of the past century, his implicit assumption was correct.

Several notes of caution should, however, be sounded. It is possible to pay too much for growth and to buy growth stocks at peak periods in the investment cycle. Apart from dollar averaging, which tends to meet this problem and is therefore highly recommended, the advantage of a low price-earnings ratio over a high one should be recognized. Several studies have pointed to the advantages of buying when price-earnings ratios are relatively low. Nicholson, for example, calculated the price-earnings ratios and returns for 100 trust investment quality stocks over various 5- and 10-year periods from 1939 through 1959. The results indicated that the lowest price-earnings-ratio stocks dramatically outperformed the higher price-earnings-ratio stocks.[5] McWilliams, using a sample of 390 listed stocks over the period from 1953 through 1964, showed that better investment performance can be obtained from a portfolio of low price-earnings-ratio stocks as contrasted to portfolios made up of high price-earnings-ratio stocks.[6] Furthermore, records of high past earnings growth cannot necessarily be presumed to forecast future earnings behavior. Based on a study of 344 companies in 12 industries in 38 different test periods between the years 1950 and 1965, Murphy found little significant correlation between relative rates of growth of earnings per share in one period and relative growth in earnings per share in the next period. Only rarely in his sample did companies which recorded superior growth in earnings per share in one period show more than an even chance of recording above-average growth in the next period.[7] Selection of growth stocks for long-term investment is, therefore, no simple task.[8]

### The Family at Midstream

When the head of a family is between 40 and 50, earning on the average from $20,000 to $30,000 a year, the focus of his investment interest tends to change. He is financially more mature and sophisticated, has paid off his mortgage, built an investment fund, and is now, because of his tax bracket, likely to be interested primarily in varied and diverse forms of pursuit of *capital gains*. This is probably his investment objective by and large and the keynote to his investment activity. His portfolio is shifted more frequently, his investment holdings changed more often, as he devotes his talents and energies to the pursuit of *capital gains*.

The average business or professional man is probably moving into the prime of his life from 40 to 50. Although his earnings are perhaps not at the highest level he will attain, yet in these years he finds himself with greater financial mobility than at any other time. Generally his house is paid for or almost so, his insurance program is well underway, and a

---

[5] S. Francis Nicholson, "Price-Earnings Ratios," *Financial Analysts Journal*, July–August, 1960.

[6] James D. McWilliams, "Prices, Earnings and P-E Ratios," *Financial Analysts Journal*, May–June, 1966.

[7] Joseph E. Murphy, Jr., "Relative Growth of Earnings per Share," *Financial Analysts Journal*, November–December, 1966.

[8] Walter R. Good, "How To Avoid Overpriced Stocks," *Financial Analysts Journal*, November–December, 1966.

comfortable cash balance is available in the bank for any emergency which may arise. It is during this period that he is in a position to use funds aggressively. He can afford a somewhat higher degree of risk because his earning power is such that he is capable of continuously adding new capital to his portfolio of investments. His ability to take risks more extensively than he could earlier enables him to pursue diversified investing.

With this greater flexibility, a wider variety of investment paths is open to him. He is in a position to consider the whole gamut of investment possibilities. He can think of a speculative capital gains portfolio, of trading in performance stocks—the market favorites of the time—or of moving into cyclical stocks at the correct stage of the business cycle. He can buy on margin to enhance profitability, sell short, look into special situations, consider convertible bonds or warrants, or rights deals. He can switch from stocks to bonds to take advantage of changes in the trend of the market and in the economic environment. In the light of his tax position, he can consider tax-exempt state and municipal bonds, tax-sheltered investments, oil and gas royalties, real estate, and stock gifts to his children. These are merely some of the possibilities. And if he has little time to sort out investment opportunities, he can turn to mutual funds which specialize in achieving capital gains and whose past performances indicate that they are likely to achieve their stated objectives.

The tax factor is an important consideration in the selection of investment choices at this stage. A long-term capital gain (over six months) is taxed by the federal government in one of two ways: either (*a*) half of it at regular income tax rates; or (*b*) all of it at 25%—whichever results in the least tax. Taxable income, for federal tax purposes, includes 50% of any excess of net long-term capital gains over net short-term capital losses. Since our head of family is likely to be in a tax bracket ranging from say 35% to 70%, the investment incentive for long-term capital gains is quite apparent. An increment of income or of short-term gain for someone in the 50% tax bracket would skim off half. If the gain were long term, only 25% would be lost to the tax collector.

Softening or overcoming the impact of taxes is an important consideration to most investors at midstream, particularly to those in the higher income brackets. At the same time, however, the tax aspect should be kept in proper prospective and should not be allowed to overshadow other investment objectives. There are three classes of securities from which investment selections can be made. The first and principal source consists of state and municipal bonds, the interest payments on which are completely exempt from federal income taxes and which also are exempt in many cases from state and local taxes in the state of issuance. (The tax exemption applies to interest income from the bond but not to any capital gain that may be realized.)

Table 16–8 suggests the extent to which an investor can benefit from purchase of tax-exempt securities. By applying the tax rate indicated for his taxable income bracket to the coupon rate of a prospective tax-exempt acquisition, an investor can easily determine the relative appeal of the

TABLE 16–8

## TAX EXEMPT VS. TAXABLE YIELDS

*Based on New Tax Rates Fully Effective in 1965*

| Taxable Income: More Than | Taxable Income: But Not Over | Tax % Rate | Follow'g Ylds. (%) on Tax-Exempt Securs. 2.75 | 3.00 | 3.25 | 3.50 | 3.75 | 4.00 |
|---|---|---|---|---|---|---|---|---|
| | | | Are Equal to Yields Below on Taxable Issues | | | | | |
| $1,500 | $2,000 | 17.0 | 3.31 | 3.61 | 3.92 | 4.22 | 4.52 | 4.82 |
| 2,000 | 4,000 | 19.0 | 3.40 | 3.70 | 4.01 | 4.32 | 4.63 | 4.94 |
| 4,000 | 6,000 | 22.0 | 3.53 | 3.85 | 4.17 | 4.49 | 4.81 | 5.13 |
| 6,000 | 8,000 | 25.0 | 3.67 | 4.00 | 4.33 | 4.67 | 5.00 | 5.33 |
| 8,000 | 10,000 | 28.0 | 3.82 | 4.17 | 4.51 | 4.86 | 5.21 | 5.56 |
| 10,000 | 12,000 | 32.0 | 4.04 | 4.41 | 4.78 | 5.15 | 5.51 | 5.88 |
| 12,000 | 14,000 | 36.0 | 4.30 | 4.69 | 5.08 | 5.47 | 5.86 | 6.25 |
| 14,000 | 16,000 | 39.0 | 4.51 | 4.92 | 5.33 | 5.74 | 6.15 | 6.56 |
| 16,000 | 18,000 | 42.0 | 4.74 | 5.17 | 5.60 | 6.03 | 6.47 | 6.90 |
| 18,000 | 20,000 | 45.0 | 5.00 | 5.45 | 5.91 | 6.36 | 6.82 | 7.27 |
| 20,000 | 22,000 | 48.0 | 5.29 | 5.77 | 6.25 | 6.73 | 7.21 | 7.69 |
| 22,000 | 26,000 | 50.0 | 5.50 | 6.00 | 6.50 | 7.00 | 7.50 | 8.00 |
| 26,000 | 32,000 | 53.0 | 5.85 | 6.38 | 6.91 | 7.45 | 7.98 | 8.51 |
| 32,000 | 38,000 | 55.0 | 6.11 | 6.67 | 7.22 | 7.78 | 8.33 | 8.89 |
| 38,000 | 44,000 | 58.0 | 6.55 | 7.14 | 7.74 | 8.33 | 8.93 | 9.52 |
| 44,000 | 50,000 | 60.0 | 6.88 | 7.50 | 8.13 | 8.75 | 9.38 | 10.00 |
| 50,000 | 60,000 | 62.0 | 7.24 | 7.89 | 8.55 | 9.21 | 9.87 | 10.53 |
| 60,000 | 70,000 | 64.0 | 7.64 | 8.33 | 9.03 | 9.72 | 10.42 | 11.11 |
| 70,000 | 80,000 | 66.0 | 8.09 | 8.82 | 9.56 | 10.29 | 11.03 | 11.76 |
| 80,000 | 90,000 | 68.0 | 8.59 | 9.38 | 10.16 | 10.94 | 11.72 | 12.50 |
| 90,000 | 100,000 | 69.0 | 8.87 | 9.68 | 10.48 | 11.29 | 12.10 | 12.90 |
| 100,000 | 200,000 | 70.0 | 9.17 | 10.00 | 10.83 | 11.67 | 12.50 | 13.33 |
| 200,000 and over | | 70.0 | 9.17 | 10.00 | 10.83 | 11.67 | 12.50 | 13.33 |
| Corporations | | | | | | | | |
| $25,000 | | 22.0 | 3.53 | 3.85 | 4.17 | 4.49 | 4.81 | 5.13 |
| $25,000 and over | | 48.0 | 5.29 | 5.77 | 6.25 | 6.73 | 7.21 | 7.69 |

NOTE: These computations are for a single person. In joint returns divide taxable income by two and read corresponding figures from table. In computing the above table, the rate applying to the top bracket of an individual's income was used, since this is the level affected each time a new investment is made.

tax-free feature. For example a municipal, purchased at par, yields 3.75%. If the investor is in the 55% tax bracket, the 3.75% tax-exempt yield is equivalent to an 8.33% taxable yield. There is a simple formula by which any investor can determine a taxable equivalent yield for his own tax bracket. It is:

Tax-exempt yield ÷ (100% − tax bracket %) = Taxable equivalent yield (federal income taxes only)

Thus if an investor in the 55% tax bracket bought New York City 4.6% tax-exempt securities, he would be obtaining a taxable equivalent yield of 10.20%:

$$4.60 \div (100\% - 55\%) = 4.60 \div 45\% = 10.20\%$$

Incidentally, it should be noted that the table and the above calculation take no account of the benefits of state and local tax exemption, which differ widely. In many cases, as for the New York City resident in the above example, the additional advantages are considerable.

The second grouping of securities with special tax features includes companies that plow back the bulk of their earnings, such as growth stocks, or what one expert has called "stingy dividend payers." Money reinvested in the business becomes more valuable to the shareholder, from a tax standpoint, than earnings paid out in dividends; the deciding factor is the lower rate of tax imposed on capital gains. Growth stocks which have consistently reinvested more than 70% of their earnings include:

Air Products & Chemical
AMP, Inc.
Automatic Data Processing
Bangor Punta Alegre
Becton, Dickinson
Barnes-Hind Pharm.
Berkey Photo
Braniff Airways
Brown Forman
Capital Cities Broadcasting
Cenco Instruments
Crown Cork & Seal
Delta Air Lines
Disney, Walt
Donnelley & Sons
Eastern Gas & Fuel
Getty Oil
Holiday Inns
Howard Johnson
International Flavors & Fragrances
Iowa Beef
Kaiser Industries
Ling-Temco-Vought
Litton Industries
Londontown Mfg.
McDonald's Corp.
National Can
Pabst Brewing
Oshawa Wholesale
Polaroid
Rexall Drugs
Roadway Express
Rohm & Haas
Steinberg's Ltd.
Texas Instruments
Tidewater Oil
Xerox[9]

A third category of stocks with tax advantages includes those whose dividends, in whole or in part, are either free from federal income taxes or are treated as capital gains. Tax-free dividends arise from three main sources. One is when companies hold securities or other disposable assets on their books at values well in excess of current values and establish enough of these losses to offset other income. The second is where mining

---

[9] Source: Leo Barnes, *Your Investments* (Rye, N.Y.: American Research Council, 1967).

and other companies engaged in extractive industries make distributions from depletion or depreciation reserves. The third is where companies pay dividends shown to be not fully earned on the books they keep for tax purposes. A number of public utility companies have been in this category in recent years largely because of accelerated amortization and depreciation charges, which are treated differently for tax purposes than on the books kept in accordance with the requirements of regulatory bodies. Thus, in 1965, in the case of Consolidated Edison Company of New York only 37% of dividends were taxable, while in the case of Pacific Power & Light 41% was taxable, 59% was nontaxable. See Table 16–9.

The nontaxable portion of dividends (see last column of Table 16–9) is a return of capital. It must be applied toward reducing the tax cost of the stock. It is not treated as income in the federal tax returns; only the taxable portion, if any, is reported. Since the tax-free dividend is used to write down the cost of the investment, it is ultimately taken into account when the stock is sold. If the securities have been held over six months, the profit is subject to a maximum tax rate of 25%.

Also given special treatment are dividends paid by regulated investment companies out of net realized profits on security investments.[10] Such dividends are shown in the third column of Table 16–9. In some cases, dividends were partly from capital gains and thus partly nontaxable. Unlike the nontaxable dividends in the case of the utility companies, capital gains distributions of regulated investment companies must be reported in federal income tax returns. The portion representing the distribution of security profits, however, is not treated as regular dividend income but as long-term capital gains, on which the tax rate is, of course, lower. For example, in Table 16–9 in the case of Dreyfus Fund, in 1965, of the $1.19 of dividends paid, 41 cents was income, 78 cents was capital gain. In the case of the Essex Fund, of the $3.86 paid, 26 cents was income, $3.60 was capital gains. For the Oppenheimer Fund, of the $1.56 paid, $0.015 was income (1½ cents), while $1.545 was capital gains.

Another tax consideration which should receive the attention of our investor at midstream is the useful impact of stock gifts to children. A married man earning $30,000 pays about $10,000 in income taxes. Assume a relative dies and leaves him $50,000 (after estate taxes). If he invests it at 5% he can keep less than half of the $2,500 income. Given to his two children either in stock gifts or in irrevocable trusts, they will each have annual incomes from it of $1,250, on which, after the personal exemption of $600, the minimum standard deduction of $300 and the $100 dividend exclusion, etc., almost no tax will have to be paid.

Under the Uniform Gifts to Minors Acts adopted in most states and

---

[10] See Chapter 17, which follows.

the District of Columbia, a parent can make a stock gift to a child. The stock can be registered in the name of the parent as custodian for the child and can be traded from time to time. Any income or capital gain is taxable to the child, not to the parent. The gift, of course, must be irrevocable; when the child comes of age he or she becomes the outright owner. Any

## TABLE 16–9

### Tax Free and Capital Gains Dividends in 1965

(Based on information available at date of publication. Status is based on determinations by the companies and is subject to audit and final determination by the United States Treasury Department. Class of stock is common or capital, unless otherwise indicated.)

| | 1965 Payments ($) | | | |
|---|---|---|---|---|
| | Total Paid | Income | Cap. Gains | Non-taxable |
| ABC Consolidated Corp | 0.725 | Status not yet available | | |
| Abacus Fund | *Stk | .... | .... | *Stk |
| *Distribution of portfolio securities with a total value of $3,358,125 per Abacus sh ($1.3325 in Jan & $2.02565 in Dec). Fair market value of shs distributed on payment date: Phila & Reading-$37.625; Sterling Drug-$29.00; Amer Tel & Tel-$61.0625; Marathon Oil-$53.6875; Peoples Gas Lt & Coke-$41.875; Radio Corp Amer-$45.9375. | | | | |
| Adams Express | 2.20 | 0.77 | 1.43 | .... |
| Advance Ross Corp. 5% Pfd. | 1.25 | .... | .... | 1.25 |
| Advisers Fund | 0.275 | 0.195 | 0.08 | .... |
| Affiliated Fund | 0.74 | 0.28 | 0.46 | ... |
| Amer Business Shares | 0.3225 | *0.1425 | 0.18 | ... |
| *Only 44% qualifies for divd exclusion. | | | | |
| Amer Enterprise Fund | 0.49 | 0.20 | 0.29 | .... |
| Amer European Securities | 1.7912 | 0.5986 | 1.1926 | .... |
| Amer Growth Fund | 0.738 | 0.115 | 0.623 | .... |
| Amer International | 1.30 | 0.45 | 0.85 | .... |
| Amer Investors Fd | 1.00 | a0.06 | a0.94 | .... |
| Amer Mutual Fund | 0.90 | *0.26 | 0.64 | .... |
| *Only 72% qualifies for divd. exclusion. | | | | |
| Amer Realty Trust | 0.72 | 0.165 | .... | 0.555 |
| Amer Research & Development | 0.21 | *0.18 | 0.03 | .... |
| *Only 17% qualifies for exclusion or credit. | | | | |
| Arizona Public Service | 0.92 | 13% | .... | 87% |
| Arkansas Western Gas | *0.60 | 85% | .... | 15% |
| *Plus stk. | | | | |
| Associated Fund Trust | 0.109 | 0.057 | 0.052 | .... |
| Atlantic City Elec | 1.08 | 54% | .... | 46% |
| Atlas Corp 5% Pfd | 1.25 | 0.50 | .... | *0.75 |
| *Represents Mar & Jun divds. | | | | |
| Axe-Houghton Fund A | 0.60 | *0.17 | 0.43 | .... |
| *Only 59.5% in Feb & 58.3% of divds in other quarters qualify for divd exclusion. | | | | |
| Axe-Houghton Fund B | 0.75 | *0.307 | 0.443 | .... |
| *Only 60.8% in Jan & 59.9% of divds in other quarters qualify for divd exclusion. | | | | |
| Balanced Income Fund | 0.45 | *0.39 | 0.06 | .... |
| *Only 68.5% qualifies for divd excl. | | | | |
| Bangor Punta Alegre Sug Pref | 1.25 | *.... | .... | *.... |
| *Mar, Jun & Sep divds 100% nontaxable. Status of Dec divd available after Sep 30'66. | | | | |
| Beacon Hill Mutual Fd | 0.08 | *0.025 | .... | 0.055 |
| *Only $0.01 qualifies for divd exclusion. | | | | |
| Belco Petroleum Corp | 0.50 | 0.50 | .... | .... |
| Belle Isle Corp | 0.92 | 0.42 | .... | 0.50 |
| Blue Ridge Mutual Fd | 1.26 | 0.312 | 0.948 | .... |
| Bondstock Corp | 0.22 | 0.11 | 0.11 | .... |
| Boston Fund | 0.65 | *0.32 | 0.33 | .... |
| *Status for divd exclusion later. | | | | |
| Bridgeport Gas | 2.00 | Status not yet available | | |
| Broad St Investing | 1.02 | 0.50 | 0.52 | .... |
| Brockton Taunton Gas | | | | |
| Common | 1.43 | .... | .... | 100% |
| $3.80 Preferred | 3.80 | 96.71% | .... | 3.29% |
| Bullock Fund | 1.06 | 0.41 | 0.65 | .... |
| Business Capital Corp | 0.36 | *0.36 | .... | .... |
| *2.1% of Jul & Oct divds qualify for divd excl, Jan & Apr divds do not qualify. | | | | |
| Canadian Fund | 1.23 | *b0.4892 | 0.7977 | .... |
| *Includes $0.0569 Canadian tax paid for stkhldrs account. | | | | |
| Canal Assets | 1.30 | 0.7071 | .... | 0.5929 |
| Canal-Randolph Corp | 0.825 | 34.48% | .... | 65.52% |
| Capital Income Fund | 2.77 | 0.35 | 2.42 | .... |
| Capital Shares Inc (Md) | 0.07 | 0.0185 | 0.0515 | .... |
| Carriers & General Corp | 2.09 | 0.966 | 1.124 | .... |
| Centennial Fund | 0.28 | 0.14984 | *0.13016 | .... |
| *Co at Jul 31'65, had undistributed cap gains of $1.553276 a sh. | | | | |
| Central Hudson G & E | 1.22 | Status not yet available | | |
| Central Louisiana Elec | 1.32 | a81% | .... | a19% |
| Central Securities | 3.50 | 0.21 | 3.29 | .... |
| Channing Balanced Fund | 0.73 | *0.40 | 0.33 | .... |
| *Only 65% qualifies for divd exclusion. | | | | |
| Channing Common Stock Fd | 0.14 | 0.05 | 0.09 | .... |
| Channing Growth Fund | 0.45 | 0.18 | 0.27 | .... |
| Channing Income Fund | 0.55 | *0.34 | 0.21 | .... |
| *Only 52% qualifies for divd exclusion. | | | | |
| Channing Intl Growth Fd | 0.72 | *b0.177 | 0.582 | .... |
| *Incl $0.039 foreign taxes pd for stkhldrs account. | | | | |
| Channing Special Fund | 0.18 | 0.08 | 0.10 | .... |
| Chase Fund Boston | 0.245 | 0.085 | 0.16 | .... |
| Chemical Fund | 0.89 | 0.24 | 0.65 | .... |
| Chesapeake Fund | 0.55 | 0.20 | 0.35 | .... |
| Chic Milw St Paul & Pac Ry Common | 1.00 | .... | .... | 1.00 |
| 5% N-C Pfd Ser A | 5.00 | .... | .... | 5.00 |
| Chicago & North West Ry | 3.00 | a25% | .... | a75% |
| Chicago Rock Island & Pac RR | 0.25 | .... | .... | 0.25 |
| City Gas Co of Florida | 0.50 | .... | .... | 0.50 |
| Colonial Fund | 0.93 | *0.41 | 0.52 | .... |
| *Only 68% qualifies for divd excl. | | | | |
| Colonial Growth & Energy Shs | 0.80 | 0.236 | 0.564 | .... |
| Columbia Realty Trust | 0.60 | .... | .... | 0.60 |
| Commonwealth Realty Trust | 0.60 | Status not yet available | | |
| Composite Bond & Stk Fd | 0.66 | *0.30 | 0.36 | .... |
| *Only 57.66% qualifies for divd exclusion. | | | | |
| Composite Fund | 0.64 | 0.22 | 0.42 | .... |
| Concord Fund | 0.47 | 0.30 | 0.17 | .... |
| Connecticut Light & Pwr | 1.46 | 85% | .... | 15% |
| Consol Edison of NY | 1.80 | 37% | .... | 63% |
| Consol Investment Trust | 0.60 | 0.38 | 0.22 | .... |
| Consultant's Mutual Invest | 0.82 | 0.23 | 0.59 | .... |
| Consumers Investment Fund | 0.145 | 0.06 | 0.085 | .... |
| Convertible Securities Fd | 0.58 | *0.36 | 0.22 | .... |
| *Status for divd exclusion later. | | | | |
| Convertible Secur & Growth Stk Fd | 0.80 | *0.07 | 0.73 | .... |
| *Status for divd exclusion later. | | | | |
| Corporate Leaders Trust | 4.72 | *.... | *.... | *.... |
| *Jun distribution taxable 9.0867% as income, 35.0392% as cap gains, & 55.8741% nontaxable; Dec distribution 18.0555% as income, 14.5273% as cap gains, & 67.4172% nontaxable. | | | | |
| Counselors Invest Fund | 0.325 | 0.195 | 0.13 | .... |
| Countrywide Realty | *0.30 | †.... | .... | †.... |
| *Plus stk in Natl Equities Inc com. Tax cost basis, corporate & non-corporate holders $95.53 a sh. | | | | |
| †Cash pd in connection with 2% stk divd; distribution in Natl Equities stk (equivalent to $3.82 per Countrywide sh); and $0.20 cash pd Mar 30'65, are 9.42% taxable as income & 90.58% nontaxable. Status of Sep 30 divd available after yr-end. | | | | |
| Crown Western Investments | | | | |
| Dallas Fd Ser | 0.135 | 0.13 | 0.005 | .... |
| Divers Fd Ser | 0.62 | 0.185 | 0.435 | .... |
| Day Mines | 0.20 | Status avail. after yr-end. | | |
| Decatur Income Fund | 0.95 | *0.48 | 0.47 | .... |
| *Only $0.28 qualifies for divd exclusion. | | | | |
| Delaware Fund | 1.10 | 0.235 | 0.865 | .... |
| Detroit & Canada Tunnel | 1.20 | 91.418% | .... | 8.582% |
| Detroit Internatl Bridge | 1.05 | Status not yet available | | |
| De Vegh Mutual Fd | 9.01 | 1.07 | 7.94 | .... |
| Devonshire Street Fd | 0.3225 | 0.18 | 0.1425 | .... |
| Diversification Fund | 0.56 | 0.56 | *.... | .... |
| *Co at 5/31/65, had undistributed cap gains of 0.052 a sh. | | | | |
| Diversified Growth Stk Fund | 0.485 | 0.115 | 0.37 | .... |
| Diversified Invest Fund | 0.695 | *0.345 | 0.35 | .... |
| *Only 71% qualifies for divd excl. | | | | |
| Diversified Trustee Shs C | 0.726 | *.... | *.... | *.... |
| *Jun divd: Income 82.75% (only 81.13% qualifies for divd exclusion); cap gains 15.78%; nontaxable 1.47%. Dec divd; income 99.94% (only 98.43% qualifies for divd exclusion); cap gains 0.06%. | | | | |
| Dividend Shares | 0.2325 | 0.1005 | 0.132 | .... |
| Dominick Fund | 1.48 | 0.48 | 1.00 | .... |
| Dorsey Corp | | | | |
| Common | 0.10 | .... | .... | 0.10 |
| 6% Pfd. A | 3.00 | .... | .... | 3.00 |
| 6% Pfd AA | 3.00 | .... | .... | 3.00 |
| Drexel Equity Fd | 0.39 | 0.186 | 0.204 | .... |
| Dreyfus Fund | 1.19 | 0.41 | 0.78 | .... |
| Duquesne Light | 1.40 | 1.1049 | .... | 0.2951 |
| Eaton & Howard Bal Fund | 0.8025 | *0.4025 | 0.40 | .... |
| *Only 64.54% qualifies for divd exclusion. | | | | |
| Eaton & Howard Stock Fund | 1.07 | 0.36 | 0.71 | .... |
| Electric Bd & Sh | 1.55 | .... | .... | 1.55 |
| El Paso Natural Gas | 1.00 | 58.5% | .... | 41.5% |
| Embassy Corp | *0.70 | †.... | .... | †.... |
| *Plus liq. | | | | |
| †Mar distribution taxable 68.2% as income and 31.8% return of cap. Jun distribution of $27.50 was liquidating distribution in entirety. | | | | |
| Energy Fund | 1.41 | 0.38762 | 1.02238 | .... |
| Equity Fund | 0.60 | 0.208 | 0.392 | .... |
| Essex Fund | 3.86 | 0.26 | 3.60 | .... |
| Eurofund Inc | 0.25 | *b0.3236871 | ... | .... |
| *Includes foreign tax credit of $0.0736871 a sh. | | | | |
| Exchange Fd of Boston | 0.63 | 0.63 | *.... | .... |
| *Co at 6/30/65 had undistributed cap gains of $0.008 a sh. | | | | |
| Fairfield Securities | 1.32 | 0.067 | 1.253 | .... |

a—Preliminary estimate. b—Does not qualify for dividend exclusion.

## TABLE 16–9 (Continued)

| | 1965 Payments ($) | | | |
|---|---|---|---|---|
| | Total Paid | Income | Cap. Gains | Non-taxable |
| Federal Street Fund | 1.00 | 1.00 | *.... | .... |
| *Co at 6/30/65 had undistributed cap gains of $1.60 a sh. | | | | |
| Fidelity Capital Fund | 2.78 | 0.40 | 2.38 | .... |
| Fidelity Fund | 1.24 | 0.44 | 0.80 | .... |
| Fidelity Trend Fund | 0.96 | 0.27 | 0.69 | .... |
| Fiduciary Mutual Investing | 0.71 | 0.24 | 0.47 | .... |
| Financial Fund Inc. | 0.74 | 0.49 | 0.25 | .... |
| Financial Industrial Fd | 0.31314 | 0.113 | 0.20014 | .... |
| Financial Indus Income Fund | 0.70 | *0.438 | 0.262 | .... |
| *Percentage qualifying for divd exclusion: Jan 71.50%; Apr 62.03%; Jul 61.37%; Oct 66.46%. | | | | |
| First Genl Real Est Tr | 0.34 | 0.0234 | .... | 0.3166 |
| First Hartford Realty | 0.05 | .... | .... | 0.05 |
| First Natl Rlty & Constr Pfd | 0.60 | 0.45 | .... | 0.15 |
| First Union Realty (Ohio) | 0.78 | b0.313 | .... | 0.467 |
| Fitchburg Gas & Elec Lt | 3.00 | Status not yet availabe | | |
| Florida Capital Corp | 0.38 | .... | .... | 0.38 |
| Florida Growth Fund | 0.445 | 0.145 | 0.30 | .... |
| Founders Mutual Fd | 0.208 | 0.2027 | 0.0053 | .... |
| Foursquare Fund | 0.84 | 0.30 | 0.54 | .... |
| Franklin Custodian Funds | | | | |
| Bond & Pfd Stk Ser | 0.15 | *0.115 | .... | .... |
| Common Ser | 0.585 | *0.11 | .... | .... |
| Income Ser | 0.305 | *0.12 | .... | .... |
| Util Ser | 0.255 | *0.125 | .... | .... |
| *Represents divds for 1st 3 quarters. Status of balance of divds available in Feb '66. | | | | |
| Portion eligible for divd excl: Bond & pfd stk, & com ser 25.15%; Inc ser 48.30%; Util ser 100%. | | | | |
| Fundamental Investors | 0.615 | 0.255 | 0.36 | .... |
| General Amer Investors | 2.47 | 0.46 | 2.01 | .... |
| General Precision Equip | | | | |
| Common | 1.20 | .... | .... | 1.20 |
| $4.75 Preferred | 4.75 | .... | .... | 4.75 |
| $1.60 Preference | 1.60 | .... | .... | 1.60 |
| General Public Service | 0.51 | 0.17 | 0.34 | .... |
| General Securities Inc (Minn) | 0.96 | 0.21 | 0.75 | .... |
| Griesedieck Co | 2.45 | 0.48 | 1.97 | .... |
| Group Securities | | | | |
| Aerospace Science Fd | 0.50 | 0.09 | 0.41 | .... |
| Com Stock Fund | 1.12 | 0.52 | 0.60 | .... |
| Fully Admin Fd | 0.755 | *0.375 | 0.38 | .... |
| *Only 67.6% qualifies for divd excl. | | | | |
| Growth Industry Shares | 1.28 | 0.395 | 0.885 | .... |
| Gryphon Fund | 0.57133 | 0.15613 | 0.41520 | .... |
| Guardian Mutual Fd | 1.85 | 0.58 | 1.27 | .... |
| Hamilton Funds Ser H-DA | 0.425 | 0.145 | 0.28 | .... |
| Hartford Elec Light | 2.00 | 1.40 | .... | 0.60 |
| Hawaiian Elec | 1.00 | 65% | .... | 35% |
| Honolulu Gas Co | 1.00 | Status not yet available | | |
| Hugoton Gas Trust | 0.51 | 0.36975 | .... | 0.14025 |
| Huntington Hall | 2.00 | 1.293 | .... | 0.707 |
| Idaho Power | 1.25 | 90% | .... | 10% |
| Imperial Capital Fund | 0.56 | 0.185 | 0.375 | .... |
| Income Fund of Boston | 0.735 | *0.485 | 0.25 | .... |
| *Status for divd exclusion to be determined later. | | | | |
| Incorporated Income Fund | 0.72 | *0.42 | 0.30 | .... |
| *Only 56% qualifies for divd exclusion. | | | | |
| Insur Investors Fd | 1.30448 | 0.79492 | 0.50956 | .... |
| Intl Bank Washington DC | 0.10 | Status not yet available | | |
| Intl Holdings | 3.42 | *1.34 | 2.08 | .... |
| *Only 67% qualifies for divd exclusion. | | | | |
| Intl Resources Fund | 0.57 | *0.085 | 0.485 | .... |
| *Only 48% qualifies for divd exclusion. | | | | |
| Intl Stretch Products | 0.225 | *.... | .... | *.... |
| *Feb, May & Aug divds are $0.00249 taxable as income & $0.04751 return of capital. Nov divd estimated $0.00375 as income & $0.07125 return of capital. | | | | |
| Interstate Power | 1.15 | 86.86% | .... | 13.14% |
| Investment Trust Boston | 0.92 | 0.34 | 0.58 | .... |
| Investors Capital Exch Fd | 1.52 | 1.52 | *.... | .... |
| *Co at Jul 31'65 had undistributed cap gains of $1.33718 a sh. | | | | |
| Investors Inter-Contl Fd | 0.37125 | *0.165 | 0.20625 | .... |
| *Only 27.33% qualifies for divd excl. | | | | |
| Investors Mutual Inc | 0.71625 | *0.42875 | 0.2875 | .... |
| *Only 59.88% qualifies for divd excl. | | | | |
| Investors Research Fund | *0.22 | 0.22 | †2.346 | .... |
| *Plus stk. †Pd in stock. | | | | |
| Investors Selective Fd | 0.5385 | *0.4975 | 0.041 | .... |
| *Only 19.38% qualifies for divd exclusion. | | | | |
| Investors Stock Fund | 0.866 | 0.55 | 0.316 | .... |
| Investors Variable Payt Fd | 0.409 | 0.16388 | 0.24512 | .... |
| Israel Development | 1.35 | *1.5347 | .... | .... |
| *Incl $0.1847 foreign taxes pd for stkhldrs account. | | | | |
| Istel Fund | 2.45 | *1.10 | 1.35 | .... |
| *Status for divd exclusion to be announced later. | | | | |
| Ivest Fund | 0.28 | 0.09 | 0.19 | .... |
| Jamaica Water Supply | 1.08 | 64.8609% | .... | 35.1391% |
| Johnston Mutual Fund | 0.91 | 0.28 | 0.62 | 0.01 |
| Kavanau Corp | 0.50 | .... | .... | 0.50 |
| Keystone Custodian Funds | | | | |
| Series B-1 | 1.01 | 0.9532 | .... | 0.0568 |
| Series B-2 | 1.12 | b1.12 | .... | .... |
| Series B-3 | 1.16 | *b0.728 | *0.182 | .... |
| Series B-4 | 0.85 | *b0.4407 | *0.2493 | .... |
| Series K-1 | 0.86 | *†0.3408 | *0.3992 | .... |
| Series K-2 | 0.79 | 0.094 | 0.696 | .... |
| Series S-1 | 3.36 | *0.3733 | *2.8667 | .... |
| Series S-2 | 1.93 | 0.4348 | 1.4952 | .... |
| Series S-3 | 1.55 | 0.3789 | 1.1711 | .... |
| Series S-4 | 0.07 | 0.07 | .... | .... |
| *Covers divds for 1st 3 quarters. Status of 4th quarter divd to be determined later. | | | | |
| †Only $0.157 qualifies for divd excl. | | | | |
| Knickerbocker Fund | 0.51 | 0.195 | 0.315 | .... |
| Lazard Fund | 1.23 | *0.38 | 0.85 | .... |
| *Only 61% qualifies for divd exclusion. | | | | |
| Lehigh Coal & Navigation | 0.60 | 0.082 | .... | 0.518 |
| Lehman Corp. | 1.92 | 0.63 | 1.29 | .... |
| Lexington Income Trust | 1.22 | *0.4814 | 0.7386 | .... |
| *Only 49.11% qualifies for divd excl. | | | | |
| Life Insurance Investors | 0.15 | *0.051 | 0.099 | .... |
| *Only 67.78% qualifies for divd excl. | | | | |
| Life Insurance Stock Fund | 0.062 | 0.014 | 0.048 | .... |
| Loomis-Sayles Canadian & Intl | 2.68 | *b0.71 | 2.14 | .... |
| *Incl $0.17 Canadian tax paid for stkhldrs account. | | | | |
| Loomis-Sayles Cap Devl Fund | 2.17 | 0.17 | 2.00 | .... |
| Madison Fund | 1.85 | 0.47 | 1.38 | .... |
| Maine Public Service | 1.07 | *.... | .... | *.... |
| *Co estimates that a portion of divds will be non-taxable, percentage will be available by Mar 1. | | | | |
| Manhattan Life Insur | *0.2632 | †0.2632 | .... | .... |
| *Plus stk. †Only $0.2065 in Apr qualifies for divd excl. | | | | |
| Mass Investors Growth St Fd | 0.369 | 0.159 | 0.21 | .... |
| Mass Investors Trust | 0.67 | 0.49 | 0.18 | .... |
| Mensh Corp | 0.82666 | .... | .... | 0.82666 |
| Mesabi Trust | 0.7328147 | *.... | *.... | .... |
| *Distributions taxable as income or capital gains. Co. in detailed letter to stockholders dated 1/3/66, has reported tax treatment for those in each of the following categories: (1) Holders who received all four distributions and whose taxable year is calendar year; (2) Holders who received one or more but less than all distributions. | | | | |
| Midwest Investment | 0.85 | *0.306 | 0.094 | .... |
| *Only 34.46% qualifies for divd exclusion. Represents status of Feb & May divds. Status of Aug & Nov divds available after 6/30/66. | | | | |
| Missouri-Kansas Pipe Line | | | | |
| Common | 5.50 | .... | .... | 5.50 |
| Cl B | 0.275 | .... | .... | 0.275 |
| Mutual Inesting Foundation | 0.95 | 0.585 | 0.365 | .... |
| Mutual Investing Foundation Growth Fund | 0.26 | 0.08381 | 0.17619 | .... |
| Mutual Invest Co of Amer | 0.69 | 0.09 | 0.60 | .... |
| Mutual Investment Fund | 0.61 | 0.26 | 0.35 | .... |
| Mutual Securs Fd Boston | 1.81 | 0.21 | 1.60 | .... |
| Mutual Shares Corp | 1.58 | 0.35 | 1.23 | .... |
| Mutual Tr Kansas City Mo | 0.25 | 0.10 | 0.15 | .... |
| Nassau Fund | 0.98 | *0.43 | 0.55 | .... |
| *Apx 65% qualifies for divd. exclusion. | | | | |
| Nation-Wide Securities | *.... | †0.40 | 0.35 | .... |
| *New-0.75; old-stk. †Only 63% qualifies for divd exclusion. | | | | |
| Natl Aviation | 3.36 | *0.79 | 2.57 | .... |
| *Only $0.2515 of Feb & $0.1996 in Aug qualifies for divd exclusion. | | | | |
| National Investors | 0.74 | 0.36 | 0.38 | .... |
| Natl Securities Series | | | | |
| Balanced Series | 1.03 | 0.417 | 0.613 | .... |
| Bond Series | 0.30 | b0.30 | .... | .... |
| Dividend Series | 0.41 | 0.205 | 0.205 | .... |
| Growth Stk Series | 0.54 | 0.116 | 0.424 | .... |
| Income Series | 0.48 | *0.265 | 0.215 | .... |
| Pfd Stk Series | 0.37 | 0.345 | 0.025 | .... |
| Stock Series | 0.69 | 0.305 | 0.385 | .... |
| *Only $0.184 qualifies for divd exclusion. | | | | |
| New Britain Gas Light | 2.60 | 37% | .... | 63% |
| New England Electric System | 1.20 | a75% | .... | a25% |
| New World Fund | 0.41 | 0.17 | 0.24 | .... |
| Newton Fund | 0.75 | *0.57 | 0.18 | .... |
| *Only 72% qualifies for divd exclusion. | | | | |
| Niagara Mohawk Power | *.... | 78% | .... | 22% |
| *Par $8-0.82½; np-0.50. | | | | |
| Niagara Share Corp | 1.00 | 0.445 | *0.555 | .... |
| *Co at Dec 31'65 had undistributed cap gains of $0.48 a sh. | | | | |
| North Amer Investment | 2.00 | 1.00 | 1.00 | .... |
| Northeast Investors Tr | 1.304205 | *0.84 | 0.464205 | .... |
| *Only 32.23% qualifies for divd excl. | | | | |
| Northwest Nat Gas | *.... | 9.21% | .... | 90.79% |
| *p$3⅛—0.22; p$9.50—0.58. | | | | |
| Ogden Corp | 0.55 | *.... | .... | *.... |
| *Co. expects that all or a portion of divds will be nontaxable. | | | | |
| Ohio Capital Fund | 0.43 | 0.43 | *.... | .... |
| *Co at fiscal yr-end had undistributed cap gains of $0.1858 a sh. | | | | |
| One William St Fund | 0.77 | 0.28 | 0.49 | .... |

a—Preliminary estimate. b—Does not qualify for dividend exclusion.

## TABLE 16–9 (Concluded)

| | 1965 Payments ($) | | | |
|---|---|---|---|---|
| | Total Paid | Income | Cap. Gains | Non-taxable |
| Oppenheimer Fund | 1.56 | 0.015 | 1.545 | .... |
| Orange & Rockland Utils | 0.84 | Status not yet available | | |
| Overbook Arms | 4.50 | 2.42685 | .... | 2.07315 |
| Overseas Securities | 2.31 | 0.26 | 2.05 | .... |
| Pacific G & E | 1.175 | 1.175 | .... | .... |
| Pacific Gas Transmission | 0.70 | a75.2% | .... | a24.8% |
| Pacific Power & Light | 1.14 | 41% | .... | 59% |
| Parvin-Dohrmann | 0.40 | .... | .... | a0.40 |
| Penn Square Mutual Fund | 2.22 | 0.44 | 1.78 | .... |
| Pennsylvania Gas & Water | 0.95 | 69% | .... | 31% |
| Pennsylvania Mutual Fund | 0.80 | 0.60 | 0.20 | .... |
| Pennsylvania Real Est Inv Tr | 0.80 | b0.290682 | .... | 0.509318 |
| Peoples Securities | 0.55 | 0.171165 | 0.378835 | .... |
| Petroleum Corp Amer | 1.80 | 0.60 | 1.20 | .... |
| Pioneer Enterprise Fd | 1.23 | 0.23 | 1.00 | .... |
| Pioneer Fund | 0.79 | 0.29 | 0.50 | .... |
| Pine Street Fund | 0.965 | 0.375 | 0.59 | .... |
| Portland General Electric | 0.95 | 42.8% | .... | 57.2% |
| Potomac Elec Power | 0.82 | 71% | .... | 29% |
| Price (T. Rowe) Growth Stk Fd | 0.94 | 0.34 | 0.60 | .... |
| Provident Fund for Income | 0.30 | 0.20 | 0.10 | .... |
| Prudential Fund of Boston | 3.60 | *1.15 | 2.45 | .... |
| *Only 61% qualifies for divd exclusion. | | | | |
| Public Service Co N.H. | 1.21 | 1.0438 | .... | 0.1662 |
| Public Serv El & Gas | 1.385 | 90.68% | .... | 9.32% |
| Puget Sound Pwr & Lt | | | | |
| Common | 1.60 | .... | .... | 1.60 |
| $4.84 Pfd | 4.84 | 40.46% | .... | 59.54% |
| 4.70% Pfd | 4.70 | 40.46% | .... | 59.54% |
| Puritan Fund | 0.55 | 0.38 | 0.17 | .... |
| Putnam (Geo) Fd Boston | 1.02 | 0.50 | 0.52 | .... |
| Putnam Growth Fund | 0.57 | 0.15 | 0.42 | .... |
| Putnam Income Fund | 0.515 | b0.245 | 0.27 | .... |
| Quarterly Distribution Shs | 0.54 | *0.24 | 0.30 | .... |
| *Only 62% qualifies for divd exclusion. | | | | |
| Ramada Inns | 0.40 | .... | .... | 0.40 |
| Republic Technology Fd | 0.08 | 0.08 | .... | .... |
| Revere Fund | 0.70 | .... | 0.70 | .... |
| Riker Delaware Corp | *0.84 | .... | .... | 0.84 |
| *Plus stock. | | | | |
| Rittenhouse Fund | 0.90 | *0.40 | 0.50 | .... |
| *Only 68% qualifies for divd exclusion. | | | | |
| Rutland Ry Corp | 3.90 | .... | .... | 3.90 |
| Savannah Elec & Pwr | 0.92 | 82.06% | .... | 17.94% |
| Scudder Intl Invests | 0.80 | b0.32982 | 0.47018 | .... |
| Scudder Special Fund | 2.84 | 0.32 | 2.52 | .... |
| Scudder Stevens & Clark Bal Fd | 1.48 | *0.56 | 0.92 | .... |
| *Only 58% qualifies for divd exclusion. | | | | |
| Scudder Stevens & Clark | | | | |
| Com Stock Fund | 0.99 | 0.30 | 0.69 | .... |
| Second Ohio Capital Fd | 0.07 | 0.07 | *.... | .... |
| *Co at Nov 30'65 had undistributed cap gains of apx $1.12 a sh. | | | | |
| Securities Fund | 0.54 | *0.24 | 0.30 | .... |
| *Only 73.74% qualifies for divd exclusion. | | | | |
| Security Diversified Shs | 0.49 | *0.26 | 0.23 | .... |
| *Only 62.82% of May & 81.62% of Nov income divds qualify for divd exclusion. | | | | |
| Security Equity Fd | 0.22 | 0.04 | 0.18 | .... |
| Selected American Shares | 0.79 | 0.24 | 0.55 | .... |
| Shareholders' Tr Boston | 0.88 | *0.42 | 0.46 | .... |
| *Only 65% qualifies for divd exclusion. | | | | |
| Shares in American Industry | 0.67 | 0.21 | 0.46 | .... |
| Sierra Pacific Power | *.... | †.... | .... | †.... |
| *Par $3.75-0.42; p$7.50-0.25. | | | | |
| †Co estimates that substantially more than 50% will be nontaxable. Actual percentage will be available in Feb '66. | | | | |
| Soo Line Railroad | 2.75 | Status not yet available | | |
| Southern Cal Water | 0.84 | a52% | .... | a48% |
| A further determination will be made in Feb. | | | | |
| Southwest Gas Corp | 0.65 | *.... | .... | *.... |
| *15% nontaxable in Jun, 100% in Sep & 78% in Dec, Mar divds were fully taxable. | | | | |
| Southwestern Elec Serv | 0.85 | *.... | .... | *.... |
| *Mar & Jun divds 49.57% nontaxable; Sep & Dec divds estimated 33.89% nontaxable. | | | | |
| Southwestern Investors | 0.59 | 0.22 | 0.37 | .... |
| Southwestern Pub Serv | 1.20 | *.... | .... | *.... |
| *Mar, Jun & Sep divds are 13.80% nontaxable; Dec divd is estimated 6.22% nontaxable. | | | | |
| Sovereign Investors Inc | 1.02 | 0.47 | 0.55 | .... |
| Standard Shares | 0.50 | .... | .... | 0.50 |
| State St Investment | 2.75 | 0.90 | 1.85 | .... |
| Steadman Investment Fund | 0.61 | 0.25 | 0.36 | .... |
| Steadman Sc & Growth Fund | 0.25 | 0.10 | 0.15 | .... |
| Stein Roe & Farnham Bal Fd | 2.43 | *1.04 | 1.39 | .... |
| *Only 41.4% qualifies for divd exclusion. | | | | |
| Stein Roe & Farnham Intl Fd | 1.05 | *0.37 | 0.68 | .... |
| *Amount of foreign taxes pd for stkhldrs account to be announced later. | | | | |
| Stein Roe & Farnham Stk Fd | 1.25 | 0.75 | 0.49 | .... |
| Sterling Investment Fund | 0.80 | *0.44 | 0.36 | .... |
| *Only 58.13% qualifies for divd exclusion. | | | | |
| Supervised Shares | 0.11 | 0.04 | 0.07 | .... |
| Television-Elect Fund | 0.59 | 0.18 | 0.41 | .... |
| Tenn Gas Transmission | *1.04 | 62% | .... | 38% |
| *Plus stk. | | | | |
| Texas Capital | 0.24 | *0.2110362 | 0.0289638 | .... |
| *Only 0.621% of Apr divd & 1.550% of Jul & Oct divds qualify for divd excl. Jan divd does not qualify. | | | | |
| Texas Fund | 0.94 | 0.26 | 0.68 | .... |
| Transamerica Corp | *0.80 | 28% | .... | 72% |
| *Plus stock. | | | | |
| Transwestern Mutual Fd | 0.23 | 0.16 | 0.07 | .... |
| Tri-Continental Corp | *.... | 100% | †.... | .... |
| *p$0.50-0.33; p$1-1.13. | | | | |
| †Co at Dec 31'65 had undistributed cap gains of $1.46 a sh. | | | | |
| 20th Century Growth Investors | 0.205 | *0.026 | 0.179 | .... |
| *Only 56.33% qualifies for divd exclusion. | | | | |
| 20 Century Income Investors | 0.35 | *0.183 | 0.167 | .... |
| *Only 63.26% qualifies for divd exclusion. | | | | |
| Unified Mutual Shares | 0.29 | 0.1566 | 0.11 | 0.0234 |
| Union Elec | 1.12 | a70% | .... | a30% |
| United Corp | 0.35 | .... | .... | 0.35 |
| United Funds | | | | |
| United Accum Fund | 0.70 | 0.435 | 0.26 | 0.005 |
| United Bond Fd | 0.30 | b0.30 | .... | .... |
| United Income Fd | 0.80 | 0.37 | 0.43 | .... |
| United Science Fd | 0.42 | 0.12 | 0.30 | .... |
| United Funds Canada | 0.13 | *b0.10 | 0.057 | .... |
| *Incl $0.027 Canadian tax paid for stkhldrs account. | | | | |
| U S & Foreign Secur | 1.32 | 1.061 | 0.259 | .... |
| Value Line Fd | 0.467 | *0.15 | 0.317 | .... |
| *Only 69.1% qualifies for divd exclusion. | | | | |
| Value Line Income Fund | 0.435 | *0.25 | 0.185 | .... |
| *Only 61.6% qualifies for divd exclusion. | | | | |
| Value Line Special Situations Fund | 0.06 | 0.03 | 0.03 | .... |
| Vanderbilt Mutual Fund | 0.49 | 0.17 | 0.32 | .... |
| Varied Industry Plan | 0.227 | 0.115 | 0.112 | .... |
| Wall Street Investing | 0.35 | 0.25 | 0.10 | .... |
| Washington Mutual Invest Fd | 0.77 | 0.36 | 0.41 | .... |
| Washington Nat Gas (Del) | 0.72 | a70% | .... | a30% |
| Washington Real Est Inv Tr | 0.40 | .... | .... | 0.40 |
| Washington Water Power | 1.08 | 0.60 | .... | 0.48 |
| Wellington Fd | 1.01 | *0.48 | 0.53 | .... |
| *Only 56% qualifies for divd exclusion. | | | | |
| Westminster Fund | 0.24 | 0.24 | *.... | .... |
| *Co at Dec 31'65 had undistributed cap gains of $0.6139936 a sh. | | | | |
| Whitehall Fund | 1.10 | *0.52 | 0.58 | .... |
| *Only 45% qualifies for divd exclusion. | | | | |
| Windsor Fund | 1.19 | 0.22 | 0.97 | .... |
| Winfield Growth Indus Fd | 0.66 | 0.09 | 0.57 | .... |
| Wisconsin Fund | 0.51 | 0.16 | 0.35 | .... |

a—Preliminary estimate. b—Does not qualify for dividend exclusion.

Information has been obtained from sources believed to be reliable, but its accuracy and completeness, and that of the opinions based thereon, are not guaranteed.

Source: Standard & Poor's, *The Outlook*, February 7, 1966.

income must be reinvested in the child's name, or used for the child's benefit, and cannot be used in such a way as to relieve the parent of the legal obligation to support the child. The fact that the child, on the income tax returns filed for him, takes a $600 personal exemption, does not prevent the parent from taking another $600 exemption for the child on the parent's income tax returns, providing the parent pays more than half the cost of the child's support in the taxable year. Stock gifts to children permit the spreading of dividend income, or capital gains, over members of the family, with a resultant lessening of tax liability.

There are numerous additional tax savings opportunities in securities transactions. There are tax savings opportunities in the form of objectives, such as postponing tax recognition of gain, converting short-term gains into long-term gains, etc. For example, an investor who wants to sell a security but defer the recognition of gain until the next year can do so by selling short an equal number of shares and covering the short sale in the following year with the shares originally held. This is commonly known as "selling short against the box." The long-term or short-term nature of the gain will be determined at the time of the short sale and therefore will not be affected by the deferral.[11]

Schneider and Wintrub indicate that an investor may wish to protect his profit in stock which was acquired on May 1, 1966, for $20 a share and which is selling on December 1, 1966, for $50. Yet he may wish to defer tax recognition of the gain until 1967. Instead of recognizing a $30-per-share long-term capital gain in 1966, the investor could sell the stock short at $50 and defer the closing of such sale until January, 1967, at which time the long-term gain of $30 per share (less transfer fees and taxes) will be recognized.[12]

The subject has many ramifications and is quite complicated. Furthermore, tax laws and rulings change frequently. Every active investor needs to prime himself annually with current up-to-date information on the wide variety of tax savings opportunities in securities transactions.

### Capital Gains Portfolios

Investing in the performance stocks, or in the popular market favorites as soon as it becomes apparent that they are becoming favorites, is one approach to capital gains. "If you want to make your pile, you have to be in style," wrote Eldon Grimm in the *Financial Analysts Journal*, pointing to the profit possibilities in changing taste patterns in the market. A "hot" issue one year may be a "dud" the next. For example, COMSAT rose from 20 to 70 in 1964 and then fell back to 36 in 1965. Financial Federation, Inc., rose from 14 to 91 and then quickly fell back to 31. Reynolds Metals went from 21 to 81 and then back to 20 again.[13] Universal Match jumped from 8 to 79 and then fell back to 10. Grimm noted that fads in common stock change almost as rapidly as women's styles. You have to be alert to changing fashions in the market, if you would achieve capital

[11] Herman M. Schneider and Warren G. Wintrub, *Tax Savings Opportunities in Securities Transactions* (New York: Lybrand, Ross Bros. & Montgomery, 1966).

[12] Schneider and Wintrub, *op. cit.*, pp. 36–37.

[13] Adjusted for stock splits.

gains, he concluded, after perceiving some of the past emotional surges of the market. For example, during World War I, Bethlehem Steel was in high fashion. It soared from $10 a share in 1914 to $200 just one year later. In the 1920's, talking pictures and radio swept the country and Warner Bros. Pictures shot up from 9¾ in 1927 to 138 in 1928. RCA rose from 12½ in 1922 to 573 in 1929. During the Great Depression, and the early New Deal days, gold and liquor stocks were in high fashion. The price of the old Homestake Mining stock went from 81 in 1931 to 544 in 1936. With the repeal of Prohibition, National Distillers zoomed from 13 in 1932 to 124 a year later. In recent years, office equipment and electronics stocks, airline and color TV shares have been very popular. The advent of the computer sent IBM from 40 to 600, Control Data from $2 to over $100, and then it subsequently fell behind, back down to 23⅜.[14] In color TV, Admiral jumped from 6 to 135. Motorola rose from 30 to 185.[15] The use of jets helped airline stocks soar. Northwest Airlines earnings rose from $1.11 per share in 1961 to $9.99 per share in 1965, and the stock went from 7 to 171. Delta Airlines earnings per share rose from 83 cents in 1961 to $3.61 in 1965; the shares rose from 5 to 97.

By following trends and styles, by investing in performance stocks, by watching lists of the most active stocks and those that make new highs, the astute investor, with sufficient funds available to enable him to take risks, may be able to achieve substantial capital gains. Close attention needs to be paid to timing, however, for unfavorable corporate developments, or a sudden market reversal, or changing styles and fashions, can quickly erase even substantial paper profits. This type of investing calls for a tough nervous system, a nonworrisome disposition, an ability to make decisions quickly and move fast. Temperament and psychological outlook must match astuteness for success in this type of trading.

For the capital gains–minded investor, numerous portfolios are made available from time to time, suggesting aggressive growth stocks, special situations, market favorites, cyclical issues coming into favor, etc. Of all the suggested portfolios in Dr. Barnes's annual *Your Investments*, the most successful have been the "Special Situation" portfolios, selected from among lists of stocks characterized as (1) "Sold-Out Stocks," (2) Stocks Selling Below "Net Quick Assets," (3) Companies Loaded with Cash, (4) Companies Selling at Relatively Low Price-Earnings Ratios, (5) Companies Changing Their Lines, (6) Companies with Major Foreign Interests, (7) Companies with Large Carry-Forward Tax Credits, (8) Possible Growth Companies of Tomorrow, (9) "Shoestring" Stocks, (10) Cumulative Preferreds with Dividend Arrears, (11) Leading Warrants Currently Outstanding, (12) "Flat" Bonds in Arrears, etc.

---

[14] Adjusted for stock splits.

[15] Adjusted for stock splits.

The "Special Situation" portfolio suggested for 1965 was as follows:

American Cyanamid
American Express
Amer.-South African Invest.
Bell & Howell
Boston & Maine 4½s, 1970
Callahan Mining
Coastal States Life
Erie 5s 2020
Ethyl Corp.
Federal Pacific Electric
International Silver
Jostens
Occidental Petroleum
Papercraft
Sunshine Mining
Texas Gulf Sulphur
Texas Instruments
Thompson Ramo Wooldridge
Universal Oil Products
Vanadium Corp.

The "Special Situation" portfolio selected for 1966 included:

Allis Chalmers
Bangor Punta Alegre
Becton, Dickinson
Bell & Howell
Case, J. I.
Endicott Johnson
Gulf & Western
Hertz
International Pipe & Ceramics
Kennametal
Laboratory for Electronics
Molybdenum Corp.
National Video
Ogden Corp.
Philadelphia & Reading
Realty Equity Warrants
San Diego Imperial
SCM Corp.
Texas Gulf Sulphur
Transitron

The "Special Situation" portfolio selected for 1967 included:

Alberto-Culver
Bangor Punta Alegre
Disney, Walt
Georgia International Life
Gulf & Western Industries
Howmet
Hunt Food & Industries
Kaufman & Broad
Laboratory for Electronics
National General
Occidental Petroleum
Pepsico
Purex
Rayette-Faberge
Reece
Stanley Warner
Sunasco Warrants
Tootsie Roll Industries
Transamerica
Twentieth Century-Fox[16]

The special situation approach fared best of all Barnes's sample portfolios over the five-year period from September, 1961, to September, 1966. For the entire period, the combined gain for five similarly constructed sample portfolios was 259%, far outpacing the 13.2% gain for the Standard & Poor 500 stock index over the same period.

The Eastman Dillon portfolio recommendations, referred to earlier, contained "Group V: Specialty Capital Gains Vehicles." This group is divided into two categories. The first is labeled "revitalized growth situations." These are companies whose past earnings did not, in the opinion of

[16] Source: Barnes, *op. cit.*, 1965, 1966, and 1967.

the Eastman Dillon experts, provide a true measure of future potential. Research indicated prospective upturns in earning power which had not at that time been reflected in the price of the stock. Thus they were regarded as especially attractive current values for capital gains. The companies listed included Atlantic Richfield, Congoleum-Nairn, Connecticut General Life Insurance, Cyprus Mines, Dresser Industries, General Dynamics, Rayette-Faberge, National Life and Accident Insurance, Sinclair Oil, and Wilson & Co.

The second major subcategory in Group V is called "unrecognized growth situations." The past records and future prospects of these issues have not been widely noted by investors and price-earnings ratios are generally quite moderate. When and if their potential receives broader market recognition, this could be reflected in prices that are substantially higher multiples of earnings. Since most of these companies are of moderate size and must retain all or a major portion of earnings to finance continued expansion, current dividend yields are low or nonexistent. Thus they are likely to appeal to capital gains investors. Companies listed in this category included Farmers New World Life, Matheson, Northwestern National Life, Swank, Inc., and Vanity Fair Mills.

Along similar lines are the stocks listed in John S. Herold's *America's Fastest Growing Companies*. Here companies are selected based on high growth rates of earnings and are dropped when growth rates show signs of declining. Herold maintains an investment vehicle, the Connecticut Capital Company, in which a hypothetical fund is invested, stocks bought, held, and sold, and performance measured against the Dow-Jones Industrial Average. As of the spring of 1966, the Connecticut Capital Company was 47% invested in 10 stocks with the remaining 53% in cash and short-term U.S. government securities. The 10 stocks held were CTS, Coffee-Mat, Delta Airlines, Famous Artists, Grumman, Koehring, Opticks, Swank, Swingline, and Unishops, Inc. This service has in the past unearthed some interesting though obscure growth companies whose earnings rates were rising rapidly. In bull markets many of the listings did very well, though some had comet-like careers, streaking brilliantly across the investment sky, and then falling beyond the horizon.

Standard & Poor's regularly publishes recommendations for capital gains. In addition to the stock of the month, which is written up once a month in *The Outlook*, the various forecast issues provide master lists and special lists of capital gains suggestions, as shown in Table 16–10. Various brokerage houses also publish capital gains portfolio suggestions. For example, in Table 16–5, the "Speculative Category" in the Merrill Lynch, Pierce, Fenner & Smith "Selected Issues" can be so regarded. The list is issued quarterly, and over the last decade the speculative recommendations have had a remarkably successful record on the whole.

A variant of the capital gains portfolio is the "Inflation Protection"

## TABLE 16–10

### Standard & Poor's Capital Gain Recommendations

**8 "WAVE OF THE FUTURE" STOCKS**

The following stocks, from the S&P 200 Rapid Growth Stocks, are favorably regarded growth situations. Their main attraction is for long-term capital appreciation.

| *Issue | Approx. Price | Indic. Divd. $ | Yield % | Earn. $ Per Share 1965 | Earn. $ Per Share E1966 | †Growth Rate % |
|---|---|---|---|---|---|---|
| Abbott Laboratories .. | 47 | 1.00 | 2.1 | 1.87 | 2.05 | 14 |
| ★Dow Chemical ..... | 62 | 2.00 | 3.2 | 3.58 | 4.05 | 13 |
| Eastman Kodak ...... | 126 | 2.15 | 1.7 | 3.07 | 3.85 | 14 |
| Grolier Inc. ......... | 51 | 1.50 | 2.9 | [1]4.02 | [1]4.40 | 15 |
| Pan Am. World Airways | 58 | 0.60 | 1.0 | 3.20 | 4.75 | 49 |
| Perkin-Elmer ........ | 47 | Nil | .. | [2]1.47 | [2]1.70 | 19 |
| Texas Instruments ... | 110 | 0.60 | 0.5 | 2.46 | 3.30 | 14 |
| Xerox Corp. .......... | 214 | 1.00 | 0.5 | 2.78 | 3.85 | 84 |

*Listed on New York Stock Exchange. ★Included in Master List. E—Estimated. [1]Incl. tax cr. [2]Yrs. to July 31, of follow. cal. yr. †1960-65.

**GROUP 2—STOCKS PRIMARILY FOR LONG-TERM CAPITAL GAIN**

| *COMMON STOCKS | 1966 Price Range | Recent Price | [7]Sh. Earn. $ 1965 | [7]Sh. Earn. $ E1966 | [4]Div. $ | Yield % | ‡P.E. Ratio |
|---|---|---|---|---|---|---|---|
| American Can -- | 59¾- 44¾ | 48 | 3.61 | 4.25 | 2.20 | 4.6 | 11.3 |
| Cities Service -- | 55⅜- 40 | 47 | 3.86 | 4.25 | 1.80 | 3.8 | 11.1 |
| Coca-Cola ----- | 89¼- 71½ | 86 | 2.66 | 3.10 | 1.90 | 2.2 | 27.7 |
| Columb's & S. Ohio | 41¼- 31⅝ | 34 | 2.31 | 2.35 | 1.52 | 4.5 | 14.5 |
| Consumers Pwr.-- | 57 - 40⅞ | 50 | 2.83 | 3.10 | 1.90 | 3.8 | 16.1 |
| Dow Chemical -- | 78 - 54 | 62 | 3.58 | 4.05 | 2.00 | 3.2 | 15.3 |
| du Pont (E. I.) -- | 242 -146½ | 151 | 8.63 | 8.50 | 5.75 | 3.8 | 17.8 |
| Ford Motor ---- | 57½- 39 | 39 | 6.32 | 5.75 | 2.40 | 6.2 | 6.8 |
| Gen. Am. Transp. | 48¼- 28½ | 33 | 2.41 | 2.65 | 1.55 | 4.7 | 12.5 |
| General Electric-- | 120 - 80 | 97 | 3.90 | 4.45 | 2.60 | 2.7 | 21.8 |
| General Motors - | 108¼- 66 | 66 | 7.41 | 6.15 | 4.55 | 6.9 | 10.7 |
| Gen. Pub. Util. - | 37¾- 26⅛ | 31 | 1.95 | 2.00 | 1.50 | 4.8 | 15.5 |
| Grant (W. T.) -- | 31½- 20½ | 22 | [14]2.52 | [14]2.60 | 1.10 | 5.0 | 8.5 |
| Gulf Oil ------- | 60⅞- 48⅝ | 59 | 4.12 | 4.85 | 2.20 | 3.7 | 12.2 |
| Illinois Power -- | 45⅞- 35⅝ | 40 | 2.12 | 2.25 | 1.60 | 4.0 | 17.8 |
| Johns-Manville -- | 61 - 44⅞ | 47 | 4.03 | 4.60 | 2.20 | 4.7 | 10.2 |
| Lone Star Gas -- | 25⅞- 18¾ | 19 | 1.22 | 1.50 | 1.12 | 5.9 | 12.7 |
| May Dept. Stores | 54⅝- 32½ | 34 | [14]3.07 | [14]3.15 | 1.60 | 4.7 | 10.8 |
| Mobil Oil ------ | 49½- 35¼ | 49 | 3.15 | 3.50 | 1.80 | 3.7 | 14.0 |
| Mont.-Dakota Util. | 39¾- 28½ | 31 | 2.34 | 2.50 | 1.52 | 4.9 | 12.4 |
| National Lead -- | 74½- 52⅝ | 54 | 5.01 | 5.00 | 3.25 | 6.0 | 10.8 |
| North. Natural Gas | 59¼- 41⅜ | 50 | 3.21 | 3.40 | 2.40 | 4.8 | 14.7 |
| Otis Elevator --- | 61⅞- 33⅜ | 38 | 3.41 | 3.30 | 2.00 | 5.3 | 11.5 |
| Owens-Illinois -- | 70 - 54½ | 58 | 3.38 | 3.60 | 1.35 | 2.3 | 16.1 |
| Phillips Petrol'm. | 58⅞- 44⅛ | 53 | 3.83 | 4.30 | 2.20 | 4.2 | 12.3 |
| Pitts. Plate Glass | 81 - 50 | 51 | 5.48 | 5.00 | 2.60 | 5.1 | 10.2 |
| Pub. Serv. E. & G. | 39¾- 28¼ | 36 | 2.23 | 2.35 | 1.54 | 4.3 | 15.3 |
| [1]Reliance Insur.- | 43 - 30¾ | 42 | [11]1.43 | [11]3.25 | 1.60 | 3.8 | 12.9 |
| Reyn'ds (R. J.) Tob. | 45⅞- 34 | 36 | 3.30 | 3.50 | 2.00 | 5.6 | 10.3 |
| Royal Dutch Pet. | 45⅝- 30⅛ | 35 | 3.87 | 4.10 | 1.79 | 5.1 | 8.5 |
| Sears, Roebuck - | 65¾- 45¾ | 49 | [10]2.12 | [10]2.25 | 1.07½ | 2.2 | 21.8 |
| Shell Oil ------ | 68 - 56¼ | 64 | 3.85 | 4.20 | 1.90 | 3.0 | 15.2 |
| Southern Co. ---- | 35 - 24¼ | 30 | 1.39 | 1.45 | 1.02 | 3.4 | 20.7 |
| Southern Pacific- | 47 - 27 | 29 | [18]3.60 | [18]3.75 | 1.50 | 5.2 | 7.7 |
| Stand. Oil (Cal.)- | 86 - 55⅛ | 66 | 5.15 | 5.50 | [28]2.50 | 3.8 | 12.0 |
| Stand. Oil (Ind.)- | 54½- 40¾ | 52 | 3.10 | 3.60 | 1.70 | 3.3 | 14.4 |
| Stand. Oil (Ohio)- | 73 - 55½ | 67 | 4.51 | 5.25 | 2.40 | 3.6 | 12.8 |
| Texaco, Inc. --- | 83 - 61¼ | 74 | 4.71 | 5.10 | 2.65 | 3.4 | 14.5 |
| Transamer. Corp. | 43⅜- 23 | 30 | [12]2.58 | [12]2.80 | [24]1.00 | 3.3 | 10.7 |
| Union Carbide -- | 70⅜- 45⅝ | 48 | 3.75 | 3.90 | 2.00 | 4.2 | 12.3 |
| Union Oil of Cal. | 60 - 45 | 54 | [27]3.47 | 4.30 | 1.20 | 2.2 | 12.6 |
| Union Pacific -- | 47¾- 33 | 39 | [18]4.03 | [18]4.65 | 2.00 | 5.1 | 8.4 |

Source: *The Outlook*, March 7, 1966. (Standard & Poor's 1966 Spring Forecast.)

portfolio. When inflation threatens the economy, as it does from time to time, such portfolios, consisting largely of natural resource companies, are suggested as a means of conserving the value—purchasing power—of wealth. They are expected to provide a sufficient advance in the price of the natural resource companies' stocks to offset at least the decline in the value of the dollar.[17]

Dr. Barnes's sample portfolio for inflation protection contained the following stocks:

| | |
|---|---|
| Amerada | First National City Bank |
| Anaconda | Gulf Oil |
| Bankers Trust Co. of New York | General Development |
| Boise Cascade | Indian Head Warrants |

[17] If, however, the natural resource is in excessive supply relative to demand, the price of the stock may not rise and the shares may not serve as an inflation hedge.

International Nickel
Kern County Land
Mobil Oil
Moore
National Biscuit
Newmont Mining
Occidental Petroleum
Standard Oil of California
Seven Arts Production
Standard Brands
Sunasco Warrants
Texaco
U.S. Plywood

The Standard & Poor's suggested list of nine stocks to outrun inflation included: Amerada Petroleum, Anaconda, Boise Cascade, Freeport Sulphur, Georgia-Pacific, International Nickel, Mesabi Trust, Texaco, and Texas Gulf Sulphur.

### Other Capital Gains Vehicles

Warrants appear above in the inflation protection portfolio because they are usually more volatile than the stock on which they are a claim. Warrants tend to rise faster in bull markets and fall more rapidly in bear markets than the stocks for which they can be exchanged.

Warrants are options to buy securities, generally common stock, at a given price. They are on occasion issued in connection with reorganizations; at other times they are offered to help the sale of securities which would not be attractive to investors without the warrants. That is, they are often attached to bonds to help "sweeten" the issue. Nondetachable warrants may be sold only along with the securities to which they are attached; detachable warrants may be sold separately. Rights are relatively short-lived, whereas warrants are good either for a period of years or indefinitely until exercised. Warrants fluctuate more than the stock to which they apply, and in this sense they are more speculative.

An advertisement about warrants begins: "$500 to $104,000 in 4 years." It tells the amazing but true story of the RKO warrant. In 1940 the Radio-Keith-Orpheum Company (RKO) reorganized after some years of bad fortune. The old common stockholders seemed to fare badly. For each old share, they received only one sixth of a share of new common stock plus one warrant good to buy one share of new common stock from the company at $15 per share. In 1942 RKO common was selling at a low of 2½ and with general pessimism rife, the chance of RKO common ever selling above $15, at which point the warrants would begin to have some actual value, seemed slim. RKO warrants were therefore selling at only one sixteenth, or 6¼ cents, per warrant. But this picture changed in four years. The RKO common stock advanced to a high of 28⅛. The right to buy RKO common at $15 per share from the company when it was selling on the open market at $28 per share was worth $13, and the warrants did sell at exactly $13. Thus you can see that $500 invested in these warrants in 1942 was worth $104,000 by 1946. The greater volatility of the warrant is apparent. Between 1942 and 1946,

RKO common went from 2½ to 28. Therefore a $500 investment in the stock appreciated to $5,625. But the warrant went from 6¼ cents to $13. Therefore a $500 investment in the warrant rose to $104,000.

Warrants are not for amateurs. Volatility on the downside is just as great and can inflict severe losses. Also, no return is earned on funds in warrants and often warrants expire, resulting in total loss to unsophisticated investors.

A convertible bond is a claim on stock, of course. Suppose a $1,000 convertible bond can be exchanged for 20 shares of stock. Suppose the stock is now selling for $50, and the bond is at par, i.e., it is selling at its conversion price. To buy $1,000 worth of this stock, or 20 shares, directly on margin would require 70% margin or $700. To buy the $1,000 bond on margin might require $200, with a bank lending $800. If the stock goes up to $55 per share, the common stock margin investor will have made $100 on an investment of $700, or 14+ %. If the bond rises simply by the increased value of the stock to which it is convertible and thus goes to $1,100, the bond investor will have made $100 on an investment of $200, or 50%.[18] From this greatly simplified example, it will be apparent that the main advantage to a capital gains–minded investor of a convertible bond is its capacity to serve as a claim on common stock at a much lower margin, and therefore with much greater percentage appreciation of capital actually invested, than direct common stock investment itself.

The sophisticated investor can take advantage of a declining market as well as a rising market. Assuming he makes a skillful appraisal of the leading economic indicators and the technical market measures and concludes that the market is about to top out and a recession set in, what can he do about it? Several courses of action are open.

He can sell short. Since short selling is a risky business, the investor should not undertake it unless both economic and technical market indicators have turned bearish. In picking stocks for short sale it is wise to choose those with poor prospects and paying little or no dividends. Avoid stocks that are closely held or companies which have only a limited number of shares outstanding. Warrants are useful for short selling because when they go down they decline sharply and they pay no dividends.

There are two ways of hedging—of protecting yourself from serious loss—on a short sale. You can buy a call option or you can place a stop-loss order. A call is an option to buy a specified number of shares of stock within a given period of time, such as 90 days or six months, at a specified price.[19] The price paid is known as a premium. The premium

[18] As the stock rises, the value of the bond will usually go to a premium above its stock conversion value.

[19] See *The ABC of Puts & Calls*, Godnick & Son, Inc., included in this book as an appendix to Chapter 12. See also Herbert Filer, *Understanding Put and Call Options* (New York: Crown Publishers, Inc., latest edition).

varies according to the stock, its price, its volatility, and the length of the option. If you sell Consolidated Hokum short when it is selling at 90 because you expect it to fall to 50, there is always the chance that it may fool you and rise to 130. If it falls to 50 and you cover, buy back at this point, fine. You sold at 90, bought back or covered at 50, and you have a 40-point profit. But suppose right after you sold short at 90 the stock starts to rise. As it rises you suffer a loss. To avoid this possibility, when you sell short at 90 you also buy a call on the stock, through a put and call broker, for six months at say $800 for 100 shares at 90. If the stock goes down to 50 and you close out the short sale, you don't, of course, exercise the call option. The cost of it, of course, lessens the gain from the short sale ($4,000 – $800 = net $3,200 less commission and transfer taxes). But should the stock rise rather than fall, the call option protects the short seller. Suppose just before the six-month call option is up, the stock has risen to 130. If you had to buy it back at that price to cover your short sale you would be out $4,000. But instead of buying back to cover, you exercise the call option and buy the stock at 90, the same price as your short sale. Your loss then is limited to the $800 cost of the call option plus commissions and transfer taxes.

The second method of hedging utilizes a stop-loss order. When you sell short at 90 you also place a stop-loss order to buy at say 95. Thus if your expectations are not realized and the stock rises instead of falling, when it reaches 95 your broker automatically buys 100 shares at 95 and you have covered, with a loss limited to 5 points, or $500. You can, of course, set your buy loss limit at any level you want. To engage in short selling without either a call hedge or a stop-loss hedge is foolish, because an unhedged short sale has a possible unlimited loss potential.

The second way you can profit by successful anticipation of a declining market is to buy put options. A put is an option to sell a specified number of shares of stock within a specified period of time at a specified price. Naturally, puts are bought mainly by people who think prices of stocks are going to decline. Suppose you expect the price of Consolidated Hokum to fall from 90 to 50 or some such level. You buy a put option on Consolidated Hokum at 90 for six months for $800. Thus you now have the right for six months to sell 100 shares of Consolidated Hokum to the seller of the option at $90 per share. You sit back and wait. Just before the end of that six months, Con Hok is selling for $60. You buy 100 shares in the market at 60 and resell them to your put option seller at $90. You make $3,000 less the $800 cost of the option. Had the stock gone up instead of down, you would not have exercised your option and would have been out its $800 cost.

A third method of taking advantage of a correct forecast of a market decline and recession is to switch out of common stocks into high-grade bonds. At the peak of a boom, common stock prices will be at very high levels, interest rates will be high, and the prices of high-grade bonds will be at low levels, considerably under par. After the turning point comes, stocks will decline, interest rates will fall, and high-grade bond prices will rise. By selling stocks and using part of the proceeds to buy high-grade bonds, say, long-term U.S. governments on very low margin, substantial additional profits can be realized as the bonds rise from below par to par and possibly go above par. For example, you anticipate a recession. You put up $10,000 and borrow $80,000 from a bank to buy $90,000 worth of long-term U.S. governments selling at 90 (10 points below par). Your recession guess is correct. Stock prices and interest rates decline and high-grade bond prices rise. After six months your U.S. governments are selling at 100. You sell them for $100,000, repay the bank the $80,000 you borrowed, and you have netted a profit of $10,000 on your investment of $10,000, 100% gain in six months and a day. It isn't quite as easy as it sounds but the technique is a valid one. Your forecasting and timing have to be very good to succeed at this.

### On the Verge of Retirement

Having considered the investor at midstream and his probable urge for capital gains and some of the various techniques and means for meeting it, let us turn now to the investor between 65 and 70, the investor at the edge of retirement. His requirements are usually very different. Now the emphasis shifts to maximizing safety and income. No longer is it possible to take speculative chances in the pursuit of capital gains. Since the prime earning years are over, there is no time left to rebuild capital and recoup possible speculative losses. Presumably, the investor on the eve of retirement will want to shift his portfolio to provide income to augment social security and other retirement benefits. The objective becomes mainly the highest income commensurate with safety rather than speculative or even long-term capital gains. At the same time it is advisable to lessen the risk element that previously could be assumed while one had a regular source of earned income.

Of course, individuals differ greatly in financial status, especially at this stage of life. In some cases financial planning undertaken in productive years will now pay off by adequately supplementing social security, insurance, and pension income. Previous success in achieving substantial capital gains may make the difference between a lean retirement and an ample one. Recipients of substantial deferred compensation and large pensions may face no problem at all. In fact, in some cases, because of a change in tax and insurance status, a person may be as well off in retirement as he was when actively employed. This may be demonstrated in very simplified form in the following way. Assume a person before retirement was earning a salary of $25,000 per year, that an investment fund accumulated over the years brought in $2,000 per annum of income and that it cost $875 in annual premiums to carry $50,000 of life insurance. Thus his situation would be as follows:

**Before Retirement**

| | |
|---|---|
| Salary | $25,000 |
| Investment income | 2,000 |
| Total Income | $27,000 |
| Tax exemptions | −1,200 |
| Standard deduction | −1,000 |
| Net taxable income | $24,800 |
| Less taxes | 5,940 |
| Net income after taxes | $18,860 |
| Less insurance premium | 875 |
| Net Income | $17,985 |

Now assume the man involved retires at half pay, receives social security of $2,750, and converts his insurance into a retirement annuity of $3,000 per year. His new financial status would be roughly as follows:

**After Retirement**

| | |
|---|---|
| Pension | $12,500 |
| Social security | 2,750 |
| Insurance annuity | 3,000 |
| Investment income | 2,000 |
| Total Income | $20,250 |
| Less nontaxable income | |
| Social security | −2,750 |
| 30% of pension income | −3,750 |
| Total nontaxable Income | $ 6,500 |
| Net income before taxes | $13,750 |
| Less exemptions* | −2,400 |
| Less standard deduction | −1,000 |
| Net taxable income | $10,350 |
| Taxes on above | $ 1,897 |
| Total income | $20,250 |
| Less taxes | −1,897 |
| Net Income | $18,353 |

* Each individual age 65 or older receives two exemptions ($600 × 2 = $1,200). Thus a married couple, both age 65 or older, are entitled to $2,400 in exemptions.

Thus it would appear, and there are cases like this, that this man will be enjoying slightly higher net income after taxes in retirement than he did before.

Less fortunate, however, are the widows whose husbands at death left lifetime accumulations of from, say, $50,000 to $100,000. These seemed like large savings when they were just surplus and the family lived on the income from the husband's salary. In fact, in an era of high prices and high taxes, the family probably had to skimp and hold back here and there in order to accumulate a surplus of this magnitude. But now suddenly the wife must live on the income from this fund plus social security plus possibly some insurance. If, with safe investment, a 5% return can be earned on, say, the $50,000 plus $25,000 of insurance funds, or a total fund of $75,000, it will yield only $3,750 per year. Add social security of $2,250 a year and the wife has $6,000 a year on which to live, less taxes on the investment part of the income. And yet even this may be better than thousands of individuals who are unable to accumulate any significant resources during their working lifetimes.

In financial planning for retirement, two important developments need to be considered. First, people are living longer now after retirement than they did before, and second, inflation is cutting into the purchasing power of their retirement income. According to annuity life tables, if you live to age 60, you'll probably live a good many years longer. An average male can expect to live another 18½ years, an average woman 22 years, more. Thus in financial planning you have to assume that you are going to live well into retirement. At the same time you have to realize that inflation is continuing to take its toll of the dollar's purchasing power and that any fixed dollar amount, weekly, monthly, or annual, that seems adequate today to take care of retirement needs, is not likely to be adequate 5 or 10 years hence.

One insurance company has for years been featuring an advertisement which in 1940 read "How I retired on $150 a month." By 1950 this had been changed to read "How I retired on $250 a month." By 1960 it read "How I retired on $350 a month." What will it have to be in 1970 or in 1980?

Prices have risen 1¾% compounded over the past 10 years. In 1965 they rose 2%. In 1966 about 3%. At 2%, prices increase 50% in 21 years and double in 35 years. Thus anyone 35 today, planning to retire at 70 and estimating that $500 a month, at today's prices, would meet retirement needs, had better revise his calculation and attempt to achieve a retirement income of $1,000 a month. In 35 years, it may just buy what $500 a month buys today. People who retired 15 years ago have seen the cost of living rise 30%. Those who retired in 1945 saw it rise 65% in their first 15 retirement years, while those who retired in 1940 experienced a 15-year rise of 91%.

Thus the combination of longer retirement life and steady decline in the purchasing power of the dollar poses a financial planning dilemma. How do you ensure that you do not lose any of your capital fund and yet hedge against inflation adequately to preserve purchasing power over 10 to 20 years ahead? How do you combine safety with an inflation hedge?

Several solutions have been suggested. One is the variable annuity. The variable annuity provides a life income, not of a fixed number of dollars, but of variable amounts keyed to an underlying common stock investment portfolio. Under a variable annuity, premiums are invested in common stocks and provide a retirement income that increases as stock prices and dividends increase and decreases as they decline. A fixed annuity, on the other hand, invests premiums primarily in bonds and mortgages and provides a guaranteed fixed dollar annuity income that does not change in amount from year to year, except as extra dividends are added.

It was fear of inflation and its debilitating impact on retirement income which gave rise to the variable annuity. The modern variable annuity was first developed by the Teachers Insurance and Annuity Association of America (TIAA). It established the College Retirement Equities Fund (CREF) in 1952, to enable college teachers who were contributing to the TIAA retirement system (buying an individual fixed dollar annuity) to have up to one half of their contribution (including the college's contribution) go toward the purchase of a CREF variable annuity, with the balance going to TIAA to purchase the fixed dollar annuity.

Based on thorough studies of investment and price trends over a previous 70-year period, the TIAA concluded: (1) It is unwise to commit *all* of one's retirement savings to fixed dollar obligations, since decreases in the purchasing power of the dollar can seriously reduce the value of a fixed income annuity. (2) It is equally unwise to commit *all* of one's retirement savings to equity investments, since variations in prices of common stocks are much too pronounced to permit full reliance on them for the stable income needed during retirement. While changes in common stock prices are by no means perfectly correlated with cost-of-living changes, they have provided considerably better protection against inflation than debt obligations. Therefore, TIAA concluded that contributions to a retirement plan which are partly invested in fixed dollar obligations and partly invested in common stocks offer promise of providing retirement income which is at once reasonably free from violent fluctuations in amount and from serious depreciation through price level changes.

How has this worked over the years since 1952? *Changing Times* recently provided an answer. If a retired professor had made a single payment in 1952 large enough to purchase an initial retirement income of $100 each month in TIAA and CREF, he would now be receiving the same $100 a month plus $12.43 a month dividends from TIAA. But his CREF units would be paying $347, for a monthly income of $459. If in the beginning he had elected to put all his contributions into TIAA and none into CREF, he would have received an initial monthly income of $200 from TIAA and he would still be getting the $200 plus a $25 dividend, a graphic example of how the addition of an equity fund can swell income.[20]

Why not buy common stock directly and provide the variable income in retirement by a systematic liquidation of your investments over your retirement period? There is one big reason why this is impossible. You can set up an investment program but you can't predict how long you will live. Therefore, after retirement you can't know how much of your principal it is safe to spend each year. You might figure on drawing down your money over say 15 years—and then live only half as long. Or you might still be hale and hearty after 20 years—but with all of your funds depleted.

Only an insurance company, spreading the mortality risk on a sound actuarial basis over a large number of people, can guarantee you a distribution of your savings over your full retirement lifetime no matter how long you may live. The insurance company can do this because, dealing with a large number of annuitants, the "losses" on those who live longer than the "average" will be offset by "gains" on those who do not live as long as the average. By enabling you to use up your principal as well as the return on it, over the retirement period, with income guaranteed for life no matter how long you may live, annuities generally provide a higher monthly return than comparable forms of direct investment. The purchase of a $100,000 fixed annuity is a much better arrangement *for retirement* than, say, the direct ownership of $100,000 worth of high-grade bonds. The purchase of a $100,000 variable annuity is a much better arrangement *for retirement* than the ownership of $100,000 worth of either common stock directly or of such ownership through mutual funds.

Of course, if resources are no problem and the device of the annuity is not needed in retirement to permit the cannibalization of capital, then the fixed dollar–variable dollar investment hedge pattern can be achieved by direct investment. Total investment funds can simply be divided into bonds and common stocks. Either a half and half pattern can be permanently maintained or the proportions can be varied in accordance with the principles set forth earlier in the discussion of formula plans.[21] Investors in higher tax brackets will wish to keep the bond part of this retirement investment portfolio in tax-exempts. Indeed, some wealthy investors can go to extremes in this respect. For example, *Fortune* reported that Mrs. Horace Dodge invested the entire estate her husband left her—$56 million —in tax-exempt state and municipal bonds and, assuming an average

---

[20] "Money Enough to Retire On," *Changing Times, The Kiplinger Magazine,* July, 1966, p. 10. A recent change in the TIAA–CREF plan permits up to three quarters of contributions to go into the variable annuity.

[21] See Chapter 15.

return of 3½%, thereby achieved an annual tax-free income of $1,960,000. Of course, bonds and preferreds can be purchased for income by those less favorably situated than was Mrs. Dodge. A sample portfolio suggested by Standard & Poor's is shown in the bottom third of Table 16–12.

As Figure 16–1 suggests, however, it is doubtful if a bond portfolio is useful for income purposes to individuals over long periods of time. Bonds are, of course, suitable for institutional investors who have only fixed dollar obligations to meet. Preferred stocks are basically unattractive, since holders have neither an enforceable claim to interest, as do holders of bonds, nor a right to share in residual profits after prior claims, as have common issues. More important is the fact that quality preferred issues now rarely provide better net yields to individual holders than do government bonds.

### Safety and Income Portfolios

The common stock half of the fund can be invested either in the traditional recommendations for retirement portfolios—"stocks for safety and income"—or in conservative growth stocks. If one can draw a distinction between the two categories, it may be said to rest in the fact that stocks for stability and income may have higher current yields in the form of dividend payments than the lower yielding conservative growth stocks. Over the longer run, however, the conservative growth stocks tend to yield a higher return when dividend yield is combined with capital appreciation.

Various sources provide portfolio suggestions for "safety" stocks or for "income" stocks. Annually, for example, the brokerage house of Paine, Webber, Jackson & Curtis publishes *Heirloom Stocks*, a tabulation of 100 companies which have consistently paid dividends from 40 to 180 years. These are highly qualified to be included in a "safety" portfolio for retirement purposes, and some, such as General Electric, Eastman Kodak, and International Business Machines, can also be classified as conservative growth stocks. The New York Stock Exchange, in a periodic publication called *Stocks on the Big Board*, provides a list of long-time dividend payers. This list of companies which have paid quarterly dividends for 40 years or more is shown in Table 16–11. Standard & Poor's *The Outlook* provides recommended issues in the safety and income categories from time to time. One such list is shown at the top of Table 16–12.

Dr. Barnes annually provides two selected portfolios: one for safety and one for high current income. Sample *Portfolio A—Common Stocks for Safety* included the following:

American Can
American Electric Power
American Home Products
American Tel. & Tel.
Coca Cola
Corn Products
Corning Glass
Eastman Kodak

FIGURE 16–1

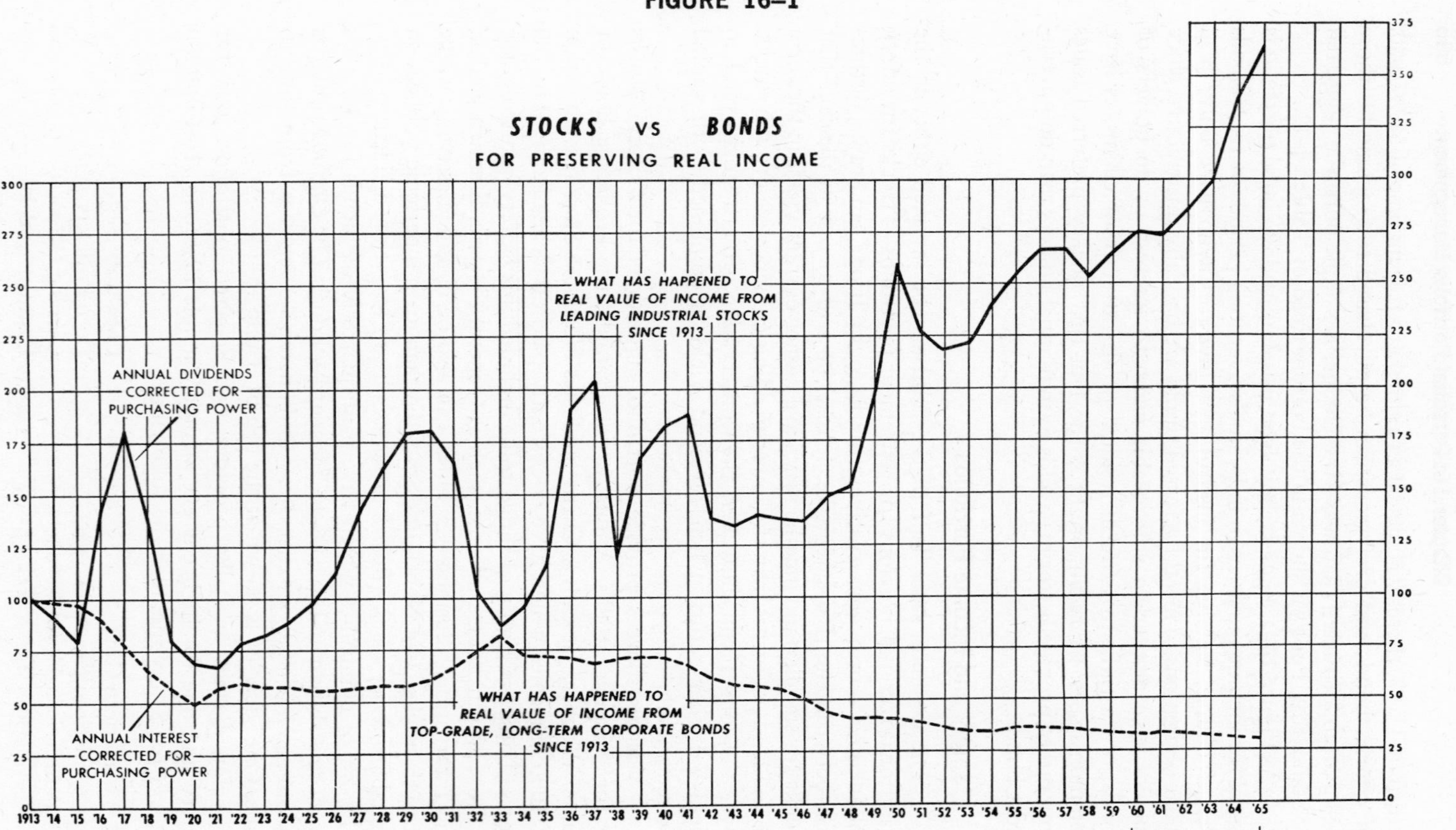
STOCKS vs BONDS
FOR PRESERVING REAL INCOME
WHAT HAS HAPPENED TO
REAL VALUE OF INCOME FROM
LEADING INDUSTRIAL STOCKS
SINCE 1913
ANNUAL DIVIDENDS
CORRECTED FOR
PURCHASING POWER
WHAT HAS HAPPENED TO
REAL VALUE OF INCOME FROM
TOP-GRADE, LONG-TERM CORPORATE BONDS
SINCE 1913
ANNUAL INTEREST
CORRECTED FOR
PURCHASING POWER
0
25
50
75
100
125
150
175
200
225
250
275
300
325
350
375
1913 '14 '15 '16 '17 '18 '19 '20 '21 '22 '23 '24 '25 '26 '27 '28 '29 '30 '31 '32 '33 '34 '35 '36 '37 '38 '39 '40 '41 '42 '43 '44 '45 '46 '47 '48 '49 '50 '51 '52 '53 '54 '55 '56 '57 '58 '59 '60 '61 '62 '63 '64 '65
1913 = 100
FRANCIS I. DU PONT & CO.
RESEARCH DEPARTMENT

## TABLE 16–11

### QUARTERLY DIVIDENDS FOR 40 YEARS OR MORE

| ISSUE | Industry | Closing Price Aug. 19 | DIVIDENDS Quarterly Payments Began | Paid 1965 $ | Ind. Rate $ | % Yld. on Ind. Rate | % Pay-out 5-yr. Av. | +Sh. Earn. Last 12 Mos. $ |
|---|---|---|---|---|---|---|---|---|
| Abex Corp. | 69 | 30 | 1904 | 1.42½ | 1.60 | 5.3 | 55 | [6]3.29 |
| Air Reduction Co. | 17 | 57½ | 1917 | 2.50 | 2.50 | 4.3 | 69 | [6]5.27 |
| Allied Chem. Corp. | 17 | 36⅛ | 1921 | 1.90s | 1.90s | 5.3 | 68 | [6]3.14 |
| Amerada Petroleum | 59 | 71⅛ | 1922 | 2.50 | 2.80 | 3.9 | 56 | [6]4.51 |
| American Can Co. | 19 | 50¼ | 1923 | 2.00 | 2.20 | 4.4 | 70 | [6]4.00 |
| Amer. Elec. Pwr. | 92 | 34⅝ | 1910 | 1.26 | 1.32 | 3.8 | 71 | [6]1.85 |
| Amer. Home Prods. | 22 | 66½ | 1926 | 1.90 | 1.95 | 2.9 | 65 | [6]3.35 |
| Amer. Natural Gas | 93 | 35⅞ | 1904 | 1.70 | 1.80 | 5.0 | 60 | [6]2.99 |
| American News Co. | 75 | 19¼ | 1864 | 1.00 | 1.00s | 5.2 | 85 | [6]1.81 |
| Amer. Tel. & Tel. | 85 | 52⅛ | 1882 | 2.00 | 2.20 | 4.2 | 60 | [5]3.54 |
| American Tobacco | 89 | 31 | 1921 | 1.65 | 1.80 | 5.8 | 58 | [6]3.11 |
| Associates Investing | 29 | 21 | 1920 | 1.40 | 1.40 | 6.7 | 57 | [6]2.47 |
| Balt. Gas & Elec. | 92 | 32⅝ | 1911 | 1.35 | 1.44 | 4.4 | 70 | [6]1.96 |
| Beech-Nut Life Sav. | 33 | 54¾ | 1903 | 1.25 | 1.40 | 2.6 | 53 | [6]2.61 |
| Borden Company | 49 | 32¾ | 1924 | 1.09½ | 1.20 | 3.7 | 55 | [6]2.06 |
| Boston Edison Co. | 92 | 38⅛ | 1892 | 1.60 | 1.76 | 4.6 | 67 | [6]2.43 |
| Brown Shoe Co. | 38 | 48¾ | 1923 | 1.87½ | 2.10 | 4.3 | 45 | [4]4.66 |
| Burroughs Corp. | 58 | 78⅜ | 1906 | 1.00 | 1.00 | 1.3 | 63 | [6]2.92 |
| Carolina Tel. & Tel. | 85 | 18¼ | 1900 | 0.55 | 0.60 | 3.3 | 66 | [6]0.96 |
| Carpenter Steel | 83 | 30⅝ | 1908 | 1.10 | 1.40 | 4.6 | 49 | [6]3.46 |
| Cent. Aguirre Sugar | 84 | 30½ | 1916 | *1.40 | 1.20 | 3.9 | y89 | 70.46[65] |
| Cent. Hudson G.&E. | 92 | 28¼ | 1903 | 1.22 | 1.28 | 4.5 | 64 | [6]2.02 |
| Central Illinois Lt. | 92 | 22⅛ | 1921 | 0.97½ | 1.00 | 4.5 | 67 | [7]1.63 |
| Chase Manh't'n Bk. | 11 | 50¾ | 1918 | 2.00 | 2.00 | 3.9 | 47 | [6]4.53 |
| Chesebrough-Pond's | 21 | 23½ | 1919 | 0.62 | 0.68 | 2.9 | 52 | [6]1.15 |
| C.I.T. Financial | 29 | 24¾ | 1924 | 1.60 | 1.60 | 6.5 | 62 | [6]2.66 |
| Cleveland Elec. Ill. | 92 | 35⅞ | 1912 | 1.32 | 1.68 | 4.7 | 59 | [6]2.46 |
| Clevite Corp. | 6 | 42⅝ | 1922 | 1.65s | 2.10 | 4.9 | 38 | [6]5.28 |
| Cluett, Peabody Co. | 86 | 18½ | 1924 | 0.70 | 0.80 | 4.3 | 44 | [6]1.65 |
| Coca-Cola Co. | 82 | 76¼ | 1921 | 1.70 | 1.90 | 2.5 | 69 | [6]2.87 |
| Combustion Engr'g. | 46 | 43½ | 1912 | 1.30 | 2.00 | 4.6 | 49 | [6]4.33 |
| Commonw'l Edison | 92 | 45⅜ | 1890 | 1.80 | 2.00 | 4.4 | 57 | [7]2.72 |
| Cons. Edison (N.Y.) | 92 | 33¼ | 1892 | 1.80 | 1.80 | 5.4 | 75 | [6]2.27 |
| Continental Can | 19 | 42¾ | 1923 | 1.47 | 1.90 | 4.4 | 54 | [6]3.55 |
| Conwood Corp. | 91 | 25 | 1903 | 1.25 | 1.40 | 5.6 | 61 | [6]2.31 |
| Corn Products Co. | 34 | 40⅞ | 1919 | 1.50 | 1.60 | 3.9 | 69 | [6]2.54 |
| Corning Glass Wks. | 57 | 314 | 1922 | 2.50 | 2.50 | 0.8 | 49 | [6]6.76 |
| Dentists' Sup. NY. | 57 | 26½ | 1923 | 1.30 | 1.45 | 5.5 | 68 | [6]2.25 |
| Detroit Edison Co. | 92 | 30 | 1909 | 1.30 | 1.40 | 4.7 | 71 | [6]2.03 |
| Dome Mines, Ltd. | 53 | 47 | 1920 | g0.90 | 0.90 | 1.9 | 58 | [6]1.56 |
| Dow Chemical | 17 | 67¾ | 1912 | 1.80s | 2.00 | 3.0 | 58 | [6]4.00 |
| Draper Corp. | 45 | 21⅛ | 1897 | 1.00 | 1.20 | 5.7 | 40 | [6]2.59 |
| Duke Power | 92 | 38¼ | 1926 | 1.00 | 1.20 | 3.1 | 66 | [6]1.70 |
| duPont (E.I.) Nem. | 17 | 174⅛ | 1905 | 6.00h | 6.00 | 3.4 | 76 | [6]8.66 |
| Duquesne Light | 92 | 29⅝ | 1913 | 1.40 | 1.50 | 5.1 | 74 | [6]1.94 |
| Eastman Kodak Co. | 5 | 121¼ | 1902 | 1.67½ | 2.05 | 1.7 | 60 | [6]3.47 |
| Elec. Storage Btry. | 6 | 44 | 1900 | 1.85 | 2.00 | 4.5 | 51 | [6]4.29 |
| Fafnir Bearing Co. | 6 | 44⅛ | 1913 | 2.30 | 2.50 | 5.7 | 63 | [6]4.59 |
| Firestone Tire & Rub | 77 | 44 | 1924 | 1.20 | 1.30 | 3.0 | 41 | [4]3.23 |
| First Nat'l Stores | 73 | 29¾ | 1914 | 2.50 | 2.50 | 8.4 | 55 | [6]1.18 |
| Foxboro Company | 26 | 37¾ | 1916 | 0.73½ | 0.80 | 2.1 | 39 | [6]2.27 |
| Garlock, Inc. | 56 | 15½ | 1906 | 0.45 | 0.60 | 3.9 | 40 | [6]1.41 |
| General Cigar | 90 | 24 | 1909 | 1.20 | 1.20 | 5.0 | 67 | [6]1.86 |
| General Electric | 24 | 88 | 1899 | 2.30 | 2.60 | 3.0 | 69 | [6]4.13 |
| General Foods | 33 | 67½ | 1922 | 2.05 | 2.20 | 3.3 | 57 | [6]3.79 |
| General Motors | 7 | 75⅛ | 1923 | 5.25 | 5.30 | 7.1 | 71 | [6]6.92 |
| Grant (W.T.) Co. | 74 | 24¾ | 1917 | 0.80 | 1.10 | 4.4 | 48 | [4]2.49 |
| Great Amer. Insur. | 94 | 51 | 1919 | 2.40 | 2.40 | 4.7 | 45 | [12]5.52 |
| Great Atl. & Pac. | 73 | 28¼ | 1920 | 1.50s | 1.50s | 5.3 | 65 | [5]2.18 |
| Great North. Paper | 64 | 37 | 1910 | 0.75 | 1.00 | 2.7 | 28 | [6]4.00 |
| Heller (Walter E.) | 31 | 8⅞ | 1921 | 0.48½ | 0.50 | 5.6 | 58 | [6]1.03 |
| Helme Products | 91 | 19 | 1912 | 1.00 | 1.00 | 5.3 | 70 | [6]1.83 |
| Hercules, Inc. | 17 | 41½ | 1913 | 1.00 | 1.15 | 2.8 | 46 | [6]2.34 |
| Household Finance | 30 | 24⅞ | 1926 | 0.85 | 1.00 | 4.0 | 42 | [6]2.24 |
| Houston Ltg. & Pwr. | 92 | 43⅜ | 1922 | 0.92 | 1.00 | 2.3 | 46 | [6]2.02 |
| Ingersoll-Rand Co. | 43 | 39 | 1919 | 2.00 | 2.00 | 5.1 | 82 | [6]3.65 |
| Interco, Inc. | 38 | 37 | 1913 | 1.20 | 1.40 | 3.8 | 59 | [5]3.42 |
| Int'l Business Mach. | 58 | 335½ | 1916 | 4.00 | 4.40 | 1.3 | 35 | [6]9.28 |
| Int'l Harvester | 41 | 39 | 1910 | 1.47½ | 1.80 | 4.6 | 51 | [7]4.02 |
| Iowa Power & Light | 92 | 31⅞ | 1916 | 1.42½ | 1.50 | 4.7 | 73 | [6]2.16 |
| Island Creek Coal | 18 | 30 | 1912 | 1.50 | 1.50 | 5.0 | 79 | [6]2.96 |
| Johnson Service | 26 | *41¾ | 1901 | 1.45 | 1.55 | 3.7 | 52 | [6]2.89 |
| Kroger Company | 73 | 24¾ | 1910 | 1.22½ | 1.30 | 5.3 | 61 | [6]2.33 |
| Liggett & Myers Tob. | 89 | 70⅜ | 1912 | 5.00 | 5.00 | 7.1 | 81 | [6]5.14 |
| Link-Belt Co. | 42 | 35¾ | 1913 | 2.15 | 2.25 | 6.3 | 69 | [6]3.83 |
| Ludlow Corp. | 56 | 44⅛ | 1886 | 1.55 | 1.64 | 3.7 | 57 | [3]3.08 |
| MacAndrews & Forbes | 64 | 11⅝ | 1908 | 0.40 | 0.60 | 5.2 | 59 | [6]1.04 |
| May Dept. Stores | 76 | 41½ | 1911 | 1.42½ | 1.60 | 3.9 | 52 | [4]3.08 |
| McCall Corp. | 67 | 29 | 1926 | 0.40s | 0.40 | 1.4 | 24 | [6]2.35 |
| McIntyre Porc Mines | 53 | 99¼ | 1924 | g2.40 | 2.80 | 2.8 | 68 | [6]3.55 |
| Melville Shoe | 38 | 30⅜ | 1917 | 1.00 | 1.25 | 4.1 | 62 | [6]3.14 |
| Minn. Mng. & Mfg. | 56 | 75¾ | 1916 | 1.10 | 1.20 | 1.6 | 50 | [6]2.44 |
| Mountain States Tel. | 85 | 21¾ | 1911 | 1.03 | 1.12 | 5.1 | 67 | [5]1.58 |
| National Biscuit | 9 | 43½ | 1899 | 1.77½ | 1.90 | 4.4 | 65 | [6]2.87 |
| Nat'l Dairy Prod. | 49 | 35⅛ | 1924 | 1.30 | 1.40 | 4.0 | 56 | [6]2.57 |
| Nat'l Fuel Gas | 93 | 28¾ | 1903 | 1.44 | 1.60 | 5.6 | 60 | [6]2.42 |
| Nat'l Lead | 16 | 54⅝ | 1906 | 3.25 | 3.25 | 5.9 | 73 | [6]5.13 |
| Nat'l Standard | 52 | 18¾ | 1922 | 0.75 | 0.90 | 4.8 | 47 | [6]2.04 |
| Nat'l Steel | 83 | 43 | 1908 | 2.12½ | 2.50 | 5.8 | 45 | [6]4.83 |
| New England T. & T. | 85 | 42⅝ | 1886 | 2.20 | 2.36 | 5.5 | .80 | [6]2.98 |
| Norfolk & West'n Ry. | 70 | 104¼ | 1900 | 6.50 | 6.50 | 6.2 | 70 | [6]9.86 |
| Norwich Pharmacal | 22 | *55 | 1925 | 1.17½ | 1.30 | 2.4 | 58 | [6]2.55 |
| Olin Mathieson Ch. | 17 | 54 | 1926 | 1.40 | 1.60 | 3.0 | 38 | [6]4.51 |
| Orange & Rock Util. | 92 | 27 | 1914 | 0.84 | 0.96 | 3.6 | 64 | [6]1.38 |
| Otis Elevator | 16 | 39¾ | 1911 | 1.92½ | 2.00 | 5.0 | 59 | [6]3.27 |
| Owens-Illinois | 19 | 66¼ | 1907 | 1.35 | 1.35 | 2.0 | 51 | [6]3.53 |
| Pacific Gas & El. | 92 | 30 | 1919 | 1.17½ | 1.30 | 4.3 | 59 | [6]2.17 |
| Pacific Lighting | 93 | 24¼ | 1909 | 1.30 | 1.30 | 5.4 | 69 | [6]2.11 |
| Pacific Tel. & Tel. | 85 | 22½ | 1925 | 1.20 | 1.20 | 5.3 | 86 | [5]1.30 |
| Parke, Davis | 22 | 28¾ | 1897 | 1.15 | 1.45 | 5.0 | 69 | [6]2.23 |
| Pennsalt Chemicals | 17 | 46¾ | 1913 | 1.00 | 1.15 | 2.5 | 50 | [6]2.37 |
| Pennzoil Co. | 60 | 83¾ | 1926 | 1.40 | 1.40 | 1.7 | 57 | [6]3.94 |
| Phila. Electric | 92 | 30¼ | 1913 | 1.44 | 1.48 | 4.9 | 75 | [6]2.02 |
| Pitts. Plate Glass | 16 | 57¾ | 1899 | 2.50 | 2.60 | 4.5 | 53 | [6]5.65 |
| Potomac Electric | 92 | 17⅞ | 1920 | 0.82 | 0.88 | 5.1 | 70 | [6]1.24 |
| Procter & Gamble | 80 | 68 | 1898 | 1.85 | 2.00 | 2.9 | 56 | [6]3.49 |
| Public Serv. E.&G. | 92 | 30½ | 1920 | 1.38½ | 1.46 | 4.8 | 62 | [6]2.26 |
| Pullman, Inc. | 69 | 50 | 1867 | 2.20 | 2.80 | 5.6 | 78 | [6]4.88 |
| Quaker Oats | 33 | 49 | 1922 | 2.20 | 2.20 | 4.5 | 59 | [12]3.89 |
| Raybestos-Manh't'n | 6 | 58 | 1898 | 2.60 | 3.00 | 5.2 | 55 | [6]5.91 |
| Rex-Chainbelt | 43 | 29 | 1922 | 1.20 | 1.40 | 4.8 | 51 | [7]3.36 |
| Reynolds Tobacco | 89 | 35⅛ | 1901 | 1.85 | 2.00 | 5.7 | 52 | [6]3.36 |
| Richardson-Merrell | 22 | 64¾ | 1925 | 1.07½ | 1.30 | 2.0 | 32 | [6]4.20 |
| Riegel Paper | 64 | 17 | 1897 | 0.80 | 0.80 | 4.7 | 46 | [6]1.98 |
| San Diego Gas & El. | 92 | 35 | 1909 | 1.46 | 1.64 | 4.7 | 62 | [6]2.73 |
| Scott Paper Co. | 64 | 26½ | 1926 | 0.92½ | 1.00 | 3.8 | 61 | [6]1.65 |
| Shattuck (Frank G.) | 75 | 13 | 1925 | 0.50 | 0.50 | 3.8 | 57 | [3]d0.23 |
| Sherwin-Williams | 16 | 45¼ | 1922 | 1.75 | 1.90 | 4.2 | 51 | [5]3.91 |
| Singer Company | 27 | 46⅜ | 1890 | 2.20 | 2.20 | 4.7 | 49 | [6]4.30 |
| South'n Cal. Ed. | 92 | 32⅞ | 1910 | 1.21¼ | 1.25 | 3.8 | 57 | [6]2.14 |
| Stand. Oil Calif. | 61 | 59½ | 1912 | 2.27½ | 2.50 | 4.2 | 44 | [6]5.28 |
| Stand. Oil (Ind.) | 60 | 46½ | 1913 | 1.55 | 1.70 | 3.7 | 50 | [6]3.44 |
| Stauffer Chemical | 17 | 39⅜ | 1915 | 1.40 | 1.60 | 4.1 | 54 | [6]3.26 |
| Sterling Drug | 22 | 34½ | 1913 | 0.76¼ | 0.80 | 2.3 | 57 | [6]1.49 |
| Sun Oil Co. | 60 | 51¾ | 1912 | 0.75s | 1.00 | 1.9 | 21 | [6]3.91 |
| Tampa Electric | 92 | 27 | 1911 | 0.52 | 0.60 | 2.2 | 56 | [7]1.14 |
| Texaco, Inc. | 61 | 65½ | 1903 | 2.45 | 2.55 | 3.9 | 50 | [6]4.91 |
| Texas Gulf Sulphur | 17 | 88¼ | 1921 | 0.40 | 0.40 | 0.5 | 43 | [6]2.45 |
| Texas Utilities | 92 | 49½ | 1919 | 1.34 | 1.44 | 2.9 | 59 | [6]2.34 |
| Timken Roller Bear. | 6 | 40¼ | 1921 | 2.00 | 2.00 | 5.0 | 51 | [6]4.78 |
| Toledo Edison | 92 | 35⅛ | 1922 | 1.12 | 1.28 | 3.6 | 55 | [6]2.10 |
| Torrington Co. | 6 | *34⅞ | 1898 | 1.55 | 1.80 | 5.2 | 45 | [6]3.71 |
| Union Carbide | 17 | 54¼ | 1918 | 2.00 | 2.00 | 3.7 | 63 | [6]4.03 |
| Union Electric | 92 | 22½ | 1918 | 1.12 | 1.12 | 5.0 | 76 | [6]1.45 |
| Union Oil Calif. | 69 | 56⅜ | 1916 | 1.05 | 1.20 | 2.1 | 38 | [6]4.09 |
| Union Pacific R.R. | 70 | 34½ | 1907 | 1.80 | 1.80 | 5.2 | 48 | [6]4.40 |
| Union Tank Car | 69 | 60⅞ | 1919 | 1.90 | 2.30 | 3.8 | 69 | [6]4.27 |
| United Eng. & Fdry. | 83 | 16¾ | 1902 | 1.00 | 1.00 | 6.0 | 56 | [6]1.56 |
| United Shoe Machy. | 45 | 53½ | 1899 | 2.50 | 3.00 | 5.6 | 50 | [5]6.52 |
| U. S. Gypsum | 15 | 49⅝ | 1919 | 3.20 | 3.20 | 6.4 | 66 | [6]4.02 |
| U. S. Pipe & Fdry. | 83 | 19½ | 1926 | 1.20 | 1.20 | 6.2 | 73 | [6]2.03 |
| U. S. Playing Card | 5 | 27¾ | 1896 | 1.35 | 1.50 | 5.4 | 83 | [6]1.99 |
| U. S. Tobacco Co. | 91 | 28 | 1918 | 1.50 | 1.60 | 5.7 | 70 | [6]2.43 |
| Upjohn Company | 22 | 75⅛ | 1921 | 1.20 | 1.48 | 2.0 | 47 | [6]2.78 |
| Washington Gas Lt. | 93 | 28⅝ | 1885 | 1.44 | 1.48 | 5.2 | 67 | [6]2.36 |
| West Va. Pulp & Pap. | 64 | 38¾ | 1895 | 1.35 | 1.50 | 3.9 | 53 | [4]4.05 |
| Westinghouse Air Br. | 69 | 32 | 1894 | 1.65 | 1.80 | 5.6 | 58 | [6]3.34 |
| Woolworth (F. W.) | 74 | 20¼ | 1912 | 1.00 | 1.00 | 4.9 | 59 | [6]2.41 |
| Wrigley (Wm.) Jr. | 81 | 106¼ | 1911 | 5.00 | 5.00 | 4.7 | 78 | [6]7.48 |

* Period ended indicated by superior number: [1]for January, [2]for February, etc.
Source: New York Stock Exchange, *Stocks on the Big Board.*

## TABLE 16–12

**S&P MASTER LIST OF RECOMMENDED ISSUES**

### GROUP 1—STOCKS PRIMARILY FOR STABILITY

| *COMMON STOCKS | 1966-67 Price Range | Recent Price | [7]Sh. Earn. $ 1965 | E1966 | [4]Div. $ | Yield % | ‡P.E. Ratio |
|---|---|---|---|---|---|---|---|
| Amer. Tel. & Tel. | 63½- 49¾ | 57 | [3]3.41 | [3]3.70 | 2.20 | 3.9 | 15.4 |
| Borden Co. | 41⅛- 27¾ | 35 | 1.98 | 2.20 | 1.20 | 3.4 | 15.9 |
| Boston Edison | 46¾- 35 | 43 | 2.35 | P2.57 | 1.92 | 4.5 | 16.7 |
| Campbell Soup | 36¾- 24⅞ | 28 | [5]1.59 | [5]1.70 | 1.00 | 3.6 | 16.5 |
| Chase Manht. Bk. | 68 - 46¼ | 61 | 4.40 | A4.71 | 2.20 | 3.6 | 12.9 |
| [2]Chem. Bk. N.Y. Tr. | 53⅛- 37½ | 46 | 4.01 | A4.14 | 2.10 | 4.6 | 11.1 |
| Clev. Elec. Illum. | 44¼- 35½ | 40 | 2.26 | P2.50 | 1.68 | 4.2 | 16.0 |
| Columbia Gas | 30⅝- 24⅛ | 26 | 2.05 | 2.15 | 1.44 | 5.5 | 12.1 |
| Corn Products | 53⅞- 35½ | 48 | 2.45 | 2.65 | 1.70 | 3.5 | 18.1 |
| [2]1st Natl. City Bk. | 58⅛- 40 | 53 | 3.52 | A3.94 | 1.80 | 3.4 | 13.5 |
| Idaho Power | 38 - 28½ | 35 | 1.84 | 2.07 | [13]1.40 | 4.0 | 16.9 |
| [2]Mfrs. Hanover | 53¾- 39 | 51 | 4.01 | A4.47 | [29]2.00 | 3.9 | 11.4 |
| [2]Morgan Guar. Tr. | 104¼- 71¼ | 92 | 6.55 | A7.02 | 4.00 | 4.3 | 13.1 |
| Natl. Dairy Prod. | 40 - 31⅜ | 35 | 2.42 | A2.55 | 1.40 | 4.0 | 13.7 |
| Natl. Fuel Gas | 33¼- 26¾ | 30 | 2.35 | 2.45 | 1.60 | 5.3 | 12.2 |
| Niag'ra M'hk Pwr. | 26½- 20⅜ | 22 | 1.58 | P1.57 | 1.10 | 5.0 | 14.0 |
| Okla. Nat. Gas | 25¼- 18½ | 21 | [12]1.56 | [12]1.65 | 1.12 | 5.3 | 12.7 |
| Pacific Lighting | 28⅞- 23⅛ | 27 | 2.09 | P2.10 | 1.50 | 5.6 | 12.9 |
| Penn. Pwr. & Lt. | 38½- 29⅛ | 35 | 2.02 | P2.14 | 1.48 | 4.2 | 16.4 |
| Philadelphia Elec. | 36⅝- 28 | 32 | 1.92 | P2.07 | 1.48 | 4.6 | 15.5 |
| Quaker Oats | 76½- 45¼ | 58 | [9]4.22 | [9]4.25 | 2.20 | 3.8 | 13.6 |
| Standard Brands | 36⅜- 27⅛ | 36 | 1.87 | P2.04 | 1.30 | 3.6 | 17.6 |
| Union Electric | 28⅜- 22 | 26 | 1.42 | P1.53 | 1.20 | 4.6 | 17.0 |

### GROUP 2—STOCKS PRIMARILY FOR LONG-TERM CAPITAL GAIN

| *COMMON STOCKS | 1966-67 Price Range | Recent Price | [7]Sh. Earn. $ 1965 | E1966 | [4]Div. $ | Yield % | ‡P.E. Ratio |
|---|---|---|---|---|---|---|---|
| •Alum. Co. of Am. | 94⅝- 66½ | 87 | 3.41 | P4.83 | 1.60 | 1.8 | 18.0 |
| American Can | 59¾- 44¾ | 48 | 3.61 | P4.18 | 2.20 | 4.6 | 11.5 |
| •Am. Home Prod. | 92½- 61½ | 90 | 3.10 | P3.65 | 2.10 | 2.3 | 24.7 |
| Cities Service | 55⅜- 40 | 47 | 3.85 | P4.16 | 1.80 | 3.8 | 11.3 |
| Coca-Cola | 97 - 71½ | 95 | 2.66 | 3.10 | 1.90 | 2.0 | 30.5 |
| Columb's & S. Ohio | 41¼- 31⅝ | 39 | 2.31 | P2.32 | 1.52 | 3.9 | 16.8 |
| Consumers Pwr. | 57 - 40⅞ | 48 | 2.83 | P3.09 | 1.90 | 3.9 | 15.5 |
| Dow Chemical | 78 - 54 | 71 | 3.58 | P4.06 | 2.00 | 2.8 | 17.5 |
| du Pont (E. I.) | 242 -143¼ | 155 | 8.63 | P8.23 | 5.75 | 3.7 | 18.8 |
| Ford Motor | 57½- 38½ | 47 | 6.32 | P5.63 | 2.40 | 5.1 | 8.3 |
| Gen. Am. Transp. | 48¼- 28½ | 34 | 2.41 | 2.60 | 1.55 | 4.6 | 13.1 |
| General Electric | 120 - 80 | 89 | 3.90 | 3.80 | 2.60 | 2.9 | 23.4 |
| General Motors | 108¼- 65⅝ | 76 | 7.41 | P6.24 | §4.55 | 6.0 | 12.2 |
| Gen. Pub. Util. | 37¾- 26⅛ | 33 | 1.95 | 2.00 | 1.50 | 4.5 | 16.5 |
| Grant (W. T.) | 31½- 20½ | 26 | [14]2.52 | [14]2.55 | 1.10 | 4.2 | 10.2 |
| Gulf Oil | 63¼- 48⅝ | 63 | 4.12 | P4.87 | 2.20 | 3.5 | 12.9 |
| Illinois Power | 45⅞- 35⅝ | 41 | 2.12 | 2.25 | 1.60 | 3.9 | 18.2 |
| Johns-Manville | 61 - 44⅞ | 58 | 4.03 | P4.50 | 2.20 | 3.8 | 12.9 |
| Lone Star Gas | 25⅞- 18¾ | 21 | 1.22 | P1.47 | 1.12 | 5.3 | 14.3 |
| May Dept. Stores | 54⅝- 31¾ | 38 | [14]3.07 | [14]2.95 | 1.60 | 4.2 | 12.9 |
| National Lead | 74½- 52⅝ | 65 | 5.01 | P5.03 | 3.25 | 5.0 | 12.9 |
| North. Natural Gas | 59¼- 41⅜ | 51 | 3.21 | 3.40 | 2.40 | 4.7 | 15.0 |
| Otis Elevator | 61⅞- 33⅜ | 45 | 3.41 | 3.30 | 2.00 | 4.4 | 13.6 |
| Owens-Illinois | 70 - 50½ | 60 | 3.38 | P3.51 | 1.35 | 2.3 | 17.1 |
| Phillips Petrol'm. | 58⅞- 44⅛ | 55 | 3.83 | P4.31 | 2.20 | 4.0 | 12.8 |
| Pitts. Plate Glass | 81 - 50 | 57 | 5.48 | P4.87 | 2.60 | 4.6 | 11.7 |
| Pub. Serv. E. & G. | 39¾- 28¼ | 36 | 2.23 | P2.39 | 1.54 | 4.3 | 15.1 |
| [1]Reliance Insur. | 43 - 30¾ | 41 | [11]1.43 | [11]3.25 | 1.60 | 3.9 | 12.6 |
| Reyn'ds (R. J.) Tob. | 45⅞- 34 | 40 | 3.30 | P3.48 | 2.00 | 5.0 | 11.5 |
| Royal Dutch Pet. | 45⅝- 30⅛ | 38 | 3.87 | 4.10 | 1.79 | 4.7 | 9.3 |
| Sears, Roebuck | 65¾- 44⅛ | 53 | [10]2.12 | [10]2.25 | 1.20 | 2.3 | 23.6 |
| Shell Oil | 68 - 56¼ | 67 | 3.85 | P4.19 | 1.90 | 2.8 | 16.0 |
| Southern Co. | 35 - 24¼ | 29 | 1.39 | P1.45 | 1.02 | 3.5 | 20.0 |
| Southern Pacific | 47 - 27 | 33 | [18]3.60 | [18]3.77 | 1.50 | 4.5 | 8.8 |
| Stand. Oil (Cal.) | 86 - 55⅛ | 63 | 4.90 | P5.25 | [28]2.50 | 4.0 | 12.0 |
| Stand. Oil (Ind.) | 55⅛- 40¾ | 53 | 3.10 | P3.62 | 1.90 | 3.6 | 14.6 |
| Stand. Oil (Ohio) | 73 - 55½ | 67 | 4.51 | P5.10 | 2.40 | 3.6 | 13.1 |
| Texaco, Inc. | 83 - 61¼ | 77 | 4.71 | P5.11 | 2.65 | 3.4 | 15.1 |
| Transamer. Corp. | 43⅜- 23 | 34 | [11]2.58 | [11]2.80 | [24]1.00 | 2.9 | 12.1 |
| Union Carbide | 70⅜- 45⅝ | 53 | 3.76 | P3.82 | 2.00 | 3.8 | 13.9 |
| Union Oil of Cal. | 60 - 45 | 52 | [27]3.47 | P4.24 | 1.20 | 2.3 | 12.3 |
| Union Pacific | 47¾- 33 | 40 | [18]4.03 | [18]A4.76 | 2.00 | 5.0 | 8.4 |

### HIGH-GRADE BONDS AND PREFERRED STOCKS FOR INCOME

| *BONDS | S.&P. Rating | Recent Price | Yield to Maturity % | †Call Price |
|---|---|---|---|---|
| [2]Amer. Tel. & Tel. 4⅜s, 1999 | AAA | 93 | 4.90 | 104.82('68) |
| [2]Pacific Tel. & Tel. 6s, 2002 | AAA | 107 | 5.53 | 104.74('71) |
| Texas Co. 3⅝s, 1983 | AAA | 86 | 4.89 | 103½ |
| [2]Niagara Mohawk 5⅞s, 1996 | AA | 107 | 5.41 | 108.04('71) |
| [2]Pac. Gas & Elec. 5¾s, 1998 | AA | 105 | 5.42 | 104.82('71) |
| [2]Pub. Serv. El. & Gas 4¾s, 1995 | AA | 93 | 5.23 | 105.36 |
| [2]Beneficial Finance 4¾s, 1993 | A | 89 | 5.53 | 103.73 |
| Liggett & Myers 6s, 1992 | A | 105 | 5.62 | 103.90('74) |

| *PREFERRED STOCKS | Recent Price | Yield % | Call Price | Dividend Dates | |
|---|---|---|---|---|---|
| American Can $1.75 | 36 | 4.9 | N.C. | JAJO | 2 |
| Armstrong Cork $3.75 | 78 | 4.8 | 102¾ | MJSD | 1 |
| Cincinnati Gas & Elec. $4.00 | 80 | 5.0 | 108 | JAJO | 3 |
| Consolidated Edison $5 | 93 | 5.4 | 105 | FMAN | 1 |
| General Motors $5 | 102 | 4.9 | 120 | FMAN | 1 |
| [1]Pacific Gas & Elec. 6% ($1.50) | 28 | 5.4 | N.C. | FMAN | 15 |
| Standard Brands $3.50 | 73 | 4.8 | 100 | MJSD | 15 |
| Union Electric $4.50 | 88 | 5.1 | 110 | MJSD | 28 |

*All issues on New York Stock Exchange unless otherwise noted. A—Actual. P—Preliminary. E—Estimated. †Figures in parentheses represent first year in which bonds become callable. ‡Based on estimated 1966 earnings. N. C.—Non-Callable. [1]American Stock Exchange. [2]Over the counter. [3]Based on average shares outstanding. [4]Includes actual or possible extras. [5]Years ended July 31. [7]Adjusted for stock splits or stock dividends. [9]Years ended June 30. [10]Years ended Jan. 31 excl. equity in undist. net of unconsolidated subs. [11]Adjusted net earnings. [12]Years ended Aug. 31, 1966 and 1967. [13]Dividends partly tax free. [14]Years ended Jan. 31 of follow. cal. year. [18]Includes tax deferrals. [24]Plus 2% stk. [27]Including Pure Oil on pooling of interests basis, and pro-forma 1964. [28]Plus 5% stk. [29]Plus 12% stk. JAJO—January, April, July, October. FMAN—February, March, August, November. MJSD—March, June, September, December. JN—June, November. AJOD—April, June, October, December. §Paid in 1966.

**Changes Since January 16, 1967: •Additions. Deletions—Mobil Oil and Montana-Dakota Utilities Group (2)**

Source Standard & Poor's, *The Outlook*, February 13, 1967.

General Electric
General Foods
Gillette
Hercules
International Business Machines
National Dairy
National Lead
Pacific Gas & Electric
Pfizer
Southern California Edison
Standard Oil of California
U.S. Gypsum

The stocks are drawn from lists including:

Heirloom Stocks
Stock Market Aristocrats
Stocks the Experts Like
Stocks Most Widely Held by Institutions
Stocks That Have Never Cut Their Dividends
Stocks with Top Quality Ratings
Stocks with Top Price Stability
Top Profit Makers in the U.S.
Favorite Holdings of Bank Managed Trusts

If by safety is meant unbroken dividend records along with price stability, then various electric utility issues would rate highly for a retirement portfolio.

Dr. Barnes's Sample *Portfolio B—Stocks & Bonds for High Current Income* provides a current return of close to 7%, but it appears to be too risky for a retirement income investor. It includes the following:

American Investment
Associates Investment
Brazilian Light & Power
Briggs & Stratton
Chicago Rivet & Machine
Continental Mortgage Inv.
General Motors
Hoskins Mfg.
Landis Tool
Liggett & Myers
Link Belt
Louisville & Nashville R.R.
National Securities & Research
Pacific Far East Lines
Phelps Dodge
Real Estate Investment Trust
St. Joseph Lead
Seligman & Latz
Trico Products
Wellington Management

Straining for maximum yield often involves greater risk and less capital appreciation. Often companies have high yields because their shares sell at low prices due to poor prospects, doubt about continuation of dividends at the then current rate, or to political risks. At times, however, yields are higher because the company is relatively obscure and unknown and has not yet attracted sufficient investor interest to push up the price of the stock. A somewhat more conservative listing of income stocks are those in the "Liberal Income" classification in Merrill Lynch, Pierce, Fenner & Smith's quarterly *Selected Issues.*

### General Portfolio Selection Considerations

It must be apparent by now that portfolio selection will vary with age, objective, resources, and temperament, to mention only a few of the elements involved.[22] Few portfolios are built all at once. Most are assembled bit by bit over long periods of time. Sometimes the investor is conscious of his objectives and his requirements. Many, however, follow fancy, tips, and whim. In either case a periodic portfolio review by an investment counselor, or a stock brokerage house, may be useful. In an appendix to this chapter we reproduce, with permission, a sample portfolio review by Merrill Lynch, Pierce, Fenner & Smith. It involves a hypothetical portfolio and is designed to illustrate the general techniques involved.

While numerous sample portfolios have been presented as illustrative of a type, few investors confine their actions to one category alone, and indeed, the average portfolio is a conglomerate. That is, the average investor is neither entirely aggressive nor entirely defensive, neither completely speculative nor completely conservative. Broad principles concerning diversification, objectives, timing, etc., may easily be set forth. They are seldom followed in practice, and indeed, in the face of this endlessly changing kaleidoscope of the investment world, an edifice of principles one time may be rubble shortly thereafter. The real world of investments eludes unchanging first principles. It is both pragmatic and empirical. Flexibility is desirable. One can say with hindsight what was wrong with a given investment program or pattern, but looking ahead, choice, decision, selection, timing, etc., are all painfully difficult. The more active one is in investments, the more humility one acquires.

### SUGGESTED READINGS

Leo Barnes. "Tax Relativity: The Missing 'X' Factor in Stock and Portfolio Evaluation," *Financial Analysts Journal*, January–February, 1965.

———. *Your Investments.* Issued annually. Rye, N.Y.: American Research Council.

W. Scott Baumann. "Investment Management," *Financial Analysts Journal*, January–February, 1966.

Nathan Belfer. "Construction of Private Investors' Portfolios," *Financial Analysts Journal*, May–June, 1965.

Editors of *Fortune*. *Fortune's Guide to Personal Investing.* New York: McGraw-Hill Book Co., 1963.

Walter R. Good. "How to Avoid Overpriced Stocks," *Financial Analysts Journal*, November–December, 1966.

---

[22] See Nathan Belfer, "Determining the Construction and Composition of an Individual Securities Portfolio," *Financial Analysts Journal*, May–June, 1965.

Benjamin Graham. *The Intelligent Investor.* 3rd ed. New York: Harper & Row, Publishers, 1965.

J. Parker Hall, III. "Toward Effective Portfolio Management," *Financial Analysts Journal*, January–February, 1966.

Charles C. Holt and John P. Shelton. "The Implications of the Capital Gains Tax for Investment Decisions," *Journal of Finance*, December, 1961.

The Institute of Chartered Financial Analysts. *C.F.A. Readings in Financial Analysis*, Part V, "Portfolio Management." Homewood, Ill.: Richard D. Irwin, Inc., 1966.

Gerald M. Loeb. *The Battle for Investment Survival.* New York: Simon & Schuster, 1965 Revision.

Harry C. Sauvain. *Investment Management.* 2nd ed. Englewood Cliffs, N.J.: Prentice-Hall, Inc., 1959.

———. "Problems of Portfolio Policy," *Financial Analysts Journal*, May–June, 1965.

Herman M. Schneider and Warren G. Wintrub. *Tax Savings Opportunities in Securities Transactions.* New York: Lybrand, Ross Bros. & Montgomery, 1966.

## APPENDIX TO CHAPTER 16

**CONFIDENTIAL PORTFOLIO ANALYSIS**

PREPARED ESPECIALLY FOR

*Mr. John Doe*

MERRILL LYNCH,
PIERCE,
FENNER & SMITH INC

RESEARCH DIVISION 70 PINE STREET, NEW YORK, N. Y. 10005

SECURITIES RESEARCH INFORMATION MEMORANDUM

JUNE 23, 1966

OFFICE MANAGERS:
ACCOUNT EXECUTIVES:

SAMPLE PORTFOLIO REVIEW

This sample portfolio review for "Mr. John Doe" supersedes the sample review dated August 11, 1965, which should be destroyed.

This review, which was prepared on the basis of an actual request, can be shown to prospects and customers as an example of the kind of review we can prepare for them. Please do not give the sample to customers or prospects. Mr. Doe's circumstances and his holdings are unique, and the suggestions made here are not necessarily the ones we would make in any other review. Instead, you can offer a review of the investor's own portfolio.

Because of possible legal restrictions, we have not enclosed copies of the Stock Appraisals and Stock Comments that were sent with the original review. You might insert a few current reports for illustrative purposes when showing the portfolio to prospects.

Please note the special footnote at the bottom of each page of the letter.

H. F. WILEY

G. L. Shinn
Attachment

70 PINE STREET
NEW YORK, N.Y. 10005
212 – WHITEHALL 4-1212
MERRILL LYNCH, PIERCE, FENNER & SMITH INC

June 23, 1966

Mr. John Doe
Main Street
Centerville, U. S. A.

Re: Account #222-12345

Dear Mr. Doe:

THE INFORMATION SET FORTH HEREIN WAS OBTAINED FROM SOURCES WHICH WE BELIEVE RELIABLE, BUT WE DO NOT GUARANTEE ITS ACCURACY. NEITHER THE INFORMATION, NOR ANY OPINION EXPRESSED, CONSTITUTES A SOLICITATION BY US OF THE PURCHASE OR SALE OF ANY SECURITIES OR COMMODITIES.

Your account executive has asked us to review your portfolio, and we welcome the opportunity to do so. As is our custom, we have tabulated your present holdings on the attached Schedule I, and have included the values and indicated annual income for each security.

We understand that you wish your portfolio to provide appreciation and growth, and that you are willing to assume a greater degree of risk with a portion of your funds by investing in issues that appear to offer promising opportunities for capital gains. Our suggestions have been made accordingly.

We find that your portfolio consists, for the most part, of quality stocks, and that you have representation in segments of the economy that have demonstrated worthwhile progress and that we believe will continue to offer attractive potential. Nevertheless, most of your securities proved to be vulnerable to the decline in the general market from the February peak in the Dow-Jones Industrial Average. Although prices have recovered somewhat since then and growth stocks such as your holdings in Kodak, Schering, and RCA made even better gains, we believe the market's performance will remain sensitive to changing business conditions and to international developments. Because business is operating at the highest capacity since the Korean War, restrictive fiscal and monetary measures have been instituted to slow the present rate of economic expansion. The nation's increasing commitment in Vietnam is placing additional demands on the economy. Therefore, in our opinion, it is important to be particularly selective in both the retention and purchase of common stocks; emphasis should be placed on issues that sell at reasonable multiples of earnings and on equities of companies that have well-defined prospects.

*This is a sample portfolio analysis intended for illustrative purposes only. The information set forth herein is not current and should not be used as a basis for making any investment decision.*

- 2 -

General Motors, your largest single stock holding, accounts for about 45% of the total value of your portfolio and we believe that this concentration of funds places too much dependence on the fortunes of a single company. As you know, this stock has been performing poorly because sales and earnings for 1966 are expected to decline below record 1965 results. We estimate that 1966 earnings will be approximately $6.50 to $6.75 a share vs. the $7.41 a share earned last year. This stock has also suffered from the psychological effects of the Congressional investigation of automobile safety. On the other hand, long-term prospects for GM are considered good, and the company recently estimated that the industry's sales will approach 13 million units by 1975. In view of the depressed price of the stock, we are limiting our proposal that you take profits in GM to 200 shares at this time, but we believe that additional profit-taking should be considered periodically to further diversify your portfolio.

We also believe that you could make better use of the funds committed to the Chesapeake & Ohio Railway because, in our opinion, the prime appeal of this stock is liberal income instead of appreciation or growth. We understand that you do not depend upon income from your investments; for this reason, we suggest the sale of this issue. The C&O has proposed to merge with the Norfolk and Western, and we realize that the operating economies, if the merger is consummated, will be significant over the long term. The shares of the C&O currently sell at a discount from the proposed merger terms. However, we expect that the Interstate Commerce Commission will not make a decision on the proposed consolidation for at least two years. In the interim, we believe that your appreciation objective could be better satisfied elsewhere.

As indicated on the attached Schedule II, we suggest that you utilize the sale proceeds to add to your commitments in Schering and Radio Corporation of America and to purchase Burroughs. You would thus have more significant representation in the favorable prospects for Schering and RCA and direct participation in the growing office-equipment field.

Schering has established itself as a strong, diversified, specialty-drug company, and management has made efforts to build a base for future growth. The company's rate of profit improvement has accelerated during the last two years and we believe that Schering will maintain an above-average earnings performance within the drug industry as a whole. Although results will be subject to general conditions in the drug industry, Schering's sales and earnings should benefit in coming months from the continued growth expected in sales of its specialty drugs and from the introduction of Garamycin ointment and cream, which has been approved by the F.D.A. While the price-earnings multiple has increased somewhat, this issue is, in our opinion, still undervalued in relation to the drug group because of good gains in earnings, basic strengthening of operations, and new products in various stages of clinical testing or awaiting F.D.A. approval. We estimate 1966 earnings at $2.10 a share, compared with $1.82 in 1965.

*This is a sample portfolio analysis intended for illustrative purposes only. The information set forth herein is not current and should not be used as a basis for making any investment decision.*

- 3 -

Color-television stocks have been weak recently as a result of price reductions on several models of color-television sets. We believe, however, that this performance is typical in the evolution of pricing for new products and that lower prices should further stimulate the already excellent demand for color-television sets. We expect sales of color-TV sets to approximate 5.3 million units this year, compared with the 2.7 million units sold in 1965. RCA has predicted that its factory sales of home instruments will double to $1 billion in 1967 compared with somewhat less than $500 million in 1965. The National Broadcasting subsidiary continues to operate at a record level, partly because almost all of its prime-time evening shows are telecast in color. The company's computer operations were profitable in 1965 for the second consecutive year, and RCA believes that they will be a major source of income by the 1970's. RCA's sales and earnings reached record levels in 1965 for the fourth straight year, and we estimate earnings for 1966 at about $2.10 to $2.20 a share vs. $1.73 in 1965.

Because of strong demand for Burroughs' commercial products and systems, we continue to regard the stock as one of the more attractive commitments within the office-equipment field for medium-to-longer term appreciation. Earnings should register another significant gain in 1966 and exceed $3.00 a share, despite an increase in the number of shares outstanding as a result of the call of the convertible debenture in March. Burroughs earned $2.37 a share in 1965, and accounting machines generated a large percentage of revenues and represented one of the most profitable and growing areas of Burroughs' operations. The company recently introduced several new members of the Burroughs 500 computer systems series. The addition of the new large-scale B-6500 computer to the company's existing line provides both new and present users of Burroughs' computers with a broad choice of equipment capable of handling basic data-processing applications by means of large, comprehensive total-information systems. Sales of computers, including military sales, presently represent about 25% of total volume, and revenues from commercial data processing are expected to grow by at least 20% a year between now and 1970. By the late 1960's and 1970's, EDP is expected to become a highly profitable part of Burroughs' business.

Turning to your remaining holdings, we believe General Telephone, Standard Oil of California, and Eastman Kodak are appropriate for your investment objectives. The areas served by General Telephone are experiencing good industrial and population growth, and its Sylvania Division offers representation in the growing field of electronics and color television. Despite an increase in the number of shares outstanding, we believe General Telephone will earn about $2.15 a share this year compared with $1.87 a share in 1965.

Eastman Kodak is expected to maintain its leadership in the photography field. In addition, the company has important operations in the chemical industry. We expect Kodak to record a good earnings gain this year to about $3.85 a share vs. $3.07 a share in 1965.

*This is a sample portfolio analysis intended for illustrative purposes only. The information set forth herein is not current and should not be used as a basis for making any investment decision.*

- 4 -

As one of the major international oil companies, Standard Oil of California is a sound holding for growth. The company has projected that demand for petroleum products in the United States will rise by 2 1/2-to-3% this year, and that demand in other areas of the Free World will be up by nearly 10%. The company has had a good exploration record; an unusually large number of discoveries in the last two or three years are contributing to the company's above-average gains in production of crude oil. We estimate that earnings for 1966 will increase to about $5.65 a share from $5.15 per share in 1965.

In summary, Mr. Doe, we suggest that you begin to reduce the size of your position in General Motors in order to permit you to participate in other attractive investment fields. We also think that your potentials for medium-term appreciation would be enhanced by exchanging Chesapeake & Ohio Railway for other issues. Although we realize our proposals will result in a capital gain on which taxes must be paid, we do not believe that tax considerations should unduly influence your investment decisions. Moreover, by following our suggestions, you would gain meaningful representation in the office-equipment, drug, and color-television industries where prospects are considered above-average.

We hope that you will find our analysis of your portfolio helpful. Because you may wish to discuss our suggestions with your account executive, we are sending a copy of this report to him. In view of ever-changing market and economic conditions, we invite you to submit your portfolio for periodic review.

Very truly yours,

Securities Research Division

Enc.

*This is a sample portfolio analysis intended for illustrative purposes only. The information set forth herein is not current and should not be used as a basis for making any investment decision.*

70 PINE STREET
NEW YORK, N. Y. 10005
212 WHITEHALL 4-1212

**MERRILL LYNCH, PIERCE, FENNER & SMITH INC**

3000 PORTFOLIO OF MR JOHN DOE — PAGE 1

SCHEDULE I PRESENT STATUS — PRICES ON OR ABOUT JUNE 21 1966

| SECURITY CLASSIFICATION | QTY. | DESCRIPTION | COST | RECENT PRICE (U-INDICATES BID PRICE) | APPROXIMATE MARKET VALUE | INDICATED ANNUAL INCOME** | FOOT-NOTE CODE |
|---|---|---|---|---|---|---|---|
| | | CASH FOR INVESTMENT | | | $ 5,000 | | |
| | | | | | 5,000 * | * | |
| | | COMMON STOCK | | | | | |
| | | | | | * | * | |
| AUTO&EQUIP | 800 | GENERAL MOTORS | 25 | 81 1 /8 | $ 64,900 | 4160 | K |
| | | | | | 64,900 * | 4160* | |
| COMMNCATNS | 400 | GEN TEL ELECTRC CORP | 24 | 43 5 /8 | $ 17,450 | 448 | |
| | | | | | 17,450 * | 448* | |
| DRUGS | 100 | SCHERING CORPORATION | 32 | 49 | $ 4,900 | 100 | E |
| | | | | | 4,900 * | 100* | |
| HOUSE SUPP | 170 | RADIO CORP AMERICA | 11 | 52 4 /8 | $ 8,925 | 136 | |
| | | | | | 8,925 * | 136* | |
| PETROLEUM | 121 | STAND OIL OF CALIF | 28 | 65 1 /8 | $ 7,880 | 303 | |
| | | | | | 7,880 * | 303* | |
| RR & EQUIP | 200 | CHESAPEAKE & OHIO RY | 61 | 71 7 /8 | $ 14,375 | 800 | |
| | | | | | 14,375 * | 800* | |
| RECREATION | 210 | EASTMAN KODAK | 11 | 138 | $ 28,980 | 389 | K |
| | | | | | 28,980 * | 389* | |
| | | | | | $ 152,410 ¤ | $ 6336¤ | |

SEVENTY PINE STREET
NEW YORK, NEW YORK 10005
WHITEHALL 4-1212

MERRILL LYNCH, PIERCE, FENNER & SMITH INC

3000 1

SUMMARY

| | % OF TOTAL | | APPROXIMATE VALUE | INDICATED ANNUAL INCOME ** |
|---|---|---|---|---|
| SAVINGS & LOAN | | | | |
| U S GOVERNMENT SECURITIES | | | | |
| WORLD BANK BNDS | | | | |
| CDN GOVT AND OR PROVINCIAL BONDS | | | | |
| FOREIGN BONDS | | | | |
| CORPORATE BONDS | | | | |
| PREFERRED AND OR GUARANTEED STOCKS | | | | |
| COMMON STOCKS | 97 | | 147,410 | 6336 |
| TOTAL | | | 147,410 | 6336 |
| YIELD ON ABOVE 4.30% | | | | |
| CASH FOR INVESTMENT | 3 | | 5,000 | |
| MUNICIPAL BONDS | | | | |
| GOVNMT SAVINGS BONDS & BILLS | | | | |
| TOTAL VALUE OF PORTFOLIO | 100% | | 152,410 | 6336 |

EXPLANATION OF FOOTNOTE CODES

** - PAID OR DECLARED IN THE LAST 12 MONTHS OR CURRENT INDICATED ANNUAL RATE.
A - ADJUSTED FOR RECENT STOCK SPLIT OR STOCK DIVIDEND OF 10% OR MORE.
B - PLUS STOCK.
B1 - STOCK DIVIDEND ONLY.
C - CANADIAN FUNDS SUBJECT TO APPLICABLE CANADIAN NON-RESIDENT'S TAX.
D - DIVIDEND OMITTED OR DEFERRED.
E - EXCLUDING EXTRAS.
F - EXCLUDES CAPITAL GAINS IF ANY.
F1 - PARTIALLY NON-TAXABLE AS ORDINARY DIVIDEND INCOME.
G - ESTIMATED MARKET VALUE FOR TABULATION PURPOSES ONLY.
H - ARREARS.
J - ASSUME ISSUE OR AMOUNT HELD.
K - INCLUDING EXTRAS.
K1 - NET AFTER APPROPRIATE UNITED KINGDOM TAX, A PORTION OF WHICH MAY BE APPLICABLE AS A CREDIT FOR U. S. INCOME TAX PURPOSES.
L - INCOMPLETE DESCRIPTION.
M - RECENT PRICE AND/OR DIVIDEND NOT READILY AVAILABLE.
N - PAID LAST YEAR
P - PROSPECTUS.
P1 - EXTENDED AT PAR FOR TABULATION PURPOSES ONLY.
Q - GROSS BEFORE DEDUCTION OF ANY FOREIGN WITHHOLDING TAX AND ADR DEPOSITARY FEE, WHERE APPLICABLE.
R - NON-TAXABLE AS ORDINARY DIVIDEND INCOME.
S - OFFERING PRICE.
T - NO DIVIDEND POLICY ESTABLISHED AS YET.
T1 - MATURED OR CALLED.
T2 - LIQUIDATED.
V - NAME CHANGE.
W - NO READILY AVAILABLE INFORMATION.
X - INCLUDING CASH VALUE OF STANDARD OIL OF N. J. STOCK DIVIDEND.
Y - PAID TO DATE THIS YEAR
Y1 - RATE VARIES ACCORDING TO ISSUE DATE.
Z - U. S. FUNDS SUBJECT TO APPLICABLE CANADIAN NON-RESIDENT'S TAX.
Z1 - U. S. FUNDS FREE OF 15% DUTCH TAX UPON FILING "DECLARATION OF RESIDENCE" WITH CHASE MANHATTAN BANK.
Z2 - PLUS STOCK IN OTHER COMPANIES.
Z3 - RESULT OF MERGER.
Z4 -

PRINTED IN U.S.A.

THE INFORMATION SET FORTH HEREIN WAS OBTAINED FROM SOURCES WHICH WE BELIEVE RELIABLE, BUT WE DO NOT GUARANTEE ITS ACCURACY. NEITHER THE INFORMATION, NOR ANY OPINION EXPRESSED, CONSTITUTES A SOLICITATION BY US OF THE PURCHASE OR SALE OF ANY SECURITIES OR COMMODITIES.

70 PINE STREET
NEW YORK, N. Y. 10005
212 WHITEHALL 4-1212

MERRILL LYNCH, PIERCE, FENNER & SMITH INC

PAGE 1

3000 SUGGESTIONS FOR MR JOHN DOE

SCHEDULE II

| SECURITY CLASSIFICATION | QTY. | DESCRIPTION | COST | RECENT PRICE (U-INDICATES BID PRICE) | APPROXIMATE MARKET VALUE | INDICATED ANNUAL INCOME** | FOOT-NOTE CODE |
|---|---|---|---|---|---|---|---|
| | | SELL | | | | | |
| | | COMMON STOCK | | | | | |
| AUTO&EQUIP | 200 | GENERAL MOTORS | 25 | 81 | 16,200 | 1040 | K |
| RR & EQUIP | 200 | CHESAPEAKE & OHIO RY | 61 | 72 | 14,400 | 800 | |
| | | TOTAL | | | 30,600 | 1840 | |
| | | EST CAP GAINS TAX | | | 3,350 | | |
| | | CASH TO INVEST | | | 5,000 | | |
| | | TOTAL TO INVEST | | | 32,250 | | |
| | | BUY | | | | | |
| | | COMMON STOCK | | | | | |
| OFF EQUIPT | 200 | BURROUGHS CORP | | 76 | 15,200 | 200 | |
| DRUGS | 200 | SCHERING CORPORATION | | 49 | 9,800 | 200 | E |
| HOUSE SUPP | 130 | RADIO CORP AMERICA | | 53 | 6,890 | 104 | |
| | | TOTAL | | | 31,890 | 504 | |
| | | YIELD 1.58% | | | | | |

CODE 90R 1-63
PRINTED IN U.S.A.

**MERRILL LYNCH, PIERCE, FENNER & SMITH**
INCORPORATED
**INVENTORY FOR INVESTORS**

FOR: Mr. John Doe
Name (Please Print)
Main Street
Address (Please Print)
Centerville, U. S. A.
City and State

ACCT. NO. 222-12345 ☐ PROSPECT

FOR OFFICE USE ONLY
DATE: June 17, 1966
FROM: ______ (Office)
MAIL REPLY TO: ☒ CUSTOMER ☐ ACCT. EXEC.
Acct. Exec. ______ No. ______
Approved by: ______ (Manager)

A WORD ABOUT THESE QUESTIONS

The information you supply in this form will be held in strictest confidence. We have just one purpose in asking for this information: to help you decide what kind of investment program may be best suited to your needs. Obviously, people's circumstances vary. And the kind of securities we suggest for a person who is dependent on dividends for much of his income will differ markedly from those that we suggest for a person who can afford to assume a greater measure of risk in the hope of increasing his capital. That is why the first question below asks you to define your investment objective as you see it yourself; and all the other questions are designed to clarify that objective—both for you and for us.

**1. INVESTMENT OBJECTIVES:** (If more than one objective, indicate order of importance.) Portfolio Reviewed Last On ______ Date

☐ Relative Safety of Principal
☐ Income of About ____%
☐ Tax Exempt Income
☒ Appreciation—Good Quality
☒ Appreciation—Speculative
☒ Long Term Growth

If our analysis indicates that bonds or preferred stocks seem suitable investments, would the client be receptive to such suggestions? ☐ Yes No ☒

**2. PERSONAL INFORMATION:**

Sex ☐ Male ☐ Female
Marital status ☐ Single ☐ Married ☐ Widowed
Age ☐ 21 - 30 ☐ 30 - 40 ☒ 40 - 50 ☐ 50 - 60 ☐ 60 - 65 ☐ over 65

Number and ages of dependents Three
Occupation or profession Marketing Executive
Name companies in the portfolio with which there is a close connection None

**3. FINANCIAL INFORMATION:**

Approximate annual income from all sources other than securities substantial
Total cash savings Entirely adequate
Amt. of total cash savings available for investment $5,000
Approximate annual savings ______
Amount of life insurance Adequate
Real Estate - Home yes
Approximate top tax bracket High %
Other ______
Other resources (pension expectations, participation in profit sharing plans, bequests, etc.) ______

Fixed obligations (mortgages, loans, etc.) ______

## LIST OF SECURITY HOLDINGS

(Include Government Bonds, Other Bonds and Preferred and Common Stocks)

A.E.'s Copy of Customer's Statement is Attached ☐

**Please give complete description of bonds, including interest rates and maturities.**

Please Supply Prices and Dividends on Local Issues

| Date of Purchase | No. of Bonds or Shares Now Held | NAME OF SECURITY (Please do not use symbols) | Unit Cost (Adjusted) | Please leave this space blank |
|---|---|---|---|---|
| Long Term | 800 | General Motors | 25 | |
| | 400 | General Telephone | 24 | |
| | 100 | Schering | 32 | |
| | 170 | Radio Corporation of America | 11 | |
| | 121 | Standard Oil of California | 28 | |
| | 200 | Chesapeake & Ohio Railway | 61 | |
| | 210 | Eastman Kodak | 11 | |
| | | | | |
| | | | | |
| | | | | |
| | | | | |
| | | | | |
| | | | | |
| | | | | |
| | | | | |
| | | | | |
| | | | | |
| | | | | |
| | | | | |
| | | | | |
| | | | | |

Additional information that will aid in making a better analysis ........................................

# 17

# INVESTMENT COMPANIES

All you need in this life is ignorance and confidence and then success is sure.

—Mark Twain

In Chapter 15 it was noted that small investors who wish to follow a dollar averaging program in a diversified list of stocks may do so via the shares of an investment company. In this chapter we will examine the nature of investment company shares, their performance record, and their suitability as an investment medium.

## Investment Companies Defined

*Open-End versus Closed-End.* An investment company sells its own securities to the public and invests the proceeds in accordance with a stated objective—income, capital gain, or both. The Investment Company Act of 1940 defines an investment company as one with over 40% of its assets in securities other than U.S. government obligations or majority-owned subsidiaries other than investment company subsidiaries. At the present time only two general types of investment companies are of any significance—closed-end and open-end "managed" companies. So-called "unit investment trusts" (which invest in a fixed list of securities and are, therefore, "unmanaged"[1]) and "face-amount certificate companies" (whose investments are similar to time deposits in a bank) are relatively unimportant in terms of assets controlled.

The distinguishing feature of a closed-end company is that its own securities—stocks and bonds[2]—are traded in the open market like any

[1] Most of the assets of unit investment trusts in recent years have been represented by companies which invest in the securities of other investment companies, mostly open-end managed companies.

[2] Closed-end companies may sell bonds and preferred stocks within specified legal limits (asset coverage of 300% is required on debt; 200% on preferred stock). On the other hand, open-end companies organized since 1940 may not have any senior securities in their capital structure.

other corporate issues. Thus, the value of its common stock, at any given time, may be above or below the value at that time of the securities held in its investment portfolio (the so-called "net asset value"). Moreover, unless the company offers a new security issue to the public, which is an infrequent occurrence, its capitalization remains static.

In sharp contrast, an open-end company—popularly referred to as a "mutual fund," a term which hereafter will be employed in this chapter to designate an open-end company—continuously offers new shares for sale and always stands ready to redeem existing shares in cash at the stockholder's request.[3] Sales and repurchases are executed by the funds at the current net asset value per share, which is recalculated at least daily, and typically more frequently. (The arithmetic is to obtain the current market value of each security in the portfolio, sum up, subtract any outstanding liabilities, and divide the resulting figure by the number of outstanding shares of the fund's own common stock.)

*Sales Charges and Operating Expenses.* The buyer of closed-end company shares pays the same brokerage commissions he would pay to acquire the shares of any corporation, say, General Motors. This is not the case with mutual funds. Most mutual funds are sold through stockbrokers and dealer organizations. To compensate the sellers, a "loading charge" is added to the net asset value. The charge varies from fund to fund, but typically falls within a range of 7% to 9% of the selling price, unless the transaction is very large (for example, $50,000), in which case the load is much lower.[4] Although a majority of funds levy sales loads, a number of funds sell shares directly to the public and make no sales charges. These "no-load funds," however, usually levy a redemption fee of 1% or 2% whereas load funds do not.

In addition to the costs of acquiring and disposing of shares, the investors in both open- and closed-end companies are charged with the expenses of operating the companies. These expenses include bookkeeping, maintenance of research staffs, sending reports to stockholders, etc. The amount of such expenses varies considerably from company to company. Perhaps three fourths of 1% of net asset value, deducted *annually* from investment income, is a fair approximation of "average" expense

[3] A few funds redeem at all times but sell new shares only occasionally—for example, Lazard Fund.

[4] Actually, the 7% to 9% is an understatement of almost 1%, because it relates the charge to the total selling price rather than to the net asset value. For example, letting sales price equal net asset value plus load, suppose the figures for a particular fund are $10.00 = $9.20 + $0.80. In the usual mutual fund terminology, the load is expressed as 0.80/10.00, or 8%. From the investor's point of view, however, 0.80/9.20, or 8.7%, is a more meaningful figure, because he is buying only $9.20 of assets. Moreover, most mutual funds also add a "custodial fee" of 1% or more to the sales load. The SEC recently recommended legislation to limit mutual fund sales loads to 5% of net asset value.

charges. Since operating expenses are deducted from investment income, it is informative to express such expenses as a percentage of investment income in addition to the traditional percentage of net asset value calculation. For example, if an investment company's expenses are three fourths of 1% of net asset value, and its interest and dividend income is 4% of net asset value, expense as a percentage of investment income is three fourths of 1% divided by 4% (.0075/.04), or 18¾%. A further charge, deducted from principal, represents the brokerage commissions incurred by the investment company when it buys and sells securities.

*Taxation.* At the outset of an investment company's operation, a basic decision must be made as to whether it is to be a "diversified" investment company or whether it is to invest substantial sums in a few enterprises where it can exercise a large degree of operating control. Tax advantages have made most managements choose the diversified form.

A nondiversified investment company (for example, Christiana Securities, and Equity Corporation) is taxed like any other corporation. That is, 100% of interest income and 15% of dividend income is subject, after deducting expenses, to the prevailing corporate tax rate. Short-term capital gains are fully taxed and long-term gains are subject to the 25% maximum rate. When such a company pays dividends to its stockholders, they are taxable as ordinary income.[5] This chapter will not deal with the highly specialized subject of nondiversified investment companies.

The law sets up special tax provisions for investment companies which meet all three of the following tests:

1. At least 75% of the assets must be "diversified"—defined to mean that no security holding within this 75%, other than U.S. government obligations, may represent over 5% of the investment company's total assets nor over 10% of the outstanding voting securities of the issuer.[6]
2. At least 90% of gross income must be obtained from interest, dividends, and security profits, but not more than 30% may be from profits earned in less than three months.
3. At least 90% of interest, dividends, and short-term capital gains,

---

[5] In the case of both diversified and nondiversified companies, however, dividends paid by companies having deficits in the surplus account due to previous losses are treated as tax-free returns of capital. The carrying cost of the stock is reduced by the amount of the tax-free dividend.

[6] Actually, the Internal Revenue Code requires that the "5% rule" apply to only 50% of an investment company's assets. But the Investment Company Act of 1940 requires that the rule apply to 75% of assets in order for a company to publicize itself as diversified. (The Act of 1940 also limits an investment company's ability to "pyramid" control of securities by limiting its right to acquire the voting stock of other investment companies.) Moreover, the states of Ohio and Wisconsin, among others, require that the rule apply to 100% of assets. Since most companies want to do business in these states, 100% diversification is more typical than not.

after deducting operating expenses, must be paid out to stockholders. Realized long-term capital gains may be retained if so desired.[7]

If a company meets these tests, it is taxed only on the amounts not paid out to its stockholders. The usual corporate tax rates apply to these amounts. (The 85% intercorporate dividend credit does not apply, however.) Stockholders receiving dividends from such companies pay their full personal rate on that portion representing interest, dividends, and net short-term capital gains, and pay the appropriate capital gains tax on that portion which represents net long-term capital gains. The investment company must inform the taxpayer of the proportionate shares of each dividend represented by the various sources of income. Where the company retains capital gains and pays a tax thereon, the stockholder is entitled to a credit if he himself would have paid a lower tax had all the income been distributed. He also can raise the cost basis of his stock by the after-tax amount of the retained capital gain.[8]

*Types of Diversification.* Assuming management chooses to operate a diversified portfolio, a decision must be made whether to include both stocks and bonds in varying proportions, or whether to invest exclusively in either bonds and preferred stocks, on the one hand, or predominantly in common stocks, on the other. If the company chooses to run a common stock fund, it has several further alternatives:

1. It may follow a policy of buying stocks in a broad cross section of the American economy.
2. It may invest in so-called "growth stocks."
3. It may specialize in the securities of a particular industry or group of industries.

Whatever investment policies are chosen must be stated in general terms in a report to the SEC. This statement also must appear in the company's prospectuses and may not be changed without consent of the stockholders. It should be noted that there has been much agitation on the part of public agencies and others to require this policy statement to be more specific than traditionally has been the case. Such requirements are opposed by investment company managers on the grounds that they need a rather flexible framework within which to operate in order to carry out

---

[7] The usual procedure for open-end companies is to pay out capital gains but to encourage shareholders to reinvest automatically in additional shares. Many closed-end companies, on the other hand, follow a practice of retaining capital gains. It has been estimated that about 70% of all capital gains realized by investment companies are reinvested in the companies, either directly by not paying them out or indirectly by stockholders' reinvestment of dividends.

[8] For example, if the investor paid $50 per share for the stock and the company subsequently realizes a $1 per share capital gain, paying a $0.25 capital gains tax and retaining $0.75 net after tax, the investor considers his stock to have cost $50.75 for purposes of calculating his tax liability when he ultimately sells the stock.

their job most efficiently under conditions of constant economic change. Policy statements of several different mutual funds are presented in Figure 17–1.

### Postwar Growth of Investment Companies

As of June 30, 1966, the SEC had on registration under the Investment Company Act of 1940 about 550 "active" companies with an estimated market value of assets of $50 billion.[9] Total registrations as of June 30, 1947, were 352 companies worth $4 billion. These figures are dramatic evidence of the growth of this industry during the years since the end of World War II.

The distribution of companies and assets within the industry is of further interest. In mid-1966 there were more than 350 active open-end companies with over $38 billion of assets. At the same time there were only a few dozen diversified closed-end companies with about $2½ billion of assets.[10] In 1947, on the other hand, the ratio of open-end to closed-end companies was less than 2 to 1 in both number and assets. Most of the growth of closed-end assets during this period came from rising prices of the stocks in the companies' portfolios, while about half of the open-end growth came from net sales of capital stock to the public and half from price appreciation.

Closed-end companies have not been able to raise much new capital, because the market prices of their stocks typically have been at discounts from net asset value during the period. It would not be fair to existing stockholders to sell new shares at a discount (except in rights offerings to the stockholders themselves), because this would dilute their equity. Indeed, the Investment Company Act restricts such transactions in order to protect the shareholders. By the same token, *new* closed-end companies cannot be promoted readily, because the public understandably is reluctant to pay net asset value or higher for a new company's shares when existing companies' shares can be bought at a discount.[11]

---

[9] There were, in addition, more than 100 "inactive" companies—i.e., not operating or in the process of being merged or liquidated.

[10] About $10 billion of additional assets were represented by nondiversified closed-end companies, including registered Small Business Investment Companies ($5 billion); unit investment trusts ($3½ billion); and face amount certificate companies ($1½ billion). These estimates and others in this chapter are derived from several sources, including SEC annual reports, the Investment Company Institute, the Wharton School study, and Arthur Wiesenberger & Co. publications.

[11] Of course, not all closed-end shares sell at discounts at all times. Lehman Corporation and Madison Fund, for example, frequently have sold at premiums. In 1966, the latter organization raised $30 million of new funds in a rather unique fashion, for investment companies—a convertible preferred stock issue. It may be noted also that the managements of the discount closed-ends frequently have been criticized for failing to buy back the companies' own stock in the open market, which would help to narrow the discount and raise the net asset value per share at the same time.

## FIGURE 17–1

### Illustrative Mutual Fund Statements of Policy

*A Conservative Balanced Fund—Wellington Fund*

Wellington Fund is designed to provide conservative investors with a prudent investment program with the following objectives:

*a*) Conservation of principal
*b*) Reasonable income return
*c*) Profits without undue risk

Wellington Management Company, the investment adviser for the Fund, endeavors to achieve these objectives for the Fund through a balanced and diversified program of investing in bonds, preferred stocks and common stocks.

*A Conservative Stock Fund—Axe-Houghton Stock Fund*

The primary objective of the Fund is long-term capital growth, but it also seeks to protect capital values. To attain its objectives the Fund's assets are normally invested in common and preferred stocks. At times when management believes that economic conditions indicate the desirability of a defensive position they may invest a large portion in bonds until the outlook for equities appears more favorable.

Management pays particular attention to industries which are expected to benefit from recent scientific developments and from new engineering methods.

*A Growth Stock Fund—Massachusetts Investors Growth Stock Fund*

The objective of Massachusetts Investors Growth Stock Fund is to provide long-term growth of principal and future income rather than current income return. To achieve this objective it is the policy of the Fund to keep its assets invested, except for working cash balances, in the common stocks, or securities convertible into common stocks, of companies believed by the management to possess better than average prospects for long-term growth, and this policy may not be changed without a vote of shareholders.

Generally speaking, such potentialities are indicated for companies which produce types of goods or services having relatively favorable long-term prospects for increasing demand, or which aggressively pursue policies of developing new and improved products or services and new and expanding markets through intensive research and resourceful management, and which normally retain a relatively large proportion of earnings for research and development and for "plowing back" into working assets.

Emphasis is thus placed on the selection of progressive, well-managed companies believed by the management to have sound promise, rather than on speculative possibilities or on concentration in a limited area.

*A "Performance" Fund—Manhattan Fund*

The investment objective of the Fund is to seek long-term appreciation of capital. The potential for capital growth will be almost the sole basis for selection of portfolio securities and any income received from such securities will be entirely incidental to the growth objective.

The Fund's policy of investing in securities believed to have a potential for long-term capital appreciation means that the assets of the Fund will generally be subject to greater risk than may be involved in securities which do not have growth characteristics. In selecting investments the Fund considers a number of factors, such as product development and demand, operating ratios, utilization of earnings for expansion, management abilities, analyses of intrinsic values, market action and overall economic and political conditions. It is anticipated that common stocks will constitute all or most of the Fund's investment portfolio, but the Fund is not restricted from investing in preferred stocks and debt securities, where opportunities for capital growth may also be found. When management believes that a more defensive or conservative position is warranted, the Fund may invest in bonds or other fixed income securities or retain cash, all without limitation.

Impetus to the steady growth of open-end company capital has come from the widespread acceptance of periodic accumulation plans. Under "contractual" accumulation plans, investors agree to dollar average in a mutual fund by purchasing a fixed dollar amount of shares on a regular monthly or quarterly basis for a specified number of years. A "voluntary" accumulation plan, on the other hand, is more flexible in its payment arrangements. Moreover, under a voluntary plan the regular sales load is deducted on each individual transaction, and there is no penalty if the investor fails to make payments. But with a contractual plan, most of the sales load for the *entire* program is deducted within the first three years, and termination of the plan is supposed to be discouraged thereby because it is so costly.[12]

Securities salesmen obviously are very attracted to periodic accumulation plans, particularly the contractual variety, since the salesman is assured of commissions whether or not the plan ultimately is completed. So aggressively have accumulation plans been promoted that their share of

[12] For example, suppose an investor contracts to pay $1,000 a year for 10 years and the sales load is 8½%, or $850 on the $10,000 contract. If, say, $500 of the $850 is deducted in the first three years, the investor will have purchased only $2,500 worth of shares with $3,000 of payments. If he terminates the plan at that point, the per-share value of the fund would have had to appreciate substantially during the three years for the investor merely to break even. Actually, in many contractual plans the so-called "front-end load" is 50% of the investor's *first 12 monthly payments*. In such cases, early termination can be extremely costly. The SEC has recently recommended legislation to abolish such front-end loads.

the total value of mutual fund accounts exceeded 30% at the end of 1963, compared with 5% in 1954. (Post-1963 data are not available, nor is there any breakdown between voluntary and contractual plans. However, the SEC estimates that at the end of 1965 there were 1.3 million contractual plans in force, in which about $3 billion had been invested.)

There is one final aspect of mutual fund growth which is important to note. For the industry as a whole there has not been a single year, since records began to be kept in 1941, when share redemptions exceeded sales of new shares. Indeed, data on quarterly inflow and outflow of capital during the postwar period reveal that new sales ranged from 1½ to 5 times redemptions, with an average sales/redemption ratio of more than 2.0. Thus, the industry's growth not only has been large in magnitude but also persistent.

## Management Problems of Investment Companies

*Unique Aspects.* A surface appraisal of investment companies suggests that they are in a rather unique position among financial institutions from an investment management point of view. Unlike banks, insurance companies, and even pension trusts, they have no liabilities to speak of and thus cannot become insolvent.[13] Although it is true that the common stock of a mutual fund is redeemable on demand, it is redeemable at whatever the net asset value happens to be at any given time rather than at a fixed price. Furthermore, mutual funds have been growing so rapidly that share redemptions in most cases can be paid with the proceeds of sales of new shares, thus minimizing the risk of having to liquidate assets under pressure. Some closed-end companies, of course, do have fixed liabilities to cover. But most of them have a wide margin of common stock equity between their assets and their senior securities—indeed, they are required by law to have a wide margin. Thus, as far as either legal or practical obligations are concerned, it would appear that the only companies having need for stability of principal are those which specifically write such an objective into their policy statements.

Since management fees and operating expenses generally amount to less than 1% of net assets, they usually can be covered by even a small income yield.[14] Therefore, the funds would appear to have as little need for stability of income as for stability of principal—unless they specifically write such an objective into their policy statement.

[13] In a strict sense, pension trusts also have no liabilities in that any deficiency of assets relative to the sponsoring corporations' pension agreements with their workers must be made up by additional contributions from the corporations. Nevertheless, at least the *corporations* have pension liabilities, and the pension trustees have this "target" before them at all times.

[14] However, it should be stressed that while 1% of net asset value doesn't sound like much, if a fund's portfolio is yielding only 3%–4%, a 1% expense rate would reduce income dividends to stockholders by 25%–33%.

In addition to these apparently favorable factors, investment companies meeting the Internal Revenue Service requirements have no significant tax problems. Thus, we have been describing what sounds like an investment manager's paradise—no tax problems, no need for stable principal, no need for stable income, no need for anything he does not choose to burden himself with. Surely life couldn't be as easy as all that. It isn't!

*The Influence of Size.* Successful portfolio management tends to be easier if the size of the fund permits (1) adequate diversification, (2) ample new money coming in to take advantage of attractive opportunities as they appear, (3) a spreading of the overhead, both clerical and research, among more accounts, and (4) an ability to pry information out of corporate executives.[15] It may be argued, of course, that *excessive* size can hamper flexibility and therefore performance. For example, some very large funds, such as Massachusetts Investors Trust, have diversified so broadly that they cannot hope to show better-than-average performance.[16] They, in effect, *are* the average. Any single wise investment selection is unlikely to have much of an impact on total results. In order to have such an impact, the purchase might have to be so large in amount as to run the risk of driving the issue's price far up when buying and far down when selling. Indeed, the size of purchase required to have an impact on overall results may be in violation of the diversification laws noted earlier, which tend to restrict an investment company from holding more than 10% of any one corporation's voting securities.

It is easy to overstate the problem of size, however. For example, suppose a fund has assets of $1 billion—i.e., it is a *very* large fund.[17] And suppose its managers decide upon a policy of keeping 2½% of assets at any given time (half the legal limit) in each of only 40 stocks which seem to have excellent prospects at that time. Two and one-half percent of $1

---

[15] Regarding point (4), it should be recognized by the reader that there may be many legal and ethical questions raised when companies reveal at private meetings information which is not available to the public.

[16] A correlation analysis by Ira Horowitz and Harold B. Higgins ("Some Factors Affecting Investment Fund Performance," *Quarterly Review of Economics and Business,* Spring, 1963) provides statistical evidence of a negative relationship between performance and size and between performance and breadth of diversification.

[17] At the end of 1965, 257 open-end companies listed in the *Investment Dealers' Digest* had the following asset-size distribution:

| | |
|---|---|
| Under $10,000,000 | 102 |
| $ 10,000,000 to $ 25,000,000 | 39 |
| 25,000,000 to 50,000,000 | 34 |
| 50,000,000 to 100,000,000 | 20 |
| 250,000,000 to 500,000,000 | 20 |
| 100,000,000 to 250,000,000 | 26 |
| 250,000,000 to 500,000,000 | 20 |
| 500,000,000 and over | 16 |
| | 257 |

billion is $25 million in each stock. If it also is decided that not more than 2½% of the outstanding shares of each issue should be acquired (one quarter of the legal limit), the investment managers can consider only issues with a market value of $1 billion or higher. But in recent years there have been approximately 100 issues on the New York Stock Exchange with a market value of $1 billion. Thus, the fund's managers would have a reasonably broad scope for exercising their skills. They would have to choose 40 stocks from a list of 100. If they were, indeed, skillful in their profession, they should be able to "beat the averages" quite handily. The major restraint on their operation would be that they could not change their minds too frequently regarding the composition of the 40 stocks, because $25 million of stock usually cannot be acquired and disposed of very easily in a short period of time.

If the advantages of size are balanced against the disadvantages, it would seem that, up to a point, large size and continued growth make the investment manager's task easier.[18] But how does an investment company grow and become large? Since investment companies have to pay out 90% of current income to remain tax exempt, the only routes to growth are retention of capital gains or sale of additional securities. The closed-end companies depend primarily on retained capital gains (realized and unrealized); the mutual funds on both new sales and unrealized capital appreciation. But in the long run, both capital gains and new sales depend upon successful investment performance.[19] So we have the beginnings of a vicious circle: Successful performance is easier if a company is fairly large, but a company usually will not get large unless it has a successful performance. Even though the industry as a whole may be growing, the *individual* company cannot count on following the industry's growth trend unless it successfully performs its functions.

The vicious circle is most vicious for an open-end company. If performance is poor relative to stockholders' objectives and expectations, share redemptions may begin to exceed new sales. The need for cash to meet net redemptions puts the portfolio manager on the defensive. Since he does not want to run the risk of having to sell stocks in a bear market in order to raise cash, he must maintain a more liquid position than he

---

[18] And one need not be a cynic to recognize that growth also means larger fees for the managers, since their compensation usually is geared to net asset value.

[19] The observation that sales depend upon successful performance is not entirely true, especially over the short run. Since the buyers of investment company shares are not as well informed as they should be about performance records, a strong sales campaign can cause even a poor-performing company to become large. The Wharton Study, for example, revealed a direct relationship between salesmen's compensation (the percentage load) and sales of new shares. But sales load was not correlated with investment performance. A slight relationship was discovered between performance and sales of new shares. For additional evidence of a lack of relationship between performance and sales of new shares, see I. Horowitz, "Popularity Versus Performance: The Mutual Funds," *Quarterly Review of Economics and Business,* Spring, 1966.

otherwise would. But liquidity reduces the portfolio's earnings, which further dissatisfies the stockholders and accelerates their tendency to redeem their shares. The problem is aggravated by the fact that investors tend to be impressed by the actions of other investors. If net new sales are high and rising, people assume the fund is good, and they buy still more. If net redemptions set in, people assume something is wrong, and the redemptions accelerate.

*"Public Relations" Aspects.* The emphasis on giving the shares of investment companies "sales appeal" often creates additional problems:

1. Unlike those of most other financial institutions, the investment activities of these companies are exposed to the constant glare of publicity. Therefore, the managers may feel under pressure to concentrate their portfolios in the securities of popular companies. These are either the glamour companies which have caught the public's fancy or the great blue-chip companies in which the public has confidence and which can be traded in large volume. The trouble is that popular securities tend to be overpriced relative to less well-known situations.[20]

2. Since income and capital gains may be reduced when funds are kept idle, and since the competition among investment companies is very strong, investment company portfolio managers often are pressured into being fully invested in common stocks during a bull market even if they believe stocks to be overpriced and due for a fall. Similarly, they may be under pressure to sell stocks on which they have capital gains, and buy others, even though the discarded stocks still look attractive, in order to provide the basis for capital gains distributions to compete with other funds.[21] If stockholders were more aware of the distinction between income distributions and capital gains distributions, there would be less incentive for these maneuvers.

How have investment companies responded to these investment management problems? What kind of investment policies do they actually follow?

### Management Policies

*Overall Portfolio Structure.* Approximately two thirds of mutual fund assets are with companies following a policy of always keeping 80%

[20] In an interesting study, "The Less Popular Stocks versus the Most Popular Stocks," W. Scott Bauman shows the following average rates of return during the period 1954–63: Popular Stocks—13.7%; Unpopular Stocks—14.9%. (*Financial Analysts Journal*, January-February, 1965, p. 62). He also shows, however, that the less popular stocks are subject to a greater degree of volatility and that the protection of diversification is, therefore, more important. At least one mutual fund—Penn Square—has made it a deliberate policy to purchase stocks in out-of-favor industries.

[21] On the other hand, they sometimes may be tempted *not* to take gains, even on stocks which have become unattractive, because distributions of these gains might not be reinvested and total assets would decline. Even if the gains were taken and retained, the company would have to pay a 25% tax, thereby shrinking the size of the portfolio.

or more of their funds invested in a diversified list of common stocks. They may stress growth of capital, current income, or a combination of both. Some 20%–25% of mutual fund assets are with companies following "balanced" or "flexible" policies. Balanced funds typically keep around 60%–75% of their funds in a diversified selection of common stocks, with the remainder in bonds and preferred stocks. Flexible funds, on the other hand, vary the bond-stock proportions widely, depending on management's view of the business and capital market outlook. As with common stock funds, both balanced and flexible funds may stress either growth, income, or a combination of both, but there is generally slightly less emphasis on growth in exchange for greater stability of principal and income.

The remainder of mutual fund assets is divided among funds specializing in (*a*) the common stocks of a particular industry or group of industries, (*b*) foreign stocks, or (*c*) bonds and preferred stocks.

The portfolio policies of diversified closed-end companies are much more difficult to classify than those of mutual funds, but some generalizations can be made. Their limited prospect of growth through new capital inflow means that they usually can make portfolio adjustments only by selling existing holdings and replacing them with more attractive securities. This is often a harsh choice to make, and as a result closed-end companies tend to have more conservative portfolio structures than those mutual funds having "all common stock" policies. However, while they usually are more conservative than common stock funds, the closed-ends as a group are not as conservative as balanced funds, which always keep 25% or more of assets in fixed income securities regardless of capital market conditions.

*Liquidity.* Regardless of their policies on overall portfolio structure, investment companies typically keep about 5% of their assets in cash and liquid investments. This liquidity position is maintained to meet unexpected redemptions (in the case of mutual funds) and to take advantage quickly of unusually attractive investment opportunities. A side result, of course, is that current income is below what it otherwise might be. It also should be noted that smaller mutual funds tend to keep a larger liquidity position than the industry average, although it is not clear whether this is by choice or necessity.

*Common Stock Characteristics.* While diversified investment companies have become increasingly attracted to over-the-counter stocks, the great majority of their holdings are in the more popular companies listed on the New York Stock Exchange. Moreover, just as the value of all NYSE–listed common stocks is heavily concentrated in a few industries (five industries—utilities, petroleum, chemical, electrical equipment, and automotive—represent about two thirds of total market value), so it is with investment companies. It is noteworthy, however, that while a fairly high industry concentration usually is present in any given investment company portfolio, the specific industries in which holdings are concentrated often differ sharply from company to company. Thus, some portfolios are heavy in chemicals, electronics, and similar "exotic" industries, while other portfolios are heavier in more "mundane" industries such as utilities and oils.

The pressure toward investing in popular stocks is reflected in the fact that a dozen or so well-known companies are represented in the portfolios of over 100 mutual funds (see Figure 17–2). Nevertheless, few investment company portfolios are concentrated in a small number of issues. The 1962 Wharton School study of mutual funds revealed that in 1952 and 1958 the top four fund holdings represented 5% and 7%, respectively, of the total value of their stockholdings, whereas the top four stocks on the New York Stock Exchange represented about 20% of the value of all listed issues. The Investment Company Institute has estimated that the stocks of over 2,500 corporations are contained in the industry's portfolios, with the typical portfolio containing almost 100 different issues at any given time. Thus, investment company managers appear to be willing to make major decisions on *industries* in which to concentrate, but they also appear to seek the safety of numbers by purchasing many *individual issues*.

*Turnover.* There is evidence in the Wharton study that mutual fund managers make a conscious effort to shift around the industry distribution of their portfolios in order to take advantage of changing prospects. But there is conflicting evidence about the *timing* of such shifts. Evidence can be cited that investment companies follow the trend of the market, buying aggressively when prices are rising and getting very cautious in declining markets. However, there also has been evident from time to time an effort to act counter to market trends, especially near the end of major stock price declines. No generalizations on this subject appear warranted.

Also unwarranted are loose generalizations regarding the *degree* of portfolio turnover by the typical investment company. Since investment company managers frequently are connected with, or are actually partners in, brokerage houses, it is easy to suspect them of frequent commission-generating transactions, known as "churning." Another reason for this suspicion is the thought that investment companies can induce brokerage houses to make special efforts to sell investment company shares by giving them a lot of commission business. The evidence, however, is not clear-cut. While some observers note that investment company turnover has been significantly greater than that of institutional investor generally,[22] other observers point out that the level and trend of investment

[22] There has been some evidence recently of an increased willingness on the part of all institutional investors to adopt more aggressive turnover policies. See S. R. Karr, "Speculative Funds," *The Wall Street Journal*, March 8, 1966.

## FIGURE 17–2

### One Hundred Stocks Ranked by Number of Investment Companies

| Rank | Stock | No. of Inv. Cos. Holding | Rank | Stock | No. of Inv. Cos. Holding | Rank | Stock | No. of Inv. Cos. Holding | Rank | Stock | No. of Inv. Cos. Holding |
|---|---|---|---|---|---|---|---|---|---|---|---|
| 1. | I.B.M. | 214 | 26. | Ford Motor | 77 | 51. | Goodyear | 57 | 76. | Union Oil of Calif. | 50 |
| 2. | General Motors | 186 | 27. | Lockheed | 77 | 52. | Avon Products | 56 | 77. | Burlington Industries | 49 |
| 3. | Std. Oil (N.J.) | 171 | 28. | Anaconda | 75 | 53. | Continental Oil | 56 | 78. | U.S. Steel | 49 |
| 4. | Texaco Inc. | 144 | 29. | duPont (E.I.) | 75 | 54. | Gillette | 56 | 79. | Armco Steel | 48 |
| 5. | A.T.& T. | 123 | 30. | Massey-Ferguson | 74 | 55. | American Airlines | 55 | 80. | Bristol-Myers | 48 |
| 6. | Xerox | 123 | 31. | Litton Industries | 73 | 56. | Atlantic Richfield | 55 | 81. | Olin Mathieson | 48 |
| 7. | Intl. Nickel | 122 | 32. | Intl. Paper | 72 | 57. | C.B.S. | 55 | 82. | Fed. Dept. Stores | 47 |
| 8. | General Electric | 115 | 33. | Sears Roebuck | 72 | 58. | Delta Air Lines | 55 | 83. | No. Amer. Avia. | 47 |
| 9. | Eastman Kodak | 112 | 34. | United Air Lines | 72 | 59. | Dow Chemical | 55 | 84. | American Can | 46 |
| 10. | Mobil Corp. | 105 | 35. | M.M.M. | 69 | 60. | Syntex | 55 | 85. | Bethlehem Steel | 45 |
| 11. | Gulf Oil | 104 | 36. | Reynolds Metals | 68 | 61. | Norfolk & Western | 54 | 86. | General Dynamics | 45 |
| 12. | Alcan Aluminium | 101 | 37. | Pan Am. World Air. | 67 | 62. | Zenith Radio | 54 | 87. | Phelps Dodge | 45 |
| 13. | Royal Dutch | 101 | 38. | Honeywell | 65 | 63. | Central & So. West | 53 | 88. | Chase Manhattan Bk. | 44 |
| 14. | Polaroid | 98 | 39. | Alum. Co. of Amer. | 64 | 64. | Continental Can | 53 | 89. | Corning Glass | 44 |
| 15. | Genl. Tel. & El. | 94 | 40. | Celanese Corp. | 64 | 65. | Pfizer (Chas.) | 53 | 90. | Magnavox | 44 |
| 16. | Chrysler | 93 | 41. | Southern Pacific | 63 | 66. | Amer. Elec. Power | 52 | 91. | Newmont Mining | 44 |
| 17. | Boeing | 90 | 42. | Texas Utilities | 63 | 67. | Goodrich (B.F.) | 52 | 92. | So. Calif. Edison | 44 |
| 18. | Westinghouse El. | 90 | 43. | Motorola | 62 | 68. | Cities Service | 51 | 93. | Amerada | 43 |
| 19. | Union Carbide | 89 | 44. | PepsiCo | 62 | 69. | Grace (W.R.) | 51 | 94. | Rexall Drug & Chem. | 43 |
| 20. | Monsanto | 85 | 45. | Sinclair Oil | 62 | 70. | Merck | 51 | 95. | Halliburton | 42 |
| 21. | I.T.& T. | 82 | 46. | Kennecott Copper | 61 | 71. | Pennsylvania RR. | 51 | 96. | Imperial Oil Ltd. | 42 |
| 22. | Northwest Airlines | 82 | 47. | Caterpillar Tractor | 58 | 72. | Florida Pwr. & Lt. | 50 | 97. | Middle South Util. | 42 |
| 23. | United Aircraft | 81 | 48. | Southern Co. | 58 | 73. | National Airlines | 50 | 98. | Reynolds Tobacco | 42 |
| 24. | Std. Oil, Calif. | 79 | 49. | Std. Oil (Indiana) | 58 | 74. | Revlon | 50 | 99. | Smith Kline & French | 42 |
| 25. | R.C.A. | 78 | 50. | Cndn. Pacific Rwy. | 57 | 75. | Texas Instruments | 50 | 100. | Genl. Public Util. | 41 |

Source: Vickers Associates, Inc., *Vickers Favorite 50*, June 30, 1966, edition.

company turnover has not been significantly greater or less than overall turnover on the New York Stock Exchange.

The Wharton study does demonstrate convincingly that turnover rates have varied *inversely* with size. This finding should not be surprising, however. Large companies usually can use new fund inflow to take advantage of investment opportunities as they arise. But small companies do not have such a regular inflow of new funds and often have to sell existing holdings to raise cash for more attractive investments. The situation is similar to that touched upon above in discussing diversification policies of closed-end companies.

## Management Performance

*Defining the Problem.* Having examined the management policies of investment companies, the next logical question is: How successful have the managers actually been? This question is by no means academic. In 1958 the Investment Company Institute surveyed holders of mutual fund shares to determine their principal reasons for investing in the funds. Number one on the list of reasons was diversification. Another survey in 1962 revealed that diversification had moved to second place among accumulation plan holders, with expert management taking over first position. Among regular account holders, diversification was still first, but management had moved from a very poor second to a challenger for first place. Convenience was cited as the third most important reason. By 1966 the survey revealed that professional management had moved to first place.

Note that what is being discussed is the performance of the *managers.* We are not, for the moment, considering the results achieved by *investors.* The latter would require that we take into account sales and redemption charges (if any), premiums and discounts in the case of closed-end companies, and an estimate of the results which a typical investor could have achieved by investing directly in securities rather than indirectly via an investment company. What is being considered now is solely the following question: Have investment company managers achieved any better results, relative to their objectives, by exercising selection and timing discretion with the net assets at their disposal, than they could have achieved by simply "buying the averages"? This involves two subsidiary questions: (1) What have the managers achieved? (2) What has been the performance of "the averages"?

*A Method of Measuring Performance.* Probably the simplest, most direct method of measuring management's overall achievement during any given year is to compute the percentage appreciation of one share of the investment company from one year-end to the next, including all dividend distributions paid during the year. The computation follows the formula:

$$\frac{\text{N.A.V.}_{\text{Dec. 31, }t} + \text{Dividends}_t}{\text{N.A.V.}_{\text{Dec. 31, }t-1}} - 1.00$$

Where: N.A.V. is per-share net asset value; *t* is the year being studied; and Dividends include distributions paid during the year from both regular income and realized capital gains.[23]

Arthur Wiesenberger's annual *Investment Companies* manual applies this formula to all investment companies of any substantial size. We have averaged these performance data annually for the years 1950 through 1965, for all companies having records of five years or longer, excluding companies investing exclusively in foreign securities or exclusively in bonds and preferred stocks. The data have been arranged under three classifications: (1) open-end companies which always keep most of their portfolios in common stocks, (2) open-end companies which were described earlier in this chapter as "balanced" or "flexible" because they keep part of their funds in stocks and part in bonds, and (3) all closed-end companies.

These annual results can be compared with similar computations for, say, the Standard & Poor's 425 Industrial Stock Price Index. The formula would be: year-end index plus dividends on the index during the year, divided by previous year-end index, minus 1.00. This would be a measure of the performance of hypothetical common stock companies which simply "bought the averages." But so straightforward a comparison would not be fair to the investment companies for several reasons:

1. The averages are, by definition, 100% invested at all times. Although an investment company which simply bought the averages would not need a cash reserve to take advantage of good buying opportunities, it would have to maintain *some* cash reserve to meet dividend payments and (for mutual funds) unexpected net share redemptions. These cash needs could, of course, be met by selling off a part of the portfolio. But such a procedure would not be very efficient. Therefore, let us assume a cash requirement of 2% when calculating the performance of "the averages."[24]

2. An investment company which bought the averages would have to invest new fund inflows like any other investment company. This involves brokerage commissions. Additional transactions and brokerage commissions would be called for when companies are added to or deleted from the particular stock market average being followed. Since the averages make no allowance for brokerage charges, assume a deduction of one fourth of 1% of the beginning value every year.[25]

---

[23] Some analysts believe that the effect of leverage on closed-end company performance should be eliminated from the computation. We do not agree, since the degree of leverage is within management's discretion.

[24] Some of this could be invested in short-term interest-earning assets, but for simplicity assume it is kept as nonearning bank balances.

[25] This is equivalent to an assumption that annual transactions amount to 25% of total beginning net assets at an average commission of 1%.

3. A company which bought the averages would need no staff of security analysts, but it would still need a clerical staff and have other overhead costs. A "typical" investment company has annual expenses of about three fourths of 1% of net asset value, including one half of 1% in salaries and fees to the portfolio managers themselves.[26] Thus, excluding management fees, since there would be no managers, one half of 1% would seem to be a generous allowance for clerical and other overhead. Therefore, assume a one half of 1% annual deduction in addition to the one fourth of 1% brokerage deduction already discussed.

4. Balanced and flexible companies should not be measured against an all-common-stock yardstick, since performance must be interpreted in the light of investment objectives. Most investors in balanced and flexible companies put heavy emphasis on safety of principal and stability of income in addition to growth. No one who has these investment objectives would keep his whole portfolio in common stocks. A substantial portion doubtless would be kept in fixed income securities. How much in fixed income issues is a question with no single correct answer; therefore, a rather arbitrary assumption must be made. For present purposes, balanced and flexible fund results will be compared with a hypothetical fund having 25% of its assets in fixed income securities. As a further simplification, it will be assumed that these securities always yield 4% in interest income—i.e., 1% of total net assets[27]—and that their market values always remain unchanged.

To summarize, the yardsticks against which investment company performance will be compared in this section are computed as follows:

*A—For "all stock" companies:*

$$\left[98\% \left(\frac{\text{S \& P } 425_{\text{Dec. 31, } t} + \text{S \& P 425 Dividends}_t}{\text{S \& P } 425_{\text{Dec. 31, } t-1}} - 1\right)\right] - \tfrac{3}{4}\%$$

*B—For "balanced" and "flexible" companies:*

$$\left[73\% \left(\frac{\text{S \& P } 425_{\text{Dec. 31, } t} + \text{S \& P 425 Dividends}_t}{\text{S \& P } 425_{\text{Dec. 31, } t-1}} - 1\right)\right] + \tfrac{1}{4}\%$$

Note: The factor 98% reflects the 2% cash reserve; 73% reflects 2% cash reserve and 25% fixed income fixed principal investment. The three fourths of 1% deduction reflects brokerage commissions and operating expenses; the one fourth of 1% addition reflects the three fourths of 1% deduction plus 1% interest income.

*Possible Criticisms of the Performance Measure.* Three criticisms may be leveled at these standards for evaluating the performance of

[26] Fund managers increasingly are accepting compensation on a sliding scale, the fee falling as asset size rises. Failure to adopt sliding scales has become a great source of criticism and controversy. See the 1966 SEC *Report on the Public Policy Implications of Investment Company Growth.*

[27] $4\% \times 25\% = 1\%$

investment company managers. The criticisms should be considered before proceeding further.

1. It often is said that "the averages" do not reflect the portfolio structure of typical investors, individual or institutional. While this statement probably is true, it really is quite irrelevant in the present context. The fact is that any given investment company's managers can, if they choose to do so, structure their portfolio in line with one of the popular price averages or indexes. If they do not choose to do so, presumably they think they can do better on their own. Thus, it is fair to test them against a standard which they consciously or unconsciously think they can outperform.

**TABLE 17–1**

**Overall Performance Measures (%)**

| | *Open-End Companies* | | | *Hypothetical Funds* | |
|---|---|---|---|---|---|
| | *Stock* | *Balanced or Flexible* | *Closed-End Companies* | *All Stock* | *Balanced* |
| 1950 | +24 | +18 | +19 | +32 | +24 |
| 1951 | +18 | +11 | +20 | +23 | +18 |
| 1952 | +12 | +10 | +10 | +15 | +12 |
| 1953 | 0 | 0 | 0 | − 3 | − 2 |
| 1954 | +48 | +33 | +44 | +54 | +41 |
| 1955 | +20 | +15 | +19 | +33 | +26 |
| 1956 | + 9 | + 4 | +13 | + 6 | + 5 |
| 1957 | −11 | − 8 | − 9 | −11 | − 7 |
| 1958 | +43 | +31 | +37 | +40 | +31 |
| 1959 | +15 | + 8 | + 8 | +12 | +10 |
| 1960 | + 4 | + 4 | + 2 | − 2 | − 1 |
| 1961 | +28 | +20 | +23 | +25 | +20 |
| 1962 | −15 | − 5 | −11 | −10 | − 7 |
| 1963 | +19 | +14 | +20 | +22 | +18 |
| 1964 | +14 | +13 | +16 | +15 | +12 |
| 1965 | +25 | +11 | +14 | +12 | +10 |
| Average rate of return: | | | | | |
| 1953, 57, 60, 62 | − 5 | − 2 | − 4 | − 6 | − 4 |
| Other Years | +23 | +16 | +20 | +24 | +19 |
| 1950–65 | +16 | +11 | +14 | +16 | +13 |
| Standard deviation around 1950–65 avg. | 16 | 11 | 14 | 18 | 13 |
| Geometric mean of 1950–65 performance relatives | +15 | +11 | +13 | +15 | +12 |

2. It also is claimed frequently that whether or not investment companies "beat the averages" is less relevant than whether they do more for the individual investor than he could do on his own. While one can be quite sympathetic with this reasoning, it nevertheless is important to know

whether investment companies could do even more for their shareholders by simply "buying the averages."

3. The S & P 425 Stock Price Index has had a faster growth rate than the Dow-Jones Industrial Average. Therefore, it may be argued that comparisons of investment company performance with the performance of the S & P 425 Index contain a statistical bias. The answer to this argument is that the S & P Index has broader coverage and is more soundly constructed than the Dow. Indeed, it is the Dow Average which contains the statistical bias. It is biased downward because of its treatment of stock splits. Each time a component stock in the Dow is split, its price falls and its effective weight in the Average thereby is reduced. This is not true of the S & P Index, because each stock's price is weighted by number of shares outstanding. Since the stocks that are split most tend to be those that are growing most rapidly, the Dow Average tends continuously to reduce the weight of its most rapidly growing components. This gives it a downward bias in comparison with the S & P Index.

*The Performance Comparison.* Table 17–1 compares the annual performance measures of the investment company groupings with the hypothetical results of companies buying the averages. On the basis of these data, three conclusions seem warranted:

1. The rate of return on investment company shares has been slightly better than that of the averages during bear markets (1953, 1957, 1960, 1962) and slightly poorer during bull markets (defined for convenience as all other years of the compilation).[28] In other words, investment company volatility has been slightly less than that of the averages.[29] The differences, however, are so small that for practical purposes it can be said that investment company performance on the whole has been almost identical to what it would have been under hypothetical unmanaged conditions.

2. As would be expected, open-end stock funds have done better than balanced or flexible funds during bull markets and worse during bear markets.

3. Closed-end company performance has been midway between that of open-end stock and balanced-flexible funds.

---

[28] Contrary to precedent, the 1965 bull market performance of stock funds was outstandingly good. It will be interesting to observe in future years whether the "new breed" of performance-oriented managers who have begun to enter the industry can succeed in maintaining such excellent results in comparison with the averages.

[29] Several recent articles on the subject of mutual fund performance measurement have emphasized the element of risk, as measured by year-to-year volatility, in addition to rate of return. See J. L. Treynor, "How to Rate Management of Investment Funds," *Harvard Business Review*, January–February, 1965; I. Friend and D. Vickers, "Portfolio Selection and Investment Performance," *Journal of Finance*, September, 1965; W. F. Sharpe, "Risk Aversion in the Stock Market: Some Empirical Evidence," *Journal of Finance*, September, 1965; and W. F. Sharpe, "Mutual Fund Performance," *Journal of Business: Supplement on Security Prices*, January, 1966.

The preceding data concerned investment companies as a group, and the finding that they merely did about as well as "the averages" should not be too surprising. After all, one should hardly expect them to do much better when one considers how broadly diversified their portfolios are. As a group, they *are* the averages.

The really surprising aspect of this investigation is revealed in Table 17–2, which shows the distribution of investment companies that typically

**TABLE 17–2**

**Dispersion of Individual Performance Measures**

| % of Years in Which Company Outperformed Group Average | | Number of Investment Companies Studied: Open-End Companies: Stock | Open-End Companies: Balanced or Flexible | Closed-End Companies |
|---|---|---|---|---|
| 0– 24 | Consistently poor performers | 16 | 2 | 0 |
| 25– 40 | | 40 | 19 | 6 |
| 41– 50 | Average performers | 29 | 13 | 6 |
| 51– 59 | | 9 | 3 | 1 |
| 60– 75 | Consistently good performers | 13 | 9 | 3 |
| 76–100 | | 5 | 0 | 0 |
| Total Companies Studied | | 112 | 46 | 16 |

did better, worse, or the same as *their own group's average performance.* Here it can be seen that there is extreme diversity in performance. For example, 18 of the 112 open-end stock companies outperformed their group 60% or more of the time. On the other hand, 56 of the 112 outperformed their group 40% or less of the time. The data are similarly skewed for balanced-flexible funds. The closed-end sample is probably too small to be meaningful, but it too shows a preponderance of poor performers.

Thus, a disproportionately large number of investment companies have been consistently poor performers. Were it not for the fact that the relatively few consistently good performers had exceptionally good results, investment companies as a group would have done worse than hypothetical unmanaged companies.[30]

*Identifying Good and Poor Performers.* An investor who wishes to determine which specific mutual funds and closed-end investment companies have been outstandingly good, or average, or mediocre performers has a substantial amount of information available to him. Figures 17–3

---

[30] However, W. F. Sharpe has shown that poorer performing funds tend to exhibit less year-to-year volatility than better performing funds. See his "Mutual Fund Performance," *op. cit.*

through 17–5, for example, illustrate the type of information provided in Wiesenberger's annual *Investment Companies* manual. Figure 17–3 shows, for different funds, a 10-year record of annual percentage gains and losses, computed as described earlier, and also shows *cumulative* performance for 1, 2, 3, etc., years ending with the most recent year. (Appendix A of this chapter discusses some of the conceptual problems involved in the measurement of cumulative performance.) Figure 17–4 presents statistics which measure the degree to which different funds were more or less "volatile" than the Dow-Jones Industrials—i.e., the degree to which they rose and fell during bull and bear market phases of the cycle, *relative to the Dow.* Figure 17–5 shows a typical page from the section of the Wiesenberger manual which reviews individual investment companies in detail. The history and portfolio objectives of the fund are summarized, supplemented by a statistical record of assets,[31] income, and expenses. At the bottom of the page is a chart which itemizes the 10-year results of a $10,000 investment in the fund, after allowing for the applicable selling charges. A transparent plastic overlay is provided which permits the user of the chart to compare the fund's performance with the results of a similar investment in the Dow-Jones Industrials.

Charts of investment company performance, together with overlays which permit comparisons not only with the broad stock price averages but also with individual well-known stock issues, are contained in *Johnson's Investment Company Charts*, a service available on a subscription basis. Monthly and quarterly reports on changes in the investment portfolios of most large funds are offered by Vicker's Associates (see Figure 17–6), Capital Gains Research Bureau, and the brokerage firm of E. F. Hutton, among others. One of the most convenient sources of performance data is *Forbes* magazine. *Forbes*, usually in its mid-August issue each year, measures individual fund performance between peaks and troughs of bull market and bear market cycles (rather than calendar years) and assigns relative performance rankings to each fund. Also shown are data on asset amounts, sales loads, expense ratios, dividend yields, and cumulative performance data. The 1966 edition of *Forbes*' mutual fund report is reprinted as Appendix B of this chapter.

In appraising investment company performance, it is advisable to keep several thoughts in mind:

1. Consistency of performance year-in and year-out is as significant as, if not more significant than, overall performance for a large number of years. Moreover, in examining annual performance data the potential investor should try to determine whether management's results—good or poor—can be traced to consistently good or poor selection of individual

[31] At the rear of the manual, the individual stockholdings of the fund at the latest year-end are reported.

## FIGURE 17–3

## Management Results: Mutual Funds

Approximate Per Cent Change in Net Assets per Share

RECORDS FOR INDIVIDUAL YEARS

| FUNDS | 1965 | 1964 | 1963 | 1962 | 1961 | 1960 | 1959 | 1958 | 1957 | 1956 |
|---|---|---|---|---|---|---|---|---|---|---|
| | ANNUAL RESULTS | | | | | | | | | |
| **I: GENERAL PURPOSE DIVERSIFIED COMMON STOCK FUNDS** | | | | | | | | | | |
| **A. Objective: Growth (Volatility: Moderately Above Average)** | | | | | | | | | | |
| Aberdeen Fund | +20.2 | +11.0 | +20.5 | −15.4 | +20.3 | −2.0 | +19.4 | +39.0 | −8.4 | +15.1 |
| American Growth Fund | +17.4 | +13.7 | +27.0 | −13.9 | +37.7 | +4.3 | +12.4 | | | |
| Chemical Fund | +27.4 | +14.2 | +29.4 | −15.4 | +19.4 | −0.2 | +22.8 | +38.9 | −0.2 | +7.1 |
| Colonial Growth & Energy Shares | +23.7 | +13.9 | +11.2 | −14.3 | +18.9 | +5.8 | −3.8 | +40.8 | −20.7 | +19.1 |
| Delaware Fund | +35.2 | +15.6 | +19.1 | −15.1 | +27.7 | −2.0 | +11.9 | +47.4 | −13.2 | +9.2 |
| de Vegh Mutual Fund | +27.5 | +11.7 | +15.6 | −12.5 | +18.9 | −4.5 | +12.0 | +44.3 | −6.9 | +19.1 |
| Dreyfus Fund | +29.6 | +16.7 | +24.8 | −13.7 | +26.1 | +6.5 | +25.3 | +53.1 | −4.4 | +16.3 |
| Energy Fund | +28.7 | +9.1 | +21.4 | −17.9 | +20.2 | +6.0 | +23.7 | +47.6 | −15.1 | +21.3 |
| Florida Growth Fund | +15.9 | +13.1 | +18.2 | −13.0 | +20.5 | +7.8 | +10.0 | +41.8 | | |
| Franklin Custodian—Common Stock | +19.7 | +10.3 | +20.2 | −15.1 | +24.6 | +7.9 | +16.2 | +47.3 | −9.4 | +9.6 |
| Growth Industry Shares | +18.6 | +11.9 | +17.9 | −21.5 | +23.1 | +5.4 | +20.6 | +48.2 | −11.8 | +13.7 |
| Imperial Capital Fund | +18.8 | +17.4 | +18.0 | −19.3 | +23.7 | +10.7 | +18.5 | +46.3 | −18.6 | −1.8 |
| Investors Variable Payment Fund | +18.7 | +14.6 | +18.5 | −17.1 | +24.8 | +1.1 | +9.6 | +48.8 | | |
| Keystone (K-2) Growth Fund | +30.1 | +12.2 | +13.8 | −19.0 | +25.0 | +7.1 | +16.3 | +51.6 | −19.8 | +18.3 |
| Keystone (S-3) Growth Common | +36.6 | +17.1 | +22.7 | −14.7 | +26.7 | −5.9 | +12.8 | +45.9 | −23.3 | +19.6 |
| Lazard Fund | +9.5 | +10.8 | +24.4 | −10.6 | +22.1 | −1.8 | +11.3 | | | |
| Loomis-Sayles Capital Development | +26.5 | +12.2 | +18.4 | −17.0 | | | | | | |
| Mass. Investors Growth Stock Fund | +24.9 | +10.0 | +18.6 | −17.3 | +25.4 | +8.5 | +15.5 | +48.9 | −12.1 | +18.7 |
| MidAmerica Mutual Fund | +19.9 | +14.3 | +12.9 | −27.1 | +20.3 | | | | | |
| Mutual Inv. Foundation—MIF Growth | +18.9 | +16.4 | +19.4 | −17.8 | | | | | | |
| National Investors Corp. | +23.0 | +11.5 | +19.1 | −15.3 | +20.7 | +12.1 | +17.8 | +47.6 | −6.6 | +17.7 |
| National Securities—Growth Stocks Series | +24.3 | +11.2 | +17.1 | −19.3 | +16.2 | +2.0 | +26.7 | +44.5 | −13.1 | +14.5 |
| Philadelphia Fund | +19.6 | +13.4 | +20.7 | −11.3 | +21.0 | +5.9 | +10.6 | +46.4 | −14.7 | +8.0 |
| Price (T. Rowe) Growth Stock Fund | +25.6 | +11.9 | +18.5 | −12.7 | +24.7 | +8.0 | +18.9 | +39.9 | −3.0 | +11.2 |
| Putnam Growth Fund | +31.3 | +11.7 | +13.3 | −21.0 | +39.3 | +19.9 | +36.5 | +48.0 | | |
| Television-Electronics Fund | +30.2 | +13.0 | +16.0 | −16.7 | +21.5 | +1.5 | +22.9 | +52.8 | −9.9 | +11.4 |
| Texas Fund | +10.8 | +13.9 | +17.5 | −5.4 | +32.4 | +6.8 | +5.6 | +38.9 | −6.0 | +9.4 |
| United Science Fund | +36.5 | +9.1 | +19.1 | −18.1 | +18.9 | −2.2 | +24.2 | +44.6 | −12.4 | +12.4 |
| Windsor Fund | +29.0 | +13.9 | +12.7 | −25.1 | +29.6 | +11.0 | +16.3 | | | |
| AVERAGES | +24.1 | +13.0 | +18.8 | −16.3 | +24.1 | +4.6 | +16.7 | +45.8 | −11.5 | +13.5 |
| **B. Objective: Growth And Income (Volatility: Average)** | | | | | | | | | | |
| Blue Ridge Mutual Fund (a) | +14.8 | +16.8 | +15.0 | −9.1 | +24.9 | +0.8 | +7.7 | +40.5 | −10.7 | +7.7 |
| Bullock Fund | +14.6 | +15.9 | +20.9 | −9.4 | +25.4 | +0.8 | +7.0 | +36.5 | −10.7 | +14.8 |
| Channing Common Stock Fund(b) | +17.0 | +15.4 | +18.0 | −13.8 | +22.2 | −4.2 | +22.1 | +38.2 | −13.7 | +7.5 |
| Commonwealth Stock Fund | +22.1 | +12.8 | +15.1 | −16.9 | +20.4 | +2.6 | +9.5 | +37.0 | −11.4 | +11.6 |
| Corporate Leaders Trust—Series B | +10.6 | +16.9 | +17.3 | −5.7 | +24.3 | +0.9 | +15.5 | +38.0 | −3.1 | +0.6 |
| Crown Western—Diversified Fund | +13.6 | +9.4 | +12.2 | −17.4 | +28.3 | +1.8 | +14.8 | +41.3 | −12.5 | +5.5 |
| Eaton & Howard Stock Fund | +13.9 | +15.2 | +17.0 | −12.1 | +27.0 | +2.2 | +9.7 | +34.7 | −9.1 | +10.8 |
| Equity Fund | +13.9 | +17.5 | +18.0 | −11.6 | +32.7 | −0.4 | +13.3 | +37.8 | −8.8 | +6.4 |
| Fidelity Fund | +18.2 | +14.7 | +24.2 | −13.3 | +25.3 | +0.4 | +10.7 | +46.4 | −16.0 | +8.6 |
| Financial Industrial Fund | +21.1 | +18.0 | +16.3 | −17.2 | +25.2 | −2.6 | +16.3 | +41.3 | −17.5 | +7.9 |
| Founders Mutual Fund | +15.9 | +19.2 | +23.9 | −13.6 | +24.1 | −0.9 | +14.9 | +46.6 | −9.9 | +9.7 |
| Foursquare Fund | +33.0 | +5.9 | +17.1 | −2.0 | | | | | | |
| Fundamental Investors | +19.3 | +17.4 | +18.5 | −11.7 | +25.9 | −2.3 | +11.1 | +43.1 | −14.1 | +13.1 |
| Hamilton Funds—Series H-DA | +16.2 | +17.1 | +12.4 | −17.2 | +23.1 | +1.5 | +12.7 | +38.2 | −8.7 | +4.5 |
| Incorporated Investors (c) | +12.4 | +12.4 | +15.6 | −17.5 | +16.1 | −8.3 | +12.7 | +46.4 | −23.1 | +13.3 |
| Investment Company of America | +26.7 | +16.2 | +22.7 | −13.3 | +22.9 | +4.4 | +14.1 | +44.2 | −11.7 | +10.7 |
| Investment Trust of Boston | +12.6 | +17.5 | +19.5 | −13.3 | +23.0 | +0.9 | +9.7 | +40.9 | −14.1 | +8.7 |
| Investors Stock Fund | +9.8 | +14.3 | +16.5 | −13.4 | +25.0 | −0.5 | +10.4 | +47.6 | −12.4 | +10.2 |
| Johnston Mutual Fund (d) | +23.3 | +12.3 | +18.5 | −16.1 | +23.1 | +14.1 | +15.2 | +27.0 | −5.3 | +6.7 |
| Keystone (S-1) High-Grade Common | +11.2 | +14.6 | +16.5 | −12.1 | +26.7 | +5.4 | +11.1 | +39.4 | −6.3 | +5.1 |

## FIGURE 17–3 (Continued)

### With Capital Gains (Reinvested) Plus Income Dividends (Received in Cash)

FOR VARIOUS PERIODS (INCLUSIVE)

| FUNDS | 1964 to 1965 | 1963 to 1965 | 1962 to 1965 | 1961 to 1965 | 1960 to 1965 | 1959 to 1965 | 1958 to 1965 | 1957 to 1965 | 1956 to 1965 | 1956–1965 Breakdown (Italicized figures are for maximum period available, if less than 10 years): % Change in Net Asset Value* | Total Income† |
|---|---|---|---|---|---|---|---|---|---|---|---|
| **I. GENERAL PURPOSE DIVERSIFIED COMMON STOCK FUNDS** | | | | | | | | | | | |
| **A. Objective: Growth (Volatility: Moderately Above Average)** | | | | | | | | | | | |
| Aberdeen Fund | +33.1 | + 59.8 | + 34.2 | + 60.9 | + 56.5 | + 86.1 | +156.6 | +131.8 | +164.1 | +138.2 | +25.9 |
| American Growth Fund | +33.2 | + 68.6 | + 43.9 | + 97.1 | +102.8 | +125.0 | | | | *+105.7* | *+19.3* |
| Chemical Fund | +45.0 | + 86.7 | + 56.6 | + 86.1 | + 84.2 | +124.4 | +208.2 | +202.4 | +219.1 | +189.0 | +30.1 |
| Colonial Growth & Energy Shares | +40.5 | + 55.5 | + 32.6 | + 56.9 | + 64.5 | + 56.5 | +118.4 | + 70.2 | +100.8 | + 74.6 | +26.2 |
| Delaware Fund | +55.5 | + 83.7 | + 54.5 | + 95.8 | + 89.3 | +109.5 | +204.1 | +156.8 | +175.0 | +140.5 | +34.5 |
| de Vegh Mutual Fund | +41.9 | + 63.3 | + 42.0 | + 68.3 | + 59.6 | + 78.0 | +155.1 | +135.2 | +177.9 | +152.5 | +25.4 |
| Dreyfus Fund | +50.7 | + 86.9 | + 59.8 | +100.3 | +111.0 | +161.7 | +295.8 | +272.0 | +326.0 | +284.1 | +41.9 |
| Energy Fund | +39.9 | + 69.1 | + 38.3 | + 66.0 | + 75.3 | +116.1 | +216.8 | +166.3 | +220.5 | +199.1 | +21.4 |
| Florida Growth Fund | +30.7 | + 53.8 | + 32.9 | + 59.5 | + 70.2 | + 85.3 | +161.6 | | | *+135.2* | *+26.4* |
| Franklin Custodian—Common Stock | +31.7 | + 57.7 | + 33.0 | + 64.8 | + 75.9 | +101.8 | +192.7 | +155.0 | +174.4 | +135.5 | +38.9 |
| Growth Industry Shares | +32.3 | + 55.4 | + 21.2 | + 48.9 | + 56.0 | + 87.2 | +174.8 | +138.0 | +166.6 | +135.9 | +30.7 |
| Imperial Capital Fund | +39.0 | + 63.3 | + 31.0 | + 61.8 | + 77.9 | +109.4 | +203.6 | +144.7 | +136.4 | +111.1 | +25.3 |
| Investors Variable Payment Fund | +35.6 | + 60.1 | + 32.0 | + 64.2 | + 65.0 | + 80.1 | +167.2 | | | *+145.7* | *+21.5* |
| Keystone (K-2) Growth Fund | +45.6 | + 64.8 | + 32.8 | + 65.5 | + 76.4 | +104.4 | +207.2 | +141.2 | +181.4 | +157.4 | +24.0 |
| Keystone (S-3) Growth Common | +59.3 | + 94.2 | + 64.1 | +106.6 | + 92.3 | +115.3 | +210.6 | +133.3 | +175.0 | +147.1 | +27.9 |
| Lazard Fund | +21.1 | + 50.2 | + 33.4 | + 62.1 | + 57.8 | + 74.8 | | | | *+ 58.0* | *+16.8* |
| Loomis-Sayles Capital Development | +41.5 | + 66.7 | + 37.0 | | | | | | | *+ 29.8* | *+ 7.2* |
| Mass. Investors Growth Stock Fund | +37.1 | + 61.8 | + 32.9 | + 66.2 | + 79.1 | +105.6 | +203.8 | +162.8 | +208.4 | +179.8 | +28.6 |
| MidAmerica Mutual Fund | +36.8 | + 53.9 | + 11.8 | + 33.9 | | | | | | *+ 23.9* | *+10.0* |
| Mutual Inv. Foundation—MIF Growth | +38.1 | + 64.2 | + 33.9 | | | | | | | *+ 26.9* | *+ 7.0* |
| National Investors Corp. | +36.6 | + 61.9 | + 36.1 | + 63.7 | + 82.4 | +113.1 | +211.3 | +185.4 | +230.9 | +195.0 | +35.9 |
| National Securities—Growth Stocks Series | +38.0 | + 61.0 | + 29.2 | + 49.9 | + 52.1 | + 91.9 | +175.0 | +135.3 | +166.3 | +143.2 | +23.1 |
| Philadelphia Fund | +35.2 | + 62.3 | + 42.7 | + 71.7 | + 80.2 | + 97.7 | +186.3 | +139.7 | +155.4 | +123.7 | +31.7 |
| Price (T. Rowe) Growth Stock Fund | +40.1 | + 65.2 | + 43.2 | + 77.8 | + 90.6 | +124.8 | +211.5 | +197.0 | +225.7 | +193.8 | +31.9 |
| Putnam Growth Fund | +46.2 | + 65.1 | + 29.7 | + 80.5 | +115.7 | +193.0 | +330.8 | | | *+307.7* | *+23.1* |
| Television-Electronics Fund | +46.4 | + 68.9 | + 39.5 | + 68.8 | + 69.9 | +107.3 | +213.1 | +175.6 | +201.4 | +166.1 | +35.3 |
| Texas Fund | +26.0 | + 47.6 | + 38.9 | + 83.1 | + 93.8 | +102.9 | +178.9 | +157.6 | +177.8 | +147.2 | +30.6 |
| United Science Fund | +48.4 | + 76.0 | + 43.3 | + 69.8 | + 64.7 | +103.6 | +191.9 | +151.6 | +178.7 | +154.0 | +24.7 |
| Windsor Fund | +46.5 | + 64.5 | + 22.8 | + 58.9 | + 75.7 | +103.1 | | | | *+ 92.3* | *+10.8* |
| AVERAGES | +39.7 | + 65.2 | + 37.3 | + 70.0 | + 77.7 | +106.1 | +198.9 | +157.6 | +188.1 | | |
| **B. Objective: Growth And Income (Volatility: Average)** | | | | | | | | | | | |
| Blue Ridge Mutual Fund (a) | +33.8 | + 52.9 | + 37.7 | + 70.9 | + 70.1 | + 81.2 | +151.8 | +119.5 | +132.5 | + 95.7 | +36.8 |
| Bullock Fund | +32.4 | + 59.1 | + 42.5 | + 77.4 | + 76.6 | + 86.9 | +152.1 | +120.5 | +149.3 | +109.4 | +39.9 |
| Channing Common Stock Fund (b) | +34.6 | + 58.0 | + 34.8 | + 63.9 | + 55.6 | + 88.6 | +156.9 | +116.8 | +129.5 | + 95.3 | +34.2 |
| Commonwealth Stock Fund | +37.3 | + 57.2 | + 29.7 | + 55.6 | + 58.7 | + 72.7 | +134.8 | +105.3 | +126.8 | +100.1 | +26.7 |
| Corporate Leaders Trust—Series B | +29.0 | + 50.4 | + 40.5 | + 73.5 | + 73.0 | + 97.6 | +168.9 | +154.9 | +151.4 | +110.8 | +40.6 |
| Crown Western—Diversified Fund | +23.9 | + 38.3 | + 13.4 | + 45.1 | + 46.7 | + 67.1 | +133.4 | + 99.6 | +107.0 | + 70.4 | +36.6 |
| Eaton & Howard Stock Fund | +30.9 | + 52.4 | + 32.9 | + 67.9 | + 70.0 | + 84.8 | +146.3 | +120.0 | +140.6 | +107.6 | +33.0 |
| Equity Fund | +33.5 | + 56.8 | + 37.6 | + 82.0 | + 79.5 | +101.7 | +175.2 | +146.2 | +158.0 | +127.5 | +30.5 |
| Fidelity Fund | +35.0 | + 66.7 | + 42.9 | + 78.0 | + 76.4 | + 93.1 | +178.8 | +128.1 | +142.9 | +105.3 | +37.6 |
| Financial Industrial Fund | +42.3 | + 64.5 | + 35.0 | + 68.2 | + 62.2 | + 86.9 | +161.0 | +109.6 | +122.4 | + 90.1 | +32.3 |
| Founders Mutual Fund | +37.7 | + 69.5 | + 44.9 | + 78.8 | + 75.5 | + 99.9 | +189.6 | +156.3 | +176.8 | +139.1 | +37.7 |
| Foursquare Fund | +40.2 | + 63.1 | + 59.3 | | | | | | | *+ 50.2* | *+ 9.1* |
| Fundamental Investors | +39.7 | + 64.4 | + 43.7 | + 79.7 | + 73.7 | + 91.2 | +170.3 | +126.8 | +152.4 | +116.8 | +35.6 |
| Hamilton Funds—Series H-DA | +35.6 | + 51.3 | + 24.1 | + 52.1 | + 53.1 | + 71.2 | +134.1 | +109.5 | +116.5 | + 82.2 | +34.3 |
| Incorporated Investors (c) | +26.0 | + 45.1 | + 18.9 | + 37.6 | + 25.4 | + 40.8 | +105.1 | + 55.0 | + 74.0 | + 47.8 | +26.2 |
| Investment Company of America | +46.5 | + 78.5 | + 53.1 | + 86.8 | + 92.8 | +117.7 | +209.9 | +167.8 | +191.7 | +155.3 | +36.4 |
| Investment Trust of Boston | +31.9 | + 56.7 | + 34.5 | + 64.5 | + 64.3 | + 78.4 | +148.0 | +107.8 | +121.7 | + 84.9 | +36.8 |
| Investors Stock Fund | +25.2 | + 45.2 | + 25.0 | + 55.6 | + 53.6 | + 68.3 | +146.1 | +111.1 | +129.4 | + 94.7 | +34.7 |
| Johnston Mutual Fund (d) | +38.0 | + 62.6 | + 35.2 | + 65.7 | + 87.5 | +113.7 | +167.5 | +147.8 | +159.7 | +126.1 | +33.6 |
| Keystone (S-1) High-Grade Common | +27.2 | + 47.5 | + 28.8 | + 62.7 | + 70.1 | + 87.3 | +158.4 | +137.4 | +145.3 | +113.0 | +32.3 |

* Including value of shares accepted as capital gains distributions.

† As a percent of asset value at the beginning of the period.

(a) Investment counsel to this fund was changed in 1964.
(b) Investment counsel to this fund was changed in 1960.
(c) Name changed to Putnam Investors Fund effective April 5, 1966.
(d) Operated as a balanced fund prior to 1959.

Source: Arthur Wiesenberger & Co., *Investment Companies, 1966,* pp. 114–15.

## FIGURE 17–4

### Price Volatility of Mutual Fund Shares

| | PRICE VOLATILITY | | | | |
|---|---|---|---|---|---|
| | Rising Period 10/25/60 to 12/13/61 | Declining Period 12/13/61 to 6/26/62 | Rising Period 6/26/62 to 5/14/65 | Declining Period 5/14/65 to 6/28/65 | Rising Period 6/28/65 to 12/31/65 |
| Dow-Jones Industrial Average | 1.00 | 1.00 | 1.00 | 1.00 | 1.00 |
| **I. GENERAL PURPOSE DIVERSIFIED COMMON STOCK FUNDS** | | | | | |
| **A. Objective: Growth** | | | | | |
| Aberdeen Fund | 1.17 | 1.22 | 0.98 | 0.91 | 1.29 |
| American Growth Fund | 1.51 | 1.10 | 1.09 | 0.89 | 1.24 |
| Chemical Fund | 1.10 | 1.26 | 1.24 | 0.80 | 1.47 |
| Colonial Growth & Energy Shares | 1.13 | 1.22 | 0.92 | 1.07 | 1.63 |
| Delaware Fund | 1.33 | 1.22 | 1.14 | 1.46 | 2.46 |
| de Vegh Mutual Fund | 1.10 | 1.04 | 0.93 | 1.29 | 1.99 |
| Dreyfus Fund | 1.30 | 1.11 | 1.11 | 1.18 | 2.08 |
| Energy Fund | 1.47 | 1.30 | 0.85 | 0.99 | 2.30 |
| Florida Growth Fund | 0.93 | 0.75 | 0.65 | 0.44 | 0.85 |
| Franklin Custodian–Common Stock | 1.60 | 1.22 | 0.87 | 1.12 | 1.51 |
| Growth Industry Shares | 1.43 | 1.37 | 0.89 | 0.90 | 1.21 |
| Imperial Capital Fund | 1.23 | 1.11 | 0.89 | 0.87 | 1.24 |
| Investors Variable Payment Fund | 1.39 | 1.27 | 0.96 | 0.95 | 1.27 |
| Keystone (K-2) Growth Fund | 1.47 | 1.30 | 0.94 | 1.42 | 2.22 |
| Keystone (S-3) Growth Common | 1.47 | 1.19 | 1.17 | 1.30 | 2.61 |
| Lazard Fund | 1.17 | 1.00 | 0.86 | 0.97 | 0.86 |
| Loomis-Sayles Capital Development | — | 1.07 | 0.96 | 1.24 | 1.63 |
| Mass. Investors Growth Stock Fund | 1.47 | 1.30 | 0.95 | 0.87 | 1.47 |
| MidAmerica Mutual Fund | 0.45 | 1.39 | 0.85 | 0.99 | 1.37 |
| Mutual Investing Foundation–MIF Growth | — | 0.92 | 0.85 | 0.91 | 1.18 |
| National Investors Corp. | 1.33 | 1.30 | 1.03 | 1.06 | 1.48 |
| National Securities–Growth Stocks Series | 1.23 | 1.33 | 1.02 | 1.24 | 1.69 |
| Philadelphia Fund | 1.17 | 1.04 | 0.98 | 1.04 | 1.26 |
| **A. Objective: Growth (Continued)** | | | | | |
| Price (T. Rowe) Growth Stock Fund | 1.27 | 1.15 | 1.02 | 0.94 | 1.42 |
| Putnam Growth Fund | 1.97 | 1.26 | 0.85 | 1.17 | 2.10 |
| Television-Electronics Fund | 1.17 | 1.15 | 0.91 | 1.09 | 1.96 |
| Texas Fund | 1.60 | 1.00 | 0.95 | 0.93 | 0.95 |
| United Science Fund | 1.13 | 1.33 | 1.04 | 1.00 | 2.05 |
| Windsor Fund | 1.83 | 1.52 | 0.99 | 1.07 | 1.82 |
| **B. Objective: Growth and Income** | | | | | |
| Blue Ridge Mutual Fund | 1.20 | 0.96 | 0.86 | 1.04 | 1.20 |
| Bullock Fund | 1.20 | 0.96 | 0.90 | 0.91 | 1.08 |
| Channing Common Stock Fund | 1.23 | 1.07 | 0.89 | 1.01 | 1.18 |
| Commonwealth Stock Fund | 1.13 | 1.19 | 0.84 | 1.05 | 1.51 |
| Corporate Leaders Trust–Series B | 1.13 | 0.96 | 0.93 | 0.88 | 0.76 |
| Crown Western–Diversified Fund | 1.47 | 1.11 | 0.63 | 1.12 | 0.95 |
| Eaton & Howard Stock Fund | 1.37 | 1.07 | 0.90 | 1.03 | 1.07 |
| Equity Fund | 1.57 | 0.96 | 0.94 | 0.88 | 0.84 |
| Fidelity Fund | 1.30 | 1.07 | 0.92 | 1.10 | 1.42 |
| Financial Industrial Fund | 1.27 | 1.19 | 0.99 | 0.99 | 1.43 |
| Founders Mutual Fund | 1.17 | 1.07 | 1.07 | 1.05 | 1.20 |
| Foursquare Fund | — | 0.64 | 0.64 | 1.02 | 2.45 |
| Fundamental Investors | 1.30 | 1.07 | 0.97 | 1.03 | 1.47 |
| Hamilton Funds–Series H-DA | 1.33 | 1.11 | 0.81 | 1.00 | 1.12 |
| Incorporated Investors* | 0.93 | 1.22 | 0.79 | 0.97 | 0.97 |
| Investment Company of America | 1.17 | 1.07 | 1.09 | 1.16 | 1.63 |
| Investment Trust of Boston | 1.20 | 1.07 | 0.93 | 0.96 | 1.04 |

Source: Arthur Wiesenberger & Co., *Investment Companies, 1966*, p. 126.

## FIGURE 17–5

## Typical Page from Section which Reviews Investment Companies in Detail

### THE DREYFUS FUND INCORPORATED

*2 Broadway, New York, New York 10004*

Originally incorporated in 1947 as the Nesbitt Fund, Inc., this company adopted its present name in 1951 when The Dreyfus Corporation took over its management and sponsorship.

The primary investment objective of Dreyfus Fund is growth of capital. Current income, though not ignored, is considered of secondary importance. The management "leans towards full investment in common stocks"; however, it has operated under a flexible policy and at various times taken substantial defensive positions. As the fund has grown in size, there has been considerable broadening of the portfolio and a tendency toward narrower changes in percentage defensive holdings.

At the end of 1965, the fund's cash position amounted to 8% of assets, an increase of 5% over the prior year-end. In the common stock sector of the portfolio, airlines were the largest industry holding (10.5% of assets). Other sizable group investments were photographic equipment (8%), oils (7.5%), auto & truck manufacturers (7%) and tobaccos (6%). Polaroid, the largest individual holding—as it has been for most of the past ten years—accounted for 8% of assets. Four other major individual commitments—General Motors, Northwest Airlines, Anaconda and American Tobacco—represented about 3% of assets each. Unrealized appreciation was 27% of total net assets.

**Special Services:** The voluntary *accumulation plan* requires a minimum initial investment of $150; subsequent periodic payments must be at least $50. *Contractual plans* (10- or 15-year payment period) with optional completion insurance are also available. Shareholders may arrange for *automatic dividend reinvestment*; income dividends are invested at asset value. A monthly or quarterly *withdrawal plan* is available without charge to accounts worth at least $7,500 at the offering price; minimum payment is $20. A *Keogh Plan* custody agreement is available.

### *Statistical History*

| | AT YEAR-ENDS | | | | | | | | ANNUAL DATA | | | | |
|---|---|---|---|---|---|---|---|---|---|---|---|---|---|
| | | | % of Assets in | | | | | | | | | | |
| | Total Net Assets | Number of Share-holders* | Cash & Equiva-lent | Bonds & Pre-ferreds | Common Stocks | Net Asset Value Per Share | Offer-ing Price | Yield | Income Divi-dends | Capital Gains Distribu-tions† | Expense Ratio | Offering Price High | Offering Price Low |
| 1965 | $1,339,359,991 | 324,000 | 8% | 1%** | 91% | $26.00 | $28.38 | 1.4% | $0.41 | $0.78 | 0.60% | $28.91 | $21.52 |
| 1964 | 800,242,497 | 267,000 | 3 | 1** | 96 | 21.12 | 23.05 | 1.6 | 0.38 | 0.44 | 0.62 | 23.69 | 20.51 |
| 1963 | 530,664,337 | 217,000 | 4 | 1** | 95 | 18.84 | 20.56 | 1.8 | 0.365 | 0.035 | 0.64 | 20.67 | 16.73 |
| 1962 | 361,265,654 | 197,000 | 6 | ... | 94 | 15.42 | 16.83 | 1.9 | 0.32 | 0.29 | 0.67 | 20.18 | 14.02 |
| 1961 | 310,746,011 | 159,000 | 15 | ... | 85 | 18.54 | 20.23 | 1.6 | 0.33 | 0.15 | 0.66 | 20.65 | 16.29 |
| 1960 | 170,898,771 | 113,800 | 17 | ... | 83 | 15.10 | 16.48 | 2.1 | 0.34 | 0.57 | 0.74 | 16.80 | 14.40 |
| 1959 | 95,086,377 | 68,700 | 9 | ... | 91 | 15.10 | 16.48 | 1.8 | 0.30 | 0.30 | 0.75 | 16.62 | 13.35 |
| 1958 | 36,622,420 | 31,400 | 3 | ... | 97 | 12.57 | 13.72 | 1.8 | 0.25 | 0.15 | 0.88 | 13.76 | 9.18 |
| 1957 | 15,231,324 | 18,000 | 25 | ... | 75 | 8.49 | 9.27 | 2.1 | 0.198 | 0.332 | 0.89 | 10.91 | 8.64 |
| 1956 | 9,972,747 | 7,100 | 2 | ... | 98 | 9.43 | 10.29 | 2.0 | 0.21 | 0.69 | 0.89 | 10.29 | 8.49 |
| 1955 | 5,639,306 | 2,200 | 5 | 3** | 92 | 9.12 | 9.95 | 1.2 | 0.12 | 0.44 | 0.88 | 9.96 | 7.95 |

* Including contractual planholders starting in 1955.
** This percentage includes a substantial proportion in convertible issues.

† Realized security profits are paid in January of the following year. $0.695 from 1965 profits paid to shareholders of record January 14, 1966.

**Directors:** Jack J. Dreyfus, Jr., Chmn.; Howard Stein, Pres.; Lester R. Bachner; Dr. Herbert M. Diamond; William P. Rogers; Harold A. Weissman; Dr. Robert B. Woodward.

**Investment Adviser:** The Dreyfus Corporation (Howard Stein, Pres.; Lawrence M. Greene, Treas.; Jack J. Dreyfus, Jr., Consultant). Compensation to the Adviser is ⅛ of 1% quarterly of the average market value of net assets.

**Custodian and Transfer Agent:** The Bank of New York, New York, N. Y.

**Distributor:** The Dreyfus Corporation, 2 Broadway, New York, N. Y.

**Sales Charge:** Maximum is 8⅜% of offering price; minimum is 1% at $500,000. Reduced charges begin at $25,000. See page 134 for details. Reduced charges are applicable to subsequent purchases on a permanent basis. Minimum initial subscription is 10 shares.

**Dividends:** Income dividends are paid quarterly in the months of January, April, July and October. Capital gains, if any, are paid the last week in January.

**Shareholder Reports:** Issued quarterly. Fiscal year ends December 31. New prospectus usually effective in February.

**Qualified for Sale:** In all states and D.C., except Wisconsin.

An assumed investment of $10,000 in this fund, with capital gains accepted in shares, is illustrated below. The explanation on page 137 must be read in conjunction with this illustration.

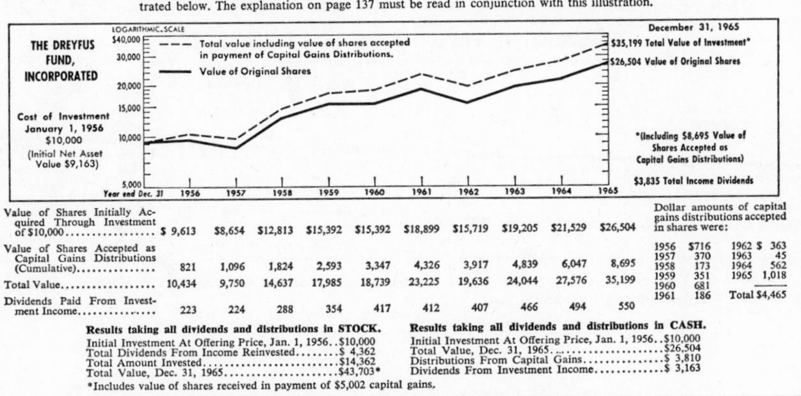


| | 1956 | 1957 | 1958 | 1959 | 1960 | 1961 | 1962 | 1963 | 1964 | 1965 |
|---|---|---|---|---|---|---|---|---|---|---|
| Value of Shares Initially Acquired Through Investment of $10,000 | $ 9,613 | $8,654 | $12,813 | $15,392 | $15,392 | $18,899 | $15,719 | $19,205 | $21,529 | $26,504 |
| Value of Shares Accepted as Capital Gains Distributions (Cumulative) | 821 | 1,096 | 1,824 | 2,593 | 3,347 | 4,326 | 3,917 | 4,839 | 6,047 | 8,695 |
| Total Value | 10,434 | 9,750 | 14,637 | 17,985 | 18,739 | 23,225 | 19,636 | 24,044 | 27,576 | 35,199 |
| Dividends Paid From Investment Income | 223 | 224 | 288 | 354 | 417 | 412 | 407 | 466 | 494 | 550 |

Dollar amounts of capital gains distributions accepted in shares were:

| Year | Amount | Year | Amount |
|---|---|---|---|
| 1956 | $716 | 1962 | $ 363 |
| 1957 | 370 | 1963 | 45 |
| 1958 | 173 | 1964 | 562 |
| 1959 | 351 | 1965 | 1,018 |
| 1960 | 681 | | |
| 1961 | 186 | Total | $4,465 |

**Results taking all dividends and distributions in STOCK.**
Initial Investment At Offering Price, Jan. 1, 1956..$10,000
Total Dividends From Income Reinvested........$ 4,362
Total Amount Invested..........................$14,362
Total Value, Dec. 31, 1965.....................$43,703*
*Includes value of shares received in payment of $5,002 capital gains.

**Results taking all dividends and distributions in CASH.**
Initial Investment At Offering Price, Jan. 1, 1956..$10,000
Total Value, Dec. 31, 1965......................$26,504
Distributions From Capital Gains...............$ 3,810
Dividends From Investment Income.............$ 3,163

Source: Arthur Wiesenberger & Co., *Investment Companies, 1966,* p. 177.

## FIGURE 17–6

## Vickers Favorite Fifty

| RANK BY $ VALUE | | | | | STOCKS | $ Value (Millions) | § No. Fds. Holding | Number Shares Held | % Outst. Stk. Held by Fds. |
|---|---|---|---|---|---|---|---|---|---|
| Dec. 31 1963 | Dec. 31 1964 | Dec. 31 1965 | Mar. 31 1966 | June 30 1966 | | | | | |
| 1 | 1 | 1 | 1 | 1 | INTERNATIONAL BUSINESS MACHINES | 1256 | 219 | 3,582,800 | 6.6 |
| 9 | 12 | 5 | 3 | 2 | XEROX CORPORATION | 534 | 124 | 2,174,100 | 10.3 |
| - | 44 | 8 | 5 | 3 | POLAROID CORPORATION | 504 | 102 | 3,549,200 | 22.5 |
| 4 | 3 | 2 | 2 | 4 | GENERAL MOTORS CORPORATION | 497 | 182 | 6,177,000 | 2.2 |
| 14 | 13 | 7 | 7 | 5 | EASTMAN KODAK COMPANY | 450 | 115 | 3,499,700 | 4.3 |
| 3 | 4 | 3 | 4 | 6 | TEXACO INC. | 449 | 144 | 6,384,800 | 4.7 |
| - | 49 | 20 | 8 | 7 | NORTHWEST AIRLINES, INC. | 424 | 80 | 3,748,300 | 41.0 |
| 2 | 2 | 4 | 6 | 8 | STANDARD OIL COMPANY (NEW JERSEY) | 418 | 171 | 6,080,100 | 2.8 |
| 10 | 10 | 6 | 9 | 9 | GENERAL ELECTRIC COMPANY | 330 | 115 | 3,112,300 | 3.4 |
| - | 22 | 18 | 14 | 10 | AVON PRODUCTS, INC. | 257 | 56 | 3,104,900 | 10.8 |
| 8 | 7 | 10 | 12 | 11 | GULF OIL CORPORATION | 254 | 100 | 5,088,300 | 4.9 |
| 13 | 11 | 13 | 10 | 12 | INTERNATIONAL NICKEL OF CANADA | 254 | 123 | 2,890,500 | 9.8 |
| 11 | 8 | 9 | 11 | 13 | MOBIL OIL CORPORATION | 253 | 105 | 5,889,500 | 5.8 |
| 6 | 5 | 11 | 13 | 14 | ROYAL DUTCH PETROLEUM COMPANY | 250 | 100 | 6,430,100 | 6.6 |
| 18 | 14 | 17 | 19 | 15 | INTERNATIONAL TELEPHONE & TELEGRAPH | 245 | 80 | 3,306,800 | 16.2 |
| - | - | 22 | 18 | 16 | BOEING COMPANY | 225 | 87 | 3,130,000 | 16.1 |
| - | - | - | 26 | 17 | PAN AMERICAN WORLD AIRWAYS | 224 | 64 | 3,167,200 | 20.4 |
| 5 | 19 | 14 | 20 | 18 | AMERICAN TELEPHONE & TELEGRAPH | 217 | 123 | 3,952,600 | 0.8 |
| - | - | - | - | 19 | *TRANS WORLD AIRLINES | 216 | 61 | 2,404,800 | 27.0 |
| 37 | 24 | 19 | 24 | 20 | GENERAL TELEPHONE & ELECTRONICS | 214 | 94 | 5,094,300 | 5.6 |
| 28 | - | - | 41 | 21 | MINNESOTA MINING & MANUFACTURING | 211 | 70 | 2,861,200 | 5.4 |
| - | - | 16 | 17 | 22 | WESTINGHOUSE ELECTRIC CORPORATION | 200 | 86 | 3,817,000 | 10.2 |
| - | - | 33 | 22 | 23 | UNITED AIR LINES, INC. | 196 | 74 | 3,060,700 | 18.9 |
| - | - | 35 | 25 | 24 | ANACONDA COMPANY | 188 | 76 | 2,256,500 | 20.6 |
| - | - | - | 30 | 25 | TEXAS INSTRUMENTS, INC. | 185 | 52 | 1,614,800 | 16.0 |
| 20 | 21 | 47 | 39 | 26 | COLUMBIA BROADCASTING SYSTEM | 185 | 57 | 3,340,800 | 16.3 |
| - | - | 28 | 15 | 27 | MOTOROLA, INC. | 183 | 63 | 1,073,400 | 17.6 |
| 29 | 20 | 15 | 23 | 28 | UNION CARBIDE CORPORATION | 181 | 85 | 3,077,100 | 5.1 |
| - | - | 39 | 35 | 29 | UNITED AIRCRAFT CORPORATION | 176 | 83 | 2,042,500 | 17.8 |
| 7 | 6 | 12 | 16 | 30 | FORD MOTOR COMPANY | 176 | 77 | 3,872,200 | 3.5 |
| 38 | 38 | 34 | 33 | 31 | MERCK & COMPANY | 173 | 51 | 2,242,000 | 6.9 |
| 21 | 23 | 21 | 21 | 32 | STANDARD OIL COMPANY OF CALIFORNIA | 173 | 79 | 2,702,000 | 3.6 |
| - | - | - | 43 | 33 | DELTA AIR LINES, INC. | 167 | 55 | 1,518,000 | 23.8 |
| - | 46 | 36 | 31 | 34 | AMERICAN AIRLINES, INC. | 166 | 58 | 2,213,100 | 24.7 |
| - | - | - | 44 | 35 | REYNOLDS METALS COMPANY | 166 | 70 | 3,030,300 | 18.2 |
| - | - | - | - | 36 | *EASTERN AIR LINES | 165 | 53 | 1,585,700 | 35.9 |
| - | - | 31 | 34 | 37 | LITTON INDUSTRIES, INC. | 163 | 70 | 2,177,600 | 10.7 |
| 26 | 25 | 38 | 49 | 38 | GOODYEAR TIRE & RUBBER COMPANY | 160 | 56 | 3,166,200 | 8.9 |
| 23 | 9 | 23 | 27 | 39 | MONSANTO COMPANY | 157 | 81 | 2,378,700 | 7.5 |
| 15 | 17 | 42 | 46 | 40 | AMERADA PETROLEUM CORPORATION | 156 | 45 | 1,942,000 | 15.2 |
| 41 | 50 | 30 | 32 | 41 | LOCKHEED AIRCRAFT CORPORATION | 155 | 76 | 2,497,600 | 22.5 |
| 16 | 16 | 25 | 36 | 42 | SOUTHERN COMPANY | 153 | 58 | 4,975,300 | 10.5 |
| 19 | 15 | 24 | 42 | 43 | CONTINENTAL OIL COMPANY | 152 | 57 | 2,435,600 | 11.2 |
| 34 | - | 40 | 29 | 44 | RADIO CORPORATION OF AMERICA | 150 | 76 | 3,037,000 | 5.1 |
| 27 | 27 | 26 | 37 | 45 | SOUTHERN PACIFIC COMPANY | 140 | 60 | 4,059,200 | 15.0 |
| - | - | - | - | 46 | **ALCAN ALUMINIUM LTD. | 138 | 102 | 3,897,300 | 12.5 |
| - | - | 50 | 47 | 47 | KENNECOTT COPPER CORPORATION | 136 | 62 | 3,758,200 | 11.3 |
| - | - | - | 48 | 48 | ZENITH RADIO CORPORATION | 135 | 54 | 1,948,600 | 10.4 |
| 36 | 45 | - | - | 49 | **LOUISIANA LAND & EXPLORATION | 135 | 37 | 2,747,400 | 15.2 |
| - | - | - | - | 50 | **DEERE & COMPANY | 132 | 44 | 1,949,000 | 13.2 |

* NEWCOMER ** RETURNEE

DISPLACED: Armco Steel Corporation - Chrysler Corporation - Pennsylvania Railroad - Syntex Corporation - Union Oil Company of California

§ The figures in this column have been adjusted for late reporting funds and may not agree completely with RANK BY NUMBER OF INVESTMENT COMPANIES.

### SUMMARY OF FAVORITE FIFTY BY INDUSTRY

dollar value of stocks by industry to total dollar value of favorite fifty

| | 6/30/66 | 3/31/66 | 12/31/65 | 12/31/64 | 12/31/63 |
|---|---|---|---|---|---|
| OIL & NATURAL GAS | 18.0% | 19.1% | 22.6% | 31.0% | 30.1% |
| OFFICE EQUIPMENT | 14.4 | 13.4 | 12.7 | 10.1 | 11.7 |
| ELECTRIC & ELECTRONICS | 12.8 | 13.5 | 10.5 | 4.3 | 6.4 |
| AIRLINES | 12.5 | 8.5 | 4.3 | 2.0 | - |
| LEISURE | 9.2 | 8.3 | 6.9 | 4.6 | 3.6 |
| METALS & MINING | 7.1 | 6.1 | 4.6 | 2.4 | 2.1 |
| CHEMICALS & DRUGS | 6.2 | 7.7 | 7.7 | 11.5 | 9.3 |
| MOTORS | 5.4 | 8.4 | 9.8 | 11.0 | 8.4 |
| MISCELLANEOUS | 14.4 | 15.0 | 20.9 | 23.1 | 28.4 |
| | 100.0% | 100.0% | 100.0% | 100.0% | 100.0% |

Source: *Vickers Guide to Investment Company Portfolios.* Copyright © 1966, by Vickers Associates, Inc. Reproduced by permission.

## FIGURE 17–6 (Continued)

### CANDIDATES

| STOCKS | $ Value (Mil.) | No. Fds Holding | Number Shares Held |
|---|---|---|---|
| Union Oil Co. of California | 129.4 | 48 | 2,435,200 |
| Texas Utilities Co. | 129.1 | 63 | 2,341,100 |
| Shell Oil Co. | 129.0 | 31 | 2,159,800 |
| Honeywell, Inc. | 127.7 | 65 | 1,507,200 |
| Florida Power & Light | 126.3 | 50 | 1,732,500 |
| Chrysler Corp. | 125.8 | 92 | 3,224,600 |
| Atlantic Richfield Co. | 124.8 | 52 | 1,659,000 |
| Aluminum Co. of America | 123.5 | 62 | 1,494,600 |
| Armco Steel Corp. | 121.4 | 47 | 2,273,600 |
| Sears, Roebuck & Co. | 120.5 | 71 | 2,176,100 |
| Magnavox Co. | 119.9 | 44 | 2,404,100 |
| Central & South West Corp. | 119.4 | 52 | 2,713,400 |
| Pennsylvania Railroad Co. | 119.2 | 53 | 2,060,400 |
| Gillette Co. | 118.1 | 55 | 3,203,700 |
| Syntex Corp. | 113.6 | 55 | 1,224,300 |

| STOCKS | $ Value (Mil.) | No. Fds. Holding | Number Shares Held |
|---|---|---|---|
| National Airlines, Inc. | 110.0 | 49 | 1,302,000 |
| Burlington Industries | 108.4 | 48 | 2,753,100 |
| W. R. Grace & Co. | 108.2 | 50 | 2,326,000 |
| Standard Oil Co. (Indiana) | 107.5 | 56 | 2,349,500 |
| International Paper | 107.1 | 70 | 3,930,000 |
| American Electric Power | 105.5 | 52 | 2,730,700 |
| Sinclair Oil Corp. | 104.8 | 62 | 1,717,500 |
| Massey-Ferguson, Ltd. | 103.5 | 73 | 3,234,400 |
| E. I. duPont | 101.4 | 75 | 540,100 |
| Fairchild Camera & Instrument | 100.6 | 27 | 597,000 |
| Corning Glass Works | 100.6 | 47 | 350,400 |
| Burroughs Corp. | 99.7 | 38 | 1,416,600 |
| Arkansas Louisiana Gas | 98.9 | 37 | 2,254,300 |
| Federated Department Stores | 98.3 | 46 | 1,545,100 |
| Chas. Pfizer & Co., Inc. | 95.3 | 52 | 1,466,600 |

### SELECTED STOCKS GAINING FAVOR

| STOCKS | $ Value (Mil.) | No. Fds. Holding | Number Shares Held |
|---|---|---|---|
| Addressograph-Multigraph | 40.9 | 32 | 639,000 |
| Allegheny Ludlum Steel | 38.3 | 20 | 814,600 |
| Armour & Co. | 45.9 | 27 | 1,232,300 |
| Canteen Corp. | 22.2 | 12 | 836,600 |
| Continental Air Lines | 24.2 | 19 | 341,500 |
| General Aniline & Film | 3.2 | 8 | 135,300 |
| General Precision Equipment | 15.0 | 13 | 293,400 |
| Gulf & Western Industries | 47.0 | 24 | 1,503,600 |
| International Harvester | 65.0 | 36 | 1,436,200 |
| Johnson & Johnson | 42.2 | 14 | 225,200 |

| STOCKS | $ Value (Mil.) | No. Fds. Holding | Number Shares Held |
|---|---|---|---|
| Kaiser Aluminum & Chemical | 66.7 | 36 | 1,502,000 |
| KLM Royal Dutch Airlines | 28.5 | 16 | 233,500 |
| Martin-Marietta Corp. | 47.2 | 26 | 1,988,700 |
| Otis Elevator | 28.5 | 17 | 615,900 |
| Parke, Davis & Co. | 41.6 | 29 | 1,335,000 |
| Pitney-Bowes, Inc. | 17.8 | 17 | 326,300 |
| Revlon, Inc. | 41.5 | 43 | 882,700 |
| SCM Corp. | 35.6 | 17 | 459,100 |
| Swift & Co. | 47.2 | 29 | 910,000 |
| Swingline, Inc. | 23.2 | 20 | 533,900 |

### COMMENTS

The 48th issue of Vickers Favorite 50 covers the common stock holdings of about 485 investment companies with combined assets of approximately $48 billion. The market value on June 30, 1966 of the 50 stocks was $12.4 billion, approximately 25% of total fund assets, against $12.6 billion as of March 31, 1966. The number of shares totalled 164 million and the average market price per share was $75¾ compared with approximately $82⅝ on March 31st and $78⅞ on December 31, 1965.

Vickers Favorite 50 Index stood at 781.23 as of June 30, 1966 against 793.29 at the end of March, a drop of 1.5%. This compares with a drop of 5.9% in the Dow-Jones Industrials from 924.77 to 870.10. Going a step further, at December '65 our Index was 728.74 and on June 30, 1965 was 600.81, representing increases to June '66 of 7.2% and 30.0%. The DJI was 969.26 at '65 year-end and 868.03 on June 30, 1965, representing a decrease of 10.2% from December to June '66 and an increase of 0.2% for the year.

TRANS WORLD AIRLINES, INC. - More investment companies bought more shares....1,559,300....of TWA in the June quarter than they have ever bought of any stock in a three-month period. At the end of the March 1966 quarter, 33 investment companies owned 845,500 shares of TWA worth $59 million, representing 9.7% of the outstanding common. As of June 30, 1966, they owned 2,404,800 shares worth $216 million, representing 27%....up 17.3%. As a result of this buying, TWA by-passed the Candidates and moved into 19th spot.

Why such interest? We contacted some of the major buyers for the answer. They were unanimous in stating that not only did they like TWA stock, but because of the size of the secondary offering they were able to buy a very substantial block at one fell swoop. These fund executives put it this way ....the market is thin on the offering side as well as on the bid side, and it is extremely difficult for a large block buyer to pick up a worthwhile quantity of a stock in which he has a real interest.

SUMMARY BY INDUSTRY - Our Summary by Industry Group shows a further decline in Oil & Natural Gas to 18%. Two leading oil stocks, TEXACO and STD. OIL (N.J.), both down approximately 300,000 shares, along with displaced UNION OIL were responsible. Airlines showed the sharpest gain from 8.5% to 12.5%, the result of two Newcomers, TWA and EASTERN AIR LINES. The total market value of the seven airline stocks now in the Favorite 50 is $1.6 billion, a dollar increase since March of $493 million or 46%. On the other hand, Motors had the sharpest drop from 8.4% to 5.4%, caused by sizable selling in G.M. (-717,300 shares), FORD (-859,000 shares) the most heavily sold stock, and Displaced CHRYSLER (-360,100 shares). This resulted in a dollar decrease since March of $390 million or 37%.

LEADERS - I.B.M.'s hold on first place is stronger than ever, with a dollar value of $1.3 billion, more than double the $534 million invested in 2nd-place XEROX. POLAROID moved into 3rd place on an increase in holdings of 239,000 shares.

LARGEST GAINERS IN RANK - M.M.M. showed the biggest gain, moving up 20 places from 41st to 21st spot, largely because of an increase in fund holdings of 568,300 shares. C.B.S. (+264,500 shares) was up 13 positions, from 39th to 26th. Next in line were GOODYEAR and DELTA with gains of 11 and 10 places respectively, both bucking the downward market trend.

LARGEST LOSERS IN RANK - R.C.A. (-262,600 shares) showed the biggest drop in rank, falling 15 places from 29th to 44th, followed by FORD, down 14 spots. MOTOROLA and MONSANTO lost 12 places each, casualties of market action.

NEWCOMERS AND RETURNEES - Newcomer TWA has been discussed above. Increase in holdings of EASTERN AIR LINES (+493,700 shares) moved it into 36th position. Returnee ALCAN, in 46th place, was one of the more heavily bought issues (+531,000 shares). LA. LAND and DEERE moved into 49th and 50th positions respectively, the main boost from good market action.

DISPLACED - Displaced stocks other than CHRYSLER and UNION OIL, mentioned above, were PENNSYLVANIA RR. (-416,500 shares), SYNTEX (-278,200 shares) and ARMCO, the latter off 10 points in market.

securities or whether one or two major holdings are the key to the performance. Prospectuses compare average acquisition costs of each issue held with market prices, so a file of several years' prospectuses is an invaluable reference source.[32]

2. Past performance is a good guide in making selections, but it is only a guide. There is no necessary reason for past performance to be repeated in the future. Therefore, it may be advisable to purchase stocks in *a few* best performing companies which have objectives similar to those of the investor, rather than to commit all one's funds to a single company.

3. An investment company's objectives, as stated in its prospectus, may put too much emphasis on the growth versus current income aspects and not enough on the safety versus risk aspects. After all, a person desiring a steady flow of current income can buy a growth fund rather than an income fund and supplement the lower dividend yield by gradually liquidating a portion of the growing principal. Indeed, there may be considerable tax advantages in such a procedure. What is really significant is the *risk* attached to one procedure as compared with the other. For example, the person who depends on investment income for living expenses is frequently one who may have to liquidate a sizable portion of his assets in an emergency. Such an individual may not be able to take the risk of having to liquidate severely depressed growth fund shares in a bear market.

4. Closed-end company share prices frequently are at deep discounts from net asset value—often 25% or more (see Figure 17–7). Purchase at deep discount can produce higher dividend yields than are available on open-end shares, and offer the prospect of greater capital gain through a subsequent narrowing of the discount to, say, 10%–15%. On the other hand, there is always the risk that discounts may widen instead of narrow. There has been some tendency for discounts to widen in bull markets and narrow in bear markets. This can cause profits to be lower from closed-end than from open-end shares.

*Causes of Good and Poor Performance.* *Why* do some investment companies have a superior performance while many more, with similar objectives and presumably expert professional investment managers, have an inferior performance? Before attempting an answer to this question, it is worthwhile to list several factors which research has indicated do *not* explain differences in performance among investment companies.

1. Performance has not been a function of selling charges. For example, "no-load" mutual funds have a record quite similar to companies charging sales loads. Some have done better than other funds with similar objectives; some have done worse; and in total they have done about as well as hypothetical unmanaged funds.

---

[32] Annual and quarterly reports always show market values on individual security holdings, and sometimes show cost data as well.

## FIGURE 17–7

### Discounts on Closed-End Investment Companies

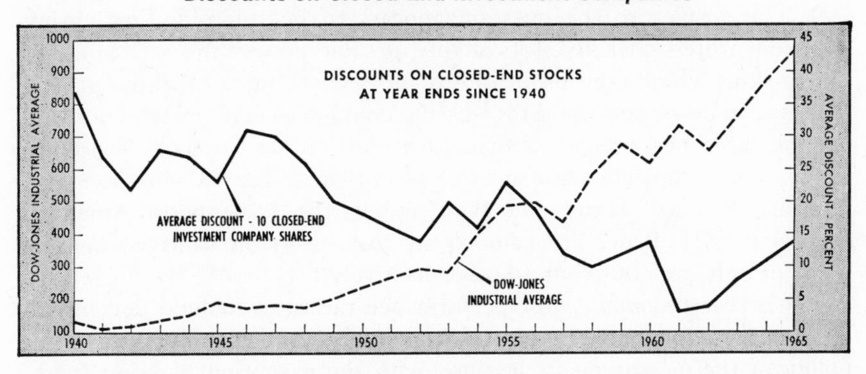


**Year-End Discounts**

| | 1965 | 1964 | 1963 | 1962 | 1961 | 1960 | 1959 | 1958 | 1957 | 1956 | 1955 |
|---|---|---|---|---|---|---|---|---|---|---|---|
| **Diversified Companies** | | | | | | | | | | | |
| *U. S. & Foreign Securities† | 33% | 26% | 24% | 19% | 16% | 22% | 18% | 13% | 18% | 9% | 26% |
| *Tri-Continental Corporation | 23 | 24 | 21 | 15 | 13 | 23 | 21 | 17 | 24 | 40 | 48 |
| Boston Personal Prop. Trust | 23 | 19 | 17 | 21 | 9 | 28 | 22 | 20 | 24 | 27 | 25 |
| International Holdings | 21 | 15 | 19 | 14 | 12 | 28 | 29 | 22 | 26 | 24 | 30 |
| *Consolidated Inv. Trust | 21 | 14 | 19 | 18 | 12 | 21 | 18 | 20 | 5 | 13 | 14 |
| Abacus Fund | 20 | 16 | 11 | 4 | P 2 | 2 | 5 | P 2 | P 4 | —Not Meaningful— | |
| *Dominick Fund | 19 | 12 | 9 | 5 | 4 | 17 | 17 | 20 | 22 | 25 | 18 |
| General Public Service | 14 | 16 | 15 | 8 | P12 | 13 | 17 | 11 | 16 | 11 | 8 |
| American International | 13 | 12 | 6 | 4 | 1 | 14 | 7 | 6 | 5 | 23 | 24 |
| *Adams Express | 12 | 10 | 9 | 4 | 3 | 14 | 8 | 4 | 11 | 20 | 17 |
| *Carriers & General | 11 | 6 | 8 | 7 | 2 | 12 | 13 | 3 | 11 | 18 | 23 |
| *Lehman Corp. | 11 | 6 | P 1 | P 4 | P 5 | P 1 | 1 | P11 | P14 | P14 | 12 |
| *Niagara Share | 8 | 0 | 6 | 3 | P 6 | 12 | 8 | 16 | 20 | 29 | 29 |
| *General American Investors | 7 | 6 | 3 | P 1 | 10 | 19 | 3 | 4 | 4 | 20 | 16 |
| *Madison Fund | P 2 | P 3 | P13 | P26 | P23 | 2 | 14 | 14 | 23 | 32 | 24 |
| Diversified Investment Company Average | 14 | 10 | 8 | 4 | 3 | 14 | 12 | 10 | 12 | 19 | 23 |
| **Non-Diversified and Specialized Companies** | | | | | | | | | | | |
| Equity Corporation‡ | 48% | 60% | 51% | 56% | 52% | 51% | 50% | 48% | 63% | 42% | 32% |
| Alleghany Corporation‡ | 38 | 46 | 36 | 10 | 31 | 36 | 46 | 52 | 54 | 48 | 37 |
| American Research & Devel. | 36 | 15 | P 6 | 21 | P 7 | 12 | 34 | 27 | 40 | 31 | 34 |
| Japan Fund | 27 | 32 | 15 | 34 | —Company commenced business in 1962— | | | | | | |
| United Corporation | 24 | 19 | 12 | 3 | 5 | 4 | 2 | P 5 | P16 | 1 | P10 |
| Eurofund | 23 | 19 | 24 | 23 | 7 | 20 | 16 | —Commenced business in 1959— | | | |
| Standard Shares | 16 | 10 | 8 | 3 | P 1 | 3 | 5 | P 1 | 5 | 6 | 0 |
| Central Securities | 11 | P 5 | P 5 | P 3 | P 5 | 12 | 19 | 27 | 30 | 19 | 26 |
| National Aviation | 2 | 10 | 2 | P 2 | 3 | P 2 | 10 | 11 | P 8 | P 8 | P 6 |
| American-South African | P 5 | 10 | 34 | 35 | 39 | 30 | 11 | 6 | –Commenced business in 1958– | | |
| Petroleum Corporation | P 6 | 3 | 6 | 5 | 0 | 0 | 6 | 6 | 10 | 10 | 17 |

* Included in Diversified Investment Company Average.
† Discounts from net asset values before deducting possible liability for federal taxes in contention.
‡ Discounts from net asset values before deducting potential liability for federal taxes on unrealized appreciation.
P—Premium.
Source: Arthur Wiesenberger & Co., *Investment Companies*, 1966.

2. Large outlays for professional management staffs produce no better investment performance than smaller outlays. Indeed, there is some evidence of a negative relationship between performance and the magnitude of management fees relative to the size and investment income of the fund.

3. Companies affiliated with brokerage houses have done no better or worse on average than companies not so affiliated.

4. There is no correlation between performance success and portfo-

lio turnover. Some successful funds are active traders and some are not; likewise with the less successful funds.

The answer to the question appears to be twofold. First, many so-called professional investors simply do not possess the selection and timing skills which they claim to possess. Second, many of those professionals who do possess the skills lack the courage to take quick action and commit large percentages of their portfolios on the basis of their judgments. The companies with superior performance records—for example, Dreyfus, Fidelity Trend and Ivest among the load funds, American Investors and T. Rowe Price among the no-loads—seem to have managers who not only are astute but who act decisively.

*Current Income.* Most performance measures include current income but are dominated by capital gains and losses. Generally, this is not a failing of the measurements because, with the exception of bond funds, most investment company buyers (and managers) seem to have long-term appreciation as their primary objective. The difference between one buyer and the next is mostly in the degree of risk he is willing to undertake in exchange for prospects of appreciation. Nevertheless, *some* investment company buyers do have current income as their primary objective, and these investors may wish to compare investment company income with income on "the averages."

If it is desired to compare dividend yields on investment company shares with average yields on bonds, stocks, or a bond-stock combination, the investor should be particularly aware of the need to adjust average yields for operating expenses. The usual investment company accounting procedure is to deduct brokerage charges from principal, and operating expenses (including management fees) from dividend and interest income. Thus, if a balanced fund's *gross* current income yield is 4% of net asset value, an operating expense ratio of three fourths of 1% of net asset value is equivalent to almost 20% of gross income. Unless some expense deduction is made from yields on "the averages," investment company income almost always will appear deficient by comparison. With an adjustment, however, investment company income yields have, on the whole, been about equal to yields on the pertinent averages. The question remains, however, whether this performance justifies the sales loads and management fees which the investor must pay. We turn to this question next.

### Concluding Observations

The groundwork having been laid, the advantages and disadvantages of investment company shares now can be evaluated from the stockholder's point of view.

*Acquisition Costs.* It is possible for the small investor in common stocks who seeks safety through diversification to obtain such diversification at a reasonable acquisition cost through the investment company medium. However, not all investment companies offer acquisition cost advantages. For example, to buy and sell *directly* 5 shares each of 10 different $50 stocks—a $2,500 investment—would cost $145 in commissions and odd-lot fees, or about 6% of the investment. Actually, the percentage might be somewhat higher since, if the stocks appreciate in price between the purchase and sale date, the selling commissions would be levied on the appreciated values, thus increasing the percentage commission on the original investment.[33]

The effective costs of acquiring stocks through the investment company medium would include, first, the commissions which the investment company itself incurs to invest the stockholder's funds. These would be relatively low—say 1% of the invested amount—because the investment company pools all funds and usually trades in 100-share units. Additional acquisition costs would depend upon the type of investment company involved.

A closed-end company's shares can be purchased and sold under standard commission schedules, and total costs on a $2,500 amount probably would be considerably less than 6%. An open-end no-load fund would involve no selling charges, but usually would involve a redemption fee of 1% or 2% of the value of the shares at the time of liquidation. Again, total costs on a $2,500 investment probably would be considerably less than 6%. Open-end load funds, however, generally would cost more than 6% to acquire. The typical load on a $2,500 investment is 8%–9%. (There usually is no redemption fee when a sales load of this magnitude is levied.)

The case is even clearer if a load fund has a high proportion of its portfolio in bonds. Since commissions on direct investments in such securities are quite low, and since diversification needs are slight if the bonds are of high quality, heavy sales loads would be quite difficult to justify objectively.

Finally, mention should be made of some of the rather odious selling techniques employed in the distribution of mutual funds on a contractual accumulation plan basis. There is plentiful evidence that salesmen fail to inform their clients of the availability of *regular accumulation plans*, on which the sales load is charged only as payments are made instead of in advance. Even if the salesman sincerely believes that a contractual plan is the best arrangement for his client (for example, because it "forces" the client to save), he should at least inform the client of the alternative.

[33] Smaller investments would involve much larger transaction costs. For example, a $1,000 investment in 2 shares each of 10 different $50 stocks would cost $130, or 13% of the investment, to buy and sell. However, although examples of this type frequently are cited by salesmen for open-end load funds, it is doubtful that a sensible investor would, in fact, seek diversification by purchasing two shares each of many different companies. He probably would be far better off, for example, if he bought a larger number of closed-end company shares.

*Convenience.* It is convenient to invest through the investment company medium. There is no need to keep detailed transaction records for tax purposes, no need to handle a large number of dividend checks of small amounts, no need to worry about safekeeping. Reinvestment of small dividend amounts is simplified (and often available without sales load[34]); stock splits and rights present no problems. Regular withdrawal plans frequently are available at death or retirement, and group life insurance is available under accumulation plans.

These surely are conveniences. But it must be recognized that the investment company hires clerks and executives to provide such conveniences, and the investor, therefore, pays for them. Yet there is reason to doubt whether the investor is sufficiently aware that he is paying for them. For example, a recent survey revealed that 30% of mutual fund buyers were not aware that they were being charged a sales load; and of those who did know, 25% didn't realize it was as high as 8% or more. If so many investors are not aware of the selling charges they are paying, one wonders how aware they are of the year-in and year-out charges they are paying for conveniences.

*Performance.* In the final analysis, the costs of acquisition and the annual management fees which are borne by purchasers of investment company shares must be weighed against the investment performance of the companies. It has been suggested in this chapter that investment company claims about providing expert management are rather exaggerated in terms of their actual performance. If, on the whole, investment company managers do only as well as the averages, one can rightfully question the wisdom of paying substantial acquisition charges, *plus* management fees of one half of 1% of net asset value—about 15% of interest and dividend income—year-in and year-out, *plus* additional charges for conveniences.

Frequently, investment company personnel will argue that average performance is nothing to be sneezed at by most laymen. It probably is true that many individuals haven't the requisite time, inclination, or skill to invest directly in common stocks and would do worse than "the averages" if they did invest directly.[35] But the question remains, why pay managers and a staff of security analysts when the same results could be obtained by a bookkeeper whose function would be to invest all incoming money in proportion to the composition of some popular stock price average?

---

[34] The SEC has recommended that all sales loads on dividend reinvestments be abolished.

[35] An interesting elaboration of this point is contained in Leo Barnes, "What Difference Does Knowledge Make to Investors?" *Financial Analysts Journal,* September–October, 1965.

Moreover, while investment companies on the whole turn in average performance, a great many do quite poorly. The industry's overall performance is pulled up by the relatively few which are consistently outstanding performers. This fact requires the investor seeking above-average results to do almost as much investigating and analyzing of different investment companies as he would have to do of different operating corporations if he were investing directly. Short of this, his safest course of action probably would be to purchase a few shares of each of many different investment companies—diversifying within the investment company field. But then his investment results almost surely would be merely average, for which results he would have incurred substantial charges.

It cannot be denied that investment companies have performed a valuable social service in conveying to the community at large the advantages of "owning a share of American industry." Nor can it be denied that some investment companies have done a truly outstanding job of managing the funds entrusted to them. But, clearly, many investment companies have not performed satisfactorily, and no intelligent investor should consider his investment problems to be solved automatically when he turns the job over to others. If he wants to let others do the job, he should carefully appraise their qualifications for the task in terms of their demonstrated performance relative to their stated objectives and to his own objectives.

## RELATED TOPICS

### The Monthly Investment Plan of the New York Stock Exchange

The Monthly Investment Plan (MIP) is designed to accommodate individuals who wish to invest relatively small amounts ($40 to $1,000) on a regular basis (monthly or quarterly) in any stock listed on the New York Stock Exchange. If he desires to purchase more than one issue, the investor may set up several plans. Or he may achieve diversification by setting up a plan to acquire shares in one of the closed-end investment companies listed on the exchange.

The price at which the MIP investor acquires his shares at each time interval is the first odd-lot price after his payment is credited. Standard commission rates are charged, but there is a 6% maximum for amounts under $100. Purchased shares may be kept in the custody of the brokerage firm with which the plan is established (any member firm).

The big advantage of MIP over the usual type of transaction is that fractional shares, calculated to four decimal places, may be acquired at 6% commission, thus facilitating a dollar averaging program. Upon liquidation of the plan, again at standard commissions with a 6% maximum, the investor receives the equivalent number of full shares and the cash value of any remaining fractions. Dividends may be taken in cash or accumulated for reinvestment.

Once having signed up for a plan, the investor is expected to continue making regular payments. There is no penalty if he does not, but the broker can refuse to continue the plan if payments are missed repeatedly. The fifty most popular stocks of monthly investment plan participants are shown in Figure 17–8.

FIGURE 17–8

**Monthly Investment Plan—Fifty Most Popular Stocks as of September 30, 1966**
(Eliminates stocks whose popularity depends on company-sponsored employe payroll deduction plans.)

| Name of Stock | Number Of Plans | Name of Stock | Number Of Plans |
|---|---|---|---|
| American Tel. & Tel.*# (1) | 12,461 | Union Carbide# (27) | 1,126 |
| General Motors* # (2) | 10,306 | Corn Products (25) | 1,059 |
| Radio Corp.# (4) | 7,429 | Communications Satellite (30) | 902 |
| General Tel. & Elec. (3) | 7,035 | Lehman Corp.# (28) | 895 |
| Intl. Bus. Machines (6) | 5,264 | Int'l Tel. & Tel. (31) | 802 |
| Sears, Roebuck (5) | 4,704 | Monsanto (29) | 789 |
| General Electric (7) | 3,345 | Sperry Rand (32) | 775 |
| Tri-Continental Corp.* # (8) | 3,058 | American Cyanamid# (36) | 686 |
| Standard Oil* # (9) | 2,848 | Long Island Lighting (33) | 650 |
| Eastman Kodak# (11) | 2,736 | Caterpillar Tractor | 626 |
| Minnesota Mining (10) | 2,678 | Chrysler (43) | 624 |
| Pacific Gas & Elec.# (12) | 2,317 | Westinghouse Electric# (34) | 598 |
| Standard Oil Calif.# (13) | 2,281 | Consolidated Edison (40) | 591 |
| Xerox (16) | 2,174 | American Hosp. Supply | 567 |
| Dow Chemical# (14) | 1,630 | Lone Star Gas (35) | 544 |
| Safeway Stores (15) | 1,606 | Honeywell (45) | 538 |
| Scott Paper (17) | 1,550 | General Foods (37) | 517 |
| Merck (22) | 1,505 | Polaroid | 516 |
| Texaco (20) | 1,483 | FMC Corp. | 509 |
| Gulf Oil# (18) | 1,398 | U. S. Steel# (39) | 506 |
| Ford Motor (24) | 1,294 | Transmerica Corp. (42) | 488 |
| Du Pont# (21) | 1,244 | Pan American Airways | 487 |
| Pfizer (19) | 1,235 | Madison Fund (44) | 482 |
| Litton Industries (26) | 1,218 | Control Data (41) | 481 |
| Phillips Petroleum# (23) | 1,129 | Columbia Gas# (38) | 474 |

* Always in top ten MIP favorites.
# Always in top fifty MIP favorites.

Figures in parentheses indicate Nov. 1965 ranking if in top fifty.

Source: *The Exchange*, Vol. XXVIII, No. 1 (January, 1967).

## Small Business Investment Companies

It was noted in Chapter 6 that some investment advisors believe that the only sound way to participate in the pioneering stage of a growth industry is to purchase a "package" of stocks. They believe that the risks involved in buying a single pioneering company, in the hope that it will be one of the few survivors, is simply too great for most investors other than "insiders." The difficulty with the package approach, however, is that most individual investors cannot afford to buy a package.

One possible way out of the dilemma is to buy the shares of a Small Business Investment Company (SBIC). Established under special federal legislation, SBIC's are nondiversified closed-end investment companies specializing in the provision of long-term financing to relatively small enterprises.[36] To encourage this type of financing the government has created various incentives to organize SBIC's. The more important incentives are as follows.

1. An SBIC, although nondiversified, is taxed like a diversified investment company as long as it distributes 90% of current investment income to its stockholders. Moreover, it is allowed to charge its capital losses against ordinary income rather than against capital gains.

2. Investors in SBIC shares can charge in full against ordinary income any capital losses incurred upon the sale of the shares. This treatment is quite different from that on other investments, where capital losses must be charged first against gains and, if any net loss remains, $1,000 a year against ordinary income.

3. Federal funds are made available to individual SBIC's at modest interest rates in amounts up to several million dollars, depending on the magnitude of the company's capital and surplus. Further leverage is permitted to be obtained through private borrowing, much of it guaranteed against loss by the Small Business Administration.

More than 700 SBIC's have been licensed, but less than 100 are publicly owned and traded. They had about $700 million of assets at the end of 1965. These companies have widely varying policies. Some limit their investments to firms operating in the field of applied science while others are broadly diversified. Some finance only enterprises with established operating records while others finance brand new companies as well. Virtually all, however, emphasize long-term growth rather than current income. To this end they purchase mostly the common stock or convertible debentures of companies in which they have confidence. But current income is not ignored; the convertible debentures usually carry interest rates around 8%–9%.

The fond hope of investors in SBIC's is to see the financed small businesses grow large and sell stock publicly. This creates a market for the shares owned by the SBIC's (directly or via conversion), which then can be sold at handsome gains or can be "spun off" (distributed) to the SBIC stockholders. The collapse of the "new issue market" in 1962 thus dealt a severe blow to the prices of SBIC shares (see Figure 17–9), most of which are still selling at prices far below book value.

The risks of SBIC ownership are considerable, not the least of which is inadequacy of information on the nature and prospects of the individual investments in the portfolio. But the risks of undiversified direct investment in young, pioneering companies often are even greater. Anyone

[36] A "small business" is defined under the legislation as one with assets under $5 million, net worth under $2½ million, and average earnings under $¼ million during the two years prior to financing. These limitations may be waived in special cases. For example, auto and tire manufacturers recently were designated "small" if they produce less than 5% of industry shipments.

FIGURE 17–9

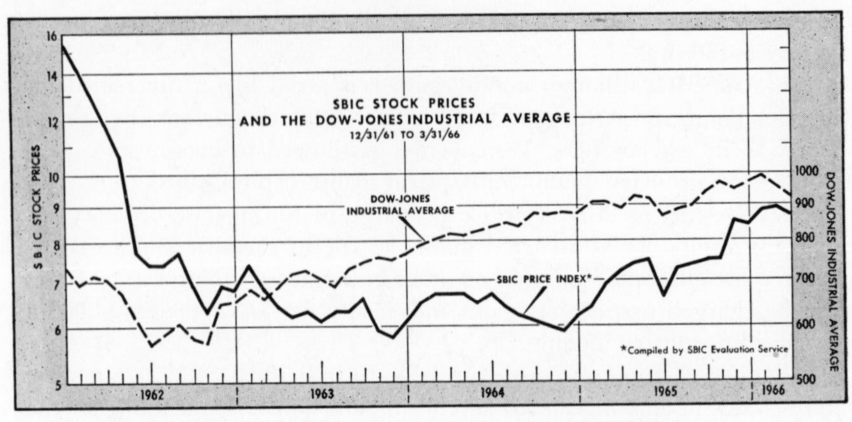


Source: Arthur Wiesenberger & Co., *Investment Companies, 1966,* p. 101.

attracted to the latter type of investment activity should give consideration to SBICs.

## Variable Annuities

The widespread sale to individuals of so-called "variable annuities" by life insurance companies is still on the horizon, pending the clarification of various legal and regulatory aspects of the subject. Nevertheless, it is worthwhile to indicate briefly the nature of variable annuities, since they already are competing for group pension fund dollars and will one day probably be in direct competition with mutual funds for individual investors' dollars.

Under a variable annuity program, contributions made to an insurance company during a person's working life are invested in a diversified portfolio of common stocks. The contributions are credited to the policyholder not in dollars but in *units,* the number of units depending primarily on the value of the stocks held at the time of each contribution. (The unit value includes automatically reinvested dividends.) This is essentially the same procedure as would be followed in a mutual fund accumulation plan.

At retirement, instead of guaranteeing a lifetime income of so many dollars per month, as in the case of a conventional annuity, the insurance company guarantees a fixed number of retirement *units* per month. The number of units to be paid is based primarily upon the total number accumulated to date and the annuitant's life expectancy. The dollar amount of the check actually mailed to the annuitant is equal to the number of annuity units multiplied by the then current value per unit. Since the unit value fluctuates with investment experience—dividend income and capital appreciation or depreciation—the benefit payments vary accordingly; hence the term "variable annuity."

It is important to bear in mind that even though the benefit payments vary in amount, the annuitant is guaranteed an income for life. He is protected against the risk of exhausting his capital. Only an insurance company is permitted to make such a guarantee.

## SUGGESTED READINGS

Hugh Bullock. *The Story of Investment Companies.* New York: Columbia University Press, 1959.

*Forbes* magazine, annual survey of mutual fund performance (usually appearing in mid-August issue).

Irwin Friend *et. al. A Study of Mutual Funds.* Prepared for the SEC by the Wharton School of Finance and Commerce and published August 28, 1962, by the U.S. Government Printing Office.

Hugh A. Johnson Investment Co. *Johnson's Investment Company Charts.* Buffalo, N.Y. (Annual.)

*Report of the SEC on the Public Policy Implications of Investment Company Growth.* Washington, D.C.: U.S. Government Printing Office, December, 1966.

William F. Sharpe. "Mutual Fund Performance," *Journal of Business: Security Prices: A Supplement*, January, 1966.

Vickers Associates, Inc. *Vickers Guide to Investment Company Portfolios.* Huntington, N.Y. (Annual.)

Rudolph L. Weissman. *Investment Made Easy.* New York: Harper & Bros., 1962.

"Why Closed-End Funds Have Come under Fire," *Business Week*, February 18, 1967.

Arthur Wiesenberger & Co. *Investment Companies.* New York, N.Y. (Annual.)

## APPENDIX TO CHAPTER 17

Since the subject of mutual fund investment performance is quite controversial, some discussion is warranted as to why we prefer to measure performance on a year-to-year basis rather than on a long-term *cumulative* basis. The reasons are as follows.

1. A single year's fabulous or abysmal results can have a disproportionate influence on cumulative results, and can create a mistaken impression of successful or unsuccessful performance.

2. It is desirable to see what happened in bull and bear markets taken separately.

3. When an investment company pays dividends from realized capital gains, its per-share net asset value is reduced below what it would be if capital gains were retained. Since a market average has no capital gains distributions, the investment company's capital gains distributions must be hypothetically reinvested if its performance is to be meaningfully compared with the averages. Otherwise there would be a statistical bias against the company. But hypothetical reinvestment of capital gains raises many problems:

*a*) The usual assumption is that capital gains distributions, if retained, would appreciate (or depreciate) by the same percentage as actual per-share net asset value. This assumes that management normally would invest the additional funds in precisely the same way as it invests the other funds. But such an assumption may not be valid.

*b*) There is a question as to *when* the reinvestment should be assumed to take place—time of distribution, year-end, or gradually during the course of the year.

*c*) There is also a question as to whether capital gains taxes should be deducted from the hypothetical reinvestment.

*d*) It might be argued that an even more meaningful measure would assume *income* reinvestment in addition to capital gains reinvestment.

4. Comparison of beginning and ending per-share values, whether assuming or not assuming dividend reinvestment, ignores the question of intraperiod cash flow arising from sales or redemptions of the investment company's own shares. In a year-to-year analysis, there is little reason to be concerned with cash flow. The results, during a single year, of investing new fund inflows, or liquidating to meet net redemptions, usually are swamped by the change in the value of the starting portfolio. But in a cumulative analysis, when cash flow is large relative to starting asset value, the situation is different. Consider the following hypothetical example, which is purposely exaggerated to bring out the point clearly.

A fund starts with $10 million and has $15 million net cash inflow during a long time period being examined. Its per-share value during the period averages $10, which also happens to be the value at both the beginning and end of the period. During the same span of time the S & P Industrial Stock Price Index starts at 50, rises sharply, and then falls back to 50, for an average value of 75.

If we compare the fund's performance with the S & P price index by the usual beginning versus ending per-share value technique, both show no change, and we conclude that the fund has done exactly as well as the index. But if cash flow is considered, the results are strikingly different.

The beginning value of $10 million is represented by 1 million fund shares at $10. Had it been invested in "the averages" it would have bought 200,000 index units at 50. The $15 million cash inflow is invested in the fund at an average price of $10, buying 1½ million shares. Had it been invested in the averages it would have bought 200,000 units at 75. The actual fund, therefore, ends the period with 2½ million shares at $10, or $25 million. The hypothetical fund, however, ends with 400,000 shares at 50, or $20 million (ignoring all expenses). Therefore, instead of concluding that the fund did exactly as well as the index, we conclude that it did $5 million *better*.

The creation of a performance measure which adequately takes cash flow into account involves all sorts of complex methodological problems, not the least of which is inadequate data on the cash flows of individual companies. The nature of these problems is too technical for this exposition. Suffice it to say that for our purposes it seems best to ignore these, and all the other problems described above, by making comparisons on a simple year-to-year basis rather than cumulatively.

## SECOND APPENDIX TO CHAPTER 17

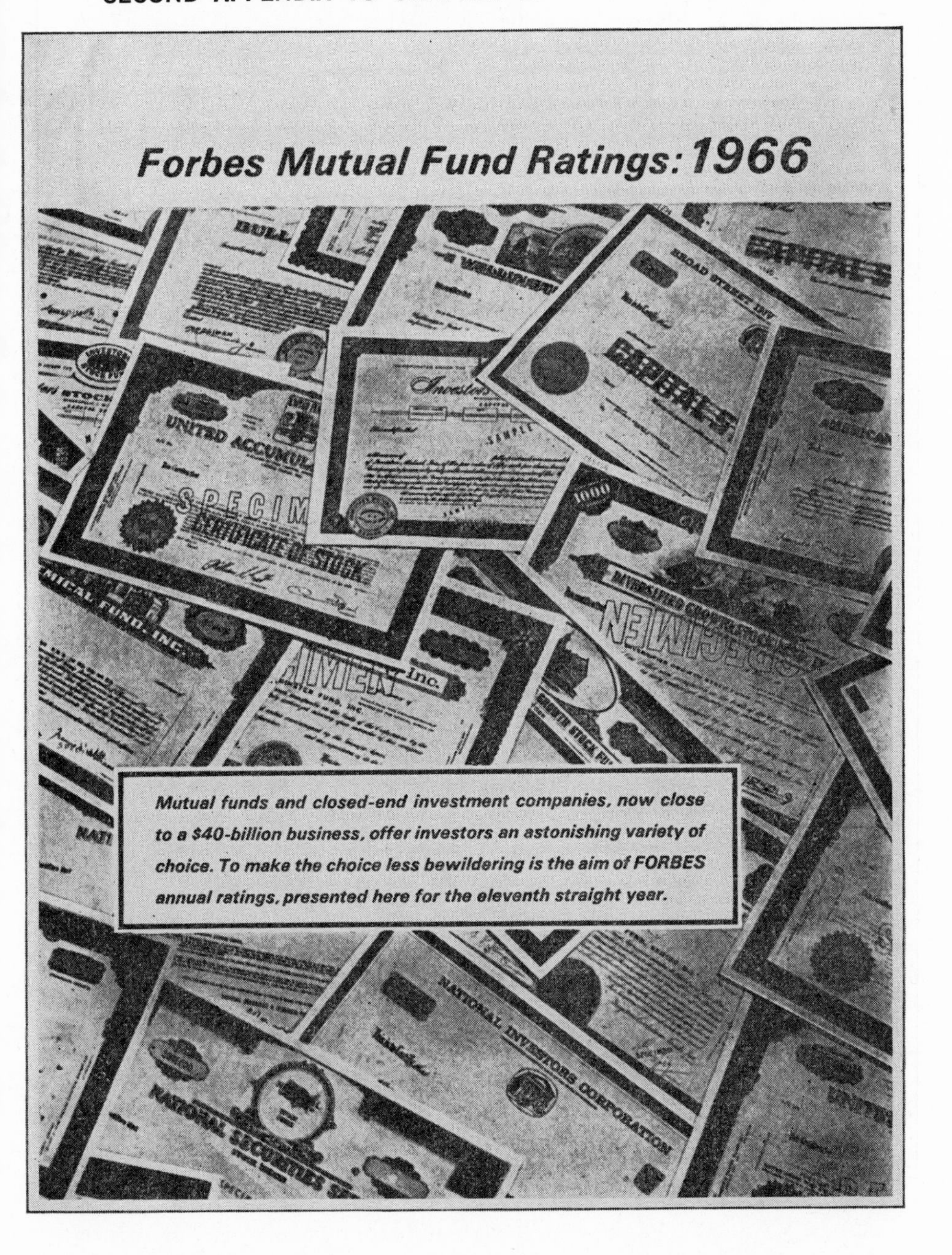

# *Forbes Mutual Fund Ratings: 1966*

*Mutual funds and closed-end investment companies, now close to a $40-billion business, offer investors an astonishing variety of choice. To make the choice less bewildering is the aim of FORBES annual ratings, presented here for the eleventh straight year.*

ALTHOUGH mutual fund sales have faltered this summer (they were down about 9% in June from the previous June), the mutual fund industry has enjoyed the best six-month sales in its history. In spite of a weak and queasy stock market during the period, the public bought $2.9 billion worth of mutual fund shares in the first six months, 37% more than in the same period of 1965. This lively sales pace put combined assets for U.S. mutual funds and closed-end investment companies at nearly $40 billion by mid-1966.

But it was, significantly enough, a very uneven kind of boom. The really big sales gains went to the so-called "performance" funds: Fidelity Trend gained 257% in sales, Channing Growth, 102%. Such big old-line funds as Wellington declined 11%, Massachusetts Investors Trust, 20%.

Isn't it only natural that funds which "perform" will sell better than funds which merely "keep up"? No it isn't. In the past, the best-selling funds have often been funds whose capital gains performances were average and no more. One reason was the sales pitch the business has generally relied upon. Most fund salesmen tended to sell not the fund or its performance, but an economic objective such as retirement, college education or a trip to Europe. What counted was professional management, diversification and "keeping ahead of inflation." Performance as such was frequently downplayed—at least by the more ethical salesmen. In addition, the funds usually hand out their brokerage business to those stockbrokers whose firms sell their fund shares. The bigger, established funds, with more brokerage business to hand out, tended to get bigger.

During the past year or so, this has changed. Perhaps the change is temporary. Perhaps not. A handful of young portfolio managers, running what have come to be known as "performance funds," have come into their own. Their opinion of traditional fund managers is harsh. "Old guys figure if a stock rises a lot it must be speculative," says Thomas Martin, president of Channing Growth Fund. George Chestnutt Jr., president of American Investors Fund, describes the typical manager of a conservative fund this way: "He lives in Darien, buys a copy of the *Wall Street Journal* on the train, and by the time he gets to Wall Street, he's an expert."

**Fashion Business**

The performance funds are increasing in number, and include such funds as Fidelity Trend and Fidelity Capital, Dreyfus, Oppenheimer Fund, Ivest, Channing Growth. The most spectacular this year was, of course, Gerald Tsai Jr.'s new Manhattan Fund. Its promoter, formerly manager of Fidelity Trend Fund, started out to raise $25 million, and ended up with over $400 million. But Tsai is not alone.

Richard Jenrette, chairman of the executive committee of the progressive young brokerage house of Donaldson Lufkin & Jenrette, says this about the new breed: "They think of themselves as being in a fashion business, and the fashions are constantly changing. They tend to go for short-term trends, unless they feel that investor fashions are becoming long term. They turn over their portfolios at a high rate, and they organize their operations simply, to give them more flexibility than the older committee-run funds."

Put differently, they are speculators—and proud of it They maintain that intelligent, clever speculation is what their shareholders are paying them for.

Says Channing's Martin, a typical member of the breed: "When you make mistakes, you get out. We bought Douglas on Monday and sold it on Wednesday."

No one denies that the performance funds have improved their performance by abandoning many of the traditional safeguards against risk, such as diversification by industry, dollar-averaging, buying stocks only for the long term and concern over preservation of capital. "As soon as some bright guy got the idea you really didn't have to own utilities in a period of rapid industrial expansion, the rules were off," says broker Jenrette.

In recent months these funds have tended to buy heavily into airlines and color TV, both of them industries considered to be at the peak of fashion and earning power (FORBES, *Aug. 1, p. 66*). Naturally, they hope to get out of such stocks quickly enough to hit whatever the next fashion will be. "We pick companies with aggressive management, ability to acquire companies on a favorable basis, and which are in interesting areas of technology," said 33-year-old W. Nicholas Thorndike, president of Ivest Fund. Ivest recently had nearly 5% of its portfolio in one speculative stock—Teledyne.

President Leon G. Levy of the performance-minded Oppenheimer Fund says, "We buy stocks that we think are going to move in a relatively short period. The traditional attitude, in contrast, is to buy a cross section of American industry, and wait for it to increase in value. That isn't management, that's being a custodian." Says D. George Sullivan, executive vice president of Fidelity Capital: "Today you don't sit still with a big-name stock if you can improve your fund's performance by selling it."

**Left-Handed Compliment**

This much is clear: The performance funds have left the older traditional funds eating dust. For the latest 12 months ended June 30, 1966, a $100 investment in two large performance funds, such as Fidelity Trend and Dreyfus Fund, reaped $162.23 and $130.16, respectively. Smaller performance funds as American Investors and Channing Special did even better, to the tune of $166.95 and $168.07. By contrast, traditional Investors Mutual and Wellington Funds, the two largest balanced funds, showed lean results—$95.05 and $95.16, both worth less than the original $100 investment. Likewise, Boston Fund did even poorer with a $92.72 performance.

Confronted with these statistics, traditional managers emphasize that performance funds are so new that no one knows how they will perform in a serious market crash, or over the long run. In a left-handed compliment, Massachusetts Investors Trust trustee, John L. Cooper, says: "If a man wants to speculate and doesn't know how, it's a good thing to have Fidelity and Dreyfus around."

There is always the danger, too, that the performance funds, acting identically, will buy the same stocks and have trouble unloading them at the same time. For example, the relatively small Northwest Orient Airlines is a performance fund favorite; all told, mutual funds own 39% of its 9.2-million share capitalization. What happens if a number of them decide to unload at the same time? It may well be that the investing policy that produced great results in 1966 may produce duds in 1967.

Joseph E. Welch, president of conservative Wellington Fund, believes that performance funds are here to stay and he has moved to acquire Ivest Fund's management company. But he doesn't feel that performance funds are going to sweep the market. The big money is still among conservative investors, not among speculators. What Wellington is looking for is the money now in banks, in savings & loans, in life insurance.

Welch has a point. For what both investors and fund managements should keep in mind is this: In the long pull, it isn't what sells best for a day or for a season that counts, but what best fits the needs of the market. It's much too early to say that the performance funds best serve the big market that mutual funds are aimed toward—or that their managers have the key to perpetual investment success.

**What the Numbers Show**

All of which brings us to FORBES' Mutual Fund Ratings. These are designed for the essential purpose of helping investors make some statistical sense out of conflicting claims. Applying a tough but carefully worked-out set of standards to fund performance, our statisticians have graded the funds on a scale ranging from "A+" to "D–". They have been rated for their performance in both rising and declining markets.

These Consistency Ratings are based on fund performance in eight distinct periods, four of rising markets and four of declining markets.* For each period, FORBES statisticians have asked: Did the fund do better than the averages? Did it merely keep up? Or did it actually fall behind the averages? Funds that just managed to keep up with Standard & Poor's 500 stock average in all four of the *up* periods received a B+ for consistency. Funds that kept up three times got a B; twice, a C+; once, a C. Funds that did poorer than the averages in all four periods received a D.

Funds with exceptionally good—or exceptionally poor performance—received modified ratings. A fund that succeeded not only in outperforming the average every time, but in outperforming it by 10% or better, rated an A+; by 3% to 9.9%, an A. A fund that was consistently *beaten* by the averages by a margin of 10% rated a D–. No ratings have been given when a fund did not exist for at least two full periods. Thus, only 221 of the survey's 304 funds are rated.

A fund in existence for only three periods could attain a maximum rating of A, and funds in existence for only two full periods a maximum of B+; poorer performances were scaled down from that point.

Note this carefully: The ratings are not based on short-run spectacular performances. They are meant mainly to measure *consistency* rather than hypothetical dollar results. Thus a fund may look better in sheer dollar figures (the sixth and seventh columns on the preceeding pages) than it does in the Consistency Ratings—or vice versa. Dollar figures are more easily distorted by one dramatic good or poor period, irrespective of when it may have come.

You can't have everything. An aggressive fund is not able to turn on a dime in down markets and outperform a conservative fund that continuously sits with large chunks of cash, waiting for declines. Keystone S3, for example, scored an A+ for consistency in rising markets, but only C in declining ones. Affiliated Fund, by contrast, scored A in declining markets and only C in rising ones.

Which is more important: consistency in up markets or in down markets? It depends on the individual. Some people prefer to eat well. Some prefer to sleep well. Since we have been in a period of rising prices in the last 13 years, a consistency in up markets has been more prevalent.

The balanced funds, specially designed for those who prefer to sleep well, are not measured against the S&P index. Instead, we have measured them against the average performance of the ten largest balanced funds in FORBES' survey. The balanced funds, with 40% or so of their assets in cash and fixed-income securities, naturally fall behind the market in *up* periods and always outperform it in *down* periods. For this reason, we have rated the balanced funds against an average of their own performance.

What about loading charges? These sales commissions typically run from 8.5% down to 1%, depending on the size of the purchase. None of the FORBES ratings takes the loading charge into account; the ratings are intended to measure management skill in handling money rather than the actual investment results. A formula for adjusting FORBES dollar figures for the effect of the loading charges appears below.† The FORBES survey also includes such features as a fund's size, its expense ratio, its maximum load and its yield. New this year is a list of tax-free exchange, or "swap" funds. These funds are not being offered for sale. They represent a one-shot combination of the assets of investors who want to diversify concentrated holdings of stock. Instead of selling such securities and thereby incurring a capital gains tax, they pool their stocks in an exchange fund, receiving fund shares in their stead. FORBES this year included their results for those investors who may be interested in participating in such funds.

Also included is a list of "no-load" funds. These funds have no sales charge, although some charge 1% upon redemption. Finally, the Survey includes a section on the closed-end investment companies. Unlike open-end funds, these do not issue their shares continuously. The investor must buy such shares in the open market, and this ordinarily creates a price discount from or premium over the actual net asset value per share. FORBES here ignores such discounts or premiums, preferring to measure the actual performance of the closed-end fund managers.

Like all the FORBES investment company ratings, these are designed to help the *long-range* investor decide whether investment companies are for him—and, if so, which ones. FORBES does so by asking—and answering—a simple question: How consistently skillful has the management been in handling the dollars entrusted to it? ■

*The four periods of rising markets: 1) Sept. 30, 1953 to June 30, 1956; 2) Oct. 25, 1957 to Dec. 31, 1959; 3) Sept. 30, 1960 to Dec. 31, 1961; 4) June 30, 1962 to Feb. 9, 1966.
The four periods of declining markets: 1) June 30, 1957 to Oct 25, 1957; 2) Dec. 31, 1959 to Sept. 30, 1960; 3) Dec. 31, 1961 to June 30, 1962; 4) Feb. 9, 1966 to June 30, 1966.

†To determine how much the loading charge affects dollar performance, simply multiply the management results figure by the loading charge, then move the decimal point two places to the left. Then subtract the resulting sum from the management results figure. For the performance ratings, an exact adjustment is impossible; but the absence of a load could change a fund's rating.

# 1966 FUND RATINGS

| Assets in Millions | Maximum Sales Charge % | Annual Expenses (Cents per $100) | | Consistency of Performance: In UP Markets | Consistency of Performance: In DOWN Markets | Management Results: 1953-1966 | Management Results: Latest 12 Months | Dividend Return % |
|---|---|---|---|---|---|---|---|---|
| | | | | | | $100 ENDED AS... | | |
| | | | Standard & Poor's 500 Stock Average | — | — | $362.91 | $100.74 | 3.4% |
| | | | Average of 10 stock funds in FORBES Index | C+ | C+ | $439.67 | $112.59 | 2.4% |
| | | | **STOCK FUNDS (LOAD)** | | | | | |
| $ 41.7 | 8.50% | $0.75 | Aberdeen Fund | B+ | C | $432.88 | $110.33 | 1.7% |
| 2.7 | 8.50 | 0.85 | Advisers Fund | C | B | 263.17 | 108.40 | 2.4 |
| 1,256.0 | 7.50 | 0.34 | Affiliated Fund | C | A | 318.21 | 104.79 | 3.6 |
| 1.1 | 8.50 | 0.87 | American Diversified Investors (started 12/64) | — | — | — | 107.08 | 2.3 |
| 10.9 | 8.00 | 1.00 | American Growth Fund (started 8/58) | •B | B | — | 112.08 | 1.6 |
| 327.2 | 8.50 | 0.62 | American Mutual Fund | B | B | 396.57 | 107.65 | 2.7 |
| 59.8 | 8.50 | 0.74 | Associated Fund Trust | D— | C+ | 236.40 | 101.77 | 2.7 |
| 7.6 | 2.00 | 0.95 | Associations Investment Fund (started 4/60) | — | — | — | 107.25 | 1.6 |
| 22.0 | 8.50 | 1.00 | Axe-Houghton Stock Fund | C | A | 409.27 | 152.98 | 1.0 |
| 30.5 | 8.00 | 0.84 | Axe Science Corp. (started 2/55) | B | B | — | 143.53 | 1.9 |
| 43.7 | 8.50 | 0.75 | Blue Ridge Mutual Fund | D | B | 331.71 | 111.01 | 2.5 |
| 13.0 | 8.50 | 0.75 | Bondstock Corp. | C+ | C | 325.51 | 122.72 | 1.9 |
| 329.0 | 7.50 | 0.17 | Broad Street Investing Corp. | D | B+ | 306.63 | 99.28 | 3.5 |
| 2.3 | 8.50 | 1.04 | The Brown Fund of Hawaii | C— | A | 253.49 | 103.36 | 1.8 |
| 111.8 | 8.67 | 0.38 | Bullock Fund | C | B | 354.90 | 105.93 | 2.8 |
| 89.1 | 8.75 | 1.04 | Capital Life Insurance Shares and Growth Stock Fund (started 1/60) | •C | •D | — | 84.10 | 0.3 |
| 100.5 | 8.50 | 0.38 | Century Shares Trust | C | C | 291.21 | 84.56 | 1.6 |
| | | | Channing Funds | | | | | |
| 36.1 | 8.50 | 0.80 | Common Stock Fund | C+ | C | 314.91 | 110.30 | 2.4 |
| 201.5 | 8.50 | 0.75 | Growth Fund | B | C+ | 435.77 | 150.43 | 0.9 |
| 18.5 | 8.50 | 0.85 | Special Fund (started 9/54) | A | C | — | 168.07 | 0.3 |
| 32.2 | 8.50 | 0.69 | The Chase Fund of Boston (started 6/58) | •B | B | — | 153.15 | 0.8 |
| 437.3 | 8.50 | 0.46 | Chemical Fund | B+ | C+ | 547.25 | 119.97 | 1.5 |
| 1.5 | 7.50 | 0.39 | Coastal Security Investment Fund (started 2/59) | •C | C | — | 103.36 | 1.6 |
| 194.8 | 8.50 | 0.60 | The Colonial Fund | D | B | 340.22 | 105.71 | 3.3 |
| 49.9 | 8.50 | 0.71 | Colonial Growth & Energy Shares | C | C+ | 304.78 | 128.61 | 1.5 |
| 7.2 | 8.00 | 0.81 | Common Stock Fund of State Bond & Mortgage Co. (started 5/62) | — | — | — | 118.13 | 1.1 |
| 35.3 | 7.65 | 0.62 | Commonwealth Fund Indenture of Trust A & B† | — | — | 241.37 | 111.61 | 3.1 |
| 33.6 | 8.50 | 0.73 | Commonwealth Stock Fund | C | C+ | 359.03 | 117.02 | 2.4 |
| 27.5 | 8.00 | 0.75 | Composite Fund | D | A | 295.12 | 112.79 | 2.5 |
| 3.1 | 8.50 | 0.75 | Consumers Investment Fund (started 6/58) | •C+ | B | — | 123.78 | 1.7 |
| 23.1 | 8.50 | 0.98 | Convertible Securities & Growth Stock Fund (started 1/54) | C | C+ | 420.17△ | 144.31 | 0.5 |
| 93.5 | 7.64 | 0.20 | Corporate Leaders Trust—Series "B" | C | C+ | 300.41 | 95.98 | 3.1 |
| | | | Crown Western Investments | | | | | |
| 1.5 | 8.50 | 1.01 | Dallas Fund (started 2/54) | C— | C+ | 286.17△ | 119.98 | 1.6 |
| 13.4 | 8.50 | 0.87 | Diversified Fund | C— | C+ | 298.66 | 108.16 | 3.0 |
| 298.2 | 8.50 | 0.73 | Delaware Fund | B | C | 417.20 | 138.40 | 1.6 |

*•Fund rated for two periods only; maximum allowable rating B+. △Fund not operating for full period.*
*†Transferred from balanced section this year; not rated.*

WHAT THE RATINGS MEAN

***We have selected eight distinct market movements over the past 13 years—four major up moves, four major down moves. For each period we have compared each stock fund's performance against that of the broadly based Standard & Poor's 500 stock average. The balanced funds have been compared against the FORBES balanced fund index. A high rating indicates a consistent ability to outperform the average; a low rating indicates a consistent inability to do as well as the average.***

# 1966 FUND RATINGS

| Assets in Millions | Maximum Sales Charge % | Annual Expenses (Cents per $100) | | Consistency of Performance: In UP Markets | Consistency of Performance: In DOWN Markets | Management Results: 1953-1966 | Management Results: Latest 12 Months | Dividend Return % |
|---|---|---|---|---|---|---|---|---|
| | | | | | | $100 ENDED AS... | | |
| | | | Standard & Poor's 500 Stock Average | — | — | $362.91 | $100.74 | 3.4% |
| | | | Average of 10 stock funds in FORBES Index | C+ | C+ | $439.67 | $112.59 | 2.4% |
| | | | **STOCK FUNDS (LOAD)** | | | | | |
| $189.2 | 8.75% | $0.71 | Diversified Growth Stock Fund | A | C | $615.51 | $145.19 | 0.9% |
| 353.8 | 8.67 | 0.44 | Dividend Shares | D | B+ | 304.98 | 98.96 | 2.9 |
| 113.0 | 7.50 | 0.89 | Dow Theory Investment Fund (started 12/54) | — | — | — | 136.50 | 1.4 |
| 1,539.8 | 8.38 | 0.58 | Dreyfus Fund | A | C+ | 786.40 | 130.16 | 1.8 |
| 239.7 | 7.50 | 0.57 | Eaton & Howard Stock Fund | C | C+ | 364.90 | 107.26 | 2.3 |
| 40.1 | 3.50 | 1.31 | Equity Fund | C+ | B+ | 364.22 | 104.03 | 1.9 |
| 10.7 | 8.50 | 1.05 | Federated Growth Fund (started 11/55) | B | C+ | — | 133.56 | 1.0 |
| 403.0 | 8.00 | 0.64 | Fidelity Capital Fund (started 5/58) | •B+ | B | — | 164.19 | 1.0 |
| 620.8 | 7.50 | 0.50 | Fidelity Fund | B | C+ | 387.18 | 116.91 | 2.4 |
| 954.4 | 8.00 | 0.63 | Fidelity Trend Fund (started 6/58) | •B+ | B | — | 162.23 | 0.9 |
| 11.1 | 8.50 | 0.72 | Fiduciary Mutual Investing Co.† | — | — | 258.78 | 99.63 | 2.7 |
| 334.0 | 8.50 | 0.67 | Financial Industrial Fund | C+ | C | 350.07 | 115.06 | 2.1 |
| 42.7 | 8.75 | 0.60 | First Investors Stock Fund (formerly Mutual Investment Fund) | D− | B+ | 212.77 | 109.95 | 2.5 |
| 2.4 | 8.85 | 1.00 | First Participating Fund—Life-Growth Stock Series (started 8/64) | — | — | — | 85.66 | 0.4 |
| 7.4 | 8.50 | 0.91 | Florida Growth Fund (started 2/57) | D | A | — | 105.02 | 1.7 |
| 1.5 | 8.50 | 0.97 | Foundation Life Stock Fund (started 5/59) | •C+ | C | — | 76.86 | none |
| 181.4 | 8.50 | 0.38 | Founders Mutual Fund | B+ | C | 418.97 | 103.18 | 2.8 |
| 10.4 | 8.50 | 0.67 | Foursquare Fund (started 4/62) | — | — | — | 135.31 | 2.4 |
| | | | Franklin Custodian Funds | | | | | |
| 8.3 | 8.75 | 0.77 | Common Stock Series | B | C+ | 421.49 | 115.92 | 2.0 |
| 30.8 | 8.75 | 0.77 | Utilities Series | C | B+ | 339.27 | 86.99 | 2.5 |
| 41.3 | 8.50 | 0.93 | Fund of America | C+ | B | 390.68 | 151.66 | 0.2 |
| 1,163.3 | 8.75 | 0.52 | Fundamental Investors | B | C | 411.44 | 115.45 | 2.1 |
| | | | Group Securities | | | | | |
| 16.0 | 8.50 | 0.72 | Aerospace-Science Fund | B | C+ | 442.19 | 150.96 | 0.9 |
| 258.3 | 8.50 | 0.72 | Common Stock Fund | D | B | 283.88 | 101.74 | 3.8 |
| 41.7 | 2.91 | 0.48 | Growth Industry Shares | A | C+ | 450.21 | 111.30 | 1.9 |
| 5.5 | 8.50 | 1.00 | Gryphon Fund (started 4/63) | — | — | — | 136.86 | 0.5 |
| 489.1 | 8.50 | 0.65 | Hamilton Funds—Series H-DA | C | C+ | 261.58 | 103.11 | 2.6 |
| 1.1 | 4.00 | 1.00 | Hampden Fund (started 7/62) | — | — | — | 105.92 | 2.0 |
| 26.9 | 8.00 | 0.85 | Imperial Capital Fund | C | C+ | 286.91 | 109.18 | 1.9 |
| 4.2 | 8.00 | 1.26 | Imperial Growth Fund (started 4/63) | — | — | — | 135.85 | 0.4 |
| 57.6 | 8.50 | 0.51 | Industries Trend Fund (started 2/65) | — | — | — | 149.05 | 0.7 |
| 1.8 | 8.50 | 0.64 | Industry Fund of America (started 3/62) | — | — | — | 128.68 | 0.8 |
| 3.9 | 8.50 | 0.80 | Insurance & Bank Stock Fund (started 1/60) | C | D | — | 83.26 | 1.2 |
| 9.8 | 8.80 | 0.98 | Insurance Investors Fund (started 6/57) | B | B | — | 103.86 | 2.7 |
| 1,215.0 | 8.85 | 0.45 | Insurance Securities Trust Fund* | — | — | 245.89 | 93.45 | 1.3 |
| 542.6 | 8.50 | 0.57 | Investment Co. of America | B+ | C+ | 508.84 | 121.85 | 2.2 |
| 91.2 | 8.50 | 0.58 | Investment Trust of Boston | C | C | 340.48 | 102.82 | 2.7 |
| 4.0 | 8.50 | 1.00 | Investors Research Fund (started 4/59) | •C+ | B | — | 163.70 | 0.8 |
| 1,730.0 | 8.00 | 0.43 | Investors Stock Fund | C+ | C | 314.06 | 99.12 | 2.8 |

*•Fund rated for two periods only; maximum allowable rating B+. *Data not provided by company; all figures FORBES estimate. †Transferred from balanced section this year; not rated.*

**EXPLANATION OF COLUMN HEADINGS**

*Annual expenses include management fees and operating expenses as a percentage of average net assets. Only funds in existence for at least four of the measured periods are given a FORBES performance rating. All capital gains distributions have been reinvested, but income dividends have not. All ratings are based on investments of net asset value and do not allow for sales charges.*

*In Management Results section, the 1953-66 period covers the period from Sept. 30, 1953 to June 30, 1966; the latest 12 months covers the period from June 30, 1965 to June 30, 1966. Dividend Return is based on June 30, 1966 net asset value and the income payout for the preceding 12-month period.*

# 1966 FUND RATINGS

| Assets in Millions | Maximum Sales Charge % | Annual Expenses (Cents per $100) | | Consistency of Performance: In UP Markets | Consistency of Performance: In DOWN Markets | Management Results ($100 ended as...): 1953-1966 | Management Results ($100 ended as...): Latest 12 Months | Dividend Return % |
|---|---|---|---|---|---|---|---|---|
| | | | Standard & Poor's 500 Stock Average | — | — | $362.91 | $100.74 | 3.4% |
| | | | Average of 10 stock funds in FORBES Index | C+ | C+ | $439.67 | $112.59 | 2.4% |
| | | | **STOCK FUNDS (LOAD)** | | | | | |
| $559.8 | 8.00% | $0.49 | Investors Variable Payment Fund (started 5/57) | A | C+ | — | $114.96 | 2.0% |
| 43.3 | 3.00 | 0.83 | Istel Fund (started 1/54) | D | A | $332.99△ | 115.73 | 2.4 |
| 34.8 | 8.50 | 1.07 | Ivest Fund (started 1/59) | •B+ | B | — | 148.03 | 0.3 |
| | | | Keystone Custodian Funds | | | | | |
| 218.8 | 8.30 | 0.58 | K-2 | B | C+ | 466.27 | 133.87 | 1.3 |
| 51.1 | 8.30 | 0.58 | S-1 | C+ | C+ | 366.45 | 102.93 | 2.1 |
| 134.3 | 8.30 | 0.58 | S-2 | C | B | 313.48 | 104.69 | 3.3 |
| 153.8 | 8.30 | 0.58 | S-3 | A+ | C | 630.29 | 131.36 | 1.7 |
| 276.8 | 8.30 | 0.56 | S-4 | A+ | C+ | 623.21 | 130.20 | 1.5 |
| 14.1 | 8.70 | 1.10 | The Knickerbocker Fund† | — | — | 212.37 | 110.98 | 2.5 |
| 5.9 | 8.70 | 1.00 | Knickerbocker Growth Fund | B | C+ | 434.38 | 147.96 | 0.4 |
| 91.7 | | 0.63 | Lazard Fund (started 7/58) | •C | C | — | 102.02 | none |
| 1.7 | 8.50 | 0.79 | Liberty Fund (started 7/56) | C | C+ | — | 101.28 | 2.6 |
| 93.3 | 8.50 | 0.59 | Life Insurance Investors (started 8/57) | C+ | C | — | 81.97 | 0.8 |
| 11.2 | 8.25 | 0.76 | Life Insurance Stock Fund (started 1/55) | C— | B | — | 79.95 | 0.3 |
| 931.0 | 8.50 | 0.38 | Massachusetts Investors Growth Stock Fund | A | C+ | 570.85 | 121.54 | 1.5 |
| 2,089.0 | 8.50 | 0.18 | Massachusetts Investors Trust | C | C | 325.87 | 98.65 | 3.1 |
| 1.7 | 8.50 | 1.00 | Mercer Fund (started 4/59) | C+ | A | — | 144.39 | 0.9 |
| 7.6 | 8.50 | 1.73 | Mid America Mutual Fund (started 1/61) | — | — | — | 119.14 | 1.6 |
| | | | B.C. Morton Funds | | | | | |
| 9.0 | 8.75 | 0.99 | Growth Series (started 2/56) | A | B | — | 150.55 | 0.5 |
| 5.7 | 8.75 | 0.99 | Insurance Series (started 2/56) | C— | B | — | 87.55 | 0.7 |
| 11.4 | 7.50 | 0.75 | Mutual Investing Foundation—MIF Growth Fund (started 2/61) | — | — | — | 113.28 | 2.1 |
| 0.9 | 8.75 | 0.71 | Mutual Investment Co. of America | C+ | C | 367.78 | 127.21 | 0.8 |
| 559.9 | 7.50 | 0.16 | National Investors Corp. | B+ | C+ | 546.59 | 118.21 | 1.8 |
| | | | National Securities | | | | | |
| 171.6 | 8.50 | 0.69 | Growth Stock Series | B | C+ | 476.70 | 120.47 | 1.3 |
| 311.5 | 8.50 | 0.69 | Stock Series | D | C | 276.55 | 103.56 | 3.9 |
| 1.2 | 8.75 | 2.75 | National Western Fund (started 6/61) | — | — | — | 82.45 | 0.7 |
| 2.7 | 1.00 | 0.93 | Old Dominion Investors Trust | C | C+ | 333.16 | 103.36 | 1.0 |
| 74.7 | 8.50 | 1.03 | Oppenheimer Fund (started 4/59) | •B+ | B | — | 148.72 | 0.5 |
| 1.2 | 8.00 | 1.31 | Over-the-Counter Securities Fund (started 6/56) | A | B | — | 137.03 | 1.1 |
| 5.1 | 8.50 | 1.00 | Paramount Mutual Fund (started 9/58) | •D | B | — | 102.23 | 3.6 |
| 20.5 | 8.75 | 0.79 | Peoples Securities Corp. (started 12/55) | A | C | — | 133.93 | 1.0 |
| 72.0 | 8.75 | 0.70 | Philadelphia Fund | B | C+ | 440.86 | 114.31 | 2.0 |
| 87.4 | 8.50 | 0.78 | Pioneer Fund | C+ | B | 379.85 | 116.65 | 2.6 |
| 373.2 | 8.50 | 0.61 | Putnam Growth Fund (started 11/57) | •B | B | — | 128.68 | 1.2 |
| 255.6 | 8.50 | 0.56 | Putnam Investors Fund (formerly Incorporated Investors) | C+ | C | 299.41 | 109.68 | 2.1 |
| 18.2 | 8.50 | 0.98 | Republic Technology Fund (started 5/55) | C— | C+ | — | 118.47 | 1.7 |
| 57.1 | 8.50 | 0.93 | Research Investing Corp. (started 6/59) | •C+ | B | — | 120.20 | 1.4 |
| 5.4 | 8.50 | 2.20 | Revere Fund (started 8/59) | •B | B | — | 147.30 | none |
| 8.0 | 8.50 | 1.00 | Security Equity Fund (started 9/62) | — | — | — | 180.73 | 0.3 |

*•Fund rated for two periods only; maximum allowable rating B+. △Fund was not operating for full period. †Transferred from balanced section this year; not rated.*

# 1966 FUND RATINGS

| Assets in Millions | Maximum Sales Charge % | Annual Expenses (Cents per $100) | 1966 FUND RATINGS | Consistency of Performance: In UP Markets | Consistency of Performance: In DOWN Markets | Management Results ($100 ended as...): 1953-1966 | Management Results ($100 ended as...): Latest 12 Months | Dividend Return % |
|---|---|---|---|---|---|---|---|---|
| | | | Standard & Poor's 500 Stock Average | — | — | $362.91 | $100.74 | 3.4% |
| | | | Average of 10 stock funds in FORBES Index | C+ | C+ | $439.67 | $112.59 | 2.4% |
| | | | **STOCK FUNDS (LOAD)** | | | | | |
| $187.6 | 7.50% | $0.61 | Selected American Shares | C+ | C | $370.09 | $122.31 | 2.0% |
| 17.8 | 7.50 | 0.68 | Southwestern Investors (started 2/54) | C— | A | 271.68△ | 107.53 | 2.6 |
| 5.3 | 8.67 | 0.80 | Sovereign Investors | D | C+ | 283.01 | 102.66 | 2.3 |
| 346.6 | * | 0.51 | State Street Investment Corp. | C+ | B | 351.25 | 116.60 | 1.9 |
| 3.7 | 8.50 | 1.00 | Steadman Investment Fund (started 8/57) | B | B | — | 107.14 | 2.9 |
| 48.5 | 8.50 | 0.95 | Steadman Science & Growth (started 12/53, formerly Atomics, Physics & Science Fund) | C | C+ | 269.22△ | 127.47 | 1.5 |
| 3.1 | 8.50 | 1.00 | Steadman's Shares in American Industry (started 12/59, formerly Shares in American Industry) | •B+ | B | — | 123.69 | 1.1 |
| 7.4 | 8.00 | 1.33 | Supervised Shares | D | B | 289.59 | 101.89 | 2.3 |
| 481.8 | 8.25 | 0.62 | Television-Electronics Fund | B+ | C+ | 523.50 | 125.77 | 1.8 |
| 93.2 | 8.50 | 0.61 | Texas Fund | C+ | B | 404.50 | 104.31 | 2.1 |
| 13.4 | 8.50 | 0.98 | Twentieth Century Investors—Growth Investors (started 10/58) | •B+ | B | — | 149.22 | 0.3 |
| 4.7 | 8.50 | 1.02 | Unified Mutual Shares (started 10/63) | — | — | — | 119.44 | 1.6 |
| | | | United Funds | | | | | |
| 1,245.4 | 8.50 | 0.41 | Accumulative | C+ | B | 402.27 | 108.11 | 2.5 |
| 661.1 | 8.50 | 0.42 | Income | C | B | 356.94 | 105.36 | 2.7 |
| 319.7 | 8.50 | 0.42 | Science | B+ | C+ | 517.02 | 127.87 | 1.2 |
| 17.3 | 8.75 | 0.81 | The Value Line Fund | C+ | B | 354.51 | 126.78 | 2.1 |
| 31.9 | 8.75 | 1.00 | The Value Line Special Situations Fund (started 4/56) | A | C | — | 157.28 | 0.4 |
| 1.7 | 8.50 | 0.65 | Vanderbilt Mutual Fund (started 5/57) | C | C+ | — | 118.35 | 2.6 |
| 6.9 | 8.00 | 1.00 | Varied Industry Plan (started 10/61) | — | — | — | 113.43 | 2.2 |
| 1.0 | 8.00 | 1.00 | Viking Growth Fund (started 9/56) | C+ | C+ | — | 112.74 | 0.6 |
| 16.1 | 8.50 | 0.76 | Wall Street Investing Corp. | D— | A | 284.01 | 104.85 | 2.3 |
| 181.6 | 8.50 | 0.68 | Washington Mutual Investors Fund | C+ | C+ | 410.14 | 104.05 | 3.2 |
| 3.9 | 8.50 | 1.00 | Western Industrial Shares (started 4/59) | •B+ | B | — | 134.36 | 0.4 |
| 95.8 | 8.00 | 0.75 | Windsor Fund (started 10/58) | •B | C+ | — | 123.86 | 1.3 |
| 15.0 | 8.50 | 0.95 | Winfield Growth Industries Fund | B | C+ | 468.26 | 143.47 | 0.9 |
| 26.5 | 8.50 | 0.66 | Wisconsin Fund | C | B+ | 313.04 | 110.10 | 2.0 |
| | | | **STOCK FUNDS (NO-LOAD)** | | | | | |
| $ 1.9 | 1.00†% | $2.69 | Leon B. Allen Fund | B | B+ | $512.18 | $130.02 | none |
| 68.6 | none | 1.29 | American Investors Fund (started 1/58) | •B+ | B | — | 166.95 | 0.4% |
| 9.3 | none | 0.90 | Consultants Mutual Investments (started 6/63) | — | — | — | 118.02 | 2.1 |
| 22.2 | none | 0.55 | De Vegh Mutual Fund | B+ | C | 559.15 | 129.57 | 1.6 |
| 1.6 | none | 0.69 | Dodge & Cox Stock Fund (started 12/64) | — | — | — | 107.55 | 1.9 |
| 49.0 | none | 0.84 | Energy Fund (started 10/55) | B+ | C+ | — | 126.74 | 1.4 |
| 4.0 | none | 1.00 | Fairfield Securities (started 6/60) | — | — | — | 157.30 | 0.2 |
| 2.1 | none | 0.87 | General Securities | C+ | C+ | 337.43 | 117.93 | 1.4 |
| 35.3 | none | 0.74 | Guardian Mutual Fund | C+ | B+ | 377.86 | 109.51 | 2.3 |
| 61.1 | none | 0.66 | The Johnston Mutual Fund** | •C+ | B+ | 361.26 | 124.48 | 1.7 |

*•Fund rated for two periods only; maximum allowable rating B+. *Fund no longer selling new shares; existing shares traded over-the-counter. †Entrance fee. **Prior to 1959 was a balanced fund; rated for subsequent periods only. △Fund was not operating for full period.*

# 1966 FUND RATINGS

| Assets in Millions | Maximum Sales Charge % | Annual Expenses (Cents per $100) | | Consistency of Performance: In UP Markets | Consistency of Performance: In DOWN Markets | Management Results: 1953-1966 ($100 ended as...) | Management Results: Latest 12 Months ($100 ended as...) | Dividend Return % |
|---|---|---|---|---|---|---|---|---|
| | | | Standard & Poor's 500 Stock Average | — | — | $362.91 | $100.74 | 3.4% |
| | | | Average of 10 stock funds in FORBES Index | C+ | C+ | $439.67 | $112.59 | 2.4% |
| | | | **STOCK FUNDS (NO LOAD)** | | | | | |
| $ 7.7 | none | $0.84 | Loomis-Sayles Capital Development Fund (started 6/61) | — | — | — | $126.08 | 1.5% |
| 2.1 | none | 0.72 | Mairs & Power Growth Fund (started 1/58) | •C— | B | — | 109.64 | 1.4 |
| 2.6 | none | 1.00 | National Industries Fund (started 6/60) | •B+ | •C+ | — | 133.89 | 1.3 |
| 3.2 | none | 2.12 | Nelson Fund (started 11/55) | •D | A+ | — | 109.11 | 0.5 |
| 2.2 | none | 0.73 | Newton Fund (started 8/60) | •D | •C+ | — | 108.77 | 2.4 |
| 231.6 | none | 0.51 | The One William Street Fund (started 6/58) | •C— | C | — | 107.92 | 1.9 |
| 142.0 | none | 0.59 | Penn Square Mutual Fund (started 11/57) | •B+ | C | — | 106.16 | 2.5 |
| 43.0 | none | 0.43 | Pine Street Fund | D | A | $334.53 | 106.17 | 3.2 |
| 20.0 | none | 1.00 | Rowe Price New Horizons Fund (started 6/60) | •C+ | •C+ | — | 149.65 | 0.3 |
| 224.1 | none | 0.60 | T. Rowe Price Growth Stock Fund | B+ | B | 585.31 | 116.51 | 1.8 |
| 42.5 | none | 0.61 | Scudder Special Fund (offered publicly 5/66) | A | C+ | — | 131.49 | 1.0 |
| 120.6 | none | 0.61 | Scudder, Stevens & Clark Common Stock Fund | C+ | B | 386.86 | 108.28 | 2.5 |
| 8.0 | none | 0.98 | Securities Fund** | — | — | 472.60 | 147.15 | 1.2 |
| 59.7 | none | 0.58 | Stein Roe & Farnham Stock Fund (started 7/58) | •C+ | B | — | 112.79 | 1.9 |
| 1.7 | none | 0.66 | Variable Stock Fund (started 1/57) | D | B | — | 104.33 | 1.8 |
| 0.6 | none | 1.76 | Wade Fund | C+ | C+ | 331.77 | 114.96 | 0.8 |
| | | | **CLOSED-END INVESTMENT COMPANIES*** | | | | | |
| $ 41.8 | — | $0.55 | Abacus Fund (started 6/57) | B+ | B | — | $107.70 | † |
| 117.8 | — | 0.37 | Adams Express | C | C+ | $302.47 | 103.34 | 2.7% |
| 53.3 | — | 0.49 | American International | C | C+ | 306.34 | 102.84 | 2.8 |
| 19.6 | — | 0.70 | Carriers & General Corp. | C+ | B | 349.39 | 92.22 | 2.9 |
| 87.2 | — | 0.11 | Consolidated Investment Trust | C+ | C | 363.91 | 99.38 | 3.1 |
| 55.6 | — | 0.47 | Dominick Fund | C | C+ | 299.17 | 116.38 | 1.9 |
| 82.0 | — | 0.75 | General American Investors | C+ | C | 355.94 | 115.98 | 1.4 |
| 94.3 | — | 0.37 | General Public Service | C | A | 326.06 | 100.20 | 2.7 |
| 88.0 | — | 0.50 | International Holdings | D | B | 260.20△ | 104.83 | 3.3 |
| 433.0 | — | 0.32 | Lehman Corp. | B | C+ | 376.62 | 112.86 | 1.8 |
| 228.6 | — | 0.49 | Madison Fund | C | C+ | 348.58 | 116.21 | 2.8 |
| 89.8 | — | 0.60 | National Aviation | B+ | B+ | 659.22 | 140.22 | 2.1 |
| 93.5 | — | 0.46 | Niagara Share Corp. | C+ | C+ | 412.46 | 110.23 | 2.0 |
| 49.9 | — | 0.33 | Petroleum Corp. of America | C | B | 304.17 | 108.97 | 3.1 |
| 55.0 | — | 0.42 | Standard Shares (started 3/56) | C | A | — | 108.13 | 2.3 |
| 531.2 | — | 0.19 | Tri-Continental | C— | C+ | 275.19 | 102.49 | 2.8 |
| 145.0 | — | 0.47 | The United Corporation | D | A | 267.51 | 104.94 | 2.8 |
| 133.0 | — | 0.43 | U.S. & Foreign Securities | C | C+ | 295.49 | 99.18 | 2.5 |
| | | | **FUNDS FOR INVESTING ABROAD** | | | | | |
| $ 51.2 | 8.50% | $0.66 | Canada General Fund (started 8/54) | D | C+ | — | $ 93.01 | 2.1% |
| 29.8 | 7.50 | 0.72 | Canadian Fund | D— | B | $245.06 | 98.66 | 2.4 |
| 9.0 | 8.50 | 0.75 | Commonwealth Capital Fund (started 5/61) | — | — | — | 143.10 | 0.8 |
| 1.2 | 8.00 | 1.00 | International Investors (started 8/55) | C— | A+ | — | 102.78 | 2.7 |
| 6.8 | 7.50 | 0.75 | Keystone International Fund (started 10/54) | C— | B | — | 119.19 | 1.6 |
| 15.6 | none | 1.02 | Loomis-Sayles Canadian & Int. Fund (started 8/59) | — | — | — | 97.03 | 2.0 |

*• Fund rated for two periods only; maximum allowable rating B+. *All data based on net asset values. †All distributions are considered a return of capital and have been reinvested. **Transferred from balanced section this year; not rated. △Fund not operating for full period.*

# 1966 FUND RATINGS

| Assets in Millions | Maximum Sales Charge % | Annual Expenses (Cents per $100) | | Consistency of Performance: In UP Markets | Consistency of Performance: In DOWN Markets | Management Results: 1953-1966 ($100 ended as...) | Management Results: Latest 12 Months ($100 ended as...) | Dividend Return % |
|---|---|---|---|---|---|---|---|---|
| | | | Standard & Poor's 500 Stock Average | — | — | $362.91 | $100.74 | 3.4% |
| | | | Average of 10 stock funds in FORBES Index | C+ | C+ | $439.67 | $112.59 | 2.4% |
| | | | **FUNDS FOR INVESTING ABROAD** | | | | | |
| $ 29.0 | * | $0.72 | Scudder International Investments (started 6/54)..... | D– | B | — | $100.56 | 2.2% |
| 14.3 | none | 0.68 | Stein Roe & Farnham International Fund (started 8/54) | D– | B | — | 94.90 | 2.4 |
| 4.9 | 8.50% | 1.08 | Templeton Growth Fund Ltd. (started 11/54).......... | B | A+ | — | 116.55 | 1.3 |
| 11.0 | * | 0.90 | Transatlantic Fund (started 4/59).......... | D– | A+ | — | 102.88 | 2.2 |
| 10.9 | * | 0.96 | United Funds Canada—International (started 8/54).... | D | C | — | 96.94 | 1.4 |
| | | | **Average of 10 balanced funds in FORBES Index** | — | — | **$241.20** | **$101.69** | **3.5%** |
| | | | **BALANCED FUNDS (LOAD)** | | | | | |
| $ 25.7 | 7.50% | $0.71 | American Business Shares.......................... | C | A+ | $190.90 | $100.81 | 3.7% |
| 55.2 | 8.00 | 0.92 | Axe-Houghton Fund A.......................... | C | B+ | 273.46 | 123.09 | 2.5 |
| 258.9 | 8.00 | 0.71 | Axe-Houghton Fund B.......................... | A | C | 271.88 | 111.61 | 3.3 |
| 2.2 | 8.75 | 0.58 | Balanced Income Fund (started 3/64)................ | — | — | — | 103.16 | 4.7 |
| 345.6 | 8.50 | 0.54 | Boston Fund.......................... | C | B+ | 250.91 | 92.72 | 3.5 |
| 2.4 | 8.75 | 1.33 | Capital Income Fund (started 2/65)................ | — | — | — | 102.51 | 5.0 |
| | | | Channing Funds | | | | | |
| 103.4 | 8.50 | 0.73 | Balanced Fund.......................... | B+ | B+ | 270.36 | 107.37 | 3.0 |
| 47.0 | 8.50 | 0.73 | Income Fund.......................... | B | C+ | 239.98 | 106.93 | 4.0 |
| 3.4 | 8.50 | 1.03 | Citadel Fund (started 1/54) (formerly Florida Mutual Fund).................... | A | C– | 205.56△ | 110.02 | 1.9 |
| 70.8 | 8.50 | 0.60 | Commonwealth Income Fund (started 11/57).......... | •D | C | — | 101.92 | 4.5 |
| 178.9 | 8.50 | 0.59 | Commonwealth Investment Co.......................... | D | C+ | 226.58 | 104.90 | 3.1 |
| 12.0 | 8.00 | 0.79 | Composite Bond & Stock Fund.......................... | C | B+ | 216.56 | 104.45 | 3.2 |
| 26.1 | 8.50 | 0.82 | Convertible Securities Fund (started 11/56).......... | D– | B | — | 117.25 | 4.1 |
| 33.3 | 8.50 | 0.73 | Decatur Income Fund (started 3/57).......... | B | B+ | — | 108.87 | 4.0 |
| 158.4 | 8.75 | 0.66 | Diversified Investment Fund.......................... | B | C | 230.40 | 105.17 | 3.6 |
| 208.0 | 7.50 | 0.55 | Eaton & Howard Balanced Fund.......................... | C | B | 210.89 | 94.70 | 3.4 |
| 12.6 | 8.50 | 0.80 | Financial Industrial Income Fund (started 7/60)....... | •C+ | •C | — | 110.09 | 3.8 |
| 2.3 | 8.75 | 0.76 | Franklin Custodian-Income Series Shares.............. | C | B | 233.01 | 103.53 | 4.9 |
| 17.7 | 8.00 | 0.61 | General Investors Trust.......................... | C | B | 207.06 | 96.34 | 4.1 |
| 20.6 | 8.50 | 0.72 | Group Securities—Fully Administered Fund.......... | C | B | 212.81 | 100.29 | 3.9 |
| 37.1 | 8.50 | 0.96 | Income Foundation Fund.......................... | B+ | C+ | 263.18 | 110.69 | 2.8 |
| 49.2 | 8.50 | 0.70 | Income Fund of Boston (started 2/55).............. | D | C | — | 99.46 | 6.0 |
| 2,838.9 | 8.00 | 0.38 | Investors Mutual.......................... | D | B | 205.68 | 95.05 | 3.9 |
| 127.7 | 8.30 | 0.56 | Keystone Custodian Funds—K-1.......................... | D– | A | 148.65 | 101.13 | 5.0 |
| 7.3 | 8.50 | 1.04 | Lexington Income Trust.......................... | D– | A | 187.07 | 102.87 | 4.9 |
| 7.7 | 4.00 | 0.80 | Horace Mann Fund (started 12/57).................. | •C | C | — | 98.60 | 3.4 |
| 140.2 | 8.50 | 0.54 | Massachusetts Life Fund.......................... | D | A | 215.89 | 100.45 | 3.1 |
| 5.8 | 8.75 | 0.99 | B.C. Morton—Income Series (started 7/57).......... | D– | B | — | 102.46 | 5.0 |
| 88.1 | 7.50 | 0.67 | Mutual Investing Foundation—MIF Fund.............. | A | B | 324.58 | 105.92 | 3.4 |
| 11.0 | 2.00 | 0.90 | Mutual Trust.......................... | B+ | D | 219.05 | 99.09 | 3.8 |
| | | | National Securities | | | | | |
| 5.3 | 8.50 | 0.71 | Balanced Series.......................... | D– | B | 172.37 | 94.40 | 3.9 |
| 92.8 | 8.50 | 0.71 | Dividend Series.......................... | B | C | 209.90 | 109.68 | 4.6 |
| 91.8 | 8.50 | 0.70 | Income Series.......................... | D | C | 193.92 | 101.37 | 4.5 |

*•Fund rated for two periods only; maximum allowable rating B+. *Funds temporarily not offering shares; existing shares traded over-the-counter. △Fund was not operating for full period.*

# 1966 FUND RATINGS

| Assets in Millions | Maximum Sales Charge % | Annual Expenses (Cents per $100) | 1966 FUND RATINGS | Consistency of Performance: In UP Markets | Consistency of Performance: In DOWN Markets | Management Results ($100 ended as...): 1953-1966 | Management Results ($100 ended as...): Latest 12 Months | Dividend Return % |
|---|---|---|---|---|---|---|---|---|
| | | | Standard & Poor's 500 Stock Average | — | — | $362.91 | $100.74 | 3.4% |
| | | | Average of 10 stock funds in FORBES Index | C+ | C+ | $439.67 | $112.59 | 2.4% |
| | | | Average of 10 balanced funds in FORBES Index | — | — | $241.20 | $101.69 | 3.5% |
| | | | **BALANCED FUNDS (LOAD)** | | | | | |
| $ 79.4 | 7.50% | $0.45 | Nation-Wide Securities Co. | D | A | $221.64 | $ 97.64 | 3.6% |
| 24.2 | 7.50 | 0.69 | New England Fund | C | A+ | 205.23 | 102.29 | 3.4 |
| 25.0 | 8.50 | 0.95 | Provident Fund for Income (started 8/60) | •C | •B+ | — | 116.25 | 4.0 |
| 480.0 | 7.50 | 0.53 | Puritan Fund | A | C | 313.01 | 111.69 | 3.5 |
| 395.9 | 8.50 | 0.44 | The George Putnam Fund of Boston | A | B | 286.00 | 106.43 | 3.0 |
| 168.6 | 8.50 | 0.40 | Putnam Income Fund (started 10/54) (formerly Incorporated Income Fund) | C | B | — | 97.59 | 4.6 |
| 9.9 | 8.50 | 0.95 | Quarterly Distribution Shares | C | D | 227.69 | 109.92 | 3.1 |
| 4.2 | 7.50 | 0.60 | Security Diversified Shares (started 11/59) | •C | •C | — | 115.12 | 2.1 |
| 85.4 | 8.50 | 0.62 | Shareholders' Trust of Boston | B | B+ | 239.59 | 110.63 | 3.7 |
| 5.3 | 7.50 | 0.67 | Sterling Investment Fund | C | B | 188.91 | 103.98 | 3.5 |
| 2.6 | 8.50 | 0.98 | Twentieth Century Investors—Income Investors (started 10/58) | •B+ | B | — | 112.62 | 2.7 |
| 90.0 | 8.75 | 0.75 | The Value Line Income Fund | C | B | 180.85 | 109.29 | 3.5 |
| 1,920.6 | 8.00 | 0.38 | Wellington Fund | D | B+ | 213.51 | 95.16 | 3.5 |
| 17.0 | 7.50 | 0.27 | Whitehall Fund | D | A | 225.83 | 100.74 | 3.7 |
| | | | **BALANCED FUNDS (NO LOAD)** | | | | | |
| $ 1.1 | none | $0.94 | Counselors Investment Fund | D | B | $180.87 | $ 96.28 | 3.8% |
| 12.6 | none | 0.64 | Dodge & Cox Balanced Fund | B+ | B | 244.99 | 105.32 | 2.8 |
| 128.2 | none | 0.61 | Loomis-Sayles Mutual Fund | C | C+ | 213.11 | 99.49 | 3.8 |
| 4.4 | none | 1.48 | Mutual Shares Corp. | B | A | 351.27 | 114.52 | 2.2 |
| 8.8 | none | 0.76 | The Nassau Fund (started 10/57) | •B+ | C | — | 103.22 | 3.0 |
| 25.2 | none | 0.71 | Northeast Investors Trust | B | A+ | 259.67 | 98.85 | 4.8 |
| 2.1 | none | 0.72 | Prudential Fund of Boston | C | B+ | 198.90 | 96.93 | 2.9 |
| 8.2 | none | 0.63 | Rittenhouse Fund | C | C | 213.92 | 101.03 | 2.9 |
| 117.8 | none | 0.57 | Scudder, Stevens & Clark Balanced Fund | B | C— | 219.93 | 100.33 | 2.9 |
| 113.0 | none | 0.55 | Stein Roe & Farnham Balanced Fund | B | A | 296.29 | 106.92 | 2.5 |
| | | | **BONDS & PREFERRED STOCK FUNDS** | | | | | |
| $ 0.3 | none | none | The Atlantic Fund for Investment in U.S. Government Securities (started 8/61) | | | — | $100.17 | 4.0% |
| 1.9 | 8.75% | $0.85 | Franklin Custodian, Bond And Preferred Stock Series | | | $ 93.60 | 98.53 | 5.6 |
| 43.8 | 7.00 | 0.47 | Investors Selective Fund | | | 109.44 | 95.66 | 5.0 |
| | | | Keystone Custodian Funds | | | | | |
| 12.1 | 4.15 | 0.29 | B-1 | | | 89.44 | 95.69 | 4.3 |
| 11.0 | 8.30 | 0.58 | B-2 | | | 98.66 | 96.34 | 5.0 |
| 59.3 | 8.30 | 0.56 | B-3 | | | 108.56 | 98.30 | 6.0 |
| 85.7 | 8.30 | 0.58 | B-4 | | | 120.64 | 99.80 | 6.0 |
| | | | National Securities | | | | | |
| 2.4 | 8.50 | 0.74 | Bond Series | | | 101.88 | 96.58 | 5.1 |
| 7.7 | 8.50 | 0.73 | Preferred Stock Series | | | 106.10 | 94.92 | 5.5 |
| | | | **NEW FUNDS & OTHERS*** | | | | | |
| $ 0.3 | 8.50% | $1.23 | All American Fund (started 2/64, formerly International & Common Market Fund) | | | — | $100.00 | 2.8% |
| 0.6 | none | 2.05 | American Enterprise Fund (started 9/58) | | | — | 113.59 | 1.9 |

*•Fund rated for two periods only; maximum allowable rating B+. *Includes funds started after 6/30/65 and all funds under $1 million which were not in existence for all measured periods.*

| Assets in Millions | Maximum Sales Charge % | Annual Expenses (Cents per $100) | 1966 FUND RATINGS | Consistency of Performance: In UP Markets | Consistency of Performance: In DOWN Markets | Management Results: 1953-1966 | Management Results: Latest 12 Months | Dividend Return % |
|---|---|---|---|---|---|---|---|---|
| | | | | | | $100 ENDED AS... | | |
| | | | Standard & Poor's 500 Stock Average | — | — | $362.91 | $100.74 | 3.4% |
| | | | Average of 10 stock funds in FORBES Index | C+ | C+ | $439.67 | $112.59 | 2.4% |
| | | | Average of 10 balanced funds in FORBES Index | — | — | $241.20 | $101.69 | 3.5% |
| | | | **NEW FUNDS & OTHERS*** | | | | | |
| $ 1.3 | none | — | American Investment Counseling Fund (started 7/65)... | | | — | — | — |
| 0.9 | none | $1.00 | American Pacific Fund (started 5/63)... | | | — | $ 81.55 | 0.3% |
| 0.4 | none | 1.00 | Beacon Hill Mutual Fund (started 12/64)... | | | — | 99.59 | 1.9 |
| 0.6 | none | 0.99 | Bridges Investment Fund (started 7/63)... | | | — | 101.73 | 2.6 |
| 0.4 | 8.00 | 1.03 | Central Mutual Fund (started 5/62)... | | | — | 84.02 | none |
| 0.8 | 7.50 | 1.30 | Commonwealth Fund for Growth (started 12/60)... | | | — | 137.44 | 0.7 |
| 0.4 | none | 1.10 | Connecticut Western Mutual Fund (started 6/64)... | | | — | 93.50 | 0.05 |
| 0.9 | 8.00 | 1.00 | Diversified Fund of State Bond & Mortgage Co. (started 7/64)... | | | — | 100.27 | 2.7 |
| 4.4 | none | 0.75 | Farm Bureau Mutual Fund (started 7/65)... | | | — | — | — |
| 0.3 | 8.50 | 2.43 | Invested Dollars Fund (started 8/63)... | | | — | 140.45 | 0.3 |
| 428.5 | 8.50 | — | Manhattan Fund (started 2/66)... | | | — | — | — |
| 0.8 | none | 0.65 | Mathers Fund (started 4/65)... | | | — | 126.48 | 0.7 |
| 0.8 | 5.00 | 0.75 | Meridian Fund (started 2/63)... | | | — | 112.94 | 2.0 |
| 0.7 | 8.50 | 0.53 | Mutual Income Fund (started 1/65)... | | | — | 100.42 | 4.3 |
| 0.9 | 8.50 | 1.00 | Mutual Securities Fund of Boston (started 5/58)... | | | — | 150.98 | 0.7 |
| 0.8 | 8.75 | 1.00 | Pilgrim Fund (started 8/64, formerly Pilgrim Financial & Growth Fund)... | | | — | 96.23 | 0.5 |
| 0.4 | 8.50 | 1.00 | Pioneer Enterprise Fund (started 7/57)... | | | — | 114.32 | 1.6 |
| 0.5 | 8.50 | 1.62 | Planned Investment Fund (started 5/61)... | | | — | 127.07 | 0.6 |
| 0.5 | 8.50 | 11.24 | Samson Fund (started 7/57)... | | | — | 208.17 | none |
| 0.6 | none | 1.03 | Trans-American Fund (started 9/60)... | | | — | 103.87 | 1.8 |
| 0.3 | 8.50 | 0.60 | Transwestern Mutual (started 6/61)... | | | — | 102.13 | 2.4 |
| 0.9 | 8.50 | 1.00 | Vanguard Fund (started 12/60)... | | | — | 124.55 | 0.4 |
| 0.4 | none | 4.10 | Venture Securities Fund (started 8/56)... | | | — | 134.09 | none |
| 0.7 | 8.30 | 5.06 | Worth Fund (started as open-end 5/60)... | | | — | 140.79 | none |
| | | | **EXCHANGE FUNDS†** | | | | | |
| $ 83.8 | — | — | Capital Exchange Fund (started 3/66)... | | | — | — | — |
| 11.3 | — | $0.62 | Centennial Fund (started 8/60)... | | | — | $108.31 | 1.6% |
| 9.9 | — | 0.63 | Second Centennial Fund (started 6/61)... | | | — | 108.41 | 1.6 |
| 45.7 | — | 0.56 | Congress Street Fund (started 4/61)... | | | — | 113.39 | 1.8 |
| 40.4 | — | 0.59 | Second Congress Street Fund (started 6/64)... | | | — | 115.31 | 1.5 |
| 83.2 | — | 0.55 | Depositors Fund of Boston (started 4/65)... | | | — | 108.81 | 1.7 |
| 27.1 | — | 0.62 | Devonshire Street Fund (started 7/61)... | | | — | 121.23 | 1.5 |
| 90.0 | — | 0.55 | Diversification Fund (started 7/61)... | | | — | 101.78 | 2.3 |
| 56.4 | — | 0.72 | Empire Fund (started 6/62)... | | | — | 111.03 | 0.2 |
| 18.2 | — | — | Second Empire Fund (started 3/65)... | | | — | 112.60 | 1.2 |
| 71.9 | — | 0.57 | Exchange Fund of Boston (started 9/63)... | | | — | 109.23 | 2.0 |
| 147.2 | — | 0.53 | Federal Street Fund (started 3/61)... | | | — | 118.80 | 1.7 |
| 16.0 | — | — | General Exchange Fund (started 8/65)... | | | — | — | — |
| 24.6 | — | 0.58 | Investors Capital Exchange (started 8/61)... | | | — | 115.59 | 1.3 |
| 7.9 | — | 0.68 | Ohio Capital Fund (started 11/61)... | | | — | 106.78 | 2.3 |
| 4.0 | — | — | Second Ohio Capital Fund (started 9/65)... | | | — | — | — |
| 16.0 | — | — | Presidential Exchange Fund (started 8/65)... | | | — | — | — |
| 70.2 | — | 0.60 | Westminster Fund (started 7/61)... | | | — | 114.05 | 1.7 |

**Includes funds started after 6/30/65 and all funds under $1 million which were not in existence for all measured periods. †Funds not offered for sale after initial offering; results are shown only for comparative purposes.*

# 18

# INSTITUTIONAL PORTFOLIO MANAGEMENT—I: COMMERCIAL AND SAVINGS BANKS

It is not a custom with me to keep money
to look at.

—George Washington

In the sections on institutional investment policies which follow, an effort will be made to organize our comments within the following framework.

### Framework of Discussion

1. What are the obligations of the particular financial institution? What is it established to do—its *raison d'être?*
2. What legal requirements apply to its investments?
3. How is investment income taxed?
4. Are there any "intangible" considerations such as politics, the psychology of the institution's clients, the character of its own personnel, etc., which act as constraints upon its investment operation?
5. How do these four factors affect the institution's investment objectives with regard to current income, capital gains, marketability, liquidity, safety?
6. How has the institution actually operated to achieve the indicated objectives?
7. What major areas for improvement are most apparent?

Primary emphasis will be placed, in the course of the discussion, on developments of the past dozen or so years. There are three major reasons for confining ourselves largely to this period without probing further backward in time. First, prior to the "Accord" between the Federal Reserve System and the U.S. Treasury, in March, 1951, interest rates had not for a decade been freely responsive to normal market forces. Second, there were several basic changes in legislation affecting institutional investments in the early 1950's. Finally, the Depression and World War II periods seem fairly irrelevant in connection with planning for the years ahead, while the 1920's are relevant but not amenable to detailed examination because of lack of space and of adequate data.

## COMMERCIAL BANKS

### Functions and Operating Environment

*Deposits and Loans.* A commercial bank has two principal functions:

1. It must provide safekeeping for depositors' money. This means that a bank at all times must be prepared to meet deposit withdrawals. The largest portion of deposits—demand deposits—are *legally* payable on demand. Even time and savings deposits, however, which are not demand liabilities in a legal sense, are expected by the customers to be paid on demand. (Negotiable certificates of deposit have a specific due date and are exceptions to this statement.)

2. It is expected to provide credit to worthy borrowers. Within the limits of its resources (which are, of course, affected by Federal Reserve policies), a commercial bank is supposed to screen loan applicants and make funds available to those deemed creditworthy and capable of repaying principal plus interest. A bank makes a loan by setting up a demand deposit in the name of the borrower. Since the borrower is, presumably, borrowing because he wants to use the money, the lending bank expects the newly created deposit to be drawn down quickly.

Banks have other functions in addition to the two enumerated. For example, they provide check-clearing facilities, trusteeship services, assistance with customers' international transactions, etc. But the two enumerated functions—meeting deposit withdrawals and making loans—are the most vital in our economy. Both of these functions, significantly, have a common denominator—liquidity.

*Liquidity.* A commercial banker has little fear that all of his depositors will demand their money at the same time. Since the advent of deposit insurance, "bank runs" have become rarities. Nevertheless, he cannot count on new deposit inflows always equaling or exceeding withdrawals. It is almost certain that there will be periods when withdrawals exceed new deposits. Even if this condition is temporary, as is likely in an expanding economy, at those times he must have "cash"[1] available to meet the net withdrawals.

[1] "Cash" in this context does not necessarily mean actual currency. More frequently, banks make payments by issuing checks against their deposits at other banks—usually at Federal Reserve banks.

A similar need for "cash" arises in connection with the lending function. When the borrower draws down his newly created deposit, some of the recipients of the funds probably will be depositors in the borrower's bank. Therefore, a portion of the withdrawn funds will return to the bank. But some will not, and for this portion the banker needs "cash." Since the term "liquidity" refers to the ability to raise cash, we say that commercial banks have a great need for liquidity because of the nature of their primary functions.

Now, most loans are illiquid. With certain exceptions, the banker cannot call up his borrowers at any time and say, "Pay up." Nor can the banker readily transfer the loans to some other party in exchange for cash. There are legal and customer relations impediments to such transactions, and even if they were possible the banker could not hope to realize the full par value of the loans. He would doubtless have to take losses.

Thus, every time a commercial bank makes a loan, with minor exceptions, the bank becomes less liquid. If it overstressed the loan aspect of its dual function, therefore, it would run the risk of becoming too illiquid to meet its deposit function satisfactorily. On the other hand, if it overstressed the deposit function, keeping all of its resources liquid, it would not carry out its social responsibility to make loans to worthy borrowers. Nor would it carry out its responsibility to its stockholders, which is to make an acceptable profit. For liquid resources typically produce little or no rate of return to their owners. And in our economic system, commercial banks are expected to be profit-making institutions.

*Safety.* The conflict between liquidity and profitability must be viewed in the context of yet another aspect of the commercial bank's operating environment. Table 18–1 presents a condensed version of the combined 1965 balance sheets of insured commercial banks, which represent 99% of the assets of all commercial banks in this country. One of the outstanding features of this combined balance sheet is the very small ratio of capital and reserves to total assets. Capital, surplus, and reserves typically represent between 7% and 9% of total assets. But even this small ratio is an overstatement, because it is a convention of the banking business that surplus is virtually as inviolable as capital. A reduction of surplus is generally looked upon in the financial community with almost the same gravity as an impairment of capital.

In seeking to earn a profit, a commercial bank must be aware of its small margin of safety. The only cushion for losses is its undivided profits and reserves—a slim 2%–3% of total assets. This means, in effect, that a bank must operate profitably not only over an extended period of time but year in and year out. If a severe net loss is sustained in any one year, the bank is washed up. The obvious concomitant of an inability to sustain sharp losses is an inability to take high risks.

*Investment Implications.* The foregoing discussion may be summa-

TABLE 18–1

**Principal Assets and Liabilities of Insured Commercial Banks, December 31, 1965**

| | *Billion $* | *% of Total* |
|---|---|---|
| Vault cash, federal reserve balances, and deposits in other banks | 60.4 | 15.9 |
| Loans and investments (before loss reserves*) | 308.8 | 81.4 |
| Bank premises and other assets | 10.2 | 2.7 |
| Total Assets | 379.4 | 100.0 |
| Demand deposits | 183.8 | 48.4 |
| Time deposits | 147.7 | 38.9 |
| Accounts payable, etc. | 14.0 | 3.7 |
| Capital, surplus, and reserves | 33.9 | 9.0 |
| Capital stock, notes, and debentures | 10.2 | 2.7 |
| Surplus | 13.5 | 3.6 |
| Reserves for loan losses* | 4.0 | 1.1 |
| Undivided profit and contingency reserves | 6.2 | 1.6 |
| Total Liabilities | 379.4 | 100.0 |

* In the original FDIC data, as in most reports of individual banks, reserves for loan losses are shown as a contra-item on the asset side of the balance sheet—i.e., loans are reported net of loss reserves. For the purpose of this table, however, which is to show the proportion of funds available to absorb operating losses, it seems more appropriate to carry loans gross, and show loan loss reserves as an addition to capital and other reserves.

Source: Federal Deposit Insurance Corp., *1965 Annual Report.*

rized as follows: A commercial bank has the dual function of meeting deposit withdrawals and making loans. This dual function requires that the bank have substantial liquid resources. But liquid resources are typically not very profitable, and a commercial bank is supposed to earn an adequate profit on the stockholders' investment. Compounding the difficulty of earning a satisfactory profit yet remaining acceptably liquid is the inability of the bank to undertake high risks because of its thin equity cushion.

This summary of the commercial bank's operating environment brings us precisely to the commercial bank's investment problem. An efficient bank must strike a compromise between an excessive loan position and an excessive cash position. The compromise is achieved via the investment portfolio. The function of a bank's investments is to earn as high a return as possible on unloaned resources while keeping these resources as safe and as liquid as possible in order to meet potential customer demands for them.

In other words, the ideal commercial bank investment portfolio is safe, liquid, and profitable. Since profitability is a goal in conflict with safety and liquidity, astute portfolio management involves a sensible balancing of opposing goals.

Lest it be thought that the commercial bank's investment problem is merely of academic interest, Table 18–2 shows that interest earned on security investments provides about one quarter of commercial bank gross operating earnings. Its contribution to net income is even greater, because the expenses of running an investment operation are proportionately lower than the expenses of a lending operation. (In this connection, we should note that mortgages are considered loans rather than investments in commercial banking terminology. While we have reservations about this classification, we shall abide by it in this chapter.) In addition to interest earned on investments, capital gains and losses are often a significant item in bank income statements. In fact, this area of activity often presents a bank's investment officers with the greatest opportunity to exercise their skills.

**TABLE 18–2**

**Income Account of Insured Commercial Banks, 1965**

| | *Billion $* | % |
|---|---|---|
| Current operating earnings | 16.82 | 100.0 |
| Interest on securities | 3.51 | 20.9 |
| Interest on loans and mortgages | 11.00 | 65.4 |
| Service charges, etc. | 2.31 | 13.7 |
| Current operating expenses | 12.49 | 74.3 |
| Net pretax operating income | 4.33 | 25.7 |
| Net security gains | 0.03 | 0.2 |
| Net loan losses and increase in reserves | (0.82) | (4.9) |
| Net before income taxes | 3.54 | 21.0 |
| Income taxes | 1.03 | 6.1 |
| Net income | 2.51 | 14.9 |
| Net income/Average capital* | 8.73% | |

* Average of capital, surplus, undivided profits and contingency reserves at beginning, middle, and end of year.

Source: Federal Deposit Insurance Corp., *1965 Annual Report*.

## Secondary Reserves

*Factors Influencing Liquidity Needs.* The first thing that should be determined by the investment officers of a commercial bank is the magnitude of the bank's liquidity requirements. Several specific factors influencing liquidity needs should be considered.

1. The seasonal pattern of deposit and loan fluctuation is, quantitatively, the most important and, fortunately, the most predictable liquidity factor. As illustrations of this factor we can cite the Christmas and other holiday cash needs of most communities, loan demands at income tax time, and the influence of crop seasons. Many of these seasonal patterns are so widespread that the Federal Reserve Board undertakes "open-market op-

erations" to help offset them. Otherwise, all banks would be drained of cash or in receipt of cash at the same time. But the Federal Reserve's operations do not put each individual bank in the same position. The larger the bank, the less important seasonal factors are, because when there is a diversified list of customers, some are likely to have peak seasonal cash needs simultaneously with the troughing of other customers' needs. But even the major New York City banks have strong seasonal liquidity requirements.

2. A bank's deposit structure is also a significant liquidity factor. Demand deposits are usually more volatile than time and savings deposits and, therefore, call for more liquidity. But different banks have different proportions of total deposits represented by demand deposits. The demand and time components, moreover, are far from homogeneous. For example, some banks are heavier than others in governmental deposits, which are often more volatile than those of businesses or individuals.[2] In addition, governmental depositors usually require that their deposits be backed by 100% or more of highest quality securities. As will be noted later, this collateral requirement significantly limits the investment options of a bank.

Some banks, especially in small communities, have a large proportion of total deposits represented by one or two businesses and are thus more vulnerable to sudden drains than banks with a more diversified clientele. As for nondemand deposits, it makes a big difference whether the major component is individual savings accounts or negotiable certificates of deposit. The latter, of course, must be considered "hot money" in comparison with the former.

3. Just as different banks have different deposit structures and thus different liquidity needs, so too are variations in bank loan structures reflected in liquidity needs. In recent years an increasing number of banks have put high percentages of their resources in business loans of 3 or more years' maturity—sometimes as high as 10 or even 15 years. The higher the proportion of "term loans," other things being equal, the greater a bank's liquidity needs. A short-term loan portfolio has more "built-in liquidity." Yet, many so-called short-term loans, with maturities of a year or less, are in reality long-term because they tend to be automatically renewed at maturity. But the renewal at least provides an opportunity for a credit review and gives the bank a choice among alternative uses of funds. Longer term loans mean more exposure to unanticipated problems. Similarly, heavy loan concentration in a particular geographic area or industry usually is indicative of greater liquidity needs.

---

[2] Not all governmental deposits are demand deposits. Increasingly, state and local governments have been keeping their funds in interest-bearing time deposits. However, since these do not represent permanently idle funds, they tend to be fairly volatile.

4. No commercial bank is flush with capital funds, but some banks are more richly endowed than others. If a bank has a fairly high ratio of capital and reserves to assets it has a greater ability to absorb losses if it should have to raise funds quickly by disposing of assets. Therefore, it is more willing to have illiquid assets than a bank which has a greater fear of running into losses if it has to sell assets to raise cash. In this connection, we might note the increasing tendency of banks to supplement stockholders' equity with issues of subordinated debentures (straight or convertible). Traditional concepts of the adequacy of equity capital relative to risk assets should be modified to reflect the fact that debt issues can supplement equity. However, a development which some observers look upon with misgivings is the apparent willingness of many bankers to view new issues of short-term promissory notes and certificates of deposit as a major source of liquidity and a substitute for long-term funds.

5. A final aspect of liquidity needs is one to which we shall refer frequently. It has to do with the impact of the business cycle on a bank's operations. In pre–World War II days, depressions were marked by financial panics—liquidity crises wherein whole communities rushed for cash at once. Since then, conditions have changed dramatically. In each postwar recession, commercial bank deposits have actually risen. Money has been pumped into the economy through the unbalancing of the federal budget, the operations of the Federal Reserve System, unemployment compensation, farm price supports, etc. Add to this the deposit insurance system and it is understandable why the public not only refrains from withdrawing bank funds but rather seeks the haven of bank deposits during periods of economic stress. Individual banks, of course, may be strained during recessions, but for the most part we may say that a commercial bank's greatest need for liquidity is during periods of boom rather than recession. In boom periods the demand for bank loans becomes almost insatiable, and idle bank deposits are kept to a minimum.

All of these liquidity factors can be quantified and planned for, in greater or lesser degree. In addition, random movements can be allowed for by examining the historical record and building in a margin for error. Let us assume, therefore, that a bank's managers decide that there is a definite need for $X$ dollars of liquidity and a possible need for $Y$ additional dollars. Part of these needs will be kept in the form of vault cash, and the balance is invested in liquid securities. The question to which we must next turn is: What kind of securities are appropriate for the liquid investment portfolio—the so-called "secondary reserves," as distinguished from the "primary," or legally required, reserves (which now can include vault cash)?

*Investing for Liquidity.* A liquid security is one which can be disposed of in substantial quantities, at short notice, with negligible capital loss. Therefore, the term "liquidity," when applied to a security, immediately implies a high degree of marketability. That is, securities to be considered liquid must have a market in which there are continuous bids and offers for large quantities, with a narrow spread between the bid and offer prices. By narrow spread we mean a maximum of about one quarter of 1% (for example, 100 bid, 100¼ asked).

In addition to a good market, the negligible capital loss requirement of the liquidity definition implies a fixed income, fixed principal, fixed maturity security entailing no credit risk. That is, the security must be a debt in form, and there must be virtually no risk that the issuer will fail to meet the interest and principal payments when they come due.

Since capital loss can occur on a debt issue as a result of rising interest rates in addition to actual defaults of payments, liquidity implies minimization of the interest rate risk. As demonstrated in Chapter 11, this risk varies directly with the length of time to maturity. Therefore, liquidity suggests very short maturity. Short maturity also protects against the purchasing power and credit risks, because there is little time within which prices can rise or the borrower get into financial difficulty.

What kinds of securities possess the liquidity characteristics of excellent marketability, unimpeachable quality, and short maturity? The answer is: (1) U.S. Treasury bills, certificates of indebtedness, and notes or bonds nearing maturity; (2) short-term issues of the independent government agencies—in particular the Federal National Mortgage Association ("Fannie Mae") and the Federal Home Loan Bank; (3) short-term general obligations of large states and municipalities; and (4) high-grade commercial paper and bankers' acceptances.[3] Of these, only short-term U.S. Treasury issues are available in the large quantities required by the banking system. Thus, the *X* dollars considered absolutely necessary for liquidity will usually be kept mostly in Treasury issues with under one-year maturity. (However, as will be noted later, more and more banks have recently been using short-term state and local issues for liquidity needs).

The possible *Y* additional dollars which may be needed for liquidity are usually kept mostly in one- to three-year Treasury issues if the short-term yield curve is sufficiently upward sloping to warrant maturity extensions beyond one year, and also in high-grade state and municipal general obligations. The yields on the latter are quite attractive when their tax-exempt status is taken into account (see discussion of tax-exempts below). When one- to three-year issues are purchased, a policy of "spaced maturities" is typically followed. For example, 20% of the issues may mature in one year, 20% in 18 months, 20% in two years, etc. In this way,

---

[3] The latter, together with other secondary reserve assets such as certificates of the Commodity Credit Corporation and call loans, show up to a large extent in the loan, rather than the investment, portion of a bank's balance sheet.

liquidity is provided as much by the fact that a large portion of the portfolio matures periodically as by the fact that the portfolio can be readily sold at face value.

The importance of short-term U.S. Treasury securities to commercial banks can be seen in Figure 18–1. In recent years, about 20% of total

**FIGURE 18–1**

**Asset Distribution of Insured Commercial Banks**

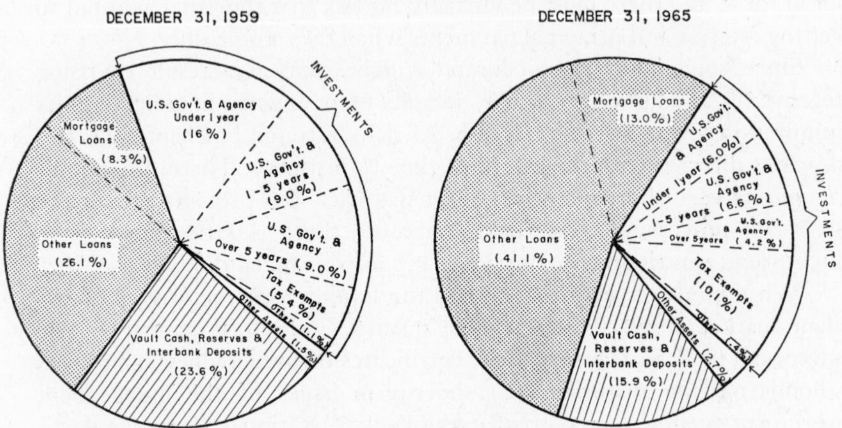


Sources: Federal Deposit Insurance Corp., *Annual Reports; Treasury Bulletin.*

assets has been represented by federal issues. Of these issues, about 80% has been under five years' maturity, with about one third under one year. As for tax-exempt security investments of commercial banks, no system-wide maturity distributions are available, but data for *National* banks at the end of 1965 show that 20% were of less-than-one-year maturity and 29% were of one- to five-year maturity.

### Other Investments

We turn next to a consideration of the potential outlets for any investable funds that may be left over after providing for liquidity needs. The first factor to recognize in this connection is the restraint imposed by the law and by the collateral requirements of governmental deposits. In addition, tax considerations must be taken into account. Finally, the pros and cons of different investment media can be compared.

*Legal Restrictions.* Commercial banks are among the most regulated financial institutions in the country. With regard to investments, the regulations of the Comptroller of the Currency, established for national banks, have generally set the tone for state banking commissions as well.

Briefly, commercial banks may invest freely in federal, state, and most municipal obligations, including the obligations of special local revenue authorities. They may not invest over 10% of capital and surplus (in some jurisdictions, undivided profits are added to the surplus base) in the securities of any one corporation, and these securities must meet at least two standards:

1. They must be fixed income, fixed principal securities. Preferred and common stocks are prohibited, except for Federal Reserve bank stock and stock in certain bank subsidiaries such as international investing corporations established under the Edge Act.

2. They may not be "predominantly speculative," which phrase is generally defined as not falling within the top four ratings of the leading bond rating agencies. Convertible bonds, moreover, may be bought only if the premium for the conversion feature is small.

Securities which are legally eligible are entitled to be carried on a bank's books at cost, with regular amortization of premiums and, if desired, accrual of discounts. Ineligible securities, on the other hand, must be carried at lower of cost or market. In a declining bond market, therefore, paper losses on ineligible investments would reduce the bank's capital adequacy ratios. As a result, banks are effectively restrained from investing in lower grade securities. This being the case, it is clear that the type of security eligible for the less liquid portion of a commercial bank's portfolio includes U.S. government obligations beyond the three-year maturity range; good-quality state, municipal, and local revenue obligations; and good-quality corporate bonds.

*Collateral Requirements.* Even this relatively limited list of securities which are legally eligible for a bank's investment portfolio is something of an overstatement. Governmental depositors usually require that banks set aside U.S. government securities or general obligations of state and local governments as collateral against their deposits. Often, the collateral requirement is in excess of 100% of the deposited amounts. It has been estimated that about one third of all commercial bank security holdings at the end of 1965 represented such deposit collateral. Thus, a bank's flexibility in managing the nonliquidity portion of its investment portfolio may be significantly restricted over and above the legal limitations described previously.

*Tax Status.* Commercial banks are taxed at normal corporate tax rates—currently 48% on ordinary net income over $25,000 and 22% on lesser amounts. Net long-term capital gains are taxed at 25%, like those of other corporations.[4] However, capital losses receive favorable treatment

---

[4] However, this applies only to gains incurred in the regular banking-investing operation. Gains of bank *dealer* departments are treated as fully taxed ordinary income.

not accorded to other investors. As is always true, capital losses must first be offset against any capital gain in the same year to determine whether there is a net gain or loss. But if there is a net loss, it may be offset in full by a bank (savings banks and savings and loans in addition to commercial banks) against regular operating income. Other corporations, on the other hand, can merely carry net capital losses forward for five years to be offset against future capital gains but can never offset them against regular income.[5] This feature of the tax law has important implications for bank investment policy, as we shall note later in the chapter.[6]

*Tax-Exempt Bonds versus U.S. Government Bonds.* During the postwar period, the flood of state and local government financing caused a sharp rise in the yields of tax-exempt obligations relative to the yields of fully taxable federal obligations. Since 1952, the yields on highest grade long-term tax-exempts have averaged about 80% of fully taxable long-term Treasury bond yields. In July, 1966, for example, Aaa tax-exempts traded at an average yield of 3¾% compared with 4¾% on long-term government bonds. Admittedly, the quoted yields on many tax-exempts is not really all tax-free, because many of these issues are selling at discounts and the yield therefore includes some taxable capital gain. Even taking this into account, however, it is clear that banks in the 48% tax bracket can earn considerably more after tax on tax-exempts than on governments. The spread widens, moreover, on investments in slightly lower rated general obligations and widens even further on good-quality revenue issues.

Traditionally, there has been a reluctance on the part of many commercial bankers to take advantage of the high after-tax yields on state and local bonds. This reluctance stems from the rather unusual nature of the market for these issues. Among the factors which have been noted by bankers are:

1. The bonds are issued by hundreds of different governmental units, many of them quite small and with little information available about them. This impairs their marketability.

2. The bonds are issued in serial form. That is, instead of selling, say, $10 million of 20-year bonds and retiring $500,000 each year through a sinking fund, a local government breaks the $10 million up into many small blocks with different maturities—1 year, 2 years . . . 20 years, etc. This is done in recognition of the segmented nature of the demand side of the market. For example, a long-term investor may hesitate to purchase a 20-year bond which may be called for sinking fund purposes long before

---

[5] *Individuals* having no capital gains against which to offset losses may offset ordinary income to the extent of $1,000 annually.

[6] The reader should be aware, however, that discussions have been held in Washington regarding a thorough overhauling of the favorable capital loss treatment received by banks.

maturity. By the same token, an investor desiring liquidity will not buy a 20-year bond, with or without a sinking fund; he wants a one- to three-year issue. But while the serial method of issue is efficient in this regard, each serial maturity is, in effect, an individual small issue and therefore has a relatively thin market.

3. Price movements in the state and local market are often quite volatile because smaller investors are important factors in the market and because many dealers in the market carry large inventories on small capitalizations and are quick to sell out at the first sign of trouble.

While these observations about the nature of the tax-exempt market are, in general, correct, in our opinion the lack of marketability has been unduly exaggerated by many bankers. Indeed, banks like the Chemical in New York and the Mellon in Pittsburgh have actually used short-term tax exempts as secondary reserves and have demonstrated that it is possible to dispose quickly of tens of millions of dollars worth of tax-exempts without disrupting the market—even in a bear market. The secret is to have a well-spaced maturity structure and an intimate familiarity with supply-demand conditions in different segments of the market. Certainly, the extra yield obtainable on these issues warrants the expense involved in developing the necessary expertise. A side advantage of owning tax-exempts, and one of the many "intangible" factors in institutional portfolio management, is the maintenance of good public relations in the local communities issuing the securities.

Figure 18–1 shows that bankers recently have been having second thoughts about their traditional attitudes toward tax-exempt obligations. The percentage of assets represented by tax-exempts has risen to 10% of all commercial bank assets from half that percentage a dozen years ago. This despite the fact that *total* investments have declined sharply as a percent of assets, offsetting the rapidly rising loan proportion.

Some observers believe that the increase in time deposit rates since 1962 has forced banks to seek higher yielding investments such as tax-exempts. Others believe that the gradual recognition of the attractiveness of tax-exempts, as well as a high demand for loans, has encouraged banks to offer higher rates on time deposits. Like the question of whether the chicken or egg came first, there probably will never be a satisfactory answer to the question of whether higher time deposit rates caused a search for high-yielding investments or vice versa.

*Corporate Bonds versus U.S. Government Bonds.* On the surface of things, corporate bonds might seem desirable investments for the nonliquidity portion of a commercial bank's portfolio, at least in preference to long-term U.S. government bonds. In the first place, yields are considerably higher. Since 1952, yields on corporate bonds of Aaa to A quality have averaged 110%–120% of long-term government bonds, and Baa's have been 5%–10% higher yet.

In addition to having higher yields, corporate bonds have been less volatile in yield and price than government bonds. Indeed, price stability has tended to vary inversely with quality. This may sound wrong to the reader, but further thought will reveal why it is not. Government bonds, having no credit risk, respond in price solely to cyclical changes in interest rates. Corporate bonds respond to both interest rate changes and credit factors, and the lower the quality, the greater the latter influence. Thus, in a recession, when the level of interest rates is falling, government bond prices rise in response. Corporate bond prices also rise, but lower quality issues seem less creditworthy in recession, and their prices rise less. On the other hand, in boom times, when rising interest rates drive government bond prices down, lower quality corporates go down less because (*a*) they previously hadn't risen as much, and (*b*) they now seem like better credit risks than they did before. Another reason for the greater price volatility of governments is that the open-market operations of the Federal Reserve and the response of the commercial banks have their initial and major impacts in this sector, spilling over into the rest of the capital market with a lag and with less force.

The combination of higher yield and greater price stability than on government bonds would seem to suggest that Baa corporate bonds would be highly desirable commercial bank investments. However, as indicated in Chapter 10, Table 10–3, there is a fairly high chance that Baa bonds will subsequently be downgraded, thus becoming ineligible under banking law, with the attendant penalty of having to mark their prices down to market. The risk of this happening even to A-rated issues is also sizable.

While Aaa and Aa corporate bonds also provide yield advantages over long-term governments, the spreads are not as great as on A's and Baa's, especially in recent years. Moreover, the banker sees other disadvantages in these issues:

1. They are not as marketable as long-term governments if they should have to be sold.
2. Government bonds are not considered risk assets by bank examiners whereas corporates are. Therefore, to maintain a given capital/risk asset ratio, more capital is necessary with a portfolio of corporate bonds than with a portfolio of governments.
3. Most important, corporate risks are already underwritten in the loan portfolio, and diversification requires that investment risks be concentrated elsewhere.

We are in general agreement with these observations. However, we would note, with regard to item (1), that the marketability of long-term government bonds is frequently not as good as commonly supposed. With regard to item (2), state and local obligations are also considered risk assets, yet their extra yield after taxes has apparently been sufficient to overcome the capital requirement factor. (Some capital adequacy formulas, however, require less capital for state and local issues than for corporates.) We are most impressed with item (3), and think it is sufficient justification for the very low proportion of commercial bank assets represented by corporate bonds (see Figure 18–1).

### Timing Considerations

*Principles.* By the nature of a commercial bank's business, the timing aspect of investment management does not really involve the question of when to be a net buyer or a net seller. A bank does not have much discretion in this regard. It buys on balance when investable funds are plentiful—usually in a recession, when interest rates are low and bond prices high. It sells on balance when loanable funds are scarce—usually in a boom, when interest rates are high and bond prices low. Thus, a bank's investing takes place in a perverse (from the bank's point of view) environment. It always tends to buy and sell at the wrong time, buying when prices are high and selling when they are low. Good timing, therefore, means making the best of a difficult situation. It boils down, in the final analysis, to the proper management of the maturity structure. Good timing means knowing when to shift from intermediate and long-term issues into shorter term issues, and when to shift back again.

If a bank's managers could predict accurately the course of the interest rate and loan demand cycles, their general investment strategy should be as follows. At the bottom of the cycle, switch the bulk of the portfolio into short-term securities. This is because the trough of the cycle will be followed by a rise in loan demands and interest rates. The Federal Reserve System, at that time, can usually be expected to cut back the rate at which it supplies reserves to the banks. Therefore, any given bank can expect to have to sell off some of its investments to raise loan funds. This being the case, the shorter the maturity of the investments being sold, the less the loss on sale during a period of rising interest rates.

By the same token, at the very peak of the cycle any remaining investment funds should be shifted into long-term securities. This is because a period of falling loan demands and interest rates can be expected to follow. If the bank has previously "gone long," it will have assured itself of high current interest income on those funds during the course of the recession and, in addition, can achieve capital gains when, at the bottom of the cycle, it sells its long-term securities and shifts into liquid issues. Furthermore, as the bank builds up additional investable funds during the recession, when the Federal Reserve is pumping funds into the system, the funds should be invested in long-terms until, as noted earlier, the bottom of the cycle has been hit, when they should be shifted—probably at a profit—into shorts.

It is clear, then, that if a bank's managers had perfect foresight they could turn the perverse environment to their advantage. The trouble is that even the most expert bankers and economists do not have perfect foresight. Unfortunately, the shape of the yield curve is such that premature shifting of portfolio maturities will hurt a bank's performance relative to that of its competitors.

*Influence of the Yield Curve.* The impact of the business cycle on the shape of the yield curve was discussed at some length in Chapter 13. To briefly reiterate, when the level of interest rates is low (usually in recession), the yield curve is usually upward sloping. That is, longer maturities yield more than shorter. As the level of interest rates rises (in a period of economic recovery), the yield curve flattens out. Yields tend to be similar at all but the very shortest maturities. Finally, when the level of interest rates is quite high (during the boom phase of the cycle, as a rule), the yield curve takes on a ski-sloped shape. Longer maturities yield less than shorter, and there may be a high "hump" at around the five-year maturity range.

Now, let us suppose that the economy is in recession. Loan demands and interest rates are low, and there is considerable pressure on the investment managers to beef up the bank's earnings through the security portfolio. The yield curve is upward sloping, so longer term securities are emphasized. All is well and good up to a point—the point when sound principles require the portfolio managers to decide when the trough of the cycle is at hand. If they estimate the timing of the trough correctly, and move the portfolio into short-term issues just at the right time, they have more than earned their salaries. Indeed, they are heroes. But suppose they are wrong, and the recession persists. Or suppose the recession does, in fact, end but the monetary authorities maintain easy credit conditions for an extended period of time, which is precisely what happened for several years following the 1960–61 recession. Here the bank will be with a portfolio of liquid, low-yielding securities, when its competitors are still in longer term, higher yielding issues. (Of course, banks in this position after 1960–61 did not fare badly, because short-term rates were maintained at a fairly high level in relation to long-term rates.)

The investment manager's dilemma is similar during boom periods. Suppose he tries to anticipate the end of the boom and moves into long-term securities. But suppose he is premature, and the boom continues. He will be earning lower yields than if his maturity structure were shorter (because the yield curve is downward sloping during booms), and he will take heavier capital losses when he has to continue selling securities to raise funds for loans.

Obviously, good timing involves a sensible balancing of the rewards to be gained by correct forecasts against the penalties to be suffered if the forecasts are incorrect.

*Swap Transactions.* Several pages back, it was pointed out that banks can charge net capital losses against ordinary 48%–taxed operating income while, at the same time, paying only 25% tax on net long-term capital gains. This unique feature of the tax law has two influences on bank investment timing policy. First, it causes banks to make a strong effort not to take both capital gains and capital losses in the same calendar year.

Since capital losses can be offset against ordinary income only after having first been offset against any capital gains for the year, the fullest tax advantage is achieved when capital losses are registered in a no-gains year. Early in every calendar year, therefore, a bank's management tries to look ahead and decide whether security transactions are more likely to result in gains or losses during the year. On the basis of the outlook, they designate the year a "loss year" or a "gains year" and try to concentrate on one or the other type of transaction during the year.

The ability to charge capital losses against ordinary income is particularly advantageous, because losses are most likely to be taken during boom periods, when securities have to be sold to raise loanable funds. During such periods, interest income from loans is rising, and any offsets are most welcome. Even if securities do not have to be sold to raise loanable funds, however, it may pay to sell at capital losses anyhow, in what is known as a "swap" transaction.

Suppose a bank has securities which it purchased at par and which are now selling at a discount in the open market. If the bank sells the securities at a loss and immediately repurchases similar, but not identical, securities at a discount from par, the following tax consequences ensue. The loss is offset against 48%–taxed operating income (if there are no capital gains in the same year), and the capital gain that will be earned when the newly purchased discount bonds mature is taxed at only 25% (if there are no capital losses the same year). The result is a saving of approximately 23% of the value of the transaction, the exact amount depending on the prices and coupon rates of the securities involved. In addition, if the transaction is undertaken at what seems to be the peak of the interest rate cycle, the opportunity can be used to lengthen the maturity of the portfolio by purchasing issues of longer maturity than those sold. (Note: the securities purchased cannot be identical to those sold or the Internal Revenue will consider the transaction a "wash sale" and not allow the loss to be offset against income.)

An advantageous swap can also be executed in a period of falling interest rates. Assume that a security which was purchased at par has gone to a premium. Sell the security, paying a 25% tax on the capital gain, if there are no capital loss offsets, and repurchase another premium issue (of shorter maturity if the bottom of the cycle seems to be at hand). In subsequent years, the amortization of premium is a capital loss which can be offset against highly taxed ordinary income if there are no capital gains in those years. The savings here are less than in the previously described transaction. Here the capital gains tax is paid immediately, and the income offsets are realized later and probably not in full (because there are likely to be capital gains in at least some of the later years), whereas in the previous transaction the offset was immediate and most likely in full, with the capital gains tax coming later. But the room for astute maneuvering should be apparent to the reader.

*Accounting Influences.* To some extent, commercial bankers have failed to take maximum advantage of timing opportunities because of a "noneconomic," yet very real, factor. We refer to the nature of commercial bank accounting practices, whereby most capital gains and losses show up as nonrecurring, "below-the-line," items and are therefore given less weight by the investment community than interest income. As a result, bankers tend to prefer interest income to capital gain, even though the net after-tax yield is higher for the latter. Some illustrations will clarify our point:

1. By moving into short-term securities at the bottom of a recession, current interest income is sacrificed (yield curve is upward sloping) in order to minimize subsequent capital losses. But since interest income is "above the line" whereas capital losses are below, a banker may be tempted to stay in longer and higher yielding maturities even if he knows he should be shortening.

2. By moving into long-term securities at the peak of a boom, current interest income is sacrificed (yield curve slopes downward) in order to maximize subsequent capital gains. But above- and below-the-line considerations may prompt the banker to stay in, say, five-year issues, which have the highest yields then available.

3. The purchase of low-coupon, deep-discount issues, in swaps or other transactions, may sometimes be discouraged because capital gain is not as "important" as coupon income.

Gradually, the accounting, banking, and investment communities are becoming aware of these paradoxes. They are recognizing that whereas capital gains and losses are extraordinary, nonrecurring items for, say, a manufacturing concern, they are quite normal for a commercial bank. Consequently, astute or inadequate management of investments should be taken into account in evaluating a bank's performance. It is now becoming increasingly common for banks to accrue security discounts (net of deferred tax liabilities) above the line, just as they have always amortized bond premiums, and for security analysts to add or deduct some average of capital gains or losses to regular operating income in computing a bank's normal earning power. Hopefully, this trend will produce a more rational management of commercial bank investments than has heretofore been observable.

*Mechanical Timing Policies.* It is apparent that basic to successful timing is an ability to discern pending shifts in business and monetary conditions. But many bankers, particularly in small towns, have admitted an inability to forecast with any degree of accuracy. Our recommendation to such bankers would be to consult their large-city correspondents who have, or should have, greater skills along these lines. Some small-town bankers do, indeed, follow such a course. But others have tackled the problem by resorting to more mechanical techniques.

One very popular approach is to set aside a normal, or average, liquidity reserve, regardless of the state of the business cycle, and to invest any remaining unloaned funds on an evenly spaced 10- to 20-year maturity schedule. That is, equal portions are invested in one-year, two-year, three-year issues, etc. In this way, 5% or 10% of the portfolio matures every year. If the funds are not needed for loans, they are reinvested in the longest maturity permitted under the program, enabling the cycle to continue. If they are needed for loans, the remaining portfolio may either be left as is, or redistributed to achieve even spacing out to the longest maturity.

The advantage of a spaced-maturity program is that regardless of the nature of interest rate fluctuations, a bank assures itself of an average rate of return on its investments without the headaches of actively managing a portfolio. Moreover, if there should be a long period of consistently upward-sloping yield curves at a constant level of rates (for example, during the pre-1951 "pegging"), a bank can convert some of its interest income into capital gain form. This is known as "riding the yield curve." It refers to the fact that if the yield curve remains upward sloping and the level of interest rates does not rise, long-term bonds go to premium prices in the open market merely through the passage of time. For example, a 20-year bond will sell, after 5 years, at the yield level of a 15-year bond, which is lower than the original yield of the 20-year issue. The lower yield means a higher price. Therefore, a bank with evenly spaced maturities can get the higher interest income available on long-term issues and can sell the long-terms at a profit after a few years and redistribute its portfolio to restore equal spacing. However, there is an ever present danger in such an investment policy that interest rates will rise and yield curves flatten, in which case bond sales would involve serious capital losses.

A question that frequently arises, both in a spaced-maturity program and in a more flexible program of switching back and forth between long-term and short-term securities, is the maximum bond maturity that should be permitted. Being highly conscious of liquidity and price volatility, many bankers are reluctant to go beyond about 15 years. In our opinion, these bankers have a mistaken notion about the price characteristics of intermediate-term versus long-term bonds. It is certainly true that long-term bonds—say, 20 years or more to maturity—are more volatile in price than shorter-term issues—say, 5 years or less. But experience suggests that 10- to 15-year bonds have little or no more price stability than 20- to 30-year issues. Since the latter usually yield about the same as, or higher than, the former (except in periods of very tight money), a good case can be made for either limiting long-term maturities to 10 years or pushing out to around 25 years. Beyond 25 years, the yield curve is usually flat, and further maturity extensions are usually worthless.

An increasingly popular technique of mechanical portfolio management is known as "allocation of assets."[7] This technique is based on the theory that a commercial bank is really a combination of four distinctive types of funds: (1) very volatile demand deposits, (2) less volatile demand and time deposits, (3) savings accounts, and (4) bank capital. Banks adopting the asset allocation technique classify their liabilities into these four segments and adopt a portfolio policy for each sector—so much percent for primary reserves, so much for secondary reserves, long-term investments, commercial loans, consumer loans, mortgages, etc. The policy is designed to provide the *maximum* necessary liquidity and is maintained under virtually all conditions.

Since the high-liquidity position of asset allocation entails reduced earnings, an attempt is made to levy various service charges on the grounds that a bank is a customer-servicing institution rather than an investing institution, and therefore customers should be willing to pay the bank for the privilege of always being able to call upon its services. The service-charge device, of course, is most feasible in communities where bank competition is limited. Many banks, it should be noted, use asset allocation as a device for setting a general policy framework but exercise considerable discretion within the broad framework. This use of the technique appeals to us in much the same way as formula planning appeals to us in managing a common stock portfolio (see Chapter 15).

## MUTUAL SAVINGS BANKS AND SAVINGS AND LOAN ASSOCIATIONS

### The Nature of the Institutions

*Organization.* Mutual savings banks operate under state charters in only 18 different states, and over 85% of their deposits are located in four states—New York, Massachusetts, Connecticut, and Pennsylvania. In contrast, savings and loan associations may be either federally or statechartered and operate throughout the nation. The savings banks are currently seeking legislation which would establish federal chartering and permit them to expand their industry.

---

[7] For greater details than presented here, see H. E. Zarker, *Allocation of Commercial Bank Funds* (Bankers Publishing Co., 1957).

Virtually all savings banks are mutual organizations. Most savings and loan associations are also mutuals. However, almost two dozen states permit the latter to be stockholder owned, and in those states, stock associations represent about 40% of all savings and loan assets (over 20% of total U.S. savings and loan assets). Stock association growth has been particularly pronounced in California, Ohio, and Texas.

Depositors in mutual savings banks and savings and loan associations either do not possess any voting rights or do not generally exercise such rights as they may possess. Management powers are usually vested in a self-perpetuating board of trustees, whose members are mostly prominent businessmen and civic leaders rather than bankers and who, therefore, elect a full-time staff of executive officers. The board confines itself essentially to policy-review functions.

The average deposit in these institutions is about $2,500, but the average is lifted by relatively small numbers of large accounts. Membership in either the Federal Deposit Insurance Corporation or Federal Savings and Loan Insurance Corporation provides deposit insurance up to $15,000 per depositor. Although there are legal differences in the two types of insurance, depositors are about equally protected under both. Depositors should be wary, however, when the insurer is an institution other than one of these two federal agencies.

*Liquidity Needs.* The law permits savings banks and savings and loan associations to require 30 to 60 days' notice of intent to withdraw deposits. In practice, however, the public has become accustomed to being able to make withdrawals on demand. Indeed, more and more savers seem to be using their savings accounts in lieu of checking accounts. For a fee of 10 cents or 15 cents most savings institutions will issue money orders or cashier's checks against withdrawals by depositors appearing in person, and some institutions levy no fee.[8] Therefore, liquidity is needed to assure the ability to meet withdrawals.

Like commercial banks, although to a lesser degree, savings banks and savings and loan associations have seasonal peaks and troughs in cash needs. For example, withdrawals have a distinct tendency to rise at the end of dividend periods, reflecting the withdrawal of dividends and the previous postponement of withdrawals in order to qualify for the upcoming dividends. In addition, as will be seen below, these institutions are predominantly mortgage lenders. As such, their cash outflows are related to the seasonal pattern of construction.

Liquidity needs are also affected by the competition of other savings media. For example, in October, 1959, when the Treasury offered its widely publicized 5%, 4-year–10-month notes—the so-called "Magic

---

[8] Savings banks in New Jersey, Maryland, and Indiana may actually offer checking account services.

Fives"—mutual savings banks lost $200 million of deposits. This was the largest monthly decline of the postwar period up to that time, larger even than the drop that took place in the summer of 1950, when consumers went on a war-hedging buying spree. Banks located in large financial centers and having the largest size accounts were hardest hit. The competition of other savings and investment media was again severe in 1966, when commercial banks began to offer high-yield nonnegotiable certificates of deposit to individuals in small denominations, and when government and government agency bonds rose in yield to 5% and higher.

Deposit withdrawals for investment in stocks, bonds, and other savings media usually occur during boom conditions and come on top of increased withdrawals for consumer durables purchases. During recession, on the other hand, consumers retrench in their spending and are reluctant to draw down savings accounts. Thus, the liquidity needs of savings institutions have a cyclical as well as a seasonal component.

Despite these apparent needs for liquidity, few savings institutions have ever been under real pressure to liquidate assets in order to meet deposit withdrawals. In general, receipts of new deposits and accrued interest left on deposit has typically been in excess of withdrawals. This has been particularly true of mutual savings banks and somewhat less true of savings and loans. On the other hand, the latter are assisted in providing for liquidity needs by their membership in the Federal Home Loan Bank System. Member associations may borrow, at quite reasonable rates, up to 17½% of their savings accounts from the FHLB, and even more in emergencies. Few associations have borrowed the 17½% limit,[9] but it is fairly common to borrow 5%–10%. Indeed, the industry as a whole is almost always in a net indebtedness position within this range of magnitude.[10] Mutual savings banks are also eligible for membership in the Federal Home Loan Bank System, but few have joined. Fewer still have ever borrowed in any form permitted by law, apparently feeling that public confidence might be sacrificed by such transactions.

*Economic Role and Earnings Pressure.* The function of a mutual savings bank is to safeguard depositors' money and to earn as high a rate of return as is consistent with that primary responsibility. Savings and loan associations have the additional function, explicitly stated in their charters, of channeling savings into residential construction. Although

[9] In 1966 several California associations reached the maximum.

[10] It may be noted, however, that in April, 1966, the chairman of the Home Loan Bank Board stated that loans should not be granted to member savings and loan associations as a substitute for permanent additions to capital. In the future, he said, loans would not be granted to savings and loan associations which fail to gear their operations to their actual expected cash flows. See *The New York Times,* April 28, 1966, p. 62.

earnings maximization is not, theoretically, the primary goal of either type of institution, intense competition for the savings dollar puts constant pressure on the managers to improve earnings. If any single savings institution's dividend-paying ability falls significantly behind that of its competitors, the institution will not only fail to maintain its share of new deposits but may face net withdrawals. This would force it to maintain an abnormally high liquidity position or to sell off high-earning assets, either of which actions would further worsen earnings and aggravate withdrawals.

A sense of the earnings constraints under which savings banks and savings and loans operate can perhaps best be conveyed by referring to their income and expense ratios (see Table 18–3). Annual operating

**TABLE 18–3**

**Principal Income Account Items of Mutual Savings Banks (Insured*) and Savings and Loan Associations, 1965**

(% of Average Deposits)

| | *Savings Banks* | *Savings & Loan Ass'ns.* |
|---|---|---|
| Interest and discount on mortgages | 4.6 | 6.4 |
| Interest and dividends on securities | 0.9 | 0.3 |
| Total current operating income | 5.5 | 6.7 |
| Current operating expenses | 0.7 | 1.3 |
| Income and franchise taxes | 0.1 | 0.4 |
| Dividends to depositors | 4.2 | 4.2 |
| Net additions to surplus | 0.5 | 0.8 |

* Representing about 85% of total savings bank assets.
Source: Federal Deposit Insurance Corp., *1965 Annual Report;* U.S. Savings & Loan League, *1966 Savings and Loan Fact Book.*

expenses and taxes for a mutual savings bank generally run about 0.8% of deposits. For savings and loan associations the figure is twice as high, primarily because of their heavier commitment to mortgages (mortgages cost more to originate and service per dollar invested than securities) and because they typically do more advertising and promotion to gain new accounts.

In addition to operating expenses, well-run institutions must build up their surplus and loss reserves in line with deposit growth. Otherwise, their ratios of surplus and reserves to deposits will decline steadily and eventually produce an untenable situation. Surplus and reserve ratios have averaged 8%–10% of deposits for mutual savings banks in recent years and 7%–9% for savings and loan associations. To maintain these ratios, annual additions to surplus and reserves have averaged about one half of 1% of deposits for savings banks and over three fourths of 1% for savings and loans.

When the necessary addition to surplus and reserves is added to operating expenses, the conclusion is reached that the gross rate of return earned on deposits must be at least 1¼ percentage points higher than the interest rate paid on deposits by savings banks, and about 2½ percentage points higher in the case of savings and loans. When most savings banks and savings and loan associations pay 4¼% on deposits, as in 1965, or higher, as in 1966, gross earnings rates on deposits have to be at least 5½% for the former and close to 7% for the latter. Making allowance for the fact that invested surplus, reserves, and borrowings also produce earnings, minimum required gross rates of return on total assets have to be at least 5% and 6%, respectively. This is no meager objective in view of the institutions' needs for liquidity and safety. And it is complicated by the fact that when competitive pressures force up the rates paid on deposits, the higher rates have to be paid on all deposits, old and new,[11] whereas only new funds plus cash inflow from amortization of existing investments are available for investment in higher yielding assets.

### Legal Restrictions on Investments[12]

In their efforts to achieve high rates of return on investments, savings institutions must stay within certain prescribed legal limits. Detailed discussion of the laws of each jurisdiction is beyond our present scope, but some indication of their nature can be given. For example, New York State mutual savings banks have the following major restrictions on their investments:

1. A maximum of 75% of assets may be placed in conventional mortgages; there is no limit on government-insured mortgages. (Note that, unlike our discussion of commercial banks, we are treating mortgages here under the heading of "investments.")

2. Insured mortgages may be taken on properties located in any area of the country, with no restriction on the percentage of the value of the property represented by the mortgages. Conventional mortgages, on the other hand, are restricted, in general, to properties located in New York and adjoining states, with a maximum loan/value ratio of 75%–90%, depending on the specific type of property. In 1966, however, legislation

---

[11] Some authorities have proposed a more vigorous application of multiple-rate policies. That is, pay a high rate on deposits of, say, three or more years old, a lesser rate on, say, one- to three-year deposits, and a low rate on deposits of less than a year. There has been some effort along these lines—especially as between under- and over-one-year deposits—but not much.

[12] The restrictions cited in this section are in addition to the general usury laws of the various states, which are applicable to the residential mortgage investments of these institutions.

was enacted allowing New York savings banks (and savings and loan associations) to invest up to 20% of their assets in conventional mortgages on properties located outside the state.[13]

3. A "legal list" is published of eligible corporate securities. To be on the list, a corporation's senior securities must meet certain earnings coverage and other tests of quality. The standards are not onerously high and, in general, savings banks have sufficient alternatives available. However, from time to time various issues are placed on or withheld from the legal list for reasons which do not make much sense to experienced security analysts.[14]

4. Common stock investments were not eligible until 1952. As the law now stands, common stock, at cost, may not exceed the lesser of 5% of assets or one half of surplus and reserves. Common stock plus preferred may not exceed the lesser of 7½% of assets or three fourths of surplus and reserves. To be eligible for purchase, a common stock must have paid cash dividends in each of the past 10 years and must be listed on a registered securities exchange.[15] Limitations are also placed on the percentage of assets represented by any one stock and the percentage which may be owned of all outstanding shares of a given company.

As for savings and loan associations, a few states permit a broad range of investments similar to the situation of mutual savings banks. Since 1964, federally chartered savings and loans may invest in high-quality general obligations of states and municipalities. Also, a movement is underway to permit certain types of consumer loans to be made. Despite these stirrings, however, savings and loan associations are confined for the most part to U.S. government securities and real estate mortgages.

Like mutual savings bank mortgage activities, conventional mortgage acquisitions by savings and loan associations are for the most part restricted in most states to the geographic area surrounding the home office. However, federal savings and loans may, to a limited extent, buy participations in loans originated and serviced by other associations outside their area and, to an even more limited extent, may lend directly outside the area. Limitations are also placed on the percentage of assets in multifamily and commercial mortgages, and permissible loan/value ratios range from 75% to 90%, depending on the type of property.

---

[13] Eight other savings bank states also permit this type of activity within limits. Most observers do not expect the build-up of out-of-state mortgages by New York savings banks to be very rapid, since it will take time to gain experience and staff for this type of lending.

[14] For an extensive discussion and critique of the philosophy and standards of legal lists, see W. B. Hickman, *Corporate Bond Quality and Investor Experience* (New York: National Bureau of Economic Research, 1958), chap. iv.

[15] Ownership of stock in commercial banks is prohibited to savings banks in New York but is permitted and is fairly widespread in Massachusetts.

### Tax Status

Until 1962 mutual savings banks and savings and loan associations were in a highly privileged tax position. Only those institutions whose surplus, undivided profits, and reserves totaled 12% or more of deposits had to pay any income tax. The tax paid was the regular corporate rate, levied on the balance of net income remaining after operating expenses *and after payment of dividends* on deposits. In effect, the tax was levied on additions to surplus. Since only a relatively few institutions were at the 12% surplus limit, the industry paid virtually no income taxes.

In 1962 Congress imposed moderately higher taxes on the industry. Institutions at or over the 12% surplus limit remained taxed virtually as before. But, in addition, institutions below the 12% surplus level also became subject to tax. Various options are open to these institutions regarding tax-free reserves which may be charged against income, so generalizations must be taken with a grain of salt. To generalize, nevertheless, it can be said that they currently pay an effective rate of about 20% on additions to surplus. Since additions to surplus each year typically represent about 10%–15% of gross investment income, the effective tax rate on gross investment income is only about 2%–3%. Thus, for most mutual savings banks and savings and loan associations, there is little or no incentive to seek fully or partially tax-exempt income or capital gains.

### Investment Policies

*Provision for Liquidity.* As shown earlier, liquidity is not nearly as vital to mutual savings banks and savings and loan associations as to commercial banks. Whereas about 15% or more of commercial bank assets are typically kept in U.S. government securities maturing in less than five years, Table 18–4 indicates that only 5% of savings bank assets and less than 3% of savings and loan assets are so invested. Including cash and deposits in commercial banks, the total liquidity position of both savings banks and savings and loans is about 6% of assets. In addition, mortgage loan amortization provides an annual cash throw-off—built-in liquidity—equal to about 8% of average assets for savings banks and about 12% for savings and loan associations.

*Mortgage Investments.* The importance of savings banks and savings and loan associations in the mortgage market may be seen in Table 18–5. During the postwar period, mortgages have gradually become the dominant investment of mutual savings banks, rising from 25% of assets at the end of the war to 75% at present. Savings and loan associations, of course, by their nature have always been predominantly in mortgages—about 85% of assets. Although the present percentages of assets represented by mortgages are similar for the two types of institutions, there are some marked differences in the composition of their respective mortgage portfolios.

1. The split between government-insured and conventional mortgages is about 60%–40% for savings banks, 10%–90% for savings and loans. Much of the insured mortgage activity of the savings banks, especially in recent years, reflects their increasing need to lend outside their own geographic area. This is because deposit inflows in the northeastern

**TABLE 18–4**

**Principal Assets and Liabilities of Mutual Savings Banks and Savings and Loan Associations, December 31, 1965**

| | *Mutual Savings Banks* | | *Savings and Loan Associations* | |
|---|---|---|---|---|
| | *Billion $* | *%* | *Billion $* | *%* |
| Cash and bank deposits | 1.0 | 1.7 | 3.9 | 3.0 |
| U.S. government and agency securities: | | | | |
| Maturing in under five years* | 2.9 | 5.0 | 3.1 | 2.4 |
| Maturing in five or more years | 3.3 | 5.7 | 4.6 | 3.6 |
| State and local government securities | 0.3 | 0.5 | — | — |
| Corporate bonds | 3.1 | 5.3 | — | — |
| Mortgages: | | | | |
| FHA–VA | 25.2 | 43.3 | 11.5 | 8.9 |
| Conventional | 19.2 | 33.0 | 98.7 | 76.2 |
| Preferred stock | 0.4 | 0.7 | — | — |
| Common stock | 1.0 | 1.7 | — | — |
| Bank premises and other assets | 1.8 | 3.1 | 7.6 | 5.9 |
| Total Assets | 58.2 | 100.0 | 129.4 | 100.0 |
| Savings deposits | 52.4 | 90.0 | 110.3 | 85.3 |
| Accounts payable, etc. | 1.1 | 1.9 | 4.0 | 3.1 |
| Borrowing from FHLB | — | — | 6.4 | 4.9 |
| Surplus and reserves | 4.7 | 8.1 | 8.7 | 6.7 |
| Total Liabilities and Capital | 58.2 | 100.0 | 129.4 | 100.0 |

* Includes nonmarketable issues.

Sources: National Association of Mutual Savings Banks, *1966 Annual Report;* U.S. Savings and Loan League, *1966 Savings and Loan Fact Book; Treasury Bulletin,* February, 1966.

United States, where most savings banks are located, have been considerably in excess of local mortgage financing requirements. Yet because of legal restrictions, out-of-state mortgage lending has been pretty much confined to insured mortgages. On the other hand, savings and loan association growth has occurred largely in areas of rapidly expanding construction activity, especially in the West, and conventional mortgage financing needs have been plentiful. In addition, it might be argued on a more philosophical plane that savings and loan associations are in business specifically to finance residential construction of all types and should be

**TABLE 18–5**

**Net Acquisitions of Mortgages, 1965**

(In Billions of Dollars)

| | *One to Four Family Residential* | *Multifamily and Commercial* |
|---|---|---|
| *Financial Institutions:* | | |
| Savings and loan associations | 6.6 | 2.3 |
| Mutual savings banks | 2.8 | 1.4 |
| Commercial banks | 2.7 | 2.6 |
| Life insurance companies | 1.6 | 3.2 |
| Private pension funds | 0.6 | * |
| Mortgage companies | 0.6 | * |
| *Other Investors:* | | |
| U.S. government | 0.4 | 0.6 |
| State and local governments | 0.4 | * |
| Households | −0.3 | * |
| Total | 15.4 | 10.1 |

* Less than 0.5 billion dollars.
Source: Federal Reserve Bank of Chicago, *Business Conditions*, August, 1966, p. 5.

expected to take the higher risks associated with conventional mortgages.[16]

2. Mutual savings banks do a relatively larger volume of multifamily and nonresidential construction financing than savings and loan associations.[17] A good portion of the savings banks' multifamily financing is in public housing programs.

*Other Investments.* Mutual savings banks have been steadily liquidating long-maturity U.S. government securities during the postwar years. In the past dozen years alone, such investments have been reduced from one quarter of assets to 6%, and the reduction will probably go on as funds continue to be shifted into mortgages. Savings and loan associations, too, have only very small holdings of long-term governments. Yields on these securities are simply not attractive enough, and their safety is not valuable enough, relative to the other investment outlets of the savings institutions.

Investment in corporate and state and local government securities is, for the most part, open only to mutual savings banks. As noted earlier, the tax exemption of state and local government bond interest is not particularly attractive to these low-taxed institutions. Nor is the 85% intercorporate dividend credit attractive at a time when common stock yields are in

[16] This statement, however, should not be interpreted as condoning some of the downright reckless loans that have been made by a few associations.

[17] Savings and loan activity in this sphere has been increasing markedly in recent years, however.

the 3% range and preferred stock yields are below high-quality corporate bond yields. As for the capital gains potentials of common stock, the competitive pressure to pay high *current* dividends on deposits has led most savings banks to conclude that a bird in the hand is worth two in the bush. It will be seen in Table 18–4 that the banks have not invested in common stocks up to their permissible legal limits. Moreover, about one third of the common stock that is owned represents Massachusetts savings banks' investments in commercial bank stock.

**FIGURE 18–2**

**Cyclical Shifts in Mortgage and Corporate Security Investments of Mutual Savings Banks**

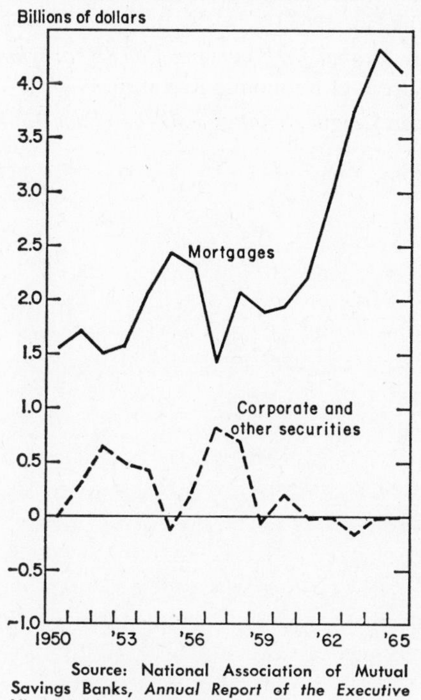


Source: National Association of Mutual Savings Banks, *Annual Report of the Executive Vice President, May, 1966,* p. 11.

Mutual savings banks do participate in the corporate bond market despite their emphasis on mortgages. To a large extent, this participation varies in direct relation to yield spreads between the two media. During most periods of economic boom and of rising interest rates, the yield advantage of mortgages has narrowed relative to that of bonds, and savings banks have stepped up their corporate bond acquisitions. The pattern then reverses during periods of stable or declining interest rates and widening yield differentials. Figure 18–2 portrays the shifting pattern vividly.

## SUGGESTED READINGS

William H. Baughn and Charls E. Walker. (eds.). *The Bankers' Handbook.* Homewood, Ill.: Dow Jones–Irwin, 1966.

Saul B. Klaman. *The Postwar Residential Mortgage Market.* Princeton, N.J.: Princeton University Press, 1961.

Roger A. Lyon. *Investment Portfolio Management in the Commercial Bank.* New Brunswick, N.J.: Rutgers University Press, 1960.

Sherman J. Maisel. *Financing Real Estate.* New York: McGraw-Hill Book Co., 1965.

National Association of Mutual Savings Banks, *Annual Reports.*

Roland E. Robinson. *Management of Bank Funds.* 2nd ed. New York: McGraw-Hill Book Co., 1962.

———. *The Postwar Market for State and Local Government Securities.* New York: National Bureau of Economic Research, 1960.

U.S. Savings and Loan League, *Savings and Loan Fact Book.* Annual.

# 19

# INSTITUTIONAL PORTFOLIO MANAGEMENT—II: INSURANCE COMPANIES AND PENSION FUNDS

Money is like an arm or leg—use it or lose it.

—Henry Ford

## LIFE INSURANCE COMPANIES

### The Nature of Life Insurance

During the early years of the life insurance business, premiums on policies were calculated on an annual cost basis. Each year an increasing premium would be required in accordance with the advancing age of the insured and the corresponding greater chances of his dying. This, in effect, was one-year term insurance, renewed each year. Experience proved, however, that this type of arrangement often caused difficulty in the middle and later years of the insured's life, when the financial burden became intolerably heavy or his health deteriorated and made him uninsurable.

To correct the defects of annual cost individual insurance,[1] a method was devised under which constant annual premiums would be levied on multiyear policies. The premium on any given policy would be higher than necessary to cover mortality risks in the early years of coverage. The excess would be built up as a reserve, and invested in income-producing assets to be employed during the later years of coverage, when the premium would be lower than warranted by the then higher mortality risks. Figure 19–1 illustrates the principle.

Numerous variations on the general idea of "level premium" insur-

[1] Group coverage still employs the annual cost concept.

FIGURE 19–1

**The Level Premium Life Insurance Concept: Schematic Diagram**

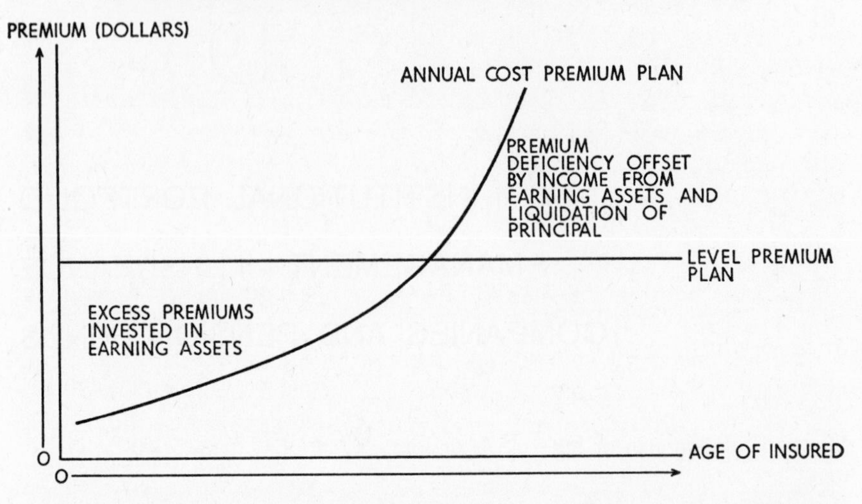


ance were devised—whole life, endowment, multiyear term, etc.—thus stimulating the industry's shift from an annual cost premium basis to a level premium basis. It was this shift which gave rise to large-scale investment activities. Under the old basis, if all the actuarial calculations were correct, annual income equaled annual outgo, leaving nothing to be invested other than, perhaps, capital, surplus, and contingency reserves. Under the new basis, a reserve for investment was deliberately established.

In modern life insurance, premiums are made up of three components: (1) the cost of pure insurance (protection against mortality risks), plus (2) a charge to cover the company's selling and operating expenses (including profit if a stockholder-owned company), minus (3) an assumed rate of return on the investment of excess premiums during the early years of policies. (Some policies, like endowments, have a fourth premium component which provides for an extra savings element.) Bearing in mind the three key components of life insurance premiums, it becomes obvious that the success of a life insurance company depends on three factors: (1) accurate calculations of mortality risks, (2) success in minimizing operating expenses, and (3) success in earning at least as high a rate of return on reserves as is assumed in the premium calculation. These factors apply whether the company is a mutual or a stockholder-owned organization (the former account for only 10% of the number of companies but 70% of the assets), except that mutuals pay dividends to policyholders when premiums prove to be higher than necessary to meet obligations.[2]

[2] Some stockholder-owned companies issue "participating" policies, which pay dividends.

### Investment Objectives

In the discussion of commercial bank investment policies in the previous chapter, it was stressed that banks have two conflicting objectives: liquidity and profitability. But while their objectives are in conflict, their problem is at least simplified by the fact that their objectives are clear-cut; banks know what they are after, although there may be considerable question about how to get it. The objectives of life insurance investment are not at all clear-cut. The immediate goal, of course, is implied by our discussion of the nature of life insurance—it is to earn, at a minimum, the rate of return assumed in calculating premiums. Beyond that, however, there is great room for differing viewpoints. Let us detail why this is so.

*Factors Suggesting Conservative Investments.* Several aspects of the life insurance business suggest that a quite conservative investment policy is advisable. In the first place, public policy places great emphasis on the safety of life company assets. Regulation of life insurance companies is diffused among the individual state legislatures and insurance commissions. However, there are many common characteristics among the different state regulations, and these characteristics are remarkably similar to the major regulations imposed on the investments of commercial banks and savings banks. This similarity suggests that from the point of view of public policy the investment portfolio of a life insurance company is in the nature of a trust fund and should be handled in accordance with conservative fiduciary principles. Chief among the regulations to which we refer are:

1. Relative freedom to invest any proportion of assets in U.S. government, state, or municipal securities, high-grade corporate bonds, or federally insured mortgages.

2. Limitation of conventional mortgage investments to a specified percentage of assets (for example, 50%) and to a specified maximum loan/value ratio. (In most cases, the maximum loan/value ratio is ⅔ or ¾, which, incidently, puts life companies at a competitive disadvantage against savings banks and savings and loan associations, since the latter can go up to 90% on most residential mortgages).

3. Requirement that companies set aside annually larger reserves on low-quality bonds and preferred stocks than on higher quality issues. (Quality tests are prescribed by the National Association of Insurance Commissioners.) These more stringent reserve requirements will reduce dividend-paying ability unless interest income is enough higher on low-quality issues to offset their impact. In addition, bonds in default and preferred stock not meeting dividend and sinking-fund payments must be marked down to market value on the owning company's balance sheet, thus cutting into valuation reserves, or even into surplus. Bonds and

preferred stock "in good standing," on the other hand, may be valued at cost.

4. Strict limitation on equity investments. New York law is among the strictest in this regard, and since companies wishing to do business in New York must "substantially comply" with that state's law, it tends to set the standard. New York limits direct real estate ownership, exclusive of property used in the insurance operation, to 5% of assets, at cost. Common stock, at cost, is limited to the lesser of 5% of assets or one half of surplus. Although the limit is based on cost values,[3] common stock must be carried on the balance sheet at market values. Realized and unrealized appreciation must be set aside in a reserve account, unavailable for dividends, until the reserve reaches one third of the common stock portfolio's market value. In addition, 1% of the value of the stock has to be set aside annually until the maximum reserve is reached. (Realized and unrealized capital losses are charged against this reserve.) Furthermore, stocks are not eligible for purchase unless they are listed on a registered exchange[4] and have paid dividends in each of the past 10 years; there are also other restrictions on top of these.[5]

It is not difficult to understand why public policy puts so much emphasis on safety. Confidence in the ability of life insurance companies to pay death and annuity benefits as they fall due is vital to the financial well-being of the community. With capital, surplus, and contingency reserves equal to only 8%–9% of the industry's assets, there is not much margin for severe losses on investments. Moreover, life insurance and annuity benefits are payable for the most part in fixed dollar amounts. There is thus no need for a life insurance company to take the risks involved in equity investments in order to hedge against inflation—unless it is selling "variable annuities" or some sort of price-related benefits.[6] In addition, the legislators and regulatory authorities are probably influenced by the fact that 10 companies out of the 1,650 in existence represent 60%

---

[3] An interesting side result of the cost basis for limiting common stock investment is that some companies are reluctant to sell overvalued stocks on which they have large unrealized capital gains, and to reinvest in undervalued stocks, because this would raise their costs basis and might put them over the legal limit.

[4] Bank and insurance stocks may be purchased even if traded over the counter.

[5] However, most state laws, including that of New York, contain a "basket clause," which permits some specified percentage of assets (3½% in New York) to be invested in any securities, mortgages, or real estate not otherwise eligible. For details of state regulations, see A. F. Brimmer, *Life Insurance Companies in the Capital Market* (East Lansing: Michigan State University Press, 1962), chap. iii. Also see H. G. Fraine, *Valuation of Securities Holdings of Life Insurance Companies* (Homewood, Ill.: Richard D. Irwin, Inc., 1962).

[6] Operating expenses do rise during inflationary periods, but this factor is not usually considered significant enough to offset the fixed dollar nature of the liabilities in choosing appropriate assets.

of the industry's $160 billion of assets. If this financial power were misused, the results could be catastrophic for the nation.

There are also some intangible factors at work which may cause life insurance companies to lean toward conservatism in their investment activities. Generally speaking, life company actuaries take few chances when calculating premiums. Assumed mortality rates are usually higher than actual mortality proves to be. (In annuity premium calculations the reverse is true; actuaries assume people will live longer than they actually do.) Assumed operating expenses also tend to be on the high side of actual; and assumed rates of return on investment tend to be on the low side of actual (although higher rates are usually offered on individual and group annuities).[7] Of course, these actuarial margins for error get returned to policyholders via the dividend route, at least in mutual companies,[8] but since the margins are relatively high, there often is not as much sense of urgency to improve investment results as there would be in the absence of such margins. Another intangible which can be cited is the fact that the senior officers and directors of the large life insurance companies have had direct personal experience with the impact of the Great Depression on investment values, and this experience is imprinted indelibly on their present decisions.

*Factors Suggesting Aggressive Investment Policies.* Whereas the senior personnel of modern life insurance companies are frequently depression oriented, a younger group is beginning to ascend the hierarchial ladder. These men look upon the 1930's as an aberration which is extremely unlikely to be repeated. And they also go one step further. Even if we have another Great Depression, they argue, what are the real risks to a life insurance company? At the very depth of the depression, in 1932 and 1933, most life insurance companies had cash inflow far in excess of cash outflow, and the need to liquidate assets in a depressed market was negligible. All that companies really had to do was sit tight and not panic, and ultimately most investment values were restored.

The liquidity needs of a life insurance company are minimal for several reasons. Most of the industry's business consists of whole-life, multiyear term life, and annuity policies. Therefore, liabilities are long term in nature. In addition, the demand for insurance is constantly growing. Unless a company's sales effort is dreadfully unsuccessful, premiums from new policies going on the books should exceed premiums terminated

---

[7] Care must be taken, however, not to confuse the typical 2½%–3% interest assumption which is used to calculate legal *reserves* with the assumptions used in calculating actual *premiums*. The latter have tended in recent years to be on a sliding scale from about 4¾% in the early life of a policy to lower rates thereafter.

[8] In stock companies the margins are not as high to begin with if the policies are nonparticipating.

due to death, lapse, surrender, etc., and total premiums should exceed total benefits and operating expenses. Not only is cash inflow in excess of outgo, but the amounts and timing of these flows is usually rather precisely predeterminable. Finally, much built-in liquidity is provided by amortization and prepayments of bonds and mortgages. Indeed, this turnover of assets provides almost as much cash inflow as the net increase in the industry's assets.

A few qualifications to the absence of liquidity needs should be made. (1) Young companies often operate at deficits because sales commissions absorb much of the initial premium income. (2) Companies which are too small to diversify their operations geographically are exposed to calamitous developments and need more liquidity than larger companies. (3) Companies whose business is heavily in group life and other short-term insurance may not be able to build up as much cash reserves as companies with a large portion of whole life insurance and annuity business. (4) Since cash surrender values are payable on demand, either upon termination of policies or as policy loans, there is a theoretical need for liquidity, although this need usually has not proven to be very significant in practice.[9] (5) While actual operating requirements may not dictate distress sales of investments, state insurance regulations demand that securities in default be marked down in price and that properties acquired in mortgage foreclosures be sold within a specified number of years (five, for example).

Point (5) warrants some additional comment. In the 1930's, state insurance commissioners interpreted the security valuation and property sale rules very liberally. Much, if not most, of the distress selling that took place reflected the panicking of insurance company executives rather than the pressure of insurance regulatory authorities. But the authorities would probably not be so liberal if a group of maverick companies struck out boldly on a policy of high risk and thereby got themselves into trouble. In the 1930's, liberality was called for because the entire industry was confronted with a situation over which it had no control.

Despite the qualifications noted above, it is generally valid to argue that life insurance companies have little need for liquidity and that this suggests an aggressive investment policy. But lack of liquidity needs is not the only argument for an aggressive policy. The new breed of managers stresses that companies which take the easy way out, and invest merely to achieve minimum required rates of return, are depriving their policyholders of the lowest possible cost of insurance. In view of the quasi-public nature of the life insurance business, do not the companies owe it to their

---

[9] In 1966, however, sharp increases in policy loans (which the public often uses in lieu of consumer credit during periods of tight money) squeezed the liquidity positions of many life insurance companies which had already made "forward investment commitments" of their anticipated cash inflows.

policyholders to strive for the maximum return consistent with the degree of safety needed, thereby enabling the cost of insurance to be minimized? Indeed, even from a selfish point of view, such a policy would seem wise. For in a highly competitive business like life insurance and annuities (especially group annuities), a company which can reduce insurance costs should be able to compete more effectively.

The income tax status of the life insurance industry gives further support to an aggressive investment policy. Under some extremely complex legislation passed in 1959, the investment income of life companies became taxed, in effect, only on the portion carried over into surplus. Income required to be earned in order to maintain actuarial soundness, and excess income paid out as policyholder dividends, were not subjected to taxation. For most companies, actual taxes paid under this legislation have worked out to approximately 10%–12% of net investment income. Thus, there is an incentive to try to earn higher income by taking increased risks, because the government does not skim off very much of the extra earnings.[10] In this context, however, increased risk taking does not necessarily infer capital gains seeking, because there is generally no tax advantage in capital gains as opposed to ordinary income.[11]

### Investment Policies

It is apparent, on the basis of the preceding discussion, that we have in a life insurance company the peculiar situation of an investing institution which is fully capable of taking substantial investment risks, but which is under no great pressure to do so and which, in fact, is discouraged by law from doing so. The end result of these conflicting influences has been what one might expect—a compromise. Life insurance company investments, as a whole, have not been particularly bold and imaginative; but neither has the industry "played it safe," especially in recent years.

*Government Bonds.* During World War II, life insurance companies invested heavily in U.S. government bonds, since other investment outlets were greatly reduced. By the end of 1945, about 45% of total assets consisted of Treasury obligations. The concentration on Treasury issues, however, did not mean that the industry was entirely lax in seeking to improve yields. Many companies, for example, showed a decided tendency to "ride the yield curve"—buying long-term government secu-

---

[10] This may somewhat overstate the point, however. The life insurance income tax is a progressive one—i.e., the higher the earnings rate the higher the effective tax rate. While it is true that even an overall earnings rate of, say, 8% is taxed at an effective rate of less than 25%, the *increment* from 7% to 8% is taxed at an effective *marginal* rate of almost 60%.

[11] Actually, the relative tax position of capital gains as opposed to interest or dividend income is far from clear-cut. The tax computation is so complex that, depending on one's assumptions, capital gains may appear to be taxed at either a higher or a lower rate than ordinary current income.

rities and selling them after a few years at capital gains, a technique that was described in the previous chapter on commercial bank investing. As long as the Federal Reserve continued to peg the level and structure of rates, profits were guaranteed. And unlike other investors who, in trying to do the same thing, exposed themselves to the risk that the Federal Reserve might remove the peg and allow bond prices to fall, life insurance companies could rest easy in the knowledge that they did not need liquidity and could, if they chose, simply hold the securities to maturity rather than sell at a loss if the peg were removed.[12]

Riding the yield curve did entail an intangible risk, however. It was the political risk of appearing to be profiting from a national emergency. This political type of risk is still present in connection with the industry's government bond holdings. As normal economic activities resumed after the war, corporations and home buyers entered the market for funds, and life insurance companies steadily shifted out of Treasury issues and into higher yielding corporate bonds and real estate mortgages. By the end of 1965, as shown in Table 19–1, Treasury issues had been reduced to 3% of total assets, mostly in maturities of over five years. Even this percentage is considered too high by many investment managers in the industry, who would prefer to continue to switch into higher yielding investments when yield spreads warrant. But they are reluctant to whittle further for fear that if their companies do not maintain at least a nominal holding of government securities there may be political repercussions.

*Corporate Bonds.* The life insurance industry is one of the most important creditors of American industry, holding over 50% of all outstanding bonds of domestic corporations. These bonds, plus some foreign issues, account for about 40% of life company assets. The great majority of life insurance company bond investments is made by the private placement technique, whereby corporations sell their bonds to a single financial institution or to a small group of institutions, rather than by the traditional underwritten public offering technique.

Since the 1930's, corporate borrowers have placed increasing reliance on direct negotiation with institutional lenders, either with or without an investment banker acting as intermediary. According to the SEC, private placements have accounted on an annual basis for between 35% and 65% of total corporate debt issues during the post war period.[13] Although no figures are available on the volume of outstanding private placements, the amount is probably close to one half of all outstanding domestic corporate bonds. Of this amount, life insurance companies probably own approximately 75%. Almost all of the industry's current hold-

---

[12] Of course, they would have sustained the opportunity cost represented by the difference between the higher level of interest rates and the interest rates on the securities held.

[13] For nonutility bonds, the share has typically been 70% or more.

TABLE 19–1

**Principal Assets and Liabilities of Life Insurance Companies, December 31, 1965**

| | *Billion $* | *% of Total* |
|---|---|---|
| Cash | 1.5 | 0.9 |
| U.S. government and agency securities: | | |
| Maturing in under five years* | 0.8 | 0.5 |
| Maturing in five or more years | 4.4 | 2.8 |
| State and local government securities | 3.5 | 2.2 |
| Domestic corporate and foreign bonds | 61.5 | 38.7 |
| Mortgages: | | |
| FHA–VA | 18.8 | 11.8 |
| Conventional | 41.2 | 26.0 |
| Policy loans | 7.7 | 4.8 |
| Preferred stock | 2.9 | 1.8 |
| Common stock | 6.3 | 4.0 |
| Real estate investment | 3.2 | 2.0 |
| Company premises and other assets | 7.1 | 4.5 |
| Total Assets | 158.9 | 100.0 |
| Policy reserves | 127.6 | 80.3 |
| Dividend and other obligations | 17.4 | 10.9 |
| Contingency reserves | 2.5 | 1.6 |
| Unassigned surplus and stock company capital | 11.4 | 7.2 |
| Total Assets | 158.9 | 100.0 |

* Includes nonmarketable issues.
Source: Institute of Life Insurance, *1966 Life Insurance Fact Book; Treasury Bulletin*, February, 1966.

ings of industrial bonds, and about half of its holdings of public utility bonds, arose through direct negotiations with the borrowers.

The increased use of the private placement technique reflects several advantages to both borrower and lender, in comparison with public offerings:

1. The borrower avoids SEC registration, which is both costly and may require the divulgence of information that the borrower prefers not to make publicly available.

2. The SEC's mandatory waiting period between the filing of registration papers and final sale of the bonds is avoided. Thus, the borrower avoids the risk that interest rates will rise during the waiting period, which would impair the salability of his bonds at the price he anticipated.

3. Investment bankers' fees, paid by the borrower, are reduced or eliminated.

4. If the borrower does not need all of the funds at once, the lending institution will allow him to draw the funds down gradually, sometimes charging a "commitment fee" of one half of 1% to 1% of the unborrowed balance. Even with the fee, however, this is usually cheaper than paying

full interest on unused funds and investing the unused funds in lower yielding Treasury bills or commercial bank certificates of deposit.

5. The lower costs to the borrower, cited above, permit him to pay a higher interest rate than on a public offering, which is, of course, advantageous to the lender.

6. The lender is able to place large blocks of investable funds in a relatively small number of individual issues, thus reducing his unit costs of security analysis and follow-up.

7. Both lender and borrower can tailor the terms of the issue to their unique requirements more readily than with a public issue. Moreover, the terms can be renegotiated in subsequent years if circumstances change—a virtual impossibility with a public issue.

The only disadvantages of private placements as opposed to public offerings would seem to be that (1) the borrower may become too dependent on a single supplier of funds, and (2) the lender has less marketability. With regard to point (2), however, life insurance companies usually don't need marketability. Furthermore, many publicly held corporate bonds are not readily marketable either, at least not in large quantities. Overall, the advantages of private placements would appear to outweigh alleged disadvantages.

It was noted above that private placements permit the parties to tailor terms to their unique requirements. In recent years, life insurance companies have placed heavy emphasis on limitations of the borrower's right to refund the issue at lower interest rates. In 1953, 55% of the industry's bond acquisitions were callable at any time by the borrower, for any reason, at specified call prices. Twenty-five percent of the acquisitions had a clause making the bonds noncallable for refunding purposes for periods ranging from 1 to 10 years; and the remainder of the acquisitions were made nonrefundable at any time. By 1957, only 15% of the acquisitions were refundable at any time, and 85% had some kind of refunding restriction.[14] Comparable data for later years are not available, but the trend has probably continued.

The reason life insurance companies are so anxious to have nonrefundability clauses in their bond investments is simple to understand. If interest rates were to drop sharply from the relatively high levels they have attained in recent years, borrowers who have unlimited call privileges would have little hesitation in calling their outstanding issues and refunding at more favorable rates. Insurers, however, could not increase premiums on existing policies, nor could they recoup the entire reduction in income through increased premiums on newly written policies. And

---

[14] *Proceedings* of the 52nd annual meeting of the Life Insurance Association of America, p. 125.

curtailment of dividends is a step they would be most hesitant to take. Therefore, they try to assure themselves of continuing high income by demanding nonrefundability, even if they have to take a lower coupon rate in order to extract this agreement from borrowers, who, of course, prefer to retain the flexibility of unlimited callability. Our only criticism of the negotiations that take place between borrower and lender with regard to callability is that they are not nearly as firmly grounded on mathematical calculations of the value of the call privilege as they ought to be.[15]

While there are no publicly available data on the quality distribution of life insurance company bond holdings, private compilations indicate that the average quality is between A and Baa. This represents a compromise between the traditionalists' emphasis on safety and the "Young Turks'" desire to exploit more fully the industry's natural risk-taking ability. The latter received important support several years ago from a study by the National Bureau of Economic Research. The study indicated that if a bond investor could have diversified broadly during the period 1900–1943, he would have received a higher net rate of return, after deducting depression-caused losses, on lower quality than on the high-quality issues.[16] Since the major life insurance companies are large enough to be able to diversify broadly, the findings of this study have been deemed quite relevant to their operations, especially in the face of ever-mounting competition among financial institutions for higher yielding investments.

In addition to offsetting risks by diversifying, some of the more aggressive companies have undertaken fairly high-risk bond investments but have shortened maturities and required rapid amortization. This leaves less time for a borrowing company's product to become obsolete or for it to get into trouble in some other way. On the other hand, the lender must be careful that he doesn't require amortization to be so rapid that it puts an unbearable financial strain on the borrower, thus hastening his downfall. Furthermore, rapid amortization exposes the lender to the risk of having to reinvest the amortization receipts at lower interest rates.

*Mortgages.* The search for higher yields has lately caused most life insurance companies to put more emphasis on mortgage lending than ever before in their history. A dozen years ago, the industry held $1.50 of corporate bonds for every $1 of mortgages. Today, the two types of

---

[15] See Chapter 11, pp. 22–24.

[16] W. B. Hickman, *Corporate Bond Quality and Investor Experience* (New York: National Bureau of Economic Research, 1958). H. G. Fraine and R. H. Mills have taken issue with Hickman's methodology. See their "Effect of Defaults and Credit Deterioration on Yields of Corporate Bonds," *Journal of Finance*, September, 1961.

investment have almost equal weight in the industry's asset structure, and we would not be surprised to see mortgage holdings surpass corporate bonds in the very near future.

Although precise comparisons of loss experience on bonds and mortgages are extremely difficult to make, such evidence as is available suggests that diversified portfolios of either type of investment have produced similar loss experience.[17] Yet yields available on conventional mortgages have traditionally been considerably higher—as much as 200 to 300 basis points higher—than yields available on corporate bonds, even after taking into account the considerably higher expenses involved in servicing a mortgage portfolio.[18] Even federally insured mortgages have typically carried much higher yields than corporate bonds. Some of the reasons often cited for this phenomenon are (1) mortgages are usually less marketable than bonds, (2) most financial institutions have not developed the specialized staffs necessary to operate effectively in the mortgage market, (3) home mortgage foreclosure proceedings have more deep-seated psychological overtones than corporate bankruptcy proceedings ("who wants to be accused of throwing widows and orphans out on the streets?"), and (4) many investors are simply ignorant of the mortgage market.

If these reasons ever satisfactorily justified sizable yield spreads between bonds and mortgages, they no longer do so. It is true that mortgages are generally less marketable than bonds. But the principal operators in the modern corporate bond and mortgage markets are not individual investors, to whom marketability is extremely important, but financial intermediaries of various types, to whom marketability is far less important. As for the necessity of specialized mortgage staffs, there has been developed in the postwar period a network of hundreds of independent mortgage bankers, who will efficiently undertake all origination and servicing for a fee only moderately higher than an institution would incur if it had its own staff. The comment about having to throw people out on the streets is a vast distortion of reality. Finally, ignorance of the nature of the largest single sector of the entire capital market is simply inexcusable.

As competition has forced investors to discard their prejudices and repair their ignorance, bond-mortgage yield spreads have narrowed. From

---

[17] For data which can be roughly compared with that of Hickman, Fraine, and Mills, see R. J. Saulnier, *Urban Mortgage Lending by Life Insurance Companies* (New York: National Bureau of Economic Research, 1950).

[18] The higher expenses reflect primarily the fact that a residential mortgage portfolio consists of a very large number of relatively small loans whereas the number of issues in a bond portfolio typically is only a slight fraction of the number in a mortgage portfolio. Since it costs little, if any, more to originate and service a large loan than a small loan, total expenses are heavily influenced by the number of loans made.

1960 to 1965, for example, conventional residential mortgages yielded 5%–5¼% after average expense deductions, whereas middle-quality corporate bonds provided 4¾%–5% and high-quality bonds 4¼%–4½%. Thus, spreads were reduced to approximately one half of 1%. This spread remained attractive to life insurance companies, however, and accounts for their increased emphasis on mortgage investments. Indeed, their interest in the mortgage field spilled over into areas formerly left to banks and private entrepreneurs, such as construction loans and loans on undeveloped land, and they are now more active than ever in income-property mortgages. The latter, which include loans on apartment houses, commercial, and industrial properties, typically carry net yields of one half of 1% or more higher than yields on residential properties. This yield differential reflects, in part, somewhat higher risks that income property values will fall in periods of adversity but also reflects great investor ignorance of the nature of the market.

About 70% of the life insurance industry's mortgage holdings is conventional, 30% government insured. This is about midway between the position of mutual savings banks (60% insured) and savings and loan associations (10% insured). Most life insurance companies utilize heavily the services of independent mortgage bankers, but some have organized their own field staffs to do much or all of the origination and servicing. The latter procedure tends to enable a company to exercise a higher degree of quality control and to keep operating expenses relatively low.

*Other Investments.* A few comments are in order about each of the other investment categories on the life insurance balance sheet. First, a paradoxical category—the policy loan. In terms of safety and rate of return, it would seem that there is no more attractive interest-bearing obligation than the policy loan. The interest rate charged is usually 5%–6%; and if the borrower defaults, the company simply cancels a like amount of insurance reserve liability. Like a savings bank passbook loan, the borrower is borrowing "his own" money, and the loan is, therefore, riskless. Yet insurance companies discourage policy loans. They do so for two reasons. First, policy loans are small in amount and are therefore very costly to administer. Their net yield is far below the interest rate charged and is not particularly attractive relative to alternative investment media. Second, and far more important, a policy loan is frequently the prelude to a lapse of the policy, and insurance companies are interested in keeping policies in force.

State and local government securities and corporate preferred stocks are generally unattractive to life insurance companies at prevailing yields, because their tax-exemption or tax-credit features are not too valuable at the relatively low effective tax rates of life companies. Moreover, a recent decision of the Internal Revenue, supported by the Supreme Court, in effect removes some of the tax exemption of state and local securities from life insurance companies.[19] However, occasional issues of revenue bonds (as opposed to general obligations) and of corporate preferred stocks yield as much as, or more than, corporate bonds, on a taxable equivalent basis. Revenue obligations account for about 75% of the state and local securities shown on the industry's balance sheet.

The question of whether common stocks are appropriate life insurance company investments is highly controversial. Hindsight makes it apparent that companies which initiated common stock programs in the early 1950's, when state laws first began to permit such investments, were wise in doing so. Dividend yields were higher than bond or mortgage yields, and a high rate of capital appreciation was received in addition, with no major market declines in the interim. It is not nearly as apparent, however, that a company which is only now beginning to consider a common stock program should actually initiate one. And there may even be questions about continuing an existing program.

Common stocks produce a current dividend yield of only 3%–4%, compared with average net yields of over 5% on a cross section of long-term fixed income investments. Even if one assumes capital appreciation of 5% or more per annum on common stocks, bringing their total effective yield to over 8%, it is appropriate to ask: Who benefits from the capital appreciation? The law requires that realized and unrealized appreciation be put into a valuation reserve, together with an annual addition of 1% of the value of the total common stock account, until the reserve equals one third of the value of the account. Thus, unless a company has had a common stock program in operation for a long enough time to be at or near the maximum reserve, capital appreciation is not directly available for dividend distributions to current policyholders. Thus, argue critics of common stock investment by life insurance companies, while some future generation of policyholders would doubtless benefit from the capital appreciation, it is questionable whether today's policyholders should subsidize future policyholders. Moreover, a stock market decline more severe than anything yet experienced in the postwar period is not inconceivable. Such a decline would eat into the surplus of companies with low reserves, since the law requires that common stock be carried on the books at year-end market value.

On the other hand, proponents of common stock investments by life insurance companies argue that current policyholder generations would not be subsidizing future generations. In the first place, they note, if *dividends* grow at a rate of 5% per annum, stocks purchased on a 3% current dividend yield basis will be yielding 5% *on cost* by the 11th year

---

[19] The case involved the Atlas Life Insurance Company. See the financial section of any newspaper dated May 18, 1965.

after the investment, and over a period of about 20 years will produce as many dollars of regular income as an equal investment in 5% bonds. Thus, existing policyholder generations will benefit *directly* from growing dividend income. As for the benefits accruing from capital gains, whether realized or unrealized, it is claimed that life company actuaries tend to give weight to the existence of the Mandatory Securities Valuation Reserve when setting dividends, and would tend to be more liberal in their current dividend declarations than one would expect simply by looking at unallocated surplus. Moreover, so-called "termination dividends," which may be paid when policies terminate through surrender, maturity, or death, are designed to redress any inequities which may have arisen among different policy classes or different policyholder generations.

Given the controversial nature of the subject, it should not be surprising that the life insurance industry as a whole has invested relatively little in common stock—indeed, less than even the strictest state law, that of New York, permits.[20] To a small extent (2% of assets) life companies have substituted direct investment in real estate for common stocks as a medium of equity investment. Life companies, for example, have pioneered in sale-leaseback financing, whereby a manufacturing or other type of company sells its plant or offices to an institutional investor, who then leases the property back to the seller under a long-term rental agreement. The annual rental charge is usually designed to amortize the entire principal during the term of the lease and to provide the investor with a rate of return of 6%–10% per annum. Hopefully, the property still has some residual value at the end of the lease period, thus providing a capital gain over and above the regular annual income. In addition to real estate investment, many life insurance companies use their private placement bond investments as an equity medium by requiring selected bonds to be convertible into common stock or to have stock purchase warrants attached.

*Investment Timing.* Most life insurance companies, and especially the larger ones, make little attempt to follow a cyclical investment timing policy, in the sense of keeping funds in short-term securities during periods of low interest rates and moving into longs when rates get higher. The feeling is that the volume of incoming funds is so large and so steady that it is difficult enough to find attractive *permanent* outlets as funds

---

[20] It is interesting to note that British life insurance companies, which are not subject to legislative or regulatory investment restrictions as are American companies, have invested large proportions of their assets in common stocks, with no significant adverse effects. On the other hand, most British life insurance companies do not make the same kinds of cash value guarantees as do American companies, and this doubtless has a bearing on their attitudes toward common stock investment. See G. Clayton and W. T. Osborn, "Insurance Companies and the Capital Market," *Three Banks Review,* March, 1958.

become available. To allow funds to pile up for months or years during a period of low rates, while awaiting a rise in rates, would make the ultimate placement of the entire amount an impossible task. Indeed, an attempt to place all the funds at once might well disrupt the entire market.

Moreover, if a forecast of higher rates proves to be wrong for a year or two, a company which refrained from making permanent investments would have lost for all that time the difference between the short-term rate and the long-term rate—perhaps as much as 2% per annum. A considerable ultimate rise in long-term rates, say one half of 1% or more, would be needed to offset a loss of this magnitude during an average loan life of 10–15 years.[21] Finally, it is vital for life insurance companies to maintain good relationships with the mortgage banking, investment banking, construction, and corporate communities. These parties, after all, supply the life companies with their bonds and mortgages, either directly or indirectly. If a company is in the market one year and out the next, its relationships with the other market participants become strained, and it may be frozen out of the market in subsequent years.

We would stress, however, that these observations apply primarily to the larger companies. Smaller companies with greater flexibility should, in our opinion, pay more attention to cyclical timing than they normally do. Not only should they consider refraining from making permanent investments in periods of relatively low rates (as long as the short-term rate is high enough to cover the actuarial interest assumption), but they should also consider selling existing holdings at premium prices. Even private placements can be disposed of, within limits. It is true that such a policy may temporarily depress earnings, and therefore policyholder dividends, relative to that of competing companies; but over a period of years the policy should pay off—unless, of course, the interest rate forecasts are consistently wrong.[22]

We do not want to leave the impression that life insurance companies, even the larger ones, are totally insensitive to cyclical factors. Companies respond to cyclical fluctuations in two ways. First, when the general level of interest rates is expected to fall, and spreads between bond and mortgage rates are expected to widen in favor of mortgages, more investment funds tend to be allocated to mortgages than if the level of rates is expected to rise and bond-mortgage spreads to narrow. Second, when rates are high and expected to decline, life companies will attempt to increase their "forward commitments," which are agreements to lend at

---

[21] The average loan life takes amortization into account. Thus a 20-year maturity bond has approximately a 10-year average life if amortized on a straight-line basis.

[22] It may be noted that Canadian life insurance companies, unlike American companies, generally follow a fairly active bond trading policy.

a future date at today's rates.[23] Likewise, when rates are low and expected to rise, forward commitments will be restricted.

## PROPERTY AND CASUALTY INSURANCE COMPANIES

### Sales Organization

Property and casualty insurance is written by many different types of organizations. Stockholder-owned companies account for only about one quarter of the number of organizations in the business, but do two thirds or more of the volume. Mutual companies account for almost three quarters of the number, but account for only about one quarter of the volume. (Note that the situation is precisely the opposite in the life insurance industry, where mutuals are in the minority in number but do the bulk of the business.) Both mutual and stock companies compete with state workmen's compensation funds, nonprofit hospital-medical associations, and life insurance companies writing various types of sickness and accident insurance.[24]

In the United States, the sale of property and casualty insurance has traditionally been carried out through independent local agents. Under this method of distribution, which is known as the "American Agency System," the insurance company—known as the "underwriter"—appoints agents who agree to represent the company. These agents are supposed to perform preliminary underwriting functions in selecting clients with whom to do business; they also collect premiums, deliver the policies, and, when losses occur, prepare initial loss reports. To recompense the agents for these services, the underwriting company pays commissions based on premium volume.

Strongly competitive methods of distribution have been developed in recent years. So-called "direct-writing" companies have centralized much of the administrative detail which is handled by agents under the traditional system. This permits compensation of salesmen (who usually are employees of the direct-writing companies rather than independent agents) to be reduced and premiums to be lowered.[25] As a result,

---

[23] Some people have argued that life companies should actually borrow from banks at such times, to raise funds which they could relend at high rates. Subsequently, when internal funds become available, the bank loans can be repaid. Most life companies, however, steadfastly reject any suggestion that they introduce leverage into their operations, largely for fear that they will run afoul of the regulatory authorities.

[24] In general, life insurance companies are not permitted to be in the property and casualty business, except for sickness and accident, but property and casualty companies can write life insurance, either directly or through subsidiaries.

[25] Critics claim that service to policyholders is reduced as a by-product.

direct-writing companies have grown much more rapidly than old-line companies.

### Underwriting Procedures and Experience

Property and casualty insurance companies are controlled by state governmental authorities in several ways, perhaps the most important being the establishment of maximum premium rates on various policy lines. Premiums are determined in the following manner. "Rating bureaus," owned by the old-line companies, gather statistical data showing industry claim-payment experience, by line of insurance, during the past three to five years, on a national, state, and county basis. To these claim data are added allowances for operating expenses, contingencies, and a margin for profit. On the basis of this information, the state insurance commissions calculate maximum premiums. No allowance is made, in setting these premiums, for income earned on the investment of any surplus or reserves!

If subsequent experience indicates to the rating bureaus that the premiums are inadequate, applications for rate increases on newly written policies are filed. These applications may or may not be granted by the regulatory agencies. On the other hand, if subsequent experience suggests that premiums are too high, the commissioners may order rates to be reduced. It should be stressed that the rates established are maximum rather than fixed rates. Therefore, efficient companies, particularly the direct-writing organizations, may offer to sell insurance at discounts from these rates.

Unlike life insurance, it is difficult to predict accurately the amount of claim payments that will have to be made on underwritten property and casualty risks. First of all, such insurance is much more exposed to catastrophes than life insurance. Citywide fires, tornadoes, and blizzards are examples of occurrences which make claims fluctuate widely from year to year. Other reasons for the difficulty in predicting claim payments are (1) the uncertain rate of change in the price level, which causes the costs of repairing damages to be uncertain, and (2) the leeway given to juries in making awards in cases involving bodily injuries. The effects of these factors are exaggerated by the typical lag between the time of an accident and the time of final settlement.

Since property and casualty insurance premiums are based on past underwriting experience, and since the past is not too reliable a guide to the future, actual experience is often considerably better or worse than anticipated when setting premiums. As noted earlier, the insurance commissioners should, in theory, lower or raise premiums when actual experience varies from assumed experience. But the motivation of insurance commissioners obviously has an important political content, so rate revisions are not usually as prompt as they should be ideally. Moreover, the revised rates apply only to new policies written, and since existing policies often have several years to run because they were originally written for three- or five-year periods, the revised rates are not reflected in underwriting income for several years. By that time, the circumstances which caused the rate revisions in the first place may have completely reversed themselves. All of this has the result that underwriting operations usually result in long waves of losses followed by profits followed by losses again. Unfortunately for the industry, in recent years the "profit waves" have simply been waves of lower losses than in the preceding loss wave. Underwriting experience for property and casualty insurance has been almost uniformly bad since the mid-1950's.

## Insurance versus Investment Operations

Table 19–2 presents summary balance sheets for stock and mutual companies. On the asset side of the balance sheets we find a diversified list of investment securities. These securities represent the investment of premiums not yet paid out to meet claims and expenses, and of capital and surplus. Interest, dividends, and profits earned on these securities have been *the* major source of property and casualty insurance company earn-

**TABLE 19–2**
**Principal Assets and Liabilities of Stock and Mutual Property and Casualty Insurance Companies, December 31, 1965**

| | *Stock Companies* | | *Mutual Companies* | |
|---|---|---|---|---|
| | *Billion $* | % | *Billion $* | % |
| Cash and bank deposits | 1.0 | 3.1 | 0.3 | 3.2 |
| U.S. government securities | 4.3 | 13.8 | 1.8 | 20.1 |
| State and local government securities | 7.7 | 24.7 | 2.9 | 32.3 |
| Corporate bonds | 1.4 | 4.6 | 1.1 | 12.5 |
| Mortgages | 0.1 | 0.2 | 0.1 | 0.9 |
| Preferred stocks | 0.8 | 2.5 | 0.3 | 3.1 |
| Common stock | 12.3 | 39.4 | 1.7 | 18.4 |
| Real estate | 0.4 | 1.2 | 0.2 | 2.3 |
| Receivables and other assets | 3.3 | 10.5 | 0.6 | 7.2 |
| Total Assets | 31.3 | 100.0 | 9.0 | 100.0 |
| Unearned premiums | 7.9 | 25.2 | 2.1 | 23.3 |
| Loss reserves and other liabilities | 9.7 | 31.2 | 4.0 | 44.5 |
| Capital and surplus | 13.7 | 43.6 | 2.9 | 32.2 |
| Total Liabilities and Capital | 31.3 | 100.0 | 9.0 | 100.0 |
| Insurance exposure ratio* | 1.01 | | 1.79 | |
| Investment exposure ratio† | 0.90 | | 0.57 | |

* Premiums written divided by capital and surplus.
† Common stock divided by capital and surplus.
Source of balance sheet data: Alfred M. Best & Co., *Best's Fire and Casualty Aggregates and Averages*, 1966 edition. (Exposure ratios calculated by authors.)

ings, especially in recent years when underwriting experience has been so poor.

Since investment earnings are not taken into account in calculating premiums, a property and casualty insurance company is, in a very real sense, two separate organizations—an insurance company and a diversified balanced closed-end investment company.[26] There is no specific investment income goal which must be met to keep the insurance end of the business sound. However, to the extent that underwriting activities are unsuccessful, the soundness of the total company depends on the soundness of the investment portfolio. Thus, the two parts of a property and casualty company are interdependent. When risks of loss are increased in one part, they must ordinarily be reduced in the other. Good investment management, therefore, facilitates the achievement of a proper balance between the two parts of the business.

### Legal Restrictions on Investments

The legal regulation of property and casualty insurance company investments is relatively lenient. In New York State, for example, the following regulations are most significant:

1. Since policyholders receive a discount for paying premiums in advance—for example, a three-year policy may be fully paid with a lump sum equal to 2½ years' premiums—the premium income of most companies contains a large "unearned" element. In New York, at least 50% of unearned premiums plus 50% of the portion of earned premiums which is set aside as a reserve for payment of losses must be invested in high-grade bonds and mortgages.

2. The balance of a company's funds, may be invested in a wide variety of bonds, stocks, mortgages, or real estate. There are a few requirements dealing with quality and diversification, however, these are easily satisfied.

3. Stocks—preferred and common—must be carried at year-end market values, other assets at cost. As will be seen shortly, this is a crucial factor.

### Liquidity Needs

It is much more difficult for a property and casualty insurance company to forecast cash inflow and outflow than for a life insurance company. Liquidity requirements are, therefore, considerably greater. It will be seen in Table 19-2 that U.S. government securities represent 15%–20% of the assets of property and casualty companies. This compares with only a few percent for life companies. Of the governments held, between one half and two thirds have maturities of less than five

[26] It is not an investment company in the legal context of the Investment Company Act of 1940, however.

years, and within this segment a policy of spaced maturities is usually followed, so that some issues are always nearing maturity. Liquidity consciousness has discouraged these companies from entering the mortgage market to any considerable extent.[27]

### Taxation

Both stock and mutual property and casualty insurance companies are taxed like other business corporations with regard to investment income: (1) They are subject to an income tax rate of 48% on net interest income. (2) The same rate applies to net dividend income—but after an 85% credit, so that the rate is really only 7 + %.[28] Long-term capital gains are taxed at 25%.

These tax factors make state and local government bonds highly attractive to property and casualty companies in comparison with corporate bonds.[29] Since dividend income is taxed leniently, preferred stock is also often preferable to corporate bonds and mortgages. Convertible preferreds may be particularly appealing. Obviously, common stock investment also takes place with taxation prominently in mind, because dividends and capital gains receive favored treatment.

### Common Stock Investment Policies

The most crucial aspect of fire and casualty company portfolio management is determining the proportion of total assets to be invested in common stock—or, more accurately, the proportion of capital and surplus to be so invested, since policy reserves and unearned premiums are largely invested in fixed income securities. We have seen that investment policy must complement insurance policy. If insurance risks are great, investment risks must be reduced, and vice versa. Common stock is the investment medium carrying the most risk, since stock prices are very volatile and the law requires stocks to be carried at market value.

When we speak of risk exposure in any business, the first thing that comes to mind is the capital position of the business in relation to those phases of its operations that carry a high degree of risk. Traditionally, the degree of risk exposure in the insurance part of a fire and casualty

---

[27] For a view that the real liquidity needs of property and casualty companies are significantly less than is commonly assumed, see W. W. Amos, "Liquidity Currently Needed by Insurance Companies," *Commercial and Financial Chronicle*, October 6, 1966.

[28] Life insurance companies get the intercorporate dividend credit also, but since only investment income which contributes to surplus is taxed, the credit, in effect, is based on that small portion of dividends.

[29] However, companies with large underwriting loss carry-forwards may not find tax-exempts so attractive. For them, higher coupon rates may be desirable, even if taxable, since the underwriting losses can act as an offset against the interest income.

company is measured by the ratio of annual premium volume to capital and surplus. (Some analysts use "premiums written" in the numerator of the ratio, others use "premiums earned"; for old, established companies the two figures are usually quite similar.) Investment risk is measured by the ratio of common stock holdings to capital and surplus. To illustrate the significance of these ratios, let us refer, first, to an extreme example, and then to a more realistic case.

Suppose a company has annual premium volume of five times capital and surplus. Obviously, if in any one year a 20% loss is suffered—that is, if claim payments and operating expenses equaled 120% of premium income—capital and surplus would be wiped out. Of course, a 20% loss is quite improbable. But a 10% loss is not so improbable, and two consecutive years of 10% insurance losses would also wipe out capital and surplus.[30] If, under such circumstances, the company had common stocks in its portfolio, and the stock market declined during the period, the stocks would have to be marked down on the books, and the company would become insolvent. The stated value of assets would be less than stated liabilities. Therefore, it is axiomatic that a company with an insurance exposure ratio of 5 to 1 could not afford to have any investment exposure.

Now, an insurance exposure ratio of 5 to 1, or even 3 to 1 is unheard of, because the risks are simply too great. As a more realistic example, let us assume the following facts: At the end of year *X*, a company has capital and surplus of $100 million, and common stock investments of an equal amount, at market value. Normal premium volume for the company is $150 million. Thus, its insurance exposure ratio is 1.5 and investment exposure is 1.0. Next, assume that during year $X + 1$, an underwriting loss of 6% is suffered, and on top of this the stock market declines 25% (measured from December 31st of year *X* to December 31st of year $X + 1$).

A 6% loss on premium volume of $150 million is $9 million, and a 25% markdown of a $100 million stock portfolio is equal to $25 million. In other words, capital and surplus is reduced by $34 million, to $66 million. If new premium volume continues at the $150 million level, the new insurance exposure ratio is 150/66, or almost 2.3. Investment exposure is 75/66, or 1.1. At this point, the company would prudently have to consider switching out of common stocks and into safer investments, because another such year would bring it to perilous straits. Another $9 million underwriting loss combined with a $19 million writedown of common stock (25% of $75 million) would reduce capital and surplus to $38 million and raise the company's insurance exposure ratio to a totally unacceptable level of almost 4.0.

---

[30] Because of the possibility of large underwriting losses, property and casualty insurance companies typically have a ratio of capital and surplus to policy liabilities which is several times larger than that of life insurance companies (see Table 19–2).

But selling stocks after a 25% price decline is a dreadful action, because the odds are high that a turnaround is in the offing. Nevertheless, prudence would require such action, because a continued price decline would have even more dreadful consequences. The moral of the example, therefore, is that an investment exposure ratio of 1.0 is probably too high for a company whose insurance exposure ratio is 1.5.

Table 19–3 presents the insurance and investment exposure ratios of 10 leading stockholder-owned fire and casualty companies at the end of 1961, the peak of a rampant bull market. The table also ranks the ratios from lowest to highest. It will be noted that there is a fairly high degree of inverse correlation; companies with the highest insurance exposure ratios tend to have the lowest investment exposure ratios, and vice versa. This is precisely what the previous discussion should lead us to expect.

**TABLE 19–3**

**Risk Ratios of 10 Leading Stock Fire and Casualty Insurance Companies, 1961**

| | *Insurance Exposure* | | *Investment Exposure* | |
|---|---|---|---|---|
| *Company* | *Ratio* | *Rank* | *Ratio* | *Rank* |
| A | 0.43 | 1 | 1.08 | 10 |
| B | 0.64 | 2 | 0.92 | 8 |
| C | 0.80 | 3 | 0.96 | 9 |
| D | 1.02 | 4 | 0.91 | 6* |
| E | 1.14 | 5 | 0.84 | 5 |
| F | 1.20 | 6 | 0.83 | 4 |
| G | 1.26 | 7 | 0.91 | 6† |
| H | 1.34 | 8 | 0.76 | 1 |
| I | 1.43 | 9 | 0.82 | 3 |
| J | 1.44 | 10 | 0.79 | 2 |

* Tied with Company G.
† Tied with Company D.

It will also be observed, however, that the correlation is not perfect. Company G, for example, ranks seventh in insurance exposure but ranks sixth rather than fourth in investment exposure. Similarly, Figure 19–2 shows that in 1965 there was a generally inverse relationship between insurance exposure and investment exposure but that the correlation was far from perfect. The absence of perfect correlation is explained by the fact that considerations other than the absolute insurance exposure ratio are important in the determination of common stock investment policy. The most important of these other considerations are:

1. If premium quality is high, more investment risk is justified at a given insurance exposure ratio than if premium quality is poor. Two companies may write the same amount of business, but one may show consistently greater underwriting profits than the other. Premium quality

FIGURE 19–2

**Insurance and Investment Exposure Ratios of 20 Stock Fire and Casualty Insurance Companies, 1965**

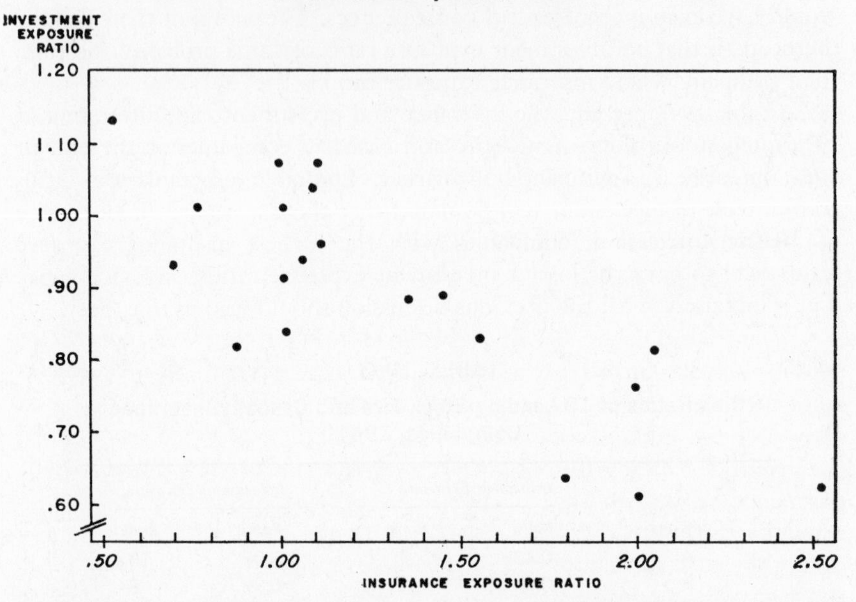


is related to such factors as type of business underwritten (auto lines, for example, are generally more risky than fire), geographic diversification of risks, and extent of reinsurance.

2. The trend of the insurance exposure ratio may be as important as its level. Young companies, which are rapidly expanding their volume of activity, usually have rising insurance exposure ratios because their capital and surplus expands less rapidly than sales. The opposite may be true of older companies with stable or declining sales. Other things being equal, the latter companies can follow a more aggressive investment policy than the former.

3. Identical investment exposure ratios do not necessarily signify identical risks. One company may stress stocks in relatively stable industries while another may put more emphasis on growth stocks or highly cyclical stocks. Furthermore, the stockholdings of many fire and casualty companies contain a large segment which is not a security investment in the usual sense of the word. Rather, it represents the ownership of subsidiary and affiliated insurance companies.

4. The underlying business philosophy of the management is important. Many companies, particularly the mutuals, reason that they are operating an insurance business first and foremost. If risks are to be assumed, they should be assumed primarily in underwriting. Many stock companies, on the other hand, reason that their stockholders are venture

capitalists who are willing, and even anxious, to take greater risks for greater potential returns. So long as the combined insurance and investment exposure does not transfer the risks to the insured—that is, so long as the probabilities of insolvency are small—an aggressive policy should be followed throughout the company. The composite insurance and investment exposure ratios for mutual companies, on the one hand, and stock companies, on the other, shown in Table 19–2, illustrate the philosophical cleavage between the two types of companies. A similar cleavage, though different in degree, exists within each of the two types of companies.

## NONINSURED PENSION PLANS

### Private Pension Plans

*Determination of Funds Available for Investment.* A competent pension actuary analyzes a company's pension benefit formula and its labor turnover, retirement, and mortality rates. Then, by incorporating an allowance for administrative expenses and assuming a rate of earnings on the investment of any funds to be set aside in advance for ultimate benefit payments, he estimates the probable net costs of the pension plan. The accuracy of this estimate will depend, of course, on the accuracy of the assumptions he makes regarding the relevant cost factors. But while pension costs are usually estimated in advance, with greater or lesser degrees of accuracy, funds do not necessarily have to be set aside in advance to meet these costs. A company may choose to operate on a "pay-as-you-go" basis, simply drawing checks on the general corporate bank account as benefits come due. Obviously, if a pension plan is on a pay-as-you-go basis, there is no investment portfolio management problem, because there is no investment of funds external to the business itself.

Since pay-as-you-go provides no security for the employees in the event the company terminates the pension plan or goes out of business altogether, this system of meeting pension costs is generally frowned upon and is not very common. More typical is some form of advance funding. The advance funding of pension costs is divisible into two major segments—funding of the "past service liability" and funding of the "current service liability" (technically referred to as "normal cost").

Past service liability mostly reflects the fact that when a pension plan becomes effective, the age of the labor force is not uniform. At retirement, therefore, different men will have worked a different number of years under the plan, yet will collect the same pension benefits, other things being equal. Accordingly, at the very outset of the plan a liability exists for workers who are then above the age of eligibility for entry into the plan. For example, if the entry eligibility age is 25 and a worker is 40 when the plan commences, there is a 15-year past service liability on his account. Similarly, past service liability arises when a company hires an older man or when benefits are liberalized. (Of course, if the benefits are geared directly to number of years worked from the commencement of the plan, or from date of hiring of a new man, there would be a past service liability only when benefits are liberalized.) Current service liability represents the annual accrual of costs after the adoption of the plan, or the hiring of a new man, or a change in the benefits.

The strictest type of advance funding involves the immediate setting aside of money equal to 100% of the past service liability plus annual set-asides in the amount of the current service liability. This is much too costly for most companies. Moreover, the Internal Revenue Service does not allow more than 10% of the past service liability to be charged against a company's income in any single year. Consequently, most companies fund the past service liability over a 20- to 30-year period and regularly fund the current service liability. The object is to have set aside enough money by the time each worker retires to guarantee him a life annuity. There are many companies, however, whose funding method is a cross between pay-as-you-go and advance funding. In effect, a worker's pension security is dependent on continued contributions by the company after he retires![31]

Clearly, the speed with which pension liabilities are funded is of vital importance to those charged with investing the funds set aside. In the first place, the funding method is the key determinant of the cash flow pattern and, therefore, of the need or lack of need for liquidity. Second, and perhaps less obvious—even to professional investment managers—the speed of advance funding affects the security of the employees. Companies can, after all, go out of business, and the more rapidly their pension liabilities have been funded, the more secure are their employees' pension rights.[32] The less secure these rights, the more questionable is a high-risk investment policy.

Once a funding method is chosen, the funds must be put under someone's control. A simple balance sheet reserve set up by the employer is unacceptable under IRS regulations, which require the funds to be outside the employer's control in order to be tax deductible. There are, basically, two things that can be done with the funds. (1) They may be turned over to an insurance company and used to purchase annuities—

---

[31] The minimum annual contribution under an IRS-approved plan is the current service liability plus interest on the past service liability. None of these comments should be interpreted as suggesting that funding is done on an individual-employee basis. It is not. However, it is helpful to think in terms of the individual employee's position should the company terminate the plan.

[32] When the Studebaker Corporation moved its auto operations to Canada in 1964, the amount of pension funds that had been set aside was too small to secure the pensions of all but the oldest workers. Younger men lost all pension rights. For a discussion of some practical aspects of pension funding methods, see C. L. Trowbridge, "ABC's of Pension Funding," *Harvard Business Review*, March-April, 1966.

either gradually during the working career of each employee or in a lump sum when each retires. (2) They may be placed with a trustee for investment and ultimate distribution of benefits—either directly by the trustee or through the medium of an insured annuity purchased by the trustee when each worker retires. The trustee under arrangement (2), often referred to as a "self-administered plan," may be a committee of company executives and/or union representatives, but more often it is a commercial bank.[33]

It is beyond the scope of this chapter to discuss the pros and cons of insured versus trusteed financing of pension plans, except to note that recent innovations in the life insurance industry have made the differences between the two methods of financing less clear-cut than in former years.[34] In any event, since insured pension plan assets are, in effect, invested the same way as other life insurance company assets,[35] and since we have already discussed life insurance investment policies, we will be concerned in the balance of this chapter with the investment of trusteed pension funds.

*Factors Influencing Investment Policies.* There are four major factors which influence the investment of trusteed corporate pension plans. (Note we are not, at this point, discussing deferred profit sharing plans or the plans of state and local governments. These will be reviewed briefly in a later section.) The four factors are as follows.

1. There are no legal restrictions on pension trust investing other than the usual fiduciary principle that a trustee must deal at arm's length with the trust, making no personal profit from its operation other than his regular service fee.[36] In addition, the Commissioner of Internal Revenue has the power to restrict the investment of pension trust assets in the securities of the employer corporation if he has good reason to believe that the trust is being used as a captive source of funds for the corporation—i.e., if purchase of the securities cannot be defended on their own

[33] Since the IRS requires pension funds to be outside employer control, some interesting questions arise when company executives act as trustees of their company's pension plan. Under general fiduciary law, individual trustees are *personally* liable for the funds under their control. But in most of the 50 states, the extent of this personal liability is not clear with regard to pension plan trustees. For example, it has been reported that the pension plan of the Textron Corporation contains a clause excusing certain officer-trustees from "any statute, rule of law or custom governing investments by fiduciaries." See J. Landauer, "Policing Pensions," *The Wall Street Journal*, March 16, 1966, p. 1.

[34] For example, in most key states life insurance companies are now permitted to segregate any portion of pension fund assets, up to 100%, and invest it in common stocks; *but only if* desired by the company sponsoring the pension plan. See J. C. Bowling, "Separate Accounts—The Quiet Revolution in Pension Funding," *The C.L.U. Journal*, Summer, 1965.

[35] Except for any portion that may be placed in a segregated common stock account.

[36] However, see footnote 33.

investment-worthiness.[37] Aside from these rudimentary controls, a trustee's investment powers are governed exclusively by the terms of the trust agreement. The most common terms are, in order of popularity:

*a*) The trustee is given complete discretion.
*b*) He is given discretion within certain prescribed limits, such as the maximum percentage of assets that may be placed in common stocks, maximum concentration of stocks in any one industry or any one company, etc.
*c*) Investments may be made only with the approval of a designated co-trustee.
*d*) Investments are to be made at the direction of the company or its investment adviser—i.e., the trustee, in effect, is merely a custodian, although he may be asked to recommend appropriate investments.

2. All income and capital gain on pension trust investments is tax exempt while in the hands of the trustee.[38] When retirement benefits are ultimately paid, the pensioner then pays an income tax.

3. There is usually a strong incentive for the trustee, where he has some discretion, to try to maximize investment return, since the employer's pension costs can be reduced, or benefits increased, by 5% or more for every extra 25 basis points earned. With labor unions constantly pressing for liberalized pension benefits, and with inflation tending to increase benefit payments automatically under plans where pensions are based on earnings (which usually rise with a rising price level), the employer's stake in improved investment performance is obvious. And the employer, after all, is usually the one who chooses the plan's trustee.

4. In seeking to maximize investment income, the trustee is usually relatively unhampered by liquidity considerations until a pension plan is quite old. The average plan which is funded in reasonably orderly fashion takes 30 or more years to "mature"—i.e., to reach the stage where benefit payments and expenses equal contributions and investment income. Plans of strong, growing companies may not mature at any time in the visible future. As long as cash inflow exceeds outgo, there is no danger of having to liquidate securities in a bear market.

We think it important to note, however, in connection with this latter point, that far too many trustees blithely assume that scheduled employer contributions will, in fact, be made. A company may very well suspend contributions, temporarily during an economic recession or permanently if it goes out of business or for some other reason, and it is our

---

[37] There is increasing feeling that some pension funds have abused the privilege of investing in their sponsor's stock. See F. L. Zimmerman, "SEC Set to Hit Firms' Purchases of Own Shares," *The Wall Street Journal,* April 21, 1966, p. 6.

[38] However, under certain circumstances the IRS may rule that the trust is actually operating a business concern via its investment, and such "unrelated business income" would be taxable.

opinion that a trustee should consider the probabilities of this occurring when he determines the extent to which he can invest in volatile, illiquid, high-risk types of securities or mortgages. At the least, it is probably good policy to keep sufficient funds in relatively safe investments to assure payments to existing pensioners.

On the other hand, we are realistic enough to recognize that the trustee may be faced with a profound conflict of interest on this score. For it may be that precisely those corporations whose financial position calls into question the certainty of continued contributions are the corporations most desirous of cost-reducing high-investment income. In that case, the trustee must balance his moral obligation to the employee beneficiaries of the trust against his bread-and-butter relationship with the employer.

*Investment Policies.* It should be clear from the above recitation that the investment managers of a pension trust usually have more flexibility than virtually any other type of investor, individual or institutional. They are unfettered by law. Their relative lack of liquidity needs enables them to seek higher yields in off-the-beaten-path investment media. Tax exemption permits them to do this without distinguishing between current income and capital gain. It also allows them to switch out of overpriced investments and into undervalued situations without regard to tax consequences. If they feel unable to "time" cyclical turning points, their steady fund inflow enables them simply to dollar average. It also permits them to restructure their portfolio by reallocating the investment of new fund inflow without being forced to sell existing holdings if doing so would upset prices.

Pension trustees have become increasingly aggressive in their investment policies with the passage of time. Twenty years ago, when the pension movement was in its infancy, safety dominated the thinking in the field, and investments were confined largely to government bonds and Aaa- to A-rated corporate bonds. Slowly, but steadily, it began to be recognized that pension trusts were ideally suited to undertake common stock investments because of the long-term nature of their liabilities and their slight liquidity needs. The trend toward common stock investment accelerated until, today, the "typical" corporate pension trust has one half of more of its assets, at market value, in common stock and most of the balance in corporate bonds (see Table 19–4). Government bonds comprise about 5% of assets, and mortgages about the same proportion. Low-yielding preferred stocks and state and local government bonds are unattractive to these tax-exempt institutions. The category labeled "other assets" mostly represents direct investments in real estate.

A frequent criticism of pension fund investment policies is that the one third to one half of assets which are invested in fixed income securities are too high in average quality. They should be more similar, it is argued,

TABLE 19–4

**Assets of Private Noninsured Pension and Deferred Profit Sharing Funds,* December 31, 1965**

(Common Stock at Market; Other Assets at Book)

| | *Billion $* | *% of Total* |
|---|---|---|
| Cash and deposits | 0.9 | 1.2 |
| U.S. government and agency securities: | | |
| Maturing in under five years† | 1.9 | 2.6 |
| Maturing in five or more years | 1.2 | 1.7 |
| Corporate bonds | 22.7 | 31.3 |
| Mortgages | 3.3 | 4.5 |
| Preferred stock | 0.8 | 1.2 |
| Common stock: | | |
| Own company‡ | 4.1 | 5.6 |
| Other companies | 34.8 | 48.0 |
| Other assets | 2.8 | 3.9 |
| Total Assets | 72.5 | 100.0 |

* Includes funds of nonprofit organizations and multiemployer plans in addition to corporate plans.
† Includes nonmarketable issues.
‡ Mostly in profit sharing funds.
Source: SEC Statistical Release No. 2132; *Treasury Bulletin*, February, 1966.

to life insurance investments, and should include more lower quality corporate bonds and more mortgages. In response to this criticism, pension trustees usually argue that higher quality fixed income securities are needed to balance the relatively high common stock proportions and that most pension trusts are not large enough to be able to diversify in the broad manner called for when lower quality bonds and mortgages are purchased. To this defense the critics reply, in turn, that the safety of diversification could be provided through specialized "common trust funds" in which the fixed income assets of smaller pension trusts could be pooled.[39] Barring this, there is always available the alternative of placing the fixed income portion of a pension trust's assets with a life insurance company under a so-called "split-funding" arrangement—although this may not be acceptable to a commercial bank from a competitive point of view.

In our opinion, the pension fund critics have the better of the argument. While we feel, as noted earlier, that safety is particularly important in situations where there is a significant possibility of contributions being terminated, we feel that the employment of common trust funds and insurance company facilities can help provide such safety. Indeed, even without resorting to these methods, over the years, pension trustees could have significantly increased earnings on fixed income in-

[39] Common trust funds are widely used for investing smaller trust fund assets in common stock.

vestments, without sacrificing safety, by the simple device of purchasing government-insured mortgages. Pension trustees have almost completely missed the boat in the mortgage field.[40] They have also been notably slow in getting into private placements in their bond operations.[41]

Pension trustees are also subject to some criticism of their common stock operations. We observe a general reluctance on their part to attempt a cyclical timing policy and a less than wholehearted attempt to ferret out relatively unknown, undervalued situations. There is not much justification for levying investment service fees if all a trustee does, in effect, is dollar average in a cross section of the stocks of large corporations. But this criticism is equally applicable, in our opinion, to most institutional investors, including life insurance companies, property and casualty insurance companies, and mutual funds.

It can be pointed out in defense of the trustees, however, that while they emphasize the stocks of large, well-known corporations and do not make much of an attempt to time the stock price cycle by switching from stocks to cash or bonds, they have increasingly made an effort to improve performance by switching out of overvalued and into undervalued "big" stocks. Table 19–5 reveals the increase, noted earlier, in the proportion of new pension fund money going into common stock (at least until 1961), but it also reveals a marked relative increase in sales transactions. Additional data putting pension fund common stock holdings and transactions

---

[40] It is noteworthy that in the relatively small number of pension plans where labor unions play an important role in investment administration, mortgages represent a much more substantial share of assets than is typical of trusteed plans. It is not clear, however, whether this is due to labor's greater recognition of the *investment* merits of mortgages or to its greater awareness of the social welfare aspects of mortgage financing.

[41] A recent Ph.D. dissertation contains the following observations:

"It was apparent from discussions with bank trust departments that the major influence on objectives of bank trusteed funds is the prudent man statute. This statute is interpreted to require that a trustee be able to justify each individual investment as being one which a prudent person would make. The principal of diversification is not satisfactory defense against the responsibility for any single investment being of insufficient quality. This causes banks to be reluctant to accept securities with unique features, to be the sole owners of private placements, or to acquire lease-backs.

"The second constraint on the range of investment alternatives is the fee schedule and the problem of staff size. Low fees as a percentage of assets administered was mentioned often by the trust departments interviewed as restricting them from committing investment, accounting and legal staff employees to the time required to process and approve non-standard investments. Several trust departments mentioned that, under the usual agreement to act as trustee for a fund, it is possible to be reimbursed for additional expenses caused by processing certain investments. However, there is a general reluctance to pass on higher fees even if the return after fee would be higher."

See R. B. Ricks, "Trends in Equity Investment in Real Estate by Institutions in the Postwar Period" (unpublished Ph.D. dissertation, University of California, 1963), pp. 156–58.

TABLE 19–5

**Common Stock Transactions of Trusteed Corporate Pension Plans**

(Dollar Data in Millions)

| *Year* | *Purchases* | *Sales* | *Net Purchases* | *Net Inflow of Funds** | *Net Purchases as Percent of Net Inflow of Funds* | *Ratio: Purchases to Sales* |
|---|---|---|---|---|---|---|
| 1953 | 513 | 74 | 439 | 1,848 | 23.8 | 6.9 |
| 1954 | 738 | 148 | 590 | 1,883 | 31.3 | 5.0 |
| 1955 | 858 | 249 | 609 | 2,122 | 28.7 | 3.4 |
| 1956 | 1,000 | 229 | 771 | 2,389 | 32.3 | 4.4 |
| 1957 | 1,186 | 208 | 978 | 2,682 | 36.5 | 5.7 |
| 1958 | 1,527 | 335 | 1,192 | 2,769 | 43.0 | 4.6 |
| 1959† | 2,207 | 544 | 1,663 | 3,270 | 50.9 | 4.1 |
| 1960 | 2,441 | 625 | 1,816 | 3,550 | 51.2 | 3.9 |
| 1961† | 3,440 | 1,170 | 2,270 | 3,636 | 62.4 | 2.9 |
| 1962 | 3,205 | 995 | 2,210 | 3,781 | 58.3 | 3.2 |
| 1963 | 3,760 | 1,555 | 2,205 | 3,946 | 55.8 | 2.4 |
| 1964 | 4,375 | 2,105 | 2,270 | 4,444 | 51.2 | 2.1 |
| 1965 | 5,585 | 2,560 | 3,025 | 5,061 | 59.8 | 2.2 |

* Employer and employee contributions plus investment and other income (exclusive of capital gains) less benefits paid and expenses.

† Slight discontinuities occur in the data at the indicated dates.

Source: Securities and Exchange Commission, *Annual Surveys of Pension Plans.*

## Deferred Profit Sharing Plans

into the broader perspective of institutional common stock investments are contained in an appendix to this chapter.

Many employers do not wish to commit themselves to the fixed obligations entailed by standard pension plans, but prefer to make contributions to an employee pension trust in relation to annual profits—for example, some percent of total profits or some percent of profits over and above a specified level. This arrangement—known as a deferred profit sharing plan—may also be used to supplement standard pension plans. That is, the company may have two plans running simultaneously. As with a standard pension plan, the employee pays no income tax on the employer's contribution until he receives a cash benefit—either in the form of a monthly annuity or a lump-sum payment (in the latter case, he pays a capital gains tax rather than regular income tax). Similarly, funds in the trust are invested *tax free.*[42] The law limits annual contributions to 15% of a company's total wages and salaries.

[42] Under both standard pension plans and deferred profit sharing plans, there are a broad variety of provisions regarding the employee's rights in the event he resigns or dies before retirement. Many deferred profit sharing plans also permit an employee to choose whether to take his share of the company's contribution on a regular annual basis—in effect, a regularly taxed bonus—or whether to let it accumulate and earn interest tax free in a retirement trust.

In several respects, the investment problems of a deferred profit sharing plan trustee are different from those inherent in standard pension plans. The major differences are as follows.

1. Since the employer's contributions are based on profits, the profit sharing trust's cash flow is far more uncertain in both timing and magnitude. The uncertainty is magnified by the choice given the employee at retirement to either take a lump-sum payment or an annuity.

2. High investment income does not reduce the employer's costs, because these costs are a function of the profits earned by the business.

3. The employer's motive in establishing a deferred profit sharing plan may be only, in part, a desire to provide his employees with a retirement income. He may, in addition, see the plan as an incentive device; if the employees know that higher profits mean higher contributions (up to the legal limits), they presumably have an incentive to work harder and more efficiently.[43]

The first two factors cited suggest a more conservative investment policy for deferred profit sharing trusts than for standard pension trusts. Since cash flow is uncertain, liquidity needs are greater. With regard to common stock investments, cash flow is not only uncertain—it is perverse. Net cash inflow tends to rise, along with the employer's profits, during periods of good business when, presumably, stock prices also tend to be high; and it tends to fall when stock prices are relatively low. An aggressive common stock program thrives on precisely the opposite cash inflow pattern—up when prices are low, down when prices are high. Moreover, since the employer's contributions are not reduced by good investment results, there is less incentive than under a standard pension plan for a trustee to strive for maximum investment income. The diminution of this incentive is reinforced by the knowledge that poor investment results directly injure the employee-beneficiaries.

While these factors suggest a conservative investment policy, if a deferred profit sharing plan is being used by the employer largely as an employee incentive device, a daring and imaginative investment policy may be advisable. Indeed, purchase of the employer's own stock may be called for to provide a triple-barreled incentive: hard work means higher profits, which result in (1) higher contributions, (2) higher dividends on the stock held in the trust fund, and (3) higher prices on the stock. Of course, such a program also places the employees in triple jeopardy.

Which of the two approaches should be emphasized in managing a deferred profit sharing plan is probably not for the trustee to determine. The basic philosophy is more the responsibility of the employer. Under some plans, the choice is given to the employees themselves. They are

[43] Whether or not the employees actually view the plan in this light is a matter of debate among students of labor relations.

permitted to specify whether they want their share of the fund to be invested in (*a*) high-quality bonds, (*b*) a balanced portfolio of bonds and common stocks, (*c*) an all-stock portfolio, or (*d*) the employer's stock. The choice may be a once-and-for-all proposition or may be periodically changeable; if changeable, the new choice may be applicable to new contributions only or to existing funds as well.

Data on the actual investment of all deferred profit sharing trusts are not available separate from data on standard pension plans. They are included in Table 19–4. However, most of the employer-company stockholdings shown in that table represent deferred profit sharing plans, in particular the plan of Sears, Roebuck.

### Pension Plans of State and Local Governments

State and local pension plan assets amounted to over $33 billion at the end of 1965, and were growing at more than a $3 billion annual rate. From an investment point of view, the most noteworthy aspect of this huge aggregation of funds has been their history of mismanagement. Their trustees have been much slower than others to move away from government bonds and into corporates. They are still not in common stock to any significant degree. And, most reprehensible of all, they have invested a large percentage of total assets in low-yielding, tax-exempt bonds, particularly the bonds of the sponsoring governmental unit.

There are several explanations for this peculiar investment behavior, some of which are understandable but most of which are deplorable:

1. Many trustees have been shackled by obsolete state laws regulating the handling of public funds.

2. The trustees are usually elected or appointed public officials rather than professional fund managers, and they have been reluctant to incur the costs of hiring professionals.

3. Private pension plans, for the most part, are private matters, but public plans are subject to examination by political partisans. This sort of atmosphere is not conducive to aggressive investment management.

4. There is a temptation to relieve strained government budgets by using pension funds as a captive buyer of the employing-government's bonds, despite their low yields.

5. Most governmental pension plans require substantial employee contributions in addition to those of the employer. Therefore, errors have a more severe impact on the welfare of state and local government employees than of corporate employees, suggesting a more conservative investment philosophy.

To an increasing degree, public pension plans are being more efficiently managed. State laws are being updated, and professional investment consultants are being retained. New purchases of tax-exempt bonds have virtually ceased, although there has not been much selling of existing holdings. It is doubtful that these plans ever will, or should, be managed as aggressively as corporate plans, but their progress is encouraging—particularly in the mortgage sphere. Mortgages represent over 10% of state and local pension plan assets compared with only 5% for corporate plans.[44]

## SUGGESTED READINGS


Victor L. Andrews. "Non-Insured Corporate and State and Local Government Retirement Funds." Study Three in *Private Capital Markets.* New York: Prentice-Hall, Inc., 1964.

Elliot Beier (ed.). *How to Increase the Investment Return of Pension and Welfare Funds.* Dornost Publishing Co., 1965.

Andrew F. Brimmer. *Life Insurance Companies in the Capital Market.* East Lansing: Michigan State University Press, 1962.

P. O. Dietz. *Pension Funds: Measuring Investment Performance.* New York: Free Press of Glencoe, 1966.

Harold G. Fraine. *Valuation of Securities Holdings of Life Insurance Companies.* Homewood, Ill.: Richard D. Irwin, Inc., 1962.

Daniel M. Holland. *Private Pension Funds.* National Bureau of Economic Research, Occasional Paper, No. 97, New York: Columbia University Press, 1966.

Institute of Life Insurance. *Life Insurance Fact Book* (Annual).

Randolph W. McCandlish, Jr. "Some Methods for Measuring Performance of a Pension Fund," *Financial Analysts Journal*, November-December, 1965.

J. W. Middendorf, II. *Investment Policies of Fire and Casualty Insurance Companies.* New York: Wood, Struthers & Co., 1954.

James E. Walter, *The Investment Process. . . . As Characterized by Leading Life Insurance Companies.* Boston: Harvard Graduate School of Business Administration, 1962.

D. N. Warters and W. M. Rae. "The Risks in Equity Investment for Pension Funds," and Discussion by panel members, 1959 *Transactions* of the Society of Actuaries, pp. 920–75.


[44] Admittedly, the emphasis on mortgages is probably motivated as much by a recognition of the social benefits of mortgage investing as by yield considerations.

Statistics on state and local government pension plans are published annually by the Bureau of the Census in a release entitled *Finances of Employee-Retirement Systems of State and Local Governments.*

## APPENDIX TO CHAPTER 19: INSTITUTIONAL COMMON STOCK HOLDINGS AND TRANSACTIONS

### TABLE 19–1A
### Stockholdings† of Financial Institutions and Others
(Billions of Dollars)*

| | End of Year | |
|---|---|---|
| | *1955* | *1965* |
| **1. Noninsured private pension funds** | **6.1** | **39.7** |
| 2. Investment companies, total | 12.1 | 41.1 |
| *a*) Open-end | 7.2 | 33.5 |
| *b*) Other | 4.9 | 7.6 |
| 3. Life insurance companies | 3.6 | 9.1 |
| 4. Property and casualty insurance companies | 5.4 | 12.4 |
| 5. Banks | .8 | 1.9 |
| 6. State and local trust funds | .2 | 2.2 |
| 7. Fraternal organizations | .1 | .2 |
| 8. Total institutions (1 through 7) | 28.3 | 106.0 |
| 9. Foreigners‡ | 9.6 | 20.0 |
| 10. All others§ (Item 11 less items 8 and 9) | 271.6 | 548.6 |
| 11. Total stock outstanding | 309.5 | 674.7 |

* Figures may not add to totals because of rounding.

† Estimated market values. Excludes investment company shares but includes foreign issues outstanding in the United States.

‡ Includes estimate of stock held as direct investment.

§ Includes individuals, personal trust funds, and nonprofit institutions. End-of-1965 holdings of personal trust and common trust funds are estimated at $75 billion; foundation holdings at $14 billion; and college endowment holdings at $6 billion.

Source: Securities and Exchange Commission, Statistical Release No. 2134 and *Report on Public Policy Implications of Investment Company Growth*, 1966, pp. 276–77.

## TABLE 19–2A

### Estimated Holdings of NYSE-Listed Stocks by Financial Institutions

(Dollar Figures in Billions)

| | *Year-End* | | | | |
|---|---|---|---|---|---|
| | *1949* | *1956* | *1963* | *1964* | *1965* |
| **Noninsured Pension Funds:** | | | | | |
| **Corporate** | **$ 0.5** | **$ 5.3** | **$ 22.6** | **$ 27.5** | **$ 31.8** |
| **Other private** | * | **0.4** | **1.3** | **1.6** | **1.9** |
| **State and local government** | * | **0.2** | **1.1** | **1.5** | **1.7** |
| Insurance companies: | | | | | |
| Life | 1.1 | 2.3 | 4.6 | 5.3 | 6.2 |
| Nonlife | 1.7 | 4.5 | 8.2 | 9.5 | 10.3 |
| Investment companies: | | | | | |
| Open-End | 1.4 | 7.1 | 18.6 | 21.8 | 25.5 |
| Closed-End | 1.6 | 4.0 | 5.7 | 6.6 | 5.5 |
| Nonprofit institutions: | | | | | |
| College and university endowments | 1.1 | 2.4 | 4.0 | 4.6 | 5.2 |
| Foundations | 1.1 | 4.1 | 8.3 | 9.5 | 10.5 |
| Other | 1.0 | 3.1 | 5.9 | 6.8 | 7.7 |
| Common trust funds | * | 1.0 | 2.2 | 2.6 | 2.9 |
| Mutual savings banks | 0.2 | 0.2 | 0.4 | 0.4 | 0.5 |
| Total | $ 9.7 | $ 34.6 | $ 82.9 | $ 97.7 | $109.7 |
| Market value of all NYSE-listed stocks | $76.3 | $219.2 | $411.3 | $474.3 | $537.5 |
| Estimated percent held by all institutions | 12.7% | 15.8% | 20.2% | 20.6% | 20.4% |

* Less than $50 million.

Source: New York Stock Exchange, *1966 Fact Book.*

## TABLE 19–3A

**Net Acquisitions of Preferred and Common Stock Issues[1] by Financial Institutions and Others**

(Billions of Dollars)*

| | 1955 | 1956 | 1957 | 1958 | 1959 | 1960 | 1961 | 1962 | 1963 | 1964 | 1965 |
|---|---|---|---|---|---|---|---|---|---|---|---|
| 1. Net acquisitions by: | | | | | | | | | | | |
| a) **Noninsured private pension funds** | **0.7** | **0.9** | **1.1** | **1.4** | **1.7** | **1.9** | **2.3** | **2.2** | **2.2** | **2.2** | **3.1** |
| b) Investment companies | | | | | | | | | | | |
| For cash | 0.5 | 0.7 | 0.8 | 1.2 | 1.1 | 1.0 | 1.6 | 1.1 | 0.8 | 1.0 | 1.4 |
| Other[2] | .. | .. | .. | .. | .. | .. | 0.5 | −0.2 | 0.1 | −0.3 | −1.2 |
| c) Life insurance companies | 0.1 | −0.1 | † | 0.1 | 0.2 | 0.3 | 0.4 | 0.4 | 0.2 | 0.5 | 0.7 |
| d) Property and casualty insurance companies | 0.2 | 0.3 | 0.2 | 0.1 | 0.3 | 0.3 | 0.3 | 0.2 | 0.2 | 0.2 | 0.2 |
| e) Other financial institutions[3] | 0.1 | 0.1 | 0.1 | 0.1 | † | 0.2 | 0.3 | 0.4 | 0.5 | 0.5 | 0.6 |
| f) Total (items 1a through 1e incl.) | 1.6 | 1.9 | 2.3 | 2.9 | 3.3 | 3.6 | 5.2 | 4.0 | 3.9 | 4.1 | 4.8 |
| 2. Net acquisitions by foreigners: | | | | | | | | | | | |
| a) Domestic securities | 0.1 | 0.3 | 0.1 | −0.1 | 0.4 | 0.2 | 0.3 | 0.1 | 0.2 | −0.3 | −0.5 |
| b) Foreign securities in U.S. market | −0.2 | −0.1 | † | −0.3 | −0.2 | −0.1 | −0.4 | −0.1 | † | 0.1 | 0.3 |
| 3. Net acquisitions by others[4] (item 4 less items 1f and 2) | 0.4 | 0.5 | 0.3 | −0.4 | −1.0 | −2.0 | −2.6 | −3.4 | −4.4 | −2.5 | −4.3 |
| 4. Net new domestic issues[5] | 1.9 | 2.5 | 2.7 | 2.1 | 2.4 | 1.7 | 2.6 | 0.7 | −0.2 | 1.4 | † |

* Figures may not add to totals because of rounding.

† Less than $50 million.

[1] Excludes net shares issued by investment companies.

[2] Reflects net effect of such transactions as the acquisition through tax-free exchange of shares, distribution of stock either through liquidation, e.g., M. A. Hanna Co., or under antitrust order, e.g., G. M.–Christiana securities.

[3] Includes state and local trust funds, mutual savings banks and fraternal organizations.

[4] Includes individuals, personal trust funds, nonprofit institutions, and certain large publicized investments by nonfinancial corporations.

[5] Sale of $340 million General Aniline Stock by Attorney-General is not included in net new issues; therefore, item 4 less items 1f and 2 do not add in 1965.

Source: Securities & Exchange Commission, Statistical Release No. 2134.

## TABLE 19–4A

### Gross Purchases, Sales and Net Acquisitions of Common Stock[1] by Certain Financial Institutions and Foreigners 1955–1965

(Billions of Dollars)*

| | 1955 | 1956 | 1957 | 1958 | 1959 | 1960 | 1961 | 1962 | 1963 | 1964 | 1965 |
|---|---|---|---|---|---|---|---|---|---|---|---|
| **1. *Noninsured private pension funds*** | | | | | | | | | | | |
| **A. Purchases** | **975** | **1,145** | **1,340** | **1,730** | **2,310** | **2,610** | **3,440** | **3,205** | **3,760** | **4,375** | **5,585** |
| **B. Sales** | **290** | **265** | **250** | **400** | **570** | **670** | **1,170** | **995** | **1,555** | **2,105** | **2,560** |
| **C. Net purchases** | **685** | **880** | **1,090** | **1,330** | **1,740** | **1,940** | **2,270** | **2,210** | **2,205** | **2,270** | **3,025** |
| 2. *Open-end investment companies* | | | | | | | | | | | |
| A. Purchases | 1,085 | 1,545 | 1,695 | 2,435 | 2,890 | 2,785 | 3,955 | 3,695 | 4,010 | 4,770 | 6,530 |
| B. Sales | 720 | 1,025 | 995 | 1,455 | 1,905 | 2,000 | 2,755 | 2,720 | 3,235 | 3,885 | 5,165 |
| C. Net purchases | 365 | 520 | 705 | 980 | 985 | 785 | 1,200 | 980 | 780 | 885 | 1,365 |
| 3. *Life insurance companies* | | | | | | | | | | | |
| A. Purchases | 230 | 225 | 255 | 275 | 360 | 385 | 605 | 555 | 575 | 790 | 970 |
| B. Sales | 175 | 215 | 205 | 220 | 240 | 220 | 370 | 240 | 405 | 455 | 575 |
| C. Net purchases | 60 | 5 | 55 | 55 | 115 | 165 | 235 | 315 | 170 | 335 | 395 |
| 4. *Property and casualty insurance companies* | | | | | | | | | | | |
| A. Purchases | n.a. | n.a. | n.a. | n.a. | n.a. | n.a. | n.a. | 675 | 710 | 765 | 760 |
| B. Sales | | | | | | | | 475 | 600 | 660 | 700 |
| C. Net purchases | | | | | | | | 200 | 110 | 105 | 60 |
| 5. *Total* (items 1–4, incl.) | | | | | | | | | | | |
| A. Purchases | 2,290 | 2,915 | 3,295 | 4,445 | 5,555 | 5,780 | 8,000 | 8,135 | 9,060 | 10,700 | 13,845 |
| B. Sales | 1,185 | 1,505 | 1,450 | 2,075 | 2,715 | 2,890 | 4,295 | 4,430 | 5,795 | 7,100 | 8,995 |
| C. Net purchases | 1,110 | 1,405 | 1,845 | 2,370 | 2,840 | 2,895 | 3,705 | 3,705 | 3,265 | 3,595 | 4,850 |
| 6. *Foreigners*[2] | | | | | | | | | | | |
| A. Purchases | 1,560 | 1,620 | 1,300 | 1,400 | 2,225 | 1,975 | 3,070 | 2,235 | 2,720 | 3,075 | 3,630 |
| B. Sales | 1,430 | 1,365 | 1,160 | 1,450 | 1,870 | 1,770 | 2,245 | 2,150 | 2,525 | 3,425 | 4,130 |
| C. Net purchases | 130 | 255 | 145 | −55 | 355 | 205 | 325 | 85 | 195 | −350 | −500 |

* Figures have been rounded to nearest $5 million.

[1] Includes only cash transactions; figures do not reflect stock dividends or splits and exclude exchanges of one security for another pursuant to conversion rights, mergers or plans of reorganization.

[2] Reflects trading in domestic issues including preferred stock.

Source: Securities and Exchange Commission, Statistical Release No. 2134.

## TABLE 19–5A

### Relative Importance of Share Volume of Institutions and Intermediaries to Total Volume

| | Share Volume per Day | | |
|---|---|---|---|
| | | Institutions and Intermediaries | |
| Period* | Total Volume (Thousands) | Shares (Thousands) | % of Total Volume |
| March, 1965 | | | 31.4% |
| October, 1963 | 12,227 | 2,921 | 23.9 |
| September, 1961 | 7,389 | 1,936 | 26.2 |
| September, 1960 | 6,607 | 1,606 | 24.3 |
| June, 1959 | 6,670 | 1,521 | 22.8 |
| September, 1958 | 8,887 | 2,036 | 22.9 |
| October, 1957 | 4,880 | 1,136 | 23.3 |
| March, 1956 | 7,121 | 1,429 | 20.1 |
| June, 1955 | 6,790 | 1,319 | 19.4 |
| December, 1954 | 7,696 | 1,346 | 17.5 |
| March, 1954 | 4,098 | 962 | 23.5 |
| March, 1953 | 4,954 | 956 | 19.3 |
| September, 1952 | 3,101 | 762 | 24.6 |

* The years 1959, 1960, 1961, and 1963 are based on transactions for one day. The previous eight studies are based on two days. The 1958 data are projections from a 10% sample. Complete information not available for 1965.

Source: New York Stock Exchange.

TABLE 19–6A
Percent Distribution of NYSE Share Volume by Institutions and Intermediaries, September 26–30, 1960, and October 21–25, 1963

| | September 26–30 1960 | October 21–25 1963 |
|---|---|---|
| ***Employee Pension or Profit Sharing*** | | |
| **Corporation** | **4.7%** | **3.5%** |
| **Government** | **0.2** | **0.3** |
| **Union** | **0.1** | **0.4** |
| **Religious** | **0.2** | **0.2** |
| **Other** | * | **0.4** |
| *Banks* | | |
| Commercial | 40.1 | 34.0 |
| Other | 0.5 | 3.5 |
| *Insurance Companies* | | |
| Life | 2.2 | 2.3 |
| Nonlife | 3.2 | 2.9 |
| *Investment Companies* | | |
| Mutual funds | 17.5 | 17.9 |
| Closed-end | 1.8 | 2.3 |
| *Educational Institutions* | | |
| Colleges and universities | 1.4 | 1.9 |
| Other schools | 0.1 | 0.2 |
| *Nonbank Trusts* | | |
| Personal trusts | 2.6 | 2.0 |
| Estates | 1.6 | 2.7 |
| Guardianships | 0.2 | 0.1 |
| *Other Nonprofit Institutions* | | |
| Religious organizations | 0.5 | 0.5 |
| Hospitals | 0.4 | 0.2 |
| Nursing homes or homes for aged | 0.2 | 0.1 |
| Health and benevolent associations | 0.1 | 0.2 |
| Foundations | 1.2 | 1.5 |
| *Miscellaneous* | | |
| Nonmember broker/dealers | 11.0 | 11.2 |
| Nonfinancial corporations | 4.6 | 5.0 |
| Personal holding corporations | 1.9 | 1.7 |
| Partnerships | 0.7 | 1.8 |
| Investment clubs | 0.7 | 1.2 |
| Other | 2.1 | 2.0 |
| All Institutions and Intermediaries—Total† | 100.0% | 100.0% |

* Less than .05%.
† Accounts for about one quarter of total NYSE share volume.
Source: New York Stock Exchange.

# 20

# THE ROLE OF THE COMPUTER

I dare to dream things that never were and
say—why not?

—George Bernard Shaw

Electronic computers have been used by stock brokers for many years to perform so-called "back office operations"—recording transactions, billing, preparing monthly statements, and similar bookkeeping routines. But investment organizations are only beginning to apply the powers of the computer to security analysis and portfolio management problems. There is increasing awareness, however, that the speed and accuracy of the computer can relieve professional investment personnel of many of their routine, repetitive chores and, probably more important, can broaden their horizons. A computer can "remember" far more factual information than a human being and can cope with difficult calculations and complex interrelationships at lightning speed—once it is "told" what to do. Thus, the human and the machine can interact to achieve a depth and breadth of knowledge about the investment process which has never before been possible.

The role of the computer in investment analysis, moreover, need not be limited to a mere handful of gigantic institutions, although it is true that to date relatively few financial organizations have used computers for analytical purposes. In the first place, it is not necessary to own an electronic computer, or even to have a long-term lease on one, in order to use one. Computer time can be rented on an hourly basis from numerous organizations. Access to moderately efficient computers can be had at an hourly cost of about $50. Very advanced equipment, which performs calculations at speeds 10 or more times faster than older equipment, can be rented for about $400 an hour. To illustrate the capacity of such an advanced computer, we would estimate that in one hour per week the routine paper work (for example, ratio analysis of income statements and balance sheets) could be processed on which a staff of six or more junior and senior security analysts and portfolio managers spend at least 25% of their time.

Second, virtually anyone with a reasonable degree of intelligence can learn to write computer programs using the FORTRAN (Formula Translator) language, or a similar programmer-oriented language. From personal experience, we can state that after about three weeks of study, and with the occasional assistance of a professional programmer (whose services are also rentable on a part-time basis), a competent investment analyst can write complex computer programs quickly and efficiently. Furthermore, at least one firm is developing a new computer language and leased computer installation specifically for financial analysis, which it claims can be effectively learned and applied in less than a day.[1] In addition, the major computer manufacturers make freely available a large assortment of programs which can either be used directly or can be modified by the user to suit his unique requirements.[2]

Third, magnetic tapes and punched cards containing a vast quantity of company income statement, balance sheet, and stock price data can be rented from Standard & Poor's Corporation, Ultronic Systems Corporation, and other organizations at relatively modest charges. Thus, a large amount of data processing and analysis can be done without the user having to expend funds and resources to develop the basic data input files.[3]

Summing up, we would argue that computer-oriented investment analysis programs can be undertaken with relatively modest increases in an organization's research budget. It would seem, therefore, that financial organizations which do not undertake such programs must fail to do so because they do not appreciate the potential advantages to be gained. The purpose of this chapter is to describe some of these advantages. To do so, the investment process has been subdivided into four component parts:

1. Screening
2. Security Evaluation
3. Investment Timing
4. Portfolio Strategy

---

[1] The firm is White, Weld & Co. The language incorporates some of the features of "teaching machines." That is, the user and the computer interact in a continuing "real-time dialogue" until the program is completed to the user's satisfaction. For a description of the concept, see J. J. Gal, "Man-Machine Interactive Systems and Their Application to Financial Analysis," *Financial Analysts Journal*, May-June, 1966. A subset of FORTRAN, known as "BASIC," has already been developed by General Electric, in conjunction with Dartmouth, and is being used successfully by financial analysts at the First National City Bank of New York.

[2] We would note, however, that it is often easier to write a new program than to modify an existing program package.

[3] It must be admitted, however, that available data banks of daily stock prices, volume of trading, and other "technical" statistics are not yet very complete.

## Screening

A very large proportion of the time spent by most security analysts and portfolio managers is in the nature of routine paperwork. Most of this work is designed to screen out from the thousands of stocks and bonds available to investors a few dozen which, at a given moment of time, are deserving of intensive study for the purpose of determining whether to buy, hold, or sell. Electronic computers can be utilized in the screening process to relieve highly trained and well-paid personnel from much of this routine work, thus freeing their time for more creative endeavors. Furthermore, the speed and accuracy of the computer can be expected to do a more efficient screening job on a larger list of securities than humans are capable of.

One illustration of the use of the computer for screening purposes is the so-called "Financial Analysis Program," developed by IBM to facilitate common stock analysis. The program generates five types of reports, utilizing as input a magnetic tape file of annual income and balance sheet data for hundreds of industrial corporations. This file, known as "Compustat," is maintained and updated by Standard & Poor's Corporation, which offers it to subscribers on a rental basis. Starting below and continued the next several pages, sample print-outs of each of the five reports are shown, together with a brief description of the purpose of each report.

### FIGURE 20–1

### Stocks Meeting Selected Criteria

REQUEST NO. 01 — FINANCIAL ANALYSIS REPORT NO. 1

REQUESTED BY JCP — 12/31/65

PAGE NO. 1

CONTROL STANDARDS —

| | P/E | | YIELD | | OP INC MARGIN | | RET ON COM | | NET PROF MARGIN | |
|---|---|---|---|---|---|---|---|---|---|---|
| | OVER | UNDER | OVER | UNDER | OVER | UNDER | OVER | UNDER | OVER | UNDER |
| | | 15 | 3.5 | | | | 12.0 | | | |

COMPANIES WHICH MEET THE ABOVE SPECIFICATIONS --

| CODE INDUSTRY | CODE COMPANY | COMPANY SYMBOL | OR NAME | P/E | YIELD | OP INC MARGIN | RET ON COM | NET PROF MARGIN |
|---|---|---|---|---|---|---|---|---|
| 1000 | 141400 | CDP | Cerro Corp. | 8 | 3.7 | 17.2 | 12.6 | 8.7 |
| 1031 | 365500 | HD | Hudson Bay Mining | 13 | 4.8 | 38.8 | 18.5 | 25.9 |
| 1031 | 636400 | SJO | St. Joseph Lead | 10 | 4.7 | 25.8 | 19.3 | 16.7 |
| 2063 | 016100 | AGM | Amalgamated Sugar | 9 | 3.8 | 19.6 | 13.3 | 8.2 |
| 2063 | 326400 | GSW | Great Western Sugar | 9 | 5.0 | 16.6 | 18.3 | 7.3 |
| 2070 | 797800 | WWY | Wm. Wrigley | 14 | 5.0 | 21.0 | 15.0 | 10.7 |
| 2111 | 037500 | AT | American Tobacco | 13 | 4.2 | 23.6 | 13.3 | 11.4 |
| 2111 | 436800 | LL | P. Lorillard | 11 | 5.7 | 20.3 | 14.1 | 9.3 |
| 2111 | 583100 | MO | Philip Morris | 13 | 4.0 | 13.8 | 12.9 | 5.8 |
| 2111 | 618200 | RJR | R. J. Reynolds Tobacco | 13 | 4.2 | 29.2 | 18.2 | 13.3 |
| 2300 | 499300 | MUN | Munsingwear | 11 | 3.6 | 10.1 | 12.8 | 4.5 |
| 2800 | 512900 | LT | National Lead | 14 | 4.6 | 15.8 | 17.5 | 7.7 |
| 3141 | 467100 | MES | Melville Shoe | 10 | 3.6 | 8.5 | 23.3 | 4.1 |
| 3331 | 379000 | IC | Inspiration Copper | 10 | 6.3 | 28.7 | 13.3 | 18.8 |
| 3331 | 406600 | KN | Kennecott | 13 | 3.9 | 33.1 | 12.2 | 15.3 |
| 3331 | 579100 | PD | Phelps Dodge | 11 | 5.4 | 24.4 | 14.5 | 14.5 |
| 3531 | 098800 | BY | Bucyrus-Erie | 9 | 4.8 | 19.2 | 20.0 | 10.1 |
| 3531 | 413400 | KOE | Kohring | 10 | 3.9 | 11.2 | 16.2 | 5.6 |
| 3533 | 059475 | BKO | Baker Oil Tools | 13 | 3.7 | 17.6 | 15.1 | 8.3 |
| 3540 | 504400 | NCM | National Acme | 10 | 6.2 | 18.4 | 14.4 | 9.8 |
| 3560 | 147700 | CGG | Chicago Pneumatic | 13 | 3.6 | 24.1 | 15.9 | 12.0 |
| 3711 | 282950 | F | Ford Motor | 9 | 3.9 | 13.4 | 16.7 | 6.1 |
| 3711 | 303010 | GM | General Motors | 14 | 5.0 | 21.6 | 27.3 | 10.3 |
| 3713 | 291100 | FTR | Fruehauf | 12 | 4.2 | 12.1 | 14.6 | 5.9 |
| 3714 | 142530 | CHM | Champion Spark Plug | 14 | 4.8 | 26.8 | 20.8 | 14.1 |
| 3714 | 203800 | DCN | Dana Corp. | 13 | 4.4 | 13.6 | 14.0 | 6.2 |
| 3714 | 237236 | ENX | Eaton Yale & Towne | 10 | 3.6 | 15.1 | 17.3 | 6.2 |
| 3714 | 259600 | FMO | Federal Mogul Bower | 13 | 4.7 | 15.2 | 14.0 | 6.9 |
| 3714 | 718900 | TKR | Timken Roller Bearing | 10 | 4.3 | 27.5 | 19.7 | 13.0 |
| 3721 | 533100 | NV | North American Aviation | 11 | 4.6 | 6.1 | 14.4 | 2.3 |
| 5322 | 294200 | GSK | Gamble Skogmo | 11 | 3.6 | 9.9 | 19.0 | 2.0 |
| 6140 | 106100 | CIT | C.I.T. Financial | 12 | 5.2 | 48.2 | 12.7 | 15.2 |
| 6140 | 296700 | GAC | General Acceptance | 11 | 5.4 | NA | 18.8 | NA |
| 6140 | 301300 | GFN | General Finance | 10 | 4.5 | 37.8 | 15.1 | 10.0 |
| 6140 | 349800 | HLR | Walter E. Heller | 12 | 4.1 | 60.1 | 12.8 | 16.0 |
| 6145 | 026801 | AIC | American Investment | 13 | 5.5 | 33.9 | 14.9 | 10.1 |
| 6145 | 255400 | FAM | Family Finance | 12 | 4.5 | 43.8 | 16.7 | 16.3 |
| 6145 | 647100 | SFC | Seaboard Finance | 14 | 4.0 | 37.4 | 21.7 | 11.8 |

NA – NOT AVAILABLE

## FIGURE 20–2

## Ten Year Statistical Record

FINANCIAL ANALYSIS REPORT NO. 2

FINANCIAL DATA

ALUMINUM COMPANY OF AMERICA
3334-015400

12/31/65

| YEAR | CASH AND EQUIV | RECEIV- ABLES | INVEN- TORIES | CURRENT ASSETS | CURRENT LIAB | TOTAL ASSETS | GROSS PLANT | NET PLANT | LONG TERM DEBT | PREFERRED STOCK | COMMON EQUITY |
|---|---|---|---|---|---|---|---|---|---|---|---|
| 1965 | 44.0 | 193.0 | 283.3 | 524.1 | 219.9 | 1,743.1 | 2,068.8 | 999.8 | 490.6 | 66.0 | 843.905 |
| 1964 | 39.4 | 169.0 | 260.8 | 474.3 | 150.3 | 1,630.0 | 1,940.7 | 939.6 | 497.6 | 66.0 | 798.020 |
| 1963 | 36.5 | 138.3 | 244.8 | 423.8 | 146.0 | 1,467.9 | 1,793.9 | 854.9 | 385.8 | 66.0 | 765.514 |
| 1962 | 40.1 | 130.6 | 249.3 | 423.7 | 120.0 | 1,377.8 | 1,726.4 | 821.1 | 358.7 | 66.0 | 742.139 |
| 1961 | 48.1 | 136.7 | 262.5 | 451.7 | 139.6 | 1,380.5 | 1,694.4 | 839.6 | 385.1 | 66.0 | 704.925 |
| 1960 | 40.7 | 115.2 | 260.0 | 421.1 | 117.3 | 1,374.1 | 1,665.5 | 868.2 | 412.2 | 66.0 | 691.802 |
| 1959 | 72.3 | 116.9 | 224.0 | 418.4 | 99.1 | 1,360.1 | 1,602.2 | 871.0 | 436.3 | 66.0 | 662.234 |
| 1958 | 78.0 | 92.2 | 209.9 | 385.3 | 92.3 | 1,337.3 | 1,560.7 | 890.9 | 462.7 | 66.0 | 615.766 |
| 1957 | 40.0 | 104.0 | 231.7 | 379.8 | 192.0 | 1,315.6 | 1,498.0 | 882.7 | 358.9 | 66.0 | 600.592 |
| 1956 | 49.9 | 96.3 | 224.9 | 375.4 | 185.8 | 1,157.6 | 1,308.6 | 743.1 | 273.3 | 66.0 | 552.014 |

| YEAR | NET SALES | OPER INCOME | DEPREC & AMORT | FIXED CHARGES | INCOME TAXES | NON- RECURRING | NET INCOME | PREF DIVIDENDS | AVBL FOR COMMON | COMMON DIVIDENDS | NO SHS OUTST** |
|---|---|---|---|---|---|---|---|---|---|---|---|
| 1965 | 1,165.6 | 223.58 | 86.17 | 23.78 | 44.00 | -1.34 | 75.59 | 2.47 | 73.112 | 29.99 | 21,423.72 |
| 1964 | 1,036.9 | 188.36 | 80.85 | 19.40 | 35.50 | -0.42 | 60.76 | 2.47 | 58.289 | 26.77 | 21,413.18 |
| 1963 | 972.1 | 167.99 | 77.85 | 15.65 | 31.60 | -2.61 | 51.08 | 2.47 | 48.604 | 25.66 | 21,386.94 |
| 1962 | 938.7 | 165.72 | 78.39 | 15.32 | 26.60 | -5.38 | 56.45 | 2.47 | 53.972 | 25.64 | 21,369.59 |
| 1961 | 853.3 | 152.61 | 80.05 | 16.52 | 19.20 | -1.60 | 43.05 | 2.47 | 40.574 | 25.61 | 21,338.94 |
| 1960 | 861.2 | 135.13 | 80.19 | 16.35 | 7.10 | -3.02 | 40.04 | 2.47 | 37.569 | 25.65 | 21,313.86 |
| 1959 | 858.5 | 174.14 | 73.06 | 17.01 | 35.00 | -0.47 | 55.57 | 2.47 | 53.096 | 25.24 | 21,038.29 |
| 1958 | 753.1 | 152.69 | 65.66 | 17.65 | 31.50 | 0.00 | 42.89 | 2.47 | 40.410 | 24.77 | 20,644.96 |
| 1957 | 869.4 | 210.79 | 57.66 | 14.64 | 69.00 | 0.00 | 75.57 | 2.47 | 73.093 | 24.73 | 20,607.43 |
| 1956 | 864.4 | 229.35 | 50.77 | 9.37 | 84.95 | -0.58 | 89.62 | 2.47 | 87.146 | 24.64 | 20,553.20 |

| YEAR | NET SALES PER SHARE | NET OP INC MARGIN | OPER INC PER SHARE | NET PROFIT MARGIN | EARNINGS PER SHARE | CASH FLOW PER SHARE | DIVIDENDS PER SHARE | PAYOUT RATIO | DIV % OF CASH FLOW |
|---|---|---|---|---|---|---|---|---|---|
| 1965 | 54.41 | 19.2% | 10.44 | 6.5% | 3.41 | 7.43 | 1.40 | 41% | 19% |
| 1964 | 48.42 | 18.2% | 8.80 | 5.9% | 2.72 | 6.50 | 1.20 | 44% | 18% |
| 1963 | 45.45 | 17.3% | 7.85 | 5.3% | 2.27 | 5.91 | 1.20 | 53% | 20% |
| 1962 | 43.93 | 17.7% | 7.75 | 6.0% | 2.53 | 6.19 | 1.20 | 47% | 19% |
| 1961 | 39.99 | 17.9% | 7.15 | 5.0% | 1.90 | 5.65 | 1.20 | 63% | 21% |
| 1960 | 40.41 | 15.7% | 6.34 | 4.6% | 1.76 | 5.52 | 1.20 | 68% | 22% |
| 1959 | 40.81 | 20.3% | 8.28 | 6.5% | 2.52 | 6.00 | 1.20 | 48% | 20% |
| 1958 | 36.48 | 20.3% | 7.40 | 5.7% | 1.96 | 5.14 | 1.20 | 61% | 23% |
| 1957 | 42.19 | 24.2% | 10.23 | 8.7% | 3.55 | 6.34 | 1.20 | 34% | 19% |
| 1956 | 42.06 | 26.5% | 11.16 | 10.4% | 4.24 | 6.71 | 1.20 | 28% | 18% |

** THOUSANDS- ADJUSTED FOR STOCK SPLITS AND STOCK DIVIDENDS
NA NOT AVAILABLE
NOTE- DOLLAR AMOUNTS IN MILLIONS EXCEPT FOR STOCK PRICE AND PER SHARE DATA WHICH IS IN DOLLARS AND CENTS AND ADJUSTED FOR STOCK SPLITS AND STOCK DIVIDENDS

FINANCIAL ANALYSIS REPORT NO. 2

FINANCIAL DATA

ALUMINUM COMPANY OF AMERICA
3334-015400

12/31/65 PAGE 2

| YEAR | BOOK VALUE PER SHARE | RETURN ON COM EQUITY | RETURN ON INV CAP | CAPITAL TURNOVER | CAPITAL EXPEND | NO OF EMPLOYEES* |
|---|---|---|---|---|---|---|
| 1965 | 39.39 | 8.7% | 5.0% | 0.8 | 162.8 | 48.2 |
| 1964 | 37.27 | 7.3% | 4.1% | 0.7 | 179.4 | 46.5 |
| 1963 | 35.79 | 6.3% | 3.9% | 0.7 | 124.2 | 46.7 |
| 1962 | 34.73 | 7.3% | 4.5% | 0.7 | 80.7 | 47.1 |
| 1961 | 33.03 | 5.8% | 3.5% | 0.7 | 64.4 | 46.1 |
| 1960 | 32.46 | 5.4% | 3.2% | 0.7 | 80.3 | 48.7 |
| 1959 | 31.48 | 8.0% | 4.4% | 0.7 | 54.7 | 47.4 |
| 1958 | 29.83 | 6.6% | 3.4% | 0.6 | 81.6 | 44.3 |
| 1957 | 29.14 | 12.2% | 6.7% | 0.8 | 207.5 | 54.6 |
| 1956 | 26.86 | 15.8% | 9.2% | 0.9 | 139.3 | 58.5 |

| YEAR | STOCK PRICE -- ADJUSTED HIGH | LOW | CLOSE | NO SHS TRADED** | P/E RATIO HIGH | LOW | P/CASH FLOW HIGH | LOW | YIELD HIGH | LOW |
|---|---|---|---|---|---|---|---|---|---|---|
| 1965 | 80 | 61 | 77 | 2,696.4 | 23 | 18 | 11 | 8 | 2.3% | 1.8% |
| 1964 | 82 | 59 | 62 | 1,712.2 | 30 | 22 | 13 | 9 | 2.0% | 1.5% |
| 1963 | 70 | 51 | 69 | 1,669.5 | 31 | 22 | 12 | 9 | 2.4% | 1.7% |
| 1962 | 69 | 45 | 55 | 1,342.0 | 27 | 18 | 11 | 7 | 2.7% | 1.7% |
| 1961 | 82 | 56 | 65 | 1,303.4 | 43 | 29 | 15 | 10 | 2.1% | 1.5% |
| 1960 | 108 | 61 | 69 | 1,167.3 | 61 | 35 | 20 | 11 | 2.0% | 1.1% |
| 1959 | 116 | 77 | 107 | 1,026.5 | 46 | 31 | 19 | 13 | 1.6% | 1.0% |
| 1958 | 97 | 60 | 93 | 1,248.8 | 49 | 31 | 19 | 12 | 2.0% | 1.2% |
| 1957 | 102 | 60 | 60 | 1,268.9 | 29 | 17 | 16 | 9 | 2.0% | 1.2% |
| 1956 | 134 | 82 | 92 | 1,084.5 | 32 | 19 | 20 | 12 | 1.5% | 0.9% |

* THOUSANDS
** THOUSANDS- ADJUSTED FOR STOCK SPLITS AND STOCK DIVIDENDS
NA NOT AVAILABLE
NOTE- DOLLAR AMOUNTS IN MILLIONS EXCEPT FOR STOCK PRICE AND PER SHARE DATA WHICH IS IN DOLLARS AND CENTS AND ADJUSTED FOR STOCK SPLITS AND STOCK DIVIDENDS

## FIGURE 20–3
## Key Financial Ratios

FINANCIAL ANALYSIS REPORT NO. 3

RATIO ANALYSIS

11/25/66

ALUMINUM COMPANY OF AMERICA
3334-015400

REQUESTED BY 236

COMPANY VS. INDUSTRY

| | COMPANY | | | | INDUSTRY 3334 | | | |
|---|---|---|---|---|---|---|---|---|
| | | -----AVERAGE OF------ | | | | -----AVERAGE OF------ | | |
| | 1965 | 3 YRS | 5 YRS | 10 YRS | 1965 | 3 YRS | 5 YRS | 10 YRS |
| PRICE-EARNINGS RATIO | 18 - 23* | 24 | 25 | 29 | 15 - 20* | 21 | 23 | 22 |
| PRICE-CASH FLOW RATIO | 8 - 11* | 10 | 10 | 13 | 7 - 9* | 9 | 9 | 10 |
| DIVIDEND YIELD | 1.8% - 2.3%* | 1.9% | 1.9% | 1.6% | 2.0% - 2.7%* | 2.1% | 2.0% | 1.8% |
| DIVIDEND PAYOUT RATIO | 41% | 45% | 48% | 46% | 39% | 45% | 47% | 41% |
| DIVIDEND % OF CASH FLOW | 19% | 19% | 20% | 20% | 18% | 19% | 19% | 18% |
| CURRENT RATIO | 2.4 | 2.8 | 3.0 | 2.9 | 2.7 | 2.9 | 3.0 | 2.8 |
| QUICK RATIO | 1.1 | 1.2 | 1.3 | 1.2 | 1.2 | 1.3 | 1.3 | 1.3 |
| NET OPERATING INCOME MARGIN | 19.2% | 18.3% | 18.1% | 19.6% | 20.7% | 19.9% | 20.1% | 21.7% |
| NET PROFIT MARGIN | 6.5% | 5.9% | 5.8% | 6.4% | 6.8% | 6.0% | 5.9% | 6.7% |
| RETURN ON COMMON EQUITY | 8.7% | 7.5% | 7.1% | 8.1% | 10.1% | 8.3% | 7.9% | 8.9% |
| RETURN ON INVESTED CAPITAL | 5.0% | 4.3% | 4.2% | 4.7% | 4.7% | 3.9% | 3.7% | 4.0% |
| CAPITAL TURNOVER | 0.8 | 0.7 | 0.7 | 0.7 | 0.7 | 0.7 | 0.6 | 0.6 |
| LONG TERM DEBT % OF TOTAL CAP. | 35% | 35% | 34% | 35% | 44% | 43% | 44% | 45% |
| COMMON EQUITY % OF TOTAL CAP. | 60% | 60% | 61% | 60% | 49% | 49% | 49% | 48% |

* RANGE

## FIGURE 20–4
## Growth Measures

FINANCIAL ANALYSIS REPORT NO. 4

GROWTH ANALYSIS

11/25/66

ALUMINUM COMPANY OF AMERICA
3334-015400

REQUESTED BY 236

TEN YEAR PERFORMANCE – COMPANY VS. INDUSTRY AND ECONOMY
BASE YEARS FOR ALL INDEXES 1957-59 EQUALS 100

| | CO. SALES | CO NET INCOME | IND. SALES | IND NET INCOME | FRB | GNP | CO SALES % OF IND | -------COMPANY PER SHARE DATA------- SALES | CHANGE | EARNINGS | CHANGE |
|---|---|---|---|---|---|---|---|---|---|---|---|
| 1965 | 141 | 130 | 154 | 146 | 143 | 149 | 35.2 | 137 | 12.3% | 128 | 25.3% |
| 1964 | 125 | 105 | 132 | 112 | 132 | 138 | 36.3 | 122 | 6.5% | 102 | 19.8% |
| 1963 | 118 | 88 | 120 | 86 | 124 | 129 | 37.4 | 114 | 3.4% | 85 | -10.3% |
| 1962 | 114 | 97 | 113 | 97 | 118 | 123 | 38.4 | 110 | 9.8% | 95 | 33.1% |
| 1961 | 103 | 74 | 104 | 79 | 110 | 113 | 37.9 | 100 | -1.1% | 71 | 7.9% |
| 1960 | 104 | 69 | 103 | 83 | 109 | 110 | 38.8 | 101 | -1.0% | 66 | -30.2% |
| 1959 | 104 | 96 | 105 | 96 | 106 | 106 | 38.1 | 102 | 11.8% | 94 | 28.5% |
| 1958 | 91 | 74 | 95 | 85 | 94 | 97 | 36.8 | 92 | -13.6% | 73 | -44.8% |
| 1957 | 105 | 130 | 101 | 118 | 101 | 97 | 40.0 | 106 | .3% | 133 | -16.3% |
| 1956 | 105 | 154 | 98 | 148 | 100 | 92 | 40.8 | 106 | 715.1% | 159 | 1.4% |

COMPANY GROWTH ANALYSIS

| | 5 YRS. | 8 YRS. | 10 YRS. |
|---|---|---|---|
| NET SALES PER SHARE | | | |
| GROWTH RATE | 7.3% | 5.0% | 2.8% |
| STABILITY FACTOR | 2.0% | 3.7% | 7.0% |
| EARNINGS PER SHARE | | | |
| GROWTH RATE | 13.2% | 6.5% | -1.9% |
| STABILITY FACTOR | 10.6% | 16.4% | 31.6% |

COMPANY GROWTH VS. INDUSTRY GROWTH

| | ----COMPANY----- 5 YRS. | 10 YRS. | ----INDUSTRY---- 5 YRS. | 10 YRS. |
|---|---|---|---|---|
| NET SALES | | | | |
| GROWTH RATE | 7.4% | 3.3% | 9.7% | 4.5% |
| STABILITY FACTOR | 2.0% | 6.8% | 2.3% | 5.8% |
| NET INCOME | | | | |
| GROWTH RATE | 12.7% | -1.3% | 14.5% | -.3% |
| STABILITY FACTOR | 10.0% | 29.6% | 11.7% | 22.6% |

COMPANY GROWTH RATES

| | 5 YRS. | 8 YRS. | 10 YRS. |
|---|---|---|---|
| DIVIDENDS PER SHARE | 3.1% | 1.2% | .8% |
| OP. INCOME PER SHARE | 9.2% | 4.1% | -.9% |
| CASH FLOW PER SHARE | 6.1% | 3.9% | 1.1% |
| BOOK VALUE PER SHARE | 4.3% | 3.8% | 3.9% |

* - INDICATES THAT 1 IN THE UNITS POSITION HAS BEEN SUBSTITUTED FOR A NEGATIVE OR ZERO VALUE IN THE GIVEN SERIES

## FIGURE 20–5

## Comparative Financial Ratios

FINANCIAL ANALYSIS REPORT NO. 5

COMPARATIVE ANALYSIS 11/25/66 PAGE NO. 1

REQUESTED BY 229

| | A | AL | AA | KLU | RLM |
|---|---|---|---|---|---|
| CURRENT PRICE | 82 | 26 | 78 | 39 | 48 |
| RANGE | | | | | |
| 1965 | 52 - 87 | 25 - 32 | 61 - 80 | 29 - 41 | 34 - 50 |
| 1964 | 40 - 59 | 25 - 32 | 59 - 82 | 29 - 42 | 32 - 44 |
| 1963 | 41 - 54 | 20 - 28 | 51 - 70 | 31 - 42 | 24 - 37 |
| 1962 | 36 - 53 | 18 - 29 | 45 - 69 | 25 - 37 | 21 - 41 |
| 1961 | 44 - 65 | 26 - 39 | 56 - 82 | 30 - 50 | 35 - 56 |
| CURRENT YIELD -%- | 4.0 | 3.8 | 2.1 | 2.6 | 1.6 |
| AVERAGE | | | | | |
| 1965 | 5.4 | 2.9 | 2.0 | 2.6 | 1.8 |
| 1964 | 5.1 | 2.2 | 1.7 | 2.6 | 1.3 |
| 1963 | 5.3 | 2.5 | 2.0 | 2.4 | 1.7 |
| 1962 | 5.7 | 2.6 | 2.1 | 2.9 | 1.6 |
| 1961 | 4.5 | 1.9 | 1.7 | 2.3 | 1.1 |
| CURRENT P/E RATIO | 11 | 15 | 23 | 19 | 16 |
| AVERAGE | | | | | |
| 1965 | 10 | 16 | 21 | 17 | 14 |
| 1964 | 9 | 20 | 26 | 23 | 19 |
| 1963 | 11 | 26 | 27 | 30 | 21 |
| 1962 | 10 | 20 | 23 | 18 | 23 |
| 1961 | 14 | 33 | 36 | 31 | 37 |
| CURRENT P/CASH FLOW RATIO | 7 | 7 | 10 | 8 | 9 |
| AVERAGE | | | | | |
| 1965 | 6 | 7 | 9 | 8 | 8 |
| 1964 | 5 | 9 | 11 | 8 | 9 |
| 1963 | 5 | 9 | 10 | 10 | 8 |
| 1962 | 5 | 8 | 9 | 7 | 8 |
| 1961 | 7 | 12 | 12 | 10 | 13 |
| CURRENT DIVIDEND PER SHARE | 3.25 | 1.00 | 1.60 | 1.00 | 0.75 |
| ANNUAL | | | | | |
| 1965 | 3.75 | 0.83 | 1.40 | 0.90 | 0.74 |
| 1964 | 2.50 | 0.65 | 1.20 | 0.90 | 0.50 |
| 1963 | 2.50 | 0.60 | 1.20 | 0.90 | 0.50 |
| 1962 | 2.50 | 0.60 | 1.20 | 0.90 | 0.50 |
| 1961 | 2.50 | 0.60 | 1.20 | 0.90 | 0.50 |

NOTE- PRICE AND DIVIDEND PER SHARE ARE ADJUSTED FOR STOCK SPLITS AND STOCK DIVIDENDS

FINANCIAL ANALYSIS REPORT NO. 5

COMPARATIVE ANALYSIS 11/25/66 PAGE NO. 2

REQUESTED BY

| | A | AL | AA | KLU | RLM |
|---|---|---|---|---|---|
| NET SALES | | | | | |
| 1965 | 993.9 | 827.8 | 1,165.6 | 576.5 | 739.8 |
| 1964 | 895.0 | 677.5 | 1,036.9 | 515.9 | 620.1 |
| 1963 | 802.5 | 619.7 | 972.1 | 437.1 | 565.6 |
| 1962 | 691.3 | 518.6 | 938.7 | 444.2 | 537.3 |
| 1961 | 624.3 | 495.7 | 853.3 | 424.0 | 478.3 |
| OPERATING INCOME | | | | | |
| 1965 | 224.76 | 216.22 | 223.58 | 107.64 | 139.51 |
| 1964 | 170.60 | 180.35 | 188.36 | 95.26 | 106.91 |
| 1963 | 152.53 | 146.10 | 167.99 | 83.46 | 87.89 |
| 1962 | 145.83 | 142.19 | 165.72 | 98.88 | 91.21 |
| 1961 | 118.63 | 133.44 | 152.61 | 94.13 | 80.83 |
| NET INCOME | | | | | |
| 1965 | 79.48 | 58.07 | 75.59 | 37.20 | 52.64 |
| 1964 | 57.24 | 46.34 | 60.76 | 28.65 | 36.64 |
| 1963 | 45.42 | 30.28 | 51.08 | 23.36 | 27.80 |
| 1962 | 48.84 | 35.06 | 56.45 | 31.15 | 26.58 |
| 1961 | 42.10 | 29.36 | 43.05 | 24.04 | 25.10 |
| NET PROFIT MARGIN -%- | | | | | |
| 1965 | 8.0 | 7.0 | 6.5 | 6.5 | 7.1 |
| 1964 | 6.4 | 6.8 | 5.9 | 5.6 | 5.9 |
| 1963 | 5.7 | 4.9 | 5.3 | 5.3 | 4.9 |
| 1962 | 7.1 | 6.8 | 6.0 | 7.0 | 4.9 |
| 1961 | 6.7 | 5.9 | 5.0 | 5.7 | 5.2 |
| OPERATING INCOME MARGIN -%- | | | | | |
| 1965 | 22.6 | 26.1 | 19.2 | 18.7 | 18.9 |
| 1964 | 19.1 | 26.6 | 18.2 | 18.5 | 17.2 |
| 1963 | 19.0 | 23.6 | 17.3 | 19.1 | 15.5 |
| 1962 | 21.1 | 27.4 | 17.7 | 22.3 | 17.0 |
| 1961 | 19.0 | 26.9 | 17.9 | 22.2 | 16.9 |
| EARNINGS PER SHARE | | | | | |
| 1965 | 7.27 | 1.79 | 3.41 | 2.10 | 2.92 |
| 1964 | 5.26 | 1.42 | 2.72 | 1.55 | 1.96 |
| 1963 | 4.15 | 0.94 | 2.27 | 1.23 | 1.42 |
| 1962 | 4.62 | 1.14 | 2.53 | 1.74 | 1.35 |
| 1961 | 3.93 | 0.96 | 1.90 | 1.27 | 1.26 |
| CASH FLOW PER SHARE | | | | | |
| 1965 | 12.44 | 3.97 | 7.43 | 4.65 | 5.48 |
| 1964 | 10.20 | 3.39 | 6.50 | 4.15 | 4.42 |
| 1963 | 8.55 | 2.77 | 5.91 | 3.82 | 3.85 |
| 1962 | 8.87 | 2.92 | 6.19 | 4.36 | 3.69 |
| 1961 | 7.55 | 2.69 | 5.65 | 4.20 | 3.43 |

NOTE- DOLLAR AMOUNTS IN MILLIONS EXCEPT FOR PER SHARE DATA WHICH IS IN DOLLARS AND CENTS AND ADJUSTED FOR STOCK SPLITS AND STOCK DIVIDENDS

FIGURE 20–5 (Continued)

COMPARATIVE ANALYSIS — FINANCIAL ANALYSIS REPORT NO. 5 — 11/25/66 — PAGE NO. 3

REQUESTED BY 229

| | A | AL | AA | KLU | RLM |
|---|---|---|---|---|---|
| **BOOK VALUE PER SHARE** | | | | | |
| 1965 | 101.25 | 16.93 | 39.39 | 17.39 | 26.81 |
| 1964 | 97.93 | 15.45 | 37.27 | 16.19 | 24.46 |
| 1963 | 94.96 | 14.58 | 35.79 | 15.30 | 23.06 |
| 1962 | 91.87 | 14.20 | 34.73 | 14.88 | 22.12 |
| 1961 | 89.11 | 14.10 | 33.03 | 14.03 | 21.24 |
| **RETURN ON COMMON EQUITY -%-** | | | | | |
| 1965 | 7.2 | 10.6 | 8.7 | 12.1 | 10.9 |
| 1964 | 5.4 | 9.2 | 7.3 | 9.6 | 8.0 |
| 1963 | 4.4 | 6.4 | 6.3 | 8.0 | 6.2 |
| 1962 | 5.0 | 8.0 | 7.3 | 11.7 | 6.1 |
| 1961 | 4.4 | 6.8 | 5.8 | 9.0 | 5.9 |
| **CURRENT RATIO** | | | | | |
| 1965 | 4.0 | 2.6 | 2.4 | 2.7 | 3.2 |
| 1964 | 4.3 | 2.7 | 3.2 | 3.0 | 3.6 |
| 1963 | 4.2 | 2.9 | 2.9 | 2.6 | 3.5 |
| 1962 | 4.6 | 2.5 | 3.5 | 3.6 | 3.7 |
| 1961 | 5.0 | 2.5 | 3.2 | 3.8 | 3.4 |
| **COM EQUITY % OF TOT CAPITALIZATION** | | | | | |
| 1965 | 93.3 | 46.6 | 60.3 | 35.4 | 45.9 |
| 1964 | 92.0 | 46.8 | 58.6 | 34.8 | 46.9 |
| 1963 | 90.7 | 44.4 | 62.9 | 36.1 | 44.8 |
| 1962 | 90.6 | 45.4 | 63.6 | 34.8 | 43.8 |
| 1961 | 93.6 | 44.7 | 61.0 | 32.6 | 43.1 |
| **L/T DEBT % OF TOT CAPITALIZATION** | | | | | |
| 1965 | 6.7 | 48.4 | 35.0 | 51.9 | 44.7 |
| 1964 | 8.0 | 47.8 | 36.5 | 51.7 | 42.4 |
| 1963 | 9.3 | 50.1 | 31.7 | 48.5 | 44.2 |
| 1962 | 9.4 | 54.6 | 30.7 | 49.8 | 44.8 |
| 1961 | 6.4 | 55.3 | 33.3 | 51.9 | 45.2 |
| **DIVIDEND PAYOUT RATIO -%-** | | | | | |
| 1965 | 52 | 46 | 41 | 43 | 25 |
| 1964 | 48 | 46 | 44 | 58 | 26 |
| 1963 | 60 | 64 | 53 | 73 | 35 |
| 1962 | 54 | 53 | 47 | 52 | 37 |
| 1961 | 64 | 63 | 63 | 71 | 40 |

NOTE- BOOK VALUE PER SHARE IS ADJUSTED FOR STOCK SPLITS AND STOCK DIVIDENDS

In Report 1, the user "asks" the computer to scan the tape file and print out the names of those companies which meet specified standards. One or more of the following standards may be set:

*a*) Price-earnings ratio is to be above (or below) any specified value.
*b*) Dividend yield is to be above (or below) any specified value.
*c*) Operating profit as % of sales is to be above (or below) any specified value.
*d*) Net income as % of sales is to be above (or below) any specified value.
*e*) Net income as % of stockholders' equity is to be above (or below) any specified value.

The sample print-out shown here screened a tape of 425 industrials, and reported those companies with a 1965 closing price-earnings ratio of less than 15, a dividend yield of more than 3.5%, and a return on stockholders' equity of more than 12%. No specifications were given for criteria (*c*) and (*d*).

Report 2 is a convenient 10-year data record for any named corporation which is on the tape—in this sample Aluminum Company of America. Major balance sheet and income statement items are shown in dollar amounts; selected items are converted into per-share terms (fully adjusted for stock splits and stock dividends); and some of the most widely used financial ratios are computed and printed.

In Report 3, more than a dozen key financial ratios are calculated and averaged for the past 3, 5, and 10 years for any specified company and for a comparative industry composite. The user can define the composition of industry groupings in any way he chooses. The sample shown compares Alcoa with the four major aluminum companies (including Alcoa) combined.

In keeping with the growth orientation of the modern-day stock market, Report 4 consists of a quite comprehensive comparative sales and earnings growth analysis for any specified company and industry group. To add further perspective, the report includes some information on the growth of the total economy. In addition to growth rates, moreover, stability ratios are calculated for sales and earnings (stability being defined in terms of average percentage deviations from trend), and growth rates are shown for company dividends, book value, cash flow, and operating income, all on an adjusted per-share basis.

Finally, Report 5 is somewhat like Report 3 in that it is a comparative financial ratio analysis. However, instead of comparing a single company with an industry composite it compares any five selected companies individually. Our sample shows the four major aluminum companies, and for possible additional interest and contrast, the Anaconda Company.

Like any prepackaged program, IBM's Financial Analysis Program probably contains many items that are not of particular interest to any given user and probably omits some items which are of great interest. Furthermore, like most other prepackaged programs, especially complex ones such as this, personalized tailoring is extremely difficult even if the services of highly trained programmers are available. Yet it should be obvious that such a program can be a useful screening tool—free of charge to the bargain. At the very least, it is suggestive of ideas for any firm wishing to develop its own screening program.

Another example of a computer-generated screening program is the "Finstat" service, which has been offered by the firm of Faulkner, Dawkins & Sullivan to its brokerage clients.[4] Finstat puts heavy emphasis on the components of return on stockholders' equity (see Chapter 8, ff. 313), and presents data in both tabular and graphic form. The graphs are transparencies to facilitate visual comparisons among companies and industries. Figures 20–6 through 20–9 are illustrative of this service. The firm of White, Weld & Co. offers a screening service which can be tailored to the unique requirements of individual subscribers.

According to a recent report, one large New York City bank has refined the screening process into a rather elaborate information system. An employee of that bank has written:

> At Bankers Trust, to use my company as an example, a system is currently being implemented which provides for the orderly storage and

[4] The service is now in the process of being terminated; but it is illustrative of what can be done.

# FIGURE 20–6

## Financial Statistics on Ashland Oil Co.

| ASHLAND OIL + REFINING CO. | | 9-65 | 9-64 | 9-63 | 9-62 | 9-61 | 9-60 | 9-59 | 9-58 | 9-57 | 9-56 | |
|---|---|---|---|---|---|---|---|---|---|---|---|---|
| STOCK MARKET DATA AND INDICES | | | | | | | | | | | | |
| 1. PRICE - HIGH AND LOW | $ | 29-19 | 21-14 | 16-13 | 14-10 | 14-11 | 12-9 | 12-9 | 9-7 | 9-7 | 9-7 | 1. |
| 2. AVG. P/E MULTIPLE | X | 12.29 | 11.49 | 12.12 | 12.07 | 12.31 | 9.74 | 10.36 | 11.37 | 6.76 | 8.20 | 2. |
| 3. AVG. DIVIDEND YIELD | 0/0 | 3.21 | 3.69 | 4.25 | 4.96 | 4.32 | 4.80 | 4.51 | 5.84 | 5.74 | 5.09 | 3. |
| 4. APPROX. TRADING/MONTH | MM$ | 4.08 | 2.92 | 1.74 | 1.33 | 1.83 | 1.01 | 2.10 | 1.33 | 1.15 | 2.11 | 4. |
| 5. SALES INDEX (1957-59=100) | 0/0 | 149.1 | 131.3 | 121.9 | 105.9 | 104.2 | 101.1 | 100.1 | 93.3 | 106.6 | 93.2 | 5. |
| 6. SALES PER SHARE INDEX | 0/0 | 114.2 | 104.7 | 97.7 | 88.1 | 92.8 | 96.2 | 98.3 | 94.0 | 107.6 | 94.2 | 6. |
| 7. EARNINGS PER SHARE INDEX | 0/0 | 199.8 | 155.8 | 118.6 | 102.0 | 105.1 | 107.8 | 104.8 | 73.0 | 122.3 | 100.3 | 7. |
| 8. AVERAGE PRICE INDEX | 0/0 | 268.7 | 196.0 | 157.3 | 134.7 | 141.7 | 114.9 | 118.8 | 90.8 | 90.5 | 90.1 | 8. |
| 9. ANNUAL CHANGE IN EARN P.S. | 0/0 | 28.24 | 31.43 | 16.27 | -2.98 | -2.47 | 2.86 | 43.60 | -40.33 | 21.85 | 39.25 | 9. |
| TURNOVER (AVERAGE ASSETS) | | | | | | | | | | | | |
| 10. SALES TO CASH + EQUIV. | X | 10.11 | 12.10 | 16.83 | 26.40 | 22.92 | 18.02 | 15.95 | 12.02 | 13.65 | 12.04 | 10. |
| 11. SALES TO RECEIVABLES | X | 8.62 | 8.39 | 9.75 | 10.26 | 10.62 | 10.92 | 11.09 | 10.41 | 11.93 | 11.35 | 11. |
| 12. SALES TO INVENTORY | X | 7.50 | 6.37 | 6.45 | 6.16 | 6.10 | 6.09 | 6.45 | 6.25 | 7.42 | 7.11 | 12. |
| 13. SALES TO NET PLANT | X | 2.74 | 2.53 | 2.82 | 2.93 | 3.02 | 3.26 | 3.41 | 3.21 | 3.82 | 3.70 | 13. |
| 14. OPERATING ASSET TURNOVER | X | 1.39 | 1.31 | 1.48 | 1.54 | 1.56 | 1.60 | 1.64 | 1.52 | 1.79 | 1.71 | 14. |
| PROFIT MARGINS | | | | | | | | | | | | |
| 15. COST OF G.S. TO SALES | 0/0 | 69.88 | 71.85 | 74.03 | 75.11 | 74.94 | 74.36 | 74.97 | 76.69 | 75.54 | 75.23 | 15. |
| 16. SG+A, ETC. TO SALES | 0/0 | 13.47 | 12.70 | 12.53 | 12.18 | 11.61 | 11.65 | 11.04 | 11.15 | 9.25 | 9.30 | 16. |
| 17. D+A TO SALES | 0/0 | 5.79 | 6.55 | 5.86 | 5.60 | 5.65 | 5.60 | 5.28 | 5.69 | 5.28 | 5.91 | 17. |
| 18. OPERATING PROFIT MARGIN | 0/0 | 10.86 | 8.90 | 7.58 | 7.11 | 7.79 | 8.39 | 8.71 | 6.47 | 9.93 | 9.56 | 18. |
| 19. LESS FIXED CHARGES | 0/0 | 0.85 | 1.04 | 0.86 | 0.50 | 0.45 | 0.37 | 0.34 | 0.41 | 0.31 | 0.32 | 19. |
| 20. PLUS NON-OP INCOME | 0/0 | 1.28 | 1.36 | 1.14 | 1.04 | 0.63 | 0.51 | 0.67 | 0.51 | 0.55 | 0.51 | 20. |
| 21. PRETAX PROFIT MARGIN | 0/0 | 11.30 | 9.22 | 7.86 | 7.65 | 7.97 | 8.53 | 9.04 | 6.56 | 10.16 | 9.75 | 21. |
| 22. TAX RATE | 0/0 | 37.56 | 34.77 | 37.05 | 37.01 | 38.85 | 42.38 | 47.20 | 43.80 | 50.15 | 50.55 | 22. |
| 23. NET PROFIT MARGIN | 0/0 | 7.06 | 6.02 | 4.95 | 4.82 | 4.87 | 4.92 | 4.77 | 3.69 | 5.07 | 4.82 | 23. |
| 24. AVAILABLE FOR COMMON | 0/0 | 6.96 | 5.91 | 4.83 | 4.60 | 4.50 | 4.45 | 4.24 | 3.08 | 4.52 | 4.23 | 24. |
| RATES OF RETURN AND EARNINGS | | | | | | | | | | | | |
| 25. OPER PROFIT ON OPER ASSETS | 0/0 | 15.11 | 11.70 | 11.18 | 10.98 | 12.15 | 13.41 | 14.30 | 9.83 | 17.75 | 16.31 | 25. |
| 26. PRETAX PROFIT ON TOT ASSTS | 0/0 | 14.64 | 11.11 | 10.55 | 10.82 | 11.32 | 12.49 | 13.89 | 9.38 | 17.10 | 15.74 | 26. |
| 27. NET RETURN ON TOTAL ASSETS | 0/0 | 9.01 | 7.13 | 6.48 | 6.51 | 6.40 | 6.52 | 6.51 | 4.41 | 7.60 | 6.83 | 27. |
| 28. TOT ASTS TO COM EQUITY | X | 2.07 | 2.22 | 2.00 | 1.79 | 1.96 | 2.06 | 2.16 | 2.32 | 2.43 | 2.47 | 28. |
| 29. NET RETURN ON COM. EQUITY | 0/0 | 18.65 | 15.83 | 12.93 | 11.64 | 12.54 | 13.42 | 14.02 | 10.23 | 18.45 | 16.86 | 29. |
| 30. EQUITY PER COMMON SHARE | $ | 10.53 | 9.68 | 9.01 | 8.61 | 8.23 | 7.89 | 7.34 | 7.01 | 6.51 | 5.85 | 30. |
| 31. EARNINGS PER COMMON SHARE | $ | 1.96 | 1.53 | 1.17 | 1.00 | 1.03 | 1.06 | 1.03 | 0.72 | 1.20 | 0.99 | 31. |
| 32. PAYOUT RATIO | 0/0 | 39.47 | 42.45 | 51.50 | 59.88 | 53.25 | 46.74 | 46.66 | 66.38 | 38.82 | 41.70 | 32. |
| 33. DIVIDEND PER COMMON SHARE | $ | 0.77 | 0.65 | 0.60 | 0.60 | 0.55 | 0.49 | 0.48 | 0.48 | 0.47 | 0.41 | 33. |
| 34. REINVESTMENT RATE | 0/0 | 11.29 | 9.11 | 6.27 | 4.67 | 5.86 | 7.15 | 7.48 | 3.44 | 11.29 | 9.83 | 34. |
| COMPOUND RATE OF CHANGE SINCE | | 9-64 | 9-63 | 9-62 | 9-61 | 9-60 | 9-59 | 9-58 | 9-57 | 9-56 | 9-55 | |
| 35. SALES PER SHARE | 0/0 | 8.65 | 7.81 | 8.64 | 5.19 | 3.43 | 2.49 | 2.77 | 0.74 | 2.13 | 3.20 | 35. |
| 36. PRETAX MARGIN | 0/0 | 20.30 | 18.16 | 13.02 | 8.73 | 5.62 | 3.72 | 7.76 | 1.33 | 1.64 | 3.36 | 36. |
| 37. TAX RETENTION RATE | 0/0 | -4.36 | -0.40 | -0.29 | 0.52 | 1.61 | 2.80 | 1.50 | 2.82 | 2.59 | 2.04 | 37. |
| 38. EARNINGS PER SHARE | 0/0 | 24.88 | 26.10 | 22.43 | 16.06 | 12.35 | 10.76 | 14.39 | 6.14 | 7.65 | 10.20 | 38. |
| 39. EQUITY PER COM. SHARE | 0/0 | 8.47 | 7.78 | 6.72 | 6.15 | 5.78 | 6.01 | 5.82 | 6.01 | 6.53 | 6.77 | 39. |
| 40. RETURN ON COM. EQUITY | 0/0 | 16.40 | 18.32 | 15.71 | 9.91 | 6.57 | 4.75 | 8.58 | 0.13 | 1.12 | 3.43 | 40. |
| 41. OPER. ASSET TURNOVER | 0/0 | 5.73 | -2.93 | -3.48 | -2.84 | -2.78 | -2.76 | -1.26 | -3.14 | -2.27 | -1.45 | 41. |
| 42. OPER. PROFIT MARGIN | 0/0 | 19.89 | 18.02 | 14.13 | 8.30 | 5.17 | 3.68 | 7.41 | 1.13 | 1.42 | 2.89 | 42. |
| 43. LEVERAGE | 0/0 | -7.08 | 1.80 | 4.88 | 1.35 | 0.09 | -0.68 | -1.64 | -2.00 | -1.95 | -1.91 | 43. |
| 44. TAX RETENTION RATE | 0/0 | -4.36 | -0.40 | -0.29 | 0.52 | 1.61 | 2.80 | 1.50 | 2.82 | 2.59 | 2.04 | 44. |
| 45. MISC. CAUSES OF CHANGE | 0/0 | 2.22 | 1.83 | 0.47 | 2.58 | 2.49 | 1.72 | 2.56 | 1.32 | 1.33 | 1.86 | 45. |

ASHLAND OIL + REFINING CO. COMPANY 48900 

| | | 9-65 | 9-64 | 9-63 | 9-62 | 9-61 | 9-60 | 9-59 | 9-58 | 9-57 | 9-56 | |
|---|---|---|---|---|---|---|---|---|---|---|---|---|
| SOURCE AND APPLICATION OF FUNDS | | | | | | | | | | | | |
| 46. NET INCOME | 0/0 | 54.9 | 47.9 | 45.8 | 46.3 | 46.3 | 46.7 | 47.5 | 39.3 | 48.9 | 44.9 | 46. |
| 47. DEPREC. + AMORT. | 0/0 | 45.1 | 52.1 | 54.2 | 53.7 | 53.7 | 53.3 | 52.5 | 60.7 | 51.1 | 55.1 | 47. |
| 48. DEFERRED TAXES | 0/0 | 0. | 0. | 0. | 0. | 0. | 0. | 0. | 0. | 0. | 0. | 48. |
| 49. CASH FLOW | MM$ | 57.5 | 49.6 | 39.6 | 33.1 | 32.9 | 31.9 | 30.2 | 26.3 | 33.1 | 30.0 | 49. |
| 50. CHNG. IN L.T. DEBT + PFD. | MM$ | -13.8 | -4.2 | 60.8 | -7.4 | -8.0 | 10.7 | -14.1 | 4.1 | 0.6 | 2.9 | 50. |
| 51. MISC. CHNG. IN COM. EQUITY | MM$ | 6.7 | -0.1 | -0.5 | 7.7 | 6.2 | 3.0 | 2.7 | 0.2 | 0.2 | 0.2 | 51. |
| 52. TOTAL SOURCE / APPLIC. | MM$ | 50.4 | 45.3 | 99.9 | 33.4 | 31.1 | 45.7 | 18.8 | 30.5 | 33.9 | 33.1 | 52. |
| 53. CASH DIVIDENDS | MM$ | 12.4 | 10.3 | 9.5 | 9.2 | 8.5 | 7.6 | 7.5 | 7.4 | 7.4 | 6.6 | 53. |
| 54. CAPITAL EXPENDITURES | MM$ | 35.5 | 37.8 | 72.7 | 16.3 | 29.5 | 26.0 | 16.9 | 17.0 | 22.6 | 25.0 | 54. |
| 55. CHANGE IN NET CUR. ASSETS | MM$ | 8.2 | 3.8 | 21.8 | 6.2 | -3.3 | 4.6 | -8.3 | 6.6 | 2.9 | -3.5 | 55. |
| 56. INVESTMENTS AND ADVANCES | MM$ | -1.2 | -4.2 | 6.8 | -1.3 | -3.6 | 7.4 | 2.7 | -0.4 | 1.2 | 2.5 | 56. |
| 57. RETIREMENTS + MISC. | MM$ | -4.5 | -2.4 | -10.9 | 3.0 | 0.- | 0.+ | 0.+ | -0.1 | -0.1 | 2.5 | 57. |
| BALANCE SHEET STRUCTURE (YEAREND) | | | | | | | | | | | | |
| 58. CASH + EQUIV. | 0/0 | 32.1 | 23.4 | 21.8 | 13.5 | 11.2 | 16.8 | 18.1 | 21.7 | 26.2 | 23.0 | 58. |
| 59. RECEIVABLES | 0/0 | 32.0 | 33.7 | 31.5 | 31.9 | 31.7 | 28.9 | 28.6 | 28.5 | 26.9 | 29.7 | 59. |
| 60. INVENTORY + MISC. | 0/0 | 35.9 | 42.9 | 46.8 | 54.6 | 57.0 | 54.4 | 53.3 | 49.8 | 47.0 | 47.3 | 60. |
| 61. CURRENT ASSETS | 0/0 | 46.9 | 44.6 | 43.4 | 43.6 | 43.0 | 45.3 | 48.1 | 48.8 | 50.3 | 49.7 | 61. |
| 62. NET PLANT | 0/0 | 46.6 | 48.0 | 47.4 | 47.7 | 49.0 | 44.9 | 44.9 | 45.3 | 43.7 | 44.5 | 62. |
| 63. NON-OPERATING ASSETS | 0/0 | 6.4 | 7.4 | 9.3 | 8.7 | 8.0 | 9.8 | 7.0 | 5.9 | 6.0 | 5.8 | 63. |
| 64. CURRENT RATIO | X | 2.13 | 2.16 | 2.24 | 2.25 | 2.02 | 2.12 | 1.99 | 2.43 | 1.96 | 2.04 | 64. |
| 65. CASH + EQUIV. RATIO | X | 0.68 | 0.51 | 0.49 | 0.30 | 0.23 | 0.35 | 0.36 | 0.53 | 0.51 | 0.47 | 65. |
| 66. CURRENT LIABILITIES | 0/0 | 22.1 | 20.6 | 19.4 | 19.4 | 21.3 | 21.4 | 24.2 | 20.1 | 25.6 | 24.4 | 66. |
| 67. MISCELLANEOUS | 0/0 | 1.4 | 1.7 | 2.0 | 0. | 0. | 0. | 0. | 0.2 | 0.1 | 0.1 | 67. |
| 68. LONG-TERM DEBT | 0/0 | 23.4 | 29.0 | 32.1 | 17.9 | 16.8 | 17.5 | 12.4 | 18.0 | 15.1 | 15.2 | 68. |
| 69. PREFERRED STOCK | 0/0 | 2.5 | 2.6 | 2.5 | 4.1 | 8.7 | 12.4 | 15.1 | 17.3 | 17.3 | 19.8 | 69. |
| 70. COMMON EQUITY | 0/0 | 50.6 | 46.0 | 44.0 | 58.7 | 53.2 | 48.7 | 48.3 | 44.4 | 41.8 | 40.5 | 70. |
| PER EMPLOYEE STATISTICS | | | | | | | | | | | | |
| 71. OPERATING ASSETS | M$ | 42.35 | 46.19 | 40.03 | 43.83 | 42.71 | 41.29 | 39.80 | 40.09 | 37.30 | 35.66 | 71. |
| 72. SALES | M$ | 58.91 | 60.68 | 59.05 | 67.68 | 66.57 | 66.02 | 65.35 | 60.89 | 66.71 | 60.85 | 72. |
| 73. TOTAL LABOR COST | M$ | N-AV | N-AV | N-AV | N-AV | N-AV | N-AV | N-AV | N-AV | N-AV | N-AV | 73. |
| 74. OPERATING PROFIT | M$ | 6.40 | 5.40 | 4.47 | 4.81 | 5.19 | 5.54 | 5.69 | 3.94 | 6.62 | 5.82 | 74. |
| MISCELLANEOUS DATA | | | | | | | | | | | | |
| 75. NON-RECUR. P.S. EXCLUDED | $ | 0. | 0. | 0. | 0. | 0. | 0. | 0. | 0. | 0. | 0. | 75. |
| 76. NON-RECUR. P.S. INCLUDED | $ | 0. | 0. | 0. | 0. | 0. | 0. | 0. | 0. | 0. | 0. | 76. |
| 77. NON-CONSOL. EARNS. P.S. | $ | -0.06 | -0.06 | -0.05 | N-AV | N-AV | N-AV | N-AV | N-AV | N-AV | N-AV | 77. |
| 78. PENSION COST TO SALES | 0/0 | N-AV | N-AV | N-AV | N-AV | N-AV | N-AV | N-AV | N-AV | N-AV | N-AV | 78. |
| 79. RENTAL EXPENSE TO SALES | 0/0 | 1.21 | 1.14 | 1.00 | N-AV | N-AV | N-AV | N-AV | N-AV | N-AV | 0.98 | 79. |
| 80. VALUE ADDED TO SALES | 0/0 | N-AV | N-AV | N-AV | N-AV | N-AV | N-AV | N-AV | N-AV | N-AV | N-AV | 80. |
| 81. IMPLIED PLANT LIFE | YRS | 14.73 | 13.88 | 15.63 | 15.74 | 15.35 | 14.77 | 14.51 | 13.60 | 12.04 | 11.16 | 81. |
| 82. PER CENT PLANT DEPRECIATED | 0/0 | 56.51 | 55.08 | 54.88 | 61.49 | 59.68 | 61.16 | 61.41 | 59.51 | 57.46 | 56.09 | 82. |
| 83. INVENTORY BASIS | | LIFO | LIFO | LIFO | LIFO | LIFO | LIFO | LIFO | LIFO | LIFO | LIFO | 83. |
| 84. TIMES RENT + FIXED CHG EARN | X | 6.49 | 5.23 | 5.23 | N-AV | N-AV | N-AV | N-AV | N-AV | N-AV | 8.50 | 84. |
| 85. TIMES FIX CHG + PFD DIV EARN | X | 8.33 | 6.18 | 5.94 | 7.39 | 6.48 | 6.39 | 5.82 | 4.03 | 6.26 | 5.67 | 85. |
| 86. CASH RETAIN TO GRS OP ASTS | 0/0 | 8.53 | 8.00 | 7.05 | 6.41 | 6.81 | 7.21 | 7.15 | 6.13 | 8.91 | 8.95 | 86. |

| | SALES FOR LAST | | | SALES P.S. FOR LAST | | | EARNS P.S. FOR LAST | | | PRICE FOR LAST | | | |
|---|---|---|---|---|---|---|---|---|---|---|---|---|---|
| LONG-TERM TRENDS | 3 YRS | 5 YRS | 10 YRS | 3 YRS | 5 YRS | 10 YRS | 3 YRS | 5 YRS | 10 YRS | 3 YRS | 5 YRS | 10 YRS | |
| 87. LEAST SQUARES RATE | 10.8 | 10.0 | 5.0 | 8.2 | 6.3 | .9 | 29.5 | 21.3 | 8.3 | 31.8 | 21.3 | 14.3 | 87. |
| 88. ONE STANDARD DEV. | 2.9 | 5.3 | 8.2 | .9 | 6.2 | 8.3 | 1.6 | 13.5 | 23.6 | 6.3 | 15.3 | 15.1 | 88. |

ASHLAND OIL + REFINING CO. — DATA FOR FISCAL YEAR ENDING SEP., 1965 (000,000)

| | | | | | | | |
|---|---|---|---|---|---|---|---|
| NET SALES | 447.7 | CURRENT ASSETS | 167.1 | CURRENT LIABILITIES | 78.5 | AVG. MARKET VALUE | 382.6 |
| OPERATING PROFIT | 48.64 | NET PLANT | 166.0 | LONG TERM DEBT | 83.4 | EMPLOYEES (000) | 7.6 |
| AVAIL. FOR COMMON | 31.146 | TOTAL ASSETS | 356.0 | COMMON EQUITY | 179.988 | SHARES OUTSTANDING | 15.861 |

# FIGURE 20–7

## Financial Statistics on a Composite of Domestic Oil Companies

| | | 1965 | 1964 | 1963 | 1962 | 1961 | 1960 | 1959 | 1958 | 1957 | 1956 | |
|---|---|---|---|---|---|---|---|---|---|---|---|---|
| STOCK MARKET DATA AND INDICES | | | | | | | | | | | | |
| 1. AVERAGE MARKET VALUE | MM$ | 18575. | 16120. | 13324. | 11258. | 12355. | 10567. | 11976. | 10961. | 11720. | 12235. | 1. |
| 2. AVG. P/E MULTIPLE | X | 13.90 | 14.36 | 12.97 | 12.68 | 14.82 | 12.48 | 15.02 | 16.40 | 13.65 | 13.72 | 2. |
| 3. AVG. DIVIDEND YIELD | 0/0 | 3.07 | 3.17 | 3.40 | 3.71 | 3.17 | 3.67 | 3.23 | 3.49 | 3.25 | 3.00 | 3. |
| 4. APPROX. TRADING/MONTH | MM$ | 117.95 | 110.22 | 105.51 | 57.53 | 64.01 | 48.89 | 65.44 | 66.29 | 66.28 | 78.40 | 4. |
| 5. SALES INDEX (1957-59=100) | 0/0 | 145.3 | 129.1 | 122.1 | 112.9 | 107.9 | 105.0 | 102.3 | 96.3 | 101.4 | 94.4 | 5. |
| 6. SALES PER SHARE INDEX | 0/0 | 142.1 | 127.3 | 121.1 | 112.4 | 107.5 | 104.6 | 101.6 | 96.4 | 102.0 | 95.2 | 6. |
| 7. EARNINGS PER SHARE INDEX | 0/0 | 167.3 | 141.8 | 130.6 | 113.2 | 106.4 | 108.3 | 101.8 | 86.2 | 112.0 | 116.5 | 7. |
| 8. AVERAGE PRICE INDEX | 0/0 | 156.1 | 136.5 | 113.5 | 96.0 | 105.5 | 90.5 | 102.4 | 94.9 | 102.7 | 107.5 | 8. |
| 9. ANNUAL CHANGE IN EARN P.S. | 0/0 | 17.94 | 8.61 | 15.40 | 6.36 | -1.77 | 6.37 | 18.09 | -22.98 | -3.92 | 5.92 | 9. |
| TURNOVER (AVERAGE ASSETS) | | | | | | | | | | | | |
| 10. SALES TO CASH + EQUIV. | X | 11.19 | 10.11 | 9.62 | 9.86 | 9.17 | 8.79 | 8.39 | 8.36 | 8.70 | 7.77 | 10. |
| 11. SALES TO RECEIVABLES | X | 6.73 | 6.85 | 7.21 | 7.20 | 7.67 | 8.38 | 8.85 | 8.93 | 10.06 | 10.08 | 11. |
| 12. SALES TO INVENTORY | X | 9.30 | 8.90 | 8.94 | 8.58 | 8.41 | 8.15 | 8.06 | 7.46 | 7.86 | 8.33 | 12. |
| 13. SALES TO NET PLANT | X | 1.28 | 1.24 | 1.24 | 1.18 | 1.19 | 1.22 | 1.23 | 1.21 | 1.36 | 1.39 | 13. |
| 14. OPERATING ASSET TURNOVER | X | 0.88 | 0.86 | 0.86 | 0.83 | 0.83 | 0.85 | 0.85 | 0.84 | 0.92 | 0.93 | 14. |
| PROFIT MARGINS | | | | | | | | | | | | |
| 15. COST OF G.S. TO SALES | 0/0 | N-AV | N-AV | N-AV | N-AV | N-AV | N-AV | N-AV | N-AV | N-AV | N-AV | 15. |
| 16. SG+A, ETC. TO SALES | 0/0 | N-AV | N-AV | N-AV | N-AV | N-AV | N-AV | N-AV | N-AV | N-AV | N-AV | 16. |
| 17. D+A TO SALES | 0/0 | 9.60 | 9.56 | 9.98 | 10.37 | 10.41 | 10.57 | 10.41 | 10.74 | 10.41 | 10.18 | 17. |
| 18. OPERATING PROFIT MARGIN | 0/0 | 10.47 | 9.05 | 9.07 | 8.38 | 8.30 | 8.81 | 8.55 | 7.22 | 9.41 | 11.31 | 18. |
| 19. LESS FIXED CHARGES | 0/0 | 0.98 | 0.92 | 0.95 | 1.02 | N-AV | N-AV | N-AV | 0.93 | 0.81 | 0.65 | 19. |
| 20. PLUS NON-OP INCOME | 0/0 | 1.28 | 1.26 | 1.38 | 1.14 | N-AV | N-AV | N-AV | 0.79 | 0.81 | 0.75 | 20. |
| 21. PRETAX PROFIT MARGIN | 0/0 | 10.78 | 9.39 | 9.50 | 8.50 | 8.33 | 8.94 | 8.70 | 7.09 | 9.42 | 11.41 | 21. |
| 22. TAX RATE | 0/0 | 22.06 | 15.75 | 19.53 | 16.61 | 16.60 | 18.95 | 19.42 | 11.70 | 19.18 | 25.62 | 22. |
| 23. NET PROFIT MARGIN | 0/0 | 8.40 | 7.91 | 7.65 | 7.09 | 6.95 | 7.24 | 7.01 | 6.26 | 7.61 | 8.49 | 23. |
| 24. AVAILABLE FOR COMMON | 0/0 | 8.18 | 7.74 | 7.48 | 7.00 | 6.87 | 7.17 | 6.94 | 6.17 | 7.54 | 8.40 | 24. |
| RATES OF RETURN AND EARNINGS | | | | | | | | | | | | |
| 25. OPER PROFIT ON OPER ASSETS | 0/0 | 9.26 | 7.77 | 7.77 | 6.94 | 6.89 | 7.45 | 7.27 | 6.03 | 8.70 | 10.54 | 25. |
| 26. PRETAX PROFIT ON TOT ASSTS | 0/0 | 8.90 | 7.50 | 7.59 | 6.55 | 6.43 | 7.07 | 7.01 | 5.65 | 8.35 | 10.22 | 26. |
| 27. NET RETURN ON TOTAL ASSETS | 0/0 | 6.75 | 6.19 | 5.98 | 5.39 | 5.30 | 5.67 | 5.59 | 4.93 | 6.68 | 7.53 | 27. |
| 28. TOT ASTS TO COM EQUITY | X | 1.58 | 1.53 | 1.52 | 1.50 | 1.49 | 1.48 | 1.49 | 1.50 | 1.51 | 1.49 | 28. |
| 29. NET RETURN ON COM. EQUITY | 0/0 | 10.67 | 9.47 | 9.06 | 8.07 | 7.89 | 8.41 | 8.31 | 7.38 | 10.07 | 11.25 | 29. |
| 30. COMMON EQUITY | MM$ | 12527. | 11862. | 11344. | 10999. | 10563. | 10060. | 9593. | 9057. | 8528. | 7925. | 30. |
| 31. AVAILABLE FOR COMMON | MM$ | 1336. | 1123. | 1027. | 888. | 834. | 846. | 798. | 668. | 858. | 892. | 31. |
| 32. PAYOUT RATIO | 0/0 | 42.72 | 45.53 | 44.12 | 47.08 | 46.98 | 45.82 | 48.50 | 57.15 | 44.39 | 41.14 | 32. |
| 33. DIVIDENDS | MM$ | 571. | 511. | 453. | 418. | 392. | 388. | 387. | 382. | 381. | 367. | 33. |
| 34. REINVESTMENT RATE | 0/0 | 6.11 | 5.16 | 5.06 | 4.27 | 4.19 | 4.56 | 4.28 | 3.16 | 5.60 | 6.62 | 34. |
| COMPOUND RATE OF CHANGE SINCE | | 1964 | 1963 | 1962 | 1961 | 1960 | 1959 | 1958 | 1957 | 1956 | 1955 | |
| 35. SALES PER SHARE | 0/0 | 10.96 | 7.96 | 7.80 | 6.97 | 6.13 | 5.58 | 5.54 | 4.14 | 4.45 | 4.60 | 35. |
| 36. PRETAX MARGIN | 0/0 | 13.91 | 6.28 | 7.92 | 6.43 | 3.69 | 3.52 | 5.91 | 1.55 | -0.76 | -0.86 | 36. |
| 37. TAX RETENTION RATE | 0/0 | -7.83 | -1.60 | -2.25 | -1.70 | -0.79 | -0.56 | -1.79 | -0.46 | 0.51 | 0.63 | 37. |
| 38. EARNINGS PER SHARE | 0/0 | 16.50 | 12.38 | 13.03 | 11.31 | 8.69 | 8.27 | 9.47 | 5.02 | 4.02 | 4.19 | 38. |
| 39. EQUITY PER COM. SHARE | 0/0 | 4.23 | 4.10 | 3.68 | 3.74 | 3.95 | 4.13 | 4.26 | 4.40 | 4.70 | 5.00 | 39. |
| 40. RETURN ON COM. EQUITY | 0/0 | 12.27 | 8.28 | 9.35 | 7.57 | 4.74 | 4.14 | 5.21 | 0.62 | -0.69 | -0.80 | 40. |
| 41. OPER. ASSET TURNOVER | 0/0 | 3.20 | 1.74 | 2.33 | 1.69 | 0.97 | 0.71 | 0.85 | -0.53 | -0.56 | -0.65 | 41. |
| 42. OPER. PROFIT MARGIN | 0/0 | 14.75 | 7.20 | 7.44 | 5.81 | 3.43 | 3.35 | 5.25 | 1.23 | -0.94 | -0.94 | 42. |
| 43. LEVERAGE | 0/0 | 3.26 | 2.04 | 1.71 | 1.45 | 1.25 | 0.98 | 0.75 | 0.59 | 0.62 | 0.49 | 43. |
| 44. TAX RETENTION RATE | 0/0 | -7.83 | -1.60 | -2.25 | -1.70 | -0.79 | -0.56 | -1.79 | -0.46 | 0.51 | 0.63 | 44. |
| 45. MISC. CAUSES OF CHANGE | 0/0 | -1.11 | -1.11 | 0.12 | 0.32 | -0.11 | -0.34 | 0.14 | -0.22 | -0.32 | -0.34 | 45. |

DOMESTIC INTEGRATED OIL AFI CS CLL MRO P SHM SUO SI L SN SOH SUN SDX TV UCL COPYRIGHT 7/7/66 BY FINSTAT, INC.
COMPOSITE NO. 430 SIDE 1

| | | 1965 | 1964 | 1963 | 1962 | 1961 | 1960 | 1959 | 1958 | 1957 | 1956 | |
|---|---|---|---|---|---|---|---|---|---|---|---|---|
| SOURCE AND APPLICATION OF FUNDS | | | | | | | | | | | | |
| 46. NET INCOME | 0/0 | 46.7 | 45.3 | 43.4 | 40.6 | 40.0 | 40.7 | 40.2 | 36.8 | 42.2 | 45.5 | 46. |
| 47. DEPREC. + AMORT. | 0/0 | 53.3 | 54.7 | 56.6 | 59.4 | 60.0 | 59.3 | 59.8 | 63.2 | 57.8 | 54.5 | 47. |
| 48. DEFERRED TAXES | 0/0 | N-AV | N-AV | N-AV | N-AV | N-AV | N-AV | N-AV | N-AV | N-AV | N-AV | 48. |
| 49. CASH FLOW (EX DEF TAX) | MM$ | 2940.9 | 2533.8 | 2419.4 | 2215.9 | 2105.3 | 2101.4 | 2003.3 | 1839.8 | 2053.2 | 1980.2 | 49. |
| 50. CHNG. IN L.T. DEBT + PFD. | MM$ | 1115.1 | 64.9 | 300.8 | 39.4 | 187.0 | 87.1 | -129.4 | 140.9 | 207.4 | 499.1 | 50. |
| 51. MISC. CHNG. IN COM. EQUITY | MM$ | -68.3 | 22.2 | -162.7 | -9.7 | 150.6 | -25.4 | 101.4 | 276.8 | 24.5 | 189.5 | 51. |
| 52. TOTAL SOURCE / APPLIC. | MM$ | 3987.7 | 2620.9 | 2557.5 | 2245.6 | 2442.9 | 2163.1 | 1975.3 | 2257.5 | 2285.1 | 2668.8 | 52. |
| 53. CASH DIVIDENDS | MM$ | 607.9 | 536.2 | 476.8 | 602.7 | 410.3 | 405.6 | 398.7 | 390.8 | 395.8 | 379.9 | 53. |
| 54. CAPITAL EXPENDITURES | MM$ | 2524.7 | 2197.5 | 1723.5 | 1765.6 | 1757.6 | 1645.3 | 1556.6 | 1468.8 | 1956.0 | 1907.1 | 54. |
| 55. CHANGE IN NET CUR. ASSETS | MM$ | 292.5 | -69.7 | 358.4 | 32.5 | 114.0 | 28.1 | -84.5 | 197.5 | -56.7 | 341.0 | 55. |
| 56. INVESTMENTS AND ADVANCES | MM$ | N-AV | N-AV | N-AV | N-AV | N-AV | N-AV | N-AV | N-AV | N-AV | N-AV | 56. |
| 57. RETIREMENTS + MISC. | MM$ | N-AV | N-AV | N-AV | N-AV | N-AV | N-AV | N-AV | N-AV | N-AV | N-AV | 57. |
| BALANCE SHEET STRUCTURE (YEAREND) | | | | | | | | | | | | |
| 58. CASH + EQUIV. | 0/0 | 27.0 | 24.1 | 30.8 | 27.1 | 29.2 | 31.1 | 32.1 | 33.9 | 30.6 | 35.8 | 58. |
| 59. RECEIVABLES | 0/0 | 42.3 | 43.0 | 38.0 | 39.7 | 37.3 | 34.6 | 31.6 | 30.8 | 29.6 | 27.9 | 59. |
| 60. INVENTORY + MISC. | 0/0 | 30.8 | 32.8 | 31.3 | 33.3 | 33.5 | 34.4 | 36.3 | 35.3 | 39.8 | 36.2 | 60. |
| 61. CURRENT ASSETS | 0/0 | 29.1 | 28.3 | 29.3 | 27.8 | 27.8 | 28.1 | 28.9 | 29.4 | 29.8 | 31.6 | 61. |
| 62. NET PLANT | 0/0 | 64.4 | 64.7 | 63.8 | 65.4 | 65.2 | 64.9 | 65.0 | 66.1 | 65.9 | 64.5 | 62. |
| 63. NON-OPERATING ASSETS | 0/0 | 6.5 | 7.0 | 6.9 | 6.8 | 7.1 | 7.0 | 6.0 | 4.5 | 4.4 | 3.9 | 63. |
| 64. CURRENT RATIO | X | 2.15 | 2.30 | 2.42 | 2.38 | 2.43 | 2.47 | 2.46 | 2.75 | 2.56 | 2.66 | 64. |
| 65. CASH + EQUIV. RATIO | X | 0.58 | 0.55 | 0.75 | 0.64 | 0.71 | 0.77 | 0.79 | 0.93 | 0.78 | 0.95 | 65. |
| 66. CURRENT LIABILITIES | 0/0 | 13.6 | 12.3 | 12.1 | 11.7 | 11.4 | 11.4 | 11.8 | 10.7 | 11.6 | 11.9 | 66. |
| 67. MISCELLANEOUS | 0/0 | 3.3 | 3.6 | 3.4 | 3.0 | 3.0 | 2.1 | 2.0 | 1.2 | 1.1 | 1.2 | 67. |
| 68. LONG-TERM DEBT | 0/0 | 16.6 | 15.5 | 16.2 | 17.1 | 17.6 | 17.7 | 17.7 | 19.5 | 19.4 | 18.9 | 68. |
| 69. PREFERRED STOCK | 0/0 | 5.2 | 3.1 | 2.9 | 1.4 | 1.2 | 1.2 | 1.3 | 1.4 | 1.5 | 1.6 | 69. |
| 70. COMMON EQUITY | 0/0 | 61.4 | 65.4 | 65.3 | 66.7 | 66.8 | 67.6 | 67.2 | 67.2 | 66.3 | 66.4 | 70. |

| LONG-TERM TRENDS | SALES FOR LAST 3 YRS | 5 YRS | 10 YRS | SALES P.S. FOR LAST 3 YRS | 5 YRS | 10 YRS | EARNS P.S. FOR LAST 3 YRS | 5 YRS | 10 YRS | PRICE FOR LAST 3 YRS | 5 YRS | 10 YRS | |
|---|---|---|---|---|---|---|---|---|---|---|---|---|---|
| 87. LEAST SQUARES RATE | 9.3 | 7.8 | 4.7 | 8.5 | 7.2 | 4.4 | 13.6 | 12.4 | 5.4 | 17.0 | 13.0 | 4.8 | 87. |
| 88. ONE STANDARD DEV. | 3.4 | 3.1 | 4.5 | 3.2 | 2.8 | 4.4 | 4.7 | 4.7 | 12.3 | 3.0 | 11.7 | 12.3 | 88. |

| AVERAGE OF 15 COMPANIES | | 1965 | 1964 | 1963 | 1962 | 1961 | 1960 | 1959 | 1958 | 1957 | 1956 | |
|---|---|---|---|---|---|---|---|---|---|---|---|---|
| STOCK MARKET DATA AND INDICES | | | | | | | | | | | | |
| 5. SALES INDEX | 0/0 | 178.6 | 155.1 | 137.2 | 124.4 | 117.6 | 113.2 | 105.0 | 96.8 | 98.1 | 91.0 | 5. |
| 6. SALES PER SHARE INDEX | 0/0 | 168.0 | 146.2 | 131.3 | 120.3 | 113.8 | 110.6 | 102.9 | 96.5 | 100.6 | 93.3 | 6. |
| 7. EARNINGS PER SHARE INDEX | 0/0 | 177.1 | 145.6 | 133.7 | 114.6 | 107.1 | 112.2 | 102.4 | 83.9 | 113.7 | 120.8 | 7. |
| 8. AVERAGE PRICE INDEX | 0/0 | 160.7 | 140.4 | 117.4 | 98.7 | 105.4 | 88.3 | 102.6 | 95.5 | 101.9 | 105.6 | 8. |
| 2. AVG. P/E MULTIPLE | X | 13.54 | 14.20 | 13.12 | 13.01 | 14.90 | 11.95 | 15.12 | -40.44 | 13.69 | 13.29 | 2. |
| 3. AVG. DIVIDEND YIELD | 0/0 | 3.09 | 3.18 | 3.41 | 3.78 | 3.40 | 3.90 | 3.28 | 3.61 | 3.47 | 3.23 | 3. |
| TURNOVER, MARGINS, RETURNS, ETC. | | | | | | | | | | | | |
| 14. OPERATING ASSET TURNOVER | X | 0.88 | 0.87 | 0.86 | 0.83 | 0.84 | 0.86 | 0.85 | 0.84 | 0.91 | 0.92 | 14. |
| 18. OPERATING PROFIT MARGIN | 0/0 | 11.08 | 9.88 | 9.88 | 9.08 | 9.05 | 9.76 | 9.47 | 8.69 | 11.09 | 12.99 | 18. |
| 22. TAX RATE | 0/0 | 22.73 | 16.85 | 19.70 | 16.96 | 16.12 | 17.13 | 16.10 | 8.52 | 16.01 | 23.01 | 22. |
| 23. NET PROFIT MARGIN | 0/0 | 8.62 | 8.28 | 8.07 | 7.50 | 7.51 | 7.94 | 7.88 | 7.52 | 9.20 | 10.17 | 23. |
| 25. OPER PROFIT ON OPER ASSETS | 0/0 | 9.58 | 8.36 | 8.18 | 7.25 | 7.31 | 8.19 | 7.94 | 7.11 | 9.50 | 11.48 | 25. |
| 28. TOT ASTS TO COM EQUITY | X | 1.70 | 1.63 | 1.59 | 1.56 | 1.55 | 1.55 | 1.55 | 1.56 | 1.57 | 1.54 | 28. |
| 29. NET RETURN ON COM. EQUITY | 0/0 | 11.25 | 10.00 | 9.50 | 8.36 | 8.33 | 9.28 | 9.21 | 8.55 | 11.23 | 12.59 | 29. |
| 32. PAYOUT RATIO | 0/0 | 42.95 | 45.04 | 45.05 | 49.39 | 50.06 | 46.38 | 49.94 | 54.79 | 45.31 | 40.94 | 32. |
| 34. REINVESTMENT RATE | 0/0 | 6.45 | 5.39 | 5.09 | 4.11 | 4.04 | 4.89 | 4.58 | 3.62 | 6.16 | 7.35 | 34. |

AGGREGATE DATA FOR FISCAL YEAR ENDING 1965 (000,000) - DOMESTIC INTEGRATED OIL COMPOSITE NO. 430 SIDE 2

| | | | | | | | |
|---|---|---|---|---|---|---|---|
| NET SALES | 16332.4 | CURRENT ASSETS | 6112.7 | CURRENT LIABILITIES | 2843.4 | AVG. MARKET VALUE | 18575.5 |
| OPERATING PROFIT | 1710.65 | NET PLANT | 13508.6 | LONG TERM DEBT | 3474.3 | EMPLOYEES (000) | 267.7 |
| AVAIL. FOR COMMON | 1336.091 | TOTAL NET ASTS | 20976.1 | COMMON EQUITY | 12874.655 | SHARES OUTSTANDING | 361.987 |

updating of practically all information related to the security analysis process. The central information file contains not only relevant past financial statement data for the companies which the bank follows, or might choose to follow in the future, but also the past estimates by the bank's analysts.

Reports which are useful to analysts in making estimates are generated according to a prearranged timetable, and analysts are notified automatically of revisions in expectations which they must supply. The system provides for periodic feedback to analysts so that they may compare their past estimates of, say, earnings to the earnings which actually transpired. It can also keep track of estimates provided by brokerage firms and outside consultants so that their contributions can be better evaluated.

For the most part, the Bankers Trust system calls for weekly updating, but at some future time, movement toward a real-time system is anticipated. While the information system is designed to provide analysts with timely information for making their estimates and also to provide them with feedback on past forecasts, these are not the only purposes. It also provides the input data for security valuation procedures.[5]

*Improvement of Screening Filters.* Just as the computer can be used efficiently in the actual screening process, which consists of putting hundreds of companies through filters and extracting a shorter list of companies worthy of more intensive study, it also can be used to help improve the underlying nature of the filters themselves. For example, the Chase Manhattan Bank and Standard & Poor's Corporation have each devoted a large segment of their computer-oriented investment research programs to this type of investigation. Essentially, what is done is to hypothesize various characteristics of a stock which may cause its price to improve more than the prices of stocks in general. Then the computer is programmed to search for these characteristics in past data records of many stocks, isolate the stocks which have exhibited these characteristics, and trace the price performance of these selected stocks in comparison with those not selected. One finding of this type of research has been that companies with *accelerating* earnings growth rates have been excellent candidates for further common stock analysis.[6]

### Security Evaluation—I: Common Stock

Having screened out a group of stocks "for further analysis," the computer has many applications in this further analysis, and particularly in evaluation procedures. In common stock analysis, evaluation consists

---

[5] J. E. Fanning, "How to Improve Investment Decisions," *Harvard Business Review*, January-February, 1966.

[6] M. Kisor, Jr., "Quantitative Approaches to Common Stock Selection," *Business Economics*, Spring, 1966. Other evidence suggests that, in addition to growth rate *acceleration*, it is desirable that the *absolute level* of a company's growth rate be above average.

## FIGURE 20–8

### Ashland Oil vs. Shell Oil

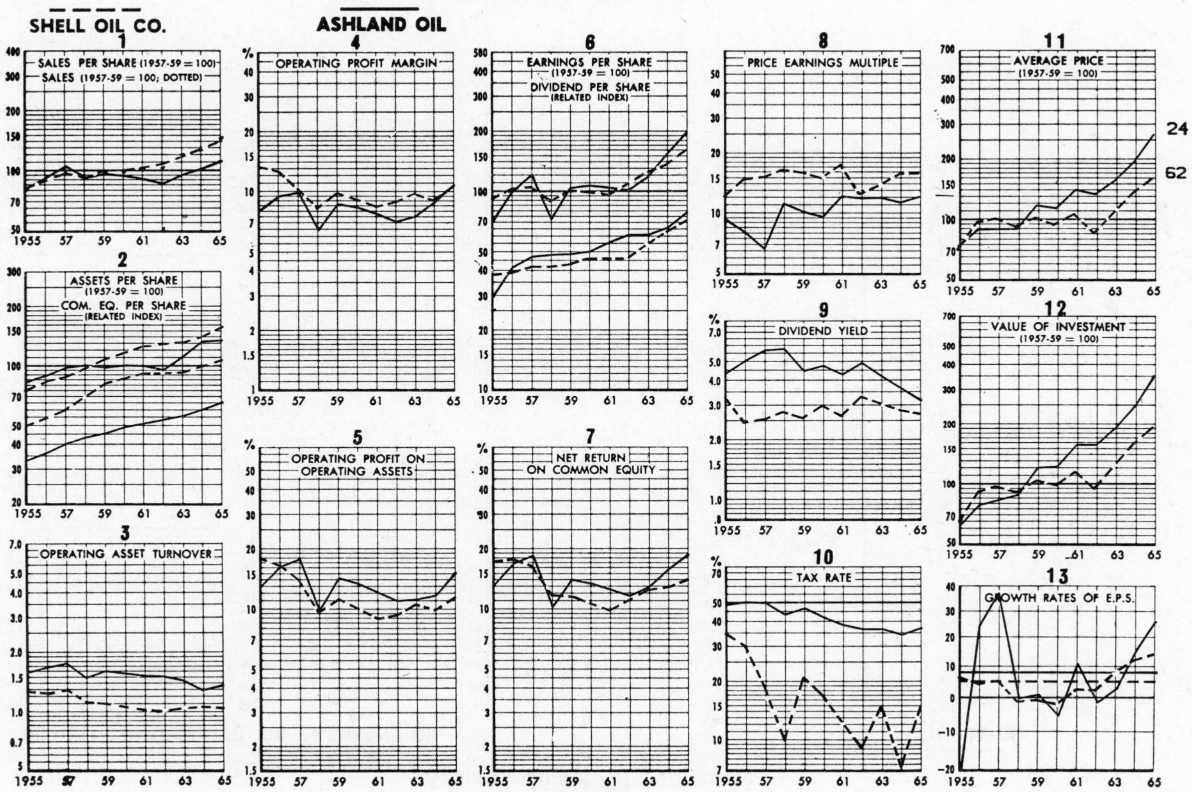

– – – – SHELL OIL CO.

——— ASHLAND OIL

1 SALES PER SHARE (1957-59 = 100)
SALES (1957-59 = 100; DOTTED)

2 ASSETS PER SHARE (1957-59 = 100)
COM. EQ. PER SHARE (RELATED INDEX)

3 OPERATING ASSET TURNOVER

4 OPERATING PROFIT MARGIN

5 OPERATING PROFIT ON OPERATING ASSETS

6 EARNINGS PER SHARE (1957-59 = 100)
DIVIDEND PER SHARE (RELATED INDEX)

7 NET RETURN ON COMMON EQUITY

8 PRICE EARNINGS MULTIPLE

9 DIVIDEND YIELD

10 TAX RATE

11 AVERAGE PRICE (1957-59 = 100)

24

62

12 VALUE OF INVESTMENT (1957-59 = 100)

13 GROWTH RATES OF E.P.S.

1955 57 59 61 63 65

INDUSTRIALS

## FIGURE 20–9
### Ashland Oil vs. Oil Composite

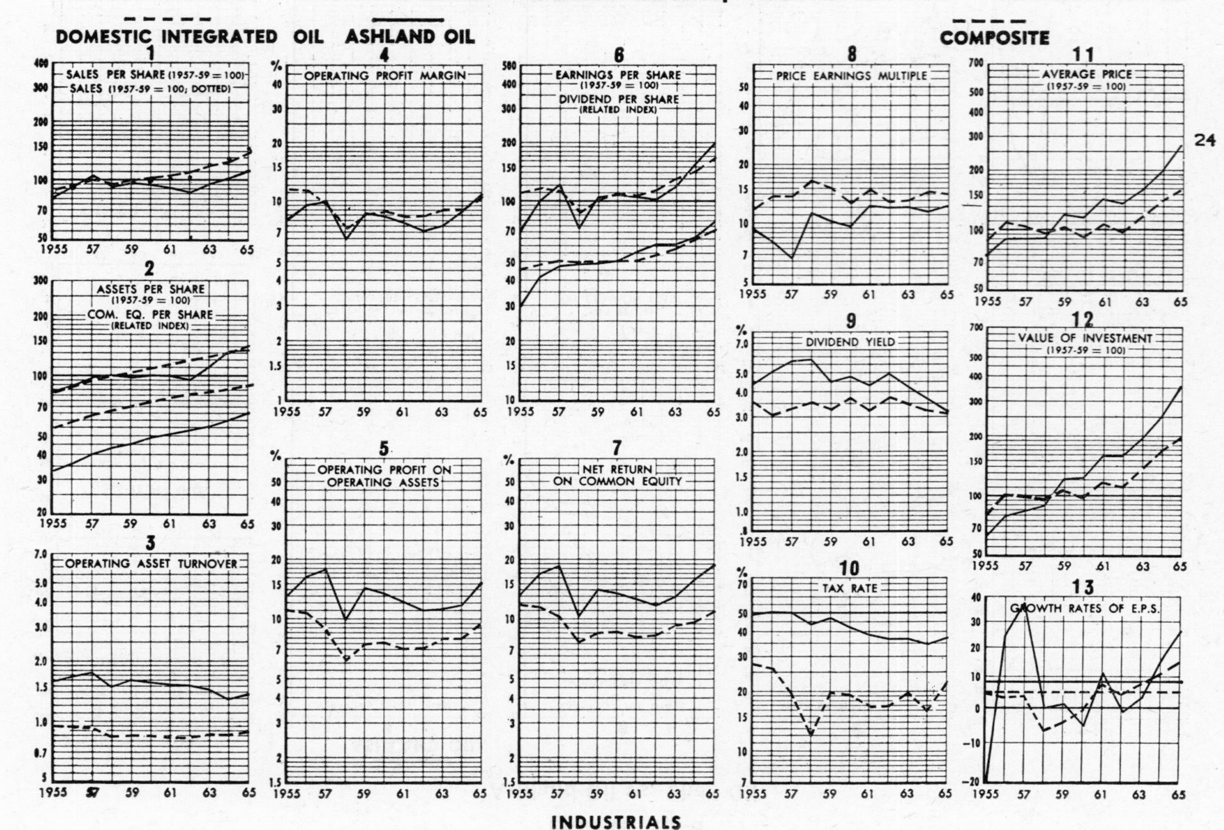


INDUSTRIALS

essentially of making projections of the growth and stability of sales, earnings, and dividends, and then applying capitalization factors to derive measures of intrinsic value. Electronic computers can make an important contribution to both the projection and the capitalization efforts of the analyst.

*Projection.* In our opinion, a major source of error in making *short-term* forecasts of corporate operating results is the tendency of security analysts to compare the data of each quarter with the same quarter a year earlier. This technique can produce very misleading impressions of current developments during periods of cyclical fluctuation. Much more informative is a comparison of each quarter with the immediately preceding quarters, after having adjusted each quarter's data for normal seasonal variations. Without the availability of a computer, seasonal adjustment is a laborious and time-consuming statistical procedure. With a computer, hundreds of series of data can be put onto punched cards or magnetic tape and seasonally adjusted quickly and accurately.[7]

A program can also be written to take in the seasonally adjusted data and calculate quarter-to-quarter percentage changes. For even greater perspective, the computer can be programmed to calculate ratios of any one company's results to those of any other company, or to all other companies. Not only can the ratios be automatically calculated, moreover, but relatively inexpensive equipment is available which can mechanically chart the results in almost any format desired by the analyst.

With regard to intercompany or interindustry comparisons, the technique of input-output analysis was discussed in Chapter 7. As noted there, presently available input-output tables show the sales of each of 80-odd industries to each other industry. This results in many thousands of entries on the table. Future input-output tables are expected to be vastly expanded in detail. Probably the only efficient way to utilize the treasure-house of material thus made available will be via electronic computers.[8]

The long-term projection of corporate growth and stability characteristics obviously involves much qualitative analysis. But it is equally obvious that the beginning point of most such analyses is a quantitative determination of past rates of change. However, one of the problems in determining past rates of change is that there is no single best measure.

---

[7] See J. Shiskin "Electronic Computers and Business Indicators," *Journal of Business*, October, 1957. Also, U.S. Bureau of The Census, *The X–11 Variant of the Census Method II Seasonal Adjustment Program* (Technical Paper 15, 1965).

[8] In May, 1966, IBM announced a new market research service which is based in large part on the input-output technique. See *The Wall Street Journal*, May 11, 1966, p. 32.

Different rates will result by varying the starting and stopping dates of the historical record being worked with. Trend lines can be either arithmetic or logarithmic, linear or curved. If curved, a number of different mathematical formulae may produce a number of strikingly different results. Or the analyst may wish to try a moving average procedure, or an advanced averaging technique such as "exponential smoothing." With the help of a computer, the analyst need not confine himself to one or two trend-fitting methods, chosen on an a priori basis and applied across the board to all companies. Rather, he can experiment with many different methods under many different circumstances, and perhaps end up with a better qualitative as well as quantitative "feel" for the data.

Finally, we would note that electronic computers provide sophisticated security analysts with the ability to break away from the elementary ratio and percentage change type of calculations and to experiment with more advanced econometric approaches to forecasting. For example, mathematical models can be constructed which relate a particular company's operations to its industry group and to the entire economy. Functional relationships between sales and other key income statement items can be developed—for example, by means of simple or multiple regression analysis techniques. And it might be fruitful to attempt an integration of income statements and balance sheets by means of a sources and uses of funds model. Of course, we do not know if these efforts would produce any better projections than are currently being produced by cruder methods, but one never knows until one tries.

*Capitalization.* In Chapter 5 we discussed at some length the theory that a common stock's value is equal to the present worth of its future dividends. A long-term projection of the dividend stream of a company is discounted at an appropriate rate, and the present values of each future dividend are summed to derive the stock's theoretical value. Several ingenious books of tables have been published in recent years to assist the analyst who wishes to make such calculations. These tables show how many dollars can be paid per dollar of today's dividends or earnings (the capitalization rate, or "multiplier") given various assumptions as to growth and discount rates. The tables are unique in that they do not require the growth or discount rates to remain constant throughout the period being forecasted. However, the number of dimensions that can be conveniently encompassed in a series of tables is necessarily quite limited. By utilizing an electronic computer, on the other hand, analysts need not be at all restricted in making discount calculations.

For example, a computer program could be written to allow the user to specify any or all of the following conditions:

1. Changing growth rates of earnings for any number of spans of years during the projection period.

2. Changing dividend payout ratios.
3. An ultimate date of sale of the stock, with an assumed price-earnings ratio or dividend yield at the time of sale.
4. Changing discount rates for different time spans of the projection period.

The discounting approach to stock valuation is designed to tell the analyst what price a dollar of current earnings or dividends should command under varying assumptions about future conditions. In Chapter 5 we applied this approach to the evaluation of the market as a whole (specifically to the evaluation of Standard & Poor's Industrial Stock Price Index). However, in dealing with the evaluation of individual stocks, we followed a different approach. Here the question asked was not what price a dollar of earnings *should* be worth, but rather what price investors have actually been willing to pay for, say, a 1% above-average (or below-average) expected growth rate of earning power and how this price is affected by differences in dividend policy, sales stability, leverage, etc.

To attempt a thorough answer to the latter type of question it is necessary to analyze hundreds of different stocks over a period of many years. Such an analysis is feasible only with the assistance of electronic computers. Just measuring the variables is a task of enormous complexity, not to mention the analysis once the measurements have been made. One project of this nature with which we are familiar involves the following work:

1. Calculation of growth rates of sales, reported earnings, pretax cash flow, and dividends for all 5-, 8-, and 10-year spans during the postwar period, for all corporations included in the S & P Industrials index.

2. Corresponding calculations of average annual deviations from fitted trend values, and of dividend payout ratios, debt ratios, market value of total capitalization, and several other financial ratios.

3. Calculation of annual price-earnings ratios, using varying definitions of earnings in the denominator—for example, actual reported earnings per share, three-year average earnings, trend value of earnings.

4. Multiple regression analysis, where the measures referred to in (1) and (2) above are correlated with various measures of price-earnings ratio. The purpose of this analysis is to isolate the variables that seem most significantly to affect price-earnings ratio. In addition to the direct use of multiple regression in this phase of the work, mechanical production of scatter diagrams and multidimensional cross-tabulations have proven helpful.

5. Interrogate professional security analysts and sift through their past memoranda to develop a record of their actual sales, earnings, and dividend growth expectations for a large cross section of stocks at various

points of time. Determine whether there are significant differences between, say, 5-year expectations and 10-year expectations.

6. Compare the actual growth expectations with the historical data that were available at the time the expectations were formulated, and try to develop a method of simulating growth expectations for stocks and for periods for which no actual expectations are available.[9]

7. Try to determine the conditions under which expectations regarding other variables—for example, stability, dividend policy, leverage—vary from the observed historical magnitudes of these variables.

8. Rerun the multiple regression studies, substituting actual and simulated expectations for historical growth and other variables, and compare results.

9. Generalize regarding the extent to which intercompany differences in price-earnings ratios can be explained by differences in history and in analysts' expectations. How much weight has normally been assigned by the market to growth, stability, dividend policy, etc., in establishing the value to place on a dollar of current earnings? Have the relative weights of each factor changed over time? Are they different in rising, level, and falling markets? Do "deviant" price-earnings ratios tend to return to "normal"?

10. Analyze in detail the characteristics of stocks whose price-earnings ratios consistently tend to depart from their regression-indicated "norms."

### Security Evaluation—II: Bonds

As indicated in Chapter 10, bond quality evaluation has traditionally consisted mostly of a retrospective calculation of various financial ratios, and a qualitative attempt to determine whether these ratios are indicative of a debtor's ability to meet his obligations in the future. Application of computers to the task of ratio calculation has been covered, in effect, in the section on screening. The qualitative aspect of the ratio analysis does not seem particularly amenable to computer assistance. However, it was indicated in Chapter 11 that recent theoretical discussions of debt-servicing ability focus on the analysis and forecasting of the entire cash flow network of debtor corporations. Here, the applicability of computers is outstanding.

First, the computer can be used to help determine past interrelationships among the major cash flow items, especially the relationships of

[9] As a part of this type of research, it might be desirable to compare analysts' forecasts with subsequent actual results and to see whether methods can be developed of correcting future forecasts for various apparent biases on the part of different analysts or for errors which are unique to the process of forecasting the results of specific companies or industries.

various expense and balance sheet categories to sales. Second, since the likelihood is that the interrelationships will not prove to have been stable over time, a relatively large number of net changes in cash balances can be envisioned at any hypothesized future sales level. When many different future sales levels are hypothesized, the number of possible net changes in cash is greatly expanded. An electronic computer is an ideal tool for calculating the impact on cash of numerous assumed interrelationships of cash flow items. Moreover, as stressed in Chapter 11, the bond analyst is interested not only in the *range* of possible cash changes but also in the *probabilities* of these changes occurring. Admittedly, the analyst must employ a good deal of subjective judgment when assigning probabilities to each individual component of the cash flow forecast. However, once these have been assigned, the task of calculating the joint and cumulative probabilities is straightforward and simple for a computer, but extremely tedious to do manually.

The application of computers to bond analysis does not stop at forecasting the borrower's debt-servicing ability. Computers are clearly applicable to bond pricing problems. One pricing area where computers have been fairly widely used is in bidding for municipal bond underwriting awards. Municipal bonds are issued in serial form, and each serial maturity can carry a different coupon, price, and yield. Since the number of possible combinations is astronomical, computers can perform yeoman service in spelling out alternatives. Likewise, investors in corporate bonds can use the computer to calculate the yields that would result under different assumptions regarding defaults, refunding calls, and reinvestment alternatives at the time of call. Commercial banks and other investors in U.S. government bonds can use computers to advantage in analyzing the probable yield gains available in advance refunding offerings and in tax-motivated "swap" transactions (i.e., sale of one security and simultaneous purchase of another).[10]

## Investment Timing—I: Economic Forecasting

We have expressed the opinion in this book that the chances of investment success can be enhanced significantly if the investor develops an ability to foresee major turning points in general economic activity some three to six months in advance. Admittedly, such an ability is largely intuitive. Nevertheless, a solid core of quantitative analysis is helpful, if not indispensable. At least two aspects of the process of economic forecasting stand out as being suited to computer application—analysis of "economic indicators" and econometric model building.

The pioneering work of Julius Shiskin, at the Bureau of the Census,

[10] IBM has made available some prepackaged programs along these lines.

best illustrates the application of computers to the analysis of the so-called leading, coincident, and lagging indicators. These indicators are statistical series which become available each month or quarter and which provide important insight into the ebb and flow of aggregate economic activity (see Chapter 13 for illustrations). Under Shiskin's direction, the Census Bureau prepares a monthly publication called *Business Cycle Developments*, which presents the indicators in various perspectives. All data are seasonally adjusted; series with highly irregular patterns of movement are smoothed with appropriate moving averages; all series are listed and charted; directions of change and incidence of new highs and lows for each series are shown; special charts compare the movements of selected indicators in the latest leg of the business cycle with their movements in corresponding phases of previous cycles; and various "diffusion indexes" are presented. Virtually all of this data manipulation and charting is done with electronic equipment!

Although *Business Cycle Developments* contains various diffusion indexes—for example, of commodity prices and profits—a notable omission is a single diffusion index based on a selected group of leading indicators. This omission, we are sure, does not stem from any lack of appreciation of the forecasting usefulness of such an index (see Chapter 13). Indeed, Shiskin has been a major participant in the diffusion studies conducted by the National Bureau of Economic Research. Rather, the omission probably reflects the unwillingness of the Census Bureau to appear to be giving official government status to a single economic forecasting index which would doubtless be widely quoted in this nation and abroad.

Given the Census Bureau's reluctance to publish a diffusion index of leading economic indicators, intelligent investors should construct their own index. The simplest way to do this is to count the number of leading indicator pluses in the monthly *Business Cycle Developments* and to express this number as a percentage of the total number of leading indicators published. This procedure, of course, does not require the use of a computer. Fingers and toes will do quite adequately. However, it is quite a nondiscriminating procedure. Some of the indicators, for example, reflect essentially similar phenomena, so there is a duplication which may be misleading. In addition, some indicators may be most significant in, say, the expansion phase of a cycle, while others may be more significant in contractions. Some kind of weighting system might improve the usefulness of the index. Perhaps it would also help to mix leading, coincident, and lagging indicators in a single index. Finally, there are various ways of defining the direction of change in a statistical series from month to month—change in the raw data, change in a short-term moving average, change in a long-term moving average, etc.

Experimentation with different methods of calculating economic diffusion indexes is warranted, and such experimentation is most feasible if electronic computers are utilized. While the National Bureau of Economic Research is continuously engaged in experiments of this nature, there is no reason why investment institutions should not carry out supplementary research projects.

The construction of econometric models of the American economy is also in the experimental stage. In essence, a model of the economy is a formal mathematical statement of the kinds of relationships which were discussed informally in Chapter 13, under the heading "GNP Model." A simultaneous equation system is constructed in which major economic variables are expressed as functions of either other economic variables or of "noneconomic" phenomena. Once a set of initial quantities is assumed, the system generates the values of all the other quantities. An econometric model can therefore be used in forecasting by assuming that set of initial quantities which the forecaster believes are likely to actually prevail in a future period. The model then generates all other quantities for that future period.

The models of the entire economy that have been constructed to date range from crude five- or six-equation systems to systems of several dozen equations. Currently, a team of scholars is working on a many-hundred-equation model. (It is known as the Brookings–Social Science Research Council, or S.S.R.C., model.[11]) Some of the existing models utilize quarterly data and were specifically designed for use in short-term forecasting, but most are on an annual basis and were designed more for basic analysis of the economic structure than for short-term forecasting. In either case, the use of electronic computers is essential to the development and utilization of the models.

To our knowledge, few investment institutions have devoted much money to research in the area of econometric forecasting models—either of the entire economy or of individual industries. Virtually all of the work has been done in universities and, to a lesser extent, in government and heavy industry. It is still too early in the development of the technique to know whether this omission is or is not a mistake. Based on some of the work we have seen, however, we would venture the opinion that it will prove to be a major gain in forecasting.

## Investment Timing—II: Technical Analysis of Stock Prices

Of all the controversies alluded to in this book, one of the most heated involves the question of whether past movements of stock prices, and related *internal* market developments, can be used as indicators of

[11] J. Duesenberry, G. Fromm, L. Klein, and E. Kuh, *Brookings Quarterly Econometric Model of the United States* (Skokie, Ill., Rand McNally & Co., 1965).

future stock prices. Our position is that so-called "technical analysis" can be somewhat helpful in the attempt to judge the probabilities of future price changes, and we have attempted to defend this position in Chapter 14. In that chapter, we illustrated the usefulness—and also the shortcomings—of breadth-of-market concepts and of such statistics as volume of trading, short selling, etc. However, we indicated that several techniques suffer from a lack of adequate supporting evidence. Chief among these "unproven" techniques is the attribution of forecasting ability to various price patterns, such as "ascending or descending tops and bottoms," "congestion areas," penetration of long-term moving averages, etc.

In our opinion, the availability of electronic computers makes it possible to test thoroughly the validity of most price-pattern theories. Precise definitions of each theory can first be spelled out. If, as in most cases, the theories are ambiguous, alternative definitions can be established. The definitions, moreover, can be elaborate enough to include data supplementary to price—for example, volume of trading or even earnings per share. After establishing the definitions, computer programs can be written which will act as filters through which the price history of hundreds of stocks can be run. For each theory it can then be determined (*a*) how many times the particular pattern occurred, and (*b*) how many times the appearance of the pattern was followed by the price behavior indicated in the theory.

We would be surprised if studies of this type revealed that in a large proportion of cases the appearance of well-defined price patterns is followed by the hypothesized price behavior. Indeed, a finding of this nature would make "value analysis" relatively unimportant. But even if the proportion is not large, as long as it is statistically significant it would be extremely useful information. For the price-pattern filter could then be incorporated in the screening process discussed earlier and could help analysts zero in on the relatively small number of stocks that are worthy of intensive study at any given point in time.[12]

Computers can also be utilized in other aspects of technical analysis. For example, it has been noted repeatedly that charts of various types are indispensable tools of the trade. Tens of thousands of man-hours are consumed each year on Wall Street to prepare price-volume charts, point-and-figure charts, and relative-strength charts. Yet much of this work could be executed mechanically, more accurately and at lower cost. Even very complex charts can be done mechanically, as illustrated in Figures 20–10 and 20–11. We must admit, however, that there is probably

[12] The reader will note the similarity between this discussion and that presented earlier under the heading "Improvement of Screening Filters." Since technical analysis can be used as a device for screening out from a large list of stocks a smaller list which is then examined in greater depth as to "fundamentals," this part of the "Investment Timing" section could well have been made a part of the section on "Screening."

**FIGURE 20–10**

**Example of a Computer-Produced Chart**

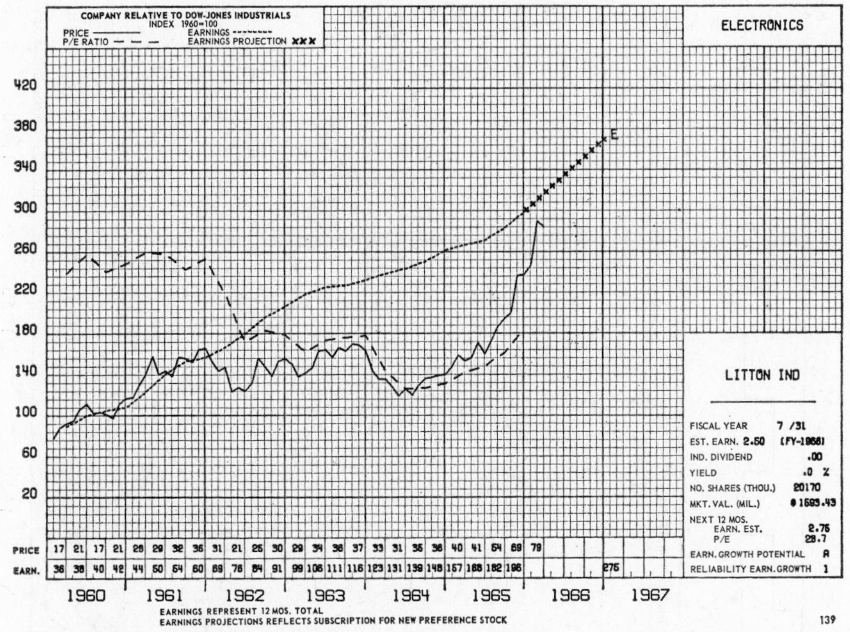


Source: Drexel, Harriman, Ripley, Inc.

some validity to the observation that when the analyst himself manually plots the points day in and day out, he gains more insight than if he is handed an already-prepared chart. Perhaps some combination of mechanical and manual charting would be ideal.

Yet another area of computer-oriented investigation of stock price behavior could be an analysis of price "covariance" to aid investors in applying the principle of diversification. One does not achieve the risk-spreading objectives of diversification by purchasing many different security issues if the prices of these issues tend to move up and down simultaneously and by similar magnitudes. Computers can be put to work in an attempt to gain insight into the interrelationship of general market price movements, industry price movements, and individual security price movements. For example, at least one academician has successfully applied the statistical technique of factor analysis to this problem, making extensive use of computers in his work.[13]

## Portfolio Strategy

To this point we have discussed the application of electronic computers to the selection and timing of individual security purchases and sales. A related, yet separate, application is to the solution of broad portfolio

[13] See B. F. King, "Market and Industry Factors in Stock Price Behavior," *Journal of Business*, January, 1966, Supplement on Security Prices.

FIGURE 20–11

Stock Market Credit: A Computer-Produced Chart

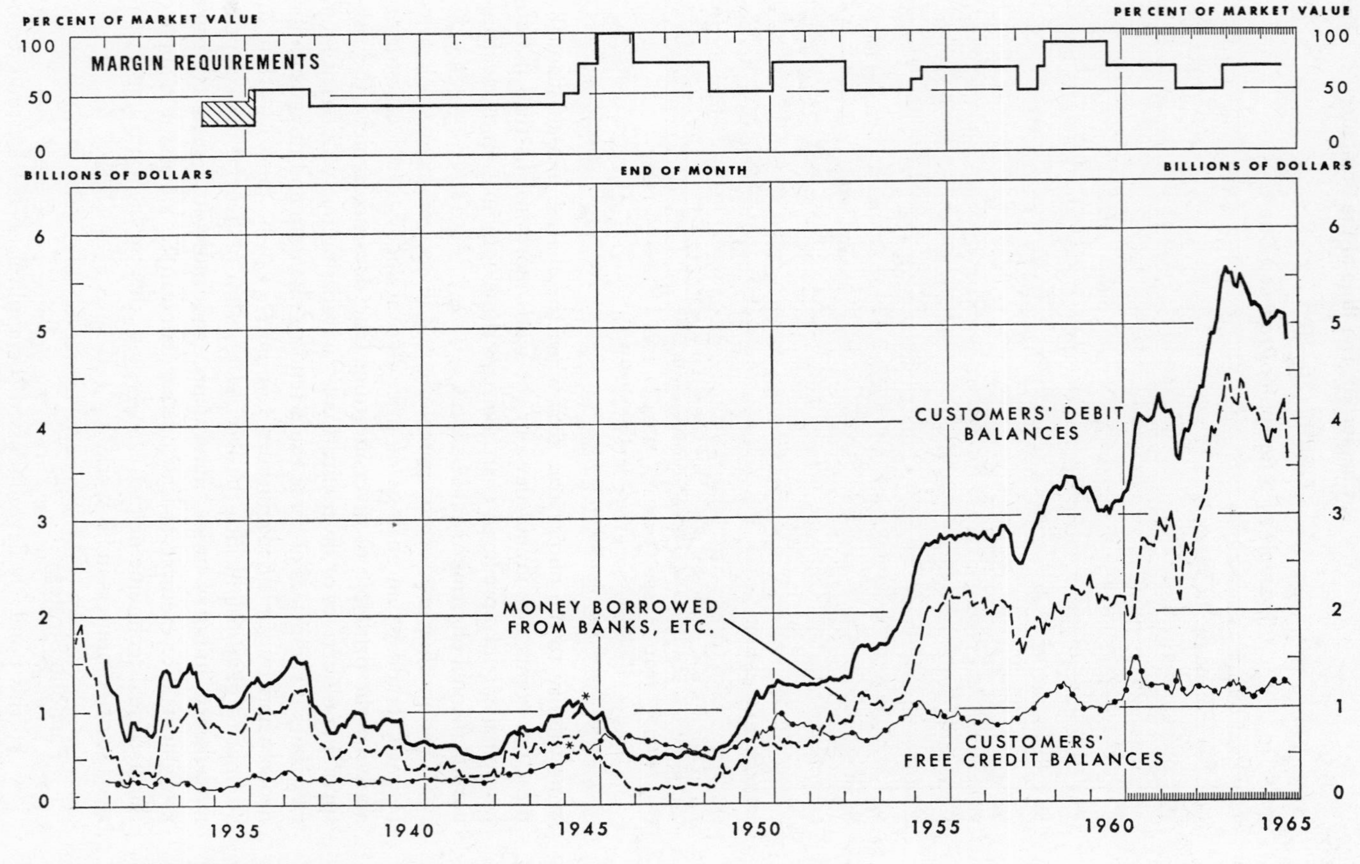


* Change in series.
Source: Board of Governors of the Federal Reserve System.

management problems. In this section we shall outline a few of what seem to us to be the most promising areas of investigation. These areas can be classified under two general headings: (1) analysis and evaluation of the portfolio manager's existing practices, and (2) attempts to improve existing practices through a deeper understanding of the consequences of alternative investment strategies.

*Existing Practices.* In a recent doctoral dissertation, Geoffrey Clarkson demonstrated that it is possible to approximate mechanically many key investment diversification decisions of a professional personal trust manager. That is, he was able to develop a computer "simulation" program which, given certain information available to the trust manager, would generate diversification decisions very similar to those actually made by the manager operating independent of the computer. The details of Clarkson's research need not be dwelt on here.[14] Essentially, however, what Clarkson did was to observe the portfolio manager at work over an extended period of time and to interview him in depth. As a result of his observations, Clarkson determined that the man—sometimes knowingly, sometimes unknowingly—was following certain rules of thumb ("heuristics") in reaching his decisions. These rules of thumb were then incorporated into a computer program which, in effect, duplicated the portfolio manager's thought processes.

Clarkson's ability to approximate mechanically a rather complex human behavioral pattern has implications far beyond our immediate sphere of interest. But even within that sphere, portfolio management, his work has great significance. We believe it would be a good idea for all portfolio managers to hire people with Clarkson's talents and ask them to try to simulate their behavior. If it can be done successfully, several advantages can be achieved. Most important are:

1. Each portfolio manager will see clearly that many of his decisions are based on thought processes of which he was only vaguely, if at all, conscious. Once these thought processes are spelled out, he can evaluate them with as much objectivity as he can muster up, and decide whether certain changes might be desirable.

2. By checking his decisions against the "decisions" of the computer, the portfolio manager can isolate any apparent inconsistencies and determine whether the unique facts of each case justify variations from his "normal" response pattern.

We emphatically do not envision computer simulation of investment behavior as a step toward the replacement of human investment managers by machines. Rather, we view it as a technique of making graphic the

---

[14] For details see, G. P. E. Clarkson, *Portfolio Selection: A Simulation of Trust Investment* (New York: Prentice-Hall, Inc., 1962).

underlying nature of one's investment behavior. And this self-knowledge, in turn, should enable one to perceive possibilities for improvement. Of course, as Clarkson points out in his publication, one does not necessarily need a computer to perform simulations any more than one needs an adding machine to perform additions. But the computer's incredible speed and accuracy certainly makes such research more feasible than ever before.

Along similar lines, we believe that the computer makes it increasingly feasible to perform the sometimes unpleasant task of measuring the true rate of return on one's past investments. The reader will probably acknowledge readily that most individual investors have little notion of what rate of return they have earned on their investments, with the probable exception of savings accounts whose rates are publicly advertised. But most readers will probably find it difficult to believe that professional investors have almost as little knowledge of their rates of return as the proverbial man on the street. Yet our experience suggests that this is truly the case.

The rate of return on any investment can be most precisely stated as the discount rate which equates the present values of all cash outlays with the present values of all cash incomes involved in the investment. (In the case of an investment which is still in the portfolio, the market value at the time of the measurement of rate of return can be treated as a cash income, after deducting applicable brokerage commissions.) This sounds simple enough. But consider what is involved in adequately measuring the investment returns of a large financial institution.

Hundreds of thousands of transactions are executed in thousands of individual stock, bond, mortgage, and other instruments. In the case of stocks, repeated new cash outlays are made as a large holding is gradually accumulated. In the case of privately placed bonds and mortgages, adjustments are frequently made in the terms of the loan during the course of its life. Income, moreover, includes not only periodic receipts of dividends and interest but also capital gains and capital losses (negative income) and perhaps various commitment fees, servicing fees, and other income. Outgo includes not only principal amounts but also servicing costs and taxes.

The bookkeeping problem inherent in keeping track of the incomes and outlays stemming from (*a*) specific investments, (*b*) broad categories of investment (including not only obvious categories such as common stocks, bonds, and mortgages but also, for example, all refunding transactions, transactions with new customers versus old customers, etc.), and (*c*) the operation of the entire portfolio, is obviously of monumental proportions. Records of such magnitude could only be kept in a technologically advanced manner—for example, on magnetic tape or disk files. Furthermore, even if proper records are kept, the only possible way of deriving the numerous discount rates which equate the cash flows is by means of an electronic computer.[15]

Thus, it is really quite understandable that attempts to measure thoroughly rates of return are rare. Yet, unless the investor faces up to the task, he has no way of judging how his performance compares with the performance of other investors and with various objective criteria such as, say, the rate of return on the leading stock market averages. He cannot even compare the success of different investments in his own portfolio. And if he cannot make such comparisons, the task of improving his performance becomes ever so much more difficult.

As an example of a policy change which can stem from a careful analysis of past rates of return, we can cite the case of a mutual fund management team which is reputed to have made such an analysis. The management had traditionally followed a policy of paying primary attention to selecting the stocks of apparently undervalued companies, with only secondary attention to the broad outlook for the industries in which these companies operated. The rate-of-return analysis demonstrated that the selection of companies within industries had, indeed, been quite good. That is, companies whose stocks were bought by the fund outperformed other companies, in the same industry, whose stocks were either sold by the fund or were not bought. However, the resulting industry mix of the portfolio proved to be rather poor, and the fund's overall performance was below management's goals. Accordingly, the managers adopted a policy of looking more intensively at industry prospects and refrained from buying stocks in unattractive industries even if the individual stocks seemed undervalued. After some years of operating under the new policy, the rate-of-return analysis will be repeated to see if performance has improved as a result of the shift in policy.

*Alternative Investment Strategies.* One of the major difficulties confronting portfolio managers is the lack of actual experience with the consequences of different investment strategies under varying economic and institutional conditions. For example, the manager of a corporate pension fund has limited direct experience with the impact of economic adversity on the flow of contributions and benefits under the plan. He has still less experience with the interaction of high-risk investments and the plan's cash flow under conditions of adversity. Accordingly, his notions of appropriate risk limits are based primarily upon intuition rather than evidence.

---

[15] For one method see L. Fisher, "An Algorithm for Finding Exact Rate of Return." *Journal of Business*, January, 1966, Supplement on Security Prices. An excellent book on the general subject of measuring investment performance is P. O. Dietz, *Pension Funds: Measuring Investment Performance* (New York: Free Press of Glencoe, 1966).

The technique of simulation, referred to previously in connection with the analysis of actual investment activities, can also be used to generate hypothetical experience under a very large number of hypothetical conditions. First a "model" of the investor's mode of operation is constructed. For example, in the case of a corporate pension fund, the market value of invested assets at the end of any given year is equal, essentially, to the value of assets on hand at the start of the period being simulated; (for example, a 25-year period), plus: employer-employee contributions, dividend and interest income, and capital gains (realized and unrealized) during the period, minus: benefits paid under the plan, operating expenses charged to the plan, and capital losses (realized and unrealized) during the period. The amount available for new investments during any year of the entire period can be defined as the change in total assets from the beginning to the end of that year, exclusive of capital gains and losses, plus the turnover of assets which were on hand at the beginning of the year. Turnover includes mandatory amortization payments by borrowers, optional prepayments by borrowers, and sales of assets by the pension fund manager. The investment "strategy" consists of the allocation of beginning assets among different investment media, the decision to sell assets, and the allocation of the periodic amounts made newly available for investment.

Once the key features of the model have been outlined conceptually, the next step is to write a computer program which incorporates these features but allows their magnitudes to vary depending on the information sought by the user. For example, a highly flexible program might specify the following:

1. A dozen different investment media are available, including three common stock categories (for example, highly volatile, moderately volatile, and fairly stable), three corporate bond categories (for example, Aaa–A, Baa–Ba, and B or lower quality), two mortgage categories (for example, low risk and high risk), U.S. government bonds, real estate equity, preferred stock, and an "all other" composite.

2. Annual interest rates, default rates (loss of interest), and capital gain and loss rates on these investment media are a function of the general level of economic activity in each year of the simulation period, plus a random variable which can be generated by the computer. The precise mathematical functions utilized are based on a study of historical experience plus judgment regarding future conditions. (The functions can be changed in successive runnings of the program but must be held constant throughout any given 25-year simulation.)

3. The general level of economic activity in each year is specified by the user each time the program is run. Likewise the rates of amortization and optional prepayment are specified for each investment category

where such rates are applicable. These factors can all be changed in successive runs.

4. The stream of employer-employee contributions is a joint function of initial actuarial estimates, the level of economic activity, cumulative capital gains or losses, and a random variable.

5. Benefit payments are a function of initial actuarial estimates plus a random variable.

6. Operating expenses are a constant percentage of asset value at the end of each year.

7. At the start of each simulation run the user specifies:

*a*) The percentage of beginning assets to be allocated to each investment category.

*b*) The percentage of new investments to be allocated to each category.

*c*) A formula timing plan for the sale of portions of each investment category. This plan can be as simple or as complex as desired. It could also be geared to alter the allocations of new investment funds *within* the simulation period.

A computer program such as outlined above could be run hundreds of times. In each run some aspects would be held constant and some would be changed. The output of each run would be 25 income statements and balance sheets for the pension fund. Assuming that each component of the program bears some semblance to reality—admittedly a monumental assumption—the pension fund manager could gain great insight into the consequences of a given investment strategy under different economic conditions and of the consequences of different investment strategies under similar economic conditions. He would also learn a good deal about the impact on income and assets of changes in assumptions regarding investment maturities, interest rates, loss rates, etc.

We have given only one illustration of the use of simulation in studying the consequences of alternative investment strategies. This illustration is entirely based on hypothetical input. But the technique can also be applied with actual historical data as input. For example, a simulation model could be constructed to indicate what the historical results would have been under different formula timing plans. Or one might simulate the results of having bought stocks with low price-earnings ratios and having sold short high p/e stocks—or vice versa.[16] The number of possible applications is limited only by the user's imagination.

There are other approaches somewhat related to these types of simulation exercises which also can be very useful in the analysis of alternative

[16] For the results of some research along these lines, see J. D. McWilliams, "Prices, Earnings, and P-E Ratios," *Financial Analysts Journal*, May-June, 1966. The same issue of this journal contains another interesting article on the subject of strategy simulation—S. P. Zobian, "Investment Decision Modelling."

investment strategies. One such approach was initially given prominence in the 1950's by Dr. Harry Markowitz[17] and has since been refined and modified by others. It applies the complex mathematics of quadratic programming to the question of how to diversify effectively a portfolio, given a choice among hundreds of individual securities, and given certain basic information supplied by security analysts and portfolio managers. The technique is feasible to apply only if electronic computers are available to perform the calculations.

The central theme of Markowitz' work is that investors are "risk averters." By this he means that for a given expected mean rate of return, investors prefer a portfolio with a minimum possible deviation from the expected return. For example, if portfolio A is expected to yield 10% plus or minus 2% (i.e., it may yield as much as 12% or as little as 8%), it is more desirable than portfolio B whose expected yield is 10% plus or minus 4%. Starting with this conception of risk and of investors' attitudes toward risk, Markowitz observes that most investors try to minimize the deviations from the expected portfolio rate of return by "diversifying"—i.e., by constructing a portfolio with different types of securities and/or the securities of different companies. But he points out that simply buying *different* issues will not significantly reduce the volatility of the portfolio's rate of return if the income and market prices of the different issues have a high degree of "covariance"—i.e., if they tend to fluctuate in similar fashion. Effective diversification is achieved only if the issues tend to fluctuate in opposing fashion, so that the volatility of the portfolio's rate of return becomes significantly less than the volatility of the individual components of the portfolio.

Markowitz proposes an approach to the problem of "efficient diversification" which requires as input the following information:

1. Projections of the most likely rate of return, including both current income and capital gain or loss, to be earned on *each security* that might be considered for inclusion in the portfolio. The rate of return may be stated either on a pretax or after-tax basis.
2. Estimates of the possible range of error of each rate of return projection—for example, 15% plus or minus 8%.
3. An indication of the interrelationships (covariances) of the error ranges among securities. That is, if something happens to cause security A's rate of return to be, say, 2% higher than the "most probable" projection, what is the likelihood that the return on security B will be similarly higher than its most probable return? What about securities C, D, E, etc.?
4. An indication of any constraints placed upon the portfolio manager,

---

[17] H. Markowitz, "Portfolio Selection," *Journal of Finance,* March, 1952; and the book by the same author, *Portfolio Selection* (New York: John Wiley & Sons, Inc., 1959).

such as maximum percentage of the portfolio to be invested in any one security, minimum number of different securities to be included in the portfolio, etc.

Given this information, Markowitz offers a mathematical technique, solvable by computer,[18] which permits the user to determine the most probable rates of return on numerous possible portfolio combinations of the individual securities and the associated possible ranges of deviation from these most probable returns. Once these calculations are made, a tabulation such as the following can be constructed:

| Portfolio | Expected Average Rate of Return | Expected Standard Deviation | Expected Range of Returns at Two Standard Deviation* Level | |
|---|---|---|---|---|
| | | | Lowest | Highest |
| 1 | 4% | ¼% | 3½% | 4½% |
| 2 | 6 | 1½ | 3 | 9 |
| 3 | 8 | 2¾ | 2½ | 13½ |
| 4 | 10 | 4 | 2 | 18 |
| 5 | 10 | 5 | 0 | 20 |
| . | . | . | . | . |
| . | . | . | . | . |
| . | . | . | . | . |
| 100 | 20 | 15 | −10 | 50 |

* The user can choose any number of standard deviations he wishes, and the results will vary accordingly. This aspect of the subject is discussed by W. J. Baumol in "An Expected Gain-Confidence Limit Criterion for Portfolio Selection," *Management Science*, October, 1963.

Depending upon the individual portfolio manager's willingness or unwillingness to risk earning a low rate of return in the effort to achieve a high rate, either portfolio 1, 2, . . . or 100 will be optimum. Different portfolio managers, obviously, will reach different decisions as to which of the various portfolios is best. However, Markowitz would argue that portfolio 4 is clearly better than portfolio 5 because both have a mean expected return of 10%, but the former is "less risky"—has a lower variance—than the latter. This assumption will be considered further in a moment.

Thus, the Markowitz approach enables the investor to repeatedly rerun the program with different assumptions regarding the returns, variances, and covariances of individual securities. In this manner, he can gain great insight into the pros and cons of alternative portfolio structures. Which of the portfolio structures he actually chooses will depend upon his attitudes toward risk versus return, and also will depend upon the costs involved in altering his existing portfolio structure. But at least he will

---

[18] IBM has programmed one version of the approach, and various modifications have been made or proposed by others—see, for example, the Sharpe article cited in the suggested readings at the end of this chapter.

have begun to clarify his alternatives. He will have forced himself to spell out his investment goals and constraints and to make explicit his ideas about the future prospects of different securities.

Several criticisms have been made of Markowitz' approach, from both theoretical and practical points of view. One criticism has to do with his assumption that rational investors are risk averters. In the illustration previously cited, it was pointed out that Markowitz considers portfolio 4, with a minimum return of 2%, a maximum of 18%, and a mean of 10%, to be superior to the portfolio 5, with a minimum of 0%, a maximum of 20%, and the same 10% mean as portfolio 4. But is this necessarily the rational choice? Why would it be irrational for an investor to be willing to chance a zero return in exchange for the possibility of a 20% return?

A closely related question is whether variance as such is the most appropriate measure of risk. Most of the work of Markowitz and his followers use normal *price volatility* to determine whether the expected rate of return from a security should be assigned a high or low expected variance. But if an investor's liquidity needs are negligible—that is, if there is little danger that he will be forced to sell at a depressed price but can wait for an upturn in price—then price volatility per se does not really pose a risk to him.[19] Conceivably, dividend volatility or purchasing power volatility is more undesirable to him than price volatility.[20] As a matter of fact, if the investor is following a policy of dollar averaging, price volatility is to be desired rather than feared! As demonstrated in Chapter 15, given two securities whose prices have the same growth *trend*, but different degrees of variations around trend, the security with the greater degree of variation will produce better dollar-averaging results.[21]

Furthermore, some very practical obstacles may lie in the way of the portfolio manager who wishes to apply the Markowitz approach. While security analysts are accustomed to thinking about expected rates of return, they are less accustomed to thinking about the possible ranges of error of their expectations and are generally totally unaccustomed to estimating *covariances* among securities. Also, it is questionable whether they conceive of the margin of error as being symmetrical—plus or minus X%—as Markowitz assumes. It is very possible that they have in mind nonsymmetrical margins of error—for example, "if things turn out right,

---

[19] Unless the investor is, say, an insurance company, which must mark down the carrying value of common stocks even if it actually has no need to sell.

[20] Other risks which may be critical are the risks of changes in tax laws, risks of callability in bonds, and intangible emotional risks. See F. E. Block, "Risk and Performance," *Financial Analysts Journal*, March-April, 1966.

[21] If the investor is a short-term trader, he may also be better off with high-volatility stocks. If he expects to catch a quick bullish swing in the market, high-volatility stocks should do better than low-volatility stocks. Of course, if his forecast of the market is wrong, high-volatility stocks should do worse.

TABLE 20–1

The Dow Jones Companies

| Company | 12/13/63 Price | Estimated 1964 Dividends | Estimated 1964 Earnings | Estimated Change in Dividends | Estimated Change in Earnings |
|---|---|---|---|---|---|
| Allied Chemical | 56 | 1.80 | 3.00 | 0.04 | 0.20 |
| Alcoa | 67 | 1.20 | 2.75 | 0.00 | 0.50 |
| American Can | 42 | 2.00 | 2.75 | 0.00 | 0.25 |
| American Tel & Tel | 140 | 4.00 | 5.95 | 0.40 | 0.00 |
| American Tobacco | 27 | 1.50 | 2.45 | 0.00 | 0.00 |
| Anaconda | 43 | 2.50 | 4.50 | 0.00 | 0.10 |
| Bethlehem | 30 | 1.50 | 1.95 | 0.00 | 0.05 |
| Chrysler | 44 | 1.00 | 3.00 | 0.58 | −1.00 |
| Du Pont | 241 | 6.75 | 9.25 | −1.00 | −0.80 |
| Eastman Kodak | 117 | 2.65 | 4.40 | 0.23 | 0.25 |
| General Electric | 86 | 2.20 | 3.35 | 0.20 | 0.20 |
| General Foods | 86 | 2.05 | 3.35 | 0.10 | 0.21 |
| General Motors | 78 | 4.00 | 5.00 | 0.00 | −0.50 |
| Goodyear | 43 | 1.05 | 2.50 | 0.05 | 0.20 |
| International Harvester | 58 | 2.40 | 4.60 | 0.00 | 0.30 |
| International Nickel | 67 | 2.40 | 3.55 | 0.15 | 0.15 |
| International Paper | 32 | 1.05 | 1.75 | 0.01 | 0.25 |
| Johns Manville | 49 | 2.00 | 3.20 | 0.00 | 0.15 |
| Owens-Illinois | 88 | 2.50 | 4.50 | 0.00 | 0.25 |
| Procter & Gamble | 80 | 1.65 | 2.95 | 0.05 | 0.20 |
| Sears Roebuck | 99 | 1.90 | 3.50 | 0.24 | 0.20 |
| Standard Oil of California | 61 | 2.00 | 4.85 | 0.09 | 0.35 |
| Standard Oil of New Jersey | 73 | 2.75 | 5.00 | 0.00 | 0.30 |
| Swift | 48 | 1.80 | 4.00 | 0.20 | 1.15 |
| Texaco | 67 | 2.25 | 4.60 | 0.25 | 0.40 |
| Union Carbide | 119 | 3.60 | 5.50 | 0.00 | 0.30 |
| United Aircraft | 43 | 2.00 | 3.60 | 0.00 | 0.50 |
| United States Steel | 52 | 2.00 | 3.00 | 0.00 | 0.00 |
| Westinghouse | 34 | 1.20 | 1.70 | 0.00 | 0.35 |
| F. W. Woolworth | 79 | 2.80 | 5.25 | 0.08 | 0.25 |
| Total | 2,149 | 68.50 | 115.75 | 1.67 | 4.76 |

Source: Lionel D. Edie & Co., Inc.

this stock can go through the roof; if not, the downside potential seems relatively small."

Given these various reservations about Markowitz' views, some people have suggested a simple linear programming approach to the portfolio management problem. Here, the portfolio manager simply tries to utilize more effectively whatever information he is already being provided. Essentially, he employs the "Minimax" approach, and tries either to (*a*) obtain the same results he is currently getting, but to obtain the results with fewer different issues and at a lesser cost, or (*b*) obtain better results than he is currently getting, at the same cost. In this context, the term "results" refers to anything the portfolio manager considers important, with whatever constraints he believes to be relevant.

Excellent illustrations of the application of linear programming to portfolio construction have been developed by Mr. Leon Kilbert, of the consulting firm of Lionel D. Edie & Co. In these illustrations, some of which are reproduced here, Kilbert deals with what is probably one of the most widespread defects of investment portfolio management, individual and institutional. It is the tendency to load up the portfolio with an excessive number of issues, thus magnifying the task of keeping track of the many developments affecting the portfolio's performance while at the same time reducing the chance that the portfolio will do "better than average" because the portfolio becomes average.

Kilbert begins with the prices of the 30 Dow-Jones Industrial stocks at mid-December, 1963, together with analysts' estimates of 1963 and 1964 earnings and dividends per share for each of the stocks. These data are summarized in Table 20–1. It will be seen from this table that if an investor at the time had put together a portfolio consisting of 100 shares of each of the 30 stocks, his cost exclusive of commissions would have been $214,900. For this outlay, estimated 1964 dividends would have been $6,850, up an estimated $167 from 1963, and estimated earnings would have been $11,575, up $476.

Kilbert then employs the computer to solve various portfolio problems with the mathematics of linear programming. The portfolio problems are as follows.

**TABLE 20–2**
**Solution to Problem 1**

| *Company* | *Number of Shares* |
|---|---|
| American Can | 355 |
| American Tobacco | 553 |
| Anaccnda | 347 |
| Bethlehem | 497 |
| Chrysler | 148 |
| General Motors | 191 |
| International Harvester | 257 |
| Johns Manville | 304 |
| Standard Oil of Calif. | 245 |
| Standard Oil of N.J. | 115 |
| United Aircraft | 347 |
| Total Cost of "Efficient" Portfolio | $149,183 |
| Cost of Complete Dow Jones Portfolio | 214,900 |
| Saving | 31% |

1. Construct a portfolio, from among the 30 Dow stocks, which will produce the same estimated 1964 earnings and dividends as 100 shares of each of the 30 stocks but at a minimum cost and with no single issue representing more than 10% of the cost of the total portfolio.

2. Construct a portfolio at the $214,900 cost of 100 shares of each of the 30 stocks, such that estimated 1964 earnings will be at least as great as if all 30 stocks were bought, and estimated 1964 dividends will be maxi-

### TABLE 20–3
### Solution to Problem 2

| *Company* | *Number of Shares* |
|---|---|
| American Can | 512 |
| American Tobacco | 796 |
| Anaconda | 500 |
| Bethlehem | 716 |
| General Motors | 276 |
| International Harvester | 371 |
| Johns Manville | 439 |
| Standard Oil of N.J. | 111 |
| Swift | 279 |
| United Aircraft | 500 |
| U.S. Steel | 413 |
| Estimated 1964 Dividends on "Efficient" Portfolio | $10,154 |
| Estimated 1964 Dividends on Complete Dow Jones Portfolio | 6,850 |
| Improvement | 48% |

### TABLE 20–4
### Solution to Problem 3

| *Company* | *Number of Shares* |
|---|---|
| Alcoa | 321 |
| American Can | 512 |
| Goodyear | 500 |
| International Harvester | 371 |
| International Paper | 672 |
| Standard Oil of Calif. | 352 |
| Swift | 448 |
| Texaco | 321 |
| United Aircraft | 500 |
| Westinghouse | 632 |
| Estimated Change in Earnings of "Efficient" Portfolio | +$2,727 |
| Estimated Change in Earnings of Dow Jones Portfolio | + 476 |
| Improvement | 473% |

Source: Lionel D. Edie & Co., Inc.

mized. Again, no single issue may represent more than 10% of the total cost.

3. Construct a portfolio at a $214,900 cost, such that estimated 1964 earnings and dividends will be at least as great as if all 30 stocks were bought, and the estimated change in earnings from 1963 to 1964 will be maximized. The 10% diversification rule is again to be maintained.

The solutions to these problems are presented in Tables 20–2 to 20–4. It will be seen in Table 20–2 that estimated 1964 earnings and dividends on the Dow could have been obtained by purchasing only 11 different issues at a cost of $149,183, a saving of 31% compared with the $214,900 outlay necessary to purchase 100 shares of each of the 30 stocks. The solution to Problem 2 (Table 20–3) shows that for the same $214,900 outlay, estimated dividends could be raised 48% above the dividends that would be earned on 100 shares of each of the 30 stocks. Finally, Table 20–4 shows that the estimated earnings improvement could be $2,727 instead of $476, for the same outlay.

### Conclusion

The electronic computer has three major roles to play in investment analysis and portfolio management:

1. To build upon and refine established procedures, carrying them out faster, with greater accuracy, and with increased comprehensiveness.

2. To solve problems which investment people have been aware of but which have heretofore been insoluble because of the sheer size and complexity of the necessary data manipulation.

3. To facilitate original research which leads to a better understanding of security price determination, thereby focusing the attention of analysts and portfolio managers on the most critical variables.

## SUGGESTED READINGS

William J. Baumol. "Mathematical Analysis of Portfolio Selection: Principles and Application," *Financial Analysts Journal*, September–October, 1966.

Charles P. Bonini. *Simulation of Information and Decision Systems.* New York: Prentice-Hall, Inc., 1963.

Richard S. Bower *et al.* "A Language for the Aid of Financial Fact Finders," *Financial Analysts Journal*, January–February, 1967.

Richard H. Chase, Jr. *et. al. Computer Applications in Investment Analysis.* Hanover, N.H.: Amos Tuck School, Dartmouth College, 1966.

Geoffrey P. E. Clarkson. *Portfolio Selection: A Simulation of Trust Investment.* New York: Prentice-Hall, Inc., 1962.

Gordon B. Davis. *An Introduction to Electronic Computers.* New York: McGraw-Hill Book Co., 1965.

Donald E. Farrar. *The Investment Decision under Uncertainty.* New York: Prentice-Hall, Inc., 1962.

Herbert E. Goodfriend. "Adjustment and Projection of Life Insurance Company Earnings Utilizing a Computer," *Financial Analysts Journal*, November–December, 1966.

Benjamin F. King. "Market and Industry Factors in Stock Price Behavior," *Journal of Business*, January, 1966, Supplement on Security Prices.

Manown Kisor, Jr. "Quantitative Approaches to Common Stock Selection," *Business Economics*, Spring, 1966.

Harry Markowitz. *Portfolio Selection: Efficient Diversification of Investments.* New York: John Wiley & Sons, Inc., 1959.

Daniel D. McCracken. *A Guide to Fortran Programming.* New York: John Wiley & Sons, Inc., 1961.

William F. Sharpe. "Mathematical Investment Portfolio Selection: Some Early Results," *University of Washington Business Review*, April, 1963.

Daniel B. Suits. "Forecasting and Analysis with an Econometric Model," *American Economic Review*, March, 1962.

# INDEX

# INDEX

## C



## D

O



P



Q



R

## S



## T

*This book has been set in 10 and 9 point Janson, leaded 2 points. Part and chapter numbers are in 30 point Caslon Open. Part titles are in 18 point Standard and chapter titles are in 14 point Standard. The size of the type page is 27 by 46 picas.*

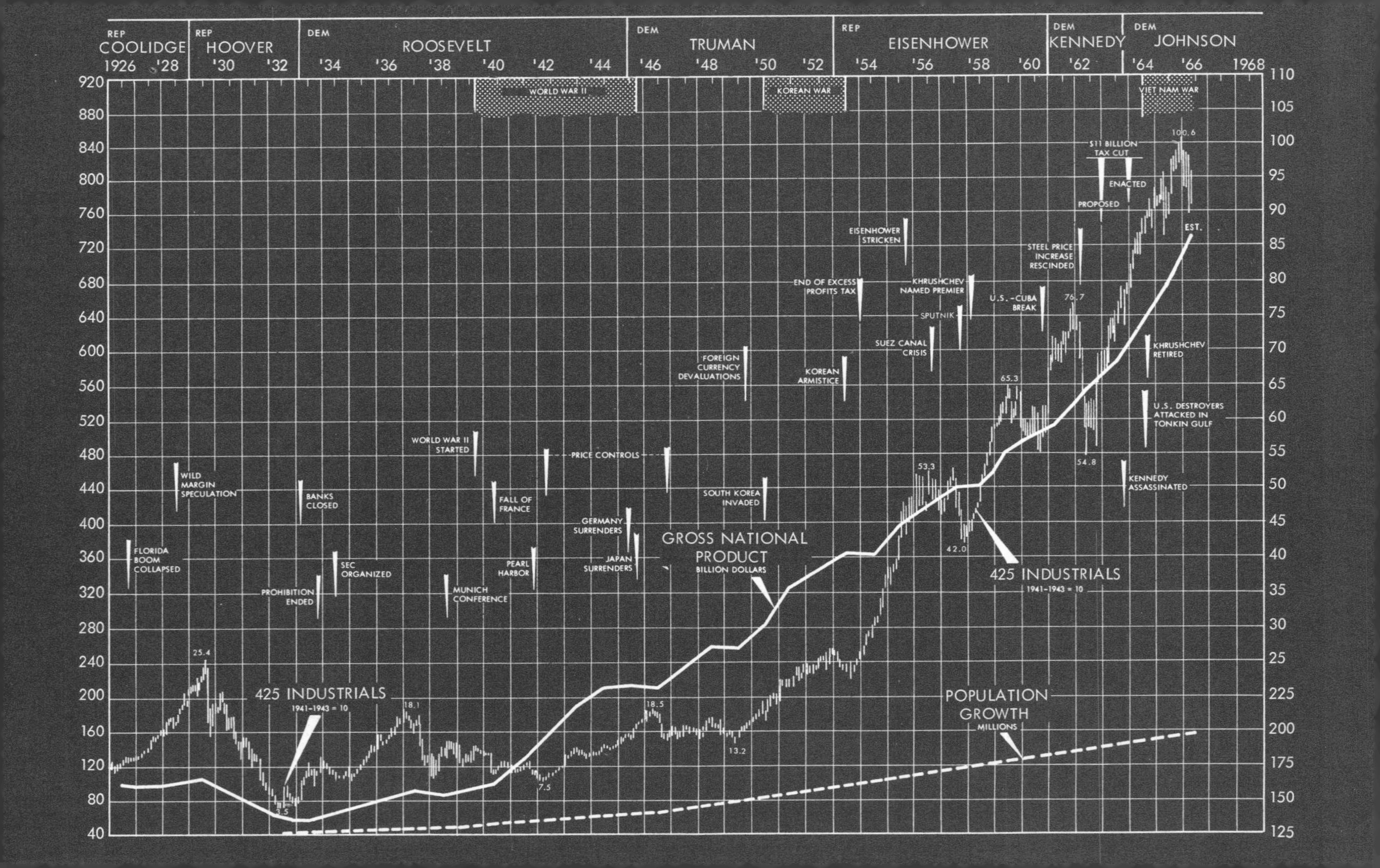

REP COOLIDGE
REP HOOVER
DEM ROOSEVELT
DEM TRUMAN
REP EISENHOWER
DEM KENNEDY
DEM JOHNSON
1926 '28 '30 '32 '34 '36 '38 '40 '42 '44 '46 '48 '50 '52 '54 '56 '58 '60 '62 '64 '66 1968
920 880 840 800 760 720 680 640 600 560 520 480 440 400 360 320 280 240 200 160 120 80 40
110 105 100 95 90 85 80 75 70 65 60 55 50 45 40 35 30 25 225 200 175 150 125
WORLD WAR II
KOREAN WAR
VIET NAM WAR
FLORIDA BOOM COLLAPSED
WILD MARGIN SPECULATION
BANKS CLOSED
PROHIBITION ENDED
SEC ORGANIZED
MUNICH CONFERENCE
WORLD WAR II STARTED
FALL OF FRANCE
PEARL HARBOR
PRICE CONTROLS
GERMANY SURRENDERS
JAPAN SURRENDERS
FOREIGN CURRENCY DEVALUATIONS
SOUTH KOREA INVADED
KOREAN ARMISTICE
END OF EXCESS PROFITS TAX
EISENHOWER STRICKEN
SUEZ CANAL CRISIS
SPUTNIK
KHRUSHCHEV NAMED PREMIER
U.S.-CUBA BREAK
STEEL PRICE INCREASE RESCINDED
$11 BILLION TAX CUT
PROPOSED
ENACTED
KENNEDY ASSASSINATED
KHRUSHCHEV RETIRED
U.S. DESTROYERS ATTACKED IN TONKIN GULF
EST.
25.4
3.5
18.1
7.5
18.5
13.2
53.3
42.0
65.3
76.7
54.8
100.6
425 INDUSTRIALS
1941–1943 = 10
GROSS NATIONAL PRODUCT
BILLION DOLLARS
425 INDUSTRIALS
1941–1943 = 10
POPULATION GROWTH
MILLIONS